1798: A bicentenary perspective

1798

A BICENTENARY PERSPECTIVE

Edited by

Thomas Bartlett
David Dickson
Dáire Keogh
Kevin Whelan

FOUR COURTS PRESS

Set in 10.5 on 12.5 point Ehrhardt for
FOUR COURTS PRESS LTD
7 Malpas Street, Dublin 8, Ireland
e-mail: info@four-courts-press.ie
http://www.four-courts-press.ie
and in North America
FOUR COURTS PRESS
c/o ISBS, 920 N.E. 58th Avenue, Suite 300, Portland, OR 97213.

A catalogue record for this title
is available from the British Library.

ISBN 1-85182-430-8

Printed in Great Britain
by MPG Books, Bodmin, Cornwall.

Contents

Maps

Preface

A five-day academic conference commemorating the bicentenary of the 1798 rebellion was held between 19 and 23 May 1998. Proceedings began in Belfast at the Ulster Museum and were later transplanted to Dublin Castle. The event brought together international scholars, local historians and specialists in a diversity of areas, all of whom were trying to understand the cataclysmic events that brought eighteenth-century Ireland to such a violent close.

The conference was extremely well supported and its sessions stirred up lively debate. Thirty-six papers were delivered in a programme that was organized around twelve plenary sessions. The present volume incorporates thirty-two of these papers (plus one that had originally been intended for delivery but could not be presented). Some of the papers were considerably modified in the wake of the conference, some extended. The exceptional length of the conference programme and the substantial and original character of many of the contributions explain the size of the present work, as well as excusing (we hope) the very long time it has taken to bring it to publication.

When it became apparent to the editors that early publication was not going to be possible, the decision was taken to organize the collection in such a way that the volume would be both definitive and self-critical. Thus we decided to commission a series of linked commentaries reflecting on the papers, on the issues they address, and on the related literature that has appeared in the recent tidal wave of publication on Ireland in the 1790s and on the revolutionary decade in the wider European and Atlantic world. Kevin Whelan has provided eight short essays, each of which introduces one of the eight sections into which the thirty-three papers have been grouped. These commentaries should be read as an extended personal review as to where '98 studies stand after the bicentennial dust has settled. And that of course means that they do not necessarily reflect the views of the editors at large, or of individual authors.

The historiography of the United Irish men and women, of their opponents, and of the 1798 rising itself will never stand still. It is our hope that this polychromatic volume captures the diversity of interpretation and perspective evident in 1998, and that it will stimulate a new cycle of research into these momentous events which had such a powerful influence on the evolution of modern Ireland. Included in this volume is a comprehensive bibliography of publications relevant to 1798 and its background that appeared between 1900 and 2002. This inventory is intended to provide a baseline for the next generation of research.

We would like to thank a number of individuals, some who contributed hugely to the smooth running of the bicentennial conference, others who have assisted in bringing the present volume to publication: Rebecca Bartlett, John Gray, Alice Kearney, Katie Keogh, and Trevor Parkhill. We would like to acknowledge in particular the contribution of Peter Collins as a member of the Conference Organizing Committee and its Belfast convenor; and of Matthew Stout who has played a heroic role as patient copy-editor, as well as being map originator and map designer for the volume.

We would like to place on record our gratitude to the patrons and sponsors of the conference whose support has made this publication possible: The Irish Government 1798 Commemoration Committee; The Cultural Relations Council, Northern Ireland; The British Council (Dublin); Trinity College, Dublin; St Patrick's College, Dublin City University; University College, Dublin; The Ulster Museum; and Allied Irish Banks plc. We would also like to thank those institutions who have materially assisted us in the success of the project: the Public Record Office of Northern Ireland; the National Archives of Ireland; the Dublin Castle Convention Centre; and last but not least, our most patient publishers, Four Courts Press.

T.B., D.D., D.K., K.W.

Contributors

THOMAS BARTLETT is Professor of Modern Irish History at University College, Dublin.

ALLAN BLACKSTOCK is a lecturer in the Department of History, The Queen's University of Belfast.

MAURICE J. BRIC is a lecturer in the Department of Modern History, University College, Dublin.

LIAM CHAMBERS is a lecturer in history, Mary Immaculate College, Limerick.

DAVID DICKSON is Associate Professor, Department of Modern History at Trinity College, Dublin.

MARIANNE ELLIOTT is Professor of History and Director of the Institute of Irish Studies, University of Liverpool.

DANIEL GAHAN is Professor of History, University of Evansville.

TONY GAYNOR is a civil servant in the Department of Education and Science, Dublin.

LUKE GIBBONS is Professor of English, Film, Television and Theatre at the University of Notre Dame.

HUGH GOUGH is Associate Professor, Department of Modern History, University College, Dublin.

TOMMY GRAHAM is Editor, *History Ireland*.

JAMES KELLY is head of the Department of History at St Patrick's College, Drumcondra.

DÁIRE KEOGH is a lecturer in the Department of History, St Patrick's College, Drumcondra.

PETER LINEBAUGH is Visiting Professor of History, at Bard College, New York.

JAMES LIVESEY is a lecturer in the Department of Modern History, Trinity College, Dublin.

IAN R. MCBRIDE is a Lecturer in the Department of History, King's College, London.

TREVOR MCCAVERY is Head of History, Regent House School, Newtownards, County Down.

BRIAN MACDONALD is an independent scholar.

ELAINE MCFARLAND is the head of the School of Social Sciences, Strathclyde University.

BREANDÁN MAC SUIBHNE is Programme Co-ordinator of the Keough Institute for Irish Studies at the University of Notre Dame.

DAVID W. MILLER is Professor of History at Carnegie Mellon University, Pittsburgh.

HARMAN MURTAGH is a senior lecturer in Law and Irish Studies at the Athlone Institute of Technology.

RUAN O'DONNELL is a lecturer in History, University of Limerick.

KEVIN O'NEILL is Professor of History at Boston College.

W.N. OSBOROUGH is Professor of Law at University College, Dublin.

JAMES QUINN is Executive Editor, Dictionary of Irish Biography, Royal Irish Academy.

N.A.M. RODGER is Professor, Department of History, University of Exeter.

GERALDINE SHERIDAN is Professor of French, University of Limerick.

BRENDAN SIMMS is Director of Studies in History at Peterhouse College, Cambridge.

BREÁNDÁN Ó BUACHALLA is Professor Emeritus, Department of Irish, University College, Dublin.

KEVIN WHELAN is Michael Smurfit Director, Keough University of Notre Dame Centre, Dublin.

DAVID WILSON is a lecturer in the Department of History at St Michael's College, Toronto.

JAMES WILSON is an independent scholar.

C.J. WOODS is Research and Editorial Assistant, Dictionary of Irish Biography, Royal Irish Academy.

SECTION I

On 31 December 1775, General Richard Montgomery died while leading his troops in the unsuccessful storming of Quebec, an action that stalled the British there for a year and allowed the Americans time to regroup.[1] Montgomery, the first member of the general staff to die in action, was quickly elevated into an American republican hero, the subject of John Trumbull's patriotic painting *The death of General Montgomery*[2] and the first revolutionary American to be honoured by a major statue when Congress erected one to him in 1787 at St Paul's church at the end of Wall Street in Manhattan.[3] When news of his massively

---

1   Hal Shelton, *General Richard Montgomery and the American Revolution: From redcoat to rebel* (New York, 1994).

2   John Trumbull (1756–1843) self-consciously set out to be America's first history painter. Encouraged by Thomas Jefferson, he embarked on an ambitious series of thirteen canvasses depicting scenes from the American Revolution, eight of which he completed, including the Montgomery one (now housed at the Yale Centre for British Art).

3   This painting was modelled on the famous *The Death of General Wolfe* (1770) by the American Benjamin West, which broke with the neo-classical orthodoxy of British painting by showing the general in a contemporary rather than classical setting. The painting is therefore a landmark in the emergence of a new republican aesthetic. Sir Joshua Reynolds had tried to dissuade West from this break with tradition. West had replied: 'The event to be commemorated took place on the thirteenth of September 1759, in a region of the world unknown to the Greeks and the Romans, and at a period of time when no such nations, nor heroes in their costumes, any longer existed ... The same truth that guides the pen of the historian should govern the pencil of the artist ... but if instead of the facts of the transactions, I represent classical fictions, how shall I be understood by posterity! I want to mark the date, the place and the parties engaged in the event': Robert Hughes, *American visions: The epic history of art in America* (London, 1977), pp 76–7. It is also possible to see the painting as an exercise in cultural nationalism: Dennis Motagna, 'Benjamin West's "The death of General Wolfe": A nationalist narrative', in *American Art Jn.* (Spring, 1981), 72–88. Remarkably, this celebrated painting was publicly displayed at Derry in 1783: 'The people of this city have lately been highly entertained by the exhibition of a beautiful painting now in Lord Bristol's house. It represents the death of the gallant General Wolfe in the famous battle of Quebec, with figures of all those distinguished personages who were present, such as General Monckton, Colonel Williamson, Colonel Barre, Surgeon Adair etc. together with a distant view of the engagement and the British fleet: the figures are drawn nearly as large as life and are all perfect likenesses. This capital piece, executed by the celebrated Mr West of London, cost 500 guineas, and is thought to be the finest ever brought to Ireland. It is intended, we hear, to

reported death reached his native Ireland, his brother Alexander and Sir Edward
Newenham wore black mourning suits in the House of Commons, and Edmund
Burke described him as 'a brave, able, humane and generous man'. Richard
Montgomery (1736–75) belonged to a north Dublin- and Donegal-based family,
settled at Abbyville.[4] As a younger man, he had been an officer in the British
army, serving in America, Canada and Martinique. Returning briefly to Ireland,
he sold his commission in 1772, before emigrating to the Hudson valley, where
he purchased an estate in 1773. He had then been elected to the revolutionary
Congress of New York and commissioned as a brigade general in the American
army in 1775, before his apotheosis into the republican pantheon at Quebec. In
1788, Sir Edward Newenham, the best-known American sympathizer in Ireland
and the correspondent of Washington and Franklin, added a tribute to him in
his '[United] State's Room' at Belcamp.[5] In alcoves around the room, Newenham
displayed busts of Washington, Franklin and Lafayette: the ceiling represented a
new dawn breaking on the political horizon. At its centre, he commissioned a
rondo plasterwork in high relief, depicting the death of Montgomery. He was
later to construct the first monument to Washington erected outside America, an
obelisk still standing in the grounds of Belcamp.[6]

The trajectory of Montgomery's career and 'The Memory of Montgomery' –
a frequent toast in Irish and Irish-American radical circles through the revolutionary period – demonstrate the complex links between Ireland and the wider
political scene in the eighteenth century.[7] This international framing is not always
sufficiently visible in treatments of Irish history. In two major books on European

be placed among His Lordship's [Lord Hervey] elegant collection of paintings and statues at
Downhill': *London-Derry Jn.*, 13 May 1783. I owe this quotation to Breandán Mac Suibhne,
Patriot Paddies: The politics of identity and rebellion in north-west Ulster, 1778–1803 (Cork, forth-
coming). The most famous painting of the 1798 rebellion, Thomas Robinson's *The battle of
Ballynahinch*, is modelled on West's painting.

4   His brother Alexander Montgomery (1720–1800) of Convoy, County Donegal, was also a British
army officer who served in India and America, where he achieved notoriety as 'Black' Montgomery for the use of scalping by troops under his command. He subsequently became Donegal's
independent MP from 1768 to 1800. A radical Volunteer officer in the 1780s, he apparently
turned down an offer from Lord Edward FitzGerald to lead the rebellion – solely on the grounds
of age.

5   Jonah Barrington sneered that Newenham was 'very deficient in talent, but very confident that he
possessed much of it; he fancied he was a great patriot … He had drawn General Washington
into a short literary correspondence with himself as to Ireland on the strength of which he affected with great importance to be an importer of the most early and authentic information from
America … a busy, buzzing, useless, intermeddling Member of Parliament and one of the most
inadvertent, feeble and fanatical of all the Irish intolerants': Jonah Barrington, *The rise and fall of
the Irish nation* (Paris, 1833), p. 228.

6   Eugene Coyle, 'From Abbyville to Quebec: the life and times of General Richard Montgomery',
in *Dublin Historical Record*, liv, 2 (2001), 146–60.

7   Note the deliberate visual reprise of Tandy as Montgomery in the *Hibernian Magazine*: Fintan
Cullen, *Visual politics: The representation of Ireland 1750–1930* (Cork, 1997), p. 64.

intellectual history published in the 1980s, the Irish presence is instructive. Ireland does not appear at all in a survey of enlightenment in national context, while it does feature in a companion volume on romanticism.[8] This pattern reflects a perception that there was no Irish Enlightenment in the second half of the eighteenth century, nothing to match its earlier intellectual vigour with Toland, Molyneux, King, Berkeley and Hutcheson,[9] and that the function of Irish radicals in the revolutionary period was to import unchanged ideas generated by the enlightened world outside. The argument presumes that Irish republicanism in the 1790s sprang directly from the Athena's head of the French Revolution. By contrast, Irish romanticism is presented as a potent home-brew of atavism, tradition and Catholicism. Enlightenment in Ireland was Protestant, cosmopolitan, and top-down; romanticism was Catholic, indigenous and bottom-up.[10] This follows the distinction made by Isaiah Berlin between Enlightenment universalism and espousal of human rights as opposed to nationalism's fragmentation and collapse into ethnocentrism: Berlin explains nationalism's sinister attraction as an emotional compensation for enlightened rationalism: nationalism is the dark, introverted, bloody reaction to the triumph of the Enlightenment.[11] A secondary distinction is between the concepts of patriotism (oriented to the state and conservative) and nationalism (oriented to the nation and anti-authoritari-

8 Roy Porter (ed.), *The Enlightenment in national context* (Cambridge, 1981); Roy Porter and M. Teich (eds), *Romanticism in national contexts* (Cambridge, 1988) [Irish chapter by Tom Dunne, 'Haunted by history: Irish romantic writing 1800–1850,' pp 68–91].

9 Seamus Deane 'Enlightenment', in W.J. McCormack (ed.), *The Blackwell companion to Irish culture* (London, 1999), pp 198–200. Jonathan Israel's recent argument redefines the debate over the origins of enlightenment. He re-positions it in time (back into the late seventeenth century) and in space (to the north and the west of Europe, away from France). Enlightenment emerged not at the centre but at the margins of Europe. This model suggests the need for a re-examination of the vigour of philosophical thinking in early eighteenth-century Ireland, and for the importance of John Toland as a transmitter of the radical enlightenment into the English language: Jonathan Israel, *Radical Enlightenment: Philosophy and the making of modernity 1650–1750* (Oxford, 2001). A valuable edition of the work of the early eighteenth-century Irish philosophers is David Berman and Patricia O'Riordain (eds), *The Irish Enlightenment and counter-Enlightenment*, 6 vols (Bristol, 2002).

10 David Berman, 'Enlightenment and counter-enlightenment in Irish philosophy', in *Archiv für Geschichte der Philosophie*, 64 (1982), pp 148–65. A modern biography of Charles O'Conor, the principal Catholic exponent of enlightenment, is badly needed. We also require an intellectual as opposed to an ecclesiastical history of the Irish colleges in the eighteenth century. See, for example, Thomas O'Connor, *An Irish theologian in eighteenth-century France: Luke Joseph Hooke 1714–96* (Dublin, 1995); Thomas O'Connor (ed.), *The Irish in continental Europe 1580–1815* (Dublin, 2000); Thomas O'Connor (ed.), *Irish migration to Europe 1601–1789: The legacy of Kinsale* (Dublin, 2003): Clare Carroll, *Circe's cup: Cultural transformations in early modern Ireland* (Cork, 2001).

11 Isaiah Berlin, 'Nationalism: Past neglect and present power', in *Against the current: essays in the history of ideas* (New York, 1980), pp 333–55. This argument has been vulgarised in an Irish context by Conor Cruise O'Brien: see, for example, *Ancestral voices: Religion and nationalism in Ireland* (Dublin, 1994).

an).[12] The figure of Burke straddles such debates. An 'Irish' Burke has emerged more forcefully in recent writings, with the recognition that his arguments (conservative in a British framework) became radical when transposed into Ireland. [13]

The conventional wisdom presupposes that there was no radical ideological potential within Irish Catholic or Jacobite cultures in the eighteenth century. Both were conservative, backward-looking and moribund.[14] This model is refashioned in the following chapters. Irish radicalism, it is argued, had indigenous roots from which to flower, that a direct link does exist between Jacobitism and Jacobinism, and Irish society mediated the American and French Revolutions in its own distinctive way rather than passively registering their effects.[15]

A legacy of Ireland's colonial situation was the precocious establishment of a 'national' consciousness among the Irish Catholic poor. Living alongside the settlers and being at the receiving end of the colonizing process accelerated their transition into political consciousness. From the late sixteenth century onwards,

12 See the effort by Joep Leerssen to apply this model to the Irish situation in the late eighteenth century: 'Anglo-Irish patriotism and its European context: notes towards a reassessment', in *E.C.I.*, iii (1988), 7–24.

13 Conor Cruise O'Brien, *The great melody* (London, 1992); Seamus Deane, 'Factions and fictions: Burke, colonialism and revolution', in *Bullán*, iv (2000), 5–26; Luke Gibbons, *Edmund Burke and Ireland: Aesthetics, politics and the colonial sublime* (Cambridge, forthcoming).

14 Sean Connolly, *Religion, law and power: The making of Protestant Ireland 1660–1760* (Oxford, 1982). Inexplicably, his recent edited collection *Political ideas in eighteenth-century Ireland* (Dublin, 2000) has no article on Jacobitism or Catholicism. In this, he follows the earlier example of R.B. McDowell, who claimed: 'The great bulk of the people were restricted by poverty and persecution to political speculations of the simplest kind': R.B. McDowell, *Irish public opinion 1750–1800* (London, 1944), preface.

15 Breandán Ó Buachalla, *Aisling Gheár: Na Stiobhartaigh agus an t-aos léinn 1603–1788* (Baile Átha Cliath, 1996); Éamon Ó Ciardha, *Ireland and the Jacobite cause 1685–1776: A fatal attachment* (Dublin, 2002); Patrick Fagan (ed.), *Ireland in the Stuart papers*, 2 vols (Dublin, 1995). Two useful studies of the manuscript tradition are Breandán Ó Conchúir, *Scríobhaithe Chorcaí 1700–1850* (Baile Átha Cliath, 1982) and Medhbhín Ní Urdail, *The scribe in eighteenth- and nineteenth-century Ireland: Motivations and milieu* (Munster, 2000). An intriguing parallel would be Robert Burns in Scotland; his blend of Jacobite/Jacobin with an intense sense of Scottishness struck a deep chord in Ireland, with popular editions of his poems printed in Belfast in 1787, 1789, 1793 and 1800: Liam McIlvanney, 'Robert Burns and the Ulster-Scots literary revival of the 1790s', in *Bullán*, iv, 2 (2000), 125–44. Another popular figure who wrote in Scots was Allan Ramsay, whose 1725 play *The gentle shepherd* was reprinted in Belfast (1743, 1748, 1755, 1768, 1792), Newry (1764, 1776, 1793) and Strabane (1789). Compare the United Irish encouragement of cultural expression in Irish and Scots with the conservative attack (*Belfast Newsletter*, 8 June 1792) on 'the disgusting gibberish of Scottish versification with which our eyes, our ears, our feelings have been so much wounded. It is strange that when so noble a language as English can be had, any writer whatever in these countries should yet have recourse to a dialect absolutely barbarous, especially as the best authors among the Scots themselves have long since abandoned it for the elegant and expressive English. I acknowledge myself to be one of those who have an invincible aversion to the Scotch language and the Scotch accent and I may say the same with regard to Irish. Happily for the republic of letters, they are both falling fast into disuse and oblivion, while the beautiful, the energetic, the admirable English language should be made the universal medium of communication throughout the British empire.'

the island's indigenous 'peasants' were already been turned into Irishmen. When one disoriented victim of the shipwrecked Spanish Armada washed up on the shores of Erris in Mayo, he asked a local man what nationality he was: 'Arkinneack' [Eireannach, 'Irish'] was the reply. Their heightened sense of national identity differentiated the Irish poor from their European counterparts, who generally had to await the intrusion of centralized nation-states before developing such a sense. This historical experience of colonization (unique among western European nations) ensures that 'invention of tradition' or prioritization of print culture arguments about nationalism do not work well in the Irish context.[16] One should also note here the tension between the social science emphasis on typology and sequence as opposed to the focus of the historian on particularity and chronology.[17] Benedict Anderson's model of the imagined community excises nationalism's positive links with the advent of democracy and socialism, while exaggerating its more troubled kinship with issues of race, religion and language. It envisages curiously inert and plastic communities, endlessly susceptible to the manipulative blandishments of their leaders. The model reduces the concept of culture to an instrumental cipher: invention or, to phrase it another way, imagination should not be theorized as consistently negative. The essence of culture is mobile, malleable, dynamic and contested, and imagination is at the heart of its creative power.

It is therefore valuable to reinsert culture into the political equation in the Irish eighteenth century. Jacobitism was one central component of popular culture. King James' flight from Ireland in 1690 facilitated his entry into a well-defined messianic niche in traditional Irish ideology – the banished rightful king destined to return and reclaim his patrimony. The seamless grafting of Stuart claims onto an older ideological stock accounts for the pervasiveness of the millenial mode in Irish discourse, most notably in the *aisling* or allegorical verse. Jacobite song was a primary vehicle of nationalist rhetoric, and poetry in the Irish language, as the main public discourse of the majority of the population, has a correspondingly high claim on the attention of historians of eighteenth-century Ireland. It secreted a latent and radical sub-text through its juxtaposition of right (*ceart*) and might (*neart*), past and present, justice and injustice, freedom and slavery, legitimate and illegitimate rule. That discourse never lost sight of the harsh realities of Irish life, remaining rooted in four primary categories – religion, race, land and language (Ó Buachalla, chapter 4).

16 Eric Hobsbawm and Terence Ranger (eds), *The invention of tradition* (Cambridge, 1983); John Gillis (ed.), *Commemorations: The politics of national identity* (Princeton, 1994); A. Smith, 'The nation: Invented, imagined and reconstructed', in M. Ringrose and A. Lerner (eds), *Reimagining the nation* (Philadelphia, 1993), pp 9–28.

17 Robert Wiebe, 'Imagined communities, nationalist experiences', in *Jn. Hist. Soc.*, i, 1 (2000), 33–63. Anderson acknowledges the tension in the 1991 edition of *Imagined communities*. We await a commentary on his native country from this Irish-born scholar.

Jacobitism bequeathed the idea of the injured nation – poor, displaced, despised, subjugated – to the majority Catholic population, especially in the southern third of the island with its close ties to the continent, its heavy 'Wild Geese' recruitment and its strongly embedded 'underground gentry', from whom Jacobite ideas percolated down to the *cos-mhuintir*.[18] It defined a cohesive community, indelibly marked by the shipwreck of the seventeenth century, and helped by its subsequent identification as 'a community of insult' in Thomas Addis Emmet's pithy phrase.[19] In Jacobite discourse, collective calamity presaged collective salvation. This discourse ramified across the categories of religion, race, land and language.[20] Its latent radicalism surfaced in the 1790s, metamorphosing into a rousing call for an overthrow of the Irish status quo. The Carlow United Irishman John Langton put it succinctly in 1798: 'The men who wore the frieze coat and the brogues purchased this kingdom with their flesh and blood. They were the first and will not be the last tho' they are kept under.'[21] The possibility existed for the transition from Jacobitism to Jacobinism in the 1790s. Long after its military threat was spent, Jacobitism persisted within popular culture, allowing it to function as the essential mode of transmission between seventeenth- and nineteenth-century versions of Irish nationalism.

Jacobitism's long-term effect hollowed out the legitimacy of Hanoverian rule in Ireland. For the majority Catholic population, this regime lacked legitimacy, opening the space for an oppositional popular culture and a distinctive moral economy. Dissenters were treated as second-class citizens, despite their commitment to the winning of the Williamite struggle, and never felt fully at ease within the Anglican ascendancy. With the exception of Anglican nodes especially in the towns, and in isolated rural pockets of dominance where Anglicanism straddled the full social spectrum, a populist Hanoverian loyalty was lacking. The Grattanite effort to expand the limits of the Glorious Revolution and to foster Irish monarchism under a dual monarchy concept foundered in the acrimonious debate over 'Protestant ascendancy' in the late 1780s and early 1790s. The vacated space, increasingly devoid of Catholics and Dissenters, generated a novel Anglican alternative in the 1790s, the Orange Order, committed to maintaining the original settlement against the claims of the majority population.

An ideology whose primary articulation was in Irish, the majority language in eighteenth-century Ireland, Jacobitism nurtured a subversive moral economy, most visibly displayed in the secret societies. There is a suggestive link between the two regions where manuscript production in Irish was strongest across the

---

18 On the underground gentry, see Whelan, *Tree of liberty*, and the agnostic review article by Toby Barnard, 'The gentrification of eighteenth-century Ireland' in *E.C.I.*, xii (1997), 137–55.
19 W.J. MacNeven (ed.), *Pieces of Irish history* (New York, 1807), p. 23.
20 Peter MacQuillan, *Keywords of the Irish language: Studies in the relationship among history, culture and language structure* (Cork, forthcoming).
21 Patrick C. Power, *The courts martial of 1798–1799* (Naas, 1998), p. 69.

eighteenth century, Munster and Airialla (Oriel), and the heartlands of the most significant secret societies, the Whiteboys, Rightboys and Defenders.[22] A cultural as opposed to an economic history of these movements is now needed.[23] These same areas were the seedbeds of Jacobite recruitment. Vast numbers of Irishmen fought with the French armies of Louis XIV and Louis XV. Where samples are available, they suggest Munster dominance: one sample has 40 per cent from Munster, 28 per cent from Leinster, 21 per cent from Ulster and 10 per cent from Connaught. The four leading counties were Cork, Limerick, Dublin and Tipperary.[24] A clear social pattern underpins these figures, correlating with the areas where an 'underground gentry' survived.

Recent work on Jacobitism has provided a counterweight to accounts of eighteenth-century Ireland which fail to register its diglossia. The simplistic notion of two pristine speech communities in splendid isolation from each other needs to be jettisoned. Like earlier 'two nations' and 'dual economies' concepts, a 'two languages' model is dangerously inadequate. We need to focus more on the hybridity and multi-lingual nature of eighteenth-century speech communities, stretching all the way from Scots Gaelic to Scots-Irish to Irish to English to Yola. Such an emphasis should help to banish the misconception that the Irish language functioned as a political contraceptive. There is now a virtual battle of the books – or manuscripts – between 'moderns' (Ó Buachalla, Buttimer, Morley, Ó Ciardha) and 'ancients' (Dunne, Ó Ríordáin, Connolly). The former argue for the dynamism and receptivity of Irish-language production; the latter stress stasis, conservatism and inflexibility.[25] A study of the most prolific Irish-language poets of this period, especially Tomás Ó Miocháin, Eoghan Rua Ó Súilleabháin and Mícháel Óg Ó Longáin, would be helpful. Attention should also be paid to

22 James Donnelly, 'The Whiteboy movement, 1761–65', in *I.H.S.*, xxi (1978–9), 20–55; James Donnelly, 'Irish agrarian rebellion: The Whiteboys of 1769–1776', in *P.R.I.A.*, C, lxxxiii (1983), 293–331. These useful accounts are too narrowly focused on newspaper evidence and completely ignore Irish-language sources.

23 Some of the building blocks for this project include Luke Gibbons, 'Identity without a centre: Allegory, history and Irish nationalism', in *Transformations in Irish culture* (Cork, 1996), pp 134–48; David Lloyd, *Ireland after history* (Cork, 1999). A study of the remarkable cycle of Irish-language poems on the judicial murder of Fr Nicholas Sheehy is now underway by Mairín Ní Dhonnacadha.

24 E. Ó hAnnracháin, 'Who were the Wild Geese?', in *Études Irlandaises*, xv, 1 (2000), 105–21. A significant work in progress by Colm Ó Conaill is counting Irish recruits to the French service 1700–1770, work conducted under the auspices of the Centre for Irish-Scottish Studies at T.C.D.

25 Breandán Ó Buachalla, 'Irish Jacobitism and Irish nationalism: the literary evidence', in Michael O'Dea and Kevin Whelan (eds), *Nations and nationalisms* (Oxford, 1995), pp 103–16; Neil Buttimer, '"Cogadh sagsana nuadh sonn": Reporting the American Revolution', in *Stud. Hib.*, xxviii (1984), 63–101; Neil Buttimer, 'Remembering 1798', in *J.C.H.A.S.*, ciii (1998), 1–26; Vincent Morley, *Irish opinion and the American Revolution, 1760–83* (Cambridge, 2002); Tom Dunne, 'The Gaelic response to conquest and colonisation: The evidence of the poetry', in *Stud. Hib.*, xx (1980), 7–30; Michelle Ó Ríordáin, *The Gaelic mind and the collapse of the Gaelic world* (Cork, 1990).

the mediators of their world-view into English, notably Denis Taaffe, Watty Cox, Bernard Coyle and James Coigly.[26] A related project is the extension of the perspectives of the 'New British History' from the seventeenth into the eighteenth century: the complex history of Jacobitism fits in this context.[27]

The welcome emphasis on Irish-language sources contributes a fresh dimension to what has been an English- and French-centred story of the transmission of radicalism (Sheridan, chapter 2). Recent research by literary and cultural historians has added depth and detail to the French connection in eighteenth-century Ireland.[28] It has extended the narrow range of literature previously examined: reading and reception have been explored and there has been closer attention to the Irish influence of Voltaire, Rousseau and Montesquieu.[29] Further work on other favourite authors of the United Irishmen, notably Volney, Raynal, Helvétius and Diderot, would be desirable.[30] This would sharpen the focus on the geography and sociology of reading, work made easier by the herculean bibliographic labours of Pollard, Fenning and the Loebers.[31] Also valuable would be sustained attention to the dynamic by which print and oral culture interacted in mutually enriching ways.[32]

The reception history of enlightenment should consider its interface with national cultures A prevalent emphasis in the literature divides Europe into 'advanced' and 'backward' regions; the temptation is then to treat the 'spread' of enlightenment as if it was a simple diffusion pattern from a single centre, in which the backward regions suffer from a geographically or culturally induced

---

26 Dáire Keogh (ed.), *A patriot priest: The life of Father James Coigly 1761–1798* (Cork, 1998).

27 A useful series of review articles can be found in 'The New British History in Atlantic perspective', in *American Historical Review*, civ (1999), 426–500.

28 Graham Gargett and Geraldine Sheridan (eds), *Ireland and the French Enlightenment, 1700–1800* (Basingstoke, 1999); Máire Kennedy, *French books in eighteenth-century Ireland* (Oxford, 2002).

29 Graham Gargett, 'Voltaire's reception in Ireland', in Gargett and Sheridan (eds), *Ireland*, pp 67–89; Michael O'Dea, 'Rousseau in eighteenth-century Irish journals', in ibid., pp 90–106; Seamus Deane, 'Montesquieu and Burke' in ibid., pp 47–66.

30 There were also many eager Irish readers of Madame de Genlis, largely because of her daughter's marriage to Lord Edward FitzGerald. Not a philosopher, she was a novelist, memoirist and deeply unreliable gossip, who was also opposed to the Revolution. Emily Lady Bellamont reported to her sister Lady Sophia FitzGerald in London on 11 Apr. 1793; 'I am deep in Madame de Sillery's *Journal of the Princes*. It is a foolish book but curiosity makes one read it on little Pamela's account and I make her tell me 100 things about them all. She confesses it was a very *sauvage* education ... Yet she talked of it with much admiration for she does quite adore Madame de Sillery and says there's no such woman upon earth'; FitzGerald papers: N.L.I., Ms 35,004 (7).

31 Mary Pollard, *A dictionary of members of the Dublin book trade, 1550–1800* (London, 2000); Hugh Fenning, 'Cork imprints of Catholic historical interest, 1723–1804: A provisional check-list', in *J.C.H.A.S.*, c (1995), 129–48; Hugh Fenning, 'Dublin imprints of Catholic interest, 1740–1759', in *Collect. Hib.*, xl (1999), 65–116; 'Dublin imprints of Catholic interest, 1700–1739' in *Collect. Hib.*, xxxix (1998), 106–54; Magda and Rolf Loeber, *A checklist of Irish fiction, 1700–1900* (Notre Dame, forthcoming).

32 Niall Ó Ciosáin, *Print and popular culture in Ireland 1750–1850* (Basingstoke, 1997).

time-lag. This conceptualization specifies the relationship between centre and periphery as that between original and copy. That conceptualization is itself rooted in enlightened thinking. In its pursuit of cosmopolitan universalism, enlightenment gave short shrift to minority or regional cultures (Gibbons, chapter 3). At best, it dealt with them elegaically, at worst with venomous ethnocidal intent. Either way, local languages and their embedded cultures were consigned to the rubbish-skip of history. The Scottish Enlightenment invented stadialism and its supercessionist model as a means of dealing with marginal cultures, most glaringly with its own Highland fringe.[33] The Ossian debate resonated in European culture because it touched on this sore point of cultural obsolescence as the price of progress.[34] Obliteration of cultural difference was evident on the aggressively expanding margins of all the powerful states of the 1790s. In France, Britain and the United States, Vendéeans, Highland Scots and Native Americans felt its cutting edge.[35] This harsh treatment was meted out indiscriminately on both the revolutionary and counter-revolutionary margins.

In political terms, the thrust of the Scottish Enlightenment was unionist: in Ireland, enlightenment was potentially separatist. It argued for cultural parity of esteem, most audibly in the public staging of the Belfast Harp Festival of 1792.[36] This initiative built on a decade of cultural retrieval of the Irish past in the English language, notably by William Crawford, Charles Vallancey, Joseph Cooper Walker and Charlotte Brooke. Barrington noted of the 1780s that 'a revolution in literature was made auxiliary to a revolution in liberty'.[37] The United

---

33 Ronald Meek, *Social science and the ignoble savage* (Cambridge, 1976); George Caffentziz, 'On the Scottish origin of civilisation', in Sylvia Federici (ed.), *Enduring Western civilization* (Westport, Conn., 1995), pp 13–36: Christopher Berry, *Social theory of the Scottish enlightenment* (Edinburgh, 1997)

34 Fiona Stafford, *The sublime savage: James Macpherson and the poems of Ossian* (Edinburgh, 1988); Hugh Gaskell (ed.), *Ossian revisited* (Edinburgh, 1991); Clare O'Halloran, 'Irish re-creations of the Gaelic past: The challenge of Macpherson's *Ossian*', in *Past & Present*, cxxiv (1989), 69–95.

35 Anthony Wallace, *Jefferson and the Indians: The tragic fate of the first Americans* (Cambridge, Mass., 1999); Allan Macinnis, *Clanship, commerce and the house of Stuart* (East Linton, 1996).

36 A.T.Q. Stewart, 'The harp new-strung: nationalism, culture and the United Irishmen', in Oliver MacDonagh and W.F. Mandle (eds), *Ireland and Irish-Australia* (London, 1986), pp 258–69. It should be noted that this treatment entirely misunderstands the nature of the cultural politics of the United Irishmen. A similar incomprehension mars Colin Kidd's account of late eighteenth-century Ireland, as when for example he describes Henry Flood's bequest to endow a chair and purchase manuscripts for the study of the Irish language at Trinity College as 'bizarre': Colin Kidd, *British identities before nationalism: Ethnicity and nationhood in the Atlantic world 1600–1800* (Cambridge, 1999), p. 176; Mary Helen Thuente, *The harp restrung: The United Irishmen and the rise of literary nationalism* (Syracuse, 1994); Carol Moloney, *The Irish music manuscripts of Edward Bunting (1773–1843): An introduction and catalogue* (Dublin, 2000). This is an indispensable guide to an under-utilized source.

37 Barrington, *Rise and fall*, p. 101. See H. Goto, 'The dawn of anti-imperialism: Irish radicals and their liberal projects for the modernisation of Ireland in the 1780s–90s' (unpublished Ph.D. dissertation, University of Dublin, 1998).

Irishmen repudiated the (divisive) colonial past and promoted in its place an (inclusive) national narrative of Ireland. They defended cultural autonomy, whether in the Irish language or Ulster-Scots mode, and sought in culture as in religion to escape the baleful binary of native and newcomer. This project accelerated in the 1790s but it was already under way from the 1770s: if a precise moment is to be identified as the origins of this new sensibility, it could be located in the adverse reaction to Richard Twiss' account of Ireland published in 1775.[38] Several thousand chamber pots were manufactured with Twiss's face on the bottom, 'painted by an eminent artist of Cork'.[39] In Ennis, County Clare, the book was publicly burned after an elaborate procession through the town led by six shoe boys, followed by six Connaught boys singing a requiem, two young sweeps with a cur dog in a coal box, the book dangling around its neck, then 'Jack Ketch' with a bundle of wet straw on his arms and finally six chimney sweeps. The procession reached the gallows at noon where the book, well smeared with soot, was burned by the common hangman, to the acclamation of several hundred spectators.[40] This nationalist turn received greater impetus from the support of many Volunteers, a finding that undermines the current treatment of the 1790s as a radical departure in Irish politics, carefully fenced off from the rest of the century.[41] The burgeoning efforts to identify a deeper Irish dimension in the 1780s are evident in contemporary historiography, in attitudes to the law, and in a redefinition of the Whig tradition in Ireland.[42] It is in the

38 Richard Twiss, *A tour in Ireland in 1775* (London, 1776).
39 *F.L.J.*, 10–14 Aug. 1776. The next issue went on: 'We hope that all apothecaries will not enhance the price of jalop [laxatives], as all the people of Ireland and elsewhere intend taking it, since Mr Twiss's picture is put in so convenient a place for the pleasure of ornamenting that false, detestable and would-be tour writer, oftener than nature requires': *F.L.J.*, 14–17 Aug. 1776.
40 *F.L.J.*, 28–31 Aug. 1776.
41 Close attention to subscription lists would show this clearly. See, for example, the lists attached to R. Pool and J. Cash, *Views of the principal buildings of Dublin* (Dublin, 1780); William Crawford, *A history of Ireland* (Strabane, 1783); *Volunteer's companion* (Dublin, 1784); Thomas Sheridan, *A general dictionary of the English language* (Dublin, 1784); William Wilson, *Post-chaise companion or traveller's directory through Ireland* (Dublin, 1786); Mervyn Archdall, *Monasticon Hibernicum* (Dublin, 1786); John Ferrar, *History of Limerick* (Dublin, 1787); Amyas Griffith, *Miscellaneous tracts* (Dublin, 1788); Robert Hitchcock, *Historical view of the Irish stage* (Dublin, 1788); Charlotte Brooke, *Reliques of Irish poetry* (Dublin, 1789); *Universal magazine* (Dublin, 1789); William Guthrie, *Improved system of modern geography* (Dublin, 1789); *The Patriot soldier* (Belfast, 1789); John Lodge, *The peerage of Ireland* (Dublin, 1789); Henrietta Battier, *Poems* (Dublin, 1791); William Beaufort, *Memoir of a map of Ireland* (Dublin, 1792); *Sentimental and Masonic Magazine* (Dublin, 1792); Ouladah Equiano, *Interesting narrative* (Dublin, 1791); Roderick O'Flaherty, *Ogyia* (Dublin, 1793); *Anthologica Hibernica* (Dublin, 1793–4); James Mullala, *View of Irish affairs since the revolution of 1688 to 1795* (Dublin, 1795); and John Ferrar, *A view of ancient and modern Dublin* (Dublin, 1796).
42 Breandán Mac Suibhne, 'Whiskey, potatoes and Paddies: Volunteering and the construction of the Irish nation in northwest Ulster 1778–1782', in Peter Jupp and Eoin Magennis (eds), *Crowds in Ireland, 1720–1920* (London, 2000), pp 45–82; Peter Smyth, 'The Volunteers and parliament 1779–84', in Thomas Bartlett and David Hayton (eds), *Penal era and golden age* (Belfast, 1979), pp

1780s, for example, that both the proceedings of the Irish parliament and Irish law reports first began to be published.[43]

Undoubtedly the horizons of the republican imaginary palpably expanded in the hothouse conditions of the American and French Revolutions. Renewed study of the Irish impact of the American Revolution is required: it has been neglected in favour of the French one,[44] accentuating an artificially sharp divide between the 1780s and the 1790s in Irish historiography.[45] A typical Ulster response was that of John Caldwell (Snr.) of County Antrim, writing to a relative in Philadelphia in 1774:

> The spirit which evinces itself on your side of the wide waters is cheering to the mind: it is pleasing to turn from the melancholy but true picture of our native country to that of your adopted country and to observe among you a revival of that opposition to tyranny, that attachment to the free and liberal principles of civil and religious liberty which animated our ancestors, but which seemed almost annihilated in the breasts of their descendants.[46]

To the top-down and anglocentric Atlantic Revolution discovered in the 1960s, we might now want to add red (bottom-up) and green (Irish) Atlantic tinges.[47]

113–36. Still useful is Patrick Rogers, *The Irish Volunteers and Catholic Emancipation* (London, 1934).

43 The *Parliamentary Register* began publication in 1784: see *The parliamentary register or history of the proceedings and debates of the House of Commons in Ireland, 9 October, 1781–18 May 1797*, 17 vols, fac. rep. (Bristol, 2001): W.N. Osborough, 'Puzzles from Irish law reporting history', in *Studies in Irish legal history* (Dublin, 1999), pp 193–212.

44 Maurice O'Connell, *Irish politics and social conflict in the age of the American Revolution* (Philadelphia, 1965), a pioneering work in its time, is now seriously dated. See also Homer Calkin, 'American influence in Ireland 1760 to 1780', in *Pennsylvania Magazine of History* and *Biography*, lxxi (1947), 103–20; Maurice Bric, 'Ireland, America and the reassessment of a special relationship 1760–83', in *E.C.I.*, ix (1996), 88–119; Marilyn Westerkamp, 'Absentee landlords and squatters rights: The Scots-Irish backcountry and the American Revolution', in J. Morgan (ed.), *The cultures of Europe: the Irish contribution* (Belfast, 1994), pp 69–86; Vincent Morley, 'The American Revolution and opinion in Ireland, 1760–83' (unpublished Ph.D. thesis, Liverpool University, 1999).

45 For the sharp emphasis on the novelty of the 1790s, see Sean Connolly, 'The United Irishmen at Trinity', in *Bullán*, i, 1 (1994), 148–50; Toby Barnard, 'Goodbye to old Ireland', in *Hist. Jn.*, xxxvi, 4 (1993), 909–28. Connolly has claimed: 'The tensions of the 1790s should not be read backwards to characterise the whole post-Williamite era' (*Hist. Ir.*, Summer 2001, p. 46). This puts enormous pressure on the impact of the French Revolution to explain Irish radicalism in the 1790s but it begs the question as to why Ireland, but not Scotland, Wales or England (which were at least as exposed to French influence) should have experienced such a massive breakdown in that decade.

46 Cited in [John Caldwell (Jnr.)], 'Exiled to New York: A United Irishman's memoirs', in *New York Irish History*, xiii (1999), 8. His sons Richard and John became United Irish officers and the whole family ended up exiled in the United States after 1798.

47 R. Palmer, *The age of the democratic revolution: A political history of Europe and America*,

Recent work has witnessed the transition from the old republicanism of Robbins and Pocock to the new republicanism of Shklar and Livesey.[48] By the 1790s republicanism had become an accepted political framework for conceptualizing modern commercial society (Livesey, chapter 1). The American Revolution eased the transition of republicanism from outmoded classical theory to modern reality. As William Sampson phrased it, 'The American Revolution had reduced the theories of the great philosophers of England, France and other countries into practice.'[49] Arthur O'Connor, in a typical reaction, described the American experiment as 'the greatest epoch that has happened from the fall of liberty in Greece and Rome'.[50]

There is room for an explicit treatment of Irish 'new republicans,' including Arthur O'Connor, Theobald Wolfe Tone, Thomas Russell, Henry Joy McCracken and James Hope.[51] This research requires a shift in emphasis, adding New British, European and Atlantic perspectives to the anglocentric focus of earlier practitioners.[52] A nuanced awareness of chronology is necessary, attending to the rapid oscillations of the French Revolution and the shifting balance of advantage in the fluid geopolitics of the 1790s. The success or failure of the republican project in Ireland in that decade ultimately depended on the wider Franco-British struggle: in 1798, that outcome was by no means self-evident to any thinking European of the period. The period between 1775 and 1824 was

     1760–1800, 2 vols (Princeton, 1959–64); Peter Linebaugh and Marcus Rediker, *The many-headed Hydra: The hidden history of the revolutionary Atlantic* (London, 2000); Kevin Whelan, 'The Green Atlantic: Radical reciprocities between Ireland and America, 1789–1812', in Kathleen Wilson (ed.), *Crossings: The new imperial history* (Cambridge, forthcoming); Nini Rodgers, 'Ireland and the black Atlantic in the eighteenth century', in *I.H.S.*, cxxvi (2000), 174–92.

48 Caroline Robbins, *The eighteenth-century commonwealth man* (Cambridge, Mass., 1959); J.G. Pocock, *The Machiavellian moment: Florentine political thought and the Atlantic republic* (Princeton, 1975); Judith Shklar, 'Montesquieu and the new republicanism' in G. Bock, Q. Skinner and M. Viroli (eds), *Machiavelli and republicanism* (Cambridge, 1990), pp 265–79; James Livesey, *Making democracy in the French Revolution* (Cambridge, Mass., 2001), pp 48–87.

49 Sampson, *Memoirs*, p. 311.

50 Hayter Hames, *Arthur O'Connor*, p. 31.

51 C.J. Woods (ed.), *Journals and memoirs of Thomas Russell 1791–95* (Dublin, 1991); Jean Agnew (ed.), *The Drennan–McTier letters 1776–1819*, 3 vols (Dublin, 1998–2000); T.W. Moody, R.B. McDowell and C.J. Woods (eds), *The writings of T.W. Tone*, 2 vols (Oxford, 1998–2001); Arthur O'Connor, *The state of Ireland* (ed.) James Livesey (Dublin, 1998). This should be read alongside its companion volume *The State of Great Britain* (Paris, 1804). A popular biography of O'Connor is Jane Hayter Hames, *Arthur O'Connor, United Irishman* (Cork, 2001). In 1807 O'Connor married Eliza, daughter of Condorcet, the leading French new republican, and he later co-edited his *Oeuvres* (Paris, 1847–49). On French new republicanism, see Richard Whatmore, *Republicanism and the French Revolution* (Oxford, 2001).

52 For an effort to broaden the interpretive frameworks for eighteenth-century Ireland, see James Livesey, 'Acts of union and disunion: Ireland in Atlantic and European contexts' in Dáire Keogh and Kevin Whelan (eds), *Acts of union* (Dublin, 2001), pp 95–105. One of the few books to treat the English context of the United Irishmen with appropriate seriousness is Nancy Curtin, *The United Irishmen: Popular politics in Ulster and Dublin 1791–98* (Oxford, 1994).

also one of imperial implosion. The British had made significant concessions in Quebec in 1774 and been ejected out of what became the United States soon after. There was a notable hiatus before the onset of the second British empire. The Spanish empire in South America subsequently collapsed, precipitating a rash of new republics.[53] William Drennan, then a young medical student in Edinburgh, observed after the battle of Saratoga: 'It is probable that future historians will date the fall of the British empire from the 16th of October [17]77. No object can be thought of more melancholy than a great empire that has thus outlived itself and is now degenerating into a state of political dotage, prophetical of its final dissolution.'[54] In the 1790s, therefore, the concepts of both monarchism and imperialism were under enormous pressure.[55] Only historical hindsight of heroic proportions has doomed the French (and with them their partners in revolution the United Irishmen) to *inevitable* defeat.

53 David Abernethy, *The dynamics of global dominance: European overseas empires 1415–1980* (New Haven, 2001), pp 64–80.
54 William Drennan to Martha McTier, 13 Dec. 1777 in *Drennan–McTier corr.*, i, p. 29.
55 Marilyn Morris, *The British monarchy and the French Revolution* (New Haven, 1998).

I

From the ancient constitution to democracy: Transformations in republicanism in the eighteenth century

JAMES LIVESEY

On 10 April 1783 the Genevan revolutionary Etienne Clavière wrote from Dublin to his friend Jacques-Louis Brissot in London. Clavière had washed up in Ireland after the failure of the republican revolution he had led in Geneva the previous year.[1] Dublin, in the aftermath of the concession of legislative independence to the Irish parliament, was an attractive place of exile for a republican, and he advised Brissot to

> Forget everything you think you know about Ireland, you can learn nothing of it from books. In fact you should write a new book about the place which would be of as much interest to the Irish as to foreigners as they try to overcome their evil history.[2]

The thrust of this letter to Brissot was to invite him to come and open an academy which would compete with Trinity College 'which has the great drawback of being in the capital, where the students are palpably corrupted'; his plan being to open another university beyond the fleshpots of Dublin which would offer a less corrupting influence to the youth of the country.[3] However, Clavière's interests in Ireland went beyond the possibilities of gainful employment for his friends or the reclamation of its youth. What he underlined to Brissot was the compatibility of the *moeurs* of the people of Ireland with their own greater political project, the creation of a modern republic:

> There is tremendous warmth in the people, everything here tends toward the greatest prosperity, in fact the population have greater need of being

1 The revolution ended with the intervention of the French for which Clavière blamed Vergennes.
2 Archives Nationales, Paris, T* 646¹.
3 A.N. T* 646¹, Clavière to Brissot de Warville, 10 Apr. 1783.

14

> restrained than encouraged, in a word, you can work here in a way that
> will bring honour to you and to the country.

He underlined his meaning with his final point: in Ireland there was all the
potential of America, without the inconvenience of going so far from Europe.

This communication between the future minister for finance of the French
republic and the future leading light of the Girondins is interesting in itself, and
for what it reveals about the possibilities of Irish politics in the late eighteenth
century, as seen by one of the most acute political minds of the era. But the correspondence, and indeed all the documents around the project to build a 'New
Geneva' in Passage East, are particularly fascinating for what they reveal about
the republican imagination in the years before the French Revolution. While
projecting their new republican microcosm, Clavière and Brissot used none of
the distinctive language or concepts of Civic Humanism, the intellectual tradition most often associated with republicanism.[4] The terms of 'real whiggery' –
the opposition of virtue to luxury, the distrust of trade and its subsequent confusion of social function, the defence of agrarian simplicity – are all absent from
this, and indeed all the subsequent texts of what became the most prolific republican publishing partnership of the 1780s.[5] In fact Clavière was so far from the
traditional republican distrust of commerce that he held that republican societies
are commercially the most successful societies. His commitment to this idea
went so far that he rejected his partner Amy Melly's scheme to compete against
the Geneva watch-making manufacture by cutting prices: no clever cost-cutting
manoeuvres would help the new colony establish itself in the watch-making
market because 'talented men seek free countries because of their pride and the
spirit of independence which their abilities inspire in them all the arts distinguish those who exercise them, those who stand out from the mass who work
only with primary materials have no other native land but that of liberty. If this
is not true then whatever we do the *négatifs* will retain the manufacture.'[6] The
arts and manufactures, trade and fashion were, we have assumed, understood to

4   The argument was most famously developed in Caroline Robins, *The eighteenth century common-
    wealthman: Studies in the transmission, development and circumstances of English liberal thought from
    the Restoration of Charles II until the war with the Thirteen Colonies* (Cambridge, Mass., 1959), and
    given definitive form in J.G.A. Pocock, *The Machiavellian moment: Florentine political thought and
    the Atlantic Republican tradition* (Princeton, NJ, 1975).
5   Their most important collaboration was, *De la France et des États-Unis, ou de l'importance de la
    révolution de l'Amérique pour le bonheur de la France; des rapports de ce Royaume et des États-Unis,
    des avantages réciproques qu'ils peuvent retirer de leurs liaisons de commerce, et enfin de la situation
    actuelle des États-Unis* (Paris, 1788). On the two see D.L. Wick, *A conspiracy of well-intentioned
    men: The Society of Thirty and the French Revolution* (New York, 1987), pp 218–23; Jean Béné-
    truy, *L'atelier de Mirabeau: Quatre proscrits Génévois dans la tourmente révolutionnaire* (Geneva,
    1962); Robert Darnton, 'Trends in radical propaganda on the eve of the French Revolution
    (1782–1788)', (unpublished D.Phil., Oxford, 1964), pp 91–232.
6   A.N. T* 646¹, Clavière to Amy Melly, 12 December 1782.

be incompatible with republican virtue. How can Clavière have imagined he could create a republican, virtuous, but commercial society?

Like Brissot with Ireland, we must forget everything we think we know about republicanism before we can answer that question. For twentieth century people republicanism is a variant of nationalism; it stands for a sovereign people representing itself through the forms of a constitution. It thus seems to derive directly from Italian civic humanism, the theory of the functioning of a free, that is to say independent, popular state.[7] This is an illusion. Civic humanism failed so spectacularly in the seventeenth century, even in the Netherlands and England, that it was not a credible theory of civil order. There was little development of republicanism as a theory in the aftermath of the failed Dutch republic.[8] Even in England, which had developed a strong and self-conscious republican movement, the settlement of 1688 marked a turning-point after which republicanism settled down into the diffuse sentiment in which a safe opposition might be articulated.[9] The common assumption of early eighteenth-century political writers was that republicanism fomented factionalism and civil discord. Civic humanist rhetoric survived only in odd places, such as the Bolingbroke circle, among American colonists or Presbyterian conservatives battling against moderate reformers; outside these fringes, the European political imagination in 1750 was dominated by monarchies and animated by the concerns of natural jurisprudence, not issues of representation and citizenship.[10] Natural jurisprudence, or modern natural law theory, approached the problems of politics by trying to work out the mutual rights and obligations between sovereign and subject.[11] The centrality of individual rights and the cosmopolitanism of natural jurisprudence, be it in the hands of Grotius, Selden or Pufendorf, was at a remove from the classical republican emphasis on the particular virtues of particular communities. Communities and individuals still understanding themselves through civic

---

7 On the Italian roots of this ideology see Quentin Skinner, *The foundations of modern political thought*, i: *The Renaissance* (Cambridge, 1978), pp 6–11, 70–107; R. Witt, 'The rebirth of the concept of republican liberty in Italy', in A. Mollo and J. Tedeschi (eds), *Renaissance studies in honor of Hans Baron* (Florence, 1971), pp 173–200.

8 E.H. Mulier, 'The language of seventeenth century republicanism in the United Provinces: Dutch or European', in Anthony Pagden (ed.), *The languages of political theory in early modern Europe* (Cambridge, 1987), pp 192–4.

9 Blair Worden, 'The revolution of 1688–89 and the English republican tradition', in Jonathan Israel (ed.), *The Anglo-Dutch moment: Essays on the Glorious Revolution and its world impact* (Cambridge, 1991), p. 269.

10 Thomas Pangle has asserted that the very idea of a coherent 'classic republicanism' makes no sense given the heterogeneity of the sources from which it is supposed to have been constructed: Thomas Pangle, *The spirit of modern republicanism: The moral vision of the American founders and the philosophy of Locke* (Chicago, 1988), pp 35–6.

11 The history of Natural Jurisprudence is heavily indebted to the work of Richard Tuck. See principally, *Natural rights theories: Their origin and development* (Cambridge, 1979) and *Philosophy and government, 1572–1651* (Cambridge, 1993).

humanist rhetoric, or variants of it, were marginal and vulnerable. The Scottish Enlightenment was fundamentally an effort by reform-minded ministers to rescue the Church of Scotland from such a debilitating antiquarianism. It is an irony of history that John Witherspoon, whose attachment to the older politics of Scottish Presbyterianism was such that he emigrated to found a new academy in the wilds of North America, should have found himself delivering 'The Dominion of Providence' to possibly the last sizeable group of Anglophones who still thought in terms of virtue, liberty and the rights of free-born Englishmen.[12] Everywhere else in the North Atlantic world, even the rhetoric of the ancient constitution was by now legal or social rather than political.[13]

Clearly, Clavière's republic had nothing to do with the antiquarianism of 'real whiggery'. But if it was not the largely discredited idea of civic humanism, what kind of civic commitment was intended by republicans? Clavière, along with other republicans of the late eighteenth century, was the beneficiary of three factors which revived, or rather reinvented, republicanism in the eighteenth century – the theoretical reformulation of political theory in the hands of Montesquieu, Rousseau and the Scottish moral sentiment philosophers; the American Revolution; and the French Revolution.[14] It would be impossible in the space available to describe the complexity of the interactions of the theoretical and practical moments of this process, but the important elements of the new theory of republicanism can be isolated, figures who participated in this development in Ireland can be identified, and the degree to which the presence of what Judith Skhlar has called 'the new republicanism' affected the development of Irish political culture can be assessed.[15]

The most obvious change in the political and social world for eighteenth century people was the emergence of commercial societies, societies in which increasing numbers of people were engaged in market relations.[16] The new republicanism directly addressed this new reality. It refocused the question of what structures would generate civic commitment among the population away from the state and toward society, itself a new object for political theory in the

12 On 'The Dominion of Providence', see R.B. Sher, 'Witherspoon's *Dominion of Providence* and the Scottish Jeremiad tradition', in R.B. Sher and Andrew Smitten (eds), *Scotland and America in the age of the Enlightenment* (Edinburgh, 1990), pp 46–64. Witherspoon was Madison's teacher at Princeton.
13 Shelley Burtt, *Virtue transformed: Political argument in England, 1688–1740* (Cambridge, 1992), pp 8–9.
14 For an analysis of the contrasts between the French and American developments, see Patrice Higonnet, *Sister republics: The origins of French and American republicanism* (Cambridge, Mass., 1988).
15 Judith Skhlar, 'Montesquieu and the new Republicanism', in Gisela Bock, Quentin Skinner and Maurizio Viroli (eds), *Machiavelli and republicanism* (Cambridge, 1990), pp 265–79.
16 For extended discussion of this theme, see John Brewer (ed.), *Consumption and the world of goods* (London, 1996).

period. The new republicanism was a theory about how society works and how it should be represented, not a theory about the structures of a virtuous republic. Its animating question was to discover the means by which the population could acquire self-command, which it understood to be good *mores*, or to use the French phrase that retains the force of the original idea, *bonnes moeurs*. *Moeurs*, a term that has dropped out of the English-language lexicon of political thought, refers to the habits and customs of a people, and their beliefs about those habits and customs; it is, in effect, political culture. Eighteenth century republicanism was a theory to define the best kind of political culture for a modern commercial nation.

Montesquieu was the first to capitalize on the perception that the languages of politics current in the eighteenth century, the available ways of understanding political life, simply did not represent the contemporary political world he saw around him. David Hume, in his essays of 1742, had come to the same idea that would animate Montesquieu's work, that a world of paper money, extensive long-distance trade, mingling of the genders, rising consumption and large unitary states did not respond to the opposition of virtue to luxury. Practice had far outstripped theory. However, for all his insight, Hume did not, or could not, escape the fascination of the ancient virtues. Even in his later *Enquiry concerning the principles of morals*, he was still deferring to 'the ancients, the heroes in philosophy, as well as those in war and patriotism, [who] have a grandeur and force of sentiment, which astonishes our narrow souls, and is rashly rejected as extravagant and supernatural'.[17] Hume thought the ancient virtues were inapplicable to modern social life, and consequently interpreted social life in terms of the utility of those engaged in it. Where Montesquieu outstripped Hume was in identifying a new way of understanding the value of modern social life without becoming trapped in an impossible nostalgia for the old, uncorrupted, world.

Montesquieu turned the assumptions of political theory on their head. The Aristotelian assumption that the character of a people was determined by the form of the political constitution under which they lived had never been seriously challenged. The *Spirit of the laws*, in a brilliant *reductio*, showed that social structure created the conditions for political constitution, that society was prior. This was a revolutionary idea, for it raised the prospect that the principles of political legitimacy were not exhausted by the old triad of monarchy, aristocracy and democracy, but might be as various as the forms of social life that humans could create.[18] Montesquieu was not content to operate a revolution in the cognitive basis of political science, but also proposed a normative revision of the basis of the understanding of liberty. Where the ancients understood liberty to be the

17 David Hume, *Enquiry concerning the principles of morals* (Oxford, 1975), pp 256–7.
18 Tzedan Todorov, *On human diversity: Nationalism, racism and exoticism in French thought* (Cambridge, Mass., 1993), p. 369.

power to participate directly in the making and the application of the law, the moderns understood it as the representation of their interests allied to their freedom to develop the private sphere of intimacy. Liberty was the duty 'to do what one should want to do and in no way being constrained to do what one should not want to do'.[19] Montesquieu concentrated on identifying the *moeurs* which were necessary to sustain the curious complexity of such a system of modern liberty. Every form of government had its principle, which gave it life and made it legitimate. For pure, that is ancient, democracies, it was virtue, for aristocracies, honour, and modern commercial monarchies were moved by the principle of moderation. The best example he found of such a system was England, and from it he derived much of what is commonly known of his theory of politics, such as the division of powers.[20] Montesquieu's description of England was effectively as a representative republic under monarchical forms, a state of liberty, but not one in which the citizen was consumed by his political rôle.

Montesquieu opened a fresh ground for political theory and generated a new understanding of republicanism; however, he was no republican himself. His direct legacy is liberalism in its many guises, not modern republicanism.[21] The work of generating a specifically republican understanding of the new world of the eighteenth century was done by Rousseau who took this new insight that modern social life demanded a specific set of *bonnes moeurs*, gave those *moeurs* a name, autonomy, and generated an argument for the institutional context necessary for autonomy, or, to use a term that was more familiar to eighteenth century thinkers working from the vocabulary of neo–stoicism, self-command. Rousseau argued that if the moral capacity of every person in modern society, the very ground of their liberty, was not institutionally protected, that capacity would be erased by the plasticity and dynamism of modern social relations.[22] The institutional context identified by Rousseau as the necessary guarantor of modern liberty was democracy, embedded in popular sovereignty. This in turn was to become the most contested ground of modern politics. Rousseau was the first thinker who specifically argued that republican democracy was the definitive political form for modern life.

Montesquieu turned the assumptions of political theory on their head, and Rousseau in turn inverted the new assumptions about social theory. He exploited a line of weakness in the fundamental understanding of the nature of modern life promoted by Montesquieu. Montesquieu had assumed that the categorical difference between political life and social life would automatically be sustained

---

19 Montesquieu, *The spirit of the laws* (Cambridge, 1989), Book 11, Chapter 3, p. 155.
20 Ibid., Book 11, Chapter 6, pp 156–66; Book 19, Chapter 27, pp 325–33.
21 See Thomas Pangle, *Montesquieu's philosophy of liberalism: A commentary on the spirit of the laws* (Chicago, 1973).
22 This was a revelation for Kant and the point of origin for his moral theory: J.B. Schneewind, *The invention of autonomy: A history of modern moral philosophy* (Cambridge, 1998), pp 487–92.

under any regime committed to law. Thus he was indifferent to the actual governing structures, though he thought monarchies more easily sustained. As long as the difference was retained, no great threat to liberty could arise from the political system. In fact at times he portrayed the sphere of politics as one of frustration and inertia, almost entirely without meaning:

> As each individual, always independent, would largely follow his own caprices and fantasies, he would often change parties; he would abandon one and leave all his friends in order to bind himself to another in which he would find all his enemies; and often, in this nation, he would forget both the laws of friendship and those of hatred.[23]

Rousseau argued that though the categories of public and private life were logically separate, the institutions of public and private life were mutually interdependent. He asserted that the space between public institutions and private life, where values were forged (an area, following Jurgen Habermas, that we have come to term 'the public sphere'), was the most important element in the constitution of a society because it was there that identity was constructed. The capriciousness that Montesquieu understood to be the sign that the real interests of moderns were ultimately expressed elsewhere than in the political sphere was understood by Rousseau to the greatest danger to the ability of modern people to be free.[24] In his novels, occasional writings and developed philosophical writings he argued that self-command could only be guaranteed by a rigorous equality. Thus, paradoxically, working from rigorously individualist premises, Rousseau was driven to denounce every concrete feature of modern social life, especially the social equality of the sexes, in defence of the principle of individual autonomy. Chapter 19 of the *Spirit of the laws* praised the modern delight in fashion as a necessary device to enhance sociability and social cohesion. Rousseau, who was a far more reflexive thinker than Montesquieu, argued that the inauthenticity of the world of fashion, to take just one target of his wrath, would eventually rob modern individuals of the sense of their individuality, of their knowledge of themselves as moral agents. The closing pages of his *Social contract* portrayed the mechanisms that would impel all commercial societies to barbarism, where the very idea of law and right had collapsed into force and power. This was the reason for his famous assertion that only poor, small, agrarian states could be virtuous. Modern individuals could only be saved if they abandoned all the distinctive features of their modern lives.

23 Montesquieu, *Spirit of the laws*, Book 19, Chapter 27, p. 326.
24 Rousseau's criticism of the creation of false needs through the system of appearances in modern life has been most fully analysed in Jean Starobinski, *Jean-Jacques Rousseau: Transparency and obstacle* (Chicago, 1988).

It might seem strange to us that Rousseau's apocalyptic vision of modern life could have been so attractive to the beneficiaries of the commercial world of the middle eighteenth century. It is tempting to see the attraction of Rousseau in a nostalgic yearning for an imagined cohesive golden age of simplicity and morality. Eighteenth-century readers were far more sophisticated in their appreciation of his texts than this. They recognized the acuity of the question he had posed; what were the structural tendencies in modern life that either promoted or destroyed the capacity for self command, for independent moral action? Adam Smith, in 1756, acknowledged that this was the central problem of the 'science of man', and that on the face of it Rousseau's description of the debilitating effects of societies without virtue was only too accurate:

> It belongs not to my subject to show, how from such a disposition arises so much real indifference for good and evil, with so many fine discourses of morality; how everything being reduced to appearances, everything becomes factitious and acted; honour, friendship, virtue, and often even vice itself, of which we have at last found out the secret of being vain; how in one word always demanding of others what we are, and never daring to ask ourselves the question, in the midst of so much philosophy, so much humanity so much politeness, and so many sublime maxims we have nothing but a deceitful and frivolous exterior; honour without virtue, reason without wisdom, and pleasure without happiness.[25]

Rousseau's antidote to the corruptions of modern life was unpalatable, but his diagnosis of the disease was impeccable. Political theory after Rousseau had at its heart the fundamentally republican question of the autonomy of the citizen.

There were many responses to Rousseau's question. Smith's own idea that the market might create disciplining structures that would inculcate civility and self-control is well known. Less appreciated is Diderot's exploration of the aesthetic as a realm that might offer grounded values to modern commercial society, though the later development of this idea by Schiller has been enormously influential. However, the most interesting, and most republican, response to Rousseau was Adam Ferguson's development of the idea of civil society. Ferguson was in some sense overdetermined as the figure to rescue civic values in a commercial age. A son of the manse, he was born at Logariat, in Perthshire, right on the Highland line. He straddled the modernizing, polite culture of Lowland Scotland and the martial world of the north. He fought, if an army chaplain fights, at the battle of Fontenoy, with a Highland regiment and was afterward professor of moral philosophy at Edinburgh University.[26] In *An essay on the histo-*

---

25 Adam Smith, 'Letter to the *Edinburgh Review*', in *Essays on philosophical subjects*, ed. W.P.D. Wrightman (Indianapolis, 1982), p. 254.

26 When the Irish Brigade broke through the British lines, he allegedly threw away his collar and went into the battle.

ry of civil society, first published in 1767, he gave a name to the particularly modern context in which the independence and vigour of the Highlander might be replicated, without the poverty and incessant warfare that bred his distinctive virtues. His effort to unite his own experience was also the most perceptive account of where and how self-command, the distinctive feature of the republican citizen, might be fostered and upheld.

Ferguson's coinage of civil society has attracted much attention of late and the idea is modish, but the recent discussion does not really replicate the eighteenth-century debate. There is no one dominant idea of civil society; liberals defend it as a completely apolitical space of association, a counter-weight to politics, while radicals develop the notion of the interdependence of a democratic political order and the existence of those associational networks.[27] However, the contemporary discussion is relatively impoverished by comparison with the eighteenth-century development of the concept; in particular the complexity of Ferguson's position still escapes it.[28] He was not celebrating private life, nor pointing out the necessity for countervailing institutions to the state; rather he was looking for the loyalties and connections that might tempt modern people out of self-interest and into commitment. He found these in associations and, most importantly, in the competition and enmity among the associations characteristic of modern social life. Ferguson ended up arguing that the greatest threat to individuality in modern conditions was concord and peace. In totally peaceful conditions, men would consult only their private interest and the individual utility of their actions. As long as there was contestation in the public sphere, individuals could be motivated to unself-regarding action. Ferguson then devoted much of his attention to understanding the conditions of limited competition and emnity in modern life. He found this linked to the extent of political liberty, arguing that modern commerce and liberty could only fully emerge if they were united with the widest and most democratic participation in political life. Nor was Ferguson under any illusion that a commercial society characterized by a large number of particular associations would necessarily be a pretty sight:

> In states where property, distinction and pleasure are thrown out as baits to the imagination, and incentives to passion, the public seems to rely for the preservation of its political life, on the degree of emulation and jealousy with which parties mutually oppose and restrain each other. The desires of preferment and profit in the breast of the citizen, are the motives from which he is excited to enter on public affairs, and are the considerations which direct his political conduct. The suppression there-

27 Ernest Gellner, *Conditions of liberty: Civil society and its rivals* (London, 1994), p. 55; M. Walzer, 'The civil society argument', in Ronald Beimer (ed.), *Theorizing citizenship* (Albany, N.Y., 1995), p. 170.
28 Jean Cohen and Andrew Arato, *Civil society and political theory* (Cambridge, Mass., 1992), p. 83.

fore, of ambition, of party-animosity, and of public envy, is probably, in
every such case, not a reformation, but a symptom of weakness, and a
prelude to more sordid pursuits and ruinous amusements.[29]

Civil society was not a system but a space for Ferguson, where the same benefi-
cial effects of independence and public-spiritedness might be generated for
modern urban dwellers as were created for Highlanders by cattle-raiding. A
social democracy of intense competition was the essential basis of liberty, but
Ferguson was silent on the actual political institutions that would represent such
a tumultuous entity. His ideas were demotic rather than democratic; political
practice would make the democratic potential actual. Ferguson accepted the
insight of Montesquieu and Rousseau that the conditions of modern liberty
were set by the *moeurs* of the people and identified a new institutional context for
the creation of political culture.

At its horizon the republican imagination of the late eighteenth century was
filled by the idea of the interdependence of a democratic political order with the
competing institutions of a healthy civil society. Yet these transformations at the
horizon of political theory might well have had no effect whatsoever on political
practice were it not for the crises that racked every North Atlantic state in the
late eighteenth century.[30] These crises were extra-ideological in origin but had
decidedly ideological consequences. The best example, because the most successful, was that of the Americans. As Bernard Bailyn has long established, the
animating ideals of the American revolutionaries in 1766 were antique and,
effectively, inadequate.[31] The Articles of Confederation, based on these original
ideals, proved a deficient base on which to construct the new polity. They were
driven to explore precisely the boundaries of political theory that we are considering here to create the framework for a modern state.[32] The gap between *The
Federalist papers* and *Common sense* is that of a century and a half of theory, even
if only twenty years in actual time had elapsed. The exact same process of ideological escalation, or rather the phenomenon of a community forced to capture
ideas in order to function, is obviously a feature of the French Revolution.
Nobody, apart from marginal figures such as Clavière, Brissot and Marat, considered an actual republic as the solution to the problems of France in 1789.
However, the thinker who most clearly articulated the ideals of the Revolution in
its early phase, Abbé Sieyès, was utterly indebted to the idea-complex of civil

29 Adam Ferguson, *An essay on the history of civil society* (Cambridge, 1994), p. 245.
30 The Atlantic perspective has not been much in vogue of late, but see the classic R.R. Palmer, *The
    age of the democratic revolution: A political history of Europe and America, 1760-1800*, 2 vols
    (Princeton, NJ, 1959–1964).
31 Bernard Bailyn, *The ideological origins of the American Revolution* (Cambridge, Mass., 1966).
32 For the definitive account of this process, see Gordon Wood, *The creation of the American
    Republic, 1776-1787* (New York, 1972).

society, commerce and popular sovereignty. It took only three years for the unthinkable institutional solution to happen, for France to become a republic.[33] The new republicanism, which sought to articulate the fact of civil society, the desire for individualism and the need for collective representations and politics, became the central ideological resource for societies in crisis. Even countries which prevented systemic collapse, such as England, developed a new republicanism. Where William Godwin understood politics in a way that would have made sense to the participants in the Putney debates, John Thelwall spoke a language that was completely novel.[34]

Republicanism was dynamic and evolving in the eighteenth century. It was a new intellectual tradition that responded to the crisis of the Atlantic revolutions and helped French, Dutch and Americans to re-construct societies and states, with varying degrees of success. Can we see any of the same tendencies in Ireland? In some ways even to pose the question as an Irish question is to start off on the wrong foot. The development of a recognizably Irish radical political culture was promoted by the position of Ireland in the complexity of the semi-federal British empire. Irish Whiggism was highly derivative and under-developed; in this it reflected the nature of whiggism generally.[35] But if the problems in which Ireland found itself located were larger than Ireland, so were the solutions. The same logic which drove other Atlantic societies toward the horizon of the political imaginary also operated in Ireland, and the same sudden sophistication of political argument happened in Ireland as in America, France and England.[36] There are many figures one might use to exemplify the new republicanism in Ireland, such as Thomas Addis Emmet or William Drennan, but Arthur O'Connor stands out as the writer and thinker who most obviously exploited this line of thought. O'Connor's writing displays the complexity of the new republicanism, has the universalist ambitions characteristic of it, and grounds its values in precisely the idea of civil society as a space of plural values and emulatory competition.

O'Connor saw Ireland and its prospects for reform through the optic of European history; as he put it in his memoirs, a successful Irish revolution would have completed the process of reform in Europe, by removing its greatest impediment:

> If the expedition of General Hoche had succeeded in separating Ireland from England, feudal Europe entire would have lost the powerful support

33 For Sieyès' political thought, see W.H. Sewell, *A rhetoric of bourgeois revolution: The Abbé Sieyès and 'What is the Third Estate?'* (Durham, N.C., 1994).

34 For Thelwall, see Gregory Claeys (ed.), *The politics of English Jacobinism: Writings of John Thelwall* (University Park, Pa., 1995).

35 Jim Smyth, *The men of no property: Irish radicals and popular politics in the late eighteenth century* (London 1992), p. 80.

36 Some of the intellectual currents that made up the new republicanism were derived from Irish sources, particularly Toland, Hutcheson and Burke.

she so long received from England who would have lost the best supply of her Navy and Army. It is from these circumstances that the events which have passed in Ireland are so important to be known by those who would thoroughly understand the history of Europe since the American Revolution.[37]

O'Connor did not expect the people of Ireland to put themselves in harm's way out of a sense of benevolence toward the other peoples of Europe. In his journalism, as editor of the *Press* but especially in his pamphlet, *The state of Ireland*, he sought to apply his understanding of the history of Europe to Ireland and to explain exactly what the interest of the population in the creation of a republic.[38] Stripped to its essentials, his argument was that only a modern, commercial republic would rescue Ireland from the cultural and structural impediments under which all its inhabitants suffered.

The new republicanism, centred on the ideal of civil society, allowed him to develop a sophisticated argument that analyzed how the deficiencies in Irish political culture and in political structure interacted to degrade the population and the country. The most striking feature of his republicanism was his distance from the languages of identity that were current on the island. O'Connor argued that the ideas of the nation used by all its inhabitants were meaningless and served to obscure the real nature of the country as a modern commercial society. The French Revolution, he argued, showed that all previous understandings of politics had to be abandoned in favour of new ideas, 'those principles to which the French Revolution has given birth, … form a phenomenon, which has never made its appearance before'.[39] He was particularly critical of the language of 'Protestant liberty'. His laconic comment on the meaning of the Back Lane parliament – 'I shall ask of no better proof that they are entitled to liberty, than their having the spirit to claim it' – was grounded in his secularized historical vision.[40] O'Connor saw no particular virtue in Catholic Emancipation in itself. His background was very anti-Catholic and his support for Emancipation, as he explained in a speech given in 1795, was because it would create an irresistible coalition in favour of reform, which in turn explained the resistance of the establishment to a measure that 'would be incompatible with their accursed monopoly'.[41] O'Connor sought to find the potential in Irish politics of the 1790s in terms other than those that the participants might themselves have used.

37 Bignon Papers, O'Connor memoirs, f. 160.
38 For a fuller consideration of O'Connor's political thought see Livesey, 'Introduction', in Arthur O'Connor, *The state of Ireland* (Dublin, 1998), pp 1–28.
39 'A Stoic' [Arthur O'Connor], *The measures of a ministry to prevent a Revolution are the certain means to bring it about* (London, 1794), p. 1.
40 'Arthur O'Connor's speech on the Catholic question, in the House of Commons, of the fourth of May, 1795', in *The beauties of the press* (London, 1800), pp 586–7.
41 Ibid., p. 583.

This critical turn was reinforced by his positive vision of the nation not as a people or *gens*, a cultural tradition, a group of language users or a body of the faithful, but as the industrious inhabitants of the island. The gap between the potential for progress in Irish commercial society and its actual state incensed him: 'shall a brave, healthy, intelligent, industrious people, be doomed to the most squalid misery at home, and be famed for enterprise, activity and industry in every country but their own, without the suspicion that they have been made prey to peculation, injustice and corruption?'[42] Industriousness encapsulated a complex of ideas for eighteenth-century thinkers, and for O'Connor in particular. Its simplest denotation was work in production, distribution, exchange or the arts of utility and agreement. However, industry also encompassed a moral ideal. Industriousness was the disposition to commit oneself to socially useful labour, and to achieve from that labour the stoic virtues of self-command: 'Liberal reward invigorates industry … it supplies the mind with constant employment, by which it attaches it to virtue, and rescues it from vice; instills a love of the country by the blessings it imparts; establishes a proud independence; and teaches the mind to account a life stained with dishonour, a burden too grievous to be longer supported.'[43] Industriousness was the central virtue of a commercial society, which otherwise could encourage egotism and ruinous dissipation in its members. Industry, the free labour that contributed to society even as it fulfilled self-interest, was the spring that drove the other elements of the mechanism of society. The acquisition of property was the rational goal of industry and its possession a symbol of industriousness. The rational self-command generated by industriousness moulded the mind of the citizen to appreciate the objective pleasures of intercourse and emulation, and so fitted him, or her since O'Connor did not have a gendered argument, for social and political interaction.[44] So central was industry to the life of the nation that the lack of it was a sure sign that the mechanism of social life was disjoint and required renovation.

O'Connor's definition of the Irish nation as a commercial society was a powerful position from which to build his critique of the state of the country. Ireland as a potentially commercial society was stifled by imperial rule and monopolizing feudal elites. The bulk of his pamphlet was given over to teasing out the terrible consequences of this distortion 'from the castle to the cabin'. Instead of a healthy public life characterized by 'emulation, collision and intercourse' in the commercial and political fields, public life was a degenerating spectacle of prostitution of talents, corruption and treason among the upper classes, indolence, demoralization and drunkenness among the lower. His analysis of the political economy of the distorted commercial society was as clear as his denunciation of

42 O'Connor, *The state of Ireland*, p. 32.
43 Ibid., p. 63.
44 See 'To Irishwomen', *Press*, No. 37, 21 December 1797, for his newspaper's argument for the rational equality of men and women.

its subjects was bitter. Ireland lacked a system of emulation because it lacked a functional economic system. Capital was constantly drawn out of the economy in useless taxes, levied to provide sinecures in the state service as a reward for political quiescence among the gentry, and in rent to absentee landlords. Without the capital to fund manufactures, the agricultural sector was overcrowded, which led to unnaturally high rents. The industrious classes were trapped in a circle of poverty from which there was no exit, and thus were entirely demoralized. The unreformed Irish state and imperial context fractured individual and collective rationality so that, to invert Mandeville, even private virtues could still lead to public vices.

At this stage of research, it would be impossible to calculate the extent to which the norms invoked by O'Connor were shared around the United Irish movement. O'Connor's work clearly shows that the processes that led to a new form of ideological politics around the Atlantic littoral were at least present in Irish contexts. There are particular features of the Irish situation which need to be addressed before we can compare the evolution of the horizons of political culture, specifically the notion of sovereignty which was an integral part of the development of French and American republicanism but was a less useful notion in the semi-federal context of the British Isles. Moreover, we have to advert to the differing fortunes of the values of republicanism in the region. The United States of America most easily integrated the ideals of a modern civism into its institutions; in France, the unfulfilled nature of the process provoked a hundred years of political instability; even Germany, dominated as it was by political romanticism, sustained a strong republican tradition; nowhere was the failure of republicanism as total as it was in Ireland.[45] So total was the eclipse of these values that the subsequent history of Ireland in the 1790s simply wrote them out in favour of the sectarian categories of political mobilization.[46] These universalist, secular and progressive values did not succeed in finding any constituency and the organizing languages of Irish politics came to be almost universally ethnic and sectarian. Given the presence of so many of the other elements of civil society in Ireland, even after 1798, the strange disappearance of a modern republicanism (as opposed to the competing versions of integrist nationalism) from Irish political life in the nineteenth century, is a problem worthy of some attention.

45 For the tortured relationship between Enlightenment republicanism and political romanticism, see Martin Thom, *Republics, nations and tribes* (London, 1995).
46 See Kevin Whelan, ''98 after '98: The politics of memory', in *The tree of liberty: Radicalism, Catholicism and the construction of Irish identity, 1760-1830* (Cork, 1996), pp 133–75.

2

Irish periodicals and the dissemination of French Enlightenment writings in the eighteenth century

GERALDINE SHERIDAN

Periodical literature published in Ireland in the late eighteenth century has received some attention in relation to the revolutionary period, but the extent of the countrywide dissemination of major texts of the French Enlightenment is only now being investigated. A recent study has catalogued eighteen periodical publications printed in Ireland in the period 1730-90 which contained literary news, and abstracts or reviews of books of European origin, mainly French. To these may be added at least one further ephemeral paper, the *Country Journal*, published by Ebenezer Ryder in George's Lane in 1735-6. Other such publications may well be recovered from oblivion with further study, which should also help to extend our understanding of the transmission of ideas through what was a relatively popular medium of communication, one that reached a wide public both geographically and socially.

The editor of the *Grand Magazine of Universal Intelligence* (issued by Hoey in Dublin) aptly remarked in his introduction to the first volume (1758) that in this kind of publication, 'many instructive precepts, many ingenious and entertaining essays, many fugitive pieces of various kinds, are preserved, which would otherwise be lost or destroyed for want of a proper repository'. The magazines offer us an insight into the contemporary tastes and interests of a wide reading public, in a manner different from that afforded by the study of books where we are limited by the vagaries of library preservation, to the detriment of the more popular, less well bound, and consequently less enduring literature of the time. Many of the magazines were within the purchasing range of people who could not have bought books with any regularity; indeed, for many years Cave's *Gentleman's Magazine*, the archetype of the miscellany, advertised on the title page that it contained 'more than any book of the kind or price'. They offered very good value for money with up to one hundred pages per issue for as little as 6*d*. (e.g. *London and Dublin Magazine*), making them much more accessible than the books they reviewed which could cost anything from 2*s*. (for an Irish reprint) to near 6*s*. for some London-printed volumes (e.g.

Buffier's *French grammar*, in 8°, listed in the *London and Dublin* in 1734 at the London price of 5*s*. 6*d*.).[1] Sixpence was the price of chap-books such as *Jack the giant killer* or *Irish rogues and raparees* which were within the purchasing reach of those Whitley Stokes referred to as the 'lower classes in Ireland' in 1799.[2] A Catholic farm labourer throughout most of the century might earn somewhere between 6*d*. and 1*s*. per day.[3] It is therefore worth asking to what extent these magazines may have penetrated socially to categories of readers not normally assumed to have any knowledge of 'highbrow' literature, such as the major texts of the French enlightenment.

The geographic distribution of some of this material spread well beyond the catchment of established bookshops, normally located within reach of major ports. Starting in 1747 and through the 1750s, the title-page of Exshaw's *Gentleman's and London Magazine* lists the contacts who distributed the magazine, and these lists include, at various times, all the following locations – Armagh, Athlone, Belfast, Cashel, Clonmel, Coleraine, Cork, Derry, Drogheda, Galway, Kilkenny, Limerick, Maryborough, Mountmellick, Newry, Roscommon, Strokestown and Waterford. Some distributors were booksellers, more were general merchants. There is a certain overlap with those known to have distributed the *Magazin à la mode*, published in French in Dublin from 1777 to 1778: this was sold through outlets in Armagh, Athlone, Ballinrobe, Belfast, Carlow, Castlebar, Clonmel, Cork, Derry, Drogheda, Dublin, Kilkenny, Limerick, Lisburn, Newry, Waterford and Wexford.[4] Interestingly, however, the dearth of outlets in the west with regard to the *Magazin* was less acute in the case of the *Exshaw's* in the earlier period with two outlets in Galway (J. Cox and Mrs E. Exshaw, probably a relation of the Dublin publisher, and the only known booksellers in the city for this period), and, for a time, Denis Mahon in Strokestown and Thomas Cuff in Roscommon, though the south-west was still poorly served. It may well have been provided for, however, by the *Magazine of Magazines, compiled from original pieces, with extracts from the most celebrated books and periodicals published in Europe*, which was reprinted from the London edition from 1751 to 1769 by Andrew Welsh in Limerick, and indicates a lively provincial market for this type of material. This was a major undertaking for a provincial printer; Welsh had imported a particular new font for the enterprise, and Joseph Sexton made a special paper for him.[5] Welsh had, in fact, been distributing *Exshaw's* in Limerick, along with Ferrar, from 1748 to 1751, and this experience must have convinced him of the profitability of reprinting for a local

---

1 Mary Pollard, *Dublin's trade in books, 1550-1800* (Oxford, 1989), pp 131ff.
2 Ibid., p. 222.
3 R.C. Cole, *Irish booksellers and English writers, 1740-1800* (London, 1986), p. 160.
4 Maire Kennedy, 'The distribution of a locally-produced French periodical in provincial Ireland: The *Magazin à la mode, 1777–1778*', in *Eighteenth-century Ireland*, ix (1994), 97–8.
5 Robert Herbert, *Limerick printers and printing* (Limerick, 1942) p. 9.

Distribution network

- • *Gentleman's and London Magazine*
- ■ *Magazin à la Mode*

Fig. 2.1   Distribution network of *Gentleman's and London Magazine* (from 1747) and *Magazin à la Mode* (1777–78)

market. Welsh's magazine was sold by C. Sullivan and Phineas Bagnell in Cork, the same booksellers who were distributing *Exshaw's*, as well as by G. Condy in Castle Street in the same city, R. James in Dame Street in Dublin, and probably other outlets not mentioned on the title-pages. Each named distributor was very likely a hub for further distribution to the surrounding post towns which had contact with the main centre two or three times a week, and where many of the booksellers had agents distributing their newspapers. Ferrar in Limerick distributed his newspaper, the *Limerick Chronicle*, to Birr, Ennis, Tipperary, Rathkeale, Sixmilebridge, Killaloe, Newport, Nenagh, and 'all parts of Kerry'.[6] Welsh would presumably have exploited similar networks for the distribution of his periodical. The advertisement placed by Finn in his *Leinster Journal* (Kilkenny) for *Exshaw's* notes that he would forward to 'gentlemen ... in town or country'.[7] Through such networks, the impact of many of the magazines reached outwards to most parts of Ireland.

One way of getting some feel for the readership of these magazines is through the birth, marriage and death announcements which many of them contained: it is very probable that those who inserted such notices had some familiarity with the particular publication. A cursory survey suggests that the *Hibernian Magazine* and *Exshaw's* show, in general, a traditional profile for bookbuyers of clergy, lawyers, army officers, nobility and gentry;[8] other journals offer evidence of a much more modest public. The *Dublin Magazine* deals with Dublin tradespeople: in January, 1762, it registers the death of Michael Clinch, brewer, and of 'Mrs Mary Kane, mistress of the Globe Coffee-house', admittedly of particular interest to the reading public who might have frequented her premises.[9] The 'Monthly Chronicle for Ireland' added into the *Grand Magazine* noted the nuptials or decease of a succession of 'eminent' farmers, farriers, linen-drapers and silk-weavers, some – John Magrath or Foghney Farrell (Jan. 1760) – very probably Catholics like the publisher Hoey himself. The Protestant majority of publishers also opened their columns – increasingly so as the century progressed – to readers from widely varied social groups, and probably all religious affiliations: John Norman in his *Weekly Magazine and Literary Review* records the marriage of 'Mr Richard Conway of Dominick-street, Gauger, to Miss Kennedy of Kilkenny' in January 1779,[10] and *Whitestone's Town and Country Magazine* in 1784 even makes bold to record the death at Ennis of 'the Revd Mr Kelly, a clergyman of the church of Rome'.[11] The notices in that magazine testify – unsurprisingly in view of the title – to a significant rural readership, as well as shopkeepers and tradespeople in Dublin such as 'Mr Barnaby O'Reilly of Dame Street, mercer' who announces his marriage to 'Miss Derham, daughter of the late Mr Derham,

6 Kennedy, 'Distribution', 90   7 Ibid., 92.
8 Pollard, *Trade in books*, pp 214–15   9 *Dublin Magazine*, Jan. 1762, 63.
10 *Weekly Magazine and Literary Review*, Jan. 1779, 99.
11 *Whitestone's Town and Country Magazine*, Jan. 1784, 56.

Merchant', or 'Mr Browne, of Abbey Street, grocer', who marries his close namesake 'Miss Brown, of Vicar Street', both in July 1784. The later *Town and Country Weekly Magazine*, which, appearing more frequently in slimmer format was presumably available at a very modest cost, also covers a wide range socially and geographically, from William Keary, a merchant in Tuam, to Thomas Glasgow, a watchmaker on Ormond Quay.[12] The *Magazine of Magazines*, printed in Limerick, contains notices for a wide range of gentry and commoners, with a significant proportion resident in the counties of Clare, Limerick and Kerry, as well as readers from the Pale, such as, in May 1761, the announcement of the marriage of 'Mr Arthur Guinness, brewer, to Miss Whitmore of Capel-Street'. There was a significant penetration of these magazines into the artisan and merchant classes across the country; given the number of titles we now know to have been circulating, the relatively wide distribution of many of these, and the fact that every copy sold was likely to have been read by several individuals – six readers for one copy was regarded as the average for newspapers,[13] with perhaps a somewhat lower figure for the type of periodical material we are considering – it is clear that these journals had the potential to make a significant impact on the contemporary reading public. The editor of the *Weekly Miscellany* was well aware of the influence of his medium:

> These sort of papers are become the fashion, and many receive all their notions in *religion* and government, all their stock of *learning* from thence; so that there seems to be no other so effectual a method of instilling proper principles, and obviating vulgar errors, as *this*; which will convey truth and knowledge into the hands of those who will neither *buy* nor *read* larger discourses.[14]

Dublin quickly picked up on the success of the new formula of miscellany-type magazine launched in London in 1731 with the *Gentleman's Magazine*, followed quickly in 1732 by its close imitator, the *London Magazine*. In January 1734 George Faulkner offered for sale the *London and Dublin Magazine, or, Gentleman's Monthly Intelligencer*, an exact reproduction, page for page, of the *London*, printed on his behalf by Samuel Powell; from April he added in a minimal amount of Irish material to justify his title. Throughout the rest of the century there would be a strong tradition of reprinting the London periodicals in this manner, and not just in Dublin, where six are recorded prior to 1789; in Limerick, Andrew Welsh reprinted the London *Magazine of Magazines* – which itself existed by openly creaming the best articles from other journals for its compendium – page for page, from 1751. In addition to the London magazines

12 Cole, *Irish books*, p. 17.
13 *Town and Country Weekly Magazine*, 30 July 1785, 384.
14 *Weekly Miscellany*, 16 Nov. 1734.

which provided the material for this publication, the cover lists several French-language journals as sources – the *Mercure historique,* the *Journal britannique,* the *Bibliothèque raisonnée,* the *Journal des savants,* as well as the transactions of the Royal Societies of Paris and other European capitals. The extent to which this claim is actually borne out calls for detailed examination, but it does alert us to the fact that, through these reprintings of London magazines, the Irish reader could hope to acquire a viewpoint on the French-speaking literary world which they would not easily find elsewhere, and which was clearly perceived as a major attraction by the bookseller who so advertised it. A wealth of French material can be found in all these periodicals.[15]

Whereas some of the reprints tended to include more original or adapted material as time went by, conversely a number of the magazines which we might class as 'original' actually contained derivative articles culled from a wide range of sources. What interests us here, however, is the selection their editors made of items which they believed would be of interest to a specifically Irish readership, and so for the purposes of this brief survey of material connected with the French Enlightenment we will confine ourselves to this particular group of periodicals as offering a more distinctively home-grown flavour.[16]

The first, and one of the most interesting to appear, was the *Weekly Miscellany.* Published simultaneously with Faulkner's reprint of the *London,* it is an unique publication, which purports to be written by one hand, appears to originate in Ireland, and has a very high proportion of material of French origin. Indeed the editor received objections to his apparent sympathy for the French – as he reports on 16 November 1734 – because '*the papists, they say, are well-wishers to* France, *they are very* uppish *on account of the success of the allies'*; in marked contrast to the majority of British periodicals, he consistently defends his own approach on the grounds that 'our good harmony with *France,* is a stronger barrier against papists, than four and twenty thousand Men'. The editor is clearly very well versed in French language and culture, and gives a particulary well-informed survey of the French-language periodical press. The very first number for 10 January 1734, advertises Voltaire's *Letters concerning the English nation* (London and Dublin 1733), one of the most influential texts of the early Enlightenment, remarking:

> Mr Voltaire who these 7 years past, has been lab'ring into fame, is now in possesion of a most establish'd character in the commonwealth of learn-

15　G. Sheridan, 'Irish literary review magazines and enlightenment France, 1730-1790', in G. Gargett and G. Sheridan (eds), *Ireland and the French Enlightenment, 1700-1800* (London, 1999), pp 21–46.

16　From a list of eight such periodicals identified (*Ireland and the French Enlightenment,* Appendix 1), we can omit the *Young Gentlemen and Ladies Magazine* (no. 18) which did not contain any French material of interest for this paper.

ing. This rare and universal genius has had the pleasure to see all his productions greedily read, I had almost said, devoured, and himself received
with great marks of distinction on t'other side the water: and since the
impression of these letters here, one could hardly go into a house of any
note, without finding them on every gentleman's table ... Perhaps ... he
thinks to secure to himself a comfortable retreat in *England*, when his
senseless affectation of libertine and irreligious principles, shall render his
own country too hot for him.

This is a striking recognition of Voltaire's impact on anglophone readers at a relatively early point in his career, of the outstanding success of the *Letters* in less
than six months of circulation,[17] and of the existence of a 'commonwealth' of
contemporary readership for what is deemed 'libertine' literature, a term which,
at the time, was used to refer as much to free-thinking in the philosophical as the
sexual domain. On 13 June, in criticizing Voltaire's *Temple of taste* which has been
published in translation in London, the author further remarks:

Poor Mr De Voltaire has been lately seized at Paris and banished by *Lettres
de cachet* to the castle of Auxone near Autun. This is no more than what I
foresaw and foretold in my first paper would be his fate if he dared in his
own country of France to vend those dangerous wares he had picked up
during his short stay in England. Deistic and libertine airs do not suit
every clime. The vain and light French as we love to call them have not
quite divested of all *seriousness* and *solidity*. They have not yet arrived at the
refinement of disgracing taste and nature, and of abandoning religion and
her august mysteries to open redicule [*sic*] and contempt.

Despite the editor's obvious interest, we already find here a number of the stereotypical views on the French which will recur throughout the magazines, coupled
with an explicit recognition of their predominating influence in all matters of culture and taste: 'those conceited *French* will be followed in everything though they
vouchsafe to imitate us in nothing'. All through the century this keen interest in
the life and activities of French writers – of whom Voltaire will remain the most
popular – will be sustained, with an enormous appetite on the part of editors for
news of their latest movements and activities, as well as the appearance and reception of their books. Notoriety, whether in the political or literary sphere, helped to
sell magazines.

This journal was more overtly Protestant in its allegiance than many of its suc-
cessors: the 'Literary News' for 17 January 1734 (continued on 21 September for
the later volumes) describes the *Histoire des Papes*, a strongly anti-Catholic satiric

17 A.-M. Rousseau, *L'Angleterre et Voltaire* [*Studies on Voltaire*, vols 145–7] (Oxford, 1976), pp
    652ff.

work published in the Hague in five volumes between 1732 and 1734; rumour immediately associated it with Lenglet Dufresnoy, but it was in fact written by an impecunious young man named Bruys. The writer of the *Weekly Miscellany* rather disingenuously claims that 'our present historian has avoided … extreams, and is valuable for the truth and sincerity of his recitals. Tho' a staunch Catholick, he assures us, that whoever reads this work, 'will be scandalized at those enormous vices he is obliged to produce.' The editor's allegiances are further highlighted in his eulogy of Limborch's *History of the Inquisition*, published in London in 1731, with a large introduction, concerning 'the rise and progress of persecution'. On 25 April the editor declares that it is 'the intention of this paper not only to advance learning and the Belles Lettres, but also to promote religion and the interest of our *Establishment*'; however, he vigorously defends himself against charges of anti-Catholic invective:

> It was the principles, but no ways the persons of *Roman Catholicks*, which have been the subject of invective in the course of this work. The author was so far from having it in his view (as has, tho' in a civil manner been laid to his charge by a certain noble person) to alarm and inflame the magistrate yet more against them; that had he a vote in the matter, I would give it not only for the mitigating, but even repealing some *Acts* lately made against them. He has liv'd long and intimately with many of the Romish communion …[18]

Relatively liberal, his tolerance does not however extend itself to the '*atheism* and *irreligion*' which he sees 'scattered up and down these kingdoms, in books and weekly papers, with a very liberal hand'.[19]

Contemporary best-sellers such as the *Spectacle de la Nature*, by the Abbé Pluche, are highlighted; this work at once epitomizes the popularization of scientific research, and the increasingly dominant assumption, 'that a principle of benevolence animates man himself and the divine order around him'.[20] A review on 21 March 1734 of the London translation (1733) asserts that 'the original garb suits much better', because 'the softnesses and delicacies of the French language do exceedingly qualify it to represent to advantage all the beauties and all the graces of nature'. Indeed, Exshaw takes advantage of the opportunity, much as Faulkner does in his periodical, to advertise this work for sale 'just imported from London […] in the original French or translated'. The response must have been significant, for Exshaw later printed his own edition in translation.[21] This high-

18 *Weekly Miscellany*, 16 Nov. 1734.
19 Ibid.; see also the review of Turretin's *Traité de la vérité*, 24 Jan., and the lead article (untitled), 20 June 1734.
20 Norman Hampson, *The Enlightenment* (London, 1990), pp 79–80.
21 See *Ireland and the French Enlightenment*, Appendix 2, nos 154–5.

lights one of the important functions of the periodicals: they were used by the booksellers to advertise and promote their bookstocks, and the information they provide on French books imported or printed in Ireland, in the original or in translation, makes a valuable contribution to our knowledge of the market for French material as interpreted by these astute businessmen.[22]

The editor of this periodical expected a substantial portion of his clients to be capable of reading the original works in French; he saw the mastery of French, and perhaps Italian, as essential accomplishments for a journalist, and as a thorough modernist he scorned the excessive place of classical learning – 'the learning of *obsolete* words and old rubbish, (call'd the classics)' – in education (16 November 1734). What few notices this paper contained suggest it was aimed at the ascendancy nobility and gentry, and a number of references to 'our university' suggest the editor may have been a person closely attached to Trinity College.

The *Country Journal*, published initially three times a week by Ebenezer Ryder in George's Lane from 5 June 1735 to 3 March 1736, with just four pages per issue, was closer in format to a newspaper, and concentrated for the main part on historical narratives (particularly extracts from the *Monastical history of Ireland*),[23] and some political news from Europe. However, Ryder, like his rival booksellers, used the pages to advertise his own publications, or those editions he was importing from England, and these included some French translations. For example, on 26 June 1735 he advertised, 'on a large paper and good letter', the serial publication of 'the eight volumes of letters writ by a Turkish spy, who lived five and forty years at Paris'. This was a translation – possibly the London edition of 1734 – of *L'Espion turc dans les cours des princes chrétiens*, by Marana, a satiric commentary on France in the reign of Louis XIV, which had been frequently reprinted in France after its first appearance in 1684.[24] On 25 July 1735 the bookseller sought to reassure his clients who subscribed for J. Templeman's translation of Rapin de Thoyras's *History of England* that the last sheets were printed in London, and could be inspected, together with some of the engravings, at his premises. This is a very unusual case, where Ryder himself would appear to have initiated the project, and the London imprint carries his name. The publication of this paper ends abruptly; it was presumably less successful than the more substantial offerings of Ryder's competitors.

From October 1744 to June 1749 the relatively well-known *Literary Journal* was edited by the Revd Jean-Pierre Droz, minister to the French Reformed congregation at St Patrick's Cathedral, and bookseller at College Green and later

22 Kennedy and Sheridan, 'The trade in French books in eighteenth-century Ireland', in *Ireland and the French Enlightenment*, pp 173–96.
23 Presumably John Stevens' *Monasticon Hibernicum* (London, 1722).
24 Chiefly remembered today as a possible source for Montesquieu's *Lettres persanes*, it is listed in Robert Darnton, *Corpus of clandestine literature in France, 1769–89* (New York, 1995), p. 62, no. 208.

Dame Street. It was the first original review-type journal in Ireland, and added analysis to the abstracts in the older European tradition. In the 'advertisement' to his first issue, Droz stated that: 'As foreign books are only known from the *French* journals, publish'd abroad, understood by few, and read by fewer, my *intention* is to give *English* abstracts of the most important foreign books, *German, Dutch, French*, or *Latin*.' Nearly half of the abstracts included in the *Journal* are translated/adapted from the *Bibliothèque raisonnée des ouvrages des savants de l'Europe*, published in Amsterdam by Wetstein, and three-quarters of all the abstracts originate from French language journals.[25] The writers associated with the *Bibliothèque raisonnée* were recruited largely from the Huguenots *réfugiés* in the Low Countries, and a number of colleagues in Switzerland and the German states (for example Haller in Göttingen): many of them came to represent the 'cosmopolitan Enlightenment',[26] the opposition to French Catholic hegemony which translates into the very different context of eighteenth-century Ireland in a somewhat surprising way. Droz probably supplied his own translations for the most part; responses by readers reinforce the impression of a scholarly, educated public eager to engage in discussion.[27] The 'literary news' in each issue listed books which were not reviewed, but had caught his attention: many of these he could supply himself as bookseller, and this contributed to the success of his periodical.

The articles in the *Journal* represent a wide spectrum of European learning, the major focus being in the areas of natural history, the experimental sciences, and contemporary history and memoirs.[28] Physics is touched on in a note on d'Alembert's *Traité de l'équilibre et du movement des fluides* which had been published in Paris in 1744;[29] Buffon and Réaumur figure large in abstracts from the *Mémoires de l'Académie Royale des Sciences* for the years 1739 and 1740. The Abbé Nollet, also a member of the said Académie, is mentioned in the 'literary news' for his *Leçons de physique expérimentale*,[30] published in six volumes in Paris between 1743 and 1748. Droz aptly comments: 'Experimental philosophy begins to prevail in France, as everywhere else, over the hypothetical way of philosophising'.[31] This interest in the experimental sciences, typical of the first half of the eighteenth century, shades over into a specifically enlightenment interest in 'philosophie' in the account of the publication in Paris ('Leyde') of the *Dissertation physique à l'occasion d'un Nègre blanc* ascribed to Maupertuis, with the comment:

25 Jean-Paul Pittion, 'A literary journal', in *Hermathena*, cxxi (1976), 129–41.
26 Elizabeth Eisenstein, *Grub Street abroad: Aspects of the French cosmopolitan press from the age of Louis XIV to the French Revolution* (Oxford, 1992), chap. 4.
27 See, for example, *Literary Journal*, Apr.-June 1745, 33–42.
28 Pittion, 'A literary journal'.
29 *Literary Journal*, ii, 2, p. 220
30 Ibid., ii, 1, p. 217.
31 Ibid.

There is lately published here a very pretty piece of sceptical philosophy in French ... All the systems about generation are there examined in a very genteel kind of pyrronism.[32]

Voltaire's description of the famous albino 'in the [sixth] Volume of his Works lately published' (Amsterdam, Ledet, 1745) is also quoted in the context of this discussion. The lively interest which Droz and his readers took in these debates of the early Enlightenment period concerning metaphysics is also reflected in the *Journal* in many references to deism: in announcing this same volume of Voltaire's *Œuvres*, Droz chooses to concentrate on the former's 'Observations on Deists in general' ('Discours sur le déisme'),[33] which would not have been available in English at the time. A passing comment by Droz to the effect that Julian the Apostate was more of a deist than a pagan provoked a lengthy and somewhat outraged refutation by his fellow Dublin pastor V. Desvœux,[34] the same who published a continuation of the *Journal* after Droz's death.[35] Desvœux attacked Voltaire's claim (as reported by Droz) that deists 'never persecuted', and therefore should be preferred 'to all other known sects', declaring it 'deserves no serious answer, till it be proved that toleration is the only duty we are bound to observe with respect to God and men, and that it agrees better with the principles of deism, than with those of Christianity'.[36] The grey world between theology and science wherein one can locate many of the heated controversies of the first half of the century, such as the debate concerning animal souls, is represented by *The theology of insects*[37] by Lesser and Lyonnet,[38] which again provoked a response from Droz's readers, this time putting Droz on the conservative side of the argument. The first, who signs 'PH—' [Paul Hiffernan?], attacks Droz's defence of the existence of a 'particular providence':

> I cannot agree with you; 'That a providence by general laws is no providence at all': on the contrary it is the only providence man has to trust to, the only one of which I believe any Interposition can be proved.[39]

This deistic position is in turn attacked by a defender of Droz in the following issue.[40]

Given the lively and enquiring tone of these debates, combined with Droz's religious, linguistic and cultural allegiances as a minister of the French Con-

32 Ibid., ii, 1, p. 213   33 Ibid., ii, 1, pp 217–18.
34 Ibid., iii, 1, p. 78   35 Ibid., iii, 1, pp 55–95.
36 Ibid., iii, 1, p. 57.
37 *Théologie des insectes . . . traduit de l'allemand de M. Lesser, avec des remarques de M.P. Lyonnet* (Paris, 1745).
38 *Literary Journal*, i, 2, pp 269–84.
39 Ibid., ii, 1, p. 34   40 Ibid., ii, 2, pp 20–34.

formed Churches, it is hardly surprising that both he and his correspondents frequently refer to Pierre Bayle as an authority.[41] Bayle's *Nouvelles de la République des Lettres* would undoubtedly have been one of the most influential models in the publishing world of the *réfugiés*, a powerful advocate for religious toleration. Bayle came to occupy a central place in European intellectual life although he was a marginal figure in every sense of the word, partly because of the decentralized transnational network of which Droz can be seen to be part.[42] Droz shows himself to be a well-informed reader and sophisticated interpreter, well aware of the political context of the philosophical debate in continental Europe. In relation to Voltaire's statement of preference for Deists 'over all other known sects whatsoever', Droz inserts a note:

> *Mr Voltaire* adds these Words (except our own church, *excepté nostre eglise*). Whether by them, he means Christianity in general, or the Roman Catholic religion in particular, or whether he did insert them by way of precaution, in case of need, is more than I can tell.[43]

Again, in relation to the review written by the *Bibliothèque raisonnée* on the *Universal history*, 1736–44, printed in London and then Dublin, Droz corrects the author for quoting Boulainvilliers as an authority concerning the danger of Spinoza's theories. He rightly points out that he was 'one of the greatest defenders of *Spinoza*', whose manuscript 'Essai de métaphysique dans les principes de B*** de S***' was published in the confusingly-titled and notorious work *Réfutation de Spinoza*:[44] Droz thus shows an impressive acquaintance with some of the most subversive philosophic material in circulation through underground channels.

The overall thrust of Droz's *Journal* is wholly consistent with his defence of 'the spirit of liberty in religious matters [which] is the right of every natural being' in the original advertisement. Although in general he professed a neutral stance as editor of the *Journal*, he was sympathetic towards deism and and aspects of the argument for toleration. Droz can be associated with a liberal, tolerant tendency evident in the writings of Molesworth (friend and patron of Toland) and his group – which included Francis Hutcheson, James Arbuckle, and Edward Synge the younger – which were published from the 1720s onward.[45] Philip Skelton, the

41 See, for example, 1745, i, 2, p. 334; ii, 2, p. 278; iii, 1, pp 67, 84.

42 Eisenstein, *Grub Street abroad*, p. 4.

43 *Literary Journal*, ii, 1, p. 217.

44 Amsterdam, 1733, edited by Lenglet Dufresnoy. Cf. G. Sheridan, *Nicolas Lenglet Dufrenoy and the literary underworld of the ancien régime* [*Studies on Voltaire*, vol. 262] (Oxford, 1989), pp 136–41.

45 David Berman, 'The culmination and causation of Irish philosophy', *Archiv für Geschichte der Philosophie*, lxiv, no. 3 (1982), 257–79: 'Irish freethinking was timid and slight when compared with that in England, Scotland and France; but there was plainly a continuing spectre of freethought which frightened Irish philosophers into producing some of the most inventive and weighty defences of religion published in the eighteenth century'.

with less favour than those of Droz; only three volumes appeared. The fact that he was not a bookseller probably told against the viability of the undertaking, making promotion and distribution more difficult, but it is possible that the more partisan, conservative bias evident in the work failed to appeal to Droz's clientèle.

The *Dublin Magazine,* published by Peter Wilson in Dame Street from January 1762 to January 1765, was the first indigenous magazine of the miscellany type, modelled on the British magazines from which it frequently borrowed. Issued monthly, with a little over sixty pages per issue, it contained more original items of Irish interest than any other magazine of the period. That Wilson aimed at a broader public than Droz is clear from articles such as those on husbandry, cures for common ailments, and short fiction, probably intended for a female audience. The publication of the *Dublin* corresponds with the peak of enlightenment publication in France: Helvétius' *De l'Esprit* had appeared in 1758, Voltaire's *Candide* in 1759; Rousseau's *Contrat social* and *Emile,* and most of the volumes of the *Encyclopédie* would appear in 1762. The section on politics always accounted for a significant proportion of the pages of each issue, with hostility to France still rumbling on in the reprintings of Wilkes' *North Briton* (a favourite of these miscellanies); however, the authority of French writers could also be invoked to back up the anti-Tory argument, the *North Briton* clearly suggesting that 'the inimitable Montesquieu' would not have written *The spirit of laws* 'had he not been conversant with that part of our statutes upon which our constitution turns'.[56] Most references to French literature and ideas came in the sections of 'miscellaneous essays', and 'literary intelligence'. In April 1764, an essay on 'The influence of liberty upon taste' explicitly evoked the ever-increasing status of French language and culture, and indicates a sophisticated understanding of the conditions governing the production and dissemination of enlightenment material in France:

> [The French] language is become almost the universal language of Europe; their productions are read everywhere: the best books of other nations are translated into French: and the most ingenious of all countries visit France. Though there are restraints upon the press at Paris, yet methods are found to elude them, and, if in some cases they fail, Holland supplies whatever they want ... Add to this, that the universality of the French language hath almost made the French citizens of the world, and put it in their power to catch the spirit, and imbibe the sentiments of the eminent men of every nation.

in Ireland, though the purchase of such a work was, of course, the preserve of the wealthy. Cf. M. Kennedy, 'The *Encyclopédie* in eighteenth-century Ireland', in *The Book Collector,* xlv (1996), 201–13; Kennedy and Sheridan, 'Trade in French books', p. 185.
56 *Dublin Magazine,* Oct. 1764, 579; see also Dec., 682.

The booksellers of Ireland were keenly aware of the extent to which the most subversive French material could be procured through booksellers outside the borders of France: Luke White, for example, was to import significant amounts of Enlightenment material from Neuchâtel in the early 1780s.[57]

The striking extent of the coverage of the 'greats' in this magazine, has been outlined in recent studies on Voltaire and Rousseau:[58] O'Dea has shown that the *Dublin* was 'strikingly sympathetic to Rousseau's religious thought',[59] and highlighted how one particularly perceptive article in February 1762 eagerly anticipates the publication of *Emile*.[60] Gargett has detailed the frequent reprintings from Voltaire's works:[61] the *Dublin* undoubtedly privileges texts which support the argument for religious toleration, such as Voltaire's analysis of the Calas affair (the arbitrary execution of a French Protestant in Toulouse in 1762 despite his evident innocence of the crime of murdering his son) in a noted letter to d'Alembert.[62] The most telling example was the famous deist 'Prayer',[63] translated from the *Traité sur la tolérance* written in defence of Jean Calas; it was a great *summa* of Voltaire's condemnation of extremism, fanaticism and sectarianism, which was to consecrate his fame as the defender of toleration throughout Europe and beyond, and it was published in English in Dublin in this year. The version in the *Dublin* was taken from the *Gentleman's Magazine* of the same month,[64] and the work's impact in England is well evidenced by a subsequent letter in that magazine, which begins:

> In conversation lately with an acquaintance of the church of Rome, he asked me if I had read Voltaire's letter on toleration, to which answering in the affirmative, he immediately said, That he hoped that it might be the means of procuring the *English* Catholics in their native country a free and open toleration of their religion.[65]

The reproduction of any part of the *Traité* in the Irish context, where the Whiteboy disturbances were at their height in Munster, and the Oakboy disruption had broken out in Ulster, could hardly be seen as anodyne:

> Thou has not given us hearts to hate one another, nor hands to cut one another's throats ... Let not the little differences between the vestments that cover our feeble bodies, between our defective languages, between our

57 Kennedy and Sheridan, 'Trade in French books', pp 183–9.
58 Gargett, 'Voltaire's reception in Ireland', in *Ireland and the French Enlightenment*, pp 74–8, and M. O'Dea, 'Rousseau in eighteenth-century Irish journals', ibid., pp 92–4.
59 O'Dea, 'Rousseau', p. 93.
60 *Dublin Magazine*, 115–21; O'Dea, 'Rousseau', p. 93.
61 Gargett, 'Voltaire's reception', pp 74–8.   62 *Dublin Magazine*, Aug. 1762, 458–60.
63 Ibid., Mar. 1764, 152–3   64 *Gentleman's Magazine*, 113.
65 Ibid., 322.

ridiculous customs, between our many imperfect laws . . . [L]et not the
many little distinctions that denote the several classes of atoms called men,
be signals of hatred and persecution. May those who litt up wax tapers at
noon day to celebrate thee, bear with those who are content with the light
of the sun thou has placed in the firmament.

Reinforcing a similar anti-sectarian message, Rousseau's 'Savoyard curate's profession of faith', which deliberately minimised the differences between Christian
denominations, was reproduced in three extracts:[66] it was to become one of the
staples of journalistic diet. In weighing the import of these extracts against a
background of religious persecution, O'Dea concludes that Rousseau's religious
vision 'evacuates sectarian difference of any relevance, while encouraging all to
remain faithful to the religion into which they were born', and may well have been
reproduced here to offer support (however indirect) to those who opposed the
exclusion of Catholics from full rights.[67]

   In many ways a successor to the successful *Dublin Magazine*, the *Hibernian
Magazine, or Compendium of Entertaining Knowledge*, was published continu-ously
from January 1771 to December 1810, and likewise shunned overt sectarianism: it
sometimes reported the death of Catholic priests, and a tolerance of Roman
Catholic viewpoints is perceptible, later issues frequently publicising the activities
of the Catholic Committee. The material is mainly derivative: a substantial
number of items are copied from the London *European Magazine* when it commenced publication in 1782. The editor had originally expected a major local contribution to his endeavour, but in May 1773 expressed disappointment at the
failure of the 'learned and ingenious of all denominations' in Ireland to furnish
him with copy.[68] In the twenty years preceding the French Revolution, the *Hibernian* bears witness to the ever-increasing dominance of France as the European
leader in gracious living and fashion, albeit that French manners and customs are
sometimes ridiculed in stereotypical fashion.[69] The increased facility in the
French language assumed of the readers is quite evident with French used in
texts without translation. In 1781, when Antoine Desca published his collection
of Voltaire's *Lettres curieuses et intéressantes* in French in Dublin, a number of
poems from the collection were reproduced in the original in the *Hibernian
Magazine*.[70]

66 *Dublin Magazine*, Oct.1762, 605–6; Feb. 1764, 107–12; Mar. 1764 177–80.
67 O'Dea, 'Rousseau', pp 103–4.
68 *Hibernian Magazine*, 1773, 219.
69 References to 'frogs' already evoke the degeneracy of French *mœurs* for the anglophone reader; see, for example, 1772, 407; 1785, 525.
70 *Hibernian Magazine*, 1781, pp 258–9. In this period a significant number of major works of
   the French enlightenment were being reprinted in Dublin for an Irish market: see Appendix
   2 in *Ireland and the French Enlightenment*.

The specifically French enlightenment material was therefore dominated by the presence of Voltaire, followed by Montesquieu, with Rousseau's popularity rather less marked subsequent to his public quarrel with David Hume.[71] Voltaire's place as European leader of Enlightenment was reflected in a striking full-length portrait of him published in 1772, and was unchallenged even after his death: throughout 1784 lengthy extracts were reproduced from the 'Memoirs of the Life of Voltaire', taken from the French work of the same title which he actually wrote himself, though this is not indicated in the magazine.[72] This piece contained the typical Voltairean side-swipes at the established churches, as, for example, in the description of Frederick of Prussia's court (where he also indulged in one of his many jibes at Frederick's homosexuality): 'God was respected, but those who in his name had imposed upon credulity were not spared. Neither women nor priests ever entered the palace.'[73] Over 80 references to the patriarch of Ferney occur in this magazine for the period 1771–83,[74] and he was followed in popularity by Montesquieu and Rousseau.[75] The major tribute which d'Alembert wrote for the Academy in Paris on the death of Montesquieu ('Eloge de M. le président Montesquieu') was reproduced in translation many years later in the *Hibernian Magazine*.[76] Montesquieu featured particularly strongly after the publication of his *Œuvres posthumes* in Paris and London (1783), which was signalled in May 1784 with the translation of an extract describing the 'character of the celebrated Duke of Berwick'. This item was of some local interest as it highlights that 'wherever [the duke] resided, all those poor English or Irish families who were related, in the most distant manner, to the exiled family, had a kind of right to introduce themselves'.[77]

Perhaps more than any other journal, the *Hibernian Magazine* bears witness in its articles to the influence of enlightenment discourse in the Irish context. Extracts from Fr Arthur O'Leary's works were reproduced at length, with the influence of French Enlightenment texts, to which he would have had access in the course of over two decades in a Capuchin monastery in St Malo, patently obvious.[78] He makes this explicit with repeated references to Montesquieu;[79] but

71 M. O'Dea, 'Rousseau', pp 94ff.
72 *Hibernian Magazine*, 1784, 388–94; 493–6; 567–70.
73 Ibid., 494.
74 Gargett, 'Voltaire's reception in Ireland', pp 79ff.
75 For the same period of the *Hibernian Magazine* there are 28 references to Montesquieu and 20 to Rousseau, but the high points of popularity did not always correspond, especially for Montesquieu who was of an older generation.
76 *Hibernian Magazine*, 1771, 312–17   77 Ibid., 648.
78 For an assessment of O'Leary's career, see J.J. Kelly, '"A wild Capuchin of Cork": Arthur O'Leary (1729–1802)' in Gerard Moran (ed.), *Radical Irish priests, 1660–1970* (Dublin, 1998), pp 39–61.
79 See, for example, 'Mr O'Leary's remarks on the Revd John Wesley's Letters in defence of the Protestant Associations in England', *Hibernian Magazine*, 1780, 304; or 'Mr O'Leary's celebrated plea for liberty of conscience', *Hibernian Magazine*, 1782, 417.

the tone, especially in 'Mr O'Leary's celebrated plea for liberty of conscience',[80] is closer to that of Voltaire, reproducing at times the imagery of the *Traité sur la tolérance*:

> My design, in the following sheets, is to throw open the gates of civil toler-
> ation for all Adam's children, whose principles are not inconsistent with
> the peace of civil society, or subversive of the rules of morality; to wrench,
> as far as in my power lies, the poniard so often tinged with human blood,
> from the hand of persecution, to sheath the sword, which misguided zeal
> has drawn in defence of a gospel which recommends peace and love; to
> restore to man the indelible charter of his temporal rights, which no earth-
> ly power has ever been commissioned by heaven to deprive him of, on
> account of his mental errors.[81]

The *Hibernian Magazine* strongly endorsed O'Leary's treatise, which was published with his *Miscellaneous tracts* in 1781 (and reproduced in full in the magazine,[82] leaving the reader in no doubt with regard to its editorial stand: in this
work, we are told, 'religious discord is banished from society, and the original
right of man to follow the dictates of his conscience, is vindicated by the most
forcible Arguments, displayed in a style that captivates the reader'.[83] Thus this
magazine reflected the extent to which arguments in favour of toleration, pioneered in France in reaction to the persecution of Protestants, were becoming
common coinage in the campaign for Catholic relief in eighteenth-century
Ireland: O'Leary emphasized the universalism of his own approach when he stated: 'I am not . . . a partial advocate. I plead for the Protestant in France, and for
the Jew in Lisbon, as well as for the Catholics in Ireland.'[84]

One of two Dublin magazines in the French language in this decade, *Le
Magazin à la mode*, published monthly by William Whitestone in Capel Street
from May 1777 to April 1778, was edited by Charles Praval, a teacher of French in
Dublin, and sold for 10s. 6d. per year with an average of over ninety pages per
issue. Praval tailored his material for the local readership to a greater degree than
his predecessor, the *Mercure de France* (1775), which had simply drawn directly on
the French periodical of the same name. It contained accounts of what was happening in the Dublin theatres, and the births, marriages and deaths announced
were mainly Irish: thus the magazine could serve some of the same functions for
its subscribers as the magazines in English, and no doubt Praval hoped to acquire

80 The treatise was serialized in six successive numbers starting in Aug. 1782 (337–41, 415–19, 466–70, 519–23, 567–70, 632–3).
81 *Hibernian Magazine*, 1782, 337.
82 Arthur O'Leary, *Miscellaneous tracts* (Dublin, 1781), pp 217–67.
83 *Hibernian Magazine*, 1781, 240.
84 Ibid., p. 337.

a wider readership in this way. Most of the notices indicate a readership of aristocracy and gentry across the country,[85] but there are exceptions: in July 1777 we are informed that 'Le Sieur Antoine ô Donnel, de Sligo, négotiant a épousé demoiselle Judith Begg, de Beature dans la Comté de Roscommon', and in December 'Le Docteur Tully, de *Tuam* dans la comté de Galway, a épousé demoiselle Dillon, *d'Ormond-Quay*'. In his preface Praval explicitly highlighted the acceptance of French as a *lingua franca* for literate Europe, adding that 'La nation Irlandaise est bien persuadé de ce que je viens de dire'. Praval invited his readership to contribute articles, and some obliged; for example one person signing 'P.L.' from Dunshaughlin, County Meath, contributed a number of 'Fables sentimentales' in French verse.[86]

Despite the fact that it is dedicated 'Aux dames', which might have signalled a more light-weight offering, the *Magazin* dealt with a considerable range of enlightenment literature. Voltaire was referred to regularly, with lengthy extracts from the *Anecdotes de la vie de M. de Voltaire*.[87] A passage describing the setting up of the East India Company in England is quoted from Raynal's famous *Histoire philosophique et politique des établissemens et du commerce des Européens dans les deux Inde*s,[88] which was immediately proscribed in France on publication in 1770, and became more radical with each subsequent edition. The proceedings of the scientific academies both of England and France were noticed. Overall, the editor showed a strong interest in Enlightenment themes, and has acquired the vocabulary of the 'Encyclopédistes'. In commenting on Marmontel's *Les Incas*, he suggested that the author's aim was to contribute towards making fanaticism more and more detestable; the Incas are described as a gentle people, who only needed enlightenment ('à être éclairé') to bring them to renounce their errors,[89] and he quoted Fénelon's injunction in his *Directions pour la conscience d'un roi*: 'Accordez à tous la tolérance civile . . .' In the October issue, we find what appears to be the only magazine extract from this book reproduced in Britain or Ireland:[90] published in Paris in this same year, *Les Incas* was rapidly reprinted in translation in London and Dublin. In April 1778 Praval published an anonymous essay 'Réflexions sur la Tolérance religieuse', clearly hostile to the prevailing enlightenment view, whose author thundered:

85 Kennedy, 'The distribution of a locally-produced French periodical'.
86 May 1777, 21; see also July 1777, 199, and June 1777, 111, for a cautionary tale submitted by 'R', and a short essay, 'Sur l'art de converser', sent in by 'P.C.'
87 *Le Magazin*, Aug. 1777, 324–31 and Sept. 1777, 420–7.
88 Sept. 1777, 393–402.
89 *Le Magazin*, Sept. 1777, 432.
90 'Histoire de la ruine de la ville de Mexico, tirée des Incas de M. Marmontel'. Robert Mayo, *The English novel in the magazines 1740-1815* (London, 1962), who found no trace of this work in his very comprehensive study of the magazines.

> J'admire la hardiesse avec laquelle tous nos déclamateurs *encyclopédistes*,
> tous nos frères *menot* de la philosophie du jour osent inviter le gouverne-
> ment Français à supprimer chez lui la distinction de tous les cultes, à
> employer les hommes sans s'informer de ce qu'ils croient.[91]

Even here the author, pleading against extreme measures of persecution, specifically denounces aspects of the penal laws in Ireland:

> En *Irlande*, la sévérité de l'intolérance va jusqu'à mettre la croyance au
> rang des qualités nécessaires pour succéder: le parent le plus prochain,
> quoique né, vivant dans le pays, est exclu, s'il n'a pas la foi du mort … C'est
> un excès déraisonnable et tyrannique.

A letter purporting to be written from Paris to the editor[92] gave a detailed account
of Voltaire's return to Paris and his reception there – he arrived on 10 February,
and died on 30 May – together with two poems which eulogize the new
Sophocles.

The last item for consideration here is the *Weekly Magazine and Literary
Review*, published weekly by John Norman in Essex Street from January to April
1779, reviving a title published in London some twenty years earlier. It contained
some original material of Irish interest, together with articles copied from the
British magazines. A letter from 'Miss N—' to a correspondent in London gave a
description of Paris and its 'amusements', including her reaction to a performance
of Voltaire's *Zaïre*.[93] The more literary offerings included the well-tried French
'moral' tale, and again a notable interest in Rousseau: there are extracts from the
Letter … to M. d'Alembert on theatre, published in English in London in 1759;[94]
from 'Reflections on, and examples of a patriotic spirit',[95] a piece which claims to
be original 'For the Weekly Magazine', and is a garbled translation of a passage
from Book I of *Emile*,[96] and 'Memoirs of the life of the celebrated Jean Jacques
Rousseau, citizen of Geneva',[97] which incorporated part of the Preamble to the
Confessions, three years before the full work was published.[98] The 'Public occur-
rences from Paris' in April included phrases in French which were not translated,[99] one being a quote from Voltaire's *Henriade*, again indicating the expectation
that a significant proportion of the readership could understand the language.

91 *Le Magazin*, 1778, 344ff.
92 Dated 16 Feb. 1778 and published in the Mar. issue of *Le Magazin*.
93 *Weekly Magazine*, 1779, 35–7.   94 Ibid., 1779, 5–7.
95 Ibid., 1779, 50–1.   96 *Œuvres complètes* (Paris, 1969), iv, p. 248ff.
97 *Weekly Magazine*, 1779, 395–8.
98 This version was almost certainly based on the translation which appeared in the London
    Monthly Review of Feb. 1779: J. Voisine, *J.-J. Rousseau en Angleterre à l'époque romantique*
    (Paris, 1956), pp 95–7. Thanks to M. O'Dea for help with identifying this piece.
99 *Weekly Magazine*, 1779, 416.

The sheer volume of French material in these periodicals, as well as in the reprints of British-printed periodicals circulating in Ireland, indicates the extent to which the works of the great figures of the French Enlightenment were popularized in the English-speaking world. The *Gentleman's Magazine* and its contemporaries established for the first time the press 'as a genuinely critical organ of a public engaged in critical political debate'.[100] While the French material was not by any means preponderant in all of these magazines, it was clearly significant; despite the populist anti-French chauvinism of the war years, it was increasingly a major cultural influence within the anglophone world. Voltaire, Montesquieu and Rousseau were accorded unique status, every detail of their lives being avidly seized on by the press. But it was also their works which were deemed to be of interest to a widespread reading public, and as the century progressed an Irish audience was increasingly exposed to ideas that challenged power structures in church and state, and appealed to a concept of universal human rights.

The debate on religious toleration was of great significance in the Irish context. 'May all men remember that they are brethren; may they abhor the tyranny that is exercised over the mind, as they execrate the violence that takes by force the fruit of labour and peaceful industry': Voltaire's powerful 'Prayer' – one of the most influential texts of the century – was reproduced not just by the *Dublin Magazine*, but also by Exshaw, who was a noted loyalist: indeed *Exshaw's Magazine*, in reprinting another extract from the *Traité sur la tolérance*, deliberately drew attention to its relevance for his potential readership.[101] These French texts fed into the debates on the question of civil toleration for Catholics which echo through the journals.

If the enduring interest in Rousseau, Voltaire and Montesquieu in these periodicals is striking, there are strong indications that the British/Irish magazine public, well-informed on the publications of the three 'giants' of the period, were left in relative ignorance of other radical thinkers such as Diderot or Helvétius. The dual factors of reputation and accessibility worked in favour of the three great names, all of whom, it must be remembered, had spent an extended period in England; their works were frequently reprinted, even in Ireland.[102] We are aware of only two Dublin editions of Diderot – *The nun* (1797), and a translation of the *Père de famille* (1751). The philosophical works, with the exception of the *Encyclopédie*, were not widely available in his lifetime; but though the *Encyclopédie* was imported and bought in Ireland, the name of the editor-in-chief seems to have remained in relative obscurity:[103] we have made only one mention of him above. The second reference to Diderot and to Helvétius occurs in a well-

---

100 J. Habermas, *The structural transformation of the public sphere* (London, 1989), p. 60.
101 *Exshaw's Magazine*, 1764, 647.
102 Appendix 2 in *Ireland and the French Enlightenment*.
103 Kennedy, 'The *Encyclopédie*'.

informed article published in the *Dublin Magazine* in 1762;[104] remarking that 'the spirit of philosophy is rising in this [the French] nation', the journalist continues:

> The name of d'Alembert, d'Aguesseau, Montesquieu, Condillac, Caylus, La Condamine, Barthelémy, Bougainville, Fontenelle, and many others, with whom we could augment this honourable list, will always reflect credit upon the age and nation to whom they belong. On the other hand France has its *minute philosophers*, whose only merit is some pert wit, and a little knowledge, blended with an abundant portion of licentiousness and impiety; such as its Diderots, its Helvétius's, with a motley crowd of abbés, counts and marquesses, too numerous to mention.

This author's viewpoint tends to confirm the 'liberal', rather than radical interest in enlightenment thought which we have discussed in relation to Droz's interest in deism in the earlier period. But there were exceptions, which should not be ignored: a radical minority of readers relishing more extreme views was referred to by Burke; as far back as 1734, the editor of the *Weekly Miscellany* had asserted that 'we see *atheism* and *irreligion* scattered up and down these kingdoms, in books and weekly papers, with a very liberal hand';[105] he went on to lament that 'the author in some papers was obliged to make use of the authority of the *ancients*, because the atheist and libertine will admit of no other.' In 1774 a doctor of Scottish origin in Cork, Patrick Blair, published his *Thoughts on nature and religion, or, an apology for the right of private judgment, maintained. By Michael Servetus, M.D. in his answer to John Calvin*. The anonymity of the piece was not surprising in view of its extremely radical content: the introduction states the author's intention to throw 'prejudice' aside, and give primacy to 'the dictates of his reason'.[106] Blair regards the narration of Genesis as purely allegorical; he denies the divinity of Christ and the immortality of the soul; in the very Enlightenment debate on the soul of brutes, he comes down clearly in favour of the argument that the animal soul is of the same nature as that of man, and therefore concludes that both perish in a like death. '[Men] cannot comprehend how matter should think'; he laments, 'they therefore deny it the power of thought.'[107] Blair's *Thoughts* quickly provoked a number of published responses, among which was one of the earliest publications of Fr Arthur O'Leary, for which he prudently sought the approval of the Protestant authorities in his area. O'Leary was quick to associate Blair's arguments with the work of French freethinkers, and in a 'free-thinkers' catechism' he cleverly indicates the origins of many of Blair's key ideas in the work of Voltaire and Helvétius, whose notorious *De l'Esprit* had shaken the Catholic establishment in France to its core at a time when O'Leary was resident there in 1758.[108]

104 *Dublin Magazine*, 1762, 176–8   105 *Weekly Miscellany*, 16 Nov. 1734.
106 Patrick Blair, *Thoughts* (Cork, 1774), p. ii   107 Ibid., p. 62.
108 D.W. Smith, *Helvétius: A study in persecution* (Oxford, 1969).

As the century progressed, the dominance of French material in the periodicals became more and more pronounced. As early as the 1730s there had been a strong interest in French literature; an extensive knowledge of the French language on the part of the readership was often assumed as in a fascinating controversy over rival translations of *Le Doyen de Killerine* in two Dublin newspapers in 1742.[109] One is always conscious of London as the metropolis; but the sphere of involvement of the educated public stretches way beyond it and the Anglophone world. Obvious examples are Dean Madden's pamphlet in 1751 reacting to a relatively unknown Jean Jacques Rousseau, or a letter from Dr Patrick Blair to *Exshaw's Magazine* detailing an interchange of ideas between Dr Connel, also of Cork, and M. Belleteste, 'Dean of the Faculty of Physick at Paris', on the subject of innoculation against smallpox, which Voltaire had turned into an Enlightenment controversy in his *Letters concerning the English nation* of 1733.[110]

The conclusion suggested by a reading of these magazines is that Irish readers of this period were not cut off from the vibrant cultures of mainland Europe. The level of interaction indicates the benefits of studying these popular forms of communication which have often been neglected in favour of book culture proper. A survey of local announcements underlines the geographic and social spread of their readership in Ireland, and gives the lie to assumptions that French language, culture and 'manners' were the preserve of the aristocracy, or the Dublin world. This substantial body of literature can certainly bear further study.

109 Pollard, *Dublin's trade*, p. 185.
110 *Exshaw's Magazine*, 1764, 177, 433–5.

3

'The return of the native':
The United Irishmen, culture and colonialism

LUKE GIBBONS

> We will not buy or borrow liberty from America or France, but manufacture it ourselves, and work it up with those materials which the hearts of Irishmen furnish them with at home …
>
> *Address of the United Irishmen to the Scottish Convention*, 1793

On 20 June 1789, as members of the newly formed National Assembly were taking the revolutionary oath in a tennis court in Paris, another strange, if less epochal, ceremony was taking place at Detroit, in the heartlands of the Iroquois nation, admitting a new chief to the famous Indian confederacy:

> I, David Hill, Chief of the Six Nations, give the name of Eghnidal to my friend Lord Edward FitzGerald, for which I hope he will remember me as long as he lives. The name belongs to the Bear Tribe.[1]

'I have been adopted by one of the Nations,' wrote FitzGerald to his mother, 'and am now a thorough Indian.'[2] The distinction conferred on the errant aristocrat came towards the end of an extended visit to America in 1788-9 which brought him into contact with the rigours of life in the wilderness. In the grip of a Canadian winter, he charted a new route, 'never before attempted, even by Indians',[3] which halved the distance between New Brunswick and Quebec, before proceeding south through the woods to Niagara and the United States. Though arduous in the extreme, the whole undertaking proved exhilarating to the young, unsettled adventurer:

---

1 Cited in Thomas Moore, *The life and death of Lord Edward FitzGerald* (London, 1831), i, p. 148. For a vivid recent account of Lord Edward's exploits in America, see Stella Tillyard, *Citizen Lord: Edward FitzGerald, 1763-1798* (London, 1998).
2 Moore, *Edward FitzGerald*, i, p. 147.
3 See Hamilton Moore's account of FitzGerald's journey, in a letter to the duke of Richmond, in Moore, *Lord Edward FitzGerald*, pp 136-8.

> There is something in a wild country very enticing; taking its inhabitants, too, and their manner into the bargain. I know Ogilvie [i.e. his foster-father] says I ought to have been a savage, and if it were not that the people I love and wish to live with are civilized people, and like houses, &c., &c., I really would join the savages; and, leaving all our fictitious, ridiculous wants, be what nature intended we should be. Savages have all the real happiness of life, without any of those inconveniences, or real obstacles to it, which custom has introduced among us.[4]

FitzGerald's encounter with the American Indians came at a time when the eighteenth-century fascination with the myth of the noble savage was slowly succumbing to the new, emergent ideologies of romanticism and racism. As the Enlightenment moved into a triumphant phase following the American and French Revolutions, the radical diversity presented by other non-western or 'primitive' cultures became a pressing political concern, and not just something to be idealized at a distance. In this new political dispensation, it gradually became apparent that universal declarations of human rights extended with greater ease to individuals than to cultures: while all human beings were equal, some cultures were less equal than others, and their destruction was justified in the name of progress. Thus the remit of the American Declaration of Independence did not extend to Indians (not to mention others such as women and slaves) and, in fact, the obdurate presence of native peoples in the 'wilderness' came to be construed as the greatest single obstacle to the untrammelled pursuit of liberty and happiness. By the same token, the treatment meted out to the peasants of the Vendée or the black Jacobins in the slave insurrection in Haiti left no doubt as the limits of the Enlightenment where other 'peoples without history' were concerned. Not only did the Enlightenment exclude 'primitive' cultures, but its whole rationale was built on their exclusion. It was left to romanticism, then, to pick up where the Enlightenment left off, offering a imaginary realm of myth and nostalgia as a consolation for those excluded from the material benefits of citizenship and progress in the real world.

In its most benign form, this romantic out-take from the Enlightenment promulgated the cult of the noble savage, and related ideologies of primitivism. These offered to radical thinkers in the West an image of 'natural liberty', a journey back in time to bear witness to the origins of natural rights. Notwithstanding the unmistakable traces of colonial condescension, native Americans were portrayed as the modern counterparts not only of primitive peoples at the dawn of European history, but also of the proud freemen of ancient Greece and Rome. The first extensive ethnographic accounts of the native Americans by the French writers, Baron de Lahontan and Joseph-François Lafitau, saw much to

---

4 Moore, *Edward FitzGerald*, i, p. 91.

admire in the Indian way of life and were enormously influential on subsequent commentators. As several recent writers have noted, such favourable accounts did not feature so prominently in the work of British officials and soldiers, but among the most sympathetic observers of the native Americans were two from an Anglo-Irish background, Cadwallader Colden (1688–1776), surveyor-general and lieutenant-governor of New York, who played a conspicuous role in the events leading up to the War of Independence, and Sir William Johnson (1715–1774), Superintendent of Indian affairs in North America and perhaps the most important strategist in bringing about the fateful alliance between Indian and British forces in their various conflicts with the colonial settlers.[5]

In his pioneering *History of the five Indian nations of Canada, which are dependent on the province of New York* (1727), the first systematic account of the Iroquois in English, Colden showed that while he was not blind to their negative qualities, such as the hideous torments which they inflicted on their enemies, native Americans had no monopoly on cruelty:

> Whoever reads the history of so famed ancient heroes, will find them, I'm afraid, not much better in this respect. Does Achilles' behaviour to Hercules' dead body in Homer, appear less savage? … witness the Carthaginians and Phoenicians burning their children alive in sacrifice, and several passages in Jewish history; and witness, in later times, the Christians burning one another alive, for God's sake.

But the analogies with classical antiquity were not entirely negative, and Colden proceeded to strike a note that accentuated the nobility of the Iroquois warrior, and lent itself particularly to subsequent idealizations of indigenous peoples by republican and Enlightenment theorists:

> The Five Nations are a poor barbarous people, bred under the darkest ignorance; and yet a bright and noble genius shines thro' these black clouds. None of the greatest Roman heroes have discovered a greater love of their country, or a greater contempt of death, than these people called barbarians have done, when liberty came in competition. Indeed, I think our Indians have outdone the Roman in this particular; some of the greatest of those have we know murdered themselves to avoid shame or torments; but our Indians have refused to die meanly, or with but little pain, when they thought their country's honour would be at stake by it; but have given their bodies willingly to the cruel torment of their ene-

---

5 Robert L. Emerson, 'American Indians, Frenchmen, and Scots philosophers', in Roseann Runte (ed.), *Studies in eighteenth-century culture*; David Noel Doyle, *Ireland, Irishmen and revolutionary America, 1760-1820* (Cork, 1981).

mies, to shew, as they said, that the Five Nations consisted of men, whose courage and resolution could not be shaken.[6]

The stoical demeanour of the Indians, in conjunction with their indomitable courage and martial valour, contributed to their image as exemplars of natural rights, of humanity in its original Edenic state of nature.[7] But as Virgil reminded those who searched for a paradise on Earth, even death is in Arcadia.[8] The fatal flaw in the primitivist love affair with the Indian was that it was essentially nostalgic and elegiac, in effect, paying homage to the simple austerities of a vanished social order. Under theories of progress adumbrated by the Scottish Enlightenment, this myth of origins was elaborated into a stages theory of history, with justice and natural rights being transferred gradually from their primordial 'natural' state to those societies at the highest stage of civilization.

While few theorists went so far as to discern in the Indian way of life the putative condition of humanity before the 'original' social contract, nonetheless the alleged freedom enjoyed by the Indian lent itself to fantasies of the abolition of society, with individuals enjoying freedom devoid entirely of social or communal obligations. Traces of this pre-lapsarian dream are evident in Lord Edward FitzGerald's reflections on his life among the Iroquois, but unlike some of his latter-day *laissez-faire* counterparts, he at least recognized that the absence of society also means the absence of property and money. Comparing the economic worries and vanities of polite society to a simple, primitive existence, he speculated that if he were brought up among the Indians 'there would be no cases of looking forward to the fortune for children, – of thinking how are you to live: no separations in families, one in Ireland, one in England; no devilish politics, no fashions, customs, duties, or appearances to the world, to interfere with one's happiness'.[9] But no sooner has he expressed these sentiments than he reveals that his utopian lifestyle is not quite so devoid of duties and obligations; rather, it possesses different and more deep-rooted social commitments than those found in corrupt commercial societies. Indian freedom does not consist in an atomized individualism but its opposite, a society suffused with communal warmth and care for others, without any of the instrumental exchanges that pass for civil society in the West:

6 Cadwallader Colden, *The history of the five Indian nations of Canada, which are dependent on the province of New York* [1727] (New York, 1902), pp x–xi, xxii. According to Robert Waite, Colden was 'the best informed man in the New World on the affairs of the British American colonies' ('Introduction', ibid., p. 36)

7 This stoic character was augmented, however unintentionally, by the appellation of the name 'Seneca' to one of the Six Nations tribes, and is a recurrent trope in descriptions of Indian bravery and self-composure.

8 For the classic discussion of the theme of 'the Golden Age' in Virgil, and its subsequent depiction in painting, see Erwin Panofsky, '*Et in Arcadia ego*: Poussin and the elegiac tradition', in idem, *Meaning in the visual arts* (New York, 1955).

9 Moore, *Edward FitzGerald*, i, p. 92.

They enjoy the love and company of their wives, relations and friends, without any interference of interests or ambition to separate them. To bring things home to oneself, if we had been Indians, instead of its being my duty to be separated from all of you, it would , on the contrary, be my duty to be with you … Instead of being served and supported by servants, everything here is done by one's relations – by the people one loves; and the mutual obligations you must be under increase your love for each other.[10]

In drawing attention to these contrary ideals – a society that is at once without duties and custom, and yet is even more saturated with mutual obligations than western societies – FitzGerald is exposing one of the main fault-lines in the appropriation of 'primitive' tribes as foundations myths for western societies. On the one hand, they are pre-social, existing an a state of nature; on the other, they are too social, living permanently in 'the shadow of each other'. The source of the confusion has to do with the ambivalence itself of the golden age: a form of life idealized and venerated at a distance, but denied and indeed actively repressed as it approximated reality, or came closer to home in the metropolitan centre. The key consideration here was distance, in both its spatial and temporal senses. For many contemporaries as well as subsequent scholars, the opening up of the New World marked a Copernican revolution in culture, de-centring the self-image of the Old World which equated humanity with Europe and its various hinterlands. As many commentators observed, epic and ethnography fused as the scale of the New World required a voyage of discovery as fundamental in redrafting the contours of the western imagination as Homer's original Odyssey.[11] This had far-reaching consequences for perceptions of time as well as space during the Renaissance, for it gradually undermined cyclical theories of history driven by a desire to restore the grandeur of classical antiquity in a modern age. New forms of the past now presented themselves which were not so amenable to restoration, opening up the possibility that history was carried forward by an irreversible flow, a river of no return.

The initial response to this disruption of the genealogy of the world was to integrate the Indians into existing accounts, even at the cost of breaking up the narrative coherence of the 'great chain of being' which had held medieval Christendom in place. American Indians were variously linked with the Lost Tribes of Israel, or with ancient Asian peoples such as the Phoenicians and the Scythians, and came to be seen as 'degenerate examples of human regression planted in their new continent after the flood and the dispersal of nations follow-

10 Ibid., p. 91.
11 See Martin Thom, *Republic, nations and tribes*, p. 133, who cites Fenelon and Chateaubriand in this respect.

ing the fall of the Tower of Babel'.[12] This facilitated another momentous shift in European sensibility, as the elaboration of natural rights and contractarian theories of society encouraged political theorists to look for evidence of pre-contractual formations to justify their models of human evolution. It is at this conjuncture that the conflicting images of pre-contractual society present themselves, oscillating from the anarchic freedom of isolated individualism to the close interdependence of archaic communalism. For Grotius, there was little difficulty in reconciling primitive, pre-contractual society with the accounts outlined in Genesis, for both shared communal property and the absence of government which made the original general contract necessary. It was left to Thomas Hobbes to link these conceptions directly to the American Indians, relating his famous picture of the state of nature, in which 'the life of man, [is] solitary, poor, nasty, brutish, and short', to the New World:

> It may peradventure be though, that there never was such a time, nor condition of war as this; and I believe it was never generally so, all over the world: but there are many places, where they live so now. For the savage peoples in many places of America, except the government of small Families, the concord whereof dependeth on natural lust, have no government at all; and live at this day in that brutish manner, as I said before.[13]

Hobbes' formulation is of note in that he still does not discern in the condition of the Indians the template for the origin of all mankind. It is this latter step, traced by Ronald Meek to the late seventeenth century and to the four-stages theory of history promulgated by the French and Scottish Enlightenments in the eighteenth century, which introduced the 'spatialization of time', the equation of distance in time with distance in space, which was so amenable to colonial ideology. Boundaries and frontiers in space became the equivalent of stages and epochs in history. This is the notion of origins which informs John Locke's important modification of Hobbes' account: 'In the beginning, all the world was *America*.'[14] The universality of the 'state of nature' was attributed at first to a common ancestry, as in the biblical story, but by relocating origins in different geographical settings, with no direct relation between them, time was given a new spatial differentiation. The Scottish historian William Robertson expressed

---

12 Zia Sardar, Ashis Nandy and Merryl Wyn Davies, *Barbaric others: A manifesto on western racism* (London, 1993), p. 54. The lost tribes of Israel and Phoenician origins were discussed – only to be dismissed – by John Ogilby in his *America: Being the latest, and most accurate description of the New World* (1671). Ogilby then opted for the Scythians, an Asian genealogy which, as it turns out, may not have been entirely inaccurate as to the origins of the Indian peoples. See Ronald Meek, *Social science and the ignoble savage* (Cambridge, 1976), pp 49ff.
13 Thomas Hobbes, *Leviathan* (London, 1651), pp 62–3.
14 John Locke, *Two treatises on government* (London, 1690), ii, 5, p. 49.

this re-casting of the origins of society in his landmark *History of America* (1777):

> A tribe of savages on the banks of the Danube must nearly resemble one
> upon the plains washed by the Mississippi. Instead then of presuming
> from this similarity, that there is any affinity between them, we should
> only conclude, that the dispositions and manners of men are formed by
> their situation, and arise from the state of society in which they live ... In
> every part of the earth, the progress of man hath been nearly the same;
> and we can trace him in his career from the rude simplicity of savage life,
> until he attains the industry, the arts, and the elegance of polished society.
> There is nothing wonderful, then, in the similitude between the
> Americans and the barbarous nations of our continent.[15]

As is clear from Robertson's formulation, the influence of Montesquieu was
crucial in promoting awareness of the effects of climate, environment and modes
of subsistence on the determination of national character and cultural diversity.
This new current in Enlightenment thought throws a less favourable light on the
tendency, endemic in homages to the noble savage, to establish affinities between
native American and other distinguished – and not so distinguished – ancient
societies, for it was by virtue of this temporal dislocation that Indians were cast
in the mould of obsolete cultures, peoples who had essentially outlived their usefulness in the modern world.

  As early as 1609, native Americans were being compared to ancient Sparta in
French writings, thus establishing a trope linking their freedom to ideals of
virtue in ancient Rome (as in Colden's account above) or, in more radical political tracts, to republican concepts of liberty. But instead of conferring cultural
prestige on the Indians and elevating them to the position enjoyed by the
Romans in western thought, the universalizing thrust of primitivism served to
divest them of all cultural specificity, in effect, denying that they were cultures at
all. Time and again, the image of the solitary Indian silhouetted against the horizon, or of individual hunters wandering through the wilderness oblivious to
each other, recurred in the Western imagination. 'The life of a fisher or a
hunter', wrote Lord Kames, 'is averse to society, except among the members of
single families. The shepherd life promotes larger societies, if that can be called a
society, which scarce hath any other than a local connection.'[16] Likewise, William
Robertson observed: 'In America, man appears under the rudest form in which
we can conceive him to subsist. We behold communities just beginning to unite,

---

15 William Robertson, *'History of America* [1777]', iv, p. 2, in *The life and writings of William
   Robertson*, p. 806.
16 Cited in Meek, *Social science and the ignoble savage*, p. 103.

and may examine the sentiments and action of human beings in the infancy of social life.'[17]

It is striking that throughout Scottish attempts to apply a developmental model to the state of nature, converting it from a state to a process, there is a recurrent anxiety about the nature of sociability, and the transition to social interaction. This is particularly noticeable in the tendency, evident in Kames' pronouncement above, to collapse the family, and related local affections, into a pre-social state, at odds with the prerequisites of civil society. What is at stake is not so much the New World and distant lands as a more immediate menace, the residual Gaelic culture and clan system of the Highlands and, of course, Ireland.[18] Roy Harvey Pearce has observed that 'American theorizing about the Indian owed its greatest debt to a group of eighteenth-century Scottish writers on man and society',[19] but it may be that this concern with primitivism was motivated by matters closer to home, the threat presented by the Scottish Highlands and Ireland to new conceptions of Britishness being forged in this century. 'Resemblances in time', as Hugh Blair liked to call them, between native Americans and native Scottish culture date to the end of the sixteenth century when Theodor de Bry, in Part One of his *America*, included illustrations of ancient Picts to accompany John White's famous ethnographic drawing of Indian life in Virginia.[20] But these at least were reassuringly removed in time from contemporary discontents in Scotland. What was less comforting, and what the whole discourse of primitivism sought to prevent, was the presence of the savage on one's native shore.

Following the logic of the new realignment of time and space, the native savage was accordingly projected back into antiquity. Instead of posing a challenge for cultural diversity in the present, Gaelic culture was presented as something superseded in the past: the Highlanders appeared, in Peter Womack's description, as 'no longer as different from ourselves, but what we *once were*'.[21] To exorcize the ghosts of Culloden, the lived experience of the recent past – the connective tissue of custom and popular memory – was dissipated, and replaced by the unattainable aura of a distant golden age. Everything that happened in

---

17 Robertson, *History of America*, iv, 8, p. 811.
18 That the threat presented by Ireland lurked constantly behind the fear of the Highlands is evident throughout the early modern period. As early as William Camden's *Brittania* (1586), Scotland is described as being composed of two cultures: 'With respect to the manners and ways of living, it is divided into the *High-land-men* and the *Low-land-men*. These are the more civilized, and use the language and habit of the English; the other more rude and barbarous, and use that of the Irish' (cited in Robert Crawford, *Devolving English literature* [Oxford, 1992], p. 16).
19 Roy Harvey Pearce, *Savagism and civilization: A study of the Indian and the American mind* (Berkeley, 1988), p. 82.
20 See Stuart Piggott, *Ancient Britons and the antiquarian imagination* (London, 1989), pp 75ff.
21 Peter Womack, *Improvement and romance: Constructing the myth of the Scottish Highlands* (London, 1989), p. 23.

between was construed as corruption and decay, as a once glorious epoch fallen into decline. A cultural legacy extending over centuries, incorporating early Christianity, the middle ages and the early modern period, was declared waste, the temporal equivalent of the Atlantic Ocean, opening up a void between then and now. As David Hume wrote to his friend David Wilkes in 1754:

> If time had permitted, you should have gone into the Highlands. You would have seen human nature in the golden age, or rather, indeed, in the silver: for the Highlanders have degenerated somewhat from the primitive simplicity of mankind. But perhaps you have so corrupted a taste as to prefer your Iron Age.[22]

For Hume and for other members of the Scottish Enlightenment there was little doubt that the source of the contamination lay not only with feudalism but with tradition and the persistence of vernacular culture (both shorthand for Catholicism and Gaelic culture). In the section on 'Rude nations' in his *Essay on the history of civil society*, Adam Ferguson argued that accounts of antiquity lack sufficient authority since they 'are made to bear the stamp of the times through which they have passed in the form of tradition, not of the ages through which their pretended descriptions relate':

> We therefore willingly quit the history of our early ancestors, where Caesar and Tacitus have dropped them; and perhaps, till we come within the reach of what is connected with present affairs, and makes a part of the system on which we now proceed, [we] have little reason to expect any subject to interest or inform the mind.[23]

It is in this context that the dim figure of Ossian emerged from the mists of the Highlands, mildewed with age but somehow transporting himself across the centuries to come within the reach of 'present affairs'. Much of the difficulty experienced by James Macpherson in vouching for the authenticity of his alleged translations derived from his reluctance to admit that such originals as existed had more to do with the vagaries of oral tradition than with the purity of manuscript sources. Howard Gaskill rightly points out, as a corrective to Dr Johnson's throwing down the gauntlet to Macpherson to 'produce the manuscripts', that on no occasion did Macpherson make the absurd claim that his originals were texts dating from Ossian's own era, or even that they were based exclusively on manuscripts.[24] Nevertheless. it is clear that Macpherson was less

---

22 Marvin B. Becker, *The emergence of civil society in the eighteenth century* (Bloomington, 1994), p. 82.

23 Adam Ferguson, *An essay on the history of civil society* [1767], ed. Duncan Forbes (Edinburgh, 1966), pp 78–9.

24 Howard Gaskill, 'Introduction', *Ossian revisited* (Edinburgh, 1991), pp 6-16.

than happy with having to rely on the debased medium of oral culture: 'Probability is all that can be established on the authority of tradition, ever dubious and uncertain.'[25] The invocation of oral tradition had its advantages, however, for it provided Macpherson with a pretext for 'improving' his raw materials or, as he preferred to describe it, restoring them to the original. As Andrew Gaillie, who worked with Macpherson on the Gaelic poems for Fingal, expressed it:

> It was, and I believe still is well known, that the broken poems of Ossian, handed down from one generation to another, got corrupted. In the state of the Highlands, and its language, this evil, I apprehend, could not be avoided; and I think great credit is due, in such a case, to him who restores a work of merit to its original purity.[26]

As to the source of the corruption, Macpherson had little doubt that the rot set in with the advent of the bardic tradition. The bards and the Gaelic order they embodied summoned up the bogey of the recent past in Scotland, but were also a painful reminder of the obduracy of Irish culture, which could not so easily be consigned to oblivion as its counterpart in the Highlands. For this reason, it was vital that their role as custodians of a distinguished culture be discredited, and ultimately destroyed:

> I have shewn how superior the probability of Ossian's tradition is to the undigested fictions of the Irish bards, and the more recent and regular legends of both Irish and Scottish historians ... It was chiefly for this reason, that I have rejected wholly the works of the bards in my publications.

Irish historians fared no better than the bardic order, as Macpherson proceeded to pour scorn on 'the improbable and self-condemned tales of Keating and O'Flaherty. Credulous and puerile to the last degree, they have disgraced the antiquities they were want to establish'.[27]

It was not just the 'undigested fictions' of the bards, but also their native allegiances and sense of belonging which caused offence to primitivist ideology. They celebrated – or excoriated – what they knew best, but never lifted their

---

25 James Macpherson, 'A dissertation concerning the poems of Ossian' [1765], in *The poems of Ossian*, 2 vols [1773 ed.] (Dublin, 1780), ii, p. 192.

26 Cited in Fiona Stafford, *The sublime savage: James Macpherson and the poems of Ossian* (Edinburgh, 1988), p. 83. Stafford adds, in her perceptive account of the manner in which the ideology of primitivism informed Macpherson's method of composition, that 'his contempt for the existing poetry of the Highlands, was the corollary of his idealized vision of Celtic Scotland ... If the existing poems were too corrupt to show off the genius of the Highlands to the outside world, Macpherson would use only the parts he considered fit and 'restore' the rest, according to his own ideas on ancient literature' (pp 83, 85).

27 Macpherson, 'A dissertation', *The poems of Ossian*, pp 192, 198-9.

eyes above their immediate horizons, which made them of little interest to other cultures: 'Their ideas, it is confessed, are too local, to be admired in another language; to *those who are acquainted with the manners they represent, and the scene they describe*, they must afford pleasure and satisfaction.'[28] In this statement, we can see one of the key contributions made by primitivism to Enlightenment thought, namely, that any kind of cultural specificity or local mode of address prevents cross-cultural communication – and, by extension, citizenship, the capacity to become a citizen of the world. Under this dispensation, as Johannes Fabian has argued, knowledge of the other can only take place across a lapse of time, so that the more distant the culture is from the here and now, the greater the appeal to cosmopolitan sensibilities.[29] Hence, as against the mere provincialism of the bards, Macpherson is at pains to point out that Ossian 'acted in a more extensive sphere, and his ideas ought to be more noble and universal; neither gives he, I presume, so many of those peculiarities, which are only understood in a certain period or country'.[30] This, as it happened, was highly convenient for Macpherson's muse, for it released him from the onerous task of having to attend to the kind of topographical details and local knowledge which were noticeably missing from the poems.

This rarefaction of the past was also bound up with another major lacuna in Macpherson's Ossian that goes to the heart of the contradictions we have earlier noted in primitivist ideology. Historians of 'rude nations' had struggled with the difficulty of reconciling the excessive sociability of savage peoples with their isolated, pre-social condition, but the relocation of the noble savage in the Scottish antiquity circumvented this problem. As Hugh Blair noted in his influential treatise on Ossian, one of the most distinctive features of the poems

> is the entire silence which reigns with respect to all the great clans and families, which are now established in the Highlands. The origins of these several clans is known to be very ancient: And it is well known, that there is no passion by which a native Highlander is more distinguished, than by attachment to his clan, and jealousy for its honour.[31]

So far from detracting from its authenticity, this was a clear demonstration that Macpherson had got it right – politically, if not historically. In laying down the cultural conditions for the transition from previous stages to the highest phase of social development, that of civility and commerce, Adam Smith had noted that the obstinacy of familial and communal attachments constitute a formidable bar-

---

28 Ibid., p. 192.
29 Johannes Fabian, *Time and the other: How anthropology makes its object* (New York, 1983).
30 Macpherson, 'A dissertation', p. 198.
31 Hugh Blair, 'A critical dissertation on the poems of Ossian' [1763], in *The poems of Ossian*, pp 355-6.

rier to the abstract, impersonal relations of the market. In his *Theory of moral sentiments*, he recalled:

> It is not many years ago that, in the Highlands of Scotland, the chieftain used to consider [i.e. show consideration] the poorest man of his clan, his cousin and relation. The same excessive regard to kindred is said to take place … I believe among all other nations who are merely in the same state of society in which the Scots Highlanders were about the turn of the present century.[32]

The anxiety induced by the dense layers of filiation in Highlands society is nowhere more evident than in Smith's agitated response to the Jacobite uprising of 1745, in which the army of invading Highlanders are stripped, in his imagination, of the raiments of society and reduced to a primal horde of savages. Decrying the lack of 'courage' and 'martial spirit' in an advanced, commercial age, he observed ruefully:

> This is confirmed by universal experience. In the year 1745 four or 5 thousand naked unarmed Highlanders took possession of the improved parts of this country without any opposition from the unwarlike inhabitants. They penetrated into England and alarmed the whole nation, and had they not been opposed by a standing army they would have seized the throne with little difficulty.[33]

It is striking how, for the most part, theories of sympathy adumbrated by the Scottish Enlightenment are based on the premise that the experience of suffering, or the expression of grievances of any kind, are incompatible with Enlightenment ideals of citizenship and fraternity, still less with human or universal solidarity. According to David Hume, although sympathy can be extended to those in need, it is pre-eminently directed at the rich and the powerful:

> Upon the whole, there remains nothing, which can give us an esteem for power and riches, and a contempt for meanness and poverty, except the principle of sympathy, by which we enter into the sentiments of the rich and poor, and partake of their pleasure and uneasiness.[34]

The 'uneasiness' generated through sympathy with the poor is little short of repulsion, and Hume anticipates Smith's neo-stoical repudiation of the right to

32 Adam Smith, *Theory of moral sentiments*, ed. D.D. Raphael and A.L. Macfie (Oxford, 1976), p. 223.
33 Adam Smith, *Lectures on jurisprudence*, ed. R.L. Meek, D.D. Raphael, and P.L. Stein (Oxford, 1978), pp 540-1.
34 David Hume, *A treatise on human nature*, ed. E.C. Mosser (London, 1969), p. 411.

complain, arguing that the poor, or the 'misfortunate', only deserve sympathy when they look for it least: 'a man who is not dejected by misfortunes, is the more lamented on account of his patience; and if that virtue extends so far as utterly to remove all sense of uneasiness, it still further increases our compassion'.[35] Adam Smith extends this to a principle that the ventilation of grievances in the public sphere is an affront to propriety which, in Smith, is shorthand for the discipline and refinement of the body which characterizes a polite, commercial age. According to Smith, 'it may be laid down as a general rule' that the kind of 'affections which tend to unite men in society' are those 'more or less agreeable to the person concerned', such as 'humanity, kindness, natural affection, friendship, [and] esteem'.[36] By contrast, experiences of pain and duress tend to shut out fellow-feeling, turning our minds and bodies in on ourselves:

> the passions which the spectator is least disposed to sympathize with, and in which, on that account, the point of propriety may be said to stand low, are those of which the immediate feeling or sensation is more or less disagreeable, or even painful, to the person principally concerned. This general rule, so far as I have been able to observe, admits not of a single exception.[37]

It is clear from this that Smith had attended a traditional Irish wake, where misfortune and distress brought out sociability to the point of excess in a community. But behind Smith's categorical imperative is an attempt to sever suffering or grievances of any kind from social interaction or concern for others – thus laying the basis for a market economy in which compassion and the alleviation of distress, even in conditions of crisis, are no longer necessary for social justice. In an ominous remark on appropriate responses to hunger, he writes:

> It is indecent to express any strong degree of those passions from a certain situation or disposition of the body; because the company, not being in the same disposition, cannot be expected to sympathize with them. Violent hunger, for example, though upon many occasions not only natural, but unavoidable, is always indecent, and to eat voraciously is universally regarded as a piece of ill manners.[38]

35 Hume, *Treatise*, p. 419. As Thomas A. Horne points out, Hume occupies a pivotal position in Western political thought in rejecting 'medieval' natural law traditions of obligations towards the poor, even questioning the role of discretionary charity as an inducement to 'idleness and debauchery': Horne, *Property rights and poverty* (Chapel Hill, N.C., 1990), p. 93.
36 Smith, *Theory of moral sentiments*, p. 243.
37 Ibid.
38 Smith, *Theory of moral sentiments*, p. 27.

In a 'Digression concerning the Corn Trade and Corn Laws' in *The wealth of nations*, this is given political expression in what might be seen as a foreshadowing of the government's response, based on Smith's authority, among others, to the Great Famine in Ireland: 'Famine has never arisen from any other cause but the violence of government attempting by improper means to remedy the inconvenience of a dearth.'[39]

The underlying assumption for Smith as for Hume is that sympathy, in the new, refined moral sense, requires the age of commerce to bestow its benefits on society. According to the natural right theories of Grotius and Pufendorf, to which Hume and Smith owed much of their intellectual formation, scarcity and want did not produce a sensitivity towards the plight of others but rather selfishness and possessiveness. For this reason, it is only in conditions of relative comfort and abundance that the refinement of the passions which permit morality takes place. This involves a conquest of physical appetite and a purging of the body from the public sphere, a form of psychic discipline which is impossible in primitive societies. Hence the paradox that for all their sociability and 'clannishness', primitive societies are incapable of sympathy, as defined in Smith's moral lexicon, on account of their constant struggle for survival. In the case of native American Indians, he asserts that 'circumstances not only habituate him to every sort of distress, but teach him to give way to none of the passions which that distress is apt to excite. He can expect from his countrymen no sympathy or indulgence for such weakness'.[40] This lays the basis for the critical argument that adversity forces us to look after ourselves:

> Before we feel for others, we must in some measure be at ease ourselves. If our own misery pinches us very severely, we have no leisure to attend to that of our neighbour; and all savages are too much preoccupied with their own wants and necessities to give much attention to those of the other person.[41]

The implications of this argument are far reaching. 'Primitive' societies, and 'the other' within – Gaelic culture,[42] the poor – are disenfranchised at the outset from the Enlightenment project as being incapable of thinking beyond themselves, or attaining that generosity of vision that comes so effortlessly to citizens of the

---

39 Adam Smith, 'Digression concerning the corn trade and corn laws', *The wealth of nations* [1776], ii, 4, v (London, 1991), p. 26.
40 Smith, *Theory of moral sentiments*, p. 205.
41 Ibid.
42 But not, of course, the imaginary Celts, as reconstituted by the Scottish Enlightenment, to provide a suitable antiquarian pedigree for 'the Athens of the North'. The primitivism of the Celts, unlike the mere Irish or the actual Highlanders themselves, was retrospectively endowed with the capacity – indeed, an excessive capacity – for sympathy. This 'sympathetic' self became, in fact, one of the defining traits of the colonial stereotype of the 'sensitive' Celt.

world. Insult is added to injury as there is not only the actual experience of hardship or suffering, but the added indignity of ostracization or isolation. Solidarity among the oppressed, particularly across cultural boundaries or between different societies with shared experiences of colonialism, is ruled out *a priori* as being beyond the reach of the primitive mind. It became imperative for this reason to widen the gap between civility and savagery – a process facilitated greatly by clearly defined 'stages' of history – to prevent primitive societies from aspiring to traits that could qualify as modern, rendering them eligible for the notions of liberty, justice and equality that were the sole preserve of advanced western societies.

If we return to Lord Edward FitzGerald's sojourn in America in the light of these observations, it can be seen that his acknowledgement of the dense networks of social ties, duties and obligations which underlie the 'natural simplicity' of primitive societies marks off the Iroquois as a fully constituted culture, not merely the denizens of a putative state of nature. For Adam Smith, as we have seen, refinements of the passions such as sympathy, not to mention the delicacy of feeling that characterizes sentimental love, are not to be found among 'the savages in North America': 'The weakness of love, which is so much indulged in ages of humanity and politeness, is regarded among savages as the most unpardonable effeminacy.'[43] But FitzGerald, not without a certain amount of wishful thinking on his part, saw the Indians as very much his contemporaries, and revelled in flirtatious exchanges with the females who accompanied him:

> They are delightful people; the ladies charming, and with manners that I like very much, they are so natural. Notwithstanding the life they lead, which would make most women rough and masculine, they are as soft, meek and modest as the best brought up girls in England. At the same time, they are coquettes au possible. Conceive the manners of Mimi in a poor squaw, that has been carrying packs in the woods all her life.[44]

Thomas Moore correctly notes, in his biography of FitzGerald, that 'much of the colouring' which he gave to 'savage life' was 'itself borrowed from civilization', but what is of interest here is the impulse (however misguided ethnographically) to bring native Americans into the modern world. For Moore, this aligns FitzGerald's republicanism with that of Thomas Jefferson, whom he cites as paying homage to 'such societies (as the Indians) which live without government' and who accordingly enjoy greater happiness than 'those who live under the European governments'.[45] But notwithstanding their admiration and enthusiasm for the American Enlightenment, leading figures in the United Irishmen

43 Smith, *Theory of moral sentiments*, p. 205.
44 Moore, *Edward FitzGerald*, i, pp 145-6.
45 Ibid., p. 102.

expressed profound misgivings over the treatment of slaves and Indians in the new land of liberty. Thomas Russell wrote, 'On every lump of sugar, I see a drop of blood.' Following the efforts of leading United Irishmen such as Thomas MacCabe to prevent Belfast becoming a centre of the slave trade, James Hope takes Jefferson to task in his poem, 'Jefferson's daughter', 'as ye trample the rights of your dark fellow men':

> Do you boast of your Freedom! peace, babblers be still,
> Unfetter your slaves, and the goddess will hear.
> Have ye power to unbind, are you wanting the will.
> Must the groans of your bondsman still torture the ear,
> The daughter of Jefferson sold as a slave.[46]

During his protracted stay in the United States, Archibald Hamilton Rowan expressed the same romantic longings for life in the wilderness as Lord Edward FitzGerald, but also shared with him the determination to include oppressed minorites with his pastoral vision. Responding to conflicting advice to settle down in Philadelphia, or to buy a small farm, he writes:

> I will do neither; I will go to the woods; but I will not kill Indians, nor keep slaves. Good God! if you heard some of the Georgians, or the Kentucky people, talk of killing the natives! Cortes, and all that followed him, were not more sanguinary in the South, than they would be in North America.[47]

One of the reasons the Enlightenment – particularly in its revolutionary Paineite form – was unable to develop a universal vision which genuinely addressed cultural diversity, and which clearly distinguished progress from colonialism and cultural domination, was its overriding concern with primitivism and the question of origins. Revolutionary upheaval called not so much for a break with the past, as with the lived experience of recent history, conveyed by custom, tradition and other forms of precedent. Thomas Paine's intention was to push aside this cultural inheritance – characterized, as it was, by monarchy, feudalism and other vestiges of privilege and inequality – to recover the true foundations of rights in their original, pristine integrity. In effect, this meant sweeping away the accumulated deposits of time and place, the distinctive features of one's culture, in order to embrace a universal brotherhood in nature. The difficulty with worshippers of the past, such as Edmund Burke, was not that they went back in time but that they did not go back far enough:

---

46 James Hope, 'Jefferson's daughter', in R.R. Madden (ed.), *Literary remains of the United Irishmen of 1798* (Dublin, 1887), p. 102.

47 William H. Drummond (ed.), *The autobiography of Archibald Hamilton Rowan* [1840] (Shannon, 1972), p. 291.

[The] error of those who reason by precedent drawn from antiquity, respecting the rights of man, is that they do not go far enough into antiquity. They do not go the whole way. They stop in some of the intermediate stages of a hundred or thousand years, and produce what was then done as a rule for the present day. This is no authority at all.[48]

The source of authority, for Paine, is not in history at all, but in nature.

For the United Irishmen, however, lifting 'the fog of time and antiquity' which hung over the intermediate stages revealed not so much a prospect of Nature as of a hidden culture, an alternative social order. In a number of declarations, they set their faces firmly against the past, but this has been erroneously taken to mean the old Irish or Gaelic order.[49] In fact, it was the *British* past which was the target of their invective, particularly the record of strife and conflict caused by the imposition of British rule in Ireland over the centuries.[50] In the crucial years 1793-6, the pressures of the revolutionary war forced British radicals into a patriotic retrenchment, moving way from Paineite declarations of universal rights to embrace versions of liberty derived from the heritage of the 'free-born Englishman'. At the same time, Irish radicals were travelling in the opposite direction, questioning the capacity of the British constitution to treat Irish people as equal subjects, let alone citizens. Defending Archibald Hamilton Rowan at his state trial in 1794, John Philpot Curran argued that 'England is marked by a natural avarice of freedom, which she is studious to engross and accumulate, but most unwilling to impart':

> In order to confirm that observation ... I should state the case of the invaded American, and the subjugated Indian, to prove that the policy of England has ever been to govern her connexions more as colonies, than as allies.[51]

In the same year, the Revd James Porter, Thomas Russell and William Sampson published anonymously a scathing satire on the revered British constitution, *Review of the lion of old England,* which professed to be a critical exegesis of a mock-heroic epic-poem on English law, and its current war policy. The target of their satire was in fact Edmund Burke in his role as high-priest of the 'ancient constitution' in England which had by then come to be seen by the more radical

48 Thomas Paine, *The rights of man* [1791], ed. Henry Collins (London, 1982), p. 87.
49 See, for example, R.B. McDowell, *Ireland in the age of imperialism and revolution, 1760-1801* (Oxford, 1979), p. 371; R.F. Foster, *Modern Ireland, 1600-1972* (London, 1988), pp 269-70.
50 See Nancy Curtin, *The United Irishmen: Popular politics in Ulster and Dublin 1791-1798* (Oxford, 1994), Chap. 7; Whelan, *The tree of liberty,* Chap. 2; Mary Helen Thuente, *The harp re-strung: The United Irishmen and the rise of Irish literary nationalism* (Syracuse, 1994).
51 Thomas MacNeven (ed.), *The lives and trials of Archibald Hamilton Rowan, and others* (Dublin, 1846), pp 91-2.

United Irishmen as the main bulwark against revolution in Ireland and in Britain.

The centrepiece of this squib takes the form of a visit to a glorious temple with the priest or 'prophet Edmund', arrayed in 'sooth-saying attire ... in which was inserted his parliamentary dagger', acting as guide.[52] As the prophet explains to the visitor 'the sublime and mysterious beauties of this venerable edifice,[53] the lion adorning the temple is so overcome 'that he involuntary [*sic*] threw his paws around the neck of the prophet, and in this manner, both one and t'other remained motionless, speechless and suspended for the space of many minutes'.[54] While 'the beautiful' and 'the picturesque' are the aesthetic styles most in evidence in the hallowed precincts of the building, a sense of terror and foreboding makes its presence felt on entering the Tudor rooms, and this intimation of the sublime casts an ominous gloom over another neglected corner of the building, where, in 'rugged niches were disposed the mouldering statues of the ANCIENT DRUIDS', or precursors of the bards. These, the prophet informs his visitors:

> are the most ancient of all our historians. Although ignorant of letters, they possessed, according to Caesar, all the learning of the Western world – with those harps which you perceive in their hands, which are indeed much decayed and disfigured by the cankering tooth of time; they were used to accompany the sweet melody of their voices, and to carol forth the praises of the virtuous and the brave ... so might they have escaped the disgraceful punishments inflicted on them in after times, by the royal mandates of the conquering EDWARD. He [i.e. the prophet] then pointed to the rude sculpture which represents the throwing them down the tremendous cliffs, where their mangled bodies were either dashed to pieces on the cliffs below – or, as the Poet says,
>
>> Precipitated headlong in the flood
>> The green wave with their crimson blood.[55]

This is Burke's image of a constitution founded on violence, 'tranquillity tinged with terror'.[56] The glories of the ancient constitution are built on the remains of

---

52 [Revd James Porter, Thomas Russell, and William Sampson], *Review of the lion of old England, or, The democracy confounded* (2nd ed., Belfast, 1794), p. 37.

53 See Burke's reference to the constitution as an edifice that has 'suffered waste and dilapidation', presumably in the seventeenth century, but which still possesses 'the walls, and in all the foundations of a noble and venerable castle': *Reflections on the Revolution in France* [1790], ed. Conor Cruise O'Brien (London, 1976), p. 121. This stands in stark contrast to his Gothic depiction of the ghostly ruins left behind in Ireland after Cromwell.

54 *Review of the lion of old England*, p. 38, fig. 8.1.

55 Ibid., p. 40.

56 Edmund Burke, *A philosophical enquiry into the origin of our ideas of the sublime and beautiful*, ed. J.T. Boulton (London, 1958), p. 136.

cultures it has shattered in the past, and this provides a cue for debunking the benefits of the 'Glorious Revolution' of 1688 as they pertain to Ireland. This radical break with the pieties of the 'ancient constitution' marked the point of no return where the United Irishmen were concerned, effecting the shift from being a reformist, Whig-inspired movement akin to the Volunteers, to a fully-fledged revolutionary organization. It is ironic, therefore, that the 'prophet Edmund' should be the butt of their satire on this count, for it was precisely Burke who argued most forcefully that measures for liberty in England turned out to be engines of oppression in Ireland – as in his famous description of the Penal Laws which followed the Williamite settlement as 'a machine of wise and elaborate contrivance, and as well fitted for the oppression, impoverishment, and degradation of a people, and the debasement in turn of human nature itself, as ever proceeded from the perverted ingenuity of man'.[57]

In fact, the radical transformation in the thinking of the United Irishmen at this juncture, renouncing the imperial remit of the English constitution and turning their attention to the rights of endangered, native cultures, can be seen as giving a specific Burkean inflection to what were otherwise Paineite conceptions of the universal rights. In the Enlightenment tradition derived from the 'Social Contract' freedom was envisaged as an original 'state of Nature', a universal realm which transcended all cultures. Culture, and by extension tradition, was seen as a fall from grace, a series of constraints upon liberty which entailed that the very concept of cultural freedom, or cultural rights, was a contradiction in terms. Hence the romantic appeal of the wilderness in which natural rights merged with the image of humanity at the dawn of creation, divested of all its cultural accretions. For metropolitan radicalism, the republic of nature presented itself as the only utopian space existing outside the constitution, as if no other cultures or societies had anything to offer in re-drawing the map of mankind.

Not least among the paradoxes of primitivism, therefore, was the fact that radically different cultures, such as those of the American Indians, were valued as an alternatives to western civilization precisely because they were not treated as cultures at all: 'the particular language', as Helen Carr writes, even when it is positive, 'ignores the Indians' own social organization'.[58] This romantic impulse, as the main vocabulary of radicalism, undoubtedly influenced the thinking of the United Irishmen, but by the mid-1790s, it was not Nature but *another culture*, the endangered inheritance of Gaelic Ireland and of the majority Catholic population, which provided a zone of critical engagement with the pieties of the English constitution. The British constitution was found wanting, in their eyes, not simply from the abstract standard of natural rights, but also in

57 Edmund Burke, 'A letter to Sir Hercules Langrishe' [1792], in Burke, *Works*, ii (London, 1901), p. 343.
58 Helen Carr, *The American primitive: Politics, gender and the representation of native American literary traditions, 1789-1936* (Cork, 1996), p. 35.

comparison to other allegedly inferior cultures such as that which they found around them, and which they also identified in America and Africa. Writing in 1796, Thomas Russell inveighed against the policies of press-ganging of up to 150,000 Irishmen – directed mainly at Catholic Defenders – into the British army in the war against France, arguing that such forms of tyranny would put so-called savage societies to shame:

> Consider beside the number of these your countrymen who have them-selves perished by disease, famine and the sword; think of the men torn, without even the form of legal process, from their destitute innocent fam-ilies under the name of defenders, by a set of detestable ruffians; crammed on board ships of war, and there to fight in a cause which, per-haps, they thought wrong. The North American savages are superior to such a practice. When they go to war, every man of the tribe who disap-proves of it is at liberty to remain at home or peaceably follow his avoca-tions of hunting … Are the Irish people aware that this contest involves the question of the slave trade, the one of the greatest consequence on the face of the earth? … Do they know that by it thousands and hundreds of thousands of these miserable Africans are dragged from their innocent families like the miserable defenders, transported to various places, and there treated with such a system of cruelty, torment, wickedness and infamy, that it is impossible for language adequately to express its horror and guilt.[59]

For Russell, the cause of the Defenders is on a continuum with that of African slaves; and the standards of civility against which English tyranny is found want-ing derive not from nature but from another culture on the receiving end of colonialism, that of the Native Americans.

This kind of argument, attentive to the rights of other cultures or religious traditions, had to await the ambivalent freedom of political exile in the United States to receive its fullest articulation in the writings of New York United Irish-men, such as William Sampson, one of Russell's co-authors on the *Review of the lion of old England*. In 1812, in a landmark case in American legal history center-ing on the secrecy of the Catholic confessional, Sampson, in his professional capacity as a lawyer, helped to establish the constitutional basis for the free exer-cise of religious worship in the United States. As Walter J. Walsh describes it:

> [This] event ranks as perhaps the earliest recorded instance of impact liti-gation in American constitutional history – a test case in which an insular

---

59 Thomas Russell, *A letter to the people of Ireland on the present situation of the country* (Belfast, 1796), p. 22.

minority deliberately sought to appropriate the courts to transform the political structure of American society.[60]

Sampson's argument was that the discrimination against Catholicism in American law was a residue of the kind of colonial repression permitted in Ireland under the British constitution in Ireland, but which had no place in a republican constitution truly devoted to liberty. This was part of the sustained campaign commenced during the 1790s in Ireland, against the delusions of grandeur entertained by those who worshipped at the shrine of the British constitution. Ridiculing English imputations of barbarism to the Irish language and Gaelic culture, Sampson proposed that the clotted language of British legal system, as eulogized by Sir William Blackstone and Sir Edward Coke, puts the Irish language in the shade:

> Indeed, [he wrote] some of the very acts of parliament, enacting penalties against those that spake Irish, or dwelt among the Irishry, are such a queer compound of Danish, Norman, hog-latin and I know not what, as to be the most biting satires upon the Englishry, and those that spake English.

And as for those who, like Coke, saw in the longevity of the ancient constitution proof of its divine status, Sampson remarks:

> All I can say of it is this, that the same panegyric will apply totidem verbis to the institutions of our red brethren, the Iroquois. The league of the five nations is similar to that of the heptarchy [into which ancient Britain was divided] ... The five nations think themselves, by nature, superior to the rest of mankind, and call themselves Ongue honwee ... ONGUE HONWEE, then say I, and away with your old barons, kings, monks, and druids ... If we look to antiquity the red men have it. If we regard duration, they have it still more, for the Picts and the Britons have long ceased to dye themselves sky-blue. The Indian paints himself for war, even to this day.[61]

What we have here is radical appropriation of some of the key tropes of primitivism and colonialism encountered earlier in this chapter. In a conscious inver-

---

60 Walter J. Walsh, 'Religion, ethnicity, and history: Clues to the cultural construction of law', in Ronald H. Bayor and Timothy J. Meagher (eds), *The New York Irish* (Baltimore, 1996), p. 55.

61 William Sampson, 'Speech in defence of the journeymen cordwainers of the city of New York; who were prosecuted for a combination to obtain an advance in wages in the spring of 1811', in *Beauties of the shamrock, containing biography, eloquence, essays, and poetry* (Philadelphia, 1812), pp 123–4.

sion of the Enlightenment equation of native Americans with ancient Picts or Britons, the very survival of the former is taken as a triumph over adversity, and a rejoinder to the myth that they are, like the Picts, doomed to extinction. The Burkean defence of the ancient constitution on the grounds that it has existed 'time out of mind' is turned on its head as applying equally to other ancient peoples, whose very longevity and political organization rivals that of their European counterparts. Sampson makes it clear that his mockery of the ancient constitution is not aimed at the British law as such, but at its claims to superiority over others: all he intends to show, he says, is that 'there are other systems as good'.[62] Among these are the legal codes of Scotland and Ireland. Even when the Scots were defeated and brought to heel by English military might, they still would not accept the superiority of English law, for all its divine wisdom:

> If, then, so important a portion of the British island can do so well without any part of the common law, can it be necessary for us to adopt superstitiously every part of it? The Irish had the common law forced on them … [They] had an ancient code which they revered. It was called the law of the judges, or the Brehon law. What it was, it is difficult to say; for with the other interesting monuments of the nation's antiquity, it was trodden under the hoof of the satyr that invaded her.[63]

He then argues that so far from disappearing in the mists of time, like the legacy of Ossian in the Highlands, the Brehon laws kept re-surfacing in the Irish political landscape until the policies of extirpation in the early modern period:

> No wonder that the 'wild natives', even in the days of Elizabeth, still kept and preserved their Brehon law, of which [even] its enemies are constrained to say, that it was a rule of right, unwritten, but declared by tradition from one to another, (like the common law,) in which oftentimes there appeared great equity, though it was repugnant both to God's laws and man's.[64]

By reinstating what Paine and the Scottish Enlightenment, in their different ways, dismissed as mere intermediate or degenerate stages in the passage from antiquity to the present, Sampson is, in effect, appropriating Burkean notions of descent for a republican project. True to Burke's vision, moreover, cultural difference is not decanted into a purely aesthetic realm, a romantic out-take, as it were, from the Enlightenment, but is integrated into the public sphere, in the form of the Brehon laws, or their social and political residues. Instead of being victims of proscription, subaltern cultures are endowed with the rights of pre-

62 Ibid., p. 160.   63 Ibid., p. 165.   64 Ibid.

scription, which take on a new critical valency in redressing the injustices of the past. Nor is this account of cultural diversity limited by the solipsism of localism or relativism which led certain strands in romanticism to construe authenticity as isolation, a withdrawal from the outside world. As if infused by the radical sensibility of Burke's sympathetic sublime, Sampson and Russell highlight the predicament of one culture by bringing it into contact with another, recasting what Walter Benjamin has called 'the tradition of the oppressed' in terms of cross-cultural solidarity. The final arbiter of a culture's worth, according to Sampson, is not just the test of time, whether it is conformed to the usages of 'Picts, Romans, Britons, Danes, Jutes, Saxons, Norman or other barbarians', but 'whether it is, or is not, an attack, on the rights of man' – as applied to cultures as well as individuals. In marked contrast to the last rites granted in valedictory accounts of primitive cultures, native peoples were now entitled to cultural rights, thus laying the basis for a more ethnographic Enlightenment which does justice to the past as well as the present.

4

From Jacobite to Jacobin

BREANDÁN Ó BUACHALLA

One of them said to me, 'Mr Owen has been favoured more than any gentleman in the barony ...' He wickedly added, that our Saviour's prophecy
was now fulfilling, when he said, 'The first shall be last, and the last shall
be first'; that *we* had been *first* long enough.[1]

It was said at Roscommon chapel, after service, 'We have lived long enough
upon potatoes and salt; it is our turn now to eat meat and mutton.'[2]

I expected that I would get what livings you, and the like of you have, for
myself ... Was it your scheme to knock the Protestants on the head, and
that you and your companions would take their places? – Yes.[3]

These, and like sentiments, are a common occurence in sources depicting, or purporting to depict, rebel attitudes and their *ipsissima verba* before and during the
1798 rebellion. There is nothing inherently novel or unique in them, either in an
Irish or in a wider context; rather they reflect a common and ubiquitous component of the millennial mode of thought: the 'reversal of roles', the belief that first
shall be last and last shall be first.[4] One finds similar sentiments in the depositions
taken down in the aftermath of the 1641 rebellion:

'I will promise you,' quoth he, 'the English shall eat no more fat beef in
this Kingdom.'[5]

One Hugh O'Ratty (late servant to Henry Manning Esqre) uttering these
words viz., 'We have been your slaves all this tyme, nowe you shall be
ours.'[6]

1 T.C. Croker, *Researches in the south of Ireland* (London, 1824), p. 355.
2 N.A.I., RP 620/22/19, p.13.
3 T.B. Howell, *A complete collection of state trials* (London, 1811–26), xxv, p. 757.
4 Y. Talmon, 'Millenarian movements' in *European Journal of Sociology*, vii (1965), 159–200,
   particularly 181, 194; B. Ó Buachalla, *Aisling ghéar* (Dublin, 1996), pp 584–6.
5 Mary Hickson, *Ireland in the seventeenth century* (London, 1884), ii, p. 137.
6 T.C.D. MS 835, p. 95.

75

> And they had a proverb among them in everyone's mouth: 'the horse had been a long time on the top of the ryder, but that now, God be thanked, the ryder had gotten on the top of the horse agaiyne.'[7]

A direct line of genetic hereditary descent need not be drawn connecting the rebels of 1641 with those of 1798, nor is a teleological progression to be assumed. But the continuity of theme and rhetoric in 'subterranean' thought, suggests that the complex background which led to 1798 cannot be adequately analyzed in terms of the extraneous and the elites alone; other forces – operating from 'within' and 'below' – must also be considered.

Given the revolutionary nature of the United Irish movement, great emphasis has been placed on its philosophical origins and in particular on the political thought underpinning the American and French Revolutions. Consequently 1798 has been seen, for the most part, in a context of change and revolution, as a 'break with the past', the notion of continuity being, more or less, eschewed. But the 'popular mind' was not a *tabula rasa* into which revolutionary and radical concepts were injected in the last decade of the eighteenth century; nor was 'popular culture' an empty vessel into which millenarian impulses automatically flowed. The influence of the 'new' revolutionary concepts cannot be gainsaid, but the ground had been well-prepared by more traditional modes of thought and it was through the 'old' that the 'new' was most effectively mediated. Furthermore, it cannot be assumed that a political lexicon which moves from one culture to another automatically maintains its original signification, let alone its intended original application. The 'freedom' for which the American colonists fought included the freedom to maintain slavery and slaves; the *egalité* of the Jacobins denoted not only social levelling but also cultural and linguistic levelling; *fraternité* would hardly have the same significance or impact in a monolingual confessional society as in a bilingual multi-denominational one. Lexical items are not autonomous but, like all linguistic components, are contextually-determined and culture-bound.

The Irish term corresponding to both 'freedom' and *liberté* is *saoirse*. It is an abstract noun formed from the adjective *saor*, that is, 'free', which, in the earlier language, regularly glosses Latin *liber*. Both the adjective *saor* and the noun *saoirse* are normally bound to the prepositions *ar* and *ó* (*saor ar* ... 'independent of'; *saoirse ó* ... 'freedom from') but they are also attested as unbound forms.[8] The earliest known examples of the noun deployed as an abstract notion in an explicitly political context occur in Irish Jacobite verse: *Atá Laoiseach* ... '*s an Prionsa* ... *ag preabadh* ... *chun saoirse a thabhairt* ... ('Louis and the Prince are moving to

---

7   T.C.D. MS 834, p. 184b. For an example of the proverb in a poem by Ó Doirnín (+1769), see B. Ó Buachalla, *Peadar Ó Doirnín: Amhráin* (Dublin, 1969), p.35.

8   E.G. Quin et al., *Dictionary of the Irish language* (Dublin, 1913–75, 1983), *s. v. doírse, saer, saírse*; Niall Ó Dónaill, *Foclóir Gaeilge-Béarla* (Dublin, 1977), *s. v. daoirse, saoirse, saor*.

grant freedom') in a poem by the Clare poet Aodh Buí Mac Cruitín; *Seo chugainn ár saoirse* ('Here comes our freedom') in a Jacobite drinking-song penned (*c.*1740) in Dublin by the scribe Tadhg Ó Neachtain; *Sin gártha ag Gaoil re haiteas, fághaid saoirse feasta* ... ('The Irish are shouting with joy, henceforth they will achieve freedom') in an *aisling* by Eoghan Rua Ó Súilleabháin.[9] In Jacobite rhetoric generally, *saoirse* is juxtaposed with *daoirse* 'servitude, oppression, bondage': the state in which the Irish found themselves and from which they were destined to be liberated.[10]

Jacobite rhetoric was the primary medium through which large sections of the community were made politically conscious by being exposed to a political lexicon which was based on concepts of legitimacy, of right as opposed to might, of freedom. Although that rhetoric was initially and primarily concerned with questions of legitimacy and hereditary right, it also concerned itself, particularly and increasingly from the 1730s onwards, with the respective condition and fate of the 'in' and 'out' categories in Irish society – those who ruled and those who were ruled. The Jacobite analysis of Irish society was presented in vivid, forceful and simplistic terms: the native Irish were in chains, ground down in abject poverty and misery, persecuted by a merciless band of foreigners and heretics; they – the descendants of Cromwell, the followers of Luther and Calvin – were a base crew who ate meat on Friday, quaffed wine, dwelt in slated mansions, and travelled in coaches, lording it over the descendants of the true nobility; their days were numbered however; 'the lease' they had on Irish land was up and their 'term' in control was nearing completion, for those who had hitherto toiled and slaved would soon rise up, depose the despotic tyrants and replace them.[11] Irish Jacobite verse provided an oppositional voice, in disparate linguistic registers, to the dominant Anglican hegemony. It provided a counter-hegemonic discourse, it expressed a focused collective consciousness, it furnished a sustaining cultural poetics for a dominated people. As Limón put it in reference to Mexican political balladry, such verse provided 'redressive symbolic action ... a poetics of maximum formal political achievement'.[12]

Irish Jacobite poetry can be categorised as a rhetoric based on and suffused with three complementary and interlocking conceits: millennialism, messianism and prophecy. I use the term millennialism not in its narrow technical signification, but in its wider general connotation, as now utilized by scholars, of 'any vision of a future golden age', 'any conception of a perfect age to come'.[13] The

---

9 Ó Buachalla, *Aisling ghéar*, pp 280, 390, 618.
10 For specific examples of the term in Jacobite poetry, see Ó Buachalla, *Aisling ghéar*, pp 271, 315, 581.
11 For specific instances of these themes and motifs, see Ó Buachalla, *Aisling ghéar*, pp 275, 308, 366, 377, 396, 426, 435, 552, 553, 561, 565, 581, 587.
12 J.E. Limón, *Mexican ballads, Chicano poems* (Berkeley, 1992), pp 152, 169.
13 S.L. Thrupp, *Millennial dreams in action* (The Hague, 1962), p. 12; R. Bloch, *Visionary republic: Millennial themes in American thought 1756–1800* (Cambridge, 1985), p. xvi.

Irish golden age, as conceived by eighteenth-century poets, would be ushered in by the return of the rightful king whose primary messianic function was to bring about the necessary 'reversal of roles':

> This English crew who are in control of Ireland and who bound our poor clergy in slavery, they henceforth will be in bondage serving the Irish.
>
> That I may see the English begging for charity and soft wet boots on them as the poor Irish used to wear.
>
> Tadhg will be happy on the bench as a powerful fine honourable judge, and Wilkes, Jones, Speed, Owens, Reed, Groves, Grant and Lane will be securely incarcerated in terror and dire bondage.[14]

The poetic delineation of the new dispensation concerned itself not only with the restoration of the ancestral lands to their rightful owners, nor with the restoration of the Catholic Church to its former status, but also with more mundane matters appertaining to food, clothing, housing and employment. Irish Jacobite rhetoric does not constitute a received canon of derived themes which was passively transmitted from generation to generation, but rather a dynamic and vibrant discourse which could accommodate and respond to changing circumstances, both locally and nationally. That rhetoric, its conservative origins notwithstanding, became in the course of the eighteenth century a corrosive radical idiom which undermined the legitimacy of the *status quo* and which foretold its eventual demise; it also became increasingly more strident and blood-curdling:

> The white mansions will be razed to the ground, noble blood will be shed by the arms of heroes, queens will be weeping incessantly and wringing their fingers on account of the elimination of their people and their earthly goods ...
>
> There will be a fire-ball of frenzy in the forehead of every young man to massacre and destroy every foreign monster; every one of them will be dejected from this year hence; we'll hang the boors and we'll burn their mansions; that we may see that and the likes of us merry ...
>
> The treacherous boors will be extinguished and vanquished; the evil progeny of Luther who never yielded to Christ will be expelled over the sea without beer, food or wine; their condition delights me ...
>
> In the lives of the saints I perceive tidings that delight me: that the rough hordes of English have used up the lease they received [in Ireland]; although I am old, I will not have long to wait now until I see the brutes

14 For the originals of these excerpts, see Ó Buachalla, *Aisling ghéar*, pp 584, 585, 589.

being cleared out of every slated airy mansion and the Irish [back] in their ancestral homes.[15]

Underlying all Jacobite rhetoric, and legitimising both its millennial vision and its messianic hope, was the all-pervasive 'validating charter' of prophecy.[16] At once a theme and a genre, political prophecy in modern Irish, more than any other literary mode, is suffused with 'a strong sense of collective calamity and a demand for collective redemption', one of the universal components of millennial thought.[17] Its clearest articulation, found as a gloss on a prophetic text in the manuscripts, presents the situation, past, present and future, in the unambiguous cryptic terms of 'them' and 'us':

Do bhíomairne agus ní bhfuilimíd,	We were and we are not,
atáidsean agus ní rabhadar,	they are and they were not,
beimídne agus éistfidhear sinn,	we will be and we will be heard,
ní bheidsean ná a dtuairisc go brách.[18]	they will not be, nor any trace of them forever.

Prophecy was not only a literary mode, it was a central and ubiquitous element in popular culture; according to William Carleton, and other writers, prophecies had a pernicious influence on 'the lower classes' and were 'subversive of the peace of the country' since they tended

> to prepare them for some great change in their favour, arising from the discomfiture of heresy, the overthrow of their enemies, and the exaltation of themselves and their religion.[19]

In utilizing and providing prophetic texts as part of their propaganda, the United Irishmen were tapping a powerful source of traditional political discourse, one which satisfied a deep need for comprehending the present within the terms of the future. Moreover, Irish political prophecy, from its earliest manifestation down to the nineteenth century, could invoke as its validatory source, an unquestionable and incontrovertible authority – the *obiter dicta* of the indigenous saints. Accordingly, Colum Cille and other saints were pressed into service to presage in 'ancient' prophecy what the needs of their modern clientele demanded and required. A thematic inventory of Irish political prophecy would include the notion of revenge, the spilling of blood, the overthrow of the ascendancy, the

15 For the original verses, see Ó Buachalla, *Aisling ghéar*, pp 425–6, 657.
16 Keith Thomas, *Religion and the decline of magic* (London, 1971), p. 503.
17 Bernard Wilson, *Magic and the millennium* (St Albans, 1975), p. 307.
18 Ó Buachalla, *Aisling ghéar*, p. 629.
19 William Carleton, *Traits and stories of the Irish peasantry* (Belfast, 1834), ii, pp 313–16.

expulsion of the English, the restoration of the Irish, the arrival of a messianic leader and the liberation of Ireland in a specific year – 1711, 1714, 1745, 1755, 1777, 1782 and later:

> Antrim John ... replied that according to a prophecy they had in the North, Ireland could not be free before the autumn of '98, when the French were to land, and then the English yoke was to be shook off for ever ...[20]

Foreign aid was a continuous and ubiquitous theme in the prophetic message; it was also central to both Jacobite strategy and rhetoric, and a commonly held view throughout the eighteenth century was that no overt miltary action could be successful in Ireland without it. When the Defenders and the United Irishmen adapted the strategy of French aid, it not only made sense in military terms, it was also meaningful in ideological terms. It invoked a potent conceit which had resonated in Irish folklore, literature and public discourse for generations. Foreign aid assumed a mythic function, in that it was perceived to be the necessary catalyst from which cataclysmic change – chaos – would flow:

> Many of the rioters ... were overheard to claim that the French would arrive shortly, that 'they should all get Estates' and that 'not one Protestant should be alive in a month' ...[21]

> 'We really did expect the French ... it was such a common phrase on everyone's mouth, that we all thought it.'[22] The great danger we were in was from the common people, who were certainly all waiting to plunder if the French should land ...[23]

> Towards the end of the year 1794, a rumour of a French invasion spread through the country, raising the hopes of the disaffected, and creating terror in all, who had any thing to lose.[24]

> A foolish prophecy went about yesterday, that on the ninth night after the French were landed here, a general massacre of the community should take place in Killalla.[25]

Given the traditional nature of the theme – and hope – of foreign aid and given its centrality to Irish political culture, it is hardly coincidental that when aid

---

20 Miles Byrne, *The memoirs of Miles Byrne* (Paris, 1863), i, p.228.
21 Marianne Elliott, *Partners in revolution* (London, 1982), p. 45.
22 Howell, *State trials*, xxvii, p. 435.
23 William Beresford (ed.), *The correspondence of the right hon. John Beresford* (London, 1854), ii, p. 128.
24 R.L. Edgeworth, *Memoirs of Richard Lovell Edgeworth* (London, 1821), ii, p. 134.
25 Bishop Joseph Stock, *Proceedings at Killalla* (Bath, 1799), p. 18.

did eventually arrive, when the French were at last 'on the sea', that their arrival was announced by the most ancient of personages in autochthonous ideology – *An tSeanbhean Bhocht*. It is hardly coincidental, either, that her function in that ballad corresponds to her function in *aisling* poetry: she is the 'authoritative figure', the source of knowledge, whom the poet-narrator encounters and engages in dialogue so that he may elicit from her the prophetic message.[26] It is not her only realization in United Irish propaganda. In 'Granny Wail's Address to the Potatoe Diggers', it is as 'your oppressed, but affectionate mother', whose potato garden 'has been trodden over, and over, by my neighbour's cattle', that she appeals to 'my dear children' to help 'an unfortunate old woman'.[27] In Whiteboy rhetoric and *aisling* poetry alike, she also appears as a mother solicitous for her children. The continuity of theme and iconography is revealing in that it furnishes concrete evidence of the elasticity of traditional Jacobite rhetoric, its potential as a medium through which later developments and movements could be mediated.

The outbreak of war in America had been seen by the Irish literati as an extension of Jacobite endeavours, a realization of traditional hopes. Although the international implications of the war were understood and commented upon, its importance was assessed entirely through Irish eyes. Accordingly, when General Arnold led American forces into Quebec in 1775, and when Washington routed the British from Boston in 1776, the poets Eoghan Rua Ó Súilleabháin and Tomás Ó Míocháin interpreted those heroic actions in familiar Jacobite terms;[28] according to Séamas Ó Dálaigh, and other poets, the prophecy which had specified 1777 as the year of liberation was now being fulfilled;[29] according to Éamonn Ó Flaithearta, *ál an fhill 's an éithigh* ('the brood of treachery and calumny') who had enslaved the Irish, were now being slaughtered by Washington and his heroes and they would not cease until they toppled the crown;[30] Eadbhard de Nógla exhorted his listeners to pray that the conflict would bring about their liberation

26 Ó Buachalla, *Aisling ghéar*, pp 528–31; A.C. Spearing, *Medieval dream-poetry* (Cambridge, 1976), p. 4.
27 [J. Porter], *Billy Bluff and the 'squire* (Belfast, 1796), pp 39–40. Cf. 'and then the Priest sang, Grawny Wail ... they are all impudent national seditious songs' (ibid., p. 5); 'Now, Billy, this is a most wicked, seditious, damnable hand-bill ... Why, Grawny Wail means Ireland, and a cursed old impudent name it is, for any man in these times to hear' (ibid., p. 39). For personifications of Hibernia and other female personages in United Irish iconography, see M.H. Thuente, 'Liberty, Hibernia and Mary Le More: United Irish images of women', in D. Keogh and N. Furlong (eds), *The women of 1798* (Dublin, 1998), pp 10-25.
28 Ó Buachalla, *Aisling ghéar*, pp 647–8; P. Ua Duinnín, *Amhráin Eoghain Ruaidh Uí Shúileabháin* (Dublin, 1901), no. 10; D. Ó Muirithe, *Tomás Ó Míocháin: Filíocht* (Dublin, 1988), no. 35.
29 *Ag Sionna na slimbharc* ... (Séamas Ó Dálaigh), R.I.A. MS 23 A 18, p. 46; see also R.I.A. MSS 23 O 35, p. 91; 23 B 19, p. 104. In this and the other excerpts quoted here, I have normalized the orthography.
30 *Ar mo leaba aréir go déanach* ... (Éamon Ó Flaithearta), R.I.A. MSS 23 M 14, p. 57, 104; 23 D 42, p. 29.

(*go saorthar sinne is gach nduine dár ndream*);[31] Uilliam Ó Lionáin regaled his audience with the new message he had received from the *spéirbhean* :

> *Do labhair 'na dhéidh sin go béasach i nGaoilge*
> *is d'aithris dom scéala do mhéadaigh mo chroí-se:*
> *go rabhadar béaraibh an Bhéarla go cloíte,*
> *gan arm, gan éadach, go traochta, gan tíortha;*
> *táid cartaithe i gcarcair 'na ndrangaibh gan treoir,*
> *faoi atuirse i nglasaibh ag Washington beo,*
> *gan ghradam, i mairg, gan charaid ná lón;*
> *'na ngrathain ag screadaigh fá heaspa na feola*
> *do chleachtadh na bathlaigh do chaitheamh gan teora.*[32]

Thereafter she spoke to me kindly in Irish and related tidings to me that raised my heart: that the English bears were vanquished, without arms, without food, exhausted, without lands; they are languishing in prison, helpless, chained in dejection by virile Washington; they are sorrowful, without esteem, or friends, or food; a rabble crying out for want of meat, which the churls used to consume limitlessly.

These poems remind us that the American Revolution was not an exercise in applied political philosophy but – like the convulsions of 1789 in France and 1798 in Ireland – a product of political circumstance. They also suggest that the impact of the American Revolution in Ireland was not primarily at the intellectual level; its crucial impact was emotional and symbolic. The poems also raise fundamental questions appertaining to the reception of revolutionary principles in Ireland. For although the dissemination of radical ideas in the last decades of the eighteenth century in Ireland has been competently dealt with by several historians, the same emphasis has not been given to the crucial questions as to how those ideas were received, mediated and applied.

A revealing insight into how the 'new' can be utilized and explained in terms of the 'old' is provided by a poem on the French Revolution which emanates from south-east Ulster and is found in a manuscript written in 1829–30.[33] The opening verses proclaim the arrival of a new dispensation which is to last forever and in which the Irish will participate:

---

31 *A éigse Mhuic-inis* … (Eadbhard de Nógla), R.I.A. MSS 23 F 18, p.74; 23 O 26, p. 76; 23 G
    20, pp 134, 393.
32 *Sealad im aonar cois Féile* … (Uilliam Ó Lionnáin), R.I.A. MSS 23 N 9, p. 111; 24 L 22, p.
    108; 23 I 48, p. 26. Meat was one of the material artifacts which had assumed symbolic sig-
    nification in Irish political poetry; others were shoes, slated houses, and the coach.
33 N.L.I., MS G 2006, pp 43–4. The poem has been previously edited by S. Ó Mórdha in *Éigse*,
    vii (1953–5), 202–4. See also *Éigse*, viii (1955–6), 150–1.

Tá na Francaigh san am so cur céim ar gcúl,
's ní bhíonn Prionsa ós a gcionn acht réil ghlan úr,
béidh Gearmanaí is Flanders is an Réin sin fúibh,
's tá mé in amhras go mbéidh Albain is Éire san dlúmh.

Ní bhíonn Laoiseach nó rí eile ón aimsir so suas
ins na críochaibh cur daoirse ar gach déa-mhac go buan,
béidh na daoine lán críonnacht gan ghéibheann, gan ghuais,
is toil shaor ag clanna Mhíle le séan go lá an Luain.

The French are now abolishing rank, and no Prince will govern them but a distinctive new dispensation; Germany, Flanders and the Rhine will be under them, and I think that Scotland and Ireland will join the confederation. Neither Louis nor any other king will henceforth impose slavery in their territories on every upright youth; the people will be full of wisdom, free from bondage and danger, and the Irish will have free will and prosperity until Judgment Day.

The following three verses relate the universal changes being heralded in the opening lines to local circumstances:

Remember the Treaty of Limerick and how you were deceived, whereby your poor children were left in bondage without property. It wasn't by birthright that Luther, or any of his progeny, acquired the fine mansions they possess from Limerick to the Boyne; the Irish will scourge those boors and they will have neither land nor residence in Ireland any longer. Munster is rising, the victorious Leinstermen are happy, the strong Ulstermen will defend the hosts and trounce the offspring of Luther – and may they not escape!

The emphasis on *clanna Mhíle* (the native Irish) and the utilization of a traditional lexicon in those verses is paralleled in other '98 poems. In an elegy written on Fr Mánus Mac Suibhne, who was hanged in Newport, County Mayo, in 1799 for his part in the rebellion, a local poet delineates in local terms, by reference to local personages, the circumstances of his execution; as a consequence *Gaeil bhochta cráite* ('the poor persecuted Irish') were lamenting his death every day. Although obviously composed for a local and sympathetic audience, the poem also encapsulates images and notions not particularly local, either in function or import; there is, in fact, a wider canvas: if Fr Mac Suibhne had lived, the 'tree of Liberty' would have been erected in Newport; it was the Orangemen who had defeated the French; but the Irish would wreak vengeance as soon as Bonaparte arrived.[34] In an

34 *Béaloideas*, x (1941), 237–8.

aisling written by Seán Ó Muláin, the *spéirbhean* proclaims that *síolrach Chailbhin uaibhrigh* ('the progeny of proud Calvin') will be destroyed once the French arrive; she concludes with a description of the French fleet on its way from Brest:

> *Tá an flít ag teacht ó chuan Brest*
> *go líonmhar lannach luaimneach,*
> *'s a gcrainn fé bhrataibh uaine*
> > *go buacach 'na mbarr;*
> *tá a dtaoiseach Mars go huaibhreach*
> *'s a chlaíomh 'na ghlaic ar luathchrith,*
> *dá mhaíomh gur gairid fuascailt*
> > *do uaisle Inis Fáil.*[35]

The fleet is coming from Brest abundantly, armed, nimbly and their masts bedecked with green flags buoyant on their tops; their leader Mars is proud with his sword quivering in his clutch, proclaiming that liberation is nigh for the nobles of Ireland.

The image of 'The Green Flag' is central to another *aisling* which, its traditional format and diction notwithstanding, presents the *spéirbhean* (*Éire céile is buime an Réacs den chine b'uaisle* 'Ireland the wife and nurse of the King of the most noble race') in a novel role: exhorting the Irish, who had been enslaved by those who hated the son of Mary, to emulate the men of the North and to unite under the aegis of 'The Green Flag':[36]

> *Cé fada fá phéin i ngéibhinn sinn*
> > *go traochta tuirseach trua tur,*
> *ag Danaraibh daora claona an oilc*
> > *ar chraos mac Muire d'fhuathaigh;*
> *is gairid a réim ar an dtaobh so mhuir*
> > *'s níl caoi acu rith tar cuantaibh,*
> *ó cheangail na Gaeil mar aon i gcumann*
> > *fá scéimh an Bhrait Ghlaisuaithne ...*

---

35 *Cois Laoi na sreabh go huaigneach...* (Seán Ó Muláin), R.I.A. MSS 23 M 14, p. 237; 24 A 34, p. 80.

36 *Maidean lae ghil gréine i ndoire* ... (Mícheál Ó Caoimh), R.I.A. MSS 23 F 18, p. 95; 24 C 26, p. 403; St Colman's College, Fermoy MS CF 7, p. 143; U.C.C. MS T8, p. 96; N.L.I. MSS G118, p. 39; G180, p. 206. Four of the nine verses of the poem have been edited and discussed by Brian Ó Cuív, 'The Wearing of the Green', in *Studia Hibernica*, xvii–xviii (1978), 107–19. 'The Green Flag, 1798' is the title of a totally different poem in R. Young, *Ulster in '98* (Belfast, 1893), p. 61. I have taken *glasuaithne* to be a compound (they appear as two separate words in the MS) and have translated the phrase *fá scéimh an Bhrait Ghlaisuaithne* rather loosely; a more literal translation would be 'under the banner (protection?) of the vivid green flag'.

A bhoirbshliocht Éibhir éachtaigh oilte,
féachaidh fir an Tuaiscirt,
ag snaidhmeadh le chéile i gcéim 's i gcion
's ag réabadh poirt is cuanta;
tuigim gur léir don taobh so anois
nach gaobhar don stoirm stuanadh,
cruinnithe in éineacht gléastar sibh
fá scéimh an Bhrait Ghlaisuaithne.

Though we are long suffering in captivity, subjugated, weary, pitiable, humourless, at the hands of base, perverse, evil foreigners who voraciously hated the son of Mary, their power will not last long on this side of the ocean and they have no opportunity of escaping over sea since the Irish have joined together in partnership under the Green Flag.

O strong descendants of powerful skilled Éibhear, look at the men of the North joining together in unison and affection and destroying ports and harbours; I perceive that it is now clear on this side that the storm is not near abating; gathered together let you arm yourselves under the Green Flag.

In an anonymous poem written 'On the Landing of the French' which is only partly preserved,[37] the combatants in the ensuing military engagement are respectively described as *na buachaillí breá Gaelach* ('the fine Irish boys') and *na bodaigh* ('the churls') who were dominant and whom God and his mother are beseeched to depose without delay. Since the early seventeenth century, *bodaigh* was one of the lexical designations of the 'other' in Irish political rhetoric; it occurs, for instance, as does its counterpart, *na buachaillí Gaelach*, in the popular verse composed in the aftermath of the battle of the Boyne.[38] But it was not only in popular verse that the traditional lexicon survived; the literati also found it indispensable in describing, explaining and validating the events leading up to and ensuing from '98.

Mícheál Óg Ó Longáin (1766–1837) is, by any standard, a major literary figure.[39] Scribe of more than 150 manuscripts, composer of more than 350 poems,

37 This is hardly surprising given that it was taken down (*c.*1830 by Robert McAdam) 'from Lane when he was blind drunk': *Dia Sathairn, mo léan, ag éirí don ghréin*, Belfast Public Library, Irish MS 31, p. 52.
38 See Ó Buachalla, *Aisling ghéar*, pp 174–77. Cf. 'As all the Boys use to meet at the exchange ... some of the Boys had wooden guns to learn ... there was a motion made to get Books and papers to enlighten the Boys ...' N.A.I., RP 620/23/59 (ii). In an introduction to one of his poems (*Aitchim tráth ar cheard na bhflaitheas*), Ó Longáin refers to his cousin Captain Steel as a *buachaill* ('boy'): R.I.A. MS 23 G 21, p. 472.
39 For his life and work, see T. Ó Murchadha, 'Mícheál Óg Ó Longáin (1766–1837)', in S. Pender (ed.), *Féilscríbhinn Torna* (Cork, 1947), pp 11–17; B. Ó Conchúir, *Scríobhaithe Chorcaí 1700–1850* (Dublin, 1982), pp 91–133; S. Ó Caoindealbháin, 'The United Irishmen

he was also, for a large part of his life, an itinerant teacher and had, accordingly, access to a wider audience than his immediate literary coterie. His verse obviously emanates from 'within', but it also constitutes a unique voice in that Ó Longáin, a member of the native intelligentsia, was also, metaphorically and literally, *engagé*: he was actively engaged, for some years at least, in the United Irishmen and had set up the organization on the outskirts of Cork city. His political verse, which comprises a wide range of subjects and concerns itself with the main political events of the period 1785–1830, assumes, accordingly, far greater importance and it warrants a more comprehensive and detailed analysis than this partial and, of necessity, inadequate summary allows.

His first poem, written, he states himself, in 1785, *An tan táinig Buachaillí Bána* ('When the Whiteboys came') is a typical Jacobite *aisling* replete with Carolus, the *spéirbhean*, the prophetic message of liberation for the Irish and defeat for *Sacsanaigh* and *fanaticks*: 'that we may drive ye Protestants to Acheron's fiery grove'.[40] In the following years he composed a series of such *aislingí* in which the same traditional message is unambiguously and clearly articulated for his clientele:

> go mbiaidh síol na nDanar tréith,
> is Gaoil i gceannas thréan,
> gan chíos, gan tax, gan phéin,
> gan daorsmacht go deo …[41]

that the seed of the foreigners will be vanquished, and the Irish in powerful command,without rent, tax or pain, without oppression forever …

> Beidh Gaoil gan easpa a mbailte 's a n-aolbhroig …
> ag tíocht go fiochmhar líonmar lanamhar …
> ag síorchur Sagsanach faon ar lár …[42]

The Irish will not be in want of their homes or their mansions, coming fiercely in numerous and full hosts incessantly knocking down the English.

> Ar theacht don Réacs réimeach go hInis Fáil,
> is ceart na nGael aosta ag seasamh lán,

in Cork county', in *Journal of the Cork Historical and Archaeological Society*, liii (1948), 115–29, particularly p. 129; liv (1949), pp 73, 81; P. Power, *The courts martial of 1798–99* (Naas, 1998), pp 174–5. There is as yet no complete edition of Ó Longáin's poetry, but some of his political poems have been edited by T. Ó Raithile, 'Mícheál Óg Ó Longáin', *An Claidheamh Soluis*, 17 Márta 1907, 3–6; R. Ó Donnchadha, *Mícheál Óg Ó Longáin* (Dublin, 1994).
40 *Lá is mé ag taisteal cois taoibh an tsrutha chiúin*; St Patrick's College, Maynooth, MS M 57 a, p. 166. The author provides his own translation. For this, and the other Ó Longáin poems, I provide but one source (an autograph copy), although other manuscript copies are available.
41 *Aisling chonarc tríom néal* …, R.I.A. MS 23 C 8, p. 414.
42 *Cois Faoinsean do ghabhas* …, R.I.A. MS 23 N 14, p. 291.

gur fairsing craobhach péacach don Bhratainn Bhán,
geallaim féin fé Inid sula dtaga an Cháisc.[43]

when the prevailing king comes to Ireland, defending fully the rights of
the ancient Irish, the White Flag will flourish widely and gaily, by Shrove-
tide, before Easter, I myself promise you.

Is me bean is buime Shéarlais,
tá ag teacht anois le scéala,
gur gearr go mbrisfear géibheann
na nGael bocht gan gó.[44]

I am the wife and nurse of Charles, who is now coming with the news that
it won't be long until the captivity of the Irish will be undoubtedly severed.

The fact that Ó Longáin did not consider the Jacobite idiom outmoded suggests
that its symbolic code was still useful for him and meaningful to his audience. It
did, after all, encapsulate a rhetoric of disaffection and revolt which was still adequate in analysing current affairs. Accordingly, this traditional idiom of Irish
political poetry is utilized by Ó Longáin throughout his work, not only in the *aislingí* but also in his occasional, epistolatory and personal verse.

The central insight informing all his work is one predicated on a powerful
binary distinction between two mutually exclusive groups in Ireland. On the one
hand were the Irish (*clanna Gael, clanna Mhíle, na Gaeil*); on the other were those
who are variously and synonomously designated in either ethnic, religious or linguistic terms as *Danair* ('foreigners', literally 'Danes'), *Gaill* ('foreigners'), *Sacsanaigh* ('English'); *aicme Lúitir* ('Luther's followers'), *sliocht Chailbhin* ('Calbhin's
progeny'), *eiricigh* ('heretics'), *fanaticks* ; *aicme an Bhéarla* ('the English'), *búir an
Bhéarla* ('English churls'); in generic terms they were nothing but *búir, daoithe*
('churls'), *meirligh* ('traitors') and *tíoránaigh* ('tyrants'). Even in depicting his personal condition or in recounting his own political activities or those of his relatives, friends and colleagues, Ó Longáin does not depart from the lexicon he
employs in delineating the general state of affairs. It was *na Danair* who pursued
him in 1798, because he had cropped his hair, and who had killed many a fine
man in 1799–1800;[45] it was *na tíoránaigh* who had banished his cousin to Botany
Bay, defeated the French at Killalla, and hanged some of his compatriots;[46] those
who had persecuted him and had deprived the Irish of their lands were *búir*.[47]

43 *Is ag taisteal im aonar* ..., R.I.A. MS 23 N 14, p. 293.
44 *Le hais na Sionna* ..., R.I.A. MS 23 G 24, p. 165.
45 R.I.A. MS 23 G 23, p. 34; Boston Atheneum, MS S 22, p. 9; N.L.I. MS G 360, p. 13. See
   n. 62 *infra*.
46 *Is atuirseach léanmhar mé le sealad*, R.I.A. MS 23 G 21, 485; R.I.A. MS 23 G 21, pp 503, 508.
   See Ó Donnchadha, *Ó Longáin*, pp 86, 96, 103.
47 Ó Donnchadha, *Ó Longáin*, pp 86, 88, 93, 103, 104, 109.

That binary classification corresponds to a parallel analysis of their respective states. The *Galla bhúir* ('foreign boors') are in total control of Ireland, they had emasculated the Irish through taxation and persecution, had vanquished them, had taken their ancestral lands from them. The condition of the Irish, on the other hand, is one of abject poverty and slavery, of degradation, subjection and suffering.[48] However, the 'prophecy of the saints', the prophetic message of the *aisling*, his own ardent wish for the future, all depicted a reversal of those respective fortunes, the expulsion of the foreigners from Ireland and the restoration of the Irish:

> *Beidh saorchlanna Éireann i gceart a shinsir ...*[49]

The noble families of Ireland will be restored to their ancestral rights.

> *Biaidh clanna Gaol gan mhoill i réim go mór is Danair díscthe a hinse Éireann leo ...*[50]

The Irish will forthwith flourish greatly and the foreigners exterminated from Ireland.

> *Biaidh an fearann so Éireann saor ó shraithibh*
> *   is Gaeil i ngradam mór,*
> *is gach scramaire bréan ler mhéin ár mealladh,*
> *   tréith ar easpa luais ...*[51]

This land of Ireland will be free of taxes and the Irish in great esteem; and every rotten grabber who wishes to delude us will be weak and bereft of vitality.

A facile approach to Ó Longáin's rhetoric dismisses it as obsessed with the past, a futile exercise in fantasy which did not address realistic contemporary issues. The past does indeed loom very large in his work, but that is hardly surprising given that a great part of his long life was spent transcribing and transmitting the literary archives of that past.[52] He was not an antiquarian, however, nor an academic pedant whose view of life was filtered through a 'backward look'. The

---

48 See, in particular, *Lá Samhna dá rabhas-sa ...*, R.I.A. MS 23 E 16, p. 279; *Maidin mhín roimh ghréin ...*, R.I.A. MS 23 C 10, p. 241; *Maidin drúchta ar startha a scrúdadh ...*, R.I.A. MS 23 E 16, p. 53; *Aréir is mé go déanach ...*, R.I.A. MS 23 N 14, p. 302; *Ar maidin an laoi ...*, R.I.A. MS 23 C 8,p. 424. See also Ó Donnchadha, *Ó Longáin*, pp 72, 74, 77, 80, 86, 88, 90, 93, 95, 96, 98, 100, 101, 103, 105, 113, 116, 121, 128, 131.

49 *A shéimhfhir bhreá Ghaelaigh ...*, R.I.A. MS 23 N 32, p. 10.

50 *Maidin aoibhinn bhíos im aonarón ...*, R.I.A. MS 23 C 8, p. 33. See Ó Donnchadha, *Ó Longáin*, p. 77.

51 *I dtairngreacht naomh is léir go bhfaca ...*, R.I.A. MS 23 G 21, p. 507. See Ó Donnchadha, *Ó Longáin*, p. 80.

52 See Ó Conchúir, *Scríobhaithe Chorcaí*, pp 91–133.

future, delineated in millennial terms, and the present loom equally large in his work. Moreover his appeal to the past was not a conservative one but one which questioned the status quo. His verse, his colophons, his glosses, his annalistic jottings and his correspondence reveal very clearly that he and his coterie were conversant with political developments, at home and abroad.[53] He alludes to his own activities during 1798, but comments also on the activities of his cousin (the famous 'Captain Steel'), of Arthur O'Connor and other activists; the disunity of the Irish, the work of informers, the capture and death of Lord Edward FitzGerald, the emergence and expected arrival of Bonaparte, the threat of the Act of Union, the famine of 1800 are all referred to.[54] In one annalistic entry, he alludes to the rise of the Peep o' Day Boys, the Defenders and the Orangemen; in another, the founding of the United Irishmen is described thus:

> *1792. Urmhór bhfear nÉireann de gach aon chreideamh do dhul i gcomhcheangal páirte re chéile d'fhonn Éire do shaoradh ó dhaorchuing na Saxan, agus do ghlaoch United Irishmen orthu féin, ag aithris ar Fhrangachaibh, dar leo, noch do shaor iad féin timpeall na huaire sin agus do rógheall dóibh cúnamh do chur chúthu ...*[55]

The majority of the men of Ireland of every faith joined together in an affiliation of affection for the purpose of liberating Ireland from the tyrannical yoke of the English and they called themselves United Irishmen in imitation of the French, they thought, who had liberated themselves around that time and who had often promised them to send them aid.

In the introduction to a poem of his, written in the prophetic mode, he explains the circumstances of its composition:

> *An tan cuireadh suas mé san mbliain 1797 i gCorcaigh mór Mumhan, is ea do chumas féin an t-amhrán beag so síos do ghríosú bhfear nÉireann de gach aon chreideamh agus go háirithe Clanna Gael, fána mbeith díleas dea-rúin discréideach i gcomhcheangal grá, páirte, cumainn agus lánmhuintearais agus i ngrá dearthaireachais le chéile, ionnas go mb'fhusaide dhóibh an cluiche seo do bhreith agus iad féin do shaoradh ón ndaorchuing sclábhaíochta féna bhfuilid le cian d'aimsir, faraor!*

When I was put up [sworn in] in Cork of Munster in 1797 I composed the following little song to exhort the men of Ireland of every religion, but

---

53 See, for instance, C.J. Buttimer, 'A Cork Gaelic text on a Napoleonic campaign', in *Journal of the Cork Historical and Archaeological Society*, xcv (1990), 107–19.

54 See Ó Raithile, 'Mícheál Óg Ó Longáin', pp 3–5; Ó Donnchadha, *Ó Longáin*, pp 80, 86, 88, 90, 95, 96, 97, 98, 101, 109, 114.

55 R.I.A. MS 23 G 21, p. 503.

particularly the Irish, to be faithful, well-intentioned, discreet, in an affiliation of love, affection, companionship, friendliness and brotherly love with
one another so that it would be easier for them to win this game and to liberate themselves from the tyrannical yoke of slavery under which they are
for a long time, alas!

The poem in question, in its opening line, relates the delightful message he had
seen *i dtairngreacht naomh* ('in the prophecy of the saints') and continues with an
exhortation to the Irish:

> *A chlanna bocht Gael tá i bpéin le fada,*
> *éiridh feasta suas,*
> *is gabhaidh go géar ag gléas bhur n-arm*
> *'s déanaidh treas gan trua;*
> *más Sagsanach é nó Quaker cruaidh,*
> *ná glacaidhse féin leis éad ná fuath,*
> *ach preabaidh le chéile in éineacht suas,*
> *ag turnadh Danar dóibh …*[56]

O poor Irish who are in distress for a long time, rise up immediately and
start diligently preparing your arms and engage in merciless battle; if he's
a Protestant or a Quaker, do not envy or hate him but let ye all rise up
together as they smite the enemy.

And although he does recognize, in those and other revealing passages, a wider
community than that encompassed by the term *clanna Gael*, his primary and
abiding concern is, as the passages also reveal, 'particularly the Irish':

> *Do bhí géarleanúin throm dhiachrach ar fhearaibh Éireann an tan sin, agus go*
> *háirithe ar Chlanna Gael …*[57]

There was heavy distressful persecution on the men of Ireland at that
time, and particularly on the Irish …

> *Gurb ansin a dúirt Mícheál Óg Ó Longáin an t-amhrán beag so ag cur mean-*
> *ma agus misnigh ar fhearaibh Éireann, agus go háirithe ar Ghaelaibh, Dia*
> *leo!*[58]

And it was then that Mícheál Óg Ó Longáin composed this short song,
instilling morale and courage in the men of Ireland, but particularly in the
Irish, God be with them.

56 R.I.A. MS 23 G 21, p. 507. See Ó Donnchadha, *Ó Longáin*, p. 80.
57 R.I.A. MS 23 G 21, p. 508. See Ó Donnchadha, *Ó Longáin*, p. 86.
58 *Déinidh go subhach, a Ghaela* …, R.I.A. MS 23 G 21, p. 512. See Ó Donnchadha, *Ó Longáin*, p. 101.

Oh Dia linn. Is mór an stoirm seo chum bhfear nÉireann san mbliain seo agus go háirithe chum clanna Gael … óir gí gur dhearbhaíodar urmhór bhfear nÉireann dá cheile fána mbeith díleas dea-rúin agus cur le chéile in gach cás chum na Banban do shaoradh ó dhaorchuing na Breataine Móire, más ea, tar a cheann san sílim gurb iad Gaeil agus an creideamh Caitlicí is mó do rinn dá ndearnadh ann …[59]

Oh God be with us. This is a great storm approaching the men of Ireland, and particularly the Irish, this year … For although the majority of the men of Ireland swore to each other to be faithful and well-intentioned and to co-operate in every respect to liberate Ireland from the tyrannical yoke of Great Britain, however, notwithstanding that, I think that it was the Irish and the Catholics [literally the Catholic religion] who did most of what was done there …

The notion of *daorchuing* ('tyrannical yoke') is central to Ó Longáin's analysis; the contemporary condition of the Irish is described by him in terms of slavery and subjection; the primary lexical items utilized by him to depict that condition are *daorsmacht* ('slavery', 'oppression'), *cuing* ('yoke'), *broid, glas, géibheann* ('bondage'):

Abair leis scéala a léigean chugham i dtráth:
an scaipfear de Ghaelaibh daorsmacht búr go brách? …[60]

Tell him to send me timely news: will the boors' oppression of the Irish ever be lifted?

Gur gairid bhiaidh Gaeil Éireann faoi ghlasaibh na mbúr …[61]

That the Irish will not be enchained by the boors for long.

Scaipfid ár mbroid is brisfear leo ár gcuing
is biaidh Danair ag rith go singil fós mar bhíos …[62]

They will sunder our bondage and break our yoke and the foreigners will yet be on the run in as poor a condition as I was.

The breaking of that yoke was equally central to his message and, thereby, the condition of the Irish to be changed to one denoted by a complex of terms ema-

59 R.I.A. MS 23 E 15, p. 24.
60 *A theachtaire shéimhse théid san dúiche tá* …, R.I.A. MS 23 N 32, p.166.
61 *Sin seascaid glan saorbhéithe* …, R.I.A. MS 23 N 32, p. 7.
62 *Sin seascaid de bhábaibh* …, R.I.A. MS 23 G 20, p. 222. In Boston Atheneum MS S 22, p. 9 and N.L.I. MS G 360, p. 13 the poem is glossed thus: 'Do bhíodar na Danair ag rith orm san mbliadhain 1798 do chionn mar do bhearras mo ghruaig' ('The foreigners were after me in 1798 because I had cropped my hair').

nating from the adjective *saor* 'free' and its derivatives, the noun *saoirse* – 'freedom', and the verb *saor* – 'to free':

> *ní deachuithe, a lao, tá ar aon chor uainn,*
> *ná teacsanna, cé gur méala mór,*
> *ach an talamh go léir bheith saor go buan* ...[63]

it isn't tithes, my dear, we want at all, nor taxes, though they are a heavy burden, but all the land to be free forever.

> *'s a séideadh ar fad i gcéin tar lear*
> *do shaoradh ár mbailte dúchais* ...[64]

and they to be expelled over the sea and our ancestral lands to be freed.

> *do bhrúfaidh aicme an Bhéarla*
> *   is do thabharfaidh saor bhur dtír* ...
> *do shúil go bhfaicfinn saor sibh*
> *   in bhur ndúchas féin arís* ...[65]

which will crush the English and make your country free ... in hope that I might see you free in your own patrimony again.

> *do réifidh snaidhm den bhuínse i nglasaibh tarla,*
> *is do shaorfaidh sinn ó chuing na nDanar ngáifeach* ...[66]

who will untie the knot from this band who are in chains and who will free us from the yoke of the terrible foreigners.

> *do shúil go n-éireodh an chuid eile d'Éirinn agus go dtiocfadh Francaigh dá*
> *gcabhair agus mur sin go saorfadaois Éirinn* ...[67]

hoping that the rest of Ireland would rise and that the French would come to help them and thereby that they would free Ireland.

> *tig gual i loing taoibh liom tar farraigí anall,*
> *'s mo bhuairt nach tíd saoirse do chlannaibh Gaol ndonn* ...[68]

coal comes in a ship nearby from across the seas, my woe that freedom does not come to the families of the fine Irish.

63 *I dtairngreacht naomh is léir go bhfaca* ..., R.I.A. MS 23 G 21, p. 507. See Ó Donnchadha, *Ó Longáin*, p. 80.
64 *Go réidh a bhean* ..., R.I.A. MS 23 E 16, p. 262. See Ó Donnchadha, *Ó Longáin*, p. 93.
65 *Déinidh go subhach, a Ghaela,* ..., R.I.A. MS R.I.A. 23 G 21, p. 512. See ibid., p. 101.
66 *Is méin liom insin daoibh* ..., R.I.A. MS 23 G 24, p. 168. See Ó Donnchadha, *Ó Longáin*, p. 105.
67 R.I.A. MS 23 G 23, p. 34.
68 *Tig fuacht i ngaoith geimhridh* ..., R.I.A. MS 23 C 8, p. 170. See Ó Donnchadha, *Ó Longáin*, p. 113.

go bhfeiceam Éire saor gan daoirse,
's an Bhratainn Uaithne in uachtar scaoilte …[69]

that we may see Ireland free without oppression, and the Green Flag
unfurled on high.

That reference to the Green Flag occurs in a poem of his written in 1798 on
the capture of Arthur O'Connor and the death of Lord Edward FitzGerald; in
another of his poems it is the White Flag that is to be victorious (see above, n. 43);
both white and green flags appear together in a verse written also in 1798 in
which he reproaches the French for not arriving as they had promised:[70]

Céad léan agus angar ar an dream sin ler mealladh sinn,
nach táinig ár bhfóirthint tar bóchna mar ghealladar;
do bhíomair ár ngruagaibh 's do bhí brait uaithne is gheala orainn,
's ní ar iarraidh do bhí ár bpící in am coimheascair is catha againn.

A hundred woes and afflictions on that crowd who deceived us, who didn't
come across the sea to help us as they had promised; we were cropped with
green and white flags over us, and our pikes weren't wanting when the
time of conflict and battle came.

The quatrain provides an illuminating microcosm of a general pattern in Ó
Longáin's verse: the confluence not so much of the 'old' with the 'new', but of
the 'residual' with the 'emergent'. For, as Limón reminds us, 'the seemingly
"new" more often consists of new transformations of older, that is to say, "residual" forms'; he elaborates: 'the residual is never quite residual and the emergent is
never quite emergent; that, in fact, the residual can be over-whelmingly present
… that the "emergent" emerges only through the incorporation of the residual'.[71]
    The challenge for modern commentators in encountering Ó Longáin's verse is
no more or no less than that presented by any corpus of historical material: to
endeavour to interpret it on its own terms, within its own parameters, and to recognize its validity, its integrity and its relevance (both aesthetic and political) for
its target audience. Ó Longáin wrote within well-established compositional
modes with their own inherent decoding mechanism, symbolic structure and ref-
erential framework. His political verse, in particular, encapsulates the traditional
motifs, themes and lexicon which had been assiduously cultivated by other poets

---

69 *Do chuala scéal* …, R.I.A. MS 23 E 16, p. 55. See Ó Donnchadha, *Ó Longáin*, p. 88.
70 R.I.A. MS 23 G 24, p. 206. Although Ó Longáin ascribes the verse in this copy and in another (St
Patrick's College, Maynooth MS M 12, p. 394) to *duine áirithe* ('a certain person'), we can assume
that he himself is the author. Cf. 'The green and white will stand upright, triumphant round our
shore …', in 'Defenders' Song' (Young, *Ulster in '98*, p. 52).
71 Limón, *Mexican ballads*, pp 42, 153.

for generations before him. He himself compiled and transcribed several collections of seventeenth- and eighteenth-century political poetry to which he added
explanatory glosses and colophons of his own and with which he integrated his
own verse and other apposite material: in a miscellaneous compilation of prose
and verse he inserts a printed copy, comprising both music and text, in French
and English, of the 'Marseilles'; he prefaces a comprehensive anthology of political verse in Irish with the ballad *Arise you gallant heroes, you sons of liberty*; in
another compilation he includes instructions, in English, for sword exercises; one
of his own political poems, he informs us, is to be sung to the air of 'The Rights
of Man'.[72]

Ó Longáin knew what he was doing, in joining and organizing the United
Irishmen, and knew what he was saying as a propagandist for them in his verse.
He was as 'rational', as 'coherent', as 'consistent', as any twentieth-century commentator. Ó Longáin counted himself among those who had been dispossessed,
not only of land and material goods, but of power, of *ceart ár sinsir* ; accordingly,
re-possession, the acquisition of power, the re-establishment of *ceart*, was fundamental to his perspective. Hence his incessant invocation of the image of the yoke
being severed and the consequent arrival of *saoirse*. In one of his verses he refers
to himself as *fear maith de chairdibh na saoirse* (a good man of the friends of freedom);[73] he composed another poem, he says, for those 'of the friends of freedom'
(*don méid de chairdibh na saoirse*) who had fallen on Vinegar Hill and throughout
Ireland;[74] his prayer was *grása na haithrí chughainn agus saoirse i dtalamh ár sinsir*
(the grace of repentance to us and freedom in the land of our ancestors).[75] If the
centrality of *saoirse* to his rhetoric, rather than other libertarian ideals, discom-
modes us, we should remember that it is no more central than 'Freedom' was to
the American colonists or 'Liberté' to the Lumiéres; and if his notion of *saoirse*
seems to us to be somewhat ethnocentric, rather homespun, it was also congruent
with other realisations of United Irishmen rhetoric:

> We will not buy nor borrow liberty from America, nor France but will
> manufacture it ourselves and work it up with those materials which the
> hearts of Irishmen furnish them with at home.[76]

> Men of Down are gathered here today, being the Sabbath of the Lord
> God, to pray and fight for the liberty of the Kingdom of Ireland. We have
> grasped the pike and musket and fight for the right against might; to drive

---

72 N.L.I., MS G 118, p. 54; R.I.A., MSS 23 C 8, p. iv; 23 N 14, pp 313, 340; 23 G 21, p. 510.
73 R.I.A., MS 23 G 21, p. 474. The verse in question (*Do fuaireas-sa tuairisc le gairid anall*) was
   obviously composed by himself.
74 *Mo bhrón, mo mhairg, mo scalladh* ..., R.I.A. MS 23 G 24, p. 167. See Ó Donnchadha, *Ó
   Longáin*, p. 100.
75 R.I.A. MS 23 G 21, p. 471.
76 Kevin Whelan, *Fellowship of freedom* (Cork, 1998), p. 31.

the bloodhounds of King George the German King beyond the seas. This is Ireland, we are Irish and we shall be free.[77]

The doctrine of the United Irishmen was not written in stone; it never constituted a canonical text which was handed down in pristine form from leaders to followers. On the contrary, once it began to be widely disseminated throughout Ireland – at various levels of society and in two languages – it acquired many accretions as it accommodated itself to local socio-cultural circumstances and as it was mediated through traditional modes. The movement advocated not only a union of Irishmen, but also the abolition of tithes, taxes and landlords; it was not only anti-monarchy, it was also anti-ascendancy, and against the status quo.[78] Jacobite rhetoric which was also vehemently and virulently 'anti-' was not only available, but was deemed eminently suitable as a channel for the radical option. The transition is almost imperceptible, helped as it was by the emergence of Bonaparte and his gradual acquisition of the messianic mantle formerly borne by the Stuarts. But Bonaparte, like the Stuarts before him, would function in Ireland not as French strategy dictated, but as Irish circumstances demanded:

Ar maidin ar drúcht is mé ag siúl go pras,
sea chonnarcsa chugham an chúileann deas,
sé labhair sí liom go cneasta is go ciúin
'nó an fada uainn an t-am ina bhfuil an dream le teacht?;
d'fhreagras go humhal an chúileann deas:
'ní fada uainn an t-am ina bhfuil an dream le teacht,
anois chuim na Samhna beidh militia fann,
is yeomen i dteannta ag Bonaparte' …[79]

One morning as I was walking briskly on the dew I saw the beautiful maiden aproaching. She addressed me mildly and quietly and asked me how long was it until the host arrived. I answered the beautiful maiden politely: 'It will not be long now until the host arrives; by November the militia will be prostrate and the yeomen entrapped by Bonaparte …

Irish political poetry oscillates within two time-frames: a linear sequence moving inexorably to its pre-ordained conclusion; and a cyclical pattern which acco-

---

77 Aiken McClelland, 'Thomas Ledlie Birch, United Irishman', in *Belfast Natural History and Philosophical Society, Proceedings and Reports*, 2nd ser., vii (1965), 24–35. The original source of the quotation (p. 31) has not been established.

78 See: 'The poor and their grievances – tithes, taxes, absentees, the cruelty of landlords and the baseness of English administrations are continually held up to view, through the medium of the print' [*Cork Gazette*]: N.A.I. 620/10/121/28. Their oath was 'To get rid of rent & tithe & to be as free as the French or Americans': N.A.I. RP 620/24/131. Cf. Jim Smyth, *The men of no property* (Dublin, 1992), p. 120.

79 *Ar maidin ar drúcht is mé ag siúl go pras*, St Patrick's College, Maynooth, MS M 9, pp 319–21.

modates both regular defeat and repetitive renewal and regeneration. Accordingly
Ó Longáin viewed contemporary affairs in a far wider perspective than the present or the punctual; rather were they part of an overarching continuum. And as
he was thus enabled to link the events and personages of '98 with those of previous eras, so did later poets relate the personages and events of their day to '98:

> In '98 you may remember
>   our dearest brethern were sent away,
> They were transported, chained and bolted,
>   we shall long remember those fatal days;
> But that time is ended and we are befriended
>   by that hero – I mean Noble Dan,
> He will gain our freedom, come let us cheer him
>   and sound his praises on Sliabh na mBan.[80]

---

80 The third verse of a macaronic song (*Éistidh sealad go n-insead scéal díobh*) in praise of
O'Connell: Cambridge University Library, MS Add. 6565, pp 24–5. Cf. G.D. Zimmermann,
Songs of Irish rebellion (Dublin, 1967; repr. Dublin, 2002), pp 206–7.

SECTION II

Looking back at the rebellion shortly after it terminated, the Mayo clergyman James Little observed: 'It is not in the poorest but the richest parts of this kingdom that sedition and a revolutionary spirit prevail and first raised their heads; an extreme degree of poverty and distress will sink the mind of man, divest him of the courage even to complain and bury in silence himself and his sufferings.'[1] The most commonly cited accounts of late eighteenth-century Ireland (Young, Campbell, Twiss) identified Munster as the 'disturbed' area of Ireland, a volatile seam stretching from Kilkenny to Limerick across the rich heartlands of the Golden Vale. Here agrarian campaigns had flared at regular intervals since the 1760s, as an expanding commercial economy clashed with a distinctive Gaelic moral economy rooted in an older cultural formation. A second seam of disturbance erupted along the Ulster fringes: centred on south Armagh, it seeped east and west through the crescent of drumlins and lakes that necklaced and insulated the province. By the 1790s, the Defenders were striking enduring tap-roots here into its cohesive if embattled Catholic community. By contrast, commentators routinely identified the most stable areas in eighteenth-century Ireland as Catholic south Leinster (especially County Wexford), a prosperous region based on a thriving tillage economy, and Presbyterian east Ulster (Antrim and Down), an area profiting from the prolonged linen boom.

Yet in the conflagrations of the 1790s, the older tinder zones in Munster and south Ulster smouldered but never caught fire, while the hitherto quiescent regions along the east coast ignited spectacularly. This raises a set of inter-related questions. Did the 1790s mark a clearcut political watershed with little continuity from the long eighteenth century? Should we seek exogenous rather than endogenous causes for the regional meltdown in the nineties? Was the geography of insurrection coincident with the geography of United Irish mobilisation? What was the relationship between high politics and the facts on the ground, and what were the filters between them?

---

1 Revd James Little, 'Diary,' p. 70.

If we turn first to Wexford (Gahan, chapter 6), the interpretative paradigm shifted during the 1990s. The older Musgrave/Kavanagh/Pakenham emphasis on a sectarian rebellion (whether provoked or spontaneous), distinguished by the absence of United Irish input, has been modified (Cullen, Whelan, Gahan, Cleary).[2] The current emphasis is on political mobilization and United Irish networks, both with complex roots in local politics. This interpretative turn reflected a new forensic sensitivity to problematic sources, especially the printed texts, and a precise calibration of the remarkably sinuous historiography of '98 after '98.[3] The Wexford work has stimulated detailed treatments of Wicklow and Kildare.[4] Instead of Pakenham's 'aimless and leaderless men', the emphasis has shifted to radical organization, the quality and continuity of leadership and links with and proximity to Dublin. The capital is now identified as the lynchpin of insurrection (Chambers, chapter 7). The geography of the rising in Leinster was intimately linked to a three-pronged United Irish plan: the taking of the capital by the city organization; a supporting crescent converging on the city (from Wicklow through Kildare to north Dublin); an outer ring of United Irish mobilization (from Wexford through Carlow, Laois and Westmeath to Meath)[5] which would rise locally and seal off the capital from reinforcements. These were expected to move east from the major military concentrations in the south, west and north, positioned to safeguard the long, indented and vulnerable Atlantic coast from a French landing.[6]

2   Despite these strictures, it should be acknowledged that Thomas Pakenham's *The year of liberty: The story of the great Irish rebellion of 1798* (London, 1969) remains the only sustained national narrative of the rebellion. When it appeared, it was a remarkably mature performance for a relatively young historian.

3   Richard Musgrave, *Memoirs of the Irish rebellion of 1798* (Enniscorthy, 4th ed. 1995); the accessibility of this crucial compendium on 1798 is massively enhanced by the provision of a detailed index, and a fine foreword by David Dickson, pp i-xiii; Patrick Kavanagh, *A popular history of the insurrection of 1798* (Dublin, 1870); Pakenham, *The year of liberty*; L.M. Cullen, 'The 1798 rebellion in Wexford: United Irish organization, membership and leadership', in Kevin Whelan (ed.), *Wexford: history and society* (Dublin, 1987), pp 269–86; K. Whelan, 'Politicisation in county Wexford and the origins of the 1798 rebellion', in Hugh Gough & David Dickson (eds), *Ireland and the French Revolution* (Dublin, 1990), pp 156–78; Kevin Whelan, 'Reinterpreting the 1798 rebellion in county Wexford', in Dáire Keogh & Nicholas Furlong (eds), *The mighty wave: The 1798 rebellion in County Wexford* (Dublin, 1996), pp 9–36; Daniel Gahan, *The people's rising: Wexford 1798* (Dublin, 1995); Brian Cleary, *The battle of Oulart Hill: Context and strategy* (Oulart, 1999).

4   Ruan O'Donnell, *The rebellion in County Wicklow 1798* (Dublin, 1998); Ruan O'Donnell, *Aftermath: Post-rebellion insurgency in County Wicklow, 1799–1803* (Dublin, 2000); Liam Chambers, *Rebellion in Kildare, 1790–1803* (Dublin, 1998). We still lack a recent account of Carlow, despite the excellent sources. A still valuable thesis is Maura Duggan, 'County Carlow, 1791–1801: A study in the era of revolution' (unpublished M.A. thesis, N.U.I. U.C.D., 1969).

5   J.G. Kerrane, 'The background to the 1798 rebellion in County Meath' (unpublished M.A. thesis, N.U.I. U.C.D., 1971).

6   Tommy Graham, 'Dublin in 1798: The key to the planned insurrection', in Keogh & Furlong (eds), *Mighty wave*, pp 65–78; For a map showing the United Irish plan, see Kevin Whelan, *Fellowship of freedom* (Cork, 1998), p. 56.

Dublin can therefore be seen as pivotal to the outcome of the insurrection (Graham, chapter 8). Curtin's 1985 study of the transformation of the United Irishmen into a revolutionary underground opened up a hugely productive debate.[7] Her account highlighted the role of Belfast, according to Dublin Castle, the 'centre of motion to the whole [United Irish] machine'.[8] Graham extended her analysis to Dublin, where mass organization developed slowly, then accelerated rapidly from late 1796.[9] Chronology is crucial here. Was there a sharp break between what some historians identify as the 'first' and 'second' United Irish organizations? Did the Fitzwilliam episode merely provide a straw man for later apologists?[10] Was there a genuine continuity of radical republicanism in Dublin as in Belfast throughout the decade? There may well be an over-emphasis on the small group (400) of early members in the capital as opposed to the 10,000 later members of the organization in 1798.[11] Can we identify the activists involved in the organizational transformation from an elite club towards a movement with a plebeian and artisanal base? How important was the infiltration of other organi-

7 Nancy Curtin, 'The transformation of the society of United Irishmen into a mass-based revolutionary organisation 1794–6', in *I.H.S.*, xxiv (1984–5), 463–92.
8 Camden to Portland, 29 July 1795, P.R.O. H.O. 100/58/171. In October 1796, John Richardson explained the contrast between the radicalism of east Derry and the conservatism of west Derry: 'This difference of disposition may be easily traced to the most obvious cause – their distance from and little trade or intercourse with Belfast for it is apparent that the disposition to rebellion is more or less in proportion to the distance from that seat of mischief': RP 620/25/171. On 26 November 1796, Edward MacNaghten of Beardiville, near Coleraine, reported to Lord Downshire that 'the town of Belfast has poisoned every county within the circuit of its commerce': Downshire papers, P.R.O.N.I., D. 607/D/348. James Hope claimed that there was 'no man of an enlightened mind who had intercourse with Belfast who did not return home determined on disseminating the principles of the union among their neighbours': Hope, *Autobiography*, p. 104.
9 An important overview is David Dickson, 'Centres of motion? Irish cities and the origins of popular politics', in Louis Bergeron & L.M. Cullen (eds), *Culture et pratiques politiques* (Paris, 1991), pp 101–22; Tommy Graham, 'A union of power? The United Irish organisation' in Dickson, Keogh & Whelan (eds), *United Irishmen*, pp 197–208.
10 Deirdre Lindsay, 'The Fitzwilliam episode revisited', in Dickson, Keogh and Whelan (eds), *United Irishmen*, pp 197–208. Fitzwilliam loomed especially large for Patriots and Catholics. Demoralized by the scale of state repression in 1793, their wilting belief in the reformability of the constitution was revivified by the advent of Fitzwilliam. His ignominious recall at the behest of an Irish faction seemed to confirm the radicals' insistence that only a clear break with the British connection could deliver change in Ireland. The Fitzwilliam episode proved that Britain would always favour 'a certain set of men' (Grattan) who could be relied on to implement her policies rather than to be guided by Irish public opinion. Thomas Moore claimed that after the recall, 'the Catholics carried their despair and their numbers into the ranks of the United Irishmen': *Memoirs of Captain Rock* (London, 1824), p. 334.
11 The bias derives partially from the accessible prosopography by R.B. McDowell, 'The personnel of the Dublin Society of United Irishmen 1791–94', in *I.H.S.*, ii (1940–1), 12–53, which is still indispensable six decades later. We await Thomas Bartlett, *Revolutionary Dublin: The letters of Francis Higgins to Dublin Castle, 1795–1801*, and C.J. Woods, 'The personnel of the Catholic Convention, 1792–1793' for similar rich archival pickings.

zations, notably the textile-based combinations, the Defenders, the Volunteers, free masons, guilds and militias?[12] Our most voluble Dublin-based witness to this period (Drennan) may not necessarily be the most helpful; we need to look more closely at the 'emerald pimpernel', William Putnam McCabe ('the right arm of sedition' according to Thomas Judkin Fitzgerald),[13] and at the activities of John 'Citizen' Burk, Richard Dry, James Hope and Oliver Bond, key figures involved in planning the underground organization.[14]

While the historiography has focused on Dublin, Cork has languished in a provincial mist (Dickson, chapter 9). Elizabeth Bowen's aphorism summarizes the received wisdom: 'In Munster, not very much happened.'[15] The strategic vulnerability of Cork as a major Atlantic port and provisioning centre for the British navy encouraged serious investment in fortification and troop concentration in the late eighteenth century. This intensified in the anxious aftermath of Bantry Bay.[16] The slow development of the United Irish organization in Cork city (at its height, its membership was only one-sixth that of Dublin) and in the wider Munster region poses questions, given the region's prior combustibility. Possible explanations for the tardiness include the cowing of Catholic leadership in the Whiteboy purges of the 1760s; the widening class divisions within the Catholic community; the predominantly Irish-speaking culture of the Munster cities, Cork, Waterford and Limerick; strategic emphasis of the United Irish leadership on Dublin (the principal Cork leaders Arthur O'Connor and the Sheares brothers operated in the capital); and the deterrent effect of military saturation of the region.[17]

12 We have no study of the Volunteers in the city, despite their undoubted significance. For the masons, see Petri Mirala, 'Freemasonry in Ulster 1733–1813' (unpublished Ph.D. thesis, University of Dublin., 1999). A flavour of their thinking is captured in the preface to a Dublin edition of their rules in 1791: 'This society is the most perfect that ever existed: in it, there is no distinction of men by the language they speak, by the dress they wear, by the rank in which they are born, or the titles they possess: the whole world is considered but as one republic, of which each nation forms a family and each individual a member: under its banner, men of knowledge, virtue and urbanity unite, its members defend the whole by their authority and enlighten each other by their knowledge.'

13 McCabe (1776–1821) was one of the most active, protean and charismatic of the United Irishmen. Fitzgerald's reference to him comes from a letter of 15 June 1798 to Castlereagh: cited in Charles Dickson, *The Wexford rising in 1798* (Tralee, 1955), p. 21.

14 We await the forthcoming biography of McCabe by John McCabe. A full scholarly edition of James Hope's autobiography (in the Madden manuscripts at T.C.D.) to replace the early truncated edition by R.R. Madden is also badly needed. Regrettably, John Messenger's 2000 edition reprints the bowdlerized Madden edition.

15 Elizabeth Bowen, *Bowen's Court* (Cork, 1998), p. 215.

16 J.A. Murphy (ed.), *The French are in the bay: The expedition to Bantry Bay, 1796* (Cork, 1997).

17 Thomas Power, *Land, politics and society in eighteenth-century Tipperary* (Oxford, 1993) is a model regional study. We await David Dickson, *Old world colony: Cork and south Munster, 1630–1830* (Cork, forthcoming). In relation to the Whiteboy fear, an indispensable treatment is W.P. Burke, *History of Clonmel* (Waterford, 1907), not least because it transcribes many documents subsequently destroyed in the Record Office fire.

And yet much of Munster still seethed in 1798, even if it never came to the boil. Was this the dying afterglow of the 'old' disaffection, the sparks of the 'new' one or some curious blend of both? While it is vital to factor in United Irish organization and political activism, it is equally necessary to emphasize the state of general politicization and the existing culture. Seen in overall context, a distinctive Munster core culture can be identified in the eighteenth century. A heartland extended from its eastern limit along Waterford harbour and the Blackstairs (Kilkenny in this interpretation is culturally a 'Munster' county), across through the midland bogs to the Shannon and its topographical western limit at Sliabh Luachra, and then pushing south to the Cork coastline. This region was also overwhelmingly Catholic in its composition. In 1798, as earlier and later, it followed its own path.[18]

From a United Irish perspective, barren ground stretched north from the bony peninsular fingers of Cork and Kerry, up through Clare (in this interpretation a 'Connacht' county) and into Connacht proper.[19] Galway was somnolent, and little seemed to be stirring in Mayo, Leitrim, or Sligo beyond sporadic Defenderism on its eastern fringes. Here were the most monolithic Irish-speaking communities and here too communal farming practices prevailed, which preserved cultural cohesion around embedded values. When some 1,000 French soldiers under Humbert unexpectedly landed on the far western fringes of this region at Kilcummin Strand in August 1798, it seemed like a classic case of 'too little, too late, and in the wrong place' (Murtagh, chapter 10). Yet over 10,000 Irish volunteers joined this tiny raiding party. Was this an impressive demonstration of latent support for the United Irish project or the deluded death-throes of a quaint Jacobitism?[20] The eighteenth-century French archives are littered with grandiose Irish invasion plans in which the lonesome west loomed large.[21] A further issue is whether the United Irishmen from Donegal to Kerry were held back by their leaders in anticipation of the projected French arrival in overwhelming force somewhere in their region.

Bonaparte was an insistent presence, dominating the song tradition of this period in both Irish and English, a further reminder not to treat the two languages as hermetically sealed. Four days before the rising broke, he set sail through the warm Mediterranean for Egypt, avoiding the cold Atlantic and his United Irish allies, and forsaking the inviting messianic niche which the Gaelic

---

18 See K. Whelan, 'Catholic mobilisation 1750-1850', in Bergeron and Cullen (eds), *Culture et pratiques politiques*, pp 235–58.

19 For Clare, see Kieran Sheedy, *The United Irishmen of County Clare* (Ennis, 1998).

20 The studies of the Humbert campaign are narrative-driven and lack analytic power. The best remains Richard Hayes, *The last invasion of Ireland: When Connacht rose* (Dublin, 1937). A competent local study is Liam Kelly, *A flame now quenched: Rebels and Frenchmen in Leitrim, 1793–98* (Dublin, 1998).

21 Indispensable here is Marcus Beresford, 'Ireland in French strategy, 1691–1789' (unpublished M.Litt. thesis, University of Dublin, 1975).

tradition had so lovingly prepared for someone like him.[22] Bonaparte became one more in a long line of lost leaders and fitted into an elegiac sense of the lost moment of the 1790s.

A further concern of these debates is the mutation of Enlightenment into romanticism, and whether a distinctive Irish variant emerged in the transition process. One response to political defeat in the 1790s was the development of a radical romanticism whose most audible if ambiguous representative was Thomas Moore.[23] This version of romanticism was radical because it sought to bring the Irish past into the present as a means of creating the future, rather than remaining a nostalgic enterprise as in the case of Walter Scott, content to leave the past safely in the past. As the public sphere was increasingly inert in post-Union Ireland, the political debate partially migrated out of the print milieu into other forms, like song and story. It then becomes important not to treat the memory of 1798 as if it was transmitted exclusively in print.[24] As late as 1845, when a repertoire of 102 popular songs was collected in the staunchly Presbyterian area of Kilwarlin in County Down, over one-third of them concerned the 1790s: ten can be found in various editions of the United Irish songbook *Paddy's resource*; twenty-nine deal with the period from a perspective sympathetic to the rebels; and there were only seven Orange songs.[25] Zimmerman noted that 'the events of 1798 were to remain for more than a century one of the principal sources of inspiration for balladmakers'.[26] The novelist James McHenry, looking back in the mid-1820s, believed that these songs 'did more to increase the numbers of the conspirators than all the

22 See G.-D. Zimmermann, *Songs of Irish rebellion: Political street ballads and rebel songs 1780-1900* (Dublin, 1967; repr. Dublin, 2002), pp 186–92; Terry Moylan, *The age of revolution in the Irish song tradition 1776–1815* (Dublin, 2000), pp 133–86. Frank Harte, *My name is Napoleon Bonaparte*, 2 CDs (Dublin, 2001) is a magnificent realization of these songs [hear also his earlier companion CD, *The year of liberty* (Dublin, 1998)]. Harte's motto is that 'the winners write the history, the losers write the songs.'

23 For the transition from enlightenment to romanticism, see especially Isaiah Berlin, *The roots of romanticism* (London, 1999); Martin Thom, *Republics, nations and tribes* (London, 1995); Katie Trumpener, *Bardic nationalism: The romantic novel and the British empire* (Princeton, 1997). For the renewed emphasis on Moore, see Emer Nolan, *Irish melodies and discordant politics: Thomas Moore's 'Memoirs of Captain Rock'* (forthcoming); Catherine Jones, 'Our partial attachments: Tom Moore and 1798', in *E.C.I.*, xiii (1998), 24–43; Tadgh O'Sullivan, 'Captain Rock in print: Literary representation and Irish agrarian unrest, 1824–1833' (unpublished M.Phil., U.C.C., 1998); Matthew Campbell, 'Thomas Moore's wild song: The 1821 *Irish Melodies*' in *Bullán*, iv (1999–2000), 83–104.

24 For comments on the folklore, see Gearóid Ó Crualaíoch, 'The French are on the say', in Murphy (ed.), *Bantry Bay* (Cork, 1997), pp 120–37; for the songs, see Tom Munnelly, '1798 and the balladmakers', in Póirtéir (ed.), *Great Irish rebellion*, pp 160–70. An important study of the folklore is Guy Beiner, *To speak of '98: Remembering the Year of the French in Ireland* (Oxford, forthcoming).

25 Hugh Shields, 'Some songs and ballads in use in the province of Ulster . . . 1845', in *Ulster Folklife*, xvii (1971), pp 3–65. See also Thomas Crofton Croker, *Popular songs illustrative of the French invasions of Ireland*, 3 vols (London, 1845–7).

26 Zimmermann, *Songs of Irish rebellion*, p. 39. In a representative local collection, 21 of 137 songs are about 1798: Paddy Berry, *Wexford ballads* (Wexford, 1982).

efforts of the French emissaries, or the writings and harangues of all the political philosophers and age-of-reason men of the times'.[27] The veteran United Irishman Andrew O'Reilly claimed that by the mid-nineteenth century 'the music of Ireland is the music of a heart-broken people: it is a collection of sighs'.[28] Many of these sighs were for the lost opportunity of 1798.

In 1884, J. Pope Hennessy investigated the reading habits of the ordinary Irish people as revealed by what they borrowed from the reading rooms (National League in the rural parishes, or the Catholic Young Men's in the towns): in the biographical section, the four favourites were Madden's *Lives of the United Irishmen*, Henry Grattan's biography by his son, Moore's *Life of Lord Edward Fitz-Gerald* and Wolfe Tone's *Memoirs*.[29] This example demonstrates how thoroughly the 1798 period penetrated popular memory. That memory increasingly sought to enter the public sphere. In 1868, young men in a Dublin procession had been arrested and tried for raising their hats as they passed the site of Robert Emmet's execution in Thomas Street.[30] In 1875, the first public 1798 memorial was erected at Bunclody in County Wexford, a discreet plaque in the local graveyard. In 1877, Dublin Fenians organised a commemoration of Fr Murphy at Boolavogue, and returned the following year to unveil a memorial to him at Boolavogue, despite concerted clerical opposition.[31] But in the 1890s a plethora of statues emerged all over the island, indicating that a seismic shift in nationalist sentiment was underway.[32]

27 James McHenry, *O'Halloran or the insurgent chief* (Philadelphia, 1824), pp 62–3. The comment follows on his vivid description of 'an old female balladeer' singing the new ballad of 'Blarris Moor' at Larne yarn market in 1797. The song described the ceremonial execution of four United Irish members of the Monaghan Militia at Blaris Moor: see Zimmerman, *Songs*, pp 129–32. Richard Musgrave noted: 'By means of songs, the passions of the multitude were very much raised': Musgrave, *Memoirs*, p. 703. The Cork yeoman Michael Joseph Barry was court-martialled for singing 'The Shan Van Vocht': Crofton Croker, *Songs of the French Revolution*, iii, p. 43.
28 Andrew O'Reilly, *Memoirs of an emigrant Milesian*, 3 vols (London, 1853), iii, p. 305.
29 J. Pope Hennessy, 'What do the Irish read?', in *The Nineteenth Century*, June 1884, p. 926. The library of Clough First Presbyterian Church in County Down in 1842 had the *Autobiography* of A.H. Rowan, and Moore's *Life of Lord Edward FitzGerald*: J.R. Adams, *The printed word and the common man* (Belfast, 1987), p.129. In 1895, when Alice Milligan founded the Henry Joy McCracken reading room in Belfast, the reading material included Tone's *Life*, Teeling's *Narrative*, Moore's *FitzGerald*, Young's *Ulster in 1798*, and Madden's *United Irishmen: Northern Patriot*, 15 Oct. 1895.
30 Unidentified newspaper cutting, 21 Feb. 1868, inserted in a copy of Madden [private collection].
31 *Dublin Evening Mail*, 3 Oct. 1878. The parish priest Thomas Connick was opposed as was the Catholic bishop Michael Warren; they succeeded in closing all the public houses in the area as the mainly Dublin crowd of Fenian sympathisers unveiled the monument near the village on 29 September 1878 (not at the graveyard, from which they were prohibited by the priest): Anna Kinsella, 'The nineteenth-century interpretation of 1798' (unpublished M.Litt. thesis, University of Dublin, 1992).
32 Nuala Johnson, 'Sculpting heroic histories: Celebrating the centenary of the 1798 rebellion in Ireland' in *Trans. Inst. Br. Geog.*, n.s., xix (1994), 78–93.

5

The rebellion of 1798 in south Leinster

DANIEL GAHAN

'South Leinster' is a nebulous term, used often to refer to the counties that make up the southern half of modern Leinster and corresponding roughly to the old kingdom of Leinster. For the purposes of this paper the term will be defined more narrowly than usual, to embrace counties Wexford, Carlow, Kilkenny and the southern parts of County Wicklow. This region was critical in the conflict that developed in Ireland in the summer of 1798. About half of the loyalist claims for compensation filed after the rebellion were made by residents of County Wexford alone.[1] The fighting in this area lasted for little more than six weeks and this, along with the fact that most of it was concentrated inside a single county, means that the rising in the south-east may have been the single most destructive war in Irish history, in relative terms at least.

The rebellion in south Leinster in general – and in Wexford in particular – has been subject to a wider variety of interpretations than has 1798 in any other region of the country. Unlike the Midlands, Mayo or Ulster, interpretations of the rising here have evolved significantly over time. Central to the debate is the question of the relative strength of the United Irish movement in the area before the rebellion and the part played by sectarian tensions in bringing the conflict about. Until the 1970s, apologists for both nationalist and loyalist traditions tended to regard Wexford and adjacent areas as very unusual in 1798, claiming (as loyalists had done) that the rebels here were engaged in a religious crusade to exterminate Protestants,[2] or arguing (as nationalists or rebel-sympathizers did) that the rebellion in the region occurred in response to a completely unjustified government reign of terror that drove the country people of Wicklow and Wexford to rebellion, in an act of self-defence and desperation.[3]

---

1 Loyalist claims for compensation, N.L.I., Mic. p 7665.
2 See especially Sir Richard Musgrave, *Memoirs of the different rebellions in Ireland* (Dublin, 1801); George Taylor, *An historical account of ... the rebellion in the county of Wexford* (Dublin, 1800).
3 See especially Patrick Kavanagh, *A popular history of the insurrection of 1798* (Dublin, 1870); Charles Dickson, *The Wexford rising of 1798: Its causes and course* (Tralee, 1955).

My purpose here is to assess why the various parts of south Leinster responded so differently to the outbreak of rebellion and to explain why the rebels in Wexford and parts of Wicklow enjoyed such stunning military success – compared with the disastrous (and brief) campaigns waged by their comrades elsewhere in the country. Moreover, we need also to consider why events such as the massacre at Scullabogue and other rebel atrocities would come to characterize the struggle in this part of Ireland more than anywhere else.

Historians like Louis Cullen and Kevin Whelan have created a very different assessment of this region in 1798 in recent years, compared with what had been standard fare for generations. They accept that sectarian tensions were very much part of life in places like Wexford and Wicklow in the 1790s; however, while they played a role in the origins of the rebellion, equally important was the politicization of large segments of the Catholic gentry and middle classes and the emergence of a liberal Protestant element which formed an alliance with them. The rise of the United Irishmen pushed this coalition towards revolution and the movement became especially formidable when it attracted tenant farmers, tradesmen and labourers, both in town and country. Cullen has shown that the United Irishmen were a powerful presence in County Wexford by the beginning of 1798 and were especially well-established in the area north and east of the Slaney.[4] The movement was equally strong in south County Wicklow and north Carlow, but was less well developed in the south-western half of Wexford, and it seems to have been present but not well developed in south Carlow and most of County Kilkenny. This distinction may be merely a matter of location; north Carlow/south Wicklow/north-east Wexford was after all more accessible to Dublin and its radicals, and to United Irish agents who came south from Ulster.[5] But this area also had a sizeable Protestant minority, the largest anywhere in Ireland outside of Ulster, and this unquestionably played an important role in the upheavals of the late 1790s. Most parishes north and east of a line from Wexford harbour to Castlecomer were at least 10 per cent Protestant in 1798, and close to half of them were over 20 per cent; a few even had Protestant minorities of over 40 per cent.[6] In contrast, the countryside that lay to the south of this line, embracing south-west Wexford, south Carlow and almost all of Kilkenny was overwhelmingly Catholic, more than 95 per cent in about three-quarters of the parishes involved, and only falling below 90 per cent in a handful.[7] If we consider this collection of counties as a coherent, well-defined region, there is no question but

4 L.M. Cullen, 'The 1798 rebellion in Wexford: United Irish organisation, membership and leadership', in Kevin Whelan (ed.), *Wexford: History and society* (Dublin, 1987), pp 269–86.

5 Kevin Whelan, 'Reinterpreting the 1798 rebellion in County Wexford', in Dáire Keogh and Nicholas Furlong (eds), *The mighty wave: The 1798 rebellion in Wexford* (Dublin, 1996), p. 16.

6 L.M. Cullen, *The emergence of modern Ireland* (London, 1981), p. 213.

7 Bruce Elliott, 'Emigration from south Leinster to eastern Upper Canada', in Whelan (ed.), *Wexford*, p. 425.

that it was made up not just of different administrative units (i.e. counties and baronies) but also of two very different worlds in terms of its religious (or ethno-religious) character, a Catholic country to its south and west (in Kilkenny, south Carlow and south-west Wexford) and a country that was essentially mixed to its north and east, even if it was still predominantly Catholic.

Unquestionably, the great preponderance of the Protestant population in the 'mixed' area stayed loyal to the government and formed a determined pro-government and anti-revolutionary faction. The presence of several Orange lodges in this area by early 1798 and the development of pronounced sectarian tensions within yeomanry units are evidence of this.[8] The religious and political divides did not coincide precisely, even in the north-east Wexford/south Wicklow/north Carlow triangle, and it is misleading to label what developed there as simply a sectarian conflict (there were far too many Catholic loyalists and far too many Protestant rebels to allow for this).[9] But the peculiar features of the religious geography of the region may still have stimulated the emergence of a strong United Irish movement here, and an especially determined one given the need for Catholic members to resist what they might have regarded as the Orange threat and for Protestant members to distance themselves from their loyalist co-religionists.

This factor looms especially large when we consider that the part of South Leinster in which the rebellion was most serious (most of Wicklow and Wexford) did not have a rich tradition of resistance to the state or its agents before the 1790s. Thus, while the Whiteboy movements of the 1760s and 1770s had affected County Kilkenny and parts of Carlow, they had little impact on either Wexford or Wicklow, apart from the western most fringes of Wexford around the villages of Killann and Newtownbarry.[10] In the 1780s Wexford produced an outspoken proponent of the patriot party, George Ogle and an active Volunteer movement but one that was more heavily dominated by Protestants than was the case in most of southern Ireland.[11] County Wexford was however rocked in the mid-1790s by two dramatic developments which, although dissimilar, did to a certain extent presage what was to come. In the summer of 1793 thousands of country people marched on Wexford town from districts to the north and west in protest against the militia draft as well as the arrest of anti-tithe agitators. The militia confronted the crowd (or ambushed them as pro-rebel historians would later put it) and shot dozens of people.[12] The riot was crushed but the event, so typical of outbursts of popular resistance in the decade of the French Revolu-

---

8 Cullen, *Emergence,* pp 214–15; Whelan, 'Reinterpreting 1798', pp 17–18.

9 Daniel Gahan, *The people's rising: Wexford 1798* (Dublin, 1995), pp 8–10.

10 Edward Hay, *History of the insurrection of the county of Wexford, 1798* (Dublin, 1803), p. 12.

11 Ibid., p. 12; Kevin Whelan, 'Politicisation in County Wexford and the origins of the 1798 Rebellion', in David Dickson and Hugh Gough (eds), *Ireland and the French Revolution* (Dublin, 1990), p. 157.

12 Hay, *Insurrection,* pp 21–7; Thomas Bartlett, 'An end to moral economy: The Irish militia disturbances of 1793', in *Past & Present,* xcix (1983), 51–3.

tion, created a precedent so memorable that in western parts of County Wexford that this event would subsequently become known as the 'first rebellion'.[13] It is difficult to determine precisely how important 1793 was to the later spread of the United Irishmen into this region, but it almost certainly gave many of the later rank and file rebels of the area some experience of resistance – as well as martyrs for the popular cause – and this only five years before the great rebellion.

The second significant development was the dramatic politicization of the Catholic population of County Wexford, in particular in the period from 1792 to 1796. Whelan has detailed this in convincing fashion and demonstrates beyond much doubt that Wexford Catholics were heavily involved in the Catholic Convention of 1792 which pressured the government to grant the relief act of 1793, giving Catholics the right to vote; he has also demonstrated that in 1795 the Wexford Catholic gentry organized a petitioning movement for the reinstatement of Earl Fitzwilliam which gained the support (through signatures) of about two-thirds of the adult male population of the county, thereby politicizing a large pro-portion of tenant farmers and even tradesmen, and unwittingly preparing such elements, once the failure of the petition left them disillusioned, for the more radical messages of the French Revolution.[14]

The Protestant population of much of south Leinster also underwent an important metamorphosis in the 1790s, one which was equally important in cre-ating a volatile mix in the region in the last years of the decade. Wexford politics had been more open than in most analagous constituencies. County elections were often fiercely contested, and Wexford town, being an open borough, was an arena for vigorous parliamentary and municipal elections. Protestants in the county had long since been divided into liberal and conservative interests. The dividing line between these two was blurred, with several landlords and mer-chants making up a floating neutral or moderate element. In the 1790s however, while many of the liberals gave at least tacit approval to the cause of Catholic relief, the conservative element consolidated itself and tightened its grip on county politics, in part inspired by the stridency with which George Ogle opposed the various relief acts, especially that of 1793. This conservative block was led by a handful of large Protestant landlords, the Rams, Tottenhams and Loftuses in particular, and was reinforced by more modest landlords and gentry such as Ogle, Hunter Gowan, Hawtrey White and James Boyd; it was under-pinned by a large portion of the Protestant tenant farmers and artisans both in south Wicklow and in most of north-east County Wexford.[15]

From early 1797 this divide between the liberal element, which had its Protestant as well as Catholic component, and the conservative element, which was initially overwhelmingly Protestant, sharpened and widened. The spread of

13 Cullen, '1798 in Wexford', p. 253.
14 Whelan, 'Reinterpreting the 1798 rebellion', p. 15.
15 Whelan, 'Politicisation', pp 158–60.

the United Irishmen into south Leinster but especially into Wicklow, north Carlow and north Wexford provided the liberals with a vehicle for organization and a radical programme which promised redress in the near future.[16] It is diffi-cult to tell if the movement spread to the ranks of the Catholic tenantry and arti-sans because of the prior presence of a Defender movement among them, as appears to have been the case in north Leinster. The Defenders may not have been well organized in this region at all in fact, but earlier traditions of resistance and politicization may have compensated for their absence.

In the summer and autumn of 1797, south Wicklow, north Carlow and north-east Wexford became the cockpit of an intense struggle between a rapidly grow-ing United Irish movement, introduced into the area by agents from eastern Ulster such as William Putnam McCabe and James Hope and which appealed mostly but not exclusively to Catholics,[17] and a pro-ascendancy block that incor-porated an emerging Orange Order, based around newly-formed lodges, especial-ly numerous in north Carlow, south Wicklow and north Wexford, on the other.[18] These competing forces were of course to be found in many regions of the coun-try, but the fact that this particular region had a large minority who were adher-ents of the established church and in whose interests the maintenance of the old regime clearly lay, ensured that the competition was especially sharp. Indicative perhaps of the strength and advanced state of the development of the revolution-ary movement in this area, local magistrates decided as early as November 1797 to declare a total of sixteen parishes in north-east Wexford to be in a state of rebellion. These parishes were located in a triangle roughly between Castlebridge, Enniscorthy and Courtown, an area that was in most respects typi-cal of the 'mixed' country north and east of the Slaney and a district that would be at the centre of open rebellion when it erupted the following summer.[19]

There was a United Irish presence in south and west County Wexford, in south Carlow, and in Kilkenny too. The Protestant population was restricted there to a few pockets, and large pro-ascendancy tenant farmers and Protestant artisans were mostly absent. For whatever reason the United movement was sig-nificantly less developed there by the spring of 1798 than it was in the north Carlow/south Wicklow/north-east Wexford triangle.[20] The area immediately to the south of Wexford town is especially intriguing since here, in a district of quite modest estates a number of Protestant landlords, gentry and merchants threw in their lot with the revolutionaries, men like Bagenal Harvey, William Hatton and Cornelius Grogan.[21]

16 Cullen, *Emergence*, pp 228–30; Whelan, 'Reinterpreting the 1798 rebellion', pp 16–21.
17 Ibid., p. 16.
18 Cullen, '1798 in Wexford', pp 267–8.
19 Whelan, 'Reinterpreting 1798', p. 19.
20 Cullen, '1798 in Wexford', pp 280–2.
21 Ibid., p. 282.

Throughout south Leinster, and even inside the hotly contested triangle, there were many moderate or even genuinely neutral elements which might, in other circumstances, have worked to bridge the gulf between the Catholic and Protestant revolutionaries and the predominantly Protestant reactionaries. As everywhere, the Catholic hierarchy and the vast majority of its priests opposed the United Irishmen,[22] even if they had encouraged the earlier peaceful efforts to end Protestant political ascendancy. Had it not been for the fact that the Protestant hierarchy and many of its clergy were so adamantly pro–ascendancy,[23] a rapprochement between the two churches directed against the revolutionaries might even have developed. There was also a floating moderate handful of liberal Protestant landlords, men who never sympathized with the United Irishmen but who, like the official Catholic Church, had at least been less than zealous in their opposition to Catholic relief. Lord Mountnorris of Camolin in north Wexford was one of these, as was Richard Carew of Castleboro in the western part of the county; the Kavanaghs of Borris, Catholic landlords who owned much of southern Carlow and leased almost all of it to large Catholic middlemen; Wexford Catholic gentlemen such as Philip Hay, who took the government side (although his two brothers, John and Edward, were United Irishmen). So also could smaller Protestant landlords and gentry from central County Wexford such as Solomon Richards, the Poundens, and Zachary Cornick.[24] Their enthusiasm for the government cause was somewhat blunted by their sense that the future for the region would have to be based on mutual accommodation of the different denominational and class interests; they took the government side nonetheless.

The pattern of the United Irish mobilization in south Leinster when the rebellion of 1798 eventually broke out reveals much about the nature of the movement in the region. In the month or so beforehand, government forces had conducted fierce anti-United Irish campaigns in east Munster and the Midlands[25] but south Leinster had escaped the worst of these for a time. Local yeomanry detachments brought elements of this campaign into the north Carlow/south Wicklow/north-east Wexford region by early May, and the North Cork militia, which came to County Wexford in April, spearheaded this effort in Wexford.[26]

In the week before the rebellion broke out in the midlands, the authorities in south Wicklow and north Wexford launched an especially fierce campaign against United Irishmen, arresting numerous suspects, most notably Anthony Perry of Inch, the United Irish colonel of the region around Gorey. This dis-

---

22 Kevin Whelan, 'The role of the Catholic priest in the 1798 rebellion in County Wexford', in Whelan (ed.), *Wexford*, pp 309–10.
23 Cullen, '1798 in Wexford', p. 268.
24 Whelan, 'Politicisation', pp 158–162; idem, 'Catholic mobilisation, 1750–1850' in Louis Bergeron and L.M. Cullen (eds), *Cultures et pratiques politiques en France et en Irlande, XVIe–XVIIIe siècle* (Paris, 1990), p. 245.
25 W.E.H. Lecky, *A history of Ireland in the eighteenth century* (London, 1892), iv, pp 265–87.
26 Cullen, '1798 in Wexford', p. 267.

rupted the movement in the Wexford/Wicklow border area to such an extent
that many of its lesser officers went into hiding in the critical days before the outbreak, Miles Byrne of Monaseed among them.[27] The militia and yeomanry were,
however, unable to identify other colonels, and were not in a position to arrest any
major United Irish figures until Perry eventually broke under torture and gave
them the names of Edward Fitzgerald, John Henry Colclough and Bagenal
Harvey, all of them United Irish officers from the south of the county (only Fitzgerald came from the area to the north of Wexford town).[28] This made Perry's
information valuable to the authorities certainly, but it also meant that they were
unable to move against the organization in the vital central part of the county. In
selecting these particular names, in other words, in spite of being under great
physical pain, Perry may have been trying to throw the authorities off the scent.

The rebel mobilization that took place in the south Leinster region between
24 and 30 May reflects both the geography of the movement at this time and the
impact of the authorities' campaign, the arrest and torture of Perry included.
But it also suggests that there was something distinctive about the United Irish
movement in the area of Wexford to the north-east of the Slaney. The mail-
coach signal seems to have been a failure, even where it was 'delivered': the coach
to Wexford was not stopped on the night of the 23rd/24th and so the signal did
not reach the area at once. Instead, the process of mobilization spread southwards from its north Kildare/north Wicklow epicentre over the course of the
24th, a parish at a time, the signal to rise in effect being the arrival of news that a
neighbouring parish had just risen. By nightfall on the 24th, it had reached the
area around Carlow town and central and southern parts of Wicklow. At this rate,
the mobilization in Wexford should have taken place on the 25th, not as it did,
late on the 26th and 27th. The arrest of Perry and the severe disruption of the
rebel command structure in the region around Gorey and Arklow, plus the arrest
and massacre of United Irishmen (or suspected United Irishmen) at Carnew on
the 25th and the disastrous rebel attacks on Hacketstown and Carlow town early
that morning,[29] seem to have created a fire-break along the entire Carlow/
Wicklow/ Wexford borderland; rather than sparking central Wexford into rebellion, it actually interrupted the process for a time. This perhaps explains why Fr
John Murphy and his men were clearly 'out' on the 25th, under the pretext of
cutting turf,[30] but made no move to openly mobilize, very likely because units in
surrounding parishes were so hesitant, being cut off as they were from the larger
Leinster mobilization. In essence then, the United Irish mobilization had to leap-
frog over this fire-break and had to be triggered locally, in places like Tincurry
and Boolavogue, without direct contact with already-mobilized units to the

27 Miles Byrne, *Memoirs* (Dublin, 1906), pp 25–6; Dickson, *Wexford rising*, pp 43–7.
28 Cullen, '1798 in Wexford', p. 274.
29 Gahan, *People's rising*, p. 11.
30 Cullen, '1798 in Wexford', p. 287.

immediate north. This may explain much of what happened in Wexford over the first five days of the rebellion, both in terms of the confusion which reigned and the particular directions the rebels took once they were in the field.

The rebellion in Wexford took off in dramatic fashion and achieved stunning military success compared with the outcome everywhere else. Undoubtedly, the fact that the north-eastern part of Wexford and south Wicklow had a well-developed and unusually determined United Irish movement played an important role in that success. In addition, it is probable that despite the efforts of the North Corks and the yeomanry the United Irish movement in many parts of Wexford had not been badly damaged by the government's disarmament campaign, certainly compared with what had happened in the midlands or Tipperary.

Another, and possibly vital, factor in the Wexford case, was the actual distribution of government forces. The militia and yeomanry were concentrated in the larger towns and villages of Wexford, as they were everywhere in Ireland, and huge tracts of countryside were effectively left to the rebels during the hours of darkness.[31] The county town happened to be located in its far south-east corner, and the largest government garrison was stationed there too.[32] The second largest garrison was at Duncannon Fort, in the far southwest, standing guard at the approaches to Waterford harbour. This deployment reflected the government's concern at the possibility of French seaborne invasion, a real threat since Bantry Bay, and something Dublin Castle believed likely in May 1798.[33] As for the rest of the county, New Ross had a very small garrison, mostly of local yeomen,[34] Enniscorthy had less than 200 men, also chiefly yeomanry;[35] apart from small yeomanry and militia detachments in Ferns, Newtownbarry, Camolin, and Gorey (most of them no more than a few dozen in number),[36] the entire northern two-thirds of the county was ungarrisoned. All told, in fact, the government side had less than 500 men at its disposal between the Wicklow/Wexford border and a line running form Duncannon Fort to Wexford town on the night of 26 May. Even more importantly there was no town or village of any size, and therefore no garrison of any kind, in the stretch of countryside between Wexford town and Gorey and between Enniscorthy and the sea, an area about twenty by fifteen miles in extent; the rebels had the luxury of an entire night to mobilize unmolested in this triangle, and therefore, the single encounter they did have with government troops at The Harrow was accidental and made little difference to their operation.[37]

31 Gahan, *People's rising*, pp 23–4.
32 Ibid., pp 54–7; Hay, *Insurrection*, p. 95.
33 Thomas Pakenham, *The year of liberty: The great Irish rebellion of 1798* (London, 1969), p. 31.
34 James Alexander, *A succinct narrative of the rise and progress of the rebellion in the County Wexford* (Dublin, 1800), p. 30.
35 Musgrave, *Rebellions*, i, pp 428–31.
36 Gahan, *People's rising*, pp 24–5.
37 Ibid., pp 181–9.

Once day broke on the 27th, the rebels were in a strong position to resist the inevitable counter-attack by government forces from Gorey, Enniscorthy or Wexford town. Their movements during the night and in the early hours of the 27th suggest that Oulart was a pre-arranged rendezvous point, with Oulart Hill as their strong-point in case of attack.[38] The hill was a natural gathering-point, one of the best available to rebels anywhere in Ireland in the crucial first forty-eight hours after mobilization. It was located almost exactly at the centre of the triangle between Wexford town, Enniscorthy and Gorey; it was the highest point in that entire district, and yet its slopes were sufficiently steep and its overall area was small enough to make it very difficult for even a large government force to dislodge them.[39] In fact, of the two gatherings of rebels that took place that first day in County Wexford, that at Kilthomas was probably the larger but had the disadvantage of being based on a long range of hills, and of being attacked by a large force of yeomanry – some from Carnew, some from Enniscorthy – early in the day, before they had much time to prepare; once the attack came, the yeoman cavalry was able to gain high ground off to the rebel right without having to fire a shot; with the high ground lost, the rebel force was scattered easily once the infantry charged them.[40] The rebels at Oulart on the other hand did not have to deal with a serious threat from government forces until about three o'clock that afternoon. Despite the disruption from which this division had suffered because of the arrest of Edward Fitzgerald, they were better prepared for the battle which took place that afternoon, in which they overwhelmed the North Cork militia, than almost any rebel force anywhere in Ireland that summer. While their victory was in part the result of resolute leadership by men on the spot, notably Morgan Byrne and Fr John Murphy, it may also reflect the fact that for several weeks beforehand the general area thereabouts had effectively been rebel country between sunset and sunrise every night.[41]

The battle of Oulart might not have been enough to give the Wexford rebels the momentum they needed to sweep into control of the entire county. Equally significant was the fact that they moved north to Carrigrew Hill that first evening and thereby drew into their ranks hundreds of rebels from Anthony Perry's district around Gorey.[42] The fact that this general area was so lightly garrisoned explains why government forces abandoned the town of Gorey at this point and fled north to Arklow,[43] and why the garrisons in the villages of Ferns and

---

38 Cullen, '1798 in Wexford', p. 291.
39 Brian Cleary, 'The battle of Oulart Hill: Context and strategy', in Keogh and Furlong, *Mighty wave*, p. 84.
40 James Gordon, *History of the rebellion in Ireland in the year 1798* (Dublin, 1801), p. 90.
41 Cleary, 'Battle of Oulart', pp 89–95.
42 Byrne, *Memoirs*, i, p. 32.
43 Gordon, *Rebellion*, p. 87; H.F.B. Wheeler and A.M. Broadley, *The war in Wexford: An account of the rebellion in the south of Ireland in 1798* (London, 1919), pp 92–3.

Camolin retreated to Enniscorthy.[44] With a single victory on Oulart Hill in east Wexford the rebels managed to sweep their enemy from the entire northern third of the county, and without having to do what the rebels in Kildare, northern Wicklow and northern Carlow had been forced to attempt, attack a well-armed garrison in a sizeable town in the first few hours of their campaign. Instead, by the time the Wexford rebels attacked a significant garrison, that in Enniscorthy, they had swelled to perhaps 6,000 men and,[45] even more importantly, they had acquired about 800 carbines and ammunition when they passed through Camolin, the day after Oulart. These weapons had been deposited there before distribution to the local yeomanry and their capture was completely fortuitous.[46] With this firepower they were able to drive Captain Snowe's garrison (70 militia-men and a little over 200 yeomanry) out of Enniscorthy on the 28th, helped undoubtedly also by the fact that Snowe had no artillery.[47]

By the end of its first forty-eight hours, the Wexford rebellion had succeeded to a degree that was unmatched elsewhere in the country. Rather than suggesting that there was anything unique about the strength of the United Irishmen in the county however, this achievement reflects the confluence of a number of fortu-itous factors, including the very geography of the county, the consequent lop-sided distribution of garrisons, the even more vital fact that Oulart Hill was such an ideal rallying point, and the chance capture by the rebels of 800 stand of firearms when they swept through the abandoned village of Camolin. The absence of any one of these factors might well have resulted in defeat for the rebels everywhere in Wexford that first day or, more likely perhaps, defeat in their attack on Enniscorthy the following day, an action that might have turned out to be equally disastrous for them as were the attacks on Naas and Carlow town by their comrades further north.

The battle of Enniscorthy is significant in that United Irishmen in the coun-tryside to the west of the town (and the Slaney) only began to mobilize in its aftermath.[48] This would be the pattern elsewhere else in south Leinster for the duration of the conflict; United Irish units could only be convinced to take the field in numbers once rebel armies had achieved a spectacular nearby victory. In contrast to the mobilization in north-east Wexford, which took place in the shad-ow of severe local setbacks, this very hesitant approach suggests that the United Irish movement here was less formidable in numbers, less mature in terms of its organization and preparation, and less committed to the rising initially, in spite of

---

44 Wheeler, *War in Wexford*, p. 86.
45 Byrne, *Memoirs*, i, p. 42.
46 William Snowe, *Statement of transactions at Enniscorthy on 28 May [1798]* (Dublin, 1801), pp 5–6; Musgrave, *Rebellions*, i, pp 428–31.
47 Gahan, *People's rising*, pp 45, 309; Cullen, '1798 in Wexford', p. 209.
48 Cullen, '1798 in Wexford', pp 255–6; Thomas Cloney, *A personal narrative of transactions in the county of Wexford during the awful period of 1798* (Dublin, 1832), pp 238–9, 268.

the fact that south-west Wexford would eventually produce some of the most celebrated rebel leaders (John Kelly of Killann in particular) and the bloodiest battle
of the entire war (New Ross).

The Wexford rebellion might still not have grown beyond a local uprising,
with the victories at Oulart Hill and Enniscorthy as its twin achievements, were it
not for the capture of Wexford town, two days after Enniscorthy. This ensured
that the Wexford rebels became the only ones that summer to seize their entire
county without French help. The county town was taken at least in part because
the Wexford garrison played into their hands. Colonel Maxwell, commander of
the garrison, had about 2,000 men at his command and had several pieces of
artillery.[49] The rebels had lost many of their best fighting men at Enniscorthy and
might have suffered enormous losses had they been forced to attack the county
town in a frontal assault,[50] and it is not at all certain that they would have been
able to carry the day. Maxwell attracted their attention to the prize of the county
seat by sending out the captured Colclough and Fitzgerald to ask them to disperse.[51] Then, in an incident of incredible ineptitude, General Fawcett of
Duncannon allowed a company of militia and several cannon to fall into rebel
hands at Forth Mountain; with that, the psychological advantage that Maxwell
held over the rebel army, in being the only one with artillery, was gone.[52] Had he
held his ground rather than withdrawing, he might still have prevailed. Instead
he abandoned the town to the rebels and in so doing allowed United Irish units in
the far south of the county,[53] spurred on by yet another rebel victory close to their
homes, to throw caution to the wind and join the movement, repeating as they
did the careful approach to mobilization followed by the movement to the west of
Enniscorthy the day before.[54]

The seizure of Wexford town by the rebels on 30 May brought the first phase
of the rebellion in south Leinster to a close. At that point the rebel army numbered well over 10,000 men and women,[55] and was drawn from almost all of
County Wexford and parts of south Wicklow. The United Irish plan had called
for their supporters in places like Wexford to seize their own counties and await
word of the formation of a new government in Dublin.[56] By that standard, the
rebels had now succeeded almost completely, the lightly garrisoned government
footholds at New Ross, Newtownbarry and Gorey being the only holdouts;[57] the

49 Hay, *Insurrection*, p. 95.
50 N.A.I. RP 620/59/98; Musgrave, *Rebellions*, i, p. 437.
51 Cloney, *Narrative*, pp 18–9.
52 Hay, *Insurrection*, p. 105.
53 Ibid., pp 109–10.
54 Ibid., p. 120; Gordon, *Rebellion*, p. 102.
55 Byrne, *Memoirs*, i, p. 46.
56 Thomas Graham, 'Dublin in 1798: The key to the planned insurrection', in Keogh and
    Furlong, *Mighty wave*, p. 69.
57 Gahan, *People's rising*, p. 87.

rebels in Wexford town may well have assumed that Gorey and perhaps Newtownbarry were ungarrisoned at this stage since the Wicklow recruits would have passed through an ungarrisoned Gorey on their way south two days earlier. The Wicklow and north Wexford rebels would also have realized that there had been severe setbacks for the cause in places like Carlow town and Carnew, and so the tendency of the Wexford chiefs to assume that all had gone according to plan elsewhere in the country may have been countered by men like Miles and Garret Byrne and Anthony Perry who were undoubtedly aware of nearby disasters.[58] However, the decisions made at Wexford town on 31 May suggest that most of the officers assumed that these were merely localized setbacks and that the movement had enjoyed success in Dublin and the Midlands. The decision to split their forces into two divisions, one to move north against Gorey and Newtonbarry, the other to march west against New Ross, is consistent with this thinking, as is the election of Bagenal Harvey as commander-in-chief and his attachment to the New Ross division, rather than his taking a post in Wexford town from which he could have co-ordinated the entire campaign.[59] The ill fortunes of the rebel movement in Dublin and Kildare had left the Wexford and Wicklow rebels alone in the field at this point, and their own good fortune to date had left them both victorious and dangerously confident of their ability to vanquish their enemy in the battles that might take place over the coming days.

In the second phase of the rebellion in south Leinster, the insurgents gradually came to realize that they were an isolated enclave in the southeast. They made extraordinary efforts both to react to this reality in military terms and to construct a make-shift local republic in anticipation of coming victory, either as a result of further successes they might gain on the perimeter of the area which they controlled, or arising from the actions of their comrades in more distant parts of Ireland, or, the ultimate hope, a French landing. This phase lasted from 1 to 21 June, an extraordinary three-week period in which this small region witnessed the creation of a republican regime for the first and only time in Ireland until 1916.

The military story of this phase of the rebellion reveals a great deal about the strengths and weaknesses of the rebel movement, and indicates at least as much about the profound difference between the movement in the north-eastern Wexford/southern Wicklow region and that which emerged out of southern and western Wexford. The campaign waged by the southern division, made up of men recruited from the lands to the south and west of the Slaney and officered and organized by, among others, a number of Protestant landlords and gentry from the area to the immediate south of Wexford town, was a strange combination of indecision and courage. From 1 to 4 June, Bagenal Harvey approached his

58 Miles Byrne had been in Carlow the day after the rebel defeat there: see *Memoirs*, i, p. 32.
59 Gahan, *People's rising*, p. 87.

task in a very casual manner, demonstrating along the way his intention of placating figures of the old establishment; he moved towards New Ross with extreme caution.[60] He and his officers appear to have been convinced for a time that the war was already won, and they did all they could to take New Ross by negotiation rather than by storm, influenced perhaps by the earlier example of the bloodless capture of Wexford town.[61] In the battle of New Ross, the southern division suffered a major early setback with the defection of a large part of their army,[62] but then went on to fight one of the most desperate battles of the entire rising, a battle in which, significantly, battalions from the barony of Bantry, the most northerly part of the south-western half of the county, were especially prominent.[63] The huge losses this division suffered here (about 2,000 dead) seem to have destroyed them as an effective fighting force.[64] For two weeks following New Ross they gradually dwindled to a small remnant and conducted no further significant actions.[65] On 20 June, as the government force under Sir John Moore pushed towards Wexford town, a rebel army came out from Wexford town and fought a stiff battle against his forces at Goff's Bridge.[66] It is significant though that this rebel force was made up in large part of companies from Wexford town itself and was not the old southern division resurrected.[67] It is notable that several groups of rebels gathered in Kilkenny on the day of the battle of New Ross, especially at Glenmore and Inistiogue,[68] and it is reasonable to assume that had the rebels been victorious in their attack on the town the same type of mobilization that had occurred in west Wexford after Enniscorthy and in south Wexford after Wexford town would have occurred across a large part of County Kilkenny.

The story of the northern rebel division was very different. They showed great decisiveness in moving north on 31 May.[69] They were stalled for a few days after setbacks in their efforts to take Newtownbarry and Gorey on 1 June,[70] but once again showed dogged determination in their reaction to the government offensive at Tubberneering on the 4th.[71] They gained control of a large part of south Wicklow and all of north Wexford as a result of Tubberneering, and their

60 Hay, *Insurrection*, pp 124–6.
61 Cloney, *Narrative*, pp 34–5; Alexander, *Narrative*, p. 70.
62 Cloney, *Narrative*, p. 37; Hay, *Insurrection*, pp 150–1.
63 Gahan, *People's rising*, p. 125.
64 Their state is revealed by Cloney in his account of a failed attack on the Market Gate, late in the battle: see *Narrative*, p. 40.
65 Gahan, *People's rising*, pp 163–4, 167.
66 Cloney, *Narrative*, pp 58–60; John Moore, *The diary of Sir John Moore*, ed. J.F. Maurice (London, 1904), i, pp 296–8.
67 Cloney, *Narrative*, pp 57–8.
68 Alexander, *Narrative*, pp 89–90; Musgrave, *Rebellions*, i, pp 511–12.
69 Hay, *Insurrection*, p. 122; Nicholas Furlong, *Father John Murphy of Boolavogue, 1753–1798* (Dublin, 1991), pp 91–2.
70 Byrne, *Memoirs*, i, pp 64–6; Wheeler, *War in Wexford*, pp 105–6.
71 Gahan, *People's rising*, pp 113–17.

failure to follow this up by seizing Arklow seems to have been in part due to a lack of ammunition.[72] It was however also due to the reluctance of some of the Wexford units to fight outside of their county, which indeed was consistent with the original United Irish plan.[73] Their eventual defeat at Arklow on 9 June forced them to engage in a fruitless stand-off against government forces until General Lake launched his general offensive against the south-eastern rebellion ten days later. But the northern division seems to have been still largely intact up to this point and might have presented Lake with a serious challenge had they remained on Kilcavan Hill,[74] just inside County Wicklow, when he moved against them.

In the third phase of the south Leinster rebellion, from 19 June until 14 July, the contrast between the south Wicklow/north-east Wexford movement and that hatched south and west of the Slaney became even more striking. When Moore and Johnson attacked Lacken Hill near New Ross, the once huge rebel army had dwindled to a tiny remnant,[75] and after the last stand at Goff's Bridge the next day the southern division practically melted away. The behaviour of officers from the south and west of the Slaney is especially instructive: Colclough and Harvey fled together to the Saltee islands, Grogan remained at Johnstown Castle, hoping the storm would pass by, and Cloney went into hiding. Fr Philip Roche, after slipping out of town with Fr John Murphy, decided to return and surrender himself. John Kelly of Killan, who was certainly a determined rebel, was unable to escape because of his wound. All these men, Cloney excepted, would lose their lives in the government terror that followed the capture of the town.[76]

In contrast, the northerners who had extracted themselves from Vinegar Hill with considerable skill, held together and almost every northern officer accompanied one or other of the two columns that slipped away from Wexford town on the 21st, one towards Peppard's Castle on the east coast of the county, the other towards Sleedagh demesne,[77] several miles south of Wexford harbour. Between 22 and 26 June, the column that escaped to Sleedagh, led by Fr John Murphy and Miles Byrne, marched across south Wexford, south Carlow and on through Kilkenny to Castlecomer and the south side of Queen's County.[78] In so doing they were making the most valiant effort yet to spread the Wexford and Wicklow rebellion to the rest of South Leinster. It was however too late to convince United Irishmen in Kilkenny to rise (apart from the coalminers of Castlecomer), and on their return towards Wexford this column was defeated and scattered at Kilcumney Hill in south Carlow on 26 June.[79] The Peppard's Castle column, which included Perry, Kyan, Roche, Fitzgerald, and Garret and Billy Byrne, (all of the important northern officers still living), reached Croghan in a day.[80] On 4

72 Ibid., p. 136.
73 Graham, 'Dublin in 1798', p. 78.
74 Byrne, *Memoirs*, i, p. 126.
75 Cloney, *Narrative*, pp 54–6.
76 Gahan, *People's rising*, p. 288.
77 Ibid., pp 221–2.
78 Furlong, *Father John Murphy*, pp 154–63.
79 Byrne, *Memoirs*, i, pp 169–72.
80 Gahan, *People's rising*, pp 226–8.

118

Daniel Gahan

and 5 July, once joined by stragglers like Miles Byrne and Fr Mogue Kearns, they struck out from their camp at Croghan for the heart of County Wicklow, and four days later marched into Kildare and Meath.[81] They were finally surrounded and defeated on the Meath/Louth border as they tried to reach the Presbyterian comrades they hoped would still join them in Antrim and Down.[82]

It would be inappropriate to label this force a 'Wexford army'. It was made up of the members of a network of United Irish cells that had emerged in the south Wicklow/north-east Wexford triangle, and while the majority of its officers and men were probably from the Wexford side of the border, it was by no means an exclusively Wexford force. This branch of rebel forces had its own internal divisions (in particular a divide over whether to stay in the mountains and await the French, or to march our and try to link up with Kildare and Ulster rebels, thereby keeping the conventional struggle going).[83] But all shared a determined effort to rekindle the movement following the collapse of the republic in the south-east which suggests a degree of dedication to the revolution that was lacking in their comrades from south and west of the Slaney. It is not perhaps surprising, and may even be very significant, even a little poignant, that these Wicklow and north-east Wexford rebels were from a part of south Leinster that had been so thoroughly prepared by William Putnam McCabe and James Hope and still included a mix of Protestants and Catholics, and would fight their dramatic last stand on 14 July as they gambled everything on an effort to reach the Presbyterian heartland of Ulster, in hopes of joining men like James Hope.

In spite of the unforgettable actions of men like the Protestant Anthony Perry and Catholics like Garret Byrne standing shoulder to shoulder at Knightstown, the rebellion in south Leinster has long been associated with sectarian hatred and the massacres conducted by the rebels at Scullabogue on 5 June, Wexford bridge on 20 June, and the less-well-known killing of about fifty loyalist refugees near Coolgreaney on 22 June which have coloured the popular image of the rebel regime which was established in the region.[84] These atrocities must be put in context. In the first place, of all Irish insurgents in 1798 the Wexford and Wicklow rebels were the only ones to gain control over a significant area for a relatively long period of time. Over three weeks they controlled almost all of County Wexford, including its two largest towns and parts of southern Wicklow. In contrast the rebellion in Antrim lasted little more than a day, that in Down for less than a week and that in Kildare for about a week also; neither the Kildare nor Down rebels gained complete control over their respective counties. The Mayo rebellion lasted longer than these, but was controlled from start to finish by the

81 Ibid., pp 284–98.
82 Luke Cullen, *Personal recollections of Wexford and Wicklow insurgents of 1798* (Enniscorthy, 1959), pp 57–9.
83 This debate began as early as 8 June: see Byrne, *Memoirs*, i, pp 91–3.
84 Gahan, *People's rising*, pp 132–3, 202–3, 227.

French. All of the three massacres in County Wexford took place in the context of battlefield disaster and what appears to have been the desire of certain factions (certainly there seem to have been distinct factions at Scullabogue and Wexford bridge) for revenge;[85] the massacre at Coolgreaney on 22 June was apparently in response to government atrocities committed in the Wicklow/Wexford border-land the day before.[86]

Beyond this, it is critically important to note that several key rebel officers were Protestant and that, in spite of Harvey's apparent demotion from comman-der-in-chief after New Ross, these men retained their position and considerable influence until the end of the rebellion.[87] There were also rumours that attacks on Protestants might take place on many occasions during the rebellion, particu-larly in the area around Wexford town,[88] but many Protestant families remained behind rebel lines in various parts of Wexford and south Wicklow and remained unmolested, including members of many landed families.[89] Not to be neglected either is the fact that the Catholic Church was unquestionably opposed to the rebels, that most of the Catholic priests who became involved in the rising were regarded as marginal characters of one sort or other,[90] and that the rebel leaders urged their followers to avoid atrocity and to pursue a non-sectarian path.[91]

In early June, probably on the 7th, Edward Roche issued a proclamation in Wexford town that was partly a response to his (and the other leaders') realisation that they were cut off and perhaps fighting alone, but is also revealing about what he thought the rising in this region was about:

> Liberty has raised her drooping head: thousands daily flock to the stan-dard: the voice of her children everywhere prevails. Let us then, in this moment of triumph, return thanks to the almighty ruler of the universe ... At this eventful period, all Europe must admire and posterity will read with astonishment, the heroic acts achieved by a people strangers to mili-tary tactics, and having few professional commanders; but what power can resist men fighting for liberty.[92]

Roche's proclamation is clearly inspired by republican thinking emanating from the Continent and seems to set a rational, and certainly a non-sectarian, agenda. Admittedly this document was issued in the aftermath of the horror of Scullabogue (in which, incidently, some Catholics were killed and at which sever-

---

85 Daniel Gahan, 'The Scullabogue massacre, 1798' in *History Ireland*, iv (1996), 30–1.
86 Byrne, *Memoirs*, i, pp 188–9.
87 Gahan, *People's rising*, p. 8.
88 *Diary of Elizabeth Richards* (N.L.I. typescript, MS 36, 486), p. 10.
89 *Recollections of Jane Barber* (N.L.I. typescript), p. 13.
90 Whelan, 'Catholic priest', pp 309–10.
91 Hay, *Insurrection*, pp 162–3.
92 Ibid., p. 162.

al Protestant rebels appear to have participated),[93] but viewed as a piece, the three weeks of rebel rule in the southeast produced a few incidents of remarkable co-operation between Catholic and Protestant rebel elements, including the important role played by Protestants in the rebel armies and in the rudimentary governmental bodies instituted in Wexford town.

The aftermath of the rebellion saw the initiation of what looked a lot more like religious war and this was unquestionably used by the authorities to aid the government side in its effort to maintain the upper hand. The initial terror, with its executions of rebel leaders on Wexford bridge and less formal punishment by soldiers rampaging through the countryside of Wexford, Carlow and Wicklow, spared neither Protestant nor Catholic rebel,[94] and a number of Protestant families who had taken no part or had remained loyal were also harassed by the soldiers.[95] In the autumn of 1798 and throughout 1799 and 1800, conditions closely resembling those of religious war came to prevail in the entire region, replete with attacks on Catholic churches, the intimidation of Catholics for the purposes of preventing them for bidding on leases, and the murder of at least one Catholic priest who had not been involved in the rebellion. Common too in those years were outbreaks of alarmism, which affected both the Catholic and Protestant communities, and which testified to the fear with which each group had now come to regard the other.[96]

How does the south Leinster rebellion fit into the larger picture of 1798? Why did the rebellion break out where it did, take the course it took and, just as importantly, why did it not break out in other parts of the region? The key to the area seems to be the north Carlow, north Wexford, south Wicklow district. Here, the United Irishmen gained many dedicated recruits early on, principally in 1797. Much of south Wexford, south Carlow and most of County Kilkenny were penetrated less effectively by the United Irishmen and required rebel victories in adjacent areas to spark them into mobilization. Thus the rebel victory at Enniscorthy roused west Wexford, and a victory at New Ross would apparently have roused much of east Kilkenny. South Carlow remained quiet throughout but the crushing defeat at Carlow town on 25 May, along with the fact that the local landlord and almost all his middlemen were Catholic and loyal to the government, may account for this.

The northern part of County Wexford was unusual then in that the rising took place there without news of a victory to its immediate north as a stimulus but in the shadow of devastating arrests in the Gorey area and defeats in Carlow

93 Gahan, 'Scullabogue massacre', p. 30.
94 Gahan, *People's rising*, p. 255.
95 *Recollections of Jane Barber*, p. 13.
96 Daniel Gahan, 'The "Black Mob" and the "Babes in the Wood": Wexford in the wake of the rebellion, 1798–1806', in *Journal of the Wexford Historical Society*, xiii (1990–1), 92–110.

town and Hacketstown, and arrests and a massacre at Carnew. The almost spontaneous nature of the rising here suggests that there was something different
about this region and that without it the rebellion in south Leinster would have
lasted no more than a day or two anywhere. Luck played an important role in
converting a strong and determined United Irish movement north and east of
the Slaney into a formidable uprising. The combination of circumstances leading
to rebel victories at Oulart, Enniscorthy and Wexford town, all of them fortu-
itous to a certain extent, made the movement here temporarily victorious. In the
end, these twists and turns in military fortunes rather than any qualities inherent
to the United Irish movement in Wicklow and Wexford were probably the main
reason that the rebellion in south Leinster became as central to the whole tragedy
of 1798 as it ultimately did.

6

The 1798 rebellion in north Leinster

LIAM CHAMBERS

The fundamental purpose of the United Irish rebellion of 1798 was the overthrow of the Irish administration based in Dublin; hence their primary military objective was the capture of the capital. This paper analyzes the rebellion in Dublin and the surrounding counties, the heart of any indigenous revolutionary endeavour. A successful rebellion depended on the participation of rebels over a wide region. Therefore an examination of an insurrection which ultimately failed must not only consider those areas where rebel mobilization occurred (Dublin, Meath and Kildare), but also the partial or non-existent mustering of those counties which contributed less to the active rebel cause (Westmeath, Queen's County and King's County).[1]

From late 1796 the internal impetus of the United Irish movement gradually shifted from Ulster to Leinster and by April 1798 the Leinster provincial had issued a set of instructions essentially designed to prepare the organization for rebellion.[2] Graham has demonstrated that a three-phase insurgency plan gradually emerged, to be executed without French military assistance, a prospect which appeared increasingly probable. Central to rebel strategy was the capture of key sites within Dublin.[3] The second phase involved the region immediately outside the capital. Francis Higgins, a government informant, reported during

---

1 For a detailed account of the rebellion in some of the counties under discussion, see Thomas Pakenham, *The year of liberty: The history of the great Irish rebellion of 1798* (London, 1969, repr. 1992), pp 88–169; for Dublin see Thomas Graham, 'Dublin in 1798: The key to the planned insurrection', in Dáire Keogh and Nicolas Furlong (eds), *The mighty wave: The 1798 rebellion in Wexford* (Dublin, 1996), pp 65–78; for Kildare see Liam Chambers, *Rebellion in Kildare, 1790–1803* (Dublin, 1998); Mario Corrigan, *All that delirium of the brave – Kildare in 1798* (Naas, 1997); Seamus Cullen and Hermann Geissel (eds), *Fugitive warfare, 1798 in north Kildare* (Clane, 1998); for Meath see J.G.O. Kerrane, 'The background to the 1798 rebellion in County Meath' (unpublished M.A. dissertation, N.U.I., U.C.D., 1971); Seamus O'Loinsigh, 'The rebellion of 1798 in Meath', in *Ríocht na Midhe*, iii–v (1966–71); for Westmeath see Liam Cox, 'Westmeath in the 1798 period', in *Irish Sword*, ix (1969–71), pp 1–15; for Queen's County (Laois), see John S. Powell, *Portarlington and 1798* (York, 1998).
2 *Report of the secret committee of the house of commons with an appendix* (Dublin, 1798), pp 233–4.
3 Graham, 'Dublin in 1798', pp 68–71.

May 1798 that it involved the rebel occupation of positions 'from Garretstown [*sic*], Naul etc. and Dunboyne and circuitously round the metropolis to Dunleary etc.' Higgins also made clear that Lord Edward FitzGerald, the United Irish 'generalissimo', was to lead a march on the capital and was to have been transported to Fingal on 20 May for this purpose, presumably to link with forces from Kildare.[4] The 'third phase' of the plan is less clearly understood but involved the remaining counties in Leinster engaging the military presence in their locality and thereby preventing the second layer of rebel mobilization coming under counter-attack.

As United Irish organization within Dublin increased in strength and military capacity during the spring of 1798, counties around the capital came under increasing strain in the form of military pacification, particularly Kildare, Queen's County and King's County. Disaster struck on 19 May when Lord Edward FitzGerald was arrested and William Lawless absconded, followed quickly by the arrest of the somewhat marginalized Sheares brothers on 21 May and of Samuel Neilson, the key remaining leader, on 23 May while involved in a mission to rescue FitzGerald, an action which illustrates the crucial importance of FitzGerald to United Irish plans. Nevertheless, plans for a rising within Dublin continued and large bodies of rebels from outside the capital had reputedly entered already. Mobilization began on the night of the 23 May following the issue of last-minute instructions by Samuel Neilson – hours before his arrest. An important reason for rebel failure at the heart of its strategy was the fact that the Dublin administration received prior information as to what was to happen and quickly occupied the rebel points of assembly, forcing the would-be insurgents to disengage and quietly return home.[5]

The rebellion as it actually occurred makes little sense outside the context of its Dublin element, the crucial central component of the overall United Irish strategy. But while the United Irishmen in Dublin failed, those in the surrounding areas rose in armed insurrection. The neighbouring baronies and counties had been kept closely informed of the developing rebel plans.[6] Samuel Sproule, an informer, reported that representatives had been sent to Kildare and Wicklow on the night of 23 May 'to raise them immediate[ly]: it is believed they will *rise tonight*'; by 9 p.m. he reported that 'Kildare is now up'.[7] All over County Dublin small parties of United Irishmen engaged with government forces. The plan to stop the mail coaches leaving Dublin, designed by Samuel Neilson to announce the rising to the country, was partially executed. The mails were stopped at Santry, attacked at Lucan, but missed at Clondalkin and Dunboyne. The Cork

4   Francis Higgins to Edward Cooke, 20 May, 30 June 1798: N.A.I., RP 620/18/14.
5   See Graham's detailed analysis of the Dublin failure: 'Dublin in 1798', pp 71–8; M.M.[?] to Mrs Helen Clarke, London, 'near 12 o'clock', 23 May 1798: N.L.I. MS 13,837.
6   Samuel Sproule to John Lees, received 15 May [1798], 19 May [1798]: N.A.I., RP 620/51/39, 27.
7   Sproule to Lees, 4:30 p.m., 9 p.m. [23 May 1798]: N.A.I., RP 620/51/18, 25.

were repulsed on 24–25 May, and Athy which (inadvertently) had not been evacuated by Colonel Campbell's force. Nevertheless, in large areas of Kildare, United Irishmen achieved their immediate objectives. Like the rebels further north they formed a number of strategically located camps near Ballitore, Kildare town, Kilcullen and Timahoe.[22]

The failure of the Dublin element of the rising left the rebels in arms in Counties Meath and Kildare stagnant and gave the rebellion a fragmentary and isolated appearance. George Lambert reported from Beau Parc on 26 May that the United Irish 'object of attack is the capital and to cut off all communications from thence to the country and from the country thither. Should they fail they may well turn about and pay us a visit, but we will do our best I promise you to resist them.'[23] The concentration of rebel forces at large camps allowed the government's forces to gather and launch counter-assaults.

However, government forces proved remarkably reluctant to launch a counter offensive; instead there was a policy of concentrating troops in Dublin. The first such assault was made by the Reay Fencibles who arrived in Dunshaughlin on 26 May en route from Cavan to Dublin and rapidly organized local yeomanry corps. Despite the strength of the rebels at Tara (at least 8,000 strong according to the official report) and the position they occupied on the hill, the government troops under Captain Blanche prevailed.[24] The battle proved decisive in ending the prospect of a more generalized rising in County Meath.[25] Indeed the identity of the leading figures on the rebel side in the area remains unclear, and Charles Hamilton Teeling believed the absence of United Irish leaders was a central aspect of the rebel defeat.

The defeat at Tara, combined with the massive reverse suffered by Carlow rebels on 25 May, resulted in the isolation of the Kildare United Irishmen. The Kildare rebellion reached its zenith by 26 May and then began to slowly disintegrate through lack of active purpose. Rebels at Kilcullen surrendered to General Dundas on 27 May. Two days later a similar surrender of Kildare town rebels was interrupted by a force from Limerick under General Sir James Duff and the ensuing 'Gibbet Rath massacre' resulted in the death of around 350 rebels. Rebels in the Ballitore area stalled in their dealings with the hard-line Colonel Campbell. He then decided to forcibly pacify south-west Kildare on 29 May. Rathangan was also retaken after two botched attempts on 28 May. In the Kildare/Meath/Dublin area, the key United Irish encampment after these defeats emerged in the Bog of Allen at Timahoe (and on its edges at Prosperous

---

22 Chambers, *Rebellion in Kildare*, pp 72–81. Dundas explained his actions to Castlereagh in a letter dated 25 May 1798: P.R.O. HO 100/76/277–9.

23 George Lambert to [Coole?], Beau Parc, 26 May 1798, part 2: N.A.I., RP 620/37/171.

24 The best account of the battle is that written by Captain Blanche: P.R.O. WO 304/11. See also G. Knox, 5 June 1798: N.A.I., RP 620/38/56, on a possible rebel commander.

25 George Lambert, Beau Parc, 27 May 1798: N.A.I., RP 620/37/180.

which remained in rebel hands) under the leadership of William Aylmer, Hugh Ware and George Lube who only entered the conflict in early June.[26]

The disintegration of rebel momentum in this region was the result of the loss of any sense of Dublin-related purpose. However, the 'outer counties' in north Leinster involved in United Irish plans had completely failed to rise, reinforcing the isolation of rebel forces in Kildare/Meath/County Dublin. The success of the rebellion in Wexford (an 'outer county') from 26 May caused an understandable shift in the focus of later narratives from north Leinster in late May. Indeed historians rarely write about why rebellions did not happen (only two pages of Musgrave's enormous tome are devoted to King's and Queen's Counties),[27] but in this case the question must be addressed with regard to Westmeath, King's County and Queen's County in any attempt to comprehend the regional significance of the 1798 rebellion in the area.

These three counties had been disturbed during the 1790s by the militia riots in 1793 and in the case of King's County and Westmeath by the Defenders in mid-decade.[28] The counties contained relatively strong United Irish organizations on paper from 1796 to 1797, though their return of figures to the Leinster provincial was irregular.[29] The arrest of the Queen's County delegates Peter Bannon and Lawrence Kelly at Oliver Bond's in March 1798 possibly explains the lack of figures for Queen's County after February 1798. Patrick O'Kelly, an Athy United Irishman, claimed the remaining Queen's County leaders 'cast the shade of indifference over the system and rendered it languid and ineffective'.[30]

The minor sparks of rebellion in Queen's County were strongly connected with events in the neighbouring counties. The colliers of the Doonane area in the south east rose on the morning of 25 May, but quickly subsided, having failed to link with the United Irishmen in either Athy or Carlow as anticipated. However, the United Irishmen of the Ballyadams/ Stradbally/Doonane area continued to pose a serious threat.[31] An attack on Portarlington was launched from the Monasterevan area on 25 May, possibly as an offshoot from the failure

---

26 Chambers, *Rebellion in Kildare*, pp 81–6.
27 Musgrave, *Rebellions*, appendix, pp 27–9.
28 Thomas Bartlett, 'An end to moral economy: The Irish militia disturbances of 1793', in *Past & Present*, xcix (1983), 49–50, 53; idem, 'Defenders and Defenderism in 1795' in *I.H.S.*, xxiv (1984–5), 373–94.
29 Westmeath: 20,000 (June 1797), 5,250 (Apr. 1798); King's County: 3,600 (February 1798), 6,500 (Apr. 1798); Queen's County: 11,689 (February 1798). Figures are extracted from *Report of the secret committee*, pp 133, 136, 177, 234.
30 Patrick O'Kelly, *General history of the rebellion of 1798* (Dublin, 1842), pp 281–2. O'Kelly may have been biased in that he blamed Queen's County United Irishmen for not supporting the Athy rebels; see his comments on the colliers of the Doonane area, p. 181.
31 Charles Asgill, Kilkenny to Lake, 25, 26 May [1798]; Coote to Henry Moore, 6 June 1798: N.A.I., RP 620/51/53, 52; 620/38/71; Chambers, *Rebellion in Kildare*, p. 79; Musgrave, *Rebellions*, p. 265.

to take the latter, but the rebels were defeated before reaching Portarlington.[32] Apparently unconnected rebel activity did take place in Borris-in-Ossory in west Queen's County, where the house of Walter Kavanagh was attacked on 25 May.[33] On 24–25 May Samuel Sproule reported that John McMahon had set off from Dublin to Wicklow and would 'call at the camps for the King's County'.[34] However despite panic in the Edenderry area and the fact that the rebels were reported to be 'in very great force in the King's County' on 30 May, no major attacks occurred.[35]

In fact it is surprising that such a widespread rebellion in Kildare did not spark a major outbreak to the west, given the close United Irish connections between these counties.[36] Indeed a Prosperous rebel was arrested in King's County shortly after the victory in the former, possibly an emissary, and a second Prosperous rebel was arrested in Athlone in early June.[37] Edward Cooke believed in late May that 'refugees from Kildare are spiriting up the [Queen's County] colliers'.[38]

Beyond a limited amount of activity the rebellion as projected did not occur in any of the 'outer counties' under discussion. One possible reason was the hesitancy of United Irishmen in these areas before a successful rebellion to the east had occurred, exacerbated by the process of pacification initiated by government forces in April in King's and Queen's Counties which had already been proclaimed under the terms of the Insurrection Act. However, a similar process of pacification occurred in Kildare, which resulted in the detachment of liberal figures from the United Irishmen but largely left the organization intact, though the government troops and local magistrates failed to coalesce in the implementation of disarming measures.

In Queen's County the pacification was better organized by General Sir Charles Asgill.[39] In Kildare the pacification resulted in a partial rebellion in the baronies of Kilkea and Moone, and East Narragh and Rheban. In the three 'outer

---

32 Earl of Portarlington, Emo, to Sir John Parnell, 25 May 1798: N.A.I., RP 620/37/161; Powell, *Portarlington and 1798*, pp 13–15.
33 Asgill, Kilkenny to Lake, 26 May [1798]: N.A.I., RP 620/51/52. See also Morgan Kavanagh, Kilcullen, [1797–8]: P.R.O.N.I., Kavanagh Papers, T.3331/22, which seems to describe the same incident.
34 Sproule to Lees [25 May 1798]: N.A.I., RP 620/51/20.
35 Edenderry Officers to Castlereagh, 27 May 1798: N.A.I., RP 620/18/11/6; R. Marshall to General Knox, 30 May 1798: N.L.I. MS 56, p. 170.
36 See for example: G. Vignoles to Robert Marshall, 1 Feb 1798: N.A.I., RP 620/35/94. Michael Doorly, brother of the rebel leader at Rathangan (John), was a leader in the King's County United Irishmen and may have infiltrated a fencible regiment in Portarlington: Confession of John Doorly [?], undated: N.A.I., RP 620/51/67; Powell, *Portarlington and 1798*, pp 10–12.
37 Examination of James Jourdan of Prosperous and Richard Morrow of Philipstown, 27 May 1798: N.A.I., RP 620/37/167.
38 Edward Cooke to William Wickham, 30 May 1798: P.R.O., HO 100/76/313–14.
39 See, for example, his careful instructions, dated 21 Mar. 1798: N.A.I., 999/37/1; Camden to Portland, 11 May 1798: P.R.O., HO 100/76/168–77.

counties' under discussion, pacification appears to have succeeded to a much greater degree. Brigadier General Dunne wrote from Tullamore on 31 July 1798:

> Altho[ugh] there has been no rising in the King's County; the reason to me appears obvious. The delegate arriving as he acknowledges, late in Dublin for a meeting held at Oliver Bond's escaped being taken, has some time since turned approver. The information received from him concerning the immediate leaders of the different baronys [*sic*] was such as to enable me to have counteracted their plans and prevent their intended attempts. Without this information, I should rather think this county would have been as bad as Kildare.[40]

The name of the delegate was possibly Flanagan, from Tullamore.[41] Musgrave recounts a similar scenario, with a religious spin, noting that the Protestant delegate (named Denis) defected after the rebellion had begun because of its sectarian nature.[42]

A comparable situation allowed government forces to prevent widespread rebellion in Queen's County. Gerard Fitzgerald writing from Maryborough in October 1798, noted that 'Carney the informant, who has stopped the rebellion in this county, and by whose information there are 36 people now indicted for treason, is in the barracks here which is a very improper place for him, for he certainly will be bribed or murdered ...' This report is vaguely consistent with Musgrave's assertion that the leading Queen's County/Dublin United Irish messenger was arrested before the rising. The key point is that the failure of these counties to rise lay in the decimation of United Irish structures before the rising commenced.[43]

An analogous degree of disorganization among United Irish leaders in Westmeath contributed to the lack of mobilization there during the last week of May. The (admittedly slim) evidence suggests the Westmeath United Irishmen did not initially attempt a rising. Renewed efforts involving the establishment of contact with Kildare rebels (through Jack Brian, an earlier Defender leader) and plans to rise on 27 May and 31 May, were scuppered by indecision and leadership differences, resulting in the arrest of Latin Fitzgerald, Michael Dardis, William Ogle and Francis Nugent, the suspected leadership core.[44]

---

40 General Dunne, Tullamore to Castlereagh, 31 July 1798: N.A.I., RP 620/4/33/6.
41 Confession of Matthias Horan and Henry Glyn, 26 May 1798; confession of John Doorly, undated: N.A.I., RP 620/37/166; 620/51/67.
42 Musgrave, *Rebellions*, p. 258.
43 Gerard Fitzgerald, Maryborough to Thomas Kemmis, 14 October 1798: N.A.I., Frazer MSS 2/94; Musgrave, *Rebellions*, p. 258.
44 General Charles Barnett, Athlone to Lord Castlereagh, 29 July 1798, with encls. incl. confession of XY, undated: N.A.I., RP 620/39/124. Similar information was reported independently by Gustavus Rochfort on 30 May 1798: N.A.I., RP 620/37/222.

At a regional level the projected rebellion in north Leinster was therefore a failure, not only at its Dublin epicentre but in most but not all country districts. The roots of such a failure in mobilization are difficult to assess but a crucial factor was the disruption of the command structure of the United Irishmen, coupled with the fact that the 'outer counties', those areas furthest from Dublin, depended on a mass rebellion (as occurred in Wexford) to encourage wavering supporters locally.

During the month of June only two major battles were fought in the entire region under discussion, at Kilbeggan on 17 June and at Ovidstown, near Timahoe in north Kildare, two days later. Narrative-driven accounts of the 1798 rebellion have tended to overlook such 'local outbreaks' even though the central focus of the rebellion remained Dublin. Within this context the north Leinster region remained crucial particularly after the setbacks suffered by the Wexford rebels at Newtownbarry on 1 June, which prevented a juncture with the rebels in Kildare, Carlow or Queen's County, and at Arklow on 9 June.[45] The letters of Francis Higgins to Dublin Castle emphasize continued rebel designs on Dublin. On 5 June he noted: 'Those infernal banditti have not abandoned their purpose of procuring a rising in the city, they hold meetings and consultations, in the vicinity of the metropolis.'[46] Contact between the Dublin leadership and rebels in the Dunboyne area is indicated by the mission of Fr John Martin, a messenger of the Dublin United Irishmen, to the Dunboyne locality in the first days of June. He was captured on 11 June while engaged in a mission to the Wicklow United Irishmen, to encourage a march on Dublin from the south, which it was hoped would draw troops out of the capital and leave it exposed to assault from Kildare and Meath.[47] Within a fortnight, however, the rebellion in south-east Meath had been effectively quelled and rebels at Garristown had even entered into a formal surrender.[48]

In early June the pivotal rebel base in the east Leinster region had emerged at Timahoe in the Bog of Allen under the leadership of William Aylmer. The camp had probably been established in the first days of the rebellion and it later provided a shelter for defeated rebels from Tara, Rathangan and elsewhere.[49] The camp at Timahoe, against which early attacks proved completely ineffective due to the terrain, maintained contact with Dublin through a number of channels. The government was well aware of the threat posed by such a large rebel camp

---

45 George Taylor, *An historical account of the rise, progress and suppression of the rebellion in the county of Wexford in the year 1798* (Dublin, 1800), p. 66.
46 Higgins to Cooke, 5 June 1798; see also letters dated 2, 4, 11, 13 June 1798: N.A.I., RP 620/18/14.
47 Dáire Keogh, '"The most dangerous villain in society": Fr John Martin's mission to the United Irishmen of Wicklow in 1798', in *E.C.I.*, vii (1992), 122–4, 133.
48 'Repentance' of the town and parish of Garristown, 31 May 1798: N.A.I., RP 620/37/236.
49 Chambers, *Rebellion in Kildare*, pp 87–92; R.J. Aylmer, 'William Aylmer of Painstown, County Kildare and the battle for the metropolis, May 1798' (unpublished paper).

not far from the capital, and, it seems dispatched the Belfast spy Belle Martin in early June. She worked as a housekeeper for Charles Aylmer (William's father) at Painstown for three weeks until 23 June, and may have passed information to government, particularly since William Aylmer used Painstown as a personal base during the rebellion. How such a notorious spy held so sensitive a position in north Kildare during the period remains a mystery; she was presumably an expert at her profession.[50]

The activities of the rebels in the Bog of Allen appear, on first inspection, to have extended little beyond intermittent pillage of the rich lands of north Kildare, hence Pakenham's comment that by late June, 'Aylmer's army had achieved only one of its aims: to stay alive.'[51] However, even the marauding activities of the rebels had a political dimension: two days after the execution of John Esmonde, the Prosperous leader, in Dublin, the property of Richard Griffith at Millicent was plundered because he had testified at the court martial.[52] The Timahoe rebels were not in fact under pressure to supply themselves with raw materials.[53] Viewed in the context of the ultimate rebel objectives (Dublin) formal rebel attacks made sense. Assaults on Kilcock (1, 4 June) and Maynooth (10, 13 June) resulted in Aylmer's force pushing small garrisons back to Leixlip and in encouraging the desertion of more yeomen to the rebel cause.[54]

On 17 June Kilbeggan on the Dublin/Galway road in south Westmeath was attacked by a large force (possibly 2,000) led by the key local activist John McManus; this was eventually repulsed. The incident was probably linked to the massing of rebels further east along the same road to Dublin on the following day. Westmeath United Irishmen were in contact with Kildare rebels in late May and a Dublin emissary was even captured in Mullingar on 31 May. John McManus himself had links to Lord Edward FitzGerald before the rebellion through Patrick Gallagher.[55] Mullingar, Mountmellick and Maryborough were all reportedly under serious threat of attack during June.[56]

50 Chambers, *Rebellion in Kildare*, pp 91–2; examination of Belle Martin, County Meath, 23 June 1798: N.A.I., RP 620/38/222.
51 Pakenham, *Year of liberty*, p. 275.
52 Musgrave, *Rebellions*, p. 242; Thomas Clere Parsons to Sir Laurence Parsons, June 1798: N.L.I. Rosse Papers, MS 13,840 (4).
53 Richard Griffith believed that they had been allowed to possess much of north Kildare: Griffith, Naas, to Thomas Pelham, 23 June 1798: B.L., Add. MSS 33,105 ff. 445–8; Oliver Barker, Clonard to Lees, 6 June 1798: N.A.I., RP 620/38/73.
54 Chambers, *Rebellion in Kildare*, pp 88–9.
55 Richard Nagle to Thomas Kemmis, 17 June 1798: N.A.I. Frazer MSS 2/82; Charles Barnett, Kilbeggan, 18 June 1798; Colonel Lytten to Cooke, 20 June 1798; Gustavus Rochfort, 31 May 1798; Court martial of John McManus, 29 June 1798: N.A.I., RP 620/38/171; 620/38/191; 620/37/238; 620/6/68/3; *Finn's Leinster Journal*, 23 June 1798.
56 Gustavus Rochfort, Beau Parc, 22 June 1798; — to Castlereagh [22 June 1798]: N.A.I., RP 620/38/213, 214; *Freeman's Journal*, 16 June 1798. On executions in Mountmellick, see William Kemmis to Thomas Kemmis, 15, 18 June: N.A.I. Frazer MSS 2/79, 80.

On Monday 18 June two mail coaches were stopped at Cloncurry on the Dublin/Galway road. The *Freeman's Journal* reported: 'The persons who stopped the coaches were well mounted and appointed with helmets etc. Parties or patrols of these insurgents were described on the hills near the road, all the way from Cloncurry to Kilcock.'[57] Furthermore, large numbers of Dublin United Irishmen (particularly from the west of the county) made their way to the Timahoe area on 18 June.[58] This massing of rebels in north Kildare is best understood within the context of continued United Irish hopes for an attack on Dublin.[59] Sproule reported new plans in mid-June both in Dublin and with the support of the Kildare and Meath United Irishmen.[60] The camp at Blackmore Hill in County Wicklow, dispersed in late May, had reassembled by 4 June under Michael Reynolds, who had led the failed attack on Naas on 24 May and was in contact with Dublin leaders. Here too, rebels were massing around 20 June, hoping to launch an attack on Dublin.[61]

This context transforms the interpretation of the battle of Ovidstown (19 June) from a localized clash into a crucial battle which prevented an attack on Dublin. On 19 June Prosperous (which had remained in rebel hands from 24 May) was attacked twice by government forces, forcing the rebels back into the bog.[62] Despite government plans to launch a serious attack on Timahoe, no such event had taken place.[63] Ongoing United Irish plans for a counter-offensive to be launched from Timahoe were destroyed on 19 June. A huge rebel army was engaged by a government force from Trim (which had arrived via Kilcock) at Ovidstown, northwest of Timahoe. The rebels were surprised and defeated (with 200 losses), though their unpreparedness for battle is a further indication that the poorly fought engagement on the edges of the bog was not what the rebels had envisaged.[64]

In the aftermath of the battle of Ovidstown, Kildare rebels continued to pose a problem for the Dublin administration, but their relationship with the Dublin

57 *Freeman's Journal*, 21 June 1798.
58 Edward Clarke, Palmerstown, 20 June 1798: N.A.I., RP 620/38/198. See also Musgrave's exaggerated account: *Rebellions*, p. 294.
59 Examination of William McConkery, 2 June 1798: N.A.I., RP 620/38/67, 96.
60 Sproule to Lees, received 16 June [1798], 22 June [1798] and 25 June 1798: N.A.I., RP 620/51/37, 36; 620/38/232.
61 William James to Cooke, 4 June 1798; Information of B [Thomas Boyle], 20 June [1798]: N.A.I., RP 620/38/42; 620/18/3; Ruan O'Donnell, *The rebellion in Wicklow, 1798* (Dublin, 1998), pp 243–4.
62 Chambers, *Rebellion in Kildare*, pp 93–4.
63 Cooke to Wickham, 15 June 1798: P.R.O. HO 100/77/163; General Grose, Kilcock, 20 June 1798: N.A.I., RP 620/38/193.
64 Seosamh Ó Muirthuile argued in 1948 that the force at Ovidstown intended to march on Dublin: *Kildare 1798 commemoration* (Kildare, 1948), p. 12. On the battle see General Grose, Kilcock, 20 June 1798; George Holdcroft, Kells, to Cooke, 21 June 1798: N.A.I., RP 620/38/193; 620/38/205. Of particular interest is the account of a captured Dublin participant, Information of Edward Whiteman, 20 June [1798]: N.A.I., SOCP 3089.

rebels may have begun to disintegrate.[65] Two factors now rendered a Kildare-based assault on the capital increasingly unlikely; first, the stationing of a regiment of Reay Fencibles in Kilcock, and second, the prospect of a reasonable surrender from Dublin Castle now under the new lord lieutenant, Cornwallis, on 29 June. The latter's arrival in Ireland resulted in the opening of channels of negotiation between the Timahoe rebels and the Dublin government.[66]

Another United Irish threat emerged in north Leinster in the form of the rebels who had migrated from Wexford and Wicklow. In the aftermath of the rebel defeat at Vinegar Hill, the United Irish forces there had separated. One force travelled north through the Wicklow mountains; the other under Fr John Murphy chose to travel northeast through Carlow, north Kilkenny and south Queen's County where they hoped to mobilize United Irish support.[67] Murphy's army camped among the Queen's County colliers at Doonane on the night of 23 June, where they received support from local rebels (who had briefly risen on 25 May). The garrison of the town retreated to Castlecomer which was attacked and temporarily occupied the following day, before the rebels returned to south Queen's County, close to Athy.[68] Murphy's ultimate objective must have been to gather a large force and proceed towards Dublin. He did receive the support of recognized local United Irish leaders, and John Wolfe, commander of the Kildare Militia, arrested three men at Balbriggan on 24 June whom he suspected of attempting to forge a link between Dublin and the rebels camped in Queen's County.[69] Around the same time the north Kildare leader John Doorly arrived in the Stradbally area from Timahoe where he planned, with local co-operation, an attack on the town, before a countermanding order was issued from Athy (possibly after Murphy's force left). Stradbally church was burned on 24 June.[70] The force under Murphy was forced to withdraw south when government reinforcements arrived in south Queen's County from Maryborough, but the colliers had already begun to desert them in any case. Most of the column eventually made it to safety in the Wicklow mountains.[71]

65 Alex Worthington, 25 June 1798: N.A.I., RP 620/38/233.
66 I.H.M. Scobie, *An old Highland fencible corps* (Edinburgh, 1914), p. 191; Chambers, *Rebellion in Kildare*, pp 95–7. The rebels continued to menace and even ambush troops under Fenton Aylmer on 4 July near Castle Browne (Clongowes Wood) outside Clane.
67 On the 'Murphy expedition', see Nicholas Furlong, *Fr John Murphy of Boolavogue 1753–1798* (Dublin, 1991), pp 136–63; Byrne, *Memoirs of Miles Byrne* (Paris, 1863; repr. Shannon, 1972), pp 200–32.
68 Furlong, *Murphy*, pp 147–51; Musgrave, *Rebellions*, pp 536–42. *F.L.J.*, 23 June 1798, claimed that Castlecomer was attacked because the Queen's County colliers had failed to join the rebels.
69 Thomas Fitzgerald, 6 August 1798, encl. court martial of James Murphy, Maryborough, 4 August 1798; Colonel Wolfe, Merrion Square, misdated 20 June 1798 [after 24 June 1798]: N.A.I., RP 620/39/147; 620/38/199. The two men arrested were relatives of the Kildare United Irishman, Malachi Delany.
70 O'Kelly, *General history*, p. 91; *Irish [Catholic] Magazine*, i (1808), 25. Stradbally rebels surrendered in large numbers around 25 July; see lists in N.A.I., RP 620/4/53/3, 7.
71 Furlong, *Murphy*, pp 152–63; Byrne, *Memoirs*, pp 225–32.

The most determined group of Wexford/Wicklow rebels entered the north Leinster region between 8 and 10 July. Under Edward Fitzgerald, Fr Mogue Kearns, Anthony Perry, Joseph Holt and others, they crossed into Kildare from Wicklow and by 10 July had linked up with the rebels at Timahoe under William Aylmer. The next day, with some Kildare support, they launched an attack on the tiny garrison at Clonard to the northwest, which was eventually repulsed. If the rebel force intended connecting with Ulster, Clonard was a strange choice of target. The idea for this move appears to have originated with Fr Mogue Kearns who had been a curate there. Contemporary records suggested Naas and Athlone as other rebel objects of attack.[72]

Following the setback at Clonard, the majority of the Kildare rebels returned to Timahoe with some of the Wexford force under Edward Fitzgerald. The general direction of the remaining Wexford/Wicklow force was eastwards towards Dublin through the south-east Meath/north Dublin territory (Dunshaughlin/Dunboyne/Garristown), which had been a rebel heartland during the first week of the rebellion. An attack on Clonard may have been a potential launching pad for an attack on the capital and it resembles Lord Edward FitzGerald's projected march along the Dublin/Galway road from a similar point of origin.[73] Francis Higgins indicated that a link-up with Dublin was planned and reported an increase in rebel traffic between the capital and Kildare/Meath.[74]

The 'Meath expedition' was however a disaster and aroused little active local support. The rebels were dispersed at Knockderrig Hill on 12 July and were forced north at Garristown. They were subsequently defeated at Knightstown Bog near Slane, and at Ballyboghill in County Dublin, on 14 July.[75] Meanwhile the Kildare rebels who had remained in the Bog of Allen reopened channels of communication with Dublin Castle and negotiated a surrender; this took place on 21 July.[76]

Those Wexford/Wicklow rebels still out successfully linked up with residual United Irish forces including those active in north Kildare and passive in south Queen's County. However, the government forces were strong enough to threaten or launch attacks on such rebels from the by now well-garrisoned towns. The

---

72 On the Wexford-Wicklow expedition, see Daniel Gahan, *The people's rising, Wexford, 1798* (Dublin, 1995), pp' 278–97; Chambers, *Rebellion in Kildare*, pp 96–8; Eamon Doyle, *The Wexford insurgents of '98 and their march into Meath* (Enniscorthy, 1997); O'Donnell, *The rebellion in Wicklow*, pp 276–83; Joseph Holt, *Memoirs of Joseph Holt*, ed. T. Crofton Croker (London, 1838), i, pp 98–101; Martin Kelly, 'Father Mogue Kearns', in *Kildare Arch. Soc. Jn.*, xvii, 3 (1996–7), 348–50.

73 Felix Rourke, the Rathcoole leader who was involved, stated that the intention was 'of marching through the different counties in order to raise them.' See F.R. Wilson [Felix Rourke] to Mary Finerty, 27 July 1798, in R.R. Madden, *The United Irishmen: Their lives and times* (3rd ser., Dublin, 1846), ii, pp 77–9.

74 Higgins to Cooke, 12, 15 July 1798: N.A.I., RP 620/18/14.

75 Gahan, *People's rising*, pp 288–97; Doyle, *Mar. into Meath*, pp 28–38.

76 Chambers, *Rebellion in Kildare*, pp 98–100.

Doonane colliers and Timahoe rebels proved more reticent about fresh conventional warfare; for the south-eastern rebels these 'marches' were desperate final ventures.

The Dublin-focused designs of the United Irishmen previous to the outbreak of the rebellion ensured that north Leinster was a crucial arena for revolutionary success or failure. Rebel failure was the result of the partial nature of the rising, isolated not only by the still-born Dublin effort but by the general inactivity outside the Kildare/south east Meath area. It is not sufficient to argue that the latter rose because they were better informed of rebel plans, since 'isolated' areas, most notably Doonane, did participate. At the root of the failure to rise was the prior decimation (through arrests) of the county-organized United Irishmen, which in turn provides a negative argument for the United-Irish nature of the rebellion where it occurred. The general failure of the 'outer counties' helped to undermine early rebel successes; rebel-occupied positions in Kildare and Meath were retaken by government forces, not from Dublin, but from positions to the west of rebel strongholds.

However, it is incorrect to argue that the movement had faded in north Leinster by 30 May. The upsurge of rebel activity around 17–20 June illustrates the continued designs of rebels on Dublin, though the battle of Ovidstown virtually ended such rebel ambition. The rebellion had been so weak in King's County that the prominent liberal Sir Lawrence Parsons was able to open a debate on the treatment of prisoners in the county as early as June.[77] The Wexford incursions into north Leinster in July were an ultimately futile attempt to stir up a widespread, conventional midlands campaign. The historian of the rebellion in north Leinster is hampered by the lack of any narrative by a major rebel commander; no equivalent of Hay, Cloney or Byrne exists for any of the six counties discussed. Nevertheless, the rebellion in this region is crucial in determining the significance, extent and reasons for the failure of the 1798 rebellion.[78]

77 'True Blue', Birr, 21 June 1798; General Dunne, Tullamore to Castlereagh, 31 July 1798: N.A.I., RP 620/38/212; 620/4/33/6; letters of Sir Lawrence Parsons: N.L.I., Rosse Papers, MS 12,840 (4).
78 My thanks to Dáire Keogh and Richard John Aylmer for their assistance while researching and writing this article.

7

The transformation of the Dublin Society of United Irishmen into a mass-based revolutionary organization, 1791–6

TOMMY GRAHAM

The title of this paper is borrowed from Nancy Curtin whose path-breaking 1985 article of similar title, minus the word 'Dublin', established beyond doubt the continuity between a so-called 'first' and 'second' Societies of United Irishmen.[1] While she convincingly established her case for the revolutionary transformation of the movement generally, her main concern was with Ulster (where underground organization first emerged) and with Belfast in particular. This paper will focus on the situation in Dublin.

Although a Dublin rising was aborted on the night of 23 May 1798, substantial United Irish organization was then in existence in the city, involving a membership of almost 10,000 (with an additional 9,000 claimed for the county).[2] Membership was concentrated in the older, poorer, western quarters of the city, with a substantial plebian and artisan element among the rank-and-file. Yet the original reformist society, had a much more restricted bourgeois membership of less than 400, only half of whom could be considered active.[3] Moreover from the early part of 1793 the society had been in decline, reflected in badly attended meetings, and it was finally dispersed in May 1794. How had this transformation of the Dublin United Irishmen from middle-class reformers into militant revolutionaries occurred in the years between the original society's apparent dissolution and the emergence of an underground organization at the end of 1796?

The first Dublin Society of United Irishmen was founded in November 1791 and its constitution envisaged basic or 'simple' societies of no more than thirty-

---

1 Nancy Curtin, 'The transformation of the Society of United Irishmen into a mass-based revolutionary organization, 1794–6', in *I.H.S.*, xxiv (1984–5), 463–92.
2 Samuel Sproule to John Lees, 14 May 1798: N.A.I., RP 620/51/40. For an account of the rising in Dublin, see Graham, '"An union of power": The United Irish organization', in David Dickson, Dáire Keogh and Kevin Whelan (eds), *The United Irishmen ...* (Dublin, 1993), pp 250–5.
3 R.B. McDowell, 'The personnel of the Dublin Society of United Irishmen', in *I.H.S.*, ii (1940–1), 12–53.

five members which would send delegates to ascending baronial, county, provincial and national committees. Outside of Antrim and Down, however, this written constitution was never put into effect and no serious attempt was made to establish a genuinely national network, although there are single references for this period to societies in Cork, Limerick, Gorey, Tullamore, Clonmel and Nenagh.[4] In Dublin, the United Irishmen continued to meet as one big society. Attendance at its monthly meetings fluctuated from about a hundred during the first half of its existence down to about forty during its final year. This decline was due on the one hand to government repression which warned off its more lukewarm members and on the other to the increasing absence of radicals who found the society's proceedings increasingly irrelevant. It was a national organization in embryo, however: 55 of its estimated 425 members were from outside Dublin, spread across 24 counties.

Mass organization was carried on through surrogate bodies in which the United Irishmen were the dominant but not the only element: in revived Volunteer corps, in masonic lodges and in the Catholic Convention of December 1792. Although the Catholic Committee and the Society of United Irishmen were distinct organizations and the relationship between the two was not without its tensions and contradictions, the overlap of membership was considerable. Numerically it was Dublin-dominated in general, and by Dublin United Irishmen in particular: many of the rural constituencies were represented by Dubliners, 127 of the 233 delegates (55 per cent) being based in Dublin. Forty-nine (37 per cent) of those were, or were later to become, United Irishmen. Their domination of the leadership was even more striking. Tone was the committee's secretary; four of the presiding ten-man sub-committee were members of the first society – John Sweetman, John Keogh, Richard McCormick and Thomas Warren; a fifth, Hugh Hamil, it was alleged, was later elected a United Irish colonel.[5] McCormick served on the Leinster executive of the underground organization until the arrests of 12 Mar. 1798; Sweetman was arrested at the same time. Keogh's involvement in the underground organization is more difficult to pin down. The informer Samuel Turner claimed he was a member of a 'National Executive' in June 1797 but ambiguously added that Keogh did not attend the meeting in question.[6] Among the Convention delegates who later held leadership positions was Edward Lewins, who became official United Irish emissary to France from 1797, and William James MacNeven, who served on the Leinster executive.

Throughout its legal existence, the Dublin Society of United Irishmen remained a rather amorphous and open organization with a rotating leadership,

---

4 R.B. McDowell, *Ireland in the age of imperialism and revolution, 1760–1801* (Oxford, 1979), p. 389.
5 Thomas Boyle to Cooke, 3 May 1798: N.A.I., RP 620/18/3.
6 Information of Turner, no date: N.A.I., RP 620/51/120; Camden to Portland (encl.), 9 December 1797: P.R.O., HO/100/70/339–48.

more akin to a debating society than a disciplined political instrument. In contrast, the northern organization was split into a number of small clubs under the direction of a secret committee in Belfast, on which Samuel Neilson was a key member. In January 1794 he visited Dublin and informed its society (correctly) that there were paid government informers among its members. He urged the society to tighten up security by appointing a 'committee of public welfare' consisting of twelve members to transact and co-ordinate its business.[7] The majority of the Dublin Society, however, were still not prepared to face up to the revolutionary implications of their radical challenge to government. The suggestion was rejected and the society was subsequently suppressed in May 1794.

Thomas Addis Emmett claimed that organization ceased at this point altogether and did not resume until late in the spring of 1795, prompted on the one hand by the recall of Fitzwilliam and the consequent dashing of hopes of constitutional reform, and on the other by the initiative of the 'lower orders' in the north, of 'mechanics, petty shopkeepers and farmers' who set up their own societies styled 'United Irishmen', which the original leadership subsequently joined.[8] In fact the northern societies continued to organize under the watchful eye of Neilson and the Belfast committee. Neither had the Dublin activists ceased to meet. As early as July 1794 the Sheares brothers, John and Henry, hosted a United Irish meeting to receive addresses from radical societies in Dundee and Glasgow.[9] In October 1794 William Drennan reported to McTier on a meeting in Henry Jackson's to discuss a proposal to divide the society into fifteen-man sections under the direction of a 'council or central committee'.[10]

By 1795 this shadowy group of former members of the original society, centred around Henry Jackson, Oliver Bond and the Sheares brothers, were known as 'the Strugglers'.[11] Francis Higgins, the spymaster, referred to them as 'the Friendly Society of Pill Lane' or 'the Pill Lane King Killers', and other associated clubs and societies crop up in reports to the Castle – 'the Spread', 'the Dexter', 'the Union', 'the States', and what Higgins sarcastically refers to as the 'Association of Eating and Drinking Democratic Citizens'.[12] At this stage they were a fairly narrowly-based elitest group, but significant nonetheless because of their links with the Catholic Committee, another focus for organization in Dublin, and more significantly because of their links with Belfast, 'the centre of motion of the whole machine'; but their crucial importance lay in the fact that

7 Curtain, 'Transformation', p. 474.
8 T.A. Emmett, 'Part of an essay towards the history of Ireland', in W.J. MacNeven, *Pieces of Irish history ...* (New York, 1807), pp 76–8.
9 Hamilton to Nepean, 14 July 1794: P.R.O., HO/100/52/159.
10 William Drennan to Mrs McTier, Oct. 1794: D.A. Chart (ed.), *The Drennan letters*, pp 214–15.
11 Camden to Portland, 29 July 1795: P.R.O., HO/100/58/181–190.
12 Higgins to Cooke, 1 Aug. 1796: N.A.I., RP 620/18/14 .

they were to provide the leadership of the mass-based United Irish organization when it did emerge in the city and across the country in 1797 and 1798.[13]

But in 1794 and 1795 the most important revolutionary development in Dublin was the penetration of the Defenders and their link-up with its many artisan political clubs. The politicization of the Defenders was confirmed by contemporaries. In June 1793 Denis Browne, MP for Mayo, attributed Defender unrest to 'the new political doctrines which have pervaded the lower classes – that ... spirit [which] has been produced by the circulation of Paine's *Rights of man*, of seditious newspapers, and by shopkeepers who having been in Dublin to buy goods have formed connections with some of the United Irishmen'.[14] The effect of United Irish and Catholic Committee propaganda in the transformation of the Defenders is now self-evident.[15] But there were more explicit links. As early as August 1792 Tone and Keogh accompanied Neilson and Alexander Lowry on a mission to Defenders in Rathfriland, County Down. This has sometimes been portrayed as a once-off 'do-gooding mission' to defuse local sectarian tensions, yet the same names crop up elsewhere in the hitherto hidden history of Defender/United Irish relations. The Teeling family played a crucial role. The father, Luke, a wealthy linen merchant from Lisburn, was a United Irishman and delegate to the Catholic Convention of 1792. Two of his sons, Charles and Bartholomew, were closely involved with the process of Defender reorganization and politicization, and a son-in-law, John Magennis, was the self-styled 'grand master' of the County Down Defenders. A third brother, George, looked after the family business in Dublin. Although not as active as his two brothers, in early 1797 he was serving on a United Irish baronial committee in Dublin city.[16] In the light of these connections it is safe to assume that there was more to the involvement of Napper Tandy, the most popular tribune of Dublin's masses, with the Defenders of County Louth, than mere 'bravado' or 'curiosity'.[17]

However, these links only involved the advanced elements of the Society and, try as they might, the authorities were unable to make charges of explicit connection stick. Defenderism first made its appearance in Dublin as early as the spring of 1793.[18] As elsewhere, the militia were a significant factor in its spread, and the Smithfield/Ormond market area north of the river was the most impor-

---

13 Camden to Portland, 29 July 1795: P.R.O., HO/100/58/181–90.
14 Denis Browne to —, 6 June 1793: P.R.O., HO/100/44/115–18.
15 J. Smyth, 'Popular politicisation, Defenderism and the Catholic question', in Hugh Gough ... David Dickson (eds), *Ireland and the French Revolution* (Dublin, 1990), pp 109–16.
16 Information of Thomas Reynolds, *Reports of the Committees of Secrecy of the House of Commons and the House of Lords of Ireland, with appendices* (Dublin, 1798), appendix dccclxviii.
17 Marianne Elliott, *Partners in revolution ...* (New Haven, 1982), p. 44. For an explanation of Defender/United Irish links, see Jim Smyth, 'Popular politicization in Ireland in the 1790s' (unpublished Ph.D. thesis, University of Cambridge, 1989), pp 111–15.
18 *Saunders News Letter*, 29 Mar. 1793.

tant neighbourhood, with its links with the cattle-producing regions of north
Leinster and of County Meath in particular, an early Defender stronghold. As
Defender trouble spread throughout the northern half of the country in 1794–5,
the narrow lanes and alleys of the metropolis became a refuge for fugitives from
Lord Carhampton's persecution, as it was again to become in the wake of the
insurrection itself. For example, in August 1795 Camden reported that fugitives
from Leitrim and Roscommon were entering the city via the Grand Canal, having found work on its barges.[19] Once in the city, Defenderism, as elsewhere,
adapted to local conditions and concerns, social and economic as well as political,
and was influenced by the experience of combination among the city's journeymen. Combination was the commonest form of illegal, autonomous, lower-class
organization and was the urban equivalent of the rural secret society.[20] This
would account for the spread of the organization south of the river into the
Liberties and also for its significant Protestant artisan membership.

Regardless of the links forged with the United Irishmen and the Catholic
Committee, the Defenders themselves had their own somewhat ill-defined agenda. They were anxious to spread their organization into Dublin. If they were
strong there, 'it was better than all they could do in the countryside' since it gave
them the possibility of striking a blow at the heart of government power.[21] In
February 1795 a Dublin Defender added to the usual vague notions of recovering
lost estates and 'sweeping clean the Protestants' the more specific object of assassinating the lord lieutenant. Another claimed later in court that a rebellion was
expected in Dublin in April.[22] During the summer of 1795 a delegation of Meath
Defenders arrived in the capital to co-ordinate a plan for seizing the capital with
their Dublin comrades.[23] At the beginning of August a spate of arms raids
occured in and around the city's northern suburbs.[24] On 22 August a mutiny
occured among regular English troops in response to the prospect of re-assign-
ment to the West Indies, a veritable death-sentence because of the prevalence of
tropical disease. The arrest and punishment of the mutineers provoked the
Dublin crowd to riot and fifty soldiers were induced to desert. They disappeared
into the Liberties where they were stripped of their weapons and accoutrements
and were provided with 'allowances of money and employment as weavers'.[25]

This deterioration of law and order in the capital provoked a decisive response from government and a number of suspected Dublin Defenders were

19 Camden to Portland, 7 Aug. 1795: P.R.O., HO/100/58/233–6.
20 For Defender/journeyman combination links, see Smyth, 'Popular politicization', p. 146.
21 'Dublin United Irishmen', no date: N.A.I., RP 620/52/183.
22 *State trials*, xxvi, pp 295, 447.
23 Information of Thomas Kennedy, no date: N.A.I., RP 620/23/59; *Morning Post*, 6 Aug.
   1795.
24 *F.D.J.*, 25 Aug. 1795; *D.E.P.*, 25 Aug. 1795
25 Camden to Portland, 25 Sept. 1795: P.R.O., HO/100/58/347.

arrested. Their trials for treason took place the following spring (1796) and revealed an unlikely plan to seize the capital. Two defendants, Patrick Hart and James Weldon, were executed; another, Thomas Kennedy, was reprieved and sent to Botany Bay. Others were either released or acquitted. The whole business was deliberately played out over several months in order to achieve the maximum intimidatory effect. Thereafter Defenderism in Dublin declined and by the end of 1796 references to it had almost ceased entirely.

In relation to the alleged conspiracy, the Rebellion Papers contain four overlapping lists of names.[26] Two, uncredited, are simply titled 'Dublin United Irishmen' and have no accompanying text. The third, also uncredited, is titled 'Defenders in the Militia' and is accompanied by a semi-literate account. The fourth is titled 'Sworn information of William Lawlor'. There are forty-four names altogether. Twelve are militiamen – six in the Fermanagh militia, four in the Longford and two in the Westmeath. Addresses are provided for twenty-eight of the remaining thirty-two who were all Dubliners: eight in the Barrack division (north-west); three in the Rotunda (north-east); six in the Green (south-east); and eleven in the Workhouse (south-west/Liberties), a fairly broad geographical spread for such a small sample but with a predictable bunching in the poorer quarters of the city north and south of the Old Bridge.

William Lawlor, an apprentice gilder from Cathedral Lane off Kevin Street, was the chief witness for the prosecution. A Protestant, he left Dublin for London in 1791 and joined the radical Corresponding Society, which gave him a letter of introduction to Archibald Hamilton Rowan, enough to secure his entry into radical circles in Dublin. There he met with John Burk, recently expelled from Trinity College for blasphemy. Burk later claimed that he was a member of the Strugglers, the revamped society master-minded by John Sheares, Jackson, Bond and others. While admiring the integrity of its members, Burk considered the new society inadequate to the task of 'making one grand association of the Irish people', and that 'more active measures were necessary'. So he formed the Athenian, Telegraphic and Philanthropic societies 'as nurseries from which to procure men of full intellectual growth and patriotism'. In addition he set on foot 'an armed secret organization divided into tens'.[27] Lawlor described its composition. Burk approached ten trusted individuals, who in turn were to recruit ten more, each of whom were to recruit five each, giving a 500–strong force for a projected attack on the Castle.[28] Burk himself claimed that at the end of 1794 an unnamed delegate despatched from Belfast reported back that 'these societies formed the sole revolutionary organization in Dublin'.

26 'Dublin United Irishmen'; 'Defenders in the Militia'; Information of Lawlor, no dates: N.A.I., RP 620/52/183–6.
27 John Burk, *History of the late war in Ireland, with an account of the United Irish association from the first meeting in Belfast, to the landing at Killala* (Philadelphia, 1799), pp 44–50.
28 *F.J.*, 25 Feb. 1796.

Lawlor's account of the liaison between the Philanthropic/Telegraphic Society and the Defenders, given in both his sworn statement and in newspaper reports of the trials, more or less corresponds with the account appended to the list of 'Defenders in the Militia'. It is probably the confession of a young apprentice glasscutter, Edward Brady, who threw himself at the mercy of the court, and from whom a semi-literate account could plausibly be expected.[29] Edward Hanlon, a fife major in the Fermanagh Militia, had administered the Defender oath to James Walsh, a tailor from Molesworth Court, Henry Flood, a silversmith from Andrew Street, to Thomas Kennedy and Edward Brady, apprentice glasscutters from Stephen's Street, all members of the Philanthropic Society, and to James Weldon of the Blackhorse Cavalry. Kennedy and Brady introduced Lawlor to Weldon, described as 'a committee man', who swore him in, along with Thomas Clayton, an apprentice cabinet-maker from Henry Street, and William Coffy from Cork Street, also members of the Philanthropic Society. Another active Defender 'committee man' was Patrick Hart, the sixteen-year-old son of Patrick senior, a skinner from Watling Street, who had previously been charged with Defenderism in his native Trim.

Eleven of the twenty-one names on Lawlor's list were members of the Philanthropic Society. All eleven were sworn Defenders as a result of the process described, at the cost of 1s. per person, and organised into numbered lodges. Meetings were held over the summer of 1795 in pubs such as 'The Churn' in Plunkett Street, where the waiter, John Cusack, was also a Defender. An emissary from outside the city called Lockingham, described as a 'captain', was the most active leader and it was he who introduced the innovation of swearing Protestants. Given the origins of the Defender movement it is not surprising that this caused tension. Patrick Hart complained bitterly about it and demanded that Lockington should be called before 'a committee of twelve' to answer for 'his crime of admitting Protestants among us'. In another outburst he demanded to know if Brady was a Protestant. In a separate trial involving fifteen members of the Royal Regiment of Artillery in a plot to seize the Phoenix Park magazine in April 1795, another Protestant Defender, Private Thomas Smith, formerly a publican from Garden Lane off Francis Street, confessed and also emphasised the anti-Protestant nature of Defenderism. He explained away his own involvement by claiming he was obliged to keep his religion secret. Many of the later confessions and informations of Protestant United Irishmen conformed to the same pattern of depicting the revolutionary movement in exclusively papist colours in order to lessen their own culpability, a version the authorities were only too willing to believe as it suited their own propaganda campaign.

A striking feature of those involved was their youth. The two who were executed, Hart and Weldon, were only sixteen. Kennedy was twenty, and he, Brady,

29 Pelham to Portland, 1 Mar. 1796: P.R.O., HO/100/63/205–6.

Clayton and Lawlor himself, were all apprentices. A month before the trial the *Freeman's Journal* denounced 'the growing depravity of the rising generation ... at least in the middle order of society', combining apprentices, and 'youths associating with [*sic*] clubs in low tipling houses, to be initiated in deism, treason and Defenderism, under the abominable mask of erudition, at which they call their philanthropic societies'. It accompanied a report on a speech by the attorney general, Arthur Wolfe, who referred to 'clubs of beardless urchins discussing politics and religion', and who blamed 'a profusion of pocket money' for the problem.[30]

A preoccupation of these Philanthropic Society/Defender meetings was the question of leadership. According to Brady, 'several of them wished they had good leaders and there was men enough[;] others said if there was a rise [*sic*] amongst them they would soon find leaders. Lawlor said they wanted leaders more than anything.'[31] According to Lawlor, the 'committee man' Weldon told Brady they would be led by 'someone from the north'.[32] The phrase is ambiguous and could either refer to the shadowy Defender leadership centred in Armagh or to United Irish leadership in Belfast. The fact that two of the four lists of names are titled 'Dublin United Irishmen' implies explicit United Irish involvement. On the other hand, there was no organization of that name active in Dublin in the summer of 1795 and none of those listed purely as 'Dublin United Irishmen' (that is, not on the other two lists) were prominent or were to become so. Nevertheless there were some links to past and future United Irish organization: Simon Maguire, a merchant from Bachelor's Walk, a member of the first Dublin society and a Catholic Convention delegate, acted as treasurer for defraying the defendants' legal expenses;[33] another member of the original society, the barrister Leonard McNally, conducted the defence. Despite his hidden role as a government spy, McNally performed credibly in court, and his character demolition of the informer Lawlor was poignant indeed! Both Patrick Hart's father and Richard Turner were involved in later United Irish organization. A defence witness, Nicholas Clare, a master tailor from Townsend Street, later served on the United Irish Rotunda district committee (1797) and the Green district committee (1798). Both Clare, a former Volunteer, and his brother, had been members of the Telegraphic Society.[34]

The most explicit link with past and future United Irish organization was in the person of Thomas Dry, whose name appears on all four lists. Dry, a clothier from Weavers' Square in the Liberties, was originally from the neighbourhood of Wexford town, and had been a member of the first Dublin Society.[35] In August

30 *F.J.*, 2 Jan. 1796.
31 'Defenders in the Militia', no date: N.A.I., RP 620/52/185.
32 *F.J.*, 25 Feb. 1796.
33 Francis Higgins to Edward Cooke, 1 Aug. 1796: N.A.I., RP 620/18/14.
34 *F.J*, 25 Feb. 1796.
35 McDowell, 'Personnel', p. 32.

1793 his brother Richard was arrested on the steps of the Royal Exchange for using seditious expressions while waving about a copy of Paine's *Rights of man* and addressing 'a number of men, not altogether of the lowest class'.[36] But there were limits to their radicalism. The previous summer (1792) both brothers were active in prosecuting combining journeymen, as were Samuel Neilson and other radicals in Belfast.[37] Thomas Dry was arrested for his part in the Defender/Philanthrophic conspiracy of August 1795 but was discharged at the end of the year. In Mar. 1796 he went to Belfast where he assumed the name Jackson. In July 1796 two emissaries from Belfast, James Hope and James Metcalfe, arrived in Dublin with letters of introduction from Samuel Neilson addressed to Edward Dunn, Henry Jackson's foreman, and Richard Dry. The following February, 1797, Richard Dry was arrested in Roscommon while on a mission to bail John O'Leary, another Philanthrophic society member acquitted in the 1795/6 Defender trial. He escaped and remained at large until May 1798 when he was arrested in County Cork. Thomas Dry, meanwhile, had been arrested in Belfast in April 1797.[38]

Nancy Curtin has suggested that the Jacobin clubs of Belfast in the early 1790s were in all probability stalking horses for radical republicanism under the direction of Neilson, Russell, McCracken etc., the 'official' United Irish leaders, and were part of a long-term strategy of building a single mass-based revolutionary organization. She has also questioned their characterization as 'plebian', pointing out that many of their key members were men of substantial means. The situation in Dublin in the mid-nineties conforms remarkably closely to the same pattern, with two more or less distinct tendencies – the Strugglers/Pill Lane society on one hand, and the Philanthropic/Telegraphic Society on the other. The comings and goings of the Dry brothers reveal a close relationship between the latter and the radical Belfast leadership. Burk's claim that he set up the Telegraphic and Philanthrophic societies in an effort to make 'one grand association of the Irish people' reveals a common strategic objective.[39] Although the rank-and-file of these societies consisted largely of artisans and apprentices, people like the Drys, Nicholas Clare and John Burk were undoubtedly men of means. But there was a difference. Whereas in Belfast the two groups were close if not overlapping, in Dublin they were separate, with the link being via the radical Belfast leadership. This would explain why the northern leaders, who were pressing the more cautious Leinster leadership for a rising in June 1797, considered going over their heads and trusting to the Dublin 'mob', and why Neilson could organize so effectively in Dublin after his release from custody in February 1798.[40]

36 Smyth, 'Popular politicization', p. 142.
37 Ibid., p. 145.
38 McDowell, 'Personnel', p. 32; Smyth, 'Popular politicization', pp 154, 160; 'J.W.' [Leonard McNally] to Cooke, 9 July 1796: N.A.I., RP 620/36/227.
39 Burk, *Late war*, p. 45.
40 Information of Turner, no date: N.A.I., RP 620/51/120; Camden to Portland (enclosure *re* Turner's information), 9 Dec. 1797: P.R.O., HO 100/70/339–8.

From as early as 1792 the radical republicans (Tone, Neilson, Russell et al.) had countenanced a close relationship with the Defenders, and an indirect liaison in the capital via its radical political clubs was a useful intermediate step. The activity of Dublin's artisan Jacobin clubs in the early and middle 1790s may not have been as autonomous from the United Irishmen (or at least the influence of *some* United Irishmen) as Curtin has suggested.[41] But they did not exercise sufficent influence to stop the Defenders and the Philanthropic/Telegraphic societies from embarking on their own insurrectionary schemes in the summer of 1795, which jeopardised plans for a United Irish rising with French help.

Dublin's lack of a structured United Irish organization in 1795 stood in marked contrast to the situation in Belfast where a disciplined network of societies was well established: the northern organization was able to make the transition underground because it had conformed to the cell-structure laid down in the original constitution, in contrast to Dublin's unwieldly, relatively open, single society. In the second place, in Belfast and in the surrounding hinterland of south Antrim and north Down the society was an almost exclusively Presbyterian phenomenon and one, moreover, in which determined radicals such as Neilson had gained an early predominance.

No such homogeneity existed in Dublin, where there were five distinct tendencies, divided by various combinations of class, religion and degree of militancy. One centred on a caucus of radicals from the original Dublin Society led by John Sheares, Oliver Bond and Henry Jackson, who had close links with the Belfast leadership. After the dispersal of the legal society in May 1794, they immediately set about establishing underground organizational structures on the Belfast model, and by early 1795 these were identifiable as the 'Strugglers' or the 'Pill Lane Society'. Standing aloof from these developments was a second group of non-Catholic reformists such as Thomas Addis Emmet, Archibald Hamilton Rowan, Simon Butler and William Drennan. They had dominated the first Dublin Society (hence the rejection of Neilson's organizational model in early 1794), but were never really happy at the prospect of revolutionary organization. Rowan, Butler and Drennan subsequently dropped out altogether, but there may have been a degree of sincerity in Emmet's at first sight implausible account of reluctant involvement in the leadership of a movement re-established underground by popular initiative. The Catholic Committee acted as a third focus of organization, led by prominent members of the first society – John Keogh, Richard McCormick and William James MacNeven.

Although organization continued underground immediately after the suppression of the legal society, it made little progress as a mass-organization. Not only was the leadership divided but there may have been a deliberate marking of time in late 1794 and early 1795 while there was a prospect of Fitzwilliam deliv-

41 Curtin, 'Transformation', p. 478.

ering on Catholic Emancipation, just as the first Society had moderated its rhetoric in the course of the Catholic campaign in 1792. Fitzwilliam's departure in Mar. 1795 dashed such hopes and left no other option but the revolutionary one. In the weeks that followed, the Catholic Committee dissolved itself, Tone was chosen as agent to seek French military assistance, and the existence of an underground organization was formalized by the adoption of a new constitution by the northern societies on 10 May 1795.

Mass organization under the control of United Irish leadership was still problematic in Dublin, however, because lower down the social scale the stage had already been occupied by the fourth and fifth identifiable tendencies, the Defenders, and their allies in the city's artisanal Jacobin clubs. Defender activity reached its peak in the summer of 1795 but was not finally crushed by government measures until early in 1796. But with growing alarm in the course of 1796 the Castle realized that its apparent 'victory' over the Defenders had merely cleared the decks for the emergence of a much more formidable revolutionary organization: a single mass-based movement led by the United Irishmen.[42] Thus it was not until late in 1796 that explicitly United Irish forms of mass-organization began to appear on the ground in Dublin.

42 Camden to Portland, 6 Aug. 1796: P.R.O., HO/100/62, 153–63.

8

Smoke without fire? Munster and the 1798 rebellion

DAVID DICKSON

The precise status of the province of Munster in the history of the 1798 rebellion remains perplexing and contradictory. On the one hand, the Rebellion Papers are rich in reports from Cork and Tipperary correspondents, from barristers on circuit like Leonard McNally and from peers, gentry and Protestant clergy, warning of local disaffection and covert United Irish organization in the years between 1795 and 1798. On the other, there is the curious silence of the region during and after the attempted French landing in 1796 at Bantry Bay and, more remarkably, little visible offensive action in 1798 itself. In terms of the national leadership of the United Irish movement, men of Munster origin were very prominent – Thomas Addis Emmet, the Sheares brothers, Arthur O'Connor – and of course 'the man from God knows where' was a native of north Cork; in addition, two of the key players in French intelligence gathering in Ireland in the 1790s were Kerrymen – William Duckett and Nicholas Madgett.[1] But, against that, no one actually resident in Munster was involved in the United Irish National Directory; nor was any provincial directory for Munster established in any of the movement's administrative re-organizations in 1797 and 1798.

Official Ireland was nevertheless convinced of the strategic importance of Munster, specifically Cork, and of its great vulnerability whether arising from a successful invasion or from a rising within the province. The course of events in Munster would, it was assumed, profoundly affect the outcome of the wider challenge to the established order; shortly after Bantry Bay, Under-Secretary Edward Cooke had baldly stated that 'England is lost if Cork be taken'; Speaker

---

1 The Emmets were a Tipperary family, but Thomas Addis was born in Cork in 1764, some years before the family moved to Dublin. The Sheares were Cork-reared. Arthur O'Connor was born in west Waterford, and educated and brought up there and in west Cork. For Thomas Russell, see C.J.Woods (ed.), *Journals and memoirs of Thomas Russell, 1791–5* (Dublin, 1991), pp 15–6. For Duckett and Madgett, see Marianne Elliott, *Partners in revolution: The United Irishmen and France* (New Haven and London, 1982), pp 58–9. John Daly Burk may also have been a Cork native; he was working in Cork city between 1790 and 1792: Michael Durey, *Transatlantic radicals and the early American republic* (Lawrence, Kansas, 1997), p. 114.

John Foster, a fortnight into the Leinster rising, warned Lord Sheffield that 'Cork and Munster are organized and ready, when Dublin draws the army from thence'; a week later Lady Londonderry, the viceroy's sister, was told confidentially that 'it depends upon the County Cork to decide our fate'.[2] This mindset was reflected in the pattern of military deployment evident from the early weeks of 1797: garrisons had been dramatically strengthened (notably in Counties Tipperary, Cork, and in Limerick city) and new camps established at Ardfinnan and near Bandon, as lessons were quickly learnt after the panic of December 1796. But crown forces within the province remained widely dispersed, a response to the crescendo of warnings from magistrates on the ground and a measure of the willingness of Camden and his civilian advisers to give credit to such warnings.[3]

Yet was all the talk of a regional United Irish organization and of an imminent southern rising little more than a mere chimera in the last analysis? Certainly those who wish to make the case for a substantial revolutionary threat have to try and explain the very modest level of subversive military activity: a check-list of incidents of collective action and political violence across Munster in 1797–8 is much shorter than one, say, of agrarian incidents as reported in 1786, the principal year of Rightboy activity. Far greater crowds appeared in '86 over a larger swathe of the province, coming out in support of 'Captain Right' and the campaign against tithes, than showed their faces in '98.[4] Yet the character of collective action was very different in the two periods: there had been a great deal of intimidation in 1786 but little actual violence and almost no loss of life; in County Cork only one man was executed on a Rightboy-related charge that year. By contrast in the far more highly charged atmosphere of 1798 at least 38 men were executed in the county on political and related criminal charges; total fatalities across the province at large reached well into the lower hundreds.[5]

Political violence in Munster between November 1797 and January 1799 was, however, concentrated in a handful of notorious incidents: a wave of assassinations of farmers in east Cork/west Waterford in the early winter of 1797; the killing of a prominent magistrate and his host in Araglin on the Cork/Tipperary

2   Kevin Whelan, 'Bantry Bay: The wider context', in J.A. Murphy (ed.), *The French are in the bay: The expedition to Bantry Bay 1796* (Cork, 1997), p. 108; John Foster, Dublin, to [Lord Sheffield], 5 June 1798: P.R.O.N.I., Sheffield papers, T.3465; 'W' to Lady Londonderry, June 1798, Kent Archives Office, Camden papers, U840/563/13.
3   See map plotting army deployments in 1797, in Kevin Whelan, *The fellowship of freedom* (Cork, 1998), p. 56.
4   J.S.Donnelly, 'The Rightboy movement', in *Studia Hibernica*, xvii–xviii (1977–8), 131–201. The most bloody Rightboy incident was when four died in an attempted prisoner rescue in Cashel in August 1786: ibid., 200–1.
5   Data on executions are taken from Colman O Mahony, *In the shadows: Life in Cork, 1750–1930* (Cork, 1997), pp 329–54. Six were convicted for the December 1786 murder of Fennor in Tipperary, but it is not clear how many were executed: Donnelly, 'Rightboy movement', 180.

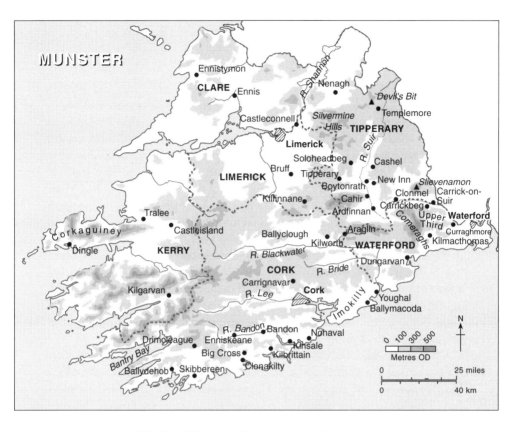

Fig. 8.1   Munster, places mentioned in the text

border in February 1798; a series of large-scale arms raids in Tipperary, and
north and west Cork in late March and April, followed by forcible official disarming campaigns; an ambush of the Westmeath Militia near Clonakilty in June,
causing several dozen deaths; the Boytonrath rally in south Tipperary and an
abortive attack on Cashel in mid-July; the Slievenamon rising near Carrick-on-
Suir later that month, again with some dozens killed; an attack on the militia at
Castleisland, Co. Kerry, in mid-August; and in January 1799 two clusters of incidents involving large crowds, the first in north-east Cork, the second and larger
one in west Clare around Ennistymon – in all, seemingly no more than a series of
forlorn demonstrations, the sidewash effects of the disastrous unwinding of an
essentially Leinster conspiracy.

    That, however, could be a misreading. Given both the level of anticipation
among contemporaries as to what was likely to happen in Munster, and the
strength of popular memory in several parts of the province as to what had nearly happened, there are grounds for arguing that a great deal was simmering

beneath the surface, much of which was never fully revealed. The purpose here is to see whether there is hard evidence to support such a hypothesis.

RADICAL POLITICS 1791–5

In most of Munster's thirty-two parliamentary constituencies there had been a vigorous recent history of electoral battle. But these contests had tended to be intimate affairs in which political argument was less concerned with the big issues of parliamentary reform or Catholic Emancipation than was the case elsewhere in the 1780s and early 1790s. One explanation for this pattern was that neither the great Leinster nor Conolly factions in the Irish parliament had Munster representatives, and although the Ponsonbys had many 'friends' in the south – no less than eight of the twenty-two MPs making up their group in 1790s sat for Munster constituencies – many of these were opponents of reform and strongly conservative on the Catholic question. In fact only a handful of Munster MPs elected to parliament in 1790 were reform-minded. And in marked contrast to the electoral warfare of previous decades the factional tensions dividing the major parliamentary interests in the region eased somewhat in the 1790s.[6] Underpinning such relative harmony at a time of gathering crisis was the pervasive conservatism of upper-class Protestants in the province.

Only in the largest urban boroughs, Cork and Limerick cities, were there (Protestant) electoral interests with strong pro-Catholic leanings – the Hely-Hutchinsons in Cork, the Perys and Maunsells in Limerick. Even in these cases, such sympathy did not extend to a general enthusiasm for political reform.[7] Many of the Munster parliamentary boroughs were ancient corporations, but none had developed the kind of guildhall-and-tavern politics which spawned Dublin's radicalism. The guilds in the southern towns were weaker in municipal terms and did not provide the framework for freemen to mobilize politically as was the case in Dublin. Indeed, parliamentary politics hardly intruded at all into some towns, notably the teeming textile centre of Carrick-on–Suir – the largest Irish urban community unrepresented in College Green.

Religious demography was inevitably a major factor in shaping the distinctive political atmosphere of Munster towns in the late eighteenth century: the wholesale merchant communities in Cork, Youghal, Waterford, Clonmel and Bandon, though still predominantly Protestant, were less emphatically so than at mid-

---

6   E.M. Johnson, 'The state of the Irish House of Commons in 1791', in *Proc. R.I.A.*, lix (1957), 1–56; Esther Hewitt (ed.), *Lord Shannon's letters to his son* (Belfast, 1982), pp lxvii–lxxiii; T.P. Power, *Land, politics, and society in eighteenth-century Tipperary* (Oxford, 1993), pp 282–301.

7   In Waterford city the two sitting MPs opposed Catholic relief in 1792, but switched to supporting the government's Catholic bill in 1793: Thomas P. Power, 'Electoral politics in Waterford city, 1692–1832', in William Nolan and T.P. Power (eds), *Waterford: History and society* (Dublin, 1992), p. 249.

century, and much of the processing trades and many sectors of artisanal production and retail trade in these towns were by now largely in Catholic hands;
Protestant mercantile wealth was noticeably weaker in Limerick, Carrick-on-
Suir, Ennis, Dungarvan and the smaller towns of the province. A Protestant
defensiveness, suspicious of the implications of Catholic relief, was natural in
such circumstances, particularly when combined with the relative strength of
the Church of Ireland within Munster Protestantism: there were a number of
powerful Quaker and Presbyterian merchant houses in Clonmel, Cork and
Waterford by that stage, but in social and political terms their moderating impact
and influence were small.

The political world of Munster Catholicism was also remarkably subdued in
the early 1790s. Although there were fairly poisonous relations between supporters of the Kerry-based Lord Kenmare and local advocates of the majority faction
in the Catholic Committee, many Munster Catholic families of potential influence were reluctant to take a public position on controversial political questions.
Thus the twenty-three Munster-based delegates at the 1792 Catholic Convention
played a surprisingly invisible role beyond chairing two plenary sessions.[8] Admittedly Bishop Moylan of Cork put in an important if probably reluctant appearance at the proceedings. County Tipperary and Limerick city were the exception
to Munster discretion: the new archbishop of Cashel, Thomas Bray, had co-operated with John Keogh in mobilizing the faint-hearted in support of the convention plan the previous July, and it is striking that five out of the seven Munster
towns listed as returning delegates to the convention were located in County Tipperary (although their delegates were Dublin residents).[9] Limerick city (unlike
Cork, Waterford, Ennis or Tralee) sent up their own group of delegates, independent of those representing County Limerick.[10]

Against such a backdrop it is perhaps surprising that radical political activity
got off the ground in Munster at all. About fifteen Munster men joined the
Dublin Society of United Irishmen, seven of them with Cork connections.

8 There were 23 convention delegates with Munster addresses, plus 17 with Dublin addresses representing Munster counties or towns: *List of the delegates who attended the Catholic Convention in
Tailor's Hall, Dublin ...* Dec. 1792 (Dublin, n.d); Thomas Bartlett, *The fall and rise of the Irish
nation: The Catholic question, 1690–1830* (Dublin, 1992), p. 131; T.W. Moody, R.B. McDowell,
and C.J. Woods (eds), *The writings of Theobald Wolfe Tone, 1763–1798*, i (Oxford, 1998), pp 325,
347. For Samuel Neilson's criticisms of the conservative posture of leading Catholics in the
southern towns, see ibid., p. 342.

9 Power, *Tipperary*, p. 293. The Tipperary towns represented were Carrick, Clonmel, Cashel,
Thurles, and Roscrea. The only other Munster towns to nominate delegates were Limerick and
Dungarvan: *List of the delegates . . . Dec. 1792* ; Jim Smyth, *The men of no property: Irish radicals
and popular politics in the late eighteenth century* (London, 1992), p. 65.

10 The leading Limerick delegate was the wealthy merchant Francis Arthur; he had chaired a
Catholic meeting in the city in October at which a strongly worded statement written by Wolfe
Tone was passed: Moody et al., *Tone*, pp 296–7. Cf. the Cork Catholic resolution: *Cork Evening
Post*, 18 Oct. 1792.

Apart from the Sheares brothers, all the known Cork members were Catholic, as were a majority of the other Munstermen who joined.[11] But there was no constitutional United Irish society established in any of the Munster cities before the war; in 1793 there may briefly have been a club in Limerick city and a furtive one in Cork city, but only in County Tipperary was there visible radical activity. In the north of that county a society was established in Nenagh and a sympathetic newspaper was printed at Roscrea, the *Southern Star*. In Clonmel, a United Irish society was quite active in 1792: indeed as a very prosperous borough with parliamentary representation monopolized by the less than inspiring Moore family, the town was perhaps the only promising radical seed-bed anywhere in the south.[12]

With the coming of the war and of Catholic relief early in 1793, the political atmosphere in the province became markedly more unsettled. Soon there were reports of an ill-defined agitation inflaming popular attitudes towards church and state and focusing attention on the issue of militia recruitment. This was not peculiar to Munster; public reaction to the raising of a militia varied greatly from county to county with no discernible regional pattern. However, the official response was marked by an uncharacteristic willingness to spill blood.[13] In Munster in the course of June and July 1793 there were two very violent eruptions of protest, both far from the centres of political life and debate – one in the remote port of Dingle, the other centred on rural south-east Limerick. In the Kerry incident military intervention culminated in about fourteen civilian deaths; in the second, up to thirty civilians were killed.[14]

The Dingle disturbances began at the end of May as news spread of the balloting system to be used for the random selection of recruits; crowds took over the town and ransacked houses on several occasions in early and mid-June, despite the arrival of regular troops from Limerick and Kinsale. A more careful-

11 Known Munster-connected members of the Dublin society were Harman Blennerhasset, Co. Kerry, barrister (admitted Jan. 1793); Edward Burke esq., Limerick (Feb. 1792); Richard Burke, Cork, merchant (Nov. 1792); David Foley, apothecary, Youghal (Feb. 1792); George Lidwell, [Co. Tipperary] (Dec. 1792); —Lew, Clonmel (Dec. 1792); Dr Moriarty, Tralee (Feb. 1792); James O'Gorman esq., Ennis (Dec. 1792); John O'Donnell esq., Cork (Feb. 1792); John Roche, Youghal, merchant (Mar. 1793); Laurence Smyth, Carrick, merchant (Dec. 1792), Jeremiah Sullivan, Cork, paper manufacturer (Feb. 1792); Henry and John Sheares, Cork and Dublin, barristers [1793]; Bryan Sheehy esq., Cork (Feb. 1792): based on R.B. McDowell, 'The personnel of the Dublin Society of United Irishmen, 1791–94', in *I.H.S.*, ii (1940–1), 20–53.

12 Confession of Timothy Conway, 13 Apr. 1799: P.R.O., PC 1/44/155; Johnson, 'House of Commons, 1791'; J.C.Hayes, 'Guide to Tipperary newspapers', *Tipperary Hist. Jnl.* (1989), 9–10; Power, *Tipperary*, pp 292–4, 304; R.B. McDowell, *Ireland in the age of imperialism and revolution, 1760–1801* (Oxford, 1979), p. 389.

13 Thomas Bartlett, 'An end to moral economy: The Irish militia disturbances of 1793', in C.H.E. Philpin (ed.), *Nationalism and popular protest in Ireland* (Cambridge, 1987), pp 191–218.

14 Edward Cooke to — , 27 June 1793: P.R.O., HO/100/44, f.184; *F.D.J.*, 20, 27 July 1793; Bartlett, 'Moral economy', pp 206–7.

ly organized protest involving thousands of country people took place on 24 June, intent, it would seem, on overpowering the still modest garrison. The results were a blood-bath. Reports reaching Dublin spoke of the role of 'diabolical incendiaries' who had been 'lurking among the people', and one local witness claimed that 'the common people of this country, this barony [Corkaguiney] particularly, have been most deluded by [and] possessed with an idea that liberty and equality should govern in future ... some of those dying claimed to expect foreign aid ...'[15] Other reports emphasized the reactive nature of the protest – against militias, tithes, taxes, and the level of rent. Sir Richard Musgrave was later to claim that 'this plot was general in the county of Kerry'.[16] What seems more plausible is that there was a general reaction in a previously under-administered county to the enthusiastic efforts of the earl of Glandore, the newly appointed colonel commander of the Kerry militia, to rush through its embodiment. Why Dingle was particularly disturbed remains unclear, but the fact that the only two Kerry delegates to travel to the Catholic Convention in Dublin six months previously had come from Dingle may be more than a coincidence.[17]

The origin of the troubles in Limerick during July 1793 seems to have been an agrarian agitation along the fringes of the Galtees, modelled on the Rightboy movement of the mid-1780s but now taking on new issues. As an oath-bound parish-to-parish movement seeking to enforce communal discipline in the payment of tithe it was nothing new; in seeking to extend this to control the bidding for land out of lease it had strong Rightboy precedents; but by linking these to resistance to the militia it assumed a more urgent and violent character. The arrest and detention in Kilfinnane jail of some of the organizers led to a spectacular rescue attempt with disastrous results: most of the village was set ablaze at the cost of five lives. As the prisoners were being escorted north to the county jail in Limerick, another rescue was attempted in the town of Bruff. The ambush was a disaster; there were probably about two dozen local fatalities, an outcome that sent shock waves across central Munster.[18] Again there were stories of external influence; it was reported that prior to the ambush 'a person dressed

---

15 *Freeman's Jnl.*, 22 June 1793; Bartlett, 'Moral economy', p. 206. For rumours of northern migrants in Dingle (which had a thriving coarse linen industry): Nancy Curtin, 'The origins of Irish republicanism: The United Irishmen in Dublin and Ulster 1791–98' (unpublished Ph.D. thesis, University of Wisconsin, 1988), p. 405.

16 *F.D.J.*, 8, 22, 29 June, 2, 13, 16 July 1793; *Freeman's Jnl.*, 20, 22 June 1793; Sir Richard Musgrave, *Memoirs of the different rebellions in Ireland* ... (4th ed., Fort Wayne, Indiana, 1996), p. 624; Bartlett, 'Moral economy', pp 206–7.

17 They were Thomas Hussey and Mathew Moriarty. The even more remote district of Erris, County Mayo witnessed an anti-militia riot in July which was at least as violent, and this suggests that in such 'frontier' communities the embodiment of the militia may have been represented in a particularly sinister and unwelcome light (Bartlett, 'Moral economy', p. 209). For Edward Cooke's suspicions as to the links between the Catholic Committee and the anti-militia agitation, see Sir Henry McAnally, *The Irish militia, 1793–1816* (Dublin, 1949), pp 36–7.

18 *F.D.J.*, 20, 27 July 1793.

as a gentleman, in a phaeton, drove through Bruff, and dispersed a number of printed papers in that neighbourhood, the purpose of which was not to pay any taxes whatever'.[19] Limerick's citizenry were reportedly in panic after the battle of Bruff in the belief that 'the Defenders in multitudes would attack them'.[20] However it is very doubtful if those involved at that stage would have described themselves as 'Defenders'. Yet the tag came to be used repeatedly in Limerick, Tipperary and north Cork over the next few years by both magistrates and newspapers seeking to describe rural collective action of any kind. Full-blown Defenderism hardly touched the province, but in time all parties colluded in the use of the term.[21]

The next wave of agrarian disturbance in Munster came in south-west Cork. In this densely settled farming district the Rightboy movement had been vigorous and successful in the previous decade; there had for example been a mass storming of Skibbereen jail in July 1786 – although with none of the disastrous consequences of the Dingle or Kilfinnane attacks.[22] In the summer of 1793 there was the threat of militia trouble in the upper Bandon valley, but the sudden appearance in February 1794 of a huge parish-based organization directed against tithe, tax and rent took the authorities by surprise. Threats of violence, even the clash between 1,500 stone-throwers and the militia at Nohaval near Kinsale which left eleven dead, would have made this agitation unexceptional but for the fact that it was the first rural movement in the province that was unambiguously political in inspiration.[23] The proximity of Bandon, 'a second Belfast', was possibly a factor in this. In the early nineties the great textile town – for all its hard old Protestant reputation – had had a radical moment. How deep-rooted this was and how far it affected its immediate hinterland remain unclear.[24] Religious dissent was weak in the town (if one excepts the embryonic congregations of Methodists), so a vital political ingredient was missing. And at least some of Bandon's radical noises were being manufactured by radically minded local gentry, notably Sampson Stawell and Arthur O'Connor's brother Roger. When in the hungry autumn of 1792 some thousands of townspeople attacked Stawell's grain-stores at Kilbrittain (as well as looting several other stores and

19 *F.D.J.*, 20 July 1793. See also Anne Kavanaugh, *John Fitzgibbon, earl of Clare* (Dublin, 1997), p. 285.

20 John Straton, Rathkeale, to Revd P. Jocelyn, 21 July 1793: P.R.O.N.I., Roden papers, vol. 18, MIC 147/9; *Cork Evening Post*, 18 July; 1, 5 Aug. 1793; *F.D.J.*, 18, 20, 23, 27 July; 3, 6 Aug. 1793; Bartlett, 'Moral economy', p. 207.

21 Smyth, *Men of no property*, p. 104.

22 Donnelly, 'Rightboy movement', 200; Diary of Robert Day, 1794: R.I.A., MS 12.W.14, pp 26–8.

23 Day diary 1794, pp 1–2, 7, 19; *F.D.J.*, 15 Mar. 1794.

24 Memorandum- and account-book of H.H. Farmar, 1795–1811: MS in private possession; Musgrave, *Rebellions*, p. 871. For a printed hand-bill of west Cork provenance, written probably late in 1793 by a gentleman radical, see *The address of the poor people of Munster, to their fellows in Ireland, with their bill of grievances annexed*: Hampshire R.O., 21MS7/A33/11.

mills in the district), conservatives smiled at the disaster: 'the first fruits of his favourite doctrine of equality'. But Musgrave claimed that what had started out as a multi-denominational food-riot split along sectarian lines before it had run its course.[25]

Whatever the role of Bandon, all commentators agreed that the 1794 move-ment-without-a-name which had manifested itself across parishes up to forty miles apart was heavily coloured by the new politics. The United Irish move-ment in Dublin, 'that horde of vipers', was quickly blamed; the local oath of association was reported to seek 'to put into execution certain resolutions, to be drawn up hereafter, by the Society of United Irishmen; to pay no tithes, or taxes, and to assess at their own pleasure what rent to pay'.[26] The Kerry barrister Robert Day was sent by the government to investigate the disturbances, and he was in no doubt that the printing presses of Cork city had also played their part: Denis Driscol's *Cork Gazette*, established in 1790, had become strongly French in its sympathies in the course of 1792, and Day claimed that in west Cork, 'Driscol's journal circulates all the sedition of the United Irishmen . . . His sedi-tious trash lighting on the sparks of insurrection which sometimes sleep but never die in the Co[unt]y C[ork] explains the unprecedented flame which has blazed out here.' Roger O'Connor, local magistrate and radical sympathiser, claimed that chapel-yard readings of the newspapers during the previous winter, particularly of 'the French debates', had turned the population of two remote west Cork parishes into 'politicians'; '[they] talked of liberty and equality [and] appointed a day to plant *the tree of liberty*'. The *Cork Gazette*'s social radicalism had indeed become noticeably more explicit in January 1794.[27]

Within six weeks the Cork flame was quenched by the actions of novice mili-tiamen from Carlow and Tipperary, at the cost of about twenty lives. The pro-testors had lacked arms, leaders, or any evident strategy, indeed had displayed an almost millenarian passivity.[28] Harsh army tactics and buoyant markets brought

25 Robert Hobart, Dublin Castle, to Evan Nepean, 5 Dec. 1792: N.A.I., OP 30/3/29; Richard Martin, Midleton, to Revd Charles Broderick, 24 Nov. 1792: N.L.I., Midleton papers, MS 8862/6; *Hibernian Chronicle*, 22 Nov. 1792; Musgrave, *Rebellions*, p. 870. Stawell, when ordering 23 firelocks with bayonets to fortify his premises, ruefully informed his brother in Dublin that 'the late attack was not marked against me as a friend to R.C. enfranchisement', and that indeed 'equality was a word used by them that is the mob in the town': Stawell, Kilbrittain to E. Stawell, 9 Dec. 1792, N.A.I., M 6954. For evidence of Bandon United Irish sympathies later in the decade, see J. Sheridan to James Crawford [21 Apr. 1795]: T.C.D. MS Dept., MIC 53/8.

26 Day diary 1794, p. 19; *F.D.J.*, 25 Feb. 1794; Statement of the Bandon town meeting, 8 Mar. 1794: *F.D.J.*, 15 Mar. 1794; Smyth, *Men of no property*, pp 110–11. Robert Connor later named Sir John Freke as one of those who had been behind the introduction of 'revolutionary princi-ples' to the district in 1794: Connor, Fort Robert, to Thomas Pelham, 31 May 1797: N.A.I., RP 620/30/265.

27 Day diary 1794, pp 7, 22–3, 32–3; Kevin Whelan, *The tree of liberty: Radicalism, Catholicism and the construction of Irish identity, 1760–1830*, p. 83; Durie, *Transatlantic radicals*, pp 113–4.

28 For John Foster's minimalist view of the Cork disturbances, see Foster to Lord Sheffield, 29

back a brittle peace to the countryside by April of that year. This peace was to last for some three years. In the next wave of rural agitation in those districts, times would be economically much harsher but firearms and pikes more plentiful. In the wake of the west Cork disturbances of spring 1794, Driscol was tried at Cork assizes for treasonable libel and sentenced to two years in jail.[29] The *Cork Gazette* however continued to appear, and its presses supplied local editions of Paine's *Agrarian justice* and other revolutionary texts which were 'sent over the country'. Noting this, Leonard McNally claimed that in the wake of Fitzwilliam's recall to London in 1795 'royalty has very few advocates in Cork, but on the contrary is traduced publicly both in songs and conversation by all the middling and trading classes'. A radical coterie continued to build on Driscol's efforts, notably the peripatetic Sheares brothers; however McNally's estimate that there were 500 members in a Cork city United Irish club in May 1795 seems implausibly high.[30] Some indication of more modest support among city freemen came at a city parliamentary by-election in November that year. Henry Sheares challenged the son of a leading merchant and was abused for supporting 'popery, sedition . . . [and] democracy'; he got a total of eighteen votes against his opponent's 306.[31] The assessment of Government by that stage was that United Irish enthusiasm in Cork city though still formidable was in decline; the continuance of the ever eccentric *Gazette* was probably seen as little threat.[32]

CONSPIRACIES AND CONTAGION 1796–7

Arthur O'Connor, MP and former high sheriff of County Cork, went on his European travels with Lord Edward FitzGerald in the summer of 1796. In managing to meet and negotiate with General Hoche at Angers in August, he secured what seems to have been the first promise of substantial French military intervention in Ireland.[33] At that moment there was little or no revolutionary capacity in O'Connor's own backyard, Ulster being far more obviously in a state of organized expectation. But Munster as a possible point of entry was always attractive to the French for naval and logistical reasons, and Cork city with its massive provisions

Mar. 1794, in [A.P.W. Malcomson, ed.], *An Anglo-Irish dialogue: A calendar of the correspondence between John Foster and Lord Sheffield, 1774–1821* (Belfast, 1975), p. 13.

29 His counsel were the Sheares brothers and T.A. Emmet: Durie, *Transatlantic radicals*, p. 114.

30 'JW', Cork to — , 13 Apr. 1795: N.A.I., OP 144/10; J. Sheridan to James Crawford [21 Apr. 1795]: T.C.D. MS Dept., MIC 53/8.

31 *C.E.P.*, 26 Nov. 1795 ; Hewitt, *Shannon letters*, p. lxx.

32 Tony Gaynor, 'The politics of law and order in Ireland 1794–98' (unpublished Ph.D. dissertation, University of Dublin, 1999), p. 182; Brian Inglis, *The freedom of the press in Ireland, 1784–1841* (London, 1954), pp 88–9. However cf. Thomas Garde, Ballinacurra, to John Heaton, 12 Sept. 1795: P.R.O.N.I., Devonshire papers, T.3158.

33 Elliott, *Partners*, pp 100–3; Paul Weber, *On the road to rebellion: The United Irishmen and Hamburg, 1796–1803* (Dublin, 1997), pp 50–1.

trade was a particularly appetizing prospect in French eyes. O'Connor returned to Ireland with Lord Edward in October, confident of an imminent French armada, and he included a visit to Cork in November in order to encourage the creation of a United Irish command structure that would be place should the French come.[34] Some assessments that autumn, including the report of Duckett, the French agent, suggested a high level of popular alienation in the southern countryside but the only new preparations on the ground seem to have been the establishment, at O'Connor's behest, of a self-appointed Cork city 'directory', initially of nine and then of five men. What this group sought to achieve in the weeks before the Brest expedition's departure is unknown.[35] There is strong evidence that those in O'Connor's confidence, including his brother Roger, were not too surprised by the dramatic Christmas news from Bantry Bay.[36] But even if storms and bad leadership had not wrecked the invasion plan and the French had landed, it is doubtful if local rural support would have presented itself in any more coherent a fashion than was to be the case in County Mayo in August 1798.

The months leading up to the coming of the French had seen the establishment across the country of the yeomanry, and the ten-day crisis at the end of the year gave some of the new corps their moment of glory. 124 yeomanry corps were eventually embodied in the six Munster counties by 1798; one of those in west Cork and two of the eight in Kerry were raised by Catholic gentry, and a scattering of other corps (including one in Limerick city and one in Cork city) had strong Catholic participation.[37] But the general pattern in Munster as elsewhere was of a frightened and deeply conservative Protestant gentry allowing or actually encouraging 'their yeomanry' to display partisan symbols that were offensive to their Catholic neighbours and tenants. The deportment of some yeomanry corps in County Cork certainly contributed not a little to the coarsening sectarian atmosphere evident during 1797.[38]

Signs of a more vigorous oath-bound United Irish movement in the province, cellular, hierarchical and disciplined, were only apparent from the spring of that

34 Elliott, *Partners*, p. 108; Weber, Hamburg, pp 53–4. Apart from his brother Roger O'Connor, a key local figure at that stage was Edmund O'Finn, a minor Catholic merchant in the city.

35 'H', Cork, to Edward Cooke, 29 Oct. 1796: N.A.I., RP 620/25/199; Conway's confession, 1799; Elliott, *Partners*, p. 115. Col. Massey's unidentified informant of Apr. 1797 implied a later date for the setting up of the Cork Directory; he was reported as saying that 'something in the nature of a directory was to be here established' and offered some of the names: Examination of Col. Massey: N.A.I., SOC 1016/8.

36 Rickard Deasy, St Helier's, Jersey, to Rickard Deasy, 20 Nov. 1845 and after: Cork Archives Institute U42, p.15. For oral tradition of men-in-the-know before the event, see Gearoid O Crualaoich, 'The French are on the say', in Murphy, *French are in the bay*, pp 131–7.

37 Deasy to Deasy, 20 Nov. 1845, p. 11; *A list of the counties of Ireland and the respective yeomanry corps in each county ... on the 1st June 1798* (Dublin, 1798); Musgrave, *Rebellions*, p.654; W.J. Hayes, *Tipperary in the year of the rebellion, 1798* (Roscrea, 1998), p. 13; Allan Blackstock, *An ascendancy army: The Irish yeomanry, 1796–1834* (Dublin, 1998), pp 71, 132–4.

38 Deasy to Deasy, 20 Nov. 1845, pp 15–18.

year, a time of gathering economic difficulty. One of the earliest areas from which
new activity was reported to Dublin Castle was the former epicentre of disturbance in 1794 – Roger O'Connor's district west of Bandon. One 1797 report spoke
of Roger as prospective 'general of Munster'; another asserted that if O'Connor
was placed under arrest 'this part of the country would be completely quiet'.[39]
Perhaps more significantly, there was clear evidence in the course of April and
May 1797 that the United men in Cork city were completely re-organizing, setting
up a series of societies (eventually three for the city) and allowing credible local
leaders to emerge; Youghal was also reporting activity. This cannot have been
Arthur O'Connor's direct doing (he was then in prison in Dublin), and there were
reports of northern and Dublin radicals active both in Cork and elsewhere in the
south around that time, notably William Putnam McCabe, Richard Dry, William
Byrne and Murtagh McCanwell; the Sheares brothers were also involved in
strengthening Cork/Dublin links at this time.[40] Roger O'Connor remained the
leading revolutionary figure resident in Cork, but he was self-evidently unsuited
for the part, both temperamentally and socially. Furthermore from the spring of
1797 he enjoyed barely three months at liberty over the next five years: he fled to
England in April, returned in June and was almost continuously in detention in
Cork and Dublin from September, ending up as a state prisoner next year.[41] Rather
it was John Swiney, a successful Catholic woollen draper, who seems to have
emerged early in 1797 to run the Cork city conspiracy and it was through him that
correspondence with Dublin, specifically with fellow woollen draper Oliver Bond,
was maintained. Swiney was to remain in the confidence of Bond and the two
O'Connors but, clever, buccaneering and at times reckless, he was always regarded
as his own man.[42] Behind him, two barristers, three medical doctors, a distiller, a
baker, a cooper, a timber merchant, a watchmaker and Sampson Stawell's cousin,
the Revd William Stawell, formed the shadowy inner group of Cork city activists.[43]

39 'Private information to Mr Beamish', *c.* 11 Apr. 1797; Lord Bantry, Cork, to — , 12 Apr. 1797;
   General Dalrymple to Thomas Pelham, 13 Apr. 1797; — , Cork, to Major Cairncross, 14 Apr.
   1797; General Coote, Bandon camp, to Pelham, 9 June [1797]: N.A.I. RP 620/29/221;
   620/29/230; 620/29/235; 620/29/277; 620/31/60; Musgrave, *Rebellions*, p. 153.
40 — , Cork, to Major Cairncross, 14 Apr. 1797; 'Information of Charles Callanan', 26 May 1797:
   N.A.I., RP 620/29/277; 620/30/196; General Dalrymple, Cork, to Major General Hewitt, 8
   May [1797]: P.R.O.N.I., McPeake papers, D.272/34C; Roger Wells, *Insurrection: The British experience, 1795–1803* (Gloucester, 1983), p. 115; Smyth, *Men of no property*, p. 158; Ruan O'Donnell,
   'Limerick in 1798' (unpublished typescript), p. 7; O'Donnell, *1798 diary* (Dublin, 1998), p. 27.
41 R.R. Madden, *The United Irishmen: Their lives and times* (2nd ser., 2nd ed., Dublin, 1858), pp
   591–97. He was briefly at liberty in Apr. 1798 when he travelled over to London.
42 Deasy to Deasy, 20 Nov. 1845, pp 19, 23–4, 34–5. It is significant that Arthur O'Connor made
   John Swiney trustee of his Irish affairs when leaving for France in February 1798: Elliott,
   Partners, p. 181; Durey, *Transatlantic radicals*, p. 135. Edmund O'Finn may have preceded
   Swiney as a principal Cork city organizer before he fled to London in or around January 1797:
   Weber, *Hamburg*, pp 53, 94.
43 Counsellors Joseph Dennis and William Webb were the barristers; Drs Bullen, Sugrue and

The regeneration of southern radical activity therefore owed much to outside stimuli. And while it might seem that Cork was a natural centre for a province-wide strategy, there is no evidence that a leading role for Cork was envisaged, either at the time when a Leinster provincial committee was being established in the autumn of 1796, or during the following year. Developments in north Munster were never seen as dependent on or subordinate to a notional provincial leadership in Cork; certainly nothing of that nature emerged. If indeed there was a strategic plan for the south in the early summer of 1797, it was to suborn the militia, present in such vast numbers in the Cork area. There were several conspiracies discovered within the Enniskeane camp west of Bandon; the most serious, supposedly involving over 200 men and involving local citizens as well as militia men, was scheduled for 2 July with the aim of capturing Bandon and then awaiting the coming of the French. The plan was rumbled, and in September four militiamen were executed in the Sheares' home-town of Inishannon; thousands of militia were required to witness the event near the public house where a United cell set up by Roger O'Connor had recently been broken up.[44]

Despite such displays of official terror, oath-taking on a large scale continued through the late summer and autumn of 1797, both by country people visiting Cork city and by folk recruited by city activists at fairs, markets and village taverns. In October General Loftus, noting the recent comings and goings of Arthur O'Connor and the Sheares, told Pelham that meetings in County Cork were 'now conducted upon the plan of the county committee of Dublin city, of 27 August last'.[45] The particular district troubling Loftus at that stage was the wealthy barony of Imokilly in south-east Cork. Throughout the autumn reports of oath-taking, secret parish committees, and Rightboy-style intimidation were coming from east Cork and west Waterford. By early November, according to the Earl of Shannon, 'few if any of the lower orders ... have not taken the United Irish oath ... the whole country is united in one league and devoted to the mandates of committees which, I understand, sit at Cork and the different bar-

Barry the medics; Robert [?] Simmons the distiller; Simon Donovan the baker (and flour factor); Thomas Gunnell the cooper; Thomas Perrott the timber merchant; Timothy Conway the goldsmith: Robert Harding, Cork, to Edward Cooke, 7 Mar. 1799: N.A.I., RP 620/52/137; Conway's confession, 1799; notebook on Munster atrocities, 1798: P.R.O.N.I., D.2085/5, pp 48–9; Deasy to Deasy, 20 Nov. 1845, pp 34, 39; Seán Ó Coindealbháin, 'The United Irishmen in County Cork [I]', in *Jnl. of the Cork Arch. Hist. Society*, 2nd ser., liii (1948), 126–8.
44 General Coote, Bandon, to [Thomas Pelham], 23, 24, 25 June 1797: B.L. Add. MS 33,104, ff. 252–7, 275, 297–9; Ó Coindealbháin, 'United Irishmen in Cork [I]', 121; 'United Irishmen in Cork – II', in *J.C.H.A.S.*, liv (1949), 72–81; 'United Irishmen in Cork – V', in *J.C.H.A.S.*, lvi (1951), 19–21; Tom Bogue, 'Cork in 1798', in Tim Crowley and Traolach Ó Donnabháin (eds), *The battle of the Big Cross* (Clonakilty, 1998), pp 5–6.
45 Major General William Loftus, Cork, to Thomas Pelham, 26 Oct. 1797: N.A.I. RP 620/32/85. For the significance of the 27 August changes, see Thomas Graham, ' "An union of power ?": The United Irish organization 1795–98', in David Dickson, Dáire Keogh and Kevin Whelan (eds), *The United Irishmen: Republicanism, radicalism, and rebellion* (Dublin, 1993), pp 248–9.

onies'.[46] The newly constituted parish committees, particularly in the lower Blackwater and Bride valleys, chose to demonstrate their strength in a massive wave of agrarian incidents, nearly all of which related to matters of tithe or farm tenancy, and there were several assassinations, mostly of persons believed to be passing on intelligence. In early December the baronies of west Waterford and east Cork became the first parts of Munster to be proclaimed under the Insurrection Act; army reinforcements had already been deployed there.[47]

Imokilly, the district closest to Cork and Lord Shannon's base, was canvassed by Swiney. Some evidence of the very high quality of his political propaganda survives – attacking the war, holding out the prospect of social amelioration to the very poor, and inclusive in its tone.[48] But local opponents there and further east detected a strongly anti-Protestant dimension to the new movement; indeed its almost Defenderist ethos in west Waterford raises the suspicion as to whether this was a United Irish movement at all. Timothy Conway, a member of the Cork Directory, tantalizingly observed in his 1799 confession that 'though the spirit of insurrection was as forward in the south as in any other part of the country, yet the difficulty of [United Irish] organization was much greater from the strong bias among the lower orders of the people in favour of Defenderism'.[49] There is certainly no evidence of a Waterford county structure emerging analogous to that in Cork city.

Apart from United Irish emissaries working out from Cork or Youghal, there were at least two other lines of political influence permeating such a region: through social intercourse with disaffected militia stationed locally; and via commercial contacts with the world outside. The Meath militia, for many months during 1797 based in east Cork, were for some a plausible source of contagion, although only a handful of cases were actually proven.[50] What no one

46 Earl of Shannon, Castlemartyr to — , 9 Nov. 1797, cited in Ó Coindealbháin, 'United Irishmen in Cork [I]', 122.

47 Thomas Knowlton, Lismore, to John Heaton, 13 Sept., 4 Oct. 1797: P.R.O.N.I., Devonshire papers, T.3158; *C.E.P.*, 5 Oct. 1797; Musgrave, *Rebellions*, pp 644, 648–9; P.M. O'Neill, *The Barrow uncrossed* (Dublin, 1998), pp 27–38. Musgrave claimed that the organization of Co. Waterford began in July and was completed by September, but this is questionable: N.L.I. Musgrave papers, MS 4,156, p. 151. On the controversy over assassination committees, see Nancy Curtin, *The United Irishmen: Popular politics in Ulster and Dublin, 1791–1798* (Oxford, 1994), p. 82.

48 See the MS hand-bill taken down from Cloyne market-house and enclosed with Lord Longueville to Charles Kippax, 16 Oct. 1797; also John Shaw, Cork, to J.S. Townsend, Dublin, 26 Dec. 1803: N.A.I., SOC 1016/15; RP 620/11/130/630.

49 Conway's confession, 1799. A local magistrate reported that the movement in Cappoquin called itself 'the Formia Brothers' at the time when an oath of loyalty to the French Convention was reportedly circulating there: Major J. Keane, Cappoquin, to [John] Beresford, 4 Nov. 1797: N.A.I., RP 620/28/130. For explicit reference to the taking of an oath to the Defenders at Ballymacoda (in Imokilly) in Oct. 1797, see O'Neill, *Barrow uncrossed*, p. 33.

50 General Dalrymple, Cork to Thomas Pelham, 17 Apr. 1797: N.A.I., SOC 1016/8; Musgrave, *Rebellions*, p. 660; O'Neill, op. cit., pp 26–7, 32–4.

commented on was the possibility of political contagion via the long-established and powerful coastal grain and potato trades operating between Youghal, Dungarvan and Dublin, yet this seems very plausible. The severe fall in grain prices in 1797 intensified pre-existing rural grievances in relation to tithe; it would seem that a 'traditional' Rightboyist protest widened to become an essentially political combination in which French-style oaths, the theft of firearms, and a rich menu of projects to attack the wealthy formed the main business.[51] The most spectacular plan was a proposal, put forward at a meeting of 'seven or eight hundred' in a field outside Dungarvan in mid-November, to capture cannon from a privateer in the harbour and to take them across country in order to level the Beresfords' great house at Curraghmore.[52] By the turn of the year support had spread eastwards into the barony of Upperthird, leading to some sixty arrests in early January of men accused of tendering oaths around Kilmacthomas and Carrickbeg.[53]

The districts involved in this autumn/winter flare-up were primarily tillage ones, badly affected by the turbulent market conditions for barley, potatoes and oats. But elsewhere across the province, wheat farmers, notably in Tipperary, east Limerick and north Cork, were hit by the cancellation of the parliamentary subsidy on the carriage of grain and flour to Dublin. And smallholders generally were experiencing the first of five very difficult years in 1797: county rates were escalating, new war taxes (notably on salt) were affecting every household, and employment in many sectors was being hit by the commercial crisis of the previous spring; even milk prices were reaching unprecedented levels.[54] The commercial textile manufacture in Munster was also in cyclical recession that year, causing distress among the weaving fraternities of Bandon, Carrick-on-Suir, Limerick and on Cork city's north side. The woollen manufacture was particularly hard hit.[55] Even in good times the woollen trade was an important channel for radical politicization between Dublin and the Munster towns; now in crisis it was doubly so.

51 Thomas Knowlton, Lismore, to John Heaton, 4 Oct. 1797: P.R.O.N.I., Devonshire papers, T.3158; *C.E.P.*, 5 Oct. 1797; Musgrave, *Rebellions*, pp 645–9.
52 Musgrave, op. cit., pp 646–9. There was also talk of using the captured artillery to see off other county gentry in Waterford.
53 O'Donnell, *1798 diary*, pp 4–5.
54 Lord Donoughmore, Cork, to Thomas Pelham, 26 Feb. 1797; Cloyne hand-bill, 16 Oct. 1797; Hand-bill from Glanmire, *c.*12 Mar. 1798: N.A.I., RP 620/28/302; SOC 1016/15; RP 620/36/14; David Dickson, 'Taxation and disaffection in late eighteenth-century Ireland', in Samuel Clark and J.S.Donnelly, Jnr. (eds), *Irish peasants: Violence and political unrest, 1780–1914* (Manchester, 1983), pp 47–52, 56–8; Power, *Tipperary*, pp 309–10.
55 General Dalrymple, Cork, to Thomas Pelham, 22 Apr. 1797, quoted in Wells, *Insurrection*, p.115; Richard Lloyd, Bandon, to Thomas Knowlton, 8 Aug. 1798: P.R.O.N.I., Devonshire papers, T3158; Shannon papers, D2707/A2/2/162A; David Dickson, 'An economic history of the Cork region in the eighteenth century' (unpublished Ph.D. dissertation, University of Dublin, 1977), p. 569.

Troubled times gave powerful arguments to the United Irishmen, and for some folk desperate circumstances may have hastened the drift into revolutionary activity. Yet economic adversity cannot be the primary factor explaining the rapid success of United Irish recruitment in parts of south Munster during 1797 or, further north, in the early months of 1798. Religious fears and animosities seem to have been an even more potent catalyst of political action. The presence now of Catholic freeholders on the voting register, first felt in the 1797 general election in the city contests in Limerick and Cork, raised the sectarian temperature. Neither Orange nor Defender lodges were then active in the region, but Orange symbols and, more ominously, rumours about the doings of Orangemen in the North were widely circulating in 1797. The partiality and loose discipline of some of the local yeomanry and their adoption of Orange markings only served to make the propagandists' work easier. Fear of Orangemen, it is clear, became the most powerful weapon for popular political mobilization in the south, a point that Swiney was later to emphasize.[56] Driscol's *Gazette* was closed down in September, and the Dublin-produced propaganda then in circulation, whether the unofficial *Union Star* or Arthur O'Connor's more literary *Press*, focused on the unsavoury excesses of the Government's Orange supporters.[57] Such stories, refracted in a Munster light, evoked old fears of an imminent communal bloodbath. The presence of Orange-tinted militia was certainly menacing to wealthier Catholics and tested their loyalty; for example, the 'band boys' of a company of the Westmeath Militia based in Clonakilty started an Orange association in the town in 1797; they were prosecuted unsuccessfully by their colonel for their activities, in the wake of which they became Protestant heroes but objects of disgust in the eyes of prominent local Catholics.[58]

1798

The Cork city United Irish organization seems to have gone from strength to strength in the early months of 1798. With Arthur O'Connor at odds with the Dublin leadership and away again on his travels, links between the capital and the Cork organization were loose but not non-existent.[59] A military structure was

56 General Dalrymple, Cork, to Pelham, 17 Apr. 1797; Information of Charles Callanan, 26 May 1797: N.A.I., SOC 1016/8; RP 620/30/196; Deasy to Deasy, 20 Nov. 1845, pp 15–17; Musgrave, *Rebellions*, pp 661–2; Ó Coindealbháin, 'United Irishmen in Cork – II', 77–8.
57 Deasy to Deasy, 20 Nov. 1845, pp 16, 19; Smyth, *Men of no property*, p. 163.
58 Deasy to Deasy, 20 Nov. 1845, pp 7–9; O Coindealbhain, 'United Irishmen in Cork – II', 78; Wells, *Insurrection*, pp 118, 120; O'Donnell, *1798 diary*, p. 28. For a concocted Orange oath circulating around Mallow in early May 1798: National Library of Scotland, MS 5750, f.133v. (I am grateful to Dr James Kelly for drawing this document to my attention.)
59 Deasy to Deasy, 'letter 5', 1845, p. 34. In this context, Benjamin Binns' recollection that Henry Jackson had sent him down to Cork in Feb. 1798 with an important message for the imprisoned Roger O'Connor is significant: T.C.D. Madden papers, MS 873/451/5.

as elsewhere attempted. Roger O'Connor continued to be actively involved from within Cork prison, while John Swiney on the outside was vigorously encouraging pike-making throughout east and west Cork.[60] On 7 March a new paper, the *Harp of Erin*, appeared on the streets of Cork, written largely by Roger O'Connor and reckless in its attacks on government. Little is known of its circulation but Musgrave claimed that it did 'infinite mischief in Munster'. It was suppressed after ten days by the Westmeath Militia.[61] At that time it would seem that the United Irish leadership in the city was quite hopeful that they were winning over segments of the military. The movement was believed to have many sympathizers in one of the two city yeomanry corps. Indeed a conspiracy within the Dublin County Militia garrisoned at Cork came to light in early March; Oliver Bond was told confidentially how much this had alarmed the local 'enemies of the human race'. Indeed his Cork correspondent (probably Swiney) spoke glowingly of local developments: 'give the people but a little time, and rest assured the progress science [*sic*] is making will astonish the world'.[62] In the event a show-piece execution of six Dublin militiamen was held on the Mardyke at the end of March; United handbills urging the militia to refuse to carry out the punishment on their fellow soldiers were circulated around the city and these coincided with plans for a city rising. How well-formed such plans were is not clear, but the upshot was the arrest of a young Protestant, Joseph Burniston; in a handbill he had denounced the government for declaring war on the people; he was later executed.[63] Burniston's arrest was followed by that of Swiney himself – on a charge of conspiring to assassinate the fiery city high sheriff, John Harding.

The detention of Swiney in 28 March, almost coinciding with the trial and unexpected discharge of Roger O'Connor (who promptly hurried over to see his brother, by then in prison in Kent), created something of a vacuum in Cork.[64] It was at this point that the Sheares brothers, whose connections with Cork had never been broken, took over – or were given – responsibility for city and county. There is no evidence that they actually came south in the following weeks, although John Sheares' concern to organize Cork was famously reported to the Castle by Captain Armstrong in mid-May on the eve of the latter's betrayal of

60 Deasy to Deasy, 20 Nov. 1845, pp 13, 14.
61 Robert Harding, Cork, to Edward Cooke, 7, 20 Mar. 1799: N.A.I., RP 620/52/137, /36/34; Deasy to Deasy, 20 Nov. 1845, 'letter 6', 1845, pp 36–7; T.C.D. Madden papers, MSS 873/248/20–21; 873/303 (indictment of John Daly); Musgrave, *Rebellions*, p. 170n.
62 Musgrave, *Rebellions*, p. 631. For a bullish late-February assessment by McNally of the Cork organization, see O'Donnell, *1798 diary*, p. 20.
63 T.C.D. Madden papers, MS 873/303 (indictment of Joseph Burniston); Deasy to Deasy, 'letter 2', 1845, pp 24–5; *Hib. Chron.*, 26 Mar. 1798; Musgrave, *Rebellions*, pp 654–5; Ó Coindealbháin, 'United Irishmen in Cork – II', 75, 79–80.
64 Bogue, 'Cork in 1798', pp 9–10. Wells has emphasized the importance of the 12 Mar. Dublin arrests on breaking Dublin-Munster communications, but this seems overstated; Swiney's arrest three weeks later was probably far more damaging: Wells, *Insurrection*, pp 129–30.

the Sheares. Swiney had no respect for the Sheares; thus, even though he remained in prison in Cork until after the rebellion, his strongly negative views of the Dublin-based Sheares must have made it extremely difficult for any of the Cork United Irish leaders to strengthen the county organization in the weeks leading up to 23 May.[65]

Despite such setbacks, the numbers sworn in County Cork during the twelve or so months before May 1798 were extremely large; Swiney was to claim that 16,000 in the city (including presumably the Liberties) had been sworn; for the whole county, he suggested a figure of 60,000 to 70,000. Such figures no doubt exaggerate. More telling were the returns of men organized: the only specific figure given for a Munster county in the January 1798 returns to Dublin Castle were of 1,100 men for County Cork; Swiney claimed that over 4,000 men had been 'organized', presumably in military discipline, by the time of his arrest in March; Daniel O'Keeffe in his affidavit after the rebellion implied that there had been around 3,000 in military command within the city; Conway stated there had been 131 splits, i.e. 1,441 'effective well-armed men, regularly sworn and organized' in the city.[66] However much such figures are cried down, one is left with the impression that in the first quarter of 1798, when there was both leadership and optimism among the Cork United Irishmen, the movement did indeed represent a formidable challenge. But by June 1798 they were not, in Castlereagh's words, 'quite so ripe'.[67]

The one Cork incident from early in the year that received national notice was the assassination of a minor landlord, Mansergh St George, in the remote valley of Araglin on the Cork–Tipperary border; this occurred on 9 February. Some accounts spoke of 'Defenders' being responsible and of their leader as being 'Captain Doe', but the city United Irishmen were well briefed about the affair.[68] St George had indeed acted with unusual vigour in his capacity as a mag-

65 Arthur O'Connor to R.R. Madden, 24 Sept. 1842: T.C.D. Madden papers, MS 873/742; Madden, *United Irishmen* (2nd ser., 2nd. ed., Dublin, 1858), p. 220; Ó Coindealbháin, 'United Irishmen in Cork – II', 78; Smyth, *Men of no property*, p. 158.

66 Conway's confession, 1799; Ó Coindealbháin, 'United Irishmen in Cork – II', 69–70, 78; O'Donnell, *1798 diary*, p. 9. In Mar. the boast had been that nine-tenths of the city were United men: Ó Coindealbháin, 'United Irishmen in Cork [I]', 123. Compare these figures with the estimates provided by Joseph Holt to government in Feb. 1799: 'there are 20,000 rebels organized at Cork and its neighbourhood': Charles Vane (ed.), *Memoirs and correspondence of Viscount Castlereagh* (London, 1848), ii, p. 186. According to Conway, Henry Sheares had had great trouble in securing an overall county return; for 'a very small part of the county' he had got figures of between 18,000 and 19,000 men, 'principally armed with pikes': Conway's confession, 1799.

67 'W' to Lady Londonderry, June 1798: Kent Archives Office, Camden papers, U840/563/13. Cf Elliott, *Partners*, p. 206, for a downbeat assessment of Cork developments. O'Keeffe's testimony about the Cork city organization being attempted, 'but so very badly attended ... it fell away' must presumably refer to the period after Swiney's arrest: Ó Coindealbháin, 'United Irishmen in Cork – II', 69.

68 Swiney and Donovan were expelled from the Loyal Cork Legion because of their refusal to be

istrate and had used the full measure of the law to threaten and to burn out suspected rebels; however the incident was murkier than it seemed as the political
loyalties of his host, Jasper Uniacke, who was also killed, were suspect. The
killings resonated around north Cork and Tipperary and seem to have clouded
the political judgment of Uniacke's notorious cousin, the Tipperary high sheriff
Thomas Judkin Fitzgerald.[69]

In Tipperary and north Munster generally, 1797 had passed off far more quietly than had been the case in Cork and west Waterford. There were rumours of
widespread oath-taking in the first half of the year around the old centres of
political radicalism in Tipperary, Nenagh and Clonmel, and there were reports
that autumn of United Irish 'suckers' reaching across the Shannon as far west as
Ennis.[70] Between January and May 1798, networks of parish committees were
created in parts of Clare, north Kerry, and across County Limerick.[71] In the
national breakdown of United Irish strength supplied in February 1798 by
Thomas Reynolds to the government, the province of Munster was credited
with a total United membership of 100,000, nearly two-fifths of the total: such a
huge rounded figure seems a little fanciful.[72] Apart from Cork, only in the case of
Tipperary is there clear evidence of the creation of a hierarchical United Irish
organization by early 1798. But assessing the level of activity in Tipperary has
always been complicated by the post-rebellion controversies surrounding Judkin
Fitzgerald's terrifying behaviour. His extreme methods of extracting confessions
during April and May 1798 became so discredited that his evidence and opinions
on all matters were totally discounted in liberal circles. However, the scale of the
Tipperary movement was probably rather closer to Fitzgerald's assessment than
has often been allowed.[73]

involved in the detention of what they claimed were innocent men. Burniston was implicated,
probably falsely, in authorizing the assassinations: Musgrave, *Rebellions*, p. 662.

69 Copy, Revd Z. Collis, Castle Cooke [Co. Cork], to 'dear Frank', 16 Feb. 1798: TCD MS 1749/1;
memoranda on Munster atrocities: P.R.O.N.I., D2085/5, p. 30; *Hib. Chron.*, 26 Feb. 1798;
Pakenham, *Year of liberty*, pp 34–5; Hayes, *Tipperary*, pp 91–2. For the case of a Tipperary
priest who had denounced the United Irishmen being threatened in early Mar. with 'the strict
laws of Arigling', see Hayes, *Tipperary*, pp 48–9.

70 'A farmer' to the Abp. of Cashel, 12 Dec. 1796: N.A.I., RP 620/26/119; Musgrave, *Rebellions*,
pp 641–2; Ignatius Murphy, *The diocese of Killaloe in the eighteenth century* (Dublin, 1991), p.
239; Power, *Tipperary*, pp 305–6; Hayes, *Tipperary 1798*, p. 17.

71 David Roche, Carass [Co. Limerick], to [Lord Carbery], 21 Dec. 1797; Edward FitzGerald,
Ballyneety, to Lord Carbery, 5 Feb. 1798: P.R.O.N.I. Carbery papers, T2966/C/3/40, /42;
Major General Sir James Duff, Limerick, to Major General Hewitt, 10 Mar. 1798: P.R.O.N.I.,
Dublin army letters, MIC 67, f.16; Wells, *Insurrection*, p. 115; J. Culhane, 'Traditions of Glin
and neighbourhood', in *Journal of the Kerry Arch. and Hist. Soc.*, ii (1969), 86–7; Power, *Tip-
perary*, p. 305; O'Donnell, 'Limerick', esp. pp 9–12.

72 Madden, *United Irishmen* (2nd ser., 2nd. ed., Dublin, 1858), p. 396. 60,000 was the figure supplied by Boyle to the Castle in January: O'Donnell, *1798 diary*, p. 9.

73 Cf. the low-key assessments of '98 by Tipperary historians Canon William Burke and Thomas
Power (Diarmuid O'Keeffe, '1798 in south Tipperary', in *Tipperary Historical Jnl.* (1990), 109;
Power, *Tipperary*, pp 303, 306), with that of Hayes, in *Tipperary*, passim.

Towards the end of 1797 the earl of Donoughmore, writing from his estate near Clonmel, had reported the influx of large numbers of armed Waterford men out of the Comeraghs and into a hitherto peaceful County Tipperary. It was however not until the following February that there seems to have a serious attempt by indigenous United Irish supporters to organize the county. Reports of large meetings around Templemore in mid-Tipperary, at which the men 'formed themselves into ranks, under officers and sergeants', began to filter out.[74] The landlord of Templemore, Sir John Carden, was complaining in early March of intimidatingly large numbers of armed men who 'march with music to cut down and take away trees'; his neighbour to the north, Cooke Otway, reported how 'thousands of Papists assemble ... under pretence of protecting themselves from Protestants or Orangemen, who they give out intend to murder them ...' What had started as nocturnal meetings in the Devil's Bit and Silvermines hills now spread far more widely; later in the month a thoroughly frightened Carden claimed that the county was 'now so bad that it should be declared in a state of *absolute rebellion*'.[75] Such a powerful and almost county-wide agitation was the result of a more than haphazard parish-to-parish process of osmosis. The government was convinced by late March 1798 that Tipperary was by then led by 'a general and inferior officers', and that 'their army are kept in the mountains ... they are extending themselves every night'.[76]

There was indeed a Tipperary general – Hervey Montmorency Morres, a young gentleman from the north of the county. Baptized a Catholic, he had married a German princess, seen military service in Austria, and briefly acted as an assistant to General Dundas. Associating with Lord Edward FitzGerald from 1796, he became a United Irishman that November. His active involvement in local conspiracy came late, possibly not until February 1798 when he was appointed, as he later put it, 'to the adjutant-generalship of Munster', but in effect in charge of Tipperary.[77] Morres narrowly missed being netted with the Leinster Directory at Oliver Bond's house on 12 March, and after that time he appears to have worked very closely with Lord Edward in reconstructing the military command of the Leinster United movement. Lord Edward himself was strongly rumoured to have come south about this time – to Tipperary, north Cork and Limerick, presumably in association with Morres.[78]

74 Musgrave, *Rebellions*, pp 669–70; O'Keeffe, 'South Tipperary', 111; Power, *Tipperary*, p. 311.
75 Sir John Carden, Templemore, to [General Duff], 7 Mar. 1798; Cooke Otway, Castle Otway to [General Duff], 11 Mar. 1798: P.R.O.N.I., Dublin army letters, MIC 67 ff.15, 17; Pakenham, *Year of liberty*, p. 56.
76 Thomas Judkin Fitzgerald to — , 28 Mar. 1798, quoted in ibid., p. 56.
77 *Castlereagh corr.*, ii, pp 94–5; E.J.Sheehan, *Nenagh and its neighbourhood* (Freshford, 1976), p. 84; Hayes, *Tipperary*, pp 18–9, 31–2.
78 Report of William Maume's intelligence to General Duff [May 1798]: P.R.O.N.I., McPeake papers, D.272/30; *Castlereagh corr.*, ii, pp 94–5; Hayes, *Tipperary 1798*, p. 32; Smyth, *Men of no property*, p. 160; O'Donnell, 'Limerick', pp 9–10. Lord Edward's presence in Munster features

At the end of March, a series of co-ordinated arms raids took place on gentry houses across Tipperary, north Cork, and the Limerick border. The town of Cahir had the unique experience of being taken over in daylight for some hours by several hundred men, their leaders neatly dressed in a uniform of blue and scarlet, during which time the town and castle were stripped of firearms. During the same week, the respectable appearance of some of the men raiding firearms around Kilworth was also noted.[79] But within a few days there were a number of more violent incidents thereabouts: two skirmishes to the west and north of Cashel took place between United men and the military, at the second of which there were several fatalities; just across the county border near Castleconnell, County Limerick, several men described as 'Defenders' were killed in an affray; and in north Cork, Lord Longueville's yeomanry killed one of '200' arms raiders at Ballyclough.[80]

This arms-gathering campaign was the most tangible evidence of Tipperary organization. Nenagh, Clonmel and probably Carrick-on-Suir were the nodal points of organization through which contact with Dublin was maintained.[81] One of Judkin Fitzgerald's victim/informants was John Fox, a Quaker miller from near Thurles, and he apparently provided details in late May of the existence of a strategic plan for a series of Tipperary risings which were to have been synchronised with events in Leinster. By that time, however, Judkin Fitzgerald's reign of terror and the extensive use by the army of free quartering had forced most of those holding illegal weapons to hand them over, and this offensive greatly weakened the county conspiracy. The high sheriff was later to claim that a massive tally of 9,500 pikes and 1,500 stand of arms were repossessed from within the county.[82]

The forceful disarming of Tipperary seized the initiative from the county's United Irishmen, although Morres was later to claim that he had had to restrain his men from going into the field in early June.[83] In Limerick city a vast army presence and an aggressive policy of corporal punishment seems to have smothered the embryonic United conspiracy there.[84] Meanwhile in south Munster in the weeks before the Leinster rising the spotlight fell back on west Cork. There

in at least two of the nineteenth-century novels set in Munster around 1798: (Anon.), *Castle Martyr: A tale of old Ireland* (London, 1839), and D.P. Conyngham, *The O'Mahony, chief of the Comeraghs: A tale of the rebellion of '98* (New York, 1879). I am very grateful to Magda and Rolf Loeber for drawing my attention to the first of these.

79 *C.E.P.*, 6 Apr. 1798; Musgrave, *Rebellions*, p. 669; Power, *Tipperary*, pp 312–4; Hayes, *Tipperary*, pp 36–7. The men attacking Cahir seem to have come from Clonmel. For evidence of a related resurgence of activity along the lower Blackwater valley during Mar. 1798, see John Musgrave, Ballyin, to the marquess of Waterford, 17 Mar. 1798: N.A.I., RP 620/36/21.

80 *C.E.P.*, 2 Apr. 1798; Hayes, *Tipperary*, pp 33–4; O'Donnell, 'Limerick', p. 15.

81 Musgrave, *Rebellions*, p. 667. General Duff believed Nenagh the best organized part of Tipperary: O'Donnell, 'Limerick', p. 15.

82 Power, *Tipperary*, p. 313; Hayes, *Tipperary*, pp 54–6.

83 *Castlereagh corr.*, ii, p. 95; O'Donnell, 'Limerick', p. 17.

84 *Clonmel Gazette*, 11–14 Apr. 1798; O'Donnell, 'Limerick', pp 16–17, 20.

a wave of pike–making and arm seizures was being reported at roughly the same time as this was happening in Tipperary, and at the beginning of May word reached Dublin of a conspiracy to seize Kinsale fort and town.[85] But the officer in command of the west Cork region since early February, General John Moore, responded in a totally different manner to Judkin Fitzgerald, carefully choreographing a counter-insurgency campaign with some 3,000 troops at his disposal. He was extremely critical of the local gentry's inflammatory disregard for due process, although he saw in Richard Townsend, the Cork high sheriff, a level-headed ally. Only after many warnings did he implement a policy of free quarters at the beginning of May. In the following days his forces swept the Bandon valley and the western coastal parishes for arms, engaging in selective house-burning. By the middle of the month some 800 pikes and a remarkable 3,400 stand of arms had been extracted from west Cork, some of which were quickly dumped off the coast.[86] Very heavy troop concentrations coupled with tight military discipline had severely weakened the offensive capability of local United Irish networks. A week after the Leinster rising General Brownrigg in Cork city was confident that all main routes thereabouts would be kept open, thanks to a smoothly functioning yeomanry and poor United Irish organization.[87]

Brownrigg's assessment was however somewhat inaccurate. It is true that the United movement in Cork city, ostensibly answerable to the Sheares brothers after John Swiney's arrest, had not recovered its early spring momentum. Conflicting reports reached Government in May as to whether or not Cork was scheduled to rise before or after Dublin, the garbled accounts suggesting a loss of clear purpose. The arrest of the Sheares' brothers themselves on the eve of the Leinster rising was the final small straw that crippled Cork city plans.[88] But in a number of districts of County Cork, notably in the Clonakilty/Skibbereen/Bantry triangle and in north-east Cork, there was a surprising United Irish resilience. The one visible demonstration of this was the battle of the Big Cross that took place about a mile north of Clonakilty on 19 June.

There had been a pitched battle of sorts further west near Drimoleague in early April between yeomanry and arms-raiders, but the ambush at Big Cross in mid-June was a far more formidable affair.[89] For days rumours had swept west

---

85 John Patrickson, Dublin to [the marquess of Downshire], 7 May 1798: Downshire papers, P.R.O.N.I., D607/F/163.

86 General Sir John Moore, Skibbereen to Major Nugent, 11 Mar. 1798: P.R.O.N.I. Nugent papers, D.2620/5/2; General Stewart, Bandon, to Nugent, 19 Apr. 1798; Capt. William Judge to Nugent, 23 May 1798: T.C.D. MS 9308/517, /518; Deasy to Deasy, 'letter 2', 1845, pp 25–7; Ó Coindealbháin, 'United Irishmen in Cork [–I]', 123–4; Bogue, 'Cork in 1798', p. 10.

87 Major-General Brownrigg, Cork, to [General Hewitt], 28 May, 1798: P.R.O.N.I., Dublin army letters, MIC 67, f.34.

88 Cf. William Maume's information (P.R.O.N.I., McPeake papers, D.272/30) with statement in the Armstrong diary, 16 May 1798 (T.C.D. MS 6409, f.60).

89 *C.E.P.*, 12, 19 Apr. 1798; Bogue, 'Cork in 1798', p.11.

Cork of preparations for some great event, inevitably linked in many minds to a return of the French. Men from Kinsale Ferry to Ballydehob were reportedly mobilized to assemble above the Bandon road in order to intercept the Westmeath Militia returning to Bandon, in the hopes it seems that such a challenge would lead to mass militia defections.[90] In the event the Westmeaths, soon joined by the Caithness Fencibles marching out from Bandon, inflicted terrible losses on the 'several hundred' rebels who had gathered. Some spoke of 150 dead, but a figure of several dozen is more likely. Sir John Freke, writing very shortly after the engagement, described it as having been 'carried on irregularly tho' with intrepidity ... the defeat ... was complete'. The leader on the day, Tadhg an Asna, 'a farming man of the name of Donovan' from near Clonakilty, was certainly one of the casualties.[91] More prestigious figures in west Cork radicalism escaped; some indeed held back or had already disappeared.[92] The plan for a west Cork rising is more likely to have been triggered by the departure for Wexford of General Moore in early June than by any fresh news of the coming of the French. Indeed Generals Brownrigg and Stewart, who both remained in Cork throughout June, were so convinced that a Munster rebellion would occur if the region's garrisons were depleted and sent to fight in Leinster that they fell out with General Lake over the issue. And on the day before the west Cork battle, Stewart, by then overruled by Lake, resigned his command. The news from Clonakilty was bitter-sweet confirmation of his predictions.[93]

But how good was these army commanders' intelligence? Their analysis was certainly correct in recognising the tactical prudence of Munster United

90 Sir Hugh O'Reilly, Clonakilty, to Col. Nugent, 13 June 1798: P.R.O.N.I. Nugent papers, D.2620/5/14; Capt. John Fiske, Ross, to Col. Nugent, 18 June 1798: T.C.D. MS 9308/519; Deasy to Deasy, letter 8, 1845, pp 53–4.

91 General Brownrigg, Cork, to [General Hewitt], 19 June 1798; General St John, Clonmel, to General Lake, 20 June 1798: P.R.O.N.I., Dublin army letters, MIC 67, ff.59, 61; Lt. Col. William Munro, Bandon, to Officer Commanding, Skibbereen, 19 June 1798; Sir John Freke, Ross, to General Nugent [19 June 1798]: P.R.O.N.I. Nugent papers, D.2620/5/16, /17; Deasy to Deasy, letter 8, 1845, p. 54; Michael Collins, 'The battle of the Big Cross', in Crowley, *Big Cross,* p. 20. Eleven Westmeath militia were however tried for treason, nine found guilty, and four executed in July: Ó Coindealbháin, 'United Irishmen in Cork – VI', 96–7.

92 Timothy O'Hea, Salamanca graduate, and Patrick Scully, poet, were involved in the battle but survived unscathed; Robert Swanton, the radical lawyer from Ballydehob, had already left the country. The level of complicity of the Stawells of Kilbrittain and of Dr William Callanan of Clonakilty remains uncertain. Another Catholic physician, Dr Bryan O'Connor of Bantry, was arrested just before Big Cross and given seven years transportation: Deasy to Deasy, letter 8, 1845, pp 56–7; 'Notes on the O'Hea family', N.L.I. G.O. MS 662, ff.6–8; Ó Coindealbháin, 'United Irishmen in Cork – V', 27–8; 'United Irishmen in Cork – VI', 97–103; Wells, *Insurrection,* p. 144; Crowley, *Big Cross,* pp 16, 39–40, 60.

93 Brig. General St John, Clonmel to [? General Hewitt], 6, 7 June 1798; General Brownrigg, Cork, to [? General Hewitt], 7, 12 June 1798; Brig. General St John, Clonmel, to General Stewart, 9 June 1798; General Stewart to General Lake, 18 June 1798: P.R.O.N.I., Dublin army letters, MIC 67, ff.44, 47, 45, 52, 51b, 58.

Irishmen in the face of full-strength garrisons, but their assessments of local revolutionary potential were at best imprecise; army commanders like Moore and
Stewart believed in the efficacy of a measured response to local subversion, but
others like General Loftus, operating through east Cork in May and June, took
no chances, and in response to a flow of rumours about a local rising made
extensive use of torture. A harvest of 1,000 pikes from the barony of Imokilly
seemed to vindicate Loftus' ruthless policy; it undoubtedly reassured the frightened local magnates who in the course of June had fortified their estate towns. In
Cork city itself an unremitting regime of whipping extracted many of the
secrets of the once-formidable county organization.[94]

Other districts across Munster were convulsed with rumours of plots and risings throughout June and July. In response General Duff instigated a regime of
repression in Limerick city, fully matched by a counter-terror in Waterford city.
In both communities wealthy innocent Catholics were seized and harshly treated, notably during periods of detention without trial.[95] In Kerry the suspected
rebel leaders were Protestant and the measures taken against them less extreme;
the very well-connected Orpens of Kilgarvan were briefly detained during June
as, to the amazement of many, was the county high sheriff, John Collis, who was
brought from Tralee to Limerick for interrogation.[96]

There were no doubts as to the loyalty of the Tipperary high sheriff; in the
course of June he turned his attentions from the north of his county to the
south, and was joined in the campaign by a triumphant Lord Kingsborough
returning from Wexford. Judkin Fitzgerald's information on radical activity in
Clonmel and Carrick seems to have been much poorer than what he had gathered for mid- and north Tipperary; once again innocent well-to-do Catholic
townsmen were scape-goated, while key figures in the conspiracy eluded the
sheriff.[97] Yet despite the crack-down in the northern half of the province, a series
of military incidents occurred between mid-June and mid-August which infused
the many rumours of local risings with heightened credibility. These incidents
were principally in County Tipperary where there were a series of hill-top meetings, one north of Annacarty on 20 June, one at Boytonrath near New Inn on 12
July – which was intercepted by the Cashel yeomanry, a fracas which led to several fatalities – and the largest at Soloheadbeg on 16 July; reports reached Cashel
the next day that 'all the country was to rise, and attack the towns'.[98] The great

94 Memoranda on Munster atrocities, pp 63–4; O'Neill, *Barrow uncrossed*, pp 50–1; 61–3.
95 Memoranda on Munster atrocities, pp 12–13; Deasy to Deasy, letter 6, 1845, pp 38–9;
   Musgrave, *Rebellions*, pp 649–53; O'Donnell, *1798 diary*, p. 43.
96 General Morrison, Limerick, to Lord Castlereagh, 14 June 1798; R.P. Mahony, Kenmare, to
   [Castlereagh], 15 June 1798: N.A.I., RP 620/38/145, 150; J.A. Gaughan, *Listowel and its vicinity*
   (Cork, 1973), pp 86–8.
97 Hayes, *Tipperary*, pp 59–69.
98 Brigadier-General F. St John, Clonmel to [? Hewitt], 6, 9 June 1798; — , Cashel, to [? Hewitt], 17
   July, 1798: P.R.O.N.I., Dublin army letters,MIC 67, ff. 44, 51b, 101; notes on Boytonrath court-

meeting of 'the mountaineers' at Soloheadbeg may well have been connected with plans by the Clonmel and Carrick United men to assemble supporters from a wide radius on the slopes of Slievenamon, presumably to attack one of the garrisons along the Suir valley. That project was set in motion prematurely as word of the inaugurating signal – hill-top bonfires – leaked out, and false signals were then used to lure United supporters to a false rendezvous: seven to eight hundred men converged on Carrigmockler on 27 July; they were easily overcome by the forces from the Waterford and Clonmel garrisons, with fatalities possibly greater than those suffered at the Big Cross.

That fiasco marked the last collective act of political violence in the province during 1798.[99] Yet reports of men in waiting, of county organizations primed, of an ugly menacing atmosphere, resonated for the rest of the year and beyond. There was a palpable sense of a boil that had not been burst. Indeed the unusually disturbed state of Clare, Cork, Tipperary and Limerick at different times over the next two years was a manifestation of this, although the very severe subsistence crisis of 1799–1800 played its part in inflaming agrarian agitation.[100]

Some elements of Munster's low-key role in the '98 rebellions are therefore clear: a once strong Cork city organization which became rudderless from early April 1798 with Roger O'Connor and Swiney out of action and the Sheares slow to fill the gap; County Cork largely disarmed by a forceful and well-resourced military command, but parish networks left intact; a late-emerging but vigorous north Munster organization, linked to Dublin not Cork, which was largely disarmed before the outbreak of the Leinster rebellion yet still resilient, not least because some of the leaders – including Morres – survived at large.

But many aspects of United Irish organization in the south remain puzzling. We can conclude that across at least half the province there was a high level of popular disaffection evident by the early months of 1798, but was that disaffection new or old, driven primarily by economic grievances, by sectarian fears, or by new notions of popular rights? The ideological penetration of republican ideas

martial: T.C.D. Madden papers, MS 873/44; Hayes, *Tipperary*, pp 73–4. For reports of a planned attack on the Tipperary/Kilkenny border village of Urlingford: George Frost, Kilcooley Abbey, to Sir William Barker, 14 June 1798: T.C.D., Barker Ponsonby papers, P/1/28.

99 Apart, that is, from the attack by 40 men on the Castleisland yeomanry barracks in Kerry on 13 August, which led to three fatalities and the seizure of the armoury: Musgrave, *Rebellions*, p. 665; O'Donnell, *1798 diary*, pp 80, 98. In the aftermath of that incident General Myers believed that there was still a prospect of a rising 'in the west of this county and the county of Kerry': Major-General Myers, Cork, to [? Hewitt], 22 Aug. 1798: P.R.O.N.I., Dublin army letters, MIC 67, f. 107.

100 Peter Walsh, Beline [nr Carrick-on-Suir], to Sir William Barker, 20 Aug. 1798: T.C.D., Barker Ponsonby papers, P2/3/5; Viscount Doneraile, Dublin, to — , 29 Jan. 1799; Edward Cooke, Dublin Castle, to General Myers, 4 Apr. 1799: N.A.I., RP 620/46/22; SOC 1/176; Musgrave, *Rebellions*, p. 642; Charles Ross (ed.), *The correspondence of Charles, first Marquis Cornwallis* (2nd ed., London, 1859), iii, pp 21, 130, 141; Ó Coindealbháin, 'United Irishmen in Cork – II', 78; Wells, *Insurrection*, p. 174; O'Donnell, *1798 diary*, pp 78, 81, 94.

and of 'the brotherhood of affection' into rural Munster was doubted even by the Cork activist Timothy Conway.[101] Yet we have seen that the circulation of printed propaganda from Cork and Dublin had been impressive, and was not by any means confined to an anglophone urban world. Was then the blood-thirsty sectarianism of parish activists something concocted by hostile local observers, most obviously by Sir Richard Musgrave? A reading of the small amount of Irish-language poetry associated with Munster in '98 would suggest the reality of anti-Protestantism, now cast as anti-Orangeism.[102] But nevertheless the leadership role of Protestant United Irishmen in Cork city and west Cork, in Tipperary and Kerry was important, perhaps even crucial, for the development of the United movement, and not least because of the conservative posture of many leading Munster Catholics. Just how crucial the organizational contribution of the northern 'emissaries' was is also unclear; Judkin Fitzgerald for one was convinced of the key role played by William Putnam MacCabe: he was 'the right arm of sedition in the whole of this province', 'he acted thro[ough] the province of Munster as principal organizer, he was styled General'. If indeed this was so, the 'emerald pimpernel' has left few documentary traces in the southern counties.[103]

Related to this problem is the difficulty over the labelling of disaffection in Tipperary, Limerick and north Cork: it is tempting to assume that the stubborn persistence of references to 'defenders' implies that the United Irish oaths, discipline and organization were heavily corrupted by the looser, more sectarian and congenial 'black oaths', rituals and structures of Midlands Defenderism. Clearly parish radicalism in Munster was a cocktail of United Irish, Whiteboy/Rightboy and possibly Defender ingredients. But the cocktail in the recently organized hill parishes of Tipperary was going to be very different from that which evolved in the deeply politicized small-farm world of west Cork.

Perhaps the most tantalizing issue remains the identity of the activists – below the fairly well documented urban or gentry participants. The Revd Horatio Townsend, west Cork magistrate and agricultural writer, saw the spoiled sons of newly prosperous farmers and retail traders as the backbone of rural disaffection: 'vulgar minds ... unable to bear prosperity'.[104] The leader of the Ballymacoda committee in east Cork, Thomas O'Neill, executed for his part in ordering the assassination of a spy in November 1797, died a very wealthy farmer with an income of £500 p.a. and was a recently enfranchised county freeholder. In

101 Confession, quoted in Elliott, *Partners*, p. 206.

102 For Patrick Scully, see Crowley (ed.), *Big Cross*, pp 25–8; pp 41–6; for Mícheál Óg Ó Longáin, Ó Coindealbháin, 'United Irishmen in Cork [I]', 128–9; Breandán Ó Conchúir, *Scríobhaithe Chorcaí, 1700–1850* (Cork, 1982), pp 102–6; Rónán Ó Donnchadha, *Mícheál Ó Longáin, file* (Dublin, 1994), pp 86–95; Breandán Ó Buachalla, 'An cúlra ideolaíoch', in Gearóid Ó Tuathaigh (ed.), *Éirí amach: 1798 in Eirinn* (Indreabhán, 1998), pp 37–9.

103 Thomas Judkin FitzGerald, Clonmel, to Lord Castlereagh, 15, 27 June 1798: N.A.I., RP 620/38/147, /247; Whelan, *Fellowship of freedom*, p. 33.

104 [Horatio Townsend], *Letters from a gentleman in Ireland to his friend at Bath* (Cork, 1798), p. 24.

Tipperary there is circumstantial evidence that Catholic farmers of substance and lineage also gave covert local leadership.[105] But what of the parish intelligentsia – the priests and teachers? In both Cork and Tipperary several Catholic clergy were harshly dealt with by the authorities, but passive sympathy rather than active involvement seems to have been their particular crime. Schoolteachers, as elsewhere, feature tantalizingly – O'Grady as the man behind the Castleisland committee in mid-Kerry, O'Hea and Collins in west Cork, and of course Ó Longáin in the liberties of Cork and Carrignavar, whose lament on the absence of Munstermen at Vinegar Hill is conventionally and rightly the starting point for the whole debate on Munster's role in '98.[106]

105 T.C.D. Madden papers, MS 873/248/64; Musgrave, *Rebellions*, pp 644, 666; O'Neill, *Barrow uncrossed*, pp 57–8; 'Reviews', in *Tipp Hist. Jnl.* (1988), 229–30; Hayes, *Tipperary*, pp 81–3.
106 For O'Grady of Castleisland: Musgrave, *Rebellions*. p. 665; for O'Hea: N.L.I., G.O. MS 662, ff. 6–8; for background on Collins: Musgrave, *Rebellions*, p. 661; Ó Conchúir, *Scríobhaithe Chorcaí*, pp 41–5; and Hugh Shields (ed.), *Ballad Research …* (Dublin, 1986), p. 221; for Ó Longáin, see fn. 102.

9

General Humbert's futile campaign

HARMAN MURTAGH

In August 1798 a little more than a thousand French troops landed in Mayo. For a fortnight they conducted a lively campaign with the support of local rebels, until they were surrounded and captured by superior government forces in County Longford as they attempted to march towards Dublin.[1] Although the French had subsequent plans to invade Ireland and the British correspondingly elaborate precautions to resist them, of which the signal and martello towers of the coastal defences and the Shannon fortifications are a visible reminder, the landing in Mayo was the sole occasion that French soldiers set foot in Ireland during the great revolutionary war of 1793–1815. However, viewed in the longer perspective, the 1798 landing was not an isolated incident, but the final act in a strategic process initiated by Louis XIV in which France, when at war with Britain, regularly sought to destabilize Great Britain by supporting the opponents of British authority in Ireland.

In 1689–91 French intervention was crucial to the Jacobite war effort against the international army of William III. Eight major French convoys sailed to Ireland in those years with extensive supplies of arms and munitions, together with a substantial number of military personnel including 6,500 troops.[2] The French had the advantage of a strong navy which, under the capable direction of Louis XIV's marine minister, the marquis de Seignelay, was well equipped and led, whereas that of the English, in contrast, was temporarily weakened by the impact of the Glorious Revolution. Although the Irish Catholics bore the brunt

---

1 General accounts include Charles H. Teeling, *Sequel to the history of the Irish rebellion of 1798: A personal narrative* (Glasgow, 1876), pp 300–22; C. Litton Falkiner, 'The French invasion of Ireland in 1798', in *Studies in Irish history and biography, mainly of the eighteenth century* (London, 1902), pp 250–350; Richard Hayes, *The last invasion of Ireland: When Connacht rose* (Dublin, 1937); Général Gastey, 'L'étonnante aventure de l'armée d'Irlande', in *Revue Historique de l'Armée* (Paris), 8th year, no. 4 (December 1952), pp 19–36; Thomas Pakenham, *The year of liberty: The great Irish rebellion of 1798* (London, 1969), pp 294ff. A shorter version of the present paper, entitled 'General Humbert's campaign in the West', appeared in Cathal Póirtéir (ed.), *The great Irish rebellion of 1798* (Cork, 1998), pp 115–24.
2 Sheila Mulloy (ed.), *Franco-Irish correspondence, December 1688 – February 1692* (Dublin, 1983–4), i, pp xlii–xliii.

of the fighting, they could never have undertaken such a war, nor sustained it for three hard years, without this strong French support.

Ireland featured again in French strategy in the eighteenth century. In 1759, for example, there were proposals for a French army to invade Ireland as part of a larger expedition to Britain.[3] During the American War of Independence, the French prepared various plans for a landing in Munster and rated an invasion of Ireland 'the most mortal blow that we can ever give to England'.[4] Remarkably, in 1778 the influential comte de Broglie even urged the creation of an Irish republic under the protection of France and Spain as the best means of encouraging the Irish to resist the English.[5] François Thurot managed to bring off a daring commando-type raid on Carrickfergus in 1760, but otherwise English naval superiority generally thwarted French plans to invade Ireland. However, it is clear that the concept of military intervention in Ireland was certainly not new to French strategic thinking when it was revived in the revolutionary period. In military terms, too, the revolution hardly altered the parameters within which the planning and execution of such an operation would have to take place.

The immediate cause of renewed French interest in Ireland in the 1790s was the efforts of the United Irishmen, chiefly through Theobald Wolfe Tone, their 'ambassador incognito' in Paris, to persuade the French government to invade Ireland and assist the republicans there to overthrow British rule.[6] Tone's negotiations resulted in Hoche's unsuccessful Bantry Bay expedition of 1796. This was on a scale which compared to Louis XIV's intervention a century earlier, but whereas in 1689 Bantry Bay had been the scene of a major naval battle – the largest ever fought in Irish waters – in which the French had come off best against the English, Hoche's expedition was a fiasco to which poor seamanship and bad equipment made a major contribution. Tone next became involved in preparations for an expedition from the Batavian Republic (Holland) to Ireland, but all hope of this was ended by the English navy's defeat of the Dutch at the battle of Camperdown in 1797.

Thereafter Ireland ranked much lower in French priorities, but within Ireland this was not immediately understood, and in 1798 the United Irish leadership fatally delayed their insurrection as they waited in vain for the expected French landing. When the Irish rebellion finally occurred, the news came as a surprise to the French government. With much of the army absent in Egypt with Napoleon, the Atlantic navy still weak and the public finances in disarray, the French were

---

3 Marcus de la Poer Beresford, 'Francois Thurot and the French attack at Carrickfergus, 1759–60', in *Ir. Sword*, x, 41 (winter 1972), 255–74.
4 Ibid., 'Ireland in French strategy during the American War of Independence, 1763–83', part 2 in ibid., xiii, 50 (summer 1977), 28.
5 Ibid., part 1 in ibid., xii, 49 (winter 1976), 288.
6 See Marianne Elliott, *Partners in revolution: The United Irishmen and France* (New Haven and London, 1982), especially parts 2 and 3.

poorly positioned to mount an effective military response. In the circumstances they did the best they could. Plans for an expedition of 8,000 men were initiated.[7] Meanwhile, in a desperate attempt to keep the Irish rebellion alive, smaller forces from Rochefort, Dunkirk and Brest were ordered to sail more or less simultaneously to the west of Ireland, where they were to link up in Donegal.

The commander at Rochefort was General Jean Joseph Amable Humbert, a thirty-year-old former skin dealer from the Vosges, whose energy, bravado and physical courage had quickly raised him to the rank of general in the heady early days of the revolutionary army.[8] He had long been involved with French plans to invade Great Britain and had sailed with the Bantry Bay expedition in 1796. Humbert lacked education – it was alleged that at one stage he had advocated invading Ireland overland – and possessed little strategic sense. But he displayed great energy in getting ready his share of the invasion force, and it was to his credit that his was the first part of the expedition to be ready. He hankered after an independent command; to the dismay of the other generals, he put to sea on 6 August, without waiting for the Brest fleet which was to carry General Hardy, the overall commander, with the bulk of the French forces.

There had indeed been political pressure to minimise delay, but by sailing when he did, Humbert forfeited the advantage of surprise for Hardy and ensured his own isolation. His precipitous departure ensured that the British naval blockade intensified, so when Hardy set out in October he was intercepted and defeated by the English navy off Lough Swilly. Theobald Wolfe Tone, who was on board, was taken prisoner and subsequently cut his throat as an alternative to being hanged. A single frigate from Dunkirk carried Napper Tandy and other Irish exiles to Donegal in September, but they withdrew after twenty-four hours, considering that the situation was hopeless. Three Dutch frigates which sailed from the Texel were also intercepted. Finally, the ships which had carried Humbert, with some others, made a second voyage to Mayo with reinforcements. They managed to run the blockade, but arrived too late to help Humbert, and the troops did not disembark. Preparations were eventually abandoned for a larger expedition from Brest under the Irish-born General Kilmaine.[9]

The three frigates under the capable Commodore Savary that carried 'the army of Ireland', as Humbert grandiloquently titled his little force, stood well out into the Atlantic to evade the English navy. This extended the time at sea, and there was some unpleasantness on board when, to ward off mutiny, Humbert was compelled to pay over a portion of the soldiers' embarkation money which he had withheld. Contrary winds prevented the squadron approaching the coast of

7   E. Desbrière, *Projets et tentatives de débarquement aux Iles britanniques* (Paris, 4 vols, 1900–2), ii, pp 69ff.

8   Jacques Baeyens, *Sabre au clair: Amable Humbert, général de la république* (Paris, 1981), passim.

9   F.W. van Brock, 'Dilemma at Killala', in *Ir. Sword*, viii, 33 (winter 1968), 261–73; Desbrière, *Projets et tentatives*, ii, pp 164–71.

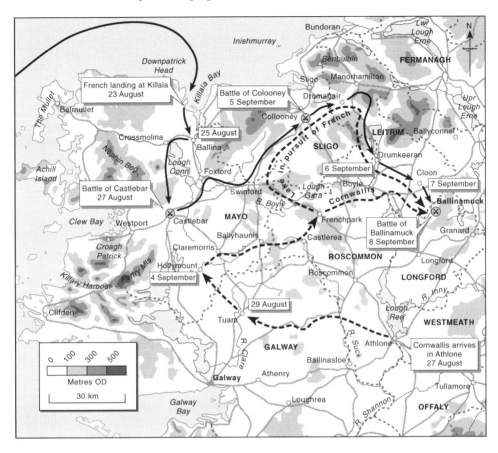

Fig. 9.1   Humbert's campaign, 25 August to 8 September, 1798.

Donegal, as planned, and off the Mullet a fresh course was plotted for Humbert to land instead at the remote beach of Kilcummin near Killala in north Mayo, and there Humbert disembarked on 22 August.

His force comprised 888 infantry, principally the second battalion of the 70th demi-brigade, together with 42 artillerymen, a staff of 35 officers and 57 cavalry mostly from the 3rd Chasseurs à cheval.[10] The artillerymen brought by Humbert were inexperienced reservists, and were reinforced by a dozen naval gunners from the ships. In the event the artillery proved more of a nuisance than an asset during the campaign, and it contributed little to Humbert's campaign beyond perhaps boosting the morale of his Irish allies and impressing his opponents. A handful of Irishmen accompanied the expedition, including Bartholomew

10 Jean-Paul Bertaud, 'Forgotten soldiers: The expedition of General Humbert to Ireland in 1798', in Gough and Dickson, *Ireland and the French Revolution*, pp 220–8.

Teeling, the radical son of the Lisburn linen merchant and Catholic politician, Tone's brother, Matthew, and the Mayo-born Captain Henry O'Keon, an ex-priest whose fluency in Irish, English and French made him invaluable. The total strength of Humbert's force was about 1,030.

Humbert's officers and men were young: the average age of the officers was thirty-four and of the rank and file twenty-six. A hostile observer noted that except for the grenadiers, in appearance 'they had nothing to catch the eye. The stature for the most part was low, their complexions pale and sallow', and the blue and grey uniforms worn by the infantry and cavalry respectively were much the worse for wear.[11] Half the officers, including Adjutants General Sarrazin and Fontaine who ranked next to Humbert, came from the rank and file of the pre-revolutionary army; the rest were from the National Guard or were army volunteers. Most were rated as capable of further promotion. Of the rank and file, some were volunteers or from the old royal army, and the rest were conscripts enrolled during the *levée en masse* of 1793. Almost all were veterans of active service on the Rhine, in the Pyrenees, in Flanders with the *armée du nord*, or in the Vendée. They were confident of the superiority of French arms, and they proved brave and resilient soldiers under fire. Disciplined, patient and hardy, it was observed that they were 'well content to live on bread and potatoes, to drink water, to make the stones of the street their bed, and to sleep in their clothes with no covering but the canopy of heaven'.[12] At first their morale was high, but hunger, fatigue, a sense of abandonment and the growing prospect of defeat combined to disillusion them as the campaign approached its climax.

The infantry was armed with flintlock muskets, best discharged in volleys of about two per minute, and with a range of less than 200 metres. The soldiers also had bayonets, and the cavalry was equipped with sabres and carbines. The artillery comprised three four-pounder field guns and their accompanying ammunition wagons. Local horses were commandeered for cavalry and transport, but insufficient numbers were available, and there are accounts of artillery and ammunition wagons being dragged by hand, using as traces the bellropes of Killala cathedral. Although there was a shortage of bread, the seizure of livestock ensured that victuals were plentiful, and the French rated the Irish beef and mutton delicious.

The rebellion in Ireland had been crushed before Humbert left France. Connacht had remained quiet throughout the disturbances of the early summer. The United Irishmen were poorly organized in the province, and their allies, the Defenders, remained weak after Carhampton's tough counter-insurgency measures in 1795.[13] However, there was widespread sympathy for the rebel cause,

11 Grattan Freyer (ed.), *Bishop Stock's narrative of the year of the French: 1798* (Ballina, 1982), p. 23.   12 Ibid.
13 Nuala Costello (ed.), 'Little's diary of the French landing in 1798', in *Anal. Hib.*, xi (1941), 64; W.E.H. Lecky, *A history of Ireland in the eighteenth century* (London, 1913), iii, pp 419–20; Patrick K. Egan, 'Progress and suppression of the United Irishmen in the western counties in 1798–9', in *Galway Arch. and Hist. Soc. Jn.*, xxv, 3–4 (1953–4), 104–34.

and in Mayo the ordinary people welcomed the French enthusiastically, kneeling by the roadside to pray for their success as they passed and greeting them with cries of *Éireann go brách* and *Vive la Republique irlandaise*.[14]

The first French victory was the capture of Killala, where Humbert made short work of opposition from the local yeomanry and established himself in the palace of the Church of Ireland bishop, Joseph Stock, who received him, in the amused words of Sarrazin, with the coolness of a 'just man who sees the sky tumbling above his head'. Stock played host to French officers for the next month, and his eyewitness account of events is a minor work of literature. The cordial relations it revealed as having developed between the bishop and the French invaders afterwards blighted Stock's ecclesiastical career. The curtilage of the bishop's palace beside the cathedral became the French camp. Humbert then issued a proclamation calling on the Irish to join him. This stated that his men were the forerunners of other Frenchmen who would shortly arrive. It claimed that the 'frightful colossus' of wealth and tyranny was everywhere 'mouldering away', and concluded with the stirring words: 'Union, Liberty, the Irish Republic, such is our shout. Let us march. Our hearts are devoted to you. Our glory is your happiness.'

A small number of Catholics of gentry and middle-class background responded to the invitation to volunteer their services and were made officers. They included James Joseph MacDonnell, the leader of the United Irishmen in Mayo, who was a lawyer of Catholic-gentry background and an old associate of Wolfe Tone and Lord Edward FitzGerald.[15] Others were John Gibbons, the county treasurer of the United Irishmen who was Lord Altamont's agent in Westport, and his sons; George Blake of Garracloon, who had been cashiered from the British army for duelling; the O'Malley brothers from Burrishoole; the Maguires, a brewing family from Crossmolina; and the self-styled Baron O'Dowda, a former Habsburg army officer, who arrived at Killala from Bonniconlon in County Sligo with a hundred or more of his tenants and dependents. Command of the Irish was given initially to Matthew Bellew, a former officer in the Russian army, who had been invalided home in a deranged state after being blown up by a Turkish mine.[16] He had the attraction for Humbert of fluency in French, but his mental instability, compounded by an addiction to drink, rendered him unfit to play a military role of any consequence. He was effectively superseded as commander of the Irish in the Killala area by Ferdy O'Donnell, a local farmer who was a former revenue official.

---

14 Richard Hayes (ed.), 'An officer's account of the French campaign in Ireland in 1798', [General Sarrazin's account] in *Ir. Sword*, ii, 6 (summer 1955), 111.

15 Hayes, *Last invasion*, pp 275–8; Sheila Mulloy, 'James Joseph MacDonnell, "The best-known of the United Irish chiefs of the west" ', in *Cathair na Mart: Journal of the Westport Historical Society*, v (1985), 67–79.

16 Richard Musgrave, *Memoirs of the different rebellions in Ireland* (2nd ed., Dublin, 1801), pp 587–90.

Bellew's appointment was a severe embarrassment to his brother, the Catholic bishop of Killala, who afterwards found it difficult to shake off allegations of collusion with the rebels, even though, like the rest of the Irish bishops, he had little sympathy with republicanism.[17] The thirty or so priests of Killala diocese were divided in their views. Some sought to dissuade their parishioners from involvement, but half a dozen or more, together with a similar number from the neighbouring dioceses, were implicated in Humbert's campaign, mainly by indications of approval and the encouragement of recruiting.[18] Discounting O'Keon, none held military command, although Fr Michael Gannon from Louisburgh, who had been a priest in France, served for a time as commissary. No Mayo Protestants joined Humbert.

In all, 6–700 volunteers enlisted with the French at Killala, and another 3,500 at Castlebar, including some captured soldiers of the Longford militia. Some said they were 'come to take up arms for France and the Blessed Virgin', which amused the agnostic French. But other motives were liberty, republicanism, hatred of the English, sectarian fear and prejudice, the prospect of loot, excitement, clothing and rations, and the universal attraction of revolution to the *sans culottes*. A decree to raise an army of 12,000 in Connacht by conscripting everyone aged sixteen to forty was never put into effect. The recruits were divided into companies of forty to fifty men. The bulk were from the poorest peasantry, and there were amusing scenes as they rushed to dress in their new blue uniforms, while a French officer banged helmets onto their heads with his fist. Forty of the Irish were mounted to supplement Humbert's meagre cavalry. The French found the process of turning such rustics into disciplined soldiers a frustrating experience.[19] Linguistic difficulties and a shortage of officers impeded drill and weapons training, while the recruits were prone to desert as soon as they had collected their uniforms and some loot. A colony of Ulster weavers, under the command of Teeling, formed the most reliable unit. They were refugees from Orange persecution who had settled around Ballina, where they were reputedly much 'addicted to speculate in politics', poisoning the minds of 'the petty shopkeepers, mechanics and servants' whom they met at 'the low tippling houses' of the town. The 3,000 muskets which Humbert distributed were almost enough to arm his Irish allies. Immense quantities of pikes were reported in Sligo and Mayo, but their use was probably mainly confined to fringe groups. A

17 Brendan Hoban, 'Dominick Bellew, 1745–1812, parish priest of Dundalk and bishop of Killala', in *Seanchas Ard Mhacha* (1972), 333–71; Patrick Hogan, 'Some observations on contemporary allegations as to Bishop Dominick Bellew's (1745–1813) sympathies during the 1798 rebellion in Connacht', in ibid. (1982), 417–25.
18 E. MacHale, 'Some Mayo priests of 1798', in *Blianiris*, ii, 5 (1991–2), 7–20; Dáire Keogh, '*The French disease': The Catholic church and Irish radicalism, 1790–1800* (Dublin, 1993), pp 182–6.
19 L.O. Fontaine, *Notice historique de la descente des francais en Irlande ...* (Paris, 1801), p. 46; Nuala Costello (ed.), 'Journal de l'expédition d'Irlande suivi de notes sur le Général Humbert qui l'a commandé' [Captain Jean Louis Jobit's account] in *Anal. Hib.*, xi, 24, 52.

green colour was unfurled, depicting the harp with the motto *Erin go bragh*.

The French landing was viewed as a serious crisis by the Irish government, especially as early reports exaggerated Humbert's strength. A veteran campaigner, Lord Cornwallis, had just been appointed viceroy and commander-in-chief. He had close to 100,000 men under his command, and a further 10,000 came from Britain in September.[20] However, only just over 10 per cent were regulars. The rest were comprised of the Irish militia, a largely Catholic force officered by Protestants; English and Scottish fencibles whose units had volunteered for service in Ireland; and the Irish yeomanry, a local defence force of part-time, volunteers. An effective part of Cornwallis' strength lay in his artillery.[21] The battalion six-pounders and curricle guns of the Royal Irish Artillery had a round-shot range of 6–800 metres, and also fired case and grape – discharges of quantities of musket balls which were devastating to massed opponents at close quarters. Scarlet was the predominant uniform colour of the government soldiers, although the artillery and some of the cavalry wore blue.

At the time of the French landing, the government had less than 4,000 troops in Connacht, largely militia and yeomanry. General Hutchinson, the commander, divided his forces and took up station with only 1,700 men at Castlebar, where he was joined by General Lake, the conqueror of Wexford.[22] Although Humbert's orders were to proceed with extreme caution, dash and impetuosity were more to his appetite, and he went on the offensive to secure the sort of military success he hoped would re-ignite the Irish rebellion. First Ballina was captured, and then, with 800 French and the same number of Irish, he boldly set out to meet the enemy head on, marching overnight, via the mountain road through Barnagehy, to arrive at Castlebar on the morning of 27 August. Lake and Hutchinson were taken by surprise with barely time to draw up their forces in traditional linear formations on the hilly ground north-west of the town.[23] Humbert attacked immediately with the Irish in the centre, flanked by the French on either side. The government artillery, positioned in front of the infantry, was well served. Humbert's Irish broke and fled before a hail of fire, while the French halted under cover of a ditch. They were rallied by Sarrazin who led them along a sunken path to threaten the flank of the government line. The militia showed their inexperience by panicky musket fire while the French were still out of range. When Sarrazin's men

20 Kenneth P. Ferguson, 'The army in Ireland from the restoration to the Act of Union' (unpublished Ph.D. thesis, T.C.D., 1980), pp 179–83.

21 G.A. Hayes-McCoy, *Irish battles: A military history of Ireland* (London, 1969), pp 282–3.

22 Statement of General Hutchinson, 21 Sept. 1798: Charles Ross (ed.), *Correspondence of Charles, first marquis of Cornwallis* (London, 1859), ii, pp 409–10; Henry McAnally, *The Irish militia, 1793–1816: A social and military study* (Dublin and London, 1949), pp 133–8.

23 See contemporary plans of the dispositions in T.H. McGuffie, 'A sketch-map of Castlebar, 27th August 1798', in *Journal of the Society for Army Historical Research*, xxvi, 107 (autumn 1948), 88–90; and W.A. Maguire (ed.), *Up in arms! The 1798 rebellion in Ireland: A bicentenary exhibition* (Belfast, 1998), p. 258.

charged forward with fixed bayonets to the cry of *Vive la République*, the government cavalry galloped away, and the Kilkenny and Longford militias fell back in disorder, abandoning the artillery. The French pressed home the attack and drove the government forces from the town in the ignominious flight that has come to be known as the 'Races of Castlebar'. Humbert lost about 40 Frenchmen killed and 80 wounded. Various conflicting claims and admissions exist as to government casualties: fatalities may not in fact have reached double figures. But the French captured five colours, with most of their opponents' artillery and baggage. Jubilantly Humbert reported to France that with 2,000 reinforcements and 15,000 more muskets, he would free Ireland within a month.

News of the French victory encouraged local insurgents to take over over Newport and Westport, and virtually the whole of Mayo came under Humbert's control. Trees of liberty were erected in the towns, and drink flowed freely in the rowdy atmosphere surrounding the celebration bonfires. With the normal forces of law and order overthrown, looting intensified, and there was widespread destruction of property. A number of big houses suffered major damage, although Westport House was preserved through the timely intervention of James Mac-Donnell. Only Wexford and Wicklow surpassed Mayo in the compensation afterwards paid to 'suffering loyalists'. Some Protestant churches were vandalized; Protestants feared for their lives, but the destruction and intimidation was probably more social than sectarian. Although Catholics wore scapulars as a badge of identity, there was not a strong tradition of religious animosity in Mayo; no Protestants died except on the battlefield, and Catholics with property also suffered, including Bishop Bellew. The French were struck by the wretched living conditions of the peasantry, and by the contrast in Ireland between rich and poor. There was a suggestion that a redistribution of land 'would communicate through the kingdom like an electric spark', but Humbert had proclaimed an 'inviolable respect' for property, and in keeping with the conservative instincts of the United Irish leadership he made no move to encourage a radical overthrow of the existing social order.[24] Some of his officers were detached for duty to the main towns, and they took an active role in restoring order. Mayo was divided into regional departments, each with a responsible local Catholic as magistrate to organize armed security patrols. Humbert set up a twelve-man provisional government for Connacht at Castlebar, tasked with organising the military power of the province and with providing subsistence for the French and Irish troops.[25] The president was John Moore, who had been educated in France and was the son of a wealthy local landowner.[26]

24 F.S. Bourke, 'The French invasion of 1798: A forgotten eyewitness', in *Ir. Sword*, ii, 8 (summer 1956), 293; John Cooney, 'Humbert's expedition – a lost cause?' in John Cooney and Tony McGarry (eds), *Post-Maastricht Europe: Papers of the 1992 Humbert Summer School* (Dublin, 1993), pp 112–13.
25 F.W. van Brock (ed.), 'A memoir of 1798', [account of Sergt. Maj. J.B. Thomas] in *Ir. Sword*, ix, 36 (summer 1970), 199–200.
26 Patrick M. Hogan, 'The undoing of Citizen John Moore – President of the provisional gov-

Humbert spent a week at Castlebar. In military terms a rapid renewal of the offensive would have been the proper course of action, but he delayed for news of his victory to trigger widespread rebellion. However, it soon became clear that Irish republicans had little appetite for fresh hostilities, certainly not until more significant forces arrived from France. Outside Mayo, there was no response even in Connacht. In Roscommon, where a strong rebel organisation was reputed to exist, the United Irish leader, an ex-French army officer named James Plunkett, lost his nerve and surrendered to the government. Leitrim had remained quiescent after the suppression of the Defenders there in 1795, despite subsequent attempts to organize the United Irishmen in the county. Sligo was still cowed after its disarmament in 1797, and in Galway the United Irishmen, who were not numerous, drilled with farm implements and waited on events.

Cornwallis was shaken by news of the Castlebar defeat, for which he severely reprimanded Hutchinson. Fearing further French landings and fresh rebellion, he took the view that it was essential to deny Humbert a second victory and warned the government commanders to avoid battle until sufficient forces were concentrated to make success a certainty. He requested reinforcements from London and placed the yeomanry throughout Ireland on permanent duty. Then, proceeding 'with extraordinary, perhaps with excess of caution', the viceroy made elaborate dispositions for his campaign.[27] Soldiers on detachment throughout Leinster were ordered to congregate at fixed stations. General Nugent moved to Enniskillen to block any thrust into Ulster. General Hewett assembled forces from the south and east at Portumna.[28] Cornwallis himself, with a force of 7,000, took personal charge of the offensive in the west against Humbert. Cornwallis had no faith in Irish troops, whom he regarded as undisciplined and untrustworthy, and he delayed his advance until Scottish and English units could join him. He reached Tuam on 2 September and consulted with Lake. It was decided that Cornwallis would move against Castlebar from the south, while the 2,500 government troops who had remained in Connacht after Hutchinson's defeat would unite under Lake at Frenchpark and advance from the east. A strong cavalry reconnaissance would precede Cornwallis, under the command of Colonel 'Black Bob' Crauford, a daredevil expert in mobile warfare. This force comprised Hompesch's Dragoon Riflemen, a German regiment in British pay, and the 1st Irish Fencible Dragoons – Lord

ernment of the republic of Connacht, 1798', in *Galway Arch. and Hist. Soc. Jn.*, xxxix (1981–20), 59–72; Sheila Mulloy, 'John Moore of Moorehall (1767–99): The general who wasn't', in *Ir. Sword*, xviii, 73 (summer 1992), 264–70.

27 *Impartial relation of the military operations which took place in Ireland in consequence of the landing of a body of French troops, under General Humbert, in August, 1798* (Dublin, 1799), pp 8–28; Carola Oman, *Sir John Moore* (London, 1953), p. 189.

28 Thomas Bartlett, 'Counter-insurgency and rebellion', in Thomas Bartlett and Keith Jeffery (eds), *A military history of Ireland* (Cambridge, 1996), p. 286.

Roden's Foxhunters – who astonished the French by jumping stone walls 'like goats'.[29]

Meanwhile, Humbert was being forced to scale down the optimistic plans he had made after the victory at Castlebar. Initially he had hoped to drive the government forces beyond the Shannon, and join with insurgents to advance on Dublin for a decisive result. Next, he considered digging in at Castlebar, making it the rallying point for Irish rebels until reinforcements came from France. But, as Cornwallis closed in, it was clear that defending Castlebar was not a realistic military proposition. Hardy had not appeared. Humbert's French were too few, and there was insufficient time to train the Irish or construct adequate fortifications. Ruling out a retreat to the western mountains, Humbert decided to break out of Mayo by a fast march through County Sligo. The idea came from Sarrazin, who claimed afterwards that from the start the objective was Dublin, which the French erroneously believed to be lightly defended. Doubtless, such a daring manoeuvre would have held appeal for Humbert. However, it seems likely that at the outset he did not exclude the possibility of heading north. In the event he adopted Sarrazin's full concept out of desperation, as circumstances developed on the march.

The French evacuated Castlebar on 3/4 September, accompanied by only 600 of the Irish under MacDonnell and Blake. Humbert slipped around General Lake who had advanced to Ballaghadereen and brushed off an attack by the local yeomanry at Tubbercurry, where he was joined by reinforcements from Ballina under O'Dowda. In thirty hours he covered the forty miles to Collooney. His men had just started to rest, when they were attacked by the Limerick militia, led by Colonel Charles Verreker, which formed part of the garrison of Sligo. A sharp, hour-long engagement ensued. Amidst noisy exchanges of cannon and musket fire, the outnumbered militia were repulsed and then overwhelmed in a characteristic flanking movement by Sarrazin. Great personal courage was displayed by Teeling in disabling one of the militia cannon. Collooney was a tactical victory for Humbert, but the engagement evidently dissuaded him from any attempt to move against Sligo.

Cornwallis was uncertain of French intentions, although he considered 'every point of direction for their march … equally desperate'. He ordered Lake to pursue and harass Humbert. Craufurd's cavalry, which had entered Castlebar, was sent to reinforce him, followed by the light infantry under Sir John Moore who was much the ablest of the English generals in Ireland. Events now took another turn with republican uprisings in support of the French in Longford and north Westmeath.[30] These were poorly organized affairs which were quickly

29 G.A. H[ayes]-McC[oy], 'Fencible corps in Ireland, 1782–1803', in *Ir. Sword*, ii, 6 (summer 1955), 140–3; M.E.S. Laws, 'Hompesch's Dragoon Riflemen' in ibid., 8 (summer, 1956), 297.

30 Liam Cox, 'Westmeath in the 1798 period' in ibid., ix, 34 (summer 1969), 1–15.

suppressed by locally available government forces. However, Humbert turned south at Dromahair in an attempt to unite with the insurgents, while Cornwallis moved east across the Shannon with his own force, and was sufficiently alarmed to order the Guards Brigade into Westmeath. The security of Dublin became a concern, and although the city was defended by six regiments and 5,000 yeomanry, barges were assembled on the Grand Canal for the transport of reinforcements, should this prove necessary.

Meanwhile Humbert pushed his exhausted column forward. All the captured artillery was dumped, and the soldiers took it in turn to ride the available horses. There was criticism among officers and men that a host of blunders had been made, their government had abandoned them and their lives were being needlessly sacrificed. It took the combined efforts of Humbert and Sarrazin to shore up the flagging morale. Craufurd's cavalry, in the van of Lake's force, continually harrassed the extended Franco-Irish column and there were several minor clashes. The country people were too terrified of retribution to give any military support, but they supplied food, and Sarrazin related that the Irish women 'showed us the care which they have for children, brothers and friends'. A promised rendezvous with the remnants of the defeated Longford insurgents failed to materialize.

Humbert's campaign ended at Ballinamuck in County Longford on 8 September. With Cornwallis blocking the French advance at Ballinalee, Lake attacked the rearguard of Humbert's column which capitulated at the first assault. Humbert drew up the rest of his force on a hillside and put up a token fight. There were casualties on both sides, but when further resistance was futile he surrendered unconditionally. The surviving 800 French were made prisoners of war, and brought to Dublin where they were feted as heroes before going on to England. The officers were soon exchanged, but it took much longer for the rank and file to be repatriated. In September and October 1798 the Paris press gave a certain amount of coverage to Humbert's expedition, but this naturally ceased once he surrendered. There was little appreciation in France of the efforts his men had made in Ireland, and it was probably as a justification of their conduct that Sarrazin, Fontaine and Jobit wrote their accounts. Humbert received no further promotion after his return and eventually emigrated to America, where he died penniless in 1823. The promotions he conferred on his subordinates in Ireland were not confirmed on their return to France.

Lake showed no mercy to the Irish who had accompanied Humbert to Ballinamuck. Hundreds were slaughtered on the battlefield or as they fled, and a large number of prisoners were hanged, including Teeling, Matthew Tone, Blake and O'Dowda. However, the Irish women who had attached themselves to Humbert's expedition were spared. They rode off, perched behind the saddles of the victorious government cavalry troopers and waving success to their former protectors. A French officer remarked ruefully that they did not seem unduly worried by their new situation.

The bloodshed continued with the suppression of the remaining insurgents in Mayo. Ballina was recaptured by Lord Portarlington, following the defeat of the pikemen of the garrison at Scurmore as they attempted to block his advance from Sligo. General Trench then led a force of 3,000 against Killala which was defended by 800 rebels under the remaining French officers. On 23 September the town fell to simultaneous attacks at both ends, and scenes of appalling carnage ensued as fencible cavalry sabred 400 rebels to death in the streets. Ferdy O'Donnell was among the casualties. The government forces ranged through Erris and Tirawley during the following week. Sixty were killed, some still naively wearing their French uniforms. Houses were burned and villages wrecked. Prominent insurgent leaders were hanged, including General Bellew and two of the priests who had supported Humbert. Others went on the run, and a few like James MacDonnell, who had escaped from Ballinamuck, got away to exile in France. President John Moore was captured at Castlebar and died in prison. O'Keon was made prisoner but eventually allowed to return to France. At first, apprehended rebels were tried by courts martial, but subsequently they were brought before the civil courts. The zeal of Denis Browne, the Mayo county sheriff and Lord Altamont's brother, in the pursuit of rebels earned him the unsavoury title of Denis the Rope. An amnesty was only finally declared in September 1799, and even then its application was selective. The total French losses were about 250, while it is estimated that 2,000 or more of their Irish allies were killed, the majority in reprisals after Ballinamuck or during the subjugation of Mayo.[31] Casualties on the government side were much less, amounting to as few as 19 killed and 116 wounded, excluding yeomanry, according to the estimate of the army's chief medical officer.[32]

The defeat of the French was followed by recriminations. Humbert was reported to have said that the Irish had deceived him abominably, robbing him of everything they could get hold of and behaving in a cowardly manner.[33] Other officers claimed the French had been misled about the extent of the support they could expect in Ireland. The truth was that Humbert's expedition was not a rational operation of war, but a foolhardy adventure, too late and far too little to assist the Irish republicans or threaten the government regime. Its small size discouraged any in Ireland, save the most naive, from joining him. It proved impossible to turn those that did into effective soldiers in the short time available. The French troops were the best soldiers on either side in 1798, and Humbert's lively campaign has always bedazzled commentators. However, there is some justice in the criticism that he was given too much rein by Cornwallis' excessive caution. It is pointless to argue that Humbert should have adopted a different strategy, or

31 Desbrière, *Projets et tentatives*, ii, p. 130; Elliott, *Partners in revolution*, p. 231.
32 Patrick M. Hogan, 'Casualties sustained by government forces during the Humbert episode, August–September, 1798', in *Galway Arch. and Hist. Soc. Jn.*, l (1998), 1–10.
33 Thomas Bartlett, 'General Humbert takes his leave', in *Cathair na Mart*, xi (1991), 102.

that another French general might have been more sucessful. A better general would not have exposed himself to isolation in the first place, but once the French had landed, the defeat of their tiny force was inevitable. Nor indeed is it very likely that a much larger French expeditionary force would have been any more successful. The whole episode proved that retaining control of Ireland was a far greater strategic necessity for Britain, especially in wartime, than 'liberating' it was for the French. In any case the disorganized and demoralized French navy was in no condition to transport a sizeable army to Ireland, or – more demanding – to sustain it there, even if such a force had been available in 1798. The impossibility of coordinating military planning between France and Ireland was a further major disadvantage. For all their diplomatic success in Paris, the United Irishmen's policy of reliance on France was a strategic mistake. The French Republic's military intervention in 1798 was puny compared to that given in 1689–91 by Louis XIV to the Irish Jacobites, who were infinitely better organized in military terms than the United Irishmen. Even then it had failed to prevent a Williamite victory. The involvement of the French raised a security threat which hardened the attitude of the British government and allied it to the most diehard and vicious forces of conservative reaction in Ireland, thereby ending all possibility of even modest political reform.

A trail of busts, plaques, monuments and commemorative nameplates marks the route of Humbert's short-lived and disastrous expedition. There has been a best-selling novel, a television drama, a successful annual summer school and even a cycling tour. But for the people of Mayo in 1798 the month of 'liberty', which Humbert brought them, was a tragedy – bloody and destructive, especially for the poorest elements in society, and the harbinger of further alienation and division in the nineteenth century, when Mayo emerged from the tragedy of the Famine to become the cockpit of the Land War.

SECTION III

Many keyboards have been tapped on the subject of 1798 in Ulster. For nationalists, the 1790s appear as the moment when the United Irishmen encouraged the settlers to lower their British blinkers, thereby allowing them to recognize the realities of their situation in Ireland. Once the sectarian scales fell from their eyes, they could see their world through the cool, clear light of a northern day rather than through the ancient lights of murky British myth. For unionists, the decade represents the classic example of what happened when Ulster Protestants lowered their guard. Their foolish flirtation with the papists had a demonstrably fatal progeny in the sectarian bloodbath of 1798, and this political experiment should never be repeated. For both dominant ideologies, the 1790s established core traditions – Tone and republicanism on one side, the Orange Order and popular defence of the Union on the other. It is not surprising therefore that the historiography of the 1790s should closely mirror these political positions, or that the late twentieth-century convulsions in Ulster should have left their mark on the work of historians.

The historiographical litmus test for orange and green has been in assigning blame for sectarian polarization in the 1790s, in particular in identifying the specific catalyst for the Armagh Troubles.[1] In response to the eruption of the Northern Troubles, a sub-Marxian interpretation was initiated by BICO (the British and Irish Communist Organisation), then adopted serially by the Official IRA, Official Sinn Féin, the Workers Party and Democratic Left. This employed crude base-superstructure models, unburdened by politics and indifferent to cultural mediation.[2] The trigger for the Armagh disturbances was sought in the distinctive socio-economic changes in the Ulster linen industry, in demographic change, in Catholic penetration of the linen industry, and the reactive resistance by plebeian Protestants.[3] As the current Troubles descended into the sombre days

---

1 A good starting point is David Miller (ed.), *Peep o' Day Boys and Defenders: Selected documents on the County Armagh disturbances 1784–96* (Belfast, 1990).

2 A representative example is Peter Gibbons, *The origins of Ulster unionism* (Manchester, 1975). The many publications of Brendan Clifford follow the same line.

3 A.T.Q. Stewart, *The narrow ground: The roots of conflict in Northern Ireland* (London, 1977); L.M. Cullen, *The emergence of modern Ireland 1600–1900* (London, 1981). Stewart and Cullen both

of bomb, bullet and Hunger Strike, a darker if equally deterministic tone infiltrated the historiography, with an emphasis on atavism, on 'intractable' ethnic division, and on the eternally divided nature of the narrow ground of Ulster.[4] This 'dreary steeples' (Winston Churchill) or 'confessional realities' (Roy Foster) model argued that those who attempted to alter this reality (like the United Irishmen)[5] were self-deluding idealists, doomed to worsen the situation they sought to alleviate.[6] Then in the 1990s, as the Peace Process tentatively developed, the historiography emphasized politicization, the link between high politics and 'ground truth,' and a more positive assessment of the radicals.[7]

Through all these twists and turns, some points have remained constant. Specialists on the period are agreed that a simple Protestant/Catholic binary is unable to accommodate the complexities of the Ulster situation or the subtle interfaces between Anglican, Presbyterian and Catholic, and the resultant patchwork mosaic of religious affiliation through Ulster (Miller, chapter 11). There was indeed no 'whole Protestant community.'[8] Thus a homogenous area like

exploit a Jungian sub-theme, arguing that the roots of modern Irish politics lay deep in atavistic myth. This approach was fashionable in the 1970s and 1980s with commentators like Richard Kearney, Leland Lyons and Conor Cruise O'Brien. It often counterposed allegedly stark binaries between British (modern, rational, cultured, Protestant) and Irish (traditional, mythic, anarchic, Catholic) values. The key text is F.S.L. Lyons, *Culture and anarchy in Ireland, 1890–1939* (Oxford, 1979). Kyla Madden, 'Ten troubled years': Settlement, conflict and rebellion in Forkhill, County Armagh 1788–1798 (Unpublished M.A. thesis, Queens University [Canada], 1998) is a good later study in the 'narrow ground' tradition.

4   David Miller, 'The Armagh troubles 1784–95' in Samuel Clark and James Donnelly (eds), *Irish peasants: Violence and political unrest 1780–1914* (Dublin, 1983), pp 155–92. The concept of a classical peasantry, with its connotations of a closed, stable, sedentary and agricultural population, does not fit easily with the proto-industrial, dynamic and open Ulster society of the late eighteenth century. A more recent collection of documents is *The formation of the Orange Order 1795–1798: The edited papers of Colonel William Blacker and Colonel Robert H. Wallace,* (ed.) Cecil Kilpatrick (Belfast, 1994). A valuable earlier pamphlet is Aiken McClelland, *The origins of the Orange Order* [Belfast, n.d.].

5   R.F. Foster, *The Irish story: Telling tales and making it up in Ireland* (London, 2001), pp 211–34. See the review by Thomas Bartlett in *T.L.S.*, 25 Jan. 2002. Among Foster's errors on the 1790s, note the muddle on David Bailie Fox (*recte* Warden), Thomas Croney (*recte* Cloney), R.R. Madden's seven (*sic*) volumes between 1842 and 1846, and the misdating of Charles Dickson's book to 1953 (*recte* 1955).

6   A principal proponent of this view has been Marianne Elliott. It is a pervading theme in her *The Catholics of Ulster* (London, 2000).

7   James Smyth, *The men of no property: Irish radicals and popular politics in late eighteenth century* (London, 1992); L.M. Cullen, 'The political structure of the Defenders' in Gough and Dickson (eds), *Ireland and France*, pp 117–38; L.M. Cullen, 'Late eighteenth-century politicisation in Ireland and France: Problems in its study and its French links', in Bergeron and Cullen, *Culture et pratiques politiques*, pp 137–57; Kevin Whelan, *The tree of liberty* (Cork, 1996); Reamonn Ó Muiri, 'The killing of Thomas Birch, United Irishman, Mar. 1797 and the meeting of the Armagh freeholders 19 Apr. 1797', in *Seanchas Ard Mhacha*, x (1989), 267–319. Miller's reply to Cullen is 'Politicisation in revolutionary Ireland: The case of the Armagh troubles' in *I.E.S.H.*, xxiii (1996), 1–17. Cullen's response follows in the same issue (18–23).

8   Terence Brown, *The whole Protestant community: The making of a myth* (Derry, 1983).

north Down (with many parishes over 95 per cent Presbyterian) reacted differently to radicalism than more religiously mixed areas to the west and south of it (MacCavery, chapter 12). The political disposition of local gentry families was also a crucial factor. In areas dominated by reform-minded magnates (Antrim and Down in Ulster; Kildare, Wicklow, Carlow and Wexford in Leinster), a distinctive pattern of politicization can be traced. While not overtly United Irish in sympathy, many of these political leaders remained visibly aloof from Dublin Castle and its policies. As tension escalated in the 1790s, the Castle sought to build its own support network under the noses of these Whigs. It was forced to rely on new men with little gravitas or experience, security hardliners and often bigots who ratcheted up the level of fear and alienation. Such men (Cleland in the Ards, Blayney in south Ulster, Judkin Fitzgerald in Tipperary, Cornwall in Carlow, Rawdon in Kildare, King in Wicklow, White, Jacob and Gowan in Wexford) drove a vicious spiral of suspicion downwards into conflict.

We also need to focus more on the internal varieties, social composition and spatial distribution of religious dissent.[9] Non-Subscribers, Covenanters, Seceders, Burghers, Anti-Burghers, New and Old Light represented the enormously fissile tendencies within the intensely democratic world of Presbyterianism, but this atomization should not be seen as weakness. It reveals the advanced level of debate, the theological sophistication and the close links to Scotland within 'the auld church, the cauld church, the church without a steeple'. Of 619 Presbyterian ministers in eighteenth-century Ulster, three (Sinclair Kelburn, William Bruce and Patrick Vance) were educated in Dublin: only twenty in total were not educated in either Glasgow or Edinburgh. Presbyterian Ulster turned resolutely away from Anglican Dublin and Trinity College. Its culture was middle-class and mercantile, rather than gentry or estate-oriented. Of those Presbyterian ministers, 71 per cent were farmers' sons, 20 per cent were ministers' sons and 4 per cent were sons of merchants.[10] Unlike the Anglicans then, the Presbyterian cultural world was Scottish rather than English in orientation, staunchly middle-class and barely tinged by aristocratic pretensions. It was also an articulate, literate and theologically alert world, which put a premium on debate within a

---

9 Ian R. McBride, *Scripture politics: Ulster Presbyterianism and Irish radicalism in the late eighteenth century* (Oxford, 1998); ibid., 'When Ulster joined Ireland: Anti-popery, Presbyterian radicalism and Irish republicanism in the 1790s', in *Past & Present*, clvii (1997), 63–93. See also Patrick Griffin, 'Defining the limits of Britishness: The 'New British history' and the meaning of the revolution settlement in Ireland for Ulster's Presbyterians', in *Jn. British Studies*, xxxix (2000), 263–87; ibid., *The people with no name: Ireland's Ulster-Scots, America's Scots-Irish and the creation of a British Atlantic world 1689–1764* (Princeton, 2001). These modify the more schematic, sociologically-derived perspective of David Miller, 'Presbyterianism and modernisation in Ulster', in *Past & Present*, lxxx (1978), 66–90.
10 The data is derived from the indispensable work of J.M. Barkley, 'The Presbyterian minister in eighteenth-century Ireland', in J.L. Haire (ed.), *Challenge and conflict* (Antrim, 1981), pp 46–71.

republican mode of internal governance.[11] Within its communities, the principal arbiters were the ministers and a group of leading families – notably the Bruces and Drennans – supplied intellectual leadership across many generations. The sermon developed as a hybridized religious/political mode of communication. In the 1780s, the publication of these dissenting sermons increased dramatically, as Presbyterian ministers became prominent in the Volunteer movement: when the United Irish movement emerged, many of these ministers – Samuel Barber, Sinclair Kelburn, William Steel Dickson, Thomas Ledlie Birch, James Porter, John Glendy – had already developed a sophisticated brand of scripture politics. Edward Wakefield (1774–1854), one of the most astute English observers of Ireland, described the Dissenters as occupying a place of preference in Irish society:

> Yet possessing all these advantages, which give them a most decided superiority over the Roman Catholics, they look upon the clergy of the established church with the most sovereign contempt; shew the utmost indifference to the government, and even a want of attachment to the soil. Every public man among them who accepts an office is detested and abhorred. They emigrate, on the slightest occasion, to their favourite land of liberty, America.[12]

These conditions cleared a space for radicalism. Three of the four dissenting ministers in Newtownards (County Down) became involved in radicalism in the 1790s, for example. There is a profound contrast between such solidly Presbyterian areas of north-east Ulster and the hybrid confessional communities which abutted them further west. We also need to emphasize more that the Dissenter-dominated Ulster communities were located primarily in the Derry hinterland; existing accounts of Presbyterianism are narrowly focused on Belfast and east Ulster. Looked at in this way, the Anglican seam separating these core areas of Dissenter dominance becomes much more prominent: this seam stretched from Belfast down the Lagan valley, girdled the southern shore of Lough Neagh and curved north towards Dungannon and on to Toome.[13]

The distinctiveness of Armagh and Fermanagh emerges from this perspective. They were the only counties where Anglicans were not heavily outnumbered by Catholics and Presbyterians, creating the social base for a hegemonic landed class and a populist loyalism that was not possible elsewhere. The Lagan valley area in north Armagh was differentiated from Fermanagh by the fact that

11 Finlay Holmes, 'The eighteenth century', in his *The Presbyterian Church in Ireland: A popular history* (Dublin, 2000) is a fine introduction, which also contains the most balanced treatment of their role in 1798.

12 Edward Wakefield, *An account of Ireland, statistical and political* (London 1812), ii, p.547.

13 See the map in Whelan, *Fellowship of freedom*, p. 4, and Miller, below, p. 207.

its Anglicans were of English descent, whereas those of the more sequestered Fermanagh had Scottish origins.[14] Armagh occupied a contested space between United Irish-dominated east Ulster and the Defender heartland of south Ulster. The wider outcome of the political struggle in Ulster was to be largely determined by which way this cockpit county swung. A detailed study of the high politics of Armagh in the 1790s is still required, and of how this related to broader social developments in the county.

Hitherto, the historians' gaze in Ulster has been directed on Belfast rather than Belturbet. In south Ulster, a predominantly Catholic swathe of territory stretched from south Down through south Armagh and into Cavan, including south Fermanagh and south-west Donegal. Here lived some of the poorest, most isolated, and most homogenous communities in Ireland, harbouring a distinct sense of themselves as bearing the crushing weight of their ancestors' defeat in the seventeenth century. Stuck in the desolate drumlins and the bleak hills, they looked north and east to the fat planter lowlands. Here too were poor Protestants, overwhelmingly Anglican, who tried to lord it over their Catholic neighbours, and to whom local elites could look for support in the yeomanry and Orangemen. This is an entirely different profile – denominationally monolithic but socially stratified – to Protestant communities in east Ulster. Resentments smouldered among Catholics, even when they had no public sphere in which to articulate them. Cavan was dismissed as 'dead to politics' by an exasperated United Irishman in the early 1790s, and indeed the scutch-grass of south Ulster proved barren terrain for the United men (MacDonald, chapter 14). The task of prosleytizing it fell to a handful of Catholic families in the region who tried to stitch the Defender and United movements together. More research is needed on these closely connected families – Magennis, Teeling, Byrne, Coigley, Coyle, Carolan, Rice, Kernan and Maguire.[15] Unlike the situation in Munster and Leinster, the class divide within Catholicism did not override confessional and cultural allegiance in Ulster, where these families' position was much less assured than that of their southern counterparts. These families were heavily involved in the Catholic Convention of 1792–3, where they forged strong links with the United Irishmen. They also supplied the leadership of the Defenders, the most secretive of the many secret societies of the 1790s (Elliott, chapter 15). To the chagrin of historians, who lust after a good informer, this organisation never produced one. Historians see them through a glass darkly or through hostile commentary from uncomprehending outsiders.[16] It is only slowly that the

---

14 Robert Bell, 'Sheep stealers from the north of England: The riding clans in Ulster', in *Hist. Ir.*, ii, 4 (1994), 25–9.

15 Representatives of many of these families – Patrick Byrne, James and Patrick Carolan, James and Richard Kernan, John Magennis, Constantine and Philip Maguire, Christopher and Luke Teeling – were at the Catholic Convention of 1792–3.

16 The most accessible source on them remains Thomas Bartlett (ed.), 'Defenders and Defenderism

Defenders have been seen in a political context.[17] We still have much to learn about their politics, ideology and internal organisation.

The north-west has also been ignored. George Douglas, editor of the *London-derry Journal*, quipped in 1792 that the Belfast managers of the *Northern Star* 'vainly imagine that their moon is a better moon than the one that shines in the next parish'.[18] Historians too have measured Ulster radicalism primarily in terms of a distance-decay effect from Belfast. A closer focus on Derry city, rendered possible by the survival of a long newspaper run, suggests that radicalism did not always have to be imported from outside: it could grow from an autonomous and regionally-specific process of politicisation[19] (Mac Suibhne, chapter 13).

The United Irishmen west of the Sperrins fitted easily into an existing Volunteer template, characterized by discipline and system. Their turn towards a broader 'Irish' as opposed to a transplanted 'British' identity gained impetus from the radicals' embrace of the American Revolution, whose separation of church and state confirmed the republican tradition of many Presbyterians. From rural Derry in 1796, it was reported that 'The Presbyterians of every different sect are a stiff, proud, discontented people. They wish to have no King but a republican government. They were all on the American side during the American war. Now they are all on the French side.'[20] Patriot politics in the north-west preceded the 1790s, having been deepened and enriched by the Volunteers. The geography of rebellion and the geography of politicization were however not necessarily co-incident and understanding of the 1790s is narrowed when we adopt a teleological perspective. We need to learn just as much about communities that did not rebel as about those that did.[21]

---

in 1795', in *I.H.S.*, xxiv (1985), 373–94. This should be read alongside the companion file on the United Irishmen in the same dossier [P.R.O., H.O. 100/58/171–90]. Splitting the file perpetuates the sense of a sharp divide between the two organisations at a time when they were explicitly drawing closer together.

17 The typical 1970s view was encapsulated in A.P.W. Malcomson's dismissive description of the Defenders as 'a popular movement, swelled by religious fanaticism and the agrarian grievances of the ignorant Catholic peasantry'. [A.P.W. Malcomson (ed.), *The United Irishmen: Facsimile documents* (Belfast, 1973), p. 20.] He reflects a long line of dismissal: Andrew O'Reilly in 1853 stigmatised the Defenders as 'a desultory, fugitive and fruitless expenditure of strength in isolated nightly attacks upon houses and persons for the mere acquisition of firearms': O' Reilly, *Memoirs of an emigrant Milesian*, iii, p. 303.

18 *London-Derry Journal*, 2 October 1792. I owe this quotation to Breandán MacSuibhne.

19 A study of Strabane, 'a nest of United Irishmen,' would be valuable, given its active publishing record and the survival of the voluminous Abercorn papers: A. Campbell, *Notes on the literary history of Strabane* (Omagh, 1902). See the preliminary discussion in Stephen Conway, *The British Isles and the war of American independence* (Oxford, 2000), pp 306–13.

20 Letter [from Derry area] to James Lenderick (Shane's Castle, Co. Antrim), [late 1796]: N.A.I., RP 620/53/23.

21 Mac Suibhne, 'Up but not out.'

10

Radicalism and ritual in east Ulster

DAVID W. MILLER

This chapter offers a new way of looking at the problem of radicalism in east Ulster in the years preceding the rebellion. Although the term 'radicalism' is now very fashionable in the historiography of this period, discussions of radicalism often proceed very briskly to the activities of particular radical groups, such as the United Irishmen. We learn a great deal about the agency exercised by radical activists, but perhaps less about the structures of popular behaviour within which they operated. To be sure, a number of recent scholars have taken note of various types of politically charged ritual performance in the 1790s, ranging from freemasonry to the ceremonial harvesting of crops of arrested radicals.[1] The relationships between such phenomena and the pursuit of radical goals tend to be presented as examples of the skills of radical leaders in organization and propaganda. While that is certainly an important perspective, we should also look upon such rituals as parts of a repertoire which had evolved over time and which might constrain as well as facilitate initiatives on the part of radicals, and indeed of their opponents.

East Ulster consists of the region depicted on the two maps in Figure 10.1. While the chief central place of the region, Belfast, was dominated by a Presbyterian mercantile elite, the rest of its lowland inner core (the Lagan valley plus the low country south of Lough Neagh) was in the hands of an Anglican landed elite which had the (for Ireland) extremely unusual advantage of a tenantry many of whom were of the same religious persuasion as themselves. Both of these elites were members of the national polity – that subset of the population which regularly contended for power in national affairs. In that contention for power, however, the Belfast elite was handicapped by various anomalies of a political structure in which even the governance of their own city was under the control of the local landlord. The main object of contention was parliamentary reform, that is, the removal of obstacles to the Belfast elite's obtaining a share of influence commensurate with their wealth over the region's parliamentary representation. Smyth's

---

1 Jim Smyth, 'Freemasonry and the United Irishmen', in David Dickson, Dáire Keogh and Kevin Whelan (eds), *The United Irishmen* ... (Dublin, 1993), pp 167–75; N.J. Curtin, *The United Irishmen* ... (Oxford, 1994), pp 228–53.

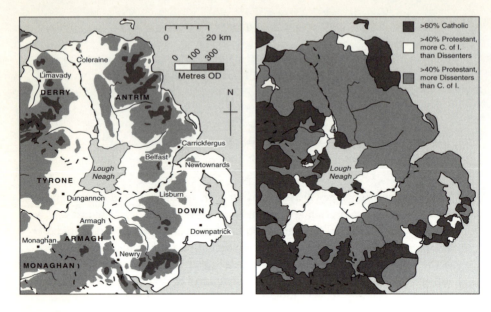

Fig. 10.1   East Ulster landforms and sectarian zones.

assertion that parliamentary reform was the focus of '[v]irtually all the political energies of radicalism' is certainly true of its Belfast adherents.[2]

We should think of the evolution of the Irish polity between 1600 and 1800 as an unsuccessful exercise in state-building.[3] The conspicuous failure of that polity to address the challenges of the 1790s led to its replacement, through the Act of Union, by a new polity of Great Britain and Ireland which, its projectors thought, might have a better chance of attaining legitimacy. In a fully legitimate modern democratic state, power consists not only of physical force (which the state, by definition, seeks to monopolize) but also of that tacit consent which most citizens, most of the time, repose in the state even if, say, they intend to vote against the current government at the next election. Nationalism and its attendant rituals contribute significantly to consent in many modern states, but in the early modern polity personalistic ties of patronage no doubt counted for more than any imper- sonal sense of 'imagined community' analogous to modern nationalism.[4] The Irish polity was routinely defended less by government forces than by the local landlord who relied for the necessary coercive force upon his able-bodied male clients. In other words, to the extent that the Irish 'state' in the eighteenth century

2   Jim Smyth, *The men of no property* (Dublin, 1992), p. 15.
3   D.W. Miller, 'Non-professional soldiery, *c*.1600–1800', in Thomas Bartlett and Keith Jeffery (eds), *A military history of Ireland* (Cambridge, 1996), pp 315–16.
4   Benedict Anderson, *Imagined communities* (rev. and extended ed., London, 1991).

enjoyed more power than the physical force at the immediate disposal of the government, it resulted not so much from popular consent as from the participation of members of the polity and their clients in the deployment of force.

The words 'state' and 'power' are here used as a political scientist might use them: power is the ability to get things done – most fundamentally to secure compliance with the state's basic political laws. But it is instructive to consider also how an anthropologist might use the words. Geertz has coined the term 'theatre state' to characterize the polity of nineteenth-century Bali. He points out that our word 'state' carries not only the connotation of governance ('statecraft') but also those of status ('estate') and pomp ('stateliness'). Concepts of public power are deficient, in Geertz's view, insofar as they neglect the latter two of these connotations and miss 'the symbolic dimensions of state power,' which in the Balinese case are paramount.[5] One reason to prefer the word 'polity' over 'state' is that it allows us to avoid an exclusive choice between a Weberian ideal type of the state which is implicit in many historians' use of the term 'state-building' and the Geertzian application of the term 'state' to political formations which are very remote from that ideal type. The failure of the eighteenth-century Irish polity to develop into a modern state invites us to think of that polity in its terminal phase, from 1780 to 1800, as a theatre state. To do so is to consider major actors in the events of that period not as the inventors of modern Irish nationalism – an ideology which would arise in response to the dysfunctions of the new polity of which they as yet knew nothing – but as players of their assigned roles on a stage they knew very well.

The government itself, of course, was a major player in the theatre state. Such events as processions of high officials, military display and the elaborate rituals associated with the viceregal court asserted the 'stateliness' of that component of the polity which manipulated the administrative levers of power from the capital. Outside Dublin the government also played important roles in political theatre such as ceremonies surrounding judicial processes in county towns, including the exemplary spectacles of corporal and capital punishment. In most parts of the countryside, however, non-governmental players probably upstaged the central administration's act most of the time in the two decades preceding the crisis of the 1790s. This was especially true in east Ulster, where four different types of non-governmental organizations which practised politically salient rituals enjoyed remarkable growth in the second half of the eighteenth century – (1) rural 'combinations' such as the Oakboys, Steelboys, Peep o' Day Boys and Defenders; (2) Volunteer units; (3) masonic lodges; and (4) the covenant-based Presbyterian sects. We should think of these very disparate phenomena in the context of the increasingly evident dysfunctions of a political system which eventually collapsed in the 1790s.

5 Clifford Geertz, *Negara: The theatre state in nineteenth-century Bali* (Princeton, 1980), pp 121–3.

TABLE I
A repertoire of political ritual:
Ideal types present in east Ulster, *c.*1760–1790

Characteristic ritual venue		
	Public	**Secret**
Leaders mainly within polity	**Patriotic** 1. Volunteering 2. Affirming 3. Patronship 4. Military force	**Illuminist** 1. Freemasonry 2. Challenging 3. Civil society 4. Reason
Leaders mainly outside polity	**Theocratic** 1. Covenant renewal, holy fairs 2. Challenging 3. Godly magistracy 4. Providence	**Communitarian** 1. Sectarian and agrarian 'combinations' 2. Affirming 3. Moral economy 4. Community solidarity

1. = examples
2. = posture toward the existing patron-client political culture
3. = political ideal
4. = method for reaching that ideal

The four growth areas in political ritual during during the period 1760–90 can be classified according to two criteria: (1) did the leadership of the bodies which practiced the ritual form fall within or outside the social boundaries of the polity; and (2) did the rituals occur primarily in public or in secret? This exercise gives us a typology of four types of political ritual which I have labelled 'patriotic,' 'illuminist,' 'communitarian' and 'theocratic,' in Table I.

'Patriotic' performance took place in public and is represented by Volunteering, whose leaders were members of the polity. By dressing up in elaborate military costume and parading with guns, the Volunteers invented rituals which defined the social boundaries of the polity in an era when the right to bear arms was a more salient mark of political participation than the franchise. No doubt these rituals drew emotive force from their gender implications. The phallic connotations of sporting a gun or sword are obvious enough, and at least one contemporary noted the utility of Volunteer participation in catching the eyes of the ladies.[6] Volunteering might highlight the claims of those males who had been unmanned by the laws and social conventions hitherto delimiting the polity, for

6   Patrick Rogers, *The Irish Volunteers and Catholic Emancipation, 1778–1793* (London, 1934), p. 49, citing Francis Dobbs, *A history of Irish affairs from 1779 to 1782* (Dublin, 1783), pp 37–8.

example by enlisting respectable Catholics or, in County Armagh, whole companies of Protestants initially considered too poor to participate.

In Ireland as a whole, Volunteer ritual primarily dramatized contention within the polity between gentry and government. In east Ulster after 1782, however, it dramatized contention between the landed and the mercantile elites. Since Presbyterians had long been welcomed in times of alarm into formal and informal military arrays (even when it had been technically illegal for them to bear arms), Volunteer display was a suitable way in which to demonstrate the discrepancy between the polity's need for their support and the barriers which electoral arrangements erected against effective contention for power by their leaders. Nevertheless, to the extent that Volunteering consisted of landlords arming their tenants, it acted out the existing patron-client political culture.

The rituals of secret societies which sought to enforce the values of the peasant community can be classified as 'communitarian'. Over the previous generation east Ulster had experienced agrarian/proto-industrial protest on the part of 'combinations' known as Hearts of Oak, Hearts of Steel and Peep o' Day Boys. The last of these metamorphosed in the 1780s into a Protestant sectarian movement whose activities in County Armagh evoked a Catholic counterpart, the Defenders. What justifies grouping these diverse phenomena together is that prior to the 1790s they do not make claims for their groups' membership in the polity.[7] Rather, they try to hold the members of the polity, their betters, to account for economic and political arrangements which are just, according to their respective lights – for fair rents or for limitation of road work, for keeping guns out of the hands of Catholics or, conversely, for preventing Protestant raids on their houses. Obviously different communities had different visions of the moral economy. In general, however, they propagated in east Ulster a repertoire of collective action and ritual performance comparable to that which flourished in many other parts of Ireland under the rubric of Whiteboyism. Despite their very different constituencies, patriotic and communitarian ritual were complementary celebrations of the social relationships implicit in the existing political culture. When Hearts of Oak or Peep o' Day Boys sought to hold landlords accountable for their obligations to their community, they were affirming the patron-client culture of local politics just as surely as did their (perhaps slightly better-off) neighbours who strutted about with their landlord's muskets on their shoulders.

The most important example of what I have called 'illuminist' ritual is freemasonry, whose proximate origins lie within the polity even though it affirmed a new sort of political culture. As Jacob has argued, freemasonry is a significant factor in the emergence of the idea of 'modern civil society' in eigh-

7 D.W. Miller, 'Politicisation in revolutionary Ireland: The case of the Armagh troubles', in *I.E.S.H.*, xxiii (1996), 13.

teenth-century Europe. Masonic lodges were intended as little polities in which, under a written 'constitution,' men committed to the priority of merit over birth met and celebrated with ceremony and sociability an enlightened vision of the social order. Thus 'the civic consciousness developed in the lodges perforce addressed the nature and purpose of the polity' in the larger sense,[8] although lodges were supposed to eschew 'politics' in the narrower sense of partisan contention. In ceremonies entailing some degree of pain and humiliation, new members were required to take an oath binding them not to reveal the secrets of the 'craft'. An important component of those secrets consisted of gestures and other signs by which a mason might make his membership in the craft known to another mason without revealing it to others present.[9] Although there was some female participation in continental freemasonry by the late eighteenth century, in Ireland the craft remained restricted to males.[10] Irish freemasonry thus promoted the bonding of males in a secret brotherhood. Perhaps even in this respect, the craft modelled the larger polity as radicals thought it ought to be, for even such an ideologue as William Drennan could dismiss the question of female suffrage as 'far-fetched' and 'speculative'.[11]

Theocratic ritual systems also affirmed a political culture very different from the dominant one in eighteenth-century Ireland. Unlike illuminist ritual which looked forward to modern civil society – albeit a male-dominated one – theocratic ritual looked backward to the political order contemplated in the sixteenth- and seventeenth-century Scottish covenants. Three Presbyterian sects, the Reformed Presbyterians and the Antiburgher and Burgher Seceders, which in the latter half of the eighteenth century erected about ninety congregations in Ulster,[12] preserved this 'old leaven' in ritual forms which had generally been abandoned by the mainstream General Synod. Seceding ministers were required to accept the continuing obligations of the sixteenth- and seventeenth-century Scottish covenants, and at least some congregations from time to time went through a ceremony of subscribing their names to a document renewing those covenants.[13] More importantly, in these wilder fringes of Scottish Presbyterianism, the sacraments were understood to be renewals of the covenants, an

---

8 M.C. Jacob, *Living the Enlightenment* (New York, 1991), p. 32 and passim.
9 David Stevenson, *The origins of freemasonry* (Cambridge, 1988), pp 125–65; S.C. Bullock, *Revolutionary brotherhood* (Chapel Hill, 1996), pp 16–7.
10 Jacob, *Living the Enlightenment*, pp 120–42. For an Irish exception which proves the rule, see J.H. Lepper and Philip Crossle, *History of the Grand Lodge* (Dublin, 1925), i, pp 38–9.
11 *Belfast politics* (Belfast, 1794), pp 142, 147.
12 David Stewart, *The Seceders in Ireland* (Belfast, 1950), pp 279–352; Adam Loughridge, *The Covenanters in Ireland* (2nd ed., Belfast, 1987), p. 135. Apparently about fourteen new general synod congregations were erected in this period: 'Increase of Congregations under the care of the General Synod of Ulster', in the *Orthodox Presbyterian*, i, 6 (Mar. 1830), 190–6.
13 For the actual document by which the Roseyards Antiburgher congregation renewed the covenants in 1764 and 1780, see P.R.O.N.I., Tennant papers, D.1748/A/2/2/1.

understanding which mainstream Presbyterian clergy were careful to eschew.[14] The Seceders' practice of open-air communions – satirized by Robert Burns as 'Holy Fairs' – which drew communicants and spectators from far afield,[15] was another ritual which challenged the status quo in the theatre state. The fact that these events recalled the days of persecution in the late seventeenth century reinforced their implicit political salience; the presence of non-communicants in a penumbra of drink, conviviality and courtship enabled the festivals to reaffirm an ethnic community broader than the constituency of these sects.[16]

As *ideal types*, the four ritual regimens did not spell disaster for the political system. Patriotic and communitarian ritual even affirmed the existing political culture. Theocratic and illuminist ritual seemed to challenge that culture only by offering utopian alternatives to the time-honoured standard of birth for the holding of political power – godliness on the one hand and merit on the other. In the actual circumstances of the polity's dysfunctions, however, the concrete manifestations of the four ideal types changed in ways which defied the neat boundaries imposed upon them in Table I, and ultimately contributed to the polity's collapse. In east Ulster two such changes were in progress before the 1790s.

Although the model for Volunteering in the late 1770s was clearly drawn from the mustering of clients by patrons in earlier times of alarm, the innovation of rank-and-file Volunteers electing their own officers in the vicinity of Belfast and other towns must have compromised the patron-client culture.[17] Moreover, once the clients had assisted their patrons to enhance the latter's own power *vis-à-vis* the government in 1782, the question whether the clients themselves might properly be part of the polity was unavoidable. Though the landed elite managed to abort the parliamentary reform initiative of 1783–4, they could not halt the shifting of the polity's social boundaries as various of their number sought allies among groups hitherto wholly or partly excluded from it: wealthy Catholics, respectable non-elite Protestants, Catholic peasants, the Protestant 'rabble'. At the same time, the complementary relationship between patriotic and communitarian ritual was in decay. Incidents in which Oakboys forced gentlemen to swear to uphold community standards in the early 1760s seem not to have recurred in the Steelboy troubles of the 1770s.[18] To the extent that the 'moral economy' atti-

---

14 T.L. Birch, *Physicians languishing under disease* (Belfast, 1796), p. 27. A denial that communion is a 'federal rite' is contained in J. Leland, J. Duchal, I. Weld, and J. Mears, *Forms of devotion for the use of families* (Dublin, 1772), pp 114–16.

15 For an example of a holy fair at Lyle Hill, see Classon Porter, *Ulster biographical sketches* (Belfast, 1884), p. 39.

16 Cf. L.E. Schmidt, *Holy fairs: Scottish communions and American revivals in the early modern period* (Princeton, 1989).

17 Rogers, *Irish Volunteers*, p. 45; A.T.Q. Stewart, *A deeper silence* (London, 1993), p. 6.

18 J.S. Donnelly, Jnr., 'Hearts of Oak, Hearts of Steel', in *Studia Hibernica*, xxi (1981), 9, 11. In his very thorough treatment of the subject, the author does not report any analogue of these Heart of Oak practices on the part of the Hearts of Steel.

tude toward the gentry was still alive among the Protestant lower orders by the 1790s, it probably took a sectarian form which aggravated the dysfunctions of the system.

The early strategy of the Belfast radicals who formed the United Irish Society included roles for both patriotic and illuminist ritual. The Volunteers would be reactivated and utilized for public advocacy of the reform agenda while a new radical society would be organized on masonic lines.[19] Little thought was given to either communitarian or theocratic rituals which were at that point beneath the notice of the enlightened gentlemen of the 'northern Athens'. A juncture of patriotic and illuminist ritual seemed practical enough, no doubt, for during the preceding decades there had been several explicitly masonic Volunteer units.[20]

At first the appropriation of patriotic ritual was quite a successful means for the Belfast elite to express its political claims, as became evident in the celebration of the third anniversary of the fall of the Bastille in 1792.[21] This and similar events demonstrated the claim of the Belfast radicals to equal membership in the polity with landlords who could display their retainers in military array. Its symbolic significance had little to do with the soldiery's ideological leanings. Theobald Wolfe Tone's famous comment that some of the country corps, especially from County Down, who participated in the 1792 Bastille day parade, were 'no better than Peep-of-day-boys' is corroborated by a correspondent of Lord Hillsborough,[22] one of the chief promoters of the Militia Bill of 1793,[23] shortly before its enactment:

> Your Lordship asks how the county stands affected round Hillsborough: I believe in general anti-Catholic and just about as well inclined for militia, but it is reported that they have hung you in effigy at or about Templepatrick. Your opponents in your own county ring the militia in the ears of the Volunteers to make you unpopular.[24]

It was precisely the fact that nearby Volunteer units could so easily be turned against magnates like Hillsborough that gave them such significance in the eyes of the Belfast elite. The aristocratic leadership of the Volunteers in the 1780s was a fact to be explained away: 'it was not Lord Charlemont that raised the Volunteers,' William Sampson would declare a few years later; 'it was the Volunteers that raised Lord Charlemont.'[25]

19 Curtin, *United Irishmen*, p. 51; Stewart, *Deeper silence*, pp 156–60.
20 Lepper and Crossle, *History of the Grand Lodge*, i, pp 246–9.
21 Samuel McSkimin, *Annals of Ulster from 1790 to 1798* (Belfast, 1906), p. 9.
22 T.W. Tone, *Life of Theobald Wolfe Tone*, ed. W.T.W. Tone (Washington, 1826), i, 157.
23 Henry McAnally, *The Irish militia, 1793–1816* (Dublin, 1949), pp. 14–27.
24 John Slade to Lord Hillsborough, 3 Mar. 1793: P.R.O.N.I., Downshire papers, D.607/B/384.
25 *N.S.*, 2–6 Jan. 1797.

Initially the formation of United Irish societies on masonic principles was less clearly successful than the revival of Volunteering. In its early form, the United movement seems to have spread only to Dublin, and to a few villages within twenty miles of so of Belfast.[26] If this experience was disappointing, the seeming failure was more than compensated for by widespread mobilisation of masonic lodges themselves in the interest of the Belfast radical agenda. In December 1792 and January 1793, despite the order's rule against partisan advocacy, resolutions by a number of northern masonic lodges in favour of reform and/or Catholic relief appeared in the newly-established Belfast radical newspaper, the *Northern Star*.[27] At the end of the year a partisan rift emerged within east Ulster freemasonry. The General Committee of the Free and Accepted Masons of County Armagh issued a declaration against reform. A meeting of masons in Dungannon responded with a declaration in favour of reform and the ringing appeal: 'Let every lodge in the land become a company of citizen soldiers. Let every Volunteer company become a lodge of Masons.' The Grand Lodge in Dublin issued a circular reiterating the rule against partisan proceedings, but northern masons had little difficulty in evading the rule, for example, by adjourning a masonic meeting into an 'Assembly of Masonic Citizens' when controversial subjects were to be acted upon.[28]

The strategy of combining the patriotic and illuminist ritual might seem contradictory since it has been suggested that generally Volunteering affirmed and freemasonry challenged the existing patron-client political culture. Actually this seeming contradiction mirrored a genuine ambiguity in the outlook of the Belfast radicals. On the one hand they longed for an enlightened political order in which a reformed parliament would accurately reflect the ideas and interests of the citizenry. On the other hand they operated within a system which demanded an answer to the question 'Who can be trusted in the defence of the polity?' Volunteering was a means of asserting that they themselves could be so trusted. In early 1793 the Belfast Volunteers took credit for protecting the town and neighbourhood from increasing threats of 'combination and outrage,' and they were especially proud of the fact that during the previous year they had assisted the sheriff of County Antrim in evicting a tenant who had voted against the wishes of his landlord despite the fact that the latter 'stood directly opposed to this town in election matters.' Indeed they went so far as to deny vehemently that in their recent growth and renovation they had any intention 'to intimidate

---

26 Stewart, *Deeper silence*, pp 162–3.
27 See resolutions of masonic meetings in Maghera, Grange, Tobermore, Hamiltonsbawn, Comber, Aughnacloy, Malone, Randalstown, Lisburn, Dungannon, Toome, Downpatrick, Clough, Castledawson, Enniskillen in *N.S.*, 15–19 Dec. 1792, 29 Dec. 1792 – 2 Jan. 1793, 2–5 Jan., 5–9 Jan., 9–12 Jan., 12–16 Jan., 16–19 Jan., 19–23 Jan., 2–6 Feb. 1793; Charles Dickson, *Revolt in the north* (Dublin, 1960), p. 90.
28 Rogers, *Irish Volunteers*, p. 288–9; Lepper and Crossle, *History of the Grand Lodge*, pp 292–8.

the legislature'. To be sure, reform was 'the first desire' of their hearts, but they only wished it 'to proceed from the general will of our countrymen'. Meanwhile they asserted, remarkably, that they were 'ready and willing to co-operate with government in opposing any party or set of men whatever, who should presume to impose any plan or wild ideas of reform upon the Irish nation.'[29]

We should take this rhetoric quite seriously. Intoxicated as they were by Enlightenment-style veneration of reason, Belfast radicals found it easy to believe that the deluded would come to their senses. Indeed, at the very moment that these words were written, the British government was coming to its senses by inducing the Irish parliament to grant Catholics the franchise. The fact that the Volunteers had won major concessions from the government a decade earlier without having to fire their guns in anger probably made it easier to suppose that public performance was enough. However, Dublin Castle was deaf to this revealing apologia, and within days a proclamation was issued to ban further Volunteer displays in Belfast and vicinity. In addition, over the next year the authorities made various efforts to cripple the illuminist half of radical strategy through prosecutions of United Irish activists.[30] The principal effect of this harrassment was to push the United Irish societies to more serious efforts to preserve secrecy than were dictated by the somewhat relaxed model of eighteenth-century freemasonry.

It was, however, the ban on Volunteer display which had the more drastic effect upon the radicalism of east Ulster. The Belfast elite was not easily reconciled to this loss of the public component of the patriotic-illuminist role they had developed for themselves in the Irish theatre state over the previous two years. When rumours of an impending Orange attack on Belfast in March 1796 prompted the doubling of military guards in the town, for example, a meeting of 'a number of those who had borne arms in the Volunteer ranks in this town' would express willingness 'to co-operate with the military ... in defence of the town and neighbourhood'.[31] Such overtures, however, were not to be honoured. From 1793 the Belfast radicals were deprived of a crucial component of the ritual repertoire hitherto available to them: patriotic performance. If they wished now to play a role more exalted than critics and prompters in the Irish theatre state, they would surely be tempted to invite members of the audience to join them in storming the stage.

So from 1793 we might well expect Belfast radicals to seek to repair their loss of access to patriotic ritual by making contact with a ritual style which originated outside the polity – theocratic or communitarian – and the most likely candidate would seem to be the communitarian Defenders. We are greatly in the debt of Louis Cullen, Kevin Whelan and Jim Smyth for their heroic labours to ferret out contacts between United Irishmen and Defenders in the borderlands of east

29 *Belfast politics*, pp 44–7, 130–5.
30 Curtin, *United Irishmen*, pp 59–61.
31 *N.S.*, 24–28 Mar. 1796.

Ulster and beyond. As our surviving documentation from the countryside is much sparser before 1795 than thenceforward, we cannot rule out the possibility of wider contacts in the early nineties than they have been able to establish. However, prior to the summer of 1795 these contacts seem to have been initiated mostly by occasional sojourners in the Belfast scene – Keogh, Tone, Russell, perhaps Coigly – rather than by Belfast-based radicals.[32] With the Armagh expulsions, however, we get quite solid evidence of Belfast purposively making and exploiting such contacts. During the expulsions, from the autumn of 1795 to the spring of 1796, one Barny McMahon, for example,

> went frequently from Belfast to the Counties of Armagh, Cavan and Fermanagh. He and his Brothers continued their Excursions and Endea-vors to make Proselytes, and Barny has lately returned to Belfast from the County of Leitrim, and other seats of Defenders, his principal business was to ascertain the number of men engaged in the Cause of Sedition and to establish a Communication between them and Belfast.[33]

Whelan's contention that the expulsions were sponsored by the government is not supported by his evidence,[34] but his metaphor for the expulsions – the 'the-atre of terror' – is apt indeed, for by condoning the expulsions a major section of the Anglican elite of north Armagh erected a stage on which their contention with the Presbyterian elite of Belfast would be acted out. By becoming the pat-rons of the Orange Order, which arose as a popular combination of the Pro-testant terrorists, Armagh gentry began a process of appropriating the patriotic ritual style for their side in this contention. Despite government misgivings, they successfully stage-managed 12th of July parading by Orangemen in 1796, thus capturing the centrepiece of the Volunteer repertoire. To be sure, their clients were parading without weapons, but the guns would come soon enough, for the gentry of north Armagh and adjacent parts of Down and Tyrone were already lobbying the government for some new armed association made up of clients they could trust – as opposed to Catholics, who predominated in the militia.[35] Orangemen were prominent in the ranks of the yeomanry formed in late 1796 as a result of this lobbying.

32 Smyth, *Men of no property*, pp 66–70; Whelan, *The tree of liberty* (Notre Dame, IN, 1996), pp 39–42; L.M. Cullen 'The political structures of the Defenders', in Hugh Gough and David Dickson (eds), *Ireland and the French Revolution* (Dublin, 1990), pp 117–38; 'Late eighteenth-century politicisation in Ireland: Problems in its study and its French links', in Louis Bergeron and L.M. Cullen (eds), *Culture et pratiques politiques en France et en Irelande, XVIe-XVIIIe siècle* (Paris, 1991), pp 137–58.

33 Andrew MacNevin to Pelham, 9 May 1796: N.A.I., RP 620/23/101.

34 Whelan, *Tree of liberty*, pp 122–6; D.W. Miller, 'The origins of the Orange Order in County Armagh', in A.J. Hughes, F.X. McCorry and R. Weatherup (eds), *Armagh: History and society* (Dublin, 2001), pp 583–608.

35 Ibid.

The distinction between what was to be created now and the force that had arisen two decades earlier, however, was not always clear even to loyalists. As the idea of a yeomanry took shape, Lord Gosford spoke of raising 'Volunteers' as a good idea, and the marquis of Hertford used the terms 'yeomanry' and 'Volunteers' as synonyms.[36] A government supporter in Omagh attended a Presbyterian meeting house to urge the congregation to unite 'as Volunteers in order to stop the hopes of our enemies'.[37] In Donaghadee an opponent of reform explained the Yeomanry bill 'as going merely to legalise Volunteers who associate for defence of country and King and constitution'.[38] Once the yeomanry was constituted, however, its distinction from the Volunteers became clear in the requirement that yeomen take the oath of allegiance, which radical propaganda interpreted as binding them to support specific obnoxious laws such as the Convention Act and the Insurrection Act.[39] This was undoubtedly the distinction that a Belfast town meeting had in mind when, in the wake of the attempted French landing in Bantry Bay, they responded to a government request that they form a yeomanry unit with resolutions calling for reform and a declaration, 'that we are ready, if permitted by Government, to arm in like manner as the Volunteers, whose memory we revere and whose example we wish to imitate'.[40]

A preoccupation with oaths and/or other forms of binding obligation had long been common to the main examples of all four types of ritual. The emphasis on oath-taking in the rituals of freemasonry and of many peasant 'combinations' was heightened as illuminist and communitarian traditions converged in the United Irish recruitment of peasants, both Catholic and Presbyterian.[41] Conversely, both Volunteering and covenanting entailed some aversion to taking oaths, in particular those prescribed by the government. In the case of east Ulster Volunteers, refusal to take such oaths was considered essential to the patriotic project, though southern Volunteer units seem to have been somewhat more relaxed on the subject.[42] Seceder objections to taking oaths by touching and kissing the book

---

36 W.N. Bell to Lees, 24 Aug. 1796: N.A.I., RP 620/24/153; [2nd Mqs of] Hertford to Downshire, 2 Sept. 1796: P.R.O.N.I., Downshire Papers, D.607/D/147.

37 James Buchanan, Omagh, to —, 19 Sept. 1796: N.A.I., RP 620/25/133.

38 James Arbuckle to [Downshire], 20 Oct. 1796: Downshire Papers, D.607/D/243.

39 Handbill entitled 'To the Yeomanry' enclosed in N. Alexander to H. Alexander, 8 Nov. 1796: N.A.I., RP 620/26/32.

40 *N.S.*, 30 Dec. 1796–2 Jan. 1797.

41 Among the peasant 'combinations' active in east Ulster, Hearts of Steel and Defenders at least seem to have practiced initiatory oath-taking comparable to that of freemasonry. The Hearts of Steel also imposed oaths upon members of their community in the interest of solidarity: F.J. Bigger, *The Ulster land war of 1770 (The Hearts of Steel)* (Dublin, 1910), pp 101, 145; Sir Richard Musgrave, *Memoirs of the different rebellions in Ireland*, ed. S.W. Myers and D.E. McKnight (4th ed., Fort Wayne, IN, 1995), pp 604–6.

42 Peter Smyth, '"Our Cloud-Cap't Grenadiers": The Volunteers as a military force', in *Irish Sword*, xiii, 52 (1978–79), 192–3.

as was customary in the Irish courts were only partially resolved by 1782 legisla-tion, and Seceding clergy continued to agonize during the 1790s over demands to demonstrate their loyalty by taking the oath of allegiance.[43] More general scruples about oath-taking extended beyond the Seceding and Reformed Presbyterian sects to mainstream Presbyterians as well, a fact which accounts for Drennan's denial, in a 1792 disputation with the New Light minister William Bruce, that the United Irish 'test' which he had composed was an oath at all.[44]

Against this background, developments in 1796–97 placed this emotionally-charged matter of oath-taking at the centre of the political stage. The Insur-rection Act of 1796 forged the authorities' principal weapon in the struggle against radicalism by making it a capital felony to administer an oath entailing membership, obedience or secrecy in such an organization as the United Irishmen.[45] As United Irish membership was rising rapidly in these years, the administration of such oaths must have been one of their most common activi-ties, especially in ethnically homogeneous areas like much of Antrim where there was little occasion for overt conflict. Moreover, from the fall of 1796 many mag-istrates began to offer people the opportunity to dispel suspicion by taking the oath of allegiance – a practice which was formalised in the procedures used in General Lake's disarming of Ulster a few months later.[46]

On both sides the swearing itself seems to have been as important as what was sworn to. Local United Irish societies seem to have been at liberty to devise vari-ations on the oath adopted in a secret convention in 1795.[47] Magistrates appar-ently felt free to improvize variations on the oath of allegiance either to remove snares for tender consciences[48] or to create them,[49] as their own sympathies dic-tated. Some gentry tried to use oath-taking to flush out persons who had already taken the United Irish oath,[50] but one magistrate claimed that such an effort had

43 Stewart, *Seceders*, pp 416–21, 102–3, 262–3; Information of John McMullen enclosed in Gen. Wilford to Pelham, 15 Aug. 1797: N.A.I., RP 620/32/50; Charles Hamilton to Pelham, 30 June 1797: N.A.I., RP 620/31/175.
44 G.V. Sampson, *Statistical survey of the county of Londonderry* (Dublin, 1802), p. 457; *Belfast poli-tics*, pp 152–3. Cf. Drennan to S. McTier, Belfast, 'about Dec.' 1791, in D.A. Chart (ed.), *The Drennan letters* (Belfast, 1931), pp 68–9.
45 R.B. McDowell, *Ireland in the age of imperialism and revolution, 1760–1801* (Oxford, 1979), p. 552.
46 See, e.g., *N.S.*, 23–26 Sept. 1796; John Richardson to —, 15 Oct. 1796: N.A.I., RP 620/25/171.
47 Anonymous, Newry, to —, 10 May 1796: N.A.I., RP 620/23/102; Curtin, *United Irishmen*, p. 247; J.L. McCracken, 'The United Irishmen', in T.D. Williams (ed.), *Secret societies in Ireland* (Dublin, 1973), p. 64.
48 Charles M. Warburton to Pelham, 4 Jun. 1797: N.A.I., RP 620/31/29. Cf. the text of the oath administered by Warburton with the official text: Stewart, *Seceders*, p. 102.
49 Wm Richardson to —, 9 Apr. [1797]: N.A.I., RP 620/29/204; Jas Arbuckle to Col. Ross, 30 May 1797: N.A.I., RP 620/30/252.
50 Copy of Knox, Dungannon, to Thomas Caulfield, 5 June 1797: P.R.O.N.I., Calendar of Pelham Papers, T.755/5.

been frustrated in his neighbourhood by the practice of radical masonic lodges admitting members, in effect, into United Irish secrets by using the masonic oath of secrecy, leaving the initiate free to swear that he had never taken a United Irish oath.[51]

The veritable frenzy of swearing was satirised in the paper supposedly found by Billy Bluff which advertised *'Oaths! Oaths! Oaths!'* for sale at the 'Humbug Office' on 'Delusion-street.'[52] One might well wonder with Dr Haliday of Belfast what good all the swearing might do. 'People that take the oath do it willingly or unwillingly. In swearing the former, where is the use, or the latter, where is the security?' The lesson which Haliday drew – that 'the practice lessens the reverence for that sacred bond of society, vitiates the mind, and miserably weakens the ties of moral and civil duty' – rests on the comfortable whiggish assumption that a consensual society did in fact exist at that point.[53] He was, however, focusing on the right issue: the bond of society. Precisely because the only social bond which this society knew – arming that share of the manhood that could be trusted – was now in tatters, all manner of folk were reduced to the illusory security of inducing or coercing one another to embrace, on pain of divine retribution, some vision of a social order which manifestly did not exist. Whatever scraps of a social bond still existed in east Ulster in 1796 were shredded beyond all recognition by the floggings, burnings and unspeakable cruelties of the spring of 1797.

We might well end here, for certainly a great many of the Belfast radicals of five years earlier now saw clearly that in their quarrel with the landed class of their region, they had been bested; their opponents would stop at no manner of barbarity to gain their point. But it would be a mistake to end here for two reasons: first because it has yet to be explained how a remnant in the east Ulster countryside remained ready to go out in '98 against all odds, and second because, paradoxically, the Belfast radicals had not been bested.

To address the first of these points, we should return to the one type of political ritual whose role in the crisis I have not yet directly addressed: the theocratic.[54] What distinguished the old leaven preached by the Seceders and Reformed Presbyterians from the message of their Methodist rivals was a focus upon the political structures of the external world, rather than upon the inner world of the sinner's heart, as the arena in which to look for providential intervention. The aversion to oaths recognizing the legitimacy of the present political order was founded upon confidence that sooner or later the Almighty would intervene to establish that godly order in the three kingdoms which the 1690 settlement had failed to secure. By the 1790s, however, the Seceding clergy were differenti-

51 Andrew Newton, Coagh, to —, 9 Feb. 1798: N.A.I., RP 620/35/133.
52 *N.S.*, 28 Nov.–2 Dec. 1796.
53 Haliday to Charlemont, 28 Jan. 1797, *HMC Charlemont*, ii, 293.
54 I have dealt with aspects of this issue in D.W. Miller, 'Presbyterianism and 'modernisation' in Ulster', in *Past & Present*, lxxx (Aug. 1978), 66–90.

ated from their Reformed Presbyterian counterparts by the fact that they had recently yielded to the temptation to accept a modest regium donum from the very government to which they still scrupled to swear allegiance. If this compromise of old leaven principles made the Seceding clergy more compliant, however, there is no reason to suppose that it had any similar effect upon their adherents. A government correspondent, reporting intelligence on the United Irishmen from a loyal Antiburgher minister, added, 'I am sorry to say the laity among Seceders are very generally infected.'[55]

We should regard all of the Presbyterian sects from the non-subscribing Presbytery of Antrim and moderatist General Synod of Ulster through the Burgher and Antiburgher Seceders to the strict covenanting of Reformed Presbyterianism as one religious system whose clergy competed for adherents from the same ethno-religious population. The temporizing of the Seceding clergy probably made their laity more receptive to the preaching of the Reformed Presbyterians, whose practice of preaching in the fields extended a component of the old leaven's ritual system beyond specifically eucharistic occasions.[56] The tenor of such open-air preaching seems to have been decidedly millenarian.[57] The more secular of the Belfast radicals no doubt were embarrassed by their own ethnic ties and common religious antecedents with the covenanting sects. Yet even such a secular figure as Samuel Neilson, editor of the *Northern Star*, realized when he received a letter containing 'a foolish old prophecy' that he must publish it 'to please his country readers'.[58] A mainstream Presbyterian minister like Thomas Ledlie Birch might dabble in millenarian speculation, which indeed flourished throughout Great Britain and Ireland during the French Revolution, but predictions of imminent providential intervention in the world tapped into a deep strain of supernaturalism in the thinking of Presbyterian country folk. A hagiographic life of the seventeenth-century covenanter, Alexander Peden, which attracted great interest in Presbyterian districts in the 1790s, prophesied not only an eventual French deliverance but various less momentous events including misfortunes which then fell on individuals who had crossed the prophet himself.[59]

---

55 Thomas Whinnery to John Lees, 13 Sept. 1796: N.A.I., RP 620/25/ 57.

56 It is probably in this context that we should try to understand the curious disavowal of 'tumultuous or disorderly meetings' by 'the Reformed Church in the Counties of Antrim and Down', in *N.S.*, 7–10 Oct. 1796. Cf. McSkimin, *Annals*, pp 37–8; Loughridge, *Covenanters*, pp 44–5.

57 McSkimin, *Annals*, p. 35. Cf. preface by the Reformed Presbyterian minister William Stavely to William Fleming, *A discourse on the rise and fall of Antichrist wherein the revolution in France and the downfall of monarchy in that kingdom are distinctly pointed out* (Belfast, 1795), pp iii–vii.

58 Curtin, *United Irishmen*, p. 190.

59 McSkimin, *Annals*, pp 32–3; *The life and prophecies of Mr Alexander Peden* (Cork, 1791), pp 30, 40–3, 45, 52, and passim.

In 1797 even a loyalist might muse, dejectedly, 'we are like the Christians in the first century, who every day expected the world would be at an end … nothing can persuade us but that some great event is at hand. God grant it may be otherwise.'[60] It should thus not be surprising that humbler county folk, who practised a ritual system which continued to affirm the imminent possibility of providential intervention in the political order, should read the signs of the times with both more optimism and more assurance. The theocratic ritual system has relatively little to do, perhaps, with the *origins* of radicalism in this region in the late eighteenth century. It can, however, help us understand how, when reason dictated to most Belfast radicals that the game was up, some of their country cousins might see matters differently. It also helps us understand why the rebel commander at Ballynahinch had to contend with the desertion of 'a great number of pious Covenanters' on account of 'irreligious expressions and profanations of the Sabbath day'.[61]

For students of Catholic society in the late eighteenth century, the point of studying radicalism in this period might well be to explicate the processes of 'politicization' which led up to the rebellion. The failure of the rebellion itself contributes to the significance of the endeavour, for the continuing existence of unredressed grievances gives explanatory power to the politicization uncovered in the 1790s – even in parts of Ireland which did not participate in the rebellion. The situation in east Ulster is different. From the standpoint of radical objectives which had been most consistently articulated there, the rebellion was not a failure, but a success. At least as late as the spring of 1797, east Ulster radicals were insisting that if only parliamentary reform and Catholic Emancipation were enacted (and the King's wicked ministers who refused such measures dismissed), everything else would come out right.[62] Precisely by playing their roles so effectively in the Irish theatre state up to that point, they dramatized the failure of the Irish polity to carry out the role assigned to it. It was for that reason that the British government enacted the first great parliamentary reform measure – the Act of Union of 1800, which eliminated the rottenest boroughs and reduced the borough representation from 79 per cent of the Irish House of Commons to 36 per cent of the Irish delegation in the united Commons. Thus, at a stroke, was abolished 'the borough system' whose preservation, according to Thomas Ledlie Birch, had been 'the great object of the dominating faction'.[63]

60 Revd. Edward Hudson to Charlemont, 5 June 1797, *H.M.C. Charlemont*, ii, p. 300.
61 Curtin, *United Irishmen*, p. 191.
62 See petition of County Antrim Freeholders, *N.S.*, 8–12 May 1797, and Address of Country Armagh Freeholders, in Réamonn Ó Muirí, 'The killing of Thomas Birch, United Irishman, Mar. 1797 and the meeting of the Armagh freeholders, 19 Apr. 1797', in *Seanchas Ard Mhacha*, x, 2 (1982), 298–9. Cf. Curtin, *United Irishmen*, p. 34.
63 Birch, *The causes of the rebellion in Ireland (1798): And other writings* (Belfast, 1991), p. 89.

Of course, actual participants in the rebellion did not immediately perceive this outcome as the fulfilment of the prime objective of their programme in the 1790s; those who lost family members to the sabre or the gallows probably never did. Nevertheless, the Union settlement created a new gap between Presbyterian and Catholic perceptions of the political system by granting the Presbyterian radicals in east Ulster at least the beginnings of what they had most earnestly desired – parliamentary reform – while withholding, at the behest of a mad king, the one thing for which Catholic radicals in Dublin and elsewhere had primarily striven – Catholic Emancipation.

'As the plague of locusts came in Egypt': Rebel motivation in north Down

TREVOR McCAVERY

A contemporary observer of the battle of Ballynahinch, the principal engagement in County Down, wrote in 1803 that 'the rebels came from the eastern part of the country as the plague of locusts came in Egypt'. Ballynahinch was in the centre of the county: Walter Harris, the mid-eighteenth-century traveller, had observed: 'Ballynahinch stands near the centre of the great roads leading from Lurgan, Dromore, Lisburn and Hillsborough to Downpatrick and from hence to the eastern coasts of Down.'[1] Here the Presbyterians from the north and north-east of the county could join with the Catholic Defenders from the south and hold the entire county for the rebel cause. Ballynahinch was also the seat of Lord Moira, a liberal peer and friend of Theobald Wolfe Tone.

The rebels who descended on the town originated from districts north and north-east of Ballynahinch. Stewart has stressed this: 'All accounts agree on one point, that though many of the insurgents came from the Saintfield-Ballynahinch direction, by far the greatest number of those subsequently involved were from the Ards, north Down and the Strangford Lough shore.'[2] This chapter considers the motivation of the 5,000 or more men from this area who challenged the crown in 1798 at Ballynahinch. A close scrutiny of the forces at work in this locality reveals that a complex combination of ideological and down-to-earth factors influenced those taking part. The community from which the rebels were drawn had been affected by those events and issues which divided the nation, and it sought in turn to affect them. However, the relationship between locality and nation was filtered by its own preoccupations and perceptions.

Radical politics in north Down and the Ards grew out of the area's Presbyterian culture, values shaped by democratic church structures, a commitment to literacy and a long experience of civil disabilities. The area had been settled by

---

1 Walter Harris, *The antient and present state of the county of Down* (Dublin, 1744, repr. Ballynahinch, 1977), pp 76–7.
2 A.T.Q. Stewart, *The summer soldiers: The 1798 rebellion in Antrim and Down* (Belfast, 1995), p. 178; W. McComb, *McComb's guide to Belfast* (Belfast, 1861), p. 138.

Scottish Presbyterians in the 'private enterprise' plantations initiated by Hugh Montgomery and James Hamilton in the early seventeenth century. By the late eighteenth century, Presbyterians made up, on average, 95 per cent of the population of the parishes of Newtownards, Dundonald, Holywood, Bangor, Donaghadee, Ballywalter and Greyabbey.[3] In Newtownards, the principal town of the area, three of the four Presbyterian ministers were allegedly associated with the United Irish movement. In all, eleven Presbyterian ministers, licentiates or clerical students from north Down and the Ards were thought to be involved in the 1798 Rebellion.[4]

The Volunteers provided many recruits for the United Irishmen and in the area there was a great attachment to Volunteering. Between 1778 and 1784, there had been over twenty Volunteer companies in north Down and the Ards.[5] Volunteering experienced a revival in the early 1790s as its members identified with the spirit of the new regime in France. At a meeting of the Newtownards Volunteers on 22 December 1792, resolutions were passed which expressed their joy

> at the emancipation of the French nation from the chains of despotism ... they have driven the armies of tyrants from their borders; we will rejoice a third time when they have established their constitution upon the broad and solid basis of the Rights of Man.[6]

Ireland's constitution, they declared, required 'thorough, adequate and effectual reform'. It was asserted that 'all power is from the people and government is but the exercise of that power in trust for the good of the whole community'; any parliamentary reform which excluded Catholics from the franchise would not be 'adequate and effectual'. Similar resolutions were agreed by the Volunteers companies in Donaghadee, Dundonald, Kircubbin and Ballywalter.[7] This was repeated by the inhabitants of the town of Newtownards, by Ballywalter Presbyterian congregation, 'Greyabbey Independent Villagers', the 'Freeholders and Inhabitants of Ballyhalbert', by 'Comber Villagers'.[8] As yet, these reformers were committed to constitutional means but, according to Curtin, it is likely that the United Irish leaders were the moving influences behind most of these resolutions. At this propagandist stage of the United Irish movement, its leaders saw no need to organize clubs where they could persuade local Volunteers corps or other groups to publicize their views.[9]

---

3 'The Newtown and Donaghadee Walks', 4 Sept. 1764: P.R.O.N.I., Groves MSS, T/808/15261.
4 Charles Dickson, *The revolt in the north: Antrim and Down in 1798* (Dublin, 1960), pp 240–1.
5 Padraig Ó Snodaigh, *The Irish Volunteers, 1715–1793: A list of the units* (Dublin, 1995).
6 *N.S.*, 22–26 Dec. 1792.
7 *N.S.*, 16 Jan. 1793.
8 *N.S.*, Jan.-Feb. 1793.
9 Nancy Curtin, *The United Irishmen* ... (Oxford, 1994), pp 52–7; Curtin, 'Rebels and radicals: The United Irish in County Down', in L. Proudfoot (ed.), *Down: History and society* (Dublin, 1997), p. 271.

There were local levers at work too. The district's major landowners, the Stewart family, fostered the development of, if not radical, at least liberal politics. In 1744, Alexander Stewart, a former Belfast linen merchant and Presbyterian elder, had bought a 20,000-acre estate of sixty townlands surrounding and including Newtownards and assumed that when he purchased the property, he would have control over the borough of Newtownards as well. This was not to be the case.[10] Having lost control of the borough's two seats in the Irish parliament, he set himself up as the leader of the popular independent interest in local politics. He chaired the first meeting of a Patriot Club which was set up in Newtownards in the spring of 1756. A contemporary, the later United Irish leader, the Revd Dr William Steel Dickson, described him as a 'man of ... principles, truly liberal in politics and religion'.[11] His son, later elevated to the peerage as Lord Londonderry, and grandson, Robert, later Viscount Castlereagh, continued the family tradition of liberal, reforming politics and contested one of the county seats against the conservative interest of the Downshires.[12]

So far only positive factors which nurtured radical opinion in the area have been identified. But from about 1792 negative influences come into play. The first was the provocative action of the Revd John Cleland, Church of Ireland minister of Newtownards between 1789 and 1809 and agent for Lord Londonderry. In 1792 he began to demand the payment of tithes.[13] This contributed to the radicalization of the locality.[14] A similar outcome followed the dramatic transformation in the political career of Robert Stewart who after 1795 opposed parliamentary reform. He and his father, Lord Londonderry, had whipped up a reforming Presbyterian interest for the 1790 general election in order to capture one of the seats from the Downshires. Once elected, the new member quickly shed his Whig views and supported the government and the status quo.

Reformers in north Down and the Ards felt let down by the volte-face of Robert Stewart. Lord Londonderry also lost his former popularity. Writing forty years later, Madden described how Lord Londonderry had become dictatorial in order to advance his interest in the county against the Downshires. Tenants learned that the way to express 'fealty' was to bring him information which concerned his electioneering interests. People were classed by Lord Londonderry as

---

10 J.T. Gilbert (ed.), *Manuscripts and correspondence of James, 1st earl of Charlemont* (London, 1891–4) i, p. 111; M. McTier to William Drennan, July 1787, in D.A. Chart (ed.), *The Drennan letters* (Belfast, 1931), p. 43.

11 W. Steel Dickson, *Narrative of confinement and exile* (Dublin, 1812), pp 6–7.

12 For details of their political activities, see Trevor McCavery, 'Reformers, reactionaries and revolutionaries: Opinion in north Down and the Ards in the 1790s', in *Ulster Local Studies*, xviii, 2 (Spring 1997), 71–7.

13 Andrew Cooper, Milecross, to Lord Hillsborough, 23 Sept 1792: P.R.O.N.I., Downshire papers, D.607/433.

14 Castlereagh, Blackrock, County Dublin, to his wife at Mount Stewart, 31 Aug. 1796: P.R.O.N.I., Castlereagh Papers, D.3030/T.

'turbulent or disaffected persons' when they differed from him politically. Dr Madden concluded:

> It is difficult to conceive the extent or the mischief of this system especial-
> ly in the county of Down at the period in question. It tended more than
> many of the political evils, which were the subject of general complaint, to
> promote the views of the United Irishmen.

The Revd James Porter, Presbyterian minister of Greyabbey, was deeply concerned at the divisive and demoralizing effect of these activities. Through a series
of fictitious letters published in the *Northern Star*, he ridiculed the espionage system and gave Lord Londonderry great offence.[15]

The locality's Presbyterianism, its Volunteering, and the positive encouragement given by the Londonderrys, followed then by their sudden political 'apostasy', helped to create and sustain radical opinion in the area. By August 1796 the
authorities regarded the situation with concern.[16] Robert Stewart (by then enjoying the courtesy title of Viscount Castlereagh because of his father's promotion in
the peerage) reported to the chief secretary that, after touring the countryside,
'there does exist a very serious affiliated conspiracy … the societies gain ground
rapidly and they have formed very sanguine and extensive hopes'.

Lords Londonderry and Downshire were 'completely alarmed' at these
developments.[17] Responding to the government's request for an alternative to the
stationing of extra troops in County Down, Downshire circulated a letter around
the proprietors of the county, inviting them to a meeting in Newtownards on 9
September 1796 to discuss the raising of a yeomanry from their tenantry. However, the county meeting did not go smoothly. Those present 'talked openly and
loudly of reform and redress of grievances previous to the consideration of
defence'. There were even some who had prepared alternative resolutions that, in
the words of one present, 'would have loosened the too lax ties of allegiance'.

Lord Londonderry attended the meeting, and was 'a good deal alarmed' at
such language in his own district. The actions he took in the autumn of 1796 may
have pushed more reformers into the hands of the revolutionaries. In September
several people in the town and neighbourhood of Newtownards received sum-
monses to appear before him to be examined upon oath to disclose all that they
knew about illegal oaths, meetings and associations. Forty bibles were ordered for
delivery to Mount Stewart for the purpose. Londonderry's actions were consid-

---

15 R.R. Madden, 'Memoir of the Revd James Porter', in *Antrim and Down in '98* (Glasgow, n.d.),
    pp 211–19; *N.S.*, 30 May 1796.
16 Marianne Elliott, *Partners in revolution* (London, 1989), pp 77–109.
17 Lord Camden to Lord [Downshire], 3 Aug. 1796: Downshire papers, D.607/D/110; Castle-
    reagh to Pelham, 23 Aug. 1796, quoted in Hyde, *Castlereagh*, p. 148; Haliday to Charlemont, 7
    Aug. 1796, in *Charlemont Corr.*, ii, p. 279; Robert Ross, Dublin, 2 Sept. 1796: Downshire
    papers, D.607/D/146.

ered arbitrary and of doubtful legality, though he claimed that he was authorised by a clause in the Whiteboy acts of 1775–6. The *Northern Star* maintained the people of the area were 'peaceable and quiet reformers,' and hinted that 'such strange devices as these prognosticate what we shall not now give a name to'.[18]

The theft of half a barrel of gunpowder and thirty pounds of three-pound grapeshot from the stores of the Donaghadee Packet Company in the early hours of 18 September confirmed Lord Londonderry's fears. One of the men suspected of the theft was considered to be a 'violent republican'.[19] On 26 September, Londonderry summoned his tenantry to Mount Stewart in order to compel them to swear the oath of allegiance. Then, possibly anticipating a low turn-out, he went to meet them. On Sunday 25 September, after the service at the Revd William Sinclair's Non-Subscribing Presbyterian meeting-house, he mounted the pulpit and addressed the congregation. The *Northern Star* satirized the episode as a 'raree show' or a cheap street performance.[20]

It was not just the *Northern Star* which was scornful of Londonderry's methods. James Arbuckle, the loyalist customs collector at Donaghadee, was 'astounded at the precipitancy and weakness of these measures', saying that they had produced a 'bad effect on the vulgar mind and proportionably encouraged the disaffected. The family is, I think, the most unpopular in the county.' He maintained that by announcing his intentions to address the congregation in the meeting-house, Lord Londonderry drew 'the ruffians of Comber and Killinchy', who filled the place, and 'his treatment was such as to have been looked for from such interlopers'.[21]

Lord Londonderry's next initiative ultimately proved more successful, but it required patient preparation. Londonderry and Castlereagh appreciated that the creation of a local yeomanry would not only be a crucial means of suppressing a rising but would be a critical test of opinion in the area, forcing men to make choices. In the parishes of Newtownards and Comber in particular, there was said to be nothing but 'discontent and sedition'. Only the parish of Donaghadee was favourable towards the idea of the yeomanry, despite the fact it was heavily tithed. As for the rest of the barony of Ards, it was said that the prospect of raising yeomanry, was 'totally out of the question at present.'[22]

The difficulty in raising a yeomanry force in the Ards peninsula is partly explained by the fact that many of the available men in that district were sworn members of the United Irishmen. Patrick Savage of Portaferry House described

18 James Arbuckle, Donaghadee, to Downshire, 11 Sept. 1796: Downshire papers, D.607/D/159.
19 Edward Hull, Donaghadee, to Downshire 18 Sept. 1796; James Arbuckle, Donaghadee Customs House, to Downshire 19 Sept. 1796: Downshire papers, D.607/D178, 182.
20 *N.S.*, 26 Sept. 1796.
21 Arbuckle, Donaghadee, to Downshire, 11, 20 Oct. 1796: Downshire papers, D.607/230, 243.
22 Arbuckle to Downshire 11 Oct. 1796; Patrick Savage, Mount Stewart, to Downshire, 19 Oct. 1796: Downshire papers, D.607/D/230, 24.

how well the United Irishmen were organized, noting that Bailie, a Belfast clock-maker living at Portaferry, had informed a United Irish meeting at Kircubbin that members were to be polled by their captains, to whom they were to swear oaths of implicit obedience:

> The privates are to meet in barns to exercise, in small parties, and 'books of discipline' are to be left with those who can read for the instruction of those who can't.[23]

There was further evidence of United organisation in the phenomenon known as 'potato digging'. Savage described how he encountered 100 men marching out of Kircubbin, 'a man with them, seemingly their captain, and two officers, playing a French tune as a quick step for them. We passed each other *sans ceremonie* ...' He believed that these 'potato gentry with their fifers' had come from Ballywalter and that they regularly marched to within a mile of his home in Portaferry.[24] Similar incidents were witnessed between Newtownards and Comber by Castlereagh:

> It was a pretty sight: a great number of young men marching along with smart girls on their arms – they were going towards Comber to dig Maxwell's potatoes.[25]

Potato digging also happened in the neighbourhood of Portaferry.[26] Such activity would explain the difficulty faced by the Londonderrys in raising a yeomanry. Savage explained the tactics used by the United Irishmen to recruit new members:

> The first step is to take an oath of secrecy and then they [the prospective members] are shown the articles of the Society in part, and are at liberty to retract under the oath taken, or go on ... Many well meaning, honest people have been drawn into believing a reform of Parliament was the object of the associations ... They [the United leaders] tell the people that many of their friends are of their party and will be at their meetings, to induce them to attend and join them ... which very often is quite false, and the first deceived are made the instruments of the others being taken in.[27]

But not everyone was a republican. Many were loyalists and were afraid to come forward, fearing reprisals. Savage believed that in this respect the state of the barony of Ards was 'miserably bad indeed.' His tenants, though loyal,

---

23 Patrick Savage, Portaferry, to Downshire, 24 Oct. 1796: Downshire papers, D.607/D/252.
24 Savage, Portaferry, to Downshire, 29 Oct. 1796: Downshire papers, D.607/D/264.
25 Hyde, *Castlereagh*, p. 165.
26 *N.S.*, 18–21 Nov. 1796.
27 Patrick Savage, Mount Stewart, to Downshire, 19–20 Oct. 1796: Downshire papers, D.607/D/232, 241, 245; Savage, Portaferry, to Downshire, 29 Oct. 1796; General Nugent, Carnbane, to Downshire, 6 Nov. 1796: Downshire papers, D.607/D/264, 289.

were afraid to come forward and show themselves, as they would be marked out by the United Irishmen and have themselves, their friends and their families destroyed; they wish to have some troops quartered at Portaferry to support them and they will then be ready to enrol themselves for the defence of their King and Constitution; they could not answer how long they would be able to withstand the solicitations and threats used to induce them or force them to join the United Irishmen. The system of terror is completely established, and the progress now making is terribly rapid, and the immediate sending of troops into this barony is the only thing can save it from total destruction of principles. I am certain it will require fifty men at Portaferry and Lord Londonderry seems to think as many will be necessary at Newtown[ards]. In my opinion there is not a moment to be lost in sending the troops to us.

Savage's reports of intimidation in the Portaferry district were corroborated at the other end of the barony: in the Groomsport area, revenue officers were in 'fear of being knocked on the head'.[28] Although Castlereagh sought to reassure his wife about his own safety around Greyabbey by telling her that 'this country[side] is as safe in daylight as it ever was', he admitted, 'certainly it would be imprudent to go out at night and therefore I shall not do it'. The Revd John Cleland was not so prudent. Castlereagh related how an assassination attempt on Cleland in Newtownards almost succeeded on Saturday 29 October 1796:

> Cleland very incautiously went out last night and was attacked by some villain who bore him ill-will. In the attack he snapped a pistol at Cleland which missed fire and Cleland fired two shots without effect at him.[29]

Another man was assassinated for taking the oath.[30] The authorities believed that a system of terror was being introduced, aimed both at those who supported only limited reform and, more obviously, at its opponents.[31] Lord Londonderry wrote to the marquis of Downshire, the governor of County Down, asking for military protection: 'in the state the country is in, my house and family are not safe without an armed force, especially if I have to act as a magistrate and become an object of resentment'.[32] Camden confirmed the tension felt by everyone living in the area: 'The terror which has been inspired by threats of assassination if they

---

28 Arbuckle to Downshire 13 Oct. 1796; Patrick Savage to Downshire, 19 Oct. 1796: Downshire papers, D.607/D/232, 241.
29 Castlereagh, Mount Stewart, to his wife [Dublin], 30 Oct. 1796: P.R.O.N.I., D.3030/T/MC 3/290; *N.S.*, 4 Nov. 1796; Londonderry to the Downshire, 2 Nov. 1796: N.A.I., RP 620/26/5.
30 P.R.O.N.I., *The United Irishmen*, Education Facsimiles, notes to No. 67.
31 Thomas Pelham, Dublin Castle, to Chichester Skeffington, collector of revenue at Belfast, 4 Jan. 1797: P.R.O.N.I., D.562/301.
32 Londonderry to Downshire, 30 Oct. 1796, quoted in Hyde, *Castlereagh*.

would not join with them was carried to such a length that scarcely one of Lord Londonderry's tenants would dare speak to him if they met him on the road or would even show him the slightest mark of respect.'[33]

The intimidation of the magistracy is another possible reason for difficulties in raising a yeomanry. Cleland was not so affected, and he complained that 'the neighbouring gentlemen and magistrates show so little disposition to be active, or commend that of others'. Arbuckle of Donaghadee also commented that the plan for raising the yeomanry had not been prosecuted 'with spirit'.[34] Blackstock has recently noted that County Down should have produced a strong yeomanry as it contained a larger than average number of minor gentry and wealthy yeomen or 'strong' farmers. But these families had grown accustomed to supporting reform movements and had traditionally opposed the marquis of Downshire, the prime mover of the yeomanry in the county, and so could not bring themselves to embrace the cause of reaction.[35] The authorities were disappointed with the attitude of Echlin of Ecclinville, Ker of Portavo, Ward of Bangor, Blackwood of Ballyleidy, Crawford of Crawfordsburn, Kennedy of Cultra and Montgomery of Greyabbey.[36]

An additional reason for hesitancy in joining the yeomanry was the success of United Irish propaganda. It asserted that those who swore the oath of allegiance were swearing that they accepted coercive legislation and would become informers. Also, a clause of the oath of allegiance said that it must be taken 'heartily and cordially', so if any man took it otherwise he would be perjuring himself in the very act of taking it.[37]

It was the task of Londonderry and Castlereagh to rebut these arguments and disabuse those who, said Castlereagh, 'had been much deceived and much threatened'. It took the whole month of November 1796 before they succeeded in raising a yeomanry. The arrival of more troops, according to Castlereagh, made 'the countenances of the people more amiable'.[38] Two companies of the York Fencibles were sent from Downpatrick to Portaferry, Kircubbin, Comber and Killinchy, and the 22nd Dragoons were sent to Newtownards and Comber.[39] On 9

33 Camden to Portland, 13 Dec. 1796, quoted in Hyde, *Castlereagh*, p. 29.
34 John Cleland, Newtownards, to Downshire, 25 Oct. 1796; James Arbuckle, Donaghadee to Downshire, 8 Dec. 1796: Downshire papers, D.607/D/253, 380.
35 A Blackstock, 'The Down Yeomanry', in M. Hill, B. Turner and K. Dawson (eds), *The 1798 rebellion in County Down* (Newtownards, 1998), pp 42–3.
36 Col J.J. Atherton to General Nugent, 20 June 1798, in W.J. Fitzpatrick, *The sham squire, and the informers of 1798* ... (Dublin, 1855), pp 347–8.
37 Pelham, Dublin Castle, to Chichester Skeffington, Belfast, 4 Jan. 1797: P.R.O.N.I., D.562/301.
38 For details of their efforts, see Camden to Portland 13 Dec. 1796, quoted in Hyde, *Castlereagh*, p. 170; McCavery, *Reformers*, pp 81–2. For the state of Newtownards opinion in the crucial month of Nov. 1796, see Castlereagh to his wife, 1, 6, 7, 19, 22, 24, 27 Nov. 1796: P.R.O.N.I., D.303/T/MC3/290.
39 General Nugent, Hillsborough, to Pelham, 31 Oct. 1796: P.R.O.N.I., T.755/3/293; General Nugent, Carnbane, to Downshire, 6 Nov. 1796: Downshire papers, D.607/D/289.

November, Castlereagh broke up a meeting of the Ulster provincial executive of the United Irishmen at Portaferry and arrested six men, and this bolstered the loyalists' confidence.

Londonderry, Castlereagh and their friends may have wrung a little comfort from the emerging loyalist movement and its expression in the new yeomanry force.[40] But this was countered by evidence of large gatherings administering oaths in the parish of Newtownards.[41] At this time, the commanding officer at Newtownards reported that the countryside about Newtownards was only in an 'apparent state of tranquillity'. He believed that 'a strong spirit of discontent prevails and only wants an opportunity to break forth'.[42] On 19 February 1797 James Arbuckle reported: 'Every appearance announces a very speedy explosion of violence in this part of the country … The preparations being made are both great and rapid … I heard today that the rebels propose to rise, even should the French not invade, in less than three weeks. Pikes and pike shafts are being made in large numbers.' He reported the cutting down of ash trees in the neighbourhood. He argued that the armed forces should be concentrated rather than dispersed throughout the area as small detachments would fall in turn and their arms taken. Also, he was worried about the security of guns and gunpowder on the packet boats.[43] Yet, despite all this activity, he was convinced that the revolutionary 'army' used conscripts rather than volunteers:

> The system of terror – to borrow, or steal a rascally tour d'expression – was never more completely organized under the Robespierrean despotism, than at this day and at this part of Ireland … Many of the United dogs have been forcibly impressed into the service of rebellion, several have been seduced, not a few repent of the engagement … the rascality of the country are wielded with such method and with most profound secrecy of operation. The last [*Northern*] Star sounded the tocsin to insurrection without any muffling whatever.[44]

The authorities decided to take no chances and tightened up in response. On 28 February 1797, Lord Londonderry asserted: 'I am seriously of opinion that nothing but the most vigorous and instantaneous measures can resist this rebellious spirit. A large body of troops must be marched into this part of the country and the inhabitants disarmed and made sensible of the efficacy of martial law, for the civil power is now set at defiance here.'[45] As Cleland was a zealous magistrate,

---

40 For the limits to their loyalism, see McCavery, *Reformers*, pp 82–3.
41 P.R.O.N.I., Cleland MSS, D.714/2/1A-B,/3/2; R. Johnston [Rostrevor] to John Lees, 24 Jan. 1797, quoted in Dickson, *Revolt in north*, p. 106.
42 Col. G.A. Chetwynd Stapleton to Gen. Lake, 14 Jan. 1797: P.R.O.N.I., Pelham MSS, T.755/3.
43 Arbuckle to Downshire, 19 Feb. 1797: Downshire papers, D/607/E/110.
44 Arbuckle to Downshire, 15 Mar. 1797: Downshire papers, D.607/E /192.
45 Londonderry to Camden, 28 Feb. 1797: N.A.I. RP 620/29/3

government secret service money was channelled through him, which would allow him fund a spy ring to provide names of those who held arms.[46] This was possibly the final factor which pushed many into revolution.

As the government hardened its attitude in County Down, ploughshares were being turned into swords – or pikes, to be more precise – and old Volunteer muskets were being dusted down. Arms had been stolen from soldiers as well.[47] 'Observator' of Newtownards reported that rumours of pike-making and oath-taking abounded.[48]

On 1 March 1797 a meeting of the magistrates of County Down at Saintfield agreed that the entire county should be placed under the Insurrection Act.[49] Accordingly on 3 March 1797 General Lake was ordered to disarm all persons who did not possess a commission, disperse all unlawful assemblies and take any measures which he thought fit for the preservation of order.[50] Lake's soldiers carried out their mission with ruthlessness and considerable brutality. He was told to 'begin with the Ards and the other side of Strangford Lough in which countries the search will be continued as long as there remains any prospect of success'. Lake found the task 'the most arduous, difficult and unpleasant service that any officer was ever employed in'.[51]

Counter-insurgency measures, in the form of arms searches, began on 13 March Between 4 and 5 a.m. on a Sunday morning, Cleland led a detachment of troops which broke into the house of William McCormick, an innkeeper in Newtownards, and arrested him and his brother-in-law without charge. They were refused an application for bail for some time. A detachment of cavalry raided the new meeting-house of the Reformed Presbyterian Church, or Covenanters, in Ann Street, Newtownards.[52] Nothing was found in this raid, but acting on information that arms were concealed at the Knockbracken meeting-house, a raid took place there on Sunday 25 June. The minister of both congregations, the Revd William Stavely, spent the next two months in prison and his property was plundered by soldiers, but no arms were ever found and no charge could be brought against him.[53]

---

46 Cleland MSS, D.714/2/1–24.
47 *N.S.* 31 Oct.–4 Nov. 1796.
48 *N.S.* 24–27 Feb. 1797.
49 Samuel McSkimin, *Annals of Ulster* (Belfast, 1906), p. 47.
50 Pelham to Lake, 3 Mar. 1797: N.L.I., Knox papers, MS 56/32.
51 Orders, and covering letter, from Thomas Pelham, Dublin Castle, to Lake, 3 Mar. 1797; General Nugent to Downshire, 11 Mar. 1797: Downshire papers, D.607/E/148, 149, 173; Lake, Belfast, to Downshire, 2 Apr. 1798: Downshire papers, D.607/F/127.
52 *N.S.*, 20 Mar. 1797.
53 Dickson, *Revolt in north*, p. 114; *Belfast News-Letter*, 27 June and Aug. 1797. For a detailed consideration of the position of Stavely and local Reformed Presbyerians, see T. McCavery, *A Covenant community: A history of Newtownards Reformed Presbyterian Church* (Newtownards, 1997), pp 35–42.

Such arrests of innocent, prominent people inevitably had the effect of turning others against the authorities. Arbuckle said: 'This disarmament, I fear, will be unproductive of intended effect – the military glean but few arms.'[54] Mrs McTier remarked on 17 March that 'Londonderry, it is said, is going to sneak into Newtown after being guarded by soldiers all the winter at Mount Stewart. His father seldom bolted his windows. Not a penny of rent is paid him'.[55]

On 13 March General Lake issued a proclamation establishing a curfew around Belfast from 10 p.m. each night. Those breaking it were to be fined five shillings and if they could not pay were to receive 100 lashes. Writing from his father's home just outside Newtownards, on 7 April, Castlereagh believed that these measures had had little effect in

> altering, the disposition of the people. The leaders of the disaffected party do not seem at all dispirited, which arises I conclude from expectations they have of another effort being made in their favour on the part of the enemy. They contrive insolently and impudently, and openly threaten those who have either withdrawn from or do not join their party.[56]

On 14 April 1797 a platoon of soldiers carried out a raid on Alexander's public house in Belfast. They arrested forty United Irishmen, who were meeting in three committees, and carried away a set of documents. Among them were 'Resolutions of the United Societies of Donaghadee and its vicinity'. The resolutions were a mixture of principles and pragmatism. They declared 'that all power is radically in the people' and when their representatives grasp at domination 'the people ought to claim their right and the power return to its proper channel'; 'at the present crisis the people, being united should also arm, choose their officers and … go forth to war'. Turning to practical matters, they urged the creation of a fund to meet the needs of 'our brethren in arms' and their families, the wounded, the widowed and the fatherless. It was to be made up from 'a contribution imposed upon the people' and the confiscated property of their enemies. Farmers would also be made to sell their surpluses. To maintain order, a force should be created. To bring these measures about, each society was to choose a delegate to a Revolutionary Committee and, acting with the Committee, were to elect magistrates for six months, 'but if a Revolution be accomplished, an annual election shall take place'. This document proves the advanced stage of politicization and of practical planning by the spring of 1797.[57]

A new phase in the conflict emerged when the time came to prosecute those who had been arrested. Castlereagh was aware that the United Irishmen would

---

54 Arbuckle to Downshire, 15 Mar. 1797: Downshire papers, D/607/E/192.
55 Mrs McTier to W. Drennan, 17 Mar. 1797: *Drennan letters*, p. 252.
56 Castlereagh to Pelham, 7 Apr. 1797, in Hyde, *Castlereagh*, pp 180–1.
57 Appendix No II to the report of the Secret Committee of the House of Lords, 1799: Linenhall Library, Belfast, N648; Donaghadee Resolution papers: P.R.O.N.I. T3465/80.

'deter the jurors summoned to the assizes from attending, in which I am appre-
hensive they will be but too successful'. The authorities responded in kind.
Cleland, as sub-sheriff, handpicked tenants of Lord Londonderry for the jury
panel. For this, said one observer, he was 'severely handled' by the prisoners'
defence lawyer, John Philpot Curran.[58] However, it must be said, according to one
present, that the juries were more intimidated by Curran himself than by United
Irishmen or the landlord's agent: 'Some would not, some durst [*sic*] not, convict
and, under the violent invective and ranting declamation of Mr Curran, almost
every prisoner was acquitted.'[59]

Failing to suppress revolutionary activity through the courts, the government
resorted to attacks on property. In June 1797, McCormick's inn in Newtownards
was burned down because some of its patrons were overheard in talk which might
have been constituted as treasonable. Dr James Jackson, a subscriber to the
Northern Star and secretary of the former Newtownards Volunteers, was robbed
and had his house burned down by the Fencibles because he was suspected of
treasonable activities, though no charge was ever brought. He subsequently
played an active role in the rebellion.[60]

Londonderry, Castlereagh and Cleland did not feel that they could relax their
efforts. In June 1797 Castlereagh told James Cleland:

> I do not consider the conspiracy as broken. Nothing but a surrender of
> arms enforced by a steady perseverance in vigorous measures can effectu-
> ally crush the spirit of a party which has had such a confidence in their
> own strength ... the [rebel] party may consider a desperate effort indis-
> pensable to keep together their alarmed and broken strength.[61]

In the summer of 1797 an itinerant priest called James McCary, after preaching at
Portaferry and in the Lecale, arrived in Newtownards. He spoke in the fields
around the town, urging the Presbyterians to 'union and fraternity [with the
Catholics] on the grounds of Christian benevolence'.[62] But the United Irish
Society were not, as Londonderry believed and as M'Cary preached, pinning
their hopes on their own strength but on external agencies – a second French
invasion borne by the revolutionary Dutch fleet. The fleet, however, was defeated
at the battle of Camperdown on 11 October 1797, with the authorities publicising
it as a telling sign of Britain's revived fortunes in the war.[63] Not to celebrate it with

58 *N.S.*, 28 Apr.; 1, 5 May 1797; Thomas Lane, Hillsborough, to Downshire, 1 May 1797: Downshire papers, D.607/E/255.
59 Thomas Lane, Hillsborough, to Downshire, 1 May 1797: Downshire papers, D.607/E/255.
60 *N.S.*, 2 Nov. 1795; F.J. Bigger, 'The builder of Stormount', in *Four shots from Down* (Belfast,
   1918); Cleland papers, D.714/3/27; Dickson, *Revolt in north*, p. 142.
61 Castlereagh to Cleland, 19, 24 June 1797: P.R.O.N.I., Castlereagh papers, D.3030/J/2, 3.
62 Richard Musgrave, *Memoirs of the Irish rebellion of 1798* (Fort Wayne, IN, 1995) p. 165.
63 Marianne Elliott, *Partners in revolution: The United Irishmen and France* (New Haven, 1982), pp
   160–1.

sufficient enthusiasm was also seen as telling, as an account from a Scottish visitor makes clear: almost every house in Newtownards had windows broken by soldiers. Cleland accompanied the soldiers.[64] Haliday told Lord Charlemont in October 1797 that he had witnessed cruel inflictions of military punishment on poor people who were not subject to martial law.[65]

Arrests of United Irish suspects continued throughout 1797.[66] Such policies may have served to spread revolutionary feeling. Certainly the movement was active in Bangor by October.[67] In Donaghadee, in January 1798, a branch of the United Irish Society was set up after the Revd James Porter and the Revd William Steel Dickson preached in the town on consecutive Sundays in December and made a return visit together in the New Year.[68]

Undoubtedly some of the membership had been goaded into revolutionary activity by the activities of such men as Cleland. The Revd Hugh Montgomery of Greyabbey called him a 'bloodthirsty hell hound', and at a United Irish meeting in 1798 lots were drawn for the job of assassinating him; this time he was to be fired on through his office window.[69] Did Cleland and his superiors push the rebels into action, and was this their intention? To what extent were those who took part in 1798 pulled into it by intimidation from local leaders? Whatever their motivation, among the rank and file at least there was still a body with considerable enthusiasm for a rising.[70] Indeed, Pakenham has suggested that 'arrests had increased the danger [to the authorities]; appeals to reason were less likely to be heeded now the moderate leaders had been removed'.[71]

The strategy adopted by General Nugent, when the rising began, also helped the rebel cause. The troops in the eastern half of Down (apart from Downpatrick) were ordered to retreat to Belfast. Nugent's plan was to give priority to

64 *The Press*, 18 Nov. 1797.
65 Haliday to Charlemont, 6 Oct. 1797, *Charl. Corr*, ii, p. 306.
66 In October, Francis Falloon, the innkeeper of Donaghadee, was arrested, accused of employing John Miskelly, blacksmith of Millisle, to make pikes, and one Robinson to shaft them. Iron was supplied by Andrew Bryson of Newtownards who purchased it from Dalzell's shop in Newtownards. The prisoners were confined to unheated and unlit cells, prohibited the use of pen and paper, and allowed no visitors. Indeed, when Falloon's stepfather applied to General Lake for permission to see his step-son his answer was that if he asked a second time he would join him in prison: Humphrey Galbraith, Donaghadee, to Downshire, 21 Oct., 1 Nov. 1797: Downshire papers, D.607/E/344, 365.
67 Galbraith, Donaghadee, to Downshire, 1 Nov. 1797: Downshire papers, D.607/E/ 365.
68 ' Old Donaghadee', in *County Down Spectator* (n.p., 1935), p. 8. The Society met in the home of Harry Angus on the corner of Sailors' Row. The leader in Donaghadee was William Bryson of Ballygrainey and pikes were made by William McGimpsey. Other Donaghadee men were McCullough, Brown, Robinson, Bunting, Purvis, Herdman, Saunders, Dunwoody. The two last named were killed at the battle of Saintfield.
69 Sworn statement [n.d., n.p.] made to the Revd John Cleland: Cleland papers; and Statement of Robert Armstrong of Falls, near Belfast, 2 July 1798: D.714/2/24, D.714 /3/11A.
70 Curtin, *United Irishmen*, pp 254–69, 277–80.
71 Thomas Pakenham, *The year of liberty* (London, 1972), p. 255.

defending the line of the Dublin road to Belfast, on the western side of County Down. He was prepared to leave the loyalists in the entire eastern half of Down to their fate.[72] This had the effect of giving the republicans in this area a false sense of confidence.[73]

From each end of the Ards peninsula came reports of a 'system of terror' organized between 1796 and 1798. By this phrase, Patrick Savage of Portaferry and James Arbuckle of Donaghadee were referring to the intimidation tactics of the United Irishmen. These were aimed not just at the local representatives of the government but also at every law-abiding citizen to prevent him rallying to the crown. Also, moderate reformers, or even uninterested individuals, were bullied into joining the revolutionary movement. Although there is plenty of evidence for such a 'reign of terror', it must be treated with caution. Some of the evidence was supplied by friends of the government who might have sought to discredit the United Irishmen and play down the discontent which existed in the area. Then there was the testimony of rebels who were arrested after the rising and wished to escape the gallows; their protests of innocence must also be treated with some scepticism. However, despite reservations about the reliability of the evidence, it is clear that much intimidation did take place and, consequently, not all who took part in the rising were inspired by revolutionary ideology. Indeed, it is likely that those who were most influenced by the movement's ideals were the leaders who were arrested before the rising.

A second, competing 'system of terror' was also established. This was the counter-revolutionary activity instigated by the Londonderrys and carried out by Cleland and the military. It was intended to suppress the United Irishmen but its brutal character may have served to push moderate men into revolution rather than scare them away from it. Each system of terror was in competition, but each may have worked in the same direction. The motivation of the United Irishmen is therefore complex: some rebels were convinced by the ideals of the movement; others were intimidated into taking part; some must have been provoked by the counter-insurgency measures. Such varied motivation may partly explain why the Presbyterians of the area eschewed revolution so swiftly after 1798 – some of them may never have been revolutionaries at all. A study of the rebels from north Down and the Ards should make us wary of over-generalized explanations and, at the same time, allows us appreciate the value of local history in giving fresh insights into the big issues of the rebellion. A local study is not just a miniature version of national events. Competing and powerful local forces shaped, and sometimes took precedence over, the political issues that have been assumed to have motivated the participants in the 1798 rebellion.

72 General Nugent, Blaris, to Lake, 10 June 1798: N.A.I., RP 620/38/121
73 For a study of how the Rising developed in north Down and the Ards after the rebel army went to Ballynahinch, see McCavery, '"A system of terror is completely established": The 1798 rebellion in north Down and the Ards', in Hill, Turner and Dawson (eds), *1798 in Down*, pp 88–98.

12

South Ulster in the age of the United Irishmen

BRIAN MacDONALD

From the overwhelmingly Catholic Fews of south Armagh, through Monaghan, Cavan and south Tyrone with their strong Presbyterian minorities, to largely Anglican Fermanagh and the southern tip of Donegal, south Ulster in its diversity tested the organizational capacity of the United Irishmen and their sectoral appeal. Of all parts of this peripheral region, Fermanagh undoubtedly represented the most significant challenge to the revolutionaries. The social and political make-up of eighteenth-century Fermanagh was forged in the upheaval of the previous century, the county's Protestant inhabitants inheriting traditions of 1641 and the military record of the Enniskilleners. Even in the late eighteenth century, the legacy of those events was used to recall Protestants to a sense of duty and obedience to the crown.

This tradition was alluded to by the United Irish leader, Thomas Russell, when he described the Fermanagh gentry as 'horrible tories' and he explained that this was 'from their being old, good *Protestants*', emphasizing the word 'Protestant' to show that he meant it in a political and not a religious sense.[1] 'This will go off', Russell added confidently, suggesting (somewhat optimistically) that, following a period of politicization, Protestants generally would embrace radicalism. Richard Musgrave similarly acknowledged the impact of a 'Protestant' political tradition, asserting that although 'both the Defenders and United Irishmen in their turn attempted to organize the county of Fermanagh ... they desisted, because they knew that the Protestants of the established Church are so numerous, so loyal, and courageous, that they would have been cut to pieces had they attempted to rise in rebellion, which was the ultimate object of their machinations ... They knew what achievements were performed in the year 1641, by the bravery and loyalty of the Enniskilleners.'[2] Musgrave's attempt to distance Fermanagh Protestants from involvement in revolutionary activity fails to stand up to scrutiny. Documentary evidence confirms that members of the Established Church in Fermanagh embraced United Irish ideology,

---

1 C.J. Woods (ed.), *Journals and memoirs of Thomas Russell* (Dublin, 1991), p. 74.
2 Richard Musgrave, *Memoirs of the Irish rebellion of 1798*, 4th ed. (Enniscorthy, 1995), p. 164.

providing effective leadership at a local level and delaying the advance of the Orange Order.[3]

From the early 1790s, the process of politicisation in south Ulster is revealed by the success throughout the region of the *Northern Star*.[4] Newspaper sales in that period generally declined as one moved west across Ulster. While this was also the case with the *Northern Star*, it had nonetheless phenomenal success when compared with rival publications such as the *Belfast Newsletter*. This relative success of the paper *vis-à-vis* its rivals should inform our assessment of the impact of radical ideas across Ulster rather than the actual numbers of papers sold in particular localities.[5]

By 1794, the *Northern Star* had virtually obliterated the *Newsletter* in County Fermanagh and, despite logistical difficulties, it had sales as far away as Ballyshannon. There was similar success in County Monaghan; in 1794 the *Newsletter* sent only ten papers to Monaghan and eleven to Clones, whereas twenty copies of the *Star* went to Clones alone.[6] Cavan was less enthusiastic and beyond Cootehill the *Northern Star* had few sales, the people of Cavan town being described as 'dead with respect to politics'.[7]

In addition to the successful distribution of the *Northern Star*, a wide range of radical literature was distributed through the region, prompting the agent of the Clones estate to remark that local Presbyterians were 'inclined much to Paine's principles' and had imbibed a dangerous democratic spirit.[8] In addition to this activity, individual United Irish emissaries were targeting various sectors of society. It was a case of horses for courses: in 1796 we find John Shaw, linen mer-

---

3   Unlike the other stronghold of the Established Church in north Armagh, most Fermanagh Protestants were not of English descent; numerically strong families such as the Johnstons, Grahams, Elliotts, Armstrongs etc. all originated as 'reivers' from the Scottish border country with England, embracing Anglicanism only after their arrival in Ireland. Given this circumstance, it is a mistake to assume that the experience and reactions of Fermanagh Protestants would mirror that of their Armagh co-religionists.

4   For an assessment of the impact of the *Northern Star* in this region, see MacDonald, 'The *Northern Star* in south west Ulster', in *The Spark Review Magazine*, ix (winter, 1995), 3–10. See also idem, 'Distribution of the *Northern Star*' in *Ulster Local Studies*, xxviii, 2 (spring, 1997), 54–68; Kevin Whelan, 'The republic in the village: The dissemination and reception of popular literature in the 1790s', in Gerard Long (ed.), *Books beyond the Pale: Aspects of the provincial book trade in Ireland before 1850* (Dublin, 1996), pp 103–40.

5   For an alternative view, see Whelan, 'The republic in the village', and John Gray, 'A tale of two newspapers: The contest between the *Belfast News-Letter* and the *Northern Star* in the 1790s', in J. Gray and W. McCann (eds), *An uncommon bookman: Essays in memory of J.R.R. Adams* (Belfast, 1996), pp 175–98.

6   Information relating to the distribution of the *Northern Star* is contained in the journey books of agents for the paper in N.A.I., RP 620/15/8/1–12, and in the correspondence of prospective local representatives in N.A.I., RP 620/19/42. Subscribers lists for the *Belfast Newsletter* are included in the Joy Papers in the Belfast Linenhall library.

7   N.A.I., RP 620/15/8/7.

8   William Mayne to Lady Dacre, 16 July 1792, quoted in P. Ó Mórdha, 'Some notes on Monaghan history', in *Clogher Record*, ix, 1 (1976), 27–8.

chant, Quaker and United Irishmen, staying among the Quakers of Cootehill.[9]
In the same period, Barney McMahon, a Catholic United Irishman, was reportedly acting as an emissary from Belfast to the remote areas of south Ulster, establishing contact with the Defenders.[10] The spread of information and of political
understanding reached even the most isolated communities. While visiting his sister in Fermanagh in April 1793, Russell learnt that people were informed of
political events even in places 'where you could not conceive that any news could
reach', in the mountains and bogs of Cavan, Fermanagh and Leitrim.[11]

By early 1793 the strength of popular politics across south Ulster was becoming apparent with widespread opposition to the formation of a militia (denounced
as a 'monster in embryo') and growing support for parliamentary reform.[12] There
was support also for the revival of the Volunteer movement and, despite government policy, some corps continued in existence well into the 1790s and these were
considered highly suspect by the authorities. In March 1794, a correspondent
from Ballyhaise, County Cavan, complained that the local Volunteer corps was
actively encouraging the spread of sedition:

> They can turn out one hundred men any time, well armed young men.
> They now think it nothing to sit down and drink the toast 'the rights of
> the people'. The county of Cavan was always quiet till now, but now the
> country entirely is on a bad understanding and ready for rebellion as any
> one part of this kingdom ... They mean in this country nothing but
> rebellion and Ballyhaise Volunteers to head them.[13]

The *Northern Star* carried several news items from Fermanagh outlining the
power struggle between the radicals and the local political elite. Most significant
was the report from Enniskillen of 'a numerous and respectable meeting of the
inhabitants of the county' on 7 January 1793.[14] This was intended to be the occasion for forming an Association for the Support of the Constitution, but became
instead an early trial of strength in which the radicals emerged victorious.
Stating that they could not support the constitution in its 'present degenerate
state', the radicals proposed an amendment in opposition to the substantive loyalist motion. Facing defeat, the establishment party abandoned the meeting, but
undaunted by what was termed 'this manoeuvre and inconvenience' the radicals,

9 [?] to Knox, 15 June 1796: N.A.I., RP 620/23/165.

10 McNevin to Pelham, 9 May 1796: N.A.I., RP 620/23/101.

11 Woods, *Russell*, p. 69.

12 Steele to Hobart, 18 Jan. 1793: N.A.I., RP 620/20/5. Steele enclosed a printed notice of a pub-
     lic meeting to oppose the formation of a militia in County Monaghan. Subsequent issues of the
     Northern Star carried reports of several such meetings, all of which articulated support for par-
     liamentary reform.

13 — to Commander-in-chief, 14 Mar. 1794: N.A.I., RP 620/21/32.

14 *N.S.*, 16 Jan. 1793.

led by young turks such as William Hamilton and Randal Kernan, emulated the example of democrats elsewhere; the *Star* reported that 'the people repaired to the Commons, no house but the court-house being sufficient to contain their number'. There, the re-constituted meeting unanimously passed a resolution urging 'a thorough and radical reform in the Commons House of Parliament, and extension of the elective franchise to every denomination of Irishmen ...' The reform demand subsequently attracted the support of fourteen lodges of Freemasons in Fermanagh, consisting of 715 members.[15]

The bitter contest between an anti-reform ascendancy party and the radicals of Fermanagh was highlighted in an incident later that year involving a member of the Fermanagh Militia responsible for the killing of Hugh Bell, a Belfast United Irishman and native of Greyabbey.[16] As pressure mounted for his arraignment on a charge of murder, the soldier 'fled' his regiment and returned to Fermanagh, where he was identified by the United Irishmen. In a revealing vignette of underlying tensions between conservatives and radicals in the county, the *Star* reported:

> They apprehended and brought him before a Reverend magistrate, who instead of committing him, threatened to commit those who took him, and forcibly took a firelock from one of the party who had him in custody, and damned the prisoner, why he did not use his bayonet and kill the rebels before he allowed himself to be taken for they were as bad as the people of Belfast, and [he] desired him to go about his business...[17]

Despite trenchant opposition, the radicals continued to make advances. On a further visit to Fermanagh in January 1794, Russell was informed that 'even the poorest people' were supportive of the French and 'quite open in their wishes for them'. 'It is a great thing in their contemplation to see haberdashers, postillions etc. etc. at the head of armys [*sic*] and they will not fail to apply the lesson.'[18] As the war with France dragged on, the United Irish leader detected a shift in the mood of Fermanagh conservatives also, Russell learning with satisfaction that even his and Wolfe Tone's old college friend, the Revd John Stack of Derryvullen, had begun to alter his views and was 'less violent against the French'.[19] In the final reference to the county in his diary, written in September

15 Ibid., 26 Jan. 1793.
16 Bell's death in controversial circumstances on Halloween 1793 soured relations between the Belfast radicals and the Fermanagh Regiment of Militia. Initial denials of military responsibility by Major Caldwell, Belfast commander of the Fermanagh Militia, were retracted when a post mortem inquiry found that a soldier named Smith was, indeed, the culprit. The controversy received extensive coverage in the *Northern Star*.
17 *N.S.*, 13 Jan. 1794.
18 Woods, *Russell*, p. 143.
19 Ibid., p. 144.

1794, Russell confidently declared that 'the spirit of liberty is daily gaining ground'.[20]

Despite the impact of the Penal Laws, a confident and well-organised network existed within the Catholic community of south Ulster, which was prepared to use its resources to challenge the establishment at a local and national level. Along with the freeholders of Monaghan, they helped ensure the return of Richard Dawson, a supporter of the Reform movement as MP for the county.[21] As further evidence of Catholic mobilization, we have a report from Fermanagh in 1795 that 'the Maguires, Karnans, Flanagins of Enniskillen [and] their friends at Carrickmacross, namely Randell McDonald ... [the] Fitzpatricks [and] Carolans ... have entered into a subscription for the purpose of supporting Major Brooke's election against Lord Cole for the County Fermanagh on the next vacancy, aided by Captain Maguire of Tempo'.[22] There was a suggestion in the same correspondence that the fees for counsel in a number of Defender trials in Enniskillen in 1795 and 1796 had been paid for by the same group.

The chief suspect in those trials was John Croker, a brother-in-law of the Kernans of Enniskillen. Family ties were an important aspect of the radicalization of Catholic opinion in south Ulster. The Carolans and McDonnells of Carrickmacross were cousins of the Kernans of Enniskillen and Ballyshannon. They were also related to the bishop of Clogher, Hugh O'Reilly, and through marriage to the Teelings of Lisburn. Members of these families were centrally involved in Catholic politics across the region, representing their counties at the Back Lane parliament, chairing meetings in support of reform, and forging links with Protestant radicals. The extent to which they succeeded was again demonstrated in the Enniskillen Defender trials where Dr James Trimble, suspected leader of the United Irishmen in the county, provided evidence on behalf of the accused, while William Hamilton, describing Croker as his 'good friend', ensured that a full report of the proceedings and of Croker's acquittal was carried in the *Northern Star*.[23]

Efforts by radical Catholics to forge a link with Presbyterians at grass-roots level were described by Norman Steele in July 1795:

20 Ibid., p. 159.
21 Richard Dawson as high sheriff for County Monaghan in 1793 chaired the public meeting which opposed the formation of the militia and supported 'a complete and radical reform' of parliament, 'including representation of all the people'. Elected as MP with the support of the independent electors, he was apparently considered suspect by government; in the summer of 1797 when arms were being distributed to Monaghan loyalists, an estimated 100 firelocks were confiscated by the military from Dawson's home at Dartrey Castle and lodged in 'protective' custody in Charlemont fort.
22 Nugent to Daly, 2 June 1796: N.A.I., RP 620/23/142.
23 Wolf [William Hamilton] to Russell, 11 Apr. 1796: T.C.D. Sirr papers, MS 868/2/f.178. For the trial report, see *N.S.*, 31 Mar.-4 Apr. 1796.

> There has been a little turbulent spirit roused by some politicians here at the head of the dissenting churches (Presbyterian and popish), who have attempted forming a coalition ... The flirtation commenced by a principal number of the Roman Catholics of Carrickmacross going in parade to the meeting house of Carrickmaclin ... and inviting the others to return the visit.[24]

The building of such links cannot have been easy, particularly in the highly charged sectarian climate of the period. From the Cavan/Monaghan border, Henry Clements of Ashfield reported that in the winter of 1794 that 'the whole of the Protestants' of that part of the country, Ashfield excepted, were 'robbed of their arms by the Defenders'.[25] There were significant Defender mobilizations throughout south Ulster; in Cavan in particular, the harsh suppression of Defenderism may have had an impact in delaying the advance of United Irish politics beyond the east of the county and those areas bordering on Monaghan.[26] Furthermore, the relative success of the Orange Order in Cavan compared with Monaghan and Fermanagh undoubtedly reinforced sectarian politics there.[27]

Throughout the region as a whole, Orangeism made few inroads, with only a handful of lodges established in Monaghan and Fermanagh prior to the 1798. Nonetheless, there were signs of a recruitment strategy in some areas. In March 1796 notices had been fixed 'on the doors of some Papists in the town and neighbourhood of Drum ... desiring the inhabitants to leave their houses or that they and everything belonging to them would be destroyed'.[28] The Orange Boys of the area sent a deputation to neighbouring areas of Cavan inviting them to join their association and, following this, notices similar to those in Drum and signed 'Oliver Cromwell' were attached to the doors of Catholics in that county. The Orange lodges of Monaghan and Fermanagh felt strong enough to hold their first walk near Drum on 12 July 1796, but more than a year later the organization had apparently failed to make any impression on the bulk of Protestants. The annals of the Order in the Roslea area record that 'the brethren would assemble at Johnston's, and at other times on a bog bank in the neighbourhood,

---

24 Steele to Shirley, 27 July 1795: P.R.O.N.I., Shirley papers.
25 Clements to [?], 20 Sept. 1796: N.A.I., RP 620/25/102.
26 Reports of radical activity in County Cavan are largely confined to the east of the county until 1798. Folklore records that the southeast of the county was organized by the Sheares brothers, and that Jemmy Hope was active in areas close to County Monaghan.
27 As late as Apr. 1797, there were as few as four Orange lodges in Fermanagh and probably a similar number in Monaghan. Cavan was better organized and in 1796 witnessed parades in Killeshandra, Belturbet and Bailieborough. The numbers of lodges began to grow from the summer of 1797 onwards, and by 1798 Cavan recorded 32 lodges, Monaghan 18 and Fermanagh 16. Even then, south Ulster continued to lag far behind Armagh and Tyrone in terms of the Order's appeal to Protestants.
28 Clements to [Dublin Castle], 7 Mar. 1796: N.A.I., SOCP 100/1015/8.

or at some unfrequented spot, to avoid the hostile visit of the disaffected and the unfriendly remarks of those from whom sympathy might have been expected'.[29]

The heightening of tension was the subject of correspondence from Henry Clements in December 1796. Reporting that the Catholics of the district were again 'collecting arms [and] ammunition', he communicated confidential information provided by the region's first informant, a Mary Quirk, of developments in the vicinity of Scotshouse and Redhills.[30] Meetings in the district at the homes of suspected Defender leaders were attended by Burke Rice, leader of the Defenderism in Monaghan. Together with named individuals from Armagh, Fermanagh, Monaghan, Cavan and Leitrim, Rice was swearing people into the United Irishmen. Quirk's evidence, in a series of affidavits, confirms the role of senior leaders in the Defender movement in facilitating and encouraging membership of the United Irishmen and also in calming those who would have engaged in sectarian reprisals.

The detailed information in Quirk's affidavits should have sounded a warning to the authorities that all was not well in south Ulster. There were other incidents which pointed to serious difficulties, not least the interception in June 1796 of a cart-load of weapons bound for Henry Jackson of Pill Lane and believed to have been manufactured by his relatives, the Jacksons of Ballybay. There were reports too of arms-training in the Roslea area of Fermanagh, while Irvine Johnston in Cavan alerted government that 'there is a certain set of men ... forming themselves into societies called United Irishmen', who 'assemble on Sundays on pretence of religious purposes and adjourn at night to bye places to learn the use of arms'.[31] United Irish military structures were in place, not least through the efforts of Jemmy Hope who wrote that

> having assisted in forming the Co. Monaghan Committee in Castle-blayney on a market day, when several very respectable linen merchants were there, we planted the Union at Maguiresbridge, Clones, Enniskillen, Ballinamore, Cashcarrigan, Carrick-on-Shannon and Strokestown ... and on our return home, formed committees in Ballyhays, Butlersbridge and Newtownhamilton.[32]

Despite evidence of intensive organisation, the authorities remained oblivious to the scale of disaffection, perhaps reassured by local correspondents such as

29 W.D. Sloan, 'Did Fermanagh lose out?', in S. Foster (ed.), *Recall: A little of the history of Orangeism and Protestantism in Fermanagh* (Enniskillen, 1990), p. 28.

30 N.A.I., RP 620/26/134; 620/26/206; 620/28/19; 620/28/42; 620/28/136–7; 620/28/158; 620/28/284; 60/28/289; SOCP 3066/1. The above papers include correspondence from Henry Clements of Ashfield to Dublin Castle, and several affidavits from Mary Quirk who was related to two prominent leaders of Defenderism in the district.

31 Johnston to Pelham, 5 Mar. 1797: N.A.I., RP 620/29/23.

32 Quoted in Sean Cronin, *A man of the people: Jemmy Hope* (Drogheda, 1964), p. 11. Given the direction he was travelling, Newtownbutler was intended here rather than Newtownhamilton.

Humphry Watt, high sheriff of Monaghan, who reported on 29 December 1796 that the county was 'in a state of the most perfect tranquillity', adding that given 'the zeal and loyalty of the inhabitants, there is every reason to hope for its continuance'.[33] The garrison throughout the region was confined for the most part to fencible regiments, the Essex regiment alone covering a district stretching from Clones to Killybegs.[34] In early 1797 General Lake issued instructions 'to send any party to Monaghan you choose', adding his view that 'a small party will be sufficient there'.[35]

In April 1797, the complacency of the authorities was rudely shattered: convinced that a French landing was imminent, United Irish activists across south Ulster began a series of arms raids. The confidence of the revolutionaries soared with the acquittal in Monaghan of those charged with United Irish activity at the Lent assizes. This news was greeted with euphoria, various correspondents commenting on the bonfires which blazed on every hill. Mary McCracken wrote that 'a gentleman who has just come through the County Monaghan says that he literally travelled through fire, as the whole country seemed in a blaze, with the bonfires on account of the universal acquittals for sedition ...'[36] The celebrations and ongoing arms raids caused consternation among government supporters. On his return to Newbliss from the assizes, Alexander Ker reported to Dublin Castle that 'the disorder and insurrection of this county has increased [to] a most alarming height', conceding that a proclamation issued by Monaghan Grand Jury could not be enforced without urgent military assistance:

> If the government do not immediately send a military force into this county, it will be impossible for the magistrates to prevent it being entirely overrun as a system of terror prevails which impels even the well affected to take part in it.[37]

Henry Clements confirmed Ker's analysis, and stressed the impact of United Irish successes in winning over even their former enemies in the Drum district:

33 Evatt to Pelham, 29 Dec. 1796: N.A.I., SOCP 100/1015/35.
34 Urquhart memorial to government, 29 Nov. 1797: P.R.O. HO 100/68. Commander of the Loyal Essex Regiment of Fencible Infantry, James Edward Urquhart claimed that 'with the assistance of the yeomanry corps', his regiment had 'been the means of timely checking the business of united Irishmen and rendering the country from Clones to Killybegs in a state of perfect tranquillity ...'
35 Lake to Knox, 4 Feb. 1797: N.L.I. MS 56 (no.24).
36 Quoted in M. McNeill, *The life and times of Mary Ann McCracken, 1770–1866* (Belfast, 1988), p. 140. Events in Monaghan and neighbouring parts of Cavan in the early weeks of Apr. are the subject of a series of letters in the Rebellion Papers including N.A.I., RP 620/29/201, 206–7, 216, 245–6, 266, 269, 271, 289, 297; 620/30/19.
37 Ker to Pelham, 9 Apr. 1797: N.A.I., RP 620/29/201.

The sentiments of the people of this country are within these last ten days totally changed from what they were. It was at that time a loyal and spirited people, determined to support their King and constitution and were bound to each other by the oath of Orangemen. But on finding they were in the exact same state with what they called the enemies of their country, the United Irishmen, both they and the freemasons, who are very numerous in this country, joined the United Irishmen and I think I do not exaggerate when I say four-fifths of the people of all persuasions are joined with them …[38]

In trying to understand what was happening all around them, Castle correspondents pointed to the inactivity of many magistrates who were themselves suspect, to the feeling among Orangemen that they had not been shown the preeminence they deserved, and to disillusionment in the ranks of the yeomanry who had not been paid since the previous December. Furthermore, the yeomanry were over-stretched, the Revd John Wright of Clones explaining that his corps were 'exceedingly harrassed by constant nightly duty of patrols and … are almost becoming dispirited through excessive fatigue and the uncertainty of their receiving any compensation for their extraordinary services'.[39]

The yeomanry had been heavily infiltrated in parts of Monaghan and Cavan in particular, and it was suggested that a successful arms raid on the stores of the Lurg yeomanry in Fermanagh may have been the result of inside help.[40] Carmen, returning to Belturbet from Newry, related their experience at a carman's inn near Castleblayney. The owner's son, a yeomanry sergeant, arrived at the inn in his uniform. Later that evening he put on a green jacket and trousers, a green handkerchief about his neck, a cap and green feather. He then took out a halbert and marched out; he was met on the road 'by a number of men who extended in ranks'. Later, he told the carmen that 'every man they saw were yeomen except three …'[41] Even in the most loyal of corps at Ashfield, two United Irishmen were discovered and dismissed. As for the Darling corps, which included Drum, Clements described himself 'at a loss what to do':

Half the corps are loyal and wish to prove themselves so, but the other half are rotten and such is the state of that immediate country that loyal men dare not declare their sentiments.[42]

38 Clements to Beresford, 10 Apr. 1797: N.A.I., RP 620/29/06.
39 Wright to Pelham, 10 Apr. 1797: N.A.I., RP 620/29/207.
40 Irvine to Pelham, 27 May 1797: N.A.I., RP 620/30/209. Irvine, as captain of the corps, wrote that the arms had been in the guard house which was 'supposed to be the most centrical and best place'. An inquiry 'sat on the guard', a point addressed by Pelham (RP 620/30/236) when he sought to establish 'what number the guard consisted [of] and what defence they made against the attack'.
41 Nixon to Pelham, 11 May 1797: N.A.I., RP 620/30/51.
42 Clements to Beresford: N.A.I., RP 620/29/269.

The aftermath of the 'battle of Crieve' near Ballybay, County Monaghan, when four members of the Armagh Militia were killed and several more seriously wounded, exposed the Kingscourt corps when they refused to march with other yeomanry corps against the people who had attacked the soldiers.[43]

Besides its implications for yeomanry, the Crieve incident showed the extent of United Irish organization in mid-Monaghan. Thousands reportedly left their work in the bleach greens of the district and, armed with muskets and pikes, confronted the soldiers who had earlier (by their own admission) killed fifteen people while searching for *poitín* stills in the nearby Ballytrain district. Nor was this rebellious spirit confined to the labouring class and small farmers; the local gentry who were present when the soldiers were killed pointedly refused to co-operate with an investigation into the incident.[44]

The United Irish strategy of generating paranoia through selective and exaggerated leaking of information was also undermining the confidence of government supporters who felt themselves increasingly isolated. Clements was warned of an army of 30,000 men being assembled in the Monaghan/Cavan borderlands and described his reaction:

> The number I thought absurd and did not mention it, but I am this day told by a person that I have no reason to think has ever deceived me as to intelligence, and was present last Friday night at their first meeting, that the number could not be guessed at, but said there was as many as would fill the whole field where they assembled could hold them. They did not meet with a hostile intention but to inspect their arms, for every man was armed ... They parted before daylight without any noise or disturbance.[45]

Papers seized in a house near Lifford in County Donegal in April gave the numbers of United Irishmen in Monaghan at 18,376, the third highest return in Ulster.[46] The figure is in excess of the 10,000 given in reports of provincial meetings published by the government's Secret Committee. Unlike Monaghan, for which specific returns were given, Fermanagh and Cavan were not represented at such meetings, so that rounded figures were entered which, in light of the evidence from correspondents, were probably a gross underestimate, particularly in

43 Holdcroft to Lees, 16 Apr. 1797: N.A.I., RP 620/29/266. Holdcroft observed that the the Kingscourt yeomanry 'can be as little depended on as any yeomanry corps in Ireland'.

44 Ker to Pelham, 27 Apr. 1797. See also RP 620/29/326. The gentry involved included all the leading linen merchants of the area, among them the Jacksons, several of whom were said to have 'gone on the run' to avoid military reprisals. It was generally agreed that those who killed the soldiers had 'gone to America' and that there was insufficient evidence against twelve men who were arrested. All were acquitted.

45 Clements to Beresford, 16 Apr. 1797: N.A.I., RP 620/29/269.

46 A list of United Irish strength in the Ulster counties and Louth from a list found by John Dun in the home of William Love, Rockhill, County Donegal: N.A.I., RP 620/30/119.

the period after April 1797. If supporters and opponents of the revolutionary movement were in agreement about anything, it was that the United Irish organization throughout south Ulster made rapid advances in the late spring and early summer of 1797 to the extent that it was generally accepted that they would soon be 'uppermost'.

There seemed to be no stopping the momentum that had been created. Worse still was the dawning realization that the women were as bad if not worse than the men. From Belleek, the Revd James Cochran warned of 'approaching insurrection ... the French system of terror aspreading by their hopeful copyists, women sworn and boys of ten and twelve years old in the train of nocturnal depredators'.⁴⁷ But if a single area was to be identified in which the revolutionary fervour had taken hold, it was Cootehill, County Cavan. Henry Clements bemoaned the change that had taken place in the sentiments of the people there:

> Every man and *woman* are now united; I almost doubt whether there is one in forty that is not. They publicly declare themselves, and such people as wished to be well effected were obliged to join them out of fear. They constantly wear the badge of their order, the men a green stock and a bit of green riband in their breasts and such as have watches, of which there appears numbers of the linen merchants in Cootehill, a green watch string. The women [wear] a green handkerchief and riband with shoe knots of the same.⁴⁸

Clements asserted that the daughter of the Presbyterian parson, Thomas Stewart, was engaged along with her father in swearing new members into the United Irish society. The radicalism of women in the area is attested to by the experience of a young doctor based in the town.⁴⁹ Although apolitical, he was anxious to secure business and accepted an invitation to a dinner party. Describing the beautiful young women who attended 'as verdant as spring; for they all wore her livery – green ribbons, green gowns, green shoes and green handkerchiefs', the doctor thought himself in clover and joined heartily in singing rebel songs 'as if he had been Napper Tandy himself'. But he was astonished when the guests responded favourably to a suggestion that a campaign of assassination should be carried out against their enemies. 'What better can they expect?', a young woman said when he innocently criticized the suggestion. Remarking to a dancing partner that assassination was not a fit subject for a girl to be discussing, she rounded on him for 'pleading the cause of his oppressors: vile wretches', adding:

47 Cochran to Pelham, 22 May 1797: N.A.I., RP 620/30/153.
48 Clements to Beresford, 18 Apr. 1797: N.A.I., RP 620/29/289.
49 J. Gamble, *Sketches of history, politics and manners in Dublin and the north of Ireland in 1810*, 2nd ed. (London, 1826), pp 207–8.

'You may wear your hair close, you may sing what songs and dance to what tunes you please, but I tell you, you are no true croppy: you reason, but a republican' said she with animation 'feels for his bleeding country – for the exile in the foreign land – for the prisoner in a dungeon – for the victim on a scaffold – for the wretched wanderer without habitation or name, whose house has been burned, and property destroyed by the vile agents of lawless and brutal power! And because I am a woman I am not to think of this: I am not to feel for their sorrows, because I cannot relieve their distresses; I am not to pursue with curses their low-minded, and soon, I hope, to be laid-low oppressors, because I am a woman – because I am weak – because I am a girl, as you were pleased to call me; but, if I am weak, God is strong, and will soon, I trust, exterminate such monsters from the face of the earth! I would not' added she, after a pause, and in a more moderate tone 'strike a dagger into one of their hearts, but I would bless and pray for the man who did it, and would take his chance of Heaven far sooner than the cold-blooded preacher who talks of virtue, but encourages vice, and tramples on and outrages innocence by affording impunity to guilt.'

The arms raids which swept Monaghan in April 1797 spread through Fermanagh and south Donegal in the early summer, reaching as far as Bundoran where the holiday home of Lord Enniskillen was burnt to the ground. With the assistance of key supporters throughout the region, the authorities initiated a counter-offensive in late May. Additional troops were deployed to the region and a two-pronged strategy implemented, offering military and judicial repression on the one hand and on the other an amnesty for those who renounced their association with the United Irishmen.

On the face of it, the amnesty seemed to work, as thousands came forward to take the required oath. But it is in the context of repression and the fear which it induced that we should examine the effectiveness of the strategy. Many who took the oath had no connection with the United Irishmen at all and simply wanted to assert their non-membership of the organization. Although three hundred took the oath before Captain William Tredennick at Belleek, only five stand of arms, one sword and three bayonets were handed in.[50]

Some who came in under the proclamation were undoubtedly associated with the United Irishmen, having at least taken the oath of secrecy. It was probably this group that was reported to be crowding into Westport, County Mayo, in mid-June. Referring particularly to the influx from Monaghan, Denis Browne claimed that 'the late immigration from the North is of those persons that came in on the proclamation and were afraid of being murdered by their former asso-

---

50 Treddenick to [Dublin Castle], 14 June 1797: N.A.I., RP 620/31/90.

ciates'.[51] Others took the oath to avoid prison sentences (as was the case of several men from Farney who, although convicted of making pike handles at the autumn assizes, were released because they had taken the benefit of the Proclamation). By 8 June Norman Steele was certainly becoming sceptical of the effectiveness of this device:

> I have not ... a doubt but that ... their coming in under the proclamation is that they may be on one hand armed against the civil power by the certificate of a magistrate and on the other against the rebellious by the signs and tokens of their societies. As to the oath itself, the security is but slender, being in constant expectation that a French invasion will dissolve those obligations ...[52]

Military repression in south Ulster began at Leysborough (now Annaghmakerrig) near Newbliss on 20 May 1797, when Alexander Ker led his troop of yeomanry and a party of the North Lowland Fencibles in an attack on a large crowd who were setting potatoes. For several weeks previous to this, hundreds of people had been going through this and neighbouring districts, carrying white flags, singing republican songs and doing the farm-work for imprisoned comrades. Eleven unarmed people were reported killed in the attack, while many more were wounded and others arrested.[53]

Although distrusted as a former supporter of reform, Lord Blayney was given permission by a deperate government to establish a 'flying camp', and on 21 May this mobile force launched its first offensive against the United Irish stronghold of Glaslough, which boasted a full regiment of the United Irishmen.[54] 'Nothing', explained Blayney, 'can be really effectual but retaliation in point of destroying property, burning houses and setting the inhabitants to the mercy of the elements, by which means you will either force them to action or make them surrender the arms.'[55] Following the success of the Glaslough operation, Pelham gave Blayney the go-ahead for similar actions, stating that 'Lord Blayney's activity and exertions are as great as those of any man I know.'[56] In an intriguing comment which suggests that the tactics in Glaslough were especially harsh, the chief secretary cautioned Henry Alexander: 'I only hope that you will temper his zeal without checking it.'[57] With government approval, Blayney's

51 Browne to [Dublin Castle], 17 June 1797: N.A.I., RP 620/31/112.
52 Steele to Pelham, 8 June 1797: N.A.I., RP 620/31/55.
53 Ker to [Dublin Castle], 22 May 1797: N.A.I., SOCP 100/1016/40; Clements to Beresford, undated: N.A.I., RP 620/34/44.
54 The strength of the United Irishmen in this part of county Monaghan is referred to in D.C. Rushe, *History of Monaghan for two hundred years, 1660–1860* (Dundalk, 1921), pp 143–4.
55 Blayney to Pelham, 22 May 1797: N.A.I., RP 620/30/148.
56 Pelham to Alexander, 26 May 1797: N.A.I., RP 620/30/149. This comment is written by Pelham on a letter he received from Henry Alexander, dated 22 May.
57 Ibid.

force struck across a wide area, from west Tyrone to south Armagh and in his own base in east Monaghan. He was clearly enjoying the free hand he had been given by the authorities, boasting about the steps he was taking to subdue the Creggan area of south Armagh around the town of Forkhill, including the burning of many houses there. Inviting Lord Glentworth to join him, he wrote: 'If you are disengaged and will take a trip down, you may see some amusement with those natives and I can give you a tent. Our quarters are uncertain.'[58]

Blayney's tactics were not universally appreciated, even by government supporters; his activities in south Monaghan, as well as the Forkhill incident, prompted a sharp rebuke from the captain of the Farney yeomanry, Norman Steele. Describing to Pelham his own methods of countering disaffection, he explained:

> By this means I am coming at all the active agitators of rebellion and restoring the more innocent to their industry, I hope without leaving an angry sore behind. I went yesterday to Castleblayney merely to make it a point with Lord Blayney that he should leave to me the curing of this district [the barony of Farney] as it does not accord with my feelings to practice the indiscriminate vengeance his lordship takes of the country.[59]

Blayney defended his activities, pointing out that his 'flying camp' was as effective as two thousand men in fixed garrisons, and had 'taken vast quantities of arms, pikes etc. and, act[ing] both in a civil and military capacity, had administered the Oath of Allegiance and bound over to security numbers', both in the counties of Armagh and Monaghan. Asserting that he had 'totally turned the mob here [in Castleblayney] against United Irishmen', he pledged to do the same in Creggan. He justified the burning of Forkhill: 'from that country proceeds all the disturbance in Louth, Armagh and part of Monaghan adjacent ...'[60]

Elsewhere in Monaghan, the assault on the United Irishmen was led by Lord Midleton's agent, Dacre Hamilton, who was appointed high sheriff for the county in 1798. There were multiple arrests in Fermanagh also, a series of affidavits testifying to the existence of widepread organization by the United Irishmen in that county among all religious denominations.[61] In County Cavan, government activity was on a more limited scale than would appear to have been the case elsewhere in south Ulster. However Henry Clements' yeomanry joined local military in Cootehill in setting fire to several houses and arresting two United Irish suspects, 'one a seceding minister, the other a linen buyer':

58 Blayney to Glentworth, undated: N.A.I., RP 620/34/45.
59 Steele to Pelham, 8 June 1797: N.A.I., RP 620/31/55.
60 Blayney to Pelham, 10 June 1797: N.A.I., RP 620/31/71.
61 N.A.I., RP 620/30.

The inhabitants of Cootehill think I have got information against them all. Twelve families ran away last night and it is supposed many more will this night. I will be out tomorrow night when I expect five or six prisoners. I have taken up 67 firelocks and some swords and pistols.[62]

The policy of burning houses spread to Fermanagh also, Captain Treddenick of the Loyal Erne corps of yeomanry arguing that in his area attacks on homes had been started by the United Irishmen.[63] Certainly there is evidence that while they may have been on the defensive, the United Irishmen were willing and able to launch counter-measures in areas of strength, particularly in 'papering' the homes of suspected informers and other enemies. In Farney, Norman Steele reported the arrest and impriorment of men charged with 'feloniously breaking open houses and cropping the heads of some individuals who had not taken the oaths of the United Irishmen'.[64]

Hundreds of prisoners were taken across the region and the jail in Monaghan was packed well beyond its capacity.[65] To relieve themselves of the problem of having to deal with alleged offenders in the courts, it was agreed to send some off to the line.[66] Thus, in early August, twenty political inmates of Monaghan jail were spirited away, most to serve in the army and several, considered unfit for military duty, to Duncannon fort in Wexford to work there as orderlies. Several prisoners were also taken from Enniskillen jail and lodged in Belfast: to the horror of the Establishment party in the county, they were subsequently released.

The Assizes in late August saw the climax of legal repression. Twelve United Irish prisoners were capitally convicted in Monaghan, most of them from Glaslough, and of these five were executed on 16 October 1797. The legal cases appear to have been less prepared in Cavan, with the result that there were no executions and the Cootehill prisoners were acquitted. At Enniskillen, however, most prisoners were discharged, but no less than eleven received the death sentence and three Roslea United Irishmen were executed. A further two men from the Clontibret district of County Monaghan were executed in 1798.

What impact did the counter-revolutionary strategy have in south Ulster? The amnesties, like the arrests, the burnings, and the executions, did not really hit the United Irishmen as hard as was at first thought, and a comment by Arthur Wolfe after the Monaghan assizes that the sentiments of the people had

62 Clements to [Dublin Castle], 12 June 1797: N.A.I., RP 620/31/81.
63 Treddenick to [Dublin Castle], 14 June 1797: N.A.I., RP 620/31/90.
64 Steele to Shirley, 1 July 1797: P.R.O.N.I., Shirley papers.
65 Wilford to Pelham, 26 July 1797: N.A.I., SOCP 3146/1. This includes a return of the names of 107 political prisoners awaiting trial in Monaghan jail (with details of the arresting magistrates and alleged offences) as well as the names of several convicted political offenders and twelve debtors. For further information on prisons and prisoners in 1797, see *Commons' Jn. Ire.*, xvii (1798), part 2, appendix.
66 Wilford to Pelham, 15 Aug. 1797: N.A.I., RP 620/32/50.

not changed was echoed by correspondents throughout south Ulster. Some became convinced that the United Irish organisation was intact and was simply biding its time, a sentiment endorsed by William Sampson in a note to the imprisoned Thomas Russell when he wrote: 'Croppies lie down is now the word and we do lie down. But God tempers the cold wind to the shorn lamb.'[67]

There were very few declarations of loyalty from religious congregations in south Ulster, not at least until the rebellion was well under way. If we look at some of the areas they came from in Monaghan (the Presbyterian congregations of Castleblayney and Frankford and the Catholic parishes of Muckno and Clontibret), we should be conscious that this was Lord Blayney's territory and in such a situation it was probably prudent to declare loyalty. First Ballybay Presbyterian church, by contrast, lay in a heartland of the United Irishmen. Again, First Ballybay's decision to publish a declaration of loyalty was undoubt-edly intended as a means of protecting themselves after their minister, John Arnold, went 'on the run' in 1797. When a new minister, James Morrell, was ordained in 1799, he was regarded as 'a government man' by a section of the same congregation: rather than accept him, they left the meeting and built their own church 200 yards away, which still stands today as a social centre for the First Ballybay congregation. Finally, the joint statement of the Catholic bishop and priests of Clogher is remarkable, not for its condemnation, but for the lack of it, for while they condemned sectarian violence, they at no point referred to the United Irishmen. Individual clergy did release emphatic denunciations of the organisation, but equally there were some who sided with the rebels, and probably a majority who simply tried to survive.

The United Irishmen of south Ulster were not defeated in 1797, but it is clear that while the conspiracy continued to work towards a rebellion, loyalist confidence had been restored, the element of surprise had been lost, and govern-ment supporters were better prepared. In late 1797, Enniskillen was chosen as one of the major military garrisons in Ulster and the yeomanry (particularly in Fermanagh) began to play an increasingly co-ordinated role in counter-insur-gency.

While the administration began to place increasing emphasis on passes over Lough Erne and on roads linking Ulster with the south of Ireland, there is no evidence to suggest that the United Irishmen regarded these as strategically sig-nificant, nor is there any evidence to suggest that an uprising was planned here. The United Irishmen of south Ulster were apparently instructed to make their way south and east to the intended centres of rebellion. This is what happened and there are folklore and documentary references to United Irishmen from the region taking part in engagements such as Ballinahinch and Tara, and in joining Humbert's expedition as it moved across the country. By far the most significant

67 Sampson to Russell, undated: T.C.D., Sirr Paper MS 868/2, f. 230.

rendezvous point was in Bailieborough demesne in east Cavan where on 26 August 1798 the United Irishmen from several parts of south Ulster and north Leinster assembled on their way to link up with Humbert. Their movements were monitored, however, and a attack was launched by yeomanry, militia and regular forces on the rebel positions, forcing a general flight. As many as 800 may have died in the battle of Rebel Hill as it came to be called, many having drowned in the Castle Lough and Castle Weir as they attempted to escape.

Even when the rebellion was crushed, there is no evidence that the conspiracy was at an end, and in the new United Irish leadership that emerged, activists from south Ulster, including Edward Carolan, were to play a prominent part. There were reports in late September 1800 'that some meetings have been held by the heads of the rebellious party towards Ballybay ...' Three years later, William Hamilton was back in Ireland along with Emmet and Russell. After a period in Rathfarnham, he headed for south Ulster to co-ordinate an uprising in an area that was still considered to have strong revolutionary potential. Following the capture and execution of both Emmet and Russell, Hamilton was eventually captured while sleeping in a cabin by the shore of Lough Egish, close to a bleach green owned by the Crawfords, a prominent United Irish family.

In the light of the recriminations which must surely follow every failed attempt at revolution, the strategy of detaching Presbyterians and radical Protestants from their union with Catholics intensified. Emerging from his church on the Diamond in Clones, the Revd John Wright was astonished to find two preachers at the foot of the church steps, inciting the mob against Catholics and then to discover that they carried a pass from Lord Castlereagh to spread what Wright termed 'their poison'. The loss of many political activists who fled to America or to France seriously weakened whatever challenge the radicals might have advanced against such tactics, which in turn were to have had such profound repercussions for the subsequent history of Ireland.

13

Politicization and paramilitarism:
North-west and south-west Ulster, *c.*1772–98

BREANDÁN MAC SUIBHNE

> Like the simple countryman, [the conductors of the *Northern Star*]
> vainly imagine that their moon is a better moon than the one that
> shines in the next parish!
>
> George Douglas, editor, *London-Derry Journal*, 2 Oct. 1792

On 3 June 1772 George Douglas (1744?–1828) printed the first edition of the
London-Derry Journal and General Advertizer in the shop of James Blyth, a
bookseller and occasional printer of chapbooks, on the Diamond of Derry.
Douglas was young, probably still in his twenties. He had served his time in the
capital where he had briefly worked in a print-shop on College Green.[1] He
pinned his hopes for the newspaper on his religious status and experience: 'The
publisher of this paper satisfies himself', he announced, 'that by his being a
Protestant; by having had experience for a considerable time in a work of this
nature in the city of Dublin; by printing this paper on an elegant new type; and
by an unceasing readiness to please, he will be so fortunate as to gain the appro-
bation and protection of every one who shall honor him as a subscriber.' In the
same edition Douglas advertised for an apprentice to the 'printing business'; the
only qualifications were that 'he must be a Protestant and well-recommended'.[2]

The *Journal*, appearing twice weekly, soon established itself as the chief
newspaper west of the Sperrins and second only to the *Belfast Newsletter* in
Ulster. Nevertheless, the collection of subscriptions and monies owed for advertisements proved difficult; in January 1773 Douglas entered into a partnership
with Blyth which lasted until October 1775 when he again became sole owner-
editor. He reduced the paper to a single weekly edition in 1781, but trouble collecting subscriptions, a new stamp duty on advertisements (which he perceived
as an attack on the 'free press'), and the fading prospect of radical parliamentary

1 R. Munter, *A dictionary of the print trade in Ireland, 1550–1775* (New York, 1998), p. 82.
2 *L.J.*, 3 June; 27 Oct. 1772.

reform, sapped his enthusiasm.[3] In May 1786 he 'disengaged from the laborious task of conducting a newspaper', and Samuel Glen, a young man who had served his time with the *Journal*, acted as editor until 1788. At that point the centenary of the siege of Derry re-invigorated radical politics and prompted Douglas (who had remained as owner) to return to the editor's chair.[4] Still, the old problems remained: he grumbled constantly about unpaid subscriptions and the government's encroachment on the press.[5] Long enthralled by America's experiment with democracy, he decided to emigrate. He sold the *Journal* and his various properties in Derry in spring 1796 and left for Philadelphia late that summer.[6]

Shortly before Douglas' departure, an *ad hoc* group of fifty-six merchants and businessmen who styled themselves the 'steady friends of merit' presented him with three silver cups to mark his contribution to civil society over 'twenty-four years in Derry'. Douglas thanked the group for the cups, and presented his friends with several bound volumes containing the back-issues of the *Journal*. In doing so Douglas evoked an image of Ireland enjoying unprecedented prosperity, and he expressed his hopes for the happiness of its people without regard to rank or religion:[7]

> To you and your posterity, they will be found a useful and entertaining registry, not only as containing an interesting history of the most awful and important transactions that have ever agitated and convulsed the world, but as a valuable deposit of the local occurrences of the City of Derry and its vicinity during a period of 24 years.
>
> In these volumes will also be discovered, among a vast collection of other momentous matter, the first dawnings of that well-regulated spirit, which has raised THIS Country to its present state of opulence and reputation. My most fervent prayer is, that this spirit may continue to be so wisely directed to the further welfare of IRELAND, that future journalists may have nothing to record, but the extension of its commerce, the increase of its riches, and the happiness of its people.

As Douglas spoke, the United Irishmen were building a paramilitary organization across north-west Ulster. Within twelve months, three of the 'friends of

3   *L.J.*, 8 May 1781; 14 Feb.; 28 Mar. 1786.
4   Ibid., 2 May 1786.
5   Ibid., 19 Jan. 1796.
6   Ibid., 26 Jan. 1796. On Douglas' career in Philadelphia, Baltimore, and also in New York where he established the *Western Star and Harp of Erin* (1812–14), see R. G. Silver, 'The Baltimore book trade, 1800–1825', *Bulletin of the New York Public Library*, lvii (1953), 193; R. Cargill Cole, *Irish booksellers and English writers, 1740–1800* (Kent, 1986), pp 166–7.
7   P.R.O.N.I., Mic. 60/6 [*London-Derry Journal*], printed account of 'a meeting of a number of Gentlemen, Citizens of Derry' on 18 Aug. 1796; 'Subscribers to cups to Mr Douglas, London-Derry, 1st Aug. 1796'.

merit' had been implicated in a plan to capture the city and make it a 'fortress for the rebels'. And by then one of the three, Joseph Orr, was on the run in Liverpool trying to make his way to France and the two others, Robert Moore and William McClintock, were in Derry gaol, charged with treason. All three were men of the highest respectability.[8] Orr, a particularly close friend of Douglas, was a wealthy brazier with a shop on Pump Street.[9] Moore was the city's leading ironmonger, and McClintock one of its best regarded haberdashers. They had all been prominent in civic life over the previous generation. Moore, the most conspicuous, had been a Volunteer officer in the 1780s and again in the 1790s; the chairman and treasurer of the city poor-house and infirmary; an active member of the Chamber of Commerce; and a delegate to the last Dungannon convention. His standing is implied in the allegation that he was remanded in custody – despite an offer of £2,000 bail – to shield Sir George Hill, one of the city's MPs, from his 'exertions and influence' in the election of August 1797.[10] Notwithstanding their respectability, Derry Corporation erased all three names from its roll of freemen in November 1798; the names of Christopher Hardy, another merchant, and Henry Grattan, an honorary freeman, were also expunged. Moore and McClintock had by then followed Douglas to America where the printer was already well-integrated into the burgeoning community of expatriate radicals, having collaborated with Mathew and James Carey in the re-publication of Grattan's *Present state of Ireland* in 1797. Orr was now in France where he was active among Irish exiles and an intimate of Thomas Paine; determined to throw the remainder of his fortune against '*la tyrannie du gouvernement Britannique*', he died in the Vendée the following year.[11]

The contrast between Douglas' narrow sectarianism in the first edition of his newspaper and the inclusive project which his friends pursued in 1796–8 points to a profound transformation in regional society: sectarian animosities were withering away and Catholic, Protestant and Dissenter were 'uniting' under the common name of Irishman. However, historians of late eighteenth-century Ireland have displayed scant understanding of political and ideological change in

8 Orr, Moore and McClintock were not the only 'steady friends of merit' exposed as republicans. In December 1796, William Beattie, an ironmonger who had contributed to the silver cups, was arrested for attempting to suborn members of the Tipperary Militia, see Bagwell, Derry, to [Cooke], 7 Dec. 1796: N.A.I., RP 620/26/104; Hill, Derry, to Cooke, n.d.: N.A.I., RP 620/26/107.

9 On Douglas' relationship with Orr, see his obituary for Orr's wife in *L.J.*, 20 Oct. 1795.

10 Ibid., 25 Feb.; 28 Mar. 1780; 6 July; 10 Aug. 1790; 24 Jan.; 6 Mar. 1792; 22 Jan.; 29 Jan.; 5 Feb. 1793; Hill, Derry, to Cooke, 17 July 1797: N.A.I., RP 620/31/262.

11 *L.J.*, 6 Nov. 1798. On Orr's participation in an aborted expedition to Ireland in 1798, see Elliott, *Partners in revolution*, p. 217. On his contact with Paine, see Paine to Couttreau, n.p., n.d. [Paris, 1798]; Muir, Paris, to Bruix, 11 Sept. 1798; Orr, Paris, to Bruix [Sept. 1798]. I am grateful to John Gray and Kevin Whelan for typescripts of these letters. On his death in 1799, see renunciation of J. Moore, D. Watt and W. Buchanan, 1 Sept. 1818: P.R.O.N.I., D.1015/2.

the north-west. The dominant analysis in the scholarship of the last two decades conceives 'uniting' as the invention of an organization, the Belfast Society of United Irishmen, and explains spatial variations in the strength and ideological coherence of that organization as a consequence of the efforts of its agents (or the circulation of its newspaper) and distance from headquarters.[12]

This paper examines republican paramilitarism in north-west Ulster in the eleven months between the presentation to Douglas, the flight of Orr, and the arrests of Moore and McClintock. It argues that within this region, 'uniting' grew out of existing beliefs, structures and networks and was not externally imposed. More particularly, it seeks to locate the United Irishmen in a protracted and regionally-specific process of politicization in which the critical period was the late 1770s and early 1780s. To illuminate causation, the chapter counterpoints developments in the north-west with the experience of south-west Ulster where 'uniting' was only a brief shaft of light, shining from outside the region into a morbidly atavistic political culture.

* * *

West Ulster is here conceived as two internally differentiated regions, one centred on Derry, the other on Enniskillen, in each of which an advantaged core zone traded with a disadvantaged periphery. In both cores, there was a substantial population of English-speaking Protestants; Irish-speaking Catholics dominated the peripheries. Despite broad similarities, there were basic differences between the two regions. First, the north-west was more commercialized with extensive proto-industrial networks for the production of linen yarn, cloth, and latterly *poitín*. Second, Presbyterians outnumbered Episcopalians in all districts in the north-western core, while the Protestant population in the south-western core was almost exclusively Episcopalian, its small Dissenting minority being composed mainly of Methodists. In a provincial context, therefore, the two regions were polar opposites: one was the only Ulster region where Presbyterians outnumbered Episcopalians in all heavily Protestant districts, the other the only region in which Episcopalians outnumbered Dissenters in all such areas.

Socio-economic and cultural differences produced radically different political cultures and set the two regions on divergent political tracks. In the north-west, binary oppositions of Planter and Gael, settler and native, Protestant and Catholic, became increasingly unstable during the eighteenth century. The eviction of Presbyterians from the polity in the early 1700s – despite their numerical

---

12 A.T.Q. Stewart, *The narrow ground: Aspects of Ulster history, 1609–1969* (Belfast, 1977, reprinted 1997), pp 107–8; N. Curtin, 'The United Irish organization in Ulster, 1795–8', in D. Dickson, D. Keogh and K. Whelan (eds), *The United Irishmen: Republicanism, radicalism and rebellion* (Dublin, 1993), p. 214; N.J. Curtin, *The United Irishmen: Popular politics in Ulster and Dublin, 1791–8* (Oxford, 1994), pp 68–70. For a critique, see B. MacSuibhne, 'Up not out: Why did north-west Ulster not rise in 1798?', in C. Póirtéir (ed.), *The great Irish rebellion of 1798* (Cork, 1998), pp 83–4.

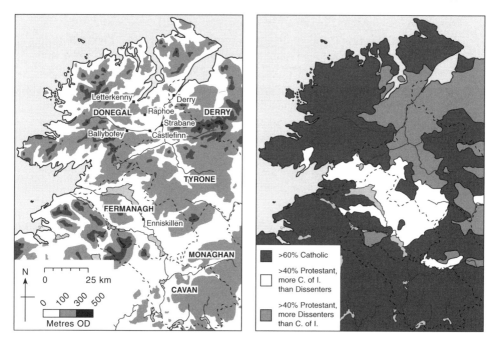

Fig. 13.1 West Ulster landforms and sectarian zones (data kindly supplied by Prof. D.W. Miller). Towns shown are those where the *Derry Journal* had an agent in 1772.

strength and wealth, and the salience of *their* siege in the 'Glorious Revolution' – generated tensions that rendered notions of a 'whole Protestant community' redundant.[13] Commercialization, meanwhile, promoted social and cultural differentiation within the Catholic community. From mid-century, English-speaking, mass-going Catholics – although still clustered in less prestigious trades – were increasingly well-integrated into the urban middle class and alienated from their Irish-speaking country cousins: shopkeepers of all denominations contributed to rewards for sharpers and coiners of all denominations, and Catholic, Protestant and Dissenter routinely united under the common name of licensed publican to shut-down shebeens. The inclusion of Catholics in such voluntary associations reflected the evolution of a social and cultural space where the zero-sum politics of Planter and Gael were out of place. Print media and the public house were central to this 'public sphere'.[14] There was a lively trade in almanacs, broadsheets and chapbooks at fairs and markets, and from mid-century village shops sold histories, political pamphlets, devotional literature, children's books and 'novels and romances'. Most importantly, the region was exceptionally well-

13 T. Brown, *The whole Protestant community: The making of an historical myth* (Derry, 1985).
14 C. Calhoun, 'Introduction: Habermas and the public sphere', in C. Calhoun (ed.), *Habermas and the public sphere* (Cambridge, 1992), pp 1–48; G. Eley, 'Nations, publics, and political cultures: Placing Habermas in the nineteenth century', in ibid., pp 289–339.

served by newspapers

served by newspapers: besides Douglas' paper (1772), one could read the *Strabane Journal* (1771) and the *Strabane Newsletter* (late 1780s).[15] Print and particularly the weekly press elevated reasoned argument, and in city, town and country where the clientele of taverns, inns and shebeens were a promiscuous mix of classes and creeds, newspapers were routinely read aloud early in the evening and people would then 'discuss politics and settle the affairs of the nation, over a cool tankard of porter and a comfortable sup of [toddy]'.[16] Conservatives complained that 'Liberty Boys' – 'coffee-house politicians' and 'frequenters of low public houses' who railed against government – dominated these assemblies, yet the critical point is that there was debate and that reasoned argument was esteemed.[17]

In the latter half of the century, the involvement of the regional economy in wider markets raised resentment against British restrictions on Ireland's trade and constitution, and there are signs that a broader 'Irishness' constructed in opposition to a British 'other' came to be imposed over the older, rickety identities of settler and native. The American War had a vital role in this process, reinforcing perceptions of Britain as selfish, corrupt and oppressive, and establishing a patriot-loyal polarity as the essential division in regional politics. A Limavady poet's lines on 'the murdering sword when haughty Britain drew/Against her faultless sons – and bid adieu/To Justice, mercy, honour, and the laws' encapsulates popular attitudes to the war: patriots opposed loyalist celebrations of British victories; Paine's *Common sense* generated a regional pamphlet controversy; and Douglas had to refute claims that the *Journal* was 'but a sort of a kind of a rebelly paper'.[18] Local connections heightened interest. General Richard Montgomery, who fell leading the Americans at Quebec, was a brother of Alexander Montgomery, Donegal's crypto-Presbyterian 'Independent' MP; he and other 'rebels' with strong north-west Ulster links, including John Dunlap, printer of the Declaration of Independence, Blair McClenaghan, a prominent Philadelphia republican, and William Stewart, a successful general, were hailed as heroes.[19] Most importantly, the war occasioned the formation of local Volunteer companies. Popular alternatives to resented British troops, these companies developed into 'the Volunteer Army of Ireland' in the winter of 1779–80 by asserting their

15 J.R.R. Adams, *The printed word and the common man: Popular culture in Ulster, 1700–1900* (Belfast, 1987), p. 35; E.R. McC. Dix, *List of books and pamphlets printed in Strabane in the eighteenth century* (Dundrum, 1908).
16 *L.J.*, 9 Oct. 1778.
17 Ibid., 18 Apr. 1777.
18 Ibid., 10 Dec. 1776; 6 May; 31 Oct.; 18 Nov.; 16 Dec. 1777; 2 Jan.; 9 Oct. 1778; 10 May 1785.
19 Both McClenaghan and Stewart were feted on their return to the north-west, see *L.J.*, 8 June 1784; 12 Apr.; 19 Apr.; 26 Apr.; 17 May 1785. On Montgomery, see ibid., 31 Jan. 1777; 12 Dec. 1786; G.S. Montgomery, *A family history of the Montgomerys of Ballyleck, County Monaghan, now of Beaulieu, County Louth, Convoy, County Donegal and ... antient history of Montgomery* (Belfast, 1887), p. 19. For an apparent reference to Dunlap, see *Strabane Journal*, 18 Oct. 1785.

equality with 'the King's troops', insisting on uniformity and silence in the ranks, instituting paramilitary funerals and court-martials, and establishing battalion and regimental structures. Through an elaborate theatre of war – field days, reviews and sham-fights in which they 'fought' – they asserted Ireland's capacity to be 'free' and, once Ireland achieved 'freedom', ships sailed from Derry under the national flag, the harp appearing beneath the Irish (radial), not the British (imperial) crown. Illuminations proclaimed George III 'the first King of Ireland'; Volunteers pronounced Irish 'our native tongue', and involved themselves in the building of Catholic chapels to 'render the people of Ireland, an united, a happy, and a powerful nation'.[20]

The notion of 'a united people' was of central importance in the patriots' ideological project: Britain, they argued, had promoted religious divisions to keep Ireland weak; 'the people' must forget sectarian narratives of Planter or Papist atrocities and reflect on the 'prouder story' of a small nation's six centuries of struggle for freedom from a selfish and oppressive neighbour. In other words the people, freeing themselves from a divisive past, would enable a future free from the British parliament. Dr William Crawford, Presbyterian minister of Strabane, gave this project its most developed intellectual expression in his *History of Ireland* (1783), a two-volume history of 'the Irish nation' from 'our Milesian ancestors' to the settlement of 1782. However, two drunken nights in Derry in 1779 illuminated the advanced character of regional ideology with equal clarity.[21] On 30 November 1779, when news reached the city that Ireland had achieved 'free trade', the 'true-born Patriot Paddies' of Derry celebrated by drinking 'Irish whiskey … in every possible modification, currant, raspberry, mixed, plain, etc., etc.' out of 'Irish naggins' and glasses from which the feet had been broken off and 'the want supplied by potatoes'; this *bouleversement* of British stereotypes of 'the Irish' defies 'revision'.[22] The second drunken night occurred a week later when the Apprentice Boys, a Volunteer company composed of tradesmen, inaugurated modern commemorations of the shutting of the gates and then entertained their officers in the town hall; 'Paddy's triumph', a song sung that night, boisterously expresses the notion of people of diverse backgrounds uniting under the common name of Irishman:[23]

> Tho' Paddy has been mock'd to scorn,
> For being poor and needy,

20 For a full discussion, see B. Mac Suibhne, 'Patriot Paddies: The Volunteers and Irish identity in north-west Ulster, 1778–86' (unpublished Ph.D. dissertation, Carnegie Mellon University, 1998), chapters 2 and 3.
21 W. Crawford, *A history of Ireland: From the earliest period, to the present time …* (Strabane, 1783). For its influence in France in the 1790s, see G. Le Biez, 'Irish news in the French press: 1789–98', in Dickson et al., *United Irishmen*, p. 256.
22 *L.J.*, 3 Dec. 1779.
23 Ibid., 21 Dec. 1779.

He has a soul can stand a storm,
From Britons rich and greedy.
Long, long, dear friends, we have been fools,
Divided in religion;
By this, to foes we have been tools,
And Paddy was their pigeon —
But Luther, Calvin, and the Pope
Now drink their jug of whiskey,
Shake hands, and join in one great hope,
And swear they'll get all tipsy!

Patriot politics went stale after the achievement of legislative independence. By 1784 Volunteer companies and battalions were fragmenting; by 1786 the movement had effectively collapsed. Significantly, however, there is no evidence that a re-emergence of old sectarian identities precipitated the movement's decline in the region. Rather, personality-driven controversies at national level over the extent of independence obtained in 1782 debilitated companies; the end of the American War and return of British troops deprived them of their *raison d'être*; the long-awaited general election in 1783 denied them fresh opportunties to bully parliament; and, finally, the emergence of the Beresford-Foster-Fitzgibbon troika in Dublin confronted them with a more resolute administration which shut off the possibility of radical parliamentary reform.[24] As the prospect of reform faded, patriots turned to practical matters: Crawford established the Strabane Academy, a multi-denominational college (1785); Derry patriots launched the Greenland Fishery Company to fish for whales (1785), and founded the Irish Cotton Manufactory (1786) where over '100 persons' worked at carding machines and spinning jennies; and 'the Castlefin Committee', a watchdog on grand-jury road-presentments, emerged from a meeting of Donegal ratepayers in the Red Lion tavern on St Patrick's Day 1786.[25] The *Journal*, meanwhile, campaigned for schools for poor children, a bridge across the Foyle at Derry, and a canal link to the Swilly. It was at this stage, when progress seemed possible on mundane matters rather than on the broad constitutional front, that a disillusioned Douglas ceased to edit the *Journal*.[26]

The siege centenary in 1788 occasioned a precocious revival of political energy. Douglas resumed editorial duties and offered a medal for the best poem on the siege; he and other patriots prodded the corporation to stage a massive festi-

24 See MacSuibhne, 'Patriot Paddies', chapter 4.
25 *L.J.*, 12 July; 16 Aug.; 13 Sept.; 20 Sept.; 4 Oct. 1785; 7 Feb.; 25 July 1786; 6 Mar. 1792; *S.J.*, 7 Mar. 1786; W. Crawford, *Regulations of the Strabane Academy and an address to the students in general* (Strabane, 1785).
26 *L.J.*, 2 May 1786.

val of liberty and to erect a commemorative arch.[27] The French Revolution boosted an already resurgent patriotism. In the election of 1790 William Lecky, a former officer in the Apprentice Boys, secured one of the city seats for the 'popular party', and ex-Volunteers were prominent in 'The Chamber of Commerce for the City of Derry' (1790) which called loudly for a reform of the corporation.[28] Similar types organized Bastille Day celebrations in Derry and country towns in 1791 and 1792, and were no doubt involved in the 'society of gentlemen' which arranged the 'anonymous' publication (by Douglas) of a 'cheap edition' of Paine's *Rights of man, Part I* in 1791 - well before any edition came from the 'Athens of the North'. Apparently subsidised by a raffle for a life-size portrait of Washington, it was sold throughout Ulster 'merely at a price which will defray the expense of printing' – 6*d*. compared to 3*s*. 3*d*. and 2*s*. 2*d*. for the London and Dublin editions.[29] By the early 1790s, moderate local figures such as Lecky and Dr John Ferguson (whose involvement in earlier patriot organizations had owed as much to their electoral ambition as to ideology) were losing control of the 'popular party' to the more driven, 'rebelly' elements.

Loyalists in the region were quick to see the Belfast Society of United Irishmen as a vehicle for revolutionary republicans, not casual reformers who might drift aimlessly towards rebellion. Within months of the society's formation in 1791, Abercorn's agent reported from Strabane that he had dined with a man just returned from Belfast who gave 'very dreadful' accounts of a 'Patriotic Society': 'Napper Tandy has been among them', he continued, and 'among the common run of their toasts after dinner at their meetings is a bloody summer and a headless king and the like; they are ripe for rebellion.'[30] In particular, the Volunteer 'revival' of winter 1792–3 – when companies were formed across the region's core – disconcerted loyalists. They insisted that the activities of the 'Nappers' – a derisive term for radical Volunteers since 1784 – and the election of delegates to the associated Dungannon convention were efforts to promote 'sedition'; they scorned the protests of opportunistic Derry aldermen, notably Ferguson, that they joined these companies merely to ensure 'moderation'; and Donegal magistrates, meeting in January 1793, felt it necessary to issue an address declaring their attachment to the constitution and their abhorrence of 'all disturbers of the public peace, sowers of sedition, and disseminators of libel-

---

27 G. Douglas (ed.), *The Poliorciad: or Poems on the siege of Derry written for the Prize Medal, 7 Dec. 1788* (Derry, 1789). This item is reprinted in G. Douglas (ed.), *Derriana: A collection of papers relative to the Siege of Derry, and illustrative of the Revolution of 1688* (Derry, 1794).

28 *L.J.*, 4 May; 6 July; 13 July 1790; 10 Jan. 1792; 26 Feb. 1793; 15 Apr. 1794.

29 Ibid., 5 Apr.; 26 Apr.; 3 May; 12 July; 19 July 1791; 19 June; 3 July; 17 July; 24 July 1792; T. Paine, *Rights of man: Being an answer to Mr Burke's attack on the French Revolution* (Derry, 1791).

30 Hamilton, Derry, to Abercorn, 4 Apr. 1792: J.H. Gebbie (ed.), *An introduction to the Abercorn letters as relating to Ireland* (Omagh, 1972), p. 171.

lous and unconstitutional doctrines'.[31] Other loyalists turned to propaganda: Alexander Knox of Derry began to produce handbills and newspaper articles attacking radicals; Dr William Hamilton, rector of Fánaid, published a series of 'letters' warning Dissenters against French democracy, and the Catholic clergy of Derry issued an address in March 1793 instructing their hearers to be loyal and obedient subjects; this was the second of three such 'instructions' that they published in the last quarter of the century – the first had appeared in November 1779 when the free trade stand-off raised the possibility of a rising, and the third in June 1798 when there was one.[32]

Haunted by the experience of 1778–82, Government forced the Volunteers to disband and established militia regiments in spring 1793. But friction between patriots and loyalists continued to spark violence: in April 1794 heavily armed loyalists openly resisted a patriot making an arrest in the cathedral town of Raphoe and the following month Strabane's chief magistrate stood idly by as members of the Wicklow Militia smashed the windows of William Ross, a prominent patriot who had refused to illuminate his house to celebrate a British victory.[33] As the war dragged on, the anti-British sentiment that had long characterized regional political discourse achieved a new virulence. Patriots applauded French victories and in spring 1795, when the revolutionary army swept through Holland and Britain seemed beleaguered, Douglas boldly announced that he had lived to see 'three great events. First, the Revolution in America – next, the French Revolution – and, on this day, the subjugation of Holland by the irresistible power of the new Republic … What an awful lesson for princes and politicians.'[34]

Developments in south-west Ulster contrasted sharply with those in the north-west. Here, a lower degree of social and cultural differentiation within both denominational blocs, but particularly within 'the whole Protestant community', ensured that religion maintained a cohesive function and that Planter and Gael remained meaningful terms. Reflecting a general ideological paralysis, Jacobitism – little in evidence in the north-west – was a central element in Catholic political culture and left a deep impression on oral history. At the same time, lower levels of commercialization stunted the development of a regional

---

31 A. Young, Derry, to Abercorn, 10 Mar. 1793: P.R.O.N.I., Abercorn papers T2541/IB1/4/16; W. Conyngham, Dublin, to Abercorn, 29 Mar. 1793: P.R.O.N.I., Abercorn papers T2541/IB3/1/17; *N.S.*, 12 Dec. 1793; *L.J.*, 22 Jan. 1793. For an early use of the term 'Napper', see Revd R. Black, Derry, to Revd W. Bruce, 6 Sept. 1784: P.R.O., Chatham papers 430/8/329.

32 A. Knox, *Essays on the political circumstances of Ireland written during the administration of Lord Camden with an appendix containing thoughts on the will of the people and a postscript now first published* (Dublin, 1798), pp iv–vii; W. Hamilton, *Letters on the principles of the French democracy and their application and influence on the constitution and happiness of Britain and Ireland* (Dublin, 1792–3); *L.J.*, 16 Nov. 1779; 5 Mar. 1793; 3 July; 10 July 1798.

33 *L.J.*, 15 Apr.; 6 May 1794.

34 Ibid., 3 Feb. 1795. For sharp anti-British rhetoric, see ibid., 20 Jan.; 29 Sept. 1795.

print-culture: the region's first newspaper was the *Enniskillen Chronicle,* established in 1808. In the 1780s Volunteering was a less widespread and more conservative movement, and there were no signs of significant ideological flux. Hence for many Catholics in the south-west the opportunity provided by the French war was not the destruction of Britain but the overthrow of the heretics, and Defenders were organising there by the mid-1790s.[35] In the north-west, by contrast, efforts by outsiders to import Defenderism proved abortive and there is nothing to suggest increased Catholic atavism.[36] Troubles in Inishowen in 1793 – 'burning houses, destroying grain, extorting money, and writing threatening anonymous letters' – had a political focus – the revenue laws – and a committee formed to suppress them was conscious of a wider context: 'the voice of disaffection agitates the public mind … seditious publications are industriously circulated, and certain wild democratic theories warmly recommended, subversive … of all good order in society'.[37] Moreover, the most horrific incident in the region – the burning alive of Brian Bacach McCloskey in 1795 – occurred in predominantly Presbyterian Bovevagh where 'Shakers' were opposing the rector's enthusiasm for tithes; McCloskey had turned informer.[38]

Although something was stirring late in 1795, a United Irish organization only emerged in north-west Ulster the following summer. Loyalists connected its emergence with the arrival of the Limerick Militia from Belfast where republicans had 'tainted' it, and with the activity locally of 'emissaries' and 'agents'. A predominantly Catholic regiment, the Limericks arrived in June 1796; five companies were headquartered in the city and smaller units deployed in country towns. Billeted with the lower class and bringing with them 'the books called the Constitution', maps of Ireland and incriminating cyphers, they immediately heightened tension. In Derry they disconcerted ultra-Protestants by parading with music to mass, and several attacked 'gentlemen' attending the assizes to give evidence against south Derry Defenders; in Strabane their officers scuffled with loyalists after a theatre performance.[39] Sir George Hill and Henry Alexander, the

---

35 N.A.I., Frasier MS II/1: 'The examination of Thomas Mulhern, Ballyshannon in the parish of Kilbarron, barony of Tyrhugh in said county servant to Michael [Hanly] of Ballyshannon aforesaid Merchant taken [before] me this 27th day of July 1795'.

36 J. Rea, Letterkenny, to —, n.d. [Aug. 1795]: N.A.I., RP 620/22/36A; *L.J.,* 25 Aug.; 1 Sept.; 15 Sept. 1795.

37 *L.J.,* 12 Feb 1793. The 'Inishowen Committee' offered a large reward for information against 'a promoter, adviser, abettor or perpetrator … worth £100 Sterling'; the 'principal' of these 'Break-of-Day Men' was apparently James Doo Butler, 'commonly called Captain Fearnought', arrested in Apr. 1793; the surnames of those arrested suggest they were mainly Catholic; see ibid., 26 Feb.; 12 Mar.; 30 Apr.; 27 Aug. 1793; 29 Apr.; 23 Sept. 1794; 14 Apr. 1795.

38 Ibid., 24 Feb.; 31 Mar.; 23 June; 28 July; 4 Aug. 1795; A. Day, P. McWilliams and N. Dobson (eds), *Ordnance Survey memoirs of Ireland: Parishes of County Londonderry, VII, 1834–5: North-west Londonderry* (Belfast, 1994), pp 26–7; 54; 59.

39 Alexander, [Derry], to [Cooke], 1 Aug. 1796: N.A.I., RP 620/24/76a; Lloyd, Derry, to the Lord Chancellor, 9 Aug. 1796: N.A.I., RP 620/24/111; Hill, Derry, to Cooke, 13 Aug. 1796: N.A.I.,

city's MPs, grew alarmed: in early August Hill warned Dublin Castle that 'there is but one idea prevails – "that every mischief is to be dreaded"; agents are indefatigable in bringing over to their plans the lower orders'. 'Agents' included Michael Byrne of Newry, a nephew of Edward Byrne, who was in Derry 'almost every week' that summer, 'in conclave' with local 'democrats', and Samuel Neilson, who visited Strabane shortly before his arrest in September, stopping with James Orr, brazier and agent of the *Northern Star*.[40] By the end of September, countrymen were openly damning the king, 'seditious notices' were going up in the Laggan, and there had been arms finds in Kilmacrenan and Strabane; in the latter town, the arms, found in Orr's house, were all licensed, yet were confiscated nonetheless.[41] By the end of 1796, Joseph Orr of Derry was on the organization's national executive, and county delegates to the provincial committee were claiming over 8,000 men in Derry, 3,000 in Donegal and 6,550 in Tyrone; in spring 1797, the figures reported were about 10,000 in Derry, a similar number in Donegal, and 13–14,000 in Tyrone.[42]

The activities of a Belfast-based leadership, the arrival of the Limericks from that town, and the ubiquity of 'Belfast agents', all gave the impression of United Irish sentiment extending itself westward, an impression that loyalist propaganda was keen to cement. In a handbill printed in Derry in December, Knox, soon to become Castlereagh's private secretary, used an epidemiological metaphor which still pervades historical writing on the organization of the United Irishmen:[43]

> Already has the mischief spread from an inconsiderable society to an
> unsummed multitude; it has gone on from parish to parish, and from

RP 620/24/112; Hill to Cooke, Derry, 15 Aug. 1796: N.A.I., RP 620/24/118; J. Hamilton, Strabane, to —, 17 Sept. 1796: N.A.I., RP 620/25/74. On the Limerick Militia in Belfast, see *N.S.*, 25 Apr. 1796.

40 Hill, Derry, to Cooke, 13 Aug. 1796: N.A.I., RP 620/24/112; [Hamilton], Strabane, to [Cooke], 1 Oct. 1796: N.A.I., RP 620/25/138. James Orr was a connection of John Dunlap (see John Dunlap, Philadelphia, to Robert Rutherford, 12 May 1785: in W.H. Crawford and B. Trainor (eds), *Aspects of Irish social history, 1750–1800* (Belfast, 1969), p. 55).

41 Hill, Derry, to Cooke, 6 Sept. 1796: N.A.I., RP 620/25/33; Sir G.F. Hill, Derry, to E. Cooke, [9 Sept. 1796]: N.A.I., RP 620/25/38; McClintock, Rathdonnell, to Cooke, 1 Oct. 1796: N.A.I., RP 620/25/139; N.A.I., Hamilton, Strabane, to —, 1 Oct. 1796: RP 620/25/138; Hamilton, Strabane, to Abercorn, 3 Nov. 1796: P.R.O.N.I., Abercorn papers T2541/IA2/6/15.

42 *Secret Committee*, p. 62. Elliott, *Partners in revolution*, p. 108, gives the other members of the executive as FitzGerald, O'Connor, Simms, McCormick, McNeven, Emmett, Teeling and Lowry.

43 'Essay XIII Addressed to country gentlemen and other persons of property in the North of Ireland, December 12, 1796', in Knox, *Essays*, p. 103. The republication of Knox's essays in November 1798 was part of wider government strategy, which he had helped to devise, to discredit surviving republican leaders; the essays purported to show that, contrary to claims by the state-prisoners, 'no fact can be more established than that the Society of United Irishmen from the first moment of its institution, has been, with respect to its leading members, a band of systematic traitors': ibid., xi.

county to county, like 'the pestilence that walketh in darkness'; and fresh numbers of the peasantry are every day catching the contagion. If no effectual check be provided, is it not self-evident that it will advance incalculably; forming still a wider and wider circle, until the malignant principle shall have diffused itself through all the lower ranks of the community?

Belying the metaphor, however, Knox and other loyalists knew well that republicanism had a distinct social base – it was strongest among Presbyterians and weakest among Episcopalians and middle-class Catholics – and that there were home-grown 'democrats' and 'republicans'; indeed, one of Hill's complaints against the Limericks was that they mixed with locals known to be 'desperate democrats'.[44] Furthermore, striking continuities from earlier organizations (particularly the Volunteers) were immediately evident in the region's United Irish movement, confirming that it was less the creation of Belfast than a relatively autonomous development from earlier networks, themselves the products of a regionally specific process of politicization in which the formative period was 1778–84.

The district in which republicans emerged first and remained most formidable – the core zone and the *poitín*-peninsula of Inishowen – was remarkably coterminous with the Volunteer heartlands: compare, for example, Donegal Volunteer companies attending the Derry Grand Review in 1781, with Dr William Hamilton's delineation of United Irish activity in the county in February 1797 (see fig. 13.2).[45] And many United Irish slogans and symbols had been heard or seen before. 'The Irish Harp new-strung that shall and must be heard' had been drunk in Derry in 1783. The potato-diggings which republicans undertook with great political effect in 1796 also had precedents: neighbours of the Scotts of Mullenan, prominent Patriots, 'voluntarily' came and harvested their crops in 1793; this 'friendly band' was composed of 'near 300 reapers, exhibiting on the right thereof thirty young women, neatly dressed in white ornamented with green ribbons'.[46] Furthermore, there were continuities at the leadership level. Moore, a delegate attending at least five provincial meetings in 1796–7, had been elected to the governing committee of the Derry Battalion in 1780 and had been conspicuous in the radical revival, chairing the meeting called to establish the London-Derry Volunteers, serving as first lieutenant of the city battalion, and

---

44 Alexander, Derry, to Cooke, 1 Aug. 1796: N.A.I., RP 620/24/76a; Hill, Derry, to Cooke, 15 Aug. 1796: N.A.I., RP 620/24/118. Knox actually published handbills in June 1796 attacking 'conspicuous figures at clubs and publick societies' in Derry: see 'Essay VII – June 16, 1796', and 'Essay VIII – June 18, 1796', in Knox, *Essays*, pp 51–63.

45 W. Hamilton, Raphoe Castle, to Cooke, 15 Feb. 1797: N.A.I., RP 620/28/269. Curtin, *United Irishmen*, p. 73, misreads Hamilton's radius as 10 miles.

46 *L.J.*, 4 Nov. 1783; 15 Oct. 1793.

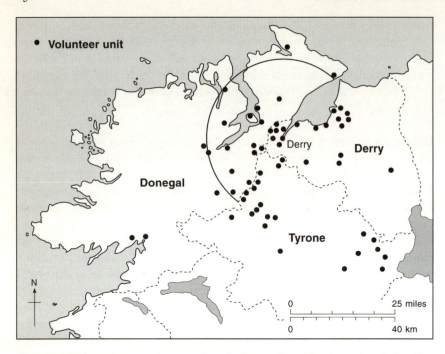

Fig. 13.2   Volunteer companies attending the Derry Grand Review, 26–27 July 1781.
The semi-circle is that delimited in Revd William Hamilton's description of United Irish
activity in Co. Donegal: 'A *semi*-circle of the county of Donegal extending 18 miles from
the city of Derry as a centre ... including the wealthiest parts of the county, and almost
½ the actual space of it, seems to include the whole of its visible disaffection and turbu-
lence. From all the enquiry I cd. make, and from my own personal knowledge, which is
not inconsiderable, there is reason to believe that the disaffection and its efforts are feeble
and ill-conducted nearly in proportion as the distance from that centre increases. And, on
careful examination it will be found that dissenting power and interest varies almost
exactly in the same proportion. Southward of the *semi*-circle, the Protestant interest and
strength is paramount; westward, that of the Roman Catholic; and hitherto each of these
tracts of country, tho' not unattempted has been quiet and seems at present not likely to
be disturbed' (*London-Derry Journal*, 31 July, 21 Aug. 1781; W. Hamilton, Raphoe Castle, to
E. Cooke, 15 Feb. 1797: N.A.I., RP 620/28/269).

attending the last Dungannon convention as a delegate of the city and liberties.[47]
Likewise, Alexander Montgomery, Donegal's MP who had been colonel of the
Raphoe Battalion in the 1780s, together with several associates including the
Dobsons of Letterkenny and Sinclairs of Holly Hill, became publicly linked to
the United Irishmen in 1796–8: he had himself released republicans from Lifford
gaol; flagrantly insulted an active yeomanry officer; taken a crowd of United

47 Ibid., 25 Feb.; 28 Mar. 1780; 22 Jan.; 29 Jan. 1793; 15 Apr. 1794; Hill, Derry, to —, 12 Sept.
    1797: N.A.I., RP 620/32/114,

Irishmen to the resulting duel; and issued a warrant for the arrest of a revenue officer who had torched republican homes.[48] These incidents and a political affiliation with Lord Edward FitzGerald – in February 1795 they formed a minority of two in opposing an address to George III – add weight to the oral tradition that he was a United Irish leader and that FitzGerald offered him 'command of the men in the North'.[49]

The connections of other leaders with Volunteering and associated political campaigns are also well-established. Near Limavady William Simpson of Ballycrum, a prominent republican in 1796–8, had been a Volunteer officer, while the family of Young John Horner of Carnet, a rebel who remained 'out' in the Sperrins for a year after the rising, had also been active in radical politics in the 1780s.[50] Elsewhere common names confuse. James Orr, the Strabane republican, was either the James Orr who had been lieutenant of the Urney Rangers and adjutant of the Strabane Battalion, or the James Orr Jr., lieutenant of the Strabane Rangers in the early 1780s.[51] Similarly, William McClintock, the haberdasher arrested with Moore, was probably once captain of the Derry Light Dragoons, a troop of horse formed in 1780; and John Scott, a republican agent in the Derry liberties, may well have belonged to the Mullenan family that had supplied principals to various radical causes.[52] While there were certainly many officers in both the 1778–84 and 1792–3 movements who never became United Irishmen and, indeed, some who became active loyalists, the involvement of key figures like Moore in Derry, Montgomery in the Laggan and Orr in Strabane reflects continuity more than change. Conversely, the emergence of Sir George Hill and, to a lesser extent, Henry Alexander as loyalism's drum-boys in 1796–8 also points to 1778–84 as a defining period; Hugh Hill and James Alexander had held the city seats at that time yet had kept the Volunteers at arm's length, accepting no offices and not attending the grand reviews staged in Derry, some of which had drawn crowds of 40–50,000 spectators.

Paradoxically, the partial replication of earlier command structures in the United Irishmen militated against Catholics becoming prominent in the regional

48 On Montgomery's association with the United Irishmen during the election, see Hamilton, Lifford, to Abercorn, 2 Aug., Strabane, 3, 6 Aug. 1797: P.R.O.N.I., Abercorn papers T2541/IA2/6/35–6, 38. On the clash with Hayes and his United Irish backing during the duel, see Hamilton, Strabane, to Abercorn, 29 Aug., 8, 17 Oct. 1797: T2541/IA2/6/44, 47, 49. For Montgomery's vindictive attitude to active loyalists, see Rea, Letterkenny, to —, 14 Jan. 1798: N.A.I., RP 620/35/36.

49 *L.J.*, 3 Feb. 1795; T.H. Mullin, *Convoy: The kirk and lands of Convoy since the Scottish settlement* (Belfast, 1960), pp 59–60; Montgomery, *Family history of the Montgomerys*, pp 23–4.

50 Mullin, *Limavady and the Roe Valley*, pp 44–9; *L.J.*, 11 Nov. 1783; 19 June 1798; Hill, Coleraine, to Cooke, 25 Aug. 1798: N.A.I., RP 620/32/48; Hill, Derry, to Cooke, 28 July 1799: N.A.I., RP 620/47/104.

51 *L.J.*, 13 May; 16 Dec. 1783; 2 Aug. 1785.

52 On McClintock and the Scotts, see *L.J.*, 3 July 1778; 24 Sept. 1779; 29 Feb.; 16 May; 29 May 1780; 24 Oct.; 31 Oct. 1786; 15 Oct. 1793.

leadership, a contrast with those areas with a less radical Volunteer tradition such as south Derry, where Catholics were promoted to cement the 'union'.[53] Larry McShane, one of the few Derry city leaders positively identified as a Catholic, had already well-established political credentials. A master shoemaker, McShane had pulled himself up by the bootstraps from the Bogside to become the owner of an extensive shop on the Diamond; he was the central figure in a mixed cartel of master shoemakers that had defied turn-outs by journeymen in 1792–3; and 'Lawrence McShane, Jr.', was the first signature on a letter signed by ten laymen in October 1792 denying an allegation that Derry Catholics had not subscribed to the Declaration of the Catholics of Ireland (implying that he was spokeman for radicalized Catholics); he was also a freemason.[54] There are similar hints of earlier activism or least dissidence outside the city: James Friel, a Fánaid schoolmaster, and Mánas Ó Dónaill, a Kilmacrenan grazier, both of whom became significant local leaders, had been 'intended for the priesthood' but failed to complete their studies, in Friel's case because of 'some certain odium' Dr Anthony Coyle, bishop of Raphoe, had had towards his father.[55]

The fact that the administration of the republican oath was almost invariably done by locals not outsiders is another indicator of the indigenous character of the movement. Significantly, the crown's first major strike against city republicans in December 1796 did not result from locals informing, but from members of the Tipperary Militia (who had replaced the Limericks in October) revealing that Billy Beattie and John Bracken, two city merchants, had attempted to seduce them from their 'duty and allegiance': Bracken was a tallow-chandler at the Ferryquay Gate and Beattie an ironmonger with a shop on Bishop Street who, four months earlier, had been one of the 'Friends of Merit'.[56] Indeed, repentant militia-men were responsible for the crown's other intelligence-based breakthroughs in the city – the detention of over half a dozen middle-level city leaders in March 1797, and the disclosure in June of aborted plans to capture Derry (which led to the flight of Orr and the arrest of Moore and McClintock).

Finally, although local loyalists fulminated against the *Northern Star*, *Billy Bluff* and *Paddy's Resource* – Knox fumed about 'the flying sheets of the enemy (those miasma of mental pestilence)' making their way 'to every farm-house and

---

53 *Secret Committee*, pp 86–7 [Appendix No. 6, Extracts from the information of Charles McFillin].
54 *L.J.*, 3 July 1787; 22 May; 5 June; 9 Oct. 1792; 19 Nov. 1793; 16 Nov 1794; information of David Dobbyn, serjeant, Tipperary Militia, 21 Mar. 1797: N.A.I., RP 620/29/99; information of Patrick Hickey, Private in the Tipperary Regt., 23 Mar. 1797: N.A.I., RP 620/29/111.
55 J. Friel, New York, to Revd J. Friel, 20 Nov. 1799: N.A.I., RP 620/57/104; R.S. Ó Cochlainn, 'Captain Manus O'Donnell', *Donegal Annual*, iii (1949), 193–203.
56 J. Bagwell, Derry, to [Cooke], 7 Dec. 1796: N.A.I., RP 620/26/104; Hill, Derry, to Cooke, Wed. night; examination of Patrick Baldwin, private in the Tipperary Militia, 7 Dec 1796; examination of George Hennessey, private in the Tipperary Militia, 7 Dec. 1796: N.A.I., RP 620/26/107; *L.J.*, 12 Jan. 1796.

to every cottage' – republicans were not dependent on 'Belfast productions'.[57] Local printers, particularly in Strabane, the main source of Volunteer publications, added to the stream of sedition: in 1795 an unidentified Strabane printer published *Prophetical extracts*, an anthology of pieces 'selected from the writings of Godwin, Jurieu, Brown, Love, Knox, Willison, More, and Gill'; in winter 1796 the provincial committee discussed '8,000 maps to be printed in Belfast and 3,000 in Strabane'; in spring 1797 *Christ in triumph, coming to judgement!*, a levelling prophecy just off the press of Andrew Gamble, a Strabane printer, was available from hawkers at fairs and markets, and as late as June 1798 the military were searching for 'Alexander of Strabane' for 'having an unlicensed printing press in his possession which certainly printed several seditious papers'.[58] Moreover local republicans, notably the Revd William Dunlop of Badoney, contributed to the *Northern Star*. And loyalists were acutely aware that several figures in the national leadership had close connections with the north-west and saw their hand in republican propaganda: Hill, for example, had 'little doubt of the style of [William] Sampson, the lawyer' and pointed it out in ballads seized in Derry and forwarded to Dublin Castle: a Derryman, Sampson had been a Volunteer in the city in the 1780s.[59]

So what was the role of 'Belfast agents'? In early April 1797 Thomas Boyle, a Dublin informer, reported that Charles Boyle, a cousin of his who kept a shop on Derry's Diamond, was then visiting the capital; his cousin, he wrote, had mentioned that there were 'people from Belfast' in Derry and Tyrone and that 'Carey and the Frenchman', two green pimpernels, had been in Ballymagrory six days earlier.[60] According to Boyle, Carey and the Frenchman had since gone

57 'Essay IX – June 23, 1796', in Knox, *Essays*, p. 68.
58 Campbell, *Literary history of Strabane*, p. 17; Mina Lenox-Conyngham, *An old Ulster house and the people who lived in it* (Dundalk, 1946), p. 139; A. Cole Hamilton, Beltrim Castle, to —, 2 Mar. 1797: N.A.I., RP 620/29/8; Cavan, Derry, to Knox, 16 June 1798: N.L.I., MS 56/195. Loyalists also had maps prepared in Strabane-Lifford: in late 1796 Generals Lake and Knox contracted William McCrea of Lifford – who, with several assistants, had been making maps for grand juries for twenty years – to provide them with a map of the province showing every townland; McCrea also allowed Captain Taylor of the Engineers to copy his maps of Derry, Tyrone, Monaghan, Donegal, Armagh and part of Fermanagh and prepared a two-inch map of Derry, Donegal and west Tyrone for Lord Cavan: McCrea, Lifford, to —, 2 May 1797: N.A.I., RP 620/30/9; Hill, Derry, to Pelham, 26 June 1797: N.A.I., RP 620/31/154; Hill, [Derry], to Cooke, June 1797: N.A.I., RP 620/31/181; McCrea, Lifford, to Pelham, 3 July 1797: N.A.I., RP 620/31/202. Note, however, that Samuel McCrea, a Strabane printer, emigrated to Baltimore about 1800 where he published the radical *American Patriot*: see Silver, 'Baltimore book trade', 251.
59 G.F. Hill, Derry, to Cooke, Wed. night [7 Dec. 1796], Monday 27 Dec. 1796: N.A.I., RP 620/26/107, 165. On Dunlop, see Classon E. Porter, *Irish Presbyterian biographical sketches* (Belfast, 1883), pp 20–23. Other figures with regional connections include Oliver Bond, Dublin (native of St Johnston; factor for Derry merchants); Dr A. Crawford, Lisburn-leader and state-prisoner (brother of Dr W. Crawford; married 'Miss Smily of Strabane' in 1783); Patrick and John Gallagher, FitzGerald's 'butlers' (Strabane); Revd James Porter, Greyabbey polemicist (native of Ballindrait); and Henry Haslett, Belfast-based editor of the *Northern Star* (native of Limavady).
60 Boyle, [Dublin], to Worthington, Apr. 1797: N.A.I., RP 620/29/224.

to Donegal 'to keep disorder in the lower people by making them believe that when the French come they will be all happy'.[61] This was a recurrent theme in reports on republican activists, both locals and outsiders, in the winter and early spring of 1796–7: when Michael Abraham of Dunhill and Thomas and William Browne of Rosnagalliagh put Richardson Boardman of Newbuildings 'up' in January 1797, they told him 'they were to join the French but to make no attempt until they came and that the taking of arms was only to prepare for it'; in February 1797, when James Hamilton, a respectable hatter and dyer in the Bogside, treated Patrick Hickey, a militiaman, in Kennedy's public house on the Diamond, he said that 'when the country was well united and the French came – which they expected – they would join them and they would no longer be oppressed', but in the meantime he should 'be seen to do his duty as a soldier alertly if he was called out on any party'; and, similarly, a report from the provincial committee discovered in William Love's house in Rockhill claimed that the executive had 'reason to expect [the French] soon again but at present cannot specify time or particulars thereof but request the provincial to [exhort] the people to patience and prudence and not to risk a well grounded hope by foolish intemperance … violent measures must ruin us'.[62] The specific role of Belfast agents, therefore, was not to build a paramilitary organization, but as outsiders to add authority to local efforts at impressing the national leadership's analysis (that the French were coming) and policy (that republicans would only rise when the French landed); in other words, whether through the distribution of tracts, the singing of songs, or the making of 'speeches or declamations', their role was as much to restrain as to 'excite the people'.[63]

The initial loyalist response to republican paramilitarism was desultory. Faced with the prospect of rebellion and aware that Lough Swilly was a likely destination for a French fleet, Hill and Alexander added their voices to calls for the establishment of yeomanry corps. Once approval was given in September 1796, the London-Derry Cavalry, a large corps commanded by Hill, was enrolled almost immediately. Yet elsewhere in the region enrolment was sluggish: in north Donegal, for instance, only ten corps had been established by the year's end and most were small, usually containing about forty men.[64] Across the north-west gentlemen were reluctant to 'step forward' as officers and would-be soldiers feared that they might be called on to serve outside their own localities.

61 Boyle, [n.p.], to Worthington, n.d.: N.A.I., RP 620/52/212.
62 Copy of information of Richardson Boardman, 29 Jan. 1797: N.A.I., RP 620/28/166; information of Patrick Hickey, private in the Tipperary Regt., 23 Mar. 1797: N.A.I., RP 620/29/111; Rea, Letterkenny, to Pelham, 20 May 1797: N.A.I., RP 620/30/119. The report dates from early 1797.
63 'Statements to secret committee, 1797', in Gilbert, *Documents*, p. 115.
64 *A list of the officers of the several district corps of Ireland, together with the dates of their respective commissions, and an alphabetical index* (Dublin, 1797).

Delays in sending arms and pay from Dublin to the first men enrolled deterred others from following their example, and in many instances the only 'good effect' of meetings convened to establish corps was to expose the extent of sedition: for example, at a meeting called in Letterkenny in October 1796, men were 'openly refusing to sign a very moderate resolution or to take the oath of allegiance' and making 'expressions of impudent disloyalty with a boldness ... arising from the expectation of an invasion'.[65]

Compounding matters, Generals Knox and Lake toured the north-west in December and decided, in Hill's words, that 'no effectual stand could be made by the fortification of Derry against cannon', and that if the French made Lough Swilly the military would actually relinquish the city and meet them further inland.[66] Loyalists, however, enjoyed one new and unexpected advantage: the regional press, proudly patriotic since the 1770s, was suddenly pro-government. Conservatives had acquired the *Journal* from Douglas – Hill called it 'our newspaper' – and the *Strabane Journal* may also have changed hands about this time.[67] Knox and John Schoales, an ambitious lawyer – both from the city's tiny Methodist congregation – penned articles to 'raise the cowardly gentry', and they produced *The farmer's friend, or A word to the wise*, a series of handbills in which a Dissenting farmer warned his neighbours of the consequences of a French landing. Hill believed these 'literary shots' were effective, and Edward Cooke was sufficiently impressed to reprint them for wider circulation.[68] The short-term consequences of the final gagging of the patriot voice in the regional press are difficult to assess, yet in a long-term perspective it formed one of the final markers in the collapse of the public sphere and the emergence of a new, more atavistic politics.

Bantry Bay completed the formation of two armed camps in the country and propelled both into action. Convinced that the French would soon return, republicans began to collect arms and pewter to make bullets; they established pike and gunpowder manufactories: and in mid-January 1797, they commenced raids on loyalist houses. Travelling to Raphoe on 19 January Dr William Hamilton 'found everywhere that houses had been robbed of arms and money, corn destroyed, turf stacks burned, windows broke, &c. but the magistrates and yeomen tho' active [are] yet destitute of proper information'.[69] The following night 'some desperate villains' torched barns containing stock, hay, corn, flax and potatoes at Cloone, near Newtown-cunningham; the owner, William Law,

65 Boyd, Ballymacool, to Justice Boyd, 5 Oct. 1796: N.A.I., RP 620/25/148.

66 Hill, Derry, to Cooke, 27 Dec. 1796: N.A.I., RP 620/26/165; see also instructions as to the allocation of military force in Ulster [n.d.; *c.* Dec. 1796; unsigned]: N.L.I. MS 56/7.

67 Hill, Derry, to Cooke, 28 Aug. 1797: N.A.I., RP 620/32/78.

68 Hill, Derry, to Cooke, Sunday [post-marked 6 Dec. 1796], Tuesday [Dec. 1796], 8 Jan. 1797: N.A.I., RP 620/26/103, 203, 620/28/69; 'The Farmer's Friend or, A Word to the Wise'; Hill, [Derry], to Beresford, [recvd. 29 Jan. 1797]: N.A.I., RP 620/28/166; Knox, Bellarena, to Burrowes, 3 Mar. 1797: N.A.I., RP 620/29/30. Also see Knox, *Essays*, XVII-XVIII.

69 Hamilton, Fanet Glebe, to Knox, 2 Feb. 1797: N.A.I., RP 620/28/195.

was an officer in the Derry Cavalry.[70] 'The face of our country has so far lost its distinguishing features', Alexander commented in the first week of February, 'that I cannot venture to describe the change.'[71] A week later, Abercorn's agent drew a similar picture: 'They go out in the night only, in large armed parties, and take up all arms and pewter they can find (the latter for bullets) and oblige every individual to swear; the arms and pewter are said to be deposited in large chests laid in quick lime and sunk in dry parts of mountains; or as some allege buried in coffins in the churchyard ... We were quiet and peaceable about a fortnight ago. It came on quite like a planet shower, and has defused itself (regularly progressive) over the two neighbouring baronies.'[72]

Leading loyalists had begun to advocate more extreme measures in the weeks prior to Bantry Bay, insisting that 'terrors adverse and contrary to those excited can alone control the activity and violence of the disaffected'.[73] Now, meetings of magistrates were hastily convened and, by the end of February, almost the entire district where republicans were active had been proclaimed under the insurrection act. Urban yeomanry corps also became more assertive. From mid-January, the Derry, Limavady, Strabane and Letterkenny corps were out at night with the regular army, scouring the countryside for arms and suspects. Operating from Derry, Hill routinely directed night searches eastwards towards Limavady and Dungiven, westwards to St Johnston, and northwards into Inishowen. Distrusting the Hamiltons of Strabane, he sent the Revd John Hill, his brother, to live in Drumquin; the latter with Colonel James Leith of the Aberdeenshire Fencibles were out 'almost every night' patrolling the Laggan and west Tyrone.[74] Similarly, John Rea took the Letterkenny corps as far north as Ards.[75] Inevitably, there were clashes. On 28 January, the Derry Cavalry and Manx Fencibles ambushed over thirty Newbuildings republicans as they raided for arms: they killed several, arrested nineteen in follow-up raids, and caused some 200 to quit their homes.[76] A few nights later, as Leith and John Hill led a joint-force to Newtownstewart to raid a county meeting, they encountered armed republicans at Derg Bridge who engaged them in a gun-battle.[77]

70 *B.N.*, 27–30 Jan. 1797.

71 Alexander, [Derry], to —, 5 Feb. 1797: N.A.I., RP 620/28/219.

72 Hamilton, Strabane, to Abercorn, 11 Feb. 1797: P.R.O.N.I., Abercorn papers T2541/ IA2/6/17.

73 Alexander, [Derry], to [Pelham], 24 Dec. 1796: N.A.I., RP 620/26/150.

74 Hill, Derry, to Cooke, 9 Feb. 1797: N.A.I., RP 620/28/241; Revd J. Hill, Strabane, to Beresford, 19 Feb. 1797: N.A.I., RP 620/28/285. For an explicit allegation that the Hamiltons were screening republicans, see Revd R. Fowler, Urney, to —, 20 Nov. 1796: N.A.I., RP 620/26/63.

75 Rea, Letterkenny, to Hamilton, 27 Mar. 1797: N.A.I., RP 620/29/116; Rea, Letterkenny, to Pelham, 12 Apr. 1797: N.A.I., RP 620/29/228.

76 Hill, Derry, to Cooke, 2 Feb. 1797: N.A.I., RP 620/28/196; Hill, Derry, to Beresford, 29 Jan. 1797: N.A.I., RP 620/28/166; *B.N.*, 3 Feb. 1797.

77 Leith, Strabane, to Pelham, 7 Feb. 1797: N.A.I., RP 620/28/228; J. Hill, Strabane, to Beresford, n.d.: N.A.I., RP 620/28/232; Stewart, n.p., to Cooke, 9 Feb. 1797: N.A.I., RP 620/28/238;

The most serious incidents occurred in Fánaid on the north Donegal coast. While other country 'gentlemen' fled to the city, Dr William Hamilton had attempted to rally 'the entire body of Protestants' whom he organized as a 'yeomanry', and compelled suspects to take the oath of allegiance; by mid-January over 250 men had taken the oath and he had informations against several leaders. Supported by an officer and twenty Manx Fencibles, Hamilton raided the homes of Alexander and Frederick McIlwaine, suspected 'principals', at 5:00 a.m. on Monday 23 January. They were 'out on a night party', yet he discovered arms, an eight-foot pike and papers naming Old James McIlwaine, their father, and Robert, their brother, as United Irishmen. He arrested both men and also Bryan Ferry, Robert's servant, and returned to the glebe-house. A 'siege' or 'insurrection' followed. At 3:00 p.m. that afternoon, the United Irishmen 'mustered their forces to the number of 150–200 … and armed with guns, bayonets and pikes, they approached [the glebe] in tolerable military order to rescue the prisoners'; they sent 'mediators' to Hamilton but he refused to negotiate; the rebels then 'went through several movements and filed off in some force to some distance'. Republicans now mobilized across the peninsula: 'the passes of the country were occupied, the boats broken and the country entirely in motion'; Hamilton's curate was taken 'prisoner' by the main group which, 'with fresh recruits from various quarters', soon numbered 800; five miles away a servant of Lord Leitrim's agent was 'taken into custody', and fourteen miles in the opposite direction two men, paid to carry a letter from the glebe to Letterkenny, were stopped and searched. In the early hours of Tuesday, Hamilton and Thomas Smyth, a revenue officer, slipped out of the glebe and, after 'routing some armed patrols … and avoiding others', reached Derry at 9:00 a.m. They returned after midnight with a party of militia; in the face of these plus reinforcements from Letterkenny, the rebels dispersed. Hamilton then combed Fánaid for arms. By 12 February, forty guns, twelve pistols, eleven bayonets, twelve pikes, sixteen swords and one small cannon had been surrendered or promised; a total of 1,125 people – '167 Established Protestants; 82 Dissenters and 876 Roman Catholics' – had taken the oath; Frederick McIlwaine and John Walker, another leader, had been handed over for service in the fleet; several others were in custody, and there were sworn informations against a further 130.[78]

Hill, Derry, to Beresford, 9 Feb. 1797: N.A.I., RP 620/28/240; Hill, Derry, to Cooke, 9 Feb. 1797: N.A.I., RP 620/28/241.

78 Hamilton, Springfield, to Marshall, 14 Jan. 1797: N.A.I., RP 620/28/99; Hamilton, Fanet Glebe, to Knox, 2 Feb. 1797, Hill, Derry, to Beresford, 7 Feb. 1797: N.A.I., RP 620/28/195; Hamilton, Fanet Glebe, to Cooke, 12 Feb. 1797: N.A.I., RP 620/28/259; list of men who have taken the Yeomanry oath of allegiance before the Revd Wm. Hamilton; list of arms in the parish of Clondavaddock acknowledged on oath before the Revd. Wm. Hamilton; list of prisoners committed. For a subsequent account of the 'insurrection', see Anon., 'A memoir of the late Revd William Hamilton', in Hamilton, *Antrim Coast*, ix-xxxv, probably by Robert Marshall.

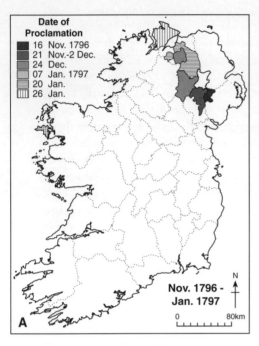

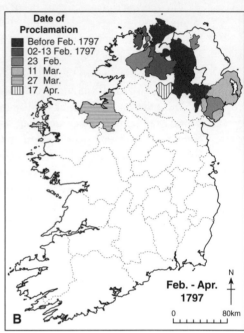

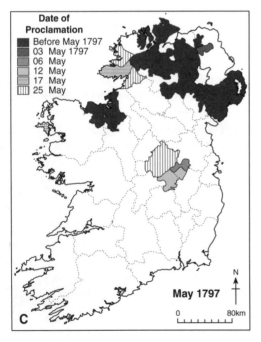

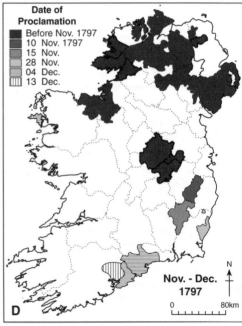

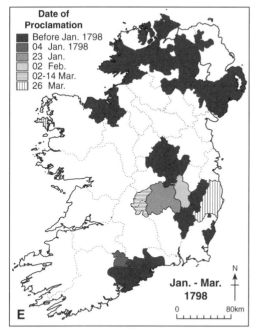

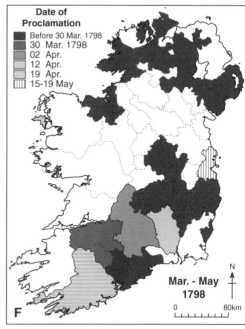

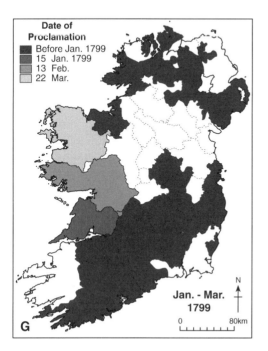

Fig. 13.3 Districts proclaimed under the Insurrection Act, 1796–1799 (*source*: 'An account of the several parts of Ireland that have been proclaimed by His Excellency the Lord Lieutenant and Council to be in a state of disturbance or in immediate danger of becoming so' [1796–1799]: N.A.I., OP, II, 990/66). Note: shaded areas represent entire parishes proclaimed under the act, parts of parishes proclaimed in Co. Antrim are not shown.

Hamilton's aggressive stance in the weeks after Bantry Bay was exceptional; active loyalty had receded to the large towns. Indeed, the range of military-yeomanry operations from these towns highlighted the failure of country corps: in Donegal, for instance, there were four largely inactive corps in Inishowen where the Derry Cavalry occasionally appeared; three in the Laggan where both the Derry and Strabane corps operated; and two west of Letterkenny where that town's corps was active.[79] Although initially attributing inactivity to Dublin Castle's tardy distribution of arms and pay, there were widespread reports from early February of republican infiltration of yeomanry corps: Rea, for example, claimed it was 'part of their system to get among the yeomen not only for the purpose of getting arms but also to get disciplined', and conceded that some men in his own corps had 'violent republican principles if they are not worse'.[80] Elsewhere, rebels targeted yeomen who lived apart from their corps, forcing them to take their oath or an oath of secrecy: John Cochran, first lieutenant in the Loyal Finwaters, was among those sworn to secrecy.[81]

Loyalists quickly lost faith in the country corps and demanded that government provide 'brave Britons' or, more specifically, 'an English force', and chomped at the legal bit: after the Newbuildings ambush Hill confided to John Beresford (his father-in-law) that he understood a break in communication with Cooke as a sign that 'Government may wish I should step out of the legal course and do something very decided but, my Dear B., the complexion of politics is too precarious and G. Hill too small to attempt anything of the sort without some previous sanction'.[82] Hill, Knox and Alexander all despaired of the yeomanry and Lord Cavan, the military commander in the region, shared their views: he refused to give country corps powder to practise firing, dismissed individual yeomen, disarmed entire corps, and disbanded others including David Ross' Cumber Cavalry; in the latter case, Hill supported disbandment as his 'principal and most useful informer' told him that they were 'united to a man except the officers … they promoted and headed the treasonable proceedings during the entire winter'.[83]

---

79 These corps were the Malin Cavalry, Moville Cavalry, Burt Cavalry and Culdaff Infantry in Inishowen; the Raphoe Cavalry, Loyal Finwater Cavalry and Burleigh and Orwell Cavalry in the Laggan, and the Ramelton Infantry and Lennan Infantry north of Letterkenny.

80 Rea, Letterkenny, to Hamilton, 27 Mar. 1797: N.A.I., RP 620/29/116.

81 Gilbert, *Documents relating to Ireland, 1795–1804*, p. 115. On the intimidation of a member of the Rathmelton Infantry, see *L.J.*, 3 July; 10 July 1798.

82 Extract from a letter on state of barony of Raphoe dated 26 Feb. 1797: N.A.I., RP 620/28/301; Morgan, Killaghtee, to Urquhart, 15 Apr. 1797: N.A.I., RP 620/29/264; Hill, Derry, to Beresford, [February]: N.A.I., RP 620/28/230.

83 Knox, Bellarena, to Burrowes, 3 Mar. 1797: N.A.I., RP 620/29/30; Alexander, Derry, to Pelham, 27 Apr. 1797: N.A.I., RP 620/29/307; Hill, Derry, to Cooke, 10 July 1797: N.A.I., RP 620/31/216; Rea, Letterkenny, to Pelham, 8 Sept. 1797: N.A.I., RP 620/32/105; Cavan, Milton, Co. Derry, to Knox, 20 Aug. 1797: N.L.I., MS 56/93; Cavan, Derry, to Knox, 14 Feb. 1798: MS 56/138.

In the midst of all, a bizarre distraction heightened loyalists' conviction that Dublin Castle did not comprehend the gravity of their situation. Over Christmas 1796, William Armstrong had arrived in Derry expecting to be appointed a military engineer.[84] A woollen-draper, Armstrong had entered business in the city in 1778, becoming a close associate of Moore and equally, if not more, prominent in radical politics; indeed, as recently as spring 1793, Armstrong and Henry Joy had been secretaries of a committee appointed by the Dungannon Convention 'to re-convoke this assembly as occasion may arise' and he and Moore had organized a militia-substitute scheme across west Ulster. However, in September 1794, facing bankruptcy, he had performed an extraordinary about-turn by accepting a commission in a regiment raised by the corporation 'in support of Government'. Although he resigned in November and left Derry, he was completely out of favour in radical circles. Consequently, his return two years later to a city 'where he [had] insulted every loyal man for ten years and practised democracy' and which it was 'the exertion of his life to disturb' made him 'the ridicule of all classes – military, loyalists and democrats', and did nothing to inspire confidence in government. Hill and Beresford badgered Dublin Castle to remove him; indeed, Beresford, labelling him 'the Napper Tandy of Derry … a most dangerous fellow', dredged up the damning gem that Armstrong and Oliver Bond had served their apprenticeships together with a Derry haberdasher. Armstrong left Derry in February and it appears that he subsequently became a general in the British army.[85]

Any doubts that senior officials may have entertained about the republican threat in the north-west and, indeed, in Ulster generally were abruptly ended at the beginning of March 1797. On 2 March Dr William Hamilton had left Fánaid to attend a meeting of magistrates in Raphoe. He decided to spend the night with Dr John Waller, rector of Raymochy, at Sharon, outside Newtowncunningham and to return home the next day. Sending his servant to call on Waller, he attended the meeting and arrived at Sharon that evening. During the night some fifty United Irishmen surrounded the house, smashed the windows and demanded that Hamilton be turned out. Hamilton fled to the cellar. The attackers fired, fatally wounding Waller's wife as she shielded her infirm husband, and then threatened to burn down the house unless Hamilton was surrendered. The servants dragged him to the door where he was 'butchered in the most inhumane manner'.[86] Hamilton's assassination rocked the establishment.

84 Hill, Derry, to Cooke, 6 Jan. 1797: N.A.I., RP 620/23/6; Hill, Derry, to Beresford, [recvd. 11 Jan. 1797]: N.A.I., RP 620/28/83.

85 *L.J.*, 13 Mar. 1778, 28 May, 4 June 1793, 26 Aug., 16 Sept., 2 Dec. 1794; Hill, Derry, to Cooke, 6 Jan. 1797: N.A.I., RP 620/23/6; Hill, Derry, to Beresford, [recvd. 11 Jan. 1797], Beresford, Custom House, to Cooke, 11 Jan. 1797: N.A.I., RP 620/28/83; Hill, Custom House, to Beresford, 5 Feb. 1797: N.A.I., RP 620/28/217; Colby, *Ordnance Survey memoir*, p. 48.

86 R.G. Hill, [Sharon], to Cavan, 3 Mar. 1797: N.A.I., RP 620/29/13; R.G. Hill, Derry, to Beresford, 4 Mar. 1797: N.A.I., RP 620/29/29; R.G. Hill, Derry, to Beresford, 12 June 1797:

Besides being a minister and a magistrate, Hamilton had been very well-connected: he had been a founding and active member of the Royal Irish Academy; a personal friend of Dr Robert Marshall, Pelham's private secretary; and a correspondent of Cooke.[87] On 3 March, the day after the assassination, Pelham ordered General Lake to disarm Ulster, orders subsequently confirmed as a declaration of martial law. 'Hamilton's fate' was almost certainly the final straw; word of his assassination having reached Derry before 4:00 a.m. on 3 March, expresses could have been in Dublin later that day.[88]

Hill and Cavan now intensified searches for arms and suspects. On 10 March detachments of Manx Fencibles and Derry Cavalry searched a number of Foyleside parishes in Derry and Donegal and returned to headquarters with some 239 firelocks, twelve pistols, large quantities of pewter, an assortment of bayonets and swords, and a few pikes. By that date militia operating out of Omagh, Strabane and Raphoe had 'ransacked most places', and it was estimated that they had taken up ten times that amount.[89] More controversially, large quantities of licensed gunpowder were confiscated in Strabane, 'a nest of the United Irishmen'.[90]

The crackdown had an uneven impact. Within two weeks, the authorities made their second strike against the city leadership when three militia-men swore informations against six middle-level figures, 'all inhabitants of this town in reputable situation and circumstances'; those arrested included Larry McShane and William Davison, Joseph Orr's cousin and commercial agent. Many of the 'lower ranks' fled.[91] Outside the city, however, paramilitary activity continued uninterrupted.

N.A.I., RP 620/31/78; Boyd, Ballymacool, to [Mansfield], 9 Mar. 1796: N.A.I., RP 620/29/46; *D.E.P.*, 30 Sept. 1797; J. Gamble, *A view of society and manners in the north of Ireland in the summer and autumn of 1812* (London, 1813), pp 268–73; Frank L. Gailey, 'The Sharon murders, 1797: A traditional account with introduction and notes', *Donegal Annual*, iii, 3 (1957), 8–16.

87 John Nowlan, Hamilton's curate, commented a few days after the assassination, that 'the reasons that brought him to that infernal spot [Sharon] were to be enabled to ans.r the question of Mr Cooke respecting the state of these parts in case of an invasion; the scene of his murder he at all times considered the worst part of the north except Belfast or its vicinity': Nowlan, Ramelton, to Knox, 7 Mar. 1797: N.A.I., RP 620/29/49.

88 Curtin, *United Irishmen*, pp 77–9.

89 Hill, Derry, to Cooke, 11 Mar. 1797; list of arms taken up by detachment under command of H. Murray Col., 2nd R.M.F. near Derry; list of arms taken up by detachment under command of Capt. Lathrop, 2nd R.M.F. near Derry: N.A.I., RP 620/29/32.

90 Hamilton, Strabane, to Hill, n.d. [Mar. 1797]: N.A.I., RP 620/29/32; Hamilton, Strabane, to Hill, 11 Mar. 1797; Hill, Derry, to Cooke, 12 Mar. 1797: N.A.I., RP 620/29/58; Hill, Derry, to Cooke, 12 July 1797: N.A.I., RP 620/31/224; J. Hill, Strabane, to John Beresford, [4–7 Feb. 1797]: N.A.I., RP 620/28/232; Revd J. Hill, Strabane, to Beresford, 19 Feb. 1797: N.A.I., RP 620/28/285; Revd J. Hill, Strabane, to [Beresford], 27 Feb. 1797: N.A.I., RP 620/28/311. Of the licensed gunpowder taken in Strabane, £10 worth was taken from Patrick Fleming, £11 from William Hamilton and £40 12s. from James Orr; a few weeks earlier, over 500 lb of powder, 57 bullet moulds and various arms on sale in Orr's shop had been confiscated.

91 Information of David Dobbyn, Derry, 21 Mar. 1797: N.A.I., RP 620/29/99; information of Patrick Hickey, private in the Tipperary Regt., 23 Mar. 1797: N.A.I., RP 620/29/111; Hill, Derry, to Pelham, [recvd. 25 Mar. 1797]: N.A.I., RP 620/29/111.

Here, croppies had easier access to arms and there were few regular troops or militiamen. Indeed, rural republicans – some of whom, having quit their homes, were permanently 'out' – responded to the crackdown with a wave of attacks. 'Every day brings us news of these fellows being in arms the night before at one place or the other,' Hill observed on 11 March. The previous evening, a fencible carrying an express to Derry had fired on a United Irishman armed with a pike 'who came down from the hills with a comrade to reconnoitre' and hit him in the calf; the soldier 'fled for it and was fortunate as to escape'.[92] A few days later, republicans destroyed eleven turf stacks belonging to an officer in the Muff Yeomanry and cut all the trees on his plantation; on the same night, a different party torched a loyalist's house six miles from Derry, and on 19 March another group disarmed the inhabitants of Buncrana.[93] Hill was convinced that the events at Sharon had 'given courage to the blackguards and alarmingly augmented the dismay of the better sort of people who are unconnected with them – many are coming into Derry and others going to England'.[94] This reaction had been immediate. Surveying his district ten days after the assassination, Cavan concluded that the subsequent flight of the loyal had extinguished 'the small spark of civil power that did remain' outside the towns.[95]

Despite a visit by Thomas Russell to Ballyshannon the previous September, a United Irish organization only now emerged in south-west Ulster.[96] On 4 March 1797 John Kincaid of the largely inactive Loyal Finwater Yeomanry traced the 'rapid progress of their [the United Irishmen's] principles' for Hill: 'except some petty circumstances in Inishowen', he wrote, 'there was not supposed to be one United Irishman in the whole county of Donegal at the commencement of winter and now three of the largest baronies are almost to a man publicly united and I am informed the party begin to establish themselves over the mountains in the Barony of Tyrhugh: to show themselves is to establish their principles'.[97] Similarly, on 21 March Leith reported from Strabane that the 'system of revolution' was 'spreading with rapidity to the south'.[98] Several months later, Peter Caveny, a United Irishman, confirmed these analyses to Bartholomew Clancy, a Castle agent: he dated the establishment of societies around Ballyshannon to March 1797 when Eneas Cammel, a trader whose business took him through several counties, had distributed 'constitutions' and 'other seditious publications … to

---

92 Hill, Derry, to Cooke, 11 Mar. 1797: N.A.I., RP 620/29/32.
93 On these incidents, see Hill, Derry, to Cooke, 12 Mar. 1797: N.A.I., RP 620/29/58; Cavan, Derry, to Pelham, 13 Mar. 1797: N.A.I., RP 620/29/62; Hill, Derry, to Pelham, 20 Mar. 1797: N.A.I., RP 620/29/96.
94 Hill, Derry, to Cooke, Thursday [post-marked 11 Apr. 1797]: N.A.I., RP 620/34/46B.
95 Cavan, Derry, to Pelham, 13 Mar. 1797: N.A.I., RP 620/29/62.
96 J.W., Dublin, to Pollock, 24 Sept. 1796: N.A.I., RP 620/25/108.
97 Kincaid, Redford Lodge, to Hill, 4 Mar. 1797; Hill, Derry, to Ld. Lt, 13 Mar. 1797: N.A.I., RP 620/29/61.
98 Leith, Strabane, to Pelham, 21 Mar. 1797: N.A.I., RP 620/29/100.

inflame the minds of the people'; Cammel had then established baronial committees – presumably for Tyrhugh, Banagh and Boylagh – in one of which he
[Cammel] was secretary.[99] Violence followed: there were arms raids in Killaghtee
in mid-March and by early May, there had been further raids there and in the
vicinity of Ballyshannon.[100]

Clear differences are evident in the character of the organization in the two
regions. Republican activity was quite chaotic in the south-west; although some
reports do indicate a concern for military form, participants in arms raids in
south Donegal were disorderly, often demanding whiskey as well as weapons.[101]
In the north-west by contrast, a Volunteer template was evident in the pronounced concern for military discipline and 'uniformity'. Republicans conceived
themselves to be soldiers in a national army, and when, for instance, they were
suborning non-commissioned officers in the Tipperary Militia, they promised
them that they would be officers in the United Irishmen's 'army' and would
receive full-pay.[102] Without the walls, rebels placed great emphasis on drill. On 19
February, Hill co-ordinated a cavalry raid on St Johnston where he expected the
United Irishmen to be on 'parade', having received 'undoubted information' that
they 'exercised' there several nights a week; two parties arrived silently at midnight – one from Derry and the other from Strabane – and completely surrounded the town, but they saw signal lights warning those who had assembled
to disperse. 'It is very harassing', Hill wrote Beresford, 'to do so much merely to
protect the property of a country that not only does not assist but betrays you'.[103]
Two weeks later Richard Cross, a Manx Fencible, observed several hundred men
drilling near the house of Shelburne Kincaid, a wealthy bleacher, at the St
Johnston and Castle Forward cross-roads: they 'had lights or lanterns fixed on
poles ... dressed as if they were camp colours ... frequently the lights were put
out and all was then quiet; ... this was done upon a whistle being given and ...
when the lights were once again raised the party all fell into ranks ... [and] he
twice heard distinctly the word of command "Halt" '.[104] Drill and the paramilitary experience that informed it produced disciplined activity. Richardson

---

99 Clancy, Dublin, to —, n.d.: N.A.I., RP 620/51/137.
100 On attacks in southern Donegal, see Morgan, Killaghtee, to Urquhart, [15 Apr. 1797]; N.A.I.,
    RP 620/29/264; Montgomery, The Mall, near Donegal, to [Urquhart], 14 May 1797;
    Cochran, Belleek, to Pelham, 22 May 1797: N.A.I., RP 620/30/72, 153; Cochran, Ross
    Harbour, to Pelham, 8 June 1797: N.A.I., RP 620/31/58; Tredennick, Camlin, to —, 14 June
    1797: N.A.I., RP 620/31/90; copy of examination of the Revd Patrick Morgan, rector of
    Killaghtee, 11 May 1797: O.P. II 990/27.
101 Cochran, Belleek, to Pelham, 22 May 1797: N.A.I., RP 620/30/153. Cochran describes a par-
    ticularly confused raid.
102 Information of David Dobbyn, Derry, 21 Mar. 1797: N.A.I., RP 620/29/99.
103 Hill, Derry, to Beresford, Sunday [post-marked 20 Feb. 1797]: N.A.I., RP 620/28/287; J. Hill,
    Strabane, to Beresford, 19 Feb. 1797: N.A.I., RP 620/28/285.
104 Examination of Richard Cross, Derry, 7 Mar. 1797; Hill, Derry, to Cooke, 11 Mar. 1797:
    N.A.I., RP 620/29/32.

Boardman, captured in the Newbuildings ambush, described how between thirty and fifty rebels were divided into 'squads' of eight men before setting out to raid for arms; the squads – a term used by the Volunteers in the 1780s – and their members were identifiable by a number, Boardman being 'number one of the third squad commanded by John Collins'.[105] Notwithstanding their frequent use of epithets such as 'villains' and 'banditti', loyalists were aware that they were dealing with a self-consciously militaristic 'system' or 'engine'. Thus reports from Strabane that republicans 'distinguish themselves by one uniform button at the top of the coat, lettered round "For My Country" with a "shamroge" in the centre; [and] they in general wear also a green silk cravat, with close cropt hair' can be credited.[106]

Republican activity escalated in early April 1797. In both regions, leaders were 'more indefatigable then ever, their communications more frequent'; there were boycotts of loyalist businesses and organized opposition to tithes.[107] Most importantly, there was an upsurge in arms raids and manufacture. In Fánaid, which had been calm since the siege in January, the United Irishmen 'openly declared themselves' in May and disarmed 'all the loyalists in that part of the country'; dressed in white shirts and caps, they surrounded Glinsk and Tamney, Episcopalian house-clusters, and demanded and received arms before 'marching off'.[108] Raids became generally more daring, particularly from late May, as republicans targeted large arms caches. There were raids on big houses at Pettigo, Ballyshannon, Belleek and Oakfield, and Lord Enniskillen's 'beautiful bathing lodge' near Bundoran was destroyed.[109] Similarly on 23 May several hundred men overwhelmed four militiamen guarding John Hill's house at Drumquin and seized several stand of arms and at least 1,000 ball cartridges.

105 Copy of information of Richardson Boardman, 29 Jan. 1797: N.A.I., RP 620/28/166; information of Richardson Boardman, 5 Feb. 1797: N.A.I., RP 620/28/241.
106 Hamilton, Strabane, to Abercorn, 11 May 1797: P.R.O.N.I., Abercorn papers T2541/IA2/6/27.
107 Hill, Derry, to Pelham, 13 Apr. 1797: N.A.I., RP 620/29/334; Cochran, Ross Harbour, to Pelham, 8 June 1797: N.A.I., RP 620/31/58; Rea, Letterkenny, to Pelham, 20 May 1797: N.A.I., RP 620/30/119; threatening letter from U.I.M. to John Rea (enclosure in Letterkenny, 7 June 1797, Rea to Pelham): N.A.I., RP 620/31/48; Patton, [Rossnakill], to Nowlan, 15 May 1797: N.A.I., RP 620/30/141; testimony of W. Atkinson: S.O.C., II 3091/1; Hamilton, Strabane, to Abercorn, 25 Mar., Omagh, 4 Apr., Strabane, 30 May, 29 Aug. 1797: P.R.O.N.I., Abercorn papers T2541/IA2/6/20–1, 29, 44.
108 Patton, [Rossnakill], to Nowlan, 15 May 1797, Murphy, Ramelton, to Nowlan, 16 May 1797: N.A.I., RP 620/30/141.
109 Cochran, Belleek, to Pelham, 22 May 1797: N.A.I., RP 620/30/153; memorandum of disturbances, 20 May 1797: N.A.I., RP 620/30/117; Aiken, Pettigo, to Barton, 7 June 1797: N.A.I., RP 629/31/52. For later references to these events, see Clancy, Dublin, to —, n.d. [July 1797]: N.A.I., RP 620/51/137; Johnston, Ashfield, to Cooke, 1 Nov. 1797; information of John Dougherty, Kinlough, Leitrim, 31 Oct. 1797: N.A.I., RP 620/33/2; Johnston, Brookhill, to Kemmis, 15 Sept. 1798: S.O.C. II 3217; Howard, Dublin, to Pelham, 4 Dec. 1797: N.A.I., RP 620/33/115.

The following week, republicans disarmed fifteen men of the Culdaff Yeomanry and cut down a 'vast number' of ash trees to make pikes.[110] By early June 'cutting trees and forging pikes' were the 'nightly occupations of numbers', and yeomen were delving gardens in Letterkenny with spits in vain searches for arms dumps.[111]

Initially, this escalation appeared to be related to the assizes held at Omagh, Lifford and Derry in the second and third weeks of April. From late March, republicans had been levying money to defray their prisoners' legal expenses and intimidating informers and potential jurors. During the assizes, they littered the county towns with handbills and raided outlying houses 'to show ... that they were strong'. A man captured in one of these raids near Newtownstewart was beaten and brought into Omagh when the court was in session; he was charged, tried before John Toler, and hanged within an hour. Hill noted that he declared he would not discover his accomplices: ' "It was", he said, "sufficient he should suffer himself and that he was determined to die like a soldier" and die he did most unfeelingly.'[112] However, convictions at all three assizes were few. Bonfires on hills outside the towns celebrated the acquittal of republicans and after the Lifford assizes, where Thomas Young, the high sheriff, refused to pack juries as had happened at Omagh and Derry, 'the mob' took the horses off Montgomery's carriage at Raphoe and drew him home to Convoy. Violence meanwhile continued: a few weeks after the assizes, an informer from 'below Letterkenny' who had testified against republicans was shot in his bed.[113]

While the assizes certainly energized the 'Unites', there was another explanation for the increased hunt for arms and their high level of activity into early June: republicans were preparing for an imminent rising, the local objectives of which were clear; at a provincial meeting in early April delegates learnt that the executive had received word of an imminent French landing; they were to return to their county committees, appoint senior officers, and finalize local plans to rise when the French landed. Derry's county committee therefore met in the city during the assizes and agreed that baronial meetings of 'captains' should be convened over the following two weeks. At these meetings, captains returned the

---

110 R.G. Hill, Omagh, to [Beresford], 25 May 1797: N.A.I., RP 620/30/180; Hill, Derry, to Beresford, [recvd. 12 June 1797]: N.A.I., RP 620/31/77; Hill, n.p. [Derry], to Cooke, June 1797: N.A.I., RP 620/31/181; Hamilton, Strabane, to Abercorn, 30 May 1797: P.R.O.N.I., Abercorn papers T2541/IA2/6/29.

111 Rea, Letterkenny, to Pelham, 20 May 1797: N.A.I., RP 620/30/119; Hill, [Derry], to Cooke, 12 June 1797: N.A.I., RP 620/31/181.

112 Hill, Omagh, to Pelham, 12 Apr. 1797: N.A.I., RP 620/29/231.

113 Hamilton, Strabane, to Abercorn, 17, 29 Apr., 17 May 1797: P.R.O.N.I., Abercorn papers T2541/IA2/6/22, 24–5. Young was a cousin of James Sinclair, a confidante of Montgomery; Tom Sinclair, James' brother, attended the assizes as a lawyer and was reprimanded by Toler for his overly 'warm' advocacy of republicans' cases. Young's refusal to pack juries occasioned a 'general jail delivery'; for republican reaction see *N.S.*, 21 Apr. 1797.

number of men in their companies, elected senior officers, and confirmed plans for disarming the 'king's forces' in country towns. Moore was to give the 'necessary instructions' for County Derry and, in a regional context, the capture of the city was the prime objective.[114]

By June, well-informed loyalists were convinced that republicans would soon turn out. In the first week of the month there were reports from 'every quarter' around Letterkenny 'that a general rising is shortly intended'; the same week, Sir Samuel Hayes came into the town to confer with Rea and Bacon after receiving similar reports from around Stranorlar. Threatening letters sent at Belleek warned that 'the moment our friends land or whether they do or not', the republicans would 'soon take the field and defy the world'.[115] The following week, Hill spent three days with the Cambridgeshire Cavalry in Inishowen – during which time he did not sleep three hours – searching for the Culdaff Yeomanry's arms; they burned two 'very good cabins' and threatened two townlands with 'destruction' if the arms were not returned. He thought the people were 'wild absolutely to turn out' and he confided to Beresford that 'we are taking such measures as will either quiet us or produce an issue. It is impossible to get up with these fellows when they keep to the mountains, and it is too tantalising to see them in large numbers beyond attack.' Back in Derry, he heard that 'one or two hitherto very loyal priests have been this last week sworn United Irishmen', which he took as another sign that the 'spirit of revolution' was about to 'ripen'.[116]

Then in the second and third weeks of June 1797 there was a sudden and general cessation of republican activity across Ulster. Rebels began to dump weapons, 'come in' and take the oath of allegiance, following the terms of a previously ignored amnesty proclaimed on 18 May. Writing from west Tyrone on 10 June, John Stewart insisted that 'the state of the barony of Omagh' was 'rapidly improving ... the tide is turned ... they are flocking to this house in crowds every morning to take advantage of the proclamation'; from Fermanagh

114 Hill, Derry, to Cooke, Oct. 1797: N.A.I., RP 620/32/196; copy of further information of Charles McFillin, Derry, 28 Sept. 1797: N.A.I., RP 620/32/144. Although these documents date from the autumn they contain details of the Apr. meetings. At that time news that 'they very lately announced the coming of the French' quickly reached Hill who believed it resulted from 'an apprehension on their part that the spirit they have excited might otherwise die away from the people becoming wearied from expectation'; the announcement was 'for no other purpose but to keep their mischief alive'; he was confident that 'the United gentry in this part' still believed that a rising would be pointless without the French, yet 'if they are assured of support from the south no man can say what they might do'; above all, he dreaded the 'middle-ranks': see Hill, Derry, to Pelham, 13 Apr. 1797: N.A.I., RP 620/29/334.

115 Rea, Letterkenny, to Pelham, 3, 7 June 1797: N.A.I., RP 620/31/26, 48; Capt. John Fearnought, Rosarber, to the Revd Dr Coghrain, (enclosure in Cochran, Ross Harbour, to Pelham, 8 June 1797), Brevery Mountain, Sunday night: N.A.I., RP 620/31/58.

116 Hill, Derry, to Beresford, [recvd. 12 June 1797]: N.A.I., RP 620/31/77; Hill, Derry, to Cooke, June 1797: N.A.I., RP 620/31/181; R. Hill, Derry, to Beresford, 12 June 1797: N.A.I., RP 620/31/78.

on 14 June, William Stewart announced that several magistrates were 'as busy as possible swearing the people and taking security for their future good behaviour'. From Letterkenny on 17 June, Rea observed 'a wonderful apparent change' since 7 June: 'not an hour passes that I am not called upon by numbers to administer the oath of allegiance'; in the last week of June alone, he would administer it to some 1,008 men; by then, he had 260 surrendered guns and received a further 132 guns, ten bayonets, eight pistols and three swords by 9 July.[117]

Leading loyalists doubted that this cessation was genuine. Hill did not see 'anything like a prospect of changing the minds of the people'; as late as 10 July he noted wryly that 'people in this country are swearing as much as may last them a century but [are] bringing in no arms' – an apparent reference to pikes not firearms.[118] Rea had 'no great faith in the sincerity of one half of those who take [the oath]' and, despite operating as far west as Rosguill and taking up guns, he received no pikes until 25 July.[119] Similarly, Alexander attributed the 'mysterious silence' to a 'confidence of success':[120]

> At present men of all descriptions are coming in and claiming the benefits of the proclamation. But I am sorry to observe all their confessions seem preconcerted in extent and nature and everything leading to crimination is suppressed, except that which can be extracted from the more unwary by their mistaking the extent of our informations ... Upon the whole I see not that sincerity which ought to induce any relaxation in your exertions or the vigor of your measures, as the crowd will go with the strongest party. His Majesty's Govt. is committed in a contest and force must suppress what fraud intends when it has collected force. You have as many men and of as true a spirit staunchly loyal as they have stiffly republican. The herd of men vacillate according to the vibrations of apparent strength and appearances will finally decide their adoption of one party or the other.

Scepticism about the cessation proved well-founded. Having elected officers and drawn up battle plans in April, Ulster republicans had become sanguine about the prospect of success without 'foreign aid'. In the first week of June, Joseph Orr had attended a meeting of the Ulster and Leinster executives in Dublin. The Ulstermen proposed an immediate rising, the Leinster leaders balked, and Orr and his colleagues returned home to 'begin the business by themselves'.[121]

117 Stewart, [Enniskillen], to Enniskillen, 14 June 1797: N.A.I., RP 620/31/91; Stewart, [Athenree], to Pelham, 10 June 1797: N.A.I., RP 620/31/67; Rea, Letterkenny, to Pelham, 17 June, 1, 9 July 1797: N.A.I., RP 620/31/111, 191, 214.
118 Hill, Derry, to Cooke, June, 10 July 1797: N.A.I., RP 620/31/182, 216.
119 Rea, Letterkenny, to Pelham, 17 June, 26 July 1797: N.A.I., RP 620/31/111, 277.
120 Alexander, Derry, to Pelham, 3 July 1797: N.A.I., RP 620/31/298.
121 Elliott, *Partners in revolution*, pp 132–3.

Hence, the 'mysterious silence' that suddenly fell across the province the next week must be seen as a ploy; rebel leaders were gambling that if they could lull the authorities into a false sense of security, large forces of pike-men, joined by militia-men and yeomen, would easily overcome regular troops.

The 'grand attempt' was never made. Leinster's refusal to rise dissuaded some Antrim leaders from taking action without foreign aid. Around 18 June (by which stage the token surrenders were underway) Moore attended a provincial meeting in Randalstown, aimed at making them reconsider, yet a majority still insisted that 'it was imprudent to act at that time without foreign aid'.[122] Against a background of uncertainty, events began to overtake the leadership at regional and provincial level. In the week ending 23 June, Col. John Bagwell of the Tipperary Militia made the 'fortunate discovery' that some fifty of his men had been suborned and were involved in plans to capture Derry city: 'it was determined to have several houses opened immediately in this town, to give drink gratis to the whole Regiment and when drunk to swear them and as soon as sufficient numbers were sworn to put Lord Cavan, Sir George Hill and me to death by surprise at night'.[123] An investigation led to Corp. Thomas Patterson, a 'remarkably respectable man in the regiment'. On 30 June Patterson revealed that Christopher Hardy, a saddler and inventor, had administered the republican oath to him. Hill was dumbfounded: he had always considered Hardy his 'friend'; indeed, Hardy was then in Dublin collecting £1,200 for government saddle contracts and Hill had to send expresses to the Castle ordering his arrest.[124] Word of the arrest reached Orr before Hill. He went immediately to Hardy's house, burned his papers and fled with 'a number of others'. Moore and McClintock were soon in custody. Meanwhile, unconnected events led to the flight of several east Ulster members of the executive and the provincial committee; the United Irishmen were in disarray across the north.[125]

Moore and McClintock spent only two months in gaol. At the September assizes John Philpott Curran, 'brought down specially' to represent them, acknowledged they had 'entered into that kind of obligation known as obligation of United Irishmen', but insisted that they had not known it was treasonable and would gladly take the oath of allegiance. Unsure of conviction, the crown dropped the charges and both men took the oath, Moore telling the court that 'it never was my wish to act in any treasonable manner against this country'.[126]

---

122 'Appendix No. 15: Extracts from the information of John Hughes of Belfast', in *Secret committee*, pp 120–2.

123 Bagwell, Derry, to —, 28 June 1797: N.A.I., RP 620/31/167.

124 Hill, Derry, to Cooke, 30 June 1797: N.A.I., RP 620/31/172. A Presbyterian, Hardy was a native of Tipperary but had been resident in Derry for several years.

125 Hill, Derry, to Cooke, 10, 17 July 1797: N.A.I., RP 620/31/216, 262.

126 *D.E.P.*, 28 Sept. 1797; Hill, Derry, to Cooke, 6 Sept. 1797: N.A.I., RP 620/32/99; Hill, Derry, to —, 12 Sept. 1797: N.A.I., RP 620/32/114.

Moore now stepped back from conspiracy; in October he rejected a request from the provincial committee to resume his role as county delegate, insisting that he would not act until they were 'in the field'.[127]

Moore's reticence is best understood in the context of developments within the county organization rather than in the region. Hill had gleaned considerable information on the south Derry organization from Thomas Ledlie, a young man arrested in August and remanded in Derry gaol. Ledlie spoke candidly on condition he was not exposed as an informer, and in September, using Ledlie's information, Hill turned Charles McFillin and Denis Lynch, both south Derry Catholics who had been delegates to the county and provincial committees; they gave extensive information on 'all the leaders in this county, delegates, &c.' Although Lynch continued to feed the authorities high-grade information for the next year, republicans were aware of McFillin's treachery by late September and betrayal at this level must have disconcerted many of the principals. The county organization crumbled: no Derry delegate attended a provincial meeting from June 1797 until March 1798.[128]

Formal county structures survived intact in Donegal and Tyrone. Delegates from both counties met their Antrim and Down counterparts in July to reactivate the provincial committee and routinely attended its meetings over the next year.[129] Still, there were changes. In north Donegal there is an impression of old political hands growing cautious. The less-rooted south Donegal movement may never have fully recovered from the arrest of Ballyshannon leaders in early summer; as in south Derry, sectarian fissures opened in south-west Ulster as Catholic informed on Protestant and vice versa.[130] Furthermore, there was no resumption of paramilitary violence: arms raids and manufacture ceased and informers returned home and lived unmolested. In the north-west, republicans only twice asserted themselves in the latter half of 1797: towards the close of polls in the August election, 'the late frenzy of the United Irishmen' revived when Montgomery released republican freeholders from Lifford gaol to vote for him, and in October 'more than 500 of Montgomery's United friends' attended his duel with Sir Samuel Hayes, and bonfires lit up the Laggan to celebrate his victory; Hayes' second was Captain Forbes of the Manx Fencibles.[131]

127 N. Mageean's report on provincial meeting of 14 Oct. 1797: P.R.O.N.I., Clelland papers D714/2/8A.
128 *Secret Committee*, pp 85–7; Hill, Coleraine, to Cooke, 14 Aug. 1797, Derry, 19 Aug. 1797: N.A.I., RP 620/32/47, 61; copy of further information of Charles McFillin, 28 Sept. 1797: N.A.I., RP 620/32/144; Mageean's report on provincial meeting of 24 Mar. 1798: P.R.O.N.I., Clelland papers D714/2/17 N.
129 Mac Suibhne, 'Up not out', pp 99–100.
130 Tredennick, Enniskillen, to Urquhart, 12 June 1797, Tredennick, Enniskillen, to Morrow, 12 June 1797: N.A.I., RP 620/31/130; Major, Ballyshannon, to Pelham, 3 July 1797: N.A.I., RP 620/31/194.
131 Hamilton, Strabane, to Abercorn, 4 Aug., 8, 10, 17 Oct. 1797: P.R.O.N.I., Abercorn papers T2541/IA2/6/37, 47–9.

Ultimately, Donegal, Derry and Tyrone did commit to rise in May 1798 and the military anticipated 'much trouble' in Fánaid, Inishowen and Donemana. However, the bungling of the orders to rise in Ulster and an escalation of counter-insurgency activity which spiralled into a terror campaign during the summer months of 1798 prevented even local outbreaks.[132] Rumours circulated of rebels assembling to attack Strabane in June, and there was a low but audible rumble of activity in late August and early September – a priest openly damning the king; some swearing of rebels – when Humbert was in Connaught and later in October during the great sea-battle off north-west Donegal. Moreover, in mid-September when Napper Tandy berthed at Rutland in west Donegal, far from the rebel heartland, local people were aware of Humbert's defeat yet still eager to join the French.[133] Would the old networks have turned out had Humbert pressed north or had Tone made Lough Swilly or, indeed, had Tandy stayed longer? One incident is suggestive: on 26 August an express reached Letterkenny ordering the militia south to meet the French; Rea requisitioned horses and carts to transport soldiers; with one exception, every horse in town was in the market-place within an hour; the only man who refused was 'Mr Dobson, agent to Mr Montgomery and indeed long suspected'.[134]

***

In November 1794 Douglas, his mind, perhaps, already set on emigrating, had published *Derriana*, 'a collection of papers relative to the siege of Derry'. In the preface to this valedictory volume, he reflected on the writing of history, a subject in which he had evinced a keen interest over the previous twenty-odd years:[135]

> Histories have been too often made up from general and uncertain information. Local and minute accounts of distinct portions and districts are necessary to form a full and authentic history of a large and populous country. Historians, also, have been too much in the practise of passing over the most useful and most numerous class of mankind, and of only noticing the sons of rank and fortune – they have dwelt too much on the prominent features, whilst they have almost entirely neglected the smaller

132 Mac Suibhne, 'Up not out', pp 89–98.
133 Hamilton, Strabane, to Abercorn, 13 June, 2, 9 Sept 1798: P.R.O.N.I., Abercorn papers T2541/IA2/7/13, 31–2; *L.J.*, 13 Nov. 1798; Elliott, *Partners in revolution*, p. 233; 'The memorial of Francis Forster of Rutland', 16 Apr. 1801: N.A.I., RP 620/10/119/4.
134 Rea, Letterkenny, to [Castlereagh]., 27 Aug. 1798: N.A.I., S.O.C. I 1017/20. Andrew Dobson was then Montgomery's agent. Thomas Dobson, his predecessor, had also been the *Journal's* first agent in Letterkenny; see *L.J.*, 3 June 1772.
135 Douglas, *Derriana*, v.

but essential lineaments of the great picture. Of late, however, authors have begun to adopt more rational and philanthropic subjects – they are gradually renouncing the 'false glory,' of battles and sieges and human slaughter, and are leading the public mind to the contemplation of the arts of peace, and the improvement of civil and domestic life.

Douglas' reflections remain relevant to the history of his own lifetime. Since the late nineteenth century, historians have focused on the rising and the 'lives' of those activists whom they have credited with arranging it – Douglas' 'battles and sieges and human slaughter' and 'sons of rank and fortune', the pulp history of militaria and political biography. In recent years, attention has shifted towards the process of politicization and the social and cultural bases of sedition. However, there remains a need for 'local and minute accounts' of the long-term changes in 'civil and domestic life' that allowed Irish society to touch the very penumbra of colonialism's shadow in the last quarter of the 1700s, only to slip backwards into the darkness in the early 1800s. The 'great picture' suggested here is that in some regions, such as south-west Ulster, the 1790s did constitute a new 'window of opportunity' as the United Irishmen mapped a course out of the anti-politics of Planter and Gael, but in others, not least north-west Ulster, this course had been set years before the foundation of the Belfast Society of United Irishmen. In this and similar regions a door had been swinging shut since the mid-1780s when the emergence of the troika in Dublin Castle had given Britain a more effective administration, one which had assiduously acted to narrow the space for reasoned discourse in Irish society. As politicization – not simply an organization and its activists – comes to replace the rising as the focus of historical inquiry, the pressure brought to bear on the mainstream press from the mid-1780s should emerge as a far more significant development than the smashing of the *Northern Star*'s office by a few drunken Monaghan-men in 1797.

14

Religious polarization and sectarianism in the Ulster rebellion

MARIANNE ELLIOTT

The 1790s marked a watershed in Irish history and set the pattern which has not yet been broken.[1] But there was nothing inevitable about its legacy of militant Catholic nationalism and Protestant loyalism, despite the intensity of the religious suspicion which existed. The decade opened optimistically, with the belief that old fears and sectarian mind-sets were a thing of the past. It ended with Irish (and particularly Ulster) society more bitterly polarized than before.

For most of the eighteenth century, a *modus vivendi*, based on recognizably different spheres, maintained the peace between Protestant and Catholic in Ulster. Paradoxically it was the breaking down of demographic, cultural and most of all political divisions which sparked the end-of-century conflict. The dramatic rise of population, which more than doubled that of Ulster between 1750 and 1790, involved significant encroachment on the kind of poorer, upland territory so often occupied by Catholics. This was particularly noticeable in Armagh – the most populous county in Ireland. As a result of the manner in which the area had been settled in the Ulster Plantation, there were unusually large numbers of lower-class Anglicans in Armagh and neighbouring parts of Tyrone.[2] The tensions created formed the backdrop to the Armagh troubles of the 1780s and '90s.[3]

The troubles, which by 1785 had produced the Catholic Defenders and Protestant Peep o' Day Boys, had built on localized faction fights and party parades over the previous two decades. Parading to Anglican or Presbyterian church services, in full military regalia, had been a particular feature of Volunteering, as had its public celebration of William of Orange. By all accounts

---

1 This paper has been largely drawn from my book *The Catholics of Ulster* (London, 2000).
2 William Macafee, 'The population of Ulster, 1630–1841: Evidence from mid-Ulster' (unpublished D.Phil. thesis, University of Ulster, Coleraine, 1987), chap. 5.
3 The religious topography of Armagh is an important topic in every work on the Armagh troubles. There is a good overview in Frank Wright, *Two lands in one soil: Ulster politics before Home Rule* (Dublin, 1996), pp 31–2. See also L.M. Cullen, *The emergence of modern Ireland, 1600–1900* (Dublin, 1981), pp 206–8.

Protestants were the original aggressors. But very soon the Catholics returned like for like. Boycotts of traders of the opposing religion (by both Defenders and Peep o' Day Boys) extended the circle of malcontents. Parades and social events became factionalized. Fights at fairs increased. New companies of Volunteers were raised on a purely Protestant basis. Neighbours began to withdraw goodwill from those of opposite religion. Converts and those in mixed marriages became particular targets of Protestant rancour, and swaggering youths were to the fore in deliberately provocative actions.

By the early 1790s the sectarian troubles of Armagh had spilled into Down, Louth, Monaghan and parts of Tyrone and intensified after the establishment of the Orange Order in September 1795. Over the next twelve months thousands of Catholics were intimidated out of counties Armagh and Down. These 'Armagh Outrages' sent hordes of Catholics into the United Irishmen. The government was fully aware of the possible consequences of alienating loyal Catholics and sought at first to curb such attacks by preventing provocative Orange marches.[4] But increasingly its emergency counter-insurgency measures seemed to give countenance to United Irish claims that such attacks on Catholics had government sanction. Certainly the United Irishmen later attributed the upturn in its membership to the 'Armagh Outrages'.

The sectarian disturbances in Armagh set the tone for future politics in Ulster. But at the outset they were highly unusual and spread only to similar cultural frontier zones. Although the northern United Irish Society would remain largely Presbyterian, outside Antrim and Down lower-class Presbyterians were more likely to become Orangemen.[5] Once again, the religious geography of Ulster is crucial to understanding what happened in the 1790s. In areas of ancient animosities, the alliance between Dissenter and Catholic was weaker. In north Down and most of Antrim (including Belfast), however, relations between Catholics and Dissenters were good. Catholics were in a minority and posed little threat. These were non-plantation counties. There had been no major land confiscations and many Catholics and Dissenters had common Scottish roots. Down had produced the most advanced Presbyterian supporters of Catholic political rights during the 1780s, even after their co-religionists elsewhere were beginning to pull back. The numerous Catholic chapels erected during these years – Belfast, Lisburn, Dromore, Saintfield, Ballynahinch, Saul, Ballee, Portaferry – were all built with substantial Protestant, and particularly Presbyterian, assistance.[6] Sectarian ten-

---

4   Camden's correspondence with Portland, Jan.-Aug. 1796: P.R.O., HO 100/62/15–19, 153–63; HO 100/64/168–72; Reports from Down, Armagh, Tyrone, Cavan and Monaghan: N.A.I., SOC 1015/6–11, 21.

5   Brendan McEvoy, 'The United Irishmen in County Tyrone', *Seanchas Ardmacha*, v (1969), 37; I.R. McBride, *Scripture politics: Ulster Presbyterianism and Irish radicalism in the late eighteenth century* (Oxford, 1998), p. 191.

6   Patrick Rogers, *The Irish Volunteers and Catholic Emancipation* (Belfast, 1934), pp 144–66.

sions would weaken the movement almost everywhere else in Ulster and provide government with its most important informers. But here prominent County Down Catholic families like the Teelings and the Magennises were fundamental to the Defender-United Irish co-operation prior to and during the rebellion. Down would become the strongest United Irish county in the country. Here, as in Dublin, there was a concentration of upwardly-mobile Catholics, ready to identify their own cause with that of the advanced reformers. It is no accident that there was a particularly high level of Catholics among the most radical United Irishmen in this area.[7]

Ulster, however, has always been a patchwork of highly localized regions. Presbyterians tended to join the United Irishmen only in areas where Catholics were in a minority. In poorer rural areas, or where old sores from confiscation persisted, where Catholics predominated or where they equalled Protestants in numbers, the tendency was for neither Presbyterian nor Catholic to join. Yet even in mid- and west Ulster, where Catholics had been relatively quiescent, a very sudden change had occurred by spring 1797. Lord Abercorn's agent began also to suspect the Catholics, though he had previously considered them ten times more loyal than either the Presbyterians or the Methodists. The main reason was the semi-institutionalization of Orange attacks.

In July 1796 – in response to a government request for advice on how to extinguish animosities – John Ogle, sheriff of Armagh, warned Dublin Castle to avoid the mistakes of the past. Catholics claimed to have taken matters into their own hands because the Peep o' Day Boys had always been acquitted by Protestant juries. 'As this [may] have been so or not, their minds were strongly impressed by it, and with the alleged oppression of their sect and having no cordiality toward a Protestant Government when they broke out under the style of the Defenders, they became a ready prey to any sort of miscreants, whether United or Disunited Irishmen.' He had not known the Catholics to show any discontent at their exclusion from government until aroused by this 'Protestant banditti', with their 'absurd bravados', not satisfied 'with the security and advantages they possess unless they may be allowed to bawl out Protestant ascendancy'.[8]

As late as 1797 even the Armagh gentry had been anxious about appearing to countenance the Orange Order. But as disaffection spread in 1796–7, and their inability to control their own areas became all too evident – to say nothing of the persistent French threat of invasion – they became increasingly dependent on

---

7 L.M. Cullen, 'The political structures of the Defenders', in Hugh Gough and David Dickson (eds), *Ireland and the French Revolution* (Dublin, 1990), pp 129–30; Cooke to Gen. Nugent [Jan. 1796]: P.R.O.N.I., D.272/149; T. Lane to Downshire, 12 Oct. 1799: P.R.O.N.I., D.607/G/200; Marianne Elliott, 'The Defenders in Ulster', in David Dickson, Dáire Keogh and Kevin Whelan (eds), *The United Irishmen: Republicanism, radicalism and rebellion* (Dublin, 1993), pp 222–33.

8 D.W. Miller, *Peep O'Day Boys and Defenders: Selected documents on the County Armagh disturbances, 1784–96* (Belfast, 1990), pp 138–9.

the ultra-loyalists. With the embodiment of the yeomanry in September 1796, which would become a predominantly Orange institution in Ulster, the reassertion of Protestant supremacy seemed complete.

The yeomanry was a part-time policing force, but it could be – and increasingly was – used like regular military at times of crisis. Fitzwilliam had hoped to embody such a force as part of a Catholic Emancipation package, uniting the propertied of all denominations who would then be expected to enrol their own tenantry. He was concerned at the prospect of a yeomanry recruited on a purely Protestant basis. At first Camden's administration shared such fears. In the absence of Emancipation and the escalating security threat, this is exactly what happened. Outside Ulster, Catholics did enrol in the yeomanry. In Ulster, however, there was fierce resistance to admitting Catholics. Entire Orange lodges were recruited, and, as time progressed and the likelihood of rebellion and invasion seemed ever more likely, increasingly with the Castle's tacit blessing. The bulk of the yeomanry were located in the north, their local knowledge and Orange sympathies adding to the perception that they were arrayed against 'papists' rather than rebels. A 1798 version of the popular loyalist tune 'Croppies lie down' had the chorus changed to 'Papists lie down'.[9] They also made it quite clear that the Catholic-dominated militia was unwelcome.[10] The militia remained a politically suspect force and increasingly the authorities came to depend on a mixed force of yeomanry and fencibles to contain the rising tide of Ulster's disaffection.[11] Both forces were heavily infiltrated by Orangemen, who ostentatiously displayed Orange emblems as they disarmed disturbed areas. The fear of Orange attack became the main reason for a sudden Catholic influx into the United Irishmen after 1796.

Some loyal Protestants protested at the growing ascendancy of Orangeism in the armoury of counter-subversion.[12] Nor was the spirit of radical reform entirely dead – many leading Protestants and Dissenters still called for Catholic Emancipation and parliamentary reform.[13] Ultimately, however, even critics had to admit that Orangeism was a necessary evil to combat disaffection, which had got entirely out of hand. Even so, the French traveller, de la Latocnaye, moving

9   G.D. Zimmermann, *Songs of Irish rebellion* (Dublin, 1967, repr. Dublin, 2002), p. 297.

10 R.R. Madden, *Antrim and Down in '98* (Glasgow, n.d.), pp 25–6: letter to Henry Joy McCracken from his brother, 26 July 1797. The United Irishmen seem to have made particular headway among the Kerry Militia; See *Report from the Secret Committee of the House of Commons,* 1797 (Appendix II of 1798 report), p. 82.

11 T. Bartlett, 'Defence, counter-insurgency and rebellion: Ireland, 1793–1803', in Thomas Bartlett and Keith Jeffery (eds), *A military history of Ireland* (Cambridge, 1996), p. 270; Allan Blackstock, 'The raising of the yeomanry in Ulster', in Dickson, Keogh and Whelan (eds), *The United Irishmen,* pp 234–43.

12 *Drennan letters,* p. 259; *Charlemont MSS,* ii, pp 294, 303.

13 W.E.H. Lecky, *History of Ireland in the eighteenth century* (London, 1892), iv, pp 62–4; R. Ó Múirí, 'The killing of Thomas Birch', *Seanchas Ardmhacha,* x, 2 (1982), 298–300; P.R.O.N.I. facsimiles, *United Irishmen,* no 62.

through Ulster towards the end of 1796, found reports of sedition in the north greatly exaggerated. When he returned the following year, however, the situation had entirely changed. A failed French invasion attempt in December-January had exposed the country's vulnerability. The military forces at government disposal were inadequate, and London refused to send reinforcements. The French attempt had boosted disaffection in the north and at the spring assizes no juries could be found to convict those arrested. A terrible change had come over Ulster. In Tyrone and Donegal whole baronies which had been quiet in January were in a rebellious state only weeks later, the United Irishmen having successfully spread among 'all religions'. Elsewhere new mansions, recently built in the heyday of Protestant confidence, were bricked up for defence.[14] In County Down, Lord Londonderry had to be guarded by soldiers at his home, when his father had rarely bolted his windows.[15] United Irish agents in France assured the French government of widespread support among the country's defence forces and there is no denying that they were having things very much their own way in the early months of 1797.[16]

In March 1797, government decided on a crackdown; martial law was proclaimed and the people were required to surrender arms and take an oath of allegiance. Infected militia units were purged and exemplary examples made of militiamen who had taken the United Irish oath, the most famous being the execution of four Catholics from the Monaghan Militia stationed near Belfast. Their fate was immediately immortalized in a popular ballad.[17] For the first time in a century Ulster was exposed to the full rigours of martial law. House-burnings and floggings became routine and prison ships were anchored off the coast to accommodate the huge numbers of those arrested. De la Latocnaye found Ulster given over to military licence, the 'poor peasant' suffering the brunt of the military campaign, the real rogues 'very careful themselves to stay behind the curtain'. He found the people in the mountainous areas near Newry had suffered far more than their neighbours, their houses routinely burned to extort information about arms. Here the most notorious regiment of fencibles, the Ancient Britons, was quartered. Certainly south-east Ulster suffered particularly harsh treatment; even the noted government supporter John Giffard observed that the Ancient Britons' route could be traced by 'the smoke and flames of burning houses, and by the dead bodies of boys and old men'. Since such atroci-

14 Ó Múirí, 'The killing of Thomas Birch', 280; J.H. Gebbie (ed.), *An introduction to the Abercorn letters* (Omagh, 1972), pp 196–9.
15 *Drennan letters*, p. 252.
16 Notebooks of John Maxwell (member of the United Irish Ulster provincial committee, appointed colonel of County Down): N.A.I., RP 620/34/54; 1798 'Black Book': P.R.O.N.I., D 272/1; Ó Múirí, 'The killing of Thomas Birch', 279, 284; McEvoy, 'United Irishmen in County Tyrone,' p. 313; Elliott, *Partners in revolution*, p. 125.
17 Zimmermann, *Songs of Irish rebellion*, pp 129–32; Elliott, *Partners in revolution*, p. 127.

ties were aired in the British parliament by Lord Moira, they have become the stock of every historical account of the period. But Lecky – a noted critic of government – accepted that the authorities were obliged to take strong measures, such was the seriousness of the situation in the north.[18]

The existence of a formal United Irish assassination committee was roundly denied by its leaders. When told about it by one of its most useful informers – Edward Newell – the government effectively incorporated it into its propaganda campaign. Newell was a weak young man, who craved approval from any quarter – blaming it all on his mother who denied him affection – seeking it in the Defenders, the United Irishmen, the Orangemen and ultimately as a government spy. But the very many informers and vigilant magistrates who met violent deaths speaks volumes, and, as Nancy Curtin has shown, Ulster was in the grip of both republican-inspired terror and government counter-terror in the year before the rebellion.[19]

Not every county experienced the lash of the Ancient Britons. In those areas which underwent the worst military license, however – notably Down, Antrim and adjacent areas of Derry – there would be major Catholic involvement in the 1798 rebellion. Although even peaceable Protestants were abused, it was the poorer Catholic populace which suffered most in the disarming of Ulster. For the first time they joined the United Irishmen in great numbers, intensified efforts having been made to woo them via specifically Defender oaths.[20] The suddenness of this Catholic transformation from passive loyalty to active subversion was a matter of comment. The final date to surrender arms was 25 June and a great flurry of activity was noticeable among the United Irishmen as they attempted to bring about a rising before their undoubted strength was eroded. The attempt highlighted the traditional animosities between Ulster and Leinster, for the leaders in Dublin (many Catholic or pro-Catholic) opposed a rising before French help arrived. However, nothing separated the Catholic United Irish leaders in east Ulster from their Presbyterian counterparts, and people like the Teelings, Coigly and Magennis were among the leading militants attempting to bring about a rebellion and French invasion.

Catholics also came forward in large numbers to take the oath of allegiance and to subscribe to the flood of declarations of loyalty orchestrated by their parish priests. The Catholic hierarchy had finally won its long campaign to show government that it was a force for conservatism, and the government's establish-

---

18 Lecky, *Ireland*, iv, pp 116–17, 141; *A view of the present state of Ireland . . . by an observer* (Dublin, 1797), pp 21–34.

19 J.E. Newell, *The apostasy of Newell* (London, 1798), partly reprinted in Madden, *United Irishmen*, 2nd ser., i, pp 345–425; Nancy Curtin, *The United Irishmen ...* (Oxford, 1994), pp 82–3; R.M. Young, *Ulster in '98* (Belfast, 1893), p. 45.

20 Information from Revd Edward Hudson of Portglenone (who was often far more sympathetic towards the Catholics than the Presbyterians): *Charlemont MSS*, ii, p. 321.

ment of a Catholic seminary at Maynooth in 1795 saw them firmly on the side of the authorities throughout the crisis of 1798. Only one Irish bishop (Thomas Hussey, bishop of Waterford and Lismore) was to speak out publicly against Orange and military atrocities, and the Ulster bishops – under Primate O'Reilly's firm anti-political lead – were the most quiescent of all. It is no accident that fewer Ulster clergy would be involved in 1798 than anywhere else in the country.[21] O'Reilly's excommunication of the Defenders, however, made little difference and the declarations of loyalty still accounted for a tiny proportion of Ulster Catholics (though it looks as if most of the Catholic middle class were among them). The United Irishmen had urged their adherents to take the oath and surrender some arms to prevent worse damage, and the evidence of Abercorn's agent was that, quite out of character, Catholics by 1797 had no difficulty in perjuring themselves.[22] There was nothing unusual in Catholic tradition in ignoring the priest who stepped outside his community, and there was no denying the widespread disaffection of the Catholic populace by 1798.

In such a conservative society, whose world had been literally turned upside down, millenarianism was rife. Defenderism made public the kind of millenarianism so common in the Gaelic poetry of south Ulster. Till now it had been the private talk of an enclosed community. But this was the era of the French Revolution and with it came an explosion of democratic print and propaganda aimed at showing that Catholics too had natural rights. The United Irishmen had industriously circulated old prophecies foretelling apocalyptic change. Presbyterians were told that the French Revolution had brought about the fall of Antichrist and inaugurated the demise of popery. For a while their ability to distinguish the abstract from the individual was a crucial element in the Presbyterian alliance with Catholics. Such diverse prophecies as those of the thirteenth-century Thomas the Rhymer, the seventeenth-century Scottish Covenanter, Alexander Peden, and the sixth-century Colmcille converged in foretelling deliverance at the hands of the French. The widespread belief in cataclysmic change was the backdrop to the dramatic, almost trance-like atmosphere of the years 1796–8.[23]

21 There is a full discussion of this political quietude of the Ulster hierarchy in my *Catholics of Ulster*, chaps. 7–8. See also 'A pastoral of Archbishop O'Reilly, 1788', *Seanchas Ardmhacha*, iv (1960–1), 176.

22 Gebbie, *Abercorn letters*, p. 200; *Castlereagh correspondence*, i, p. 206; Charles Dickson, *Revolt in the north: Antrim and Down in 1798* (Dublin, 1960), p. 240.

23 J.R.R. Adams, *The printed word and the common man: Popular culture in Ulster 1700–1900* (Belfast, 1987), pp 88–9, gives a good idea of the huge numbers of these prophecies rolling off the presses in Ulster in these years. See also Curtin, *The United Irishmen*, pp 188–9; S.J. Connolly, *Priests and people in pre-Famine Ireland, 1780–1845* (Dublin, 1982), pp 109–10; Lecky, *Ireland*, iv, pp 125–6. And see *Report from the Committee of Secrecy of the House of Commons of Ireland* (Dublin, 1798), appendix no. xxvi, and *Beauties of the press* (London, 1800), pp 152–3, for reports of Orange oaths to massacre all Catholics. J.S. Donnelly Jr., 'Propagating the cause of the United Irishmen', *Studies*, lxix (1980), 15–21, shows how the

But the power of prophecy – particularly in times of distress and dislocation, and particularly in poorer rural communities – lies in its ability to interpret or foretell whatever the community wants to hear. Whilst it served to unite at the height of United Irish confidence, ultimately it fed the increasing sectarian polarisation. The Defenders operated at many different levels, their chameleon character and transmutation over time confounding historical efforts at explanation. In their south Ulster heartland, however, they acted as the bridge linking the prophetic vision of the poetry with the political ideas of the 1790s. The idea of a French saviour picked up the old Jacobite message and translated it for a new age. The Messiah was France rather than the Stuarts, but the message of a radical overthrow of the existing order was the same.

> The French at this time are relegating rank,
> and there'll be no prince over them but a pure new regime;
> Germany, Flanders and the Rhine will be subject to them,
> and I suspect that Scotland and Ireland will be in the bloc.

> There'll be no Louis or any other king from now on
> in the countries forever oppressing each fine son;
> people will be full of wisdom, unfettered, unthreatened,
> and the children of Milesius will have free will
> and prosperity until Judgement Day.

> Remember the conditions the Gaill gave you at Limerick, my woe!
> you were betrayed, and no mistake, since the time of King William
> which left your poor children in distress, without property but in pain
> like a blind beast running for a prize while its guide has no reins.

> Not by inheritance did Luther or anyone of the descendants obtain
> all the bright new courts from Limerick to the Boyne
> a scourge will come on these boors from the Gaels in battle
> and they'll have no estate or fortress in Ireland any more.

> The province of Munster is restraining its multitudes
> and every famed man among the victorious Leinstermen is happy
> the mighty, active Ulster men will be defending the hosts
> as they rout the race of Luther, and may they not escape them.[24]

---

northern United Irishmen in particular were adept at exploiting popular millenarianism. See also *Prophetical extracts, particularly such as relate to the Revolution in France, and the decline of papal power in the world* (Strabane, 1795).

24 N.L.I., MS G.200 (b), *'Ollamh Éigin. An Revolution. The French Revolution. By an uncertain author'*. It seems to be from the Dundalk area, for the scribe was Pádraig ó Gallóglaigh of Dundalk. See also Séamus P. Ó Mórdha, 'Dán Faoi Mhuirthéacht na Frainnce', *Éigse*, vii (1953–4), 202–4, on this poem.

French help would 'get [them] the conditions of Limerick', prospective Defenders were told; 'that the Protestants had the power of the country long enough, and that they would have it as long more'.[25]

The main United Irish leaders and the Catholic middle class (however radical) distanced themselves from the increasingly sectarian readings of the prophecies. But many others were not immune from playing on the fears of Orangeism or of Catholic hopes for a reversal of the land settlement as a means of swelling their ranks. The United Irish press became much more shrill after the destruction of the *Northern Star* in May 1797. The prophecies of Colmcille, foretelling a dreadful massacre of the Catholics, which had circulated in 1641 and would do so again in the next century, gained particular currency. Catholics in Antrim, Derry and Donegal were reported to have fled to the hills because of the prophecy.[26] In Armagh, de la Latocnaye thought it was put about by Orangemen to force the Catholics to flee to the west.

> The poor folk, who are after all the most timid and credulous of the universe, with their families and small remains of furniture, started in crowds to put themselves in safety on the other side of the Shannon. I myself have met often these wandering families moving to the line of safety … It was in talking to some of these on the road that I learned of the prophecy of St. Columba.[27]

At first widespread intimidation swelled the ranks of the United Irishmen – 'designing men who buzzed in our ears Catholic Emancipation, and the danger of being massacred by Orangemen' – as the parishioners of Arboe, County Tyrone, told their priest in June 1797.[28] Certainly the ease with which Ulster was disarmed suggests that many had enlisted through fear rather than commitment. Neighbours were now perceived as potential murderers, where once they had lived in peace.[29] Even converts to Protestantism were suspect. Thomas Macan – who converted in 1751 – was a Volunteer captain and sovereign of Armagh until 1794. But he retained a liberal attitude towards the Catholics. His son Arthur succeeded him as sovereign and was a yeoman commander. He was nevertheless nicknamed 'Papist Macan', and it

25 Howell, *State Trials*, xxv, c. 754; also, McEvoy, 'United Irishmen in County Tyrone', 11.
26 Samuel McSkimin, *Annals of Ulster*, E.J. McCrum (ed.) (Belfast, 1906), p. 65.
27 De Latocnaye, *A Frenchman's walk through Ireland*, ed. John Stevenson (Belfast, 1917), pp 263–4.
28 Dáire Keogh, *'The French disease': The Catholic Church and radicalism in Ireland, 1790–1800* (Dublin, 1993), p. 163. N.A.I., SOC 1016/30 tells a similar tale from the Polls area of the Meath/Cavan/Monaghan borders.
29 W.S. Dickson, *A narrative of the confinement and exile of William Steele Dickson, DD* (Dublin, 1812), pp 30–31.

looks very much as if his departure for India in December 1797 was for his own safety.[30]

By 1798 the prophecies were adding to the sectarian polarization of Ulster. Outside Antrim and Down, many United Irishmen had become Orangemen and yeomen, even moderates joining the extremists. Since spring 1797 Ulster was effectively a military camp, and many of the troops were billeted on the people. The other provinces did not experience martial law till the spring of 1798 and the terror induced was a major factor in the outbreak of the rebellion. As a result of military repression and sectarian polarization, little of the united movement survived in Ulster outside Antrim and Down by 1798. The United Irishmen still expected support from movements once strong in parts of Donegal and Derry. But in the event only Antrim and Down rose in June 1798, an attempted turn-out at Maghera, County Derry, collapsing on news of the approaching troops.

By the last week in May 1798, nearly all the main United Irish leaders were in prison, and confusion reigned in Ulster when the planned rebellion finally erupted in Dublin on 23 May. The entire country had been proclaimed at the end of March and as the floggings, torture and house-burning – made infamous by the disarming of Ulster – now spread south, affected counties witnessed a similar upsurge in sectarian tensions.

'I am happy to be enabled to assure your Lordship', wrote Abercorn's agent in Strabane, 'that the zeal and loyalty of almost all ranks in this part of the North have of late been increasing in proportion to the disaffection of the South. The Presbyterians (however late) now plainly see that the disaffection to government which originated with their party, must, without a speedy check, end in the total annihilation of them, in common with the church establishment … they will now fight in earnest to keep down the Catholics.' He now looked upon the Catholic populace as the most disaffected – only months after he had reported the exact opposite – and apprehended 'a rising of the Catholics in the wild parts of Donegal … [where they were] as numerous as sand', to say nothing of the 20,000 or so then gathering at Lough Derg only sixteen miles from Barons Court (Abercorn's seat). News of the rising in Antrim and Down came as a shock: 'so long as it appeared a Catholic business I was quite easy about the North, but Antrim is quite a Protestant county'.[31]

By June 1798 more arrests had decimated the original Ulster leadership. The Down commander, the non-subscribing Presbyterian minister of Portaferry, the Revd William Steele Dickson, had been taken on 5 June. In Down the succession of leaders friendly towards the Catholics (Russell, Dickson and finally Munro)

---

30 Miller, *Peep O'Day Boys and Defenders*, p. 62; Réamonn Ó Muirí, 'The killing of Thomas Birch, United Irishman, Mar. 1797 and the meeting of the Armagh freeholders, 19 Apr. 1797', *Seanchas Ard Mhacha*, x (1982), 289–90. See also Dickson, *Revolt in the north*, p. 103 for more examples of sympathetic Protestants being harassed.

31 Gebbie, *Abercorn letters*, pp 204–5.

had ensured an unusual unity right through the tensions of 1797–8. In Antrim, the last-minute assumption of command by Henry Joy McCracken in June 1798 would have had the same effect and ensured a high Catholic turnout. Along with Russell, McCracken was one of the few highly placed United Irishmen who was popular with the common people of all denominations. McCracken had been central in the United Irish/Defender alliance, and, according to Hope, was chosen by the Defenders shortly before the rising as their deputy for communication with the United Irish Society.[32]

But the omens were bad. Many of the Antrim colonels refused to act, and it was younger men, occupying positions of less social prominence, who were pushed to the fore. Martial law had been intensified and spies at the very heart of the United Irish command were feeding the military commander, General Nugent, with accurate information about their plans. The Antrim rising began on 7 June, with perhaps as many as 22,000 turning out in battles at Randalstown, Antrim and Ballymena, and countless skirmishes in almost every other town and village.[33] But the rebels were ill-armed and poorly-led and after initial victories they succumbed to Nugent's forces. When one of the military commanders offered an amnesty, McCracken's rebel army melted away.

Much has been made of religious dissensions among the rebels. Indeed, given the atmosphere of the time, their absence would have been unusual and there was much greater dissension among the rebels generally. But most of the incidents reported come from the pens of two hostile writers, Richard Musgrave and Samuel McSkimin – a yeoman in 1798 – and should be treated accordingly. The early stages of the Antrim rising had a carnival atmosphere. Old banners, flags and ensigns were resurrected (many from former Volunteering days). Columns sang the *Marseillaise* en route to the battlefield, and in his excitement, Larry Dempsey, an army deserter from Munster, allegedly exclaimed: 'By J——s, boys, we'll pay the rascals this day for the Battle of the Boyne'.[34] The story is McSkimin's, but is not improbable given the bad relations between the Orangemen and southern soldiers sent to Ulster. 'The great Orange fear' of 1798 tended to assume greater proportions the further removed from Ulster itself. But threading through McSkimin's account of the rising in Antrim and Down is a suggestion of separate Defender forces, very often involved in dissensions with the rest.

As the largely Presbyterian leadership began to fall apart, there is some evidence of escalated recruiting among Catholics – United Irishmen capitalising on the Orange scare by using specifically Defender oaths to entice them to join.[35] James Hope, the Presbyterian weaver from Templepatrick (and still something

32 Madden, *Antrim and Down in '98*, pp 42–3.
33 Curtin, *United Irishmen*, p. 267.
34 McSkimin, *Annals of Ulster*, pp 74–5.
35 Hudson to Charlemont, 3 May 1798, *Charlemont MSS*, ii, p. 321; Madden, *Antrim and Down in '98*, p. 13.

of a folk-hero in those parts), was McCracken's closest aide in the recruitment of Defenders. 'Charles Teeling was labouring ... to unite the Defenders and Catholics of the smaller towns of Ulster', he told Madden, 'and joining in sworn brotherhood, they became United Irishmen. At a later period, Henry Joy McCracken advised and assisted in the special organization of a body of 7,000 men, *originally* of the Defenders, to act as a forlorn hope, in case of necessity, out of the 21,000 that were returned fighting men in the county of Antrim'.[36] This is an intriguing passage, suggesting a later strategy in tune with Hudson's comment. It receives further endorsement from David Bailie Warden's account of events in these crucial days of early June. Warden – a young Presbyterian schoolmaster and trainee minister – was one of the commanders in north Down. On 3 June he was present when an express arrived from Antrim announcing: 'That the Colonels of United Irishmen in the County of Antrim were averse to action but that the Defenders were 5,000 all ready for action.'[37] On 1 June the Ulster commander in chief, Robert Simms – one of a very few of the original United Irish leaders still at liberty and, along with most leaders of that vintage, adamant against rising without the French – resigned. On the 2nd – as the remaining commanders still vacillated, when faced with demands from the inferior officers for immediate action – McCracken was raised to the command, his elite force of Defenders apparently becoming part of the argument for action.

However, the image of Catholics and Presbyterians fighting under different banners can only be taken so far. When the so-called 'regenerated Defenders' emerged after the collapse of the United Irish rebellion, it is clear that their new leaders had actually been United Irishmen in the rebellion year.[38] Catholics only seem to have coalesced in separate Catholic divisions when the demography of their particular area was exclusively Catholic and such would have been the case in parts of County Down. Predictably it is from here that the main case of religious division is reported for, more than any other county in Ulster, huge numbers of Catholics in County Down joined the standard of rebellion.

In the split of 1797 over the timing of the rising, a large meeting took place near Newry at which over 1,000 were said to have attended. Prominent among those calling for immediate rising were John Magennis and Alexander Lowry and they appear to have won their case, for it was a minority (some 300) who withdrew in protest.[39] Thereafter the same group took the initiative in the north,

36 Madden, *Antrim and Down in '98*, pp 98, 116, for 'old' Defenders being sworn as United Irishmen.
37 'Narrative of the Rebel Army within County Down': N.A.I., RP 620/4/41. See A.T.Q. Stewart, *The summer soldiers* ... (Belfast, 1995), p. 271, for the identification of Warden as the author.
38 Elliott, *Partners in revolution*, p. 342; Elliot, 'The Defenders in Ulster', in Dickson, Keogh and Whelan (eds), *The United Irishmen*, pp 222–33.
39 [J. Lee] to George Anderson, 20 June 1797: N.A.I., RP 620/31/128.

in support of a militant faction within the Dublin leadership. Their immediate strategy – apart from avoiding arrest (a distinct possibility for warrants were out against them) – was to organize supporters in Britain and France. They were joined by Coigly, Anthony McCann from Carlingford, Pat and John Byrne from Dundalk, and the only Teeling still at liberty, Bartholomew. By now, Down was the United Irishmen's most organized county and the most vocal in pushing for rebellion.[40] With most of the main leaders either out of the country or in prison, it is difficult to keep track of the vicissitudes among the leadership. Yet even after the great Orange scare which immediately preceded the rising, Catholics were well-represented among the United Irish leadership: a list of six colonels of April 1798 included three Catholics – Patrick McDonnell, the priest Bernard Magennis, and Hugh O'Hanlon of Newry.

Down and Antrim were to have risen on the same day, but McCracken's message had not arrived and most of the commanders had been arrested. The first news of the Antrim rising was brought by William Kane from Belfast, who crossed Belfast Lough to Holywood. Whom he told is unclear, for David Bailie Warden, one of the commanders in north Down, only heard of it from Mageean on 6 June. But on 7 June when he turned up at the expected rendezvous – Scrabo Hill, west of Newtownards – no one was there. The rising in Down started with an attack on Saintfield on Saturday 9 June. Warden 'having gone through several stages of promotion' in one day, was made commander of the Ards brigade. By the following day the Ards peninsula was in rebel hands – but Warden could barely contain the disposition among his ill-trained men to flee, arms and all, at the slightest rumour of attack. The insubordination escalated *en route* to the main rebel camp. This had been established at Creevy Rocks – just south of Saintfield on the road to Ballynahinch – but as yet it had no overall commander. On Sunday Henry Munro was 'appointed by acclamation, to the chief command'.[41] Munro was a young linen draper from Lisburn, a member of the Established Church, a mason, a former Volunteer with a known interest in military tactics and an established reputation as a reformer. Ironically he was the direct descendant of the same Major-General Munro who, sent to quell the 1641 Ulster rising, was defeated by Owen Roe O'Neill at Benburb and is claimed to have introduced Presbyterianism to Ireland.[42]

In the religious geography of Ulster, the Down rebellion had been a largely Presbyterian one until now. But the Ards men hoped to cross Strangford Lough to link with the Defenders in an attack on Downpatrick.[43] The main battle occurred at Ballynahinch on the 11th. On its eve, 'the mutinous disposition …

40 *Report from the Committee of Secrecy of the House of Commons of Ireland* (Dublin, 1798), pp 162–65.
41 Madden, *Antrim and Down in '98,* p. 129 seq.
42 Stewart, *Summer soldiers* p. 206; Dickson, *Revolt in the north,* pp 227–31.
43 Stewart, *Summer soldiers,* p. 190.

[and] spirit of insubordination', which Warden found among the foot soldiers from the outset, had reached such a height that entire units, officers and all, threatened to decamp and return home. The rebels were poorly armed and ill-equipped and Munro hesitated. Troops converging from Belfast and Down-patrick could be tracked by the plumes of smoke on the horizon, for towns taken by the rebels were torched by the military and a statement put out by General Nugent offered a choice of clemency on surrender, or utter destruction. Whether it was this or clear indecision among the rebel command which caused it, there can be no doubt about the hundreds defecting on the eve of battle. The twelve-year-old James Thompson watched the battle from a neighbouring hill, where his family had sought refuge, and in later life left a vivid account of the day's proceedings. 'The chief injury sustained by the rebels … consisted in the gradual desertion of a great part of their army … we distinctly heard their more determined fellows shouting to stop the runaways … during every hour of the night fugitives were seen passing our station.'[44] Musgrave claimed that these were Catholics.[45] This cannot be proved. Nor can the continuing speculation that John Magennis had returned on the eve of the rebellion and that it was he who had argued with Munro and withdrawn with the Catholics from Ballynahinch.[46] Such were the stories still circulating in 1834 about the defection of the Catholics, that Hope felt compelled to confront them.

> A party, which was assembling near Rathfriland, was advised to disperse by John O'Neil, of Eight-mile Bridge; they did so and traitors represented them as Catholics who had deserted the people. There was another false report that was industriously spread, and which is current to this day, that Maginnis had gone to Ballinahinch, with a body of Catholics, but in consequence of a dispute with Munro, had abandoned the people, and taken away his party with him. Maginnis was not there at all, nor any body of men, exclusively Catholics; the Catholics that were there were mixed with the Dissenters, and fought side by side with them, in a com-

44 Cited in Dickson, *Revolt in the north*, pp 227–31; C.H. Teeling, *Personal narrative of the Irish rebellion of 1798* (Shannon, 1972, reprint of 1876 edn.), p. 136.

45 Musgrave, *Memoirs of the different rebellions in Ireland*, 2nd ed. (Dublin, 1801), p. 557. Musgrave claimed that as many as 2,000 Catholics defected and watched from the Seaforde road with satisfaction as the Protestants were destroying each other.

46 See L.M. Cullen, 'The internal politics of the United Irishmen', in Dickson, Keogh and Whelan (eds), *United Irishmen*, pp 194, 344. Cullen, in a revision of his earlier conclusions in 'The political structures of the Defenders', in Gough and Dickson (eds), *Ireland and the French Revolution*', pp 133–4, argues that Lowry and Magennis did return to Ulster on the eve of the rising. If this can be proved, it would significantly alter our understanding. There is a rumoured report by Leonard McNally on 2 June that 'Lowrie and another from France are in the North': N.A.I., RP 620/10/121/108. However, since he signed a petition in Paris on 16 June, it is unlikely that he can have been in Ulster on the eve of the Down rising. See Elliott, *Tone*, pp 379, 469.

mon cause … the Killinchy people were the men who deserted, and they were Dissenters.[47]

The story first surfaced in information given to Fr James McCary – a curate in Carrickfergus – in September 1798. He had it from a Felix Conroy or Converoy from Armagh, who had it from Mr Clark, a Lisburn innkeeper and cotton manufacturer, said to be one of the rebel commanders at Ballynahinch. Clark blamed the defeat on 'an ambitious and religious contest' between Munro and someone called Magennis. The dispute over who should lead the forces was decided in Magennis' favour by the toss of a coin. But Munro drew his sword, crying out that 'his intentions was [*sic*] to establish a Presbyterian independent Government' – unlikely, given his Anglicanism – and called to his side all who supported him. Magennis did likewise and that night they left the rebel camp. Several hundred Catholics who were to have joined the camp the next day, heard of Magennis' departure and failed to turn up.[48]

In the south of the county a military council was held to decide whether to march north to join Munro at Ballynahinch, or to capture Newry, extend along the Armagh/Louth borders and cut the north off from Dublin. After much time-wasting, the latter strategy was adopted. But before it could be implemented, news arrived of the defeat at Ballynahinch. It may well have been from these forces that young Charles Teeling escaped into the mountains of south Ulster, his journey charting the widespread military license and destruction which had occurred since the previous year. But of any sectarian quarrels among the Down rebels, Teeling is silent. Catholic rebels also set out from Monaghan to join the Down men and, as with the Derry men who tried to reach Antrim, others too may have been stopped in their tracks by news of the swift suppression of the rising in the two counties.[49] It is difficult to know what to make of the Magennis story, for Clark was clearly no bigot and seems to have used his business dealings to spread the United Irish system among the Defenders of Connacht. It does not at all square with what we know of Munro; and yet there is a strong possibility that the aforementioned Bernard Magennis was 'out' in the Down rebellion – certainly he was arrested and imprisoned after the Battle of Ballynahinch.[50] A far more reliable witness – David Bailie Warden – blamed their defeat on a failure of command, 'the arrestment of most of our principal officers – the neglect or ignorance of the next superiors [all accounts agree on Munro's courage and honour, but absence of military acumen], the disordered embodiment of the people

---

47 Madden, *Antrim and Down in '98*, p. 240.

48 Information contained in MacCary to Edward Cooke, under-secretary at Dublin Castle, 8 Oct. 1798: N.A.I., RP 620/40/140.

49 D.C. Rushe, *Monaghan in the eighteenth century* (Dundalk, 1916), p. 37; Teeling, *Sequel to the history of the Irish rebellion in 1798* (Shannon, 1972), pp 202–3.

50 Keogh, *French disease*, pp 197–8.

and the too great eagerness in General Munro for engaging – together with some improprieties committed at Ballynahinch'. In his long account of the Down rising, he does not single out religious dissension as a major factor in its failure.[51]

Hope may be guilty of excessive pleading. But in the aftermath of 1798, there was no shortage of those trying to shift the blame onto the other side and the tendency was actively promoted by government supporters. Indeed the Ballynahinch incident – like so many from the events of 1798 – was blown up to suit party purposes. Frank Wright was told of it by the Protestants of Newtownards in the late 1980s. The point of such stories, he reflected 'is that they create a picture of a United rising that really had very little to do with the Catholics, and which was anyway seen as a mistake later … They dispose of the romantic rubbish about how the 1798 Republicans were 1916 rebels little over a hundred years before their time.' To paint the 1798 Ulster rebels as somehow deluding themselves until Wexford had alerted them to the real threat of Catholic power is, concluded Wright perceptively, 'to accept uncritically the claims of later political actors who wanted to destroy the very idea that there might be any unity of purpose between Protestant and Catholic'.[52] The reality was that in those areas where the rebellion did erupt, Catholics were too few and too insignificant to appear in any other guise than the victims of military and Orange atrocities. Such Catholics were beholden to the Presbyterians, who at every stage had supported them.

Government had long sought to drive a wedge between Catholics and the far more dangerous Dissenters. The withdrawal of the propertied Presbyterians on the eve of the Ulster rising caused intense bitterness among lower-class Catholics throughout Ireland. Their action, Hope reflected, 'gave our enemies an opportunity of shaking the confidence of our countrymen in the other provinces, by constantly reminding them how the Dissenters of the north began the business, and in the time of need were the first to abandon it'.[53] The truth, as ever, probably lies somewhere in between. The institutional Catholic Church in Ulster was almost totally united in its condemnation of disaffection and, outside those areas which provided an interdenominational leadership, there is little sign of the leadership (Presbyterian or Catholic) required to turn discontent into rebellion. The *Belfast News Letter* took comfort from its analysis of the inaction of the bulk of Ulster Catholics during the rebellion:

> The different character maintained by the Catholic of the north and the
> Catholic of the south is well understood by everyone acquainted with
> Ireland. God be praised the former has better information than the latter

---

51 'Narrative of the Rebel Army within C. Down': N.A.I., RP 620/4/41; Stewart, *Summer soldiers*, p. 271.

52 Wright, *Two lands on one soil*, pp 42–3.

53 Madden, *Antrim and Down in '98*, p. 131. See Elliott, *Partners in revolution*, pp 237–8, for the many examples of this feeling throughout the country.

and has we believe a degree of liberality with which the other is unacquainted.[54]

Given the religious demography of the rest of Ireland, it was inevitable that
the foot soldiers of the rebellion elsewhere should have been largely Catholic.
The possible consequences of this seems to have struck various Presbyterians at
different times. In an oft-quoted declaration immediately prior to his execution,
the Antrim leader James Dickey allegedly claimed 'that if the *north* had been
successful, *they* would have had to fight the battle over again with the Catholics
of the *south*'.[55] The propertied of all denominations had steadily withdrawn from
the United Irishmen after the military clampdown, and lack of leadership and
continued military licence, more than any dissension, were responsible for the
steady stream of defections. Disillusionment was widespread. James Orr – the
folk-poet of Ballycarry, whose entire village was out in '98 – graphically
described the motives which decimated the main rebel camp at Donegore Hill in
Antrim. Many were half-hearted:

> Repentant Painites at their pray'rs,
> An' dastards crousely craikin',
> Move on, heroic, to the wars
> They meant na to partake in,
>   By night, or day.

And when the soldiers appeared, they took flight:

> For Nugent's red-coats, bright in arms,
> An' rush! the pale-fac'd randies
>   Took leg, that day.

> The camp's brak up. Owre braces, an' bogs,
> The patriots seek their sections;
> Arms, ammunition, bread-bags, brogues,
> Lye skail'd in a' directions.

> Come back, ye dastards! – Can ye ought
> Expect at your returnin',
> But wives an' weans stript, cattle hought,
> An' cots, an' claughin's burnin?
> Na, haste ye hame: ye ken ye'll 'scape,
> 'Cause martial worth ye're clear o';
> The nine-tail'd cat, or choakin' rape,

54 *B.N.L.*, 24 July 1798, cited in R.B. McDowell, *Ireland in the age of imperialism and revolution,
1760–1801* (Oxford, 1979), p. 643.
55 *B.N.L.*, 24 July 1798, cited in Curtin, *United Irishmen*, p. 277; Musgrave, *Rebellions*, p. 558;
Joy, *Belfast politics*, p. xi.

Is maistly for some hero,
    On sic a day.
Better he swing than I, on
    Some hangin' day.

What might have been, asked Orr, 'Had they no been deserted'; but flesh is weak and:

In tryin' times, maist folk, you'll fin',
Will act like Donegore men.[56]

The terrible bloodshed and suffering of the 1798 period alienated many reformers, but it had not yet destroyed their belief in natural rights and a genuinely tolerant Irish society. James Orr's continued support for Catholic Emancipation well into the nineteenth century was not untypical though, as his editors suggest, it might not have survived its link with O'Connellism, which for some Ulster Presbyterians came to symbolize the kind of Catholic tyranny allegedly forecast by Dickey.[57] But the idea of a cross-religious revolutionary movement survived in Antrim and Down for longer than anywhere else – as late as 1814 Sir George Hill reporting such among 'a few Protestant traitors, a remnant of the views and projects of 1798' in the hinterland of Belfast.[58] As long as a possibility of French aid survived – which it did, at least theoretically, until 1815 – many who had been 'out' in 1798 and escaped execution or transportation were willing to rise again. Even after the collapse of the 1798 rebellion there are signs of fence-sitting by some and the desired French invasion – even as late as 1811, when it was again on offer – might well have shown the presumed collapse of the old alliance to have been illusory.

Yet the general statement of disaffection being predominantly lower-class Catholic in character would remain true for much of the century after the collapse of the 1798 rebellion – a totally new development in the history of Ulster Catholicism. Castlereagh, always an astute observer of long-term trends, though despised by the Presbyterian reformers because he had originally been one himself, described the transformation which had occurred in popular politics by the end of the eighteenth century thus:

The Protestant Dissenters in Ulster have in a great degree withdrawn themselves from the Union, and become Orangemen. The northern Catholics always committed in feeling against the Presbyterians, were

56 D.H. Akenson and W.H. Crawford, *James Orr, bard of Ballycarry* (Belfast 1977), pp 10–11, 39–40.
57 Akenson and Crawford, *James Orr*, p. 16.
58 Hill to Peel, 9 Mar. 1814: N.A.I., SOC 1567/10.

during the early period of the conspiracy loyal – the religious complexion of the Rebellion in the South gradually separated the Protestants from the Treason, and precisely in the same degree, appear'd to embark the Catholics in it – defenderism was introduced, and it is principally under that organization ... that whatever there is of Treason in the North, is at present associated. They are destitute of Leaders, and the people of substance, manufacturers as well as farmers have withdrawn from them.[59]

Within months of the collapse of the Ulster rising, the main flow of the disaffected was into a revived Defenderism.

The legacy of '98 in Ulster is much more confused than anywhere else in Ireland. In Antrim and Down there is still a pride in certain Ulster Presbyterian circles that their ancestors were 'out' in '98, still that intense distrust of Britain which so characterised the Presbyterian radicalism at the core of the United Irishmen, still a Presbyterian tradition that they had shunned the Orangemen. In the decades immediately following the 1798 rebellion there was a widespread belief among the Catholics that they had been abandoned by the Presbyterians at that time.[60] By the twentieth century such bitterness had been replaced by a romantic nostalgia of the time when the Presbyterians had been allies.[61] However, Presbyterian radicalism shrank in proportion to the inclusion of elements of the United Irish story in nationalist mythology. The rejection of Theobald Wolfe Tone is a case in point. The story of 'Betsy Gray and the Hearts of Down' was once a favourite with the people of County Down – Catholic and Protestant alike. It was immortalized in the 1896 novel of W.G.Lyttle, a liberal newspaper editor in Bangor, north Down. The short novel became a minor classic and I remember my father retelling the story as late as the 1960s and '70s. It is the story of Elizabeth Gray, who had joined her brother and lover at the battle of Ballynahinch – all three being killed by yeomen in the aftermath of the defeat. Far into the nineteenth century, the descendants of these yeomen were shunned at Anahilt Protestant church and their children stoned at school. But when Home Rulers tried to use Betsy's grave for the 1898 centenary, local loyalists smashed it to pieces to prevent its takeover by nationalists.[62]

59 Castlereagh to the duke of Portland, 3 June 1799: P.R.O., HO 100/87/5–7.
60 John Gamble, *A view of society and manners in the north of Ireland, in the summer and autumn of 1812* (London, 1813), pp 116–7; Elliott, *Partners in revolution*, p. 238.
61 U.C.D., I.F.C., MS 1925/9 and 1922/58. For the continuing tradition among northern nationalists that there may be remnants of 'old' radicalism among the Presbyterians, see also Ulster Folk and Transport Museum, transcripts of field recordings, vol. 16/5 and 20 (Tape R76.1), vol. 7/132 (Tape R.80/55).
62 W.G.Lyttle, *Betsy Gray or The Hearts of Down* (Newry, 1968), appendix 162–3. A synopsis of the story is in Stewart, *Summer Soldiers*, 227–9. See U.C.D., I.F.C., MS 976/346 for an example of how Betsy Gray has been incorporated into the nationalist canon.

SECTION IV

In 1798, Laurence McDonald, a weaver's reed-maker from Stratford-on-Slaney in County Wicklow, was twenty-seven years old. His passion was for fighting cocks, and he was a famous handler and 'feeder' (the skilled task of throwing the cock into the main at the right moment, trajectory and angle), and well regarded by the local gentry as a result. The day after the rebellion started, a drummer from a regiment stationed at Stratford-on-Slaney grabbed his favourite fighting cock. McDonald retrieved the cock and flung the drummer in the ditch. The infuriated drummer came back later with six soldiers to arrest McDonald who fled to the Glen of Imaal and joined the rebellion.[1] What is the historiographical moral of this vignette from 1798? Is this a case of pre-politicized motivation, a trivial story of cocks and robbers? Or does it reveal how broader issues of asymmetrical power surfaced in the daily routines of life?

The vexed issue of sectarianism still dominates most versions of 1798. As yet, the concept has been deployed in mechanistic, facile or even coarse ways, with little effort to see how such a catch-all term meshes with other categories of explanation.[2] Sectarianism remains (as Louis Cullen has described it) the *deus-ex-machina* of 1798 studies.[3] Because eighteenth-century Ireland was a confessional state, a clear line of separation cannot readily be drawn between 'sectarian' and 'political' motivation. Any opposition to the state could then be construed as motivated solely by sectarianism. It is precisely the strength of religious affiliation among an array of interrelated factors that is the relevant issue. Given that land was the basis of political power, that Protestants owned the bulk of the land, and that their ownership rested on a relatively recent victory in the pro-

---

1 *Personal recollections of Wexford and Wicklow insurgents of 1798 as collected by Revd Brother Luke Cullen O.D.C., 1793–1859* (Enniscorthy, 1960), pp 82–3. McDonald fought through the whole campaign, including that in Meath. He was arrested and consigned to the 'Croppy regiment'-the Irish fencible corps in the 89th regiment. He then reluctantly participated in the Egyptian campaign. He eventually got back to Dublin where he died in 1826.

2 From among a plethora of his recent articles restating this view, see Tom Dunne, 'Rebel motives and mentalities: The battle for New Ross, 5 June 1798', in *Éire-Ireland*, xxxiv (1999), 5–27.

3 L.M. Cullen, 'The United Irishmen: problems and issues of the 1790s', in *Ulster Local Studies*, xviii (1997), 15.

tracted struggles of the seventeenth century, it is practically impossible to separate the sectarian, agrarian and political dimensions of, for example, the secret
societies of the late eighteenth century. In these circumstances, Cullen has
observed that 'the facile description of the Defenders as sectarian becomes hope-
lessly naive'.[4] Indeed, one surprising conclusion could be drawn from 1798: the
closest circumstances to a religious civil war was the conflict between Presbyterians and Anglicans in Ulster. The involvement of clergymen on both sides in
Ulster was far greater than in the Leinster phase of the rebellion, despite the historiographical blind eye on it. The surprisingly active role of Anglican clergymen (many of them magistrates and yeoman officers) is another feature that has
been almost universally ignored.

Why then were contemporaries so besotted with Protestant/Catholic interpretations of what had happened to their society in 1798? One reason is that the
existing models of historical understanding offered a ready template into which to
set the events of 1798. For the Anglican loyalists who produced the early accounts,
1798 could be inserted into an Irish narrative that stretched back to 1690 and
1641, to the well-known accounts of King and Temple. Beyond that, it fitted into
a British narrative originating with Foxe's *Book of martyrs* and (in a wider European frame) into the Protestant martyrology of the St Bartholomew's Day massacres, the revocation of the Edict of Nantes and the persecution of the Vaudois
and Albigensians.[5] For conservative Protestants, the temptation to see the 1790s in
terms of the 1640s and the 1690s was well-nigh irresistible: '1641 renewed' was
FitzGibbon's abrupt summary (Kelly, chapter 15). An explanatory model which
viewed their role in Irish society as an enlightened vanguard of British values reinforced their self-appointed civilizing and Protestantising mission.[6]

The 1780s and 1790s strengthened and buttressed this mode of interpretation
within conservative Irish Protestantism, as the parent British state retreated
from its Protestant constitutional carapace under the twin pressures of the
expansion of empire into Catholic Canada and the pressing need to recruit Irish
Catholics as military fodder.[7] During the 1780s, the state had silently jettisoned
the old emphasis on 23 October (the anniversary of the outbreak of the 1641
rebellion) in its sectarian calendar in favour of the more ecumenical and politically neutral 17 March, St Patrick's Day.[8] The tight bundling of liturgy, com-

4 Ibid., p.16.
5 Tony Claydon and Ian McBride (eds), *Protestantism and national identity: Britain and Ireland c.1650–c.1950* (Cambridge, 1998).
6 Thomas Bartlett, 'A people made rather for copies than originals: The Anglo-Irish, 1760–1800', in *Int. Hist. Revd*, xii, 1 (1990), 12–25.
7 J.R. Hill, 'Religious toleration and repeal of the Penal Laws: An imperial perspective, 1763–1780', in *Archiv. Hib.*, xliv (1989), 98–109; Bartlett, *Fall and rise*.
8 Toby Barnard, 'The uses of 23 October 1641 and Irish Protestant celebration', in *E.H.R.*, cvi (1991), 889–920; James Kelly, 'The glorious and immortal memory: Commemoration and

memoration and politics which had held the Protestant political consensus together was stealthily unravelling. In the middle of the decade, Henry Grattan led the first sustained critique of the rights and privileges of the Established Church, notably on tithes.[9] The aggressive riposte by the church, spearheaded by Bishop Richard Woodward, precipitated a polemical warfare, enthusiastically joined by Presbyterians and Catholics, out of which crystallized the defensive concept of 'Protestant ascendancy.'[10] This re-stated the imperative that the British state must at all costs back the Established Church, 'the sheet-anchor of the constitution,' against the disruptive forces ranged around it. The conservative newspaper editor John Giffard concluded: 'There was but one sound principle of attraction which held Ireland in spite of all these disturbing forces: the Protestants, descendants of Englishmen, and united to them by religion as by blood, saw in the connection with Britain their own safety.'[11] This zero-sum sectarian thinking was summarised by George Ogle: 'Everything you grant in compliance with the claims of the Catholics is just so much lost to the Protestants.'[12]

Intellectual shifts in the 1780s encouraged an engagement with the Irish past that radically recast the standard Temple/King line. Grattan claimed that his conversion to supporting Catholic claims to citizenship followed a reading of John Curry's abrasive attack on the standard Protestant versions of 1641.[13] Efforts by William Crawford, Joseph Cooper Walker, Charlotte Brooke and others to detach Protestant Ireland from a restrictive colonial reading of its own history provoked a conservative backlash led by the Revd Edward Ledwich, who published a staunchly Protestant version of Irish history in 1790.[14] But the very

---

Protestant identity, 1660–1800', in *R.I.A. Proc.*, C, xciv (1994), 25–52; Bridget McCormack, *Perceptions of St Patrick in eighteenth-century Ireland* (Dublin, 2000); J.R. Hill, 'National festivals, the state and "Protestant ascendancy" in Ireland 1790–1829', in *I.H.S.*, xxiv (1984), 30–51.

9 Maurice Bric, 'The tithe system in eighteenth-century Ireland', in *R.I.A. Proc.*, C, lxxxvi (1986), 271–88; David Dickson, 'Taxation and disaffection in late eighteenth-century Ireland', in Clark and Donnelly (eds), *Irish peasants*, pp 37–63.

10 Historians of the eighteenth century have generally backed James Kelly's arguments rather than those of W.J. McCormack in relation to the origins of the concept and phrase: James Kelly, 'Eighteenth-century ascendancy: A commentary', in *E.C.I.*, v (1990), 173–87, references other articles in this sequence.

11 A.H. Giffard, *Who was my grandfather?* (London, 1865), p. 24.

12 Cited in E. Johnston-Liik, *History of the Irish parliament, 1692–1800* (Belfast, 2002), v, p. 392.

13 John Curry, *A brief account ... of the causes of the Irish rebellion ...1641* (London, 1747); on Grattan's conversion, Madden, *United Irishmen*, first series, second ed, [1858], i, p. 174. Ian Paisley in 1972 gave his audience a history lesson; 'I want to tell you something. Do you think God delivered the people of Ulster in 1641 to let Ulster perish in 1972? I don't. Do you think that God delivered us in 1798 to let us perish in 1972? I don't': Ian Paisley, *United Ireland. Never!* (Belfast, [1972]).

14 Joep Leerssen, *Mere Irish and fior-Ghael* (Cork, 1996). Ledwich later advised Musgrave.

outbreak of these battles of the books signalled that seismic cultural and political shifts were underway well before the 1790s. Presbyterians, buoyed up by the spectacular American experiment in separating church and state to the advantage of Dissenters, were willing to challenge the Erastian status quo. From 1779, radical Volunteers sought to broaden the Williamite tradition, presenting William of Orange as a defender of civil and religious liberties for all, rather than just for the Anglicans. This more pluralist William allowed Catholics to join publicly in the centenary celebrations at Derry and Drogheda in 1788 and 1789. There was also a renewed Whig emphasis on the shutting of the gates against the despot (which invited a radical interpretation) as opposed to the breaking of the siege, an episode that deprived the local community of agency.[15] Thus the siege commemoration moved to celebrate its Irish as opposed to its British dimensions, demonstrating that 'the better republicans were inside not outside the gates'.[16]

The United Irishmen astutely promoted Bastille Day (14 July) to downplay the divisive 12 July. This redefinition of the sectarian basis of the state provoked a conservative defence of William as an exclusively Protestant hero in the mid 1790s, most obviously in the newly formed Orange Order of 1795. This explains the enormous appetite that conservative Protestants displayed for Richard Musgrave's version of 1798, which reinvigorated the discredited Temple/King line. His Gothic history was soon to be joined by its fictional correlative – Protestant Gothic.[17] Musgrave's work was aimed more at British than Irish opinion; it drew from as it fed into the strengthening evangelicalism of Protestantism (the most significant British cultural response to the French Revolution) and it strengthened anti-popish elements.[18] The Ulster Evangelical Society was found-

15 This interpretation is not evident in two recent accounts of this episode: Ian McBride, *The siege of Derry in Ulster Protestant mythology* (Dublin, 1997); Brian Walker, 'Remembering the siege of Derry', in *Past & Present: History, identity and politics in Ireland* (Belfast, 2000), pp 1–28.

16 Comment by Joseph Johnston in 1939 [cited by his son Roy, *Irish Times*, 12 Nov. 2001].

17 An important work in progress is James Shanahan, 'Jacobins, Jacobites and jacqueries: The 1798 novel in the nineteenth century'. In poetry, United Irish production straddled three linguistic groups: Mícheál Óg Ó Longáin and Riocaird Bairéad in Irish, Henrietta Battier, John Corry, William Drennan and William Hamilton Drummond in English, James Orr in Ulster-Scots.

18 The justly celebrated statement on this is E.P. Thompson, *The making of the English working class* (London, 1968). In one sense, Linda Colley's *Britons* is a long footnote to Thompson's argument. For Thompson's own response to Colley, see his 'Which Britons', in E.P. Thompson, *Making history: writings on history and culture* (New York, 1994), pp 319–29. It is regrettable that Colley, following the advice of Roy Foster (p. 8), excluded Ireland from her already classic account. We have nothing of a comparable quality or sweep in Irish history: J.R. Hill, *From patriots to unionist: Dublin civic politics and Irish Protestant patriotism, 1660–1840* (Oxford, 1997) is a modestly conceived institutional history. David Hempton and Myrtle Hill, *Evangelical Protestantism in Ulster society, 1740–1890* (London, 1992), while exceptionally useful, sticks closely to a religious rather than a broader cultural history.

ed in 1798. Methodism also spread rapidly in this same period. Between 1791 and 1864, Anglican churches increased from 1,001 to 1,578. A similar impulse underpinned the 'Second Reformation' of the 1820s, which should be seen as a delayed response to the French Revolution. Similarly, the determined effort by state and church to regain control of popular education via national education stemmed from the belief that the 1790s had indicated the political danger of allowing a flourishing informal education sector (the 'hedge schools') to exist with minimal supervision. The pervasive role of schoolmasters in the United Irish organization at local level was one of the most disturbing aspects of the 1790s for conservatives: 'From this it follows then that education is your only resource; 'tis this alone can open to you all channels of instruction, and this will enable you to meet the enemy, who has secretly got possession, not only on equal terms, but with superior advantage.'[19] In this respect, the National School system was a riposte to the success not the failure of the hedge schools.[20] It suited both church and state that these schoolmasters be demonised as a prelude to gaining control over them, hence the surge of polemical writing which emphasized the lurid reading material, the inappropriate pursuit of Latin and Greek, and the character defects of the pedagogues themselves; none of this should be taken at face value.

In the 1790s, Irish evangelical families like the Tighes, Trenchs, Hams and Barnards were most prone to make a reflexive retreat to seventeenth-century apologetics when faced with the contemporary challenge. Musgrave shared this sensibility and preached that the British drive to relax the Penal Laws over the heads of more knowledgeable Irish Protestants had been a fatal mistake, whose evil fruit was the 1798 rebellion. Similarly, Irish Presbyterians were self-deluding in making common cause with Catholics, and Musgrave strove to widen the gap between them.[21] Rather than Burke, Musgrave was favoured by the Tories in the decades after the rebellion. The influence of his tome contributed to delaying the concession of Catholic Emancipation for three divisive decades.[22]

This strategic sectarian wedge was not just a paper product of Musgrave's

---

19 *Essay on the present state of manners and education among the lower class of the people of Ireland and the means of improving them* (Dublin, 1799), p. 7.

20 L.M. Cullen, 'Patrons, teachers and literacy in Irish 1700–1850', in Mary Daly and David Dickson (eds), *The origins of popular literacy in Ireland* (Dublin, 1990), pp 15–44.

21 Recent work on Musgrave includes; Dickson, preface to fourth edition; Whelan, *Tree of liberty*, pp 135–40; James Smyth, 'Anti-Catholicism, conservatism and conspiracy: Sir Richard Musgrave's *Memoirs of the various rebellions in Ireland*', in *Eighteenth-century Life*, xxii (1998), 62–73; M. Ó hÓgartaigh, 'Nineteenth-century interpretations of 1798', in Bull et al. (eds), *Ireland and Australia*, pp 24–33.

22 J.J. Sack, *From Jacobite to conservative: Reaction and orthodoxy in Britain, c.1760–1832* (Cambridge, 1993). Burke's rise to prominence as a conservative thinker dated to the Victorian period when Gladstone, primed by John Morley and Matthew Arnold, adopted a Burkean perspective on Irish affairs – that Ireland would have to be governed on 'Irish' rather than 'British' lines.

prodigious hyperactivity. On the ground in mid-Ulster by the mid 1790s, it became one of the most devastating weapons in the arsenal of counter-insurgency (Blackstock, chapter 16; Wilson, chapter 17). The yeomanry, after much government agonizing, was raised in 1796. The state's misgivings stemmed from their fear of unleashing a new and equally uncontrollable Volunteer army – 'a self-raised host of patriot soldiers'.[23] Yet the government desperately required amenable allies. Their solution was to retain centralized control over the new force and to monitor closely those to whom units were entrusted.[24] Having a local force to deal with low-intensity, sporadic and scattered insurgency allowed regular troops to be concentrated so as to meet the anticipated French invasion. The yeomanry provided an additional bonus to conservatives: it stiffened loyalist morale, counteracting the weather-vane tendencies of communities to follow the line of least resistance and to support whichever faction seemed dominant at any particular time. In mid-Ulster, there was a spectacular break-through when General John Knox, the army commander there, built an alliance with the local Orangemen. This drove a paramilitary wedge between the strongly United Irish areas to the east (in Antrim and Down) and the north-west (the Foyle/Mourne valley of west Tyrone, east Donegal and Derry), and the Defender territory of south Ulster.[25] The staunchly conservative area in the Lough Neagh crescent prevented what seemed all too possible in 1795 – an Ulster popular politics dominated by a homogeneously radical popular coalition from the Ards to Ardara. For the first time, conservatives spearheaded a non-elite organization with paramilitary capabilities and solid support across the social spectrum.

In considering the yeomanry, it is important however not to view them from an exclusively Ulster perspective. In that province, it faced initial antipathy, as they were painted as a betrayal of the province's cherished independent Volunteering tradition.[26] Elsewhere, there was much less opposition: the liberal gentry sponsored corps, with Catholics and United Irishmen joining them in substantial numbers. This pattern is clear in counties controlled by the Whigs (Kildare, Wicklow) or where they had a visible presence (Carlow, Wexford). Here one can identify Catholic officers as well as substantial rank and file membership. A sizeable segment of Catholic opinion, especially among the burgeoning propertied

---

23 Barrington, *Rise and fall*, p. 25.

24 Allan Blackstock, *An ascendancy army: The Irish yeomanry, 1796–1834* (Dublin, 1998).

25 See the map in Whelan, *Fellowship of freedom*, p. 44.

26 Ó Snodaigh's insistence on family continuity from Volunteer to yeomanry corps misses this crucial distinction: Pádraig Ó Snodaigh, *The Irish Volunteers, 1715–1793: A list of the units* (Dublin, 1995). This is profitably consulted alongside James Kelly, 'A secret return of the Volunteers of Ireland in 1784', in *I.H.S.*, cii (1989), 268–92.

27 Maureen Wall, *Catholic Ireland in the eighteenth century* (Dublin, 1989) is the appropriate starting point for this discussion. However, one should not over-emphasize the docility of Catholics; as many as one quarter of the *c*.300 members of the Back Lane parliament ended up joining the United Irishmen. See also Patrick Fagan, *Catholics in a protestant country: The papist constituency in eighteenth-century Dublin* (Dublin, 1998).

and mercantile interest, was solidly conservative.[27] Dublin in particular had a significant conservative Catholic presence.[28] In counties that had a moderate political tradition (Kilkenny, for example, under benign Ormonde tutelage), Catholics remained aloof from the United Irishmen and were prominent in the yeomanry. In counties where the government sought to undermine Whig leadership through promoting countervailing conservative elements, the composition of the yeomanry became a flash-point, culminating in the disbanding of liberal units, the expunging of Catholics, and the increasingly heavy-handed deployment of conservative-controlled units. In Kildare, Wicklow, Wexford and Carlow in the tense spring of 1798, this pattern appeared.[29] Only in April of that year did Dublin Castle feel sufficiently confident to introduce Knox's mid-Ulster innovation at national level. The incorporation of Orangemen as additional supplementary yeomen marked their transition from 'a bigoted set of men' to 'a political party' (Knox's term). We have a detailed description of the process in action in Belfast in 1797 from the United Irishman Thomas Potts, writing after the first Orange parade in the town in July:

> On Wednesday last, we witnessed one of the most extraordinary spectacles that ever was seen in the town of Belfast – a procession of Orangemen in favour of the Battle of the Boyne. All the people belonging to that party, men, women and children to the space of twelve or thirteen miles around, were assembled on the occasion, introduced as a show of strength and respectability of that class of people who attach themselves to government. Great preparations were made for several days and loyal expectation was wound up to the highest pitch. Everything was done by those in power to make the business as consequential as possible … We were told for several days that there would be at least twenty or thirty thousand of these respectable king-and-constitution men in the procession and that General Lake would review them … At length the twelfth of July old-style arrived and with it eighteen hundred and forty three Orangemen and about one hundred women, boys and girls, composed of the foulest dregs of meanness and corruption, a motley banditti fit only for 'treasons, spoils and strategems.' In truth, there was not one in a hundred worth five pounds and the greater part of their leaders were notori-

28 An under-utilized source is George Little (ed.), 'The diary of Richard Farrell, barrister-at-law, 1798', in *Capuchin Annual*, xv (1944), 326–38. The institutional church is well treated in Dáire Keogh, *'The French disease': The Catholic Church and radicalism in Ireland, 1790–1800* (Dublin, 1993).

29 L.M. Cullen, 'Politics and rebellion in Wicklow in the 1790s', in Ken Hannigan and William Nolan (eds), *Wicklow: History and society* (Dublin, 1994), pp 411–502. Although ostensibly about Wicklow, this article is also an indispensable account of the situation in Kildare.

ous and professional rascals. The real friends of government were so much ashamed of them that they endeavoured to circulate a report that they were only the lower orders of the Orangemen who assembled (though it is well-known that almost every soul of that class over a country containing a population of upwards of three hundred thousand persons were turned out). There were no spectators for the inhabitants all kept within their houses ... There was not anyone to be seen in the streets the whole time of the procession but boys, blackguards and Orangemen. These Orangemen are of the same banditti that disgraced Ireland but the county of Armagh in particular about three years ago where their devastations are yet to be seen as monuments of reproach and infamy to the government and misery and misfortune to the unhappy and persecuted Catholics, who were the object of their cruelties, till the information of the *Northern Star* and the mild principles of the United Irishmen put a stop to their depredations in that quarter and forced the most villianous part of them to seek their safety in flight, as appeared at the trials of some of the United Irishmen at Omagh last assizes. I am certain that if the Northern Star had still been in circulation, these miscreants would not have ventured to show themselves here, for before its suppression, they carefully concealed themselves like murderers and robbers, as they were sure to see their principles and their actions gazetted up for the execrations of mankind in the 'Paper of the People.' They were full of rage and disappointment, as they came here full of expectation that they would get money, drink and compliments from General Lake but he was most grossly deceived in them as well as in other matters by the liars and sycophants that communicate intelligence to him, for they had always been represented to him as being numerous and respectable ... no matter how illegally they act, provided they cry 'Church-and-King.'[30]

In looking at the partial link-up between the Orange Order, the military and the yeomanry, the danger exists of over-emphasizing the manipulative and top-down side of Orange organization (Wilson, chapter 17). Despite the historiographical consensus to the contrary, the Order in its early Ulster years was

30 Thomas Potts, Belfast, to Mr Atkinson, attorney, London, 14 July 1797, intercepted letter: N.A.I., SOC, II, 3097.
31 Robert Ogle Gowan (1803–1876) in Canada first stressed the genteel basis of early Orangeism in his *Orangeism: Its origins and history*, 3 vols (Toronto, 1859–60). His efforts to elevate the social status of early Orangeism (and with it that of his notoriously louche father John Hunter Gowan) stem from the soap-opera qualities of his own precipitate flight from Dublin to Toronto in 1829. Ogle, illegitimate son of Hunter Gowan and the god-child of George Ogle, forged his dying father's will in 1824. Hunter Gowan had sixteen children, three of them (including Robert Ogle) illegitimate sons born after his wife's death, and excluded from public participation in the family. Robert Ogle used local Orangemen belonging to his father's yeomanry corps

neither hierarchical, gentry-led nor Dublin-controlled: it retained a fraternal, autonomous, rural and local character.[31] The early leaders came from the mid-dling ranks of Ulster Anglican society (publicans, farmers, weavers, militia sergeants) who devised 'a system of their own creation'. The Order can be seen as a democratic manifestation, evolving out of the distinctive world of the Lough Neagh crescent where Anglicans were unusually well represented at every level of society. They retained a sense of their English origins, and saw no reason to dismantle the Williamite settlement that had positioned them at the top of the sectarian pecking order in Ulster. Their existence also meant that the state (coached by local notables) knew where to find unquestioning support when it needed it. Barrington believed that the reform project was deliberately under-mined by the injection of 'barbarous sectarial discord, a weapon without which the British government would have ever found Ireland too proud for the influ-ence of power and too strong for the grasp of annexation'.[32]

Emphasizing these points does not absolve historians from a responsibility of analysing how the Order fitted into the wider political context. The founding of the Order can be interpreted as a direct response to a complex power struggle within Armagh politics which resolved itself into a three-sided battle by the mid-1790s.[33] One faction was the moderate Charlemont interest, espousing the older Volunteer tradition of independence; it endorsed the Protestant interest but was not virulently anti-Catholic. A more radical group, spearheaded by Robert Cope, dismissed Charlemont as the increasingly out-of-touch leader of

to forge the will and bound them to secrecy with the Orange oath. He tested the accuracy of his forgery of his father's signature by sending a letter to Major Sirr, which fooled him. The ensu-ing court case raked up everything from incest (Hunter Gowan's grand-daughter married his son) to robbery (Robert Ogle stole one of the silver cups presented to his father for services ren-dered in 1798 and was prosecuted by his brother) in the Gowan family. The lurid details can be found in *Interesting trial: Hopkins against Gowan, Wexford spring assizes, Mar. 14 and 15 1827* (Dublin, 1827) [N.L.I., J.P. 997]. Gowan subsequently became the first grand master of the Orange Lodges of British North America. For an unintentionally hilarious effort by a historian to novelize Gowan's life, see D.H. Akenson, *The Orangeman: The life and times of Ogle Gowan* (Toronto, 1986). The Grand Orange Lodge of Ireland re-printed unchanged chapters from Gowan's 1859 history as *Murder without sin: The rebellion of 1798* (Belfast, 1996). No editorial or historiographical matter was provided, indicating that Gowan's views were still considered applicable in the 1990s.

32 Barrington, *Rise and fall*, p. 84.

33 This high political dimension to the Armagh Troubles has been emphasised by L.M. Cullen and Kevin Whelan. See Réamonn Ó Muirí, 'Killing of Thomas Birch'; ibid., 'Lt. Col. Lindley St Leger, United Irishman', in *Seanchas Ard Mhacha*, xi (1984), 133–200. For the precise details of the by-election, see C.F. McGleenon, 'Lord Gosford versus the 'Patriots': The Armagh by-election of 1794–5 and its sequel', in *Seanchas Ard Mhacha*, xvii (1998), 55–9.

34 Hugh White to W. Barber, Feb. 1797: N.A.I. RP 620/28/276. Jonah Barrington described Charlemont as 'too smooth and gentle to turn the vast machinery of revolution': *Rise and fall*, p. 73. He also observed that 'the moderate and cautious party in general followed the indecisive

the discredited remnants of 'the old rotten aristocratic Volunteers'.[34] Cope's faction supported the radical Volunteers and the Grattanite Whigs, opposed Dublin Castle, and flirted with the United Irishmen.[35] On the other side of Charlemont, a more hard-line group was led by Lord Gosford: it supported Dublin Castle, espoused 'Protestant ascendancy,' and flirted with the Orange Order.[36] The celebrated description of the Orangemen marching through Gosford's demesne on 12 July 1796 needs to be seen in this explicitly political context.[37] The Armagh by-election of 1795 produced a strong showing for Cope. He lost by only eighty votes. Conservatives subsequently depended on the emergent Orange Order to shore up their electoral support in the 1797 election. Opinion polarized and Charlemont was now marginalized.[38] Thus in the mid-1790s, compelling political and strategic reasons led Dublin Castle and local conservatives to view the Orange Order as a potentially crucial ally in treacherous territory.

The speed with which the Order had penetrated the militia demonstrates the success of the fledgling alliance; the partisan administration of law is another; their co-option into the yeomanry a third. While it would be unwise to give the government all the credit for sponsoring the Order's establishment and early growth, there is no doubt that it turned a conveniently blind eye to their excesses. This policy differs markedly from the state's earlier robust response to the predominantly Presbyterian Oakboys and Steelboys.[39] Prior to the rebellion, the

and feeble counsels of Earl Charlemont', and he criticised 'the slow and almost courtly approach of the Charlemont system': *Rise and fall*, p. 11.

35 We now need an update of the beautifully written but depoliticised biography of Charlemont by Maurice Craig, *The Volunteer earl* (Dublin, 1948). For more recent perspectives (still too partisan in their uncritical admiration), see Michael McCarthy (ed.), *Charlemont and his circle* (Dublin, 2001).

36 Hugh White described the resulting 'arming of the Orangemen or midnight robbers and burners [who] are completely organized and officered by government hacks': White to Barber, 15 Feb. 1797: N.A.I. RP 620/28/276. James Hope claimed that government functionaries like the Revd Philip Johnston of Lisburn 'organised a faction of intolerant, turbulent men into lodges like freemasons called the Loyal Orange Institution.' He also claimed that the institution in 1797 was 'under the nursing care of the magistrates' and that its members boasted that 'the government protected its institution and that judges were friendly to it': Hope, *Narrative*, p. 102.

37 This letter was first published in W.H. Crawford and Brian Trainor (eds), *Aspects of Irish social history, 1750–1800* (Belfast, 1969), p 179. This fine book established the study of late eighteenth-century history on much more solid archival footing. A similarly influential interpretative volume was Thomas Bartlett and David Hayton (eds), *Penal era and golden age: Essays in Irish history, 1690–1800* (Belfast, 1979).

38 Barrington jibed that Charlemont 'lived just long enough to experience and to mourn the fallibility of his predictions': *Rise and fall*, p. 74.

39 James Donnelly, 'Hearts of Oak, Hearts of Steel', in *Studia Hib.*, xxi (1981), 7–73; Eoin Magennis, 'A Presbyterian insurrection? Reconsidering the Hearts of Oak disturbances of July 1763', in *I.H.S.*, xxxxi (1998), 165–87; ibid., 'County Armagh Hearts of Oak', in *Seanchas Ard Mhacha* xvii (1998), 19–31, which brings together a useful collection of documents.

Order's spread had been confined to the Anglican corridor of the Lagan valley. It made little head-way in the Presbyterian districts in Antrim, Down, Derry and Donegal, where its church-and-king politics cut little ice with the Dissenters. Only some time after the rebellion (as late as the 1810s) did the Order become a genuine umbrella organization, militating against the notoriously fissiparous tendencies within Protestantism as a whole. A closer study of the relationship between Presbyterians and the Orange Order over its first generation is now badly needed, as is a study of its popular historiography. The revisionist treatment of Irish unionism is long overdue.[40]

A danger in focusing on United Irishmen and Orangemen in the 1790s is that the substantial sections of Irish opinion that were organizationally unattached tend to be discounted. Within Protestantism, a solid, quieter middle ground existed, equally distanced from Dublin Castle and from the United Irishmen. It despised the sectarian crudities of a FitzGibbon, a Musgrave or a Duigenan. This middle ground supported Cornwallis when he abandoned the hard-line policies of the previous Castle cabinet, and its acquiescence was vital to the passing of the Union. Less strident and epistolary than the shriller positions on either side of it, this constituency is easy to ignore: yet its quiet voices, like Maria Edgeworth and Mary Leadbetter, may be a truer guide to mainstream Protestant opinion than the endlessly quoted FitzGibbon, Foster and Downshire (O'Neill, chapter 18).[41] Mary Leadbetter, a well-placed, balanced and humane voice, abhorred the violence of the state as much as that of the United men. Her Quaker convictions of a shared identity, based on equality and community, offer an arresting counterpoint to the emphasis on a society irredeemably riven by sectarianism.[42] The middle-ground Protestant consensus on the political need to incorporate the

---

40 A laudable exception is Alvin Jackson, 'Unionist myths 1912–1985', in *Past & Present*, cxxxvi (1992), 164–85; see also Ian McBride's forthcoming work on the Presbyterian memory of 1798. Curiously the Orange Order is better served by two histories of its role in Scotland and Canada: E.W. McFarland, *Protestants first: Orangeism in nineteenth-century Scotland* (Edinburgh, 1994); Cecil Houston and W.J. Smyth, *The sash Canada wore* (Toronto, 1980).

41 A cautionary word is necessary on the Rebellion Papers, Dublin Castle's retrospectively compiled archive of the revolutionary period. This liberal Protestant perspective is almost totally missing: Deirdre Lindsay, 'The Rebellion Papers: An introduction to the Rebellion Papers collection in the National Archives, Bishop Street, Dublin', in *Ulster Local Studies* xviii (1997), 28–42.

42 Kevin O'Neill, 'Mary Shackleton Leadbetter: peaceful rebel', in Keogh and Furlong, *Women of 1798*, pp 137–62; Kevin O'Neill, 'Almost a gentlewoman: Gender and adolescence in the diary of Mary Shackleton', in Mary O'Dowd and Sabine Wichert (eds), *Chattel, servant or citizen*, pp 91–102. We await O'Neill's monumental editions of the diaries of a woman who has serious claims to be the best documented in the world for her life span (1758–1826). The most authoritative account of Edgeworth is the 'General Introduction' by Marilyn Butler, in Marilyn Butler and Mitzi Myers (eds), *The novels and selected works of Maria Edgeworth*, 9 vols (London, 1999), pp vii–lxxx.

Catholics survived the cataclysm of 1798, even in counties at its very epicentre like Wexford.[43] A predominantly Protestant electorate in that county consistently elected pro-Catholic candidates in the aftermath of 1798, most obviously in 1806.[44] Indeed the Protestant losers from the rebellion were those who pursued doctrinaire politics.[45] Hitherto dominant players like Fitzgibbon, Downshire, Ely and Ogle faded remarkably quickly into marginality.[46] Ogle was squeezed out of Wexford and lost the Dublin election of 1802: Lord Auckland claimed that 'it was the papists and the rebels that brought in La Touche, not for his sake but in opposition to Ogle, whom they hate above all men'.[47] Castlereagh was ignominiously booted out of the representation of County Down in 1805 as the Presbyterians took their revenge on him. Elsewhere support for Emancipation among mainstream Protestantism held up well until 1829. Once that delayed part of the Union compact was delivered, and once the tithe issue (a major

43 Three good examples of the liberal perspective can be found in the following pamphlets: Whitley Stokes, *Projects for re-establishing the internal peace and tranquillity of Ireland* (Dublin, 1799); William Bingley, *An examination into the origins and continuance of the discontents in Ireland, and the true cause of the rebellion* (London, 1799); Robert Bell, *A description of the conditions and manners as well as the moral and political character, education etc of the peasantry of Ireland such as they were between the years 1780 and 1790* (London, 1804).

44 A celebrated example of the liberal perspective was Judge Fletcher's 'Charge' to the Wexford grand jury in 1814, which excoriated the behaviour of its predecessor in 1798: *Judge Fletcher's charge to the Wexford grand jury of the county of Wexford at the summer assizes of 1814* (Dublin, 1814). The controversial Alcock–Colclough duel of 1806 which claimed the life of John Colclough of Tintern Abbey was also part of the fall-out from 1798 at the gentry level in Wexford.

45 The biggest losers were the Grattanites, who believed in an Ireland free of coercive British influence, political corruption and religious intolerance, and argued that their aims could be achieved in classic Whig style by political means and the force of public opinion alone. Grattan himself endured a rocky ride. Barrington described three phases in his reputation – 'Glory, Calumny, Resurrection' (Barrington, *Rise and fall*, p. 55). Trinity College commissioned a portrait of Grattan when his popularity was at its height in the early 1780s. The ecclesiastical fellows turned against him when he subsequently addressed the tithe issue in the late 1780s, refusing to allow the picture to be hung: 'When Lord Fitzwilliam went over, then up went Grattan; Lord Fitzwilliam being recalled, down again came Grattan. When the picture was up, it was neither a credit to Mr Grattan nor to the College – a mere daub, a twenty pounds portrait, and although a miserable thing of its kind, there were more boards called, more controversy over putting up and taking down poor Grattan's picture than on any questions of mathematics or natural philosophy that ever were argued in the university. It is said to be untrue that the portrait has been destroyed but it is papered up and stands behind the Provost's chair, ready for another exhibition when times change': Bingley, *Examination*, p. 20. According to William Sampson, the portrait had been consigned 'to a privy-house': Sampson, *Memoirs*, p. 214. W.E.H. Lecky revived Grattan's reputation at Trinity with his sympathetic coverage in *The leaders of public opinion in Ireland* (London, 1871), which provided the stimulus for the fine statue by John Henry Foley erected outside T.C.D. in 1876.

46 'Lord Clare was no longer consulted. His importance had expired with the Irish parliament': Barrington, *Rise and fall*, p. 15.

47 Cited in Johnston-Liik, *Irish parliament*, v, p. 393.

Presbyterian grievance) was largely resolved, liberal Protestantism refused to back the subsequent Repeal project, repudiated the confessional O'Connell and aligned itself with the centralizing state against Anglican and landlord privilege. Jonah Barrington put it succinctly: 'The protecting body of the country gentlemen have evacuated Ireland and in their stead we now find official clerks, griping agents, haughty functionaries and proud clergy.'[48] As the state pursued non-denominational education, centralised as opposed to local control of law and order, and eventually disestablishment of the Anglican church, liberal Protestantism slowly shifted from an anti-state stance to an increasingly unionist one. These shifts had all reduced Anglican dominance, tempered gentry arrogance and diminished the grounds of friction between Anglican and Dissenter, making possible a more homogeneous Protestant political stance. The first Home Rule crisis of the 1880s fatally wounded Ulster liberalism. Partition finally buried it.

48 Barrington, *Rise and fall*, p. 2.

15

'We were all to have been massacred':[1] Irish Protestants and the experience of rebellion

JAMES KELLY

Describing the capture on 28 May 1798 of the town of Enniscorthy, Lord Shannon reported to his son that it had been followed by 'a massacre of ... Protestants'. Shannon did not possess the full details, but his information that the dead included '4 clergymen and their families, ... [and] several gentlemen', and that 'women and children [were] not spared' suggested to him that the object of the rebels was to extirpate Protestants.[2] These were slim grounds upon which to adduce the apocalyptic language of 'massacre'. But as alarm spread through the Protestant community, conservatives like Shannon resorted reflexively to this claim, and to the conviction, reinforced by reports of the discovery on John Sheares a few days prior to the rebellion of a proclamation instructing rebels to 'spare no blood' and by rumours that the success of the rebellion in the capital 'depended on servants murdering their masters', that massacre was central to the insurgents' strategy.[3] Even those like Bishop Thomas Percy of Dromore who remained convinced during May that the prompt actions of the authorities had prevented a 'general uprising' reached the same conclusion. Reports from Wexford that 'hardly ... a Protestant' was left 'alive' and the discovery of a rebel oath in which they 'have openly avowed to spare no heretics, by which they mean Protestants' ensured that by early June Percy and many others concurred with Shannon that the rebellion was prompted by a 'popish plot' to clear the country of Protestants.[4]

---

1 Mrs Brownrigg's journal, 10 June 1798, in H.F.B. Wheeler and A.M. Bradley, *The war in Wexford* (London, 1910), p. 179.
2 Thomas Bartlett, *The fall and rise of the Irish nation: The Catholic question, 1690–1830* (Dublin, 1992), p.235.
3 M[aria] N[—] to Helen Clarke, 23 May: N.L.I., MS 13,837; G.A. Little (ed.), 'The diary of Richard Farrell', in *Capuchin Annual*, xv (1944), 332; Thomas to Anne Percy, 25 May 1798: B.L., Percy papers, Add. MS 32,335, ff 23–4. Sheares' proclamation actually stated that 'many of the tyrants have already bled; many more will bleed by the decrees of the revolutionary tribunals which will immediately be established' (idem., f. 24).
4 Thomas to Anne Percy, 21, 25, 26, 28, 29 May, 8 June 1798: B.L., Percy papers, Add. MS 32,335, ff 21–2, 23–4, 25, 27, 29–30, 33; Nancy Curtin, 'The origins of Irish republicanism:

Given the non-sectarian ideals of the United Irish leadership, it is tempting to dismiss this as a deliberately malicious construction by ideological opponents of the United Irish enterprise. However, because atrocities could be demonstrated, and because of the conviction, based on historical experience and quasi-theological enquiry, that Catholics were committed to the bloody extirpation of heresy, it was an interpretation many Irish Protestants had no difficulty accepting. Their readiness to do so was informed by their belief that many of their forebears had been massacred during a similar insurrection in 1641. Their sensitivities on this point were heightened by intermittent rumours, significantly prolific in the run-up to the rebellion, that Irish Catholics were intent on repeating their bloody enterprise. However, in 1798 it was reports from Wexford and Wicklow of rebel atrocities that convinced Protestants that this was actually happening. Already strongly established before the end of 1798, this interpretation became the orthodoxy of a reinvigorated conservative Protestantism in Britain as well as Ireland with the publication by Sir Richard Musgrave in 1801 of his monumental chronicle of the Protestant experience of rebellion, *Memoirs of the Irish rebellion of 1798*.

The readiness of Irish Protestants in 1798 to interpret the rising as a sectarian massacre derived in the first instance from the conviction of successive generations from the mid-seventeenth century that the Catholic population aspired to that end. This originated with the events of 1641 when hundreds of thousands of Protestants supposedly succumbed to the murderous intentions of Catholics. Modern analyses of 1641 challenge the contemporary Protestant contention that the insurrection was part of a European-wide 'Catholic war' aimed at eradicating heresy.[5] However, their experiences of flight, harassment and bereavement convinced Protestants otherwise, and the combined impact of emotive atrocity literature and hugely inflated estimates of the number of casualties left a deep impression, which the inauguration of an official commemoration sustained. Commemoration of the events of 1641 was authorized initially by an Irish act of state on 14 October 1642 which directed that a prayer service should be held 'in every cathedral and parish church or other usual place for common prayer' to thank God for 'deliverance'. But it only took concrete form in 1661 following the Irish parliament's decision that the Church of Ireland clergy should conduct a memorial service every 23 October in which an account of the 1641 rebellion was delivered stating that 'many thousands' of Protestants were massacred and attributing their demise to the actions of 'malignant and rebellious papists and … popish clergy'.[6] This partisan interpretation was derived from Sir John

The United Irishmen' (unpublished Ph.D. thesis, University of Wisconsin-Madison, 1988), p. 720; Little, ed., 'Farrell diary', pp 329, 330.

5 See, for example, Nicholas Canny, 'Ireland in the first British empire', in Bernard Bailyn and P.D. Morgan (eds), *Strangers within the realm: Cultural margins of the first British empire* (Chapel Hill, 1991), pp 54–7.

6 *An Act of state made by the Lords Justices and Councill of Ireland for the observation of the three and*

Temple's seminal *History of the Irish rebellion* (London, 1646), which also provided much of the raw material that was worked into the anniversary sermons
that were a highlight of both the liturgical and commemorative calendar of Irish
Protestantism.[7] It is notoriously difficult to measure the communal acceptance of
any belief. But the frequency with which reference was made by Irish and
English Protestants in the 1660s, 1670s and 1680s to 'the late Irish bloody massacre' and to the 'inhuman butchery' of 1641, and the scares animated in 1672,
1674 and 1680 by rumours that Catholics had determined anew 'to massacre ...
Protestants' suggest that this interpretation of the 1641 rebellion was firmly
embraced.[8]

Certainly, the accession to the throne in 1685 of James, duke of York, a
Catholic, prompted a palpable increase in reports that Catholics conspired to 'fall
upon' and massacre Protestants.[9] The unease to which this attested burgeoned
into anxiety and finally panic when Jacobites took control of Ireland following
James II's deposition in 1688. There is no evidence from Jacobite sources to suggest that a massacre of Protestants was contemplated. But Protestants in
England as well as Ireland were so persuaded this must ensue that, in a repeat of
what happened in the 1640s, broadsides with accounts of 'horrid and bloody
massacre[s] ... of several thousand of Protestants' streamed off the London
presses.[10] Few of the 'barbarous murders' and instances of 'revenge upon the

twentieth day of October yeerly to be a day of thanksgiving for the discovery and prevention of the hor
rible conspiracy and plot of the Papists to massacre all the Protestants in that kingdom (London,
1642); James Kelly, 'The glorious and immortal memory: Commemoration and Protestant identity in Ireland 1660–1800', in *R.I.A. Proc.*, C, xciv (1994), 27.

7 T.C. Barnard, 'The uses of 23 October 1641 and Irish Protestant celebrations', in *E.H.R.*, cvi
(1991), 889–920; Robert Eccleshall, 'Anglican political thought in the century after the revolution of 1688', in D.G Boyce et al. (eds), *Political thought in Ireland since the seventeenth century*
(London, 1993).

8 *The Irish colours displayed in a reply of an English Protestant to a late letter of an Irish Roman*
Catholique ... (London, 1662), p. 12; *A looking glass for England, being an abstract of the bloody*
massacre in Ireland ... (London, 1667); *A collection of certain horrid murthers in several counties of*
Ireland committed since the 23 of October 1641 ... (London, 1679); David Fitzgerald, *A narrative*
of the Irish Popish Plot for the betraying that kingdom into the hands of the French, massacring all
English Protestants there ... (London, 1680); 'Extracts from the journal of Thomas Dinely', in
Journal of the Kilkenny and South East of Ireland Archaeological Society, n.s., iv (1862–3), 40; [—]
to Dudley Loftus, 26 Nov. 1682 in *J.R.S.A.I.*, 4th series, iv (1876–8), 176; John Hanly (ed.),
Letters of Oliver Plunkett (Dublin, 1979), p. 317; John Oldmixon, *Memoirs of Ireland from the*
Restoration to the present time, containing ... a conspiracy to massacre the Protestants in 1674 ...
(London, 1716); *Anal. Hib.*, ii (1931), 91.

9 Christchurch letter, 31 Aug. 1786: B.L., Add. MS 15,894, f. 158; William King, *The state of the*
Protestants of Ireland under the late King James's government (London, 1692), p. 188.

10 *An account of a late horrid and bloody massacre in Ireland of several thousand of Protestants, procur'd*
and carry'd on by the Lord Tyrconnel and his adherents (London, 1688); *An account of the late bar*
barous proceedings of the earl of Tyrconnell and his soldiers against the poor Protestants in Ireland,
with them killing and driving some thousands out of Cork and Lymerick stark naked in the cold, their
besieging Bandon in taking the Hon. Captain Boyle and their bloody association to destroy all the
Protestants in that kingdom (London, 1689).

heretick' reported were based on real events. But the proliferation of reports of a general massacre and the panic engendered by the 'Comber letter', which maintained that Catholics intended 'to fall on and to kill and murder' Protestants on 9 December 1688, threats to blow up Protestant prisoners in 1689, and persistent rumours that the defeated Jacobites planned to burn the city of Dublin and put 'Protestants to the sword' heightened their fears that this was imminent.[11]

More worrying still was William King's conclusion that a Roman Catholic king was '*obliged … to destroy* his Protestant subjects'. This was not widely believed, perhaps. But the implication – that Protestants must be active in the defence of their Protestant constitution in church and state – was reinforced in the first half of the eighteenth century through regular reprints of Temple's *History*, incendiary annual 23 October sermons, cautionary lessons derived from reports of the persecution of Protestants in Polish Prussia in the 1720s and, most dramatically, through panics engendered by rumours of impending massacres such as were reported in 1705, 1714–15, 1726, 1739, 1743 and 1745.[12] The diminution of the Jacobite threat thereafter produced fewer reports of this ilk, but the conviction that Catholics merely awaited an opportunity continued to resonate. It is readily identifiable, for example, in Sir Richard Cox's passionate appeal to the electors of Dublin in 1749 to 'remember 23 October, 1641' in response to Charles Lucas' controversial assertion that England was complicit in the outbreak of rebellion in 1641; in Walter Harris's decision to entitle his refutation of John Curry's Catholic interpretation of that event, *Fiction unmasked* (1752); in the annual 23 October warnings about Catholic bloodthirstiness; and in the publication of massacre literature of which John Lockman's *A history of the cruel sufferings of the Protestants and others by popish persecutions* (1753) is a fine example. Combined, these served to convince mid-eighteenth Protestants that the extirpation of heretics remained a Catholic aspiration, as can be shown by further rumours, such as that reported from County Kerry in 1762, 'that a massacre was intended by the papists of Ireland ag[ain]st the Protestants of the kingdom'.[13]

11 *Full and true account of the late horrid and most barbarous massacre of the Right Reverend Bishop, and the reverend the Dean of Waterford …* (London, 1689); R. Gillespie, 'Irish Protestants and James II 1688–90', in *I.H.S.*, xxviii (1992), 128–9; George Bennett, *The history of Bandon* (Cork, 1869), pp 297–301; 'Diary of William King, D.D. Archbishop of Dublin', in *J.R.S.A.I.*, xxxiii (1903), 275, 279 and passim; *A true account of a plot lately discovered in Ireland for fireing the city of Dublin, and putting all the Protestants to the sword* (Dublin, 1690).

12 As note 7; Jacqueline Hill, *From patriots to unionists: Dublin civic politics and Protestant patriotism 1660–1840* (Oxford, 1997), pp 63–4; Gerard McCoy, 'Patriots, Protestants and papists', in *Bullán*, i (1994), pp 107–8; H.M.C., *Portland*, iv, 165–9; B.L., Stowe MS 229 (ii), ff 164, 195; Patrick Fagan, *Sylvester Lloyd* (Dublin, 1993), pp 81–3; Devonshire to [ ], 21 Sept. 1739: P.R.O., SP 63/402; M.B. Buckley, *Life and writings of Arthur O'Leary* (Dublin, 1868), pp 45–6; W.P. Burke, *The Irish priests in the penal times* (Waterford, 1914), p. 292.

13 J.G. McCoy, 'Court ideology in mid-eighteenth century Ireland' (M.A. thesis, St Patrick's College, Maynooth, 1990), pp 48–55; Eoin Magennis, 'A beleaguered Protestant: Walter Harris

The 'prodigious alarm' that this 1762 report generated in the south-west was due in no small part to Protestant anxiety at the activities of the Whiteboys and to the perception that they were being promoted by 'ffrench money and ffrench schemes'.[14] This fear eased with time. So too did the apprehension of massacre in the more tolerant atmosphere of the 1770s and 1780s. Encouraged by this, the popular Capuchin, Arthur O'Leary, and the young activist Matthew Carey were emboldened to suggest at the beginning of the 1780s that the reconstruction of 1641 as an anti-Protestant massacre 'should be effaced from the records of the nation as well as from the memory of man', but this was asking too much. Conservatives opposed to Catholic relief cited the papal boast that 'popery now is, and ever has been the same in all ages' in support of their conclusion that Irish Catholics would perpetrate 'the most horrid cruelties and massacres on the persons of Protestants' if they were given an opportunity.[15] There was less support for this point of view at that moment than at any point since the 1640s, but the reinforcement of conservative Protestantism prompted in the late 1780s by the perception that the Rightboys sought to undermine the Church of Ireland and, thereby, to weaken the 'the Protestant constitution in church and state' contributed to its rehabilitation. The key figure was Richard Woodward, Church of Ireland bishop of Cloyne, because he gave renewed respectability and substance to traditional anxieties about Catholic intentions by drawing attention to the presence in the consecration oath taken by Catholic bishops of the phrase *hereticos persequor et impugnabo* as evidence of the hostility of Catholic intent towards Protestants. This was not a licence to Catholics to massacre Protestants, but few conservatives chose to interpret it otherwise. As a result, not alone did the late 1780s witness the beginnings of the emergence of a more ideologically combative Protestantism determined to secure its 'ascendancy', it also witnessed the reanimation of the debate on massacre.[16]

The impact of this became apparent in the 1790s as the threat posed to the security of Protestant authority by popular movements like the Defenders and republican revolutionaries like the United Irishmen produced a flurry of reports of intended massacres in Ulster. One, dating from 1791, centred on a supposed plan to burn Newry town. This was followed in the winter of 1792–3 by a more general alarm prompted by rumours of a 'popish conspiracy' to massacre all

and the writing of *Fiction unmasked*, *Eighteenth-century Ireland*, xiii (1998), 86–111; John Brady, *Catholics in the eighteenth-century press* (Maynooth, 1966), p. 125; Lauder to Bandon, 10 Apr. 1762: T.C.D., Crosbie papers, MS 3821/248.

14 Lauder to Bandon, as note 13; Colles to Colles, 5 Apr. 1766: N.A.I., Prim collection, 87/91.

15 Arthur O'Leary, *Remarks on Mr Wesley's letter* (Dublin, 1780), p. 78; R.D. Edwards, 'The minute book of the Catholic Committee', in *Archivium Hibernicum*, ix (1942), 61; *F.J.*, 25 June 1778.

16 James Kelly, 'Interdenominational relations and religious toleration in late eighteenth-century Ireland', *Eighteenth-century Ireland*, iii (1988), 52–60; idem, 'The genesis of 'Protestant ascendancy', in G. O'Brien (ed.), *Parliament, politics and people* (Dublin, 1989), pp 93–127.

Protestants on the night of 15 February 1793.[17] Neither came to pass, but the readiness of Protestants to 'stand in arms all night' in 1793, and the articulation by Charles Brodrick in 1794 and Lady Louisa Conolly in 1795 of their fear that they would be 'guillotined', bear witness to mounting unease.[18]

Following the adoption by the United Irishmen of a revolutionary strategy in 1795, the apprehension of Protestants that they were targets for massacre heightened appreciably. It was fuelled by testimony offered at treason trials, such as James Weldon's in December 1795, that radicals contemplated 'massacring all ... Protestants', and that the Defenders employed passwords which committed them to this very action.[19] The fears became so acute that, in the late summer of 1796, Protestants in Ulster 'dare[d] hardly to go to bed at night', while the earl of Clare attested to official concern when he conceded to Lord Camden that if 'the opportunity were to offer, we should see the scenes of 1641 renewed'.[20] The anxieties which prompted such responses were fed by the 'horrid unheard of brutality' Protestants observed round them, by 'great talk of blood' and, in particular, by arms raids because they brought the threat of 'massacre' into their homes. This is vividly illustrated by William Clancy's observation in his report of an attack by Defenders on his home at Ballymount, County Dublin, that the expectation he would 'be murdered ... wrought a great change' in the political outlook of his erstwhile liberal cousin.[21]

As the level of disorder in society intensified in the spring of 1798, Protestants became increasingly disposed to conclude that a massacre was imminent.[22] For example, the report that a 'general rising' and massacre was to take place on St Patrick's Day 1798 caused many in mid-Ulster to remain on the alert overnight and to prompt the doubling of the guard at Derry. There is less information on the reaction elsewhere, but rumours of a 'design ... to exterminate the Protestants' were widely circulated, as were destabilizing counter claims from radicals that the oath taken by Orangemen committed them to 'exterminate' Catholics.[23] Concern was most acute in Dublin because of information

17 L.M. Cullen, 'The United Irishmen: problems and issues of the 1790s', in *Ulster Local Studies*, xviii, 2 (1997), 23–5; Hill, *From patriots to unionists*, p. 239; Curtin, *United Irishmen*, p. 373; C.J. Woods (ed.), *Journals and memoirs of Thomas Russell* (Dublin, 1992), p. 70.

18 D. Jenkins, 'The correspondence of Charles Brodrick', in *Irish Archives Bulletin*, ix–x (1979–80), 46; E. Burgess, 'Lord Edward's aunt: How Lady Louisa Conolly and her sisters faced the rebellion', in D. Keogh and N. Furlong (eds), *The women of 1798* (Dublin, 1998), p. 166.

19 *Walker's Hibernian Magazine*, 1796, pp 77, 79; Curtin, *United Irishmen*, p. 166. The password referred to is Eliphismatis.

20 Clare to Camden, 28 Aug. 1796: K.A.O., Camden papers, U840/0183/6.

21 Anne to John Bewley, 19 Nov. 1797: Friends Historical Library, Dublin, Bewley papers; William to James Clancy, 22 Aug., 1797, 25 Jan. 1798: N.L.I., Clancy papers, MS 20,626. I am grateful to Dr Dáire Keogh for the first reference.

22 William to James Clancy, 15 Feb., 12 Mar., 4 Apr. 1798: N.L.I., Clancy papers, MS 20,626.

23 [—] to Anne Tottenham, 12 Mar.: La Touche papers, N.L.I., Reports on private collections, no 174, pp 1896–7; Jones to O'Hara, 30 Mar.: N.L.I., O'Hara papers; Tighe to Ponsonby, 21 Apr.

received by the authorities on 12 May that the United Irishmen were recruiting servants to gain access to the houses of 'the principal people' to assassinate them. As a result, before the first reports of atrocities were received from Wexford in late May, Protestants were predisposed to believe that they were targets for massacre and, by implication, to interpret any violence against them in equivalently apocalyptic terms.[24]

Given this background, it is not surprising that the atrocities reported from Wexford following the outbreak of rebellion there caused widespread panic among Protestants throughout the kingdom. Like their predecessors in 1689, those who could left. There was such an exodus that it was reported from Waterford on 6 June that 'there is not a female in the rank of a gentlewoman that has not fled', and from Newry, four days later, that 'the barbarities in Wexford occasion'd a most precipitate flight of ... gentry and clergy'. These are exaggerations, but it is clear that a combination of parental and paternalistic solicitude ensured that all ships heading east carried an unusually high complement of worried women and frightened children, and that they travelled, as Edward Hatton of Cork observed, with the belief that they had left their husbands and fathers at 'the mercy of the insurgents'.[25] Fear of death also prompted ten clergymen from the diocese of Ferns to take refuge in Wales, and caused the primate and the bishops of Ossory, Ferns, Clogher, Kilmore and Down either to take flight or to despatch their families to safety in early June.[26] All left bearing 'alarming reports'. Some of these were little more than the outcome of the inconveniences normally experienced by civilians in conflict zones, but they were given impetus as well as piquancy by the apprehension, vividly articulated by one of Bishop Percy's servants, that he 'expect[ed] death' when the rebels reached Dromore.[27]

In fact, for all the reports of 'terrible panic', the rising in Antrim and Down caused local Protestants only a *soupçon* of the 'terror' felt by their brethren in

---

1798: N.L.I., Wicklow papers, MS 4813, partly printed in G.H. Bell, (ed.), *The Hamwood papers* (London, 1930), p. 292; Orangeman's oath dropped at Mallow, 8 May 1798: National Library of Scotland, Lothian papers, MS 5750, ff 133–4.

24 Information of Thomas Kennedy, 12 Mar.: N.A.I., RP, 620/23/59; Hill, *From patriots to unionists*, p. 256; Thomas to Isabella Barnard, 15 May 1798, in A.D. Powell (ed.), *Barnard letters, 1778–1824* (London, 1928), p. 86.

25 Cook to Sutton, 6 June: N.L.I., Reports on private collections, no. 218; Warburton to Fitzwilliam, 10 June 1798: Sheffield City Library, Fitzwilliam papers, f. 30; St Leger to Hutchinson, 9, 16 June: N.L.I., Hutchinson papers, MS 8925; Hatton to Eliot, 6 June 1798: Eliot Hawood (ed.), *Eliot papers* (2 vols, London, 1895), i, pp 105–6; A.T.Q. Stewart, *The summer soldiers: The 1798 rebellion in Antrim and Down* (Belfast, 1995), pp 194–9.

26 Thomas to Anne Percy, 11, 13 June, 13 July: B.L., Percy papers, Add. MS 32,335, ff 37–8, 42, 64; Cleaver to Grenville, 8 June 1798: B.L., Grenville papers, Add. MS 41,855, ff 156–60; Percy to Anderson, 16 Apr. 1800: W.E.K. Anderson (ed.), *The correspondence of Thomas Percy and Robert Anderson* (New Haven, 1988), p. 24; Little (ed.), 'Richard Farrell's diary', p. 332.

27 Thomas to Anne Percy, 13 June, [—] to Percy, 12 June: B.L., Percy papers, Add. MS 32,335, ff 42, 44–5.

south Leinster, as their experiences in May and June attest.[28] One of the most vivid illustrations of this is provided by the diary of Elizabeth Richards of Rathaspick, Clonard, County Wexford. Though from a liberal family, Elizabeth Richards was seized by deep alarm as the 'dreadful intelligence' of rebel victories in late May was accompanied by the claim that 'every Protestant is to be murdered'. Imagining 'the infernal pikes ... at our breasts', she and her female relatives remained awake for most of the night of 30 May contemplating death and jumping with 'terror' each time they heard 'shouts or rather yells of joy' from rebels in nearby Clonard.[29] That night passed without incident, but claims by 'people who had flown from Wexford ... that a massacre of the Protestants was intended and would undoubtedly take place', and from a 'papist' that the strategy was 'first [to] murder the Orangemen' ensured that Richards continued to fear the worst. 'Several Protestants' close to her were so 'terrified' that they 'abjured their faith and suffered themselves to be christened by Romish priests' in order to secure letters of protection. Elizabeth came under pressure to do the same. On being informed on 1 June that 'the massacre of the Protestants would take place that night' and that she would die 'unless [she] consented to be christened', she met with a priest but, unlike her mother, she remained faithful to her beliefs.[30] She was marked by the episode, however. Following the arrest of Colonel Le Hunte for possessing an orange firescreen, she categorically rejected the rebels' claim that they targeted Orangemen and not Protestants. 'This Orange business is only a pretext for murdering Protestants', she noted bitterly before concluding fatalistically that she and others of her family would 'be murdered ... if we cannot effect an escape'.[31]

Elizabeth Richards survived the rebellion unscathed. Indeed, unlike some Wexford Protestants, she appears not to have witnessed a killing. Those like Isabella Brownrigg of Greenmount who did needed little persuasion that the 'plundering and butchering every Protestant ... not absolutely favourable to their cause' was integral to the 'religious war' being pursued against them. Given that she felt it necessary to assure her daughter that she would die before her on the commencement of the massacre at Wexford Bridge, and believed she only escaped being piked by the arrival of the military, such a conclusion is not unexpected.[32] It was echoed by Barbara Lett, though she used the term 'massacre' more sparingly. She applied it to the 'carnage' that took place at Wexford Bridge, where her father died. And it is clear from her account of her harrowing experiences in *postbellum* Enniscorthy (where her life was threatened because of her Orange connections, where she witnessed the brutal murder of John Pounden of

28 Thomas to Anne Percy, 13 June, 13 July 1798: B.L., Percy papers, Add. MS 32,335, ff 42, 64.
29 Elizabeth Richard's diary, pp 2–3, 7–9: N.L.I., Mic. p. 6486.
30 Ibid., pp 10–13.
31 Ibid., pp 28–9
32 Mrs Brownrigg's journal, pp 166, 175, 179, 185–92 and passim.

Daphne and where she was encouraged to convert to Catholicism to save her life), from her description of the insurgents as 'our bloodthirsty enemies', and from her relief at being 'set free from the yoke of Popish persecution' following the battle of Vinegar Hill, that she accepted the general conclusion of Protestants in the county that their very existence was threatened.[33]

Indeed, what is striking about the accounts by Wexford Protestants of their experiences in May and June 1798, whether they were written at the time or compiled later, is their virtual unanimity that the rebels were motivated by anti-Protestant as well as anti-Orange sentiments. Occasionally, attempts are made to distinguish between the two. This is certainly the implication of the claim in one anonymous account that individual insurgents explicitly sought to send 'an Orange man to the Devil' because it would guarantee them 'eternal reward'. However, the threat the rebellion posed to their lives, the frequency with which relatives, friends and acquaintances are reported as having met their death, and the repeated reference to the atrocities perpetrated at Wexford Bridge, Sculla-bogue and the camp at Vinegar Hill ensured that this distinction was not upheld. Based on their experiences and observations, most concluded that the object of the rebellion was 'to kill' Protestants whatever their political views, and that this evil design was only prevented by their military failure. There is a certain incon-sistency within and between some accounts as to whether the rebels' preference was to 'massacr[e] every Protestant man' or 'to massacre all Protestants without distinction of age or sex', but most do not entertain such refinements.[34] Indeed, it is an indication of how convinced Wexford Protestants were that they were targeted for massacre that though Quakers were seldom victimized, one of their number, Joseph Haughton, interpreted the appearance at Wexford on 20 June of the controversial flag bearing the letters MWS, which Protestants translated to mean 'Murder Without Sin', as the signal for the commencement of 'a massacre of every class who were not of the Romish Church'.[35] In this context, it is hardly surprising that those of more orthodox religious views defined the rebellion as a 'popish plot' and attributed the deaths of the estimated '7 to 8,000 [that] fell in the cause of loyalty' to Satan and popery as well as to the 'savage murderers' that perpetrated the killings.[36]

Someone who shared this interpretation in the broad sense was the Church of Ireland bishop of Ferns, Euseby Cleaver. A political as well as religious conserva-

33 'Mrs Barbara Newton Lett diary', *The Past*, v (1949), 119–42.
34 As note 33; S.L. de Montfort (ed.), 'Mrs Pounden's experiences during the 1798 rising in Co. Wexford', in *Irish Ancestor*, viii (1976), 4–8; [—] to Murray, [1798], in McMurray letters (in private possession); J.E. Vincent (ed.), *The memories of Sir Llewelyn Turner* (London, 1903), p. 42; Jane Adams narrative: B.L., Add. MS 21,142; Stewarts Kalendar for 1798, May 1798: N.L.I., Hatch papers, MS 11,994; Wexford in 1798: N.L.I., MS 25,004; Brownrigg's journal, pp 191–2.
35 Joseph Houghton's narrative of events during the Irish rebellion, 1798: N.L.I., MS 1576.
36 Diary of Richard Hobart, pp 148–9: N.L.I., microfilm p. 7363.

tive, Cleaver observed the rebellion from the safety of Dublin, where he anxious-ly queried the fate of his Protestant servants and gleaned to his dismay that the episcopal palace upon which he had expended £13,000 was 'reduced to a skele-ton'.[37] Like most of his religion and background, Cleaver did not doubt the reports he received from Wexford that the rebels' object was 'Protestant blood' as he attested by informing Thomas Grenville on 1 June that 'the Protestants ... have been horribly massacred'. A week later, as he readied his family to depart these 'scenes of murder', reports of priestly involvement caused him to portray it as 'popish' and to imply that most Catholics were complicit. Citing 'docu-ments found in the possession of prisoners and traitors who have been seized' and 'confessions' elicited by the 'rigour of military law', he gloomily informed Grenville 'that there is not one Papist in one hundred who has not confederated under the most solemn sanction to extirpate the whole race of heretics from the island'.[38]

This reductivist interpretation was informed by Cleaver's deep suspicions of Catholicism as well as by his conviction that 'the repeal of the Popery laws' was a mistake. Given that five of his clergy died in the rebellion and that he had con-cluded by late July that the 'chief injuries' he had sustained were perpetrated by Catholics 'indebted to my good offices', some of whom, he informed the earl of Egremont, 'expressed much impatience to murder both me and Mrs Cleaver', his embrace of the massacre thesis is unsurprising.[39] This is not the construction placed today on the pattern of random, and essentially opportunistic atrocities perpetrated upon Protestants,[40] but Cleaver's response was that preferred in Protestant circles in the summer of 1798.

One powerful figure who readily accepted that this was the correct conclusion was the speaker of the House of Commons, John Foster. He explained to his old friend Lord Sheffield on 5 June that 'the whole is ... a Popish conspiracy' and that 'Protestants young and old' were being 'massacre[d] all through the coun-try'.[41] Less well-connected but at one with Foster in her reading of events, Sara Tighe of Rosanna, County Wicklow, was persuaded by reports that 'many have perished' to conclude 'that the tragedy of 1641 is acting over again'. Indeed, as

---

37 Cleaver to Grenville, 31 May, 7, 8 June: B.L., Grenville papers, Add. MS 41,855, ff 148–9, 152, 156–60; Cleaver to Egremont, 6 July: Petworth House, Egremont papers; Thomas to Anne Percy, 22 June 1798: B.L., Percy papers, Add. MS 32,335 f. 59.

38 Cleaver to Grenville, 1, 7, 8, 11 June: B.L., Grenville papers, Add. MS 41,855, ff 150, 152, 156–60, 161; Cleaver to Hawkins Browne, 25 June 1798: Beinecke Library, Osborn Collection, Cleaver letter.

39 Patrick Comerford, 'Church of Ireland clergy and the 1798 Rising in Wexford', in Liam Swords (ed.), *Protestant, Catholic and Dissenter: The clergy and 1798* (Dublin, 1997), pp 232–5; Cleaver to Grenville, 8 June: B.L., Grenville papers, Add. MS 41,855, ff 156–60; Cleaver to Egremont, 24 July [1798]: Petworth House, Egremont papers.

40 Daniel Gahan, *The people's rising: Wexford 1798* (Dublin, 1995), passim.

41 Cited in Bartlett, *Fall and rise*, p. 235.

well as 1641, she linked it with the St Bartholomew's Day massacre in France.[42] The ease with which Tighe fitted events in Wexford, and Wicklow into this familiar Protestant gazetteer of Catholic massacres could not have occurred if she did not believe this was always likely. But of greater consequence was the alleged discovery, upon the body of Fr Michael Murphy after the battle of Arklow on 9 June, of a letter which spoke of administering 'a tincture of poison and pike … against heretics' and a document entitled the 'articles of popish faith' which affirmed 'that the late holy massacre was lawful; and justly put into execution against Protestants', and that 'we are bound to drive heretics out of the land with fire, sword and faggot'.[43] The authenticity of these documents may be questioned, but proliferating reports that Protestants in County Wicklow were murdered because they were 'heretics' or 'Orangemen', and that there was 'not one of the Romish religion that has not taken the oath to destroy us' suggest that few Protestants were seized by doubts.[44] Sara Tighe was certainly convinced. As her mental landscape filled up with 'stories about … murders [and] escapes', with images of the difficulties faced by the thousand 'fugitives' that 'fled from Wexford', and the strain of 'wretched night[s]', she had little difficulty crediting reports from Waterford and Cork that a systematic and 'diabolical plot' was afoot 'to destroy all the Protestants'.[45]

Sara Tighe's reaction was shaped by her knowledge of events in County Wicklow. The apprehension of massacre was less keenly felt in those areas where the rebellion was less severe. Nonetheless, incidents like that at Rathangan where 'several Protestants were murdered' coalesced with reports of the discovery of 'oaths … in the pockets of people kill'd … pledging themselves to Jesus Christ and the Virgin to murder every heretic till they were up to their knees in blood' also created a mood of acute foreboding. Arising out of this, Protestants, like the wife of the dean of Kildare, were willing to believe that Catholic apothecaries were preparing 'doses of poison … to sell to the servants of the great families' and for 'mix[ing] in the officers' messes'.[46] Indeed, Protestant susceptibilities were so heightened that the Church of Ireland bishop, William Barnard, report-ed from Limerick, which remained largely undisturbed, 'that a general massacre

42 Tighe to Ponsonby, 4 June 1798: Bell (ed.), *The Hamwood papers*, p. 294; N.L.I., Wicklow papers, MS 13,615.
43 Lambert to Edward Bayly, June: Bayly papers, N.L.I. Reports on Private Collections, no. 96, pp 949–50; Articles of Popish faith found on the body of Priest Murphy killed at the battle of Arklow, [1798]: N.L.I., Musgrave papers, MS 4156, f. 49.
44 [—] to Tottenham, 27 July 1798: La Touche papers, p. 1897; *The trial of Billy Byrne of Ballymanus* (Arklow, 1996), pp 6, 11, 18–9, 22, 24–5, 26, 27, 45.
45 Tighe to Ponsonby, 12/13, 16, 20 June, 2 July, 8 Aug.: Bell (ed.), *Hamwood papers*, pp 295–300; N.L.I., Wicklow papers, MSS 4813, 13615.
46 John to Francis Trench, 8 June: Trench papers, N.L.I., Reports on private collection, no. 439 p. 3003; Trench to Cooke, 19/20 June 1798: T.R.F. Cooke-Trench, *A memoir of the Trench family* (privately printed, 1897), pp 81–7.

was to have accompanied the conflagration' local rebels had in mind.[47] Barnard's apprehensions on this point soon eased, but in common with most Protestants he remained distinctly nervous throughout the summer months. Certainly, rumours, such as those reported by Anne Bewley in July that local rebels promised that 'if they get Rathangan again in their power they will not leave a Protestant alive', or that condemned by Bishop Caulfield of Ferns in September 'that the Roman Catholics intended an immediate rising and general massacre of the Protestants' predisposed them to justify the ruthless tactics employed in putting down the rebellion.[48]

With the defeat of the rebellion in Wexford, public reference to massacre diminished. Protestants remained uneasy, however, as 'murders and other outrages' continued to take place.[49] Despite this, the most remarkable feature of their response to the news of the arrival of a French expedition at Killala on 22 August was the calm with which it was received: Sir Richard Musgrave reported to Bishop Percy that 'this intelligence has not created the smallest alarm'.[50] Concern mounted as the French force forged an alliance with local rebels and embarrassed the crown forces at Castlebar, but the absence of reference to massacre along the lengthy route the rebel force followed ensured this was kept within proportion.[51] This is not to say it did not exist. The wife of one Protestant clergyman clearly felt her end had come because she later attributed her 'miraculous escape from the intended massacre' to 'that great and omnipotent being, the ruler of the universe'.[52] This perception was reinforced by the alleged discovery of a notice, affixed to church doors in County Westmeath, addressed to local Protestants warning them that 'the earth shall no longer be burthened with bloody heretics'. Reports by captured French officers that they were urged by

47 William to Isabella Barnard, 3 June 1798: Powell (ed.), *Barnard letters*, pp 89–91.

48 Thomas to Isabella Barnard, 16, 18, 24, 29 June: Powell (ed.), *Barnard letters*, pp 91, 95, 97, 98; Anne to Samuel Bewley, 7 July 1798: Bewley papers; Caulfield to the clergy of Ferns, 13 Sept. 1798: P.F. Moran (ed.), *Spicilegium Ossoriense* (3 vols, Dublin, 1874–84), iii, p. 572; Thomas to Anne Percy, 17 June, 23 July: B.L., Percy papers, Add, MS 32,335, ff 50, 68; Patrick to James Clancy, 30 June: N.L.I., Clancy papers, MS 20,626; Druitt to Eliot, 18 July: Howard (ed.), *Eliot papers*, i, p. 107.

49 Honora to Morgan Kavanagh, 5 July: Kavanagh papers, N.L.I., microfilm p. 7155; Thomas to Anne Percy, 4 July, 7 Aug.: B.L., Percy papers, Add. MS 32,335, ff 60, 73; Roche to [—], 1798: N.L.I., Roche letter, MS 24,549; Thomas to Isabella Barnard, 17 Aug. 1798: Powell (ed.), *Barnard letters*, p. 101; Patrick to James Clancy, 9 July, William to James Clancy, 16 Sept: N.L.I., Clancy papers, MS 20,626.

50 Musgrave to Percy, 24, 27 Aug. 1798: N.L.I., Musgrave papers, MS 4157, ff 85, 87.

51 Eliza Edgeworth's Journal, Sept. 1798: N.L.I., Edgeworth papers, MS 18,756; C.A. Webster, *The diocese of Cork* (Cork, 1920), pp 339–40; Trumbull to Wadsworth, 20 Sept.: Yale University, Sterling Library, Trumbull papers, MS 506/1/3; Tweedie to Minto, 27 Aug., Woodford to Minto, 27 Aug., 1, 5 Sept.: National Library of Scotland, Minto papers, MS 11,194, ff 116, 118, 124, 128; Malone to Burney, 6 Sept. 1798: Folger Library, Washington, Burney papers, MS C.a.2 (2).

52 [—] to [Anne —], 10 Oct. 1798: N.L.I., MS 8283.

their Irish allies, whom (Protestants reported with satisfaction) they deemed 'the greatest savages they ever met', 'to murder the Protestant clergy' confirmed them in their conviction that their escape was providential.[53]

As this attests, the fear of massacre ensured, as the year's end approached, that Irish Protestants regarded Catholics and Catholicism with palpably greater antipathy and suspicion than had been the case before the outbreak of rebellion. One suggestive indicator is provided by their increased disposition to employ the term 'savages' when referring to the Catholic population.[54] The implication – that the massacre of Protestants was and remained a Catholic objective – was underlined by Sara Tighe. Angered by continuing unrest in County Wicklow in the late autumn, arising out of which a number of Protestants were 'cruelly and treacherously killed', she linked what transpired in Ireland in 1798 with the 'crusade' that had resulted in the premature death of 70,000 Albigensians and Waldensians in 1209, the St Bartholomew's Day massacre in which 25,000 Huguenots were killed in 1572, and the 1641 rebellion 'which took away the lives of 100,000 in this country'. On the basis of this, she concluded severely that 'there is something anti-Christian in the Roman Church'.[55]

Sara Tighe's inability to offer any estimate of the number of Protestants that had fallen victim to 'massacre' in 1798 is striking. The 'melancholy distress' reported by Protestants in south Leinster, once the initial elation occasioned by their delivery from the fear of destruction evaporated, was intensified by their continued scarcity on the ground in south Leinster and by anger and resentment that the government seemed determined 'to gloss over our misfortunes and the massacres of Protestants'. Like Edward Hardman of Drogheda and many others, Tighe singled out Lord Cornwallis for aspersion because of the failure of 'the public prints to relate the injuries done to his majesty's loyal Protestant subjects', as a result of which, one of Bishop Percy's correspondents opined, 'we know not the hundredth part of the dreadful scenes that have happened'. In this context, Tighe expressed the widely shared conviction when she argued that a salutary purpose would be attained if 'the cruelties exercised by the Roman Catholics against the Protestants' were 'collected and given to the public'.[56] Sir Richard Musgrave, MP for Lismore, concurred. A committed advocate of 'Protestant ascendancy', he was determined that the lessons of the 'savage barbarity' of the rebellion would not be lost. With this in mind, he undertook to write a history of the event which, like its exemplar Temple's history of the 1641 rebellion, was to

53 Balfour to Cooper, 9 Sept.: N.L.I., Townley Hall papers, MS 10,362/5; Thomas to Anne Percy, 27 Oct. 1798: B.L., Percy papers, Add. MS 32,335, f. 94.

54 As note 53. See also Edward to Lambert Bayly, 14 June: Bayly papers.

55 Tighe to Ponsonby, 9 Oct., 20 Nov. 1798: N.L.I., Wicklow papers, MS 4813.

56 Tighe to Ponsonby, 20 Oct. 1798: N.L.I., Wicklow papers, MS 4813; Hardman to Minto, 25 Nov. 1798: Minto papers, MS 11,194, ff 196–9; H. W[aring] to Percy, 15 Mar. 1799: N.L.I., Musgrave papers, MS 4156, f. 34.

be grounded upon documented experiences in anticipation that this would galvanise Protestants to rally to the defence of the 'Protestant constitution'.[57]

Musgrave was not the only supporter of 'Protestant ascendancy' to recognise that the events of May and June 1798 provided them with a glorious opportunity to promote their political agenda. Within days of the outbreak of the rebellion, the pages of the *Dublin Journal* reverberated with accounts of rebel atrocities and priestly participation in support of the contention that the rebellion was a 'popish plot' against Protestantism. This claim was endorsed by Patrick Duigenan in an attack on Henry Grattan, and implicitly sustained by Musgrave himself in two publications – an anonymous defence of the stern security actions taken by the state in 1796–7 as necessary to 'subdue a ferocious and sanguinary spirit that would have disgraced the Tartars and Saracens' and a commentary, published under the penname Verax in the *Dublin Journal* in August 1798 – in which he accused the Catholic clergy of complicity in the massacre of Protestants.[58]

Musgrave's primary purpose, he explained to Bishop Percy, was 'to vindicate the Protestant church' and to defend 'the constitution in church and state' by demonstrating that the rebellion was intrinsically sectarian.[59] In order to do this, he had to show, as Temple had done, that Protestants were targeted for elimination. With this in mind, he applied to witnesses, clergy, soldiers and country gentlemen for statements and information as a result of which he assembled a 'volume of affid[av]its' which allowed him to commence 'composing the Wexford part of my history' in October 1798; he borrowed and collected correspondence and documents; and he studied 'trial proceedings' and such 'notes' as he was permitted access by general officers. The cumulative impact of 'the thousand curious anecdotes of the atrocities of the Co[unt]y Wexford' he gathered not just confirmed his conviction that Protestants were targeted, but affirmed his belief as to 'the sanguinary principles inherent' in Roman Catholicism.[60] His conclusions on this point were reinforced by continuing attacks on loyalists as well as by reports from Connacht, following the French invasion, of 'plans to butcher Protestants'. These were disputed, but Musgrave was unpersuaded by contrary opinion. He likened the insurgents in Connacht on one occasion to 'vermin … whose object is blood'; and he was convinced by the fact that captured French officers 'speak dreadfully of the Irish savages', and by the informa-

57 Bartlett, *Fall and rise*, p. 238; Musgrave to Percy, [Oct. 1798]: N.L.I., Musgrave papers, MS 4157, ff 91–2; David Dickson, 'Foreword' to Sir Richard Musgrave, *Memoirs of the Irish rebellion of 1798* (4th ed., Fort Wayne, Indiana, 1995).
58 Dáire Keogh, '*The French disease*' (Dublin, 1993), pp 205–6; [Sir Richard Musgrave], *To the magistrates, the military and the yeomanry of Ireland* (Dublin, 1798), p. 20.
59 Musgrave to Percy, 22 Sept., 22 Dec. 1798: N.L.I., Musgrave papers, MS 4157, ff 89, 79.
60 Musgrave to Percy, 20 Aug., 22 Sept., [Oct.], 1, 8, 13, 26 Oct, 16, 30 Nov., 6 Dec. 1798, 2, 15 Jan., 15 Feb. 1799: N.L.I., Musgrave papers, MS 4157, ff 83, 89–90, 91–2, 93, 95, 97, 99, 101, 103, 81, 77, 7–8, 20–22. N.L.I. MS 4156 contains copies of materials, notes, information and correspondence to Bishop Percy that informed Musgrave's work.

tion he gleaned that a local physician at Castlebar had appealed to the French officers for 'one hour's revenge against the Protest[an]ts for 100 y[ea]rs of cruelty and oppression' that his was the correct interpretation.[61]

He was so convinced of the rectitude of his conclusion that, following the publication by the Catholic bishop of Ferns, James Caulfield, of a defence of the priests of Wexford, he vowed in October 1798 to produce a 'rejoinder which will expose the ludicrous features of popery and prove the guilt of not only the vulgar herd of priests but even of their bishop'. Musgrave was induced to do this by the realization that his 'history' was going to 'take longer than expected', and by his wish that 'some of the most striking features of the rebellion' and 'the abominations of popery' should be made public without delay. He embarked on this work with some trepidation because of his fear that he would be 'assassinated' if it became known what he was undertaking. However, he had his *Concise account of the material events and atrocities which occurred in the present rebellion* ready by January 1799, and he realized he had struck the right note when it quickly sold out three Dublin editions and a Cork imprint following its initial publication in March.[62]

The thesis of *A concise account* was that the 1798 rebellion was a 'popish rebellion' instigated and advanced by the Catholic clergy in order to bring about 'the extirpation of heretics' because this was the 'sanguinary' mission of Roman Catholicism. In support of this argument, Musgrave cited evidence he had collected in the course of his research into the Wexford rebellion which attested both to the participation of Catholic clerics and to their failure to prevent atrocities. He was scornful of Bishop Caulfield's claim that those Protestants who suffered did so because they were Orangemen; this was, he thundered, nothing more than 'an artful attempt to hide the grim, the hideous, the gorgon visage of Popery, with a political mask, while fanatical fury against Protestants in general fomented'. Indeed, Musgrave contended, citing Archbishop Troy of Dublin on the unchanging nature of Catholic tenets, this was how Catholicism was and how it had always been:

> we find them equally destructive against the Albigenses and Waldenses in the 13th century, against the Protestants of Paris in the 16th, in the expulsion of the Moors from Spain, in the Irish rebellion in 1641, against the Protestants of France in 1791, in the massacre on Vinegar Hill, in the barn of Scullabogue, on the bridge of Wexford, and in the general carnage of protestants which took place in that once-peaceful and happy country.

61 Musgrave to Percy, 22 Sept., [Oct.], 1, 8, 13 Oct., 30 Nov. 1798, 15 Jan., 15, 25 Feb., [late Feb.], [early Mar.] *c.*8 Mar. 1799: N.L.I., Musgrave papers, MS 4157, ff 89–90, 91–2, 93, 95, 97, 103, 7–8, 20–22, 27, 29, 31, 35.
62 Musgrave to Percy, 8 Oct., 22 Dec. 1798, 2, 28 Jan., [early Mar.], 5 Mar., [Mar.] 1799: N.L.I., Musgrave papers, MS 4157, ff 95, 79, 77, 1, 31, 33, 39.

Though superficially simply a restatement of a familiar argument, Musgrave's explicit linkage of the Wexford rebellion with previous Catholic 'massacres' amounted to the modernization of classic Protestant massacre theory to embrace the events of 1798. The fact that the extensive evidence he supplied to sustain the rebellion's inclusion was presented in a text which traced this policy from the Lateran Council, and that he documented his contention 'that many doctrines of the popish church, not only encouraged but even recommended persecution and bloodshed, ever since the beginning of the twelfth century' gave his argument authority with the Protestant readership towards whom it was directed. It provided them with a rationale for the conclusion many had already reached instinctively that the 1798 rising was 'a popish rebellion against Protestantism', and that those Protestants who were massacred died for the same reason that their forebears had died in 1641 – because 'the spirit of Popery, as ravenous as the grave, and as relentless as death, dictated their destruction'.[63]

The writing of *A concise account* distracted Musgrave from his primary task of producing a Protestant history of the rebellion. But his readiness to incorporate corrections, suggested by Bishop Percy and Edward Ledwich, into the second and third editions which appeared during the summer of 1799, indicate that he was gratified by its impact.[64] He continued to collect information for his history regardless from, among other sources, courts martial and witnesses to the Wexford Bridge massacre. These reinforced his perception that the rebels acted with clerical approval. The quality of the new information he gathered also persuaded him that he had been right not to rush his history, though he was, even now, short of basic materials relating to events in Ulster – a problem he sought to resolve by appealing for information to clerical and lay supporters who agreed with him on the importance of 'writing in defence of the constitution in church and state'.[65]

Musgrave also appealed to clerical allies for accounts of 'the factions and insurrections' (which was how he described the agrarian movements that had dominated the Irish rural landscape for several decades) with which he intended to commence his narrative.[66] This reflected his long-held conviction, and that of other conservatives, that the 1798 rebellion should not be viewed in the short temporal context of the 1790s; it was rather the logical outcome of intensifying disorder that could be traced back to the late 1750s. It also indicated that, in con-

---

63 Veridicus [Sir Richard Musgrave], *A concise account of the material events and atrocities which occurred in the present rebellion with the causes which produced them, and an answer to Veritas's Vindication of the Roman Catholic clergy of the town of Wexford* (3rd edition, Dublin, 1799), passim, but especially pp 2, 16, 19, 33, 41–42, 48.

64 Musgrave to Percy, [Mar.], postmarked 9 Mar., 19 Apr., 13 May, June/July 1799: N.L.I., Musgrave papers, MS 4157, ff 39, 37, 69, 66, 57.

65 Musgrave to Percy, [Mar.], 10, 13, 21 May, 6, 25 June, [June/July], 2 July 1799; Musgrave to Sturrock, 2, 22 July: N.L.I., Musgrave papers, MS 4157, ff 39, 67, 64, 62, 51–5, 57, 47, 49, 75.

66 Musgrave to Pery, 25 June 1799: N.L.I., Musgrave papers, MS 4157 f. 54.

trast to *A concise account*, his history would focus on the events of the rebellion and on Ireland, and so avoid the more overtly polemical approach demonstrated in that pamphlet.

This is not how Musgrave's *Memoirs of the Irish rebellion of 1798*, the first edition of which was published in the spring of 1801, is perceived today. But due acknowledgement should be paid to the author for the lengths to which he went to gather and to collate testimonies 'in order to avoid the smallest aberration from truth'. It was virtually unprecedented for a work of this kind and time, and it gives the *Memoirs* an authority that none of its rivals possess. Written in England, whither Musgrave had repaired in July 1799 after he had sorted his materials and 'sketch'd' his outline,[67] his *Irish rebellion* is an elaborately detailed, vigorous statement of the conservative Protestant thesis that the rebellion was prompted by the age-old sectarian ambition of Irish Catholics to extirpate Protestantism. Though the literary style is unremarkable and the exposition mechanistic, the book still resonates because of the high emotion with which the 'sanguinary' intent of those in rebellion and the bloody fate of their Protestant victims is related. Interpretively, it offers little not previously provided in *A concise account*. But factually it dwarfs the earlier account in scope and in scale because Musgrave consciously sought to provide as full and expansive a chronicle as he could construct of the fate of those Protestants who fell victim to the rebellion, and a detailed exposition of the excesses of the rebels and of the complicity and involvement of Catholic clergy.[68]

Because it provided the account many believed the authorities were intent on occluding and because it 'proved' that they had been targeted for decimation, Musgrave's *Irish rebellion* was warmly received by conservative Irish Protestants. Its acceptance was aided by continuing disorder which ensured that Protestants remained visibly uneasy as to Catholic intentions.[69] Musgrave certainly possessed few doubts as to their anti-Protestant purpose. In May 1801, he interpreted the unconnected murders of a number of 'zealous loyalists' as a manifestation of Catholic determination 'to cut off all the Protestants one by one; or to expel them from Ireland by a system of terror'.[70] In this context, Musgrave's enthusiastic support for the Act of Union is immediately comprehensible. Indeed, he delayed publishing his history, on the duke of Portland's request, 'till the union question was finally decided'. However, once the book was in print he took the necessary steps to ensure it sold well in Britain because he was no less eager to make it clear to Protestants there as well as in Ireland that 'the Protestant religion' was 'the only

67 Musgrave to Pery, 21 May, 2, 12, 15 July: N.L.I., Musgrave papers, MS 4157, ff 62, 47, 111, 45.
68 Musgrave, *Memoirs of the Irish rebellion*.
69 See, *inter alia*, P. Power, 'A Carrickman's diary, 1787–1809', in *Journal of the Waterford and South-East of Ireland Archaeological Society*, xvii (1914), 14; Garde to Heaton, Apr. 1800: P.R.O.N.I., Chatsworth papers, T3158/1801.
70 Musgrave to Loftus, 16 May 1801: N.L.I., autograph letters, MS 3009, f. 51.

bond of union' binding Ireland to Britain.[71] The outcome exceeded his expectations. Musgrave's *Irish rebellion* was widely reviewed in the conservative periodical literature of the day and the virtually unanimous conclusion was that he had proven conclusively that the purpose of the 1798 rising was to exterminate Irish Protestants and that Catholics remained as committed as ever to this policy. As a result, Musgrave's *Rebellion* became, as Sack has shown, one of the defining texts of the new British right and in the words of William Bennett, afterwards bishop of Cloyne, of 'the utmost service' in prompting the palpable shift that took place within the British establishment from favouring Catholic relief in the late eighteenth century to upholding the Protestant constitution in the early nineteenth.[72]

This was a most welcome development for Irish Protestants for whom the events of 1798 provided complete proof of the folly of diluting the Penal Laws.[73] Certainly, the combined impact of the rebellion and of Musgrave's reconstruction of it as a popish massacre prompted an increase in the passion with which Protestants vowed to oppose Catholic Emancipation and tithe reform, and a comparable increase in their determination to sustain the Church of Ireland which, 'in these days of revolution', Euseby Cleaver tellingly observed, was 'the sheet anchor of the constitution'.[74] In a more explicitly religious sense, the experience of '98 strengthened the convictions of doctrinal conservatives who, believing that their escape from destruction was a sign of divine favour, advocated intensified evangelization to ensure the triumph of 'pure, ... rational, and enlightened religion' and the forging of a harmonious society in which 'the principle of subordination' was accepted.[75]

Some Protestants at least believed that the prospects for this were better than they had been in the 1690s, when similarly optimistic sentiments were expressed, because the massacre of Protestants in 1798 had shattered the Dissenter-Catholic alliance that the United Irishmen had endeavoured to construct. This alliance was never as secure as Protestants concluded, but when things looked bleak in the summer of 1798 they consoled themselves with the news from Ulster that the reports of massacre and murder from south Leinster had 'turned all the Dissenters', and that they were now 'desirous to join with the Protestants of the Established Church'.[76]

---

71 Ibid.; Musgrave to Devonshire, 24 Apr. 1800: P.R.O.N.I., Chatsworth papers, T3158/1802; Musgrave to Stockdale, 11 June 1801: H.M.C., *Laing MSS*, ii, 685–6.

72 J.J. Sack, *From Jacobite to conservative: Reaction and orthodoxy in Britain c.1760–1832* (Cambridge, 1993), pp 96–7, 240–42; Bennett's notes on Musgrave's History: N.L.I., MS 637.

73 Patrick Duigenan, *A fair representation of the present political state of Ireland* (Dublin, 1799), p. 35.

74 Cleaver to Egremont, 30 Apr. 1801: Petworth House, Egremont papers; Cleaver to O'Hara, 3 Oct. 1800: N.L.I., O'Hara papers, MS 20,396.

75 Joseph Liechty, 'Irish evangelicalism, Trinity College, Dublin, and the mission of the Church of Ireland at the end of the eighteenth century' (unpublished Ph.D thesis, St Patrick's College, Maynooth, 1987), pp 274–5, 292–5, 301–2.

76 Kevin Whelan, *The tree of liberty* (Cork, 1996), pp 133–4; Percy to Percy, 28 May, 11 June 1798:

That such a transformation was wrought attests to the impact of the 1798 rebellion on Irish Protestants. This is vividly illustrated on an individual level by the conclusion of one Wexford Protestant in 1799 that 'here is no place for a Protestant'; it can also be identified in the 'great horror of this country' expressed by Catherine Cleaver and in her husband's request for a translation to a bishopric, no matter how impoverished, in England or Wales in preference to Ferns.[77] Such strong sentiments were ameliorated by time, but the legacy of suspicion and antipathy left by the events of 1798 ensured that a deep, and in many cases an unbridgeable, gulf divided the bulk of Irish Protestants and the bulk of the Catholic population thereafter. Emmet's rebellion contributed to this. But the most convincing evidence that their experiences in 1798 were the main reason is provided by the frequency with which Protestants, not all of whom were 'zealous loyalists', recalled the 1798 rebellion. By this means, they reminded themselves that if providence ensured that they had escaped massacre in 1798, others had not been so lucky and that Catholic 'readiness to resort to the sword or faggot for effecting [this] object' represented a continuing threat to their existence.[78]

B.L., Percy papers, Add. MS 32,335, f. 27; Curtin, *The United Irishmen*, p. 723; Musgrave to Percy, *c.*16 May 1799: N.L.I., Musgrave papers, MS 4157, f. 71.

77 W[aring] to [Percy], 15 Mar. 1799: N.L.I., Musgrave papers, MS 4156, f. 34; Cleaver to Egremont, 19 Mar. 1799, 26 Jan. 1806: Petworth House, Egremont papers.

78 O'Beirne to Castlereagh, 25 Apr. 1799, in *Castlereagh correspondence*, iii, p. 28; Bartlett, *Fall and rise*, pp 275–7; Robert Day's diary, 1807–15, pp 5, 7 13: Beinecke Library, Osborn Collection; Andrew Bigelow, *Leaves from a journal, or Sketches of rambles in North Britain and Ireland* (Edinburgh, 1824), pp 77, 128–9; T.P. Cunningham, 'Catholic rent lists from Kilmore', in *Breifne*, ii (1962–3), 212; E. Gillett (ed.), *Elizabeth Ham, by herself* (London, 1945), pp 87–8, 136–7.

16

The Irish yeomanry and the 1798 rebellion

ALLAN BLACKSTOCK

When Lord Cornwallis arrived in Ireland in late June 1798 as the new viceroy and commander-in-chief, he was horrified by what he found. Though astounded by the ferocity of all species of troops he was to command, Cornwallis reserved his most pointed censure for the locally-raised Irish yeomanry. But while Cornwallis hated amateur soldiers of this kind, his professionalism allowed him to make a balanced judgement about the yeomanry. 'These men' he said 'have saved the country, but they take the lead in rapine and murder.'[1] Although Cornwallis certainly saw the licentiousness traditionally associated with the yeomanry, he also begrudgingly recognized that they had served a purpose. Like their opponents, the yeomen have until relatively recently suffered from over-simplified accounts, enlisted by post-rebellion polemicists either as heroes or villains. Given that so little is known about what even Cornwallis acknowledged was a vital element in the 1798 configuration, it is essential to examine this force, the heart of local opposition to the United Irishmen.

The years between the outbreak of war in 1793 and the formation of the yeomanry in October 1796 is a necessary context for exploring their origins. The Irish government faced a dilemma in these years: it had to guard against two intimately related dangers – invasion from France, and domestic insurrection by the United Irishmen – which made competing demands on its military resources.[2] The regular army garrison was depleted by the French war and replacements for it were of dubious quality. The Irish militia, raised in 1793 and largely Catholic in its rank and file, was considered susceptible to United Irish and Defender infiltration. Fencible regiments drafted over from Britain from 1795 were considered poor quality troops.[3] The usual wartime option of locally-

---

1 Cornwallis to Ross, 24 July 1798: National Army Museum [hereafter: N.A.M.], Cornwallis papers, 6602/43/3/f 5.

2 P. Stoddart, 'Counter-insurgency and defence in Ireland, 1790–1805' (unpublished D.Phil. thesis, Oxford, 1972); T. Bartlett, 'Defence, counter-insurgency and rebellion: Ireland, 1793– 1803', in T. Bartlett and K. Jeffrey (eds), *A military history of Ireland* (Cambridge, 1996).

3 These were troops raised for wartime service only. Their terms of service confined their duty to Great Britain and Ireland.

raised resident home defence was nullified by the suppression of volunteering in 1793. The immediate backdrop to the formation of the Irish yeomanry was the growing strength and military capability of the United Irishmen, now in alliance with the Defender movement, and intelligence reaching government of the preparation of a French invasion fleet destined for Ireland.

The viceroy, Earl Camden, initially hesitated over the decision to use a locally-raised force, still haunted by the spectre of 1782 when the Irish Volunteers exploited Britain's weakness during the American war to force political concessions for the College Green parliament. However, in September 1796 Camden took the crucial decision to go ahead with a new local force, the Irish yeomanry, hoping that the safeguards of pay and commissioned officers would keep it under the government's control. The actual raising of yeomanry was entrusted to the major county interest, usually the county governor, who was empowered to convene a magistrates' meeting in order to elicit offers to raise corps. Offers of service were sent to the Castle, usually accompanied by loyal resolutions. After vetting, commissions were issued for the captain and lieutenants to embody and discipline the men while arms, accoutrements and uniforms were issued from government stores. Yeoman infantry corps averaged 100, while cavalry troops averaged between forty and fifty. All yeomen took the oath of allegiance and commited themselves to train two days a week, in return for regular army rates of pay; they were bound to support civil magistrates when required. Their duty areas were limited to their home district. If necessary, they could make a further offer of emergency full-time military service, which came to be known as 'permanent duty'.[4]

Official membership policy was denominationally inclusive but, in reality, with selection delegated to the local gentry, the yeomanry was a largely Anglican force, though it also included some Presbyterians and Catholics in cavalry corps and in areas of sparse Protestant settlement in the south and west. Although the government tried to keep the yeomanry clear of politics, this was like dropping iron filings into a ring of magnets and expecting them to remain static in the conditions of the mid-1790s. Even before the first yeoman got his gun, the force was embroiled in the politics of the Catholic question, as a largely Catholic yeomanry had been mooted in 1795 by Fitzwilliam, Camden's predecessor as viceroy, as a potential benefit of emancipation. Orangeism was present in some of the first northern corps, though overall the Volunteer movement was the most important influence in the new force, which was often raised from the same groupings as had served in the Volunteers.[5]

Motivations for joining varied. In some areas where the threat of disorder was minimal, there was an undoubted element of fashionable foppery. Lord Shannon

---

4   37 Geo III sections 1–5; A.F. Blackstock, *An ascendancy army: The Irish Yeomanry, 1796–1834* (Dublin, 1998), pp 72–4.
5   Blackstock, *Ascendancy army*, chap. 4.

complained that many MPs refused the government's frugal standardised uniform to clothe themselves in more flamboyant style. Daniel O'Connell borrowed money from his uncle to keep up with the counter-revolutionary *chic* of the Lawyers' Artillery, whose lavish uniform cost double the official allowance. In parts of the north, poverty played a role. The marquis of Downshire complained that men would join 'for the sake of getting a suit of clothes'.[6] However, fear and prejudice were also motivating factors. Around Newry, an area of Defenderism, Downshire had offers from men whose conditions were that they would not serve with Catholics.[7] In areas of mid-Ulster where Orangeism was formally established and where the gentry were connected with them, the yeoman corps was selected from the lodge; the best documented instance is William Blacker's account of assembling around 1,000 men and selecting 100 for his yeomanry. In other cases, conservative old Volunteer corps, which functioned like the proto-Orange Boyne Societies, re-constituted themselves as yeomanry corps.[8] The door was not closed on radical ex-Volunteers or reformers either. In the British Volunteer Infantry, the nearest equivalent to the Irish yeomanry, non-partisan loyalty to principles of constitutional order was a bigger feature of that movement than its connections to the earlier chauvinistically anti-radical Reevesite Loyal Associations.[9] Though the background was different, this patriotic model of motivation was encouraged by the Irish government, and evidence of it occurs frequently enough to be considered significant. Lord Castlereagh and his father were only able to raise yeomen by changing the usual standard loyal resolutions to include a get-out clause for men who did not want their yeomanry offer to preclude them 'from seeking every constitutional method of obtaining a repeal of many laws which we consider as obnoxious and indeed [are] encroachments on the very spirit and essence of the constitution'.[10] Lord Charlemont, ex-Volunteer commander-in-chief, was courted by the government because of his Volunteering influence. Charlemont defined his stance succinctly: 'Would I refuse to bear a hand in stopping a leak in a sinking vessel because I hated the commander?'[11]

6 Shannon to Boyle, 20 Oct. 1796: P.R.O.N.I., Shannon papers, D2707/A3/3/22; D. O'Connell to M. O'Connell, 3 Jan. 1797: M.R. O'Connell (ed.), *The correspondence of Daniel O'Connell* (Shannon, 1972–80), i, pp 26–8; Downshire to Camden, 4 Nov. 1796: Centre for Kentish Studies, Pratt papers, U840/0160/8.
7 Downshire to Pelham, 24 Nov. 1796: N.A.I., RP 620/26/77.
8 Cited in H. Senior, *Orangeism in Britain and Ireland, 1795–1836* (London and Toronto, 1966), p. 58. The flag of the Killeavy Volunteers, 1778 (Boyne Orange Society, no. 153) is on display in Armagh County Museum. For an illustration see W.A. Maguire (ed.), *Up in arms: The 1798 rebellion in Ireland ...* (Belfast, 1998) p. 142.
9 A. Gee, 'The British Volunteer movement, 1793–1807' (unpublished D.Phil. thesis, Oxford, 1989), p. 336.
10 Newtownards Yeomanry Resolutions, Nov. 1796: P.R.O.N.I., D1494/2/24.
11 Charlemont to Haliday, 12 Sept. 1796: H.M.C. *Charlemont MSS*.

Therefore the yeomanry of October 1796 appears as anything but a one-dimensional political force. It embraced northern farmers and weavers, Dublin professionals, Armagh Orangemen and Boyne Society men, Catholics, whiggish reformers, and a leaven of radical Volunteers to boot.[12] All, however, had taken the oath of allegiance and were, as far as could be ascertained, not United Irishmen. Yeomanry flags give a clue to the broad focus of this loyalty. While some bear the motto 'For King, Laws and Constitution', others proclaim their allegiance locally and domestically with 'For Hearth and Home'.[13]

This yeomanry force crucially functioned as an agent of counter-revolution in the period 1796–8. Hindsight shows us the importance of 31 October 1796, the day the first yeomanry commissions were signed. Up to that point there would have been little or no locally-organized resistance to the United Irishmen, and the proposed rising would have been more of a revolution and less of a civil war. It is vital to chart accurately the sequence of events during this period as one circumstance provides the context for the next in a deepening spiral of action and reaction which threatened to drag the whole country into the abyss. The United Irishmen had already been trying to prove themselves the strongest group to boost their military expansion, vital if the French were to be persuaded that Ireland was a viable invasion option. When yeomanry corps were first mooted, battles for local dominance developed. A prominent Tyrone magistrate, Thomas Knox of Dungannon, aptly noted that 'the first up will carry the day'.[14] Initially it seemed that the United Irishmen and Defenders would be the early risers. Bantry Bay, rather than a discouragement, actually served as a morale boost for the United men by proving that France was deadly serious about invasion, an accretion of confidence further augmented by the Irish army's totally inadequate response.

Yeomanry morale plummeted. A campaign to win over Orangemen and infiltrate the yeomanry was begun by United Irishmen, who had changed their name to 'Liberty Men', highlighting a word charged with significance in the Williamite tradition, and consequently downplaying the 'United' context, which implied union with the Catholic Defenders.[15] Some isolated yeomen were afraid to appear on drill or duty. The Newry yeomen were reportedly terrified into inaction in March 1797.[16] For a time it looked as though the yeomanry would fail completely. In December 1796, Thomas Knox summed up the relative positions of the United Irishmen and the authorities: 'they have nearly subdued the coun-

---

12 Blackstock, *Ascendancy army*, pp 88–90; Revd W. Richardson to [Arthur Wolfe], 26 Sept. 1796: N.A.I., RP 620/25/118.
13 See, for example, the guidons (pennants) of the Lower Iveagh Yeoman Cavalry and the Londonderry Cavalry in the Ulster Museum.
14 W. Richardson, *The origins of the Irish yeomanry* (Dublin, 1801), p. 14.
15 J. Knox to Lake, 11 Mar. 1797: B.L., Pelham papers, Add. MS 33,013, ff 265–6.
16 Magistrates' memorial, 18 Mar. 1797: B.L., Pelham papers, Add. MS 33,103, ff 249–50.

try by a system of terror and we shall be wise in taking a lesson from them and terrifying in return'.[17]

By early 1797, many parts of Ulster were proclaimed under the Insurrection Act, giving magistrates unprecedented powers to search for arms. To help them they could use yeomen or request military aid. The first searches were often ineffectual, as the United Irishmen knew in advance what was happening and either hid their weapons or handed in unserviceable ones. Reports grew about yeomen and indeed some Orangemen defecting to the United Irishmen. In these circumstances, Thomas Knox's brother General John Knox, who commanded at Dungannon, took a decision which was to have wide ramifications. Knowing the inefficiency of searches under the Insurrection Act, he decided that all searches in his district would be carried out by yeomen – with instructions to disarm selectively.

In an oft-quoted letter to the chief secretary, Thomas Pelham, written in Mar. 1797, John Knox justified his actions. Local yeomen were to leave unregistered arms in the hands of Orangemen, but to seize United Irish guns. This was to be done, he told Pelham, not with any realistic hopes of disarming insurgency, but rather 'to increase the animosity between the Orangemen and the United Irishmen ... Were the Orangemen disarmed or put down, or were they coalesced with the other party, the whole of Ulster would be as bad as Down or Antrim.'[18] There were sound strategic reasons for this policy. Knox's military district had the natural defensive features of Lough Neagh and large rivers, the Bann and Blackwater, with easily monitored crossing points. If he could thwart United Irish attempts to enlist Orangemen and infiltrate the yeomanry, he could make his area function as a strategic wedge between east and west Ulster.

John Knox had earlier spoken of the need for 'spiriting up' opposition to the United Men to 'oppose violence to violence',[19] and his encouragement of the Orangemen in the spring of 1797 was done not only by winking at Orange guns but by indicating that Orangemen were welcome in local yeomanry corps. Knox got specific permission from Pelham to add Orangemen as supplementary men to James Verner's yeomanry and to create a new corps entirely from Orangemen, under Joseph Atkinson of Crowhill. This Orange connection was advertised by Knox, allowing the yeomen to sport Orange ribbons in their uniforms at a review in the park of his father (Lord Northland) in Dungannon.[20] Knox's dilemma was how to cast Orangeism in a sufficiently favourable light to the government to achieve the sanction he needed to harness it to the yeomanry, while simultaneously to 'spirit up' wavering loyalists. The latter was done by a deliber-

17 T. Knox to [?Cooke], 12 Dec. 1796: N.A.I., RP 620/26/117.
18 J. Knox to Pelham, 19 Mar. 1797: B.L. Pelham papers, Add. MS 33,103, f. 263.
19 J. Knox to Pelham, 2 Jan. 1797: N.A.I., RP 620/28/13.
20 J. Knox to Pelham, 19 Apr. 1797: B.L., Pelham papers, Add. MS 33,103, ff 379–80; Lake to Knox, 19 Apr. 1797: N.L.I., Lake papers, MS 56/f. 53.

ate resurrection of the Williamite tradition of 1690, casting the conflict in apocalyptic terms and inserting an ideology which could counteract the United Irish
appeal of 'liberty'. The obstacle presented by the government's reluctance was
more formidable. Remembering the Armagh outrages of 1795–6 and the political handle they gave to the Foxite whig opposition, Pelham was understandably
nervous. He initially refused Knox's overtures regarding the Orange-yeomanry
link-up. However, Knox navigated this by adopting a dual approach, with separate central-local emphases, epitomized in his second and successful approach to
Pelham. He engineered Orange resolutions, specifically for Castle consumption,
stressing that they would keep within the law. However, there was one huge
problem: how to stir up the 'spirit' of counter-revolution while, at the same time
keeping the counter-revolutionaries orderly. The inherent incompatibilities of
this approach are illustrated in print. The local Orangemen's published answer
to the United Irishmen's overtures was strictly for local consumption. This was
very much in the context of 'spiriting up', and concluded belligerently: 'We
gave you only a taste at the Diamond, but the next time we come to blows, you
shall have a bellyful'. Coincidentally, this sanguinary riposte was published the
very same day, 21 May 1797, as Knox's anodyne Orange resolutions were posted
to Pelham.[21] Some days later Knox assured Pelham about the Orangemens' credentials: 'They were originally a bigoted set of men, who were ready to destroy
the Roman Catholics. They now form a political party and are the only barrier
we have against the United Irishmen.' Recognizing the chief secretary's dilemma, Knox said that he did not want the Orangemen given open encouragement
but rather that it should be done 'silently by permission to enrol themselves in
the district corps [yeomanry]'.[22] However, this did not answer the inherent problem of squaring active loyalism with promises of keeping within the law.

The answer was not to square the circle at all but to change the rules. John
Knox had little faith in the Insurrection Act as a counter to insurgency and was
an early advocate of more severe methods. In May 1797 he summed up martial
law ruthlessly as 'authorising the general officers to declare war upon property
until the surrender can be made – arms may be hid, ringleaders may conceal
themselves, but houses and barns cannot be removed'.[23] This was in effect
counter-terror and it was certainly not confined to property. Individuals suffered
too. Henry Joy McCracken's brother John told of Tyrone yeomen hanging suspects by the heels and lashing them with belts.[24] In July 1797, an infamous inci-

---

21 J. Knox to Pelham, 21 May 1797: B.L., Pelham papers, Add. MS 33,014, f. 91; Answer of the
    Armagh Orangemen to the address of the United Irishmen, 21 May 1797: P.R.O.N.I.,
    T1689/21.
22 J. Knox to Pelham, 28 May 1797: B.L., Pelham papers, Add. MS 33,104, ff 139–40.
23 J. Knox to Pelham, 2 Jan. 1797: N.A.I., RP 620/28/13; J. Knox to Pelham, 28 May 1797: B.L.,
    Pelham papers, Add. MS 33,104, f. 140.
24 J. McCracken to M. McCracken, 26 July 1797: T.C.D., Madden papers, MS 873.

dent near Newry saw the murder of defenceless civilians, including children, by local yeomen and by members of a Welsh fencible regiment, the Ancient Britons, under the pretext that the district was one of strong United Irish support. The wanton and gratuitous ferocity of this incident was enough to make even loyalists blanche. John Giffard, then a captain in the Dublin militia and later a prominent Orangeman, complained to Cooke about the incident.[25]

In reality martial law, by imposing *de facto* war conditions, was stealing a march on the United Irishmen whose intention of armed insurrection had been clear for some time. However, if martial law was the last resort of the pragmatist, given the background of rising tension, it would inevitably also be the first refuge of the rogue and the revenger. It is notable in this context that the Newry yeomen, virtually overwhelmed in early 1797, were involved in one of the worst atrocities of the whole disarming campaign, pointing to the symbiotic nature of the conflict in the crucial lead-up to the rebellion. With the spread of the United Irish military system, the establishment of yeomanry, the growth of Orangeism and the subsequent struggles for allegiance, more and more people were becoming involved. All were drawn into the escalating conflict. In affected areas, grievances and fears were perceived communally and local people did not have to look further than their own parish boundaries to find reason to fight. Political ideology, republican or Williamite, was a means to a military end.

John Knox subsumed his private views. The public face of a ruthlessly pragmatic general disguised the fact that he privately disliked the Orangemen, was an early advocate of legislative union, and maintained a correspondence with the United Irishman, Arthur O'Connor. Indeed, at the very time he was drilling yeomen in Tyrone in late 1796, he was being secretly investigated by the government: an intercepted letter to O'Connor turns up in the Rebellion Papers. Knox's radical correspondence continued right into 1798. The under-secretary, Edward Cooke, called Knox 'a man of speculation … and independency of spirit' who would once have been attracted by the 'democratic novelties of the French Revolution'. Camden considered Knox's position very seriously, but eventually decided that, coming from a propertied background, his natural instincts made him reliable.[26] Cooke was right in one thing however. Knox certainly had an active mind and his political open-mindedness was mirrored by military innovation: in his thinking he was looking beyond the destructive horrors of martial law at a more constructive measure.

John Knox recognized immediately that the yeomanry, organized in small isolated corps, would be useful against local disorder and for defending property,

25 W.E.H. Lecky, *A history of Ireland in the eighteenth century* (London, 1913), iv, pp 41–2.
26 J. Knox to A. O'Connor, 26 Dec. 1796: N.A.I., RP 620/15/3/8; Portland to Camden, 7 Mar. 1798: P.R.O., HO 100/75 f. 177; Cooke to Wickham, 10 Mar. 1798: HO 100/75 ff 191–2. See also Lecky, *Ireland*, iv, pp 234–6.

but was quite incapable of acting in a wider military capacity without resources for concerted action. Bantry had proved that if the regular troops, militia and fencibles had to move to meet an invasion, individual yeomanry corps could be cut off piecemeal. Various plans were mooted, but in September 1797 Knox got Pelham's approval for a new plan which promised more flexibility. In January 1798 he was summoned to the Castle to provide details of all yeomanry stations in Ulster. Knox's idea was to establish an emergency plan, whereby the scattered yeomanry corps could go on permanent duty under the overall direction of a military brigadier, and gather in large brigades in defensible towns from which a network of patrols and mini-garrisons could be dispatched into the countryside. These could either prevent insurgents gathering or, if met with overwhelming force, retreat to fall-back positions in the major garrisons.

This necessitated plenty of yeomen and backups. Knox had been working towards this in his home district with the Orange-yeomanry liaison, and this local connection set the precedent for a much wider linkage in April 1798, when thousands of additional supplementary yeomen were raised from Orangemen both in Ulster and Dublin.[27] The idea was that when the yeomen were on per-manent duty, the supplementaries could guard the home parish, or retreat into the garrison towns as a last resort.[28] This yeomanry brigade system was adopted and adapted throughout Ireland; other criteria were used to determine the relia-bility of citizen volunteers, and undoubtedly Catholics were used, particularly in the south and west. Each county was given a yeomanry brigade major to superin-tend and act as an administrative liaison between the yeomanry captains and the regular brigadier. New standing yeomanry orders were issued from the Castle on 15 May 1798 and reprinted locally.[29]

This sequence of events leading up to the rebellion provides the context in which to analyse two issues which have an important bearing on our understand-ing of 1798: the build-up of local pre-conflict tensions, including the vexed question of official manipulation of sectarianism, and the yeomanry's actual role during the insurrection. Cornwallis later noted that indiscipline was worst among his indigenous forces, particularly the yeomanry. The fact that the yeomen, relative to the militia and fencibles, had little military training and less actual experience as military corps goes some way to explain this. However, another cogent reason is the reality that the yeomen, like their opponents, fought on and for familiar ground near their own homes. This military localism was characterized by subjective fears about survival. When the 'smothered rebellion' of 1796–7 erupted spectacularly in 1798, abstractions like 'King, Laws and Constitution' took second place to tangible realities like hearths and homes.

27 A.F. Blackstock, 'A dangerous species of ally: Orangeism and the Irish yeomanry', in *I.H.S.*, xxx (1996–97), 393–405.
28 Blackstock, *Ascendancy army*, pp 144–61.
29 *Standing orders for the yeomanry of Ireland, 15 May 1798* (Derry, 1798), [B.L. 8827 aaa 43].

This raises the issue of the official exploitation of sectarianism. John Knox's manoeuvring is often cited as an example,[30] and there is no doubt that Knox pragmatically pumped up atavistic fears. Did John Knox and Pelham cynically deploy the sectarian shades of 1641 and 1689 to break the unity of the 'Union'? Much depends on the perspective from which one views the position. We should be wary about loading late eighteenth-century central government with more local control and knowledge than it had, as Camden's convulsions about canvassing the yeomanry plan prove.[31] However, the perspective of the yeomanry, which has interlinking central and local, military and civil foci, offers an alternative thesis. The precedent is the accepted tradition of giving local army commanders discretion to arm loyal citizens in an emergency. When a small French force landed in Pembrokeshire in 1797, 750 local citizens were given arms.[32] However, although disaffection in Britain was minimal compared to Ireland, there were parallels: military delegation was a natural and traditional emergency response of civil administrators in both countries, and Pelham and Camden instinctively thought in these terms. Knox already had discretion to augment yeomanry from December 1796.[33] The fact that these men were now being armed, not as Orangemen *per se*, but were being brought under the pay and discipline of the yeomanry system, and that Pelham had the local commander's guarantee that they were law-abiding meant, from Pelham's standpoint, that this was not a policy to link the government with the Orangemen, so much as an *ad hoc* partial and local emergency measure with political and military safeguards built in.

If we accept that delegation was the convention in Britain and Ireland and view matters from this perspective, the manipulation of fear inherent in John Knox's counter-revolutionary Orange liaison appears in its contemporary context as another stage in the pre-conflict manpower struggle. Another way of reading Knox's strategy is to see a tactical chess-game; his brother Thomas' remark about taking a lesson from the 'conspirators' is pertinent here. There is no question that people's fears were enlisted as recruiting sergeants by both sides. Panics were created by the United Irishmen, playing upon attacks on Catholics in Armagh in 1795 and 1796, to promote the Defender alliance. In May 1796 Dr Haliday told Charlemont of scares about mythical Orangemen in Antrim: 'a report was circulated that a number of Orangemen (from the moon I suppose) were to be there [at a fair] to fall upon the C[atholics]'.[34] Similarly the United Irishmen tried to represent the entire yeomanry as an Orange force, well before the Orange Order had spread either geographically or significantly into the yeomanry, claiming, for example, in February 1797 that 'the Orangemen or

30 K. Whelan, *The tree of liberty* (Cork, 1996), p. 119.
31 Blackstock, *Ascendancy army*, chapter 3.
32 I.F.W. Beckett, *The amateur military tradition* (Manchester, 1991) p. 78.
33 J. Knox to Pelham, 28 Dec. 1796: N.A.I., RP 620/26/175.
34 Hudson to Charlemont, 29 May 1796: H.M.C. *Charlemont*, ii.

midnight robbers and burners are completely organized and officered by the government hacks, the yeomen'.[35] Miles Byrne admits that he and others rode into villages at night posing as Orangemen in the spring of 1797, while later that year rumours were spread that Orangemen would attack worshippers at the Christmas Eve masses in Dublin.[36] John Knox's tactics were, at one level, part of the same cynical game. In this way, as with the earlier organization of the yeomanry itself in local corps, the counter-revolutionary response mirrored the tactics of its adversaries. Indeed, from a manpower perspective, the military harnessing of Orangeism was a mirror image of the United Irishmen's own alliance with the Defenders. Now that there were two recognizable 'sides' to the contest, given this torrid background of fear, manipulation, oaths of secrecy, infiltration, legalised terror under martial law, it is scarcely surprising that the hand that 'set the heather blazing' ignited an explosive combination which had been gathering since 1796.

Although the yeomanry brigade model was initiated by the Orange-yeomanry linkage, this should not be understood simply as the government blatantly arming one side against the other. The discrepancy can be seen clearly when it is realised exactly what *could* have happened if the government had actually embarked on a policy of arming the Orangemen. In Mar. 1798 the Orange leadership offered its entire manpower to the government (which it extravagantly reckoned at 100,000, but Camden more conservatively trimmed to 40,000), to serve as armed auxiliaries. The then commander-in-chief, Sir Ralph Abercromby, wanted this offer held in reserve. This remained the official line even after Abercromby's departure. Lord Auckland later noted that 'These Orange Boys, as they are called in Ireland, are growing numerous and are most inveterate against the United Irishmen. They are a dangerous species of ally; however, to a certain extent, it is necessary to use them.'[37] The organization of 5,000 Orangemen for emergency use as supplementary yeomen (they too were not to get guns until the very last moment) was in reality a compromise. This would continue to obscure the Orange connection to watching Whigs and bring the Orangemen under the control of yeomanry system. This still left the majority of Orangemen *outside* the yeomanry system and, although individual commanders were given discretion during the rebellion to arm as many non-aligned Orangemen as they thought fit, this was never carried to its full potential. Just how last-minute even this limited application was can be seen in Coleraine where loyalist citizens, much to the disgust of the Methodist John Galt, were not armed until the precise moment the commanding officer moved his soldiers and regular yeomen out

35 White to Stephenson, n.d. [February 1797]: N.A.I., RP 620/28/276 (14).
36 S. Gwynn (ed.), *The memoirs of Myles Byrne* (Dublin, 1907), p. 8; M. Elliott, *Partners in revolution* (New Haven and London, 1982), p. 173.
37 Auckland to Mornington, 22 Apr. 1798: B.L., Wellesley papers, Add. MS 37,308, f. 132.

of the town against the United Irishmen.[38] As late as 11 June, Camden was still agonising about 'how impolitic and unwise it would be to refuse the offers of Protestants to enter the yeomanry ... yet how dangerous [is] even any encouragement of the yeomanry spirit, whilst our army is composed of Catholics as the militia generally is'.[39] Nugent, although he armed Downpatrick Orangemen, remained opposed to a general armament until the 'last extremity' as, once started, he realised 'it must be total'. Indeed, Nugent had *discouraged* the arming of Orangemen as much as possible. Although all further arming of civilians, Orange or otherwise, was stopped by the arrival of Cornwallis, Nugent's stance was not just post-Cornwallis trimming. His views on the Orangemen pre-date Cornwallis, as he had supported Castlereagh's plan of 10 June 1798 to control and regularize the arming of loyalists by embodying them into 'skeleton regiments'. This notion was not dissimilar to the supplementary plan; indeed Nugent consulted John Knox on it.[40] The Orangemen themselves, though they boasted later of what they saw as official approval, were frustrated at the time by the reluctance of the authorities to give them their head. In the middle of the rebellion, Lord Shannon noted that 'the Orangemen call aloud for guns and to be let loose'. Orangemen on the Hertford estate near Lisburn were refused arms and took matters into their own hands; they reportedly sank boats on the Lagan Canal to prevent communication between United men in east Antrim and south Derry.[41]

This is not to say, however, that the armed Orangeman of 1798 was a bogeyman dreamed up by United Irishmen, but merely to reflect that what both Camden and many of the generals saw as a dangerous liaison was, in practice, as limited a link-up as they could make it. Like so much about 1798, the reality of events on the ground was distorted by the polemicists and balladeers who took up pens almost as soon as the pikes were put down. A song was published in 1800 entitled 'The Orange yeomanry', to be sung to the tune of 'Rule Britannia' in all Orange lodges, with a flagrant disregard for chronology. It claimed:

> When rebel schemes first did unfold
> were to o'erwhelm this happy land;

---

38 John Galt's Diary, 11 June 1798: P.R.O.N.I., D561/1/47.
39 Camden to Portland, 11 June 1798: P.R.O., HO 100/77, f. 132.
40 Castlereagh to Nugent, 10 June 1798: N.A.M., Nugent papers, 8807/174/ff 459–62; Nugent to J. Knox, 15 June 1798: N.L.I., Lake papers, MS 56/193; Nugent to Cooke, 19 June 1798: N.A.I., RP 620/38/175.
41 Nugent to Hewitt, 4 Sept. 1798: Charles Vane (ed.), *The memoirs and correspondence of Viscount Castlereagh* (London, 1848–53), i, pp 322–3; Shannon to Boyle, 9 June 1798: P.R.O.N.I., Shannon papers, D2707/A3/3/80; Dr Cupples to Foster Archer, 21 June 1798: N.A.I., RP 620/38/202.

'Twas then our yeomen,
Our yeomen great and bold
Did nobly for their country stand
'Hail courageous, hail Orange yeomanry
Traitors ever spurn from thee'.[42]

The second major issue concerns the yeomanry's role during the rising itself. Their activity should not just be seen solely in terms of the undoubted mayhem and cruelties of martial law, or the post-conflict atrocities Cornwallis noted. Indeed, as the yeomanry was a national force, investigation of this role needs to extend beyond the areas which actually saw fighting. What Cornwallis meant when he said that the yeomanry had saved the country was not just the fighting in Antrim or Wexford, but that Knox's yeomanry brigade system had enabled the entire military response to be co-ordinated. By integrating the yeomanry into the military system, the old counter-insurgency/defence circle was squared. From April 1798 when the supplementaries were first organized, the government had at last a system with the flexibility to respond to invasion, insurrection and threatened insurrection. All three contingencies were tested in 1798. Despite arrests and informers, the United Irishmen still had the natural advantage of surprise as well as numbers. A successful defence system, if it could not be locally preventative, had to function as a holding measure and stop areas affected by major risings passing completely from the government's hands until a full response could be marshalled. The yeomanry brigade system was intended to facilitate both prevention and cure. The latter is best illustrated by looking at County Down.

The key garrison positions for Down were Belfast, Blaris Camp, Downpatrick and Newry. These were to be defended at all costs and function as fall-backs, if the smaller garrisons were attacked. The Castlewellan Yeomanry provided detachments for small garrisons in Castlewellan itself and also at Ballynahinch, Rathfriland and Bryansford. Their fall-back was Newry. Those at Portaferry had instructions, if attacked in force, to cross the narrows of Strangford Lough to the town of Strangford, with an eventual fall-back to Down-patrick.[43] This worked well. The Castlewellan yeomen at Ballynahinch lost seven men captured when the United Irishmen over-ran the town on the Saturday before the battle, but the remainder dropped back to Hillsborough. The garrisons of Newtownards, Comber and Saintfield withdrew to Belfast, following a take-over by United Irishmen.[44] Things could go wrong. The ambush and *de facto* defeat (though Nugent never acknowledged it as such) of government forces under Colonel

42 *Loyal Songs no. 2 as sung in all the Orange Lodges* [B.L. 11622d2].
43 Nugent to Lake, 10 June 1798: N.A.I., RP 620/38/121.
44 McKey to Downshire, 10 June 1798; Lane to Downshire, 10 June 1798: P.R.O.N.I., Downshire papers, D607/F/219, 221.

Stapylton at Saintfield was due to his having left Comber before he received Nugent's order to fall back. Whether this was due to foolhardiness on Stapylton's part, or a break-down in communications, cannot now be established, but Stapylton and his mixed force of fencibles, yeomen and civilian volunteers did eventually limp back to Belfast after their mauling at Saintfield on 9 June.[45]

Portaferry's yeomanry garrison fared better. Occupying the Market House, and using the swivel guns of the revenue cruiser waiting in the harbour for their escape, they beat off an attack with little loss and crossed over safely to Strangford. As they withdrew, the United Irishmen, who lost around forty men, abandoned the assault and retreated. Nugent's emphatic suppression of the Down rising at Ballynahinch was a textbook implementation of the new defence system. Having gathered his strength at Belfast, Blaris and Downpatrick, he counter-attacked by co-ordinating forces, including many yeomanry corps, to march from these centres to trap the insurgents at Ballynahinch.[46] The system worked less well in the south, particularly in Wexford where the numbers (Wexford yeomanry totalled only 1,800 *after* the rebellion whereas their opponents gathered well over 10,000 for the attack on New Ross), speed and surprise of the United Irish mobilization initially caught the yeomanry and other forces cold. It worked better in Dublin where 5,000 yeomanry were organized, giving coverage so significant Camden noted that, although the Dublin United men planned to rise, 'the yeomanry are so alert that I think it is impossible it can be effected'.[47]

There is also clear evidence that the yeomanry brigade system actually *prevented* risings in other parts. A gathering of insurgents in County Leitrim was quickly dispersed by local yeomanry units.[48] John Knox's own district, which included Cavan, Fermanagh, Tyrone and parts of Armagh, was not only held totally by its yeomen but also provided a surplus.[49] When rumours spread that a rising was planned in Cavan for midsummer, he marched a large force of Fermanagh yeomen from Enniskillen to link up with the Cavan yeomanry brigade to ensure that nothing happened.[50] Earlier he had sent yeomanry reinforcements from Tyrone to aid Nugent with the Antrim rising.[51] Although the

45 Nugent to Lake, 10 June 1798: N.A.I., RP 620/38/121.
46 Stephenson to Downshire, 12 June 1798, 13 June 1798; Galbraith to Hull, 13 June 1798: P.R.O.N.I., Downshire papers, D607/F/226, 235, 236; General Nugent's printed dispatch, 14 June 1798: B.L., Percy papers, Add MS 32,335, f. 40.
47 Cooke to Wickham, 2 June 1798: Camden to Portland, 4 June 1798, P.R.O., HO 100/77, f. 21, ff 25–8; Ross to Downshire, 24 June 1798: P.R.O.N.I., Downshire papers, D607/F/ 271.
48 Camden to Portland, 1 June 1798: P.R.O., HO 100/81, f. 1.
49 J. Knox to Adjutant General Hewitt, 31 May 1798: P.R.O.N.I., Dublin Army Letters, mic 67, f. 39.
50 J. Knox to Nugent, 17 June 1798: N.A.M., Nugent papers, 6807/174, ff 465–9.
51 Nugent to J. Knox 6 June 1798: N.L.I., Lake papers, MS56/178; Nugent to Castlereagh, 8 June 1798: P.R.O., HO 100/81, f. 41; Richardson, *Origins of the yeomanry*, pp 41–2; Nugent to J. Knox, 15 June 1798: N.L.I., Lake papers, MS 56/193.

yeomanry corps which faced Humbert at Killalla were no match for French veterans, the national force was put on permanent duty, enabling Cornwallis to
assemble a huge army to crush the invasion. Within days of Humbert's defeat,
Cornwallis established a new defence system by dividing his force into stationary
and moveable brigades. Cornwallis' system remained the foundation of Irish
defence policy for the rest of the war. The yeomanry featured largely in the stationary part of that system, and their remit was based on the 1798 yeomanry
brigade system, a practical endorsement of Cornwallis' earlier remarks about the
yeomanry's role in saving the country.[52]

The critical point about the yeomanry is the primacy of military localism,
both in 1798 and in the maelstrom of terror and counter-terror leading up to it.
Although the yeomanry brigade system certainly helped hold the country and
equally certainly saved lives by preventing collateral risings, by that stage the die
was cast. The high-risk manpower-raising and propaganda strategies of both the
United Irishmen and the authorities ensured that in parts of Ulster and
Leinster, a popular contemporary prophecy was fulfilled and 1798 was indeed 'a
bloody summer'.[53]

52 Blackstock, *Ascendancy army*, p. 159.
53 I would like to thank the following individuals and institutions for permission to draw on
   archival material in their keeping: the Deputy Keeper of the Records, P.R.O.N.I.; the National
   Library of Ireland; the National Army Museum, Chelsea; the National Archives, Ireland; the
   Centre for Kentish Studies; the British Library; the Public Record Office, London (the Home
   Office Papers are Crown Copyright); the Board of Trinity College Dublin.

17

Orangeism in 1798

JAMES WILSON

'To consider the best mode of organizing the Orangemen of Ireland and [to] render them more effective in support of their King and Glorious Constitution': with this pragmatic aim and object, eighteen members of the Orange Society met on 8 March 1798 in Dublin, probably in the town house of James Verner.[1] The make-up of the group reveals much about the social structure and control of Orangeism at this time: at least fifteen of those present held rank either in the militia or the newly formed yeomanry; eleven were titled as sergeants or non-commissioned officers, suggesting that they were not gentlemen but belonged to the middling group of tenant farmers, estate agents and linen traders, callings that were deemed respectable.[2] In keeping with contemporary practice, little record of debate, dissent or discussion was minuted. But the original record of four agreed resolutions does survive; the first has been quoted above; the second stated that 'it is advisable a grand lodge should be formed ... to be held in Dublin'. The subsequent creation of the Grand Lodge of Ireland marks out Orangeism as unique among the various plebeian solidarity groups that had emerged from rural Ulster in the eighteenth century. Surprisingly this uniqueness has not attracted close academic study.

The general historiography of Orangeism has currently but one entry – the publication by Hereward Senior in 1966, a work which failed to stimulate much debate, indeed perhaps the reverse.[3] However, if frequent reference is made to Senior's work in this paper, it is not to create a straw target. Rather it is a desperate attempt to open up a dialogue and to initiate the debate that the subject richly deserves. Orangeism in its long history after 1798 succeeded in uniting

1 Grand Lodge of Ireland, Belfast, MS GOLI/A/A/98, minute book, p. 1.
2 Ibid. The minute book records names and lodges: William Blacker – No. 12; Major Molesworth, Capt. Moore – No. 154 (Cavan Militia); Thomas Verner – No. 176; Capt. J.C. Beresford (Royal Dublin Cavalry); Sergeants Hughes, Hamilton and Gilchrist – No. 177 (Cavan Militia); Sergeants Little, MacClean and Holmes – No. 222 (Armagh Militia); Sergeants Douglas and Sinclair – No. 235 (Armagh Militia); Edward Ball, Isaac Dejoncourt – No. 413 (Dublin); Lt. Col. Rochford – No. 414 (Carlow); Sergeant-Major Galloughly, Sergeant Price – No. 415 (Fermanagh Militia).
3 Hereward Senior, *Orangeism in Ireland and Britain, 1795–1836* (London, 1966).

disparate Protestant elements; it negotiated a new social contract within the Reformed confession and helped produce an enduring cultural identity which embodies many elements of fraternalism via ritualized male bonding. But to interpret the essence of the early Orange Society we must begin by discarding any present-minded concepts of the contemporary institution that is its heir and successor. Eighteenth-century Orangeism is not a topical subject; no appreciation of the fears, ambitions or collective passions of Atkinson, Verner and Winter can be gained from an observation of Drumcree churchyard or the Ormeau Road. A failure by both historians and polemicists to be sensitive to periodization is a characteristic of the early (and some contemporary) historiography.

The first detailed study of the Orange movement escapes this criticism. The 1835 House of Commons Select Committee report was compiled not by historians but by politicians. It did not claim to be a history; rather, as it plainly asserts, it sets out the evidence presented to the Committee and its findings. This investigation did not focus on the events of the 1790s but on the contemporary activities of a secret society which was operating illegally within the British army. The report was accepted by the movement's early leadership as a reasonably factual and balanced account of Orangeism's genesis. Indeed William Blacker refers the reader of his 'Day Book' journal to its narrative.

> This beginning of the Orange organisation, with the pass words and regulations, have, through a medium of parliamentary reports, become matters of historic record. A reference to those reports does away with my going over the same ground again.[4]

Blacker's 'Day Book' was his account of the events of 1795–8. It is in the form of a reflective journal, penned some forty years later. The years may have mellowed Blacker's fervour, for the first county grand master of Armagh was at pains to censure his Orange brethren for their acts of retribution against the Roman Catholic community in the aftermath of the Diamond skirmish.

> Happy had it been for the Protestant name if Protestants had been content with the defeat of their enemies at the Diamond and the formation of a protective society. Unhappily it was not so, and a spirit of vengeance and retaliation had sunk too deeply in their minds to be thus easily satisfied.[5]

4 P.R.O.N.I., T2595/4, Col. William Blacker, 'The day book' (1836), p. 17 [now published in [Cecil Kilpatrick (ed.),] *The formation of the Orange Order, 1795–98: The edited papers of Col. William Blacker and Col. Robert H. Wallace* (Belfast, 1994)].
5 Ibid., p. 19.

Blacker further endears himself to the historian by confining his account to those matters that he can vouch for personally. He frequently qualified his account with the admission that as a Trinity College student there were times when he 'escaped being any sort of witness' to crucial events.[6] In view of this degree of concern with verifiable fact and the private nature of the journal (there is no evidence that it was ever intended for readership outside the Blacker family), some of the passing comments within the Day Book can be taken as unwitting testimony:[7] Blacker makes reference to the involvement of the Peep o' Day Boy in early clashes with Defenders; he portrays the Peep o' Day Boys as an *ad hoc* grouping with no 'systematic affiliation'; furthermore he does not attempt to cover up Orange-inspired sectarian violence or classify it as Peep o' Day Boy activity; and finally (in stark contrast to the later orthodoxy) he denies widespread involvement in Orangeism by the 'resident gentry'.[8]

Both the Select Committee report and Blacker's 'Day Book' are, strictly speaking, primary source material. The 'true' secondary accounts of the nineteenth century must be understood against the backdrop of the '98 rebellion. Historians were at pains to attribute blame for this localized bloodbath and, depending on perspective, Orangeism was characterized as having either actively helped provoke the atrocities (through the severity of repressive measures taken by the 'Orange' yeomanry or militia),[9] or Orangeism was seen as a crucial factor in checking the murder and mayhem of the rebels,[10] (and a few writers like Edward Hay made little reference to Orangeism or to its contribution to the crisis at all).[11] In general terms, this flurry of histories in the wake of the rebellion was based on accessible source material. The element of bias and subjective prejudice was uncomplicated and is easy to discern. But in 1825, however, Ogle Robert Gowan, former acting grand secretary of the Loyal Orange Institution, wrote a history of the movement that had the effect of distorting much subsequent Orange historiography.

Gowan, son of the former Wexford 1798 magistrate John Hunter Gowan, may have been prompted to write a defence of Orangeism following the dissolution of the Grand Lodge (1825). His book established a *genre* for Orangemen who wrote their Order's history in that it began with a protracted account of the Williamite war and Glorious Revolution. This back-drop was to become an almost mandatory prologue and had the effect of entwining the birth of

6 Ibid.

7 Armagh Public Museum, Blacker papers (1836), p. 241.

8 Blacker, 'Day book', p. 18.

9 R.R. Madden, *The United Irishmen, their lives and times* (2nd ed., Dublin, 1857–62); Francis Plowden, *The history of Ireland from its invasion under Henry II to its union with Great Britain* (London, 1805).

10 Sir Richard Musgrave, *Memoirs of the different rebellions in Ireland* (London, 1802).

11 Edward Hay, *History of the Irish insurrection of 1798* (Dublin, 1798).

Orangeism directly with the 'glorious memory' which it dedicated itself to per-
petuating. There are, however, more serious innovations in the Gowan version,
deviations that have profoundly warped the received views of early Orangeism
down to the present. There is no evidence to indicate that Gowan was ever in
County Armagh, nor that he had ever bothered to record the testimony of any
survivors of the Diamond. His extraordinary conclusion was that the Peep o'
Day Boys were 'deluded Presbyterians [who] ... joined with Roman Catholics in
harassing the Protestants of the Church of Ireland', and that these Peep o' Day
Boys were part of the Defender attacking-force at the Diamond on 21 September 1795.[12] This raises doubts as to his reliability as a collator of source material.
Either Gowan was completely ignorant of the preconditions and events of the
Diamond battle – or he had just disclosed Orangeism's best-kept piece of esoteric knowledge. The former conclusion is more probable and this should have
alerted Gowan's readership to his habit of creating fictions when his scant and
selective research failed to yield solid fact.

Yet the alarm bells did not ring. When Hereward Senior wrote his account of
Orangeism in 1966 he commended the work of Ogle Gowan.

> His [Gowan's] is also an official history, but is better organized and closer
> to the event ... Gowan is an intelligent if partial observer ... There is a
> little offered in the works of other Orange historians ... that cannot be
> found in Gowan ...[13]

There was indeed unique material to be found in Gowan, material that does not
tally with any other contemporary source. A good example is Gowan's treatment
of the Grand Lodge. In tracing its evolution he related in great detail a meeting
that was alleged to have taken place on 12 July 1798 which supposedly resulted
in a series of resolutions and the appointment of Grand Officers:

> 1st Resolved – That all lodges shall pay an annual sum of three pence for
> each member, to defray the various expenses incurred by Mr Atkinson in
> the issue of warrants.

> 2nd Resolved – That no lodge shall be held without a warrant to be
> signed by Mr Wolsey Atkinson, and a seal with the likeness of King
> William affixed thereto.

> *Grand Officers (appointed 12 July 1798)*
> Captain William Blacker, GM Armagh
> Thomas Verner Esq, GM Tyrone, Derry, Fermanagh

12 Ogle R. Gowan, *Annals and defence of the Loyal Orange Association of Ireland* (Dublin, 1825),
   p. 45.
13 Senior, *Orangeism*, p. 289.

Doctor William Atkinson, GM Antrim
Thomas Seaver, GT Armagh
David Verner, GS Armagh
William Hart, GS Antrim
Wolsey Atkinson, Acting Grand Secretary.[14]

All this conveys the image of a harmonious institution, with those of lower social rank such as Wolsey Atkinson being given some status within the Grand Lodge before absolute control was placed in the hands of those of higher station. In Armagh, this process would appear to have been well underway with David Verner already grand secretary. However the reality was that Wolsey Atkinson was the grand secretary of the Grand Lodge of Armagh from 12 February 1798 until January 1800.[15] There is no evidence that he ever attended a meeting of the Grand Lodge of Ireland, nor that the Grand Lodge sat at any time between 18 May and 28 September 1798.

In 1859, Gowan, then living in Canada, published his second work on Orangeism.[16] Not only did it confirm his basic ignorance about the origins of the movement but it allowed him compound his earlier fiction with a spurious account of early Orangeism in Dublin and Wexford.[17] We are told that his father, John Hunter Gowan, introduced the first warranted lodge to Wexford on 10 February 1798. This, Gowan claimed, was LOL 406, and this warrant 'marched' throughout the rebellion with the Wingfield yeomanry. It was, he added, signed by Wolsey Atkinson, J.C. Beresford and Thomas Verner. This was a fabrication. First, warrant 406 was working in Longford in 1798. Second, Wexford's first officially recorded warrant was LOL 650, issued on 4 December 1798.[18] And finally, the complicated counter-signing agreement for warrants was not brokered until 11 February 1799.[19] A warrant issued as early as 10 February 1798 would have been signed by James Sloan of Loughgall.[20]

By the stage when Gowan's account reached the formation of the Grand Lodge, his powers of fabrication showed no limit; using his inside knowledge, he was able to construct a plausible record of meetings that was to deceive later historians. The extract below contains his account of a completely fictitious Grand Lodge session in which Gowan's father is referred to as 'Grand Master of Wexford' and Wolsey Atkinson is transported from Portadown.

14 Gowan, *Annals*.
15 *B.N.L.*, 23 Feb. 1798.
16 Ogle R. Gowan, *Orangeism, its origins and history* (Toronto, 1859).
17 Ibid., p. 138.
18 Grand Lodge MS GOLI/A/M/98, pp 30–8.
19 Ibid.
20 Ibid.; *B.N.L.*, 23 Feb. 1798.

> The meeting being duly organised calling Mr Thomas Verner to the chair, appointing Mr Atkinson Secretary, some discussion ensued as to the proper mode of proceeding. The Right Hon. Mr Ogle, in a very eloquent and impressive speech seconded by Captain Blacker, proposed that Thomas Verner be the First Grand Master of Ireland. Before putting the motion, Mr Verner said, as he had no objection in view, but the good cause and security of the Kingdom he thought that the first Grand Mastership should be offered to the Earl of Athlone, or Marquis of Drogheda, as the only remainder of King William's Generals ... The Earl of Athlone and Lord Drogheda declined respectfully the proffered honour, stating that no man could have greater or even so great a claim as Mr Verner. Major Sirr proposed and Captain Gowan seconded the appointment of Sir Richard Musgrave for Grand Treasurer.[21]

Gowan goes on to relate the events of 1798, particularly the heroism of his father and of the role of 'the Orangemen of Newtownbarry' in defeating the rebels. No trace of this extract – or indeed of any of Gowan's documentation – can be found in the Grand Lodge minute book. We must conclude that between 1825 and 1859 Ogle Robert Gowan fabricated a highly misleading account of early Orangeism. This prompts three questions: Why did Gowan compile such fiction? Secondly, why did both contemporaries and later historians choose to believe it? And, most seriously of all, how did this naïve acceptance of the Gowan material distort the received view of the role and function of Orangeism in 1798?

Why did Gowan do it? One possible motive stemmed from the fact that after emigrating to Canada, he pursued an active career in colonial politics. To win his seat in the legislature of Canada, he had to make full use of his position as first grand master of British North America. There was a growing constituency of Ulster Protestants settling in Ontario, and how better to win their votes than to present himself as a son of a true Orange hero and founder member?[22] Why was Gowan's account unchallenged? In the case of his peers, some mitigation can be offered. First, his rank as grand master provided him with a position of authority, coupled with the fact that he had been a former acting grand secretary to the Grand Lodge of Ireland. It could be presumed that he was a well-informed source. Second, it is clear that Gowan was plying a version of Orangeism's origins that Orangemen wanted to hear: it was flattering to know that the great Williamite dynasties of Athlone and Drogheda had graced the Institution and somehow imparted a higher legitimacy to Orangeism. It is more difficult to find excuses for Senior's acceptance of Gowan's fiction. True, he did not have access

---

21 Gowan, *Annals*, p. 60.
22 Rory Fitzpatrick, *God's frontiersmen: The Scots-Irish epic* (London, 1989), p. 209.

to the Grand Lodge minute book which effectively settles the issue, but conflicting evidence from the *Belfast News Letter* should have made him question
whether Gowan was indeed just an 'intelligent if partial observer'.

Finally, what damage did the acceptance of Gowan's falsification do to our
understanding of early Orangeism? Gowan can be credited with the introduction of two false elements which are still taken as part of the accepted historical
record. First was his incorporation of major gentry families into the thick of the
early action. The belief in high-level patronage of Orangeism was flattering to
later Orangemen, and was a useful precedent for Ulster Unionists during the
Home Rule crisis when both middle and upper classes flocked into the Orange
fold. Senior, it must be said, did craft a more accurate picture as to the level of
gentry support.[23] He nevertheless accepted Gowan's model of an Orange Society
which originated with the 'peasantry' and quickly passed to 'gentry' control.
This model is no longer credible in the light of newly available primary material,[24] and the recent reassessment of eighteenth-century Ulster society.[25]

From the 1850s there were two aspects of the development of Orangeism
which stimulated interest in its origins and provoked the addition of elements to
the historiography which had a clear polemical purpose. First, there was Orangeism's indispensable links with Ulster Unionism; second, its international dimension reflected Ulster emigration to the empire. Thus when Fr H.W. Cleary's *The
Orange Order* was published in 1899, its primary purpose was to expose the
Order's sectarian record in Australia and New Zealand, but coupled with this was
a scathing accusation that, back in Ireland, the gentlemen and respectable middle-
class Unionists of the day were in open association with an organisation founded
by an unreformed gang of Armagh cut-throats.[26] Cleary centered much of his
case on the material in the House of Commons Select Committee Report. He isolated the evidence of James Christie and, in what was a very selective presentation
of his testimony, made a seemingly strong case for seeing the original Orangemen
as nothing more than the Peep o' Day Boys operating under a new cloak of convenience. This resurrection of the Peep o' Day Boy–Orange continuum was difficult to refute since both movements appeared to share a common period and
location; indeed much of Cleary's model can be recognized in the received image
of the Orange genesis. The following passage by J.C. Beckett serves as a good
illustration of just how accepted this concept became.

> This [sectarian strife] reached a crisis in September 1795 when a pitch-
> ed battle between Peep o' Day boys and Defenders took place at the

23 Senior, *Orangeism*, p. 94.
24 Grand Lodge MS GOLI/A/M/98.
25 Kevin Whelan, 'Settlement and society in eighteenth-century Ireland', in Gerald Dawe
   and John Foster (eds), *The poet's place* ... (Belfast, 1991), p. 46.
26 H.W. Cleary, *The Orange Order* (London, 1899), p. 57.

Diamond in County Armagh. The defenders were completely routed, and that evening the victorious Protestants established an 'Orange Society'.[27]

Senior's treatment of the Peep o' Day Boy–Orange continuity is interesting. Conscious that there was a clear dichotomy in the activity patterns of the two groups,[28] he cautiously concluded that Peep o' Day Boys probably fought at the Diamond, hence their exclusion from the Orange Society would have been difficult.[29] This more nuanced gloss on Peep o' Day involvement in early Orangeism made little impact. The orthodoxy remained – the Peep o' Day Boys had collectively decided on 21 September 1795 to become Orangemen.[30]

Shortly after the centenary of the Order, Colonel Robert Wallace brought together a remarkable collection of pieces on Orange history – remarkable not least in that it was to lie unexamined for ninety years before being published.[31] Wallace was a busy man; in addition to being senior partner of the family law firm, he was county grand master of Belfast at the height of the Independent Orange crisis. He was no professional scholar; indeed much of his work, particularly where reference to the Grand Lodge in Dublin is concerned, is a mere borrowing from Gowan. Yet Wallace's account is of interest for three reasons. As a prominent member with an Oxford education, Wallace was a popular touring lecturer within the Institution. This brought him into contact with the sons and associates of the original Orangemen.

> ... (warrant) No. 5 went to Robert Irwin of Kinnego ... My informant was his son James ... who said his father was initiated behind a ditch.[32]

This contact with the grass roots, made a mere generation from the founders, endowed Wallace with a sense of the 1790s that is lacking in the work of later histories. He identified some of the elements of character and social structure of early Orangeism that current research is only now confirming:

> The farmers and linen manufacturers to whom we owe the Orange Society were God fearing men ... therefore the humble men who did not aspire to represent pocket boroughs in the Irish House of Commons and never expected to be in employment of the state decided on a system of their own creation.[33]

27 J.C. Beckett, *The making of modern Ireland* (London, 1966), p. 257.
28 Senior, *Orangeism*, p. 14.
29 Ibid., p. 19.
30 See for example D.J. Hickey and J.E. Doherty, *A dictionary of Irish history since 1800* (Dublin, 1980), p. 449.
31 P.R.O.N.I., D1889/6/4/1–2, Wallace papers [now published in *Formation of the Orange Order*].
32 Ibid., p. 49.   33   Ibid.

Wallace, as Belfast's senior Orangeman, was tactfully aware of the growing strength and value of Presbyterians within the Institution. He was the first writer to recognize Orangeism's unique function as a Protestant umbrella group.

> The Dyan men were all, or nearly all, Presbyterians; the Loughgall men were all, or nearly all, Episcopalians; they had fought together, they were determined to cling together. All things considered, the grandest feature of the Orange Society is the catholicity of its constitution.[34]

Wallace constantly reworked his script and it was obviously intended for eventual publication.[35] He was however living in an age when Ulstermen were making history rather than writing it. His involvement with the UVF probably caused him to shelve any plans to publish, and it was during this period that an 'official history' of Orangeism, written by R.M. Sibbett, began to appear in serial form in the *Belfast Weekly News*. Sibbett's commission to write an official history may have deterred Wallace from the publication of a rival account; there is indeed some evidence of corroboration between them.[36] Sibbett's survey was published in 1915, an impressive two-volume work. At one level, it is a valuable record: he transcribed oral traditions that would have been lost; his work was not coloured by any ulterior motive – other than perhaps to depict Orangeism in a completely respectable light. But it is pure narrative with little offered by way of analysis.

Sibbett expressed the firm conviction that most Protestant gentry of the 1790s were staunch Orangemen. Thus we find contemporary critics such as Gosford and Charlemont presented in such a way as to suggest that they might well have been closet supporters of the movement.[37] Sibbett's self-imposed obligation to portray Orangeism as the great fraternal catch-all movement made him oblivious to even the most outlandish of Gowan's claims. With the background of the Home Rule crisis and the fledgling state of Northern Ireland, the image of an Orange Society which in times past had enjoyed the patronage of the great and good was a useful prop for promoting membership within middle-class Ulster. Apart from an anonymous update of Sibbett's work in 1939, Orange historiography lay dormant for some forty years until Senior's study was published in 1966. This was – and is still – the only scholarly study of the Institution. Aside from a critical reading by T.W. Moody, the work is very much an outsider's piece of research, both in methodology and in its analytical presentation.[38] Despite a highly impressive bibliography for its time, there is no indication that Senior ever consulted the Grand Lodge of Ireland, and thus he may

34 Ibid., p. 49.
35 P.R.O.N.I., D1889/6/4/1. There are signs of proof-reading and correction on pp 101, 103.
36 R.M. Sibbett, *The formation of the Orange Order* (1st ed., Belfast, 1914–5), ii, p. 23.
37 Ibid. (2nd ed, London, 1939), p. 269.
38 Senior, *Orangeism*, preface, p. iv.

have been completely unaware of the existence of the eighteenth-century minute book.

In the light of fresh archival material and of three decades of research on Ulster's social and political history since Senior's study appeared, we can pick out several major limitations in Senior's analysis. First, we now have a more nuanced appreciation of the society out of which Orangeism emerged. It was no simple monolithic peasant world but one of very considerable social complexity, compounded by the impact of rural industrialization in Armagh and east Tyrone – the very cradle of Orangeism.[39] The massive growth of linen manufacture had dramatic effects on the social and demographic structure. In 1770 Ulster had 42,000 weavers; forty years later this had reached 70,000; thus in 1792 the pamphleteer 'John Byrne' observed: 'We may justly say that the county of Armagh is a hot bed for cash for the industrious farmer and weaver.'[40] What recreation and social activity was open to the industrious farmer and weaver? In County Armagh of the 1790s such men would have found two avenues for fraternal recognition and advancement. The Freemasons were at their zenith. The appeal of such a body was universal: for one night in the month one could find escape from the everyday and aspire to rising status. The obligations of the brotherhood, the secrets, passwords and degrees, all helped create an alternative world where mundane lifestyles could be exchanged for exciting – often frightening – experiences that were rewarded with access to esoteric knowledge and the conferral of rank. The annual parades to church gave an opportunity to wear the sash and ribbon.

A second social activity offering status improvement was closely affiliated to masonry – Volunteering. It gave a more overt opportunity to be noticed and created scope for social encounter with the gentry. Again there was the opportunity for parades and ceremony. The Armagh weaver/farmer could swagger along behind a flute band to the air of *The Boyne Water* and feel considerable fulfilment. Thus the role and function of the Volunteers as a precursor of Orangeism cannot be underestimated.[41] There are three well documented accounts of a long-running conflict between Defenders and Volunteers. The first is by the Revd W. Campbell: on 21 November 1788 the Benburb Volunteers marched to Sunday worship at Armagh Cathedral:

> On their march they were assaulted by a large body of Papists who took a bayonet from one of the lads, and pursued them with stones. As the corps only had their side arms, and being apprehensive for their safety on their

39 Whelan, 'Settlement and society', p. 46.
40 J. Byrne, *An impartial account of the late disturbances in the county of Armagh* ... (Dublin, 1792), pp 34–9.
41 David Miller, 'The Armagh troubles, 1784–95', in Samuel Clarke and J.S. Donnelly (eds), *Irish peasants: Violence and political unrest, 1780–1914* (Manchester, 1983), p. 173.

return, they borrowed some firelocks from friends of this town, and got I am told eight. The company was commanded by Lieutenant Young.[42]

This report to the earl of Charlemont relates that on the return journey the Volunteers were attacked with stones and were forced to shoot one of their attackers.[43] Another contemporary report, written after the inquest, suggests a sectarian motive for the assault: 'that the reason for the intended attack on the Volunteers was, their playing tunes that were an insult to Catholics ... 'The Protestant boys' and 'The Boyne Water' were the tunes alluded to ...'[44] This clash at Drumbee was minor in the context of the riots of the time. There were two recorded Catholic fatalities. But the consequences however were, it seems, far-reaching. The funerals of Dennis and Finnegan were attended by immense crowds, and the coroner's inquest at the Lent assizes brought the affair into public focus;[45] in the words of Byrne, 'the battle of Drumbee was the whole discourse that occupied most people's attention'.[46]

The Volunteers were now perceived by the Defenders as legitimate targets, and a series of attacks was launched against their homes and workplaces.[47] Thomas Prentice wrote to Charlemont that 'this unfortunate business has given the deepest concern to every man who wishes well to the peace and happiness of this country, as it may probably rekindle that animosity between the lower rank of Protestants and Catholics, which appeared to be subsiding for some time past'.[48] Prentice's concerns were well-founded. The Lent assizes of 1789 and the subsequent Summer assizes recorded a sharp upturn in violent sectarian crime, assault and use of firearms. In two well documented incidents, the Volunteers clashed with Defenders on St John's Eve (23 June) 1789,[49] and later at Lisnagade, where a five-hour gun battle was waged.[50] A second crucial aspect of Prentice's testimony is that it suggests that prior to Drumbee sectarian animosities appeared to have been subsiding. This observation does not sit comfortably with Byrne's account, which highlights continuous Peep o' Day Boy activity until the early 1790s; for example, Byrne places the Goodfellow murder in 1790, whereas court records list the case as being dealt with at the Lent Assizes of April 1789. This discrepancy in Byrne's narrative casts doubt on the mortality figures for the 'Armagh disturbances' suggested by Miller.[51] On the basis of pre-

42 Revd W. Campbell to the earl of Charlemont, 26 Nov. 1788: H.M.C., *Charlemont MSS*, ii, p. 78.
43 Other contemporary evidence suggests two fatal shootings.
44 Thomas Prentice to Charlemont, 28 Nov. 1788: *Charlemont MSS*, ii, p. 80.
45 P.R.O.N.I., Armagh Assizes indictment book, bill 21, 1788.
46 Byrne, *Impartial account*, p. 40.
47 Robert Livingston to Charlemont, 17 Dec. 1788: *Charlemont MSS*, p. 83.
48 Thomas Prentice to Charlemont, 28 Nov. 1788: *Charlemont MSS*, p. 80.
49 Byrne, *Impartial account*, pp 40–1.
50 John Moore to Charlemont, 15 July 1789: R.I.A., Charlemont papers, MS 12/R/15/56.
51 Miller, 'Armagh troubles', p. 173.

sent evidence it seems that the principal power struggle in Armagh in the late 1780s and early 1790s was one between those associated with the Volunteers and the Defenders, and did not involve the Peep o' Day Boys.

The year 1793 heralded two events that altered the local power balance and created an environment for Orangeism. First the new militia act sounded the death knell for Volunteering. The militia was to be raised by local levy; inherent in this was the possibility that those with Defender or revolutionary sympathies would be drafted and armed. The second event was the Catholic Relief Act, which raised the political awareness of Catholics and stimulated a surge in both the membership and activity of Defenders. Their contact with the United Irishmen introduced the concept of revolutionary change which was translated into a Catholic nationalism endorsed by millenarian prophecy; they came to be organised into a national network of lodges, and were sustained by the firm hope of foreign assistance in the event of an actual rising. Protestants and former Volunteers in Armagh and east Tyrone were in dire need of an umbrella organisation that could define their loyalism to the crown and provide an effective counter to what was perceived as a growing Defender challenge. We have the first recorded meeting of an Orange-style society in the locality taking place early in 1793;[52] this group, composed of 138 members, demonstrated a clear distance from the covert activities of Peep o' Day Boys. It clearly had some form of structure, held formal meetings, and published its resolutions concerning duty, collective action and loyalty in the *Belfast News Letter*.[53] The first recognized warrant to constitute an actual Orange Lodge would eventually be issued to this group at the Dyan in east Tyrone.[54]

By 1795, a confrontation between the embryonic Orange movement and the Defenders was to some degree inevitable. A local dispute at the Diamond was to provide the catalyst.[55] In late September the Defenders exercised their efficient lodge network and mobilized at least 500 men to meet at the location in order to show solidarity with local Catholics. The Orange party also mobilized. At first, local peacemakers were confident that the highly ritualized stand-off could be contained and would pass off without bloodshed as had happened the previous June, but the late arrival of Defender reinforcements from Tyrone destroyed a fragile truce.[56]

> The newcomers spurned at any idea of anything like a truce or treaty and resolved not to return home empty-handed. Accordingly, on Monday

52 *B.N.L.*, 29 Jan. 1793.
53 The Orange Club at Dyan were clearly operating in the mode of the later Orange Societies; it had a Master and made loyalty to the king its public resolution.
54 Grand Lodge MS GOLI/A/M/98.
55 Dr Richard Allott to Henry Pelham, 17 June 1795: N.A.I., RP 620/22/9.
56 Revd William Richardson to the duke of Abercorn, 14 Feb. 1797: P.R.O.N.I., Abercorn papers, D623/A/156/4.

morning, the 21st they fired down from their position on Tullymore (or Faughard as it is sometimes called) upon the little hamlet of the Diamond – the principal object of their attack being the house of a farmer named Winter … the Protestants … marched rapidly back to their position on Grangemore where they arrived just in time …[57]

Dr William Richardson supplied a detailed account of the encounter:

Both [sides] were eager for action, the Catholics relying on vast superiority of numbers, the others on better arms and the old Volunteer discipline …[58]

Nor was the Diamond an isolated incident but rather part of a series of show-downs between the over-confident Defenders and the former Volunteers who, for a group disbanded two years earlier, were displaying a striking degree of cohesion:

A final blow having been given to the Defenders, about Bann foot, by some of your Lordship's Veterans – the Protestants here as they call themselves, being too weak for their opponents sent to Maghera craving assistance – two score of the old Volunteers march'd off at midnight and the next morning closely attacked a body of three hundred who had thrown away their fire and completely routed them.[59]

To contemporary observers this situation was new and not just another round of Peep o' Day Boy and Defender feuding. This was the baptism of a new Protestant solidarity grouping which drew powerfully on the Volunteer tradition. Orangeism was quick to formalize and develop a structure as the smoke cleared from Ruddocks Grange:

The Catholics though in proportion of ten to one were defeated … the battle was called the Battle of the Diamond and in commemoration of it, the first Orange Lodge was founded on the 21st September 1795, the name of Orangemen having been adopted a year before …[60]

The local gentry and landowners were clearly in full support of the former Volunteers at the Diamond and Bannfoot. From the tone of Blacker's apology, it is probable that this social group remained aloof from the revenge attacks that

57 Blacker, 'Day book'.
58 Richardson to Abercorn, 14 Feb. 1797.
59 Dr Haliday to Charlemont, 18 Oct. 1795: R.I.A., Charlemont papers, MS 12/R/18, p. 79.
60 Thomas Verner and J.C. Beresford, *Orange vindicated, in a reply to Theobald McKenna* (Dublin, 1799), p.7.

followed the victory of the Orange party. There is however one allegation that the Verner family condoned reprisals.[61] At the Lent assizes of 1796 some thirty of those listed in the Armagh Indictment Book would appear to be connected with Orangeism. The enforcement of the law and the intervention of Lord Gosford on behalf of William Trimble and Francis Winter, saving them from the gallows, may have chastened Orangeism.[62] But by July 1797 Holt Waring was advising Cooke of an attractive dimension to the new movement:

> I must beg to observe to you that a distinction must be made between these Orangemen and those of Co. Armagh under that denomination who have wrecked and wrecked and made such a horrid waste.[63]

This distinction was marked by the discipline of oath-bound obligations, including 'to ... protect existing laws'; there was also a conscious strategy to recruit 'the gentleman of property'.[64]

There is no evidence that any of the major landed families joined the Society, but to the minor gentry and officers of the militia and yeomanry Orangeism with its system of oath, test and proof of loyalty was a godsend. William Richardson succinctly defined the weakness of loyalism in the face of the dynamic appeal of the United Irishmen;

> All parties were now ready to rise but the loyalists, who having no system or point of union or method of showing themselves, were supposed by many and asserted by the United Irishmen not to exist.[65]

In Orangeism loyalists found many of these needs being met. By the spring 1798, the crisis in the country resulted in the posting of many Ulster units of militia and yeomanry to Dublin. Using the system, passwords and 'point of union', a group of young officers and sergeants met to consider 'the best mode of organising the Orangemen of Ireland'. The proposal was the formation of a Grand Lodge.[66]

It is now beyond contention that the group who met in Dublin on 8 March 1798 were in social status far removed from the flattering picture constructed by Gowan. The circumstances which had brought about the meeting and set its mood were in stark contrast with the received view. No 'acting secretary' from

61 Owen Crilly to Thomas Burgh, 20 June 1797: N.A.I., RP 620/31/131.
62 Earl of Gosford to Sackville Hamilton, 23 July 1796: N.A.I., RP 620/23/115; Armagh Assizes indictment book.
63 Revd Holt Waring to Edward Cooke, 23 July 1796: N.A.I., RP 620/24/46.
64 Resolutions of the Armagh Convention, *B.N.L.*, 29 May 1797.
65 Richardson to Abercorn, 14 Feb. 1797.
66 Grand Lodge MS GOLI/A/M/98, p. 1.

Armagh was present and there was no mandate or official sanction from any county for the action that was discussed. In the absence of such approval the group were wise enough to initiate a canvassing letter to each known working lodge in Ireland. The letter was penned by Thomas Verner on 10 March and enclosed the resolutions of the meeting. He took care to describe what had happened as 'a meeting of several orange lodges now in Dublin' and hoped that they 'had not presumed too far in forming this association'. The key resolution referred to the formation of a Grand Lodge in Dublin. Although Thomas Verner styled himself as 'Grand Master of Tyrone, Fermanagh, and Londonderry', there is no evidence of any district or county structure in these areas at this time. Armagh had indeed elected its first county grand officers some twenty-four days earlier.[67] Yet County Grand Master Blacker, a student at Trinity who attended the Dublin meetings, was not recorded as having been given an official view from that county. Blacker registered at only one subsequent meeting. What is more surprising is that the Dublin group chose to ignore the office of the Armagh grand secretary, Wolsey Atkinson, and to canvass each lodge. Atkinson had inherited the Orange warrant registers from James Sloan of Loughgall, and was thus in a position to supply the name and address of every Orange lodge in Ireland.[68] Without this information, the consultation process would have been haphazard and incomplete. The lodges in the district of Portadown chose to ignore it completely.[69]

The replies to Verner's letter, incomplete as they are, give an overall picture of the state of Orangeism in 1798. On paper there is a muster of at least 11,876 men spread over seventeen counties. The stronghold was of course Ulster: Armagh had 75 recorded warrants, Tyrone 58, Down (including south Antrim) 49, Cavan 24, Fermanagh 20, Monaghan 18, Londonderry 7, and Donegal 3. Outside Ulster, Dublin had five lodges, and the rest were scattered through Longford, Westmeath, Limerick, Carlow, Leitrim and Wicklow. Five warrants 'marched' with the regular British army in addition to those held by militia and yeomanry corps which appear to have been lumped with their county at this time.[70]

When the Dublin group met again on 9 April, it styled itself as 'Grand Lodge'. Meeting again on 21 April, the ten-man group appointed Thomas Verner as grand master and J.C. Beresford as grand secretary. The same meeting resolved to order a 'copper plate ... for the purpose of striking warrants', that 'in future all warrants for holding lodges ... do issue from the Grand Lodge ... [and] ... a letter be written to Wolsey Atkinson of Portadown for the books [the Warrant Registers] and the last issued by him and presenting him with a silver medal'.[71]

67 *B.N.L.*, 23 Feb. 1798.
68 Ibid.
69 Grand Lodge MS GOLI/A/M/98, pp 4–17.
70 Ibid.   71   Ibid., p. 20.

The Grand Lodge never got the books and Wolsey Atkinson got no silver medal. A dispute with the Grand Lodge of Armagh lasted until February 1799, at which time Verner and another Dublin official travelled to Armagh and met Atkinson. The minutes of the meeting and the associated correspondence shows that the concept of brotherhood through the Orange system presented opportunities for men like Atkinson. He treated Verner with respect but not deference, and politely reminded the grand master of Ireland that in Armagh at least Orangeism was democratic. Even a grand master must await the formal decision of the County Armagh lodge.[72] The resolution displayed by Atkinson clearly had a profound effect on Verner. Perhaps he grasped that the body that he had helped to establish was not some hierarchical system and that as a 'brother' Orangeman he was under a fraternal obligation to afford them respect and treat them as brethren, irrespective of their humble social rank. Verner went as far as to make the concession in writing:

> The object of the Grand Lodge of Ireland has been to give equal representation to the Orangemen of the whole kingdom, wherefore every Master of a lodge, or his representative was and is considered a member thereof with equal powers to assent or dissent any proposed measure.[73]

This was a major revision of the resolutions of 8 March 1798, which had offered only limited suffrage. Verner effectively dispensed with the special status of the Dublin lodges. In Atkinson's reply to Verner, we see a masterly composition couched in the Lockean lexicon of covenant and contract that even Thomas Paine would have found familiar.

> The Grand Lodge of Armagh acknowledges the Grand Lodge of Ireland held in the city of Dublin, so long as it shall continue to allow the same precedent to the County of Armagh as it now doth.[74]

The Grand Lodge of Ireland acquiesced in full to Armagh's demands. Atkinson's conditions were minuted with a note that 'without delay' they would agree to his request for 300 new warrants.[75] The Grand Lodge met ten times from 25 April 1798 until 18 December of that year. During the two meetings in the month of May, they appointed a new secretary and published a declaration of loyalty. They did not meet again until 28 September, when they resolved to print a secret oath and articles. The rest of the meetings that year were devoted to the dialogue with County Armagh and the new rules and regulations. At the meet-

72 Ibid., pp 62–3.
73 Ibid., p. 60.
74 Ibid., p.63.
75 Ibid.

ing of 4 December the first lodge in Wexford was formally established and issued with warrant number 650.[76]

So what then was the role and function of Orangeism in 1798? First, we can dismiss the notion that the Grand Lodge of Ireland was active in directing operations. The small coterie who had gathered in Dublin were not in a position to exercise control or to develop a national strategy. The sum total of the Grand Lodge of Ireland's contribution to the defeat of the rebellion was to publish a resolution of loyalty. Any deeper involvement in conspiracy was wishful thinking by Ogle Gowan. At the local level Orangemen did their duty in the ranks of crown forces. It is true that the Ulster Orangemen had lobbied in 1797 for the creation of an Orange corps of supplementary yeomen.[77] Some groups that were to come under the Orange umbrella, such as the Loyal Association of Antrim, started out, in the absence of the yeomanry, as paramilitary in style. The idea of an Orange regiment was however not accepted, and by the following year there were signs that the Armagh rank and file had opted to develop Orangeism as a fraternal brotherhood and not as a paramilitary grouping:

> a letter of ... Master of Lodge 346 being read stating ... the conduct of Wolsey Atkinson in issuing more than one number to one person without the proper certificates and without knowing the name of the persons to whom the numbers were delivered and refusing direct command with the Grand Lodge as being a military body.[78]

It is pertinent to note the strength of Orangeism in 1798. Portland made an estimate of 170,000 persons in Ulster alone.[79] But it must be borne in mind that the very visible and public events often attracted the whole force of 'Orange Boys, Orange wenches and Orange children'.[80] A look at the returns to the Verner letter in March of that year shows some Armagh lodges with as few as seven members and some with as many as one hundred and seven. The average membership for some private lodges in Armagh and Tyrone was forty members. On the basis that there were at least 470 warrants in circulation by March 1798, the total Orange strength in Ireland would have peaked at between 18,000 and 20,000. This prompts the question as to how such a relatively small group could make such a powerful impact on events at large.

Two factors help explain the Orange impact. First, a disproportionate number of Orangemen entered the ranks of the yeomanry and militia. If a trooper was known to be an Orangeman, then he was considered a sound loyalist and

---

76 Ibid., p. 53.
77 George Knox to Pelham, 22 May 1797: B.L., Add. MS 33,104.
78 Grand Lodge MS GOLI/A/M/98, p. 18.
79 Duke of Portland to the earl of Camden, 2 Apr. 1798: N.A.I., RP 620/40/6.
80 Haliday to Charlemont, 13 July 1797: Charlemont papers.

free from the temptation of sedition. Such units as the North Corks who carried warrant No. 441 had a high profile in Wexford,[81] whilst the Armagh Militia, who were to humiliate General Humbert and his French demi-brigade in the wastes of Ballinamuck, contained no fewer than five Orange lodges.[82] The second element establishing Orangeism's reputation was the sheer weight of the black propaganda that had been generated. By 1798, the 'Orange bogey' was widespread; the mere rumour that Orangemen were coming was sufficient for a village population in County Carlow to flee their homes.[83] In Wexford, the tendency to see Orangemen behind every bush greatly inflamed the situation.[84]

If Orangeism did make one decisive contribution in 1798, it was to make loyalism far more attractive. It took the Williamite myth of 1688/90 – its theme of collective persecution, affliction, solidarity, providence and eventual deliverance – and fashioned it into a system of unique collective cultural identity. It redefined loyalty as a holy virtue: 'Honour all men. Love the brotherhood. Fear God. Honour the king.'[85] Fearing God was the cornerstone of the Reformed faith, honouring the king was defined as being an obedient subject of George III, and the brotherhood was the Loyal Orange Association. Endorsed by the King James Bible, Orangeism could redefine loyalty as legitimate and yet inject it with all the excitement of secrecy usually reserved for sedition. Oath-taking and an initiation into esoteric mysteries were based on symbols and icons already familiar through the Bible, *Pilgrim's progress*, and freemasonry. Orangeism was open to all of the Reformed sects, and had enough covenant theology to attract Presbyterians.[86]

This ability to make sense of the events of 1798 in a manner that endorsed loyalty and made it an attractive alternative to revolution was the lasting contribution of Orangeism. By the end of the first quarter of the nineteenth century, the Grand Lodge had dissolved and Orangeism had reverted to its origins in rural Ulster. Here it developed as a reformed masonry, serving as a culture bearer and as a solidarity group for ritualized brawling with its sectarian counterpart, the Ribbonmen.

81 Grand Lodge MS GOLI/A/M/98, pp 4–17.
82 Ibid. The Cork Militia it seems 'lost their warrant in action at Enniscorthy': ibid., p. 56.
83 *F.D.J.*, 13 Jan. 1798. See also Cooke to Pelham, 23 Dec. 1797: B.L., Add. MS 33,105.
84 Henry Alexander to Pelham, 26 July 1798: B.L., Add. MS 33,106.
85 1 Peter, 2:17.
86 Charles McCartney to —, 20 Nov. 1797: N.A.I., RP 620/33/74.

18

'Woe to the oppressor of the poor!': Post-rebellion violence in Ballitore, County Kildare

KEVIN O'NEILL

On 24 May 1820 Mary Shackleton Leadbeater took the occasion of the anniversary of the rising of 1798 to write to her daughter, Elizabeth, who had been six years old when the United Irishmen of Ballitore, County Kildare, rose in rebellion.

> My dear Eliz[abeth]
> Hast thou any recollection of this melancholy, miserable day? ... & often I thought [of] that still more terrible day to us, the following 27th when blood & devastation deformed our till then lovely village.[1]

At first sight her sentiments hardly seem surprising for a member of the Society of Friends who followed the Society's principle of peace.[2] Yet, when we consider the priority of terror explicit in this communication between a mother and daughter who knew the different nature of these two May days, the meaning of 1798 becomes problematic. By characterizing the first day of a popular rebellion proclaimed by some as a Catholic assault upon Protestants as 'melancholy' and 'miserable', and the day upon which Protestants were supposedly delivered from the hands of these Catholics as 'still more terrible,' Mary presents us with a sectarian conundrum.

An understanding of her pre-rebellion politics helps to explain why, in 1798, her sympathies were with the politics, if not the violent action, of the United Irishmen.[3] But familiarity with Mary's post-rebellion writings upon the subjects of political violence, authority and change – which were morally and politically

---

1 N.L.I., MS 5985, 24 May 1820.
2 The Society of Friends is the official name of the religious society conventionally referred to as Quakers. In this paper 'Friends' will be used as the proper noun, and for sake of convenience 'Quaker' will be used as the adjective.
3 See Kevin O'Neill, 'Mary Shackleton Leadbeater: Peaceful rebel', in Dáire Keogh and Nicholas Furlong (eds), *The women of 1798* (Dublin, 1998), pp 137–62.

conservative and didactic – might lead us to expect a less liberal perspective in
1820. A simple explanation is available to explain why Mary and her family saw
state violence as more terrible than rebel violence: it was. By any objective standard the people of Ballitore suffered far more from the actions of the state than
of the rebels. Before, during, and after the rebellion, the forces of the state
showed little consideration for the rights, property or lives of the people of
Ballitore. For the Leadbeater family this was very direct experience. The rebel
army that occupied Ballitore on 24 May contained many members of the community and was led by one of the Leadbeaters' close friends, Malachi Delany.
These United Irishmen treated the people of Ballitore village with respect and
caused only minor damage before their withdrawal. Conversely, the army was
responsible for a savage assault upon an undefended village. The Suffolk Fencibles burnt most of the village and murdered several of its inhabitants, including Frank Johnson, another member of Mary and William Leadbeater's intimate
circle. Surely this alone could explain the sentiments that Mary shared with her
daughter in 1820?

Yet even such a straightforward explanation raises several issues of interest to
those who wish to understand the long-term meaning of the rebellion of 1798. If
Mary's pre-'98 politics were radical, and her personal experience of violence
during 1798 reinforced her belief that the real terror of Irish society was carried
out by the state, how do we explain her apparent transition to a post-'98 didactic
position that accepted the legitimacy of the state and resisted radical reform?
Initially I sought the explanation for this transition in the post-rebellion violence
that, on cursory examination, seemed to be sectarian: it is plausible that protracted sectarian violence would alienate liberal Protestants and dissenters who had
supported the goals of the United Irishmen before the rebellion. This direct
personal memory of rural sectarian violence would have been congruent with
the characterization of the rebellion by Protestant polemicists as a sectarian
jacquerie, and might well account for the transformation of someone like Mary
Shackleton Leadbeater from sympathy with Godwin and Wollstonecraft to a
pattern of moralizing and didactic writing in harmony with Maria Edgeworth
and Hannah More.

This was a nice thesis. But a careful re-reading of her description of these
events challenges the assumption that sectarianism was central either to Ballitore's experience, or to Mary's subsequent efforts to find meaning in this critical
moment of her life. By following Mary Shackleton Leadbeater's own narrative
of violence, and by offering a review of post-rebellion violence set in its local
context, we can offer some preliminary observations about the significance of
sectarianism in Ballitore and Mary's political transformation.

Ideally a review of the violence of 1798 should explore the substantial pre-
rebellion violence in Ballitore. But for the sake of compression the final day of
the rebellion in Ballitore, 27 May 1798, serves well to set the stage for the ensu-

ing post-rebellion chaos. The events of that day reverberated through the years that followed. Its impact was so great upon Friends that Quaker children soon began to refer to this day as 'Bloody Firstday'.[4]

The diary record that Mary Shackleton has left us of that day captures the brutal nature of the moment and its casual terror.

> [May] 27 First-day.
> About 3 in the morning we were roused by undoubted notice that the army was at hand. I took up the children & drest them, by wch time a great party of horse & foot entered: they asked here for milk and water desired us not to be frightened, & were very civil ... I thought the bitterness of death was past, settled my parlour, & got the cows milked, when behold another party headed by Colonel Campbell came in. Ah! they came breathing vengeance ... My mind can scarce arrange the transactions of one eventful hour ... I was told our cupboard was about to be broke & I went to open it for two soldiers who were in the kitchen; one walked quietly away, the other said he only wanted to break it, & in a rage asked me were any united-men in the house last night. I answered there were ... he cursed me I think, & presented his gun at me. I desired he would not shoot me & ran away just as he began to dash the things about the kitchen, & broke the window ... After this one of them told me they were going to hang Dr Johnson. I had seen him just before walking with them, & he did not appear to me dejected, nor did I suppose him in danger, nor could I think what was told me true. I ran upstairs to my children whom I had in the room over the dairy, the Burrough was now on fire, the crash of breaking windows was heard, & the trumpets sounded just then ... the Dr was shot. I ran out into our room, & beheld him lying on his back his arms extended, & his life flown: then terror & distress seized on me. A[nne] Doyle took me from the windows...[5]

This military terror was exercised against the loyal and unarmed people of the village; those involved in the rising were long gone to seek out other surviving United Irishmen. The harshness of the treatment which the innocents received framed the dynamic of rural terror which would dominate the area over the next two years.

The weeks immediately following the defeat of the south Kildare United Irishmen were marked by confusion, rumour and continuing violence. Mary and

---

4 Friends rejected the common nomenclature of the days of the week and instead numbered them, beginning with the sabbath. Hence 'Bloody Firstday' = 'Bloody Sunday.'
5 N.L.I., MS 9322., 27 May 1798. In order to understand the impact of what she describes, it is useful to know that the Dr Johnson referred to was a childhood friend and the medical doctor who delivered two of her children. In May 1798 Frank Johnson, his wife Maria, and their daughter Eliza, were the closest friends of the Leadbeater family.

William travelled to Carlow town on 6 June to attend the Friends' Monthly Meeting. Mary records in her diary that 'the town appeared in much bustle' some of the inhabitants looking very sad, a great deal of military about the streets, & a report circulated that an attack of the mob was expected that night. We were ready to wish ourselves in Ballitore'. There was another reason that Mary and William were uncomfortable in Carlow. She records that during this visit 'we scarcely dared to utter humane sentiments, the tide ran so strongly' against the United Irishmen.[6]

During the month of June 1798, Mary records the deaths of four people known to her, two the victims of the popular party, two shot down by soldiers. Both of those who fell by the hands of the popular party had distinguished themselves as active supporters of the government during the pre-rebellion era. On 25 June the first of what would come to seem an endless number of attacks upon Ballitore homes took place. The house attacked, Boakefield, was one of the two big houses in Ballitore and were occupied by Epharim Boake, a Quaker descendent of one of the founders of Ballitore.

> This night a party [of United Irishmen] came to Boakefield, demanding arms, finding there were none, they asked for whiskey, & got some; desired a newspaper, but there were none of a late date. They wanted them to swear they had no arms, but did not insist on it: Ephm. refused letting them in, & they said they would not break the door.[7]

The very tentative nature of this encounter serves well to illustrate the beginning of a shift from rebellion to banditry in the Ballitore area. The United Irishmen demand arms, but accept Ephraim Boake's claim that he has none. They want him to swear to it, but do not insist. They want him to open the door, but refrain from breaking it when he refuses. Their desire for a newspaper adds a touch of pathos – defeated on their own battle field, they now sought anxiously for word of what was happening to United men elsewhere. In action and words, these are still United Irishmen, not robbers; but just as clearly, they were struggling to maintain their military and political integrity while facing annihilation.

July was marked by arrests and executions of South Kildare men. On 12 July, Mick Toole and Greg Tisdal of Ballitore were hanged in Athy. Six days later, two more neighbourhood youths were hanged. One, Daniel Welsh of Mullaghmast, was the second son of a widow to be executed since May. The steady drumbeat of the executions was accompanied by continued arrests of local men. On 23 July, Pat 'Ley' [Lyons] and Terry Dillon of Ballitore were taken by the yeomen. On the 24th, along with news of the execution of another Ballitore

6 N.L.I., MS 9322, 7 June 1798; 'Mary Leadbeater's Annals of Ballitore', in *The Leadbeater papers* ... (London, 1862), i, p. 254.
7 N.L.I., MS 9322, 25 June 1798.

man, word came that Hugh Cullen and Mick Kennedy were taken as prisoners to Athy. These last arrests raise an intriguing possibility. The history of the Catholic Church in Ireland might have evolved differently if it had not been for the strong connections between Catholics and Friends in Ballitore. One of Hugh Cullen's brothers, Paul, had already been sentenced to death, and Ephraim Boake – whom we have already met defending his house against United Irishmen – was determined that the father of these boys would not lose another son. The elderly Boake travelled to Dublin to successfully seek mercy for Hugh Cullen, father-to-be of Paul Cullen, prince of the church.[8]

Other Ballitore neighbours were busily engaged in trying to save their friends from execution. Mary wrote several letters of character urging mercy for Ballitore men. In at least one case she was successful. She recorded with glee that shortly after his release from prison 'Pat Lyons told me that a note which I wrote ... on their behalf lay on the table.' The general of the court martial was about to ignore the letter because it was from a woman and 'women did not care what they said but on seeing the [unusual nature of the] date, [the general] reckoned it was from a Quaker & that Quakers do not tell lies, on wch attention was paid to it & Pat says it got him his liberty'. There were other signs that summer that perhaps life could begin to return to normal. In the middle of the month Mary reported that the fair was 'well attended. It was pleasant to see so many men alive, they rejoiced to see each other.'[9]

But the return to normality was not to be so easy. Not every United man had a Friend to plead for them, and few United men could safely return home. Mary and William's first rather innocuous taste of what the future months would bring in more bitter draughts came on 17 August. They were awakened at 2 a.m. by men seeking wine. After William handed them out two bottles of wine through a window, they warned him, 'not a word of this in the morning'.[10]

A month later, more men returned to the Leadbeater household again looking for wine, this time in broad daylight. As Mary records:

> About 10'clock [*sic*] this morning some men came to the house, rapped loudly & frequently, & demanded two dozen of wine. Wm got them off with 11 bottles ... The fright seemed to affect my body more than mind, & I staid at home all day.[11]

Mary's reaction signals the beginning of a depression that affected many Ballitore people. There was good reason for it. The bandit force was growing more desperate. In the following days they attacked the mail coach, burned it, and

8 N.L.I., MS 9322, 12, 18, 24, 25, 27 July 1798.
9 N.L.I., MS 9322, 15 Aug. 1798.
10 Ibid., 17 Aug. 1798.
11 Ibid., 16 Sept. 1798.

stole horses throughout the neighbourhood. Perhaps this was a desperate attempt to duplicate the original signal for the rising? Perhaps it was a preparation for an effort to break out of the trap which the Wicklow/Kildare refuge was becoming. The rebel's desperation was no doubt fuelled by the news of the defeat of the French invasion force, and with it, any realistic hope of reversing their fortunes.[12]

On 24 September the most violent of the post-rising incidents took place. Again, Mary's diary records the event in stark, terse words:

> A fine moon-light night, but marked with death & destruction. Hannah Manders (a widow whose house had been plundered very lately) had her house burnt tonight, herself, 2 sisters & nephew & another woman killed Rawsons house at Glassealy burnt we hear. John Farmer's attacked & his papers burnt.[13]

And two days later word reached Ballitore of:

> an attack made … Mary Lecky & Sally Pim very roughly handled by 4 robbers who tied a rope around each of their necks, dragged M. Lecky several times up & down stairs, struck her & seemed near taking her life.[14]

These acts of violence and terror call for some explanation. Hannah Manders and John Farmer were Protestants and Mary Lecky and Sally Pim were Friends, so perhaps these were overt sectarian attacks. But Mary records that the assault upon Hannah Mander's household was widely thought to be provoked by a member of the household giving information about those who had robbed the house on a previous occasion.[15] The Manders family had also been involved in resisting the growth of the Defenders in Ballitore in 1794.[16] John Farmer had been active in local loyalist circles, and had accepted a position as adjutant in the militia regiment raised by the local landlord, Maurice Keatinge. He may well have been involved in the purging of suspect Catholics from militia ranks.[17] These fragments of information, together with Mary's apparent disinclination to identify these attacks as sectarian, suggest that they were rather a continuation of the rebellion's political violence. They were assaults upon individuals or families identified as leaders of the anti-United party, and in particular on those who

12 Ibid., 19 Sept. 1798.
13 Ibid., 24 Sept. 1798. Rawson is the infamous Thomas Rawson of the Athy yeomanry and author of the *Statistical survey of Kildare*.
14 Ibid., 26 Sept. 1798.
15 *Annals*, p. 260. Also see Thomas Bartlett 'Bearing witness: Female evidences in courts martial convened to suppress the 1798 rebellion', in Dáire Keogh and Nicholas Furlong (eds), *The women of 1798* (Dublin, 1998), p. 71.
16 N.L.I., MS 9319, 17 July 1794.
17 Ibid., 22 Apr. 1794.

had been responsible for the deaths of United men. The eyes of the victims invariably saw any attack upon those supporting the government as sectarian. Such a perspective is important to understand the larger picture, but it is equally important to recognise that the motivations of the surviving rebels were still aggressively tied to their goals of an independent egalitarian society, and that there is no evidence at all of attacks being made upon Protestants because they were Protestants. We can however also note the obvious; the rules of behaviour were changing, and Mary's use of the word 'robber' rather than 'United Men' or 'insurgents' to describe the former United men who attacked the Lecky household signals an important shift taking place in her perception of who and what they were.

We have another perplexing question here: why were women such prominent victims of the most extreme violence? The insurgents clearly directed violence against those who tried to deny them entry to their homes. Perhaps these female-headed households were more likely to resist trespass. Perhaps the male assailants were participating in some form of gender-based revenge against women who had violated rules of gender behaviour. Perhaps men who had failed in their efforts to use violence to reshape the rules of authority *vis-à-vis* their social superiors wished to buttress and demonstrate the gender authority that they did possess. But if this does represent some sort of reassertion of patriarchy over transgressive women, it is a most unusual one. In all of the events Mary records, there is no hint of rape or any other form of more overtly sexual violence (This is not because of a reluctance on Mary's part to discuss rape; she does record an apparent attempted rape of a Ballitore woman by a soldier.)

Mary and her family would shortly learn more than they wished to know about this more desperate and violent class of bandit. On 4 October, just three weeks after their last experience, they had another close encounter. At this time she and her family had moved in with her mother to provide mutual support in disturbed times. Returning from an evening with the widow of the murdered Dr Johnson, they called in at their own house to see how their house mates, Anne and Mary Doyle, were faring in their absence. Mary describes the encounter:

> It was a star-light night ... near A[nne] Doyle's we met a man, & at her door I think 3 more, we suspected them, but had scarcely entered the shop, when they were in with us, & with arms in their hands demanded money, several times threatening, Mary [Doyle] especially ...Wm went out backward ... to alarm the neighbourhood. I stood in the shop, & saw them empty the tills of silver & halfpence & take away some of the shop goods ... One of them affected to speak broken French. After they were gone, I suffered a good deal of anxiety about Wm. ... when Wm came back...we went home, & found mother & the girls about the house, & the four children partly drest, the parlour strewed with clothes & papers the

two desks & clothes press broke, ... the robbers questioned & threatened
Eliz: to tell where her father kept his money: the poor child cried & said
she did not know. 'I know' says Jane, 'Where, Honey '—'In his breeches
pocket'. They ... broke Sally's writing desk to pieces ... My mother's
nice mahogany cabinet broke, ... they ... broke the desks & clothes press
& a little trunk, tho' Eliz begged they would not as her Grandfather's letters were in it ... In breaking the press the gun or pistol went off, & past
thro the foot of Jane's bed in wch she lay; her danger frightened the robber who went to see was she hurt ... Elizth. was greatly frightened. We
got a little disturbed sleep. My mind was much deprest all day ...[18]

Just two days later, the robbers returned:

I was knitting in the parlour, when I heard them demand Wms watch,
which he gave them, they desired him not to be afraid, he told them he
was not, ... I desired they would not disturb the children who were
asleep, & they seemed careful not, they did not ... search me, nor ask my
watch; but one who was unarmed threatened to go out for a blunderbuss,
the other would not allow it ... Then one of them put fire in the alcove to
extort more money but soon let Wm take it away, & behaving with more
civility than might be expected went away, leaving us very calm. They
then went to Mary & Anne who would not open the door for them, then
they broke in the kitchen window & beat them & Jenny Miles severely,
taking from them about a guinea.[19]

This second attack confirms the basic pattern of the bandits' behaviour. Those
who did not resist were treated with a rough 'civility', those who did resist were
treated severely. Again, women received the most violent treatment, and there
was no sign of sectarian motive.

After this second, more brutal attack, the Leadbeaters and a number of other
Quaker families decided to leave Ballitore and seek a more secure haven.

The treatment of our friends seemed to affect our minds more than what
we had met with. We set about packing the house-linen &c to send away
... We seemed carried away by the tide of apprehension, tho' solicited to
go to Athy ... we thought Carlow the safest road ... On the road I was
very thoughtful lest we had done wrong in removing, & that this want of
faith was reprehensible ...[20]

Mary's doubts about abandoning her larger community in its time of distress
continued upon their arrival in Carlow town. Despite the kindness of their

18 Ibid., 4 Oct. 1798.   19 Ibid., 6 Oct. 1798.   20 Ibid., 7 Oct. 1798.

friends in Carlow, William returned to Ballitore the following day, and Mary determined upon doing so as soon as her mother and children had made some recovery from their shock.

Despite news from Ballitore of other attacks, Mary and her two eldest children returned home after only a week's respite. Their spirits were anything but confident. Mary described herself and her neighbours 'like weak trees supporting one another against the storm ... We anticipated with too much certainty the dread and the dangers of that which now approached, and scarcely dared to look beyond it. In fact, all about us was gloom'.[21]

The most ambitious assault on Boakefield house took place on 31 October. Mary and her family could see the flames and hear the firing of volleys of musket fire as they

> strove to wait our fate patiently. The firing continued, the flame blazed much. We got into the room over our kitchen without a candle, the window open ... At length the firing & shouting ceased. All was quiet – we were almost afraid to hope no lives were lost. After a while the dogs barked & presently we heard the band approaching. Poor Nancy trembled & wished it over: my mind was tolerably tranquil. I believe we all felt our situation awful. A horseman galloped along, & fired a shot wch we thought was at Brother's gate, & that his house was attacked ... Presently their tongues & feet were heard near us, & we found they had past by. Relieved on our own account from the terrour of a visit from those who perhaps came raging from having committed murder, burning & robbery, our anxiety for our neighbours prevailed ... We sat up till midnight.[22]

The following day Mary went to Boakefield to assist, and to learn of the particulars:

> This armed band on desiring admittance assured them they would do no harm, & on every refusal fired a volley with the regularity of disciplined men ... At length they got in at the back kitchen window, & one who appeared their commander accosted John Thomas, 'I am Capt. Smith, I know my doom, & I scarce care what I do. Why would not you let us in?' He was answered they took them for the gang of robbers ... 'We are no robbers, & yet what else can you call us?'[23]

'Capt. Smith's' ambiguous denial of his identity as a robber underscores the pathos of the situation these men found themselves in. Trying to hold to their identity as the army of the people, they were nonetheless forced to confront the

21 *Annals*, p. 266.   22 N.L.I., MS 9322, 31 Oct. 1798.   23 Ibid., 1 Nov. 1798.

doom so clearly recognized by Captain Smith who would be captured within the week.

Mary records one other item of interest about this assault. During the height of the attack upon Boakefield, one of the house's defenders had slipped out of a window and run to Timolin where a garrison of soldiers was stationed. The soldiers refused to come to the assistance of the Ballitore householder; they had been told to 'leave the devoted hole to itself'.[24] The possibility that the military authorities were leaving Ballitore purposely undefended is difficult to assess, but the language of the soldiers resonates with the sort of advice that the army was receiving from local elites. As early as 27 May, Lord Aldborough, one of the most influential local notables, had written to the authorities and characterised Ballitore as 'the nest [of] traitors of that district'. He urged the government to respond quickly and severely to the rising: 'I hope the murderers will be brought to speedy punishment & the rest sent abroad ... as it would be fatal to Protestants to let them join their friends & be suffered to live any more in the Country.'[25] It is striking that it was the elite perspective of Lord Aldborough which saw these events in simple sectarian terms. From his isolated position (he relied upon his servants for information about his neighbours) he offered a simple and sectarian view of the conflict.

Regardless of actual military intentions or plans, the strong military presence evident during July and August, the days of arrests and executions, had given way to a different security situation; there was now a clear correlation between the absence of the military in a locality and the incidence of banditry. The low profile of state authority and the growing desperation of the surviving rebels increased the Ballitore villagers' sense of isolation and vulnerability. And the autumn of 1798 was about to yield to a winter during which 'the darkness of the winter nights was illuminated by the fires of the houses'.[26]

But first Mary and her family had to face a darkness of their own – a family tragedy that matched their community's anguish. The burden which Mary had carried through this summer and autumn was enormous. In addition to her normal work load in the household, dairy and shop, she faced the added physical and emotional burden of caring for her three-year-old daughter, Deborah, who had contracted smallpox, and for her mother, who had become severely mentally disoriented by the chaos that surrounded her. These burdens were made all the more debilitating by the sleepless nights occasioned by constant alarms. On the evening of 29 November, after a day of anxious nursing of Deborah, the exhausted mother relaxed her vigilance for a moment and allowed her four-year-old Jane an unusual independence.

> Just then my sweet Jane told me she wanted to go upstairs, & I most unfortunately, stupidly & carelessly trusted the wax taper with her, tho' I

24 *Annals*, p. 268.   25 N.A.I., RP 620/87/182.   26 *Annals*, p. 269.

thought me not, & then again that she was so steady, & tho' I am mostly attentive to danger of fire she went not into Mother's room but into the one over the parlour, & setting down the candle on the floor I suppose when she rose from the pot it caught her. I heard her cries, & immediately apprehended the cause. We found Molly Webster endeavouring to put out the fire … I lay with her & tho'surprized at her coldness & want of pulse still was not enough aware, she was fine & cheery desired I would buy a coach for Deborah at the fair … but added, 'I am too lazy.', she mentioned again being lazy, said the bed was cold…[27]

The following day Jane died in her mother's arms.

The depth of Mary's grief and guilt is beyond the scope of this paper, but it compels us to consider the complexity of individual experience at a time of public calamity. Though Jane was not a casualty of war, Mary would never be able to disassociate the public and private tragedy of this time. And reflection upon the domestic nature of this rebellion might suggest that we direct more attention to such effects upon rural society. An entry from Mary's diary a few days later catches the juxtaposition of the personal and the public tragedy that 1798 was for her.

Ah my lovely child; her round blue eyes, her dented nose, her rosy cheeks & white teeth all rise to my idea, & I feel inexpressibly my loss. I was vain of her I believe, & cherished hopes from her stability & affection to me more I think than from the rest, except my poor dear Eliz: whose feelings just at first seemed acute, but very soon subsided, even while her sister lay dead; yet why should I wish her tender mind to feel the smart which has so often tortured mine ? This night we saw the fire of Wilson's & Gilthorp's houses burning. My W[illiam] L[eadbeater] seemed poorly to-night, low & strangely affected, & in fear of a fever, taking some spirits relieved him.[28]

But private grief did not bring relief from public woes. On 23 December the Leadbeater home was again invaded and robbed.

About eleven last night the robbers entered the town I suppose; attacked both O'Hara's & P. Murphy whom they robbed to a considerable amount I suppose. After twelve we heard them at this shop-door, I got a little clothes on, & strove to hide my watch, a little money, & some clothes of Wm's. which I had but done when a robber entered the room. A[nne] D[oyle] had opened the shop door for them, yet they had broke the

27 N.L.I., MS 9322, 29 Nov. 1798.   28 Ibid., 11 Dec. 1798.

kitchen window. Eliz. had before ran into her G[rand]mother's room. I
was obliged to give the money, the robber got the watch under the bed
where I hid it, also Wms. new breeches, & some of his shirts out of a
clothes bag. I unlocked the drawers, out of which I believe they got little
but my mother's watch. Little Deborah lay quiet & when I brought her
into her G[rand]mother's room, she said 'Grandmother don't speak'.
Eliz. wished it would please the Lord to send us day-light. My darling
Jane escaped this trial. A man with a gun came into Mother's room after
having broke open M[ary] Doyle's box, but on her expostulating did not
take all her clothes. The robber behaved civilly & was searching my desk
rather gently when another came & told him the soldiers were coming.
'Then we will have a slap at them' says he, & away they went.[29]

Again, even though Mary's anxiety and sense of 'trial' dominate this description,
she still manages to note the civility of the robbers. Her recording of the combative bravado with which these men choose to confront rather than flee the
approaching soldiers underscores that even at this late date their actions were
still as transgressive as they were predatory.

Soldiers were becoming a more regular feature in the village in the New Year.
On 9 January 1799, soldiers were billeted upon the Leadbeater and other Ballitore households. The uninvited presence of soldiers in Ballitore homes had been
the cause of much pre-rebellion discord, and though their presence now brought
some respite from the midnight attacks, they were by no means seen as saviours.
The Leadbeaters' were not immune from the problems with military indiscipline
that plagued most Ballitore homes. In February 1799 one drunken soldier
returning to his quarters in the Leadbeater home caused a great uproar; when he
frightened seven-year-old Elizabeth to tears, William tried to put him out of the
house, but the soldier abused and struck him; the soldier also struck and knocked
down a neighbour, Bob Hudson, who came to assist William; Mary's brother,
Abraham Shackleton, also came to William's assistance but he was driven out of
the house by the soldier threatening him with a musket. Order was only restored
when the corporal in command was threatened with a report to higher command.[30]

There were other incidents of friction between the people and the occupying
soldiers, but by far the most serious incident occurred in May 1799. A soldier
taunted a carter from Kilkenny passing through Ballitore. When the taunts
exposed the fact that the Kilkenny man had a stammer, the soldier

told [the carter that] he was badly made, adding, but 'I'll finish you', presenting a pistol which he thought was …uncharged … The poor young
man from the bloom of health & gaiety was instantly a bloody corpse on

29 Ibid., 23 Dec. 1798.   30 N.L.I., MS 9323, 27 Feb. 1799.

the floor ... An inquest sat, & ... acquitted [the soldier] of murder. But the people are enraged.[31]

While anger over the military presence was constant through the late winter and spring of 1799, we also have evidence of a new dynamic developing: the people of the Ballitore area began to take an active and organised role in resisting the banditry that plagued their community. On 17 February Mary recorded that, 'the country people [are] searching for robbers some of whom they took ...'[32] From this moment the larger Ballitore community was aligned against those insurgents who still remained on the run and assisted in apprehending them.

Eventually, the presence of soldiers in Ballitore and the new activism of the villagers sharply curtailed attacks upon village homes. But the Leadbeater house had one more attack to endure at the beginning of Mar. By now the family had developed a drill:

About two Wm jumped out of bed ... We got on some clothes, alarmed the family, I got the children into mother's room. Wm called out of the window & desired them to wait till the door should be opened ... but they had burst in the parlour window, & they came upstairs ... loudly calling for Leadbeater. He ... stood his ground and answered them with great courage. They desired him to go with [them], he refused, desired them to do what they would to him, but he would not leave his family ... I sat still pretty composed, & thinking that their noisy threats were but to terrify. Pretty soon one asked Wm what o'clock it was. 'I was robbed of my watch'; 'Do you call us robbers? – We are no robbers– we want no watch – we only want some money ...' Wm offered them his purse, wch containing only a few shillings they rejected with disdain, & insisted on a guinea note; finding he had not it, they became more furious, threatening his life, snapped a pistol & raised a sword, as if to cleave his scull; the pistol burnt priming, & the sword struck the wainscot in the narrow lobby; the clatter of the arms, & the cries of the women made me run out; just then Wm burst from them, & ... got out of the house. This escape relived us; but such a scene! ... Anne, holding her head, came into my mother's room, telling me she believed she was killed, while blood poured down her neck ... M[ary] Doyle almost distracted exclaimed they had killed her sister, two blows were aimed at her; & one of them hit her ... One of them ... shewed concern, he came in once or twice, looked at her, said she was not killed ... I told one of them to go for the Dr (but alas what Dr have we!).[33]

31 Ibid., 20 May 1799.   32 Ibid., 17 Feb. 1799.   33 Ibid., 1 Mar. 1799.

The following day the Clare Militia came to garrison Ballitore and their continued presence in the village effectively ended the activity of bandits in the village
proper, though violence in the surrounding area did not end for over a year.

Perhaps the best place to conclude this narrative of communal chaos is with
Mary's reflection offered several months later, in August of 1799, when there
were rumours that all military forces were being withdrawn from the area:

> Talk of the soldiers going & robbers coming [back] sunk me too much & I
> am grieved & angry with myself to give way to fear, & consequently place
> dependence on armed force.[34]

This Quaker sensitivity to the shifting nature of her own perspective on the
army and the insurgents is an important indication of a transition in her thinking, a reassessment in which the preservation of the peace became paramount to
all other considerations. This was consistent with Quaker teaching; yet, as
Mary's voice indicates, the Leadbeaters could not calmly accept the new situation. Both William and Mary continued to push themselves to ensure that they
did not become part of the system of inequalities that had in part motivated the
rebellion. When the Captain Doyle who had been responsible for at least three of
the invasions of the Leadbeaters' house was finally apprehended in Ballitore in
December 1799, William went to the gaol in Naas – not to offer evidence against
him – but to console the bandit captain.

Mary Shackleton Leadbeater's narrative presents us with a perspective upon
these events that is both compelling and strikingly objective. Her descriptions of
these incidents are remarkably free of any overt condemnation of the rebels. She
does condemn their violence, but a careful reading reveals that her critique of
violence places the behaviour of the former rebels in a broad context. She rejects
a sectarian characterization of both the rising and its aftermath. Instead, she
offers other explanatory variables that locate the source of violence in revenge for
economic exploitation, traditional land disputes, and the pressure of impossible
circumstances faced by the defeated rebels. All these could be subsumed into a
definition of 'sectarianism', but Mary, a Protestant witness of this violence, was
acutely aware of the polemical power of such definition and strove to contain
meaning within a narrative of causality that was congruent with her experience.
Perhaps the most striking annunciation of her understanding of the rebellion
and its meaning is to be found in her discussion of the tragedy at Scullabogue,
County Wexford. This massacre of loyalists became the touchstone for those
who saw the rebellion in sectarian terms and was surely the most compelling evidence for such an interpretation. But when Mary came to discuss it in her
Annals she rejected any such interpretation, and was no doubt reading that distant event through her own experience; she explained that it was

34 Ibid., 27 Aug. 1799.

not the work of the whole body, but abhorred by them, and was done by a party maddened after the defeat of Ross. Women & children were spared, and Quakers in general escaped; but woe to the oppressor of the poor, the hard landlord, the severe master, or him who was looked upon as an enemy![35]

Mary would spend the remaining twenty-five years of her life rethinking and rewriting the story of 1798. As the days of violence drew to a close in 1801, she was already framing the simple truth that would be the focal point of her future. As the Act of Union was being debated, Mary reported that some in Ballitore supported it, and some opposed it. Her own comment upon it was remarkably simple, yet prophetic of her future life: 'I longed only for peace & quiet, and to behold once more our fields cultivated and our poor fed.'[36]

Leadbeater and her neighbours would spend the rest of their lives trying to find ways to live in peace and to ameliorate the poverty that surrounded them. After this great and violent political upheaval she would also do all that she could to prevent a return to local political confrontation. These two goals would define her future, and not the reactions to any hostility, real or imagined, from her Catholic neighbours.

35 *Annals*, p. 255.　　　36 *Annals*, p. 294.

SECTION V

In 1798, just after the battle of Ross, James Alexander interviewed the defeated United Irishmen as to their motivation. Their replies focused insistently on their economic miseries, inflicted on them through the agency 'of gripping and oppressive landlords', but equally on the partisan nature of the law: 'the connivance of normal justice at all their suffering, which they perceived to proceed from no other reason than their being Roman Catholics'.[1] It is a revealing example of how the older 'Whiteboy' grievances had now been joined by a newer concern with the politics of law, the intrusion of the state, and the clear interplay between the sectarianism of that state and the administration of justice, conceived of not just in abstract terms but with a vivid sense that these issues pressed on their daily lives in intolerable ways. The politicization of the 1790s intersected with the lives of ordinary people caught up in extraordinary circumstances.

One novel facet was the militarization of the 1790s in response to the wider European theatre of war: Volunteers, militias, yeomen, fencibles, Hessians fol-

---

1 James Alexander, 'To all whom it may concern,' in *Walker's Hibernian Magazine*, Nov. 1798, p. 793. Alexander emphatically rejected the idea of sectarian motivation: 'The present rebellion is not founded upon any religious principle whatsoever. They [loyalist victims] did not suffer as Protestants but as being staunch friends of the constitution. What Protestant or Dissenter known to be an enemy to the constitution was ever hurt by the rebels in person or property or troubled on the score of religion?' (p. 795). A classic liberal, he then claimed that the real necessity was 'to gain a victory over their [the defeated rebels] hearts and minds as well as their bodies' (p. 796). James Alexander (ob. 1815) was a native of Harristown, County Kildare, who became a soldier, sailor, Methodist preacher, actor, excise officer and author. He was town-major of New Ross during the insurrection. Among his works were *Some account of the first apparent symptoms of the late rebellion in the county of Kildare ... with a succinct narrative ... of the rebellion in the county of Wexford especially in the vicinity of New Ross* (Dublin, 1800) and *An amusing summer-companion to Glanmire near Cork* (Cork, 1814), a book which shows an intimate knowledge of the local people. He also projected a millenarian book to be published in Dublin in 1800, *The whore of Babylon detected from her characteristic marks in the Book of Revelations with large and important illustrations from Roman Catholic commentators, particularly Signor Pastorini whose arguments to prove that by the whore spoken of is signified Rome in her heathen state are completely confuted, with much assistance from himself.*

lowed one another with breathless rapidity.[2] A second feature was the inexorable advance of the central state as the gentry lost their grip on local communities. A third was the state's assaults on the public sphere through convention acts, secret committees, show trials, assaults on the press, suspension of *habeas corpus*, and eventually martial law, and the United Irishmen's efforts to withstand the pressure of the state by appealing to public opinion.[3] In the early 1790s, long before there was a military threat from the United Irishmen, the Irish state had systematically abandoned civil liberties – freedom of speech (Press and Stamp acts), the right of assembly (Convention Act), the right to bear arms, trial by jury (Secret Committee of 1793). To save the constitution, the constitution itself was progressively sacrificed, leaving Irish Whigs caught between a rock and a very hard place. By 1797, all Grattan and the Whigs could do was to abandon the parliament altogether. The state's efforts to close the space for reasoned political discourse forced the United Irishmen to develop new modes of expression: they believed, as Samuel Neilson expressed it, that 'you must govern by public opin-

2   An essential overview is Thomas Bartlett, 'Defence, counter-insurgency and rebellion: Ireland 1793–1803', in Thomas Bartlett and Keith Jeffery (eds), *A military history of Ireland* (Cambridge, 1996), pp 247–93. The complexity of this militarization can be illustrated by even a brief note on the North Cork Militia. These were mainly recruited from around the Doneraile and Mitchelstown areas, especially on the King estates. Lord Kingsborough offered the first 244 recruits in 1794 a small farm for life at a low rent, provided they were Protestant [Henry McAnally, *The Irish militia, 1793–1816* (London, 1949) , p. 48]. Many were the Irish-speaking sons of Protestant converts to Catholicism, Orangemen bearing Gaelic and Norman surnames. The bitter reaction to them in Wexford in part derived from this knowledge, reflected in the stories of the beaten North Corks reciting Catholic prayers in Irish. According to Thomas Crofton Croker, 'The [North] Cork Militia were especially Orange': [p. 179]. The song 'The Groves of Blackpool' commemorates their return to Cork after 1798:

>   With our band playing before us in order/We played coming into the town
>   We'd up with the old 'Boyne Water'/Not forgetting 'Croppies lye down'
>   Because you might read in the news/'T was we made the rebels so cool
>   Who all thought like Turks or like Jews/To murder the boys of the 'Pool.

Their leader Lord Kingsborough (1770–1839), later third earl of Kingston, earned an unenviable reputation in 1798 as a sexual predator and bigot. By the 1820s, he had mutated into a supporter of Catholic Emancipation. In a gothic moment, he went mad in his own house, the grandiose Mitchelstown Castle (1823–5), after summoning his Catholic tenants there to account for their refusal to back his candidate in an 1830 election. As he faced the throng in his great hall, he screamed: 'They are come to tear me to pieces; they are come to tear me, to tear me to pieces!' Big George subsequently died in a lunatic asylum in London: Elizabeth Bowen, *Bowen's Court*, p. 258. A fine account of the building of his *folie de grandeur* is Frederick O'Dwyer, 'A noble pile in the late Tudor style: Mitchelstown Castle', in *Irish Arts Review*, xvii (2002), 31–44.

3   On the opening of the public sphere, see James Donnelly, 'Propagating the cause of the United Irishmen', in *Studies*, lxix (1980), pp 5–23; Curtin, *United Irishmen*, chapter seven; Whelan, *Tree of liberty*, chapter two. These treatments all rely on the conceptual model developed by Jurgen Habermas in his *Structural transformation of the public sphere*. For a recent critique of this model, see T.C. Blanning, *The culture of power and the power of culture: Old regime Europe, 1660–1789* (Oxford, 2002).

ion and not by force'.[4] Among these new forms were the satire (like *The lion of old England* and *Billy Bluff*), the prophecy (essentially a form of political allegory), the catechism, and direct court reports.

These issues collectively raise a further one. Did the 1790s present an entirely novel situation, imported into Irish society under the external agency of the American and French Revolutions? Or did the decade expose structural flaws in the eighteenth-century Irish state, hitherto decorously veiled by the gorgeous mask of its Georgian veneer?[5] Are historians entitled to see the 1790s as casting a Burkean dark shadow back to the origins of this society in the Glorious Revolution, conventionally celebrated as a fundamental advance in civil liberties in Britain, but in Ireland having the opposite effect of fully excluding 80 per cent of the population (the Catholics) and partially excluding another 10 per cent (the Dissenters) from formal political participation? The archival record which is used by historians to explore this issue is itself skewed: only the chance survival of the Rebellion Papers has allowed us to look in detail at the 1790s in a way not now possible for the rest of the eighteenth century, given the destruction of the Public Record Office in 1922. Nineteenth-century historians with access to those records, like Mary Hickson and James Anthony Froude, revelled in exposing the violent underbelly of Irish life.[6] Contemporary historians are denied these sources: one result is the normalising tendency evident in the work of S.J. Connolly and Toby Barnard who present eighteenth-century Ireland as a quiescent society.[7] Absence of evidence may not constitute evidence of absence.[8] The resurgence of nationalism after the fall of the Iron Curtain is a contem-porary example of how cultures seemingly compliant and silent under an oppressive regime can articulate their real feelings once political space to do so becomes available again. As Eoghan Rua Ó Súilleabháin's biting couplet expressed it:

> Ní ins an ainnise is measa linn bheith síos go deo
> Ach an tarcaisne a leanas sin i ndiaidh na león.[9]

---

4 Neilson, *Brief statement*, p. 35.
5 The 'gorgeous mask' quotation is from Denis Taaffe, *Ireland's mirror* (Dublin, 1796), p. 14.
6 J.A. Froude, *The English in Ireland in the eighteenth century*, 3 vols (London, 1881); Mary Agnes Hickson, *Selections from old Kerry records, historical and genealogical*, 2 vols (London, 1872–4).
7 Connolly, *Religion, law and power* is the most considered statement of the quiescence model. With a greater level of archival penetration, he reinstates the core arguments deployed in J.P. Mahaffy's corruscating if coat-trailing introductory essay to volume v of *Georgian Society records of eighteenth-century domestic architecture and decoration in Dublin* (Dublin, 1913). Connolly's treatment of Irish-language sources is criticized by Vincent Morley, '"Tá an cruatan ar Sheóirse' – folklore or politics?', in *E.C.I.*, xiii (1998), 112–20.
8 It is surprising that such a sophisticated historian as Toby Barnard, whose work derives great authority from its archival depth, has chosen to set aside Irish-language material *tout court*.
9 Seán Ó Tuama and Thomas Kinsella (eds), *An Duanaire: Poems of the dispossessed* (Dublin, 1990), p. 29. [It is not being constantly sunk in misery that is the worst for us but the contempt that follows it after the loss of our leaders].

A starting point for re-examining these issues must remain the seventeenth-century transition in land-owning in Ireland which effectively removed the existing gentry. They sacrificed all as a result of their Catholicism in a disaster that embraced equally descendants of Norman and Gael, and makes a mockery of attempts to describe their politics then or in the eighteenth century as a narrowly ethnic 'Gaelic nationalism'.[10] (This crudely reductive phrase should be banished from the lexicon of scholars of eighteenth-century Ireland.) Under the cosh of colonialism, Catholics from diverse and hitherto antagonistic cultural backgrounds constructed a pluralist vision of an absorptive 'Irish' identity that transcended the old ethnic binaries.[11] It also deployed an anti-colonial narrative, the declension of a high native Irish civilization after the Norman onslaught. Charles O'Conor was later to rework Séathrún Céitinn's schema into an Irish version of the English Whig 'Norman Yoke,' revealing an Irish 'ancient constitution' in the pre-Norman period.[12] This provided a usable past for late eighteenth-century radical nationalists.

In the long term, the eradication of the existing gentry was the single biggest factor working against the acceptance of the British project in Ireland. In Scotland, for example, their own trusted indigenous gentry led the bulk of Scots into acquiescence with the new constitutional dispensation in the eighteenth century; the Welsh gentry were similarly compliant; in Ireland, there was a gaping hole. The sweeping Cromwellian reforms utterly modernised the legal and fiscal aspects of Irish landowning, leaving none of the customary protections which insulated European peasantries from the full blast of commercialism. There was no need for a later enclosure movement in Ireland as there were no 'traditional' rights to be legally confiscated.[13] Their absence was surely decisive in generating the (unique in British terms) secret societies which sought to assert an Irish moral economy as commercialization swept unimpeded across the land, backed by the coercive power of the state, with devastating consequences for the legally defenceless rural poor.[14] The absence of a sheltering moral economy facilitated this penetration, and left the Irish Catholic poor among the most marginalised social groups anywhere in the eighteenth-century world, comparable to the fellahin in Egypt or the American slaves. They themselves were well aware of this. Travelling through Roscommon in 1796, Arthur O'Connor and Lord Edward

10 Breandán Ó Buachalla's *Aisling gheár* is the standard treatment here and see now Éamonn Ó Ciardha, *Ireland and the Jacobite cause, 1685–1766...* (Dublin, 2002).
11 Mícheál Ó Siochrú, *Confederate Ireland, 1642–49: A constitutional and political analysis* (Dublin, 1999).
12 See Kevin Whelan, 'Foreword', in Claire Connolly and Stephen Copley (eds), *The wild Irish girl* (London, 2000), pp xix-xxi, for development of this idea.
13 J.H. Andrews, 'The struggle for Ireland's public commons', in Patrick O'Flanagan, Paul Ferguson and Kevin Whelan (eds), *Rural Ireland* (Cork, 1987), pp 1–23.
14 Kevin Whelan, 'Ireland in the world system 1600–1800' in H.J. Nitz (ed.), *The early modern world system in geographical perspective* (Frankfurt, 1993), pp 204–18.

FitzGerald met a group of labourers. One of them, a former schoolmaster, answered a query about their awareness of politics: 'Look at these wretched styes built in the bog on your right and see those flocks of bullocks on your left in fine grass up to their knees and ask yourself if we men can value life, not to risk, when we are treated worse than the brute beasts.'[15]

Writing in 1793, George Knox pinpointed this lack of hegemony as the fatal flaw in Irish society, attributing it to the oppressive legacy of 'the colonising system':

> It is the misfortune of Ireland that the rich and poor form two such distinct bodies, having different languages, habits, religion and objects, the consequences of the colonising system. The whole country has not grown up together as in England where a sort of relationship subsists among all classes of the people. There the rich and poor are separated from each other by such a gradation that they can neither be addressed and worked on as a body. Here, there is a strong line drawn between them and they feel that their interests are distinct. The only influence of the rich is from the servility and timidity of the poor but he has none from attachment or feudal feelings. The consequence is that any cunning low man can win the peasant from his landlord with the greatest ease and in times of public commotion will certainly do so.[16]

These conditions also left the Irish poor naked in legal terms before the landed class. The resulting sense of isolated impotence was even stronger among communities where the Catholic 'underground gentry' were present. This created a further difficulty: there was no moral economy, no hegemony, no possibility of a consistently harmonious relationship.[17] The *Press* contrasted England with Ireland:

> Where the great body of the people have no interest whatever in the soil: there are not many so far from absolute poverty as to have anything absolutely worth defending. The religion professed by government and established by law is not that of the majority of the people. Much landed property is held by the tenure of forfeiture and confiscations. The chief magistrate is not a native: the ministers who compose his council are not natives. They have an interest to take care of separate from and possibly incompatible with that of the country which they govern and which they may prefer. They can, of course, have no common cause with the people and have not a shadow of security in their affections.'[18]

---

15 Hayter Hames, *Arthur O'Connor*, p.127.
16 George Knox to Abercorn, 16 Mar. 1793, Abercorn Papers, P.R.O.N.I., T2541/IBI/4/17.
17 Terry Eagleton, 'Ascendancy and hegemony', is a useful starting point. See his *Heathcliff and the Great Hunger* (London, 1995), pp 27–103.
18 *Press*, 28 Sept. 1797. The style is that of Arthur O'Connor.

The Irish landlords had powers that astonished outside observers (Arthur Young, for example) and which distanced them from their own tenantry.[19] Into the resulting social gulf came the Catholic priest and the Presbyterian minister as accepted authority figures.[20] When the beaten rebels trudged into New Ross to surrender, they walked behind their priests rather than their landlords. In Ulster it was a vociferous conservative complaint that the Dissenting minister rather than the Anglican landlord controlled local communities. A 1720 list of the 540 Ulster landlords divided them into 'Churchmen, Dissenters and Papists': of these, only forty (7 per cent) were Dissenters, only nine (less than 2 per cent) were Catholic.[21] Despite their dominance, Anglican landlords could not presume to insulate their Presbyterian tenants from the influence of their ministers.[22] Archbishop King as early as 1719 believed that the fate of Ulster depended on 'whether the Presbyterian ministers, with their synods, presbyteries and lay elders in every parish, shall have the greater influence over the people to lead them as they please, or the landlords over their tenants'.[23] When the political temperature reached scalding point in the 1790s, the landlord class had no reservoir of hegemony to cool the situation: hence their panic-stricken appeals to Dublin Castle to protect them from their own servants and tenants, increasingly objects of intense fear. The British elite looked on aghast at what they saw as Irish landlords' monumental dereliction of duty: the Act of Union would be the price exacted for their failure.[24] From the viewpoint of the Irish poor, the 1790s witnessed a novel political exposure to the rigours of state power, with a highly

---

19 Arthur Young, *A tour in Ireland with general observations made in the years 1776, 1777 and 1778*, 2 vols (London, 1780), ii, p. 54. 'A landlord in Ireland can scarcely invent an order which a servant, labourer or cottar dare to refuse to execute. Nothing satisfies him but an unlimited submission ... A poor man would have his bones broke if he offered to lift a hand in his own defence. Knocking down is spoken of in the country in a manner that would make an Englishman stare. Landlords of consequence have assured me that many of their cottars would think themselves honoured by having their wives and daughters sent for to the bed of their master; a mark of slavery that proves the oppression under which such people must live'. Another instance was the treatment of Catholic women who sometimes tried to evade 'Purification' money, demanded as a small tithe in the eighteenth century: 'It is necessary to prove the woman to have had a child and that she was then in the way of nursing, and that the dues to the established church had not been paid. To elude a search, women often attempted to conceal from the prying eye of the proctor or tythe farmer, their infants and the cradle: should, however, a suspicion arise, these gentry, without ceremony, examine their breasts to discover whether they are in the way of nursing or giving suck': Bingley, *Examinations*, p 18.

20 Patrick Corish, *The Catholic community in the seventeenth and eighteenth centuries* (Dublin, 1981).

21 'A list of the nobility and gentry who are generally esteemed to have one hundred pounds a year and upwards in the province of Ulster, as divided into Churchmen, Dissenters and Papists' [*c.*1720], Lambeth Palace Library, MS 1742.

22 This theme runs through many of the documents in Crawford and Trainor (eds), *Aspects*.

23 Cited in W. Maguire (ed.), *Kings in conflict* (Belfast, 1990), p. 168.

24 Thomas Bartlett, 'Britishness, Irishness and the Act of Union', in Keogh and Whelan (eds), *Acts of union*, pp 243–58. The state's rapid assumption of control of the yeomanry is one good example.

visible and intrusive state apparatus lined up as a partisan weapon against them.[25] According to William Sampson, 'every man who shared the public plunder was government. Every man in a red coat was government. Every turn-key was government. Every hired informer was government. Every Hessian soldier was government. Every sentry-box was government.'[26]

When professional British officers like Abercromby, Moore or Cornwallis saw the Irish gentry at close quarters, they were appalled at their failure of nerve, their blood-lust and the undisciplined ferocity and sectarianism of the yeomanry and militia under their command.[27] The Abercromby incident arose precisely from this milieu (Gaynor, chapter 19). Abercromby's analysis was that Dublin Castle (the agent of a weak centralized state) pandered excessively to local elites who viewed the military as an instrument to be deployed to their own ends of patronage, electioneering, property protection and the peevish pursuit of private vendettas. Petty politics took primacy in setting the military agenda, with ruinous consequences for strategy, discipline and performance.[28] A series of weak lords lieutenant (Westmorland, Fitzwilliam, Camden) had lost control to a local 'cabinet' of Foster, Fitzgibbon, Agar, Beresford and Parnell.[29]

25 The introduction by Breandán MacSuibhne and David Dickson to *The outer edge of Ulster: A memoir of social life in nineteenth-century Donegal* (Dublin, 2000) offers penetrating insights on this theme.

26 Sampson, *Memoirs*, p. 101.

27 Charlemont reports that he personally heard the earl of Carrick declare after he had first involved his very young son (Lord Ikerrin) in hunting Whiteboys: 'I have blooded my young dog. I have fleshed my bloodhound': Lecky, *Ire.*, ii, p. 40. [The original is in R.I.A. Ms 12/R/7, p. 50]. In 1798, Lord Londonderry's yeomen, under the command of the Revd John Cleland, called themselves 'croppy hounds': Madden, *United Irishmen*, Fourth series, 2nd ed., p. 36: The 89th Foot were known as 'Blayney's bloodhounds' after their exploits in 1798: E. Cobham, *Brewer's dictionary of phrase and fable* (London, 1895).

28 Tony Gaynor, 'The politics of law and order in Ireland 1794–1798 (unpublished Ph.D. thesis, University of Dublin, 1998); see also his 'The legal challenge to the Irish government in the 1790s', in *Ir. Jurist*, xxxiv (1999), 300–37.

29 Gillian O'Brien, 'Camden and the move towards union 1795–1798', in Keogh and Whelan (eds), *Acts of union*, pp 106–25, seeks to rehabilitate Camden. The recent accession to a public archive of Agar's papers is an important breakthrough: A.P.W. Malcomson, *Archbishop Charles Agar: Churchmanship and politics in Ireland, 1760–1810* (Dublin, 2002). We also require a full study of Edward Cooke, the pivotal Castle administrator. He was the son of the master of Eton College 'and a scholar of the first order; he was passionately fond of the English poetry, more particularly Shakespeare, Milton and Gray': A.H. Giffard, *Who was my grandfather?* (London, 1865), p. 27. What was the psychological state of a man whose office at Dublin Castle is described in the following terms in 1798?: 'It was full of those arms which had been at different times and in various parts of the country wrested from the hands of the unfortunate peasants. They were chiefly pikes of a most crude workmanship and forms the most grotesque: green crooked sticks cut out of the hedges, with long spikes, nails, knives or scythe blades fastened on to the end of them, very emblematic of the poverty and desperation of these unhappy warriors and showing in a strong light the wonderful effects of despair and the courage it inspires. Never did human eyes behold so curious an armory as this secretary's office': Sampson, *Memoirs*, p. 24. The United Irishmen described him as 'a duck-nosed looking cuckold' in Apr. 1798: N.A.I., RP 620/10/121/98.

An English commentator believed that the 'English viceroy' had become 'a mere cypher in the state'.[30] These powerful politicians supported their local allies whenever possible. Fitzgibbon, for example, packed the magistracy with hardliners from the mid-1790s in counties not amenable to Dublin Castle control, even adding military officers, thereby circumventing the requirement for them to work through a restraining local magistracy.[31] This was a flagrant violation of the principle of the separation of powers.[32] Moderates identified a link between anti-Catholic politics in parliament and harsh law-and-order measures at local level. County Louth is the obvious example. In the brief interval of the Fitzwilliam lord lieutenancy, it seemed possible that a more Burkean approach might be adopted. However, the 'cabinet' quickly saw off Fitzwilliam and they undermined Abercromby, 'the Scotch beast', when he tried to reassert centralized military control of the army. He was replaced by the mediocre, blustering Englishman Gerard Lake, putty in the hands of the Foster clique.[33] Cornwallis, with a joint position as lord lieutenant and commander-in-chief, and with the unambiguous backing of Pitt, was able to wrest control back from the discredited 'Irish cabinet'. Foster's resulting sulk rushed him into the anti-Union camp, joining some strange bed-fellows like Grattan, hitherto his implacable opponent. The Irish elite felt that the Union would represent a return to the *status quo ante* but instead it witnessed their marginalisation. The hypocrisy at the heart of the union was that it was simultaneously sold to Catholics as a defence against the Protestants and to Protestants as a defence against the Catholics.[34]

30 Bingley, *Examinations*, p. 8. For senior administrators, the Irish parliament had become a liability after the re-arrangement of 1782; Castlereagh described it as 'the plaything of their independence': *Castlereagh corr.*, i, p. 441.

31 Ann Kavanaugh, *John Fitzgibbon, earl of Clare: A study of personality and politics* (Dublin, 1997).

32 J.P. Swan, 'The justices of the peace of the county of Wexford 1661–1800', in *J.R.S.A.I.*, series v, iv (1894), 65–72; H. Berry, 'Justices of the peace for the county of Cork 1661–1800', in *J.C.H.A.S.*, iii (1897), 58–65; 106–112. These conveniently list the dates of appointments of magistrates in the eighteenth century from records subsequently destroyed. The inability to get Antrim and Down proclaimed in 1796 shows the extent of the alienation from Dublin Castle. See the valuable series of maps in Mac Suibhne, above, pp 278–9. There were also many more magistrates, including a noticeable accession of clergy and military men in the 1790s – they comprised *c.*20 per cent by 1798. The number per decade newly created in County Cork oscillated from 98 (1760–69), 89 (1770–79), 59 (1780–89) to 151 (1790–99). Of 55 magistrates created in 1787–98, 3 were Anglican clerics, 21 were military officers. Between November and December 1797, in what was obviously a concerted policy, all the senior army officers in Cork were created magistrates. In Wexford, the new magistrates were almost uniformly unpopular in 1798: John Hunter Gowan, A.H. Jacob, James Boyd, Richard Bookey, J.H. Lyster, Revd Thomas Handcock, Standish Lowcay, Charles Tottenham and Richard Kerr.

33 Gerard Lake (1744–1808) was born in Middlesex. He served in America, India, Holland and Ulster, before being made a lieutenant-general in Ireland in 1797. He was elevated to commander-in-chief in 1798 and subsequently served as commander-in-chief in India, where (with Wellington), he prosecuted the Maharta war.

34 Kevin Whelan, 'The other within: Ireland, Britain and the Act of Union', in Keogh and Whelan (eds), *Acts of union*, pp 13–33.

As George Douglas put it, the Union was 'a state expedient,' dictated by 'the hug of policy, not the embrace of love'.[35]

The state had become visible at local level as the exposed gentry looked to it, and as the state itself sought for the first time to recruit Irish Catholics for the war effort. The rule of law became more politicized as the United Irishmen responded to the avalanche of coercive measures. It is crucial to note that this coercion developed between 1793 and 1795, before the full onset of the paramilitary phase of the radical movement. The radicals sought to put the law itself on trial through their star legal performers, most notably Curran,[36] but also through their own members like William Sampson,[37] Thomas Addis Emmet, Richard Newton Bennet,[38] Mathew Dowling and the informer Leonard MacNally.[39] Lawyers were active members of the United Irishmen, notably Arthur O'Connor, Bagenal Harvey, Simon Butler, John Sheares, William Todd Jones and Theobald Wolfe Tone.[40] They staged some major propaganda coups: even when they seemingly lost, as with the execution of William Orr, they still reaped benefits by exposing the chicanery and vindictiveness of the state itself.[41] They were experts at turning the courtroom into a moral theatre. Curran was a justly feared shredder of the motley crew of informers that mushroomed in the 1790s, and community odium added to the isolation of informers (Bartlett, chapter 20). The two most notorious Ulster informers, Edward Newell and John Bird, were 'turned' by the United Irishmen in 1797, with humiliating propaganda and practical effects on a crest-fallen Castle.[42] An outstanding aspect of the 1790s was the ability of the Irish radicals to withstand the fierce legal pressure exerted on them by

35 George Douglas, *Paddiana: or A dissertation philosophical and analytical, critical and satirical on Irish bulls to which is added a collection of blundering songs and sayings* (Baltimore, 1803), p. vii.

36 A study of Curran's legal and political career is badly needed. Among his many lapidary phrases was 'The price of freedom is eternal vigilance.'

37 A fine example of what can be achieved by a legal scholar is Walter Walsh's two studies of William Sampson: 'Redefining radicalism: A historical perspective', in *George Washington Law Review*, lix (1991), 636–82; 'Religion, ethnicity and history: Clues to the cultural construction of the law', in Ronald Bayor and Timothy Meagher (eds), *The New York Irish* (Baltimore, 1995), pp 48–69.

38 Richard Newton Bennett (b.1769), a Wexford Protestant educated at Trinity and the King's Inns, was active with United Irish prisoners in 1798 and 1803. He was one of Daniel O'Connell's closest friends in this period when O'Connell had briefly joined the United Irishmen.

39 Thomas Bartlett, 'The life and opinions of Leonard MacNally, playwright, barrister, United Irishman and informer', in Hiram Morgan (ed.), *Information, media and power through the ages* (Dublin, 2001), pp 113–36.

40 Of the original Society, 39 were attorneys, 26 were barristers.

41 F.J. Bigger, *William Orr* [facsimile reprint, orig. ed. 1906] (Belfast, 1998). An ancillary publication is R.H. Foy, *Remembering all the Orr: The story of the Orr families of Antrim and their involvement in the 1798 rebellion* (Belfast, 1999).

42 Edward Newell, *The apostacy of Newell containing the life and confessions of that celebrated informer . . . written by himself* (London, 1798) [N.L.I., J.P. 5853]. A practical result was that the government were forced to release the high-profile Ulster United Irishmen in January 1798.

the state. Their success depended on a high degree of public support, reflected in the surprising acquittal rates in court. Between 1796 and the spring assizes of 1798, the acquittal rate for political offences was 70 per cent.[43] Dublin Castle had then to resort to jury-packing and other extra-legal manoeuvres, bringing the rule of law into ever greater disrepute. By contrast, the Scottish reform movement wilted quickly under pressure from Dundas and Braxfield in 1793–4;[44] in England, radicalism was easily cowed in 1796–7.[45] In both these jurisdictions there was popular 'church and king' support for the harsh legal treatment of radicals, to a degree never replicated in Ireland.

The 1790s also saw the development of the republican funeral. Closely modelled on classical precedent, as in the Periclean oration, and building on the recent example of the Volunteer paramilitary funeral, a republican genre of public death ritual emerged in the 1790s.[46] This was secular; it emphasised merit rather than birth; it fused the exemplary greatness of the republican hero with his representativeness of the wider community; it emphasised proximity between the living and the dead, and it asserted the triumph of memory over oblivion. The carefully choreographed funeral of the Presbyterian martyr William Orr in 1797 was the finest but by no means the only example of such a republican event in the 1790s. One can also see at this stage the mutation of the older eighteenth-century 'gallows speech' into an explicitly political form.[47] A further innovation was the development of accurate trial reports, pioneered by William Sampson, which provided a way of circumventing censorship and government-inspired bowdlerised versions. These remarkable speeches inspired other radicals, as, for example, Frederick Douglass (1817–95), who specifically visited Ireland in 1845 to pay homage to O'Connell.[48] A further literary form pioneered by the radicals at this stage was the political catechism, modelled on

43 Gaynor, 'Legal challenge,' p. 305.
44 E.W. McFarland, *Ireland and Scotland in the age of revolution* (Edinburgh, 1994).
45 The treatment of John Binns in Birmingham in 1796 is an apposite example: John Binns, *Recollections of the life of John Binns* (Philadelphia, 1854), pp 66–72; Jenny Graham, *The nation, the law and the king: Reform politics in England, 1789–1799*, 2 vols (New York, 2000).
46 See the suggestive analysis in Avner Ben-Amos, *Funerals, politics and memory in modern France, 1789–1996* (Oxford, 2000).
47 James Kelly deliberately excludes these political versions from his collection *Gallows speeches from eighteenth-century Ireland* (Dublin, 2001). It is precisely this innovation that distinguishes the Irish versions from the British genre and which also becomes the precursor to the 'Speeches from the Dock' versions of the nineteenth century. See Whelan, *Fellowship of freedom*, p. 99 for a striking Wexford example.
48 He was inspired by the speech of Arthur O'Connor in the Irish House of Commons on 4 May 1795 in favour of Catholic Emancipation, reprinted in *The Columbian orator* (Philadelphia, 1798). Douglass misremembers the speech as being by Richard Brinsley Sheridan. His error is repeated by Fintan O'Toole in his article on Sheridan, *Irish Times*, 30 October 2001. See also Alan Rice and Martin Crawford (eds), *Liberating sojourn: Frederick Douglass and transatlantic reform* (Athens, Ga., 1999).

versions produced in the French revolution, notably Volney's *Catechism of a French citizen* [1792].[49] The genre also allowed for easy fluidity between printed and oral forms and invested political instruction with the authoritative form of ecclesiastical precedent.

While the focus on the flow of information has been exclusively on that directed at Dublin Castle, much flowed in the opposite direction. Incredibly, the man responsible for opening seditious mail at the post office, William St John, subsequently turned out to be a United man.[50] For all its notoriety as an 'assassination sheet', Watty Cox's *Union Star* was often accurate. Francis Higgins, Edward Newell and Belle Martin are three figures well known to historians whom he targeted.[51] Maria Edgeworth's *Castle Rackrent* deploys the porous door as an image of the dangerous all-knowingness of servants in eighteenth-century Irish life. The credulous stupidity of the Rackrents in allowing the insidious Thady Quirk to eavesdrop on all their private conversations gave him the opportunities to undermine them in favour of his son Jason, in a classic example of 'sly civility'. The Rackrent house is physically perforated – broken windows, missing slates and shingles, doors with no locks, broken bolts, cracked mirrors. This encourages Thady to slink through back corridors, and skulk at the doors, covertly acquiring the necessary information to destroy his masters.[52] The rebellion released a pent-up torrent of fear of servants, especially among isolated loyalist women, which can only be seen as a symptom of a colonial psyche.[53]

The relative effectiveness of informers is a more open question than is assumed in the standard accounts. Certainly the incredulity at the French descent on Bantry Bay, the absence of any high-grade intelligence on the Defenders, the failure to identify County Wexford as a likely insurrection centre (despite Jonah Barrington's best – or worst – efforts), and the shock at the Emmet insurrection in 1803 do not suggest an omniscient Dublin Castle.[54] The

---

49 K. Whelan, 'Introduction to "The poor man's catechism"', in *Labour History*, lxxv (1998), 22–37. Volney's catechism first appeared as a supplement in the 1792 edition of *The ruins or a survey of the revolutions of empire*, one of the favourite texts of the United Irishmen.

50 St John, according to a London informer, was 'a person in the letter department of the post office in Dublin. He used to have the care of searching suspicious letters. He joined the rebel camp at Wicklow and was a chief ... St John is a very desperate man for whom it is imagined the Irish govt. are in search': Information given by H.M. [November?] 1798: N.L.I., MS 33,043.

51 It would be extremely useful to have an edition of the eight issues of the *Union Star*. Not all Cox's advice was followed. Among those he identified as an active spy was the brewer Arthur Guinness. He vainly warned: 'United Irishmen will be cautious of dealing with any publican that sells his drink.'

52 Maria Edgeworth, *Castle Rackrent*, ed. George Watson (Oxford, 1981), pp 61, 65, 84.

53 John Beatty (ed.), *Protestant women's narratives of the Irish rebellion of 1798* (Dublin, 2001).

54 There is a palpable and sustained antipathy to Barrington in Madden, *United Irishmen*, first series.

emphasis on informers intensified in the mid-nineteenth century: Madden, Fitzpatrick and Kavanagh dwell at length on the theme. All were eminent Victorians: Madden a high-ranking imperial official (Woods, chapter 24); Fitzpatrick a Dublin Catholic gentleman; Kavanagh a leading cleric in the rapid march of the Irish Catholic church to respectability. The new threat of the oath-bound Fenians dominated their work as did a concern for respectability.[55] Fitzpatrick justified his work on 1798: 'nor is the story without a moral. The organizers of illegal societies will see that, in spite of the apparent secrecy and ingenuity of their system, informers sit with them at the same council-board and dinner-table, ready at any moment to sell their blood, and that the wider the ramifications of the conspiracy, the greater becomes the certainty of detection'.[56] The plebeian origins of the informers appears as a worse crime than the betrayals of their associates, and there is much sententious moralising on the dangers of drink.[57] Ultimately the refusal of the best-placed informers (MacNally, Turner, Magan) to testify in open court proved a serious impediment. Suspects could be jailed but not tried, thereby exposing the Castle to charges of abusing the law. Overflowing gaols and an inability to prosecute led to embarrassing releases of well-known prisoners like the Ulster leaders. The most effective informer was Thomas Reynolds because he was prepared to testify in open court, and was sufficiently brazen to withstand a withering character assault by Curran. It is also important not to focus exclusively on the major informers: lethal damage may have been inflicted on United Irish morale by continuous low-level informing, which sapped the confidence of the rank-and-file.

Against this backdrop, the decision of the United Irish leaders to accede to the 'Kilmainham Treaty' remains puzzling (Quinn, chapter 21). Their willingness to admit publicly their part in a long-running conspiracy with France was a propaganda windfall, as Fitzgibbon, Cooke and Castlereagh instantly recognised. It eased the government off the hook as to how to deal legally with their notoriously high-profile prisoners. Cooke gleefully reported: 'We get rid of seventy prisoners, many of the most important of whom we could not try and who could not be disposed of without doing such a violence to the principles of law and evidence as could not be well justified'.[58] It rehabilitated the disgraced

55 R.R. Madden, in his prospectus to the 1861 edition of his series of volumes, claimed that one purpose of his work on the United Irishmen was 'to convince the people of the folly of entering into secret associations'. Good examples of the enduring Irish obsession with informers are John Adey Curran, *Reminiscences of John Adye Curran* (London, 1915); J.G. Swift MacNeill, 'The agent provocateur in Ireland', in *Contemporary Review*, 635, Nov. (1918), 527–36; Liam O'Flaherty, *The informer* (London, 1925).

56 Fitzpatrick, *Secret service under Pitt*, p. vi.

57 Note the prurient avoidance of sex in favour of drink as a source of moral weakness.

58 Cited in Gaynor, 'Legal challenge,' p. 335. FitzGibbon advocated summary executions: 'civil and military forms of trial are too slow for the times and all culprits should be executed on the instant … We should put to death ten for every one': E. Hewitt (ed.), *Lord Shannon's letters*, p. 80.

Dublin 'cabinet' in England, retrospectively justifying their harsh methods in the 1790s. It seriously discomfited leading Whigs like Fox, Sheridan, Moira and Burdett who had ostentatiously supported O'Connor in a blaze of publicity at his sensational trial at Maidstone in Mar. 1798.[59] The willingness of the United Irish leaders to sign the treaty left them vulnerable to the charge of saving their own necks, after having incited thousands of their own rank and file to die just a few months earlier. As the informer John Bird had astutely pointed out in 1796, the best way to undermine the United Irishmen would be to 'destroy the only bond that holds them together, namely mutual confidence'.[60] Fitzgibbon turned up the heat by publishing a cunningly doctored version of their evidence in the report of the Committee of Secrecy in August 1798, to howls of useless protest from the out-manoeuvred United leaders. Too late, Samuel Neilson concluded that 'their primary object was to blast our reputations'.[61] That their capitulation and the taint of moral cowardice bothered them is seen by the wave of subsequent self-justification. The extraordinary emotion released five years later by Robert Emmet's exemplary behaviour in the courtroom and on the scaffold exorcised the accusing ghost of Kilmainham. Emmet expiated the United Irishmen (including his elder brother Thomas Addis who had allegedly wept like a child while giving his evidence) by his exemplary sacrifice. His unflinching willingness to face the consequences of his political choice (like Orr's legendary calm as he sang the 23rd psalm before his execution,[62] Tone's Senecan suicide, and Russell's bravery at Downpatrick)[63] elevated Emmet into the republican pantheon in a way denied to those tainted by Kilmainham. This is not to argue that Tone, Russell or Emmet courted a sacrificial death: the rank-and-file simply responded to their willingness to face death in the same way that so many of those that they had recruited faced death, thereby insulating them from the accusation of double standards.

59 Both Fox and Burdett (by marriage) were relatives and friends of Lord Edward FitzGerald; Sheridan a high profile Irish dramatist; Francis Rawdon (1754–1826), second earl of Moira, was a County Down landowner, army officer and leader of fashion, dismissed by Gifford in 1813 as 'the king of the coxcombs': Giffard, *Who was my grandfather?*, p. 77. Moira ended up as governor-general of India.

60 John Bird to Skeffington, 21 Apr. 1796: N.A.I., Fraser MSS 2/17c.

61 The extent of the damage to the United Irishmen is indicated by the fact that even the ultra-secretive Neilson felt compelled to write about the treaty: Samuel Neilson, *Brief statement of a negociation between certain United Irishmen and the Irish government in July 1798* (New York, 1802), p. 38. One of the few surviving copies of this pamphlet is in the library of Thomas Moore at the Royal Irish Academy [MR 16/I/12].

62 'Yea tho' I walk in death's dark vale,/yet will I fear none ill.' He had then read the 31st Psalm, emphasizing the words 'In thee O Lord, I put my trust/shamed never let me be ... And sith thou art my strength therefore/pull me out of the net/which they in subtility for me/so privily have set/Unto thy hands I do commit/my spirit for thou art He/O thou, Jehovah, God of Truth/that hath redeemed me.' He had then read from 1 Corinthians, 16:54: 'O Death, where is thy sting? O Grave where is thy victory? The sting of death is sin and the strength of sin is the law. Therefore my beloved brethern, be ye steadfast, unmoveable.'

63 James Quinn, *Soul on fire: A life of Thomas Russell, 1767–1803* (Dublin, 2002).

If we look at the 1790s as a whole, a key question has to be responsibility for the violence that convulsed the decade. While there is no consensus on the number who died, the most common figure to be quoted recently is 20,000. Of that figure, a maximum of 2,000 died on the loyalist side.[64] The stark reality is that at least 90 per cent of the killings were by the state, either directly or through groups it sponsored. It is important to stress this imbalance as so much discussion of violence in the 1790s proceeds on the assumption that the revolutionary forces were the principal agents of death. The shocking scale of state killing (Madden believed that it 'ranked among the worst outrages on humanity that have ever been committted by civilised men'[65]) raises the question: was it justified, in terms of the magnitude of the threat they faced? It also raises tough questions about the rule of law itself (Osborough, chapter 22). By 1797, the Grattanite Whig argument was that the constitution had been so retrenched that there was no point in indulging the fiction that normal parliamentary politics were possible. Grattan acerbically commented that there were obviously two times when the state could not be reformed – in times of peace and in times of war. When Camden declared national martial law on 30 March 1798, it was an illegitimate use of the prerogative but there was no one left to oppose it. Martial law, attainder acts and indemnity acts drew on legal precedents which had been exercised in Ireland since the period of intense colonialism in the late sixteenth century but which had long fallen into desuetude in Britain.[66] The rule of law fell into such disrepute in Wexford in 1798 that rebels actually opted to be tried by courts martial rather than by a local jury. After the humiliating 1796 assizes, juries were being packed in County Antrim as early as spring 1797.[67] The indemnity acts screened those who had violated civilised norms of behaviour, like the unbalanced Thomas Judkin Fitzgerald in Tipperary.[68] The compensation avail-

---

64 The most comprehensive and accurate list of loyalist dead is to be found in *A list of the subscribers to the fund for the relief of widows and orphans of yeomen, soldiers etc. who fell in suppressing the late rebellion* (Dublin, 1800). [N.L.I., J.P. 2216]. It lists by name, for example, the 106 members of the North Cork Militia annihilated at Oulart Hill. Overall figures for deaths in the rebellion have oscillated dramatically: Marsden in 1798, 20,000; Newenham in 1805, 15,000; Madden in 1860, 70,000; Pakenham in 1969, 30,000; Bartlett in 2001, 10,000. A good technical discussion of the issues can be found in L.M. Cullen, 'Rebellion mortality in Wexford in 1798', in *Jn. Wex. Hist. Soc.*, xvii (1998–9), 7–29.

65 Madden, *United Irishmen*, first series, second edition, p. xi.

66 Ronan Keane, 'The will of the general: Martial law in Ireland, 1535–1924', in *Ir. Jurist*, xxv-xxvii (1990–92), 150–80. Martial law was essentially an imperial concept: Charles Townshend, 'Martial law: Legal and administrative problems of civil emergency in Britain and the empire 1800–1940', in *Hist. Jn.*, xxv (1982), 167–95.

67 For the evidence from Antrim, see R.M. Young, *Ulster in '98: Episodes and anecdotes now first printed* (Belfast, 1893), p. 88. The trial of Fr James Coigly in 1798 set the precedent which still stands in the UK for permitting an unlimited amount of peremptory challenges to potential jury members by the crown: E.P. Thompson, 'In defence of the jury', in *Making history: Writings on history and culture* (New York, 1994), pp 141–66, esp. pp 156–7.

68 The nickname 'Flogging' Fitzgerald followed him to his grave. His obituary in the *Irish*

able after 1798 was rigidly confined to active loyalists: it was not enough just to be neutral. Conservative cliques vengefully excluded those whom they deemed insufficiently pro-active in 1798.[69] The sudden (65 per cent) post-rebellion boost in the numbers enrolled in the yeomanry - from 43,221 on the eve of the rebellion to 66,082 in 1799 - had much to do with this imperative to parade one's loyalty as a preliminary to claiming compensation. To this day, a significant component of the housing stock of the south Leinster region dates to the great re-building after 1798, when the housing style shifted from the thatched single-story dwelling to substantial, stone-walled, two-story slated houses.[70] The four counties with the greatest yeomanry increases were however all in Ulster – with numbers jumping by over 2,600 in Tyrone, 1,900 in Fermanagh, 1,800 in Cavan and 1,500 in Down.[71]

Despite honourable efforts by many lawyers, the long-term effect of the 1790s was to reinforce the long-standing Catholic conviction that the law was not a neutral instrument. They were taught by bitter experience that the law was a friend to their enemies, while it was consistently operated in a partisan way against them. As Thomas Moore phrased it : 'You may track Ireland through the statute book of England, as a wounded man in a crowd is tracked by his blood.'[72] The failure to incorporate Catholics fully into the new state in 1801 convinced them that there was a close link between their political impotence and their legal isolation. Daniel O'Connell was to be the ultimate beneficiary of this politicization of the law in the eyes of Irish Catholics. It was no accident that his rise to political dominance in the Catholic community followed on his spectacularly successful legal career.

Magazine noted 'The history of his life and his loyalty is written in legible characters on the backs of his countrymen; his enormities were so various and the fertility of his imagination in devising new modes of desolation and torture were truly original': *Irish Magazine*, Oct. 1810, 482. One of his many innocent victims, Mathew Scott of Carrick-on-Suir, eventually committed suicide in 1811.

69 On narrower studies of the results of courts martials, compensation claims and Cornwallis' interventions, see Thomas Bartlett, 'Clemency and compensation: The treatment of defeated rebels and suffering loyalists in the administration of Lord Cornwallis', in Smyth (ed.), *Revolution*, pp 92–127; Michael Durey, 'The United Irishmen and the politics of banishment, 1798–1807', in Davis (ed.), *Radicalism*, pp 96–109; Power, *The courts martial of 1798–1799*.

70 'The farmers' houses around Gorey exhibit a remarkably neat appearance which Mr Beaumont ascribes to their having been erected since the rebellion. At that time, great numbers were burnt, and those since built are constructed in a superior manner as they consist of stone walls with slated roofs': Edward Wakefield, *An account of Ireland, statistical and political* (London, 1812), i, p 409.

71 Numerical strength of the yeomanry, 1797 to 1799, N.A.I., RP 620/48/56.

72 Thomas Moore, *Memoirs of Captain Rock, the celebrated Irish chieftain, with some account of his ancestors* (London, 1824), p. 368.

19

The Abercromby affair

TONY GAYNOR

The winter of 1797 witnessed a struggle in Ireland to decide who should control the formation of military policy in the kingdom. This resulted in the resignation of the commander-in-chief, Sir Ralph Abercromby, only two months before the outbreak of the rebellion of 1798. Abercromby's attempts to reverse some of the policies implemented by his predecessors had aroused the wrath of a law-and-order lobby that had been pivotal in the adoption of those policies in the first place. This lobby, composed of a powerful group of loyalist politicians, represented the fears and aspirations of the loyalist community at large in the kingdom, and their control over the lord lieutenant, Earl Camden, and his chief secretary, Thomas Pelham, was near absolute. Before Abercromby's arrival on 2 December 1797, they had become accustomed to dictating military policy to the commander-in-chief. Their endeavours in this respect were more easily crowned with success by the presence of active sympathizers among the army command, in particular General Gerard Lake, the commanding officer of the northern district, and Brigadier General John Knox who served under him in mid-Ulster. Together these men had succeeded in prioritizing the needs of counter-insurgency over those of preparation against a possible French invasion. This amounted to a policy of dispersing the troops through the country in small detachments in response to the alarms of frightened loyalists, and then employing them in vigorous measures against the disaffected. The arrival of the French fleet in Bantry Bay in December 1796 shattered the illusions of Irish loyalists that the British admiralty would protect them from invasion, which had been pivotal in the formation of this tough security policy. The dangers if the French actually effected a landing, and the boost given to United Irish numbers by the appearance of the French, prompted the Irish 'cabinet' to force Camden into employing the military in a more direct manner against disaffection in the kingdom. This initiative resulted in the disarmament of Ulster in the spring of 1797 and the proclamation issued in May 1797 by the lord lieutenant and council which directed the military to act without waiting for the authority or sanction of the civil magistrate. With troops out in small parties searching the countryside for concealed arms, often with no officer supervision, and authorized to act independently of the civil authority, military excesses inevitably increased.

This situation confronted Sir Ralph Abercromby when he reluctantly accepted the Irish command in the autumn of 1797. He had spent twenty years in the kingdom earlier in his career, during which time he had grown to dislike the manner in which the country was governed and the mode by which the military establishment was entirely dominated by the civil authorities. His reluctance to return arose from his apprehension that the policies he favoured would meet with strong hostility from the loyalist lobby which effectively governed the kingdom. With this in mind, he endeavoured to obtain assurances from the British cabinet before leaving London in October 1797 that his decision on army affairs would be final. He went so far as to tell Pitt that opposition to his command would result in his resignation. In response, he was assured by the London government that he should labour under no difficulty or restraint and that in time of war the control of the army (with the exception of patronage) would lie entirely under his command. Despite these assurances, it was not long after his arrival in Ireland that Abercromby began to voice complaints about the obstacles placed in his path by the civil authorities which prevented him from moulding the army in the fashion he desired. On 25 December, only three weeks after his arrival in the kingdom, he demanded from William Elliott (military under-secretary at Dublin Castle) an explicit declaration as to who actually controlled military policy; he felt that divided authority was not conducive to an efficient command, and that it was vitally necessary that either the lord lieutenant should take sole command with the senior officer acting as his lieutenant general, or the command should be delegated to the commander-in-chief.[1] General John Moore, a confidante of Abercromby's, observed that in peace-time the commander-in-chief had been little attended to in Ireland, and the army had been considered as little more than an instrument of corruption in the hands of the government. He believed that this had been so much the custom that even at that critical period, with the country facing internal and external threats, Abercromby would require all of his temper and moderation to maintain his authority.[2] The reason for the frustrations he encountered in establishing his authority over the armed forces in Ireland lay in the opposition to the policies he sought to implement.

Abercromby believed that the policy of dispersing the troops throughout the country in small detachments had to be reversed. Defence against possible French invasion had to take priority over counter-insurgency measures, and he was not long in the country before he made his sentiments known. On 13 December 1797 he instructed Lake to concentrate the forces under his com-

---

1 General Ralph Abercromby to William Elliott; to the earl of Camden, 25 Dec. 1797, 15 Mar. 1798: P.R.O., HO 100/75229–30, 315–6; James, Lord Dunfermline, *Memoir of Sir Ralph Abercromby, 1793–1801* (London, 1861), p. 74.
2 J.F. Maurice (ed.), *The diary of Sir John Moore* (2 vols, London 1904), i, p. 270.

mand in the northern district. Abercromby appreciated how difficult it was for the government to resist the applications of individuals for protection, and felt that in some cases they ought not to be resisted. But he was convinced of the absolute necessity of contracting 'to a *certain degree*' the quarters of the troops. In their present state they were exposed to be corrupted, disarmed and made prisoner. They could not be easily assembled, and if called away suddenly to face an enemy in the field, a general dismay would occur in the country.[3] The concentration of the troops would not only facilitate their training and rapid mobilization in the event of a French invasion, but it would also allow for the imposition of regular military discipline, one of the consistent themes throughout Abercromby's career.[4] His tour of inspection to the south of Ireland in January 1798 convinced him of the necessity of withdrawing troops from their dispersed detachments, where discipline suffered 'exceedingly'. The country appeared to him to be tranquil, and he could see no reason for them to be so scattered. The dispersed state of the troops was, in his opinion, ruinous to the service, and he informed the government that the best regiments in Europe could not long stand such usage; many of the regiments would be unable at that moment to take the field because of their various shortages, and these could not be known or made good until the troops were brought together.[5]

Abercromby admitted that dissatisfaction and disaffection existed in the south of Ireland, and acknowledged that it would take a watchful eye to preserve internal tranquillity, but he tended to dismiss these disturbances as traditional agrarian grievances endemic in that part of the country. He questioned the necessity for sending troops to protect frightened loyalists, and was extremely discriminating in responding to requests for military assistance.[6] The maintenance of law and order in the interior of the kingdom was the proper domain of the local gentry and magistrates, assisted by the yeomanry. The concentration of the troops and their withdrawal from counter-insurgency duties should encourage gentlemen to exert themselves for the preservation of domestic peace, and oblige them to rely on the yeomanry, on whom they would have ultimately to depend if the army were called away to face a foreign enemy.[7] His previous experience in Ireland prejudiced him against the country's ruling oligarchy, and this sentiment only increased during his second sojourn in the kingdom. He considered the magistrates and country gentlemen to be imperfectly educated, devoted to political intrigue, and negligent of the duties imposed on them as landlords.

3 Dunfermline, *Abercromby*, pp 79–80.
4 *Diary of Sir John Moore*, i, p. 270; Dunfermline, *Abercromby*, p. 18.
5 Abercromby to Camden, 18 Jan. 1798: K.A.O., Pratt papers, U840 0166/9; Dunfermline, *Abercromby*, pp 85–6.
6 Dunfermline, *Abercromby*, pp 84–5, 92–3; N.L.I., Kilmainham papers, 1014/73, 78.
7 Abercromby to Camden, Pelham, 18 Jan., 21 Feb. 1798: K.A.O., U840 0166/9; B.L., Add. MS 33,105, 345–8; Dunfermline, *Abercromby*, pp 85–6.

He criticized them for not taking responsibility upon themselves for local law enforcement. Most importantly, however, he held them responsible for under-mining the discipline of the troops by calling upon them on every occasion to execute the law and to afford them personal protection, in the words of Colonel Hope, 'purchasing momentary quiet by the ruin of the army'.[8] While he did not object to the troops being employed by the civil authority in cases of emergency, he guarded against 'any excess in the execution of their duty'. Without this dis-crimination, he believed that the discipline of the troops would have been com-pletely ruined, and they would have been led into 'a thousand irregularities' contrary to law. He complained from Bandon on 26 January that the gentry pro-claimed districts out of the king's peace without just cause and then instigated the troops to burn houses and other illegal activities.[9]

Abercromby's general orders of 24 December 1797 summarised the policy he was endeavouring to implement in Ireland, focusing on the need to concentrate the troops, restore discipline to their ranks and regulate their conduct. The dom-inant theme of the orders, however, was their emphasis on the need to keep the military within the boundaries of the law.

> In this country it too frequently happens that the troops are called upon in aid of the civil magistrates, to support the peace of the country. Although on all occasions they ought to behave with firmness, yet they must not forget that they are only called upon to support the laws of the land, and not to step beyond the bounds of them. Any poutrage or excess, therefore, on their part is highly culpable, and they are strictly enjoined to observe the greatest moderation and the strictest discipline when they are called upon to execute this part of their duty. Even in time of actual war, among all civilised nations, it is considered as disgraceful and subversive of all discipline, if soldiers are allowed to be licentious.[10]

These orders have been overshadowed by the more famous 'general orders' of 26 February 1798, but it is evident that long before that date Abercromby had made known his military policy. The heavier emphasis in the February orders on the need to discipline the troops was occasioned by a combination of factors: the observations he had made during his tour to the south, his growing dissatisfac-tion with the results of his earlier initiatives and, more immediately, by the rape of a servant girl by two military officers. Catherine Finn had been a servant to

---

8 Col. Alex. Hope to Dundas, 3 Apr. 1798: N.L.I., Dundas papers, MS 54A, 132; Aber-cromby to Camden, 15 Mar. 1798: P.R.O., HO 100/75/229–30; Dunfermline, *Abercromby*, pp 74, 84–5, 92–3.
9 Abercromby to Camden, 26 Jan. 1798: K.A.O., U840 0166/11.
10 National Army Museum, Nugent papers, MS 6807/174/325–31; Kilmainham papers, 1081/266, 277–8; Dunfermline, *Abercromby*, pp 108–10.

Jasper Uniacke, who had been murdered along with Mansergh St George in
County Cork in early February. Taken into custody in the hope of being able to
identify those involved, she was raped by two lieutenants. This outraged Abercromby, who regarded it as a clear manifestation of the want of discipline in the
army which he had been attempting to eradicate.[11] This helps explain the
unequivocal forcefulness of the February orders which declared that the frequency of courts martial and the many complaints of irregularities of the troops
in Ireland had 'unfortunately proved the army to be in a state of licentiousness
which must render it formidable to everyone but the enemy'. In consequence, he
ordered all commanding officers to exert themselves and compel from those
officers under their command the strictest and unremitting attention to the discipline, good order and conduct of their men. He directed observation to be
paid to the standing orders of the kingdom which forbade the troops to act,
except in case of attack, without the authority of the civil magistrate. In those
cases where they were called into action by a magistrate, the most clear and precise orders were to be given to the officer commanding the party.[12]

By thus restricting the military to the standing orders of the kingdom,
Abercromby hoped to improve their discipline and to force the country gentlemen to trust to their own exertions, with the assistance of the yeomanry, in the
maintenance of law and order in their neighbourhoods.[13] This was a direct contradiction, however, of the proclamation which had been issued by the lord lieutenant and council on 17 May 1797, authorising the military to act without
waiting for directions from the civil magistrate in dispersing any tumultuous
assemblies of persons threatening the peace of the realm and the safety of the
lives and property of his majesty's loyal subjects.[14] Those loyalists whose
attempts to grant the military a free hand in suppressing disturbances had been
frustrated by Abercromby's policies saw this as their opportunity to undermine
his authority. They were not familiar with a commander-in-chief who was actually determined to assert control over the army under his command, and they
seized upon his contradiction of the proclamation of May 1797 as a means to
discredit him and his policies on both sides of the Irish sea.[15]

Abercromby's absence from Dublin for crucial periods allowed the opposition to his command to consolidate under two stalwarts of Irish loyalism, John
Foster and John Parnell. After the issue of his general orders of December 1797,
Abercrombie had set off upon a tour of inspection to the south of the kingdom,
and following the February orders he departed on a similar tour of the north. In

11 Kilmainham papers, 1014/120.
12 *Diary of Sir John Moore*, i, p. 283.
13 Dunfermline, *Abercromby*, pp 112–14.
14 *Diary of Sir John Moore*, i, p. 285.
15 Crawford to Wickham, 28 Mar. 1798: P.R.O., HO 100/66/198–205; Dunfermline, *Abercromby*,
   p. 117.

his absence, the exponents of a firm security policy consulted together and intrigued against him. Their endeavours were assisted by the opening of the new parliamentary session in January 1798, which drew MPs back to the capital from their country seats. From early February, criticism of his policies began to emerge.[16] This opposition was particularly vocal in the southwest of the kingdom, where two of the commanding officers were Generals John Moore and John Hope, two Scotchmen who shared Abercromby's principles and who had followed him from the West Indies. General Hope had made himself objectionable to local loyalists by declaring that the government did not want any more houses burned. Lord Longueville asserted in response that house-burning would cease when the outrages of the disaffected were at an end. Another commanding officer in the region Major General Sir James Stewart, was also censured for his adherence to the policies of the new commander-in-chief.[17] Stewart had issued orders, condemned by Edward Cooke as a 'ridiculous imitation of Sir Ralph', designed to guard against military excesses and to forbid military officers from acting as magistrates. This defeated the design of the law-and-order lobby who had appointed certain military officers as magistrates, in order to enable them to act in this double capacity, thereby obviating the need for the authority of a civil magistrate.[18]

During Abercromby's absence from the capital, Foster convened a meeting of prominent loyalists which censured the February general orders and sent a deputation to Chief Secretary Pelham, conveying this opinion and their determination to bring it before parliament.[19] The militia officers were informed that the orders of 26 February were an insult to the character and discipline of their corps, and this resulted in the resignation of Lord Abercorn from the command of the Tyrone regiment on 12 March. Abercorn demanded that the government expressly disavow the general orders, and force Abercromby to give the Irish regiments and their commanding officers a reparation as public as the insult he had offered them.[20] The commander-in-chief's policy of refusing troop reinforcements to individual noblemen and gentlemen added to the hostility against his command.[21] In addition, Beresford, Cooke, Fitzgibbon and John Lees communicated their complaints to the duke of Portland and Lords Auckland and Westmorland in England. Cooke informed Auckland on 12 March that the gen-

16 A. Newton to [—], 9 Feb. 1797: N.A.I., RP 620/35/130.
17 Opinions of Shannon: K.A.O., U840 0166/10; Longueville to C. Kippax, 14 Feb., 3 Mar. 1798: N.A.I, SOC 1017/5, 7.
18 John Beresford to the earl of Westmoreland, 20 Mar. 1798: William Beresford (ed.), *Correpondence of the rt. hon. John Beresford* (London, 1854), ii, pp 153–5; Beresford, Cooke to Auckland, 24 Mar. 1798: P.R.O.N.I., Pelham papers, T.3229/2/31–32.
19 *Diary of Sir John Moore*, i, pp 286–8.
20 Abercorn to Camden, 12 Mar. 1798: K.A.O., U840 0186/6; Dunfermline, *Abercromby*, pp 97–8.
21 Kilmainham papers, 1014/74, 78, 80, 81, 83, 108, 114.

eral orders were 'a fatal blow to the government'.²² Robert Ross and General
Lake lobbied Lord Downshire. Ross expressed the wish that Abercromby had
stayed with the natives in 'Martinico' and predicted that the kingdom would be
lost if he remained in command.²³ A smear campaign was also initiated, accusing
the commander-in-chief of political designs, and in particular attempting to
implicate him in complicity with the charges which the Whig peer, Lord Moira,
had made against the conduct of the military in Ireland only a week before the
issue of the February orders. Robert Ross even accused him of keeping company
not only with Moira but also with the rebel chief Lord Edward FitzGerald.²⁴
The extent and intensity of the plot against Abercromby was revealed by John
Lees, secretary to the general post office, who dined with eighteen of 'the first
men in the kingdom' on 2 April, whose disposition inclined them to have the
commander impeached for his conduct.²⁵

The successful manipulation by the Irish cabinet of their loyalist allies in
Britain provoked the duke of Portland to raise the subject of the general orders
with Camden for the first time on 11 March.²⁶ The lord lieutenant had at first
attempted to avoid adverting to them in his dispatches to London, and when the
furore among his supporters in Ireland made mention of them unavoidable, he
endeavoured to explain them away by placing a purely military interpretation on
them. He privately regarded the orders as 'most injudicious and almost criminal', but he was reluctant to reveal publicly his views for fear of provoking
Abercromby's resignation. He valued his military talents and more importantly,
his resignation in such circumstances would substantiate Whig criticism of the
manner in which the army in Ireland was being employed.²⁷ Camden's fears that
Abercromby would resign in the face of the opposition to his command were
realized on 15 March. In an interview that day, the commander-in-chief denied
any political agenda and declared that his general orders had been issued
expressly for the purpose of correcting abuses, supporting stricter discipline and
stimulating the exertions of the gentlemen of the country. He did acknowledge
that he had believed the proclamation of the previous May to have been aban-

---

22 Cooke to Auckland, 12 Mar., 24 Mar. 1798: P.R.O.N.I., Sneyd papers, T.3229/2/28, 32;
   Beresford to Auckland, 13 Mar., 24 Mar. 1798: *Ibid.*, T.3229/2/29, 31; Fitzgibbon, John Lees to
   Auckland, 23 Mar., 2 Apr. 1798: B.L., Auckland papers, Add. MS 34,454, 185–6, 197–8;
   Beresford to Westmorland, 20 Mar. 1798: *Beresford correspondence*, ii, pp 153–5.
23 Ross to Downshire, 27 Mar., 2 Apr. 1798: P.R.O.N.I., Downshire papers, D/607/F/108, 127;
   Lake to [—], 28 Mar. 1798: N.A.I., RP 620/36/94).
24 Fitzgibbon to Auckland, 23 Mar. 1798: B.L., Add. MS 34,454, 185–6; Ross to Downshire, 27
   Mar., 5 Apr. 1798: P.R.O.N.I., Downshire papers D/607/F/108, 131A; *Beresford correspondence*,
   ii, pp 153–5.
25 J. Lees to Auckland, 2 Apr. 1798: B.L., Add. MS 34,454, 197–8.
26 Portland to Camden, 11 Mar. 1798: P.R.O., HO 100/75/193–4.
27 Camden to Portland, 20 Feb., 14 Mar. 1798: P.R.O., HO 100/75/100, 225–8; Camden to Pitt, 17
   Mar. 1798: K.A.O., U840 0156/28.

doned through disuse, but argued that the interpretation and execution of that proclamation could not have been left to officers of all ranks without great danger to the discipline of the armed forces. He informed Camden that if he did not possess the confidence of Camden's advisors he must impede the operation of his government, and therefore tendered his resignation. Until the appointment of his successor, however, he would temporarily retain the command.[28]

Faced with this dilemma and failing to comprehend that the debate over the general orders was but a manifestation of a deeply-rooted conflict between two rival military policies, Camden endeavoured to achieve the contradictory goals of placating his supporters while retaining Abercromby in the military command. Camden's advisors lobbied for the adoption of a tougher law-and-order policy, criticising the timidity of the administration and associating together in parliament in order to force the hand of the lord lieutenant towards a more vigorous policy.[29] Camden endeavoured to placate his supporters by two measures: he ordered the arrest of the United Irish leaders in Leinster, despite having received advice 'somewhat like a remonstrance' from Portland against the proposal; secondly, he directed Abercromby on 14 March to implement disarmament of the disaffected in Kildare, King's and Queen's counties. As a further concession to loyalist pressure, the military involved in this campaign were authorized to act, in direct contradiction of the orders of 26 February, without waiting for the sanction of the civil authority.[30] Camden was confident that by these means, in addition to interpreting the February orders in a purely military light, he would satisfy demands for vigorous measures and defuse the intensity of the campaign against the commander-in-chief.[31] In the meantime he endeavoured to persuade Abercromby to retain the command. The viceroy had been pleased with his acknowledgement that he had not considered the proclamation of May 1797 as still in force, and mistakenly interpreted this as an admission by the commander-in-chief that his censure on the Irish armed forces had been ill deserved. Fuelled by this self-deception Camden endeavoured on 22 March to convince Abercromby of the necessity of his remaining in Ireland. Although he expressed sympathy with Abercromby's goals, and acknowledged that he was above 'manoeuvre and intrigue', he absolutely insisted that the proclamation had to be acted upon. Camden wanted something he could use to placate those calling for Abercromby's resignation. This amounted to an explicit disavowal by the commander-in-chief of his orders of 26 February. The authority granted to the

28 Abercromby to Camden, 15 Mar. 1798: P.R.O., HO 100/75/229–30; Dunfermline, *Abercromby*, pp 106–10, 112–4, 125–7; *Diary of Sir John Moore*, i, pp 282–5.
29 Camden to Portland, 8 Feb., 6 Mar. 1798: P.R.O., HO 100/75/71–4, 162–9.
30 Camden to Portland, 10 Mar., 11 Mar. 1798, Elliott to Abercromby, 14 Mar. 1798: P.R.O. HO 100/75/187–8, 195–210, 239–50.
31 Camden to Portland, Pitt, Abercorn: 14 Mar., 17 Mar. 1798: P.R.O., HO 100/75/225–8; K.A.O., U840 0156/28, 0186/12.

military to act without the civil magistrates, granted by the orders of 14 March, was confined to the three counties which were in the process of being disarmed, and Camden wanted Abercromby himself to extend this order to the rest of the kingdom.[32]

Camden's attempt to conciliate his supporters with vigorous measures, while endeavouring to keep Abercromby in the command, failed in the first instance because of Abercromby's persistent refusal to implement military policy in the manner desired by the law-and-order lobby and, secondly, by their realisation that there would be no change in the implementation of such policy as long as the command rested where it did. While implementing the disarmament of Kildare, Queen's and King's County, in consequence of the orders of 14 March, Abercromby ensured that the military were kept on a tight rein. He gave the most precise and positive instructions to the officers under his command that perfect order was to be observed at all times by the troops and that no party was to be despatched without an officer. He insisted that they maintain every possible degree of regularity and that no unnecessary act of violence was to be committed.[33] This had the effect of considerably weakening the intended severity of the measure and intensified the opposition to Abercromby's command.[34] In response, Camden's advisors sabotaged his endeavour to reach a compromise solution through negotiations with the commander-in-chief. One of the principal leaders of the cabal, John Foster, speaker of the House of Commons, used the occasion of his speech at the bar of the House of Lords on 24 March, while presenting the money bills, to inflame the situation. Foster's speech was a direct and public riposte to the charges made by Abercromby against the military. He expressed admiration for 'the order and alacrity' which the army had shown on every occasion, and praised 'the courage, the vigour and the discipline of these forces', which 'must render them formidable to the enemy and ensure his defeat, should he be desperate enough to attempt invasion'.[35] Even Cooke believed that it was imprudent and improper to make the allusion to the orders of 26 February when the government had determined to avoid the issue, but he admitted that the sentiments expressed by the speaker accurately reflected the general feeling of parliament.[36]

Foster's speech only served to fix Abercromby in his determination to resign, and revealed to Camden the depth of the hostility to his command. In consequence, he agreed to accept the reality of the resignation on 26 March and to appoint a new commander-in-chief.[37] Once Abercromby's resignation had been

32 Camden to Portland, to Abercromby, 14 Mar., 22 Mar. 1798: P.R.O., HO 100/75/225–8, 303–6.
33 Adj. Genl. Hewett to Dundas, 16 Mar. 1798: P.R.O., HO 100/75/247–50.
34 John Lees to Auckland, 2 Apr. 1798: B.L., Add. MS 34,454, 197–8.
35 Camden to Portland, 26 Mar. 1798: P.R.O., HO 100/75/319–14.
36 Cooke to Auckland, 24 Mar. 1798: : P.R.O.N.I., Sneyd papers, T.3229/2/32.
37 Abercromby to Camden, 24 Mar., 25 Mar. 1798: P.R.O., HO 100/75/307–8, 311–12; Camden to Portland, 26 Mar. 1798: P.R.O., HO 100/75/299–302, 319–24.

finally accepted, the loyalist lobby pressed for an explicit disavowal of his policy. They claimed that the disturbances in the country, including an attack by a considerable body of 'insurgents' on the town of Cahir in Tipperary, had increased because of Abercromby's policies. Their persistence was rewarded by a proclamation issued on 30 March which authorized the military throughout the kingdom to act independently of the civil power, and allowed them to treat any disturbances as actual rebellion. Despite pressure from his supporters, Camden only agreed to this measure after a personal appeal on his behalf had secured Abercromby's consent to enforce the new proclamation.[38] This revived Camden's faint hopes that his advisors might be reconciled to the commander-in-chief if he exerted himself in enforcing this new measure.[39] Besides being unenthusiastic about the prospect of General Lake becoming commander-in-chief, Camden was politically anxious to have Abercromby personally endorse the proclamation, in order to reveal to the world that he had no political objection to the military policy being pursued in the kingdom.[40] Abercromby was far too shrewd, however, to become a political pawn, and in order to dissociate himself from the policy he was about to implement, he publicly announced his resignation before leaving for the south of the kingdom on 2 April, thereby signifying that he would not remain in the command on any account.[41] In addition, he endeavoured to soften the force of the proclamation. In response to pressure from Camden to adopt the strongest possible measures if the disaffected did not surrender their arms, he issued a notice from his headquarters in Kildare on 3 April, to be distributed throughout Kildare, King's and Queen's counties.[42] It stated that in consequence of the proclamation of 30 March and Camden's 'particular orders thereon', the people were given ten days to surrender the arms they had stolen from the well affected. If they complied with the notice, they would receive the protection of the military, if they failed to do so, the troops would be sent to live at free quarters among them. If the disturbances did not stop, the military would then resort to 'other very severe means'.[43]

Abercromby's recourse to free quarters did not indicate a change of policy on his part. On the contrary, by placing emphasis on free quarters conducted under tight officer supervision, he was in effect rejecting both house burning and other illegal measures conducted at the discretion of local officers. The measure was rejected by Irish loyalists, who claimed that it did not allow for sufficient dis-

38 Camden to Portland, 30 Mar., 31 Mar. 1798, Proclamation of 30 Mar. 1798; Castlereagh to Abercromby, 30 Mar. 1798: P.R.O., HO 100/75/343–50, 349–52, 359–62, 363–5; Dunfermline, *Abercromby*, pp 116–8.
39 Camden to Portland, 5 Apr. 1798: P.R.O., HO 100/75/23–4, 76/25–30.
40 Camden to Portland, 5 Apr. 1798: P.R.O., HO 100/75/23–4.
41 Camden to Portland, 2 Apr. 1798: P.R.O., HO 100/76/7–10; Dunfermline, *Abercromby*, pp 116–18, 125–7.
42 Correspondence of Camden and Abercromby, 1 Apr., 3 Apr. 1798: K.A.O. U840 0166/17–18.
43 *D.E.P.*, 7 Apr. 1798.

crimination between the innocent and guilty.[44] While they wanted the army dispersed through the country actively repressing the disaffected, they wanted their own property and that of their tenantry strictly exempted from the consequences of such conduct. In addition, the ten days' notice allowed for the surrender of arms delayed the imposition of any repressive measure against the disaffected.[45] Robert Ross succinctly voiced loyalist grievances in a letter to Downshire on 6 April:

> You see, he carefully avoids the words of our proclamations, calls rebellion insubordination, and gives Lord Moira's innocents ten days to commit fresh outrage, and instead of summary meas[ures] to quell rebellion, he threatens to send troops to live at free quarters among them, where they'll find nothing to eat. From such a commander, good lord deliver us.[46]

Throughout the implementation of free quarters, Abercromby was anxious to maintain discipline and regulation. He informed Lt. General Dundas on 12 April that the measure was to be conducted 'with all possible regularity'. General Wilford was ordered to begin operations in the barony of Kilkea, County Kildare, with 'prudence and discretion'.[47] Free quarters, therefore, far from being an aberration from Abercromby's military policy, was in fact an extension of it. Throughout his command in Ireland, Abercromby maintained a consistent military policy. Even his final reports to Camden on the state of the country in April 1798 were 'intermixed with observations upon the impolicy of suffering the military to act without waiting for the civil magistrate, and his opinion of the advantages of resorting to the civil power'. He still believed adamantly that the troops should be kept in concentrated bodies, and continued to discredit the extent of the danger facing the state, the number of arms which had been stolen, and the outrages committed by the disaffected. Until his departure from Ireland in late April, he remained convinced that Camden had been ill-advised to proclaim the kingdom in rebellion and establish 'something more than martial law'. While it might have been proper to take measures in those districts where the greatest outrages had been committed, and where the magistrates had fled their duty, he was convinced that a writ could be executed at that time in any part of the country.[48] His persistent refusal to acquiesce in loyalist demands to allow the military

---

44 Camden to Portland, 23 Apr. 1798: P.R.O., HO 100/76/122–9.

45 Asgill to Abercromby, 17 Apr. 1798: Marquis of Londonderry (ed.), *Memoirs and correspondence of Viscount Castlereagh* (London, 1848), i, pp 184–5; Agar to Auckland, 5 Apr. 1798: B.L., Add. MS 34,454, 204.

46 Ross to Downshire, 6 Apr. 1798: P.R.O.N.I., Downshire papers D.607/F/131B.

47 Abercromby to Dundas, 12 Apr., 16 Apr. 1798: K.A.O., U840 0166/26, 28.

48 Abercromby to Castleragh, 11 Apr. 1798: K.A.O., U840 0166/24; Camden to Portland, 20 Apr., 23 Apr. 1798: P.R.O., HO 100/76/97–106, 122–9; Camden to Pelham, [Apr. 1798]: B.L., Add. MS 33,105, 353–6; Abercromby to Camden, Camden to Portland, 8 Apr., 17 Apr. 1798: K.A.O., U840 0166/21, 27; Dunfermline, *Abercromby*, pp 127–8.

free reign in the country earned him their enduring resentment, and led to the appointment of General Lake as his successor. Camden did not believe that Lake was equal to the post at such a critical time, but conceded that his appointment would satisfy those calling for a vigorous military policy.[49]

The Abercromby crisis marks the culmination of a struggle over the mode in which the military were to be deployed and employed, which had been building since the outbreak of war with France in 1793. Abercromby's departure from Ireland in April 1798 marks the triumph of the local law-and-order lobby in re-asserting their control over the formation of military policy. His successor, General Lake, was closely allied to the group that had successfully campaigned against his command. With the Irish 'cabinet' unopposed in its dominance of the civil administration in late April and May, and with a commander-in-chief proving himself extremely receptive to their demands for vigorous counter-insurgency measures, the conflict between the civil and military establishments temporarily receded. In consequence, until the arrival of Lord Cornwallis in the dual capacity of commander-in-chief and viceroy in July, the military enjoyed a much greater freedom in repressing disaffection and rebellion in the Irish countryside than they had under Abercromby. The appointment of Cornwallis in this dual capacity had been advocated by Abercromby even before his arrival in Ireland in November 1797. He had pointed to the absolute necessity to appoint a viceroy with direct control of the army. This was essential, he had argued, in order to guard against subjecting military policy to political considerations. The divisions between the Irish cabinet and the military command were however, soon to reappear after it had became apparent to Irish loyalists that Cornwallis' policies were ill-suited to their agenda. But with Cornwallis acting in the dual capacity as head of both the military and civil departments, he had the independence and authority to withstand the influence of the powerful cabinet which had managed to dominate his political and military predecessors.

49 Camden to Pitt, 29 Mar. 1798: K.A.O., U840 o156A/28; Portland to Camden, 31 Mar. 1798: P.R.O., HO 100/75/357–8; Camden to Downshire, [late Apr./early May 1798]: P.R.O.N.I., Foster papers D.607/F/153.

20

Informers, informants and information:
The secret history of the 1790s re-considered

THOMAS BARTLETT

In the 200 years that have elapsed since the 1798 rebellion, the reasons for its failure have been frequently addressed by historians. Some have claimed that the failure of the French to intervene in large numbers in the early summer of 1798 contributed greatly to, may even have been decisive for, the rebels' defeat. No insurrection in the Atlantic world in the previous 200 years had succeeded without substantial foreign assistance: the English rebels of the 1640s had had to bring in the Scots to help them against Charles I, and more recently, the Americans had needed French and Spanish support in their struggle against Britain. A substantial French force in Ireland would have offered discipline, leadership, weaponry, recognition and perhaps an overall strategy; its absence denied the rebels all of these. Again, it could be argued that the rebels' failure to take Dublin at the outset of the rebellion was crucial, for the fall of the capital would have allowed the rebels to seize the organs of government, and perhaps set up some form of representative assembly. With Dublin remaining in 'enemy' hands, the rebellion thereinafter lacked a focus, with the staggered outbreak of the rebellion further playing into the government's hands. 'We may be thankful', wrote one loyalist at the time, 'that the insurgents have acted so little in unison and have presented us with the means of beating them separately.'[1] Lastly, historians have generally agreed that Dublin Castle emerged as victor in the intelligence wars of the 1790s. The Castle's high-placed spies, agents and informers within the ranks of the United Irishmen, we are told, kept it well-briefed on what they were up to and thus enabled it to take decisive counter-measures. James Hope, Antrim weaver, United Irishman and long-time radical, confided sadly to the annalist of the United Irishmen, R.R. Madden in the 1840s that 'we were all beset by spies and informers',[2] and on the basis of his researches, Madden himself concluded that through their 'infamous agency ... every

---

1   Lord Auckland to archbishop of Cashel, 14 June 1798: P.R.O.N.I., T3719/C32/83.
2   R.R. Madden, *The United Irishmen, their lives and times*, 3rd ser. (Dublin, 1846), ii, p. 215.

important proceeding of the United Irishmen was known to the government'. 'Some of [these spies],' continued Madden remorselessly, 'were high in the confidence of the [United Irishmen's] directory; others [were] not sworn in but trusted in its concerns, learned in the law, social in their habits, liberal in their politics, prodigal in their expenses, needy in their circumstances, loose in their public and private principles.'[3] The late nineteenth-century writer, W.J. Fitzpatrick, concurred with this judgement. He devoted years of research to the hidden history of the 1790s and in his *Secret Service under Pitt* (London, 1866) he detailed the extensive nature of the Castle's intelligence sources. Nor did he neglect to point out the lesson: 'secret conspiracies can do no good, ... informers will always be found to betray them'.[4]

This clear unanimity as to the efficacy of the Castle's intelligence network has appeared to render unneccessary a re-appraisal of its spies and agents in the 1790s. Such an undertaking, however, may now be timely, given the range of new material bearing on this problem that has come to light, and given the historians' heightened appreciation of the importance of 'information' to early modern governments.[5]

Even a cursory examination of the war on subversion in the 1790s turns up spectacular intelligence successes by Dublin Castle, and these have certainly contributed to its reputation for omniscience. The swoop on the Leinster Directory of United Irishmen at Oliver Bond's house on 12 March 1798 was made possible by precise information from Thomas Reynolds, a United Irish protegé of Lord Edward FitzGerald.[6] Two months later, Lord Edward himself was arrested on foot of information disclosed by the Dublin barrister, Francis Magan, to his 'controller', Francis Higgins ('the Sham Squire') who in turn passed on his hiding-place to the Castle.[7] Throughout 1797–8, Nicholas Mageean of Saintfield kept Lord Londonderry and his agent, the Revd John Cleland, well informed on the deliberations of the United Irishmen in counties Down and Antrim.[8] And perhaps most valuable of all, in October 1797, Samuel Turner of Newry divulged to Lord Downshire full details of the United Irishmen's 'French connection': in par-

---

3　Madden, *United Irishmen*, 1st ser. (London, 1842), i, pp 147, 407, 149.

4　W.J. Fitzpatrick, *The Sham Squire and the informers of 1798* (6th ed., 1872), preface to the 3rd ed., p. xvi.

5　C.A. Bayly, *Empire and information: Intelligence gathering and social communication in India, 1780–1870* (Cambridge, 1996). This book has greatly influenced my approach to this topic.

6　See 'The voluntary information of Thomas Reynolds of Kilkea Castle in the county of Kildare', 9 May 1798: P.R.O., HO 100/76/178–89.

7　Thomas Bartlett, 'The prime informant: The life and times of the 'Sham Squire', Francis Higgins (1746–1802)', in Cathal Póirtéir (ed.), *The great Irish rebellion of 1798* (Cork, 1998), pp 125–136; see also, Stella Tillyard, *Citizen Lord: Edward FitzGerald, 1763–1798* (London, 1997). Gabrielle Warnock has written a fine novel based on Francis Higgins: *The silk weaver* (London, 1998).

8　A.T.Q. Stewart, *The summer soldiers: The 1798 rebellion in Antrim and Down* (Belfast, 1995); see also Nancy Curtin, *The United Irishmen* (Oxford, 1994).

ticular, he broke the news that Theobald Wolfe Tone was in Paris, and not in the United States.[9] Moreover, these are only the better known of the Castle's informers, informants, spies and spymasters. A trawl through the Rebellion Papers in the National Archives, and other private papers, will uncover many lesser known, though possibly equally important, agents. Captain Andrew MacNevin and Serjeant John Lee of Carrickfergus kept Dublin Castle well apprised of the doings of the alleged disaffected in south Antrim.[10] From all parts of the country, 'J.W.' – Leonard MacNally – a leading barrister for the United Irishmen, wrote regularly to the Castle from the mid-1790s, advising it of the mood of the country and, as defence lawyer for some of the leaders of the United Irishmen, divulging the legal strategies of his clients.[11] For Dublin, Samuel Sproule's numerous telegrammatic letters bore witness to his tireless pursuit of information on the United Irishmen there, and surrounding areas,[12] and so too did those of the 'Sham Squire', who wrote scores of letters to Under-Secretary Edward Cooke on the goings on of the United Irishmen and their Catholic allies in the capital.[13] The Boyles, father and son, Thomas and Edward, likewise scribbled copious notes, conveying information to the Castle about the United Irishmen in Dublin and surrounding areas.[14] There was at least one 'Mata Hari'-type of spy: Belle Martin was in government pay in Belfast (keeping an eye on disaffected militia men), and later in County Kildare (watching the United Irishman, William Aylmer).[15] Lastly, there were the hundreds of informations – sworn statements – collected by magistrates throughout the country which, along with the voluminous correspondence of local worthies and busybodies, enabled Dublin Castle in theory to have precise knowledge of the spread and organization of the United Irish conspiracy.

In addition, Dublin Castle, had valuable sources of information beyond that supplied by informers and informants. The Irish post office was in essence an official, though secret, intelligence-gathering institution whose agents, under the leadership of the secretary to the post office, John Lees, intercepted, read, and copied the correspondence of suspected subversives. These were not new powers of surveillance given to the Irish post office because of the revolutionary crisis of the 1790s: on the contrary, throughout the entire eighteenth century and probably before, lords lieutenants were given warrants on their appointment to open the mail of those whom they had reason to suspect.[16] Few, if any, chief gov-

9 For Turner, see W.J. Fitzpatrick, *Secret Service under Pitt* (London, 1892), passim.
10 For MacNeven and Lee, see their letters scattered throughout N.A.I., RP 620/25 and 620/46.
11 Thomas Bartlett, 'The life and opinions of Leonard MacNally: Playwright, barrister, United Irishman and informer', in Morgan (ed.), *Information, media and power*, pp 113–36.
12 See the Sproule papers in N.A.I., RP 620/51.
13 For Higgins' papers, see N.A.I., RP 620/18/14.
14 For the Boyle papers see N.A.I., RP 620/18/3.
15 For Martin, see her statement, 23 June 1798: N.A.I., RP 620/32/222.
16 See, for example, Lord Harrington to duke of Newcastle, 20 Oct. 1747: P.R.O., SP 63/410; my thanks to James Kelly for this reference.

ernors scrupled to do so. By the 1790s, Dublin Castle had an experienced network in place. Thomas Whinnery, post-master in Belfast, kept Lees informed on the United Irishmen in that town and on their correspondents. He sent on letters from Henry [Joy] McCracken and Thomas Russell, and he identified a Mr Jordan as a United Irish agent in Liverpool.[17] It was a similar story throughout the country: everywhere the village postmasters were fully expected to be vigilant. For examples, James Kellett, in charge of the post office in Dunshaughlin, County Meath, kept Lees informed on rebel activities in that county; George Holdcroft, postmaster in Kells, did likewise for his area.[18] It was intercepted letters in Dublin that brought about the conviction of the French agent, the Revd William Jackson, in 1795,[19] and by opening the correspondence of Archbishop Troy, the Castle hoped to exert subtle pressure on him to enjoin loyalty on his flock.[20] It was surely no accident that the United Irishmen proposed to signal their rebellion by the seizure of the mail coaches departing Dublin on the night of 23 May 1798.

Other officials of the Irish government played their parts in intelligence-gathering. Those who worked in the various stamp offices in the major cities could keep a close eye on the circulation of radical (and loyalist) newspapers, and given the explosion in print in the 1790s (26 provincial newspapers as well as 11 in Dublin) there was much to note, and to notice.[21] Customs officials, too, were ordered to pay attention to unusual cargoes – the Landwaiter at Belfast, Colin MacKay, was particularly active in uncovering attempts to import the ingredients for making gunpowder – and collectors in British ports, notably Portpatrick, Whitehaven, Chester, Cardigan, and Fishguard, were instructed to keep their eyes open for suspicious travellers to and from Ireland.[22] Magistrates were expected to be vigilant where strangers were concerned, and in general they were; on occasion, excess of zeal led to errors: two wretched Turks – Mahomet Di Ego

---

17 Thomas Whinnery to John Lees, 29 Oct. 1796, 13 June 1798, 29 Mar. 1799: N.A.I., RP 620/25/57; 620/38/138a, and P.R.O. HO 100/86/226. The 'Mr Jordan' mentioned by Whinnery was probably Francis Jordan, identified by John Hughes as a Belfast merchant and treasurer for the Antrim United Irishmen: 'Examination of John Hughes', in *Report from the Committee of Secrecy of the House of Lords* (Dublin, 1799), p. 25.

18 James Kellett to [John Lees?], 28 Aug., 13 Sept. 1798: N.A.I., RP 620/39/224; 620/40/47. For Holdcroft, see the sample of letters among the Camden Papers in K.A.O., U840 148.

19 Lord Hobart to John King, 25 Apr. 1795: N.A.I., OP 30/5/4.

20 One of Troy's letters from the papal nuncio, Charles Erskine, was opened in the post office in Dublin and it was revealed that Erskine had been urging Troy to use his position to influence the Irish Catholic clergy in support of loyalty. Troy, in Camden's opinion 'a very timid and time-serving man', had, again in the Castle's view, neglected to take this opportunity and it was decided to speak to Erskine again to put further pressure on Troy to speak out: Camden to Portland, recvd. 20 Apr. 1797; Wickham to Cooke, 21 Apr. 1797: P.R.O., HO 100/76/91–4, 114–15.

21 Curtin, *United Irishmen*, p.176.

22 Colin Mackay to — , Oct. 1796: N.A.I., RP 620/26/1; letters from the various ports, Apr.-June 1798: P.R.O. HO 100/66/82, 99, 104, 105; Robert Carmichael to John Lees, 14 Sept. 1798: P.R.O. HO 40/51.

and his wife Sarah – found themselves clapped in Nenagh gaol on suspicion of being French spies;[23] and two Persians – the Effendi brothers – were locked up in Cork gaol pending further enquiries.[24]

Armies have always and everywhere been information-gathering organizations, and army officers in Ireland in the 1790s routinely involved themselves in such work.[25] The continuous production of military maps, defence plans, and coastal charts throughout the eighteenth century,[26] and the demand by officers 'in the field', under the terms of the Insurrection Act (1796), that a list of the inhabitants be posted on each house, all testify to the army's resolve, if not to its success, to 'know the country'.[27] Sometimes, army officers ran their own agents: Generals Dalyrmple and Coote, serving in Munster and Connacht respectively, had their own network of informers.[28] Moreover, the military authorities themselves managed in the summer of 1797 to infiltrate and then destroy the United Irish circles in various regiments. On occasion, as in Counties Antrim and Down, army officers co-operated successfully with local magnates. In these counties, Colonel Lucius Barber, in charge of intelligence for the northern military commander, General Nugent, had a good working relationship with John Pollock, crown solicitor and confidential advisor to Lord Downshire, and this was valuable, for both Pollock and Downshire, in their turn, were privy to a variety of intelligence sources. It was, for example, Lord Downshire to whom, in October 1797, the renegade United Irishman, Samuel Turner first unbur-dened himself about that organization's links with revolutionary France; and 'J.W.' was a frequent correspondent of Downshire's.[29]

23 Information of John Proscer, keeper of the Bridewell, Nenagh, County Tipperary, 9 Oct. 1796: N.A.I., RP 620/25/158. Di Ego and his wife were reduced to begging for food through the bars of the prison.

24 'Supplication of Keram and Abdula Effendi', 9 Oct. 1796: N.A.I., RP 620/25/149. Matters scarcely improved: Aron Philip was taken up as a spy in Galway in 1803. He had used certain expressions to disguise the fact that he was a Danish dentist and a Jew: N.A.I., Prisoners' Petitions, no. 789.

25 See Bayly, *Empire and information*, pp 155–6, where he describes the Indian army as 'a large accumulation of institutional knowledge'. See also N.J. Austin and N.B. Ranker, *Exploratio: Military and political intelligence in the Roman world* (London, 1995). Christopher Andrew has traced the origins of the modern secret service in Britain not to the Foreign Office but rather to the Victorian War Office, and before that to the short-lived Depot of Military Knowledge set up in 1803: C.M. Andrew, *Secret Service: The making of the British intelligence community* (London, 1986), p. 29.

26 For examples of these, see P.M. Kerrigan, *Castles and fortifications in Ireland, 1485–1945* (Cork, 1995), pp 150–247.

27 See 'Notice from General Lake', Clonmel, 13 Sept. 1799: P.R.O., HO 100/89/213.

28 Thomas Pelham to Lt. General Dalymple, 2 June 1797, in Sir John Gilbert (ed.), *Documents relating to Ireland, 1793–1804* (Dublin, 1893), pp 118–19.

29 See the letters from Leonard MacNally (J.W.) in P.R.O.N.I., Downshire papers, D607/C/ and D607/G; also in P.R.O., Pitt papers, 30/8/327.

In addition, Dublin Castle, in its search for information, could profit from the United Irishmen's enthusiasm for propagating their cause. In essence, the United Irishmen defined themselves by their publications, but their determination to extend and democratise print culture inevitably meant that through their newspapers, the *Northern Star*, the *Press*, even the *Union Star*, and through their printed addresses and pamphlets, much useful information about their plans, objectives and divisions was revealed to Dublin Castle.[30] Indeed, the very bookshops themselves in which these publications were sold offered opportunities for surveillance of the United Irishmen. The Sheares brothers, John and Henry, were undone when, considering him to be a fellow revolutionary, they befriended Captain John Warmsford Armstrong in Byrne's 'radical' bookshop. They took him into their confidence, he promptly betrayed them, and they paid with their lives.[31] Booksellers themselves were an additional source of danger. John Hughes, the prominent Belfast United Irishman and bookseller, turned government informer in late 1797, testified before the Secret Committee of the House of Lords, and named many of his former associates.[32] Much less spectacular, though still worthy of notice, is the case of Mary Ann Martin. She petitioned government for financial reward in 1799, pointing out that during the previous two years, she had been the proprietor of a small bookshop in Britain Street, Dublin, where she had 'sold a paper called the *Press* and some other seditious papers' as well. In support of her memorial, she alleged that from 1797 to 1798 she had given 'private information to government' on her customers: this claim was confirmed with the marginal comment, 'she did so'.[33]

Furthermore, it may be suggested that the very openness of their society made the United Irishmen particularly vulnerable to infiltration and discovery. Almost from the Society's first meeting in Dublin in late 1791, until its suppression in May 1794, the Castle was in receipt of detailed information on the persons admitted to membership, and on its proceedings, particularly its relations with sister clubs in Britain.[34] Moreover, in the years after 1794, when the Society had been re-constituted as a secret oath-bound organization dedicated to achieving an Irish republic with French assistance, its very reliance on oaths – one for secrecy, one for admission – was in itself a potentially fatal flaw. As R.R. Madden wrote:

30 J.S. Donnelly, 'Propagating the cause of the United Irishmen', in *Studies*, lxix (spring, 1980), 5–23; Curtin, *United Irishmen*, chap. 7.
31 R.B. McDowell, *Ireland in the age of imperialism and revolution, 1760–1801* (Oxford, 1979), pp 601–2.
32 Hughes's examination, *Report of Secret Committee of House of Lords*, pp 23–32.
33 Petition of Mary Ann Martin, n.d. [*c.*1799]: N.A.I., OP, 89/39.
34 Thomas Collins supplied reports of United Irish meetings in Dublin during the 'open' or constitutional period of the society, 1791–94: R.B. McDowell (ed.), *Proceedings of the Dublin Society of United Irishmen* (new ed., Dublin, 1998).

It seems to be one of the necessary results of efforts to establish secret societies that the more the secrecy of their proceedings is sought to be secured by tests and oaths, the more danger is incurred of treachery and the more difficult it is to guard against traitors: the very anxiety for concealment becomes the immediate occasion of detection.[35]

In short, a mass-based secret society – such as that of the United Irishmen – was effectively a contradiction in terms.[36]

Lastly, for an avowedly secret society – at least from 1795 on – the United Irishmen showed little aptitude for learning the secrets of the 'enemy', and no flair for counter-intelligence. From an early date, they were well aware that their organization had been infiltrated, that 'there were members ... in the habit of betraying the secrets of the society to government', and worse, 'that Mr Pitt's infamous system of having spies in all companies and in all societies, had made its way into this country', but they seemed relatively powerless to do anything about it.[37] Scarcely any of the major informers was unmasked in his lifetime, fewer still met untimely ends as a result of their treachery.[38] Arthur O'Connor did assert in his examination before the Secret Committee of the House of Commons that the executive directory of the United Irishmen had 'minute information of every act of the Irish government', but this claim appears to have been mere bravado.[39] Admittedly, the leisurely hunt for Lord Edward FitzGerald was hampered by leaks of information from workmen employed in Dublin Castle; and the United Irishmen undoubtedly did have friends in high places, but it is not clear what use, if any, they made of them.[40] We may suspect that the United Irishmen regarded spying as a tool of a corrupt government rather than as one that they might usefully adopt. If so, such principled fastidiousness was to cost them dear.

35 Madden, *United Irishmen*, 1st ser. (London, 1843), ii, p. 407.
36 Nancy Curtin, 'The transformation of the Society of United Irishmen into a mass-based revolutionary organization, 1794–6', in *I.H.S.*, xxix (1984–5), 463–92.
37 Collins's reports, 15 Feb., 10 May 1794 in McDowell, *Dublin Society of United Irishmen*, pp 110, 126.
38 E.J. Newell was probably, and Michael Phillips, a priest, was definitely murdered by the United Irishmen in Belfast. By contrast, Armstrong, who betrayed, and testified against, the Sheares brothers, enjoyed his pension on his estate in King's County until his death in 1858. Thomas Reynolds who was known to have betrayed the meeting at Bond's house lived openly in Paris for many years. Samuel Turner who revealed the details of the 'French connection' seems to have been killed in 1810 in a duel on the Isle of Man. Francis Higgins, Leonard McNally and Francis Magan were in receipt of pensions for the remainder of their lives, their treachery only being uncovered after their death. For much colourful detail see Fitzpatrick, *Secret Service*, passim.
39 Madden, *United Irishmen*, 1st ser., i, p. 149.
40 Tuite, a carpenter working in the Castle, allegedly alerted Lord Edward's friends of an impending raid: Fitzpatrick, *Secret Service*, p. 121. William St John, who at one time was charged with opening suspicious letters in the Irish post office, was subsequently revealed to be a United Irishman (see above, p. 389).

Given the apparent inability of the United Irishmen to root out informers from its ranks and given the huge amount of information pouring into Dublin Castle throughout the 1790s, it is scarcely surprising that earlier historians of the doomed conspiracy have placed great weight on the effectiveness and 'reach' of the Castle's intelligence network as a prime cause of the United Irish failure. And yet, is this emphasis justified? Surely questions concerning the use and deployment of information need to be addressed before a conclusive answer can be given? In intelligence work, the collection of information, while obviously important, is by no means the whole of the matter. Information must be processed in order to become intelligence. This means that when a security problem is identified, information will first be gathered from all sides. Once this information is processed (collated, evaluated and interpreted) it becomes 'intelligence' which can then be disseminated to those who need to know or who are required to act. In turn, this will lead to the formulation of new questions which in their turn will call for the collection of fresh information, and so on. Dublin Castle undoubtedly had impressive information-gathering capabilities in the 1790s, but did it have the necessary system in place for processing that information, supplied by its informers and informants, into *intelligence*? In this latter respect, the suggestion may be made that the Castle's reputation for omniscience has been much exaggerated.

The judgement of nineteenth-century historians such as R.R. Madden and W.J. Fitzpatrick on the effectiveness of Castle intelligence in the 1790s cannot be accepted without question. Madden had his own motive for compiling his works on the United Irishmen. He was certainly moved by a hatred of oppression – he was an anti-slavery activist all his life – and he pointedly remarked on the inconsistency of those who were moved by the sufferings of the lashed and shackled slave in the West Indies, but yet could turn a blind eye to the excesses of the 1790s in Ireland. However, in his writings, his primary object was to 'convince the people of the folly of entering into secret associations with the idea of keeping plans against oppression unknown through the instrumentality of oaths and tests'. The ubiquity – and depravity – of the informer was a constant theme with him:

> They fear death and they have good reason to be afraid of it; they love their ease and they take it after their own fashion; they pamper their appetites, they live grossly; they are given to gluttony or debauchery or avarice; they have sacrificed their sworn friends, their former principles, their future hopes for gold.[41]

W.J. Fitzpatrick, too, had his own agenda. He was a pious Catholic who wrote and revised most of his work on the secret history of the 1790s at the time of the

41 Madden, *United Irishmen*, 1st ser., ii, p. 436.

Fenian conspiracy, a movement which the Catholic Church bitterly denounced. Yet, for those who admired the 'men of '98', the Church's condemnation of the Fenians posed something of a dilemma. Might it not be legitimately claimed that the Fenians were merely following in the footsteps of the United Irishmen? One answer to this difficulty was to downplay, if not denigrate, the role of lay leaders in the 1798 rebellion and to highlight the role of the priests such as the Fathers Murphy. Viewed in this light, it had been the priests who had come to the rescue of their flock and taken on a leadership role in 1798; it had been the lay leaders who had sworn them in, but who had then abandoned them when the trial came, and who had ultimately betrayed them. For Fitzpatrick, this near certainty of betrayal was 'the true moral which I have sought to inculcate':

> The organisers of illegal societies will see that in spite of the apparent secrecy and ingenuity of their system, informers sit with them at the same council board and dinner table ready at any moment to sell their blood and that the wider the ramifications of conspiracy the greater becomes the certainty of detection.[42]

This notion was one which the Catholic Church found serviceable in its campaign to keep its members out of conspiracies. For its part, the British government, too, found the alleged ubiquity of Irish informers useful, for the threat of discovery might possibly help deter recruits from joining secret societies. In any case, the supposed 'specialty of the Celtic character', the alleged Irish propensity to betray one another, fitted well into that clutch of negative stereotypes (along with fecklessness, improvidence, laziness, murderousness and inconstancy) that coloured British attitudes towards the Irish in the late nineteenth century.[43] J.A. Froude, predictably, made much of this trait, while Fitzpatrick had to defend himself against the charge 'that I have sought to dishonour Ireland by showing it as always abounding in spies, betrayers etc.'[44] In this last respect, it might be argued that the secret societies themselves found reassuring the rumoured prevalence within their ranks of those in government pay, for the presence of these informers offered valuable confirmation of their own importance. In addition, the hunt for these renegades gave members something to do while they awaited the great day of insurrection. On all sides, then, there was general agreement on the notion of 'Informers Everywhere' – as Fitzpatrick alarmingly titled his final appendix;[45] but once again, the effectiveness, if not the ubiquity, of such turncoats has been rather assumed than demonstrated.

---

42 Fitzpatrick, *Secret Service*, pp v-vi.
43 Fitzpatrick, *Sham Squire*, p. 375.
44 J.A. Froude, *The English in Ireland in the eighteenth century* (3 vols, London, 1881), iii, p. 404; Fitzpatrick, *Sham Squire*, p. xvii.
45 Ibid., pp 375-7. Martha McTier caught well the fevered atmosphere of Belfast during the period of E.J. Newell's informing: 'At present all here is detestable plot and low cunning – suspicion

Moreover, we should note that while Dublin Castle undoubtedly had its intelligence successes in the 1790s, it certainly had its failures too. For most of the decade, it had little concrete information on the Defender phenomenon; the well-known government digest of 1795 on that secret society testifies to its ignorance about the Defenders' activities.[46] Nor did matters improve: the Castle's attempt to infiltrate a priest, Michael Phillips, into their ranks came to an abrupt end when he was found murdered in Belfast in early 1796.[47] Again, neither Theobald Wolfe Tone's true whereabouts nor his mission to France was discovered by Dublin Castle until late 1797, eighteen months after his arrival in Paris – and nearly two years after his friends in Belfast (who kept the secret) were apprised of it. So far as Dublin Castle officials were concerned, it had no reason to disbelieve the assurance of its apparently well-placed informer, 'John Smith' (i.e. William Bird): 'Tone keeps quite quiet [in the United States]. Study is his object and he is preparing a work for the press.'[48] As a result of this intelligence failure Dublin Castle (and the Admiralty) were caught totally off-guard in late 1796 when a French invasion fleet of approximately 14,000 men and some 50 ships was assembled at Brest in western France. In addition, as is well known, the French fleet, with Tone on board, managed to sail out of Brest, evade the blockading ships, make its way to Bantry Bay, and then, unable to effect a landing, limp back to its home port largely unchallenged.[49] In the gravest threat faced by the British state between the Armada of 1588 and the threatened German invasion of 1940, the much vaunted British (and Irish) intelligence networks were found wholly wanting. Lastly, Dublin Castle despite its apparently impressive store of knowledge on subversives in Ireland, was very poorly informed on United Irish organization in County Wexford in 1798, or else it had been easily misled about the true situation there. In either case, the rising in that county in late May 1798 came as a huge shock to the Castle, all the more unwelcome because it served to re-ignite a rebellion which had shown sure signs of petering out elsewhere in Leinster.

and ineffectual secrecy where both sides gain much true information, yet both are betrayed – not a word or look on any subject above the weather or the card table that is not noticed, and I believe there are few in this town who have not some sort of spy on them': McTier to Drennan, May 1797, cited in Mary McNeill, *Life and times of Mary Ann McCracken, 1770–1866* (Belfast, 1960), p. 170.

46 Bartlett, 'Select Documents, XXXVIII: Defenders and Defenderism in 1795', in *I.H.S.*, xxiv (1984–5), 373–94.

47 'We have at present a real clue to Defenderism if we can follow it home', wrote Cooke to Pelham, 4 Dec. 1795: P.R.O.N.I., Pelham transcripts, T755, with reference to Fr Phillips. In Jan. 1796, the priest's body was fished out of the River Lagan: Cooke to Nugent, n.d. [Jan. 1796] (National Army Museum, Nugent papers, 6807/174/149.

48 Bird to [Edward Cooke?], 26 July 1796: P.R.O., HO 100/62/149. It was Samuel Turner who in Oct. 1797 broke the news that Tone was in Paris.

49 See J.A. Murphy (ed.), *'The French are in the bay': The French expedition to Bantry Bay in 1796* (Cork, 1996).

The reality was that for most of the 1790s the Irish government faced what amounted to an 'intelligence famine' where the United Irishmen and Defenders were concerned, for its information-gathering arrangements throughout the decade were wholly inadequate. For example, two of the Castle's prime inform- ers in the Belfast area, William Bird himself, and Edward Newell, a miniature portrait painter, eventually broke cover, and denounced their controller, causing huge embarrassment to Dublin Castle. In the process, they handed the United Irishmen a substantial propaganda victory. The activities of these men are worth scrutinising for the light they shed on the Castle's management of informers and agents, and its deployment of the information supplied by them.

Bird was a bankrupt London merchant who fetched up in Belfast in late 1795 in search of a fresh start. Initially befriended by the radicals in that town, he turned violently against them when they denied him financial assistance. Rumours then began to circulate that he was a government informer: incensed by his treatment, Bird made contact with the collector of Belfast, Charles Skeffington and embarked on his career as a spy. His reports to the Castle throughout 1796 were on occasion perceptive: he claimed, for example, that the best way to cripple the United Irishmen would be to publish their secrets, 'for this would most effectually destroy the only bond that holds them together, namely mutual confidence',[50] a suggestion that Cornwallis would later implement in his bargain with the state prisoners in July 1798.[51] Again, he shrewdly urged the authorities to strike before the United Irishmen had matured their plans: 'It would be good policy to drive them to a pre- mature revolt, for then, unprepared – divided – and betrayed – they would be easi- ly subdued.'[52] Lastly, his dismissive remarks about the 'men of B[elfast] [who] are wealthy, wiley [sic] and avaricious' were also, as time revealed, quite well-founded:

> The King's party in B[elfast] is I am certain 5 times stronger than the
> public in general imagines. It is evident that the democrats are false to
> each other and afraid to act. They are too tenacious of life and property to
> move themselves whatever they may effect by means of others, and how-
> ever they may bravado, they will never dare to act decisively till they are
> aided by the French.

This last statement, however, was rather spoiled by Bird's rider, 'and of that there is at present no talk', a remark that surely indicates Bird's distance from the centre of United Irish affairs, for the leading Belfast United Irishmen were by then well aware of Tone's mission to France, and of the prospect of a French landing.[53]

50 Bird to Skeffington, 21 Apr. 1796: N.A.I., Fraser MSS 2/17c.
51 For Cornwallis' negotiations with the State Prisoners, see McDowell, *Ireland in the age of imperi- alism and revolution*, pp 655–6 and below chap. 24.
52 Bird to [Cooke?], n.d. [c. 30 Aug. 1797]: N.A.I., Fraser MSS, 2/37.
53 Bird's information, 15 July 1796: P.R.O., HO 100/62/137–8.

In the end, for all their apparent 'insight', Bird's reports consisted of little more than cheap tittle-tattle that reveal him to have been an opinionated know-all with an ear for scurrilous gossip. His 'information' cannot have held much more than a certain entertainment value for Dublin Castle. His assessment of the United Irishmen in Belfast then in custody, and their relationships with their wives and lovers, was almost entirely worthless. He strongly advised that Daniel Shanaghan be confronted with his pregnant wife – 'a perfect termagant, ignorant, vain and avaricious' – before whom 'he cowers as a chicken beneath a kite' and he forecast that she would get him to come forward with information. By contrast, he urged that under no circumstances should Bartley's wife (according to Bird, currently the lover of both Young, the tavern-keeper, and James McCracken) be allowed to visit her husband because she had 'a most sovereign contempt' for him and 'she would to a certainty tell him that a glorious death is preferable to an ignominious life, in order to be rid of him'. Bird had an abiding interest in the trivial and the prurient: he insisted, for example, on recounting a drinking toast (despite it being 'too indecent to be repeated') proposed by his fellow subversives: 'May the hair of the Queen's c—t be manufactured into ropes to hang the King and all the royal family'. In any case, on its own, Bird's own cheerfully noted fondness for drink must surely have ruled him out as a really effective agent:

> There is one thing wherein they [the United Irishmen] puzzle me which is, they seldom say much until they are nearly drunk and by the time I get them in that plight, I am little better myself and tho' they were to open their hearts ever so liberally I stand a fair chance of forgetting it by morning.[54]

A flat refusal to testify in open court further diminished Bird's worth. Summoned as a witness before the House of Commons Secret Committee in 1797, he feared for his life, hastily made contact again with the United Irishmen, and then prudently wrote a series of letters in the *Press* denouncing 'the great phalanx of monsters' who supplied information to the government.[55] As MacNally put it, Bird had let 'the cat out of the bag' by exposing Dublin Castle's intelligence operations to public gaze.[56] Strapped for cash, he remained an irritant to Dublin Castle for some time: on one occasion, he threatened Lord Camden that he would place in the hands of the leading Castle critic, Lord Moira, 'such documents as shall strike your boldest orators dumb! and raise through the three kingdoms a tornado of execration', on another, he declared his intention to publish a tell-all 'Book of

54 Bird's information, *c*.25 July: P.R.O., HO 100/62/143–4.
55 McDowell, *Ireland in the age of imperialism and revolution, 1760–1801*, pp 531–2.
56 Quoted in Fitzpatrick, *Secret Service*, p. 178.

his life' for which he expected to make £1,000. The United Irishmen, John Stoyte, was rightly scathing: 'I told him not to build too much on it as my opinion was he would not make three pence by it.' In the event, the work does not appear to have been published, if it was ever written.[57]

Like Bird, Edward John Newell – described by Madden as 'the worst, the most thoroughly debased, the vilest of the vile' – was an informer in Belfast who steadfastly refused to give evidence in court.[58] Initially an ardent United Irishman – by his own account, 'I gloried in, I revered the cause of liberty' – he parted company with his associates when he fell under suspicion of being less than whole-hearted, and he promptly decamped to Dublin where he secured an interview with no less a personage than Edward Cooke, under-secretary in Dublin Castle.[59] After being de-briefed by Cooke over several sessions, he returned to the north on General Carhampton's staff and, throughout 1797, accompanied by an armed guard, and with his face blackened, or covered with a handkerchief, Newell conducted numerous raids on United Irish meetings in the Belfast area.[60] He also alerted the authorities to the disaffection among the Monaghan Militia stationed at Blaris camp, near Lisburn.[61] Later, as with Bird, he was called as a witness before the House of Commons Secret Committee: but then, again like Bird, he renounced his actions and fled north to his former associates in the United Irishmen. His final letter to Camden was eloquent in its bitterness. 'In return for the fifty guineas I received on Saturday,' he wrote, 'I shall give you the truest information I have ever done, and one which it would be highly necessary to attend to – my Lord, the people execrate you!'[62] In Belfast, Newell, unlike Bird, did in fact write a book about his career as informer in which he accused Cooke, among other charges, of forcing him 'to enter in my lists [of suspects], men with whose very names I was unacquainted'. With the publication of this book, Newell had clearly outlived his usefulness to both sides: he disappeared in late 1797 and was never seen again. He was very possibly murdered by the United Irishmen.[63] All in all, neither the services of Bird nor those of Newell should be rated major intelligence coups for Dublin Castle.

57 Bird to Lord Camden, n.d. [early 1798]: K.A.O., U840/0197; Cooke to Wickham, 11 Mar. 1799: P.R.O., HO 100/86/134; J. Stoyte to [—] , 3 July [1799]: N.A.I., RP 620/51/196.
58 Extracts from Newell's *Narrative* were re-printed by Madden, *United Irishmen* (2nd ed., Dublin, 1857), i, pp 538–80.
59 Newell's *Narrative*, in Madden, *United Irishmen*, pp 540–1.
60 Newell's disguise was hardly convincing: Mary Ann McCracken told her brother Harry that when her house was raided by soldiers led by a man 'dressed as a cavalry officer with a handkerchief tied across his mouth … everyone in the family instantly recognised [him] to be Newell': McNeill, *McCracken, 1770–1866*, p. 118.
61 Newell's statement, enclosed with Camden to Portland, 15 Apr. 1797: P.R.O., HO 100/69/275–9.
62 Newell to Camden, 21 Feb. 1798: K.A.O., U840/0197/3.
63 In her novel, *The green cockade* (Dublin, n.d. [1920?]), pp 375–6, Mrs M.T. Pender, probably drawing on local tradition, has Newell drowned at the Gobbins, near Whitehead, County Antrim.

In general, for most of the 1790s, Dublin Castle was much too reliant on local initiative for gathering information on subversives in the various counties: where this was not forthcoming, the Castle was at a loss to know how to proceed. This passivity may account for the almost total lack of information on the United Irishmen in County Wexford, or on Defenderism everywhere: in neither case had Dublin Castle the necessary agents in place, nor did it appear to have the expertise to recruit these. The Castle was never pro-active enough in placing its own men in areas where the resident gentry or magistrates were signally failing to transmit relevant information. Hence, the Castle's dependency on unreliable 'walk-ins', like Bird and Newell, or on garrulous cranks such as George Holdcroft in Kells, or Captain Andrew McNevin in Carrickfergus, both of whose letters figure prominently among the Rebellion Papers. Hence also its vulnerability to approaches from those for whom dabbling in espionage offered a splash of colour to an otherwise monochrome existence. 'If you think this worthy of notice', wrote one informant who had just denounced a neighbour, 'you will please to mention something of it in the *Freeman's Journal*';[64] another declared that he would have signed his letter 'but for the uncertainty of the post' and he proposed by way of acknowledgment: 'Put into the *Evening Post* that 'Edward's has received a letter';[65] a third, 'A.B', asked for an advertisement to be placed in the *Dublin Journal* giving him further instructions how to proceed.[66] All were well aware of the risks run in embarking as an informer – or in gaining the notoriety of being one. 'I should let you know who I am', wrote 'Justice' to Pelham, 'but for fear of being assassinated in the dark'; while Captain John Lyster who had testified against Archibald Hamilton Rowan, found himself as a result – so he claimed – drummed out of his regiment. 'I am looked upon here and called a government spy in every coffee house I go to. It is true I always take up the cause of government, and always shall,' he stoutly maintained, 'but I have never been a spy or an informer although I have got the name of both.'[67] Yet, for all the risks, there was the satisfaction of a job well done, and the clear prospect of reward. The Parker brothers from Limerick claimed that by their 'vigilance ... not noisy and ostentatious but as much otherwise as it could be', they had prevented Limerick falling into the hands of the rebels in December 1797. They therefore sought positions in government, anything in 'the military, ordnance [or] commissariat departments as well as in the civil' would be acceptable.[68] Similarly, the Revd Patrick Morgan from Killybegs, County Donegal, sought a Commission of the Peace in County Down for himself (and a lieutenancy in the Marines for his son) for his exertions in the north-west in 1797: 'By the various ramifications of

64 'A friend to Government' to [Cooke?], 1 June 1798: N.A.I., RP 620/38/16.
65 Anon., Galway to [Cooke?], 25 Jan. 1799: N.A.I., RP 620/46/18.
66 A.B. to Thomas Pelham, 29 Sept. 1796: N.A.I., RP 620/25/144.
67 Lyster to [Cooke?], 1 June 1798: N.A.I., RP 620/38/16.
68 Statement of Lewis Parker and brother, 14 Oct. 1798: N.A.I., OP 54/19.

private intelligence in my possession', he wrote, 'I have been the means of suppressing speedily the rebellion in this district in 1797.'[69] Claims such as these – and they were, as Cooke claimed, 'voluminous' – no doubt raised a wry smile in Dublin Castle, but unwittingly, they point towards a central truth about official information-gathering in the 1790s. Even if the information coming in had been 'solid gold', it seems certain that, in the absence of an effective information-processing structure, the Castle might not have been able to recognise its quality or make the best use of it. Edward Cooke, at the centre of the Castle's intelligence-gathering was, in effect, a one-man agency, and espionage was only one of his many responsibilities. Throughout 1797 and 1798 he was in receipt of anything from 150 to 200 letters a month and, while he performed heroically at his task, it was surely impossible for him to obtain a clear picture of what the United Irishmen were about. During these years, Dublin Castle was suffering from an information overload which, in the absence of a proper processing structure, produced an intelligence 'famine'. In short, up until early 1798, the Castle could neither know nor understand what intelligence it had. It is easy for historians to direct a snigger of derision at the exaggerated reports flooding into Dublin Castle from nervous magistrates concerning phantom armies, assassination committees planning mass poisonings, and the ubiquitous Thomas Paine, but the whistle of appreciation for the truly striking piece of information may be equally inappropriate. Consider this letter: on 7 June 1795, Rowland J. O'Connor at the stamp office in Belfast, wrote to William Sackville Hamilton, Cooke's predecessor as under-secretary in Dublin Castle:

> I think it my duty as well as inclination to inform your government that there is now here a Counsellor Tone pretending to go to America but that his real design is to go to France and that one Russell who formerly had been in the army and who is one of the most violent democrats on the face of the earth, is going with him. Tone has been paid the greatest compliments here and a subscription of £1,500 raised for him; Sam[uel] Neilson, Rob[ert] and Will[iam] Simms, Coun[sellor William] Sampson, Dr Randal MacDonnell, John and William McCrackens [sic] and many others have private meetings with him and have often gone with him to visit diff[eren]t parts of the coast and taking plans of it; if his and Russell's papers were examined, I would forfeit my existence if some useful discoveries were not made. There are now in this town sixteen diff[eren]t societies of United Irish and the generality of the people here wish and are very ripe for a revolution. I believe Tone will sail in 3 or 4 days. I have the honour to be etc.[70]

69 Revd Patrick Morgan to Alex. Marsden, 2 Aug. 1803: N.A.I., OP 153/57.
70 O'Connor to Sackville Hamilton, 7 June 1795: K.A.O., U840/0147/4/1.

In just under 200 words, O'Connor had described the future strategy of the United Irishmen, and he had correctly identified the major figures within that organization in Belfast, many of whom would be active in 1798. However, no notice whatsoever appears to have been taken of this letter either at the time or subsequently. O'Connor's comment that Tone's ultimate destination was France was completely ignored; and even his remark that Tone and his companions were taking plans of the coast, presumably with a view to a future French landing, went unflagged. The conclusion seems inescapable: for most of the 1790s, Dublin Castle had no clear way of distinguishing quality information from the hysterical drivel sent in by panic-stricken magistrates or by the many adventurers within the United Irishmen (or on the fringes of that organization).

That said, there is some persuasive evidence that Cooke did in fact begin to build some sort of intelligence-processing structure from mid-1797 on. He had taken over from the lethargic Sackville Hamilton as under-secretary for Civil Affairs in June 1796,[71] but it took the French invasion scare at the end of that year to alert him to the gravity of the threat posed by the United Irishmen in France, Britain and Ireland. In early 1797, he began systematically to draw up lists of alleged subversives, whose names were then cross-referenced in a very large 'Book of Suspects'.[72] Steps were taken to co-ordinate military and civilian intelligence, with Cooke, Castlereagh, Cleland, Pollock and Downshire liaising with Generals Nugent and Lake in targeting leading United Irishmen particularly in Antrim and Down. Furthermore, in Dublin, Major Charles Henry Sirr was given a free hand (and, in effect, unlimited cash) to buy information.[73] All of this was certainly an advance on former practice. However, the limits of these innovations should also be recognised: there was still no sign of a proper card-indexing system; astonishingly, it was not until July 1798 that there was talk of a regular exchange of information between London and Dublin magistrates;[74] and, as noted above, during 1797 there occurred the embarrassing débâcles with Newell and Bird. Nonetheless, from mid-1797 on, there was a purposefulness about the Castle's intelligence-gathering that is striking. In May 1797, Cooke revealed, possibly on information supplied by Francis Higgins, that Edward Lewins who 'speaks French like a native' was on his way to Paris to act as United Irish agent there.[75] The revelations of the Hamburg-based United Irishman, Samuel Turner (a.k.a. Richardson or 'Lord Downshire's friend') were carefully

71 J.C. Sainty, 'The secretariat of the chief governors of Ireland, 1690–1800', in *Proc. R.I.A.*, C, lxxvii (1977), 1–33.
72 'Book of Suspects': N.A.I., RP 620/1.
73 Sirr is worth a study in his own right. See TCD MSS 868–9 for the Sirr papers.
74 Castlereagh to Wickham, 17 July 1798: P.R.O., HO 100/81/233.
75 Cooke to Greville, 20 May 1797: P.R.O., HO 100/71/342. See Higgins' letter to Cooke mentioning Lewins: [Francis Higgins], Stephen's Green, Dublin, to 'Dear Sir' [Edward Cooke], 27 June 1797: N.A.I., RP 620/18/14.

digested and used as the basis for further enquiries into the organization's links with France. In addition, the detailed information supplied by two other key informers, Thomas Reynolds of Kildare, and Francis Magan of Dublin, transformed the Castle's understanding of the ramifications of the conspiracy in Ireland, and enabled it to act decisively in the spring of 1798. The Leinster Directory was arrested in a swoop on Oliver Bond's house; Lord Edward FitzGerald himself was soon taken; and the Sheares' brothers, aptly described by R.B. McDowell as 'very energetic, courageous, and incompetent conspirators' were betrayed by Armstrong.[76] There was undoubtedly much room for improvement: the Castle still did not possess anything like a modern secret service and this was dramatically revealed when Cooke himself resigned unexpectedly in 1801. His intelligence network promptly fell apart because its efficiency had to a large extent depended on his controlling presence. In Cooke's absence, Dublin Castle was to be caught out badly at the time of Robert Emmet's attempted insurrection in July 1803.[77] In 1798, however, Dublin Castle had won the intelligence war, and that was what counted: but it had been a close-run thing.

---

76 McDowell, *Ireland in the age of imperialism and revolution*, p. 602.
77 Charles Abbot, Castlereagh's successor as chief secretary, was furious at Cooke's resignation, probably because he well recognized what a loss he would be to the Castle's intelligence network: Abbot to Hardwicke, 1 July 1801: B.L., Add. MS 35,711/67. For Abbot's not very successful attempt to make his office 'the depot of all information respecting the affairs of Ireland', see Abbot to Hardwicke, 20 June 1801: B.L., Add. MS 35,711, 49.

21

The Kilmainham treaty of 1798

JAMES QUINN

It was one of the ironies of the 1798 rebellion that many of those who had done so much to bring it about played so little active part in it. Most of the United Irish leadership had already been arrested prior to its outbreak, some as early as the autumn of 1796, others in the raid on Oliver Bond's house on 12 March 1798, and a substantial part of the remainder was rounded up in the early days of the insurrection. After the initial success of the Wexford rebels, it must have been with some trepidation that the imprisoned leaders heard news of the rebel defeats in June. Their anxiety was further increased when early in July the government began the trials of those United Irish leaders against whom it had hard evidence. Convictions were easily secured: John and Henry Sheares were hanged on 14 July and John McCann on the 19th.[1] With William Michael Byrne and Oliver Bond condemned to suffer the same fate, and several others unsure of their own, some of the prisoners began to consider coming to terms with the government.

The first move came from Samuel Neilson, whose attorney, James Crawford, also attorney to Byrne and Bond, advised him in mid-July that since the rebellion had been defeated, any further resistance was pointless, and it was now time to conclude a treaty to end unnecessary bloodshed. Neilson broached the matter with his fellow prisoners, most of whom agreed with Crawford.[2] The prisoners then applied to the Whig magnate Lord Charlemont to act as guarantor of any agreement. Charlemont approved of the measure but pleaded infirmity and appointed his friend Francis Dobbs, MP for the borough of Charlemont, as a mediator; Dobbs was assisted by Henry Alexander, MP for the city of Derry, a relative of Oliver Bond.[3] Neilson informed Alexander that if the terms of the prisoners were met he would reveal to them 'every muscle, sinew, nay, fibre of the internal organization', and Alexander urged him to put his proposal in writing.[4]

1 R.R. Madden, *The United Irishmen, their lives and times* (2nd ed., London, 1860), iv, p. 60.
2 Thomas Russell to John Russell, 10 Dec. 1800 [copy]: T.C.D., Madden papers, MS 873/655, ff 11–12; C.H. Teeling, *Sequel to a personal narrative of the 'Irish rebellion' of 1798* (Belfast, 1832), pp 294, 307; William Sampson, *Memoirs* (New York, 1807), p. 25.
3 Madden, *United Irishmen* (1860), iv, pp 62–3.
4 Henry Alexander to Thomas Pelham, 26 July 1798: Lecky, *Ire.*, v, p. 32n.

On 24 July, the day before Byrne was due to be executed, Dobbs called on the chief secretary, Castlereagh, with a written proposal signed by most of the prisoners. In exchange for the lives of Byrne and Bond and an assurance that other prisoners would not be prosecuted, they agreed to give full details of the organization and aims of the United Irishmen and to submit to banishment for life in a neutral country, although they would not implicate any named individuals.[5]

The recently appointed lord lieutenant, Cornwallis, was immediately attracted to the offer, which fitted in well with his aim of restoring peace through a policy of firmness tempered by leniency. In early July he had issued a proclamation offering a general pardon to rank-and-file rebels who surrendered their weapons and took the oath of allegiance, and he had already formed the opinion that banishment was the most suitable punishment for the leaders.[6] But he knew that such an apparently lenient step would infuriate loyalists, who were in such a mood that 'nothing but blood will satisfy them'.[7] Although he was supported by Castlereagh, he was reluctant to proceed without securing additional backing. The following day he discussed the offer with his chief legal officers, who unanimously opposed it. They noted that several of the leading state prisoners, including Arthur O'Connor, had not signed the paper, that there was nothing to prevent exiled prisoners making their way from a neutral country to France, and that such leniency would greatly damage loyalist morale.

In the polarised atmosphere of Ireland in the summer of 1798, there was little mood for compromise. Most loyalists were baffled by Cornwallis's readiness to negotiate with the leaders of a defeated rebellion that had brought about such bloodshed and destruction of property. Popular Protestant feeling in Dublin and prominent ascendancy stalwarts such as John Foster were ranged against any negotiations with the United Irish leadership, and many yeomen threatened to lay down their arms should the agreement go ahead.[8] Not wishing to isolate himself, Cornwallis allowed the execution of Byrne to go ahead on 25 July.[9]

Byrne's execution concentrated the minds of the prisoners, and most of those who had refused to sign the agreement were persuaded by their colleagues to do so.[10] On 26 July Dobbs called on Castlereagh and informed him that the dissidents, including O'Connor, were now willing to sign, and that they agreed to leave the time and place of their liberation to the discretion of government, so long as they were not to be transported as felons.[11]

5 [24] July 1798: N.A.I., RP 620/39/231.
6 *Castlereagh correspondence*, i, p. 149; Cornwallis to Portland, 8 July 1798: *Cornwallis correspondence*, ii, p. 359.
7 Cornwallis to Portland, 26 July 1798: *Cornwallis correspondence*, ii, p. 374.
8 Cooke to Pelham, 9 Aug. 1798: B.L., Add. MS 33106, ff 49–50; Clare to Auckland, 1 Aug. 1798: Bishop of Bath and Wells (ed.), *The journal and correspondence of William Eden, Lord Auckland* (London, 1861–2), iv, p. 39.
9 Cornwallis to Portland, 26 July 1798: *Cornwallis correspondence*, ii, pp 372–4.
10 Arthur O'Connor to Castlereagh, 4 Jan. 1799: Teeling, *Sequel*, p. 297.
11 28 July 1798: N.A.I., RP 620/4/29/15; *Castlereagh correspondence*, i, pp 347–8.

Cornwallis again summoned his law officers, who on the basis of this new offer agreed to postpone Bond's execution to 30 July.[12] In the meantime he found the support he needed from an unlikely quarter. When the lord chancellor, Clare, returned to Dublin from his Limerick estate, he threw his weight solidly behind the agreement, stating in parliament that it would have been 'inexcusable' for the government not to take advantage of the prisoners' offer. The support of Clare, a rock of the Protestant ascendancy, proved decisive in muting the opposition of anti-Catholic zealots to any compromise.[13]

Although loyalists continued to grumble at his moderation, for Cornwallis the Kilmainham treaty (taking its name from the prison where most of the negotiations were conducted) had more to do with expediency than leniency. He claimed that if he had had any real evidence that could have convicted the rebel leaders, he would have gone ahead and hanged them, but he realized that (with the possible exceptions of Neilson and MacNeven) all the prisoners were likely to escape punishment.[14] Much of the evidence they had against them was vague and came from informers who were anxious to retain their anonymity, and the Castle had seen in the past how skilful defence counsel could tear reluctant or vague witnesses to pieces. It was unlikely that they could even establish the guilt of Neilson, who had been caught red-handed planning an attack on Newgate jail, and every acquittal would be a victory for the rebels.[15] The agreement, therefore, offered the Castle a convenient means of getting rid of a large number of troublesome agitators who otherwise would have to be detained indefinitely without charge.[16]

Cornwallis regarded comprehensive confessions from the United Irish leaders as 'more important than the lives of twenty such men as Oliver Bond'.[17] By establishing the existence of a widespread conspiracy, the government would justify its draconian security policy of recent years; the confessions might also damage relations between the United Irish leadership and the rank-and-file, and drive a wedge between the United Irishmen and France, destroying the prospects of any future invasion. To this end the government tried particularly hard to get the prisoners to reveal the names of French agents they had been dealing with, knowing that if they did so the French would never trust the United Irishmen again. Crucially, all of this would be accomplished without the Castle having to reveal its informants. Moreover, Arthur O'Connor's accession to the

---

12 Cornwallis to Portland, 26 July 1798: *Cornwallis correspondence*, ii, p. 374.
13 A.C. Kavanaugh, *John Fitzgibbon, earl of Clare* (Dublin, 1997), p. 347; Cooke to Pelham, 9 Aug. 1798: B.L., Add. MS 33106, ff 49–50; Clare to Auckland, 1 Aug. 1798: *Auckland correspondence*, iv, pp 38–9; Cooke to Wickham, 28 July 1798: *Cornwallis correspondence*, ii, p. 378.
14 Cornwallis to Pitt, 25 Oct. 1798, Cornwallis to Portland, 26 July 1798: *Cornwallis correspondence*, ii, pp 425, 372–4.
15 Cooke to Pelham, 9 Aug. 1798: B.L., Add. MS 33106, f. 48.
16 Cooke to Wickham, 28 July 1798: *Cornwallis correspondence*, ii, p. 378.
17 26 July 1798: *Cornwallis correspondence*, ii, p. 374.

agreement was a particular prize, since the government hoped that his testimony would discredit opposition politicians in both Dublin and Westminster, men such as Grattan, Fox and Sheridan who had endorsed his political principles and stood as his character witnesses during his trial for high treason at Maidstone. All in all, Cornwallis thought the agreement 'the most complete triumph both in England and Ireland'.[18]

For the United Irish prisoners there were also sound reasons for coming to terms with the government. They had already seen colleagues, in some cases relatively junior colleagues, go to the scaffold and, with little idea of just how vague the government's evidence against them was, the prospect of a mass execution of the United Irish leadership loomed before them. But this was more than just an exercise in self-preservation; some of the leaders had also been uneasy about the levels of bloodshed unleashed during the rising, and hoped to end the sporadic violence still occurring in parts of the country. Thomas Addis Emmet, for example, lamented that during the rising there was an absence of 'men of talents, firmness and integrity to direct its energies and control its excesses'.[19] However, not all the United Irishmen were enthusiastic about the agreement: Arthur O'Connor and William Sampson signed only after the execution of Byrne; William Dowdall and Roger O'Connor never signed, and some such as Thomas Russell (who expressed 'great repugnance' at the idea of treating with the government) signed with strong reservations. All who assented to the agreement insisted that their only motive was to save the lives of others, and maintained that they had made 'a great personal sacrifice'.[20] The very fact that several of the prisoners kept detailed accounts of the progress of the agreement betrays a wariness about treating with the government and an awareness that they might be called on to vindicate themselves in the future.[21]

But some United Irish leaders argued that the treaty could be turned to their advantage, in that it could be used to gain maximum publicity for their cause.[22] Significantly, prisoners in Kilmainham, Newgate and the Bridewell chose three of their most able propagandists, Thomas Addis Emmet, William James Mac-Neven and Arthur O'Connor to represent them, and at a meeting with Castle-

18 Cornwallis to Ross, 30 July 1798: *Cornwallis correspondence*, ii, p. 381; Clare to Auckland, 1 Aug. 1798: *Auckland correspondence*, iv, pp 38–9; Wickham to Castlereagh, 13 Aug. 1798: P.R.O., HO 100/66/359; 15 Aug. 1798: N.L.I., Melville papers, MS 54A/145.
19 T.A. Emmet to — , 22 Sept. 1798: B.L., Add. MS 22130, f. 39; see also Boyle, Aug./Sept. 1798: N.A.I., RP 620/18/3.
20 Thomas Russell to John Russell, Fort George, 10 Dec. 1800 [copy]: T.C.D., MS 873/655, ff 7v-9v; W.J. MacNeven, *Pieces of Irish history* (New York, 1807), p. 191.
21 Neilson's account is in Madden, *United Irishmen*, 2nd ed. (1860), iv, pp 60–76; Russell's in T.C.D., MS 873/655/II, ff 7–13; O'Connor's in Teeling, *Sequel*, pp 294–327; MacNeven's in MacNeven, *Pieces*, pp 142–73.
22 MacNeven, *Pieces*, p. 188.

reagh and Clare they agreed to give a detailed written history of their movement to the government.[23] This narrative was presented to Cornwallis on 4 August. It portrayed the United Irishmen as moderate reformers forced into republican separatism by an intransigent and repressive government. They claimed that the United system only began to make headway among Catholics after the recall of Fitzwilliam, and that the unchecked sectarian pogroms in Armagh had clearly demonstrated collusion between the authorities and Orange societies. In contrast the United Irish movement had curbed popular passions by exerting a restraining force on Defenderism and opposing random violence. There had been no general plan of insurrection prior to the arrest of the Leinster delegates on 12 March 1798, but after this the severity of military repression made recourse to arms inevitable. The prisoners admitted negotiating for a French invasionary force, but compared themselves to the English revolutionaries of 1688 who had also allied with a foreign power to liberate themselves from tyranny. They claimed that continuing repression could only serve to alienate the Irish people from the government and the connection with Britain, and grimly warned the government that 'you must extirpate or reform'. The tone was one of defiance rather than contrition: they made clear that although they wished to end unnecessary bloodshed, their principles remained unchanged.[24]

Not surprisingly, the authorities were unhappy with the memoir. It smacked too strongly of a 'controversial pamphlet', and was seen as more 'a justification of their treason than a statement of facts'.[25] Cornwallis instructed Cooke to return it to the prisoners, with a request that it be altered, but the prisoners refused to change a word.[26] They did, however, agree to appear before parliamentary secret committees, when they again stated their continued commitment to the principles of the United Irishmen. All the prisoners openly stated their belief in the feasibility of Irish independence, Emmet claiming that 'if Ireland were separated from England, she would be the happiest spot on the face of the globe'.[27] However, despite the defiant tone of the examinations, the secret committees unanimously agreed that the prisoners' evidence 'was given freely and without reserve and that they had fairly adhered to the spirit of their engagement'.[28]

In claiming that they had agreed to the treaty in order to exploit the propaganda opportunities it opened up, the prisoners were to some extent making a virtue of necessity. But disseminating information had always been an essential

---

23 Castlereagh to Wickham, 30 July 1798: *Castlereagh correspondence*, i, p. 248.

24 *Memoir of the Irish union* (n.p., n.d. [1802?]).

25 Cornwallis to Portland, 7 Aug. 1798: *Cornwallis correspondence*, ii, pp 382–3; *Castlereagh correspondence*, i, p. 352.

26 MacNeven, *Pieces*, pp 301–2.

27 *Memoir of the Irish union*, pp 29–31, 65, 69.

28 *Castlereagh correspondence*, i, p. 352.

part of the United Irish strategy, and the society had generally shown more talent as propagandists than insurrectionists. Having been defeated in the field, the
United Irish leadership was now engaged in a propaganda war with the government, and knew that it was important to portray themselves as a party that had
made a tactical compromise rather than one that had simply capitulated. They
believed that a clear and honest statement of their motives would open the eyes
of the people 'to the indispensable necessity of political liberty, and to all the
rapturous prospect of self-government'.[29] In response to claims that he had
betrayed the cause, Emmet replied that

> I trust in God I have advanced it by the very disclosures I have made. My
> cause is the promotion of Irish liberty and happiness... [we] will show to
> every reflecting man that such a cause must triumph in the end; and will I
> hope induce every honest man to forward it with his best endeavours, and
> to bring to its aid morality and virtue... we were something more than
> disinterested in what we did.[30]

For their part, the government hoped that the treaty could be used to pacify
the country. They permitted Francis Dobbs and a delegation of United Irishmen
to go to County Wicklow to persuade rebels there to surrender, and this mission
had some success.[31] The terms were offered to the United Irishmen in Ulster, but
all the main leaders in custody refused it outright, apparently confident in the
knowledge that government would not find it easy to convict them.[32]

The negotiations between the prisoners and the government were difficult
and complex and were plagued by suspicion and bad faith. As in most propaganda wars, truth was an early casualty. The prisoners' memoir was suppressed, since edited accounts of their statements before the secret committees
served the government better. The versions of the examinations published by
government and prisoners differed substantially. The government versions,
published as an appendix to the report of the parliamentary secret committees
on 22 August, blurred the subtleties and nuances of the prisoners' answers,
and stressed the United Irishmen's transformation into a military organization and their negotiations with the French for an invasion force.[33] The
version published by the prisoners, although generally frank about their preparations for insurrection and their dealings with the French, repeatedly
stressed how government severity and intransigence had left them with no
alternative but armed revolt. Negotiating for a French invasion was also por-

29 MacNeven, *Pieces*, p. 187.
30 T.A. Emmet to —, 22 Sept. 1798: B.L.., Add. MS 22,130, f. 39.
31 HMC *Charlemont MSS*, ii (London, 1894), pp 331–2; MacNeven, *Pieces*, p. 189.
32 N.A.I., RP 620/39/172, 197, 203, 205.
33 *Reports of the committees of secrecy of the House of Commons and House of Lords of Ireland* (London,
   1798), pp 225–36.

trayed as a responsible step, which would enable the United Irishmen to accomplish their aims quickly and with little bloodshed, and save the country from a prolonged civil war.[34] But the accuracy of the prisoners' versions is also questionable. They were composed from notes committed to writing after their examinations, and some of their replies, particularly O'Connor's rambling discourses, look more like answers they wished they had given than answers they actually gave.[35]

Clare was particularly unscrupulous in using the prisoners' evidence to his own ends – something he candidly admitted to MacNeven.[36] He claimed that the testimony of the United Irishmen proved they would be happy with nothing less than 'the subversion of all ecclesiastical establishments, Protestant or Popish', the separation of Ireland from the British crown, and a democratic House of Commons. He also claimed that the prisoners had admitted that Catholic Emancipation had been a 'mere pretence', and MacNeven's claim that he would as soon establish 'the Mahometan' religion as the Catholic was distorted into an assault on all Christian religion.[37]

Extracts of their testimony which appeared in some Dublin newspapers towards the end of August were also mangled.[38] These claimed that the military organization had begun in 1795 rather than 1796 (several months before the introduction of a draconian insurrection act rather than several months after), and comments by Emmet and MacNeven on the attitude of the masses to parliamentary reform and Catholic Emancipation were edited to imply that the United Irish leadership were contemptuous of the understanding of ordinary people.[39] Significantly, the names of their United Irish colleagues Tone, Lewins and Lord Edward FitzGerald also appeared in their testimony.[40]

The prisoners claimed that it was in response to these inaccuracies and misrepresentations that they were forced to publish a notice in the press, which was also widely distributed in handbills.[41] It claimed that the published versions of their testimony were a 'gross and … astonishing misrepresenta-tion', bearing no real relation to the evidence they had given, and they specifically denied that they had implicated any of their colleagues.[42] Given that rumours had begun to circulate that the prisoners had secretly revealed the names of their comrades,

34 *Memoir of the Irish union*, pp 31–3, 39; *Reports of the committees of secrecy*, p. 230; MacNeven, *Pieces*, p. 199.
35 MacNeven, *Pieces*, p. 190.
36 *Memoir of the Irish union*, p. 67.
37 *Lords jn. Ire.*, viii, 144; for MacNeven's version, see *Memoir of the Irish union*, p. 72.
38 *D.E.P.*, 25 Aug. 1798; *F.J.*, 23 Aug. 1798; *F.D.J.*, 23 Aug. 1798.
39 *Reports of the committees of secrecy*, p. 230; 29 Aug. 1798: P.R.O., Chatham papers 30/8/325; MacNeven, *Pieces*, p. 237.
40 *D.E.P.*, 25 Aug. 1798.
41 John Beresford to Auckland, 30 Aug. 1798: *Beresford correspondence*, ii, p. 176.
42 *S.N.L.*, 27 Aug. 1798; *Hibernian Journal*, 31 Aug. 1798.

this was a charge to which they were particularly sensitive.[43] Informers had always been excoriated in United Irish propaganda and the leaders were aware they were treading dangerous ground in giving information. In their offer to the government they had specified that 'the prisoners are not by names or describing to implicate any person whatever'.[44] They regarded this as a cornerstone of the agreement and claimed that they had already resisted pressure by the government to get them to reveal names in the early days of the agreement.[45] Giving general information, information that the prisoners suspected the government already knew, was one thing, but informing on colleagues would have stripped them of all honour and discredited the entire agreement.[46]

However, loyalists were outraged at the conduct of the prisoners. William Conyngham Plunket, one of the few Whigs still remaining in the Commons, condemned their ingratitude and 'libellous and insolent language'. Some members maintained that the agreement had been broken and that the prisoners should immediately be tried by martial law.[47] Even William Pitt notified Castlereagh of his displeasure at the prisoners' statement.[48] The government was furious that by denying the unauthorised statement of the secret committee's report in the newspaper, the prisoners had managed to deny the validity of the report itself. The fact that it had been inserted immediately after news of a French landing in Mayo was not seen as a coincidence, but as an incitement to rebellion.[49] They were curtly informed that unless they changed their conduct, they would be understood to have violated the agreement.[50]

The prisoners, however, maintained that they had done nothing wrong. They claimed they had insisted in earlier negotiations on the right to publish in full any information they might give and specified that they would refute anything published against them, and that in publishing the notice they were simply exercising a right already agreed upon.[51] At Pitt's suggestion they were re-examined by secret committee on 7 September. They made no effort to retract the evidence they had already given, but rather confirmed it, and expressed the hope that government would publish their entire testimony, rather than selective portions of it.[52]

43 Henry Alexander to Pelham, 4 Aug. 1798: B.L., Add. MS 33,106, f. 40; Arthur O'Connor to Castlereagh, 4 Jan. 1799: Teeling, *Sequel*, p. 304; MacNeven, *Pieces*, p. 191.
44 29 July 1798: N.A.I., RP 620/39/126.
45 Madden, *United Irishmen*, 2nd ed. (1860), iv, p. 64; MacNeven, *Pieces*, p. 180.
46 MacNeven, *Pieces*, p. 185.
47 *F.D.J.*, 28 Aug. 1798; Lecky, *Ire.*, v, 52.
48 1 Sept. 1798: *Castlereagh correspondence*, i, p. 329.
49 Beresford to Auckland, 30 Aug. 1798: *Beresford correspondence*, ii, p. 176.
50 Castlereagh to William Wickham, 27 Aug. 1798: *Cornwallis correspondence*, ii, p. 392; *Castlereagh correspondence*, i, pp 347–8.
51 State prisoners to Castlereagh, Aug. 1798: N.A.I., RP 620/15/3/34; Arthur O'Connor to Castlereagh, 4 Jan. 1799: Teeling, *Sequel*, pp 299–300, 304.
52 Castlereagh to Pitt, 7 Sept. 1798: *Castlereagh correspondence*, i, p. 336; MacNeven, *Pieces*, p. 193.

Relations between the two sides deteriorated further when a draft of the proposed banishment bill appeared in the English newspaper, the *Courier*, on 6 September, alleging that the state prisoners 'had acknowledged their crimes, retracted their opinions and implored pardon'. Now it was the prisoners' turn to be outraged. Neilson informed Castlereagh that he intended to write to the *Courier* to make clear that the state prisoners had neither changed their principles nor begged pardon, but had entered into an agreement with government as an equal party to bring about an end to unnecessary bloodshed. He was immediately visited by Cooke and Alexander Marsden, the Castle under-secretaries, who threatened that such a step would annul the agreement and bring about a resumption of executions.[53] The prisoners were not prepared for such a drastic step and a vague compromise was reached whereby Neilson would forgo writing to the *Courier* and Cooke would attempt to have the wording of the bill softened. However, this came to nothing and the bill was passed stating that the prisoners 'being conscious of their flagrant and enormous guilt, have expressed their contrition for the same, and have most humbly implored his majesty's mercy'.[54] Clearly, both sides were playing to their respective constituencies throughout these months, and just as the United Irishmen sought to show themselves as defiant and unrepentant, so the government wished to portray itself as merciful but firm, and only willing to pardon those misguided subjects who had at last seen the error of their ways.

Many of these problems arose because of the ad hoc nature of the agreement. The Kilmainham treaty was no carefully worded document but evolved from a loosely worded initial offer, which was not particularly well defined in subsequent discussions. Therefore both sides tended to put their own interpretation on the agreement – an interpretation usually at odds with that of the other party. There were also the difficulties involved in using intermediaries. In his anxiety to bring about an agreement, the well-meaning Dobbs may have misrepresented the prisoners' offer to make it as acceptable as possible to the government. He maintained that the prisoners were prepared to leave the timing and destination of their banishment entirely to the discretion of the government, provided they were not to be transported to Botany Bay, and were not detained after the end of the war.[55] The offer signed by the prisoners, however, did not give such powers to the government but simply stated that they were 'ready to emigrate to any country as shall be agreed on between themselves and government'.[56]

Most of what passed between the two parties was verbal, and so it is difficult to be certain about its precise nature, but the prisoners believed that they would be offered a period of bail to settle their affairs prior to emigration and some say

53 Madden, *United Irishmen*, 2nd ed. (1860), iv, pp 73–4.
54 38 Geo. III c. 78: *Stat. Ire.*, xviii, 1129.
55 Francis Dobbs to Castlereagh, 28 July 1798: N.A.I., RP 620/4/29/15.
56 Teeling, *Sequel*, p. 305; N.A.I., RP 620/39/126.

in their place of exile. But they received neither of these concessions. They claimed that the government's interpretation of the agreement had never been explicitly specified in any interviews, and that this interpretation had been repeatedly changed to suit the government as circumstances changed. Emmet complained that the government began by promising prisoners 'the utmost liberality and good faith', that it continued the same language until the prisoners had fulfilled their undertaking, and then it acted with pettiness and vindictiveness.[57] As the months in custody dragged on with no sign of their release, the prisoners grew increasingly bitter about their treatment. It is likely that they were also bitter at the weakness of their position. They were well aware that once they had given information and agreed to their banishment, they had played all their cards. Government held the upper hand and could bend its interpretation of the agreement as it wished. One important consequence of the treaty was that when Theobald Wolfe Tone lay under sentence of death, his fellow United Irish prisoners could do nothing to save his life, knowing that any attempt to intervene on his behalf would prove fruitless since they now had nothing left to bargain with.[58]

Although the government was adamant that no definite time for the release of the prisoners had been laid down, it was aware that it would seem an obvious breach of faith on its part if the prisoners were detained indefinitely. Moreover the government wanted to be rid of them, believing that the 'state would be subjected to much inconvenience and some danger' if they continued to be held in Ireland.[59] The cost involved in supporting almost 400 United Irish prisoners was a further incentive to expel them, Castlereagh complaining that 'the expense of this regiment of traitors exceeds five-fold that of the best regiment in the king's service'.[60] Of the ninety prisoners who eventually signed the Kilmainham treaty, Cornwallis believed that only fifteen of these were sufficiently important for their place of exile to be a matter of any real concern.[61] In December most of those who had signed the banishment act were given permission to emigrate to neutral countries, and many of those not included in the act who had already been convicted by courts martial were later transported to Prussia to serve in her armies.[62] But the problem remained – where to send the leaders? Their preference was to emigrate to a neutral German state, but since this would give them easy access to France, they were told they must go to America.[63]

57 Teeling, *Sequel*, pp 308–9; T.A. Emmet to Cornwallis, 11 Oct. 1798: N.A.I., RP 620/15/2/13; Bridewell prisoners to Cornwallis, 17 Sept. 1798: N.A.I., RP 620/40/65.
58 T.A. Emmet to Thomas Russell, [Nov. 1798]: N.A.I., RP 620/15/2/15.
59 Cornwallis to Portland, 29 Oct. 1798: *Cornwallis correspondence*, ii, pp 427–8.
60 Castlereagh to Wickham, 29 Oct. 1798: *Castlereagh correspondence*, i, p. 414.
61 29 Oct. 1798: *Cornwallis correspondence*, ii, pp 427–8; for a list of prisoners included in the terms of the agreement, see 38 Geo. III c. 78: *Stat. Ire.*, xviii, 1129–30.
62 Castlereagh to Wickham, 2 Jan. 1799: P.R.O., HO 100/85/7; Samuel Neilson to Thomas Russell, 5 Dec. 1798: N.A.I., RP 620/16/3; *Cornwallis correspondence*, ii, p. 427.
63 Cornwallis to Portland, 29 Oct. 1798: *Cornwallis correspondence*, ii, pp 427–8.

Most of the active United Irish leaders were opposed to this, regarding the current American government as no better than the British, and the Federalist president John Adams as an American version of Pitt.[64] But if the United Irish prisoners had misgivings about going to the United States, the United States had equal misgivings about receiving them. Cornwallis had his doubts about how the Americans, who had recently passed swingeing Alien and Sedition Acts, would react to receiving this 'cargo of sedition',[65] and such doubts proved well-founded. The American ambassador in London, Rufus King, claimed that the principles of the United Irishmen were 'so dangerous, so false, and so utterly inconsistent with any practicable or stable form of government' that they should not be sent to the United States.[66] On 16 September Alexander Marsden informed the prisoners that the American government would not allow them enter the country: pressed for a reason, he answered that 'perhaps Mr King does not desire to have republicans in America'.[67] With the option of sending them to America blocked, Portland decided that there was no viable place of banishment for them, and advised Cornwallis to keep the leading prisoners in custody 'as long as the war lasts, or it is thought necessary'.[68]

While negotiations were going on there were persistent rumours that the United Irishmen were attempting to revive their organization. One informer reported that the state prisoners had been engaged in mischief since the day they had signed the agreement. He claimed that the prisoners were encouraging their colleagues still at large and telling them that 'it is now that the real business is beginning'.[69] In the aftermath of the rising much of the Irish countryside had remained disturbed, the counties in the neighbourhood of Dublin particularly so.[70] The severe reprisals by crown forces had left behind a legacy of sullen resentment among many Catholics; several rebel bands continued to hold out in isolated regions, and the expectation of a French invasion was widely held.[71] Parts of Antrim and Down were reported to be preparing for a new insurrection, the counties of Wicklow and Wexford remained disturbed, and government saw the hand of the United Irishmen in recurrent agrarian violence in the south and west.[72]

---

64 T.A. Emmet to Cornwallis, 11 Oct. 1798: N.A.I., RP 620/15/2/13; Castlereagh to Wickham, 29 Oct. 1798: *Castlereagh correspondence*, i, p. 414.
65 13 Sept. 1798: *Cornwallis correspondence*, ii, p. 403.
66 Rufus King to Portland, 13 Sept., 17 Oct. 1798: P.R.O., HO 100/66/369, 373–4.
67 T.A. Emmet to Rufus King, 9 Apr. 1807: MacNeven, *Pieces*, p. 291.
68 12 Nov. 1798: *Cornwallis correspondence*, ii, pp 435–6.
69 Boyle, [Sept. 1798]: N.A.I., RP 620/18/3.
70 John Brown to — , 29 Aug. 1798; Boyle, 8 Sept., 22 Dec. 1798; John Sidwell to Cooke, 3 Jan. 1799]: N.A.I., RP 620/39/227; 620/18/3; 620/46/3.
71 Cornwallis to Portland, 16 Jan., Mar. 1799: P.R.O., HO 100/85/87–8, 195–6; Buckingham to Grenville, 11 Mar. 1799: HMC, *Dropmore MSS* (London, 1892–4), iv, pp 496–8.
72 Cornwallis to Portland, 14 Feb. 1799: *Castlereagh correspondence*, ii, p. 174.

Undoubtedly some of the state prisoners in Dublin, believing that the pact made with the government had been violated, were attempting to capitalise on this widespread disaffection. Leaders such as Russell and Arthur O'Connor, who had been reluctant adherents to the agreement in the first place, saw their misgivings confirmed and were to the fore in attempts to revive the movement.[73] The new organization was based on an acceptance that the United Irishmen were not in a position to mount an effective insurrection themselves, but that they should await the arrival of the French.[74] The new movement had a simplified, pared-down structure, designed to be difficult for informers to penetrate and to be activated rapidly when required. There was to be no hierarchy of committees; instead the Dublin-based directory would appoint a number of colonels throughout the countryside, who would in turn form local regiments which they would call out once the French had landed.[75]

The government was kept well informed of the conspiratorial activities of the state prisoners by their attorney, James McGucken, and on the morning of 16 January 1799 their cells were searched and their papers seized.[76] Among these papers were found notes of a conversation held by Russell, Neilson and a number of their colleagues at Newgate repudiating the agreement and discussing the 'probable success' of an insurrection given the disturbed state of the country.[77] The seizure of their papers, however, seems to have done little to disrupt the prisoners' organizational efforts. Reports continued to arrive at the Castle claiming that preparations for insurrection were continuing in east Ulster and the counties around Dublin, and were being orchestrated by an executive that met in the prisons of Kilmainham and Newgate.[78] Cornwallis observed that the United Irishmen 'look on with pleasure' at the growing disturbances in the country 'and are whetting their knives to cut the throats of all the nobility and gentry of the island'.[79]

Government anxiety was further increased by United Irish attempts to form an alliance with Orangemen disaffected by government proposals for a legislative union between Great Britain and Ireland.[80] Many loyalists saw the proposed abo-

---

73 Marianne Elliott, *Partners in revolution: The United Irishmen and France* (New Haven, 1982), p. 247.

74 James McGucken, 3 Jan. 1799, 7 Feb. 1803: N.A.I., RP 620/7/74/2, 8; Wickham to Castlereagh, 28 Feb. 1799: P.R.O., HO 100/85/281–3.

75 Elliott, *Partners*, p. 248; McGucken, 29 Dec. 1798; 29 Jan., 2 Feb., 15 Feb. 1799; Boyle, 13, 17 Mar. 1799: N.A.I., RP 620/3/32/19; RP 620/7/74/5, 7, 11; 620/18/3.

76 Thomas Russell to John Russell, 10 Dec. 1800 [copy]: T.C.D., Madden papers, MS 873/655, f. 12.

77 Madden, *United Irishmen*, 3rd ser. (1846), ii, pp 184–5.

78 Robert Henry, 27 July 1799; McGucken, 29 Jan. 1799; Boyle, *c.* Mar. 1799, 13, 17 Mar. 1799: N.A.I., RP 620/47/100; 620/7/74/5; 620/18/3; Thomas Wright: P.R.O., HO 100/86/301–2.

79 13 Feb. 1799: *Cornwallis correspondence*, iii, p. 60.

80 Hereward Senior, *Orangeism in Ireland and Britain, 1795–1836* (London, 1966), pp 122–4.

lition of the Irish parliament as betrayal by the British government, the yeomanry in particular regarding it as a poor reward for their vigorous efforts in quashing rebellion the previous summer. Members of the Dublin yeomanry proposed that they should stage a mass resignation in protest, while some rural corps threatened open revolt.[81] United Irish prisoners in Newgate were reported to be encouraging their friends at the bar to support the union 'to inflame the Orangemen'. The ever optimistic Thomas Russell believed that 'the Orangemen of Dublin have offered arms to the United Irishmen and are going about in order to destroy all parties [and] factions and have a common cause'. United Irish propaganda now called on the Orangemen to renounce their past 'errors' and to form an alliance to defend Ireland's independence.[82]

Although the prospect of this alliance was not a complete chimera – there were complaints to the Orange Grand Lodge that some members had sought to make common cause with the United Irishmen[83] – the Orange Society as a whole adopted a position of neutrality to the union, and the yeomanry remained loyal.[84] The unlikely alliance of Orangemen and United Irishmen came to nothing, but it was an example of the difficulties the prisoners could cause. For a government that had enough on its hands in attempting to pass the union, it was an irritant they could do without. Since the prisoners were proving resourceful in communicating with the outside world, including disaffected groups in Britain, Cornwallis was instructed that they should be removed from Ireland.[85] He therefore decided to implement the recommendation that he had made months earlier, and to pack the leading prisoners off to the Scottish Highlands.[86] On 19 March they were dispatched to Fort George, near Inverness. To prevent them leaving behind instructions, they were given only a few hours notice of their impending departure and were not told of their final destination.[87]

Without its leadership, and dependent on outside help, the United Irish movement practically ground to a halt. By the middle of May 1799, even a normally alarmist informant noted that 'nothing is now doing among the disaffected – they are completely down'.[88] Several years of relative tranquillity followed, and in that sense the Kilmainham treaty of 1798 was a success for the government,

---

81 Castlereagh to Portland, 2 Jan. 1799: *Castlereagh correspondence*, ii, p. 81; Cornwallis to Portland, 16 Jan. 1799: P.R.O., HO 100/85/87; Senior, *Orangeism*, p. 126.
82 McGucken, 3 Jan. 1799; 29 Jan. 1799; 19 Feb. 1799: N.A.I., RP 620/7/74/2; 620/7/74/5; 620/7/74/12.
83 'J.W.' [Leonard McNally] to — , 20 Jan. 1799: N.A.I., RP 620/10/121/124; *Castlereagh correspondence*, ii, p. 169.
84 Senior, *Orangeism*, p. 127.
85 Portland to Cornwallis, 5 Mar. 1799: P.R.O., HO 100/86/9; 26, 28 Jan. 1799: P.R.O., PC 1/43/152;Wickham to Castlereagh, 26 Mar. 1799: *Castlereagh correspondence*, ii, p. 238.
86 Cornwallis to Portland, 13 Sept. 1798: *Cornwallis correspondence*, ii, p. 403.
87 Castlereagh to Wickham, 19 Mar. 1799: P.R.O., HO 100/86/163–4.
88 Sproule to Lees, 16 May 1799: N.A.I., RP 620/47/26.

particularly in depriving Irish republicanism of its most able leaders. Although some militants such as Thomas Russell and William Dowdall would play an important part in the Emmet rising of 1803, most of the remaining leaders would never return to Ireland and henceforth played a peripheral role in Irish affairs. With their flank secured from political disaffection, Cornwallis and Castlereagh were now in a position to concentrate all their efforts on passing the Act of Union.

In contrast the United Irishmen seem to have gained relatively little from the treaty. Ironically, Oliver Bond, the one man who was certainly saved from the scaffold by the treaty, died of natural causes only five weeks after it was concluded. The agreement prevented the wholesale executions of leaders which they had feared, but the leadership was nullified for another two or three years by their detention in Fort George, and the propaganda benefits they had hoped for proved largely illusory. Aware that they had gained little from the treaty, the United Irishmen fell back on the claim that they had been betrayed by the government.

So was it a mistake for the prisoners to deal with the government at all? The United Irish prisoners in Belfast, for example, did not accept the terms of the agreement and most of them were released and allowed to return to Ireland in December 1801.[89] But none of the northern prisoners were under immediate sentence of death, and one must allow that the Dublin state prisoners were operating under conditions of great strain as they saw colleagues going to the gallows. Had they known just how little real evidence the government had against them, they probably would have been far more wary about concluding an agreement. It would be unfair to criticize them for this, but they do deserve some criticism for their naiveté in negotiation. They had no reason to trust the government, having regularly criticized them in the past for their unscrupulous attitude to the rule of law, yet the pact they made smacked almost of a gentlemen's agreement. They seem to have had little appreciation that skilled politicians such as Cornwallis, Castlereagh and Clare might for reasons of state bend a flexible agreement as they wished. More skilled negotiators would have recognized the weakness of their position and insisted that a binding and detailed treaty be published. Instead they put themselves at the mercy of the government's good faith, and complained bitterly when this good faith was not forthcoming. It was perhaps out of a belated recognition that they had been out-manoeuvred that in nationalist historiography the Kilmainham treaty of 1798 became another in a long list of acts of British treachery.[90]

89 Hardwicke to Pelham, 31 Oct. 1801: P.R.O., HO 100/104/216; Thomas Russell to Margaret Russell, 20 Dec. 1801: T.C.D., Sirr papers, MS 868/1, ff 291–2.
90 MacNeven, *Pieces*, p. 188; William Sampson, *Memoirs*, pp 40–1; Madden, *United Irishmen*, 2nd ed. (1860), iv, pp 142–9.

22

Legal aspects of the 1798 rising, its suppression and the aftermath

W.N. OSBOROUGH

On 24 May 1798, a proclamation was issued in Dublin by the Irish lord lieutenant, Earl Camden. Over the names of members of the Irish privy council, it read as follows:

> His Excellency, the lord lieutenant, by and with the advice of the Privy Council, has issued orders to all the general officers commanding His Majesty's forces to punish all persons acting, aiding, or in any manner assisting in the rebellion which now exists in this kingdom, and has broken out in the most daring and violent attacks upon His Majesty's forces, according to martial law, either by death o otherwise, as to them shall seem expedient for the punishment and suppression of all rebels in their several districts; of which all His Majesty's subjects are to take notice.[1]

Prior to the onset of actual rebellion, the deterioration in the situation as viewed from Dublin Castle had generated other official announcements of varying seriousness, each one of which nevertheless bore witness to the deepening Irish crisis. The privy council, for instance, had promulgated a succession of decrees 'proclaiming' counties or parts of them under the provisions of the Insurrection Act, an exercise which brought in its train the enforcement of curfew and the curtailment of other rights of George III's Irish subjects.[2] The mili-

---

1 *Commons' Jn. Ire.*, xvii, pt. 2, p. dccccxii.
2 36 Geo. III, c.20, as amended by 37 Geo. III, c.38. Once a district was proclaimed, curfew-breakers risked being dubbed 'idle and disorderly' and of being forcibly drafted into the navy or (after 1797 and the naval mutinies of that year) into the army. Magistrates were given special powers of search and seizure, especially in respect of arms; public meetings were restricted. Other provisions dealt with the registration of arms and with the administration of unlawful oaths, the latter crime being made punishable by death. The principal act of 1796 was precipitated, according to the report of the Committee of Secrecy of the Irish commons (*Commons' Jn. Ire.*, xvii, pt. 2, p. dcccxxix), by 'the outrages committed by common bandits, calling themselves Defenders, in the counties of Roscommon, Leitrim, Longford, Meath, Westmeath and Kildare, together with a religious feud prevailing in the county of Armagh'. In the early stages

tary, too, had been far from idle. Commanders in the field had been issuing orders demanding the surrender of arms, accompanying the more recent of these with the threat, by no means a fanciful one, of the billeting of troops local-ly at free quarters in the event of non-compliance.[3] For all these signs of hectic and awesome governmental and military activity, the proclamation of 24 May betokened an official initiative of an immeasurably graver sort – the trial of civil-ian rebels by panels of military personnel who might even, should they see fit, sentence such rebels to death. Self-evidently, the stakes had been raised to a very high level indeed.

Trial by court-martial, as sanctioned by the May proclamation, was to become commonplace: the arrangement was copperfastened under the Suppres-sion of Rebellion Act of 1799.[4] It was not just, as early statistics demonstrate with sombre exactitude, a deadly serious business;[5] trial by court-martial pro-

of the gathering unrest, the legislation was principally to be invoked in respect of areas in the North, as the Committee of Secrecy related (ibid.): 'Many districts in Ulster in which outrages prevailed occasioned by the active and persecuting spirit of the United Irishmen were in the course of the winter of 1796 and the spring of 1797, put under the provisions of the act.' Late in 1796 Charlemont made successful representations to Camden to have one district in Co. Armagh excepted from a proposed Insurrection Act proclamation: Camden to Charlemont, — Nov. 1796: H.M.C. *Charlemont MSS*, ii, 289–90. How this body of draconian legislation was viewed from the United Irish perspective may perhaps be gleaned from evidence that emerged at a court-martial of dissident Dublin militiamen held in Cork in Mar 1798. A plan to murder a crown informer had apparently been aborted because the incident would have provoked an immediate meeting of magistrates leading in turn to the inevitable 'proclamation' of Cork, something that would have made it much more difficult for the local United Irishmen to organ-ise themselves: *Commons' Jn. Ire.*, xvii, pt. 2, p. dccccii. Legal confusion surrounded the pre-cise date of expiry of the 1796 Insurrection Act, a fact that the legal advisers of William Orr, executed at Carrickfergus in September 1797, hoped – vainly – might have saved Orr: William Drennan to Martha Mc Tier, — Aug. 1797: D.A. Chart (ed.), *The Drennan letters* (Belfast, 1931), p. 261. Payments to newspapers to publish proclamations under the Insurrection Act constituted a hidden form of press subsidy: Brian Inglis, *The freedom of the press in Ireland, 1784–1841* (London, 1954), pp 62–63, 74. For post-1797 Insurrection Act developments, see 38 Geo. III, c.21: measures to prevent the manufacture and distribution of pikes and pikeheads; 38 Geo. III, c.82: rules on the licensing of blacksmiths. In s.5 of 39 Geo. III, c.36 will be found authorisation for those dubbed 'idle and disorderly' to be forcibly recruited into the armies of friendly foreign powers. The creation of such an authority had been suggested in a letter from the Prussian chargé d'affaires; see Castlereagh to Wickham, 28 Feb. 1799: *Cornwallis correspon-dence*, iii, pp 70–1. For a general overview, see R.B. McDowell, *Ireland in the age of imperialism and revolution, 1760–1801* (Oxford, 1979), pp 552–56.

3   See *Commons' Jn. Ire.*, xvii, pt. 2, p. dccccxi. For the 'offensive' of the spring of 1798 that threatened the billeting of troops, see McDowell, *Ireland*, pp 57–79; Thomas Pakenham, *The year of liberty: The great Irish rebellion of 1798* (London, 1969), p. 63f.; Thomas Bartlett, 'Defence, counter-insurgency and rebellion: Ireland, 1793–1803', in Thomas Bartlett and Keith Jeffery (eds), *A military history of Ireland* (Cambridge, 1996), p. 274. For the texts of other relevant proclamations, see, e.g., *Commons' Jn. Ire.*, xvii, pt. 2, pp dccclv–viii, dccccxi.

4   39 Geo. III, c.11; and see below.

5   Lake to Castlereagh, writing from Wexford, 23 June 1798: *Castlereagh correspondence*, i, p. 224: 'I really feel most severely the being obliged to order so many men out of the world; but I am

vides the focus for an examination of legal and constitutional questions that are of both transient interest and enduring significance. The practical problem arose straightaway of how exactly the military panels foreshadowed by the proclamation should set about their task. The conduct of courts-martial of persons subject to army discipline was regulated by a long series of annually re-enacted Mutiny Acts.[6] An oath was laid down to be taken by all officers chosen to serve. These officers themselves had to be of the rank of captain or above. A court of thirteen officers was obligatory and nine votes were required to support a death sentence. A judge-advocate was to be present. Proper records of trials were to be kept and made available, too, for the benefit of those proceeded against.[7] For the courts-martial of civilian rebels, on the other hand, the legal environment was very different. At first, indeed, legislative control was non-existent: the Suppression of Rebellion Act 1799 was thus content to leave all matters connected with the constitution and functioning of such courts-martial to the discretion of the lord lieutenant. Legislation thereafter did concern itself with a few important details. In 1800 it was stipulated that the courts were to consist of commissioned officers of the line, fencible or militia regiments or yeomanry corps. The maximum number of officers to sit on any court was set at thirteen, the minimum at three. In 1801 an act of the United Kingdom parliament raised the minimum to seven and prescribed a two-thirds majority for any death sentence awarded.[8]

Imbalance in the amount of legislative regulation as between the two kinds of court-martial remains striking. Understandably, in the early days of the rising, such few critics as there were of the major legal experiment then afoot urged the officers manning the courts-martial set up to try rebels, *faute de mieux*, to observe the detailed rules laid down in the Mutiny Acts.[9] The Mutiny Act-style prosecutions of soldiers for their United Irish sympathies, for administering unlawful oaths and for spreading general disaffection furnished a helpful recent parallel.[10] It is notorious, even so, that such 'advice', was not to be heeded, at least

convinced, if severe and many examples are not made, the Rebellion cannot be put a stop to.' The report on Irish prisons for 1798 (published in 1799) reveals that in 1798 in County Wexford 27 men sentenced to death by court-martial had been executed: *Commons' Jn. Ire.*, xviii, pp cccxlii-iii. In the country at large, between late August 1798 and the end of February 1799, of 380 persons tried by court-martial, 131 had been sentenced to death; there had been 90 executions – Cornwallis to Portland, 28 Feb. 1799: *Cornwallis correspondence*, iii, p. 70.

6 For the first in the series of Irish Mutiny Acts, see 19 & 20 Geo. III, c.16; for the last, 40 Geo. III, c.7.

7 Mutiny Act 1798, 38 Geo. III, c.27.

8 39 Geo. III, c.11, s.1; 40 Geo. III, c.2, s.2; 41 Geo. III, c.14, s.2 (U.K.).

9 This inference can be drawn from the questions directed in August 1798 at General Cradock who had presided at the court-martial of Cornelius Grogan two months earlier and from the account, published in 1801, of the court-martial of Sir Edward Crosbie. See further the sources mentioned at nn. 12 and 13 below.

10 For accounts of such courts-martial, see *Commons' Jn. Ire.*, xvii, pt. 2, pp dcccxcix–dccccii.

not initially. Some of the early courts-martial of apprehended 'rebels', in consequence, attracted much unfavourable publicity, lending sustenance in fact to the jurist's frequently expressed dim opinion of martial law – that the latter is nothing more than 'the lawyer's equivalent of the physicist's anti-matter, a kind of juristic black hole, into which are sucked all the cherished principles which normally guarantee life and liberty'.[11] At the court-martial of Cornelius Grogan held in Wexford on 26 June 1798, the panel consisted of only seven officers; no oath had been subscribed by any of them; and no judge-advocate had been in attendance.[12] The court-martial of Sir Edward Crosbie held in Carlow earlier in the same month is mainly remarkable for the acute difficulties his widow subsequently encountered when endeavouring to lay hands on some account of the proceedings which had resulted in her husband being sentenced to death.[13]

The actual conduct of these two high-profile trials, presided over by General Cradock and Major Dennis respectively, has attracted other criticism besides – for instance in relation to decisions on evidence and to reject applications for suggested adjournments. In retrospect, it seems that, during at least this one critical month – June 1798 – corners were indeed cut; scarcely surprising given that the paramount, unambiguous and unashamed military objective at the time was to make examples, and to do so fast. When the forces of the crown had established their ascendancy and the rising had obviously been crushed, a different, more sober, picture emerges. From this slightly later period the evidence leads one to conclude – however hazardous any generalisation in the area must be – that the understandable determination among military men to punish the rebel would not necessarily triumph over the conscientious resolve to do justice in the individual case.[14] An isolated item of evidence that bears on the same broad question deserves to be related. In one phase of the aftermath of the rebellion in County Wexford, captured rebels came close to enjoying the effective option of trial by court-martial or trial in the ordinary courts. Most, according to Edward Hay in describing this episode, preferred trial by court-martial.[15] The proclivity of a

---

11 Ronan Keane, ' "The will of the general": Martial law in Ireland, 1535–1924', in *Irish Jurist*, xxv–xxvii (1990–92), 180.

12 This information is to be gleaned from Rowe's published account of the inquiry held by the Irish commons in August into the proposed attainder of Grogan: 'Minutes of evidence, etc.' in R.R. Rowe, *Reports of some interesting cases ... with a treatise on martial law* (Dublin, 1824), pp 1–142. See also Paul O'Higgins, *A bibliography of Irish trials and other legal proceedings* (Abingdon, Oxon., 1986), p. 172 (s.v. *R. v. Grogan*).

13 *An accurate and impartial narrative of the appeal, trial and execution on the 5th of June 1798 of Sir Edward William Crosbie, bart.* (Bath, 1801); Victor Hadden, 'The trial and death of Sir Edward Crosbie, '98', in *Carloviana*, xii (1963), 8.

14 R.B. McDowell, *Ireland*, pp 660–3. Some useful data is assembled in Rowe, *Reports of interesting cases*, pp xv–xxxvii, and in P. Power, *The courts martial of 1798–9* (Naas, n.d. [1997]), but a thorough investigation of all the surviving evidence is clearly needed.

15 Edward Hay, *History of the insurrection of the county of Wexford* (Dublin, 1803), pp xxvii–viii, 281, 296–97. Courts-martial enjoyed greater flexibility in the admission of evidence, which

Wexford jury invariably to convict, even against the weight of the evidence, rendered no other expression of preference either intelligible or intelligent.

The proclamation of 24 May 1798 raised a much more fundamental question – its very legality judged by current constitutional doctrine. The contention that it was unconstitutional, and thus invalid and of no legal effect, did rather more than rob the emperor of his clothes: the ramifications were both startling and far-reaching. The assault itself comprised a two-pronged attack.

The first challenge was attractive in its simplicity. In the circumstances which had arisen in Ireland, it was entirely legitimate for the government to declare martial law and to prescribe trial by court-martial but – and this was the key contention – if this was to be done, it had to be done by legislation. The royal prerogative, the power of which Camden had chosen to avail, could not be validly exercised for these purposes.

McDowell musters the arguments for the opposing view that Camden's invoking of the prerogative was completely legitimate.[16] Blackstone in the *Commentaries* is cited for his claim that 'eccentrical remedies' might be needed 'when the contracts of society' were 'in danger of dissolution'. The single contemporary utterance that McDowell managed to track down, is a speech of Speaker Foster in the Irish Commons in August 1798. Martial law, Foster averred,

> was a principle founded upon public exigency for the suppression of rebellion ... under which the king gave power to his generals to punish with immediate death all persons acting in rebellion. The general on his own view of the guilt, might of his own authority order such persons to be put to death, but sometimes in order to ascertain more effectually the guilt of the party, the general called for the aid of his own officers on a military tribunal, to enquire into the guilt of the party and examine the evidence.

A diametrically opposed school of thought (ignored by McDowell) argued vociferously that the subjection of civilians to martial law had to be validated prospectively by statute. In this light, Camden's proclamation of May 1798 was not only unwarranted but patently unconstitutional. In 1803, in the wake of Emmet's rebellion, Lord Redesdale (Clare's successor in the post of Irish lord chancellor) told Lord Hardwicke (now lord lieutenant) in forthright language that Camden's proclamation had been wrong. It represented no precedent: if, Redesdale argued, the administration wished to employ martial law, they would first have to secure the passage of legislation legitimising it.[17] Two years later, in

could have helped to tip the scales in their favour (this is really a reflection of how insanely biased Wexford juries had become after 1798).

16 McDowell, *Ireland*, p. 660.

17 Redesdale to Hardwicke, 3 Aug. 1803, Hardwicke to Charles Yorke [his brother], 11 Aug. 1803: E.B. Mitford, *Life of Lord Redesdale* (London, 1939), pp 114, 271–2.

1805, the question was explored by Francis Hargrave, recorder of Liverpool and well-known legal antiquary.[18] Hargrave had been invited by the surviving brothers of Cornelius Grogan to advise on how to secure the reversal of Cornelius' attainder by act of parliament in 1798.[19] Central to Hargrave's brief, as he saw it, was the need to advance an authoritative reasoned opinion on the constitutionality of Grogan's court-martial, the court-martial that had been followed by his execution. Primarily through reliance on English constitutional history, Hargrave concluded that legislative endorsement of martial law was an essential prerequisite and that this had been lacking. In the first published version of his opinion, Hargrave went on to say, however, that another critical factor entered into the equation. The Suppression of Rebellion Act 1799, which undoubtedly authorized trial by courts-martial, could extend retrospective validity back to May 1798 to their use and probably, in addition, as signalling the existence in Ireland at this late date of a distinct and as yet unmodified tradition of constitutional logic. Several years afterwards, this crucial qualification by Hargrave of what had been his initial conclusion attracted the ire of the Irish barrister, Richard Radford Rowe. In 1824, Rowe insisted that Hargrave's doubts were founded on a complete misreading of the Suppression of Rebellion Act, the precise aims of which Rowe himself then proceeded to set forth in typically idiosyncratic style.[20] In mounting his attack, Rowe was unaware, however, that in 1811 Hargrave republished his original opinion; in this second version he added a new introduction which conveys the clear impression that Hargrave was changing his mind once again. The leading precedents, Hargrave writes here, were all against the untrammelled use of the prerogative power. He himself

> saw the right of putting rebels to death in battle whilst the battle lasted. He also saw the right to arrest those found in actual rebellion or duly charged with being traitors, and to have them imprisoned for trial and punishment according to the law of treason.[21] But he could not see, that punishing and trying rebels according to martial law was, when Mr Grogan was tried and put to death, part of the English law, as it was administrable in England, or even as it was administrable in Ireland. On the contrary he saw such a prerogative doctrine to be inconsonant with

18 Francis Hargrave (1741?-1821). He acquired his reputation in the celebrated *habeas corpus* case involving the black plaintiff James Somersett in 1772. He was made recorder of Liverpool in 1797. His invaluable collection of manuscripts and printed books was purchased by the government for the British Museum.

19 The outcome is his 'Opinion in Irish case involving martial law': Francis Hargrave, *Jurisconsult exercitations* (3 vols, London, 1811), i, p. 399; Rowe, *Reports*, pp xliii-xlviii.

20 Ibid., pp xlviii-l.

21 As was done after the Jacobite rebellion of 1745: see, e.g., 168 Eng. Rep. 1 (Foster's *Crown Cases*).

several recitals and one enactment in that grand act of parliament, the petition of right, in 16th of Charles the first. He saw it also to be irreconcilable with the opinions declared by some of the greatest lawyers of that time, to a committee of the whole house of commons sitting on martial law.

Hargrave then names a distinguished roll-call of lawyers – Coke, Noy, Rolle, Banks and Mason. And, for good measure, he adds that 'such a latitude of martial law' was 'equally crossed by the doctrines of Lord Chief Justice Hale'.[22]

The reservations of Redesdale, Hargrave and Rowe date from after 1798; that no immediately contemporary reservations over Camden's proclamation, whether in Ireland or England, are recorded is itself noteworthy. No one wished to hamstring the conduct of actual courts-martial by the application of new-fangled libertarian doctrines. Lord Clare, sitting in the court of exchequer chamber in 1793, had viewed this prospect with unadorned contempt. 'If the sentence of a court-martial', Clare had then argued,

> were examinable upon its merits in the superior courts of law, what would protect the soldier who executes, or the judges, who pronounce it from action or indictment, at the suit of the party condemned? It must of necessity subvert the whole system of British jurisprudence.[23]

In the autumn of 1798, the boat was indeed to be rocked long after it had set sail and rocked most vigorously, if not quite in the manner and for the reasons later espoused by Redesdale, Hargrave and Rowe. The difficulty that arose in the autumn of 1798 over trial by court-martial at that time had been anticipated by the liberal MP Arthur Browne in January.[24] For the duration of the rising itself and beyond, the ordinary courts of the land remained open. There were few exceptions: for instance, no assizes were held in either Wexford or Wicklow in the summer of 1798, nor were there spring assizes in the latter county in 1799.[25] For confirmation that the ordinary courts continued to sit, one need only mention the major treason trials conducted in customary fashion by the special commission composed of senior judges that sat in Dublin in June and July 1798.

The government, in bringing to trial at this specific juncture, the Sheares brothers, John McCann, William Michael Byrne, Oliver Bond and Samuel Neilson, wished to make an example of the ringleaders of disaffection.[26] In

---

22 Hargrave, *Jurisconsult exercitations*, i, 400.
23 *Gahan* v. *Maingay* (1793), Irish Term Reports, p. 74.
24 McDowell, *Ireland*, p. 597.
25 Ibid., pp 659, 664–65.
26 Abraham Lincoln sought to justify the morality of such preemptive strikes in the midst of the American Civil War. 'Must I', he demanded rhetorically, 'shoot a simple-minded soldier boy who deserts, while I must not touch a hair of a wily agitator who induces him to desert? … I

Dublin in the summer of 1798 four of the six were executed, following conviction on treason charges – the two Sheares brothers, McCann and Byrne.

Specific legislation was passed enabling the Dublin city and county commission to sit during the law term,[27] and it was before this commission of senior
judges that the six accused appeared for trial,[28] when the grand jury returned
true bills on 26 June. On 4 July, the first trial – of Henry and John Sheares – was
scheduled to begin.[29] Straightaway their counsel, Leonard MacNally, contended
that the indictments were invalid: an alien, John Decluzeau, had served on the
grand jury, in contravention of what McNally reckoned was a constitutional bar.
Protracted debate followed until Viscount Carleton, the chief justice of common
pleas, dismissed McNally's point out of hand. A week's adjournment was, however, sanctioned to enable the accused to summon witnesses.

The trial proper finally began before Carleton, Judge Crookshank and Baron
George on 12 July. It lasted all day and through the following night; the jury
returning their verdict of guilty, after a brief retirement, just before 8 a.m. the
next day. The death sentences were pronounced at 3 p.m. There was no reprieve,
and the two Sheares brothers were executed in front of the courthouse in Green
Street the following day.

Despite the fact that the evidence against Henry and John Sheares was
extremely strong, the defence lawyers did not lack for arguments that might con-
ceivably have swayed a jury. The brothers had been charged with 'compassing
the death of the king', a standard accusation in the treason indictments of the
period. The phrase had been glossed down the years to include using force to
alter the form of government. Counsel argued nevertheless for the acceptance of
a more literal interpretation, linking that to another forlorn contention that
when the king was not resident in Ireland, as George III never was, it was impossible 'to compass' his death by the mere act of rebelling in Ireland. The Sheares'
counsel also dwelt on a major difference in the law of treason as between
England and Ireland. In England, statute law since the 1690s had insisted that in
proof of treason any so-called overt act had to be corroborated by no less than

think that in such a case, to silence the agitator, and save the boy, is not only constitutional, but,
withal, a great mercy': Lincoln to Erastus Corning, 12 June 1863, quoted in Sherrill Halbert,
'The suspension of the writ of *habeas corpus* by President Lincoln', in *American Journal of
Legal History*, ii (1958), 104.

27 38 Geo. III, c.38.

28 Viscount Carleton, chief justice of common pleas; Judge Crookshank, second justice of common pleas; Judge Chamberlain, third justice of king's bench; Baron Smith, third baron of
exchequer; Baron George, fourth baron of exchequer; and Judge Day, fourth justice of king's
bench. The ensuing trials proceeded before three-judge courts.

29 *A report of the whole proceedings in the trial of Henry Sheares and John Sheares, esqrs. for high
treason* (Dublin, 1798); T.B. Howell, *A complete collection of state trials* (33 vols, London,
1816–24), xxvii, col. 255; K.R. Brady, 'The brief for the defence of the trial of John and Henry
Sheares in 1798', *J.R.S.A.I.*, lxvii (1937), 1. Counsel in treason cases in Ireland had been
allowed since 1765: 5 Geo. III, c.21.

two witnesses.[30] In April 1795 in the Irish Commons, John Philpot Curran urged that Ireland should adopt this change. He garnered no support. Wolfe, the attorney general and future Viscount Kilwarden, remarked that the difference 'did not arise from casual omission but from serious consideration'.[31] In his summing-up in the Sheares' case, Carleton dealt with this line of argument stressing the absence of any corroboration rule was clearly the law in Ireland, as had been confirmed on two recent occasions by the courts. Equally damning was Carleton's conclusion, on the evidence produced against the two brothers, that one overt act could certainly be corroborated by a different overt act.[32]

The trials of McCann and Byrne threw up no new significant legal arguments. The informer, Thomas Reynolds, was a key witness for the crown and much time and energy were expended by the defence team in the attempt to impeach Reynolds' credibility. Both accused were convicted, and subsequently executed, Mc Cann on 19 July, Byrne on the 28th.[33]

Oliver Bond was to be blessed with better fortune, though he did not live long to enjoy it. His trial, fated to be the last in the series, was unusual in that four of the petty jurors chosen to try him did not exactly come fresh to the task: one had sat on the jury that convicted Henry and John Sheares, a second on the one that had convicted McCann, and a third and a fourth on the one that had convicted Byrne.[34] The course of the trial did not run smoothly. A clerical error in the original indictment meant that a fresh indictment had to be prepared. Curran, Bond's counsel, objected in vain to damaging publicity in the press. There was uproar in court, too, when soldiers in attendance took umbrage at the tenor of Curran's observations. Drama took place even after the jury had retired when Bond sought the leave of the court to send in to the jury fresh documentary evidence. This was a declaration signed by McCann stating that Bond had been ignorant of the purpose behind the critical meeting of the United Irish leadership that had been held in the latter's house. The request was turned down.[35]

Bond was convicted and sentenced to death. The sentence was deferred but ultimately was never carried out. Following the adoption on 29 July of the 'Newgate' (or 'Kilmainham') treaty, Bond gained an indefinite respite. Under this accord, an assortment of state prisoners still untried, in return for promise

30 Treason Act 1695, 7 & 8 Will. III, c.3, s.2 (Eng.).
31 *Parl. reg. Ire.*, xv, 29 Apr. 1795. The discrepancy was finally ended by statute in 1821: see 1 & 2 Geo. IV, c.24 (U.K.).
32 Howell, *State trials*, xxvii, cols. 387–88.
33 Howell, *State trials*, xxvii, col. 399f; *The trial of John McCann for high treason* (Cork, n.d. [1798?]); Howell, *State trials*, xxvii, col. 457f.; *The trial of W.M. Byrne, esq., for high treason* (s.l. [Cork], 1798).
34 Sir Thomas Lighton, Richard Jackson, William Pike and Joshua Manders, respectively. Howell's *State trials* conveniently lists the petty jury panels in the four trials.
35 Howell, *State trials*, xxvii, col. 523f.; *The trial of Mr Oliver Bond, merchant of the city of Dublin for high treason* ([Cork], 1798).

of their lives, agreed to confess their guilt and accept banishment and exile.[36] Bond himself died, apparently of natural causes,[37] on 6 September, whilst still in custody, and awaiting transfer out of the country.[38]

The ordinary courts of the land thus remained open for business and this stark fact, however much it was later to be played down,[39] constituted the second prong of the attack on the government's resort to the prerogative to install martial law and trial by court-martial. In January, Arthur Browne had warned that martial law could not be availed of 'in time of peace when the king's courts are open'.[40] The warning was sedulously ignored until in November, in dramatic cir-

36 On the background to the accord of 29 July, see Cornwallis to Portland, 26 July 1798, Edward Cooke to William Wickham, 28 July 1798: *Cornwallis correspondence*, ii, pp 372–4, 377–8; 'Narrative', sent by Cornwallis to Portland, 14 Sept. 1798: *Castlereagh correspondence*, i, pp 347–53; Pakenham, *Year of liberty*, pp 287–9; McDowell, *Ireland*, pp 655–8. McDowell is in error in stating that Bond's trial was, in consequence of the accord, not proceeded with (ibid., p. 656). It was Neilson's that was affected. The consequential Banishment Act is discussed below.

37 Samuel Neilson was never brought to trial, but did have 'his day in court' when he gave evidence at the inquest on Bond. The evening before Bond died, both of them had dined on sheep's heart and other food and had downed, in the company of two others, a bottle of wine. They had played 'matches of ball' in the prison yard until dusk. Then there had been more drinking – of spirits and punch. According to Neilson, Bond complained he was still hungry, and, accompanied by yet more drinking, had eaten more sheep's heart 'dressed for supper' as well as some cold mutton: *Irish Builder*, xxx (1888), 124.

38 Both before and after the Rising proper, there were many more treason trials in the ordinary courts (as well as trials on rebellion charges before courts-martial). Details of these other treason trials are a good deal less accessible, if extant at all. There were some acquittals. Edward Hay, reflecting on his own treason trial at the 1799 Wexford summer assizes, drew attention to a further difference that then existed between the law in England and that in Ireland. Whereas in England the accused enjoyed the privilege of not being confronted by witnesses other than those named in advance, that was not the position in Ireland in his experience: Hay, *Insurrection of county of Wexford*, pp xxx–xi. Besides creating martyrs for the pantheon of Irish republicanism, the Dublin treason trials of June–July 1798 bequeathed a legacy of a very different kind. It long remained a mystery whence was derived the formula universally employed by the trial judge in criminal cases when directing the jury, that there has to be 'proof beyond a reasonable doubt'. In 1876, an American scholar advanced the claim that the formula was invented by counsel in the 1798 Irish treason trials defence team, Leonard McNally, one of the Razumovs of the period. See *McCormick on evidence*, 2nd ed. (St Paul, Minn., 1972), p. 799, n.88. I am grateful for this reference to Paul O'Connor.

39 Notice, however, the views of Cornwallis in late July – Cornwallis to Major-general Ross, 24 July 1798: *Cornwallis correspondence*, ii, p. 371. 'Except in the instance of the six state trials that are going on here, there is no law either in town or country but martial law, and you know enough of that to see all the horrors of it, even in the best administration of it'. Note, too, the claim put forward on behalf of pacification in the preamble to the Suppression of Rebellion Act, enacted in Mar 1799, 'Whereas by the wise and salutary exercise of his majesty's undoubted prerogative in executing martial law, for defeating and disarming such armed and rebellious force, and in bringing divers rebels and traitors to punishment in the most speedy and summary manner, the peace of this kingdom has been so far restored as to permit the course of the common law partially to take place ... '

40 McDowell, *Ireland*, p. 597.

cumstances, the court of king's bench decided to pay heed to it, forcing the government to adopt remedial measures which thereafter rendered trial by court-martial legally impregnable.

Following his capture off the Donegal coast, Theobald Wolfe Tone was tried by court-martial in Dublin on Saturday 10 November, convicted and sentenced to death. Tone himself did not question the competency of the court-martial to try him. Two days later, on the Monday in the king's bench, John Philpot Curran sought a writ of *habeas corpus* to enable the legality of the detention of Tone (then about to be executed) to be tested. Viscount Kilwarden, the chief justice, granted the writ to the plain discomfiture of the military. The exercise was to prove abortive: Tone had already cut his throat and died in prison on 19 November.[41]

In his argument before the judges of king's bench, Curran contended that, as Tone held no commission under the crown, no court-martial could have cognisance of his case whilst the ordinary courts lay open. He went on:

> In times when war was raging, when man was opposed to man in the field, courts-martial might be endured, but every law authority is with me, while I stand upon this sacred and immutable principle of the constitution – that martial law and civil law are incompatible, and that the former must cease with the existence of the latter.[42]

Kilwarden, in acceding to the motion to grant *habeas corpus*, clearly signalled that there was a great deal to be said for Curran's point of view.

More than a flutter occurred in the legal dovecotes as a result of Kilwarden's decision.[43] The suspension of trial by court-martial was ordered and other steps taken to avoid a clash of jurisdictions.[44] The impasse prompted, quite literally, a return to the drawing-board. With the passing into law of the Suppression of Rebellion Act on 25 Mar 1799,[45] Cornwallis and the government believed that

---

41 See, conveniently, Howell, *State trials*, xxvii, col. 614f. For further accounts of Tone's trial, see O'Higgins, *Bibliography of Irish trials*, p. 175.

42 Howell, *State trials*, xxvii, col. 625.

43 McDowell, *Ireland*, pp 664–5. Cf. Cooke to Wickham, 12 Nov. 1798: *Cornwallis correspondence*, ii, pp 434–5. Cooke, the very day of Kilwarden's decision, wrote to the under-secretary of the Home Department in London that the Castle now feared a flood of *habeas corpus* applications, especially from prisoners detained on board tenders. Four days later, Castlereagh, in a lengthy and measured comment, drew out the full implications in a fascinating review of government policy on the use of courts-martial since May – Castlereagh to Wickham, 16 Nov. 1798: *Castlereagh correspondence*, i, pp 445–8. See, too, Cornwallis to Portland, 10 Dec. 1798: *Cornwallis correspondence*, iii, pp 10–11.

44 McDowell reports a contemporary rumour that if Tone's conviction by court-martial had been nullified and the attempt had then been made to re-try him before a civil court, his lawyers would have argued a violation of the principle against double jeopardy: *Ireland*, p. 663. That principle had recently been upheld in celebrated Irish criminal proceedings: *The King* v. *Foy* (1788), Vernon & Scriven, p. 540.

45 39 Geo. III, c.11.

they had found the right solution to their various difficulties. This major piece of legislation, however difficult its birth, applied across a very broad front indeed.[46] It regularised resort to trial by court-martial, and thus, at one fell swoop, answered those critics who had insisted all along that a statutory foundation was an essential requirement. Intriguingly, Castlereagh, in explaining the measure, by no means accepted that criticism; he argued that it was the success of the process of normalisation that necessitated the securing of a parliamentary mandate:

> Upon every great emergency the executive government was bound not to wait for the previous sanction of the legislature, but boldly to meet the emergency for the safety of the Kingdom, relying upon its own responsibility, and trusting to the future approbation of Parliament; but that this principle disappeared when the emergency was not transitory, and when the mischief to be obviated was permanent, and that a new principle then arose, which was, that the Parliament never ought to suffer for any long period a continued deviation from the ordinary practice of the Constitution, but that it ought entirely to create such a deviation if improper, or to legalise it if necessary.[47]

The Act addressed itself to the specific argument raised in Wolfe Tone's case by stipulating that trial by court-martial remained legal, and thus immune from challenge, even where the ordinary courts remained open. No doubt, either, was to attach to the scope of the remit which courts-martial enjoyed. They were given seisin of

> all offences committed in furtherance of the said rebellion, whether such persons shall have been taken in open arms against his majesty, or shall have been otherwise concerned in the said rebellion, or in aiding, or any manner assisting the same.

Recourse to the court of king's bench or any other common law court to challenge actions taken by the military under order of the lord lieutenant for the suppression of rebellion was also forbidden. And, for good measure, the same Suppression of Rebellion Act also sought to curtail the availability of *habeas corpus*, a device to which, in the vacuum created by Kilwarden's decision, counsel acting on behalf of a number of prisoners and detainees had chosen increasingly to resort, as, indeed, had originally been feared would turn out to be true.[48]

46 See Cornwallis to Portland, 14, 23, 28 Feb., 12 Mar. 1799: *Cornwallis correspondence*, iii, pp 60–3, 66–70, 74–6; and also Castlereagh to Portland, 28 Feb. 1799: *Castlereagh correspondence*, ii, p. 189. The original draft bill had been prepared in Dublin. It was to be amended to avoid the creation of the impression (which London had detected) that doubt surrounded the legality of Camden's proclamation of 24 May.
47 As related in Cornwallis to Portland, 28 Feb. 1799: *Cornwallis correspondence*, iii, pp 68–70.
48 Suppression of Rebellion Act 1799, ss.1,2,3,5.

The provisions of this major piece of legislation remained in force, following various extensions, down to June 1802,[49] at which date the rising and its aftermath was officially pronounced at an end. The legislation itself, where it purported to regularise the use of courts-martial, lay at the heart of the quarrel between Rowe and Hargrave on the legitimacy of the use of the prerogative by Camden in his proclamation of martial law on 24 May. For Rowe, the main thrust of the Suppression of Rebellion Act was not the provision of retrospective validity for trial by court-martial, but rather the institution of an efficient mechanism for inflicting condign punishment on 'rebels' who continued to perpetrate criminal offences. Sadly, in his estimation, trial by jury had been found wanting

> because ... the country was so universally disaffected, the contagion of rebellion and the United Irishmen had spread so far, that on some trial a rotten sheep, a tainted member of the community got on the jury, and no conviction could, in such case, take place. The encouragement it gave was appalling. There was no remedy to save the country, but the appointment of another tribunal in which no tainted member, no rotten sheep could insinuate himself. The legislature selected the military and martial law; and rebels, and their crimes, were, by its operation, swept from the face of Ireland.[50]

Rowe's analysis, drawn up in 1821 and published three years later, is not contradicted by the contemporary justification supplied in the preamble to the Suppression of Rebellion Act itself, although the latter is noticeably coy over the precise criticisms being levelled at the ordinary courts. The preamble included the following passage:

> And whereas many persons who have been guilty of the most daring and horrid acts of cruelty and outrage, in furtherance and prosecution of the said rebellion, and who have been taken by his majesty's forces employed for the suppression of the same, have availed themselves of such partial restoration of the ordinary course of the common law [as has taken place] to evade the punishment of their crimes, whereby it has become necessary for parliament to interpose.

Naturally, it is possible to interpret the allusion as being directed as much at the perceived liberality of the courts in granting *habeas corpus* as at the phenomenon of corrupt and perverse petty juries. If there was implicit in the govern-

---

49 40 Geo. III, c.2, 41 Geo. III, cc.14, 61 (U.K.).
50 Rowe, *Reports*, p. 1. Edward Hay's evidence for County Wexford, it will be recalled, paints a very different picture of jury trial there: *Insurrection Wexford*, pp xxvii-viii.

ment's whole approach indications of a marked preference for the use of courts-martial, the reputation of the latter in this last phase of the normalisation of conditions could not remain unalloyed. An anecdote recounted by Martha McTier as regards County Antrim merits being set beside Edward Hay's more sanguine evaluation of matters in County Wexford which has already been noted:

> Some weeks ago one of the men condemned by a court-martial here to be hanged was taken for that purpose to Ballymena, where on the market day he was brought out. He was near 70 years of age. Two men, taken up on suspicion of being concerned in the whipping of an informer who died of it, were ordered to hang the old one. Both refused, and in consequence were struck and cut in a most inhuman manner, when the old man, beseeching them to put the rope about his neck to save themselves since it was impossible he could escape, one of them appearing to consent, his father burst from the surrounding crowd and commanded his son to meet death at the foot of the gallows first. He was then struck and sent to prison, and the affair concluded for that day by the condemned putting the rope about his own neck, knotted so as by getting a pull his thread of life was broken for ever ... How my infant mind revolted at the praises I heard daily bestowed on the mildness of our laws, though their praise dropped from my father's mouth.[51]

Under attack here was not so much court-martial itself but the entire system for maintaining law and order in which this species of tribunal, albeit temporarily, filled so conspicuous a role.

In October 1798, three crucial legislative initiatives spawned major legal and administrative difficulties in the months ahead. Each originated in the resolve of the crown to visit retribution upon those individuals judged to be principally responsible for the rebellion. A link between the three statutes in question is forged by a fourth which, paradoxically, carries the imprint of a professedly merciful and beneficent sovereign. The latter is known as the General Pardon Act.[52] Another statute promising a general pardon is to be found in the Irish legislative record back in the reign of James I, but that seventeenth-century example displays rather different characteristics.[53]

The General Pardon Act, along with a large number of other statutes still to be examined, received the royal assent on 6 October.[54] Cornwallis had succeeded Camden as lord lieutenant in June, holding that post in tandem with that of

51 Martha McTier to William Drennan, May 1799: *Drennan letters*, p. 292.
52 38 Geo. III, c.55.
53 11, 12 & 13 Jas. I, c.9.
54 Delay in the enactment of the Pardon Act and the linked Attainder Act, attributable to the need for both measures to receive George III's prior approval, had been anticipated from an

commander-in-chief. The measure reflected Cornwallis' determination and that of the government to return the country, and especially those districts most caught up in the rising, to something approaching normality as swiftly as possible. Its main features had been well advertised in advance. A key clause declared that all treasons, felonies and seditious acts perpetrated in the prosecution of the rising or in the suppression of it, up until 24 August, were 'pardoned and discharged'. Straightaway, however, important exceptions to this pattern of generosity were highlighted. Two other aspects of the broad legislative scheme merit a mention: first, the relationship of the measure to the principle that underlay existing acts of indemnity does not seem to have been thought through;[55] secondly, the legislation explicitly did not capture future events nor did it touch anything done by either rebel or crown forces after 24 August.

The preamble to the General Pardon Act is cast in language which affords a glimpse into the government's thinking at yet another critical juncture in Irish affairs. The government remained aware, the preamble asserted, that some people were still bent 'on the ruin of the country'. The generosity of the legislative package would 'raise a sense of gratitude' and prevent such persons from 'committing like acts of treason in future when mercy may not be expedient for the public welfare though that would be agreeable to his majesty's inclinations'; in short, that all would be 'induced with more cheerfulness and affection to apply themselves to the discharge of their duties to his majesty'.

The orotundity of diction may have come from the pen of a sycophant. Nevertheless, it would be wrong to dismiss the crown's policy as plain wishful thinking. An identical philosophy had been espoused at an early date by the crown's military commanders; rebel rank and file had chosen to rely on it; and, after the latter had suffered their first reverses in the field, surrenders had been secured with comparative ease. All this then speaks for itself. Whatever about the degree of acceptance the promise of a general pardon did in fact evoke either at the time or subsequently, attention for present purposes must necessarily focus on the recital by the General Pardon Act of the various persons who were to be excepted from its scope. It is no brief inventory: in all, twelve categories are listed, together with 31 named individuals.[56] Included are:

> all officers in the rebel army;
> all members of executive committees of the United Irishmen at national, provincial or county level;

early date – Cornwallis to Portland, 8 July 1798: *Cornwallis correspondence*, ii, pp 358–61. See, too, *Castlereagh correspondence*, i, pp 243–6, 252–7, 260–2, 312–14.
55 The omission was rectified in the statute 39 Geo. III, c.50. But see, too, Wickham to Castlereagh, 9 Aug. 1798, Castlereagh to Wickham, 12 Aug. 1798: *Castlereagh correspondence*, i, pp 256, 261.
56 38 Geo. III, c.55, s.5.

all persons detained since January 1795 on treason charges (an allusion to
all those who continued to be held under the various *habeas corpus*
Suspension Acts);[57]

all rebels among the crown forces;

all persons convicted by court-martial since 24 May of being concerned in
the rising (some of whom had already been sentenced and executed);

all persons concerned in the rising and still out on their keeping who
were to surrender themselves by the appointed day – a cross-reference
to the Surrender Act which would go into detail and name names; and

all persons to be attainted of treason by act of parliament – a cross-reference to the Attainder Act which again would go into detail and identify
the three individuals being attainted (all of whom were already dead).

A subsequent clause in the legislation stipulated that all 'excepted persons'
might have 'the benefit of pardon upon condition of banishment or otherwise'.[58]
This, in turn, was an allusion to the Banishment Act passed into law the same
day, which supplied the statutory confirmation of the July treaty entered into
between the government and the leading United Irish state prisoners.

Borrowing a strategy with an impressive historical pedigree – in Ireland it had
been employed under Elizabeth to deal with rebels[59] and earlier in the eighteenth
century with notorious outlaws[60] – the Surrender Act identified fifty-one persons by name and declared that, unless they surrendered themselves to the civil
authorities before 1 December 1798, they would be deemed attainted of high
treason.[61] If subsequently apprehended, they would be deemed liable to be sentenced to death without further inquiry. 'Civil authorities' were defined as a
judge of the court of king's bench or any magistrate.

The Surrender Act provoked a celebrated lawsuit in the case of one of the 51
persons listed – James Napper Tandy.[62] Tandy had been arrested in Hamburg
late in November 1798 with the permission of its senate and at the request of the
British envoy. He was still in custody there on 1 December and had not thus vol-

---

57 These acts provided for the indefinite detention of persons charged with treason, suspicion of
   treason or treasonable practices. Warrants had to issue from the lord lieutenant, the chief secretary or privy council. See 37 Geo. III, c.1, 38 Geo. III, c.14, 40 Geo. III, c.18.
58 38 Geo. III, c.55, s.8.
59 See 12 Eliz. I, c.5.
60 Neal Garnham, *The courts, crime and the criminal law in Ireland* (Dublin, 1996), p. 188.
61 38 Geo. III, c.80. For evidence of early planning of such a measure see Lord Grenville to [—],
   9 May 1798: *Castlereagh correspondence*, i, pp 201–4. For the drawing up of the actual list of
   names, see *Commons' Jn. Ire.*, xvii, pt. 2, p. dccccxlii.
62 *Proceedings in the court of king's bench ... on an issue joined between the rt. hon. John Toler, A.-G.,*
   on the part of the king, and James Napper Tandy and Harvey Morris ... (Dublin, 1800); Howell,
   State trials, xxvii, col. 1191; Rowe, *Reports*, p. 472; R.J. Coughlan, *Napper Tandy* (Dublin,
   1976), p. 152.

untarily surrendered in Ireland by the prescribed date. Toler, the attorney general, took his stand on the strict letter of the statute. Following consultation with the prime serjeant and the solicitor general, he initiated proceedings in the king's bench in February 1800 to have Tandy and his associate, Harvey Morris (also detained in Hamburg), formally sentenced to death. Toler relied on the short argument that the terms of the legislation had not been complied with. Curran, Tandy's counsel, maintained that there was a lacuna in the legislation since compliance had for Tandy been a complete impossibility; the only just outcome was to let Tandy stand trial for treason.

Curran may have exaggerated when he claimed that the proceedings were 'fascinating to Europe'. They were certainly strange. The court left it to a jury to decide whether Tandy had or had not complied with the Surrender Act. The latter, doubtless impressed by the curious twist events had taken as much as by the pleas of Curran, returned a verdict in Tandy's favour after a few minutes. Toler immediately accepted that this verdict disposed of the Harvey Morris case as well.[63]

No government action taken in the wake of the rising generated so much controversy as the decision, announced on 27 July, to bring in a bill of attainder against Lord Edward FitzGerald, Beauchamp Bagenal Harvey and Cornelius Grogan.[64] A considerable interval had elapsed since the Irish parliament had last been invited to pass such a measure; this had been in 1715 in respect of the Old Pretender, his adherents and abettors.[65] Under the law still in force, forfeiture of one's real and personal estate to the crown followed inexorably from conviction of treason at common law. Special legislation was thus necessary to work an attainder in all three instances: FitzGerald had never been tried, let alone convicted, having died in Newgate on 4 June; Harvey and Grogan's convictions of rebellion had been returned by court-martial sitting later the same month in Wexford. Other names might have been added to the government's short-list, but the choice of these three prominent individuals, each possessed of an amount of landed wealth, propagated the cryptic message that the Castle was particularly eager to convey: the wealthier landowner who joined the rebels was to be left

---

63 Tandy was finally tried on a charge of treason at the Donegal spring assizes in Apr. 1801. Pleading guilty, he was sentenced to death but reprieved on condition of his agreeing to go into exile. Following the Peace of Amiens, Tandy sailed for Bordeaux from Dublin in Mar 1802: Coughlan, *Napper Tandy*, pp 197, 209.

64 *Commons' Jn. Ire.*, xvii, pt. 1, p. 356. The duke of Leinster registered an early protest, a harbinger of what was to come – Duke of Leinster to Cornwallis, 6 Aug. 1798, Cornwallis to Leinster, 11 Aug. 1798: *Cornwallis correspondence*, ii, pp 384, 385.

65 2 Geo. I, c.4. For still earlier instances, see 28 Hen. VIII, c.1 (earl of Kildare and others), 11 Eliz. 1, sess. 3, c.1 (Shane Oneile), 12 Eliz. I, sess. 2, c.1 (Thomas Queverford), 13 Eliz. I, c.3 (John FitzGerald), 27 Eliz. I, c.1 (James Eustace, Lord Baltinglas), 28 Eliz. I, c.7 (earl of Desmond and others), 28 Eliz. I, c.8 (John Brown and others), 11, 12 & 13 Jas. I, c.4 (earl of Tyrone and others), 5 Jas. II, c.30 (divers rebels).

in no doubt that he ran the risk of having his property seized, with all the serious repercussions that that entailed for his family. An additional consideration was the attraction to government of being able to raise a sum of perhaps £30,000 to £40,000 to help defray general government expenses or satisfy the compensation claims of loyalists that the government had just decided to meet. Treasury loans and the sale of quit rents[66] would furnish a portion of the finance required, but to let slip the opportunity to secure windfall income from the sale of estates of attainted rebels, apart from affronting the sensitivities of loyalists, would have appeared to border on negligence.

In the excitement of these summer months, the attainder bill secured an easy passage through both the Irish Commons and the Irish Lords. An attempt to kill the measure off at the bill's third reading in the commons on 27 August failed miserably, on a vote of 9–63.[67] In the lords, opposition was even more derisory. Parliamentary time expended on the progress of this single measure, nevertheless, was to be substantial. Witnesses were called to give evidence on the courts-martial of Harvey and Grogan and to establish the treasonable activity of Lord Edward. Testimony was also received from the high sheriff for County Wexford as well as from the solicitor for forfeited estates, presumably in order that light might be shed on the nature and extent of the lands scheduled for appropriation.[68] Parliamentary discussion, moreover, was protracted by oral hearings into the large number of petitions presented against the attainder bill itself by those its provisions threatened with substantial losses of income: widows, children and other next of kin. Petitions came from, among others, Lady Pamela FitzGerald and her three children,[69] from Bagenal Harvey's widow and his surviving brother James.[70] The two surviving brothers of the bachelor Cornelius Grogan also entered their protest: John, a lieutenant in the 5th and 15th regiment of dragoons, wounded when covering the retreat from Enniscorthy on 27 May, and Overstreet, a barrister. Thomas, another brother (as John and Overstreet's petition did not fail to point out) was a captain in the Castletown yeomanry cavalry, and had been killed at the battle of Arklow.[71]

As happened with the act of attainder directed at the regicides in England in 1660, transfers of interests in land before certain prescribed dates effected by those attainted were exempted from forfeiture.[72] An early draft insisted, as in the

---

66 For special legislative enactments in these areas, see 38 Geo. III, cc.58 and 72.

67 *Commons' Jn. Ire.*, xvii, pt. 1, p. 369.

68 For lists of witnesses summoned by the commons, see *Commons' Jn. Ire.*, xvii, pt. 1, pp 359, 361, 363 and 364 (9–18 Aug. 1798).

69 *Commons' Jn. Ire.*, xvii, pt. 1, p. 358 (9 Aug.); *Lords' Jn. Ire.*, viii, p. 137 (29 Aug.). For Curran's address in support of Lady Pamela's petition, see Leslie Hale, *John Philpot Curran: His life and times* (London, 1958), p. 203.

70 *Commons' Jn. Ire.*, xvii, pt. 1, pp 359, 360 (9–14 Aug. 1798).

71 *Commons' Jn. Ire.*, xvii, pt. 1, p. 357 (31 July 1798).

72 12 Chas. II, c.30 (Eng.).

case of the regicides and in that of the Irish attainder of Viscount Baltinglas in 1585,[73] on the registration of these transfers, but at some undisclosed stage this requirement was dropped. Other changes made to the draft bill were relatively minor.[74] The critical dates from which the three parties' treasonable activity was to be reckoned were eventually fixed at 1 December 1797 in the case of Fitz-Gerald, 5 June 1798 in that of Harvey and 1 June 1798 in that of Grogan.

By late August it was plain that no parliamentary pressure applied in Ireland would force the abandonment of the attainder bill. Rebuffed in Ireland, Lord Edward's family and their Whig connections in England drew up a petition to the king, urging him to withhold his assent. George III was resident in Weymouth at the time; this petition reached him on 29 September, the day after he had authorized Cornwallis' commission for attaching the royal assent to the various Irish parliamentary measures that were to receive it on 6 October.[75] This late initiative may have proved abortive, but the text of the petition itself, dealing as it does with questions of major constitutional significance, makes instructive reading.[76] Its author, Sir Arthur Pigott,[77] in a document of great length, emphasized that within the English constitutional tradition, it was virtually unheard of to pass an act of attainder against anyone who had never been convicted of anything – Lord Edward's situation in fact. True, there appeared to be a precedent in 1660 in the case of certain of the regicides, but the circumstances obtaining then, Pigott argued, were markedly different.

With the passing of the Attainder Act, the estates of FitzGerald, Harvey and Grogan stood forfeited to the crown. The exact extent of the sanctioned forfeiture proved contentious, and litigation ensued. Citing irregularities in the escheators' conduct of the inquisitions held in counties Wexford and Carlow into the Harvey and Grogan estates, James Harvey moved to have the result of the inquisition into his brother Bagenal's property set aside. Wrangling continued in the courtroom. Toler, the attorney general, availed of an argument also aired in 1617 in relation to the Desmond attainder of 1586: in Ireland, unlike in England, the complainant could not proceed by a simple traverse, but would have to sue out a petition of right.[78] A procedural agreement then thrashed out

73 See 27 Eliz. I, c.1.
74 Clauses were added to save the rights of Lord Edward's younger brother, Lord Robert FitzGerald, to any dignity he might inherit and to facilitate the partition of lands that Lord Monck held in common with Cornelius Grogan.
75 See the further petition addressed to the king by Emily, duchess of Leinster, Lord Edward's mother, adverting to these matters, which was presented to the king by the duke of Richmond on 24 Oct. 1798: Thomas Moore, *The life and death of Lord Edward FitzGerald* (new ed., London, n.d. [1932]), pp 268–9. Moore's biography of Lord Edward first appeared in 1831.
76 For the full text see Moore, *Life and death of Lord Edward FitzGerald*, pp 257–67.
77 Pigott (1749–1819) served as attorney-general in 'the ministry of all the talents' 1806–7, was knighted in 1806 and conducted an unsuccessful impeachment of Henry Dundas, 1st Viscount Melville, in the same year: see entry in *D.N.B.*
78 Rowe, *Reports*, pp 149–57; *Cal. S.P. Ire., 1615–1625*, p. 181.

led to a trial at bar in Dublin in November 1800.[79] Here, the jury held in favour of the crown on one facet of the ongoing dispute – the validity of a conveyance supposedly executed by Bagenal in Wexford gaol on 28 or 29 May 1798, i.e. just a few days short of the critical date upon which his treason was deemed to have commenced. A new inquisition was sped, however, and on this second occasion, the outcome was much more to James Harvey's liking: lands which it was now accepted Bagenal had bought in trust for his brother in 1794 were adjudged to be exempt from forfeiture.[80]

The Grogan brothers, satisfied (largely on the strength of their own loyalist credentials) that they too had been hard done by, pressed for amelioration of their lot, going so far as to seek the historical advice of Francis Hargrave in 1805 on how to reverse the attainder on their brother Cornelius.[81] The plan was not pursued, but, after a decent interval, the lands seized under the Harvey and Grogan attainders were apparently quietly restored.

More information is immediately forthcoming on the fate of Lord Edward's inheritance. Following the attainder, his Kildare estate was sold in Chancery under foreclosure of the mortgage, to which the attorney general was himself a party. The purchaser, who paid £10,500, was William Ogilvie, Lord Edward's stepfather. Ogilvie's competent management enabled all the judgment debts against the estate and the mortgage itself to be paid off, and the estate was ultimately resettled on Lord Edward's son, Edward Fox FitzGerald, with annuities charged on it in favour of his daughters Pamela and Lucy. The Attainder Act itself had applied the medieval doctrine of 'corruption of blood' to Lord Edward's progeny, a corollary of the legislation that was to be attacked by relatives and friends of the United Irish leader in 1799 and again in 1815, but to no avail.[82] Finally, however, the stigma was removed in a private act of parliament introduced by Lord Liverpool in 1819.[83] The prince regent had earlier intimated his acquiescence.[84] This contentious, and often postponed, remedial measure thus at long last added Lord Edward's children to the select list of all those who

79 Harvey had moved successfully for the trial of this compromise action, *Flint* v. *Reeves*, to be transferred to Dublin 'on account of the great prejudices at that time prevailing in the county of Wexford': Rowe, *Reports*, p. 157.

80 Ibid., pp 158–66.

81 Hargrave, *Jurisconsult exercitations*, i, p. 399.

82 Moore, *Lord Edward*, pp 275–9.

83 59 Geo. III, no. 3 (U.K.). This is a private Act which is not printed. For the immediate background, see Moore, *Lord Edward*, pp 277–9.

84 It was to the latter that Byron addressed a celebratory sonnet on receiving the news at Ravenna in July of the same year: 'To be the father of the fatherless,/To stretch the hand from the throne's height, and raise/His offspring, who expired in other days/To make thy Sire's sway by a Kingdom less/This is to be a Monarch, and repress/Envy into unutterable praise': 'To the Prince Regent – on the repeal of the bill of attainder agst Ld. E. FitzGerald July 1819', Lord Byron, *The complete poetical works*, ed. J.J. McGann (7 vols , Oxford, 1980–93), iv, p. 242 (no. 337).

in Ireland's constitutional past had likewise obtained an identical statutory 'restitution of blood'.[85]

The Banishment Act, the third government initiative, and likewise operative from 6 October 1798, gave express effect to the Newgate/ Kilmainham treaty of 29 July.[86] Ninety named individuals, having shown, as it was put, 'contrition for their rebellion', and having sought mercy, were pardoned on condition of their agreeing to be transported, exiled or banished. These ninety, made up of those obviously viewed by the crown as the more dangerous revolutionaries, formed a special category within the body of the General Pardon Act. The definitive list of names had been drawn up over the summer, members of the lords proposing their own additions during discussion of the draft bill in August.[87] Covered by the legislation, in addition to the ninety named individuals, was an indeterminate further group comprising such persons as had been convicted by court-martial and ordered to be transported or banished.[88] Banishment meant departure from his majesty's dominions; to return exposed the offender to the risk of a treason trial and a capital sentence. Moreover, passing into any country at war with his majesty constituted constructive treason and was punishable as such. The legislation accordingly forbade those to be banished from proceeding to France, Spain, the United Provinces or anywhere under the control of France or Spain.

The original idea had been to ship the contingent of United Irish prisoners who were signatories to the treaty off to the United States. President Adams, however, refused to admit them, whereupon, in April 1799, after some further delay, they were transferred to Fort George in Inverness-shire.[89] Situated at the end of a narrow spit of land jutting into the Moray Firth, the fort, an irregular polygon with six bastions, was defended on the landward side by a ditch, a covert way, a glacis, two lunettes and a ravelin. The area was destitute of houses and trees, which made it easy to keep the prisoners in safe custody without imposing upon them 'any restrictions prejudicial to their health'. A clause was inserted in United Kingdom legislation of 1801 to prevent the mounting of any legal challenge to this transfer of state prisoners to Scotland.[90]

---

85 From the reign of Elizabeth I, the young earl of Kildare, his brother and sisters, Laurence Delahide and Taaffe's wife; from the reign of James I (seemingly), the daughters of the earl of Desmond; and from the reign of James II, William Ryan: 11 Eliz. I, sess. 4, c.2; 27 Eliz.I, c.2; 28 Eliz.I, c.7; Mary Hayden, 'The origin and development of heads of bills in the Irish parliament', in *J.R.S.A.I.*, lv (1925), 113; 5 Jas. II, c.35.

86 38 Geo. III, c.78. On the background to the 'treaty' see above, n. 36.

87 *Commons' Jn. Ire.*, xvii, pt. 2, p. dccccxiv.

88 An amending statute in 1799 (39 Geo. III, c.36) filled an apparent lacuna in the authority to deal with those in this group who, pending banishment, had been released on bail.

89 *Castlereagh correspondence*, i, p. 413; McDowell, *Ireland*, p. 657; Pakenham, *Year of liberty*, pp 350–51.

90 Ibid., ii, p. 377; D.L. Macnie and Moray McLaren (eds), *The new Shell guide to Scotland* (London, 1977), p. 390; 41 Geo. III, c.26, s.7 (U.K.). In June 1802, after the Peace of Amiens, the prisoners were permitted to proceed to France. Many of the more eminent among them did subsequently emigrate to the United States: Pakenham, *Year of liberty*, pp 350–1.

The remaining legal questions thrown up by the rising and the manner of its suppression, related to two isolated topics: the limits of the indemnity concerning the civil and military authorities, and the mechanism for deciding claims under the scheme put in place to compensate suffering loyalists for property losses.

It was a sure sign of the growing unrest in the 1790s that legislation designed to indemnify civil and military personnel in respect of the excesses of their conduct was already in place long before the outbreak of the rising proper.[91] Such exceptional legislation could not operate prospectively, which explains the need, after May 1798, for a series of statutes regularly reiterating the principle of indemnity but confining its application on each occasion to different periods of time. There was one such statute in 1798, two more in 1799, and one in 1800; a fifth act followed in 1801 from the United Kingdom parliament.[92] The second act in the series, introduced in Mar 1799, furnished a grim acknowledgement of the sorts of conduct it was intended to cloak with legal immunity. Offenders and suspects, it recited, had been transported out of Ireland and offenders had been punished 'even with death', all without due authority.[93] Once it was shown that the actions it was sought to impugn had been carried out 'in order to suppress the said insurrections and rebellion and for the preservation of the public peace', those responsible were rendered exempt from legal suit.

That the scope of the protection afforded was by no means as broad as it seemed was laid down in an important case decided at the Clonmel spring assizes in Mar 1799: *Wright v. Fitzgerald*.[94] Bernard Wright, a teacher of French, had been flogged in June 1798 on the orders of Thomas Judkin Fitzgerald, then the Tipperary high sheriff. Under threat of a similar flogging, another individual had falsely identified Wright as a United Irishman, and the latter was then savagely beaten in what proved a fruitless endeavour to extort from him the names of other members of the movement.

The psychopathic zeal displayed by Fitzgerald on this occasion and, indeed, on others evoked considerable official unease,[95] but the language of the relevant Indemnity Act made it appear improbable that he could be successfully brought to book. However, in directing the jury on Wright's claim for assault, Judge

---

91 36 Geo. III, c.6.

92 38 Geo. III, c.74 (covering the period 1 Nov. 1797–5 Oct. 1798); 39 Geo. III, c.3 (6 Oct. 1798–25 Mar. 1799); 39 Geo. III, c.50 (8 Dec. 1797–31 May 1799); 40 Geo. III, c.89 (1 June 1799–31 July 1800); 41 Geo. III, c.104 (U.K.) (25 Mar. 1799–1 July 1801).

93 Cf. the reference of Cornwallis to 'the numberless murders that are hourly committed by our people without any process or examination whatever': Cornwallis to Major-General Ross, 24 July 1798: *Cornwallis correspondence*, ii, p. 371.

94 Howell, *State trials*, xxvii, p. 759. For a good deal of what follows I am indebted to Paul O'Higgins, '*Wright v. Fitzgerald* revisited', *Modern Law Review*, xxv (1962), 413.

95 See, e.g., Major R.T. (?) Wilson to Lord William Bentinck, 4 July 1798: P.R.O.N.I., *Irish official papers: private collection*, i (Belfast, 1973), p. 185. On FitzGerald, see McDowell, *Ireland*, pp 579–82.

Chamberlain clearly indicated that gratuitous cruelty – one possible interpretation of Fitzgerald's behaviour – would receive no protection from the courts. To
avail of any indemnity, the person claiming it would have to show that he had
seriously examined the conduct of the supposed rebel, and that in his dealings
he had been exclusively motivated by the desire to establish guilt, and not to
inflict torture. Above all, the judge continued, there was to be 'no deviation from
the common principles of humanity'. Chief Baron Avonmore concurred in
Chamberlain's direction. The jury returned a verdict in Wright's favour and
awarded him £500 damages. At the same assizes Fitzgerald again failed with a
defence based on the Indemnity Act, when successfully sued in slander by one
Porter, for having accused the latter of 'disloyalty'.[96]

Further lawsuits were pending at the time of these courtroom defeats and,
not surprisingly, Fitzgerald became alarmed. In May, he moved unsuccessfully in
the Exchequer to have the verdict in Wright's case set aside.[97] The month before,
he had also petitioned the Irish commons, craving relief.[98] At the time of
Wright's flogging, Fitzgerald contended that he was in possession of secret
information which he had not been at liberty to disclose, but now he dreaded the
consequences likely to flow from the two verdicts recorded against him. More
lawsuits over his exertions 'in repressing rebellion' were threatened, and money
was being collected locally (Fitzgerald alleged) to finance them. Initially, this
petition fell on deaf ears, but that was by no means the end of the matter: in the
third statute of our series, the Indemnity Act which came into force from June
1799, parliament widened considerably the protection that would be available to
civil and military authorities alike for the future. This represented an important
change, the full benefit of which Fitzgerald, in time, was to receive.

The new law laid it down that a plaintiff, in pressing any claim against a civil or
military authority, would have thenceforth to persuade the jury, before the latter
could reach any adverse verdict, that such authority had acted 'maliciously, and not
with the intent of suppressing rebellion or insurrection, or for the preservation of
the public peace or for the safety of the state'. The identical requirement was
repeated in the next Indemnity Act, that of 1800. Both these measures enshrined
another associated innovation, the introduction of an extremely short limitation
period – a mere three months – to apply universally in respect of four kinds of
civil action: claims for assault, battery, false imprisonment and slander. Once again,
a curb on unwelcome and distracting litigation was the unmistakable object.[99]

Insistence on proof of special malice signalled a critical new departure, raising fresh difficulties for plaintiffs as a class, a point that was straightaway dis-

96 For the identification of this second plaintiff as Porter, see Robert Day, 'Grand jury charges' (6
    vols, R.I.A.), ii, pp 237–40.
97 O'Higgins, '*Wright* v. *Fitzgerald* revisited', 416.
98 *Commons' Jn. Ire.*, xviii, pp 101–2.
99 39 Geo. III, c.50, 40 Geo. III, c.89.

cerned by another of Fitzgerald's adversaries, Matthew Scott, a merchant from Carrick-on-Suir. In June 1798, Fitzgerald had accused Scott of concealing pikes in a consignment of oats sent to New Ross and had been instrumental in incarcerating Scott in Clonmel gaol, from which the latter had only been freed on giving £20,000 bail. The military, after due deliberation, declined to press charges against Scott, whereupon the latter opened proceedings against Fitzgerald for assault and false imprisonment late in 1798. Twice in the spring of 1799, whilst his action remained unheard, Scott petitioned the Irish commons against any alteration in the law on indemnity, arguing that, if implemented, it would deprive him of his legal rights.[100] But to no avail. Scott's fears were subsequently realised when his action against Fitzgerald, heard before Judge Kelly at Clonmel, failed. Fitzgerald triumphed again in a further suit brought against him in 1801 by Francis Doyle, another Carrick merchant, also adjudicated upon in Clonmel.[101]

Fitzgerald was not the sole person to benefit from this change to the indemnity legislation. In the summer of 1801, Baron George applied it in favour of two Tipperary magistrates, Cooke Otway and Heron, in the concluding instalment of a saga that had split the magistracy in the county down the middle.[102] Otway had taken a leading part in convicting thirteen men for felling trees to manufacture pike heads. Thomas Going, a fellow magistrate, believing that these convictions had been obtained on false evidence, secured from the courts in Dublin an order of *certiorari* to have them quashed. Victory in the Four Courts spurred on the thirteen men to seek further redress against Otway and his allies. Baron George finally ruled that the errant magistrates had throughout been solely motivated by a desire to preserve the peace of the county. There had been no malice, and the magistrates accordingly were protected by the indemnity legislation.[103]

When the Irish parliament passed the earlier Indemnity Act of 1796, Grattan raised his voice in protest. He asked to be told the precise circumstances that had persuaded the government of the need to extend a blank cheque to civil and military authorities. Serjeant Stanley retorted that if Grattan had gained personal knowledge of the west of Ireland as he had from his own recent service there as a judge of assize, Grattan would not have made so foolish an intervention. It was not the case, Stanley continued, that when indemnity legislation was passed at

---

100 The details on the background to the dispute are derived from Scott's two petitions: see *Commons' Jn. Ire.*, xviii, pp 116–7 (19 Apr. 1799), pp 124–5 (27 Apr. 1799). There are subtle differences between the texts of the two petitions.

101 O'Higgins, '*Wright v. Fitzgerald* revisited', pp 417–19; *A report of an interesting case wherein Mr Francis Doyle ... was plaintiff, and Sir Thomas Judkin Fitzgerald ... defendant* (Dublin, 1803).

102 The report relates again to assizes at Clonmel.

103 Rowe, *Reports*, pp 406–9, 563. Cf., too, the case against Uniacke, id., pp 596–602, where *certiorari* was granted to quash convictions that members of the magistracy, in the opinion of king's bench, had conspired to obtain.

Westminster in the wake of London's Gordon Riots in the summer of 1780,[104] things were held up until some committee reported.[105] The bitterness of this exchange demonstrates how easily passions could be aroused over the indemnity issue. How English critics viewed the critical changes wrought by the second Irish Indemnity Act of 1799, or the manner of their introduction or their timing can only be conjectured. In 1801, when the parliament of the United Kingdom enacted the last Indemnity Act of the series, it chose to drop the requirement of special malice.[106]

Notice of a scheme to compensate loyalists in respect of property losses was given by Cornwallis in July 1798.[107] Planning went ahead at once, though the scheme itself only received statutory approval in October.[108] Important modifications to the original scheme were made by further legislation in 1799 and 1800.[109] Only losses occasioned by 'suffering loyalists' qualified for compensation. Commissioners were established with power to investigate claims and to make awards, although from the beginning it was envisaged that many decisions would be entrusted to local juries. In the early months, awards might be made in the form of interest-free secured loans but, following the introduction of specific scales of compensation in 1799, awards thereafter appear in all instances to have been outright payments. There were special clauses in the statutory scheme to combat perjury and the presentation of inflated claims. Difficulties arose over reinstatement conditions attached to awards made in respect of property destroyed or damaged. In 1800, the relevant rule was amended to provide an exemption in ease of landlords whose property losses could be blamed on disloyal tenants.[110]

A second change introduced in 1800 facilitated the launching of legal proceedings to force the repayment of compensation paid over erroneously.[111] Clearly targeted were individuals who could not be regarded as 'loyalists', however much they too may have suffered. These were times when certain individuals proved themselves unusually adept at establishing 'loyalist' credentials for compensation purposes but, equally, when others, cognisant of an award made in favour of a neighbour they viewed as an inveterate rebel, would conceive it their duty, without too much hesitation, to assume the role of informer.[112] Several decisions to grant compensation became the focus of controversy, none more so,

104 20 Geo. III, c.63 (G.B.).
105 *Hibernian Monthly Magazine*, 1796, pt. 1, p. 361.
106 41 Geo. III, c.104 (U.K.).
107 *Commons' Jn. Ire.*, xvii, pt. 1, p. 349.
108 38 Geo. III, c.68.
109 39 Geo. III, c.65, 40 Geo. III, c.49.
110 40 Geo. III, c.49, s.5.
111 Id., ss.9, 10.
112 Other factors operated, as is clear from Cornwallis' assessment of the machinations of 'loyal friends', penned in late 1799: 'The vilest informers are hunted out from the prisons to attack by the most barefaced perjury the lives of all who are suspected of being, or of having been,

perhaps, than that in favour of Captain Philip Hay in County Wexford. Championed by the earl of Kingston, the former Lord Kingsborough, Hay's adversaries commenced a suit against Hay to compel him to hand back his award. Their key contention was that in the course of the rising in Wexford, Hay had deserted the crown forces and became a rebel commander. The challenge did not prosper: quarter sessions in Wexford and the court of Exchequer in Dublin successively dismissed the suit against Hay – largely on procedural grounds, although neither court is likely to have been unimpressed by the fact that Hay had previously been tried by court-martial. Hay, in contrast to Cornelius Grogan, had successfully advanced a defence of duress and had, in consequence, been cleared of subversive conduct.[113] Kingston treated the decision of the military tribunal with contempt, regarding it as a blatant miscarriage of justice, and pursued his individual vendetta. Hay retaliated in kind, challenging Kingston in 1804 in broad daylight in a street in London to fight a duel.[114]

The records of the Suffering Loyalists Compensation Commission were destroyed in 1922. The main business of the commissioners had been concluded by 1804, though they continued to sit for two more years.[115] Two reports on their work, printed in the *Commons' journals*, contain a great deal of valuable information. The brief first report, produced in April 1799,[116] reprints guidance to the commissioners from Castlereagh on how to prioritise their investigations into claims and how to allocate compensation moneys among different categories of claimant.[117] The report furnishes details of some early awards, and concludes with an illuminating comment from the commission's secretary:

> Many applications have been laid before the Commissioners for rebuilding houses, for re-establishing manufactures, and for replacing cattle and implements of husbandry upon which they have been obliged to postpone making any grant, finding the state of the country in the respective places to be such that the houses, manufactures and cattle could not at the same time be protected from destruction or plunder.[118]

disaffected; and indeed every Roman Catholic of influence is in great danger.': Cornwallis to Ross, 16 Nov. 1799: *Cornwallis correspondence*, iii, pp 144–5.

113 *Proceedings of a court-martial held upon Captain Philip Hay, of the third regiment of foot* (Dublin, 1798).

114 George, earl of Kingston, *A narrative of the proceedings of the commissioners of suffering loyalists in the case of Capt. Philip Hay of the 18th Light Dragoons* (Dublin, 1807); *Cork Hist. Soc. Jn.*, x (1904), 190.

115 Herbert Wood, *A guide to the records deposited in the Public Record Office of Ireland* (Dublin, 1919), pp 143, 193.

116 *Commons' Jn. Ire.*, xviii, pp 106–7.

117 Castlereagh's letters of guidance are dated 3 July and 18 Sept. 1798, well before the commission was formally established by statute, or, in the case of the July letter, even announced.

118 *Commons' Jn. Ire,*, xviii, p. 107.

A second report, dated February 1800 and filling 340 pages in the *Commons' journals*,[119] is an exhaustive inventory of all claims submitted in a second batch, listing these by county, name of applicant, location of property and nature of loss. The adjudication of the commissioners, where one had been handed down, is added. As might have been anticipated, Wexford lodged the largest number of claims, grossing in value £315,191. Of that sum, the lesser amount of only £171,802 was ruled allowable, resulting, when adjustments were made to take account of the published compensation scales, in an actual payment out of £65,396. The largest single claim was that submitted by the marquis of Downshire: he claimed over £10,000 in respect of destruction of houses and furniture at Blessington, Co. Wicklow. The countess of Ormond (in the bill she submitted for over £8,000 of property loss at Castlecomer, County Kilkenny) cited destruction of 'house, plate, wines, furniture, library, paintings'. Prominent among the many large claims submitted from Wexford was one from the Church of Ireland bishop of Ferns. He sought £5,663 in respect of losses entered up as consisting of 'house, offices, demesne, furniture, plate, china, library, wines, banknotes'. Among more modest claims presented were three in respect of musical instruments lost or destroyed: a guitar, a violin and a set of bagpipes.

The first report records awards of £26,599, plus one-year repayable loans totalling £6,734. The second report grosses allowable payments out at £165,184. Claims in excess of £309,000, handed in before the closing date, were still outstanding in February 1800; here allowable payments (after the necessary adjustments) were in the region of £80,000. The total cost to the crown of compensating property loss can be extrapolated from these figures. Such success as the crown enjoyed in compelling the repayment of awards from individuals not deemed to have been suffering loyalists at all would produce a further figure; this would then have to be subtracted.

A new head of expenditure, in aid of suffering loyalists but distinct from property loss, was inaugurated under the amending legislation of 1799 and 1800 – rewards for 'discoverers' (informers) and annuities for widows and orphans of deceased loyalists.[120] The sum involved was relatively meagre – a mere £6,000. The salient statutory provisions indicate that the lion's share of this was earmarked for discoverers.

---

119 *Commons' Jn. Ire.*, xix, pt. 1, pp clviii–ccccxcviii. The details given in the *Commons' Jn.* should be collated with those supplied in the various printed notices of claims submitted per county which were previously circulated by the commissioners. The Trinity College Dublin library possesses a bound collection of these notices, presented to it in 1800 by one of the commissioners, the Revd Chamberlain Walker. I am grateful to Charles Benson for bringing this volume to my attention.

120 39 Geo. III, c.65, s.19 (discoverers); 40 Geo. III, c.49, s.11 (widows and orphans; discoverers). For details of awards made to discoverers (informers), see *Cornwallis correspondence*, iii, pp 319–21. It is to be noted that s.8 of the later Act also authorises a waiver of fees in the case of the administration of estates of poor deceased loyalists.

In the countdown to the rising and in the months after the rising's failure, the amount of Irish parliamentary legislation linked to the continuing crisis was, on any view, substantial. In addition to the laws surveyed above, there was a host of other statutes of no less intrinsic importance. The year 1797, for instance, witnessed the passing into law of a measure which authorized the embodying of the yeomanry corps[121] – an innovation boastfully recalled, in the post-mortem carried out by the commons committee of secrecy, as evidence of the resolute watchfulness of Irish parliamentarians[122] – and 1798 itself of a measure providing for the government of English militia units volunteering for service in Ireland.[123] Doubtless of minor significance, yet symptomatic of the close attention accorded to detail, a further statute, enacted the next year, had the twin objectives of saving money for the government and improving the manoeuvrability of troop formations: it exempted soldiers on the march from the obligation to pay a toll when passing through turnpikes or crossing bridges.[124]

The official legislative response to the problems created by the rising proper was marked out well in advance. Long before May 1798, space had been commandeered in the Irish statute-book for exceptional legislation that tackled an array of pressing contemporary questions, legislation recognizable from the designations customarily attached – the Insurrection, Indemnity and Habeas Corpus Suspension Acts. Re-enactments of the statutes in this group, sometimes with amendments, followed at regular intervals: none of the original legislative initiatives in the several fields concerned were destined for early jettisoning. The rest of the official legislative response – a group containing some new, often some dramatic, departures – engages one's particular attention, for reasons that are immediately obvious. Key words of the accompanying statutory vocabulary cast their own unmistakable allure: 'pardon', 'surrender', 'attainder', 'banishment', 'suffering loyalist'.

Two statutes, one from each group, merit additional remarks. The second Indemnity Act of 1799,[125] in force from June, and the Suppression of Rebellion Act of the same year,[126] in force a little earlier, from March, are only comprehensible if the strong constitutional undertones of each are thoroughly recognised. Both measures reflected a reaction to events, any repetition of which they were deliberately fashioned to prevent. Their principal business was to redefine spheres of jurisdiction and areas of competency as between the traditional courts,

---

121 37 Geo. III, c.2.

122 *Commons' Jn. Ire.*, xvii, pt. 2, p. dcccxxix.

123 38 Geo III, c.46. This act followed in the wake of a British act which authorized the service of such units in Ireland: 38 Geo. III, c.66 (G.B.).

124 39 Geo. III, c.59. Of 83 statutes passed by the Irish parliament in 1798, 22 can confidently be linked in some fashion with the continuing political and security crisis.

125 39 Geo. III, c.50.

126 39 Geo. III, c.11.

on the one hand, and the government (in its role as the civil and military authority), on the other. The timing of the legislative reaction is crucial: recent decisions of the courts, unexpected possibly but not totally surprising, had thrown into complete disarray the limits of the respective spheres of jurisdiction and areas of competency. There can be little doubt that the reverses which Thomas Judkin Fitzgerald suffered in the courts in the early spring of 1799 helped to inspire the wording of the new Indemnity Act: Castlereagh himself explicitly makes the connection.[127] It was a change in which Fitzgerald reaped the direct benefit but one from which, in time, others likewise were to derive distinct legal advantages. The implications of the Suppression of Rebellion Act were even more significant. The act cloaked with an aura of legality Earl Camden's proclamation of martial law on 24 May 1798. In more practical terms, it signified an unambiguous resolve to ensure that the common law courts kept their distance, a geographical strategy which those courts, left to themselves, even before Wolfe Tone's case in November 1798 and Kilwarden's celebrated intervention, had shown little inclination to adopt. Interference in the mechanics of military justice and thus, albeit obliquely, in the programme of counter-insurgency was identified as a luxury that the country – so this line of thought proceeded – could ill afford. The Suppression of Rebellion Act thus deprived those in custody of the principal argument upon which an application for *habeas corpus* might have been expected to succeed: courts-martial could not constitutionally co-exist alongside the ordinary courts. The legislation stated in the bluntest possible language that they could. Further provisions in the act curbed recourse to *habeas corpus* more generally. The courts were strictly prohibited from entertaining applications for release where individuals were held in military custody that was officially certified as such.[128] Taken in conjunction with the Habeas Corpus Suspension Acts which remained in force,[129] Dublin Castle and the military now possessed, both on paper and in actuality, a battery of formidable legal powers restrictive of the liberty of the subject.[130]

The willingness of the ordinary courts to attach magistrates for exceeding their powers,[131] to grant *certiorari* to enable convictions to be quashed (as in the affair of the thirteen men from Tipperary), to form the opinion they did of the actions of Thomas Judkin Fitzgerald, to adopt the stance they did over the Napper Tandy business, and their refusal to intervene in the dispute over compensation that pit-

---

127 Castlereagh to Portland, 26 Apr. 1799: *Castlereagh correspondence*, ii, p. 279.

128 39 Geo. III, c.50, s.5.

129 Notice, too, the flexibility accorded the authorities in respect of choice of place of detention under the Habeas Corpus Suspension Act of 1800 (40 Geo. III, c.18, s.2).

130 A court might order release on a *habeas corpus* application, but this could effectively be nullified where Dublin Castle then issued a certificate warranting detention under the Habeas Corpus Suspension Acts. For an illustration see Hay, *Insurrection*, p. xxiii.

131 McDowell, *Ireland*, pp 550–1 (case of two Westmeath JPs, Jan. 1796).

ted Captain Hay against the earl of Kingston, all demonstrate that the courts possessed political muscle which they did not shirk to employ on the appropriate occasion. But such cases were relatively infrequent. Of immeasurably greater significance, both practically and symbolically, was the strong attachment of the courts to the philosophy that underpinned the remedy of *habeas corpus*.[132] In all instances where *habeas corpus* was applied for, the judges would uniformly demand of the salient civil or military authority clear, unvarnished proof of the legality of the applicant's detention. Procedural requirements and the critical formulae to which returns to the writ had to conform introduced a number of hurdles which military personnel in particular did not always find it easy to surmount, even when they were prepared to be co-operative. From the language used by the judges charging the juries in the state treason trials of July 1798, there is not the whisper of a suggestion that the judiciary were in any way sympathetic to the cause of the United Irishmen. Yet these same individuals functioned within a professional culture that had elevated the safeguarding of the liberty of the citizen into a solemn judicial duty, a commitment that produced, albeit fitfully, bonuses for rebel and innocent alike. That culture had come to foster an attitude of mind nowhere better exemplified than in a controversy that arrived before the king's bench in 1795 and which centred on the gross mishandling of the case of Edward Ryan, a soldier from the Royal Leinster regiment, accused of desertion: *The King* v. *Earl Mountnorris*.[133] The judicial attitude towards *habeas corpus* evinced in this case was to be carried over into 1798 and beyond: a united bench critical of attempted avoidance of process, critical, too, of inadequacies in the reasons for detention set forth in the return to the writ; a bench that did not shrink from accusing the military to its face of sharp practice, obduracy and a failure to respect the law. In the Ireland of 1798, Cicero's oft-repeated observation, 'Silent etiam leges inter arma', could not, and did not, entirely apply.

The vigour of the judicial response may have owed something to the values of the Enlightenment but its manifestation in Ireland at this juncture owed rather more to the facts in specific cases which had bred in the judges a distrust of the military. In applications for *habeas corpus* during these years, avoidance of service of process, a conspiratorial silence over some person's actual place of detention, and resort by the military to other kinds of legerdemain emerge as recurring features in a seemingly endless game of cat-and-mouse, which no less frequently incur expressions of judicial displeasure and provoke a succession of judicial complaints.[134]

132 The remedy itself was of long standing. The 'act for better securing the liberty of the subject', otherwise known as the Irish Habeas Corpus Act (21 & 22 Geo. III, c.11), radically reshaped the governing procedures.
133 (1795) Irish Term Reports, 460. Ryan's counsel included the leading United Irishmen at the Irish bar: Simon Butler, Beauchamp Bagenal Harvey, Thomas Addis Emmet.
134 McDowell supplies these details of *habeas corpus* cases – Nov. 1795: writ granted where return omitted to state that Armagh Defenders proceeded against as 'deserters' had enlisted: *Ireland,*

This turf war between soldier and judge was not restricted to quarrels over *habeas corpus*. Interference with the standard arrangements for the administration of criminal justice could quickly match one against the other. An experience of Judge Downes in the autumn of 1798 was not untypical. Presiding at the Waterford assizes in October, Downes learnt, to his consternation, that six of the prisoners in the list of those scheduled to be tried by him had (by order of the local military commander) been taken out of the gaol and transferred into military custody that very morning. The six had been deliberately removed from the scope of Downes' commission as a judge of assize 'to deliver the gaols'. Downes' letter of complaint to Castlereagh carried a warning of the consequences should such clashes of jurisdiction continue to be tolerated by the government:

> The law cannot appear to the public to be weak, without losing that respect which it ought to have with the people especially if they shall feel only its terrors, and shall believe it is not strong enough to extend benefits to them.[135]

Posthumous tribute has been paid the judicial bench of the 1798 period. In 1923 McSwiney, one of last of the Irish serjeants, was to aver that

> the most brilliant era of the old Irish judiciary was in the immediate pre-Union times and during the rebellion of 1798, when the judges showed great courage in resisting the claims of the military ...[136]

p. 551; 1796–98: writs granted in cases of 'idle and disorderly' persons (from King's County, Westmeath, Londonderry, Carlow) transferred to naval tender or army depot where return failed to show requirements of Insurrection Act satisfied: ibid., p. 556; 1796: Captain Lees, naval regulating officer at Belfast, attached for refusing service of writ: ibid., p. 557; May 1797: writ granted in respect of Peter Evans, then detained on tender in Belfast Lough: ibid., pp 573–4; Nov. 1797: writ granted in favour of thirteen men, General Lake asserting all thirteen covered by chief secretary's warrant under Habeas Corpus Suspension legislation, but court ruling artillery barracks, actual place of detention, not a prison and detention therefore unlawful: ibid., p. 574. Hay supplies details of a *habeas corpus* case respecting a thirteen-year-old boy – Jan. 1799: writ granted to a Master James Lett, Dublin Castle electing to avoid obloquy that it would have incurred by issuing warrant under *habeas corpus* suspension legislation against someone so young: *Insurrection*, pp xix-xxi; 'from the child's appearance' in king's bench in Dublin, Hay wrote, 'it was thought he wanted the superintendence of a nurse more than a gaoler'. Rowe details several more – 1799/1800: attachment proceedings against Col. Cameron in respect of Arthur Poland and John Magee, escapees from New Geneva barracks, County Waterford, later apprehended in Down, for ignoring writ of *habeas corpus* and altering place of detention of escapees after service of writ: *Reports*, pp 585–7; 1799–1800: attachment of General Merrick for sending prisoner to Prussia after being served with writ of *habeas corpus* not proceeded with, the general's actions having been founded on a mistake: ibid., p. 550; 1799–1800: attachment of Major Uniacke, in case of Coleman, for conspiring to procure his conviction, ignoring writ of *habeas corpus*, altering place of detention, etc.: ibid., pp 596–602.

135 Downes to Castlereagh, 25 Oct. 1798: *Cornwallis correspondence*, iii, pp 14–5.
136 Serjeant McSwiney, 'Memorandum respecting the new judiciary in Saorstat Eireann to the Judiciary Committee in 1923'. Private collection.

McSwiney's accolade is excessive. Besides, in the face of perhaps 30,000 dead, amidst the idealism, the confusion and the bitterness, the courage, the carnage and the shame, to call attention in whatever fashion to the side-show that proceedings in the courts must of necessity have resembled, risks dismissal as at best insensitive. Nevertheless, in 1798 and the months following, the courts were not irrelevant: the serjeant's remarks indicate the need for a modern assessment of the work of the Irish judges of that period. The present furnishes an opportune moment.[137]

137 See n. 134, above.

SECTION VI

The Scottish soldier Archibald M'Laren, a sergeant in the Dunbarton Highlanders, described a scene at Vinegar Hill to which he was an eyewitness:

> After the battle some soldiers got hold of a croppie's wife whom they dragged into a house and shame to say four and twenty of the brutes (ambitious to disgrace a redcoat) had connection with her. Even the blind-eyed Michael Horgan . . . meant to have been one of the number. As I passed, I saw him coming out at the door and exclaiming 'blood and wounds I've lost my turn'. I began to expostulate with him upon the impropriety of his conduct, knowing that he had a wife and six children in Dublin but he cut me off short with a 'blood and wounds man, Kitty and I have made an agreement; she gives me liberty to do what I please and I give her the same when I'm from home'. I could not help laughing.[1]

This is a horrific vignette of a gang-rape. The United Irish army prided itself on leaving non-combatants unmolested and that obviously included women and children. The absence of rape in the volatile conditions of the summer of 1798 is one of the achievements of the rebel army, and a rebuttal of the argument that they were primarily motivated by sectarianism. By contrast, their adversaries routinely used rape as a weapon of war, and participation in it extended to high-ranking officers like Lord Kingsborough of the North Cork Militia and Major Siddons in Antrim.[2]

---

1 Archibald M'Laren, *A minute description of the battles of Gorey, Arklow and Vinegar Hill together with the movements of the army through the Wicklow mountains in quest of the rebels who were supposed to have been encamped at the Seven Churches to which are annexed the capture and execution of several traitors, four of whose heads are exposed to public view in Wexford interspersed with many curious anecdotes worth the readers notice* ([Dublin?], 1798), p. 39 [N.L.I., P. 5329].

2 Kingsborough personally released suspects if their wives agreed to sleep with him. In Kildare, the North Cork Militia 'had their will of the men's wives and daughters': Sampson, *Memoirs*, p. 23. Siddons proposed to permit Paul Douglas back to Ireland from America if his wife agreed to sleep with him. She eventually consented and Douglas was allowed to return: Robert Young, *Ulster in '98* (Belfast, 1893), p. 41. The English lawyer Francis Plowden observed of the crime of rape: 'It is universally allowed to have been exclusively on the side of the military': Plowden,

In the aftermath of the rising, women were relegated below the horizon of historical visibility (Keogh, chapter 25). From a conservative standpoint, the idea of politically active women, either loyalist or republican, was repugnant, a violation of the concept of separate spheres which regulated thinking about the proper behaviour of women in the eighteenth century.[3] From a radical perspective, only thinkers like James Barry, John Burk and Thomas Russell were able to see beyond the still restricted gender perspectives of the 'Rights of Man' as promulgated by the American and French Revolutions.[4] Undoubtedly there were many radicalised women in the 1790s: some examples drawn from the elite layers of the society include Elizabeth Bond (wife of Oliver and daughter of Henry Jackson), the poet Henrietta Battier, Margaret Munro, Mary Ann McCracken and Martha McTier.[5]

The 1790s also sees the symbolic role of woman in play. Out of the allegorical tradition of the *aisling* poetry, the *sean bhean bhocht*, *Granúaile* and other personifications of Ireland re-crystallized.[6] Despite a long-standing convention of seeing the *aisling* as dewy-eyed, dream-world escapism, a hard-edged politics was embedded in what should more accurately be seen as sophisticated allegory, instantly recognized in commentary on Pope, Dryden or Swift but ignored in their contemporaries Ó Rathaille and Ó Bruadair.[7] In drawing on its conventions, the United Irish movement was not regressing into intellectually mushy romantic nationalism.[8] Rather they were expanding an engagement begun under

History of Ireland, iv, p. 339. Francis Plowden (1749–1829) was a lawyer and clergyman who also wrote in defence of English Catholicism.

3   For separate spheres, see Amanda Vickery, 'Golden age to separate spheres: A review of the categories and chronology of English women's history', in *Historical Jn.*, xxxvi (1993), 383–414: Hannah Barker and Elaine Chalus (eds), *Gender in eighteenth-century England: Roles, representations and responsibilities* (London, 1997).

4   Nancy Curtin, 'Women and eighteenth-century Irish republicanism', in Margaret McCurtain and Mary O'Dowd (eds), *Women in early modern Ireland* (Dublin, 1991), pp 133–47; ibid, 'Matilda Tone and virtuous republican femininity', in Keogh and Furlong (eds), *Women of 1798*, pp 26–46. The painter Barry was ejected from the Royal Academy in 1799 for among other things having publicly kept company with Mary Wollstonecroft. Burk's play *Joan of Arc* of 1798 is considered the earliest depiction of a strong female political character on the American stage. Thomas Russell, who was sensitive to women and much loved by them, appears in Pat Murphy's pioneering feminist film *Anne Devlin* [1984] as an appalling chauvinist.

5   *Drennan-McTier correspondence*. After a close reading of the 1,500 letters of Martha's correspondence with William Drennan, one can scarcely avoid the conclusion that she had a sharper and more pragmatic political intelligence than her better-known brother. Mary MacNeill, *The life and times of Mary Ann McCracken, 1770–1866* (Dublin, 1960) is a pioneering and still useful volume.

6   M.H. Thuente, 'Liberty, Hibernia and Mary Le More', in Keogh and Furlong, *Women of 1798*, pp 9–25.

7   There is now no excuse for those without Irish ignoring these poets, given the superb modern translations by Michael Hartnett in Ó *Bruadair* (Loughcrew, 1995) and Ó *Rathaille* (Loughcrew, 1998).

8   Stewart, 'The harp new-strung.'

the Volunteers. They welded established and fresh motifs together in a clever splicing of this figure onto the separatist harp image, to create their potent icon of the maiden harp. In general, as Anna Clark has vigorously argued, the 1790s was a defeat for feminism as well as for political radicalism.[9] With that defeat, the public profile of women in politics and their role in the revolutionary decade disappeared. It now requires considerable ingenuity to recover their hidden history in the 1790s, as in Thomas Bartlett's dissection of their evidence at courts martial.[10]

If women were sidelined within the historical record, so too, if less completely, was the Presbyterian role in 1798 (McBride, chapter 23). Their involvement in the United Irish project became an increasingly difficult issue: in 1998, one flag at Drumcree read 'Croppies lie down'. However this carefully cultivated amnesia has itself a history. Unlike the situation in Wexford, there was surprisingly little public writing about 1798 in Ulster. Presbyterian ecclesiastical leaders sought to put clear blue water between their communities and their murky green past.[11] Presbyterianism had damagingly split in the 1790s. The loyalist faction, led initially by the Revd Robert Black and later by the Revd Henry Cooke, scapegoated the radicals. Cooke added a further sectarian twist: Presbyterian croppies were all lumped together as members of New Light congregations who had fallen into flagrant political error as a result of their theological backsliding.[12] As Presbyterianism in general became more evangelical and reverted to a stricter Calvinism, its Arian fringes were seen as dangerous. In a mirror-image of institutional Catholicism's dismissal of its rebel priests (Bishop Caulfield's 'very faeces of the church'),[13] New Light ministers were held accountable for all the political sins of their congregations. The political establishment, expertly coached by Castlereagh who understood Ulster Presbyterian thinking, used the ecclesiastical leaders to re-align their fiercest critics with the conservative consensus. As Alexander Knox wrote to Castlereagh in July 1803:

> Never before was Ulster under the dominion of the British crown. It had a distinct moral existence before, and moved and acted on principles of

9 Anna Clark, '1798 as the defeat of feminism: women, patriotism and politics' in Terry Brotherston, Anna Clark and Kevin Whelan (eds), *These fissured isles* (Edinburgh, forthcoming); Anna Clark, *The struggle for the breeches: Gender and the making of the British working class* (Berkeley, 1995).

10 Thomas Bartlett, 'Bearing witness: female evidences in courts martial convened to suppress the 1798 rebellion' in Keogh and Furlong (eds), *Women of 1798*, pp 64–86.

11 Ian McBride, *Scripture politics: Ulster Presbyterians and Irish radicalism in the late eighteenth century* (Oxford, 1998).

12 James Seton Reid, *History of the Presbyterian church in Ireland* (ed.) W. Killen, 3 vols (Belfast, 1867). The rebuttal is David Miller, 'Presbyterianism and "modernisation" in Ulster', in *Past & Present*, lxxx (1978), 66–90. The deterministic sociological model deployed by Miller has not aged well. The strain on the Presbyterian leaders is perhaps reflected in Black's suicide in 1816; that Castlereagh also paid a price is suggested by his suicide in 1822.

13 Keogh, *French disease*, p. 205.

which all we could certainly know was that they were not with the state; therefore when any tempting occasion occurred, ready to act against it. Now the distinct existence will merge into the general well-being, the Presbyterian ministers being henceforth a subordinate ecclesiastical aristocracy, whose feelings must be that of zealous loyalty, and whose influence upon their flock will be as surely sedative when it should be so, and exciting when it should be so, as it was the direct reverse before … This is perhaps a more favourable moment for forming a salutary connection between government and the Presbyterian body of Ulster than may again arrive. The republicanism of that part of Ireland is checked and repressed by the cruelties of the Roman Catholics in the late rebellion and by the despotism of Buonaparte. They are therefore in a humour for acquiescing in the views of government beyond what they ever were or (should the opportunity be missed) may be hereafter. How much then is it to be wished that, while the tide of their wrong passions is so unusually low, a mound should be raised that will for ever after be a safe restraint to them.[14]

Castlereagh believed that the Regium Donum would be 'a natural engine of authority' but that it would also be necessary to encourage a 'schism' within the Presbyterians: 'it is only through a considerable internal fermentation of that body, coupled with some change of system, that it [Presbyterianism] will put on a different temper and acquire better habits'.[15] That split was delayed until the 1820s.[16] Cooke finally gained the ascendant (according to Montgomery) by 'uniting evangelicanism with Orangeism and the countenance of the aristocracy with the applause of the multitude'.[17] The Orange Order served as a detoxification chamber for the politically tainted. That role may have been delayed for a decade, and continuing radicalism in Presbyterian areas was still evident for some years after 1798.[18] In 1804, Thomas Robinson was unable to sell his large painting *The review of the Belfast yeomanry by the lord lieutenant the earl of Hardwicke, 27 August 1804*: he only found a purchaser when he changed its title to *A procession in honour of Lord Nelson*.[19] A robust pride in their involvement in

14 Alexander Knox to Lord Castlereagh, 15 July 1803: *Castlereagh corr.*, iv, pp 287–9. Knox was Castlereagh's private secretary.
15 Castlereagh to Addington, 21 July 1802: *Castlereagh corr.*, iv, pp 224–5.
16 R.F.G. Holmes, 'Controversy and schism in the synod of Ulster in the 1820s', in Haire (ed.), *Challenge and conflict*, pp 116–33.
17 Cited in Holmes, 'Presbyterian minister,' p. 125.
18 James Patterson, 'Continued Presbyterian resistance in the aftermath of the rebellion of 1798 in Antrim and Down', in *Eighteenth-century Life*, xxii (1998), 45–61. James Hope, from the Covenanting stronghold of Templepatrick, died at Brown Square off the Shankill Road in 1846, still a staunch United Irishman.
19 Among the painters of the period associated with the United Irishmen were Adam Buck, James Petrie and Henry Brocas (Snr). Buck was listed among United Irish activists in London in 1799:

1798 is still clearly evident in the interviews conducted by the Revd Classon Emmet Porter of Larne with veteran United men. Consider the material he gathered from the Presbyterian weaver, soldier, Defender, freemason and United Irishman James Burns of Templepatrick, the 'old croppy'. Porter's work followed the pioneering oral history of the Carmelite Brother Luke Cullen in Wicklow and Wexford. The evidence amassed by these two writers facilitates assessment of rank-and-file motivation in 1798.[20]

Presbyterian liberalism remained strong in the first three decades of the nineteenth century.[21] It lingered on until the first Home Rule crisis in 1886[22] and was finally finished off only by partition.[23] A re-working of 1798 occurred in the period 1886–1922, as the origin myths of Ulster unionism were refurbished and related to a new set of political circumstances. 1886 is the pivotal transition year in the history of the Presbyterian memory of 1798, just as 1829 is the crucial one in the Catholic version.[24] But as always with 1798, there can be no simple narrative here. Even as the wider Presbyterian community recoiled from 1798, Francis Joseph Bigger (1863–1926) laboured to reclaim it. Bigger, a key figure in the northern axis of the Irish Literary Revival, has been airbrushed out of the cultural history of Ulster. He revamped the *Ulster Journal of Archaeology* in 1894, prodded and prompted Presbyterian ministers to collect 1798 lore, and researched a series of memoirs of the Ulster leaders, self-consciously modelled on Madden's earlier endeavours.[25] Bigger, like so many other Ulster nationalists, lapsed into silence

Petrie was arrested and jailed as a United Irishman: he painted Tandy, Curran, Robert Emmet, Michael Dwyer, and Henry Howley. Brocas (1762–1837) was responsible for the celebrated cartoons in the *Irish Magazine*: Patricia Butler, *The Brocas collection* (Dublin, 1997). It is suggestive that Pietro Bossi, designer of the distinctive inlaid marble (scagliola) chimney pieces, disappears from Dublin in 1798: Conor O'Neill, 'In search of Bossi' in *Ir. Arch. and Dec. Studies*, i (1998), 146–75.

20 The Classon Emmet Porter material is housed in P.R.O.N.I.; it was liberally drawn on by Young. The Luke Cullen material is divided between N.L.I. and T.C.D.; see the new edition (with superb footnotes) of a portion of it: Ruan O'Donnell (ed.), *Insurgent Wicklow 1798: The story as written by Luke Cullen* (Bray, 1998).

21 Only Ballymena presbytery voted against Catholic Emancipation in 1829: *Northern Whig*, 24 Feb. 1829.

22 The Revd Hugh Hanna claimed in 1888 that there were only three known Orangemen and a dozen conservatives among the 550 members of the Presbyterian General Assembly: Hugh Hanna, *Ulster, Scotland and Home Rule* (Belfast, 1888), p. 6.

23 The absence of this liberal strain was to prove a weakness to unionism as it sought to deal with the new politics of Northern Ireland after the ending of the Stormont in 1972 and of republican armed struggle in 1994. This is well demonstrated in Norman Porter's *Rethinking Unionism: An alternative vision for Northern Ireland* (Belfast, 1996). See also Norman Porter (ed.), *The republican ideal: Current perspectives* (Belfast, 1998). A longer-term perspective can be found in Flann Campbell, *Dissenting voice: Protestant democracy in Ulster from plantation to partition* (Belfast, 1991).

24 Jackson, 'Unionist myth, 1912–1985'.

25 For Bigger, see Roger Dixon, 'Heroes for a new Ireland: Francis Joseph Bigger and the leaders of the '98', in Trefor Owen (ed.), *From Corrib to Cultra* (Belfast, 2000), pp 29–38. Madden col-

with partition, but 1798 remained a fascination for some who came from within the Unionist tradition. Dissent from the Unionist mainstream encouraged exploration of the 1790s as a decade of lost opportunity and potential recuperation by a diverse group of northern Protestants. This interest can be traced from Bigger, Alice Milligan and Bulmer Hobson through Denis Ireland, Thomas Carnduff and John Hewitt to Stewart Parker, Tom Paulin, Derek Mahon and Stephen Rea.[26] There remains an enduring tendency on the nationalist side to dwell on the alleged apostacy of the Presbyterians, generating a didactic tale of how Belfast oscillated from being 'the cradle and then the grave of public spirit'.[27]

A sharp contrast exists between the different tenses of nationalism and unionism: unionism preferred the past tense, spooling backwards relentlessly from 1798 to 1690 and 1641. Nationalism promulgated the future perfect tense, scrolling forward through the teleology of 1798, 1848, 1867, 1916, 1969 to that future day when the nation would finally have come into being. This is the tense, for example, of Robert Emmet's peroration, directed not to the present but to the future and to those who would complete and perfect his vision (in *Finnegans Wake*, Joyce coined the term the 'past prophetical' to describe this common Irish mode of thinking).[28] If unionism and nationalism derived different temporalities from 1798, space as well as time bifurcated. For unionists it was crucial to quarantine 1798 into a little corner of Ulster: 'Hearts of Down' displaced United Irishmen. For nationalists, the whole point was that the rebellion stretched nationally from Antrim to Wexford to Mayo. The duration of Presbyterian radicalism was also at issue. Unionists stressed the limited stamina of the 'summer soldiers' or 'sunshine patriots'.[29] For nationalists, 1798 in Ulster represented the

lected but never published the materials for a series on the northern leaders of the United Irishmen; it survives in manuscript (private collection).

26 For Alice Milligan, see Catherine Morris, 'From the margins: Alice Milligan and the Irish cultural revival 1888–1905' (unpublished Ph.D. thesis, University of Aberdeen, 1999); for Denis Ireland, see the biography by Risteard Ó Glaisne, *Denis Ireland* (Baile Átha Cliath, 2000); for Thomas Carnduff, see John Gray (ed.), *Thomas Carnduff: Life and writings* (Belfast, 1994); for John Hewitt, see Damian Smyth (ed.), *Two plays: The McCrackens, The angry dove* (Belfast, 1999); for Tom Paulin, see *The liberty tree* (London, 1983); for Parker, see forthcoming biography by Marilyn Richtarik; for Rea, see his 'Introduction' to Stewart Parker, *Plays 2: Northern star, Heavenly bodies, Pentecost* (London, 2000), pp ix-xii. Rea's brilliant production of Stewart's *Northern star* was a cultural highlight of the bicentenary. His aim was 'to get Belfast people to understand what 1798 was about, especially given the stifled and amnesiac memory of that pivotal experience in the life of the city. It is a part of their history that Belfast people had lost touch with but that they need. The republican tradition of eighteenth-century Presbyterianism dealt with in the play had been buried. The play touched a spot. Belfast people need to face their actual history to release them from it. I wanted to help the city emerge from the great, awful, ingrown energies of loyalism': 'Stephen Rea in conversation with Luke Gibbon and Kevin Whelan', in *Yale Journal of Criticism*, xv, no. 1 (2002), 12.
27 Madden, *Autobiography*, i, p. 184.
28 J. Joyce, *Finnegans wake* (London, 1992) p. 11.
29 R.M. Sibbett, *The sunshine patriots: The 1798 rebellion in Antrim and Down* (Belfast, 1997). This is a reprinted edition by the Grand Orange Lodge of three chapters from Sibbett's *Orangeism in*

'true' instincts of Presbyterians, who had succumbed (both before and subsequently) to a false consciousness deliberately inculcated in them by the British
state for nefarious 'divide and rule' purposes.

On the nationalist side, Madden was obviously the towering figure in the
nineteenth century. His writings separated the earlier apologist tradition of
Catholic writing from the more explicit recognition that the United Irishmen
represented the core of 1798, and that it was indeed a full-blooded insurrection,
not a defensive Catholic response to sectarian provocation. While Catholic
Emancipation remained to be attained, 1798 was a touchy issue for Catholics.
There is a palpable nervousness in the early memoirs of Edward Hay, Thomas
Cloney and Charles Teeling.[30] This disappears with Madden in 1842. Like others who became fascinated with the rebellion, Madden's intense interest possibly
stemmed from the simple fact that he was born in that fateful year, on the very
day that Major Sirr was searching his father's house at Wormwood Gate
(Woods, chapter 24).[31] A very widely travelled man with an extraordinary range
of intellectual interests, he lived for extended periods in Dublin, Paris, Naples,
London, Lisbon, Constantinople, Alexandria, Jamaica, Havana, West Africa and

Ireland and throughout the empire 1688–1828, 2 vols (Belfast, 1938). Robert Mackie Sibbett
(1868–1941), born in Portglenone, County Antrim, was a journalist, a Presbyterian elder and
official historian to the Orange Order. Sibbett portrays the alliance of Presbyterians with
Catholics as an 'unnatural friendship' (p. 52); 'it was utterly impossible in the nature of things
that real co-operation could exist between them' (p. 9); 'there was no real bond of union, no real
harmony of sentiment, no tie of friendship, and no feeling that could be called fraternal' (p. 9);
1798 was 'foolish and regrettable' (p. 52); 'the great motive behind the rebellion in Ulster was
irreligiousness, blatant infidelity' (p. 120). Cf. A.T.Q. Stewart, *The summer soldiers: The 1798
rebellion in Antrim and Down* (Belfast, 1995). There is a revealing interview with Stewart in
Susan McKay, *Northern Protestants: an unsettled people* (Belfast, 2000), pp 292–5. Stewart
locates 1798 in a struggle over territory, linking this to current politics: 'You don't start with reconciliation. If you belong to a state, you subscribe to its law and order but you also expect it to
protect you. Until that is resolved, you'll not end violence. You need to strengthen the majority
position … I think the government has taken sides. Unfortunately not the Protestant one. It
worked like clockwork. They got rid of Stormont, they got rid of the B Specials, they got rid of
the UDR. Now the last defence of the state of Northern Ireland is about to go. They are getting
rid of the RUC … This state was supposed to provide a shelter for Protestants.' Stewart then
asks if the Ulster Protestant still retained 'an intuitive blood knowledge of history'. He wondered if there was in Portadown a 'Jungian folk-memory of massacres', while acknowledging
that 'admittedly, it is hard to see how the drug-taking, disco-attending, couldn't-care-less
youngsters of today could be influenced by 1641 … People say the sides have to come together.
No. One side or the other has to surrender. Maybe it's my siege mentality.' Stewart's book *The
narrow ground*, a classic 'dreary steeples' version of the history of Northern Ireland, was much
admired by Ian Paisley. Stewart's two books on the United Irishmen in Ulster deal with the
years leading up to their foundation in 1791 (*A deeper silence*), and with four weeks in 1798
(*Summer soldiers*), ignoring the difficult years in between.

30 Margaret Whelan [Ó hÓgartaigh], 'Edward Hay "styled Mr Secretary Hay" and Catholic politics 1792–1822' (unpublished M.A. thesis, N.U.I. U.C.G., 1991).

31 Thomas Crofton Croker, John Banim and James Seaton Reid, three other figures with strong
1798 interests, were also born in the fateful year.

Western Australia. The abolition of slavery was an abiding concern: he oversaw
its abolition in Jamaica in 1833–4 and he was the star witness at the celebrated
Amistad trial in New Haven in 1839.[32] His approach to the United Irishmen was
simple. They were a predictable product of bad government that (as a high-
ranking colonial official himself) he instantly recognized. Madden, a classic liberal, constantly emphasized the necessity for equality before the law, comparing
Irish Catholics to other groups who found themselves at the wrong end of an
adversarial system such as slaves, Native Americans, Jews and Muslims.[33] This is
not to paint Madden as a radical.[34] His political instincts were conservative: he
endorsed and participated in the British imperial system as long as it operated
within the restraints of British law and permitted full access to Catholics.
Madden, at a stretch a 'Castle Catholic,' fits more easily into the mould of the
earlier (Grattanite) or later (Redmondite) Home Ruler. In this sense, he was heir
to the cautious political traditions of the Dublin Catholic merchant class from
which he sprang. His father Edward participated in the Back Lane parliament
(Madden was very proud of that), but he had never become a United Irishman.

Madden's antipathy to organized underground radicalism dictated his
approach to the history of the 1790s. Rather than narrate and analyse the political history of the United Irishmen, he reduced his focus to the biographical
level. His eleven-volume series is structured around personal memoirs (fifty-
seven in all), in which the moral rather than the political qualities of his subjects
are scrutinised. A dogmatic Victorian moralism permeates his account: there is
little analytic vigour or originality. Even his historical introduction was written
by 'a friend'(William Cooke Taylor).[35] The enduring value of his work remains

32 Stephen Spielberg's *Amistad* film completely ignores Madden's role. See Madden's own account
    in *Autobiography*, pp 92–4. Madden was 'groaned' at as 'a friend of niggers' in New York in
    1839 (*Autobiography*, p. 110).

33 Madden compares the treatment of the Irish in 1798 to that of American and West Indian
    slaves, Native Americans, and Jews in Damascus: Madden, *United Irishmen*, first series, first edi-
    tion, vol. 1, pp 336–7. His personal involvement in anti-slavery work opened his eyes to the Irish
    situation: 'The struggle against slavery, whether in the West Indies or on the shores of Africa
    served in my case as an apprenticeship to the cause of freedom and tended to make contrasts
    between personal and political slavery familiar to me': *United Irishmen*, first series, second ed.
    (Dublin, 1848), p. x.

34 Miles Byrne vigorously attacked Madden's treatment of the United Irishmen: *Memoirs of Miles
    Byrne*, ed. Stephen Gwynn, 2 vols (Dublin, 1906), i, p. 313. Madden despised Thomas Paine,
    offering the phrenological opinion after examining a cast of Paine's head that he was 'a sneering
    man who had no sympathy with humanity': Madden, *Autobiography*, p. 104.

35 William Cooke Taylor (1800–49) was the author of *History of the civil wars of Ireland from the
    Anglo-Norman invasion till the Union of the country with Great Britain* (Edinburgh, 1831), whose
    final two chapters are a classic statement of the liberal Protestant perspective on 1798. In 1833,
    William Sampson expanded Taylor's account in a New York published version of the *History*.
    Taylor was born in Youghal and after graduating from T.C.D., he became a journalist, editor
    and author in London from 1829 onwards. Among a wide range of publications, he edited
    Cicero, wrote a *Popular history of British India* (1842, 1851, 1857) and published extensively on

its unrivalled accumulation of biographical detail and original documentation, emanating mainly from the United Irishmen themselves or their families (Madden acknowledged 'the fidelity of female friendship' as the crucial bearer of the memory of the dead). These volumes offer evidential redress to the imbalance in the Castle sources, themselves not neutral but gathered and organized as part of the political process and therefore already coded to bear out the officially sponsored narrative. Madden's indefatigable collecting helps historians to evade the cyclopean eye of the state apparatus, thereby widening their range of vision of the 1790s.

education, free trade and the 'condition of England' question. A Whig, he was appointed government statistician in Ireland by Clarendon, the lord lieutenant, in 1847 and strongly supported his controversial Famine policies. Taylor himself became a victim of the Famine, dying of cholera in Dublin in 1849.

23

Memory and forgetting: Ulster Presbyterians and 1798

IAN MCBRIDE

Forgetting, as Ernest Renan observed in his germinal essay 'Qu'est-ce qu'une Nation?' (1882), is an essential factor in the construction of national identities, and this is one reason, he suggested, why historical investigation poses a threat to the principle of nationality.[1] The inchoate form of nationalism which emerged among Ulster Protestants after 1886 may be aberrant in many respects, but this is not one of them. Since the publication of Hobsbawm and Ranger's paradigm-setting book *The invention of tradition* in 1983, historians in Ireland as elsewhere have become better attuned to the complicated processes of selection involved in the maintenance of social memory.[2] Those interested in the evolution of loyalist mentalities are now able to consult a series of studies which have investigated the function of emblematic dates such as 1641, 1690 and 1916.[3] In the analysis of collective identities, however, silences are often as revealing as the exemplary personalities, actions and utterances which have been assembled to produce a usable past. Renan noted that 'every French citizen has to have forgotten the massacre of Saint Bartholomew, or the massacres that took place in the Midi in the thirteenth century'.[4] In the same way, the construction of a distinctive 'Ulster' identity has meant that while certain anniversaries have been noisily commemorated, others have been studiously ignored.

At first glance the subject of this essay – Presbyterian attitudes to the rebellion of 1798 – may appear to be an unpromising field of inquiry. After all, it is commonly supposed that the United Irishmen left no permanent traces in the cultur-

---

1 Ernest Renan, 'What is a nation?', transl. by Martin Thom, in H.K. Bhabha (ed.), *Nation and narration* (London, 1990), p. 11.
2 E. Hobsbawm and T. Ranger (eds), *The invention of tradition* (Cambridge, 1983). See also J.R. Gillis (ed.), *Commemorations: The politics of national identity* (Princeton, 1994), pp 3–24; P.H. Hutton, *History as an art of memory* (Hanover, NH, 1993); *Representations*, xxvi (spring 1989) [a special issue devoted to memory and counter-memory].
3 See Ian McBride, *The siege of Derry in Ulster Protestant mythology* (Dublin, 1997) and the works cited ibid., p. 9, note 2.
4 Renan, 'What is a nation?', p. 11.

al formation of Protestant Ulster. Although the Protestant community is renowned for its fetishization of the past, there have been no re-enactments of the Battles of Antrim and Ballynahinch, no statues raised to Henry Joy McCracken, no heroic scenes from '98 painted on the gable walls of east Belfast's housing estates. On the contrary, the political rhetoric, public ritual and iconography of Ulster Unionism has descended from the opposing, counter-revolutionary tradition of the 1790s embodied in the Orange Order. Yet it is possible, through a sensitive use of the evidence, to shed some light on the ways in which the traumatic upheavals of '98 were erased by nineteenth-century historians. This process is explored in the first two sections below, which examine the political and ideological constraints which shaped Presbyterian attitudes in the immediate aftermath of the rising.

The disappearance of the '98 from popular memory was not entirely passive: as with Renan's French citizens, Ulster Protestants have sometimes engaged in a process of remembering to forget. Some of the strategies used are explored in section three below. But the United Irish movement made a more lasting imprint on the Presbyterian mind than is commonly recognized in the existing historiography. The fourth part uncovers the survival of a 'hidden' history of the '98 in the Ulster countryside, later retrieved by historians such as R.R. Madden and the contributors to the *Ulster Journal of Archaeology*. If we turn from the written record to local folklore, recollections of 'the turn-out' concentrated around particular personalities and events, and legends attached to features of the Ulster landscape. A century after the rebellion itself, when a number of clergymen began to record the stories passed down by their congregations, it was still possible to preserve the last vestiges of a rich oral tradition. Many Presbyterians were not afraid to speak of '98, but preserved a carefully qualified pride in the actions of their rebellious forefathers. Increasingly, however, they were anxious to disconnect the unique experiment of the 1790s from a unilinear narrative of nationhood that was moving, via 1848 and 1867, towards the terminus of 1916. By 1898, as the fifth section argues, a rearguard action was already being mounted to reclaim Antrim and Ballynahinch as part of a specifically *Ulster* tradition.

I

Nationalist and Unionist attitudes to 1798 hardened into their modern forms during the long struggle for self-government that took place between 1886 and 1922, but the lines of divergence can be traced back to the year of liberty itself. For all radicals – Protestant, Catholic or Dissenter – the end of the eighteenth century brought military defeat, martial law and loyalist reprisals. Apart from the physical costs of failure, there was the psychological impact of repression: the re-assertion of government authority involved such notorious acts as the public execution of the Revd James Porter at the gate of his Greyabbey meeting-house. In Belfast, Lisburn, Ballymena and other northern towns the severed heads of rebels were fastened on spikes and placed on market-houses where they remained until August. For several years after the turn-out, those republicans who had escaped hanging, imprisonment or exile sought above all to avoid attention. Against the background of continuing war with France suspected rebels were targeted by the predominantly Protestant yeomanry, which doubled its numbers from around 30,000 in 1797 to almost 60,000 in 1805.[5] The use of intimidation and terror was common throughout the disaffected regions; yet the northern and southern experiences of insurrection also differed in important respects, and these differences were vital in determining popular attitudes in the immediate post-rebellion period.

In the current state of research we know little about these crucial years, but the loyalist reaction in Ulster differed in both nature and extent from that in Leinster. Presbyterian communities certainly suffered during the rebellion. In Maghera, for example, two alleged rebels were hanged and beheaded; the Tipperary Militia took up quarters in the meeting-house and then burned everything in it except the Bible.[6] Nevertheless, there is little evidence of the sort of victimisation and violence which continued in north Wexford between 1798 and 1801, where thirty-three Catholic chapels were burned and innocent priests harassed by the yeomanry. This imbalance merely reflects the fact that the insurrections in Antrim and Ballynahinch had been overshadowed by events in Wexford. A rough idea of the relative scale can be formed from the claims for compensation submitted by loyalists in October 1798. Over half of the total came from Wexford and Wicklow alone, with another 25 per cent from the counties around Dublin and north Connaught; less than 5 per cent came from Antrim and Down.[7]

These figures highlight the divergence in the development of the northern and southern organisations. The northern United Irishmen, who supplied the backbone of the republican movement, were in a sense victims of their own success. The key year in the mobilization of Ulster was 1797 when numbers peaked following the appearance of the French in Bantry Bay; from the spring of that year General Lake began his brutal pacification of Ulster, drawing on the regular troops, the militia, and the recently embodied yeomanry. Martial law was declared at the end of March. Thousands rushed forwards to take the oath of

5   Thomas Bartlett, 'Defence, counter-insurgency and rebellion: Ireland, 1793–1803', in Thomas Bartlett and Keith Jeffery (eds), *A military history of Ireland* (Cambridge, 1996), p. 292.
6   R.L. Marshall, 'Maghera in '98', in S.S. McFarland (ed.), *Presbyterianism in Maghera* (Maghera, 1985), p. 175.
7   R.B. McDowell, *Ireland in the age of imperialism and revolution* (Oxford, 1979), p. 604.

loyalty and surrender weapons as house-burnings, floggings and other forms of torture were employed to subdue the rebels. Above all, the cellular organization was disrupted as the authorities removed the top tier of the military command, leaving in charge subordinate leaders whose influence and talents were limited. By the beginning of 1798 Dublin had replaced Belfast as the focus of the conspiracy, and the centre of gravity within the movement had shifted decisively to Leinster. When the signal came to rise, the northern movement was paralysed. 'The arresting of a colonel threw the whole battalion into disorder', as David Bailie Warden commented; 'instead of the forces meeting at any point in collected and organized bodies, they met rather by accident than by design; and they were in no better order than *a mere country mob*'.[8]

The critical fact in shaping immediate memories of the insurrection was not just that it failed, but that the movement had already entered decline. 'The road to rebellion in the north', as Nancy Curtin has written, 'had been strewn with ... the obstacles of cowardice, timidity, and outright betrayal.'[9] The natural sequel to the appalling failure of nerve on the part of the Ulster leadership was the catalogue of desertions and defections recorded during and after the turn-out. At courts martial, chastened rebels publicly recanted, while respectable figures described how they had been forced to assume leadership roles by popular pressure. Writing in the 1840s, James Hope warned that the historian must avoid 'suspicion and surmise', recalling how 'the men who flinched and fell away from our cause, grasped at any apology for their own delinquency'.[10] History is written by the winners; the problem for the northern radicals was not just the totality of the defeat, but the perception that so much of the damage had been self-inflicted. Given this inglorious descent into recrimination, it was difficult to reconstruct the turn-out as a heroic failure. The shame and humiliation that followed the rebellion is captured by the 'rhyming weaver' and United Irishman James Orr, who described the confusion and demoralization after the rebel camp at Donegore Hill broke up:

> What joy at hame our entrance gave!
> 'Guid God! is't you? fair fa' ye! -
> 'Twas wise, tho' fools may ca't no brave
> To rin or e'er they saw ye.'
>
> 'Aye wife, that's true without dispute,
> But lest saunts fail in Zion,
> I'll hae to swear — forc'd me out;

8 Narrative of 'William Fox': N.A.I., RP 620/4/41.
9 N.J. Curtin, *The United Irishmen: Popular politics in Ulster and Dublin 1791–1798* (Oxford, 1994), p. 260.
10 R.R. Madden, *The United Irishmen, their lives and times* (3rd ser., Dublin, 1846), i, p. 222.

Better he swing than I, on
Some hangin' day.'[11]

In Wexford, too, the middling ranks claimed to have joined the insurgents under duress, but the rank–and–file sense of betrayal seems to have been strongest in the north. Among the Presbyterian radicals, moreover, the post-rebellion recriminations had an added sectarian edge. Before the Presbyterian attorney James Dickey was hanged at Belfast, he allegedly declared that 'the eyes of the Presbyterians had been opened too late' and that the massacres in Leinster had shown that a successful rebellion would have been followed by civil war. This macabre piece of political theatre, probably orchestrated by the authorities, was reported in the popular historical accounts of Sir Richard Musgrave and Henry Joy.[12] Musgrave in particular seized upon any evidence of tensions within the United Irishmen; his aim was to emphasize the unnatural character of the alliance between papists and Dissenters and to show that the Wexford massacres had 'evinced the secret designs of the Romanists, and, by opening the eyes of the Northern Presbyterians, completely disunited them'.[13] In a similar vein were reports that the Catholics of Glenarm had refused to serve under the local Presbyterian minister, Robert Acheson, and that the Defenders had deserted the rebel forces the night before the battle of Ballynahinch.[14] Although the Victorian historian Richard Madden found that these tales were not true, they are popularly believed in the north-east, even today.[15]

II

The opening years of the nineteenth century constituted a formative period in Irish historiography.[16] In contrast to the half-century after 1745, a period characterised by the development of relatively consensual views of the Irish past, the decades after '98 witnessed a revival of partisan scholarship in which the responsibility for the rebellion and the shape of the union settlement became key issues. The hardline loyalists, led by Musgrave, compiled reductionist narra-

11 D.H. Akenson and W.H. Crawford (eds), *Local poets and social history: James Orr, bard of Ballycarry* (Belfast, 1977), pp 39–40.
12 *B.N.L.*, 24 July 1798; Sir Richard Musgrave, *Memoirs of the different rebellions in Ireland* ... (Dublin, 1801), pp 184, 558; Henry Joy (ed.), *Historical collections relative to the town of Belfast* (Belfast, 1817), p. xi.
13 Musgrave, *Memoirs*, pp 181,189. 194, 558.
14 Ibid., pp 181, 557.
15 Frank Wright, *Two lands on one soil: Ulster politics before Home Rule* (Dublin, 1996), p. 42.
16 Donal MacCartney, 'The writing of history in Ireland 1800–30', *I.H.S.*, x (1956–7), 347–62; Oliver MacDonagh, *States of mind: A study of Anglo-Irish conflict 1780–1980* (London, 1983), chap. 1.

tives which joined together 1641, 1688–91 and 1798 in an attempt to demonstrate the unchanging treachery of papists. The liberal Protestants, led by the
Revd James Gordon, played down the scale of Catholic disaffection and condemned the excesses of the loyalist backlash. Catholic apologists such as Edward
Hay took a similar line, attributing Catholic disloyalty to loyalist persecution and
fear rather than organized conspiracy. All these accounts were written at a time
when the apportioning of blame for the rebellion was inseparable from the continuing discussion of government policy in Ireland – most obviously the questions of union and emancipation.[17] Unsurprisingly, then, the debate was
dominated by Wexford, the subject of books by Charles Jackson (1798), George
Taylor (1800), James Alexander (1800), James Gordon (1801, 2nd edn 1803),
Edward Hay (1803) as well as Musgrave himself. Other memoirs of Leinster
insurrectionists such as Thomas Cloney (1832) and Joseph Holt (1838) later
found their way into print; the last was Miles Byrne's three-volume *Memoirs*,
published posthumously by his widow in Paris in 1863.

Set against this literature the silence from Ulster is deafening. The notable
exception was Thomas Ledlie Birch, who had been convicted of treason after
the battle of Ballynahinch but through the influence of his brother, a captain of
the Newtownards Yeomanry, had received permission to emigrate to America.[18]
His *Letter from an Irish emigrant to his friend in the United States* (1799), written
soon after his arrival in Philadelphia, set the turn-out in the long-term context of
the religious persecution suffered by Irish Presbyterians since the restoration of
Charles II. Given his audience, it is not surprising that he emphasized the politicization of Ulster Presbyterians during the American War of Independence or
that he appealed to the memory of the Hearts of Steel, many of whom had emigrated in the early 1770s.[19] With nothing left to lose, Birch was also free to
expound his own brand of republican millenarianism and to boast that if the
Belfast leaders had not hesitated, the province of Ulster would have been carried
in a single day.[20] Free of the need for self-censorship, his American pamphlet
perhaps provides some indication of the feelings of many others. In Ulster itself,
however, the only apologias for the United Irishmen came from Catholics:
Charles Hamilton Teeling's *Personal narrative of the Irish rebellion of 1798* (1832),
and *The life of the Revd James Coigley* (1798), edited by Valentine Derry.

---

17 See L.M. Cullen, 'Late eighteenth-century politicization in Ireland: Problems in its study
  and its French links' in L.M. Cullen and Louis Bergeron (eds), *Culture et pratiques en France
  et en Irelande XVIe-XVIIIe siècle* (Paris, [1991]), pp 137–57; Kevin Whelan, ''98 After '98:
  The Politics of Memory', in Kevin Whelan, *The tree of liberty: Radicalism, Catholicism and
  the construction of Irish identity 1760–1830* (Cork, 1996), pp 135–8.
18 T.L. Birch, *A letter from an Irish emigrant to his friend in the United States* (Philadelphia,
  1799), pp 19–22.
19 Ibid., pp 2–3.
20 Ibid., pp 9, 86–7.

The conspicuous silence of Ulster Presbyterians is easily explained. At a time when the church authorities were engaged in negotiations with the government over the future of the *regium donum*, the predominant loyalist party led by Robert Black of Derry ensured that 'all allusion to the events of 1798 was wisely and liberally avoided'.[21] An inquiry launched by the Synod into the behaviour of the ministers and probationers under the care of its presbyteries hastily concluded that a 'comparatively small number' had been implicated in the insurrection and that there was no ground for suspecting the loyalty of the Synod as a body.[22] A very different picture, however, could be found in Musgrave's massive *Memoirs of the different rebellions in Ireland* (1801) which, although remembered primarily as a milestone in the history of anti-Catholic invective, contained damning information on Presbyterian participation. He listed eighteen ministers involved in the rebellion, and singled out well-known radicals such as Sinclare Kelburn, Thomas Ledlie Birch, William Steel Dickson, Samuel Barber, Robert Acheson and Archibald Warwick for particular censure.[23] Though he pointed out repeatedly that most Presbyterians outside Antrim and Down had remained loyal during the insurrection, Musgrave observed that only the Established Church was steady in its loyalty to king and constitution; the Presbyterian Church, on the other hand, had emerged from a republic, and its members had tended towards that form of government throughout Europe.[24]

It was a profoundly embarrassing for the Synod, therefore, when Steel Dickson was released from Fort George in 1802. Many ministers had been accused of complicity in the rebellion; many had been imprisoned for short periods of time and had quietly resumed their pastoral duties. But Dickson was another matter. Although he had never been brought to trial, it was widely believed that he had held the rank of adjutant-general of the rebel army of County Down, and he was the only Presbyterian clergyman to have been made a state prisoner. Following his release, Dickson was re-admitted to the Synod, though many individuals were strongly opposed to his membership and had acquiesced only 'on the ground of avoiding painful discussions'.[25] In 1805, however, this uneasy silence was broken when Dickson began to complain about a resolution passed in 1799 which had described him as 'implicated in treasonable and seditious practices', and about the exclusion of his new congregation, Second Keady, from a share of the *regium donum*. Eventually, in 1812, he produced a long vindication of his political career which attacked 'the *pious* and *loyal* servili-

---

21 Robert Black, *Substance of two speeches, delivered in the General Synod of Ulster at its annual meeting in 1812* (Dublin, 1812), p. 5. The *regium donum* was a grant paid by the state to the Presbyterian clergy since 1672.
22 Ibid., p. 221.
23 Musgrave, *Memoirs*, pp 80, 111, 124, 178, 181, 557, appendix ix.
24 Ibid., pp 120, 182.
25 Black, *Substance of two speeches*, p. 3.

ty of a small, but, latterly, a dominant party' in the Synod.[26] It is significant that around this time Dickson delivered speeches to Catholic meetings in Dublin, Armagh and Newry, and that he went to the press with the encouragement of a group of Dublin Catholics rather than his own co-religionists in the north.[27]

Dickson's *Narrative* described the making of a Presbyterian radical from his enlightened education at Glasgow University to his anti-government stance during the American war, his involvement in the election campaigns of the independent interest in 1783 and 1790, and his support for parliamentary reform and Catholic Emancipation in the 1790s. About his United Irish career Dickson said only that he had taken the society's test in 1791 and was frequently in the company of United Irishmen, that he visited the Kilmainham prisoners, and that he had helped organize the legal defence of some members of his congregation.[28] Much space was taken up in describing Dickson's movements in the days before his arrest. While he went to great lengths to disprove the statements of the informers John Hughes and Nicholas Mageean regarding his appointment, he did not explicitly deny them. Regarding his supposed position as adjutant general, he would say only that 'I have neither acknowledged, nor denied the charge; and, I am fully convinced that there is not a man on earth capable of proving, either its truth, or its falsehood.'[29] He offered no defence of revolutionary republicanism, and described the insurrection merely as the 'partial insurrection into which it [Ireland] had been *somehow seduced* or *provoked* in 1798'.[30] While the controversy provoked by his remarks showed that there were still deep political divisions within the Synod, it also revealed the determination of conservatives to marginalize and eliminate the most visible reminder of 1798, and the reluctance of their opponents to discuss the real origins of the rebellion.[31]

The other Presbyterian writer to broach the subject was Henry Joy, in his *Historical collections relative to the town of Belfast* (1817). A former editor of the *Belfast News-Letter*, Joy was a veteran reformer who had played a leading role in the Volunteer movement in the 1780s. The preface to his book, essentially an apologia for the moderate faction which had opposed the Belfast republicans in the 1790s, sought to reinstate the old whiggish interpretation of Presbyterian history which asserted the continuing fidelity of the church to the principles of the British constitution under Charles I, Cromwell and James II, its defence of the Hanoverian monarchy in 1715 and '45, and its support for the 'revolution' of

---

26 W.S. Dickson, *A narrative of the confinement and exile of William Steel Dickson, D.D.* (Dublin, 1812), p. 2.
27 Black, *Substance of two speeches*, p. 42.
28 Ibid., pp 23–4, 37–9.
29 Ibid., p. 314. See also pp 72, 207.
30 Ibid., p. 270.
31 See also *Analytical review of a pamphlet lately published by a person styling himself the Revd Robert Black, D.D.* (Belfast, 1813); W.S. Dickson, *Retractions* (Belfast, 1813).

1782. Some of Joy's old radicalism could still be detected in his description of the war against revolutionary France as a 'detestable confederacy', and his enthusiasm for the revival of the English reform movement in 1817.[32] His continuing commitment to constitutional change, however, was circumscribed by his fear of the Roman Catholic masses. The cautious approach to emancipation which he had advocated in the early 1790s had apparently been vindicated by the Wexford revolt, when the Catholics had displayed 'all the bigotry and intolerance of the middle ages'.[33] Consequently, Joy gave unhesitating support to the Union as the only security for Irish Protestantism. His advocacy of reform within the new United Kingdom supplies the link between the old Northern Whig club and the Ulster Liberalism of the nineteenth century – which declared itself in favour of Catholic Emancipation but always remained suspicious of Catholic mobilization, and consistently dismissed the repeal of Union as romantic and impracticable.

III

In the eighteenth century neither the Synod of Ulster nor its non-subscribing offshoot the Presbytery of Antrim had produced an ecclesiastical history of Presbyterianism in Ireland. Materials had been gathered for the task by the Revd William Campbell, whose manuscript notes are preserved in the Presbyterian Historical Society of Ireland. His sympathetic account of 1790s radicalism describes an essentially loyal, industrious community driven into insurrection by the withholding of reform and by the reign of terror enforced after 1796. 'As to the rebellion that was raised in Ulster', he wrote, 'it was the act not of the body of Presbyterians, but only of a part made mad by unexampled oppression: which appeared to have been contrived by the prevalent faction ... to ruin the nation and make way for the Union'.[34] Campbell's manuscript was never completed, however, and it was not until much later that the Synod found its historian in James Seaton Reid, professor of church history at Belfast Academical Institution (1837–41) and Glasgow University (1841–51). His monumental three-volume history was published between 1834 and 1853 – the last volume completed after his death by W.D. Killen – and remains the essential starting point for historians.[35] By that stage however, the political situation had changed dramatically;

32 Joy (ed.), *Historical collections*, pp iv–v. See also [James Thomson] 'Recollections of the Battle of Ballynahinch', in the *Belfast Magazine and Literary Journal* (1825), pp 56–64; and [Samuel Edgar], 'Recollections of 1798', ibid., pp 540–8.

33 Joy (ed.), *Historical collections*, p. x.

34 William Campbell, 'History of the Presbyterians in Ireland': Unpublished MS, Presbyterian Historical Society, Belfast, pp 100–1.

35 For Reid, see Robert Allen, *James Seaton Reid: A centenary biography* (Belfast, 1951).

the views of Reid and Killen reflect very different theological and political priorities from those of Campbell's generation.

The 1820s had been a watershed decade for Ulster Presbyterians. The rise of O'Connell's Catholic Association as a powerful political force was accompanied by an internal ferment within the Presbyterian church as a new evangelical spirit revitalised the forces of orthodox Calvinism. After almost half a century of theological ceasefire, the interlinked questions of Trinitarian orthodoxy and subscription to the Westminster Confession erupted once again, and the old conflict between New Light and Old Light was only resolved by the withdrawal of the Arian minority from the Synod in 1829 and the reassertion of the church's Calvinist identity. The architect of the Old Light victory was Henry Cooke, in whose person theological conservatism, anti-Catholicism and Tory politics were powerfully conjoined. Born in Maghera, Cooke had been baptized by the radical clergyman John Glendy, and had witnessed the burning of his meeting-house by the Tipperary Militia. Although only a child of ten, he later wrote of that year that 'impressions were left in my mind that I have never forgotten'.[36] According to Cooke's own testimony, indeed, '98 had been the controlling experience in shaping his political creed. In his most famous speech, an attack on Repeal, he warned Daniel O'Connell, that 'the unhappy men and women who fell victims at Scullabogue barn and Wexford Bridge have been the political saviours of their country ... They live in our remembrance – their deaths opened the eyes of many thousands in Ulster.'[37]

It is clear that Cooke did not speak for all Presbyterians. Praised by his colleagues as the hero who had purified his church from heresy, his political connections with the Tory aristocracy were nevertheless rejected by the majority of ministers who saw the natural position of the Presbyterian church as protector of the tenant farming class against the tyranny of Anglican landlordism. Cooke's arch-opponent, the New Light leader Henry Montgomery, was not only a prominent supporter of Catholic Emancipation, but one of the few ministers who had supported Dickson within the Synod. He had his own memories of 1798: his two eldest brothers fought at Antrim and his home had been looted and burned by the yeomanry.[38] 'The truth ought not to be concealed', Montgomery wrote from the safe distance of 1847; 'the Rebellion, at the close of the last century was, in its origin and almost to its end, an Ulster rebellion and a Presbyterian rebellion'.[39] Yet Montgomery, who had been a close friend of William Drennan, was careful to distinguish between the 'pure and moderate purposes'

36 Finlay Holmes, *Henry Cooke* (Belfast, 1981), p. 4.
37 Wright, *Two lands on one soil*, p. 51.
38 Robert Allen, 'Henry Montgomery, 1788–1865', in H.A. Cronne, T.W. Moody and D.B. Quinn (eds), *Essays in British and Irish history in honour of James Eadie Todd* (London, 1949), p. 255.
39 Henry Montgomery, 'Outlines of the history of Presbyterianism in Ireland', *Irish Unitarian and Bible Christian*, ii (1847), 330.

of the original societies and the 'mad schemes' of insurrection adopted by their younger, weaker, and more extreme followers.[40] His bold statement that during the previous forty years he had found his best friends 'among the United Irishmen of 1798' hints at the survival of a radical circle in Belfast who not only dissented from conservative politics but refused to accept the orthodox interpretation of '98 itself.[41]

It was of vital importance that the first histories of Irish Presbyterianism, including Reid's pioneering research, took place in the context of the subscription controversy, for the neat equation of religious liberalism and radical politics asserted by both Cooke and Montgomery had a distorting effect upon views of the eighteenth century. Reid, like most Presbyterian intellectuals of the nineteenth century, was a staunch Whig and an opponent of the Tory-Anglican politics of the Orange Order, but he was also hostile to both the latitudinarianism and the republican politics of the late eighteenth century. In a sermon preached to the Synod in 1828 on the text 'Remember, therefore, from whence thou are fallen', he recalled his colleagues to what he saw as the true Presbyterian tradition represented by seventeenth-century Calvinism.[42] The 'New Light' or liberal theology which had emerged in the 1720s and triumphed in the 1770s was seen as a deviation from these foundations; the last quarter of the century was a dark period when 'error was avowed by its advocates in Presbyterian Ulster with a degree of boldness which they had never hitherto ventured to assume'.[43] Reid and his Victorians looked desperately to the less glamorous Old Lights and to the breakaway Seceders as the carriers of a continuous 'evangelical' tradition.

While Reid's work (as completed by Killen) sought to play down Presbyterian participation in the rebellion, his particular aim was to absolve the orthodox ministers of any blame. He chipped away at Musgrave's figures, pointing out that four of the eighteen rebel ministers he had listed were probationers (clerical students) and that many of the others had never been convicted of any crime. More specifically, he noted that a large proportion of those involved in rebellion were 'the noted abettors of New-Light principles'.[44] Naturally this identification of disaffection with theological error was simplified and distorted by Reid's lesser imitators. In 1871 the nephew and biographer of Henry Cooke confidently asserted that only a few clergymen, mostly Arians, had joined the rebels while the loyalists were orthodox to a man – an entirely misleading statement.[45] Similarly, the historians of the Reformed Presbyterian or Covenanter church, whose

40 Ibid., p. 334.
41 Ibid., p. 335.
42 J.S. Reid, *The history of the Presbyterian Church, briefly reviewed and practically improved* (Belfast, 1828).
43 J.S. Reid, *History of the Presbyterian Church in Ireland*, ed. W.D. Killen (3rd ed., Belfast, 1867), iii, p. 368. Killen took up the narrative at 1738, using materials gathered by Reid.
44 Ibid., iii, pp 396–7.
45 J.L. Porter, *The life and times of Henry Cooke* (London, 1871), pp 12–5.

members were more deeply involved in insurrectionary activity than any other Presbyterian group, sought to prove the innocence of their forebears.[46] By highlighting the prominence of the New Light ministers – now a spent force – Reid and Killen were thus able to suggest that the brand of 'scripture politics' preached by men like William Steel Dickson had been an aberration, essentially alien to the Presbyterian tradition. 'There has seldom been a national commotion', he concluded, 'in which religion was so little concerned.'[47]

IV

While the official pronouncements of church leaders are easily accessible to the historian, it is much harder to gauge popular attitudes. The eclipse of the Belfast reformers – vilified in election squibs as the '98 set' – was complete by 1832.[48] The enlightened, philanthropic, and clubbable market town of the late eighteenth century was now a burgeoning industrial city and port, an integral part of the expanding British economy, already disfigured by the sectarian divisions imported from the countryside by migrant workers. From 13,000 inhabitants in 1782, its population had grown to 50,000 by 1831. When the nationalist journalist Charles Gavan Duffy settled there in 1839, he noted ironically that his bitterest enemies were found among the descendants of those who had surrounded Tone and Russell fifty years before.[49] Rapid industrialization was erasing much of the past, both physically and culturally. Several decades later, the local historian George Benn claimed that among 'the majority in this young, busy, commercial community' the ideals of the Volunteers and the United Irishmen had little appeal. 'The life of the eighteenth century', he remarked, 'so quaint in our eyes when a glimpse of it can be recovered, has been pushed to the well of forgetfulness.'[50]

Belfast, as the focal point of nineteenth-century migration, was exceptional in this respect yet, even here, the erosion of late eighteenth-century memories, and of the social structures which reproduced them, was not as total as Benn suggested. When Thomas MacKnight, editor of the liberal *Northern Whig*, arrived in Belfast in 1866 he found that the scenes of battles and executions were still pointed out.[51] The descendants of William Drennan preserved his valuable correspondence and jealously protected his reputation against appropriation by nationalists.[52] Other relatives, often widows and daughters, also acted as guar-

46 Samuel Ferguson, *Brief biographical sketches of some Irish covenanting ministers* (Londonderry, 1897), pp 26–62.
47 Reid, *History*, iii, p. 384.
48 *The Down squib book* (Belfast, 1831), p. 61.
49 Charles Gavan Duffy, *My life in two hemispheres* (1898, repr. with intro. by John H. Whyte, Shannon, 1969), i, p. 61.
50 George Benn, *A history of the town of Belfast* (London, 1877), pp 666, 668.
51 Thomas MacKnight, *Ulster as it is* (2 vols, London, 1896), i, p. 23.
52 See the letters of the Drennan family in P.R.O.N.I., D.729.

dians of republican lore, and perhaps enjoyed enhanced status among erstwhile United Irishmen. It was to the 'fidelity of female friendship', demonstrated by Mary Ann McCracken, the daughters of Samuel Neilson and others, that Richard Madden owed much of the biographical material which appeared in his memoirs of the United Irish leaders in the 1840s.[53] Many relics of the rebellion period, perhaps hidden after the rebellion, also resurfaced in the nineteenth century. When two members of the Belfast Natural History and Philosophical Society assembled an exhibition of Irish antiquities in 1852, they received, in addition to bronze swords and flint arrowheads, several collections of iron pike-heads of '98, a United Irish ribbon and a silver medal with 'Remember Orr' engraved on it.[54] They were deposited in the Belfast Museum, where Henry Joy McCracken's volunteer uniform is still displayed.

In the countryside, however, oral tradition was much more tenacious. Memories coalesced around well-known features of the local landscape such as 'Madman's Leap' near Larne, the scene of a daring escape, McCracken's Well at Slemish, said to have been discovered when the Ulster commander prodded the ground with his sword, or the Bochill, a standing stone at the back of Divis, where United Irish meetings were held.[55] By a similar process the drama of 1798 became personalized: a good example is the legend of 'Bloody Castlereagh', which had particular significance in County Down where the apostate Robert Stewart had betrayed not only his country but the independent interest and the Presbyterian church. Legends naturally centred around fantastic episodes such as the disarming of five Tay Fencibles by the servant George Dickson, subsequently nicknamed 'General Halt'.[56] And sometimes the past was literally dug up, as when the remains of a hanged United Irishman were discovered during the construction of a new water-supply for Ballymena in 1883.[57]

Stories concerning the concealing of rebels, executions, and the atrocities committed by the yeomanry in the aftermath of the insurrections were passed on in vivid detail.[58] In the middle decades of the century, the Revd Classon Porter of Larne interviewed survivors such as 'the old Croppy' James Burns of Templepatrick, and collected anecdotes and stories for publication in the *Northern Whig*.[59] Similar materials were preserved by the Carrickfergus antiquarian Samuel

53 Madden, *United Irishmen* (2nd ser., London, 1843), i , p. 74; ii, p. 389.
54 *Descriptive catalogue of the collection of antiquities, and other objects, illustrative of Irish history, exhibited in the museum, Belfast, on the occasion of the twenty-second meeting of the British Association for the Advancement of Science, September 1852* (Belfast, 1852).
55 A.T.Q. Stewart, *The summer soldiers: The 1798 rebellion in Antrim and Down* (Belfast, 1995), p. 95; R.M. Young, *Ulster in '98* (Belfast, 1893), pp 30, n. 32.
56 Young, *Ulster in '98*, pp 46–7.
57 W.S. Smith, *Memories of '98* (Belfast, 1895), pp 63–4.
58 In addition to the sources already cited see *Old Ballymena: A history of Ballymena during the 1798 rebellion* [Ballymena, 1857], pp 13–56.
59 Young, *Ulster in '98*, pp 18–65.

McSkimmin, a Presbyterian and former yeoman.[60] When the *Ulster Journal of Archaeology* was revived in 1894 under the direction of the indefatigable Francis Joseph Bigger, its prospectus explicitly called for '98 material. With Bigger's encouragement, the Revd W.S. Smith of Antrim published a collection of stories concerning lucky escapes, pike making, and daring exploits passed on by the members of his congregation with 'strange indifference'.[61] In addition to the 'rebellion crazy' Smith,[62] Bigger found other allies among the Presbyterian clergy. The Revd Andrew James Blair of Ballynure, County Antrim, whose predecessor Adam Hill had been a United man, took great pride in the fact that William Orr's body had been dressed in his meeting-house.[63] J.W. Kernohan, a founding member of the Presbyterian Historical Society, found references to another radical preacher, John Smith, in the session book of the Kilrea congregation. Interestingly, he encountered opposition from the Kilrea minister, and warned Bigger that Smith's descendants might cause trouble. 'One of them', he wrote, 'I would call litigious.'[64] Local poems, ballads and songs from the '98 period, invariably proclaimed to be on the verge of extinction, were also collected by amateur antiquarians.[65] Others continued to be written, such as William McComb's 'Bessie Grey', a popular ballad which sat rather uneasily with his verses celebrating the life of Henry Cooke, the evangelical revival of 1859, and the Royal Navy.[66]

Can the survival of these tales be taken as evidence of ideological dissent? It seems possible that they helped to sustain an alternative set of values which bolstered Liberalism by underlining the continuing distance between Presbyterians and the Tory elite. James Porter's classic satire *Billy Bluff* (1796) was republished in 1868 and 1879, with a preface reminding the 'sickly Presbyterians' of their forefathers' struggle against landlordism.[67] But the evidence considered above suggests that where 1798 continued to feature in Protestant mentalities, it did so in a localised context, largely detached from political meanings. This is true even of the most famous literary memorial to the Ulster rebellion, W.G. Lyttle's, *Betsy Gray: or Hearts of Down*, first published in 1886. Lyttle was a Liberal newspaper editor from Newtownards who had interviewed relatives and descendants of those who had suffered during the rebellion. Although the United

---

60 His unfinished history of the rebellion, posthumously published as *Annals of Ulster, or, Ireland fifty years ago* (Belfast, 1849), would repay further study.

61 Smith, *Memories of '98*, p. 7. The work was originally serialised in the *U.J.A.* (1894–97).

62 Smith to Bigger, 8 Feb. 1894; n.d. [Feb.] 1894: Belfast Education and Library Board, Bigger papers, SM8/1, 3.

63 Blair to Bigger, 6 Aug. 1907: B.E.L.B., BL4/5.

64 Kernohan to Bigger, [1907]: B.E.L.B., KE 17/1.

65 Several can be found in Young, *Ulster in '98*.

66 *The poetical works of William McComb* (Belfast, 1864), pp 357–8. See also John Bell, *The humours of 99: A tale of times after the turn-out* (Larne, 1841); T.C.S. Corry, *The battle of Antrim: A reminiscence of 1798* (Belfast, 1875).

67 *Billy Bluff and Squire Firebrand* (Belfast, 1868), preface.

Irishmen may have been 'foolish and misguided', he observed, the present generation spoke 'leniently and reverently' of them.[68] Despite a vague sense of Irish patriotism, his portrait of the County Down insurgents was a depoliticised one which avoided criticism of the Orange Order. Equally significant was the fact that Lyttle's insurgents went down in legend as 'the Hearts of Down'. The story had first been serialized in his paper, the *North Down Herald and Bangor Gazette*, and the Betsy Gray story was recollected as a celebration of local community ties rather than commitment to the national cause.[69]

The 'Ulsterization' of 1798 had begun much earlier, with the writings of the Larne doctor James McHenry. His three-volume *The insurgent chief: or, O'Halloran* (1824) failed to acquire the popularity of *Betsy Gray*, but it occupies a much more interesting position in Irish literary history. *O'Halloran* clearly belongs with the 'national tale' genre which evolved in the early decades of the nineteenth century, as writers began to construct a distinctive cultural personality for Ireland, usually derived from Gaelic antiquity.[70] It is a well-known trajectory that takes us from Maria Edgeworth's *Castle Rackrent* (1800) to Sydney Owenson's *The wild Irish girl* (1806) and Charles Maturin's *The Milesian chief* (1812) to Thomas Moore's *Memoirs of Captain Rock* (1824) and eventually to the poetry of Young Ireland. Like these writers, McHenry set out to explain the enigma of Ireland to an ignorant metropolitan audience, and like them he located the source of Irish difference in her Gaelic roots. That he was aiming for the 'wild Irish' style of Owenson is suggested both by the title and by the fact that *O'Halloran* was to be the first of a series of 'national narratives' which would centre on the rebellions of the previous 250 years.[71] His hesitation between romantic fiction and documentary history is also typical of Irish writing at this time.[72] Yet the wild Irish genre, fixated on the exotic west and peopled by rakish Anglo-Irish squires and Milesian peasants, had little room for the Ulster Scots middle classes. In addition to his indignation at 'partial and inaccurate' accounts of the northern United Irishmen, McHenry took exception to the unflattering comparison between north and south made by Owenson. His aim was to present 'a fair statement of the manners of the people of Ulster, and of the part they had taken in the late rebellion'.[73] His next tale, *The hearts of steel* (1825) attempted to

---

68 *Betsy Gray; or Hearts of Down: A tale of Ninety-Eight* (3rd edn., Bangor, 1894), p. 165.

69 See also Jack McCoy, *Ulster's Joan of Arc: An examination of the Betsy Gray story* (North Down Borough Council, 1989).

70 Joep Leerssen, *Remembrance and imagination* ... (Cork, 1996).

71 [James McHenry] *The Hearts of Steel: An Irish historical tale of the last century* (3 vols, London, 1825), i, p. v.

72 He came to regret the title as 'too romantic ... for the matter-of-fact statements it contains', and planned to produce a second expanded edition under the 'more appropriate' title of 'The United Irishmen': ibid., i, p. v.

73 Solomon Secondsight [James McHenry], *The insurgent chief: or, O'Halloran, an Irish historical tale of 1798* (3 vols, London, 1824), i, pp xviii, xix, xx.

correct the impression that the Irish were all 'Papists and bog-trotters' by draw-ing attention to the industry, prosperity and intelligence of the northern province.[74] Sadly the last in the series, an account of the Enniskilleners during the Williamite wars, was never written. It was already apparent, however, that McHenry's 'national narratives' were actually regional in character; though he set out to write an Anglo-Irish novel, the result was a portrait of the honest Ulsterman *avant la lettre*. His awkward literary career provides some idea of what would happen as Irishness was redirected away from civic patriotism towards a more ethnocentric conception of the nation.

V

By 1886, when the first home rule bill was introduced, '98 had been subsumed into the story of a self-consciously Catholic Ireland. Just two years previously, an investigation of Irish popular reading matter had found that the Catholic Young Men's Societies were nourished on a diet consisting of Madden's *United Irish-men* and Wolfe Tone's *Life*, alongside the popular histories of Gavan Duffy, John Mitchel, D'Arcy McGee and A.M. Sullivan.[75] The rebellion of 1798 was also the subject of controversy among the political elite, including the prime minister himself. Lord Rosebery remembered how on a visit in 1891 Gladstone 'lost con-trol of himself (for the third time in my experience) in speaking of the Irish rebellion of 1798. In vain did I try to keep him off and turn the subject'.[76] In 1886 John Redmond published *The truth about '98*, an attack on the Unionist propagandists who had refurbished the Musgrave interpretation. What really brought the United Irishmen to the forefront of nationalist consciousness, how-ever, was the 1898 centenary celebrations organized by the Irish Republican Brotherhood and patronized by the different factions of nationalism. In Belfast the moving spirit was Alice Milligan, who helped found the Henry Joy McCracken Literary Society (1895), contributed articles on the Ulster rebels to the *Northern Patriot* and the *Shan Van Vocht*, and organized visits to the graves of '98 men.[77]

For most Unionist writers, the assimilation of 1798 to an unbroken tradition of Irish national resistance merely confirmed their own instincts. A centenary parade held in Belfast on 6 June 1898 was answered by rioting in the Shankill area, while the *Belfast Newsletter* expressed outrage that rebellion and sedition

74 [McHenry], *Hearts of Steel*, i, pp vii–viii.
75 D.G. Boyce, *Nationalism in Ireland* (2nd ed., London, 1991), p. 247.
76 Jonathan Bardon, *A history of Ulster* (Belfast, 1992), p. 404.
77 Brighid Mhic Sheáin, *Glimpses of Erin: Alice Milligan, poet, Protestant, patriot*, supplement with *Fortnight*, 326 (Mar. 1994); T.J. O'Keefe, 'The 1898 efforts to celebrate the United Irishmen: The '98 centennial', *Éire-Ireland*, xxiii (1988), 51–73.

should be celebrated within the capital of loyalism.[78] Perhaps the most interesting and certainly the most idiosyncratic Unionist propagandist was Lord Ernest
Hamilton, one of the chief myth-makers of the pre-partition period. A captain
in the 11th Hussars and MP for Tyrone between 1885 and 1892, Hamilton had
produced books on all the great landmarks of loyalist mythology from the plantation to the Western Front. His masterpiece, however, was *The soul of Ulster*
(1917), which advanced an acerbic colonialist interpretation of the Irish question
in which conventional anti-popery was reinforced with racial theory. For
Hamilton there was no difference between the atrocities on the Bann in 1641 and
those at Wexford Bridge in 1798 save that 'the latter showed a distinct advance in
brutality'.[79] Ignoring Antrim and Ballynahinch, he presented the rebellion as a
holy war, led by priests and carried out with the accompaniment of prayers, gen-
uflections and holy water. At bottom the driving force, as always, was race-hatred
of Protestants: 'They were aliens, and the elimination of aliens has always been
the first item on the official Nationalist programme. They take up room.'[80]
Other, less colourful writers also portrayed 1798 as a sectarian war of extermination, focusing on Scullabogue and Vinegar Hill to the exclusion of Antrim and
Ballynahinch.[81]

    The heirs of the Presbyterian liberal tradition were not so happy to concede
'98 to Catholic Ireland. Ulster Liberals such as James Shaw, former professor of
political economy in the University of Dublin, had been brought up to 'respect
the memory of those who took up arms against intolerable oppression, and
struck a blow for freedom'.[82] These writers employed several strategies to distinguish the patriotism of the 1790s from nineteenth-century nationalism. Firstly,
the secular, rational, and cosmopolitan ideology of their forefathers was contrasted with the parochial, romantic, and sectarian republicanism of the Fenians.
Thomas MacKnight, who wrote on behalf of 'the old hereditary Liberals in the
North', declared that the Presbyterian radicals of the 1790s were not nationalists,
but that 'the most advanced of them contemplated setting up a cosmopolitan
republic based on the principles enunciated in Paine's *Rights of man*.'[83] Secondly,
the Presbyterians were depicted as reluctant rebels: it was only when they saw no
hope of attaining their aims through an Irish parliament that they had taken up
arms; their method had been 'open warfare' rather than 'dynamite and daggers';
and they had learned the lesson that constitutional means for redress must be
used.[84] Finally, they contrasted the political circumstances of Grattan's parlia-

78 *B.N.L.*, 7 June 1898; 15 Aug. 1898, editorial.
79 E.W. Hamilton, *The soul of Ulster* (London, 1917), pp 104–5.
80 Ibid., p. 40.
81 Averell Lloyd, *Letters written during the period of 1798* (Dungannon, 1914).
82 J.J. Shaw, *Mr Gladstone's two Irish policies* (London, 1888), p. 9.
83 MacKnight, *Ulster as it is*, i, pp 19, 23.
84 James McFerran, *The rebellion of 1798 and sketches and incidents of the battles of Randalstown
    and Antrim* (Belfast, 1898), p. 30; W.T. Latimer, *Popular history of the Irish Presbyterian*

ment with the Union, pointing out that the grievances of which the United Irishmen had complained – the oppressive demands of parson and squire – had been redressed by the imperial parliament.[85] As W.T. Latimer insisted, in his *Ulster biographies relating chiefly to the rebellion of 1798* (1897), 'little of what applied to the political position in 1798, has any relevance to it now'.[86]

From this optimistic standpoint, the Act of Union constituted a new beginning, a fresh contract which cancelled out past wrongs by abolishing commercial and manufacturing restrictions and (eventually) sweeping away civil and religious disabilities.[87] In an address to the Antrim Workingmen's Constitutional Association in 1898, James McFerran imagined Henry Joy McCracken returning to Belfast to admire the benefits of 100 years of British rule – from railways, the electric telegraph and the shipyard to the extension of the franchise.[88] The Union, after all, had extinguished the bigoted and corrupt parliament of the Protestant ascendancy; Liberals now complained that a Catholic ascendancy was being erected in its place. The threat of resistance was made explicit by the prominent Liberal and Belfast businessman Thomas Sinclair at an anti-Home Rule demonstration in 1886: 'Would it be a triumph of civilisation if, after having, by eighty-six years of gradual justice, transfigured the Ulster rebels of '98 into the most loyal and devoted subjects of the realm, she [England] were now, by a grand act of injustice, to turn back the shadow on the dial and invite the return of hours of darkness and despair?'[89]

VI

The period between 1880 and 1914 was a golden age of invented or rediscovered traditions, when anniversaries, jubilees, and national festivals proliferated as never before. Like their nationalist enemies, Ulster Unionists promoted the literary celebration and public commemoration of a heroic past, as they sought to mobilize their people in a new age of mass politics. Turning back to the seventeenth century, they found in the 1641 massacres and in the Williamite wars the images of endurance and resistance required to sustain an increasingly embattled loyalism. Inevitably, the premium placed on unity and continuity meant that divisive

Church (Belfast, 1897), p. 13; Thomas Witherow, *A historical sketch of the Presbyterian Church in Ireland* (Belfast, 1858), pp 34–5.

85 W.T. Latimer, *Ulster biographies relating chiefly to the rebellion of 1798* (Belfast, 1897), preface; Robert MacGeogh, *Ulster's apology for being loyal* (Belfast, 1888), passim.

86 Latimer, *Ulster biographies*, preface. See also his *The Ulster Scot: His faith and fortune* (Dungannon, 1899), p. 27.

87 J. MacDermott, *Grattan's parliament, and 90 years of union* (Belfast, 1892), esp. pp 18–19.

88 McFerran, *Rebellion of 1798*, pp 26–7.

89 Quoted in R.F.G. Holmes, 'United Irishmen and Unionists: Irish Presbyterians, 1791 and 1886', *Studies in Church History, 25: The Churches, Ireland and the Irish* (1989), 188.

episodes such as '98 were edited out. Long before the home rule crisis, the political conditions and social contexts necessary to sustain collective memories of the turn-out had been destroyed. Indeed, the circumstances surrounding the disastrous rebellion itself had effectively disabled the heritage of Ulster radicalism.

Yet the turn-out was never entirely obliterated from either the written record or from folk-memory. First, Protestant attitudes were often more complicated and ambivalent than a simple repudiation of the United Irishmen would suggest. Even the *Belfast Newsletter*, which violently objected to the construction of the Wolfe Tone monument in 1898, could not help observing that a monument raised to the memory of Dr William Drennan might not be a bad idea.[90] Secondly, the admittedly limited success of Ulster Liberals in contesting the dominant conservative strain in Unionism allowed alternative readings of the Protestant past to survive. Although they seldom attempted a wholehearted defence of the United Irishmen, they dissented from orthodox loyalism in their insistence that a large share of the responsibility for the rebellion rested with the Ascendancy class and the British government. By stressing the differences and discontinuities between the United Irishmen and later republicans, and by claiming that radical goals had been achieved peacefully under the Union, Liberals were able to square their continuing sympathy for the men and women of '98 with their rejection of Home Rule. The pattern was thus set for the twentieth century, when John Hewitt and other left-wing intellectuals would value Presbyterian radicalism not so much as a bridge to mainstream republicanism as a non-sectarian alternative to it.

The third Home Rule crisis is a fitting point to end this discussion. The dispute over the ownership of the United Irish heritage, brought into focus by the '98 centenary, shows how memories of the rebellion continued to unsettle both Unionist and Nationalist readings of the Irish past. As Ulster Presbyterians once more prepared for an armed struggle against the British government, the curious echoes of the 1790s were detected by the novelist George Birmingham who explored the northern rebellions of 1798 and 1912 in *The northern iron* (1907) and *The red hand of Ulster* (1912) respectively.[91] Such ironies were no doubt lost on the majority of Protestants who enrolled in the Ulster Volunteer Force after 1912, but some Liberals were prepared to locate Unionist defiance in the older tradition of Presbyterian resistance to authority. It is perhaps not entirely inappropriate, then, that among weapons collected by the UVF were some old relics from 1798, hidden after the rebellion and later preserved as souvenirs: a return of the repressed indeed.[92]

---

90 *B.N.L.*, 15 Aug. 1898, editorial.
91 Tom Paulin, 'Nineteen Twelve', in Tom Paulin, *Ireland and the English crisis* (Newcastle upon Tyne, 1984), pp 120–5.
92 Alvin Jackson, 'Unionist Myths 1912–1985', *Past & Present*, cxxxvi (1992), 182.

24

R.R. Madden, historian of the United Irishmen

C.J. WOODS

Richard Robert Madden was born in the year 1798, on 20 August, on the day the town major, Charles Henry Sirr, searched the Dublin house of his father, Edward Madden, a silk manufacturer.[1] He was the youngest of a very large, comfortably-off family that had property in south County Dublin. None of his relations was a United Irishman with the sole exception of a cousin, John Madden, who played a minor role in Robert Emmet's rebellion. His father had, however, been a member of the Catholic Convention that had met in 1792 and 1793.

By training and profession R.R. Madden was a medical doctor, a good example of a physician who pursued many interests outside his professional field. On completing his apprenticeship in Ireland, he went to France for the benefit of his health and worked in Paris as an assistant to an apothecary in the Boulevard des Italiens. Perhaps his travels and residence in France kindled and stimulated his interest in the links between Ireland and France. One of his master's patients was an Irishman, the poet Thomas Moore who resided in the French capital from 1819 to 1822 and who was to publish some years later his *Life and death of Lord Edward FitzGerald*. After six months Madden moved on to Naples, where he practised for two or three years. During two extended visits to England he managed to gain experience at St George's Hospital, London, become a member of the Royal College of Surgeons and engage in journalism for the *Morning Chronicle* – thus demonstrating an extraordinary ability to get things done even from a base remote from the centre. In 1824 he was practising in Constantinople and then, for two years, in Alexandria, during which time he sent articles to the *Chronicle*,

---

[1] The main primary source for Madden's career is autobiographical matter supplemented by contemporary documents and intended for publication. Chaotic and repetitive, it was published serially in the *Limerick Reporter* (dates not established), cuttings from which, bound together under the title 'Autobiography', are in the National Library of Ireland, Ir.92.m.157. His son Richard More Madden edited and published extracts under the title *Memoirs* (Dublin, 1886). Apart from James McMullen Rigg's article on Madden in the *D.N.B.*, there is a full-length biography in Irish by Leon Ó Broin, *An Máidineach: Staraí na nÉireannach Aontaithe* (Dublin, 1971), an article in English by the same author, 'R.R. Madden, historian of the United Irishmen', in *Irish University Review*, ii, 1 (1972), 20–33, and a biographical sketch in J.B. Lyons, *Brief lives of Irish doctors* (Dublin, 1978), pp 74–8.

republished later as *Travels in Turkey, Egypt, Nubia and Palestine* (2 vols, London, 1829). In 1828 he moved to England and married a woman whose father had owned properties in Jamaica. He practised on the Sussex coast and in the Mayfair district of London, thus acquiring considerable respectability. But he was distracted by other concerns, in particular the abolition of Negro slavery. Eventually he gave up practice. In 1833 and 1834 he was a special magistrate in Jamaica, one of those appointed to administer the statute abolishing slavery. Next he toured the United States of America, taking the opportunity to collect information about fellow countrymen who had been involved in the United Irish movement in Ireland thirty or forty years before. Between 1836 and 1840 he was in Cuba as superintendent of liberated Africans, in 1840 (after some home leave) in Egypt with Sir Moses Montefiore, in 1841 (briefly) in West Africa as a special commissioner of inquiry into allegations that slave factories there were being supplied from Britain, between November 1843 and August 1846 (after a stay in Ireland) in Lisbon as correspondent of the *Morning Chronicle*. In 1847 he moved to Western Australia where until 1850 he was colonial secretary, finally returning to Ireland to the relatively undemanding post of secretary of the Loan Board. It does not seem possible that during this time he managed to compile a *magnum opus*, his eleven-volume *The United Irishmen, their lives and times*, published in three instalments between 1842 and 1846 with further instalments between 1857 and 1860,[2] and also to write over a dozen other books of lasting value.[3] Yet Madden did so.

Just when Madden began collecting information for his *magnum opus*, the first two volumes of which were published in the early summer of 1842, is unclear. In the preface to the volume that appeared in 1857, he wrote: 'twenty-two years have elapsed since the collection of the materials for this work was commenced … in the United States of America'. There, in the winter of 1835–6, he met survivors of the Irish rebellion of 1798 (most significantly the medical man William James MacNeven, who shared his views on slavery) and collected information for his work. But there is also evidence in the work itself that he had been collecting information since the early 1830s, encouraged no doubt by the favourable reception given to Moore's *Life and death of Lord Edward FitzGerald*, published in 1831.

'The main object for undertaking this work', wrote Madden in 1857, 'has been to claim a hearing in England for a truthful relation of the struggle in which the United Irishmen engaged, the sufferings and the wrongs which the Irish people endured at the hands of a bad government, a base oligarchy, a bigoted and corrupt parliament, and an army let loose upon them'. He sought to

---

2   R.R. Madden, *The United Irishmen: Their lives and times* (1st ser. in 2 vols, London, 1842; 2nd ser. in 2 vols, London, 1843; 3rd ser. in 3 vols, Dublin, 1846). The 2nd ed., so-called, is in 4 ser. in 4 vols: 1st ser. (Dublin, 1857); 2nd ser. (Dublin, 1858); 3rd ser. (London, 1860); 4th ser. (London, 1860).

3   Eighteen are listed in the *D.N.B.* According to Madden's son, Thomas More Madden, he published over forty books.

rehabilitate the United Irishmen, to lend them respectability and to explain their rebellion as an inevitable consequence of bad government. By implication he was warning the government of his own day of the dangers of unpopular policies. It was not his purpose to examine the movement comprehensively – to investigate external influences such as the Glorious Revolution, the Scottish Enlightenment, the revolt of the American colonists, the French Revolution, or to consider the ideas, policies and differences of the United Irishmen. Nor did he intend depicting them with warts and all – there was nothing on the drunkenness of Napper Tandy and Samuel Neilson, or the parsimoniousness of Hamilton Rowan towards the boatman who secreted him away to France.

Madden set about his research on the United Irishmen with quite remarkable drive and determination that overcame the obvious difficulties of working on an Irish subject when living overseas. An insight into how he coped is to be found in a letter he wrote from Havana in Cuba ('this outlandish place') on 15 January 1837 to a bookseller in Dublin. He wished to purchase a set of the *Northern Star* as well as books on Tone, Robert Emmet and MacNeven, the goods to be shipped via Liverpool. He also asked the bookseller, William Powell (whom he knew personally), to pass on requests to friends in Ireland to do things for him there. He mentioned, perhaps to reassure Powell about payment, that he had a large house and an income of £1,200 per annum.[4] Over the years Madden acquired vast numbers of books, but on two occasions he sold substantial parts of his collection by public auction (2,000 volumes in 1846, 3,500 volumes in 1865), almost certainly in order to pay off the debt he had incurred in the publication of *The United Irishmen*. After his death in 1886 what remained of his library was auctioned off in 1,864 lots.[5]

Later in his researches Madden sent out printed questionnaires to persons he believed could help, a sample of which is to be found in the Madden papers at Trinity College, Dublin. The information he requested on United Irishmen was dates of birth and death, names of parents, place of abode, profession and position, age at death, place of burial, religion and 'remarkable data in career'.[6] He also wrote personal letters. Evidence of the sort of questions he put is to be found in the reply of a certain Captain Hester respecting a government agent named Hugh Wheatley:

> No. 5 – What character? Not a very good one, being dissipated. He swore to one woman being his wife, although we knew to the contrary;
> No. 8 – Was he a temperate man? I never saw him drunk.[7]

---

4 R.R. Madden to William Powell, 15 Jan. 1837, printed in *Limerick Reporter* (see above, n. 1). See also Ó Broin, 'R.R. Madden', pp 24–5.
5 The auction catalogues are in N.L.I. and R.I.A.
6 T.C.D., Madden papers, MS 873/302.
7 *United Irishmen*, 2nd ed. (1857–60), i, p. 487.

Madden depended heavily on his friends and relations in Ireland. Foremost among these was his wife, Harriet, who transcribed his drafts, dealt with matters when he was away from home and generally shared his interests.[8] Only in 1842 and 1843 was he able to spend much time in Dublin. There he befriended the Young Irelander Thomas Davis, who introduced him to the Catholic publisher, James Duffy; Duffy in turn obliged him by undertaking the publication of the third series of *The United Irishmen* (1846), the first and second series having been brought out by James Madden, a London publisher unrelated to himself. When Madden was in Portugal as correspondent of the *Morning Chronicle*, the manuscript of the third series was in Ireland in the hands of Davis, who had agreed to see it through the press. After Davis's sudden death on 16 September 1845 his brother kept it for some months before passing it on to Duffy through Madden's nephew, W.H.F. Cogan.

In 1847 Madden stated that much matter 'of a documentary kind' had been left over and would appear in a 'future supplemental volume' but for his difficulty in getting subscribers.[9] Ten years later it began appearing in four supplementary volumes (discussed below). Referring then to his 'mode of publication at different intervals', he stated that materials had come to hand at different times and from various places.[10]

Madden's approach to his subject was to identify prominent United Irishmen and to compile a biography – what he called a 'memoir' – of each in turn, introducing all the information and especially the documents he had discovered. The first two volumes, however, are largely given over to background material – what Madden called 'historical introduction'. In it he delineates Catholic grievances and relates the rise of secret societies in the second half of the eighteenth century, culminating in the formation of the United Irishmen and Defenders. His treatment of individual United Irishmen in the first series was slight compared with what was to come in the succeeding series. It seems likely that Madden, who could sometimes be cautious, was testing the ground for the reception of an apologia for the United Irish movement. The second series – published in O'Connell's 'year of Repeal' (1843) – also began with an 'historical introduction'. But the frontispiece, 'Mrs Tone and her sons Theobald Wolfe and Matthew', was one that was likely to stimulate affection as well as interest. The introduction was followed by a lengthy memoir not of Tone but of Samuel Neilson – an example of the almost chaotic arrangement that was a characteristic of all Madden's work. The second volume, which depicted Thomas Addis Emmet in its frontispiece, had lengthy articles on Emmet, W.J. MacNeven, Arthur O'Connor, William Sampson and Henry Joy McCracken. The genies were out of the bottle. Readers had to await the third

8 Ó Broin, 'R.R. Madden', pp 26–7.

9 R.R. Madden, *Life and times of Robert Emmet, esq.* (Dublin, 1847), preface p. x. This book is a reprint of vol. iii of the third series with additional appendixes.

10 *United Irishmen*, 2nd ed., i (1857), p. ix.

series (1846) for Madden's memoir of Tone. Altogether, in the eleven volumes published between 1842 and 1860, some seventy United Irishmen were subjects of memoirs or of notices. The notices were usually of United Irishmen of lesser importance and appeared within memoirs of eminent men with whom they were associated. For example, Thomas Russell's nephew-in-law William Henry Hamilton, on whom the tattered mantle of the United Irish leadership fell after 1803, is given two or three pages within the memoir of Russell.

Madden's analysis is indiscriminatingly laudatory of all United Irishmen. It draws no distinction between the earlier and later stages of the United movement, between democrats who joined political clubs called societies of United Irishmen in 1791 or 1792 and insurrectionists who took up arms in or after 1795, or between the Emmet and O'Connor camps in Fort George and Paris. It draws no distinction between the good, the bad and the indifferent. Madden's praise is withheld only from those United Irishmen who, unknown to their confreres, passed on compromising information to the government. His biographer, the late Leon Ó Broin, refers to his 'almost pathological obsession with spies and informers'.[11] These Madden denounces, notwithstanding his stated preference for the rule of law. C. Litton Falkiner, in his study of Robert Emmet, refers to 'Madden's persistent attribution to his heroes of impossible perfection in character and to their opponents of equally unobtainable depravity'.[12]

Madden is not a reliable authority on the United Irishmen's political aims. He equates United Irish objectives with promotion of the Catholic interest and with what he calls 'patriotism' – by which he seems to mean the same thing. He ignores the reality that many United Irishmen – William Drennan and William Stavely are examples – were radicals who harboured deep suspicions of Catholics; he ignores the reality that many Catholics – for example the archbishop of Dublin, John Thomas Troy, and the chairman of the Catholic Committee, Edward Byrne – were, for that very reason, opposed to the United Irish movement. Although he has several chapters on the Sheehy affair of the 1760s (in which few United Irishmen took any interest), he says very little of the influence of the French Revolution, something most historians take for granted as central to a proper understanding of the United Irish movement.

It must be borne in mind that Madden moved in rather conservative Catholic circles and was no revolutionary. In the preface to the first volume of the so-called second edition (1857), he dismisses 'the formation of Utopian theories of government based on notions of the perfectibility of human beings and the practicability of substituting model republics, constructed on the most approved principles of modern constitution-mongers'. He rejects revolts and revolutions as harmful. On the contrary, he believed in 'deterring rulers who would be tyrants from pursuing

11 Ó Broin, 'R.R. Madden', p. 32.
12 C. Litton Falkiner, 'Robert Emmet', in *Essays relating to Ireland* (Dublin, 1909), p. 119.

the policy of 1798 and men of extravagant or lightly weighed opinions from ill-considered projects against oppression, whose driftless, unsuccessful efforts against misrule never fail to give new strength to despotism'. The final volume, published in 1860, was dedicated to his nephew, W.H.F. Cogan, whose name in the disturbed 1880s was a by-word for 'Castle Catholic' and whose property in County Wicklow passed to Madden's son.

On what can be described as the darker side of the United Irish movement, Madden is acutely aware of atrocities committed by the forces of law and order but blind to those committed by United Irish rebels. He either refuses to acknowledge, or makes light of, assassinations carried out by United Irish rebels in 1796 and 1797.[13] He lists Catholic chapels 'destroyed by unknown persons' (almost certainly persons on the government side),[14] but does not mention damage done to Protestant churches by rebels.[15]

Madden's *United Irishmen* was published in three series followed by what he describes as a second edition. The first series (in two volumes) appeared in 1842, the second series (also in two volumes) in the following year, the third series (in three volumes) in 1846. Eleven years later appeared another volume, identified on the title-page as 'First series – second edition'. It does not however correspond in any way to the first series published in 1842. Similarly the so-called 'Second series – second edition' published in 1858 bears no resemblance to the second series published fifteen years previously. And the so-called 'Third series – second edition' and 'Fourth series – second edition' (both published in 1860) were not new editions of earlier volumes. The so-called second edition, the version of Madden's *United Irishmen* most commonly cited by Irish historians, *does* contain a large amount of material already published between 1842 and 1846; moreover this material was revised, corrected and added to by Madden during the interval, an example being his lengthy memoir on Tone. What needs to be recognized is that of the 73 United Irishmen who are the subjects of memoirs or notices by Madden only 17 appear in the so-called second edition as well as in an earlier series; 32 appear only in an earlier series; 24 appear only in the so-called second edition – more correctly called a new series. To give some examples, James Coigly, James Hope, William Putnam McCabe, Henry Munro, Felix Rourke, Thomas Russell and Bartholomew Teeling are all subjects of lengthy articles in the third series (1846); but they do not reappear in any later volume. McCracken appears in the second series (1843) but not in any of the volumes published between 1857 and 1860 – despite the accumulation by Madden of a number of letters received from his surviving sister, Mary Ann McCracken, and now part of the Madden papers at

---

13   *United Irishmen*, 2nd ser. (1843), i, pp 353–8. Cf. Samuel McSkimin, *Annals of Ulster* (Belfast, 1849), passim.

14   *United Irishmen*, 1st ser. (1842), ii, pp 261–2.

15   Cf. Patrick Comerford, 'Church of Ireland clergy and the 1798 rising', in Liam Swords (ed.), *Protestant, Catholic and Dissenter: The clergy and 1798* (Dublin, 1997), pp 234–5.

Trinity College.[16] Another United Irishman, Thomas Cloney, is only very briefly mentioned by Madden, but in the Madden papers there are some useful documents relating to him.[17]

As an historian of the United Irishmen, Madden ranks very high. The sheer size of his *United Irishmen* – eleven substantial volumes together with his *Literary remains of the United Irishmen* (1887) – makes it important as a source. Its strength lies in the many contemporary documents Madden prints in full; in the personal reminiscences and lore of survivors, relations and associates which he records in the text and in extensive footnotes; and in his precise attention to detail when giving genealogical information. Madden attached great importance to dates, places and family connexions. He preserves for posterity a vast amount of information that but for him would have been lost. Deservedly his reputation has survived the many criticisms that can be levelled at his work.

The severest criticism made of Madden's *United Irishmen* in recent years – by Leon Ó Broin – is that he 'tended to utilise a mass of material with scanty regard for order and reliability'.[18] Certainly the shortcomings of the work are immediately evident to any one who turns to it as a source. The contents lists and chapter headings are inadequate and for the first seven volumes there is no index. The reader has therefore to read through all eleven volumes in order to be sure of finding what he is looking for. Madden has a tendency to drift from one subject to another and back again. One example is his memoir on Robert Emmet. In the middle of his treatment of Emmet's expulsion from Trinity College he inserts a large amount of information on Emmet's fellow students who were expelled at the same time. For good measure, he adds a chapter on the apple of Emmet's eye, Sarah Curran, and having dealt with Sarah Curran he goes on to deal with her father, brothers, sisters and husband, supplying all the information he has gathered on their lives and deaths.[19] Indiscriminatingly, Madden throws into his memoirs every piece of information he has found, scattering it around without much thought about its appropriate place. His attempts to analyse and assess produce very little of interest to the modern reader. A fault only to be expected from an historical work produced in Madden's day is partisanship: testimonies of surviving United Irishmen and their friends were sought, heard and believed without question; other witnesses were excluded.

Indeed, with these defects and the lengthy, insufferably tedious historical introductions, Madden's *United Irishmen* would read like a bad undergraduate essay, except for one redeeming feature never found in even the best of these – it is replete with primary material, both documents and reminiscences, totally unavailable elsewhere.

16 See esp. T.C.D., Madden papers, MS 873/70–89, 135–63. They are the basis of Mary McNeill, *The life and times of Mary Ann McCracken* (Dublin, 1960).
17 T.C.D., Madden papers, MS 873/1–134 .
18 Ó Broin, 'R.R. Madden', p. 31.
19 *United Irishmen*, 2nd ed. (1857–60), iii, pp 268–74.

APPENDIX I

Synopsis of R.R. Madden's *The United Irishmen, their lives and times* (1842–60)

[First series] in 2 volumes (London: J. Madden, 1842)
Volume i (pp i-xvii, 1–452)

'Dedication' dated 10 May 1842 (p. v)
'Preface' (pp vii-xvii)
'The United Irishmen, their lives and times: historical introduction' (pp 1–437)
Chapters I–III (pp 39–119)
Chapter IV (pp 120–52)
    Illegal societies. On p. 134 drifts from Defenders to United Irishmen.
Chapter V (pp 153–67)
    Tone and United Irishmen.
Chapter VI (pp 168–77)
    Lord Edward FitzGerald.
Chapter VII (pp 178–204)
    Belfast radicals incl. several documents.
Chapter VIII (pp 205–53)
    Informers esp. Thomas Reynolds.
Chapter IX (pp 254–97)
    Mainly on arrest of Lord Edward FitzGerald as related by Nicholas Murphy.
Chapter X (pp 298–332)
    Informers esp. John Hughes.
Chapter XI (pp 333–78)
    On 'barbarities that disgraced this calamitous conflict … on the part of ultra-loyalists'.
Chapter XII (pp 379–437)
    Esp. Bagenal Beauchamp Harvey, Cornelius Grogan and John Henry Colclough.
'Index to the first volume', i.e. list of contents (pp 439–52)

Volume ii (pp [i], 1–451)

'The United Irishmen, their lives and times' (pp 1–287)
Chapters I–XIV (pp 1–287)
    Substantially on Henry and John Sheares. Asides on others esp. Walter Cox (pp 55–80).
'Appendix' (pp 289–442)
    'No. I: Origin and dissolution of the Volunteers' (pp 289–95); No. II on a short-lived Catholic political society set up Oct. 1791 (pp 296–303); No. III on the early societies of United Irishmen (pp 304–41); 'No. IV: Religion professed by the leading members of the United Irish society' (pp 342–3); 'No. V: A complete copy of one number of the Union Star' (pp 343–9); 'No. VI: From *Faulkner's Journal*: Lord Edward FitzGerald's address to the electors of the County Kildare' (pp 350–53); 'No. VII: Sir John Moore' (pp 354–7); No. VIII on John Colclough (pp 358–60); 'No. IX: Roman Catholic chapels destroyed by unknown persons during and since the late rebellion' (pp 361–2); 'No. X: Revd Dr Hamill's account of Dr Duigenan' (pp 363–8); 'No. XI: Essay on forgiveness written by Mr Henry Sheares the elder' (pp 369–72); 'No. XII: Test, signs and emblems of the United Irishmen' (pp 372–6); 'No. XIII: Edward Lambert Hepenstal' (pp 376–7); 'No. XIV: Major Sirr and "his people"', i.e. spies etc. (pp 378–414); 'No.

XIV: Items copied from "Account of secret service money" applied in detecting treasonable conspiracies'" (pp 415–42).
'Index to the second volume', i.e. list of contents (pp 443–51)
'J. Madden & Co.'s list of recent publications (pp [1–4])

Second series in 2 volumes (London: J. Madden, 1843)

Volume i (pp [i-vii], i-c, 73–440)

'Mrs Tone and her sons Theobald Wolfe and Matthew' (frontispiece)
'Dedicatory letter' dated 16 May 1843 (pp [iii-v])
'Historical introduction' (pp i-c)
'Memoir of Samuel Neilson' (pp 73–344, portr.)
Incl. William Michael Byrne (pp 209–11), Oliver Bond (pp 212–14), John Sweetman's narrative of journey to Fort George (pp 220–7), and Edward John Newell (pp 347–80).
'Appendix' (pp 345–431)
'Index to the first volume', i.e. list of contents list (pp 433–40)

Volume ii (pp [i-iii], 1–538)

'Thomas Addis Emmet' (frontispiece)
'Portraits illustrating this work', i.e. list of portraits (p. [iii])
First volume: 'Mrs Tone and her sons, Theobald Wolfe and Matthew', 'Samuel Neilson', 'Theobald Wolfe Tone in his Volunteer uniform', 'Henry Sheares', 'John Sheares', 'Hamilton Rowan', 'James Hope', 'Edward Newell, the informer'; second volume: 'Thomas Addis Emmet in 1798', 'James Napper Tandy', 'Lord Edward Fitz-Gerald', 'Thomas Addis Emmet in 1803', 'Henry Jackson', 'William James Macneven', 'Arthur O'Connor', 'Henry Joy McCracken'.
'Memoir of Thomas Addis Emmet' (pp 1–208)
Incl. William Duckett (pp 66–72).
'Memoir of William James Macneven' (pp 209–88)
'Some data for a memoir of Arthur O'Connor' (pp 289–334)
'Memoir of William Sampson' (pp 335–88)
'Memoir of Henry Joy McCracken' (pp 399–506)
'Appendix' (pp 507–32)
Incl. lists of persons named in the fugitive and banishment act (pp 521–2) and United Irishmen and Irish refugees in the French Service (pp 524–30).
'Index to the second volume', i.e. list of contents (pp 533–8)

Third series in 3 volumes (Dublin: James Duffy, 1846)

Volume i (pp i-xi, 1–418)

'R.R. Madden' (frontispiece)
'Dedication to the Right Hon. Lord Cloncurry' (p. iii)
'Contents' (p. iv)
'Notice' (p. v-xi)
Introduction (pp 1–14)
'Memoir of William Corbet' (pp 15–62, portr.)
'Memoir of James Napper Tandy and James Bartholomew Blackwell' (pp 63–87)
'Memoirs of the leaders of the Society of United Irishmen who co-operated with General

Humbert' (pp 88–120) esp. James O'Dowd (pp 100–2), James Joseph McDonnell (pp 102–4), Patrick Barrett (pp 104–9), Matthew Bellew (pp 109–12), Henry O'Kane (pp 113–16).

'Memoir of Theobald Wolfe Tone and Matthew Tone' (pp 121–84, portr. W.T.W. Tone)

'Memoir of Bartholomew Teeling' (pp 185–217, portr.)

'Autobiographical memoir of James Hope' (pp 218–95, portr.)

'Memoir of William Putnam McCabe' (pp 296–359)

'Memoir of the Revd James Porter' (pp 360–77)

'Memoir of Henry Munro' (pp 378–401)

'Memoir of Benjamin Pemberton Binns' (pp 402–18)

Volume ii (pp i-iii, 1–350)

'Cap^n Russell, father of Thos Russell' (frontispiece)

'Contents' (p. iii)

'Memoir of the Revd James Coigly' (pp 1–50)

'Memoir of John Tennent' (pp 51–63)

'Memoir of Hugh Wilson' (pp 64–74)

'Memoir of Felix Rourke and some of the subordinate leaders in the Kildare and Wicklow movement' (pp 75–136)

 Chap. II (pp 96–136) headed 'Narrative of Bernard Duggan and notices of his associates'.

'Memoir of Thomas Russell' (pp 137–283, portr.)

 Incl. William Henry Hamilton (pp 210–11, 217, 226).

Appendix (pp 285–350)

 Esp. J. W. Armstrong, Thomas Reynolds, James O'Brien, Sirr and 'Orange atrocities'.

Volume iii (pp i-vii, 1–318)

'Robt Emmett' (frontispiece)

'Contents' (pp iii-vii)

'Memoir of Robert Emmet' (pp 1–318)

 Chapters numbered but untitled. Deals with Emmet and his associates esp. John Allen (pp 135–9), William Dowdall (pp 139–41), Henry Howley (pp 141–4), Denis Lambert Redmond (pp 144–8), Michael Dwyer (pp 148–59, portr.), Thomas Brangan (pp 159–61) and John Hevey (pp 161–2).

Second edition in 4 vols (Dublin: James Duffy, 1857–8; London: Catholic Publishing Co., 1860)

Vol. i (1857) (pp i-xx, 1–596)

'Edwd Newell the informer' (frontispiece)

T.p. reads 'First series – second edition'. Each volume in the second edition is described as a 'series'. There is no correspondence with the series of the first edition.

'Dedication to ... Henry, Lord Brougham and Vaux' (pp v-vii)

'Preface' (pp ix-xvi)

 Discusses work of collecting material. Began 22 years ago in U.S.A. Says 'mode of publication at different intervals' brings faults, as materials came to author's hands at various periods and from various places. States purpose – 'a hearing in England for a truthful relation of the struggle in which the United Irishmen engaged'. Compares Irish Catholics with Negroes and American Indians.

Vol. ii (1858) (pp i-xi, 1–619)

'Theobald Wolfe Tone in his volunteer uniform' (frontispiece)

T.p. reads 'Second series – second edition'.

Incl. notices of William Drennan with list of his writings (pp 262–70), Walter Cox (pp 270–88) and John Brenan (pp 288–90).
'Memoir of Lord Edward FitzGerald' (pp 359–551 portr.)
Incl. brief notice of Nicholas Murphy (p. 431).
'Memoir of the Revd William Jackson' (p 552–68)
'Memoir of Leonard MacNally, Esq.' (pp 569–89)
'Memoir of Roger O'Connor, Esq.' (pp 590–612)
'Appendix I: the mode of governing a country constitutionally by buying up patriots and buying off political opponents' (pp 613–17)
'Appendix II: Joel F. Hulbert' (pp 617–18)
'Appendix III: Theobald Wolfe Tone' (p. 618)
'Appendix IV: experience of Sir Ralph Abercrombie and Sir John Moore of the Orange regime and the Ascendency faction' (pp 618–19)

Vol. iii (1860) (pp i–x, 1–616)

T.p. reads 'Third series – second edition'.
Dedication 'to William H. F. Cogan, Esq., M.P.'.
'Contents' (pp v–x)
'Memoir of Thomas Addis Emmet' (pp 1–196)
Portr. made in Paris in 1803 facing p. 1.
'Memoir of William James MacNeven' (pp 197–256 portr.)
'Memoir of Robert Emmet' (pp 257–545 portr.)
Notices of John Patten (pp 340–41), Michael Quigley (pp 368–9), Philip Long (pp 374–50), David FitzGerald (pp 375–8) and Sarah Curran (pp 502–45); portrs of Michael Dwyer (facing p. 407) and James Hope (facing p. 408); death-mask of Emmet (facing p. 458).
Appendix I: manifesto of 'the provisional government to the people of Ireland' (pp 546–56)
Appendix II: 'Report in manuscript of Robert Emmet's speech' (pp 556–63)
Appendix III: 'Observations on the conduct of Mr W. C. Plunket' (pp 564–89)
Appendix IV: 'Official vindication of Lord Hardwicke's administration' (pp 589–609)
Appendix V: 'Testimonial to the late Lord Plunket' (pp 609–13)
Appendix VI: 'Secret service revelations' (pp 613–16)

Vol. iv (1860) (pp iii–xviii, 1–664)

'Thomas Addis Emmet in 1798' (frontispiece)
T.p. reads 'Fourth series – second edition'.
'To the people of England' (pp v–xxvi)
'Contents' (pp xxvii–xxx)
'Memoir of Samuel Neilson' (pp 1–183)
Incl. notices of John Sweetman and his narrative of journey to Fort George (pp 94–5, 170–83), William Michael Byrne (pp 161–3), Oliver Bond (pp 163–70) and Henry Jackson (pp 165–9).
'Memoir of Henry and John Sheares' (pp 184–390)
Incl. notices of William Lawless (pp 254–6) and Captain John Warneford Armstrong (pp 341–90).
'Memoirs of Wexford leaders' (pp 391–572)

Incl. notices of Bagenal Beauchamp Harvey (pp 461–94), John and Michael Murphy (pp 474–5), John Colclough (pp 495–8), Cornelius Grogan (pp 502–13), Matthew Keugh (pp 513–17), John Kelly (pp 517–18), Edward Roach (pp 519–20), Edward and John Hay (pp 520–37), Anthony Perry (pp 537–42), Esmonde Kyan (pp 542–50), Edward FitzGerald of Newpark (pp 550–63), Jeremiah Fitzhenry (pp 564–9).
Appendix I: 'Notice of Mr Francis Higgins' secret service money dealings' (pp 573–89)
Appendix II: 'T. W. Tone' (pp 589–90)
Appendix III: 'From *Memoirs and correspondence of Marquis Cornwallis*' (pp 590–92)
'Index to the first, second, third and fourth series' (pp 593–663).

APPENDIX II

Index to biographical memoirs and notices in
R.R. Madden's *The United Irishmen, their lives and times* (1842–60)

The 73 United Irishmen who are the subjects of biographical memoirs or notices in R.R. Madden, *The United Irishmen* (11 vols, Dublin and London, 1842–60), are indexed below. Of these, 32 appear only in the first, second or third series (1842–6), 24 appear only in the so-called 2nd edition (4 vols, Dublin and London, 1857–60), and 17 (indicated by an asterisk) appear in the so-called 2nd edition as well as in an earlier series.

Tandy (James Napper), 3rd ser. (1846), i, pp 63–87
Teeling (Bartholomew), 3rd ser. (1846), i, pp 185–217
Tennent (John), 3rd ser. (1846), ii, pp 51–63
*Tone (Theobald Wolfe), 3rd ser. (1846), i, pp 121–84; 2nd ed. (1857–60), ii, pp 1–173

Wilson (Hugh), 3rd ser. (1846), ii, pp 64–74

25

The women of 1798: Explaining the silence

DÁIRE KEOGH

Few aspects of the 1798 rebellion have been so consistently neglected as that of the role of women in the events of that year. Contemporaries drew upon their experience, but for the most part the voice of private women was smothered beneath the public priorities of partisan commentators. There was little enthusiasm in the immediate aftermath of the rebellion for an accurate record of events since both loyalists and the rebels played down the politicization of the 1790s. Conservatives interpreted the rising as a *jacquerie* or popish plot; the United Irishmen minimized their culpability, presenting themselves as 'reluctant rebels' or as moderating elements in a spontaneous rebellion provoked by unrelenting terror.

It was difficult to accommodate women's experience within those partisan frameworks which encouraged the de-politicization of women and their relegation to secondary roles. This tendency is immediately apparent in the mammoth loyalist history of the insurrection, Musgrave's *Memoirs* (1801).[1] This account characterizes women as victims, mourners or raving fanatics. Depositions recalled their sufferings and few are more moving than that of Elizabeth Dobbyn of Old Court, County Wexford, whose husband and two sons were among the one hundred killed in the atrocity at Scullabogue. She recalled going to the barn to collect their remains:

> She found the barn burnt and full of dead bodies, all in a standing posture, some of them with their limbs burnt off, and others with their bowels hanging out, and others with their faces and features disfigured with the fire. That deponent could not distinguish the bodies of her husband and sons from the other dead.[2]

By contrast, Musgrave presents the rebel women as bloodthirsty extremists, devoid of the natural inclinations of their sex. While the flames engulfed the

---

1 Sir Richard Musgrave, *Memoirs of the different rebellions in Ireland* ... (4th ed., Indiana, 1995).
2 Ibid., p. 778.

prisoners at Scullabogue one rebel woman allegedly called out, 'Do they want water? Give them poison.' When prisoners on Vinegar Hill pleaded for mercy, Mary Redmond insisted that they be put to death.[3]

Musgrave also records Madge Dixon of Castlebridge inciting the crowd in Wexford: Madge and her husband, Captain Thomas Dixon, discovered an Orange lodge in the home of Colonel Le Hunte of the Shelmalier yeomanry corps where the Orangemen had plotted for the 'extirpation of the Roman Catholics'. Taking an orange-painted fire screen from the house, the couple rode into town urging the crowd to take the colonel.[4] On that occasion their anger was restrained by Bagenal Harvey, Matthew Keugh and Cornelius Grogan, but mercy was not shown to the ninety-seven prisoners who were piked to death upon Wexford Bridge. Once again, Madge Dixon was to the fore – according to Musgrave, her 'thirst for Protestant blood was insatiable'; she urged the rebels to save their ammunition and 'to give the prisoners plenty of piking'.[5]

Accounts such as Musgrave's were clearly propagandist, but they also reflect late-eighteenth century attitudes and distinctions between male and female roles which emerge from contemporary debate about femininity and female consciousness. It is an irony of the Enlightenment *philosophes* that their reflections on gender perpetuated the subordination of women; for women continued to be excluded from the public realm, refused the vote, and denied the right to serve as jurors. Particularly well known are the writings of Jean-Jacques Rousseau (1712–78), especially *Emile* (1762*)* and *La Nouvelle Héloïse* (1761), which expressed a complex interpretation of woman's nature.[6] From such reflections emerged the 'separate spheres' theory – the concept that men and women existed in separate orbits; 'females, young and old alike, lived out their lives within the metaphorical or literal confines of domestic walls'.[7] Great emphasis was placed upon a

3 Ibid.
4 Transcript of diary of Elizabeth Richards: N.L.I. MS 36,486; Marie de Jong-Ijsselstein (ed.), *The diary of Elizabeth Richards 1798–1825* (Amsterdam, 1999).
5 Captain Dixon remained with the rebel army and was present in Meath in July 1798: E. Doyle, *The Wexford insurgents of '98 and their march into Meath* (Enniscorthy, 1998). George Taylor's *Rebellion in Wexford* (Dublin, 1800), p. 193, records that the couple never was captured despite the offer of a large reward. There is, however, a postscript outlined by Anna Kinsella. In 1898, a letter addressed to *The People* newspaper by the Revd Robert Leech, whose wife's grandfather had been a prisoner of the Dixons; he attributed their fury to revenge for her rape by soldiers: A. Kinsella, 'Women in folk memory and ballads', in Dáire Keogh and Nicholas Furlong (eds), *The women of 1798* (Dublin, 1998), p. 189.
6 J. Grindshaw, 'Mary Wollstonecraft and the tensions in feminist philosophy', in S. Sayers and P. Osborne (eds), *Socialism, feminism and philosophy: A radical philosophy reader* (London, 1990), p. 14.
7 R. Lettert, *Music and image: Domesticity, ideology and socio-cultural formation in eighteenth-century England* (Cambridge, 1988), pp 29–31. For a critique of the binary opposition of separate-sphere theory, see L. Klein, 'Gender and the public/private distinction in the eighteenth century: Some questions about evidence and analytic procedure', *Eighteenth-century Studies*, xxix, 1 (1995), and D. Goodman, *The republic of letters: A cultural history of the*

woman's virtue, but her reputation was of paramount importance. 'Worth alone will not suffice,' Rousseau believed, but 'a woman must be thought worthy':

> A man has no one but himself to consider, and so long as he does right he may defy public opinion; but when a woman does right her task is only half finished, and what people think of her matters as much as what she really is ... 'What will people think' is the grave of man's virtue and the throne of a woman's ... A woman's education must therefore be planned in relation to man. To be pleasing in his sight, to win his respect and love, to train him in childhood, to tend to him in manhood, to counsel and console, to make his life pleasant and happy, these are the duties of a woman for all time.[8]

Yet while women were not believed to be capable of abstract reasoning or of general principles, the complementary nature of the sexes was accepted; 'but for her contemplating sex,' Rousseau asserted, 'a woman is a man'.[9]

Nevertheless, if such qualifications accepted the mental equality of the sexes, their spheres or orbits remained distinct and women's activity was confined to the private realm where she should exercise 'a gentle and improving sway over her husband and [forge] the next generation, breast-feeding and brainwashing her children into patriotic virtue'.[10] Mary Beth Norton has discussed the practical implications of such concepts in the context of the American Revolution. In what is believed to be the first known exchange in American history on the subject of women's rights, Abigail Adams wrote to her husband in March 1776, requesting the congressman to 'remember the ladies' in the nation's new code of laws, reminding him that 'men would be tyrants if they could'.[11] Her request was for simple legal protection, not political rights or admission to the franchise, but even this John Adams jokingly dismissed:

> As to your extraordinary code of laws, I cannot but laugh ... Depend upon it, we know better than to repeal our masculine systems. Although they are in force, you know they are little more than theory ... We have only the name of masters, and rather than give up this, which would

---

French Enlightenment (Ithaca, 1994); A. Vickery, *The gentleman's daughter: Women's lives in Georgian England* (New Haven, 1997).

8 Cited in Grindshaw, 'Wollstonecraft', p. 14.

9 See M. Crampe-Casnabet, 'A sampling of eighteenth-century philosophy', in N. Zemon Davis and A. Farge (eds), *A history of women in the west: Renaissance and Enlightenment paradoxes*, iii, (London, 1993), pp 315–47.

10 L. Colley, *Britons: Forging the nation, 1707–1837* (London, 1992), p 239. See also P.R. Backscheider and T. Dykstal (eds), *The intersections of public and private spheres in early modern England* (London, 1996).

11 M. Beth Norton (ed.), *Major problems in American women's history* (Lexington, 1989), p. 83.

completely subject us to the despotism of the petticoat, I hope General Washington and our brave heroes would fight.

Abigail Adams conceded that while the 'government of states and kingdoms' was the concern of men, 'domestic government' was 'best administered by the female'. That said, in a later exchange in 1799 Abigail declared that she 'will never consent to have our sex considered in an inferior point of light. Let each planet shine in their own orbit … if man is Lord, woman is *Lordess*.'[12]

In the French Revolution, too, there was a similar ambivalence towards the role of women. There are the classic images of women's involvement; the Parisian women rioting for bread; their activism during the 'October days' when, armed with pikes and clubs, they returned the royal family to the city; Charlotte Corday plunging her knife into Marat's heart; and the eventual emergence of Liberty or Marianne as symbol of the Revolution.[13] The fate of Queen Marie Antoinette, too, lies at the heart of the Revolutionary narrative. Yet, in this case, we also witness Enlightenment attitudes and evidence of 'the problem of the feminine in the French Revolution'.[14] From his counter-revolutionary perspective, Burke highlights abuse of the queen as a metaphor for the unnatural corruption of the Revolution:

> It is now sixteen or seventeen years since I saw the queen of France … and surely never lighted on this orb, which she hardly seemed to touch, a more delightful vision … glittering like the morning star, full of life, and splendour, and joy. Oh! What a revolution! … Little did I dream that I should live to see such disasters fallen upon her in a nation of gallant men, in a nation of men of honour and of cavaliers. I thought ten thousand swords must have leaped from their scabbards to avenge even a look that threatened her with insult - but the age of chivalry is gone - the age of sophists, economists and calculators has succeeded and the glory of Europe is extinguished forever.[15]

The female revolutionaries are, by contrast, characterised as 'furies of hell in the abused shape of the vilest of women'. Yet, significantly, a great deal of the rhetoric employed by Revolutionary polemicists was rooted in a similar Enlightenment

12 Cited in J.H. Wilson, 'The negative impact of the American Revolution', in Norton (ed.), *Problems*, p. 99. See R. Hoffman and P. Albert (eds), *Women in the age of the American Revolution* (New York, 1988).

13 O. Hufton, 'Women in revolution, 1789–1796', *Past & Present*, liii (1971), 108; G. Rudé, *The crowd in the French Revolution* (Oxford, 1959); K. Offen, 'The new sexual politics of French Revolutionary historiography', *French Historical Studies*, xvi, 4 (1990), 909–22.

14 L. Hunt, 'The many bodies of Marie-Antoinette: Political pornography and the problem of the feminine in the French Revolution', in P. Jones (ed.), *The French Revolution in social and political perspective* (London, 1996), pp. 268–84.

15 Edmund Burke, *Reflections upon the Revolution in France* (London, 1968), pp 169–70.

understanding that men would be forever vulnerable to women's beauty, wit and wiles, powerless in the face of their charms. Thus Marie Antoinette's conviction in October 1793 was secured upon the grounds that she had used her sexual body to corrupt the body politic through her scheming intimacies with the king, his ministers and his army.[16]

In a curious way, however, this 'separate sphere' theory was being formed at the very time when its underlying assumptions were being seriously challenged.[17] This conflict between theory and practice was immediately apparent in the French Revolution, where the radicals were content to harness the energies of the 'blood sisters' while at the same time excluding them from the political sphere. This tension is illustrated in a series of extracts from the *Révolutions de Paris*, which in February 1791 called upon '*citoyennes* of all ages, all ranks' to leave their homes:

> all of you at once, rally from door to door and march towards the city hall ... station yourself at the head of each battalion ... armed with incendiary torches, stand before the gates of the palace of your tyrant.

Yet once the emergency had passed they were instructed to return home, to 'take up the accustomed yoke of domestic duties ... reign sweetly inside your households, teach the rights of man to the stuttering child ... but do not compete with us'. Subsequently, the paper issued a stern instruction; 'women from now, come out only with us or when we instruct you'.[18]

Such mentalities did not go unchallenged and the Revolution marked the beginnings of organised female participation in politics. Indeed the *Declaration of the rights of man and the citizen* gave rise to an immediate debate as to whether women enjoyed comparable rights. The principal feminist declaration, Olympe de Gouges' *Droits de la femme* published in September 1790,[19] demanded a more radical resolution of women's exclusion from the political process:

> All women are born free and remain equal to men ... The aim of all political associations is the preservation of the natural and inalienable rights of women and men ... The nation is the union of women and men ... Law is the expression of the general will: all female and male citizens

---

16 Hunt, 'Marie-Antoinette', p. 271; E. Colwill, 'Just another *citoyenne*? Marie-Antoinette on trial, 1790–1793', *History Workshop Journal*, xxviii (1989), 63–87; D. Outram, *The body and the French Revolution: Sex, class and political culture* (New Haven, 1989).

17 J.B. Landes, *Women in the public sphere in the age of the French Revolution* (Ithaca, 1988).

18 Darline Gay Levy, 'Women's revolutionary citizenship in action, 1791: Setting the boundaries', in R. Waldinger, P. Dawson and I. Woloch (eds), *The French Revolution and the meaning of citizenship* (London, 1993)

19 See J. Wallach Scott, ' "A Woman who has only paradoxes to offer": Olympe de Gouges claims rights for women', in S.E. Melzer and L.W. Rabine (eds), *Rebel daughters: Women and the French Revolution* (Oxford, 1992), pp 102–21.

have the right to participate personally, or through their representatives, in its formation.[20]

Women attended the Cordeliers and Jacobin clubs, they were active among the elective *Section* assemblies, and presented numerous addresses to the Assembly seeking legislation with regard to education, legal and economic rights and divorce.[21] Their cause had been advanced by the Girondin *Cercle Social*, which in October 1790 founded the first political club that formally admitted women. Three years later female militants founded their own Société des Citoyennes Républicaines Révolutionaires which was associated with the *Enragés*; this placed the feminist agenda at the heart of the broader campaign for democracy and social equality. The foundation of such groups, making explicit demands for female citizenship, sets the French Revolution apart from the English Civil War of the 1640s or the American Revolution where there was little public discussion of women's political rights.[22]

In time, however, as the Revolution struggled for stability and legitimacy, women were progressively excluded from political activism. In October 1793, following the execution of the queen, the National Convention outlawed women's clubs. This blow to female participation in popular politics was intensified in the Thermidorian reaction when, after the uprisings in the spring of 1795, women were barred from the galleries of the National Convention. Subsequent legislation placed Parisian women under a type of house arrest, forbidding them from assembling in groups of more than five under pain of dispersal by force and arrest.[23]

Even the language of the Revolution was steeped in the ambiguous rhetoric of the Enlightenment. While universal in its reference to 'man', it was at the same time gendered and exclusive of women. And while the societal head, the king, was replaced by the female Marianne, she was a mirror in which men projected their expectations.[24] In a very brutal sense, as Joan Landes has observed, 'the Republic was constructed against women, not just without them'.[25]

20 Olympe de Gouges, *Droits de la femme* (Paris, 1790).
21 J. Abray, 'Femininism in the French Revolution', in P. Jones (ed.), *The French Revolution in social and political perspective*, pp 237–40. See also O. Hufton, *Women and the limits of citizenship in the French Revolution* (Toronto, 1992).
22 L. Hunt, 'Male virtue and republican motherhood', in K. Michael Baker (ed.), *The French Revolution and the creation of modern political culture*, iv (London, 1994), p. 204; A. Fletcher, *Gender, sex and subordination in England, 1500–1800* (New Haven, 1995); A. Plowden, *'Women all on fire': The women of the English Civil War* (London, 1997).
23 J. Abray, 'Feminism in the French Revolution', in Jones, *The French Revolution in social and political perspective*, p. 248.
24 S. Desan, 'Women's experience of the French Revolution: An historical overview', in C. Montfort (ed.), *Literate women and the French Revolution of 1789* (Alabama, 1994), p. 26; J. Landes, 'Representing the body politic: The paradox of gender in the graphic politics of the French Revolution', in Melzer and Rabine (eds), *Rebel daughters*, pp 15–27.
25 Landes, *Women in the public sphere*, p. 12.

Mary Wollstonecraft compared the denial of women's political rights to the condition of slaves.[26] Her *Vindication of the rights of women* (1792), the founding text of British feminism, raised the question of female citizenship, arguing that women needed a civil existence within the state. 'Women', she argued, 'ought to have representation, instead of being arbitrarily governed without having any direct share allowed them in the deliberations of government.'[27] Yet as Nancy Curtin has illustrated, the United Irishmen, for all their lofty talk of liberty, refused to entertain the possibility of the admission of women to the political process.[28] This is perhaps unsurprising, given their intellectual debt to the Enlightenment and the French Revolution. Indeed, the contradictions present in France were also witnessed in Ireland where the women's role was largely confined to that of 'muse or madonna'. This, however, did not mean that women were uninvolved; indeed, given the convulsions of the decade, it would be naive to believe that women of all classes could remain uninvolved or unaffected by the tumult around them. Despite their exclusion from the programme of the United Irishmen (and from their 'paramilitary homosociability'), Ireland's 'rebel daughters' played an active role in radicalism of the decade, as in France where women's participation was necessary to the success of the Revolution.[29] Many took the secondary United Irish 'oath of secrecy' and a Society of United Irishwomen, on the French model, was it seems established in Belfast by 1796.[30]

There were prominent female activists like 'Mrs Oliver Bond' whose trojan efforts in propagating the United cause were brought to the attention of the Dublin Castle authorities. Some shared Pamela FitzGerald's role, acting as couriers, while others sought to convince men of the necessity of embracing women's rights. Mary Ann McCracken, for example, reminded her brother that 'there can be no argument produced in favour of the slavery of women that has not been used in favour of general slavery'.[31] In a curious way, however, their high profile reflects the acceptability of aristocratic and bourgeois political activity, where the comforts of their class allowed them to enter the public realm while remaining discreetly 'private'. Aristocratic female involvement in British high politics of the later Georgian period is well documented; Peter Jupp des-

---

26 I. Coltman Brown, 'Mary Wollstonecraft and the French Revolution, or feminism and the Rights of Men', in S. Reynolds (ed.), *Women, state and revolution: Essays on power and gender in Europe since 1789* (London, 1986), pp 1–25.
27 Wollstonecraft, cited in B. Caine, 'Women', in I. McCalman (ed.), *An Oxford companion to the Romantic Age* (Oxford, 1999), p. 46.
28 N. Curtin, 'Women and eighteenth-century Irish republicanism', in M. MacCurtain and M. O'Dowd (eds), *Women in early modern Ireland* (Dublin, 1991).
29 N. Curtin, 'Matilda Tone and virtuous republican femininity', in Keogh and Furlong (eds), *The women of 1798*, p. 31.
30 *Northern Star*, 17 Oct. 1796.
31 Mary Ann McCracken to Henry Joy McCracken, 16 Mar. 1797: P.R.O.N.I., McCracken papers, T1210/7.

cribes these years as 'a phase ... when conditions were particularly suited to women playing a role'.[32] Stella Tillyard's *Aristocrats* effectively communicates the atmosphere of the period, while the celebrity of Georgiana, duchess of Devonshire, resulted not because she canvassed in the 1784 election, but because she broke the bounds of respectability, campaigning for one outside her family, Charles James Fox, and doing so in the public gaze of Westminster.[33]

Mary Ann McCracken provides an excellent Irish example of bourgeois participation. In private, her radicalism exceeded that of her brother, yet in public she fulfilled the expectations of republican femininity: removing his broken body from the scaffold, vainly attempting to revive him, and then caring for his daughter, Maria, throughout her life.[34] The esteem for such behaviour reflected an attitude, present among the French revolutionaries, that a woman's moral authority would remain strong only if she left the tainted business of politics to men.[35] Such notions were expanded in the nineteenth century when in the evangelical revival women were increasingly cast as the moral guardians of society, 'anchors of both domestic and public life'.[36]

For the most part, the women of 1798 are recorded in a supporting role.[37] In the years after the rebellion the women's contribution was largely ignored; as Thomas Bartlett has observed, 'women could be symbol or model or victim but the role of actor, activist or combatant – *in a political context* – was denied them'.[38] There was, too, a sense present in both the American and French Revolutions that those who actually fought had betrayed their feminine nature; they had assumed unwomanly roles, becoming 'unsexed' in the process; traditional male and female roles had broken down. Society was embarrassed by images of women fighting, swearing, sweating and killing, behaviour deemed to be incompatible with concepts of virtue; such women were thus no better than prostitutes. Once more, class distinctions are important in this respect; just as the *femmes célèbres* dominate the history of the women in the French Revolution, posterity has not been kind to the memory of Ireland's female *sans coulotterie*. It

32 P.J. Jupp, 'The roles of royal and aristocratic women in British politics, c. 1782–1832', in M. O'Dowd and S. Wichert (eds), *Chattel, servant or citizen: Women's status in church, state and society* (Belfast, 1995), p.103.

33 S. Tillyard, *Aristocrats: Caroline, Emily, Louisa and Sarah Lennox, 1740–1832* (London, 1994); A. Foreman, 'A politician's politician: Georgiana, duchess of Devonshire and the Whig party', in H. Barker and E. Chalus (eds), *Gender in eighteenth-century England: Roles, representations and responsibilities* (London, 1997), pp 179–205.

34 M. McNeill, *The life and times of Mary Ann McCracken, 1770–1866: A Belfast panorama* (Dublin, 1960).

35 S. Desan, 'Women's experience of the French Revolution', p. 27.

36 B. Cain, 'Women', p. 43.

37 See detail from 'The battle of Wexford', G. Thompson, August 1798, preserved in the National Army Museum, Chelsea.

38 Thomas Bartlett, 'Bearing witness: Female evidences in courts martial convened to suppress the 1798 rebellion', in Keogh and Furlong (eds), *The women of 1798*, p. 67.

must be also be acknowledged that what was recorded of women's activity in the 1790s reflected male *expectations* of female behaviour; in this way, contemporary stereotypes have served to filter historical memory.[39]

These attitudes were also enshrined in the law, which denied married women a separate legal persona. Wollstonecraft had gone so far as to argue that marriage imprisoned women, depriving them of all rights not only to their property but also to their children and to their own bodies. This denial may explain why women do not figure prominently in the legal proceedings which followed the rebellion. With the exception of General Henry Munro's sister Margaret (who was incarcerated for twenty-three weeks in Carrickfergus) no woman was held as a state prisoner.[40] None were executed, sent to Fort George, or included in the Banishment Act; indeed, few women appear to have been tried before courts martial. Perhaps they were victims of less formal justice – rape or other atrocities?

During the course of the nineteenth century, however, gestures were made to incorporate the women of '98 in the various waves of literature and ballads which reflected the changing interpretations of the rebellion itself. For the most part these accounts are based on slender evidence; Wicklow's heroine Suzy Toole, for example, first appears as late as 1838 in a passage interpolated into Joseph Holt's *Memoirs* by their bowdlerizing editor, Thomas Crofton Croker. His characture of the Annamoe blacksmith's daughter is less than flattering:

> [She was] 5' 8" tall when she stood upright, which was not often for by the habit of sledging she had acquired a stoop; but her shoulders, though round were broad and her limbs strong and sinewy. Her face when young was broad as a full moon and her nose nearly flat to her face, having been broken by a stone in a faction fight ... and this certainly made her anything but an inviting object. Her eyes were black and sparkling. What they would have been in a handsome face, with a decent nose between them, I will not venture to say. She had an extraordinary ability to change her whole appearance ... With her dirty pepper and salt coloured frieze cloak, her stoop and dropped jaw, she could appear a decrepit miserable *baccagh* scarcely able to crawl, but when it was necessary to act with vigour, her powerful muscles and brawny limbs made her more than a match for many men. A blow from her clenched fist was like the kick of a horse ... She was quick in expedients and ready with a reason for all occasions.[41]

39 M. Myers, '"Like the pictures in a magic lantern": Gender, history, and Edgeworth's Rebellion Narratives', in *Nineteenth-century Contexts*, xix (1996), 373–412.
40 R.R. Madden, *Antrim and Down in '98: The lives of Henry Joy McCracken, James Hope, William Putman McCabe, Revd James Porter, Henry Munro* (Glasgow, 1888), p. 246.
41 T. Crofton Croker (ed.), *Memoirs of Joseph Holt*, 2 vols (London, 1838), i, p. 49; R. O'Donnell and B. Reece, '"A clean beast": Crofton Croker's fairy tale of General Holt', *Eighteenth-century Ireland*, vii (1992), 7–42.

While Holt may have been assisted by a woman known as 'the moving magazine', Suzy Toole is an invented character, based upon the numerous camp followers who aided and supplied the rebel army.

Similar heroines are associated with each of the major theatres of action, but in these cases, too, their renown is based on scant evidence.[42] Mary Doyle of Castleboro, for example, receives mention in Thomas Cloney's *Narrative* (1832) for her determined stand at the battle of New Ross:

> I must not forget to make honourable mention of the female faggot-cutter, the gallant point of war, Miss Doyle. When I was preparing to mount my horse at the Three Bullet Gate in the evening, in a very desponding state indeed, in company with our Commander-in-Chief, the point of war came up to me and asked 'could I think of going and leaving our dear little cannon behind, which had cost the lives of some heroes to obtain'... 'Well', said the amazon, seating herself on it, 'here shall I remain to be shot sooner than leave it behind, and eternal shame be to you if you do not procure me assistance to carry it away.'[43]

Fr Patrick Kavanagh refers to 'an amazon named Doyle, who marched with the insurgent army and bore herself as gallantly as the most courageous man'.[44] Her fame, however is largely based upon William Rooney's late nineteenth-century poem 'Mary Doyle, the heroine of New Ross' in which she is depicted urging on the United army with a wave of her scythe:

> Then a figure rose before us, 'twas a girl's fragile frame,
> And among the fallen soldiers, there she walked with eyes aflame,
> And her voice rang o'er the clamour, like a trumpet o'er the sea,
> 'Whoso dares to die for Ireland, let him come and follow me!

Further embellishments of the Mary Doyle legend intimate that she was betrothed to John Kelly, 'the Boy from Killanne'.[45]

The North Leinster campaign had its heroine in Molly Weston. In this case evidence is equally sparse and her reputation is based primarily on the research of Patrick Archer, the chronicler of Fingal who wrote in the 1930s.[46] A native of Woganstown, near Oldtown in north County Dublin, she was alleged to have been

42 S. Ó Saoithraí, *Heroines of 1798* (Bray, 1998).

43 T. Cloney, *Personal narrative of those transactions in the county of Wexford in which the author was engaged during the awful period of 1798* (Dublin, 1832), pp 41–2.

44 P. Kavanagh, *A popular history of the insurrection of 1798* (Cork, 1898), p. 151.

45 R. Roche, *Here's their memory: A record of the United Irish of Wexford in 1798* (Wexford, 1997), p. 73.

46 Patrick Archer, 'Fingal in 1798', *Béaloideas*, ix (1939), 191–6.

active in recruiting United Irish members prior to the rebellion. Once the fighting began, she rode into battle upon a white horse dressed in green and braid, sporting a plume in her green cocked hat. Her bravery was renowned and legend recalls how she took charge of a field piece. With this, she inflicted heavy casualties upon the Reagh Fencibles, but victory was denied the United Irish army; Molly and her four brothers were among the casualties of the battle of Tara.[47]

There are striking similarities between this and the legend of 'Ulster's Joan of Arc', Betsy Grey of Gransha, County Down, who fought at the battle of Ballynahinch alongside her brother and her lover, William Boal. Mounted on a white horse she inspired the men, leading them on with a green flag, or in some accounts a sword, until she was cut down by a party of the Hillsborough yeomanry cavalry. The earliest documentary reference to Betsy is contained in an account written by Mary Ann McCracken, appended by Dr Madden to his memoir of Henry Munro, but her reputation is based largely upon the Ballad of Betsy Gray, and Wesley Greenhill Lyttle's *Betsy Gray, or The hearts of Down*, published in 1886.[48] In his preface to a recent edition, Aiken McClelland acknowledged the influence of Lyttle's novel:

> Fact and fiction are intertwined in Betsy Gray ... For many years after the publication this was a standard book in almost every County Down home, and although a vast number of books has been written about the Rebellion of 1798, many have gleaned their knowledge of the insurrection solely from Betsy Gray. This may be regrettable from a purely historical viewpoint, but the average reader cares little about the complex political and economic factors which underlay the insurrection. He is content to read with pride how his poorly-armed ancestors defeated the English troops at Saintfield, and to thrill with horror at the murder of poor, defenceless Betsy Gray.[49]

Such priorities are reflected in the folkloric accounts of the women of 1798, many of which are contrived and follow the universal motifs of heroism. The most common trope within the tradition is the story of the lone woman killing the soldier.[50] This has been described as an Irish version of the Old Testament legend of Jael and Sisera. Eleven versions of this fable appear in Ballinamuck tradition, while County Wicklow lore recalls how Susie O'Toole (Suzy Toole?) killed a yeoman who had attempted to molest her.[51]

47 Peadar Bates, *1798: Rebellion in Fingal* (Loughshinny, 1998), pp 66–8.
48 Madden, *Antrim and Down in '98*, p. 244.
49 A. McClelland, 'Preface', in W.G. Lyttle, *Betsy Gray or Hearts of Down* (Newcastle, 1968), pp vii–viii, cited in S. Ó Saothraí, *Heroines of 1798*, p. 35.
50 Maureen Murphy, ' "The Noggin of Milk": An Old Testament legend and the Battle of Ballinamuck', in Keogh and Furlong (eds), *The women of 1798*, p. 182.
51 Ibid.

Within another popular trope, the woman acts not to save her own virtue but to protect her men from the enemy. The story of 'Mrs Grace and the Redcoats' reflects the characteristics of the genre:

> Mrs Grace was living opposite to where Wat Furlong of Carigeen is liv-
> ing now ... Things were settling down this time. She was out spreading
> clothes she was after washing. It was a rale [*sic*] warm day and she noticed
> one of the Burkes running from the direction of Furlong's and the sol-
> diers after him. She saw him running down through the land. The sol-
> diers came into the yard.
>
> 'Warm day,' they said.
> 'It is', says she, 'and I think you should come in and I'll give you a
> drink to refresh you.' She did this out of cleverality to give Burke a
> chance to escape. The soldiers all got noggins and drank a big tub of
> cream on her. But when they were leaving, one of them turned; 'for the
> toss of a pin, I'd shoot you, me auld dame', says he.
> 'For what?' she says.
> 'I know what you did', says he, 'you brought us in here to let the crop-
> py get away.'[52]

Within popular tradition, too, there is a tendency to stress the image of women as camp followers, which has led to the predominance of the 'mother courage' image which emphasizes women's role in the feeding and nurturing of combat-ants on both sides. Such depictions reflect the old-fashioned images of women, present in the memory of both the American and French Revolutions where they are portrayed as 'termagants or shrews preoccupied with food'; they ignore that fact that female support was very often involuntary and that women were frequently press-ganged into service by both sides in 1798.[53] Elizabeth Richards recalled in her diary such an incident when a rebel rode into their yard:

> He demanded or rather commanded that provisions should be sent to the
> camp. 'We are starving Ma'am,' said he to Mrs Hatton, 'send us provi-
> sions or —' he struck his sword with violence on the head of a pump near
> which he had stopped his horse, and without remonstrance from Mrs
> Hatton.
> 'Government may confiscate my property for assisting rebels.'

52 Recorded in 1954 from Mrs Elizabeth Byrne of Milltown, Grange (aged 87), Department of Irish Folklore, M Ms 1344, cited in D. Ó Muirithe and D. Nuttall (eds), *The folklore of County Wexford* (Dublin, 1999), p. 8.
53 S. Elson Roessler, *Out of the shadows: Women and politics in the French Revolution, 1789–95* (New York, 1991).

'If you do not comply we shall be murdered' was the reply by all. An old man was dispatched to the Three Rocks with a car loaded with bacon, potatoes, &c &c, for which Mrs Hatton received thanks from the rebel chiefs.[54]

Popular memory was also tailored to fit the Catholic nationalism which dominated the centenary commemorations of the rebellion. A selective revival of folkloric traditions emphasized the importance of female support for the United Irish rebellion. The account of 'Paddy Roarke' is typical of this development. Captured at the battle of Oulart he was offered his life in return for information; his mother, however intervened urging him to 'die like a man, and never be an informer'. The old woman knelt on the street of Bunclody, bore her breast, and called out, 'Now you murdering yeomen, shoot me and let me die with my son'.[55] Likewise, less attractive aspects of women's activities in 1798 were summarily dismissed. Accordingly the rebel activities of Bridget 'Croppy Biddy' Dolan, arguably the best documented woman of the campaign, was forgotten once she turned informer; she was instead castigated as a libidinous wretch, a rural prostitute without even the anonymity of city streets.[56]

This 'nationalization' reached its climax with the publication of Helena Concannon's *Women of 'Ninety Eight* in 1919. This was an important though dated history in which the secondary role of the subjects was implied by the chapter titles which included 'The mothers of '98' and 'The wives of '98'. The volume was intended as an inspiration for her contemporaries, specifically engaged in the Anglo–Irish War. Notwithstanding these reservations, it highlights the need for a thorough re-evaluation of the dynamics of male-female relationships and remains 'exceptional and ... worthy of reconsideration'.[57]

Nancy Curtin's pioneering investigation of the place of women within eighteenth-century Irish republicanism has recently provided a sophisticated theoretical framework within which it is possible to assess the relevant sources.[58] A variety of female narratives of the rebellion survive, seven of which deal specifically with events in the south-eastern theatre. While their perspective is principally loyalist and Protestant, they reflect the broad spectrum of political opinion;

54 Diary of Elizabeth Richards, p. 32.
55 A. Kinsella, 'Women in folk memory and ballads', in Keogh and Furlong (eds), *The women of '98*.
56 R. O'Donnell, 'Bridget "Croppy Biddy" Dolan: Wicklow's anti-heroine of 1798', in Keogh and Furlong (eds), *The women of 1798*, pp 87–112.
57 M. Cullen, 'United in struggle: The women of 1798', in Enda Finlay (ed.), *Radicals and revolutionaries: Essays on 1798* (London, 1998), p. 21; MacCurtain and O'Dowd (eds), *Women in early modern Ireland*, p. 1.
58 N. Curtin, 'Matilda Tone and virtuous republican femininity', in Keogh and Furlong (eds), *The women of 1798*, p. 31; idem, 'Women and eighteenth-century Irish republicanism', in M. MacCurtain and M. O'Dowd (eds), *Women in early modern Ireland*.

from the liberal commentary of Elizabeth Richards to the conservative, anti-Catholic stance of Barbara Lett of Killaligan, County Wexford. Several of these were recorded during the rebellion, but the majority were written long after the event and bear the embellishments of time and reflection.[59] Of enormous significance, too, are the accounts written by Quaker women who were neither loyalist nor rebels. The diary of Dinah Goff of Horetown contains vivid images of rebels encamped on their lawn, and of particular interest in this context is her description of a menacing band of women gathered outside their windows intent on plunder. Similarly, Mary Shackleton Leadbetter's diary reflects the experiences of a 'peaceful rebel' and indicate the extent of her political engagement.[60] Beyond the south-east, significant records include *The diary of Anne, countess dowager of Roden, 1797–1802* (Dublin, 1870), and Maria Edgeworth's account published in the *Memoirs* of her father.[61] No such narratives appear to survive from those who embraced the rebel cause in the summer of '98.

Contemporary correspondence also provides many insights.[62] The exchanges between the Lennox sisters, for instance, furnish intimate perspectives which become particularly poignant following Lord Edward FitzGerald's capture. In one moving passage Louisa Conolly described the meeting in the Phoenix Park at which she begged Lord Camden for permission to see her mortally wounded nephew: 'I have knelt at his feet and the Brute has refused to let me see my dying Edward.'[63] Further aristocratic observations may be found in the papers of Elizabeth Lady Moira, Anne, countess dowager of Roden, Elizabeth Tighe and the Countess Londonderry.[64]

At a bourgeois level, the correspondence of Mary Anne McCracken, especially the letters written to the state prisoners at Kilmainham in 1797, present a unique account of the evolution of a Belfast female radical.[65] Indeed her impassioned letter to 'Harry' in March 1797 has been described as the fullest articulation relating to the rights of women in late eighteenth-century Ireland:

> Is it not almost time for the clouds of error and prejudice to disperse and that the female part of Creation as well as the male should throw off the

---

59 Several of these narratives are now in print: John Beatty (ed.), *Protestant women's narratives of 1798* (Dublin, 2001).

60 M. Leadbetter, *Leadbetter papers*, 2 vols (London, 1862); K. O'Neill, 'Mary Shackleton Leadbetter: Peaceful rebel', in Keogh and Furlong (eds), *The women of 1798*, pp 137–62.

61 R. Lovell Edgeworth and Maria Edgeworth, *Memoirs of Richard Lovell Edgeworth begun by himself and concluded by his daughter*, 2 vols (London, 1821). Extracts from this and Lady Roden's diary are included in Beatty, *Protestant women's narratives*.

62 See *The United Irishmen and the 1798 Rebellion: Sources checklist* (Belfast, 1998); D. Lindsay, 'The Rebellion papers', *Hist. Ir.*, vi, 2 (1998), 18–22.

63 P.R.O.N.I. T3048/B. See Eleanor Burgess, 'Lord Edward's aunt: How Louisa Conolly and her sisters faced the rebellion', in Keogh and Furlong (eds), *The women of 1798*, pp 163–76.

64 Granard papers: P.R.O.N.I., T3765; Roden papers: P.R.O.N.I., MIC/147/9.

65 McCracken papers: P.R.O.N.I., T1210/7; Madden papers: T.C.D.

fetters with which they have so long been mentally bound? ... It is reserved for the Irish nation to strike out something new and to shew an example of candour, generosity, and justice superior to any that have gone before them.[66]

The most significant source of this kind, however is the voluminous correspondence between Martha McTier and William Drennan, written over a period of thirty years. Composed of 1,500 letters, this invaluable collection has now been reproduced in full with a complete apparatus by the Women's History Project. The great triumph of this edition is the resurrection of Martha McTier (1742–1837) and her record presented in these pages. Through her eyes we gain a fascinating perspective on many subjects. Prefaced by the editor's introduction and Maria Luddy's superb 'Domestic History', the Drennan–McTier correspondence contains reflections upon Irish society, politics, attitudes, medical practices, domestic arrangements and rare insights into love and the intimacies of marriage.[67]

The variety of such sources, however, reflects again a feature present in the historiography of both the American and French Revolutions, namely the class issues which have shaped historiography. Beyond the aristocratic and bourgeois voice, a discernment of a more democratic sense of female participation in 1798 proves more problematic. There are, nevertheless, a number of sources which may prove fruitful. The records of the courts martial, convened to try rebels and to repress rebellion, provide an unexpected source for women's history. Few women were tried before the courts, but at least 25 per cent of the witnesses called before the officers were women.[68] Their evidence provides a unique source for the history of the 'ordinary women' of 1798. There are cases, too, which challenge many notions concerning the role of women in rebellion and its suppression. Similarly, there are reports which reflect the opportunity provided in the post-rebellion period for settling old scores. Mary Redmond of Gorey, for example, was convicted before a court martial in May 1799 for the murder of Henry Clinch on the evidence of two females, the victim's widow Sally and her neighbour Mary Forde. The latter swore that on the

---

66 Mary Anne McCracken to Harry [Henry Joy McCracken], 16 Mar. 1796, cited in McNeill, *Life and times of Mary Anne McCracken*, pp 125–8; M. Luddy, 'Introduction', in J. Agnew (ed.), *Drennan–McTier letters*, 3 vols (Dublin, 1998–9); see J. Gray, 'Mary Anne McCracken', in Keogh and Furlong (eds), *The women of 1798*, pp 47–63.

67 Agnew (ed.), *Drennan–McTier letters*. Edited extracts were published by D.A. Chart as *The Drennan letters* (Belfast, 1931).

68 Thomas Bartlett, 'Bearing witness: Female evidences in courts martial', in Keogh and Furlong (eds), *The women of 1798*, pp 64–86. The majority of these records are found in the National Archive, Rebellion Papers, but the National Library houses a smaller collection of courts martial transcripts.

second day after Gorey was taken, I was just outside the town and I saw Henry Klinch on his knees begging for his life from a party of rebels. Some were for bringing him to the camp, the prisoner at the bar insisted he should be killed there … on that the prisoner's husband shot Klinch who immediately fell, the prisoner then took up a stone, struck Klinch as he lay on the ground saying, 'You orange rogue, you will watch no more.' Another shot was fired at Klinch by one Philips.[69]

As the trial progressed, questions were raised about the timing of the allegations. It was suggested that later accusations of theft made by Mary Redmond against Mrs Clinch's son heavily influenced her evidence. Mary Redmond was condemned to death, but the court 'in consideration of her sex and being a mother of three children' commuted her sentence to transportation for life. She was subsequently transported to Australia on board the *Atlas I*, and in 1810 was in possession of a beer licence in Sydney.[70]

The transcripts of the courts martial furnish further detail of human suffering. At the trial of John Haughran, for example, Sarah Smith of Saltmills (Tintern) recalled the death of her husband, brother, sister and niece in the flames at Scullabogue.[71] Domestic concerns and arrangements, too, feature in the evidence and many of the female witnesses implicate themselves in rebellious acts. A case in point was Mary Henry of Prospect, County Wexford, who defiantly informed the court that she had joined the rebel army 'of her own free will and accord'.[72]

The surviving records of compensation paid to 'suffering loyalists' in the wake of the rebellion reflect material losses experienced by women.[73] An indication of the hardships endured by the vanquished in the wake of the rebellion may be gleaned from the voluminous petitions directed to the Lord Lieutenant on behalf of the state prisoners. Significant numbers of these are lodged by women on behalf of their menfolk; certainly they are constructed to elicit leniency and sympathy, but the frequency to which these supplications refer to the hardships endured by women and children provides a telling indication of the brutal human consequences of rebellion.[74]

Re-examination of such sources illustrate what has long been suspected, the involvement of women in so many roles, not alone as symbol, victim and observer, but as activist and combatant in Ireland's attempted revolution. Women remain the lost constituency in the events of 1798, hidden behind the complex

69 N.L.I., MS 17,795/1.
70 I am grateful to Dr Ruan O'Donnell for this information.
71 N.L.I., MS 17,795/1.
72 N.A.I., RP 620/2/8/10, cited in Bartlett, 'Bearing witness', p. 69.
73 *Commons' Jn. Ire.*, xix, pp clviii–ccccxcviii (7 Feb. 1800).
74 N.A.I., State prisoners petitions.

web of eighteenth-century male-female relationships, stereotypes and later polemic. Identification of this lacuna will of itself suggest possibilities. The response to this challenge will complement recent scholarship and perhaps contribute to a more nuanced interpretation of 1798.

SECTION VII

Denis Taaffe (1759–1813) was a familiar figure in the Dublin of the 1790s. Born in County Louth, he joined the Franciscans, studied at Boulay and Prague, acquired a formidable array of linguistic skills (Irish, Latin, Greek, Hebrew, French, German, Italian and Dutch)[1] returning to Ireland on his ordination in 1786. Two years later, lured by the prospects of a professorship in Trinity, he conformed to Protestantism. The post never materializsed and Taaffe sank into the nether regions of Dublin life. Living in squalor and alcohol-induced poverty, he worked as a tutor, pamphleteer and writer. In 1797, as the United Irish leaders pondered the possibilities of a French invasion, they sought out this remarkable man. He advised them: 'seek French co-operation but take care what you are about'. Without careful planning, the French would use Ireland cynically and then betray her: 'you will be swopped for some sugar island'.[2]

Modern historians have sometimes come to a similar conclusion (Gough, chapter 26, Simms, chapter 27). The relevant issue then becomes to explicate the changing relationship of the United Irishmen with the French.[3] Undoubtedly in the heady days of the early 1790s, there was an unbridled enthusiasm for the Revolution and the serene promise of its export to oppressed neighbouring states, including Ireland. By the mid-1790s, those outside France and sympathetic to the Revolution developed a more realistic sense of the limits and of the

---

1   See his advertisement in *D.E.P.*, 20 Oct. 1791.

2   Andrew O'Reilly, *Reminiscences of an emigrant Milesian*, 3 vols (London, 185 3), ii, p. 227. Taaffe published a striking anonymous pamphlet during the Bantry Bay crisis: *Observations occasioned by the alarm of an invasion propagated by authority addressed to the people of Ireland* (Dublin, 1796) [R.I.A., Halliday collection, vol. 709]. He was subsequently denounced as 'a coffee-house orator': [*F.D.J.*, 14 Jan. 1797]. He went on to fight in the rebellion itself, claiming credit for the tactics at Ballyellis. He wrote anti-union propaganda, and was arrested for it on 14 Mar. 1799. As well as eight known (and often impressive) pamphlets, he published a *History of Spain* (1808), and a four-volume *History of Ireland* (1809–11). O'Reilly (1782–1862) was born in County Westmeath. A United Irishman, he exiled himself in Paris after 1798, where he eventually became the Paris correspondent of *The Times*.

3   The classic study is Marianne Elliott, *Partners in revolution: The United Irishmen and France* (London, 1982). Richly rooted in the archives, this book established a new standard for the study of the United Irishmen and remains one of the indispensable books on the 1790s.

price of the proferred help. Sober assessments were generated by the fall-out from the Terror and by the indubitable evidence of French external aggression. The perception of the French changed from partners in revolution to potentially arrogant conquerors.

Tone and others insisted that they did not want to shed one colonial power simply to be annexed by another. The ravages of the French army as they swept outside the hexagon through Belgium, Holland, the Rhineland and Italy to what they perceived as their natural frontiers were well known. So was their betrayal of the radicals in these countries, who turned quickly against their new French over-lords (Simms, chapter 29). There was an obvious transition in French policy by 1796–7 - from exporting the Revolution to safeguarding it behind its natural fron-tiers, insulated by a buffer zone of client states.[4] Castlereagh noted that in a short period, 'no fewer than five newly created republics have started up, in order to defend, together with the Rhine, the most vulnerable parts of the frontier from the Mediterranean to the ocean'. But as well as natural defence, these republics were 'so many craters which the grand volcano has thrown up on its sides to del-uge with its doctrines and reduce under its dominion (or protection as it is called) every neighbouring state'.[5] Italy offered a cautionary example of French ambi-tions. For the United Irishmen, the crucial question became whether the French would treat Ireland similarly, bleeding it white in requisitions, installing a puppet regime or cynically abandoning it to Britain as an opportune bargaining chip?[6]

By the close of 1796, the United Irish leadership wavered as they sought to clarify French intentions and to limit their exposure to annexation. Their anxi-ety was reflected in serious discussions about the scale and levels of payments to an invasion force, the powers and composition of a transitional government, and the exact relations between the United Irishmen and their allies.[7] Lord Edward FitzGerald frequently 'expressed a desire that Ireland should accomplish its own liberation rather than leave it to a foreign power'.[8] The intention was to retain control of the revolution in Irish hands and to set precise limits to French ambi-tions. The clear danger was that the United Irishmen would be swept aside in

4 Hugh Gough, 'Anatomy of a failure: Bantry Bay and the French invasion of 1796' in Murphy (ed.), *Bantry Bay*, pp 9–24.
5 *Castlereagh corr.*, i, p 443.
6 An intriguing counter-factual is how the French would have treated Irish culture. A hint is sup-plied by J.J. Marcel, *Alphabet Irlandais, précedé d'une notice historique, litteraire et typographique* (Paris, 1804). Marcel became one of the cultural group attached to the French campaign in Egypt, which contributed significantly to advances in Egyptology.
7 There are (necessarily elusive) hints that some Irish Whigs (Grattan, Curran, Ponsonby) had tentatively agreed to participate in a post-revolutionary government. William Sampson in 1797 was acting as a broker between the Whigs and the United Irishmen: Sampson, *Memoirs*, pp 214–5. An important thesis in progress at Cambridge University by Daniel Mansergh ('Grat-tan's failure: parliamentary opposition and the people in Ireland 1779–1800') argues that the links between the Whigs and the United Irishmen have been seriously underplayed.
8 Neilson, *Brief statement*, p. 33.

the aftermath of a successful invasion by an autocratic, despotic and imperial France. Tone was equally certain that he would never be an 'accessory to subjecting my country to the control of France, merely in order to rid her of that of England'.[9] Robert Emmet reiterated that concern so vehemently in his 'Speech from the dock' that Dublin Castle was able to produce a doctored version as a piece of anti-French conservative propaganda.[10]

Faced with this dilemma, the United Irish leadership agonised. The moderates (Thomas Addis Emmet, William Drennan) argued for French support to discipline popular insurgency in Ireland when it came to be unleashed. More radical elements (Arthur O'Connor, Lord Edward FitzGerald, Samuel Neilson) promulgated a revised strategy to limit United Irish exposure to the French.[11] This debate assumed a renewed urgency after Bantry Bay. Until that astonishing moment, a French invasion fleet remained a theoretical and distant possibility: now it was proximate and probable. The French would most likely return and the implications of that had to be thought through. The radicals thrashed out a fresh plan focused primarily on internal resources. Rather than providing a paper army of lightly organized sympathizers designed to support the professional French soldiers engaged in the actual fighting, the United Irishmen now sought to mobilize a disciplined underground army, capable of delivering a successful revolution with minimal French help.

This necessitated a switch in the core areas of United Irish support. Up to that time, east Ulster was heavily organized, given the expectation that the French would land at Lough Foyle or Lough Swilly and then sweep east across Ulster to coalesce with their Irish allies. The 'indigenous' strategy demanded that the movement deliver the decisive blow in the capital: to achieve that, a strong organization in Leinster was necessary.[12] Building the organization in Dublin and in the surrounding counties became crucial: an inner crescent embraced Kildare, Wicklow and Meath, and an outer one ran from Westmeath to Wexford. Thus in 1797 some of the best field organizers (McCabe, Hope, Neilson, Metcalfe) switched their formidable organizational energies to Leinster

---

9 W.T.W. Tone, *Life of Theobald Wolfe Tone*, ed. Thomas Bartlett (Dublin, 1998). It is important to treat Tone's consistently laudatory comments on France while in Paris with extreme caution. He had already learned in Ireland how incautious words could incriminate. In the notoriously suspicious atmosphere of Tone's Paris, nothing should be expected in his diaries except politically correct commentary on France, and this should not be taken at face value. He was well-aware that his diaries could be picked up by the paranoid French at any time. Tone achieved remarkable success as a diplomat amid the fractious émigré coteries in Paris, skilfully navigating exceptionally turbulent waters.
10 This is the well-known engraving of Emmet in the dock, accompanied by a version of his speech; see N.G.I., 11,352.
11 Kevin Whelan, 'Bantry Bay: The wider context', in Murphy (ed.), *Bantry Bay*, pp 95–119.
12 Tommy Graham, 'Dublin's role in the 1798 rebellion' in Póirtéir (ed.), *Great Irish rebellion*, pp 5 8–71.

(Graham, chapter 7). The needs of the capital and its hinterland assumed precedence over sustaining the morale and momentum of the Ulster organization. Rather than seeing the obvious tensions between the Ulster and Leinster organizations as evidence of a deep-seated sectarian rift, it is more accurate to view them in this wider context of a struggle between radicals and moderates.

This transition was accompanied by a debate over attitudes to popular revolution. Moderates favoured a French invasion in order to ensure a disciplined insurrection, not trusting the Catholic poor to rise above the level of a vengeful *jacquerie*. Radicals trusted the revolutionary potential and discipline of the Irish poor, a trust deepened by the successful merger with the Defenders in south Ulster, negotiated by Samuel Neilson, Henry Joy McCracken and Charles Teeling. By late 1797, social issues emerged in much sharper focus in the propaganda of the organization.[13] It is important here not to see this as classic bourgeois deception of a gullible working-class by a manipulative leadership. In the conditions of the 1790s, it was impossible to separate issues like religion and land-ownership from ones relating to the structure of political power. An Erastian state had deliberately excluded Catholics and only grudgingly admitted Dissenters. Land ownership, the basis of political power, rested on sectarian foundations of relatively recent origin. Any challenge to the political establishment could be presented by conservatives (and later historians) as only motivated by crude agrarian or sectarian concerns but this was a distortion. Take the issue of land confiscation: the estates of those that had actively supported the old regime militarily and politically would surely have been sequestered followed a successful insurrection.[14] But there is little likelihood that this would have extended to neutral or Whig landowners. In County Down, for example, estates like Castlereagh's and Downshire's would have been confiscated, but not Moira's or Rowan's. An amusing passage in Tone's *Life* has him and Thomas Russell baiting Beresford, allowing him to overhear a conversation in which they talked about which of them would get his Curraghmore estate.[15]

France remained the bell-wether of radical hopes. Edward Cooke had noted that 'our atmosphere varies with French successes,' and everyone realised that the outcome of the wider British-French struggle would determine the fate of the United Irish project.[16] A longer chronological perspective suggests that all

13 On the social issues, see James Quinn, 'The United Irishmen and social reform', in *I.H.S.*, xxxi (1998), 188–20; Smyth, *The men of no property*; Kevin Whelan, 'Introduction to *The Poor Man's Catechism*', in *Labour History*, lxxv (1998), 22–37.

14 James Donnelly, 'Propagating the cause', argues that the expropriation of *all* landed estates would have been an inevitable corollary of revolution.

15 Bartlett (ed.), *Life of Tone*, p. 170. William Sampson attacked the Beresfords as carpet-baggers: 'The grand-father of the Beresfords came from England to follow his trade as an inkle-weaver in Coleraine and the enormous fortunes of that family are nothing but the plunder of the miserable Irish': Sampson, *Memoirs*, p. 379.

16 Edward Cooke to Auckland, 9 Feb. 1797: P.R.O.N.I., Auckland transcripts, T 3229/2/22.

the major crises of British-ruled Ireland (the 1640s, 1690s, 1790s, 1860s, 1920s, 1960s and 1990s) occurred against a backdrop of instability in the international political system. The United Irishmen understood that their stock would rise or fall with the wider struggle. They also knew, as St Just had aphorized, that 'those who make half-revolutions dig their own graves'. Their historical reputation would be sealed not by some abstract calculus of merit but by the brute reality of success or failure. Tone lectured his court-martial: 'Washington conquered, Kosciuszko fell,' and that alone determined how history would ultimately judge them.[17] Tone remained an inspiration for many subsequent generations of republicans.[18] Roger Casement, visiting John Quinn in New York before his

17 Bartlett, *Life of Tone*, p. 877. Michael Davitt made the same point: 'If only the men of '98 had won as they deserved, the world of today would link the name of Wolfe Tone to that of George Washington as the successful soldiers of liberty and mankind': cited in N. McLachlan, 'The road not taken', in *T.L.S.*, 12 Feb. 1999, 14. The megalomaniac Arthur O'Connor also compared himself to Washington: 'He succeeded and I failed … Washington is a great man, a great patriot and hero, and deservedly, and I, in the eyes of the world, a traitor': Hayter Hames, *Arthur O'Connor*, p. 276.

18 Tone is a vivid example of Joseph Lee's aphorism that modern revisionism is about the tyranny of the living over the dead generations. The rise and fall of Tone's reputation is a diagnostic of wider attitudes to Irish republicanism. Thomas Davis revived his reputation in the 1840s, and erected his first gravestone at Bodenstown. The Fenians also promoted him and inaugurated the Bodenstown pilgrimage. They refurbished the grave site in 1875. In the last quarter of the nineteenth century, at the zenith of the Home Rule movement, he was eclipsed in popularity by Henry Grattan. Between 1846 and 1910, only two editions of his writings appeared. Before independence, Tone was presented as an exemplary Irish Protestant nationalist, who appealed especially to those of that ilk – Alice Milligan, Bulmer Hobson, Roger Casement. In the 1930s, Tone became a central figure in establishing a respectable republican ancestry for the new state. See the establishment by Brian O'Higgins of the *Wolfe Tone Annual* in 1932, the superb Irish translation of the memoirs by Pádraig Ó Siochfhrádha in the same year, and the biographies by Aodh de Blacam (1935), Denis Ireland (1936), Sean Ó Faoláin (1937) and Frank MacDermott (1939) as well as the manically hostile treatment of him as anti-clerical by Leo McCabe (1937). (In a proleptically revisionist moment, McCabe rewrote the words of the 'Boys of Wexford' as the 'Boys of Kilkenny' praising the men of that county for not rising in 1798. The new version never caught on, even with Kilkenny people). The originator of modern revisionism, Sean Ó Faoláin, presents Tone (as he presents Hugh O'Neill and Daniel O'Connell with de Valera in mind) as a hard-headed moderniser trapped by the sentimental atavisms of Irish culture. Ó Faoláin covertly acknowledges the help of T.W. Moody, who also wrote about Tone in the 1930s. The 1930s appropriation of Tone by the new state led to a bitter Republican riposte, the *Wolfe Tone Weekly* (1937-9), which was eventually suppressed. After this flurry of sustained intellectual interest in the 1930s, Tone's reputation faded until the 1963 bicentenary of his birth. The Wolfe Tone Society, founded in that year, became an important precursor of the civil rights movement. It also marked a turn-away from treating Tone as a physical force separatist to presenting him as an anti-sectarian social activist among 'the men of no property.' This re-examination of Tone's legacy (seen in the writings of Seán Cronin, Derry Kelleher and Roy Johnson) was a proxy debate for the switch in the IRA in the 1960s from militarism towards Marxism ('salvaging the basic enlightenment secular republican democratic tradition from the various overlays of Catholic nationalism, Fenian conspiracism and quasi-Stalinist centralism which have infected it', to quote Johnson: Obituary of Derry Kelleher, *Irish Times*, 12 November 2001). In 1966, after Nelson's Pillar was blown up, some at least thought of re-erecting it with Tone on top, but worried if he might be 'too controversial' (*Hist. Ir.*, Winter 1998, 21). In 1967, the turgid official statue ['Tonehenge'] erected at Stephen's Green marked the

departure to Germany, 'constantly referred to the Tone thing and several times he said "I am Wolfe Tone. I am the reincarnation of Wolfe Tone." '[19]

A fundamental issue therefore remained the ability of Britain to win its titanic conflict with France. Here a long-term perspective on the emerging eighteenth-century composite and imperial British state is worth noting. As a state that was almost continuously at war between 1689 and 1815, it required fiscal innovation to finance it. Four crucial concepts – 'the square of power' – lay at the heart of the British military/fiscal state: excise tax, a representative parliament, national debt, and the Bank of England.[20] Thomas Paine had identified these as early as 1796.[21] The tax bureaucracy (educated, trained and impartial), the expansion of parliamentary representation to lend legitimacy to heavier taxation, the growth of a state-backed debt, and the evolution of a reputable central bank as a means of stabilizing credit and exercising fiscal discipline all grew out of the need to finance war. Collectively, they expanded the reach and authority of the state, and brought complex financial markets to maturity. This paved the way for Britain's supremacy in the first industrial revolution and in nascent global monetary systems. British hegemony was not just the product of economic forces but rested on the capacity to develop and adapt appropriate institutional frameworks within which they could operate. The 'sinews of state' were shaped by this sustained war effort, which also fed as it benefited from the expansion of empire.[22] By

congealment of the state's version of Tone. As the Northern troubles erupted, Tone came off his plinth again. His statue was blown up by loyalist paramilitaries on 8 February 1971. His historical reputation came under equal assault. Tom Dunne in 1982 painted him as a deluded and deluding opportunist who was neither an original thinker nor a genuine republican at all. Marianne Elliott was so determined to detach Tone from the modern republican movement that she allowed a present-centred approach colour her 1989 biography. In the 1990s of the Peace Process, Thomas Bartlett restored a more balanced perspective, situating Tone within eighteenth-century republicanism and acknowledging his originality. The legacy of Tone was recalled by Dean Victor Griffin of St Patrick's Cathedral in opposing the 1983 abortion amendment as an infringement of the core republican principle of the separation of church and state: 'Remember Emmet, remember Tone! God save the Republic. Vote No': *Irish Times*, 21 Feb. 2002. A recent survey of the historiography is James Quinn, 'Theobald Wolfe Tone and the historians', in *I.H.S.*, xxxii (2000), 113–28.

19 John Quinn, reported in memorandum of Captain Thwaite, 2 June 1916, P.R.O. MFPO 2/10664. The copy of Tone's *Life* (the London edition of 1828) in Casement's possession in Brixton was presented to the N.L.I. by Alice Stopford Green [N.L.I., Ir. 92 T 9]. John Quinn (1870–1924), a wealthy cosmopolitan New York lawyer and bibliophile, was famous for his patronage of modernist writers (Pound, Conrad, Joyce, Yeats) and painters (Picasso, Matisse, Cézanne). Among his collection were all the manuscripts of Conrad and the draft of *Ulysses*. In politics he was a Democrat (USA) and a Redmondite Home Ruler (Ireland): Judith Zilczer, *The noble buyer: John Quinn, patron of the Avant-Garde* (Washington, 1978).

20 Lawrence Stone (ed.), *An imperial state at war: Britain from 1689 to 1815* (London, 1994); Brendan Simms, 'Reform in Britain and Prussia 1797–1815: (Confessional) fiscal-military state and military-agrarian complex', in *Proceedings of the British Academy*, C (1999), 79–100; Martin Daunton, *Trusting Leviathan: The politics of taxation in Britain 1793–1914* (Cambridge, 2001).

21 Thomas Paine, *The decline and fall of the British system of public finance* (London, 1796).

22 Niall Ferguson, *The cash nexus: Money and power in the modern world, 1700–2000* (London, 2001); John Brewer, *The sinews of power* (London, 1989).

1815, no fewer than one in five adult British males were in uniform. The British victory in what was the first modern war (modern in the sense that it was fought for ideological as opposed to tactical or dynastic reasons, and that it was global in scope) depended on a century-long preparation.

The United Irishmen understood that there could be no such thing as an Irish republic alongside an English monarchy. The radical project needed to succeed in England, Scotland and Wales: the United Irish built alliances there with sister organizations, the United Britons and United Scotsmen (McFarland, chapter 28). There were obviously close links between Ireland and Scotland in the eighteenth century: Ulster Presbyterianism remained connected to a wider Scottish cultural world,[23] while Jacobitism provided a common cause for many people in both cultures.[24] Scottish radicalism in the 1790s was incomparably more muted and reticent than its Irish equivalent, easily intimidated by harsh judicial measures.[25] Scottish fencible regiments, largely recruited from the Highlands, became a significant component of crown forces in Ireland. The susceptibility of those crushed by the expanding British state and empire – Highland Scots, Gurkhas, Indians – to be absorbed as foot soldiers of empire remains a little explored chapter in the cultural history of imperialism.[26] Another reciprocity went in the opposite direction: the successful transplantation of the Orange Order from Ireland to Scotland.[27] In the longer term, the impact of the 1790s bifurcated Scottish as well as Irish society into two sectarian monoliths, formations still evident in both societies two centuries later.[28]

The stability of English society under the pressure of political change in the revolutionary period was an impressive testament to the legitimacy of its political institutions, a legacy bequeathed by the Glorious Revolution. Ironically, as Arthur Young had pointed out in 1780, 'The [Glorious] Revolution did not

23 Between 1690 and 1809, 1,846 Irish – overwhelmingly Ulster – students graduated from Glasgow university (close to one-fifth of the total number): McFarland, *Ireland and Scotland*, p. 5. At least 322 of 35 0 Presbyterian ministers ordained in Ireland between 1720 and 1775 had been educated at Glasgow, where the dominant intellectual influence was the Ulster-man Francis Hutcheson: J.M. Barkley, 'The Presbyterian minister in eighteenth-century Ireland', in J.L. Haire (ed.), *Challenge and conflict* (Antrim, 1981), pp 46–71.

24 The Jacobite element is entirely ignored in the standard accounts which treat Ulster as if it contained only an anglophone Protestant population in the eighteenth century: A.T.Q. Stewart, *A deeper silence: The hidden origins of the United Irishmen* (London, 1993); E.W. McFarland, *Ireland and Scotland in the age of revolution: Planting the green bough* (Edinburgh, 1994); McBride, *Scripture politics*. On the Jacobite common culture, see Vincent Morley, 'Idé-éolaoícht an tSeacaibíteachais in Éirinn agus in Albain', in *Oghma*, ix (1997), 14–24.

25 J. Brims, 'The Scottish democratic movement in the age of the French Revolution' (unpublished Ph.D. thesis, University of Edinburgh, 1983).

26 Victor Kiernan, 'Scottish soldiers and the conquest of India', in Grant Simpson (ed.), *The Scottish soldier abroad* (Edinburgh, 1992).

27 T.M. Devine (ed.), *Scotland's shame: Bigotry and sectarianism in modern Scotland* (Edinburgh, 2000).

28 E.W. McFarland, *Protestants first: Orangemen in nineteenth-century Scotland* (Edinburgh, 1990).

extend to Ireland' where its impact had drastically curtailed rather than enhanced civil and religious liberties.[29] Thus in the 1790s, a brittle Irish political system came apart along its seventeenth-century seams. Concessions in the 1790s to the majority Catholic population can be viewed as a classic case of too little, too late.[30] By contrast, English society remained sufficiently cohesive to see off the radical challenge for another generation. In essence, the concession of Catholic Emancipation in 1829 and the 'Great' Reform Act of 1832 brought the English eighteenth century to a belated close.[31]

The degree to which English radicalism in the 1790s constituted a real threat remains a controversial issue. The most famous incident, the immobilization of the Channel fleet in the naval mutinies of 1797, has spawned multiple explanations (Rogers, chapter 27). Naval historians have downplayed radical and especially United Irish involvement in favour of emphasising internal naval issues.[32] A closer focus on Irish involvement in the British navy suggests that one-quarter were Irish-born:[33] of those, one-fifth was considered to be 'evilly disposed' politically. With 119,000 men in the entire navy in 1797, at least 6,000 may have had United Irishmen sympathies. George Douglas pointed out that 'Ireland is considered as the grand nursery of sailors and soldiers for the British fleet and armies'.[34] This impressive figure provides a context for known United Irish involvement in single-ship mutinies or conspiracies in 1797–98 – the *Pompée, Mars, Caesar, Defiance, Glory* and *St George*.[35] United Irish involvement in the Nore and Spithead mutinies remains

29 Young, *Tour*, ii, p. 249.

30 Mathew Carey noted sardonically that 'imminent danger is a wonderful liberalizer of oppressors': Mathew Carey, *Vindiciae Hibernicae*, 2nd ed. (Philadelphia, 1823), p. 475 .

31 Frank O'Gorman, *The long eighteenth century: British political and social history 1688–1832* (London, 1997).

32 See N.A.M. Rogers, *The wooden world: An anatomy of the Georgian navy* (London, 1986). For a different perspective on the capacity for radicalism in the eighteenth-century naval world by an American-based historian, see Marcus Rediker, *Between the devil and the deep-blue sea: Merchants, seamen, pirates and the Anglo-American maritime world 1700–1750* (Cambridge, 1987). There is also a pronounced anglocentric element in considerations of England in the 1790s. Even E.P. Thompson succumbed, as is suggested by the title of his classic, *The making of the English working class*. A useful corrective is Roger Wells, *Insurrection: The British experience 1795–1803* (Gloucester, 1983). For astute commentary on the anglocentric bias in historiography, see Norman Davies, *The Isles: A history* (London, 1999), but judging by his serial inaccuracies on Ireland, he is not immune to the trait himself.

33 Irishmen composed one-quarter of the men below decks in the ships of the line at the Battle of Trafalgar in 1805: R.B. McDowell, *Ireland in the age of imperialism and revolution* (Oxford, 1979), pp 493–4.

34 Douglas, 'A brief sketch of the history of Ireland', in *Forensic eloquence: Sketches of trials in Ireland for high treason etc.*, 2nd ed. (Baltimore, 1805), p. 16.

35 *Report of the Committee of Secrecy of the House of Commons of Great Britain on the papers sealed up respecting the conspirators of the United Irishmen, presented to the House by Mr Secretary Dundas* (Dublin, 1799), pp 85–94. See also Albert Goodwin, *The friends of liberty: The English democratic movement in the age of the democratic revolution* (London, 1979).

entirely plausible. The numbers of known Irish involved – 106 out of 462 mutineers – matches their overall share in the fleet. William Sampson had no hesitation in calling it 'Carhampton's mutiny' as a result of the large numbers summarily despatched to the fleet following Carhampton's infamous sweep through Connacht and North Leinster.[36] Other mutinies inspired by the United Irishmen followed, like that on *L'Impétueux* in May 1799 when 176 men also took the opportunity to desert.

Ultimately, however, Britain's wooden walls remained impervious to internal and external assault. The French could never match the naval resources deployed against them. Even Napoleon baulked at the challenge of launching an invasion of Britain, although this remained a real fear for British strategists throughout the revolutionary period. Not for nothing did Dublin erect its most elaborate memorials to Nelson in 1808[37] and the Dublin-born Wellington (James Joyce's 'one-handed adulterer') after 1814.[38] Irish towns acquired a plethora of street names named after events in the French wars. In Derry, for example, there were Waterloo, Blucher, Nelson and Alexandra Streets. The memoirist Hugh Dorian lived on Alexandra Street and died on Nelson Street. Contemplating the most tangible physical reminders of that period, the early warning system of Martello towers and signal forts whose squat profiles ringed the Irish coast, Dorian mused on this great fear:

> No wonder the English took good care of the wonderful hero after he had surrendered to them for by that act he relieved them of many a restless day and sleepless night. Such was their dread while Bony conquered that if an extraordinary large seagull's wings appeared on the horizon, it was in the hurry of the moment taken for French canvas, and the telescope was adjusted.[39]

Similarly, James Joyce, a master of the *magnum in parvo*, began his Irish epic *Ulysses* in the setting of the Martello tower at Sandycove, a small circle, which he then sets in the mirroring circle of Dublin Bay before extending out to the ever wider circles of the British empire and Roman Catholicism, and ultimately the globe itself.

36 Sampson, *Memoirs*, p. 32.
37 *Nelson's Pillar: A description of the Pillar with a list of the subscribers* (Dublin, 1811).
38 The Halfpenny bridge, erected in 1816, was originally called Wellington bridge.
39 Breandán MacSuibhne and David Dickson (eds), *The outer edge of Ulster: A memoir of social life in nineteenth-century Donegal* (Dublin, 2000), p. 66. On Martello towers and signal fortifications, see Paul Kerrigan, *Castles and fortifications in Ireland, 1485–1945* (Cork, 1995). *The Nation* described them as 'a line of saucy absurdities drawn around our coast, a cordon of insulting follies encircling our native land': *Nation*, 29 July 1843, 664.

26

The crisis year: Europe and the Atlantic in 1798

HUGH GOUGH

Seventeen ninety-eight was a crisis year for Ireland, creating a founding myth for republicanism and unionism in much the same way that, nine years previously, 1789 had created a founding myth for both left and right in France. Looked at in its wider perspective, however, 1798 was also a crisis year in Europe as a whole, affecting the Swiss, the Italians, the Belgians, the Dutch and the Egyptians too.[1]

This had not been predictable when the year began as, at first sight, 1798 should have been a year of peace rather than war. On 18 October 1797 the treaty of Campoformio, negotiated by Napoleon Bonaparte with the Austrians, ended the First Coalition that had been created in the spring of 1793, so bringing to a close five and a half years of armed conflict in continental Europe. Only Britain was now left at war and France was well placed to bring her to the negotiating table, with over 340,000 troops under arms and much of western Europe under her control: the United Provinces had been transformed into the Batavian Republic since 1795, Belgium annexed from Austria, the German Rhineland placed under military occupation, and two satellite republics created in northern Italy – the Cisalpine (centred on Milan) and Ligurian (centred on Genoa). Prussia had abandoned its possessions on the left bank of the Rhine in 1795 to retreat into neutrality, while Spain had been a French ally since October 1796. With Britain troubled by naval mutinies at Spithead and Nore, and by protests against the cost and length of war, a peace to copperfasten French hegemony of continental Europe seemed distinctly possible.[2]

Yet it was not to be. Instead, peace talks between France and Britain broke down at Lille in late October 1797, and 1798 turned out to be a year of whirlwind rather than of calm. In February French troops assisted a revolt in Switzerland that led to the creation of a new Helvetian Republic. In the same

---

1 For a rather dated overview, see R.W. Postgate, *Story of a year: 1798* (Harlow, 1969); for an excellent concise account of the main military and diplomatic developments, see P.W. Schroeder, *The transformation of European politics, 1763–1848* (Oxford, 1994), pp 150–200.

2 S.T. Ross, *Quest for victory: French military strategy, 1792–1799* (New York and London, 1973), chap. 5, passim.

month the papal states were invaded and transformed into the Roman Republic, while in the following December Naples was invaded and became the short-lived Parthenopean Republic. In the following spring of 1799 Piedmont and Tuscany were annexed, completing the French domination of Italy. In the meantime Bonaparte had sailed to Egypt with 36,000 troops in the spring of 1798 and conquered Alexandria and Cairo. 1798 was very much the year of the French, Humbert's defeat at Ballinamuck being one of the rare blemishes on a series of French victories. Why was France so dominant a power in Europe in 1798? What were her aims, and why was Ireland the exception to a run of military success?

These questions can best be analysed by focusing on three basic elements in French activity which combined to shape the year's events. The first of these was official foreign policy which it is tempting to regard as the main driving force behind military activity. The events of 1789, after all, had seen the affirmation of popular sovereignty in the Declaration of the Rights of Man, the centralization of political control in Paris and the transfer of power from king to Constituent Assembly. These developments wrenched foreign policy away from the privacy of ministerial cabinets into the glaring light of public politics. Sovereign governments control their own foreign policy, as the National Assembly officially declared in the summer of 1790, and France initially declared its intention of living at peace with *ancien régime* Europe.[3] Yet Girondin bellicism in 1792 changed that; the optimism of Brissot and his colleagues, with their euphoric vision of a European revolution to overthrow an *ancien régime* based on superstition, despotism and oppression, catapulted the revolution into a war with Austria that rapidly ballooned into an expansionist European venture. The Girondins proclaimed a moral foreign policy, based on a cosmopolitan belief in the universal validity of the rights of man and the superiority of French ideology. This led directly to the first propaganda decree of 19 November 1792, promising support to revolutionary minorities elsewhere on the continent.[4] In late November 1792 the president of the National Convention declared to a deputation of Irish and English petitioners:

> It will not be long now before Frenchmen will be going to congratulate the National Convention of Great Britain. Royalty has either been destroyed in Europe or is expiring on feudal ruins; and the Declaration of the Rights of Man, placed beside thrones, is a raging fire which will consume them.[5]

---

3 T.C.W. Blanning, *The origins of the French Revolutionary wars* (Oxford, 1986), pp 73–4.
4 Ibid., chaps 3 and 4, passim.
5 *Convention Nationale: Adresse des Ecossais et des Irlandais résidens et domiciliés à Paris à la Convention Nationale, et réponse du Président. Séance du 28 novembre 1792* (Paris, 1792), p. 3.

Some thrones were certainly consumed by the equivalent of a raging fire in the following years, including that of France, but it was the Girondins who were to be fatally consumed. Many were guillotined during the summer of 1793 because of the heavy defeats brought about by their diplomatic naivety and the ambiguity of their republican commitment. Yet their optimism had preceded them to the grave, as defeat in Belgium and the Rhineland during the winter of 1792–3, combined with the threat posed by the formation of the First Coalition during the spring, persuaded the Convention to withdraw its threat of expansion on 13 April 1793. When French armies pressed forward again in the summer of 1794, they had been reorganized and transformed into a mass army of almost a million men by the Committee of Public Safety. Yet they were now used in the service of a more pragmatic foreign policy, which appeared to abandon universal revolution in favour of strengthening revolutionary France by acquiring the so-called 'natural' frontiers of the Pyrenees, Alps and Rhine.[6] Victories in the field quickly led to peace with several members of the First Coalition – Tuscany in February 1795, Prussia in the following April, the United Provinces in May, and Spain in July. Yet it also led to the annexation of Belgium and the prince-bishopric of Liège, and the military occupation of the Rhineland. Beyond the Rhine, victory created a satellite republic in Holland, the Batavian Republic, which housed and fed a sizeable French army.[7]

The five-man Directory was divided over how to exploit this position of strength when it took office in October 1795. Moderates such as Lazare Carnot, friend of Theobald Wolfe Tone and patron of the ill-fated Bantry expedition, were ready to abandon some of the territorial gains in return for a negotiated peace that would facilitate a return to political stability.[8] Others, including La Revellière-Lépeaux, Barras and the highly influential Jean-François Reubell, favoured the more expansionary alternative of the natural frontiers.[9] This required the annexation of large chunks of territory, including Savoy, the German Rhineland and Belgium. Reubell was the specialist within the Directory on foreign affairs: reticent, irascible and frequently plagued by gout and kidney problems, he was a native of Alsace determined to safeguard the Rhine frontier for the security that it provided to the eastern frontier. To achieve that he envisaged a trade-off with Austria, in which she would give up her claims on Belgium (which had belonged to the Habsburgs since 1713) and the Rhineland territories

---

6 Bernard Nabonne, *La diplomatie du Directoire et Bonaparte, d'après les papiers inédits de Reubell* (Paris, 1951), chap. 2.

7 Simon Schama, *Patriots and liberators: Revolution in the Netherlands, 1780–1813* (London, 1977), pp 201–10.

8 M. Reinhard, *Le grand Carnot: L'organisateur de la victoire, 1792–1823* (Paris, 1952), ii, pp 212–23.

9 J.-R. Suratteau and Alain Bischoff, *Jean-François Reubell: L'Alsacien de la Révolution française* (Colmar, 1991).

of the Holy Roman Empire, in return for Napoleon's conquests in northern Italy where French armies had conquered large areas of Lombardy. The Directory's instructions to General Clarke, who was sent to Italy to negotiate peace with the Austrians at Léoben in the spring of 1797, were for him to concede Lombardy in return for the Rhineland:

> The Directory would certainly have wished to ensure freedom for all peoples who have shown themselves to be friends of our principles; but it feels more strongly the need to procure peace for the French people. It therefore authorises you, albeit with regret, to agree to the abandoning of this country.[10]

During the summer of 1797 Carnot lost the political argument. More importantly he lost the political struggle and was denounced as a crypto-royalist in the *fructidor* coup of September 1797 which forced him from office and into exile in Switzerland. Moderate left-wing republicans were now in the driving seat and the natural frontiers policy appeared secure. However, Britain remained undefeated. She had been the main driving force behind the military struggle against France since 1793, and during the terror had been declared by the Convention the 'enemy of the human species'. She had certainly profited from war, particularly on the naval front, capturing most of the French Caribbean islands in 1794, the Cape of Good Hope from the Dutch in 1795 and Spanish Caribbean islands in 1797. She had dominated the French on the high seas, trounced the Spanish at Cape St Vincent in February 1797 and defeated the Dutch fleet at Camperdown on 7 October, capturing seven ships of the line. Yet the cost of war was increasingly problematic and unpopular, based as it was on high borrowing levels by the Bank of England and on rising taxation. Peace negotiations had already broken down once at Paris in December 1796 and again at Lille in September 1797, partly because Britain was not prepared to see France retain her huge continental gains. Yet there had been reservations on the French side too, as Reubell believed that peace would allow the British to consolidate their economic superiority and colonial gains. The war therefore continued, and French plans turned towards a direct invasion across the channel, which led to the decision to form an *armée d'Angleterre* at Boulogne in late 1797. Ireland formed a subsidiary part of that invasion plan, with provision for a small force at Brest intended for an Irish landing.[11]

Yet this strategy was also affected by the views of the generals, who exerted their own influence on foreign policy decisions. For if Reubell was the dominant member of the Directory on foreign policy matters, both he and his colleagues had to contend with rivalry from a new breed of political generals. The high

---

10 Nabonne, *La diplomatie*, p. 46.
11 Marianne Elliott, *Partners in revolution: The United Irishmen and France* (New Haven and London, 1982), pp 158–60.

command of the French army, almost totally made up of nobility prior to 1789, had been transformed during the course of the 1790s. Many officers had emigrated to join the ranks of counter-revolution before war began, while others had defected subsequently, including Lafayette and Dumouriez.[12] During the Terror, over eighty generals were guillotined for incompetence or failure and a younger generation of officers replaced them, including Hoche, Moreau, Kléber, Jourdan, Pichegru and Bonaparte. Their prestige grew, as military success contrasted with the failings of civilian government. Financial considerations boosted that prestige too, as the wages and material needs of revolutionary armies could only be met by a systematic policy of requisitioning and looting in the areas that they conquered. This was certainly the case in Belgium and in the Rhineland, where the devastation that military occupation brought in its wake aroused serious opposition.[13] Yet it was particularly significant in the rich plains of northern Italy after Bonaparte's invasion in the spring of 1796, for Lombardy was a region of substantial wealth, not only in the form of money, but also in precious objects and art treasures. These French generals systematically stripped, either for their own benefit or to send back to Paris. As La Revellière-Lépeaux wrote to Bonaparte in early 1797, 'You make a hundred times more money with your bayonets than we do with all the financial laws imaginable.'[14]

The Convention had already been aware of the problem of military looting in 1795 and had appointed civilian commissaires to work with generals; but their authority was difficult to assert in the field against self-confident generals. Bonaparte certainly sent them packing from the army of Italy in 1796. As a result, many generals wielded near autonomous power in their zones of conquest and followed their own political agenda. Pichegru, who helped conquer Holland in 1795, was a secret royalist who resigned his command in 1796 to become a deputy in the Council of Five Hundred. He was eventually arrested after the *fructidor* coup that removed Carnot in September 1797. Most of the others were republicans of various shades who owed their careers to the Revolution and to the republic, and frequently used the freedom that victory and distance from Paris gave them to take their own political initiatives. In the Cisalpine Republic, set up by Bonaparte in the summer of 1797, his successor Brune, who had served his political apprenticeship as an ally of Danton in the radical Cordeliers district of Paris during the early days of the Revolution, played a leading role in a series of *coups d'état* in 1798, intervening consistently in favour of radical democrats. In the spring of 1798, under orders from the Directory, he

12 S.F. Scott, *The response of the royal army to the French Revolution* (Oxford, 1978), pp 97, 108–10.
13 T.C.W. Blanning, *The French Revolution in Germany: Occupation and resistance in the Rhineland, 1792–1802* (Oxford, 1983), passim.
14 A. Fugier, *Histoire des relations internationales publiées sous la direction de Pierre Renouvin*, IV: *La Révolution française et l'empire Napoléonien* (Paris, 1954), p. 100.

ensured the removal of moderates from the Cisalpine government. He then obstructed the Directory's agent, Trouvé, who carried through a second *coup* in August 1798 which restored the moderates and restricted the franchise, and had his revenge when Trouvé was replaced by Joseph Fouché in the autumn, carrying out a third *coup* which removed moderates. For this he was recalled to Paris in November. Similar friction between the Directory and its generals took place in the kingdom of Naples when it was invaded in the winter of 1798–1799. The French general in charge of the invasion, Jean Etienne Championnet, responded to the demands of Neapolitan Jacobins by occupying the city of Naples and supporting the establishment of the Parthenopean Republic, in direct contradiction to the Directory's instructions, which were to minimize military commitments by retaining the army just north of the city. The Directory's *commissaire civil*, Faipoult, set about reining Championnet in, but after a series of confrontations Championnet had him arrested and sent back to Rome. He too was then recalled and arrested, but the status of his Parthenopean Republic was not resolved until it finally collapsed in the following spring.[15]

The most prominent 'political' general was Napoleon Bonaparte. From the spring of 1796 onwards, when he took command of the demoralised army of Italy and turned it into an effective fighting force in the plains of Lombardy, he showed a carefully directed political ambition. Deliberately cultivating his image in the military and Parisian press, he laid the foundations for a legend that was to achieve its posthumous recognition in the Invalides in Paris. Part of that image was his foreign policy which differed in significant ways from the Directory's own. Bonaparte certainly supported the principle of territorial expansion for France, but he was not a straightforward supporter of the natural frontiers policy as articulated by Reubell and his colleagues. Instead, as a Mediterranean man, he wanted to extend French power to the south. During the peace negotiations with the Austrians at Léoben in the spring of 1797, he hurried talks on so that the main deal could be completed before General Clarke, the Directory's representative, arrived from Paris with instructions to abandon Lombardy in favour of consolidating the natural frontiers. Instead he persuaded the Austrians to concede Belgium, the Rhineland and Lombardy to France, and to accept in their place the city of Venice and the territories of Dalmatia and Istria. For France he kept the Ionian islands, including the strategically important island of Corfu, and later incorporated the mainland territories of Venice into a newly created Cisalpine Republic.[16] By selling the deal – and the cynical betrayal of the Venetian Republic – to French public opinion as a triumph that ensured peace, he not only consolidated French influence in the Mediterranean but also forced

15 J. Godechot, *La grande nation: L'expansion révolutionnaire de la France dans le monde de 1789 à 1799* (Paris, 1983).
16 Guigliemo Ferrero, *The gamble: Bonaparte in Italy, 1796–1797* (London, 1961), chaps 13–18.

the Directory to accept the *fait accompli,* much to the annoyance of Reubell who regarded Italy as a source of future trouble. The essentials of Léoben were then confirmed in the peace of Campoformio in the following October.[17]

Bonaparte's personal role was also evident in the Egyptian expedition. After Campoformio and the collapse of the Lille negotiations with Britain, the Directory appointed Bonaparte commander of the projected invasion of England. Yet he was never fully committed to the project and on 23 February 1798, after a short tour of inspection of the *armée d'Angleterre* near Boulogne, he reported that the naval preparations were well behind schedule, with insufficient craft and inadequate naval cover to provide protection against the British navy. He recommended instead an expedition to Egypt, which did not come as a bolt from the blue. He had already annexed the Ionian islands at Campoformio, and Corfu had then been garrisoned and given a constitution similar to the Directory. He had also proposed the capture of Malta in the summer of 1797 and some weeks later had written to the minister of foreign affairs, Talleyrand, urging the capture of Egypt to strengthen French trading positions in the Levant.[18] When tentative proposals for an Egyptian expedition began to circulate from the autumn of 1797 onwards, he was one of their warmest supporters, and when he proposed it in late February as a substitute for the ill-fated English expedition, the Directory endorsed it rapidly. On 5 Mar., orders were issued to assemble an army at Toulon. Bonaparte was made commander and on 19 May he set sail for Egypt with an army of 36,000 men, just four days before the outbreak of the United Irish insurrection in Dublin.

If Bonaparte supplemented government control of foreign policy, nudging its focus towards Italy and the Mediterranean from the summer of 1796 onwards, local political activists and pressure groups were influential too. This is a third influence on revolutionary foreign policy, extensively explored by R.R. Palmer and Jacques Godechot in the 1950s and 1960s, and recently reshaped by a number of excellent monographs, including Marianne Elliott's work on the links between the United Irishmen and France.[19] The Revolution in France had come in the wake of political crisis in several European states which ensured that, from 1789 onwards, Paris became a centre for political refugees anxious to return with French ideals to their homeland. Dutch patriots, Genevan democrats, Belgian and Liègeois statists and vonckists, formed political clubs, lobbied the French for support and accompanied French armies into their country from 1792 onwards as agents of revolutionary change.[20] The Irish were conspicuous at first by their absence from these

17 Blanning, *French Revolutionary wars*, pp 177–9.

18 Ross, *Quest for victory*, chap. 7; *Mémoires du prince de Talleyrand, publiés avec une préface et des notes par le Duc de Broglie* (Paris, 1891), i, pp 259–61.

19 R.R. Palmer, *The age of the democratic revolution*, 2 vols (Princeton, 1959–63); Godechot, *La grande nation*; Elliott, *Partners in revolution*.

20 For a dated but still relevant account, see Albert Mathiez, *La Révolution et les étrangers: Cosmopolitisme et défense nationale* (Paris, 1918).

groups, because the relative liberalism of British and Irish politics enabled reform activity to be carried out at home, until the gravity of war and the fear of treason from 1794 onwards tipped the balance towards repression.

The most successful exile group, the Dutch patriots, were able to set up their own government in the Batavian Republic in 1795 after French armies had expelled the stadtholder. Yet in this case, as in others, exile activity was not always harmonious, as most groups were split on personality and policy lines. The French for their part complicated matters by creating their own propaganda agencies to harness refugee enthusiasm – the *agence française* in Belgium or the *comité espagnol* for Spain – which operated according to a French agenda. In addition, the links that many exiles initially enjoyed with the Girondins worked to their disadvantage when Brissot and his colleagues were arrested in the summer of 1793. During the terror the Committee of Public Safety was deeply hostile to most foreign groups, convinced that they were all involved in a vast foreign conspiracy to subvert the revolution. As a result, after 1795 the Directory's attitude towards foreign support was deliberately cautious, using exiles' enthusiasm when it suited (as Carnot did with Tone) but reining them in when they threatened to get out of control.

In the Batavian Republic, for example, which was nominally independent after 1795 and run by pro-French patriots, the Directory intervened on several occasions to encourage political purges and enforce its own policies.[21] The case of Switzerland is similar. The Swiss Confederation of 13 cantons was neutral in the eighteenth century and the early years of the Revolution, but from 1795 came to be suspected, with good reason, of being a base for English agents of counter-revolution. Reubell was intent on preventing this, while Bonaparte had his eye on strategic passes that would strengthen his Cisalpine Republic. Both were helped by the fact that many Swiss supported the ideals of the Revolution. Among their leaders were Pierre Ochs in Bale and Frédéric-César de La Harpe who had lived in exile for over ten years. In early December 1797, at a meeting with Reubell and Bonaparte in Paris, La Harpe agreed to launch reform agitation in Bâsle and the Pays de Vaud as a prelude to a French invasion and the establishment of a unitary Swiss republic. Berne resisted change, but the Directory placed the Vaudois under French protection, and sent in French troops during February, capturing the city in early Mar. In April 1798 a constitution for a new Helvetian Republic was inaugurated, initially drawn up by Ochs but heavily amended by the Directors Reubell and Merlin to conform to French requirements. In essence it was similar to the Directory's own constitution, but with reinforced powers for the executive. Three months later, on 19 August, an imposed Franco-Helvetian alliance brought to an end 300 years of Swiss neutrality and the government undertook to raise the country's first army for over 300 years.[22]

21 Schama, *Patriots and Liberators*, chaps 6–7.
22 *Corréspondance de Frédéric César de La Harpe sur la république helvétique* (Neuchâtel, 1982), i, pp 16–22, 267–8; R. Guyot, *Le Directoire et la paix de l'Europe* (Paris, 1912), pp 624–69; 740–7; 772–7.

In the Swiss case the availability of local patriots willing to plan and support French intervention was important. The same was true in Italy. The prospect of a French invasion there in the spring of 1796 attracted the interest of Italian exiles in France, and particularly in Nice. Among them was Filippo Buonarroti, who proposed to the French foreign minister, Delacroix, that French intervention should follow on an insurrection in Piedmont and facilitate the establishment of a republic, whose provisional government could then negotiate with the French as the Batavian exiles had done in the previous year. After this, he envisaged a general uprising throughout the peninsula that would lead to the creation of a democratic Italian republic. This never happened for two reasons. First, Buonarroti was a member of the democratic Pantheon club in Paris which was closed down by the Directory in February 1796 because of its radicalism and its links with Gracchus Babeuf, whose planned *coup d'état* to establish a communist society was nipped in the bud in the spring. Second, neither Bonaparte nor the Directory had the slightest interest in promoting a united Italian republic on France's southern frontier. The Directory wanted no permanent involvement in Italy, while Bonaparte preferred to carve out smaller political units.[23] So Bonaparte defeated Piedmont in 1796 but refused to recognise the republic that patriot exiles proclaimed and concluded an armistice with the government in Turin instead, which allowed the monarchy to continue for another three years. Meanwhile he set up the Cispadane and Cisalpine republics, carved out of territory conquered from the Austrians and based on Milan. Yet patriots in Turin still wanted to get rid of the Piedmont monarchy, and the French general and ambassador, Brun and Ginguéné, supported them against the wishes of the Directory in Paris. In the summer of 1798 Ginguéné forced the king to accept a French garrison in Turin, but problems then broke out between French troops and the local nobility. The Directory, worried by Ginguéné's radicalism, replaced him in September but his successor, Eymar, followed a confrontational policy and ordered the military occupation of the whole of Piedmont in December. The king abdicated to Sardinia and local patriots promptly demanded unification with the Cisalpine Republic. However, the Directory instead offered independence or annexation, and in February 1799 a referendum produced a vote for annexation. Piedmont then became incorporated into France.

Meanwhile, in the Cisalpine Republic, Milan had acted as a centre for radicals who, like Buonarotti, wanted the French to revolutionize the whole peninsula. After Bonaparte's departure in the autumn of 1797, they hovered around generals such as Brune, Joubert and Championnet, egging on Brune in particular to defy the Directory's orders to purge radicals from the Cisalpine government in

---

23 J. Godechot, 'Les français et l'unité italienne sous le Directoire', in J. Godechot (ed.), *Regards sur l'époque révolutionnaire* (Toulouse, 1980), pp 303–27; Godechot, *Grande nation*, pp 219–22.

1798. Some of them moved south to Rome, where they supported calls for reform of papal government. The Directory had little interest in this because of the danger that any attack on Rome would bring Austria back into war, but on 28 December 1797, after a political demonstration during which papal police invaded the French embassy, the French military attaché was shot dead. He was the second French official to be murdered in five years, so the ambassador, Joseph Bonaparte, was recalled and French armies under General Berthier invaded in February 1798. As they did so, political prisoners released from jail proclaimed a Roman republic and Pius VI went into exile. The new republic's constitution was modelled on the constitution of the Year III of the French Directory, but with the provision that all officials were to be nominated by French civil *commissaires*.[24]

These examples are enough to suggest that French foreign policy during the Directory was shaped by the conflicting aims and policies followed by government, generals and local patriots alike. It was an unstable but powerful cocktail which changed both the map of Europe and its political complexion. The Dutch became a republic, the Belgians and inhabitants of the Rhineland became French, Swiss neutrality vanished and Italian states were transformed into translucent copies of directorial France. Although some of these changes disappeared with French defeats in the summer of 1799, most were to return under Napoleon and survived to leave a permanent mark on Europe in the nineteenth century. Yet what impact did the expansion of French power, particularly during 1798, have on Ireland; and why does Ballinamuck stand out as the exception to a string of French successes? In 1796 a combination of government policy, ambitious generals and political exiles had come together in the forms of Carnot, Hoche and Tone to launch the ill-fated Bantry Bay expedition. Yet in 1798 the polity (defined by Reubell), the general (Bonaparte) and the exiles (now divided and increasingly out of touch with events at home) failed to combine effectively at all. Reubell's strategy was more continental in its emphasis and aimed directly at Britain. Bonaparte's successes in Italy and decision to strike for Egypt, on the other hand, nudged the geographical focus of war away from northern Europe and towards the Mediterranean. Ireland was not a country where he could enhance his reputation: Italy and Egypt were. For their part, the United Irish exiles, increasingly divided and unsure of events on the ground in Ireland, believed in the possibility of a successful domestic insurrection and limited their expectations of France to the sending of a small military expedition and a large supply of arms. The Directory therefore expected the Irish to make their own rebellion. That strategy might have been different if a charismatic general had made the United Irish cause his own, as Hoche had done in 1796–7. Yet Bona-

24 E.Y. Hales, *The emperor and the pope: The story of Napoleon and Pius VII* (New York, 1961), pp 112–15; Guyot, *Directoire et la paix*, pp 601–24.

parte was the only feasible candidate for such a role and his ambition took him southwards. As a result Ireland was destined to become a side show in a much wider global conflict between Britain and revolutionary France.

If French assistance had arrived in any significant numbers, it is doubtful that it would have done anything to alter the final outcome. Certainly a force the size that Hoche took to Bantry Bay, had it landed successfully in late April, could have ensured the rising's success. But that scale of intervention was never on the cards: the French were not prepared to provide it and the United Irish leadership never asked for it. Yet, as Humbert's courageous but futile efforts showed, any smaller contingent had little or no chance of success, while British naval power ensured that reinforcements for any initial landing would always be difficult to secure. Given the virulent opposition that French military occupation encountered in Belgium, the Rhineland and Italy, from a Catholic and rural population very similar to the kind that it would have encountered in Ireland, the failure of the French to arrive in numbers in 1798 may have been fortunate rather than disastrous. Shortly after Humbert's surrender at Ballinamuck a bitter peasant revolt erupted in Belgium – throughout Flanders and Brabant – against French taxation and anticlericalism, and the following year saw a violent rebellion throughout much of the Italian peninsula.[25] Perhaps the real relevance of the European context to the events of 1798 in Ireland therefore lies not in considering what might have happened if the French had arrived, but in analysing what French invasions brought with them elsewhere. The rebellion itself failed because it was poorly planned, inadequately supported and launched too late. Yet, as many analysts have recently pointed out, the various groups that took part in the rising, as well as those that resisted it, conform to a European pattern of political polarization between reformers and conservatives that stretched from Warsaw to Naples and from Geneva to London. That polarization had some of its roots in previous domestic political conflict, but gained much of its dynamism from the inspiration of the French Revolution and the aggression of its foreign policy. No European country in the 1790s except France had its own successful revolution, and Ireland is no exception to that. Yet, France in the 1790s, with its cosmopolitan culture, its mixture of Enlightenment ideals and its historical political arguments, its conflicts and civil war reflect the tensions evident in most other European countries at a time of crucial change and development.

25 E. Kossman, *The Low Countries, 1780–1940* (Oxford, 1978), pp 24–6.

27

Mutiny or subversion? Spithead and the Nore

N.A.M. RODGER

For a number of reasons, it is – or at least, it ought to be – still difficult to write about the 1797 naval mutinies. The first problem is the lack of research. Until relatively recently naval historians tended to be uninterested in social history and somewhat embarrassed by the great mutinies themselves. Historians in general during most of the twentieth century have not been much interested in the Navy. The 1797 mutinies were spectacular events, not to be ignored, and scholars have been ready enough to cite them in support of their arguments, but rather less ready to undertake any serious research into them. The result is that the first, and nearly the last, serious study of these mutinies was published in 1913.[1] Only in recent years has scholarly interest revived, and most of the recent research is still unpublished.[2] Moreover several of the most important categories of evidence are still unexploited,[3] and the social history of the Navy in this period has still not been extensively studied.[4] The time is therefore not yet ripe to attempt any serious reconsideration of the significance of the mutinies.

1   Conrad Gill, *The naval mutinies of 1797* (Manchester, 1913). Since then two further studies have been published. G.E. Manwaring and Bonamy Dobrée, *The floating republic: An account of the mutinies at Spithead and the Nore in 1797* (London, 1935) use documents and add some material facts, but they are less than impartial, and their underlying purpose is evidently to comment on the 1931 Invergordon Mutiny; James Dugan, *The great mutiny* (London, 1966) is not without merit, but romantic, unhistorical and wildly partisan.

2   I refer in particular to the (as yet unpublished) papers given at the two '1797' conferences organised by Ann Coats and Philip MacDougall. I am extremely grateful to Miss Coats, Dr MacDougall and Dr Doorne for the chance to read these papers in advance of their publication. See also the theses of Neale, Oprey and Doorne, referred to below.

3   Notably the ships' musters (Coats' and Doorne's work excepted), and the bulk of the admiralty intelligence records.

4   Michael Lewis, *A social history of the navy, 1793–1815* (London, 1960) was a pioneer effort, but Lewis was mainly interested in officers, and scarcely used documents at all. J.D. Byrn, *Crime and punishment in the Royal Navy: Discipline on the Leeward Islands station, 1784–1812* (Aldershot, 1989) is solid and useful. Brian Lavery, *Nelson's navy: The ships, men and organization, 1793–1815* (London, 1989) deals intelligently but briefly with social history. Dudley Pope, *Life in Nelson's Navy* (London, 1981) is a good popular account based on wide reading and some documentary research. John Masefield, *Sea life in Nelson's time* (London, 1905) still has its admirers, but none among those who know anything at all of the subject.

This may not be a subject which inspires much research, but it certainly inspires interest, commitment, and sometimes passion. A number of those who have written about the 1797 mutinies have been more or less explicitly applying their history to support modern political or social causes;[5] and at least one is candid enough to admit that he has selected his evidence accordingly.[6] In Irish history likewise, objectivity has not always been regarded as a virtue, and the intersection of the two subjects in the 1797 mutinies makes it particularly difficulty to maintain ones balance while standing firmly on the evidence.

Fortunately this does not mean that it is impossible to say anything at all about the 1797 mutinies. Before attempting to do so, however, it may be well to sketch briefly the actual events. It is customary to speak of two great naval mutinies, at Spithead and the Nore, but it would be more accurate to distinguish four – the first and second Spithead mutinies, the Nore mutiny, and the mutiny of the North Sea Squadron off Yarmouth which subsequently joined the Nore mutiny. These mutinies differed significantly from one another, and it is not safe to assume that they all had the same origins; indeed, it has been for some time usual among naval historians to draw a clear distinction between the 'unpolitical' (benign, morally justified) Spithead mutinies, and the 'political' or 'revolutionary' (malign and dangerous) mutinies on the East Coast.[7] It is also relevant to look briefly at a number of single-ship mutinies or conspiracies later in 1797 and in 1798, because they were possibly connected with the Irish rebellion, and because several historians have deduced from them evidence of widespread underground movements.[8]

The Channel or Grand Fleet, which was the principal British squadron, had been commanded from the outbreak of war by Lord Howe, under whose command it won the battle of 1 June 1794. Howe was by this time sixty-eight and

5   Roger Wells, *Insurrection: The British experience 1795–1803* (Gloucester, 1983), with its frequent references to the 'Peace Movement', hints at such an engagement. Joseph Price Moore III, '"The greatest enormity that prevails": Direct democracy and workers' self-management in the British naval mutinies of 1797', in Colin Howell and R.J. Twomey (eds), *Jack Tar in history: Essays in the history of maritime life and labour* (Fredericton, N.B., 1991) pp 76–104, makes no secret of it: 'In the late capitalist world, the story of the meanings we have been trying to locate here is still, despite many of our battles lost, very far from having ended': p. 103.

6   Jonathan Neale, *The cutlass and the lash: Mutiny and discipline in Nelson's Navy* (London, 1985), p. 12 n.7. The author acknowledges (p. x) the encouragement of the Socialist Workers' Party; a healthy corrective to the quarter-deck view, perhaps, but not without some risk of another bias. Cf. the introduction to the same author's 'Forecastle and quarterdeck: Protest, discipline and mutiny in the Royal Navy 1793–1814' (unpublished Ph.D. thesis, University of Warwick, 1990). But in his thesis especially, Neale's handling of the evidence he has chosen to use is exemplary, and his work is highly useful even to those who do not share his politics.

7   This interpretation derives from Manwaring and Dobrée, *Floating republic*, implicitly commenting on the 1931 Invergordon Mutiny. Ann Coats in 'Spithead Introduction' argues that the contrast has been over-drawn.

8   Wells, *Insurrection*, pp 145–50; Marianne Elliott, *Partners in revolution: The United Irishmen and France* (New Haven, 1982), pp 138, 143.

anxious to retire, but the king was reluctant to part with him, and for three years he remained officially in command though for much of the time he was actually ill ashore, while his second-in-command Lord Bridport took the fleet to sea. This uncomfortable arrangement might have strained the warmest friendship, and the two admirals were not on good terms. Howe, unlike Bridport, had long been a believer in distant blockade, keeping the main fleet safely at anchor, especially in winter, while frigates watched the enemy ports until their observations, combined with intelligence from other sources, gave warning that the enemy was preparing to sail. In principle there was much to be said for this strategy, but it depended on good intelligence and communications.[9] Its disadvantages were well illustrated by Hoche's midwinter expedition to Ireland, which the Channel Fleet altogether failed to intercept; Bridport was generally blamed for this failure, though the fault was arguably Howe's, and Vice-Admiral Colpoys was actually commanding part of the fleet at sea at the time.[10] The strategy also involved keeping the main fleet at anchor for long periods, which saved damage and danger to the ships but gave the men much leisure to think and talk about their situation. In February and March 1797, Howe, convalescing at Bath, received a number of anonymous petitions purporting to come from various ships of his fleet (which was then at sea), requesting higher pay. On his own account he did not take them very seriously, but he made some enquiries in the fleet, apparently without informing Bridport, and unofficially passed the petitions to the admiralty. Similar petitions had already been received there, and ignored. In this case Lord Spencer, the first lord of the admiralty, sent the petitions to Bridport for his comments.[11]

By the time he received them it was too late. The fleet returned to Spithead on 30 Mar. After waiting two weeks for a reply, the seamen put their plans into motion. Only in the last few days did it become obvious to their officers that something was afoot. Bridport from the start advised negotiation and conciliation, but the admiralty's reaction to the rumour of discontent was to order the fleet to sea. This gave the signal for the outbreak of the mutiny on Easter Sunday 16 April.[12] The mutiny was essentially a collective refusal to obey the order to weigh anchor. For the next week the fleet was immobilized by the mutineers while a body of elected delegates, two from each ship, negotiated first with

9 A.N. Ryan, 'The Royal Navy and the blockade of Brest, 1689–1805: Theory and practice', in Martine Acerra, José Merino and Jean Meyer (eds), *Les marines de guerre Européennes, XVII-XVIIIe siècles* (Paris, 1985), pp 183–4; John Barrow, *The life of Richard, Earl Howe, K.G.* (London, 1838), pp 216–18.

10 Richard Saxby, 'Lord Bridport and the Spithead mutiny', in *Mariner's Mirror*, lxxix (1993), 170.

11 Gill, *Naval mutinies*, pp 7–12. One of the petitions is printed with other documents by D. Bonner Smith, 'The naval mutinies of 1797' in *Mariner's Mirror*, xxi (1935), 428–49; xxii (1936), 65–86.

12 Gill, *Naval mutinies*, pp 16–21; Saxby, 'Lord Bridport', pp 171–3.

Bridport, and later with the board of admiralty itself led by Lord Spencer. Although a few unpopular officers were sent ashore, no violence or disorder occurred, and the mutineers did not interfere with the ordinary routine of their ships. On 19 April, indeed, the grand duke of Württemberg, in England for his marriage to Princess Charlotte, paid a state visit to the fleet accompanied by Spencer and the lords of the admiralty, the mutineers politely manning the yards and firing the appropriate salutes.[13] The mutineer delegates insisted throughout on their readiness to sail immediately if the French fleet put out from Brest, and would not allow frigates and convoy escorts to join them, lest trade should suffer. They strongly denied any political motives and proclaimed their loyalty to the king. Their principal demands were for an increase of wages, together with various improvements in the quality and quantity of victuals and the treatment of the wounded. Most of these were eventually conceded, and with the arrival of a royal pardon on Sunday 23 April the first Spithead mutiny was officially over.[14]

The necessary legislation was now set in motion, but the motions of parliament were too slow for the seamen, who became increasingly suspicious that they had been deceived. On 7 May the mutiny broke out anew. This time there was violence, though not from the mutineers: Colpoys ordered the officers of his flagship, the *London*, to fire on the mutineers, several of whom were killed. The enraged men nearly hanged the admiral and one of his officers in retaliation, but were dissuaded by two of the leading delegates. Colpoys, Vice-Admiral Gardner, ten captains and one hundred other officers (about one-fifth of the total) were now sent ashore and the mutineers took effective command of the fleet, but the remaining captains and admirals, including Bridport, remained aboard. Two days later the necessary act of parliament finally passed the Lords and received the royal assent. Lord Howe had at last been allowed to resign his command in April, but he now came to Portsmouth on behalf of the king to persuade the mutineers that their demands really had been granted. In addition they now insisted that a list of named unpopular officers (about half of those who had been sent ashore) should be replaced, and this Howe conceded. The reconciliation was completed with ceremonies on 15 May, culminating in a banquet given by Howe for the delegates of the fleet. Two days later Bridport was able to sail to take station off Brest.[15]

Meanwhile another mutiny had broken out among the ships at the Nore. This anchorage off Sheerness dockyard, at the junction of the Thames and Medway, was a focal point where ships coming from Chatham and the river yards, or those returning from sea, often spent a few days. It was also a major distribution centre for new recruits, and an old line-of-battleship, the *Sandwich*, lay permanently off Sheerness as 'guardship', which in practice meant floating barracks. A flag offi-

13 Manwaring and Dobrée, *Floating republic*, p. 54.
14 Gill, *Naval mutinies*, pp 360–76, prints the main documents bearing on these negotiations.
15 Ibid., pp 55–82.

cer, Vice-Admiral Buckner, supervised the business of the port, and flew his flag on her. There was no fleet at the Nore, accustomed to operating together, simply a small, transient population of ships most of which stayed there only briefly. When mutiny broke out there on 12 May, it initially aroused little alarm, and virtually no official reaction. Only after twelve days, when it became clear that the concessions made at Spithead were not going to satisfy the new mutineers, did the admiralty react. The Nore mutineers demanded not only the same concessions given at Spithead (which in reality had already been granted to the whole Navy), but more regular pay, advance wages for pressed men, a right to leave in port, a more equitable distribution of prize money, a standing pardon for returning deserters, and an effective veto on the appointment of officers.[16] (Neither at Spithead nor the Nore did the mutineers mention either impressment or flogging as grievances, and the mutineer leaders themselves flogged men for drunkenness.)[17] To cement their cause the mutineers imposed rigorous discipline, stopping all communication with the shore in order that the men should not discover the concessions made at Spithead, and not hesitating to fire on ships which offered to leave the anchorage.[18]

The board of admiralty arrived on the scene on 28 May, but from the beginning they refused to make further concessions, and stopped shore supplies to the mutineers. They must have known that the new mutiny had little of the public support of the old and virtually none of the leverage. The Channel Fleet was the country's principal strength and only safeguard against invasion; the small group of ships at the Nore had limited opportunity to do mischief, and several of them were visibly reluctant to remain in the mutiny. On 30 May the frigates *Clyde* and *San Fiorenzo* escaped under fire from the mutineers. The Nore mutiny was then on the verge of collapse, but it was saved by the mutiny of Admiral Duncan's North Sea Squadron off Yarmouth on 27 May, after which most of the squadron sailed to join the Nore mutineers. This was another crisis, potentially worse than the Spithead mutinies, for Duncan's task was to blockade the Dutch fleet in the Texel, which (unlike the French in Brest) was known to be ready for sea and preparing for an expedition. For some days Duncan was reduced to keeping up a pretence of blockade with two ships only. Moreover the reinforced Nore mutineers became increasingly extreme in their attitudes as their situation grew more difficult. For three days they attempted a complete blockade of the Thames, and when that failed they discussed sailing their ships to an enemy or neutral port. But supplies were short, the navigation buoys had

16 The mutineers do not seem to have known that their demand to be paid up to six months in arrears on sailing was already law under the 1758 Navy Act. See Stephen Gradish, *The manning of the British navy during the Seven Years War* (London, 1980), pp 88–96.

17 Gill, *Naval mutinies*, pp 43, 278–81; Dugan, *Great mutiny*, p. 477.

18 Gill, *Naval mutinies*, pp 107–41; D. Bonner-Smith, 'The mutiny at the Nore, 1797', *Mariner's Mirror*, xxxiii (1947), 199–203.

been removed, more and more ships found means to desert the mutineers, and when they gave the signal to sail on 9 June no ship obeyed it. After fighting on board, all the mutinous ships had been recaptured by loyalist seamen by 13 June, and the last of the great mutinies was over.[19]

There were however a number of mutinous incidents in individual ships over the next few years. Besides those on overseas stations, they included the conspiracy that same month aboard the *Pompée* of Bridport's fleet, in which a number of men apparently planned to seize the ship and, possibly, hand her over to the French at Brest;[20] and the discontent aboard the *Mars* that summer which led to another court martial.[21] In the summer of 1798 undoubted United Irish plots were detected aboard the *Caesar* and *Defiance*, and a possible one aboard the *Glory*.[22] At the same time individuals aboard several other ships were convicted of using 'mutinous or seditious expressions'.[23]

Broadly speaking, four different explanations have been offered for the 1797 mutinies. The first might be called the traditional naval historians' explanation, except that there is no strong tradition among naval historians of studying the mutinies. According to this understanding, the Spithead mutinies were in part what they pretended to be, a strictly professional movement for purely naval ends, conducted and resolved with good sense on either side; a regrettable incident but one demonstrating the English virtues of moderation and tolerance. Behind them, however, and much more clearly in the East Coast mutinies, we can detect the evil influence of outside agitators working on the simple sailors in the interests of the country's enemies – even though here, too, good sense eventually triumphed when the loyal majority overthrew the troublemakers.[24]

It is implicit, and often explicit, in this interpretation that the seamen were essentially loyal but unsophisticated men, whose generous sympathies were easily perverted by designing landsmen without whose malign influence politics would never have corrupted the Arcadian simplicity of naval life. Certainly the Spithead mutineers had grievances and were justified in bringing them to the authorities' notice, but their mutiny was not a political action. The Navy's principal fleet remained undefiled by civilian politics. At the Nore it was different,

---

19 Gill, *Naval mutinies*, pp 151–240.
20 Dugan, *Great mutiny*, pp 340–1; Gill, *Naval mutinies*, pp 84, 117, n.2; Wells, *Insurrection*, p. 101.
21 Ibid., p. 101; Dugan, *Great mutiny*, p. 366.
22 Ibid., pp 427–8; Neale, 'Forecastle and quarterdeck', pp 332–4; Wells, *Insurrection*, pp 149–50. Doorne, who has studied these incidents in detail, regards the evidence of United Irish involvement as circumstantial, but strong.
23 Dugan, *Great mutiny*, pp 427–8.
24 Manwaring and Dobrée, *Floating republic*, pp 14–17; Lewis, *Social history*, pp 123–6. Of these three authors, Manwaring (a librarian) had written a good deal of naval history, Dobrée was a Professor of English, and Lewis was Professor of History at the R.N. College, Greenwich. Gill, *Naval mutinies*, pp 300–46, takes essentially the same line with rather more sophistication.

and the question was how and whence the evil influence of civilians had penetrated the Navy.

There was an obvious answer, already proposed at the time, and subsequently
adopted by most historians – the Quota Acts.[25] During 1795 and 1796 the government passed a series of five acts which laid obligations on local authorities in
England, Wales and Scotland to provide fixed numbers of recruits for the Navy
or army. These recruits were implicitly to be volunteers, since no mechanism for
compulsion was provided in the acts, only the means to raise money with which
to pay bounties. Those authorities which failed to meet their quotas were to pay
fines instead.[26] The 1795 acts, which coincided with a time of dearth and unem-
ployment, appear to have been successful, but the 1796 acts proposed much
smaller quotas, and produced so few men that the scheme was then abandoned.
The suggestion usually made is that these acts had introduced numbers of
landsmen – and what was worse, landsmen of some education – whose evil influence had corrupted the simple sailors; 'the pernicious leaven working, or striving
to work, in the healthy lump'.[27] One outstanding piece of evidence supports this
argument; Richard Parker, the leader (or in some interpretations, figurehead) of
the Nore mutiny, was a Quota man, and a former pupil of Exeter Grammar
School who at one period in his life had kept a school – though he was also a
professional seaman and a former inferior officer in the Navy.[28] The Quota Acts
have served subsequent historians as the perfect vehicle for every theory, each
proposing their own favourite candidates as the Quota men who must have
inspired the mutinies.

For the naval historians it was sufficient that the Quota men were, or could be
assumed to be, outsiders, landsmen, alien to the naval character. Non-naval historians, however, have found it needful to identify the Quota men with an appropriate category ashore. The first of these interpretations is what we might call
the romantic socialist view. It may be conveniently summed up in a quotation
from E.P. Thompson:

25 Ibid., pp 315–17; Manwaring and Dobrée, *Floating republic*, p. 16; Lewis, *Social history*, pp
    121–3; Wells, *Insurrection*, p. 94.
26 The Quota Acts were: 35 Geo.III c.5, which levied all English and Welsh counties for the Navy
    (9,420 men in total); 35 Geo.III c.9, which levied English, Welsh and Scottish seaports for the
    Navy (19,866 men in total, each able seaman to count as two); 35 Geo.III c.29, which levied
    Scottish counties, cities and burghs for the Navy (total 1,814 men); 37 Geo.III c.4, which levied
    English and Welsh counties, some for the army and some for the Navy (naval total 6,146 men);
    and 37 Geo.III c.5, which levied Scottish counties, cities and burghs for either service at the
    volunteers' choice (total 2,219 men). In addition there were several amending and explaining
    acts.
27 Lewis, *Social history*, p. 123.
28 Gill, *Naval mutinies*, pp 124–8. Parker's own account of his life is printed in *Private papers of
    George, second Earl Spencer*, J.S. Corbett and H.W. Richmond (eds), Navy Records Society (vols
    xlvi, xlvii, xlviii and lix [1913–24]), ii, 160–73.

It is foolish to argue that, because the majority of the sailors had few political notions, this was a parochial affair of ship's biscuits and arrears of pay, and not a revolutionary movement. This is to mistake the nature of popular revolutionary crises, which arise from exactly this kind of conjunction between the grievances of the majority and the aspirations articulated by the politically conscious minority.[29]

The true meaning of the mutinies was nothing so trivial as naval affairs, which Thompson had no idea of investigating; they were to be understood as a significant moment in that most significant of all historical movements, the rise of the English working class. As an extension of this interpretation, it has since been argued that the mutinies were the product of a native English 'peace movement', centred on the Corresponding Societies and learning from the French example, whose objective was to drive Britain out of the war and Pitt out of office, if not to engineer another English republican revolution.[30] Pitt's 'reign of terror' was on this interpretation thoroughly justified (pragmatically if not morally) for exactly the reason with which he and his supporters justified it; the real and grave threat posed by English revolutionaries to the survival of the regime.[31] But not everyone agrees that the English were capable of revolution unaided, and the same 1797 mutinies have been adduced as prime examples of the work of the United Irishmen. Again it is argued that outside agitators were at work; again the Quota Acts are offered as the mechanism by which they were introduced into the Navy. In this case the outsiders are United Irishmen, their first target was the large numbers of Irishmen in the Navy, and the 1797 mutinies join the list of Irish revolutions which nearly worked.[32]

It has also been argued that Thompson was insufficiently rigorous in his Marxism, that romantic notions of working-class solidarity are no substitute for pure dialectic, and that the only way to understand the life of the Navy is in terms of the struggling proletarians striving to escape the shackles of the capitalist mode of production. This tends to the unusual, almost unique, conclusion that the seamen were not an isolated profession needing outsiders to teach them their revolutionary responsibilities, but members of a radicalized working class quite capable of mounting their own insurrection without the instruction of the Quota men.[33]

29 E.P. Thompson, *The making of the English working class* (London, 1978), p. 184.
30 Wells, *Insurrection*, pp 81–150.
31 Ibid., p. 28.
32 Elliott, *Partners in revolution*, pp 135–44.
33 Neale, 'Forecastle and quarterdeck', pp 13–30, 329–31, 494, though he deals primarily with mutinies other than those of 1797. Moore, 'The Greatest enormity', is not far from this position, but he offers an eschatological interpetation of the mutinies and their significance in terms of Marxist salvation history; he has no clear view of their origin.

This, however, remains an eccentric position. Almost all historians who have written about the mutinies are agreed that they can only be explained by outside influence, and for all but the naval historians, it is clearly this which lends the subject its attraction. A purely naval mutiny, 'a parochial affair of ship's biscuits and arrears of pay', could be of no interest unless it involved an issue of historical importance, if not a cause worthy of the historian's commitment. Little writing, and less reading, have been bestowed upon the social history of the Navy itself, and historians have been happy to believe the most unlikely facts. The Spithead mutineers, for example, demanded the abolition of what they claimed to be the 'totally new' rating of landsman. It is an interesting question what they meant by this, but there is no question whatever that the rating of landsman and its equivalents ('landman' in the older form, and before that 'grommet') had been in continuous use in the Navy since the sixteenth century,[34] as anybody would know who had any acquaintance with the subject, but nobody does know who has actually published about it.[35] Almost without exception, the historians of the 1797 mutinies have preferred a leap of faith to a painful trawl through the naval archives.[36] Even Gill, the first and most scholarly student of the mutinies, who was interested in them for their own sake, was prone to abandon his notes in favour of assumptions unsupported by evidence or argument,[37] and his example has been willingly followed by those whose real interests lay elsewhere.

Three related aspects of the question may be used to support this charge; the leadership of the mutinies, the Quota Acts, and the sources of naval recruitment. Clearly if the mutinies were really led by Quota men, it is important to identify the leaders. In the case of the Spithead mutineers, there is no difficulty in doing so, for the delegates of the fleet put their names to documents and negotiated publicly. We know not only who they were, but their ages, ratings and places of

---

34 In sixteenth-century references, it is not always easy to distinguish a formal rating from a loose description, but 'grommets' are listed in the 1626 scale of sea pay, midway between seamen and boys; cf. *The naval tracts of Sir William Monson*, M. Oppenheim (ed.), Navy Records Society, vols xxii–xxiii, xliii, xlv, xlvii [1902–14], iii, 185–6.

35 Gill, *Naval mutinies*, p. 32; Manwaring and Dobrée, *Floating republic*, p. 52; Wells, *Insurrection*, p. 86; John Ehrman, *The younger Pitt: The consuming struggle* (London, 1996), p. 21, n.5. Even Lewis, *Social history*, pp 85, 94, is adrift on this point, though he did know something about the Navy.

36 I emphasise the *naval* archives; many of these writers have done admirable research into the subjects central to their interests.

37 Gill, *Naval mutinies*, for example – 'the secret societies to which many of the seamen belonged': pp 305–6; 'a widespread and dangerous conspiracy': p. 310; 'I have treated sedition and the belief in revolutionary theories as synonymous terms', (the evidence for 'revolutionary theories' being the use of language reminiscent of Paine): p. 314, n. 1; quota men 'as a rule, either debtors or men who had been convicted of petty fraud ... persons of comparatively good education ... [with] a slight and mischievous knowledge of the new political theories': pp 315–16; 'it is probable that several of the ringleaders at Spithead and at the Nore had been sent into the navy by the civil authorities': pp 316–17.

birth.[38] Moreover all this information has been in print since 1935, and it could easily be amplified from the available documents.[39] It has been ignored because it does not support any of the popular theories. Without exception the delegates were able seamen or seamen petty officers, ratings which they could not have reached without long experience at sea; none of them was a Quota man, and only four out of thirty-three were Irish.[40] Though the fact was long since disproved, it is still frequently repeated that Valentine Joyce, the delegates' spokesman, was a Belfast tobacconist and a Quota man.[41] In fact he was born in Jersey, had been a professional seaman all his life, and on his own statement had served in the Navy since he was eleven. His family lived in Portsmouth where his father was serving in the garrison.[42] It is only possible to believe that the mutiny was really led by Quota men if one believes that the delegates were straw men concealing the real leaders[43] – or the real leader, that shadowy Macavity of the Channel Fleet, the mysterious genius who 'must' have organized the mutiny but who covered his tracks so perfectly that no evidence of his existence survives.[44] Here we are in the presence of the conspiracy theory in its purest form, in which the entire absence of evidence only serves to prove the fiendish cunning of the conspirators.

In fact the most plausible candidate for a straw man is Richard Parker, an undoubted Quota man but not certainly the true leader of the Nore mutiny.[45] At present, however, we have little hard evidence about his colleagues. For obvious reasons the leaders of this mutiny were not keen to be identified afterwards: some escaped, others concealed themselves, and we cannot be sure that those executed were the true leaders. Captain Bligh of the *Director*, to name one deeply-involved ship of the North Sea squadron, prevented any of his ship's company being hanged.[46] Though the names are known of at least some of the most active mutineer leaders at Yarmouth and the Nore, no systematic attempt has been made to trace their origins.[47] All that can be said at present is that Parker is the only identified Quota man among them. We now have, however, an

---

38 Ibid., pp 361–2.

39 Manwaring and Dobrée, *Floating republic*, pp 262–3, but they did not attempt to trace the delegates' previous careers.

40 Ann Coats, 'The Delegates: A radical tradition'.

41 Elliott, *Partners in revolution*, p. 143; Dugan, *Great mutiny*, pp 63–4; Neale, 'Forecastle and quarterdeck', p. 317.

42 Coats, 'The Delegates', pp 18–19.

43 Lewis, *Social history*, pp 124–5.

44 Manwaring and Dobrée, *Floating republic*, pp 16–17.

45 Gill, *Naval mutinies*, pp 249–50; Philip MacDougall, 'The East Coast mutinies, May–June 1797', argues that he was a moderate who tried unsuccessfully to restrain the extremists. Christopher Doorne, 'A floating republic? Conspiracy theory and the Nore Mutiny of 1797', discusses the same question.

46 Neale, 'Forecastle and quarterdeck', pp 325–6, where the name of the ship is mistaken.

47 MacDougall, 'The East Coast mutinies', and 'Mutiny and the North Sea squadron' assembles the evidence, but has not used the ships' musters.

analysis of all men accused at court martial of mutiny or sedition anywhere in the Navy during the year 1797, which shows that 43 out of 462 were identifiable as Quota men, plus another 40 or so volunteers who, from the date of their appearance on board, might possibly have been recruited under the Quota Acts.[48]

It remains to consider how the Navy was recruited, what effects the Quota Acts had, and in particular how many Irishmen were serving in the mutinous squadrons of 1797. The eighteenth-century Royal Navy was largely demobilized in peacetime, and there was no form of continuous or career service for ratings. It followed that the Navy had to draw its seamen from the general pool of seamen and seafaring men, so that there were relatively few pure 'men-of-warsmen', but very many with experience of merchantmen and fishing boats. Professional seamen, above all topmen, were very scarce in wartime. Their skills took many years to learn, normally starting in boyhood, and the existing supply could not suddenly be increased on the outbreak of war. Since wartime demand (from the Navy and merchant service together) exceeded supply by at least two to one, both the Navy and merchant shipping had a permanent manning crisis, and all ships had to resort to a substantial dilution of skill by recruiting landsmen.[49]

The Navy initially mobilized during 1793, when its total strength rose from 16,600 to nearly 70,000. The total reached 87,000 in 1794, 96,000 in 1795, 114,000 in 1796, and nearly 119,000 in 1797 (12,000 more than the maximum number attained in the last year of the American War).[50] This voracious demand for manpower was the background to the Quota Acts, which, it has been claimed, wrought 'something of a revolution in the social composition of the lower deck'.[51] They certainly would have done that, were it true that 'in 1797 over 100,000 of the 120,000 to 135,000 strong naval force had been recruited in the preceding three years, primarily products of the Quota Acts'.[52] That would imply that the English, Scottish and Welsh local authorities had outperformed their quotas by three fold – an astonishing patriotic excess for which there is no precedent, and no evidence.[53] It would also oblige us to account for the disappearance of most of the 100,000 or so men who were already serving before the

---

48 C.J. Doorne, 'Mutiny and sedition in the Home Commands of the Royal Navy, 1783–1803' (unpublished Ph.D. thesis, University of London, 1998), tables 6.1, 6.2 and 6.3.

49 D.J. Starkey, 'War and the market for seafarers in Britain, 1736–1792', in L.R. Fischer and H.W. Nordvik (eds), *Shipping and trade, 1750–1950: Essays in international maritime economic history* (Pontefract, 1990), pp 25–42.

50 Christopher Lloyd, *The British seaman* (London, 1968), pp 288–9. These are averages of the monthly totals borne; numbers mustered were somewhat lower. Note that the table in Lewis, *Social history*, p. 119, is based on the numbers voted by parliament, which were an accounting fiction.

51 Wells, *Insurrection*, p. 83. Wells actually writes 'lower decks', which I take to be a printer's error.

52 Elliott, *Partners in revolution*, p. 136.

53 The total naval recruitment from all the five acts together would have reached 39,465 if every quota had been completely filled; no able seamen had been entered under 35 Geo. III c.9, and no volunteer had elected for the army under 37 Geo. III c.5.

first Quota men reached the fleet. In fact the net increase in the manpower of the Navy from 1795 to 1797 was only 22,000 men,[54] though the gross recruitment was certainly much greater. We do not have accurate figures for the wastage or turnover of the Navy, but a figure between 20 per cent and 25 per cent per annum would be a plausible guess.[55]

Fortunately the evidence for the Quota Acts allows us to do considerably better than plausible guesses. Although the naval muster books have not yet been analysed to give overall figures for the Navy, records of the workings of the Quota Acts survive from at least thirteen English counties, and possibly from the seaports and from Scotland as well.[56] The best estimate is that the 1795 acts recruited about 31,000 men, the 1796 acts much fewer.[57] Possibly no more than one sixth were seamen,[58] but the remainder were overwhelmingly young working men from a cross-section of the usual trades, mostly from the counties they were recruited for or nearby. Though there were some from more distant parts, only 3 per cent were Irish. There is no evidence at all of the disqualified attorneys, cashiered excisemen, fraudsters, debtors, bankrupts, vagrants, beggars, poachers, pickpockets, Sunday-school pupils, schoolmasters and other undesirables supposed to have been recruited by these acts.[59] All the evidence is that these

54 Lloyd, *British seaman*, p. 289.

55 N.A.M. Rodger, *The wooden world: An anatomy of the Georgian navy* (London, 1986), pp 148, 203; R.G. Usher, 'Royal Navy impressment during the American Revolution', *Mississippi Valley Historical Review*, xxxvii (1950), 673–88. These estimates apply to earlier periods, but at present we have none better.

56 Clive Emsley, A.M. Hill and M.Y. Ashcroft (eds), *North Riding naval recruits: The Quota Acts and the Quota Men, 1795–1797* (Northallerton, 1978). This is essentially two publications in one: an analysis by Emsley of returns from Kent, Leicestershire, Lincolnshire, Northumberland, Nottinghamshire and Sussex; and a transcript (by Hill and Ashcroft) of returns for the North Riding of Yorkshire; Christopher Oprey, 'Schemes for the reform of naval recruitment, 1793–1815' (unpublished M.A. thesis, University of Liverpool, 1961), considers records from Lancashire, Kent, Essex, Nottinghamshire and London; for Lincolnshire, see also F.W. Brooks, 'Naval recruiting in Lindsey, 1795–7', *English Historical Review*, xliii (1928), 230–40. To my knowledge the returns for Essex, London and the Isle of Wight in the Public Record Office (ADM 7/361–362 and ADM 30/63/8) have never been studied.

57 Oprey, 'Naval recruitment' – the most extensive study of these acts – is cautious about committing himself to figures, but implies (p. 127) that the 1795 quotas (total 31,100) were more or less achieved, at least in England.

58 This, however, is based on Emsley and Oprey, who have analysed only county records. The 1795 Port Quota Act (35 Geo. III c.9) called for 19,866 men (or half that number of able seamen), to be levied by committees of shipowners. This means that half the notional product of the Quota Acts was not to be raised by local authorities, and that half was obviously meant to be seamen. Until records of this Act have been studied, therefore, it is better not to be dogmatic about the proportion of landmen to seamen, but see Oprey, 'Naval recruitment', pp 221–7, for the Port Act in Liverpool.

59 Gill, *Naval mutinies*, pp 315–16; Manwaring and Dobrée, *Floating republic*, p. 16; Lewis, *Social history*, pp 117–18; Wells, *Insurrection*, pp 81, 84–5; *The private correspondence of Admiral Lord Collingwood*, ed. Edward Hughes, Navy Records Society, vol. xcviii (1957), p. 85. Cf. Coats, 'The 1797 mutinies'.

were not educated trouble-makers, but respectable working men in need of employment.[60]

The Quota Acts did not apply to Ireland, and brought in only a few Irishmen. It is often argued, however, that the proportion of Irishmen in the Navy was very high. We are told that there was 'a huge Irish contingent, reinforced further by political prisoners',[61] meaning those sent to sea under the 1796 Insurrection Act. Another historian, referring to the same act, tells us that, 'the proportion of Defenders or United Irishmen sent to the navy in those years must consequently have been considerable', but prudently avoids explaining what proportion, of what, or how much might be 'considerable'.[62] There does not at present appear to be any evidence to prove that 'thousands' of men were sent into the Navy under this act.[63] In November 1796 Thomas Pelham incautiously offered that 15,000 men had been recruited in all for the Navy in Ireland since the outbreak of war, but he was later obliged to withdraw this as an exaggeration.[64] It has been suggested that 25 per cent of the Navy was Irish,[65] and Theobald Wolfe Tone believed the figure was two-thirds or more.[66] Though no one is so incautious as to say outright that all Irishmen were United Irishmen, it is freely insinuated that United Irish leadership, or at least participation, can be assumed wherever large numbers of Irishmen can be identified. The *Mars* of the Channel Fleet, for example, is described as 'manned principally by Irishmen', and as 'one of the most militant ships at Portsmouth'.[67] The *Defiance*, we are told, 'the most troublesome ship at Spithead, had an unusually large component of Irish sailors'.[68] It has been claimed that the ships which mutinied in 1798 were 50 per cent manned by Irishmen.[69]

It is not possible to replace these figures with satisfactory evidence until the ships' musters are systematically analysed, but some things can be said with confidence. In the ships which sent delegates to the Spithead mutiny, an average of 26 per cent of the crews were Irish-born, though as we have seen the proportion

60 Emsley, in *North Riding naval recruits*, pp 7–20; Oprey, 'Naval recruitment', pp 155, 159, 170, 263.

61 Wells, *Insurrection*, p. 84.

62 Elliott, *Partners in revolution*, p. 138.

63 Wells, *Insurrection*, p. 82.

64 Elliott, *Partners in revolution*, p. 138; Wells, *Insurrection*, p. 82, adopts the figure uncritically. I take it to be the unnamed source for Manwaring and Dobrée's claim that 16,515 Irishmen were recruited during this period: *Floating republic*, p. 101. Note that recruits in Ireland are not the same as Irish recruits; professional seamen in particular were very likely to have been pressed at sea.

65 Wells, *Insurrection*, p. 82.

66 Elliott, *Partners in revolution*, pp 331–2.

67 Wells, *Insurrection*, p. 101.

68 Elliott, *Partners in revolution*, p. 143.

69 Ibid., p. 138, apparently citing Lewis, *Social history*, p. 129, which contains nothing to the purpose.

among the leaders was much lower. The *Mars*, so far from being 'manned principally by Irishmen', had the lowest figure of all (15 per cent), while the highest (72
per cent) came from the *Monarch*, which did not initially participate in the
mutiny.[70] Of the total of 462 men who were charged at court martial with mutiny
or sedition in home waters during 1797, 106 had been born in Ireland.[71] There are
also some indications of the level of Irish recruitment for the Navy as a whole. A
sample of ships commissioning at Plymouth during the American War had 20 per
cent Irish ship's companies; in a similar sample from 1804–5, this had risen to 29
per cent.[72] Since Plymouth was the nearest dockyard port to Ireland and the one
to which recruits from Ireland usually came, the figures for the Navy as a whole
would presumably have been lower, though a sample of ships which served on the
Leeward Islands station between 1784 and 1812 shows 30 per cent Irish.[73] What
proportion of these Irishmen may have been disaffected is a matter of too much
speculation, though it is worth noting that the captains in the Channel Fleet who
in 1798 were invited by the admiralty to state what proportion of the Irishmen
serving in their ships were 'evilly-disposed', returned a figure of 21 per cent.[74]

Overall we can certainly assume the presence of Irishmen in most ships, and
the presence of United Irishmen is likely in some ships in 1798, but we are far
from establishing any clear connection between the United Irishmen and the
1797 mutinies.[75] The mutinies took the United Irish leadership as completely by
surprise as they did the French.[76] The fact that the mutineer leaders enforced the
swearing of oaths does not in the least establish an Irish connection, particularly
as the form of the oaths was quite different from those used by the United
Irishmen.[77] After the event, according to Dublin Castle's intelligence, the United
Irish leadership discussed the possibility of fomenting discontent in the fleet,
but this is no proof that they tried, still less succeeded in doing so.[78] The most
that can be said is that there are strong suggestions of United Irish involvement
in some of the 1798 incidents.[79] By that stage the first target of some United

70   Coats, 'The Delegates', table 1. There are no figures for the *Defiance*.
71   Doorne, 'Mutiny and sedition', tables 6.2 and 6.3.
72   N.A.M. Rodger, 'Devon men and the navy, 1688–1815', in Michael Duffy et al. (eds), *The new
     maritime history of Devon*, 2 vols (London, 1993–4), i, pp 213–14.
73   Byrn, *Crime and punishment*, p. 76, n.2.
74   328 seamen out of 1,517, and 83 marines out of 460: Wells, *Insurrection*, p. 150.
75   *Pace* Wells, *Insurrection*, p. 84: 'Although the sources are not very revealing … there can be no
     question that the United Irish started its offensive in the navy prior to the mutinies.' Cf. Elliott,
     Partners in revolution, pp 140–2.
76   Gill, *Naval mutinies*, pp 336–8.
77   Coats, '1797 mutinies', and 'The Delegates'.
78   Gill, *Naval mutinies*, p. 334.
79   Wells, *Insurrection*, pp 145–7; Doorne, 'A floating republic'. In September 1798 William Nugent
     of the *Minerve* was court-martialled for 'having declared himself to be a United Irishman with
     many other improper expressions', and assaulting the master-at-arms: Roger Morriss, *Cockburn
     and the British Navy in transition: Admiral Sir George Cockburn, 1772–1853* (Exeter, 1997), p. 43.

Irish plotters was said to be Protestants rather than officers, and their plots were swiftly betrayed by other Irishmen.

What then, can we say about the 1797 mutinies? Much less, is the answer, than has been said; but not so much as might be said if the needful research were to be done. There is no reason to argue that seamen were political innocents incapable of collective organization without outside help. It is certainly true that the occasions on which the ratings of the Navy had directly participated in national political events were relatively few, though by no means unimportant: in the seventeenth century, the Navy had made and unmade several régimes.[80] More relevant to the great mutinies is the fact that the seamen were the heirs of a native political tradition of shipboard organization, which went back as far as our evidence allows us to see it. In the middle ages, maritime law expected a ship's company to take collective decisions in matters of commerce and navigation, and held the seamen jointly liable with the master for the consequences of decisions in which they were assumed to have participated.[81] Much had changed since then, but by no means everything. Seamen in merchant ships were still liable to bear the cost of damaged cargo, and no doubt many men serving in the Navy in 1797 had previously suffered deductions from their wages in consequence.[82] The old traditions of consensus were probably strongest in fishing boats and coasters rather than deep-sea merchantmen or the Navy, but many of the 1797 mutineers would have had experience of one or both, and even in the Navy the law still required that the ship's company give their consent in certain cases, notably to the disposing of their common property in prizes. Within recent memory it had still been customary in certain circumstances for the captains of men-of-war to consult their men on critical decisions.[83] Professional seamen like the delegates of the fleet at Spithead were the heirs of an ancient tradition which owed nothing to outside tutelage. Arguably the harsher attitude towards collective protest adopted by the admiralty since the 1780s had forced the men to tighten up their organization, but they did not have to invent or borrow a tradition of collective action.[84] The whole experience of shipboard life was an education in teamwork and initiative. Men like Valentine Joyce who had passed their boyhood afloat and aloft were steeped in the complex machinery of a sailing ship, in which everyone's safety depended on co-ordination and mutual trust, and in which the topmen in particular had to

80 Bernard Capp, *Cromwell's Navy: The fleet and the English Revolution, 1648–1660* (Oxford, 1989), pp 115–51; Hans-Christoph Junge, *Flottenpolitik und revolution: Die Entstehung der Englischen seemacht während der Herrschaft Cromwells* (Stuttgart, 1980), pp 81–107.
81 Dorothy Burwash, *English merchant shipping, 1460–1540* (Toronto, 1947), pp 61–2; Sir Travers Twiss (ed.), *The black book of the admiralty* (London, 1871–6), i, pp 89–94; Jacques Bernard, *Navires et gens de mer à Bordeaux (vers 1400–vers 1550)* (3 vols, Paris, 1968) ii, pp 638–9, 642–6.
82 Ralph Davis, *The rise of the English shipping industry in the seventeenth and eighteenth centuries* (2nd edn, Newton Abbot, 1972), pp 144–5.
83 Rodger, *Wooden world*, pp 136–7, 235–6.
84 Ibid., pp 237–44; Neale, 'Forecastle and quarterdeck', pp 49, 330–1.

think for themselves for the survival of all. As petty officers and leading hands they had been trained to carry responsibility. They knew far more about collective organization than shopkeepers or schoolmasters.

All this should make us pause before we attempt to impose interpretations on events which have to be understood in their own terms before they can be interpreted in any other. Much remains to be discovered about these mutinies, but whoever undertakes research into them will have to be prepared to understand naval life itself, and not simply treat the Navy as a blank screen onto which to project a favourite plot. When we have a complete social history of the late eighteenth-century Navy, we may be able to see more clearly in what respects the 1797 mutinies differed from naval tradition, and in what ways they may, perhaps, have been influenced from outside. Until then, modest caution best becomes us.

28

Scotland and the 1798 rebellion: The limits of 'common cause'

ELAINE McFARLAND

The sea-crossing which divides Portpatrick in the Rhins of Galloway from Donaghadee in County Down is only twenty-one miles, a closeness which has encouraged the emergence of complex reciprocal ties of ideology, kinship and commerce between the west of Scotland and the northeast of Ireland. Already by the late eighteenth century, this geographical and cultural proximity had been reinforced by an apparently similar coincidence of economic advance and political stasis in the two societies. Not surprisingly, when radicals in Ireland and Scotland embarked on the struggle for reform in the 1790s, they learned to view their efforts in terms of a 'just and common cause'.[1] This alliance of 'brother-friends' was to be tested repeatedly during its short lifetime, but it was the 1798 rebellion which displayed in starkest relief the constraints operating upon an outward-looking strategy of mutual assistance. For all the stimulus offered by United Irish links, Scottish radicals were granted an essentially restricted stage for democratic mobilization. Eighteenth-century Scotland escaped the levels of sectarian tension and social polarization exhibited in Ireland, and lacked the destabilising potential of a directly colonial relationship with England. These structural realities ultimately outweighed the politics of enthusiasm and fraternity.

The structural differentiation between the situations of Ireland and Scotland was not apparent to contemporary observers and participants in the Rising. They inhabited a volatile climate of Europe-wide revolution which challenged 'the dying embers of national prejudice' and in which all things seemed possible.[2] In the summer of 1798, boatmen on the Downshire packet from Carrickfergus whispered that 'the people in Scotland were as hostile to government as those in Ireland and were up in great numbers'; they were merely repeating commonplace radical rhetoric that the Scots would take their place in

---

1 The phrase was first used by William Drennan in his *Address to the delegates for promoting a reform in Scotland* (1792), reprinted in T.B. Howell and T.J. Howell (eds), *A complete collection of state trials* (London, 1809–28), p. xxiii, cols. 154–60.
2 *Glasgow Advertiser*, 7 Mar. 1794.

the battle line when the revolutionary alliance was called into action.[3] In January 1798 the Scottish emigré Thomas Muir assured his potential patrons in Paris in bombastic style that the cause of liberty could expect the assistance of 50,000 Scottish highlanders, and 100,000 Scottish patriots in all.[4] The following month, the Dublin-based *Press* tried to boost popular morale in Ireland by publicising a rather more modest estimate: 'the Highlands which hitherto had been the habitation of prejudice and oppression, have added numbers to the fraternity ..., and there is talk of the United Scotsmen being FORTY THOUSAND in number'.[5]

These claims were the product of expediency. While radical leaders in the Britain and Ireland attempted to bind the various national strands of their movement into an effective vanguard, militants within the United Irishmen, such as Arthur O'Connor and Lord Edward FitzGerald, used British developments to press their case for a rising independent of French assistance.[6] Such confidence also reflected a commitment to international brotherhood evident even during radicalism's constitutional phase, and drawing on French revolutionary concepts of fraternity.

Contact between the United Irishmen and the Scottish Friends of the People began within weeks of the Scottish group's establishment in July 1792.[7] Warm personal links and formal correspondence culminated in the United Irishmen's *Address sent to the Friends of the People's inaugural national convention* in December 1792. This 'Irish Address', however, revealed the difficulties implicit in trying to build bridges between movements which were at differing levels of tactical and ideological maturity. The United Irishmen were an openly advanced body, drawing on the economic contradictions of Ireland's colonial status and the uncertainty of Anglo-Irish constitutional relations. They were also able to use the organizational infrastructure of established Irish reform movements such as the Volunteers. In contrast, the Scottish Friends of the People were a more cautious and restrained grouping, aiming to channel the tide of popular protest in order to build a comprehensive national reform movement. This reticence reflected the less well-developed infrastructure for middle-class political protest in a society where the landed elite enjoyed a decisive political and social hegemony, buttressed by the parliamentary union of 1707.

A highly coloured rhetorical piece, typical of United Irish productions of the early 1790s, the Address was intended as a fraternal greeting to boost the Scots' timid spirits.[8] In the event, it received a hostile reception from the more moder-

---

3   R. Carmichael to R. Dundas, 31 June 1798: University of Edinburgh, Laing papers, II, 500.
4   Archives des Affaires Etrangères (AAE), Memo et Documents (Angleterre), II, ff.153–72.
5   *The Press*, 3 Feb. 1798.
6   Marianne Elliott, *Partners in revolution: The United Irishmen and France* (London, 1982), pp 172–85.
7   N.A.I., RP 620/19/97.
8   M. McTier to W. Drennan, 8 Dec. 1792: P.R.O.N.I., T.765, no. 356.

ate section of Scottish radicalism, while it also provided the authorities with a pretext for striking against the fledgling democratic movement with the full weight of the Scottish judicial system.[9]

The pace of political life was swift in the 1790s. Following the suppression of open constitutional protest in Scotland by early 1794, the initiative shifted from middle-class reformers to a revolutionary underground drawn largely from the 'lower orders' in weaving centres and manufacturing villages, such as Maybole and Cupar.[10] The grouping which emerged, the United Scotsmen, offered a systematic new approach to the organization of radical activity and the dissemination of democratic ideas. Again an outward-looking strategy remained vital both for democrats in Scotland and for the United Irishmen in Ulster where resentment was growing over the inactivity imposed by their centralized Dublin leadership.[11]

The authorities were uncomfortably aware of 'how exactly' the United Scotsmen had copied not only their Irish counterpart's name, but also their organizational precepts.[12] The remarkable similarity of their tests, resolutions and constitutions indeed represented a planned reworking of Scottish radicalism in the Irish mould.[13] Activists adopted the Irish constitution when it was presented by Ulster delegates in Glasgow in the summer of 1796, explaining the move to an oath-bound society on the grounds that secrecy and the means of mutual recognition were essential in a climate of government repression.[14] Ideologically some distance remained between the movements. Issues of national self-determination, for example, were of less concern to Scottish radicals than their Irish counterparts, although the 1799 *Secrecy report* believed a plot had been at work to separate Scotland as well as Ireland from England so as to found three distinct republics. The rationale of 'a distinct society of United Scotsmen' owed as much to logistics and geographical realities as to conscious nationalist convictions. Instead, the concept of 'Uniting' and the rejection of man-made barriers between peoples remained a fundamental point of principle. The United Scotsmen's *Resolutions and constitution* asserted:

> Mankind are naturally friends to each other; and it is only the corruptions and abuses in government that make them enemies. We profess ourselves friends to mankind, of whatever nation or religion. National and

9 R. Dundas to H. Dundas, 15 Dec. 1792: Scottish Records Office (S.R.O.), RH2/4/362.

10 John Kennedy, Declarations, Aug. and Dec. 1799: S.R.O, JC 26/298; Earl of Eglington to H. Dundas, 26 June 1798: S.R.O, Melville papers, GD 51/1/899.

11 Elliott, *Partners in revolution*, pp 144–5.

12 R. Dundas to duke of Portland, 13 Jan. 1798: S.R.O., RH 2/4/83, f.21.

13 For the United Scotsmen's 'Tests and Constitution', see *Report from the Committee of Secrecy of the House of Commons relative to the proceedings of different persons and societies in Great Britain and Ireland engaged in a treasonable conspiracy* (1799), app. 15, pp 67–9.

14 *State Trials*, xxvi, cols. 1135–79; D. Cameron: Declaration, S.R.O., RH 2/4/81, f.201.

party distinctions have been created and supported by tyrannical men, on
purpose to maintain their unjust usurpations of the People.[15]

Irish agents, and familiar Irish tactics – such as the diffusion of radical principles through the medium of songs and ballads – were employed in spreading the
new organization beyond its initial strongholds of Glasgow and Ayrshire during
the spring of 1797.[16] For their part, the United Irishmen were sometimes less
than impressed by the 'spirit' of their junior partners, and friction also arose with
United Irish agents in France who worried that the Ulster Committees' freelance
efforts at spreading their system might dissipate their own attempts to win support for a French expedition to Ireland.[17] However, by autumn 1797, missionizing
in Scotland had increased United membership to over 3,000.[18] This vanguard of
committed activists bore Ulster radicals' hopes of a diversionary Scottish rising.

When the long awaited rebellion in Ireland finally broke out at the end of May
1798, Scots did play a key role, not as democratic allies, but as members of the
crown forces ranged against the United Irishmen. Furthermore, the bloody
course of the rising itself tested the resolve of Scottish sympathizers and severely
damaged the United Scotsmen's self-belief and wider reputation. Highland fencible units in particular and Scottish regiments in general formed a disproportionate number of the 30,000 strong regular force stationed in Ireland on the eve
of rebellion, numbering thirteen out of twenty regiments.[19] Later reinforcements
also drew heavily on Scottish military reserves, with local enthusiasm greeting the
embarkation of regiments such as the Royal Scots and the Sutherland Fencibles.[20]
Scottish troops figured subsequently in the major engagements of the campaign
such as the battles of Ballynahinch and Vinegar Hill.[21] This contribution reflected
the broader pattern of British military recruitment at the end of the eighteenth
century in which the role of the Scottish Highlands was crucial. Landowners,
tempted by government bounties, spearheaded recruitment, thus assisting their
rehabilitation in the eyes of the state in the aftermath of '45.[22]

---

15 *Secrecy Report* (1799), app. 15, pp 67–9.
16 J. Smyth, *Men of no property: Irish radicals and popular politics in the late eighteenth century*
   (Dublin, 1992), pp 161–2.
17 W.T.W. Tone (ed.), *Life of Theobald Wolfe Tone* (Washington, 1826), ii, p. 432.
18 At a county meeting at Downpatrick, County Down, in October 1797, an agent who had just
   returned from Scotland was able to show his colleagues a Scottish constitution, which was
   'word for word as is the Irish, only the words North Britain put in for Ireland', and inform them
   that he had been present at a National Meeting in May in Edinburgh, when the number of
   United Scotsmen returned was 2,871; he had also been present in September when a further
   653 were enrolled: N.A.I., Lowry papers, D.1494.
19 *Glasgow Advertiser*, 15 Jan. 1798.
20 *Glasgow Courier*, 14 and 21 June 1798.
21 Gen. Nugent to Gen. Lake, 13 June 1798: N.A.I., RP 620/38/129; N.L.Scot., MS 5750,
   Marquess of Midlothian's notebook.
22 A. Mackillop, 'Military recruiting in the Scottish Highlands, 1739–1815: The political, social
   and economic context' (unpublished Ph.D. thesis, University of Glasgow, 1995).

Despite the public accounts of Scotland's conversion to the democratic cause in the radical press, some Irish radicals privately admitted that the Scots might well lend their weight to the struggle in this hostile capacity. Scottish regiments had already proved themselves fearsome opponents during the disarming of Ulster in 1796 and 1797; according to one Belfast United Irishman, there were only three things his men were dreading: 'a bad harvest, the exportation of vict-uals, and the importation of Scotch soldiers'.[23] In these circumstances, the pres-ence of the Scots became a useful propaganda tool for the United Irishmen. O'Connor's *Press* had already sensed the historical irony implicit in their con-duct. Recalling the events of Culloden and the activities of the Butcher Cumberland, he commented that 'Scotchmen remember those scenes with national horror! and yet they become the journeymen of *other butchers* in similar scenes perpetrated upon this hapless country.'[24]

Meanwhile the loyalty and steadfastness of Scottish troops was a watchword for the authorities, with 'Scotch Fencibles' eagerly sought by hard-pressed com-manders.[25] There were very few examples of Scottish soldiers being persuaded to take the United oath, and some were even reported to have spontaneously agreed to subscribe a portion of their pay to the War Fund.[26] When under strong command, Scottish troops strictly adhered to the rules of war over the treatment of prisoners and non-combatants: the Fifeshire Fencibles at Bally-castle were complimented on their good conduct and given three cheers on their departure, while the Scottish officers engaged in the disarming of Kildare, for example, were 'most humane', not doing any more than was absolutely necessary from their orders.[27] The historian Madden similarly commented that 'of all the King's troops in Ireland during the rebellion of 1798, the Scotch invariably behaved with the most humanity towards the people'. He considered this fact, 'well worthy of the attention of those of my countrymen … who indulge in occasional sallies against Scotch settlers'.[28] However, where leadership was less certain, the Scots could rival the Ancient Britons and the Hessians in their undisciplined conduct. In the aftermath of the defeat of government forces at Castlebar, the uncontrolled violence of Frazier's Highlanders 'raised a spirit of discontent and disaffection which did not before exist in that part of the coun-

---

23 N.A.I., Frazier papers, II/24.

24 *Press*, 18 Nov. 1797. It also printed a letter from 'A Highlander' in similar vein: 'The outrages committed by my countrymen, shew that they have already forgot the scenes of devastation exhibited in their own country but a few yeas ago': *The Press*, 9 Nov. 1797.

25 For examples see M. Wainright to J. Pollock, 7 May 1795: N.A.I., RP 620/30/29; General Lake to General Knox, 31 Jan. 1797: N.L.I., Lake correspondence, MS 6.

26 *Glasgow Courier*, 29 Mar. 1798.

27 T. Moore, *The life and death of Lord Edward FitzGerald*, 2 vols (Dublin, 1832), ii, p. 95; N.L.I., Melville papers, 54a–55b.

28 R.R. Madden, *The United Irishmen: Their lives and times* (second edn., London and Dublin, 1857–60), 3rd ser., iii, p. 283n.

try'.[29] Even for those who did not participate in these episodes, there seemed to be little sympathy for an unorthodox and 'unmilitary' enemy.[30] Indeed, in a compelling mirror image of the United Irishmen's earlier missionising effort, Scottish regiments returning from active service in Ireland introduced the Orange Order into Scotland in 1799.[31]

The extent of Scottish military involvement explains the greater impact that the 1798 rebellion had on public life in Scotland compared with England.[32] The pro-government press, for example, were quite emphatic in stressing the contribution of the Scottish regiments who 'had distinguished themselves by their activity and spirit'.[33] The unfolding of the rebellion shifted the positions of newspapers, such as the *Glasgow Advertiser*, which had previously flirted with reform. Despite previously criticizing the Irish administration, they grew outraged by the 'dreadful list of murder' and 'the horrid system adopted by the traitors ... which violates all the obligations of human society'.[34]

The geographical proximity of Scotland to the Irish unrest had a further energising effect on the Scottish authorities. Drawing on their experience of a previous refugee wave as a result of the disturbances in Ulster during 1797, they realized 'how *tenty* we ought to be this side of the water'.[35] By the second week of June 1798, Campbeltown was fast filling with refugees from Antrim, while the more familiar reception point of Portpatrick was so crowded that there was no shelter left.[36] The pressing problem was how to separate 'genuine' loyalist refugees from those who had been involved in the planning and execution of the rebellion. The screening of arrivals at Portpatrick was intensified and 'swarms' sent back to Ulster, but these measures were insufficient to check the crowds landing clandestinely along the south-west coast and melting into the interior of the neighbouring counties.[37]

In contrast to the voice of literate opinion and the activities of government agencies, the response to the 1798 rebellion of those committed political radicals associated with the United Scotsmen is much less well-documented. The *Secrecy report* of 1799 suggested that while the rebellion was at its the height, there were those on the mainland, 'who so strongly manifested their desire to support the rebels, that they became the object of criminal prosecution', but in

---

29 J. Taylor to Lord Castlereagh, 31 Aug. 1798: P.R.O, Cornwallis correspondence, ii, p. 396.
30 Marquess of Midlothian's notebook, for a triumphalist Scots soldiers' song of the 1798 Rebellion.
31 E.W. McFarland, *Protestants first: Orangeism in nineteenth-century Scotland* (Edinburgh, 1990), pp 49–51.
32 Thomas Pakenham, *The year of liberty* (London, 1972), pp 233–4.
33 *Glasgow Courier*, 30 Oct. 1798.
34 *Glasgow Advertiser*, 8 June 1798.
35 J. Carmichael to R. Dundas, 29 Nov. 1798: University of Edinburgh, Laing papers, II, 666–7.
36 *Edinburgh Advertiser*, 12–16 June 1798.
37 General Drummond to R. Dundas, 26 June 1798: University of Edinburgh, Laing papers, 500–1.

Scotland such cases were isolated.[38] In Glasgow sympathisers tried to persuade reinforcements not to leave for Ireland in June by thrusting 'very seditious papers' under the barracks gate, thus spreading 'worrying misrepresentations', while in Ayrshire during the same month Irishmen who had managed to infiltrate the Volunteer Corps fired on troops who were escorting their fugitive countrymen from the Carrick coast.[39] The Dunfermline weavers Black and Patterson attempted to convert a soldier of the West Lowland fencible regiment by 'inflammatory harangues' so that he would 'turn his arms against his king and country'. Sorrowing for British military successes and French failures, both 'had the audacity to vindicate the unnatural rebellion which has broken out in Ireland, and to represent the Irish insurgents as groaning under oppression, and struggling in defence of their just rights': this vindication played an important role in their eventual trial for sedition in September 1798.[40]

Beyond these instances, the silence from Scotland during the summer of 1798 is in itself significant. For a movement which had consistently struggled to build a mass base at home, external stimulus was vital. While some Scottish democrats took strength from the government's initial panic, the rising was ultimately a costly defeat and intensified sectarian tension. This seemed to betray the inspiring vision of universal brotherhood which their United Irish brethren had originally set before them.

It was not only the actual outcome of the rebellion which dealt a blow to the United Scotsmen. Their organization had been severely compromised by the well-tried security measures of the Scottish authorities from the spring of 1797. Indeed, the work of dispersing the societies had begun even earlier than in England. From May 1797 reports from loyal citizens were increasingly reinforced by information from the official intelligence network to the effect that secret oath-based societies in correspondence with 'the disaffected in Ireland' had indeed been established in the southwest.[41] Frustrated by the impenetrable secrecy of the new radical procedures, the response was strengthened co-operation between Edinburgh, Whitehall and Dublin, mirroring the increasing co-ordination of their opponents in the underground movement.[42]

As government surveillance in Scotland became more determined, the authorities made use of the information of spies and deserters from the movement.[43] A systematic campaign to crush the movement was forestalled by the arrest of George Mealmaker at Dundee in November 1797, but further arrests

---

38 *Report from the Committee of Secrecy* (1799), app 15, p. 27.
39 R. Dundas to duke of Portland, 24 June 1798: S.R.O., RH 2/4/83ff., 366–7; Earl of Eglington to H. Dundas, 20 June 1798: S.R.O., Melville papers, GD 51/5/29 f.38.
40 *State Trials*, xxvi, col. 1183.
41 Earl of Eglington to H. Dundas, 16 Mar. 1797: S.R.O., Melville papers, GD 51/5/29.
42 R. Dundas to J.King, 6 May 1797: S.R.O., RH 2/4/81, f. 212.
43 J. Orr to R. Dundas, 18 Nov. 1797: S.R.O., RH 2/4/81, f. 230.

of activists followed in Perth, Dundee and Edinburgh in December.[44] Within weeks details of the business and progress of the Society were available to newspaper readers: 'the oaths of secrecy similar to the United Irishmen', 'their system of communicating intelligence', and even their tactics of 'studiously trying to gain over the military'.[45] Mealmaker was brought to trial in January, his sentence of fourteen years' transportation serving as a clear warning to other erstwhile reformers.[46] A further wave of mass arrests followed in April with the United centres of Glasgow, Cupar and Ayrshire targeted.[47]

Similar reversals had beset the United Irishmen in Mar. 1798 when the government swooped on the Leinster Directory, but these did not break the momentum of rising popular alienation or prevent the outbreak of rebellion in the Irish countryside.[48] In contrast, the relative ease with which the threat from the United Scotsmen was contained is eloquent testimony as to the chronic limitations which Scottish conditions imposed upon them. These constraints and the unequal potential for mass protest in the two societies are well illustrated by a comparison of the militia riots which had swept Ireland in 1793 with those in Scotland during the summer or 1797 which gave the United Scotsmen perhaps their best political opportunity.

Both sets of disturbances were geographically widespread and socially inclusive. In Ireland all four provinces were involved and almost every county; in Scotland, riots ranged over seventy counties from New Galloway to Strathtay. Rioters were not simply drawn from the lowest social groups, but included artisans and shopkeepers, as well as weavers and colliers in the manufacturing villages.[49] Their immediate grievance was against the element of compulsion implied in the raising of the militia. The most dramatic contrast with Ireland lay in the degree of violence which accompanied the protests. The Irish riots were distinguished both by the brutal force employed by troops to suppress them, and by the readiness of mass formations of rioters to open fire on the military in response. 'In just eight weeks', comments Bartlett, 'as many as 230 lives had been lost ... over five times the number of casualties sustained in the previous thirty years of agrarian disturbances': in Scotland the total fatalities numbered eleven.[50]

This divergence reflects in turn the distinctiveness of social and political life in the two countries. The Irish militia riots were evidence not only of pre-exist-

44 N.A.I., JC 3/4; *Glasgow Courier*, 14 Nov. 1797; *Scots Chronicle*, 10–14, 14–17 Dec. 1797.
45 *Glasgow Courier*, 7 Dec. 1797.
46 *State Trials*, xxvi, cols. 1135–64.
47 *Glasgow Advertiser*, 16 Apr. 1798; *Glasgow Courier*, 14 Apr. 1797.
48 *Glasgow Courier*, 22 Mar. 1798. The Dunbartonshire Fencibles were used in the raid.
49 *Edinburgh Advertiser*, 7–11 July, 3–8 Aug., 8–12 Sept. 1797.
50 T. Bartlett, 'An end to moral economy: The Irish militia disturbances of 1793', in *Past & Present*, xcix (1983), 58. The Scottish casualties were the result of a single incident when soldiers fired on a crowd: 'Narrative of events at Tranent': S.R.O., RH 2/4/81, f. 49.

ing, deep-seated fissures in Irish society, but also of the escalating estrangement between lower-class Catholics and the Irish ascendancy. Viewed as the final bankruptcy of the Irish 'moral economy', the disturbances reflected the rising expectations and eventual sense of betrayal experienced by the Catholic masses in the aftermath of the relief acts of the early 1790s. This deep distrust was fuelled by the savagely coercive response of the authorities to the protests, and in the longer term was to be channelled into Defender and United Irish activity.

For some government supporters, the Scottish militia riots represented a similar crisis for traditional mechanisms of control.[51] The circumstances seemed favourable for political radicals to mould sharp popular discontent into support for their own vision of sweeping constitutional change and to lay the base for a future rising.[52] But, while the military situation was at times delicate in Scotland, official nervousness under-estimated the underlying stable political culture and social homogeneity which could have been drawn on by the Scottish authorities. Having escaped direct colonization and with an intact civil society, Scotland in the 1790s was a country where religious identity served as a unifying force binding ruler and ruled. The government, for example, had no 'Catholic question' to wrestle with: a policy of official aid and conciliation had been adopted towards Scotland's small Catholic community during the 1790s for which their leaders 'were fulsomely grateful, as if it had given them opulence and power into the bargain'.[53] Unlike Ireland, the greater flexibility of power relationships permitted a more subtle and effective strategy in which determined military action to stamp out unrest was combined with energetic attempts to 'educate' and win acceptance for the provisions of the Militia Act.

The combination of these approaches had a positive effect and ultimately constrained radicals' room for manoeuvre. The United Scotsmen were, it is true, able to use the riots to extend their presence into rural areas, but this still did not result in the construction of a mass movement.[54] For all the efforts of their activists, the men and women who had taken part in the Scottish militia riots were not an impoverished and alienated population awaiting the signal to rise. A century of continuous, balanced economic growth following the Union had produced higher general living standards than in Ireland and the impact of market relations in the countryside was cushioned.[55] The comparative restraint of official measures to deal with the disturbances did not contribute to the attempts at mass politicization. By the end of 1797 even those material and political factors which had previously helped the radicals were now diminished. Trade was reviv-

51 A. Gordon to duke of Portland, 23 Aug. 1797: S.R.O., RH 2/4/80, f. 154.
52 J. Brims, 'The Scottish democratic movement in the age of the French Revolution' (unpublished Ph.D. thesis, University of Edinburgh, 1983), pp 560–6.
53 Duke of Portand to J. Hippisley, 27 July [1795]: University of Edinburgh, Laing papers, II, 580.
54 N. Meikle, *Scotland and the French Revolution* (Glasgow, 1912), p. 187.
55 McFarland, *Ireland and Scotland*, pp 54–5.

ing, especially in textile areas, and the fortunes of war were turning, accompanied by a rising wave of popular loyalism which found expression in the Volunteering movement.[56] The tide for the United Scotsmen had already turned well before the outbreak of rebellion in Ireland. In these conditions, the persistence of radical cells stood as testament to their continuing faith in a wider revolutionary movement which crossed national boundaries.

The impact of the 1798 rebellion on Scotland by no means ended with the episode itself. Even after the last resistance had been extinguished, the remnants of radical organization in Ireland and Scotland struggled on, albeit in a confused state. The new United Irish system revolved around a compact national executive which now deliberately detached itself from the need to cultivate grassroots support. Instead, the movement was to be kept primed by a few travelling agents until the arrival of a French invasion force.[57] The formal links between Irish and Scottish radicals therefore remained in place, but these became increasingly overshadowed by the efforts of individuals from among 'the Irish disaffected' who arrived in increasing numbers in Scotland after 1798, despite the best efforts of the authorities. A 'considerable immigration of Irish poor' had been in motion in the south-western counties since the 1780s, but contemporary observers in Ayr, Kilmarnock and Renfrewshire were in agreement that the '98 had given a decisive boost to this movement which by 1800 had become a constant presence.[58] Here political and economic motivations were intertwined. By January 1799, the Scottish newspapers were filled with accounts of the generally unsettled state of Ireland.[59] Within months, the extra-legal activities of the soldiery and magistrates intensified the economic crisis in the Irish countryside as the harvest failed and employment slumped.

Scotland was by no means an automatic choice for asylum. Beyond British jurisdiction, it was America, 'the lamp of liberty', which appealed to middle-class United Irish leaders. Scotland was the poor man's best option, either for a speedy and reversible exit to escape persecution or for permanent settlement. Initial conveyance was cheap and employment opportunities were widening as Scottish manufactures advanced. As one observer explained:

> The Rebellion was coincident with the first attempts to introduce the spinning of cotton by power in the West of Scotland; ... the master spinners of Paisley and Glasgow were glad to employ the Irish as being the only persons who would work with them.[60]

56 *Glasgow Courier,* 17 Oct. and 21 Nov. 1797.
57 Elliott, *Partners in revolution,* p. 248.
58 *Report from the second enquiry into the condition of the poorer classes in Ireland,* Appendix G: *Report into the Irish poor in Great Britain,* Parl. Papers, 1836, XXXIV, pp 64, 130, 164.
59 *Glasgow Courier,* 1 Jan. 1799; *Glasgow Advertiser,* 6 Aug. 1799.
60 *Report into the condition of the poorer classes in Ireland,* p. 64.

By no means all the migrants arriving at Portpatrick were United Irishmen, or, if they had previously sworn the oath, many were willing to forego their radical careers in the new environment. While some Ulstermen made a crucial contribution to the diffusion of the Orange lodges, others joined with Scottish Jacobin cadres to revive the spirit of disaffection. During the riots at Paisley in spring 1800, for example, one of the main ringleaders had left Ireland following the rebellion, and was 'generally considered as of bad and seditious principles and conduct'.[61] Local groups also continued to look beyond their immediate situation and cultivate external links. When democrats in Fife regrouped in 1802, they were in contact with an United Irish cell in the Forth dragoon guards garrisoned locally who assured them that 'the boys in the morning' were numerous at home and were anxious for their co-operation.[62] By May 1803 'Scotch reports' had again become a regular feature at United Irish meetings in Ulster.[63]

While objective conditions in Scotland appeared on occasion favourable, they continued to impose limitations on such revivals. Britain and Ireland suffered a scarcity of grain supplies from 1800, with dramatically rising prices for consumers. Prices in the England escalated without respite, leading to a 'hypercrisis' by the end of 1800, while in Ulster an industrial recession dealt a blow to linen production. The Scottish case, however, saw dramatic fluctuations, but eventually followed a downward trend. Recovery was underway by 1801, though food prices remained higher than at any stage in the previous twenty years.[64] Distress was blunted by paternalistic responses to emergency relief: these were probably most effective in rural areas and in smaller towns such as Maybole – which had been United centres.[65]

Well-directed official repression remained the final challenge for insurrectionary activity. During the 1790s, the Scottish authorities had developed a more measured conception of the radical threat and tailored their response accordingly. Realizing that sworn members were not a threat simply on the basis of numbers, they believed that determined activists might nevertheless be dangerous in the event of a French invasion attempt. In addition, post-rebellion Irish migration was itself increasingly viewed as a 'security problem'. For the authorities, the Irish were 'instinctive rebels', their numbers in Scotland growing in tandem with the blossoming of disaffection. By 1803, there were reckoned to be 10,000 Irish in Glasgow and the vicinity, 'almost all of the most suspicious character, and very many of them known to be old rebels and not the least reformed'.[66]

---

61 J. McDowell to R. Dundas, 10 Nov. 1799: S.R.O., RH 2/4/86, f. 283–5.
62 C. Hope to Lord Pelham, 2 Apr. 1802: S.R.O., RH 2/4/87, f. 153.
63 M. McDonagh, *The viceroy's postbag* (London, 1904), p. 275.
64 R. Wells, *Insurrection: The British experience* (Gloucester, 1983), p. 179; K. Logue, *Popular disturbances in Scotland* (Edinburgh, 1979), pp 18–53.
65 *Glasgow Courier*, 6 Feb. 1800.
66 C. Hope to Lord Pelham, 4 Aug. 1803: S.R.O., RH 2/4/88, f. 231.

The United Irish leader William Steel Dickson complained in 1812 that the persistent image of '98 in Scotland had been that of a 'real Popish Rebellion'.[67] Yet, while the subtleties and complexities of the United Irishmen's movement were lost on most Scots, its self-confident spirit had for some years been an inspiration to their own struggling organization of Scottish democrats in the 1790s. While unable to mount a parallel insurrectionary attempt, democratic politics in Scotland outlasted the failed hopes of 1798. Nor could strategies of mutual assistance and fraternal links be unlearned. As the new century progressed, Scotland developed rapidly as an industrial society on more solid and broad-based economic foundations than did Ireland. Economic and social change in turn ushered in an increasingly antagonistic phase of social conflict. In political and industrial protest movements which developed in the new manufacturing districts, Irish personnel and methods of organization continued to make a distinctive contribution to the construction of a reborn 'Scottish' radical tradition.

67 W.S. Dickson, *The narrative of the confinement and exile of William Steel Dickson D.D.* (Dublin 1812), pp 115–16.

29

Continental analogies with 1798:
Revolution or counter-revolution?

BRENDAN SIMMS

We send you a list of the famous relics taken from the rebels: 1, The head of St Charles Borromu. 2, Blessed stuffs, found in the shrine of St Denis … The perusal of this list produced much laughter.

> Letter from the Army in the West [Vendée] read to the French in
> National Convention, 15 Dec. 1793, in *Northern Star* (Belfast),
> 30 December 1793.[1]

For sale. Two red slippers of his Holiness the Pope; a bit of the toenail of St Januarius … Theatrical gentlemen would do well to attend this auction, for the purpose of increasing their wardrobes, which are useless to their present owners, who are becoming plain citizens …

> Advertisement by Dublin radical and United Irishman John Burk,
> in *Polar Star and Boston Daily Advertiser*, 13 October 1796.[2]

---

1 Cited in Brendan Clifford, *Belfast in the French Revolution* (Belfast, 1989), p. 122. The full quote reads 'We send you a list of the famous relics taken from the rebels: 1, The head of St Charles Borromu. 2, Blessed stuffs, found in the shrine of St Denis. 3, Papers to prove that the relics of St Vincent are genuine. 4, A tooth of the lower jaw of St Vincent. 5, A bit of the head and hair of St Guingelot. 6, A piece of the robe of the Holy Virgin. 7, A piece of the frock of the infant Jesus. 8, The skull of St Sebastian. 9, The grid-iron of St Laurence. 10, A piece of the true cross. 11, Two vials of the milk of the most holy virgin. The perusal of this list produced much laughter.'

2 Cited in Kevin Whelan, *The tree of liberty: Radicalism, Catholicism and the construction of Irish identity 1760–1830* (Cork, 1996), p. 102. The full quote reads 'For sale. Two red slippers of his Holiness the Pope; a bit of the toenail of St Januarius; a scrap of the garment of Ignatius Loyola; inquisition racks, just from the inquisition; crowns, sceptres, and crosses of St Louis; cardinals' hats, ducal coronets etc. together with all the wardrobe of royalty. Theatrical gentlemen would do well to attend this auction, for the purpose of increasing their wardrobes, which are useless to their present owners, who are becoming plain citizens. Also a few Pope's bulls with gilt horns.'

> The contrast with regard to religious sentiments between the French and
> their Irish allies was extremely curious. The atheist despised and affront-
> ed the bigot; but the wonder was how the zealous papist could come to
> any terms of agreement with a set of men who boasted openly in our
> hearing, 'that they had just driven Mr Pope out of Italy, and did not
> expect to find him again so suddenly in Ireland'.
>
> Bishop Stock [of Killala], *Narrative*.[3]

One of the more poignant scenes in the *Memoirs* of Miles Byrne, the former
rebel leader in Wexford, is his encounter with a Spanish priest while serving in
Napoleon's army in the Peninsula campaign. 'This worthy patriotic ecclesiastic',
Byrne wrote, 'told them he had studied at Salamanca and had been acquainted
there with many of my countrymen, both students of the Irish college, and officers of the Irish regiment in the Spanish service; he added that he thought there
was a great similitude in many respects between the people of our respective
countries, their sufferings etc. I answered that there could be no comparison, as
in his country, at that moment the inhabitants were not persecuted and deprived
of their civil rights on account of the religion they professed.' This may have
seemed an odd statement in a country where the French and their local allies had
already massacred far more priests than the crown forces ever had in Ireland, but
it did not stop Miles Byrne from delivering a lengthy homily on the justice of
the French cause in Spain. The Spaniard, however, stood his ground, and by the
end of the debate, Byrne conceded: 'I could not help admiring the patriotism of
this enthusiastic ecclesiastic: he reminded me of the virtuous clergymen who
suffered torture and death, as martyrs both in the field and on the scaffold, in
Ireland in 1798, endeavouring to set their country free from the cruel foreign
yoke.'[4]

The Spanish analogy, initially so furiously rejected by Byrne and then grudgingly accepted, was not the first, and certainly not the last comparison between
the rebellion of 1798 and broader European developments.[5] More than thirty
years ago, R.R. Palmer wrote in his famous study of the 'Democratic Revolution': 'Atlantic civilisation was swept in the last four decades of the eighteenth
century by a single revolutionary movement, which manifested itself in different

3 Grattan Freyer (ed.), *Bishop Stock's 'Narrative' of the Year of the French: 1798* (Ballina, 1982),
   p. 63.
4 *Memoirs of Miles Byrne* (Paris, 1863), ii, pp 90–93. See also Thomas Bartlett, 'Miles Byrne:
   United Irishman, Irish exile and *Beau sabreur*', in Dáire Keogh and Nicholas Furlong (eds), *The
   mighty wave: The 1798 rebellion in Wexford* (Dublin, 1996), pp 124–5.
5 The broader context has already been stressed by Marianne Elliott, *Partners in revolution: The
   United Irishmen and France* (New Haven and London, 1982), p. xix, et passim; L.M. Cullen,
   'The 1798 rebellion in its eighteenth-century context', in P.J. Corish (ed.), *Radicals, rebels and
   establishments* (Belfast, 1985), pp 91–113; Whelan, *The tree of liberty*, p. ix et passim.

ways and with varying success in different countries, yet in all of them showed similar objectives and principles ... this forty-year movement was essentially 'democratic' and ... these years are in fact the Age of the Democratic Revolution ... [which] signified a new feeling for a kind of equality, or at least a discomfort with older forms of social stratification and formal rank.'⁶ Palmer's democratic Atlantic Revolution was thus the progenitor of more recent interpretations, such as Kevin Whelan's 'Three revolutions and a failure', which sees events in Ireland within a broader framework stretching back via the French and American Revolution to the Glorious Revolution of 1688.⁷ 'What happened in Wexford or Antrim, Kildare or Armagh', he argues, 'cannot be separated from what was happening elsewhere in the Atlantic world at this stage'; we should 'adhere to the international perspective of the United Irishmen – to link Bunker Hill, the Bastille and Boolavogue ... an Irish echo of the distant drums of the Atlantic Revolution'.⁸

The prototype of the Atlantic Revolution was the early Batavian (Dutch) republic; it was often cited by other revolutionaries, including the United Irishmen, as a model of what they wanted to achieve in their respective countries.⁹ The 'Patriot' opposition to the Orangeist quasi-monarchical stadholderate which emerged in the early 1780s included such diverse groups as Roman Catholics and the (mainly Mennonite) 'Dissenters', that is, those Protestants excluded from the established Dutch Reformed Church. Through campaigns of petition and especially through their impressive parades of militia – the 'Free Corps' – the patriots demanded representative government, a constitution, an end to corruption and to religious discrimination. Socially, the patriots were a blend of intellectuals, merchant princes and the 'middling sort', small traders and prosperous artisans determined to protect property against the threat from below; they were political, but not social radicals. In 1785, the patriot movement reached its apogee, when a vast assembly of Free Corps militia swore an Act of Association to defend a 'true republican constitution' against threats from within and without. Two years later, however, an attempted Patriot *coup* collapsed after Prussian intervention to restore the Stadholder.¹⁰

It was not until 1794, on the coat-tails of the victorious French Revolutionary armies, that the fugitive patriots were able to return and implement their programme of reforms. The whole panoply of pre-1787 activity – clubs, publishing

6 R.R. Palmer, *The age of the democratic revolution: A political history of Europe and America, 1760–1800* (Princeton, N.J., 1964), i, p. 4.

7 Kevin Whelan, 'The Glorious American, French and Irish Revolutions: The context of 1798', Paper to Cambridge Group for Irish Studies Conference, 20 Mar. 1998.

8 Kevin Whelan, 'Reinterpreting the 1798 rebellion in County Wexford', in Keogh and Furlong (eds), *The mighty wave*, pp 11, 35.

9 Palmer, *Age of the democratic revolution*, ii, pp 179–80.

10 See Simon Schama, *Patriots and liberators: Revolution in the Netherlands, 1780–1813* (London, 1992), pp 78–95.

houses, parades and so on – was now resumed. The prince of Orange was deposed, liberty trees were planted, the Dutch Reformed Church was disestablished, torture and noble hunting rights were abolished, albeit the latter against compensation. A patriot elite of lawyers, academics, Roman Catholic notables, and dissenting clergy was elected on a near-universal franchise to the assembly of the new Batavian Republic; at first only those in receipt of charity were deprived of the vote.[11] Very soon, however, the republic was shaken by crisis. There was a strong social radical challenge from below, sometimes in alliance with Orangeist elements. The French forces of occupation helped to maintain domestic order, not least because the French Directory feared that the Dutch social radicals might be part of a broader European movement allied to their own radicals like Babeuf and Buonarroti.[12] But French help came at a price. The tone had been set by General Sauviac, when he observed that it was not patriot valour, but French arms that had made the Batavian Republic possible: 'there can be no reason to treat her any differently from a conquered country'.[13] Hence the Treaty of the Hague of May 1795 involved the cession of Maastricht, Venlo and Dutch Flanders, the payment of a massive indemnity, and obligation to join the war against Britain.

In January 1798, a French-backed coup purged the assembly and seized power. The new government introduced an 8 per cent income tax to be levied on all provinces, narrowed the franchise, imposed a unitary constitution by referendum, and generally threw itself into the task of preparing a sea-borne assault on Great Britain. Six months later another firmly unitarist but more socially conservative coup followed, continuing the domestic drift towards authoritarianism, which led to the proclamation of the Kingdom of the Netherlands under Napoleon's brother Louis Bonaparte in 1806 and finally to direct annexation by France in 1810. In the long run therefore, the Dutch found themselves both internally more repressed than they had ever been, and externally tied firmly to Napoleonic imperialism.

By contrast with the initially relatively autonomous Dutch experiment, the Italian republics of the 1790s were direct French creations. The Cisalpine (Lombard) (1797), the Ligurian (Genoese) (1797), the Roman (1798), and the Parthenopean (Neapolitan) (1799) republics all sprang up in the wake of advancing Revolutionary armies. Indeed, the occupation of Rome in February 1798, the deportation of Pope Pius VI, and the establishment of a Roman Republic were emblematic of the wave of French-sponsored anti-clericalism that swept the peninsula. Local middle-class Jacobin governments were often more hostile to Catholicism than even the French occupiers; and politically they were more radical than either the Directory or the rising star Napoleon Bonaparte.[14] For many of them, the new dispensation was a chance to take up where the centralizing

11 Ibid., pp 171–247.
12 Ibid., p. 255; Palmer, *Age of the democratic revolution*, ii, 185.
13 Schama, *Patriots and liberators*, p. 201.
14 Owen Chadwick, *The popes and European Revolution* (Oxford, 1981), p. 458.

and enlightened reforming absolutists had left off on the eve of revolution.[15] All over Italy religious processions were banned, secular oaths were imposed, and church property was confiscated. Perhaps the most poignant testimony to this process is a note in the baptismal register of the church of St Cassian at Imola in Lombardy dated 28 July 1798:

> By order of the Cisalpine Commissioners, who have created in Milan a republic alleged to be democratic, they have moved the Poor Clares of St Stephen to the Capuchin nunnery, and the Augustinian nuns called the Madeleines to the Dominican nunnery. They have suppressed St Charles and all the brotherhoods, abolished bequests, imprisoned eleven of the cathedral canons in the castle. So democracy, that Liberty and Equality of the Republicans and the French, robbed our Italy.[16]

The policies of the revolutionaries in France, and those of the French Revolutionary armies and their local collaborators outside France, produced a furious backlash throughout the 1790s, most famously in the Vendée region of western France but also among the *chouans* of Normandy and Brittany, the southern *departement* of the Gard, and in southern Italy. It is with these counter-revolutionary risings – rather than with the preceding revolutions – that the Rebellion of 1798 is sometimes compared. 'Along with the Vendée', Louis Cullen has written, '[Wexford] was the last rural civil war in western Europe north of the Pyrenees, and it is no accident that both events, though widely different in background and purpose, took place in the traumatic decade of the 1790s.'[17]

From the mid 1790s onwards, the French Revolution took on a markedly anti-clerical character. The tone was set by the Civil Constitution of the Clergy in 1790, which effectively turned the clergy into oath-bound civil servants of the state; more than 30,000 non-juroring priests chose exile rather than submit. In 1793–4 the situation worsened: an aggressively secularizing government introduced calendar changes and new feast days designed to render the old religious customs obsolete; the churches were effectively forced underground.[18] This religious oppression was central to the Catholic royalist peasant risings of the Vendée and the Breton-Norman *Chouannerie* which shook the republican government to its very foundations in the mid-1790s.[19] It was also a key factor in southern French royalism.[20]

15 See T.C.W. Blanning, *The French Revolutionary Wars, 1787–1802* (London, 1996), p. 202.

16 Cited in Chadwick, *Popes*, p. 451.

17 Cullen, 'The 1798 rebellion in its eighteenth century context', p. 91.

18 Chadwick, *Popes*, p. 446.

19 On the centrality of religion in the Vendée, see Robert Garnier, *Lazare Hoche ou l'Honneur des armes* (Paris, 1986), p. 187; on *Chouans* see Roger Dupuy, *De la Révolution à la Chouannerie: Paysans en Bretagne, 1788–1794* (Paris, 1988), pp 322–3.

20 Gwynne Lewis, *The second Vendée: The continuity of the counter-revolution in the Department of the Gard, 1789–1815* (Oxford, 1978), p. 16.

The peasantry were not counter-revolutionary *per se*. At first most peasants, and indeed many lower clergy, had joined the challenge to the *ancien régime*; after all, the Revolution in the countryside had been characterized by the burning of chateaux and manorial records in the summer of 1789. It was only after the introduction of conscription and the assault on their traditional religious practices that they began to make common cause with local aristocratic elites against the Revolution. This process was accelerated by the counter-productive policy of 'disarming' ordered by Paris, which began in 1792 and involved raids on households, ransacking, torture, deportations and random killing.[21] In this way the same areas that had once sacked chateaux now rioted against conscription.[22] The western revolts thus began as part of the revolution itself; they were as much 'anti-' as 'counter'-revolutions.[23]

In the late 1790s, the focus of counter-revolution shifted to Italy.[24] As in the French revolts, religion, especially the desecration of places of worship by the French revolutionary armies and the abolition of traditional practices, played a key role in inflaming the peasantry against the Revolution. Reforming 'Catholic democrats', such as Cardinal Chiaramonti (who praised Rousseau in his Christmas homily and averred that he did not 'believe that the Catholic religion is against democracy'), were a small minority in the church.[25] All over the peninsula, the clergy found themselves thrust to the forefront of a popular rising against the French.[26] Liberty trees were cut down; visions were reported; and statues began to weep.[27] In June 1796, Napoleon Bonaparte inveighed against 'the priests and monks, who with a crucifix in one hand and a dagger in the other roused the people against us'.[28] At the beginning of the following year, in southern Italy, Cardinal Ruffo led his 'Christian Army of the Holy Faith' – Sanfedisti – to victory against the Parthenopean Republic, which collapsed with the fall of Naples in June 1799. They also attacked those liberal constitutionalist elements in the church who had made their peace with the new regime. This produced some poignantly paradoxical scenes, such as the murder of the pro-French Giovanni Serrao, bishop of Potenza in Calabria and believer in married clergy,

---

21 Tilly, *Vendée*, pp 308, 317.
22 Dupuy, *Chouannerie*, p. 330.
23 Ibid., p. 337.
24 J.A. Davis, 'Les Sanfédistes dans le royaume de Naples (1799): Guerre sociale ou guerre civile?', in Francois Lebrun and Roger Dupuy (eds), *Les resistances à la Révolution* (Paris, 1987), p. 311.
25 Cited in Chadwick, *Popes*, p. 456.
26 On the role of religion and the clergy in European counter-revolution, see T.C.W. Blanning, 'The role of religion in European counter-revolution, 1789–1815', in Derek Beales and Geoffrey Best (eds), *History, society and the churches* (Cambridge, 1985), p. 195; Chadwick, *Popes*, pp 471–2.
27 Micheal Broers, 'The parochial revolution: 1799 and the counter-revolution in Italy', in *Renaissance and Modern Studies*, xxxiii (1989), 174.
28 Cited in Blanning, *Revolutionary wars*, p. 165.

who went to his death shouting 'Long live the faith of Jesus Christ! Long live the Republic!'[29]

But perhaps even more than was the case in France, the religious dimension interacted with other considerations in Italy. Few historians would now share Gaetano Cingari's interpretation of the *Sanfedisti* rising as a popular 'class war' against the incursions of a new capitalist Jacobin economy.[30] For one thing, the course of the revolt was often determined by purely local factors: family vendettas, *campanilismo* between towns or villages, secular and regular clergy, contemplative and working orders, and so on.[31] As Michael Broers points out: 'whoever was weaker tended to turn to the French and the new Republican regimes for support and above all for protection';[32] advisedly he speaks in the plural of the 'revolts' of 1799.[33] Nevertheless, it is broadly true that the conflict divided centralizing Jacobins from localist counter-revolutionaries, especially when the satellite republics became the agents for French monetary exactions. It is no accident that the Jacobins called themselves 'federalists' in recognition of their supra-regional loyalties, whereas the royalist rebels often included the very same groups that had previously opposed the centralizing measures of the enlightened absolutist *ancien régime*.

Both the Italian and the French risings of the 1790s were savagely suppressed. By the turn of the century the Tuscan and Neapolitan rebels had been crushed; the length and breadth of the peninsula was marked by wrecked churches and massacred peasants and clergy. Likewise, the royalist bands which periodically reduced south-east France to anarchy were dealt with by Napoleon; almost 2000 priests were deported. Henceforth Napoleon's rule in the Gard rested largely on the support of the patriotic revolutionary Protestant *haute bourgeoisie*.[34] But it was in the Vendée that the French state reacted with its most notorious brutality. By and large, the rebels were known for their leniency to prisoners;[35] not so their republican adversaries. In a proclamation to the western army in 1794, the Convention adopted a frankly exterminatory rhetoric: 'Soldiers of liberty, it is necessary that the brigands of the Vendée be exterminated before the end of October'.[36] The resulting brutality has been graphically outlined by the revolutionaries themselves. As one soldier of General Turreau's *colonnes infernales* wrote to his mother in January 1794: 'we shall set off in fourteen columns to lay waste the *departements* of Deux Sèvres and the Vendée. We

---

29 Cited in Chadwick, *Popes*, p. 475.
30 Davis, 'Les Sansfédistes', p. 312.
31 Ibid., p. 313; Broers, 'The parochial revolution'.
32 Ibid., p. 164.
33 Ibid., p. 161.
34 Lewis, *Second Vendée*, p. 224.
35 Tilly, *Vendée*, p. 333.
36 Cited in Garnier, *Hoche*, p. 189.

shall bear with us iron and fire. We shall carry the musket in one hand and the torch in the other. Men and women alike, all will be put to the sword, except the little children.'[37] Another witness described the massacre of rebel prisoners thus: 'they were made to get down on their knees and were ordered to shout 'Long live the Republic!' All refused to do so, made the sign of the cross and were then shot.'[38] Very soon the revolutionary commanders, Thureau and Bourbotte were able to report to Paris: 'The Vendée no longer exists.'[39] The casualties ran to several hundreds of thousands. Among those involved in the pacification of the Vendée were Humbert and Hoche, later commanders of French expeditions to Ireland.[40]

Clearly, none of the revolutions and counter-revolutions outlined above mirror the Irish experience in 1798 in every respect. The town-country divide so characteristic of the revolts in France and Italy, though present, was not acute; nor was the division between centralists and federalists – common to the French, Dutch and Italian situations – an issue in Ireland, though it might have become one in the aftermath of a successful rising. Finally, none of the countries occupied and revolutionized by the French in 1790s was saddled with the peculiarly poisonous heritage of dispossession and colonization which characterized the eighteenth-century Protestant ascendancy in Ireland.

Nevertheless, there are clear parallels. The United Irishmen themselves professed an affinity to the early Batavian Republic, and it is easy to see why. Both countries had developed remarkably similarly from the early 1780s. In both cases demands for reform had spawned a 'patriot' movement against the Protestant ascendancy and Orangeist establishments, respectively. The Dutch Free Corps militia corresponded to the Irish Volunteer movement, though the denominational inclusiveness of the former body throws the sectarian nature of the latter into sharper relief. Similarly, the emigration of defeated Dutch patriots to Paris – and their quest for French help to overturn the status quo at home – echoes the strategy of the United Irishmen after the banning of their society in 1794. Finally, the Dutch patriot 'coalition' of Protestant dissenters and Roman Catholics bears an uncanny resemblance to the projected United Irish union of Protestant, Catholic and Dissenter.

But perhaps the most striking analogy between European revolutionaries and the United Irishmen lies in their commitment to secularism and anti-clericalism. Like bourgeois Jacobins in France and Italy, the United Irishmen sought to subvert the confessional establishment, in this case the Protestant ascendancy.

---

37 Blanning, *Revolutionary wars*, p. 97.
38 Ibid., p. 197.
39 Garnier, *Hoche*, p. 191.
40 Jean-Paul Bertaud, 'Forgotten soldiers: The expedition of General Humbert to Ireland in 1798', in Hugh Gough and David Dickson (eds), *Ireland and the French Revolution* (Dublin, 1990), p. 222.

However, their antipathy also and increasingly extended to the Roman Catholic church, not least because the Irish hierarchy faithfully followed the conservative line laid down by the pope, who condemned the Revolution as a 'French disease';[41] Tone warned the French that Irish priests 'hated the very name of the French revolution'.[42] This anti-Catholic animus was fuelled by the strong Ulster Presbyterian influence among the United Irshmen. They had seen the French Revolution specifically as a 'Catholic' event, and interpreted it as a signal that 'papists' too could aspire to liberty; it was only on this basis that they countenanced an alliance. Thus the *Northern Star* reported approvingly, but not without irony, that at a party of the 'principal Roman Catholics of Belfast' a toast had been made to 'Mr Paine and the Rights of Man … [and] (by the Revd Hugh O'Donnell, Parish Priest) Religion without priestcraft'.[43] Yet residual suspicions of and contempt for Catholicism remained. In 1791, the Northern Whig Club in Belfast showed itself bitterly divided on the question of emancipation.[44] The curious blend of pessimism and pragmatism underlying Presbyterian radical views of the Catholic mind was summed up in September 1793 by William Drennan as follows: 'It is a churlish soil but it is the soil of Ireland and must be cultivated, or we must emigrate.'[45] Tone, an active supporter of Catholic Emancipation, was no friend to the institutional church.[46] When in 1795 the French proposed to dispatch a clerical emissary to Ireland, Tone expressed his 'strong objection to letting priests into the venture at all'.[47] Nor was this hostility to the Catholic Church confined to Protestant United Irishmen; many Catholic middle-class republicans shared their secularist suspicions of clerical conservatism. In 1792 it was none other than John Keogh, chairman of the radical rump of the Catholic Committee, who warned of uncooperative clergy that 'the people seem well inclined to give them the French cure'.[48]

At first sight, the United Irishmen seem even purer 'bourgeois revolutionaries' than most of their continental counterparts. The French and Italian revolutions, for example, were initially strongly supported by the privileged orders. What can be said with some degree of certainty is that the United Irishmen

41 See Dáire Keogh, '*The French disease': The Catholic Church and Irish radicalism, 1790–1800* (Dublin, 1993).
42 Cited in Liam Swords, 'Irish priests and students in Revolutionary France', in Liam Swords (ed.), *Protestant, Catholic and Dissenter: The clergy and 1798* (Dublin, 1997), p. 32.
43 Cited in Clifford, *Belfast in the French Revolution*, p. 34.
44 See Elliott, *Partners in revolution*, pp 137–8. See also the bleakly realistic assessment of community relations in O.P. Rafferty, *Catholicism in Ulster: An interpretative history* (London, 1994), pp 92–5.
45 Ian McBride, 'William Drennan and the dissenting tradition', in David Dickson, Dáire Keogh and Kevin Whelan (eds), *The United Irishmen: Republicanism, radicalism and rebellion* (Dublin, 1993), pp 60–1.
46 Keogh, *French disease*, p. 58.
47 Cited in Swords, 'Irish priests and students', p. 32.
48 Cited in Keogh, *French disease*, p. 57.

came largely from the 'middling' sections of society. As Nancy Curtin has pointed out, artisans, merchants, and publicans made up over 60 per cent of United
Irish membership in Dublin and Belfast, even in its most radical phase between
1795 and 1798.[49] Tom Dunne has argued that for one prominent leader,
Theobald Wolfe Tone, 'radicalism involved little more than a middle-class take-
over of the political system'.[50] Insofar as the United Irishmen had a social programme it was 'unformed', 'contradictory', and 'instrumental'; its main purpose
was to 'secure a mass following'.[51] Indeed, the leadership looked to their French
allies to rein in potential socially radical forces. As MacNeven subsequently testified to government investigators, one of the reasons for the French connection
had been to 'cheque [*sic*] the *chouennery* [*sic*] of the country ... and give the
[United Irish] Executive time to form a provisional government'.[52]

If the United Irish leadership may generally be compared – and it compared
itself – to the European revolutionaries of the 1790s, the rural rebel rank and file
of 1798 bear a remarkable resemblance to the counter-revolutionary movements
of the decade. Take for example the policy of 'disarming', by which crown
forces and the French revolutionary armies both sought to 'pacify' the countryside and which, according to older interpretations, goaded the peasantry into
uncoordinated and premature revolt. Indeed, the British commander-in-chief in
Tyrone, General Knox, explicitly compared his task to that of the French in the
Vendée and recommended the same tactics, 'namely spreading devastation
through the most disaffected parts'.[53] Another obvious comparison can be made
between the apparent prominence of Catholic priests as leaders in the Vendée,
southern Italy, and in Wexford. Finally, in purely optical terms, the men of
Wexford must have resembled the Vendéens – and Ruffo's *Sanfedisti* – with their
pikes, staves, scythes, pitchforks, occasional blunderbuss, religious insignia and
all the other paraphernalia of peasant revolt. Consider the following picture of
the Vendée: 'behold how their peasants, in mere russet and hodder, with their
rude arms, rude array, with their fanatic Gallic frenzy and wild-yelling battle-cry
of *God and the King*, dash at us like a dark whirlwind, and blow the best-disci-
plined Nationals we can get into panic and "sauve qui peut".'[54] If the slogan

49 Nancy J. Curtin, *The United Irishmen: Popular politics in Ulster and Dublin, 1791–1798* (Oxford,
   1994), pp 264–6.
50 Tom Dunne, 'In the service of the Republic', in John A. Murphy (ed.), *The French are in the
   bay: The expedition to Bantry Bay, 1796* (Cork and Dublin, 1997), pp 74–5.
51 Jim Smyth, *The men of no property: Irish radicals and popular politics in the late eighteenth century*
   (London and Basingstoke, 1992), p. 165; Curtin, *United Irishmen*, p. 283.
52 Cited in Elliott, *Partners in revolution*, p. 165.
53 Cited in Smyth, *Men of no property*, p. 171.
54 Thomas Carlyle, cited in Tilly, *Vendée*, p. 336. For peasant fury in Italy see M. Broers,
   'Revolution and Risorgimento: The heritage of the French Revolution in nineteenth century
   Italy', in H.T. Mason and William Doyle (eds), *The impact of the French Revolution on European
   consciousness* (Gloucester, 1989), pp 85–7.

'Erin go Brath' were substituted for 'God and the King', Carlyle's stirring description might equally be applied to the rebel concourse on Vinegar Hill.[55]

The past decade, however, has seen a move away from simplistic views of 1798 and the French counter-revolutions as spontaneous sectarian *jacqueries*.[56] Lewis has written: 'it is all too easy to dismiss the Catholic royalist reaction under the Directory simply as a *bouilabaisse* of frondeur petty nobles, feudal curés, and psychopathic killers. They centrally figure ... but the larger themes must be borne in mind', especially the 'degree of planning and organisation'.[57] Similarly, Cullen's work has shown that the Wexford rising, far from being a spontaneous sectarian *jacquerie*, was in fact the culmination of several years of intense politicization in the county, spearheaded by the confessionally mixed United Irish leadership, including some local Catholic notables.[58] Smyth took this re-interpretation a stage further by condemning the sectarian view of the Wexford rebellion as 'inadequate and patronising', and 'essentially a propagandist creation'.[59] Whelan argues for the 'essential unity of the 1798 insurrection: what happened in Wexford was of a piece with what happened in Antrim and Down'.[60]

Yet the politicization of Wexford – indeed of much of the whole island – was more *counter*-revolutionary than revolutionary in character. The concern of the rebellious minority of Catholic 'underground gentry' was not only, or even not primarily, the creation of a French-style republic, but the overturning of the religious and land settlements in Ireland of the previous century.[61] They may have been 'secularized',[62] to the extent of collaborating with radical Protestants in order to bring down the government or of ignoring episcopal demands for loyalty, but that does not mean that they had forgotten past glories. The difference between the counter-revolutionary Catholic gentleman in Wexford and the Vendée was thus chronological rather than fundamental: the one had been dispossessed over a hundred years earlier, the other much more recently; both were bent on restitution. Thus when Miles Byrne of Monaseed spoke of plans to

55 Thomas Bartlett, 'Religious rivalries in France and Ireland in the age of the French Revolution', in *E.C.I.*, vi (1991), 57–76.
56 Tilly, *Vendée*, still stressed the element of 'aimlessness': p. 318.
57 Lewis, *Second Vendée*, pp 82, 98.
58 His most trenchant statement of the 'politicization' thesis can be found in L.M. Cullen, 'The 1798 rebellion in Wexford: United Irishman organization, membership, leadership', in Kevin Whelan (ed.), *Wexford: History and society* (Dublin, 1987), pp 248–95.
59 Smyth, *Men of no property*, p. 179.
60 Whelan, 'Reinterpreting the 1798 rebellion in County Wexford', in Keogh and Furlong (eds), *The mighty wave*, p. 34.
61 On the 'underground gentry' see Whelan, *Tree of liberty*, pp 3–58; C.C. Trench, *Grace's card: Irish Catholic landlords, 1690–1800* (Cork, 1997); Karen Harvey, 'The family experience: The Bellews of Mount Bellew', in T.P. Power and Kevin Whelan (eds), *Endurance and emergence: Catholics in Ireland in the eighteenth century* (Dublin, 1990), pp 171–98.
62 See Kevin Whelan, 'The role of the Catholic priest in the 1798 rebellion in County Wexford', in Kevin Whelan and W. Nolan (eds), *Wexford, history and society* (Dublin, 1987), p. 297.

confiscate church lands and those of emigrants, the parallel with the French Revolutionary *biens nationaux* of secularized church property and confiscated noble estates is deceptive. Byrne was really referring to the dispossession of the Protestant ascendancy and the (Anglican) Established Church, and the restitution of Catholic landowners like himself. For in the next breath he spoke of how his father had shown him 'the lands that belonged to our ancestors now in the hands of the descendants of the sanguinary followers of Cromwell'.[63] This highly charged context led to a settling of scores after the outbreak of the rising,[64] and is in some respects analogous to the vendettas which have been identified as an important part of the Italian counter-revolutions.

Sectarian grievances and dispossession were also at the heart of the politicization of poorer Catholics, especially the Defender movement with which the United Irishmen were in uneasy alliance. Most of them had never actually owned land, but thought they had, or felt they ought to have. They too sought to reverse the Glorious Revolution of 1688. In Ulster especially, as Marianne Elliott has pointed out, the restitution of property and lost status loomed large in Defender consciousness.[65] Their millenarian expectations of liberty and confessional vindication were summarised in the famous Defender catechism which acknowledged the debt to Revolutionary France and then called upon the taker 'To quell all nations, dethrone all kings and plant the true religion that was lost since the reformation'.[66] Similarly, Defenders taken prisoner after a skirmish in County Meath in 1793 spoke of 'equal distribution of property', 'assistance from France' and their determination 'to destroy the Protestant religion'.[67] And in 1794 one Defender on trial in County Louth confessed a plan 'to knock the Protestants on the head, and … take their places'.[68]

In short, the comparative perspective shows us that the rebellion of 1798 was both a revolution *and* a counter-revolution. The tension between the middle-class secularist United Irish leadership and the Catholic rural foot-soldiers of 1798 has often been remarked upon.[69] It is best summarised by the much-quoted scene of General Humbert's Mayo levies setting out to fight for 'France and the Blessed Virgin'; and by Lord Castlereagh's description of the rising as a 'Jacobin conspiracy with popish instruments'.[70] These contradictions were encapsulated

63 *Memoirs of Miles Byrne*, p. 7.
64 See Kevin Whelan, 'The religious factor in the 1798 rebellion in County Wexford', in P. Flanagan, P. Ferguson and K. Whelan (eds), *Rural Ireland, 1600–1900* (Dublin, 1987), pp 72, 75.
65 Marianne Elliott, 'The Defenders in Ulster', in Dickson, Keogh, and Whelan (eds), *The United Irishmen*, p. 224.
66 Cited in Smyth, *Men of no property*, p. 113.
67 Cited in Elliott, *Partners in revolution*, p. 43.
68 Ibid., p. 42.
69 E.g. Smyth, *Men of no property*, p. 183; Gearóid Ó Tuathaigh, *Ireland before the Famine: 1798–1948* (Dublin, 1972), p. 29.
70 Ibid., *Ireland before the Famine*, p. 29.

in an incident on the eve of the rebellion in Ulster, when a Catholic deserter from the south allegedly announced to his assembled men: 'By Jesus boys, we'll pay the rascals this day for the battle of the Boyne,' much to the consternation of their Presbyterian allies standing by.[71] Hence over-arching themes like the 'Atlantic' or 'Democratic' Revolution obscure more than they illuminate. The agrarian rank and file rebels in Wexford – as opposed to the United Irish leadership – were not part of the same movement as the middle-class Belfast Presbyterians, any more than Cardinal Ruffo's peasants bands were part of the bourgeois Jacobin *internationale*. What the repoliticization of 1798 gains in 'inclusiveness', it risks losing in explanatory power.

The unifying theme linking the revolutions and counter-revolutions of the 1790s was the primacy of foreign policy. Ireland was not so much the theatre of an ideological war as a sideshow, albeit a periodically very important one, in the struggle for mastery in Europe, pitting Revolutionary France and its satellites against British-led continental coalitions. Developments in Ireland, Holland, Southern Italy and the Vendée were thus determined by this 'Second Hundred Years War' between Britain and France. The Batavian republic and the Irish rebellion of 1798 essentially shared a role in French grand strategy against England. Indeed, French support for the Dutch patriots as a lever against Britain predated the Revolution; the policy of the 1790s was part of the many continuities from the *ancien régime*. Similarly, the strategy of using Ireland as the back door to England had been a classic French strategem well before the Revolution; and it was not so much ideological affinity as power politics which prompted the Revolution to take up where the Bourbons had left off.

Throughout Europe, this broader struggle for European hegemony interacted with local situations. In Ireland, it did so with the struggle between Presbyterians and the Anglican establishment in Ulster; the conflict between Catholics and the Protestant ascendancy in the island as whole; the continuing desire of the dispossessed Catholic gentry for restitution and political participation; and with the stance of the Roman Catholic hierarchy against the rampant forces of secularism and revolution. In practice this interaction led all sides to make compromises: power-political advantage, not ideological coherence, was decisive. The secular, essentially middle-class United Irishmen sought an alliance with the largely sectarian Catholic Defenders and, more vaguely, with social radicalism.[72] Whilst maintaining a distance from the institutional Catholic Church, they took advantage, as Dáire Keogh has pointed out, 'of the many proselytising opportunities offered by its structures'; religious processions and funerals – which the revolutionary French and their local allies had banned across the lengths of occupied Europe – were utilized for radical displays.[73] In order to stimulate a mass follow-

71 Cited in Curtin, *United Irishmen*, p. 276.
72 Ibid., pp 284–5.
73 Keogh, *French disease*, pp 12, 125.

ing, the United Irishmen did not hesitate to disseminate stories of an Orange 'extermination oath'. As Smyth comments: 'these were Enlightenment rational-ists who pedalled millenarian fantasies; apostles of a union of Irishmen of all creeds who stoked the fires of sectarian hatred'.[74] Similarly, the British govern-ment consciously, if reluctantly, put its burgeoning rapprochement with the Catholics on hold and played the sectarian card of Orangeism in order to defeat the United Irishmen in mid-Ulster. But perhaps the most cynical and dramatic gambit was undertaken by the French themselves: initially they planned unleashing a *chouannerie* in Ireland; the French minister for war, Lazare Carnot's scheme was to turn Ireland into 'England's Vendée'.[75] Tone, much to his irrita-tion, found the French obsessed with Irish Jacobitism and clericalism:[76] in the short term, the more traditionally royalist and anti-Protestant Ireland was, the greater the danger she would pose to Britain.

The result was a series of paradoxical alignments within Ireland and across Europe. Revolutionary France found itself locked in mortal combat with Catholic peasants at home, but supported them in Mayo and Wexford. Conversely, the British government savagely suppressed Catholic peasants in (parts of) Ireland, while supporting Catholic peasant risings almost everywhere else in Europe.[77] Hence the Neapolitan Bourbon Queen Maria Carolina's exhor-tation to Admiral Nelson, who was besieging the capital of the Parthenopean republic in alliance with Ruffo's Catholic army in 1799, to 'treat Naples as if it were a rebel town in Ireland'.[78] Given the fact that Ruffo's peasants resembled nothing so much as the agrarian rebels in Wexford, this has a curious resonance in the Irish context. The man appointed to command the British-backed 'Catholic Army of the Midi' was the emigré Irish Catholic Thomas Conway; he put his ideological loyalty to the Bourbons and the Catholic Church above the hereditary struggle against England. The global struggle against France pro-duced equally paradoxical scenarios in Ireland itself. For while the need to mobilise resources for struggle in Europe powered Catholic Emancipation, espe-cially the Relief Act of 1793, the contest against French-backed subversion locally demanded compromises with the sectarian impulse. It was thus the same British government which collaborated with the Orange Order to defend the Protestant ascendancy in Armagh and deployed Catholic militia against Pres-byterian rebels in Down and Antrim; there were arguably more Catholics on the crown side at Ballynahinch than among the opposing United Irishmen.[79] Con-

---

74 Smyth, *Men of no property*, p. 172.
75 Elliott, *Partners in revolution*, p. 87.
76 Ibid., pp 81–5; Swords, 'Irish priests and students in Revolutionary France', p. 32.
77 Harvey Mitchell, *The underground war against revolutionary France: The missions of William Wickham, 1794–1800* (Oxford, 1965).
78 Palmer, *Age of the democratic revolution*, ii, p. 388.
79 John Biggs-Davison and George Chowdharay-Best, *The cross of St Patrick: The Catholic Unionist tradition in Ireland* (Abbotsbrook, 1984), p. 86.

versely, there may have been proportionately more English speakers on the rebel than on the government side in Wexford. Indeed, there was no army in Ireland more multi-lingual, multi-ethnic or pan-confessional than the crown forces of 1798: in its ranks (German) Hessians rubbed shoulders with Welsh-speaking Ancient Britons and Gaelic-speaking Scottish fencibles. And where else were the many traditions of the island more inclusively synthesised in all their inherited complexities than in the North Cork Militia, with its Orange leadership and confessionally-mixed often Irish-speaking rank and file?

But the comparative approach allows one to go a step further and attempt an informed speculation about the outcome of a successful rebellion. It was often claimed at the time, and has been since, that the result would have been a massacre of Protestants. Given the experiences at Scullabogue and Wexford bridge, this seems a plausible prediction, especially for mid-Ulster and other areas where Defenderism was strong and where the United Irish leadership might have had difficulties re-establishing order. To quote Kevin Whelan, 'the rebels tried, or claimed to try, to distinguish between "Orangemen" and "Protestants" in general, but a purely sectarian motive was evident in many of the killings'.[80] More recently, Whelan has relativized this view: 'The United Irishmen continued to believe passionately in the power of the national concept to harmonise the internal discordances of Ireland. Their mistake was not, as is frequently alleged, a narrowness of sympathy, but an over-simplistic and therefore false, inclusiveness.'[81] According to this interpretation, the United Irish project was a 'window of opportunity' which opened the prospect of a relatively painless transition to secular modernity.[82] This was certainly the picture painted by John Stuart Mill in his pamphlet *England and Ireland*, where he claimed that a successful French invasion under Hoche would have solved the agrarian problem in Ireland: 'At that moment it was on the cards whether Ireland should not belong to France, or at least be organised as an independent state under French protection. Had this happened, does anyone believe that the Irish peasant would not have become even as the French peasant? … Ireland would then have been in the condition in which small farming and tenancy by manual labourers are consistent with good agriculture and public prosperity.'[83] Variants on this benign scenario include a strong social radical dimension, United Irish support for Gaelic culture,[84] and a liberal national 'democratic Gallican' alternative to London and Rome in church-state relations, which neatly squares the circle:[85] not Irish and republican merely, but Catholic and constitutional also.

80 Whelan, 'Religious factor', p. 75.
81 Whelan, *Tree of liberty*, p. 128.
82 Ibid., p. ix.
83 John Stuart Mill, *England and Ireland* (London, 1868), p. 20.
84 See the contribution by Luke Gibbons in this volume.
85 Clifford says of Roman Catholic United Irishmen that 'democratised Gallicanism was intelligible and acceptable to them': *Belfast in the French Revolution*, p. 34.

In fact, there was nothing in French policy towards Ireland, in the balance of forces within the island, and in the experience of the rest of occupied Europe to suggest that the outcome of a succesful rising and invasion would have been anything other than a murderous bourgeois secular satellite state, subservient to the needs of French foreign policy.[86] Such an outcome seems inescapable for 1796: as Kevin Whelan has pointed out, events elsewhere in Europe 'did not offer a comforting parallel for Ireland'.[87] Indeed, a recent volume on the Bantry Bay expedition is remarkable for the reserve with which the contributors regard the outcome of a successful invasion.[88] Few would now argue with Palmer's assessment that 'had the French occupied Ireland for any length of time, it may be doubtful that a viable Irish Republic would have resulted. The Directory might even have traded Ireland away at the peace table.'[89] In 1798, when the local input was much larger, and the French commitment greatly reduced, the situation was different. It has therefore been argued that, since its retention was not central to French security, 'there was every indication that Ireland liberated in 1798 would have escaped the later fates of satellite republics'.[90] Yet Napoleon hung on to remote Egypt, also captured in 1798, and reinforced it when possible until forcibly ejected by the British in 1801. There is no reason for thinking that he would have treated Ireland any differently. Had the projected descent on Britain been successful, Bonaparte might even have federated the two islands – perhaps as 'the Republic of the Atlantic Archipelago'; after his imperial coronation in 1804, it might have been rechristened a kingdom under one of his brothers.

Indeed, the United Irishmen themselves were chastened by the fate of the once-admired Batavian Republic. In 1795, horrified by the treatment of the Dutch revolutionaries, Tone noted defiantly in his journal: 'The French had conquered Holland, and had a right if they wished to throw it into the sea, but it was not so with Ireland. We rather resembled the situation of America in the last war.'[91] A year later he insisted somewhat frantically: 'I for one will never be accessory to subjecting my country to the control of France, merely in order to rid her of that of England'; and on the eve of the expedition to Bantry Bay he observed: 'I see we have a little army of commissioners who are going to Ireland to make their fortunes.'[92] Yet in January 1798, Tone was once again defending

86 See also T.C.W. Blanning, *The French Revolution in Germany: Occupation and resistance in the Rhineland* (Oxford, 1983), especially the chapter 'The alienation of the left'. Robust scepticism about the outcome of a successful rebellion has also been expressed by Kevin Myers, 'Irishman's diary' in *Irish Times*, 2 Aug. 1997, 24 Jan. 1998, and 26 Mar. 1998.

87 Kevin Whelan, 'Bantry Bay: the wider context', in Murphy (ed.), p. 111.

88 Murphy (ed.), *The French are in the bay*. Counter-factual perspectives are also suggested by Hugh Gough, 'Anatomy of a failure', pp 9–10, 23; Tom Dunne, 'In the service of the Republic?', pp 73, 81.

89 Palmer, *Age of the democratic revolution*, ii, p. 499.

90 Elliott, *Partners in revolution*, p. 166.

91 Cited in Dunne, 'In the service of the Republic?' in Murphy (ed.), *The French are in the bay*, p. 80.

92 Ibid., pp 79–80.

French interference and exactions in the Batavian Republic. The reason for this United Irish indulgence towards Revolutionary France was not so much naiveté as brutal pragmatism. They were always going to be dependent on the French, not only to dislodge the British, but to implement their reforming blueprint within the island of Ireland itself. They needed French support to rein in the very *jacquerie* and social radicalism which both parties had encouraged in the struggle against the Protestant ascendancy; and Hoche's instructions in 1796 were to do exactly that.[93] Hence, once the British had been defeated, the result would have been a bourgeois terror against threats from below. The character of this putative struggle may perhaps be inferred from the clashes between the landless 'Caravats' and the middle-class 'Shanavests', themselves remnants of the old United Irish organization, in early nineteenth-century Tipperary.[94]

But perhaps the most spectacular result of a successful rising would have been a protracted conflict between the French-backed United Irish executive and the Catholic majority. Only in the short-term – for so long as it took to defeat Britain – were the French prepared to countenance a Catholic monarch. In the long run they were extremely suspicious of Irish Catholicism because, as Hoche's instructions put it, 'its doctrines are opposed to the healthy institution of philosophy and morality and to the progress of knowledge'.[95] Indeed, French wariness towards Catholicism surfaced almost immediately after the landing in Connaught and has most famously been described by the Church of Ireland bishop of Killala, Joseph Stock.[96] Nor should one set too much store by the prospect of an enlightened democratic Irish Gallican church along the lines of the French Revolutionary constitutional church, or the later Napoleonic compromise. Irish Gallicanists had always been, as one might expect, Bourbon royalists; they were horrified by the revolution and the execution of the King. Besides, by the late eighteenth century, Gallicanism was on the decline: the romanization of the Irish church was progressing steadily and would culminate in the nineteenth century under Cardinal Paul Cullen. The church in Ireland under the influence of Archbishop Troy of Dublin followed the line laid down by Pius VI very closely; and one of the senior Gallicanists, Bishop Patrick Plunkett of Meath, showed himself a zealous opponent of the Revolution, touring his diocese and drawing attention to the plight of the pope in the face of French aggression.[97] As Keogh has shown, the well-publicised role of priests in the rising has been much exaggerated: only a tiny proportion of the lower clergy

93 Elliott, *Partners in revolution*, pp 93–4.
94 P.E.W. Roberts, 'Caravats and Shanavests: Whiteboyism and faction-fighting in East Munster, 1802–1811', in Samuel Clark and J.S. Donnelly (ed.), *Irish peasants ...* (Manchester, 1983), pp 72, 88–9.
95 Cited in Gough, in Murphy (ed.), *The French are in the bay*, p. 23.
96 Stock, *Narrative*, pp 46–7, 63.
97 Keogh, *French disease*, pp 145, 151–2.

were involved. The church as a whole would almost certainly have sided against the French occupiers, especially given the pope's exile and the renewed wave of pre-Concordat state-sponsored anti-clericalism which followed the failed royalist plots of the late 1790s. Within Ireland, therefore, as across Europe, the clergy would have become, in effect, British agents in the struggle against France. There is no doubt that some, though by no means all of their flock would have followed them. And even if Hoche himself had been relatively restrained in the Vendée,[98] there is no reason to believe that the French and their local collaborators would have treated Irish Catholic counter-revolutionaries any differently than proved to be the case in the rest of Europe.

Irish Protestants, on the other hand, would probably have fitted into the new regime very well, and indeed did so as the experience of Mayo Protestants showed.[99] If the king could no longer be loyal, the *empereur* might be. Besides, the French had always regarded the Ulster Presbyterians as the vanguard of the ideological revolution in Ireland. The *Moniteur* of February 1792 referred to 'the Catholics, who have numbers and misfortunes on their side, and are opposed to the French Revolution … and the true patriots, the Presbyterians, who keep and nourish the sacred flame of freedom'.[100] There had always been a strong element in support of foreign aid among the Belfast Presbyterians, loathe to risk their middle-class prosperity through rebellion but dependable revolutionaries once the French had taken over.[101] Who can doubt that these Presbyterians would have formed the bedrock of the new Ireland, reinforced by disorientated Anglicans and secularized bourgeois Catholics? Together they would have made short work of the very Catholic peasants and local elites who had spearheaded the initital rebellion. They would certainly have rejected any attempts to reverse the seventeenth-century land settlement, at least in Ulster; indeed, they would have been more likely to have expropriated the remaining Catholic landowners along with the Protestant ascendancy: these *biens nationaux* would have paid for the liberation and for the forthcoming invasion of Britain.

In France, many of the rebels of 1789 became the counter-revolutionaries of 1794; it might have been no different in Ireland. As James Dickey, a prominent rebel leader in Antrim, was reported as saying before his execution in Belfast: 'he knew well that had the *north* been successful, *they* would have had to fight the battle over again with the Catholics of the *south*'.[102] It can thus be argued that it was a mere matter of chance and chronology that the Catholics of 1798 did not rise against the French occupiers and their Presbyterian allies. For, like all eman-

98 Dupuy, *Chouannerie*, p. 336; Garnier, *Hoche*, p. 195.

99 Stock, *Narrative*, pp 54, 57.

100 Cited in Gilles le Biez, 'Irish news in the French press: 1789–98', in Dickson, Keogh and Whelan (eds), *United Irishmen*, p. 257.

101 Curtin, *United Irishmen*, p. 264.

102 Ibid., p. 277.

cipatory movements, that of the United Irishmen and the Revolutionary armies was predicated on an optimistic and hegemonic assumption of integration and assimilation which was often disappointed. In short, the result of a successful rising and French invasion would have been more massacres, not so much of those unwilling to forego the link with Britain or the Protestant ascendancy, as of social radicals, the old underground gentry, and anti-secularist Catholic peasants: hell hath no fury like fraternity spurned.

All of this was quite obvious both to the old Catholic gentry, whose horizons had always extended well beyond the bounds of the island, and to the hierarchy of the universal church. It is therefore not surprising that – mavericks notwithstanding – both groups should have sought in the 1790s to accelerate a rapprochement with the British state, begun some years earlier, and of which Edmund Burke had been a most eloquent advocate. The involvement of propertied and even of poor Catholics in the British war effort at home and abroad thus betokened neither sycophancy nor false-consciousness. Thanks to their broader and more European perspective, they could see – as so many of the rebels of 1798 could not – that the triumph of a French-backed revolution would have meant not the end of an old trauma for Catholic Ireland, but the beginning of a new one.[103]

103 I wish to thank Professor T.C.W. Blanning, Dr Declan Downey, and Dr Mike Broers for their comments on the first draft of this paper.

SECTION VIII

On 5 July 1803, some hardline magistrates in north Wexford received an anonymous warning about the likelihood of their actions inciting a second rebellion:

> It is horrid to think of joining a second rebellion whilst it can be prevented with ease by the gentlemen. Let them not think that we will stand to be cut like dogs while others are slurping and feasting on the industry of the poor … We were destroyed these five years past by tyranny and they want to send away the industrious people of the country to the field of slaughter whilst their fellows will remain persecuting the remainder at home. If they want good men let them go and bring them back from Botany Bay, from the East Indies and all other parts of the world they were dispersed to.[1]

It was an acute commentary on the diaspora to which the 1790s had given rise. There was possibly two hundred Defenders among the eight hundred and fifty Irish convicts transported between 1791 and 1800, notably on the ships *Cornwallis* and *Britannia*. Four hundred United Irishmen were among the 1,196 convicts despatched between 1800 and 1806, especially on the *Friendship II*, *Minerva*, *Anne I*, *Atlas I*, *Atlas II*, *Hercules I*, *Tellichery* and *Rolla*.[2] Three hundred and fifty prisoners ended up in the Prussian army, some destined to perish in the salt mines of Silesia. At least 1,500 were conscripted into the 'condemned regiments' and were despatched (effectively a death sentence) to the pestiferous West Indies. Nine hundred more 'volunteered' to serve in the British army. Four hundred were legally banished, scattering especially to France and America.[3]

---

1 B.L. Ms 35740/60.

2 Anne Marie Whitaker, *Unfinished revolution: United Irishmen in New South Wales 1800–1810* (Sydney, 1994); Ruan O'Donnell, 'Marked for the Botany Bay: The Wicklow United Irishmen and the development of political transportation from Ireland 1791–1806' (unpublished Ph.D. thesis, Australian National University, 1996); Peter O'Shaughnessy (ed.), *A rum story: The adventures of Joseph Holt, thirteen years in New South Wales 1800–1812* (Perth, 1998). An important corrective on Holt is provided by Ruan O'Donnell and Bob Reece, 'A clean beast: Crofton Croker's fairy tale of General Holt', in *E.C.I.*, vii (1992), 7–42.

3 Michael Durey, 'Marquess Cornwallis and the fate of Irish rebel prisoners in the aftermath of the

Thousands more, mainly drawn from Ulster, were forced out or left in more anonymous circumstances, destined principally for America. No wonder that Cornwallis, with political and administrative responsibility, felt wearied: 'the same wretched business of courts-martial, hanging, transporting etc, attended with all the dismal scenes of wives, sisters, fathers kneeling and crying'.[4]

A political penumbra shadowed this diaspora. Those involved, as in the 1798 rebellion generally, were young, literate, articulate (the 'amazing eloquence' of the shipboard United Irishmen was noted in 1804), and above all politicised.[5] They added a republican, democratic and egalitarian tinge to every society where they ended up. In Newfoundland, they instigated a mutiny among the fencible regiments in 1799.[6] In Australia, they backboned the 'Vinegar Hill' uprising of 1804 (O'Donnell, chapter 30). In England, they were active in radical politics (Sir Francis Burdett's celebrated campaigns for the Middlesex seat in 1802 and 1804 were actively supported by them).[7] They formed a bridge to the Chartism of the 1830s and 1840s, effectively a second-generation United Irish movement, appropriately led by the son of a United Irishman.[8] In Scotland, they built up labour radicalism in Glasgow (one report has 10,000 'old rebels' there in 1803) and in Paisley, Ayr and Kilmarnock.[9]

1798 rebellion', in James Smyth (ed.), *Revolution, counter-revolution and Union: Ireland in the 1790s* (Cambridge, 2000), pp 128–45. See also Michael Durey, *Transatlantic radicals and the early American republic* (Kansas, 1997).

4   Cornwallis to Castlereagh, 26 Sept. 1799 in *Castlereagh corr.*, ii, p. 406. There is now a need for a general study of the Cornwallis viceroyalty. His position as a pivotal figure in the British Empire in the late eighteenth century has been re-emphasized by Simon Schama, *A history of Britain: The British wars, 1603–1776* (London, 2001), pp 394–424. Barrington, with his previous American experience in mind, dismissed him as 'the chosen instrument for oppressing heroic nations': Barrington, *Rise and fall*, p. 11.

5   Whitaker, *Unfinished revolution*. A colonial official reported that they 'were keen to recite the miseries and injustice of their punishment and the hardships they suffer' (p. 36). For the age of those involved in 1798, see bar-chart in Whelan, *Fellowship of Freedom*, p. 99.

6   On Newfoundland, see John Mannion, 'Transatlantic disaffection: Wexford and Newfoundland 1798–1800', in *Wex. Hist. Soc. Jn.*, xvii (1999), 30–61; John Fitzgerald, 'The United Irish rebellion in Newfoundland 1799–1800' (unpublished paper, 1998).

7   M.W. Mathewson, *Sir Francis Burdett and his times* (London, 1931). A detailed study of Burdett's many Irish links would be timely. Among his Irish associates were Lord Edward FitzGerald, Arthur and Roger O'Connor, Valentine Lawless, Peter Finnerty, and John Philpot Curran. See also the career of Francis, son of Roger and godson of Burdett: James Dunkerley, 'The third man: The career of Fransisco Burdett O'Connor and the emancipation of the Americas', in *Warriors and scribes: Essays on the history and politics of Latin America* (London, 2000), pp 145–67.

8   I. McCalman, 'Erin go bragh: The Irish in British popular radicalism, 1790–1840', in Oliver MacDonagh and W.F. Mandle (eds), *Irish-Australian studies* (Canberra, 1989), pp 168–84; Dorothy Thompson, 'Ireland and the Irish in English radicalism before 1850', in *Outsiders: Class, gender and nation* (London, 1993), pp 103–43.

9   Martin Mitchell, *The Irish in the west of Scotland, 1797–1848: Trade unions, strikes and political unrest* (Edinburgh, 1998).

Nowhere was the United Irish presence more formative than in Australia (O'Donnell, chapter 30). Given an estimated European population of 4,500 in the colony at the time of their arrival, 600 United Irishmen and Defenders represented at least 10 per cent of the total. They had signalled their intent by staging mutinies on the *Anne* (July 1800) and *Hercules* (May 1801), and the Castle Hill uprising of March 1804 was the last concerted stand of the Irish republicans globally in the age of revolutions. One of them opined that 'It was much better to die ... than live in a state of bondage ... they had ventured their lives for their freedom before and would now again venture.'[10] Often misunderstood or dismissed by earlier anglocentric scholarship, the role of Irish political prisoners despatched to Botany Bay is only now being recovered. As a founding generation, they left an indelible mark on Australian education, labour and politics, adding tangible qualities of 'mateship' to an enduring republican strain in what was otherwise an imperial society.[11]

In America, the political eclipse of the Irish who embraced federalism and loyalism was almost total in the first quarter of the nineteenth century (Wilson, chapter 31). While a significant loyalist strain endured in Canada, the war of 1812 marked its death-knell in the United States.[12] The Orange Order never flourished in the United States, with its unambiguous separation of church and state, written republican constitution and pursuit of a meritocracy. That failure offers a revealing insight into its success in Ireland. Canada attracted a sizeable influx of Irish loyalists, many motivated by their anxieties over the rebellion. A Wexford loyalist noted in 1822: 'Since 1798, great numbers [of Protestants] have emigrated which has thinned the ranks of our once-numerous yeomanry and I say it with great regret that in a few years hence, a Protestant yeomanry in the county will not be found'.[13] Canada never experienced the first or second 'Great Awakenings,' which softened the Anglican/Dissenting divide, establishing the basis of a common evangelical American Protestantism.[14] That second revival affected especially the burned-over areas where the Irish had settled in the densest numbers.

The war of 1812 marked the point at which the United Irishmen were absorbed into the American mainstream. The war against Great Britain in 1812 was a perfect opportunity and the 'Republican Greens,' officered and recruited by

10 John Washington Price, *Minerva* Journal, 8 October 1799, cited by O'Donnell; see below p. 641.
11 Robert Hughes, *The fatal shore: A history of the transportation of convicts to Australia, 1787–1868* (New York, 1986); Thomas Kennealy, *Memoirs from a young republic* (London, 1993).
12 David Wilson, *United Irishmen, United States: Immigrant radicals in the early republic* (Dublin, 1998).
13 Cited in Daniel Gahan, 'The "Black mob" and the "Babes in the woods": Wexford in the wake of the rebellion 1798–1806', in *Wex. Hist. Soc. Jn.*, xiii (1990–91), 106. On the general pattern, see Bruce Elliott, 'Emigration from south Leinster to Eastern Upper Canada', in Whelan (ed.), *Wexford*, pp 422–77; Bruce Elliott, *Irish migrants in the Canadas: A new approach* (Belfast, 1988).
14 Nathan Hatch, *The democratization of American Christianity* (New Haven, 1989).

veteran United Irishmen, joined up in droves.[15] As on many other occasions (the Indian wars, the 1770s, the Civil War, the First World War) the Irish were integrated into civic life not only by becoming white, but by becoming soldiers. From Richard Montgomery expiring on the heights of Quebec to the glamorous navy captain and war hero Jack Kennedy in the Second World War, full-blooded participation in America's wars became the most public proof possible of Irish eligibility for citizenship, office-holding and social acceptance. Joseph O'Conway, son of a United Irish veteran Matthias, became a surgeon in the US navy and was present at the battle of New Orleans; he described to his father how the Americans, Native, French, Irish – 'a free, united and good people' – 'stood like a rock' against 'the plundering banditti'; 'a heterogenous description of farmers, merchants, lawyers, boatmen, taylors, doctors and clerks' beat the British veterans of the Peninsular campaign. After the success, O'Conway dined at the celebratory ball with Generals Jackson and Humbert, where he sang the song about a United Irish émigré, 'The exile of Erin' 'with every satisfaction to everyone present'.[16]

Far more significant than the muffled Irish loyalist strain in America was the radical republican one (Bric, chapter 32). In the 1790s alone, 60,000 Irish entered the United States, many of them ideological immigrants. They became influential advocates of republicanism and anti-Federalism, especially in Philadelphia, capital of the USA between the revolution and 1800 and hub of its national politics.[17] Through their pivotal role in print culture, they created a national profile for Jeffersonian republicanism. From vantage points in newspapers, law and politics, the United Irishmen added sophisticated propaganda, organisational know-how and the political muscle of the disciplined block vote: all of these had been honed by their prior apprenticeship in the adversarial and abrasive Irish politics of the 1790s, of which they had fallen victim. This was not just a chauvinistic ethnocentrism: their adherence to republicanism gave their politics an international language and reach. These skills helped to see off

---

15 See the extensive coverage in the *Irish Magazine* for 1812 and 1813; also the United Irishman's Thomas O'Connor, *An impartial and correct history of the war between the United States of America and Great Britain declared by a law of Congress ,18 June 1812, and concluded by a ratification and exchange of a treaty of peace at the city of Washington, 17 February 1815* (New York, 1815).

16 Joseph O'Conway (New Orleans) to Mathias O'Conway (Philadelphia), 19 Apr. 1815, N.L.I., MS 21,553. The Galway-born Mathias (1766–1842) had gone to the West Indies in 1783 and from there to New Orleans and eventually Philadelphia, where he described himself as a 'linguist and interpreter' in English, French, Spanish, Latin, Italian and Portuguese; he also compiled an important dictionary of the Irish language. He knew Humbert both from his Irish campaign and his stay at Philadelphia. Joseph (1789–1833), born in New Orleans, joined with Miranda's republican army in Venezuela as a surgeon in 1812, where his brother James (1791–1812) fell fighting with the Barlovento regiment at the battle of Portachuelo de Cuayca on 11 June 1812. He became a US navy surgeon 1814–21 and died at Zacatecas in Mexico in 1833.

17 Maurice Bric, 'Ireland, Irishmen and the broadening of the late eighteenth-century Philadelphia polity' (unpublished Ph.D. thesis, John Hopkins University, 1990).

the incipient nativism of the Federalists, most notably the Alien and Sedition Acts of 1798, which were themselves an explicit response to the rebellion in Ireland. Their powers of arbitrary deportation, internment and press gagging have been seen as the greatest threat to an evolving American tradition of civil and political libertarianism.[18] In a narrower Irish-American context, it was the Federalists who first popularized the term 'Scotch-Irish' as a means of establishing their anti-democratic respectability, through distancing themselves from what they called the 'Wild Irish' who were supporting the republicans.[19]

The United Irishmen espoused Thomas Jefferson, 'the first man for purity of character, talents and amiable manners in the republican world.'[20] His victory in the presidential election of 1800, seen by some contemporaries as a second American Revolution, answered the Federalist, anglophile and loyalist challenge.[21] It also clarified the American debate on national character. The Federalist 'One America' position, with its distaste for 'the multifarious heterogenous compound,' had to yield to a more pluralist conception of America as a composite mosaic of cultures unified by equality under republican law, the integrity of citizenship, and meritocracy, rather than Erastian, culturally homogenous and socially conservative values. The Irish espousal of a strong sense of their own national identity in the public sphere was crucial to the development of a multi-cultural, cosmopolitan society and to the emergence of a bi-polar party system (Gibbons, chapter 4; Linebaugh, chapter 33).[22] This is seen clearly in the work of the United Irish advocate William Sampson, the first 'cause' [civil rights] lawyer in America and an impassioned advocate of American codification rather than the mechanical transposition of the British common law tradition.[23] Thus the United Irishmen may be seen as catalysts of the new politics of the United States in the 1790s, the decade which witnessed the protracted birthpangs of American bi-polar party politics.

18 J.M. Smith, *Freedom's fetters: The Alien and Sedition laws and America's civil liberties* (Ithaca, 1966); J. Miller, *Crisis in freedom: The Alien and Sedition Acts* (Boston, 1952).
19 This is a point developed by Kerby Miller in *To ye land of Canaan: Letters, memoirs and other writings by immigrants from Ireland to colonial and revolutionary America, 1675–1815* (New York, forthcoming).
20 Watty Cox, *Advice to emigrants* (Dublin, 1802), p.11. On Washington, Cox opined that 'he was as cold as a dog's nose'. He 'so regretted the mischief he had done to England that he would not after the first explosion of the French Revolution allow a French or Irish gentleman to be admitted to his levees'. He had 'ordered Mr [Archibald Hamilton] Rowan from the porch of his dwelling and at every subsequent opportunity he never failed to express his marked dislike at the introduction of Irishmen into the United States': Watty Cox, *The snuff box* (New York, 1820), p. 13.
21 Bernard Weisberger, *America afire: Jefferson, Adams and the first contested election* (New York, 2000).
22 Maurice Bric, 'The Irish and the evolution of the new politics in America', in P.J. Drudy (ed.), *The Irish in America: Emigration, assimilation and impact* (Cambridge, 1985), pp 143–67. See also Peter Onuf, *Jefferson's empire: The language of American nationhood* (Virginia, 2000); Joyce Appleby, *Inheriting the revolution: The first generation of Americans* (Harvard, 2000); Joanne Freeman, *Affairs of honour: National politics in the new republic* (New Haven, 2001).
23 Walter Walsh, 'Religion, ethnicity and history: Clues to the cultural construction of the law', in Bayor and Meagher (eds), *The New York Irish*, pp 48–69.

The American context helps provide an answer to another puzzle of Irish politics after 1798: the seemingly rapid subsidence of Presbyterian radicalism.[24] In 1797, faced with an inability to prosecute Ulster radicals successfully because of jury resistance, local magnates like John Knox in Tyrone[25] and George Hill in Derry[26] implemented an informal policy of releasing United Irishmen if they entered into recognisances to banish themselves voluntarily to America for the duration of the French war. Presbyterian United Irishmen were treated more leniently after 1798 than their Catholic counterparts. The canny Castlereagh, himself from a family with a very recent dissenting background,[27] lanced the Presbyterian boil by forcing radicals out, thereby fundamentally altering the political complexion of Ulster. The Presbyterian share of the province's population, especially in the linen triangle of north and mid-Armagh, west Down and east Tyrone, dropped after 1798, as judged by figures from 1766 and 1831.[28] This area was the epicentre of Anglican loyalism and Orangeism in the 1790s; the

24 The standard account is by A.T.Q. Stewart, *Narrow ground*. For a more recent treatment, see Finlay Holmes, 'From rebels to unionists: The political transformation of Ulster's Presbyterians', in R. Hanna (ed.), *The Union: Essays on Ireland and the British connection* (Newtownards, 2001), pp 34–47; D. Thompson, 'Seceding from the Seceders: The decline of the Jacobin tradition in Ireland 1790–1850', in *Outsiders*, 134–63; James Patterson, 'Republicanism, agrarianism and banditry in the wake of the great Irish rebellion of 1798' (unpublished Ph.D. thesis, Fordham University, 2001).

25 John Knox (1758–1800), second son of Viscount Northland, had a meteoric rise in the army; after serving in India in 1783, he was quickly elevated to captain, colonel and eventually brigade-general on the Irish establishment (1796–7), with special responsibility for mid-Ulster. Appointed governor of Jamaica, he was lost at sea on his way to take up the post in 1800.

26 Sir George Hill (1763–1839) was the son of Sir Hugh Hill. He married a daughter of John Beresford and was thereafter a prominent supporter of Dublin Castle. Hill strongly resisted the claims of the Catholics. He was so successful in managing Derry that Cornwallis complimented him in 1798: 'Derry, under its present guidance has long been the counterpoise to Belfast, and the rallying point for the loyalty of the north': *Castlereagh corr.*, i, p. 33. He was appointed governor of St Vincent (1830–3) and Trinidad (1833–9).

27 In 1776, Robert Stewart (Snr.) [1739–1821] of Mount Stewart (created Lord Londonderry in 1789) was one of only three MPs (alongside Clotworthy Upton and Hercules Langford Rowley) with Dissenting backgrounds in the Irish parliament. His wealth came from his mother, a nabob heiress. The family were squeezed out of the representation in a bitter contest with the Hill (Downshire) family in 1783 (*Historical account of the late election ... for the county of Down* ([Belfast?], 1784). In 1790, his son Robert Stewart (jr.) [1769–1822], a member of the Northern Whig Club, won a famous victory in one of the longest and most expensive Irish election contests. His election agent was Samuel Neilson and the radical Dissenters backed him vigorously. When he subsequently accepted office under Pitt (serving as chief secretary to his step-uncle Camden), helped put down the rebellion and promoted the Union, he was indelibly fixed in the Dissenter imagination as a traitor to his religion, politics and country. They unceremoniously ousted him in the 1805 Down by-election. Cornwallis described him in 1800 as having 'cold and distant manners in private society.'

28 I owe these observations to recent work by Kerby Miller, based on comparisons of the 1766 religious census with the returns furnished to the Commission on Public Instruction in 1831 (and published in 1834). See his *To ye land of Canaan*.

subsequent drop in its Presbyterian component reflects the triumph and consoli-dation of loyalist conservatism. Rather than Ulster Presbyterians shedding their ephemeral republicanism as mere 'sunshine patriots' or 'summer soldiers,' its radicals were disproportionately siphoned off to America, where they were read-ily assimilated, given the extent of prior emigration from within their communi-ties. This elegant explanation provides a different context for the lack of a vibrant public memory of 1798 within the Ulster Presbyterian community: it too had been transferred to America (McBride, chapter 23).

Looking at the 1790s as a whole, a republican triangle linked America, France and Ireland. Many activists visited all three countries.[29] Serious United Irish-related incidents broke out in Jamaica, Newfoundland, Guernsey, South Africa, Botany Bay and the United States. The international horizons of the United Irishmen and their sense of participation in a cosmopolitan political project to transform the entire global order is crucial to a full understanding of them (Linebaugh, chapter 33). Thus we need a wide-angle lens to encompass the world of the United Irishmen, which should include in one frame of vision Hesse and Haiti, Bantry Bay and Botany Bay, Fort George and Fort MacHenry.[30]

Among the absorbing issues of the day for the radical enlightenment were slavery and the fate of indigenous peoples. The slavery issue had been a conspic-uous motif in the early United movement and remained an abiding concern for many of them when they had to grapple with the reality as opposed to the theory in the United States.[31] A flaw in Enlightenment generally and in republicanism specifically was an inability to safeguard cultural as opposed to individual rights. Republican thought was unable to break out of the prison of gender; there was little concern for the rights of women alongside the rights of (a carefully abstract) man (Keogh, chapter 25). It was generally accepted that the specifity of

29 Benjamin Franklin, Mathew Carey, Lord Edward FitzGerald, Archibald Hamilton Rowan, Eleazer Oswald, Theobald Wolfe Tone, John Swiney, John Chambers, Thomas Addis Emmet, Joseph Humbert, James Napper Tandy, William Putnam McCabe, Luke Lawless, James Joseph MacDonnell, William James MacNeven, William Sampson, Patrick O'Kelly, David Bailie Warden, Valentine Derry and Richard McCormick, among others.

30 The Hessians were an important component of the mercenary troops of 1798. The United Irish leaders were interned at Fort George in the Scottish Highland between 1799 and 1803. Fort George itself had been built in the aftermath of the '45 to pacify the Highlands. At Fort MacHenry in the 1812 war, Francis Keyes was inspired to compose 'The Star spangled banner', based on a United Irish song and tune which itself was modelled on an earlier O'Carolan tune.

31 On the United Irishmen and slavery, see the unduly hostile treatment in Durey, *Transatlantic rad-icals*. For broader perspectives, see Nini Rodgers, 'Equiano in Belfast: A study of the anti-slavery ethos in a northern town', in *Slavery and Abolition*, xviii (1997), 73–89; Nini Rodgers, 'Two Quakers and a utilitarian: The reactions of three Irish women writers [Maria Edgeworth, Mary Leadbetter, Mary Birkett] to the problem of slavery 1789–1807', in *R.I.A. Proc.*, C, (2000), 137–57; Richard Twomey, *Anglo-American radicalism in the United States 1790–1820* (New York, 1989); Michael Durey (ed.), *Andrew Bryson's ordeal: An epilogue to the 1798 rebellion* (Cork, 1998).

local cultures had to yield to the superior forms of a wider, rational cosmopolitanism. Thus while there could be sympathetic ethnographic and imaginative engagement with 'savage' or regional cultures, European Enlightenment judged that these cultures could have no legitimate claim on the modern public sphere and were accordingly doomed to necessary obsolescence in the name of progress (Gibbons, chapter 3). Madden visited Indian reservations in 1835 and was astonished by the vehemence with which his suggestion about the need to treat them fairly was met:

> The uniform answer given in the United State to any inquiry on the subject of the alleged efforts made to civilise the Indians is 'All efforts made to civilise them have failed utterly', 'It is impossible to civilise them', 'There is no use in any efforts made for their preservation', 'It is opposing the designs of Providence to make such attempts', 'The red man must die out', 'The red man must fly before the face of civilisation', 'The red man must be replaced before the civilised white men.'[32]

It is of interest to see how Irish republicans engaged with these issues. (Linebaugh, chapter 33). They were better equipped to do so, given the long-standing issues of colonialism and the treatment of the majority Irish-speaking population. Thomas Russell, Lord Edward FitzGerald, Edward Marcus Despard, John Dunn, John Nevin and William Sampson all grappled with the issue. These men met such Indian leaders as Joseph Brant (Thayendanega) of the Mohawks, David Hill of the Iroquois and Little Turtle of the Miami, all of whom were engaged in a united Indian policy that resonated with the United Irishmen.[33]

John Dunn was interested 'in the gradual degenerating and wasting away' of the Indians, but unlike Jefferson and other enlightened commentators, he was not convinced of the desirability or inevitability of their obsolescence.[34] Acutely

---

32 R.R. Madden, *Autobiography*, i, p. 141 [N.L.I. Ir. 92 M 157].

33 Ian Kelsay, *Joseph Brant, 1743–1807: Man of two worlds* (Syracuse, 1984). See also Richard White, *The middle ground: Indians, empires and republics in the Great Lakes region 1650–1815* (New York, 1991): Daniel Richter, *Facing east from Indian country: A native history of early America* (Cambridge, Mass., 2002).

34 John Dunn, 'Notices relating to some of the native tribes of North America', in *R.I.A. Trans.*, ix (1803), 101–37 [quotation at p. 103]. John Dunn (1752–1827) was from an Ulster Dissenting background. Like many of the leading United Irishmen (Oliver Bond, William Drennan, Samuel Neilson), he was 'a son of the manse'. His father William, a native of Armagh, a Presbyterian minister at Lurgan, and then at the Cooke and Strand Street congregations in Dublin was chaplain to the Irish Brigade Volunteers. His mother belonged to the Bruces of Belfast, one of the leading intellectual dissenting families. John was educated at Glasgow (1769–73), then of the Middle Temple (admitted in 1775) before being called to the Irish bar in 1778. A Volunteer, he became a successful barrister and politician, entering parliament as MP for Randalstown in County Antrim under the patronage of the Whig John O'Neill. A supporter of Grattan and Catholic Emancipation, Dunn moved in radical circles in the 1790s. He figures prominently in

aware of the politics of representation (some United Irishmen had actively sought to bring Gaelic culture in from the enlightenment cold), Dunn noted that 'it is part of the destiny of an unlettered people to write their memorials with the pen of a stranger. They have no alternative – imperfect representation or blank oblivion.'[35] He stressed that the Indian is 'a man, a real man', not the hideous barbarian of the prevalent stereotype.[36] The Indian was fully aware of what lay ahead, not just some passive victim of an impersonal and progressive historical process: 'He sees his approaching ruin: he sees it appalled, it haunts him in his solitude, it fills him with bitterness, when he beholds his devoted children'.[37] Dunn offered an intellectual defence of the indigenous people of the Great Lake basin, at precisely the moment when other republican thinkers like Jefferson could offer them nothing but an America cleansed of their stain, a white republic free 'of either blot or admixture on that surface'. On 18 February 1803, Jefferson was only able to see Indians in terms of 'the various ways in which their history may terminate'.[38] Russell, FitzGerald, Dunn and Despard are examples of an incipient Irish enlightened thinking which could navigate past the Jeffersonian cul-de-sac. Their defeat in the revolutionary period was to close down this appealing vista.[39]

A further way of exploring reciprocities across the 'Green Atlantic' of the eighteenth-century is to envisage gains to the American political system as balanced by losses to the Irish one.[40] An entire generation of gifted political leadership was extirpated from Ireland in the 1790s by hanging, transportation, exile, by what Stephen Rea has termed 'the Cull.' The United Irish leadership cadre was scattered to America, to the Irish legion of Napoleon's army, to Botany Bay, to the Silesian coal mines, to the 'condemned regiments' of the West Indies. We

his old classmates William Drennan's correspondence and hosted the dinner in May 1791 with Drennan and Samuel Neilson after which Drennan penned his celebrated letter setting out the United Irish project. His parliamentary career abruptly terminated in 1798 and his subsequent American journey may have been precipitated by a desire to escape his radical connections.

35 Ibid., p. 106.
36 Ibid., p. 107.
37 Ibid., p. 106.
38 Peter Linebaugh, 'The red-crested bird and black duck – a story of 1802: Historical materialism, indigenous people and the failed republic', in *The Republic*, ii (2001), 104–25.
39 Linebaugh and Rediker, 'The conspiracy of Edward and Catherine Despard', in *Many-headed hydra*, pp 248–86; Peter Linebaugh, *Edward Marcus Despard*, (Cork, forthcoming); Stella Tillyard, *Citizen Lord: Edward FitzGerald, 1763–1798* (London, 1998); Kevin Whelan, 'New light on Lord Edward FitzGerald', in *Hist. Ir.*, vii, 4 (1999), 40–4; Thomas Russell, *A letter to the people of Ireland on the present situation of the country* (Belfast, 1796); on Russell, see C.J. Woods, *Journals and memoirs of Thomas Russell* (Dublin, 1991); Denis Carroll, *The man from God knows where: Thomas Russell, 1767–1803* (Dublin, 1995); James Quinn, *Soul on fire: A life of Thomas Russell, 1767–1803* (Dublin, 2002). Séamus Mac Giolla Easpaig, *Tomás Ruiséil* (Baile Átha Cliath, 1957) is still useful.
40 Whelan, 'Green Atlantic'; Linebaugh and Rediker, *Many-headed hydra*; Nini Rodgers, 'Ireland and the Black Atlantic in the eighteenth century', in *I.H.S.*, cxxvi (2000), 174–92.

are still in the early stages of piecing together the shattered debris of this diaspora. In Ireland this cull led to the collapse of radical political organisation for a
generation. Given the lack of an available public sphere, politics contracted into
sectarian channels, seen in the nasty Orange/Ribbon disputes of the 1810s.[41]
William Drennan wrote of Belfast in 1807: 'The north seems dead and rotting,
like its flax when steeping in holes and ditches.'[42] Richard Lalor Shiel famously
described political activists in the first two decades of the nineteenth century:
'We sat down like galley slaves in a calm. A general stagnation diffused itself over
national feelings. The public pulse had stopped, the circulation of all generous
feeling had been arrested, and the country was palsied to the heart'.[43] The leadership vacuum created the space into which Daniel O'Connell (himself carefully
covering his United Irish tracks) was to expand and dominate Irish politics for
three decades with a new brand of politics which merged Catholic confessional
solidarity with a conventional Whig ideology. He thereby narrowed the global
scope of United Irish ambitions to a more insular British perspective, abandoning their principled non-sectarianism for a Catholic stance. Instead of rising
above the sectarian political arrangements foisted on Ireland with the Act of
Union, O'Connell chose instead to play the sectarian game which the British
establishment had begun, with devastating consequences in terms of a retreat to
the zero-sum sectarian politics from which the United Irishmen had sought to
extricate their country.

41 Similarly the rise of Islamic fundamentalism can be traced to the closing down of opposition politics in the Middle East in the 1970s and 1980s.
42 William Drennan to Martha MacTier, 17 Apr. 1807 in *Drennan–MacTier corr.*, iii, p. 595.
43 Cited in Bartlett, *Fall and Rise*, p. 304. William Sampson talks of the 'sullen peace' in the 'cruel
   empire' of post-Union Ireland: *Memoirs*, pp 325–6.

30

'Liberty or death': The United Irishmen in New South Wales, 1800–4

RUAN O'DONNELL

In March 1804 Irish convict Andrew Doyle described his fellow countrymen who had recently arrived in the penal colony of New South Wales as 'deamons ... banished from happiness'. Doyle was writing just four days after 300 or so Irishmen had risen in arms against the colonial authorities and fought an engagement with the military in modern western Sydney. That the site of the clash has been known ever since as 'Vinegar Hill', after the Wexford battle of that name, indicates the identity of the vast majority of the 'demons', namely United Irishmen who had been transported to New South Wales between 1799 and 1802. At least 400 and probably more than 600 Irishmen had been sent out to the colony for complicity in the 1798 rebellion and seditious crimes connected with the United Irishmen. The same people, therefore, were not only partly responsible for the most concentrated explosion of bloodletting in Irish history but also for the most serious insurrectionary challenge directed against the Australian state.[1]

The crushing of the Irish rebellion of 1798 left the government with an enormous problem of prisoner disposal. An unknown number of men, probably over ten thousand, had been captured or arrested in the course of the insurrection. Their detention exacerbated conditions in a penal system which had already been overwhelmed by the coercion campaigns of April/May 1798, despite the best efforts of the Dublin Castle administration to create auxiliary facilities. Before the turning of the tide against the rebels in north-eastern Ulster in mid-June and in Leinster by mid-July, prisoners were rarely taken by the forces of the crown. Indeed, Lieutenant-General Gerard Lake issued specific 'no prisoners' orders to his subordinates on more than one occasion. Wounded rebels and camp followers were routinely put to the sword when encountered by the mili-

---

1 Andrew Doyle to anon., 9 Mar. 1804: B.L., Add. MS 35644/292. See also Ruan O'Donnell, '"Desperate and diabolical": Defenders and United Irishmen in early New South Wales', in Richard Davis et al. (eds), *Irish Australian studies ... Hobart, July 1995* (Sydney, 1996), pp 360–72.

tary on the battlefields of Arklow, Antrim, Ballinamuck, Enniscorthy, New Ross, Newtownmount-kennedy and Newtownbarry (Bunclody). Many more were summarily executed in the general vicinity of major battle sites, and massacre consequently rivalled combat as the chief cause of what may have been 30,000 violent deaths to that year.[2]

As irregulars in a world still unaccustomed to the phenomena of organised mass revolutionary movements, captured United Irishmen were not deemed prisoners of war and were subjected instead to the summary sanctions traditionally reserved for guerilla fighters. Detention and trial, however, became increasingly likely after the Wexford battle of Vinegar Hill on 21 June 1798; it was a major tactical victory which disposed government agents to seize their defeated enemies alive in much greater numbers than before. While it was by no means the decisive military encounter sought by the army, Vinegar Hill occurred in the midst of improving circumstances for the government. Active rebels who lived long enough to be transported were therefore something of an elite group in view of their survival, if nothing else. The small minority who passed through the convict depot system to Australia were aware of their relative good fortune as they approached their new lives in the southern hemisphere.[3]

Cornwallis took viceregal office in mid-June 1798 with a keen appreciation of the ignominy of defeat; he had surrendered the British army at Yorktown to American revolutionaries in 1783. He also espoused moderate politics and favoured pacifying Ireland by the twin approaches of achieving absolute military ascendancy, and of offering pardon to the vast majority of participants. Other than the abberations occasioned by the French invasion of August 1798 (which led to the execution of over 400 prisoners in Longford on 8–10 September 1798), the new policy was highly effective. Once the military question had been settled, the vast majority of outstanding insurgents and fugitives became eligible for a series of generous clemency initiatives. Proclamations offering conditional pardons to those willing to swear the oath of allegiance were followed by the promulgation of the Amnesty Act (October 1798).[4]

One category of prisoner excluded from the near general pardon were those who had been imprisoned before the rebellion: the Amnesty Act was not retrospective. In practice this meant that United Irishmen were sent abroad for relatively minor crimes such as possession of arms, whilst neighbours who had remained at large to kill government forces during the rebellion were entitled to return home. The purpose of these surprising exemptions was to prevent the release of key political prisoners who had been sentenced by the pre-rebellion civil assizes. Such convictions had often been difficult to procure, and liberating

2 For the 'no prisoners' policy, see Major-General Nugent to General Knox, 26 May 1798: N.L.I., MS 56, p. 165.
3 See *F.J.*, 7 July 1798; *S.N.L.*, 8 Aug. 1798.
4 *F.J.*, 30 Aug., 6 Sept. 1798; *F.L.J.*, 15, 26 Sept. 1798.

assize defendants risked unravelling the carefully constructed fabric of exemplary justice. There were, furthermore, complex constitutional issues stemming from the unnatural co-existence of civil and martial law which were not fully resolved until all concerned were beyond redress.[5]

A considerable proportion of suspected United Irishmen could not be accommodated in the overcrowded prisons and were instead held on dismasted ships known as 'hulks', or on the better appointed small coasters and tenders.[6] The first tender was placed in Belfast Lough to cope with the post-Mar. 1797 dragooning of Ulster and by summer 1798 was augmented by the *Alexandria, Postlethwaite, William and Mary, Columbine, John and Esther*, and *Brunskill*, all of which were normally moored in Dublin Bay off Ringsend. The *Princess Charlotte* moved between Cove and Duncannon Fort from September 1797, the *Ravensworth* was moored at Duncannon from July 1798, and the *Lovely Kitty* (a coal ship commandeered in Wexford harbour) and another vessel were anchored off New Geneva in Waterford. The combined capacity of the tenders exceeded 3,000 prisoners.[7]

In July 1798 it was discovered that over 70 per cent of the 282 men crammed onto the *Princess* had been improperly committed, an indication that the sweeping powers of the Insurrection Act had been liberally employed.[8] United Irishman Edward Hay complained that the Wexford hulk was 'so damp and noisome' that he soon 'was affected with a paralytic stroke which he scarcely survived'. This may very well have been the reason why Wexford's loyalist Committee of Prosecution had sent him on board. For some it was worse; Edward Roche of Garrylough, one of Wexford's most effective insurgent leaders, died awaiting transportation overseas. His fate was shared by John Moore of Moore Hall, president of the short-lived Connacht Republic, who died in Waterford.[9]

Extant documentation cannot show the precise proportion of prisoners who were bailed, released or pardoned after conviction; it also remains unclear how many were actually sent to Australia. It would seem that only one in ten of those formally and specifically sentenced by courts martial to terms of transportation

5   See Ruan O'Donnell, ' "Marked for Botany Bay": The Wicklow United Irishmen and the development of political transportation from Ireland, 1791–1806' (unpublished Ph.D. thesis, Australian National University, 1996), pp 161–8.
6   See *F.L.J.*, 25 Aug. 1798.
7   Captain Lambert Brabazon to Edward Cooke, 6 Jan. 1801; Major-General Fawcett to Castlereagh, 26 July, 12 Aug. 1798, 17 July, 11 Aug. 1799: N.A.I., RP 620/10/116/2, 620/10/116/2, 620/39/120, 620/4/29/20, 620/7/79/22, 620/7/79/23; Fawcett to Castlereagh, 1 May 1801: P.R.O., HO 100/106/47.
8   1 May 1801: P.R.O., HO 100/106/40–51, and R.B. McDowell, *Ireland in the age of imperialism and revolution, 1760–1801* (Oxford, 1979), p. 670.
9   Petition of Edward Hay, 29 July 1799: R.I.A., MS 23.K.53/12. See also Charles Teeling, *The history of the Irish rebellion of 1798 and Sequel to the history of the Irish rebellion of 1798* (new ed., Shannon, 1972), pp 50, 109; Charles Dickson, *The revolt in the North, Antrim and Down in 1798* (Dublin, 1960), p. 183.

in New South Wales ever embarked. The vast majority were diverted into the ranks of those regiments which controlled the places of detention where court-martialled prisoners were confined, prior to the implementation of their sentences.[10] Most prisoners held in New Geneva and Duncannon Fort under sentence of transportation before 1800 were entitled to volunteer to 'serve abroad' with the 'condemned' regiments posted in the West Indies. Indeed, they were strongly encouraged to do so, not least owing to the prohibitive cost of transportation to New South Wales and the urgency of army manpower requirements. The fourth battalion of the 6oth regiment, the 30th, 38th, 41st, 87th and 89th infantry and the Ancient Irish Fencibles all received sentenced rebels into their ranks. Additionally, nearly 400 United Irishmen were drafted into the Prussian army in early 1799 and sent to Emden in September of that year.[11]

Transportation to New South Wales was however resorted to more and more in the pressured atmosphere of 1799–1800 when the operation of the jail-clearing Rebellion Act of March 1799 was in full swing. A narrowing of alternative outlets seemingly caused an upsurge in convoys bound for Port Jackson (Sydney) between 1800 and 1802: during that time six ships sailed in comparison with the two transports sent out in 1796–8. A major factor explaining the rising numbers was the stream of courtmartialled convicts that were quite unsuited for military induction. When seditious and military offenders were being drafted, the only two standards rigidly enforced by the inspector general of recruits (Major-General Henry Johnson) were those of reasonable physical health and a blanket exclusion of murderers.[12]

The indent of the *Atlas II*, which sailed from Waterford on 30 May 1801, is indicative: its convicts included the depot sick list from which deserters were almost invariably removed and to which rebel killers and officers were added.[13] In every case those guilty of 'murder' were expressly forbidden from entering military service, and the twenty-one men rendered ineligible were embarked. The only two 'murderers' held in Waterford who are recorded as arriving in New South Wales probably died on the trip out.

Leadership status was evidently a consideration as appears to have been the case for *Princess* inmate Patrick McHale of Crossmolina, 'a rebel leader [imprisoned for] levying money for the rebels'. An inspector declared McHale physical-

10 Lord Castlereagh to William Wickham, 7 Apr. 1798; Anon. to Lieutenant-General Sir Peter Craig, 2 Jan. 1799; Anon. to Major-General Myers, 20 Jan. 1799; Hardwicke to Pelham, 11 May 1802: P.R.O., HO 100/80/185, 100/86/104, 100/86/113, 100/108/151. Petition of Mary Murray, n.d., 1799: N.A.I., State Prisoners Petitions, 745.

11 *F.J.*, 7 Aug. 1798; O'Donnell, 'Marked for Botany Bay', pp 283–306.

12 Major-General Henry Johnson to Castlereagh, 31 Mar. 1799; 2 Apr. 1799: N.A.I., RP 620/7/79/4, 620/7/79/6; Earl Hardwicke to Thomas Pelham, 10 Nov. 1802: P.R.O., HO 100/110/340.

13 *Atlas II* log: India Office (London), L/MAR/B/27F, pp 11–3; *Atlas II* indent: Archives Office of New South Wales (Sydney), MS 4/4004.

ly 'fit' for service, along with fellow Mayo rebel officer, Thomas Rigney of Ballymanagh (Killala), although the pair were instead put on board the *Atlas II*. They joined the singularly 'unfit' jailbreaker Michael Callaghan of Tipperary and Neil Smith of Dublin, who possessed only two arms between them, two convicts under 5' 2" and 'idiot[s]' John Connor of Limerick and Denis Sullivan of Waterford.[14]

The results of concentrating scores of politically dangerous, highly motivated men can best be seen in the unprecedented disturbances experienced on board ships en route to New South Wales. Exceptionally violent and deadly mutinies struck the *Anne* and *Hercules* in 1801–2 while serious plots, hitherto discounted or ignored, were suppressed on the *Minerva* and *Atlas I*. The reputedly peaceful *Friendship* of 1799 and *Atlas II* of 1802 were by no means immune from rebel-sponsored intrigue. Taken together, the six consecutive voyages from Ireland after August 1799 comprised the most concerted bout of convict unrest in the history of penal transportation and set the tone for Irish machinations after their arrival in the colony. The mutinies are also significant in that the surviving participants were dramatically over-represented in the ranks of New South Wales plotters between 1800 to 1804.

It has generally been accepted that the voyage of the *Minerva*, the first transport to leave Ireland after the Rebellion in August 1799, was a sedate affair. This is a misconception as is evident from the journal kept by the ship's Clonmel-born surgeon and from the captain's log. There was in fact a plot to kill Tipperary informer Dudley Hartigan and at least two other bids to take the ship. One of the compromised plotters declared that 'it was much better to die … than live in a state of bondage, that they had ventured their lives for their freedom before and would now again venture'.[15] This is a variant of the Republican battle cry 'death or liberty' – one which was heard in its original form on more than one occassion in early colonial Australia. The ship-board actions of the prisoners lent credence to the May 1799 warnings of Wicklow rebel General Joseph Holt, who apprised an associate that the *Minerva* rebel convicts intended to 'begin in Bottany [*sic*] [Bay] the same business'.[16]

Any hope entertained in Dublin and London that the disquiet on board the *Minerva* had been an abberation was dispelled by the mutiny on board the *Anne* on 29 July 1800. Captain Stewart, his first mate and his gunner were ambushed after they descended into the prison hold to supervise its fumigation by men following the north Kerry rebel leader Manus Sheehy (a nephew of the executed alleged Whiteboy leader Fr Nicholas Sheehy). Thirty or so prisoners who had been permitted on deck rushed their guards on Christopher Grogan's signal,

14 1 May 1801, P.R.O., HO 100/106/49–50.
15 Journal of John Washington Price, 8 Oct. 1799: B.L., Add. MSS 13,880, p. 45.
16 Joseph Holt to William Colthurst, 18 May 1799: N.A.I., RP 620/47/38.

once the commotion below decks and the call of 'death or liberty' were heard. The crew responded to the emergency with unexpected vigour and quickly repelled their virtually unarmed attackers, killing one and wounding three others in the process.[17]

The alleged rebel Cork priest, Fr Peter O'Neil, was enlisted to secure the safe release of Stewart and his companions who had remained prisoners of Sheehy's men in the hold. With no prospect of taking the ship, Sheehy surrendered after two hours of tense negotiations and was shortly afterwards summarily executed by firing squad. Grogan, a Kildare rebel, escaped with the relatively light punishment of 250 lashes. No record has survived of the punishment inflicted on the Kerry/Tipperary United Irish officer Philip Cunningham, who was stated in 1804 to have been 'remarkably active in the mutinous transactions' on board the *Anne*.[18] Cunningham went on to lead the Castle Hill revolt of Mar. 1804 at which time he allegedly repeated the famous call for 'death or liberty'.[19] News of the *Anne* mutiny helped shape Governor Philip King's description of the 137 male convicts who had landed in his colony as 'the most desperate and diabolical characters that could be selected throughout that Kingdom'.[20]

However disturbing to the colonial authorities, the events on board the *Anne* were quickly surpassed by a bloody mutiny on the *Hercules* on 29 December 1801 which claimed eighteen lives and contributed to the deaths of twenty-six more. Captain Luckyn Betts had learned of a plot on 30 November from two unenthusiastic Ulster convicts but responded complacently; he was surprised when convicts who had been granted deck access to exercise rushed the quarterdeck. The mutineers numbered half the total male complement on board and were led by Westmeath man James 'Key of the Works' Tracey. A desperate struggle resulted in the deaths or mortal wounding of eighteen prisoners, one of whom was personally accounted for by Betts. The exceptionally harsh ship-board regime then introduced by the captain undoubtedly helped see off nearly twice that number. A non-political prisoner, Sir Henry Brown Hayes, alleged that Betts had 'starved' the convicts 'from the Cape of Good Hope to N[ew] S[outh] W[ales]' with a daily allowance of 'one pint of boiled rice' and very little water.[21]

---

17 Sheedy papers, Mitchel Library (Sydney) MS 1337, p. 130; Stewart to —, 28 Aug. 1800, quoted in Harold Perkins, *The convict priests* (Melbourne, 1984), p. 78; Charles Bateson, *The convict ships, 1787–1868* (Sydney, 1983), p. 159,

18 *Sydney Gazette*, 18 Mar. 1804. See also *Remonstrance of Revd Peter O'Neil*, cited in P.F. Moran, *History of the Catholic Church in Australasia* (Sydney, n.d.), p. 47; Phil O'Neil, 'The convict priests of '98 in Australia', in *Catholic Bulletin*, x (Sept., 1920), 540.

19 *Sydney Gazette*, 11 Mar. 1804.

20 King to Portland, 10 Mar. 1801: *Historical Records of Australia*, iii, p. 9.

21 Quoted in *Historical Records of Australia*, iii, pp 537–8. See also Sergeant Trotter, 'Extracts from a journal of an action which happened on board the ship Hercules with a party of the N[ew] S[outh} W[ales] Corps commanded by Captain Ralph Wilson ... Dec[embe]r 28 1801': P.R.O., CO 201/29/358.

The arrival of so many Irish rebels understandably alarmed the small, isolated and instinctively paranoid colonial administration. Security was an obvious problem given that the republican newcomers numbered at least 10 per cent and possibly as many as 25 per cent of the total population of less than 4,500. This ratio compares with a peak strength of the United Irishmen on paper of one-in-twenty (280,000) in their home country in 1798.

Gross irregularities in the keeping and transmission of records ensured that the New South Wales authorities were often left ignorant of the precise crimes, identities and sentences of those disembarked. Such uncertainties were unsettling: Mrs Elizabeth Paterson, married to a senior New South Wales Corps officer, expressed her fears of 'private assassins breaking into our houses in the dead of night in which they were but too successful in their own country'.[22] Her information was not entirely hearsay in view of the fact that members of the Grose, Gore and other leading establishment families had seen action against the insurgents in 1798, and stories concerning real and alleged rebel atrocities preceded the 'United' ships. Most commentators were less hysterical than Paterson but a consensus existed that the Irish community was an exceptionally troublesome and threatening importation.[23] Joseph Holt noted that he and his fellow *Minerva* rebels 'had such a name of United [Irish] criminality, as filled the inhabitants with … dread'.[24]

Nervous colonists would not have been mollified by Holt's early and public clash with Judge-Advocate Robert Dore nor by his instant friendship with the 'Scottish martyr', Maurice Margarot. These were portentous events as they indicated that at least some of the newly arrived United Irish leaders were not so embarrassed by their situation that they had tired of defending what they perceived to be their rights. The Wicklowman, protected by his status as a voluntary exile, persisted in wearing military style dress and kept both his hair and his beard cut in the style favoured by Irish republicans of the 1790s. He also acknowledged the title of 'general' and clearly relished his association with the owner of the 'most seditious house in the colony'.[25]

A similar impression was probably elicited by the early visit of United Irishman Fr James Harold to the Revd Thomas Fyshe Palmer, another 'martyr' with whom he reportedly sang republican songs. Palmer was a pariah in British offi-

---

22 Elizabeth Paterson to — , 3 Oct. 1800: Mitchel Library, Ap/36/6. See also Peter O'Shaughnessy (ed.), *A rum story: The adventures of Joseph Holt, thirteen years in New South Wales (1800–12)* (Perth, 1988), p. 47.

23 See Philip Gidley King to John King, 9 May 1800: *Historical Records of Australia*, ii, p. 507; William Gore to William Bligh, 24 May 1808: *Historical Records of New South Wales*, vi, p. 647. The phrase 'United ships' was used in the colony in 1804, see Doyle to anon., 9 Mar. 1804: B.L., Add. MS 35644, p. 452.

24 O'Shaughnessy, *Adventures of Joseph Holt*, p. 47.

25 Ibid., p. 50. See also Ruan O'Donnell, 'General Joseph Holt', in Bob Reece (ed.), *Exiles from Erin: Convict lives in Ireland and Australia* (Dublin, 1991), pp 27–56.

cial circles and was something of a marked man for having sent highly critical reports of Governor John Hunter's New South Wales administration to London.[26] Meetings and openly political expressions of this kind were proscribed in Ireland under successive versions of the Insurrection Act and could have resulted in the transportation of anyone obliged to answer such a charge. *Anne* convict Hugh Mohan of Waterford had actually been sent out for 'singing treasonable songs', an offence that did not exist in his place of exile.[27]

The general perception was that the colony was under-garrisoned and poorly defended. Fear of the all-conquering French army was at times pervasive and in April 1799 a prophesy predicting an invasion moved one convict to throw down his hoe and give 'three cheers for liberty' in front of an initially enthusiastic crowd of labourers at Toongabbie. This must have been a somewhat unsettling harbinger of what could be expected when the anticipated influx of rebel veterans took place, augmenting United Irishmen and Defenders who had been sent out prior to 1798 on the *Marquis Cornwallis* and *Britannia*. Apocalyptic and millenarian fixations were evidently no less prevalent in New South Wales than in Ireland and may even have been exacerbated by the nautical drama of 'crossing the line' into the southern hemisphere.[28]

The fact that the unilateral seizure of such a struggling colony would be an almost meaningless act offered little comfort to Governors John Hunter and Philip Gidley King. Victory, at best, offered the insurgents temporary respite from penal servitude, unless sufficient bodies of French troops could be landed to hold out against the inevitable counter-attack. A successful convict revolt, however, promised access to whatever shipping happened to be in port and the chance to effect a clean escape to America, France, Batavia or even Mauritius. Leaving the continent altogether may have been suggested by the demoralizing experiences of the Irish *Queen* absconders who had demonstrated in the early 1790s that the interior did not offer any refuge where Europeans might prosper.[29]

An undercurrent of dissent was omnipresent in Irish circles as late as 1810. In its most extreme form this defiance was manifested in repeated efforts to rise in arms against jailers who had automatically assumed the oppositional role of oppressors. Adherence to a specific republican ideology is intrinsically undocumentable but extant correspondence and trial proceedings establish that many United Irishmen regarded themselves as political prisoners. Seditious meetings, organised mass break-outs, the resurrection of command structures and the sub-

26 Harold Perkins, 'Father Harold: The story of a convict priest', in *Journal of the Australian Catholic Historical Society*, iii (1971), part three, 6.
27 A.O.N.S.W., 2/8242, p. 111.
28 David Collins, *An account of the English colony in New South Wales* (repr., Sydney, 1975), ii, p. 77.
29 O'Donnell, 'Marked for Botany Bay', pp 389–92; Watkin Tench, *Sydney's first four years* (Sydney, 1979), p. 144.

orning of the military were all common practices for rebel prisoners that bore the characteristic hallmarks of the revolutionary *modus operandi*. One of the most explicit statements regarding self-defined political status was dispatched to Governor Hunter by Fr Harold in April 1800. Harold, in expectation of the cessation of the Anglo-French War, made a case for his repatriation to Ireland as if he were a regular captured combatant.[30]

United Irish prisoners drawn from the liberal professions were encouraged to set themselves apart by the unofficial conferral of status as 'special' or 'gentleman' convicts. Given that United Irish officers were greatly over-represented in the colonial population, it is not altogether surprising that they formed a distinct cohort of better educated, wealthier and law-abiding prisoners than their avowedly criminal counterparts. The 'United ships' of 1800–2 landed three Catholic priests (Frs O'Neil, Harold and Dixon), a Church of Ireland clergyman (Revd Henry Fulton), two ex-army officers (Captains John St Leger and Henry Alcock), one former high sheriff (John Brennan), two doctors (Bryan O'Connor and William Redfern), and many lawyers, teachers and surveyors. When not implicated in seditious plotting, such men were an invaluable addition to the talent-starved administration into which they were co-opted at the earliest opportunity. Hostility between 'politicals' and 'criminals' gained impetus from their often differing social backgrounds and the unusual circumstances which had occasioned the presence of the United Irishmen in New South Wales.[31]

The first signs of serious insurgent unrest in Australia became apparent in February 1800 when some recently arrived United Irishmen plotted to seize the Port Jackson magazine and to steal the docked *Minerva* transport. Most of those implicated had been in Port Jackson less than a month when they contemplated stealing the very ship which had conveyed them into exile. On 15 May 1800, information that the Irish political prisoners were again conducting 'seditious correspondences, and holding unlawful meetings' resulted in a co-ordinated series of raids upon suspected households. Nothing incriminating was recovered, but it marked a new approach towards the rebel community by the authorities. Rumours of pike making and of Fr Harold's alleged 'seditious conversations' were also carefully investigated but nothing was substantiated.[32]

Far from reassuring the magistracy, the failure to uncover concrete details of Irish plots was interpreted as a sign that rebel solidarity was strong. An informer who retracted a deposition regarding the concealment of pikes in Sydney harbour was consequently 'severely punished' and suspected of having endured

---

30 Fr Harold to Hunter, 23 Apr. 1800: *Historical records of Australia*, ii, p. 504. See also O'Donnell, 'Marked for Botany Bay', chap. 9.

31 See Robert Eastwick, *A master mariner* (London, 1981), p. 199.

32 Collins, *Account*, ii, pp 209–10. For a full discussion of this and other United plots, see O'Donnell, 'Marked for Botany Bay', pp 382–431, 469–521; Anne Maree Whitaker, *Unfinished revolution: United Irishmen in New South Wales, 1800–1810* (Sydney, 1994).

flogging to avoid incriminating his 'confederates'. This scare was followed by more plausible revelations regarding the manufacture of pikes by United Irish blacksmiths and the swearing of recruits for a major convict rebellion in September 1800. Sufficient information was obtained by the authorities to launch a pre-emptive strike in which five men were singled out for corporal punishment and re-transportation to Norfolk Island. When further investigations were completed, many lesser figures were obliged to spend time on the hellish Pacific outpost, mostly United Irishmen who had come out on the *Minerva, Britannia* and *Friendship*.[33]

A magistrate's inquiry in Port Jackson reported that the ringleaders of the insurrection plot were Farrell Cuffe, Martin Short, Richard Byrne, Michael Byrne and Michael Cox. Short refused to co-operate when examined on 4 September, but the Wicklow man Richard Byrne admitted having been in Parramatta on 31 August 'with disaffected persons – that the subject of their conversation was a Revolt – but refuses to declare the particulars'.[34] This dispelled any suggestion that the plot was simply a matter of loose conversation. Cuffe and Byrne were known to be influential prisoners who had been named in the Banishment act (1798) and who had been key proselytizers in Ireland, as was their adopted leader and friend, Holt. Short's position in the United Irish movement was not so exalted, but he was an experienced arms raider whose stalwart conduct on the way out on the *Minerva* had distinguished him as a man of action. His home was later used in the planning stages of the Mar. 1804 Castle Hill revolt.[35]

An attempt to revive the insurrection plan in September 1800 was discovered even as judicial investigations into the initial plot were ongoing. Several men were severely flogged in early October in the main population centres of Toongabbie, Parramatta and Port Jackson. Holt evaded direct punishment but was forced to witness the 300 lashes inflicted on the twenty-year-old Kerry United Irishman Patrick Galvin. He recalled: 'There was two floggers Richard Rice and John Johnson, the hangman from Sydney. Rice was a left-handed man and Johnson the right-handed so they stood at each side, and I never saw two threshers in a barn move their strokes more handier than those two man killers did ... though I was two perches from them, the flesh and skin blew in my face as they shook off of the cats [o' nine tails]'.[36] The Revd Samuel Marsden, a hard-line magistrate, observed that Galvin 'would have died on the spot before he would tell a single sentence'. By no means all compromised plotters were as staunch as the Kerryman under interrogation, but the sense of difference between the Irish political sub-group and those deemed criminals was further emphasized.[37]

33 Collins, *Account*, ii, p. 209.
34 *Historical Records of Australia*, ii, pp 575–6.
35 *F.J.*, 25 Aug. 1798; G.W. Rusden, *Curiosities of colonization* (London, 1874), p. 78.
36 O'Shaughnessy, *Adventures of Joseph Holt*, p. 62.
37 Samuel Marsden to King, 29 Sept. 1800: *Historical records of Australia*, ii, p. 637.

The prisoners sent to Norfolk Island for the September/October plots proved that they were not cowed by their punishments: several died for conspiring to take control of the Pacific outpost in mid-December. Betrayed at a late juncture, two ringleaders were identified and summarily executed on the orders of Major Joseph Fouveaux. Twenty-two of those deemed less culpable received up to 500 lashes each on backs that had not fully healed from their earlier floggings; Sligoman John Burke endured his 2,000th lash in under two years. Laurence Davoran, an Irish lawyer turned forger, noted one year later that the suspects had been 'flagellated beyond all human conception, and have been kept in irons at work to this day'. As another plot, centred on Parramatta, New South Wales' second settlement, was discovered in December 1800, it is possible that a co-ordinated uprising had been uncovered by Fouveaux.[38]

The Castle Hill revolt of March 1804 is arguably the most serious uprising in Australian history and, among other claims to fame, elicited the first declaration of martial law on the continent. A high proportion of convicts on the government farm at Castle Hill were United Irishmen who had survived the high mortality and abortive mutinies on board the *Anne, Hercules, Atlas I* and *Atlas II*. Placing these men in the comparatively remote environs of a territory lying north-west of Port Jackson represented a deliberate ploy to weaken their seditious potential. This policy was vindicated during 1802 and 1803 when violent rebel gangs attempted several mass break outs from the settlement.

The 1804 incident was however a far larger and more threatening affair than anything which had preceded it in New South Wales and was carried out under the leadership of three United Irish officers: Phil Cunningham, William Johnson of Tyrone, and Samuel Hume of Antrim. The trio led approximately 300 prisoners, mostly Irish, who easily overcame the defences of the lightly guarded government farm on the night of 4 March. They rallied at nearby Constitution Hill to hear a rousing speech by Cunningham before moving off through the Seven Hills/Baulkham Hills district in search of firearms and recruits. The crux of the plan was the formation of a body of sufficient strength to capture the town of Parramatta before moving on Port Jackson.

Two Wicklow leaders, Holt and the 'inflexible anarchist' Thomas Brady, were responsible for organizing a supporting revolt in the vicinity of Parramatta but they pulled back from the plan when they learnt that its basic details had been leaked. Holt was so dismayed by the course of events that he resisted Hume's attempts to co-opt him at Brush Farm and correctly surmised that disaster lay in the offing.[39] A more junior Wicklow rebel, Nicholas Bryan, claimed that 'all the County Wicklow men had refused having anything to do' with revolt, although several were deeply involved, including Holt's aged servant and fellow United

38 Reprinted in *F.D.J.*, 11 May 1802. See also Whitaker, *Unfinished revolution*, pp 56–8.
39 *Sydney Gazette*, 5 May 1804.

Irishman John Byrne of Seven Churches.[40] Holt later boasted that he would have made 'a short job' of it had he commanded; well-grounded suspicions of his complicity in the planning stages resulted in his deportation to Norfolk Island on the *Betsy* in early April 1804.[41]

The climax of the rebellion had occurred when a small but well-armed body of the New South Wales Corps under Major George Johnson, aided by the yeomanry 'Sydney Association', confronted the more numerous rebels at their camp on 5 March. The clash took place on the rising ground occupied by the modern Castlebrook cemetery off the Windsor/Baulkham Hills road, quickly to be christened 'Vinegar Hill'. Transported Wexford priest Fr James Dixon remonstrated with the insurgents, urging them to surrender, but they were determined to make a stand with the twenty or so poor-quality guns that they had stolen and their meagre pike-like farming implements. Arms-raiding rebel patrols may well have over-estimated the number of available weapons in the hands of emancipists and free settlers which turned out to be far scarcer than was the case in their native country.

The fortuitous presence in Port Jackson of visiting sailors and marines freed Major Johnson's column to approach the rebel lines with unexpected speed. The major announced his intention to initiate negotiations, but this was revealed to be a ruse when the unarmed Phil Cunningham and William Johnson were seized under the flag of truce. The garrison further signalled its disdain for their adversaries by simultaneously opening fire. Between seventeen and twenty-two insurgents were killed without any government fatalities, a decisive blow which shattered the morale of the rebels and ended their resistance. Ten prisoners were capitally convicted by rapidly convened courts martial of whom eight were executed in pursuance of sentence. Ten more were given between 200 and 500 lashes each, all but three of the twenty men tried being Irish if not United Irish. Scores of those deemed less culpable were sent in chains to the hard-working road gangs and a few dozen were re-transported to the new Coal River (Newcastle) outpost and to Norfolk Island.[42]

Castle Hill marked the zenith of rebel intrigue in New South Wales and was the last armed stand of the United Irishmen worldwide. Although small-scale escapes and unrealized shadowy plots continued for some years, co-ordinated resistance to the will of the colonial government apparently collapsed. The factors underlying this apparent collapse include the gradual dispersal of the most dynamic leadership figures, the lure of early emancipation for good behaviour and, perhaps, a sense of futility stemming from repeated military failure in the

40 Petition of Joseph Holt, n.d. [1804], quoted in Rusden, *Curiosities of colonization*, p. 83.
41 O'Shaughnessy, *Adventures of Joseph Holt*, p. 79.
42 O'Donnell, 'Marked for Botany Bay', pp 490–96; R.W. Connell, 'The convict rebellion of 1804' in *Melbourne Historical Journal*, v (1965), 27–37; and J.G. Symes, *The Castle Hill rebellion of 1804* (Sydney, 1990).

context of extreme geographic isolation. Also important was the notably benign attitude exhibited towards the Irish prisoners by Governor Lachlan Macquarie whose lengthy reign commenced in 1810. It was during the 'Macquarie era' that the substantial, if increasingly diluted, United Irish community established themselves as an integral part of colonial society and were to display impressive feats in the fields of business, surveying, construction and exploration.

31

Ireland, America and the transformation of US politics, 1783–1800

MAURICE J. BRIC

On 8 July 1776, John Nixon read the proclamation of American independence in Philadelphia. It was to be the capital of the new republic until 1800, the city where Americans sought to develop structures of government and society that would be stable and free from the political troubles and social and religious schisms that characterised contemporary Europe. However, the old world was not rejected as a matter of course and the founding fathers drew on the ideas of both classical republicanism and the traditional British polity to develop the basis of their own political experiment in America. Ever since the Pilgrims had landed in 1620, this balance between old and new had given America its peculiarity. Now that the Peace of Paris had formally recognized American independence in 1783, many felt that this characteristic would be harder to promote as an 'awakened democracy' moved, in Carl Becker's well-known words, from considering 'who should rule' to 'who should rule at home'. The new political community would be dynamic, less exclusive, and led not just by those men whose inherited wealth and status made them 'natural leaders'. The case can be made that Irish immigrants in the American capital city, and the group making up the American Society of United Irishmen in particular, were major catalysts in the invention of the 'new politics' in America and the reinvention of the republic.[1]

Since the beginning of the eighteenth century, more Irish immigrants flowed into Philadelphia than into any other destination in North America. During the 1770s their political experience, sense of organization and commitment to patriotism made many of them natural and active supporters of the American Revolution. After 1783, however, these same traits were less attractive in a coun-

---

1 Carl Becker, *The history of political parties in the province of New York, 1760–1776* (Madison, 1960), p. 22; J.F. Jameson, *The American Revolution as a social movement* (Princeton, 1926), p. 11. The substance of this paper is discussed in greater length in M.J. Bric, 'Ireland, Irishmen, and the broadening of the late eighteenth-century Philadelphia polity' (unpublished Ph.D. thesis, Johns Hopkins University, 1990). For their comments, I would like to thank Thomas Bartlett, David Dickson and James McGuire.

try that wanted to settle into its independence. National consolidation demanded that ethno-cultural peculiarity and organization should come second to what one observer called 'the establishment of ... the national character of America'. For Thomas Jefferson, immigrants should not promote 'the principles of the governments' from which they came in Europe. Otherwise, 'these principles, with their language, they will transmit to their children ... and infuse into [American legislation] their spirit, warp and bias its directions, and render it a heterogenous, incoherent, distracted mass'. Thus, the objective of the founding fathers was, in George Washington's words, a country that would 'soon become one people'.[2]

The political corollary was to see the polity as a single interest. This had been central to the British system and implied that the political establishment, however defined or limited, was 'morally superior' to everybody else and as such, could represent the interests of society as a whole. Although the various colonial establishments were broadened during the course of the eighteenth century, this old world view of representation and government did not: in Pennsylvania, it dominated political thinking into the 1790s. It was also central to George Washington's denunciations of 'party' politics, the best known of which he included in his 'farewell address' in 1796:

> Combinations and associations ... [were] potent engines ... by which cunning, ambitious, and unprincipled men will be enabled to ... [agitate] the community with ill-founded jealousies and false alarms; [kindle] the animosity of one part against another; [and foment] occasionally riot and insurrection.[3]

The tranquillity and security of the new republic could be undermined by enemies from within as well as from without.

As the most obvious sign of diversity, immigrants became for many the anti-heroes of the new republic. During the 1780s Pennsylvania's dominant political faction, the Constitutionalists, were 'outsiders' not just because they were 'new' but because they were led by the Dublin-born George Bryan and his 'Irish colonels'. Bryan's critics castigated the state's new leaders as 'upstart' immigrants who were unfamiliar with government, of poor circumstances and education, and violent and troublesome. It was a short step from characterizing these

2 *National Gazette*, 12 Dec. 1792; Thomas Jefferson, 'Notes on Virginia' in Andrew Lipscomb and Albert Bergh (eds), *The writings of Thomas Jefferson* (Washington, 1905), ii, pp 120–1; Jared Sparks (ed.), *The writings of Washington* (Boston, 1834–7) xi, p. 2. For the Irish and the American Revolution, see M.J. Bric, 'Ireland, America and the reassessment of a special relationship 1760–1783', in *Eighteenth-century Ireland*, xi (1996), 88–119.

3 R.A. Ryerson, 'Republican theory and partisan reality: Toward a new view of the Constitutionalist Party', in Ronald Hoffman and P.J. Albert (eds), *Sovereign states in an age of uncertainty* (Charlottesville, Va., 1981), p. 114; W.C. Ford (ed.), *The writings of George Washington* (New York, 1889–93), xxxv, pp 214–38.

Irish leaders as 'numsculs' to deeming them to be 'unpatriotic' and 'unreliable' midwives of the new government. They were, as George Clymer put it, 'men of narrow souls, and of *no natural interest in society*, who can only support themselves by sacrificing to the vulgar and sordid motives of the populace'. Against this background, an ethno-cultural language was developed to attack a political enemy as well as articulate more general criticisms and insecurities about the nature and pace of change in the new republic. Thus, Benjamin Rush concluded in November 1782 that the contemporary 'horrors of a civil war to gratify ... ambition and personal resentments [in Pennsylvania] ... is the consequence of strangers and vagrants intermeddling in our politics'.[4] It did not matter that Bryan was as committed as any of his colonial predecessors to the notion of the single-interest polity, or that he sought to work within the established boundaries of political behaviour.

Bryan's views were also reflected in the constitution of the Society of the Lately Adopted Sons of Pennsylvania, with which the Constitutionalists and their Irish supporters were identified. The preamble made the general point that 'jealousies, engendered by national distinctions ... invariably [weakened] ... the principle of common attachment, which is the firmest support of every country'. Article V specifically rejected 'the idea of forming a separate class from the body of the people', while article VI prohibited any 'collective influence' to 'induce the members of this association to adopt the sentiments and support the measures of any particular party'. Other commentaries also cautioned against making distinctions between 'adopted sons' and 'old inhabitants'.[5] The Sons disparaged the views of people such as Rush and underlined the fact that the Irish-born leaders who were involved in building the new state and nation were as cautious and conventional as any native-born with roots a generation or two in the colonial past.

Philadelphia's Friendly Sons of St Patrick also believed that they neither did nor should have a public role. This society had been founded in 1771 by wealthy merchants who were tied by family and business links. After 1790, however, 'new Irish' immigrants emerged in the city who were less deferential and more politically experienced than their pre-revolutionary cousins. They were also more self-assured and rejected the notion that any kind of assertiveness, whether this was expressed in 'ethno-cultural' or political terms, would disturb 'domestic tran-

4   George Clymer to George Fitzsimons: Historical Society of Pennsylvania (H.S.P.), Gratz collection, case 1, box 19; Rush to George Montgomery, 5 Nov. 1782: L.H. Butterfield (ed.), *Letters of Benjamin Rush* (Princeton, 1951), i, pp 291–3. The characterizations of the Constitutionalists and their Irish supporters are taken from Bric, 'Philadelphia polity', ch. 3. For Bryan's views on the polity and political organization, see J.S. Foster, *In pursuit of equal liberty: George Bryan and the revolution in Pennsylvania* (University Park, Pa., 1994).
5   [Philadelphia] *Independent Gazetteer*, 28 Jan. 1786; *Pennsylvania Evening Herald*, 9 Nov., 10 Dec. 1785.

quillity', create distinctions between the native and foreign-born, 'raise sedition' and convey the very 'highest ingratitude to the country in which we receive our bread'.[6] Therefore, the Hibernian Society which was founded in 1791, and the American Society of United Irishmen which was active in the city from 1796 or so, evolved a character that was quite different from that of the Friendly Sons. The 'new Irish' saw no contradiction between criticisms of the established government on the one hand and, on the other, of the general political and social progress of the new republic.

During the 1790s, such people found a natural home among Jeffersonian republicans who, at the level of high politics, were also rejecting the single-interest polity and the politics of accommodation. For Jefferson and his supporters the 'genius of republican liberty' was that 'all power derived from the people', not from background, birth or class, as was the case in much of the Old World. However, Federalists such as John Jay were loath to give too much power to those who were 'unused to public affairs', or if born outside the United States, had not experienced 'a long residence in the country … to appreciate the genius of the American government'. Accordingly, Jay suggested in the *Federalist Papers* that the indirect election of the president and senate would guarantee more 'virtue' and objective concern for 'the public good' than any representative who was chosen by the people in their 'collective capacity'. The result was a system of indirect election whereby the president was chosen by an Electoral College and senators nominated by their respective state legislatures.[7] However, the differing views on the active as opposed to the rhetorical role of the citizen in the new republic did not cease with the adoption of the constitution. The sneer that to be 'true Federalists, we must be at once deaf, dumb and blind; we must hear nothing, say nothing, see nothing' echoed among Philadelphia's 'new Irish' for whom the Federalist stress on stability, harmony, homogeneity and 'natural leadership' did not provide a comfortable home, either temperamentally or politically.[8] In contrast, the Jeffersonian emphasis on the integrity of the citizen above all else would enable new structures to be invented and justified at both ethno-cultural

6 *Pennsylvania Packet*, 2 Dec. 1785. For a discussion of Irish immigration and Philadelphia's ethno-cultural organizations after 1783, see M.J. Bric, 'The Irish emigration to America after the Peace of Paris', *Journal of Interdisciplinary History* (forthcoming). I am taking my characterisation of these societies as 'ethno-cultural' rather than 'national' or 'ethnic' from the work of A.W. Tully; see especially his 'Ethnicity, religion, and politics in early America', in *Pennsylvania Magazine of History and Biography* (1983), 431–536. Tully regards the term 'ethno-cultural' as preferable to any other as it suggests 'a far greater range of characteristics than the religion or ethnicity with which writers have largely been concerned', ibid., p. 492n.

7 Jonathan Elliot (ed.), *Debates on the adoption of the Federal constitution* (Philadelphia, 1861), v, pp 398–9; M.N.S. Sellers, *American republicanism* (London, 1994), pp 238–40.

8 The quotation is from J. M. Smith, *Freedom's fetters: The Alien and Sedition Laws and American civil liberties* (Ithaca, 1956), p. 177. For a short discussion of the theme of 'natural leadership' under the first Federalist administrations, see T.P. Govan, 'The rich, the well born, and Alexander Hamilton', in *Mississippi Valley Historical Review*, xxxvi (1949–50), 675–80.

and political levels, and allow the 'new Irish' to interact with the 'new politics', to the advancement of both.

This process is usually, if somewhat narrowly, described as 'the rise of the first party system'. In Philadelphia it was signalled by a contested Congessional election in 1794 when ('to the astonishment of all parties') John Swanwick defeated the incumbent, Thomas Fitzsimons in, as James Madison put it, a 'stinging change for the aristocracy'. This election is significant in a number of ways. The first is implied in the following criticism of what Fitzsimons had earlier dismissed as the 'new style' of politics:

> The friends of the candidates had previously been satisfied to use their influence, in private, among their own particular friends; whilst the objects of their choice, observing a reserve and decorum, evinced a becoming respect for public opinion and permitted it to take its own direction without an unfair bias.

For Fitzsimons, candidates for office were 'unworthy of the station *if they would stoop to solicit it.*' This was not Swanwick's view of the path to success and his campaign was taken by some as pandering to the 'awakened democracy' and giving it a hold over elected representatives that was anathema to the city's established political arrangements. 'It is not in a crowd', warned one Federalist observer, 'that the small voice of reason is held.'[9]

Fitzsimons was also a member of the 'aristocratic junto' which had run Philadelphia for several years as well as being a Friendly Son. Swanwick was neither. Instead, he was a member of the Hibernians and appealed to the 'outs' of the city and in particular, to the 'new Irish' immigrants who were arriving in America from the politically-charged atmosphere at home. Moreover, his election established what were to be the most enduring pockets of Jeffersonian electoral strength in Philadelphia: the areas of 'new Irish' settlement in the city's northern and southern Liberties and the peripheral wards of North and South Mulberry.[10] As such, the election revealed the changes that were taking place in the city's overall political style as well as in the nature, leadership and political culture of Philadelphia's Irish community.

It also challenged the received wisdom of traditional political behaviour in at least one other way. Swanwick had urged the Administration to retaliate against

9   Samuel Clark to Jones, 15 Oct. 1794: H.S.P., U.C. Smith-William Jones Correspondence; Madison to Jefferson, 16 Nov. 1794: quoted in M.I.J. Griffin, *Thomas Fitzsimons* (Philadelphia, 1887), p. 19; Fitzsimons to Rush, 12 May 1790: *Gazette of the United States (G.U.S.)*, 3, 11, 13 Oct. 1794. For the evolution of party, see W.N. Chambers and Walter Burnham (eds), *The American party systems: Stages of political development* (New York, 1975).
10 E.E. Rasmusson, 'Democratic experiment – aristocratic aspiration', *P.M.H.B.*, xc (1966), 155–82; Richard Miller, *Philadelphia, the Federalist city: A study of urban politics, 1789–1801* (Port Washington, 1976), pp 93–4.

Britain for its treatment during searches of America's 'neutral' vessels on the high seas. These calls were tough and uncompromising, and although they addressed an important area of public policy, they also helped to revive anti-British slogans as a system of political protest in the United States. In narrower terms, however, these catchwords were interpreted in their own ways by the 'new Irish' and became part of their emerging vocabulary of ethno-cultural expression in America at a time when Republicans were trying to demonstrate that they were making common cause with the 'new Irish' against a corrupt and despotic British belief system.[11] As Swanwick consolidated the Irish sub-set of his electoral coalition, the 'new style' language of his campaign and his politics suited both the social and political aspects of Jeffersonian republicanism.

In the event, Swanwick's appeals to government were not heeded and in 1795 Jay's treaty was concluded between Britain and the United States. However, most Jeffersonians argued that the treaty had given too many concessions to the former mother country. As such, it was widely denounced in Philadelphia where many Irish leaders, including the United Irish emigré Archibald Hamilton Rowan, organized meetings and petitions against the treaty as it was being discussed in Congress during June and July 1795. The presence of Irish immigrants at the anti-treaty meetings was widely commented upon; Rowan was described as having '[recently] taken refuge among us, from the despotism of his native country'. Given his recent career and reputation, Rowan had a powerful influence on his listeners. In Philadelphia, he shared a house with a number of congressmen and was befriended by powerful figures such as George Logan, John Dickinson, Caesar Rodney and, as Carey put it, 'thousands of kindly souls, who sympathize in his sufferings'. He was also said to 'amuse himself with the politics of America, and [here] is as busy, as sincere, and as zealous as he was in Kilmainham jail'. Indeed, the encouragement 'that every good citizen … [should] kick this damned [Jay's] treaty to Hell' was often cited afterwards as an example of the disruptive influence of the Irish immigrant on American politics.[12]

From a 'new Irish' point of view however, the Federalist administrations of Washington and John Adams were under 'a very strong British influence … [which] alarms the sensible and observant friends to general freedom'. Therefore, even before the anti-treaty protests of 1795 and the unfolding of the Jeffersonian movement, many Federalists in the nation's capital were reported to

11 Washington signed the Declaration on Neutrality on 22 Apr. 1793. For the policy of American neutrality at a time of international conflict, see A.H. Bowman, *The struggle for neutrality: Franco-American diplomacy during the Federalist era* (Knoxville, 1974), and Alexander DeConde, *The quasi-war: The politics and diplomacy of the undeclared naval war with France, 1777–1801* (New York, 1966).

12 Mathew Carey to John Chambers, 19 June 1794: H.S.P., Lea and Febiger collection, letterbooks (1792–7); *G.U.S.*, 27 July 1795; [Philadelphia] *Aurora*, 29 July 1795; *N.S.*, 27 July 1795; Free Library of Philadelphia, Carsan collection; Miller, *Philadelphia*, p. 72.

be 'very uneasy' at the 'flocking out' to America of 'such numbers' of Irish migrants. Moreover, once they arrived and became politically active, they fed and fed off the developing ethno-cultural vocabulary and rhetoric that was becoming an ever more prominent feature of the 'rage of party'. In this context, some suggested that the 'new Irish' were 'un-American'. As one writer put it, they were 'aliens by birth, [and] enemies to America in principle' and as such, could never become 'good citizens'.[13]

In the context of the times, however, it was easier to stigmatise immigrants by focusing on their organized clubs and associations than dismissing them in stereotype. Between 1796 and 1800 the most pointed of these attacks were reserved for the American Society of United Irishmen which was headquartered in Philadelphia. The original society had been founded in Belfast in October 1791. However, after it was proscribed in May 1794, some of its more influential leaders, including Rowan, Theobald Wolfe Tone, James Reynolds and James Napper Tandy, emigrated at least temporarily to Philadelphia. There, given the international nature of their networks and republican ideology, they were exiles rather than immigrants. Accordingly, a United Irish 'entertainment' in the city in July 1795 toasted '*The Emigrant Irish Republicans* – soon and successful be their return'.[14]

It is difficult to say when precisely Philadelphia's United Irishmen were founded; the society was acknowledged in St Patrick's Day toasts in the city in 1795. The organization was an important addition to Philadelphia's volatile politics because it combined international networks with domestic populism, and it was a loud and strong voice steering the votes of the Irish community towards the developing Jeffersonian coalition. As a result, the term 'United Irishman' evolved in Federalist Philadelphia as one that was associated with international conspiracy and political agitation. The society was for 'vagabonds, and renegades of Ireland, outlaws, assassins, traitors and fugitives from justice of every description'. However, Federalists regarded the United Irishmen as not only 'disaffected Irishmen' but as a group of men 'disaffected with the government of the United States' who would 'aid the French [and] if occasion should serve, [act] against the Government of the United States'. To this extent, the radical Irish could never become 'truly American':

> Believe one whose country is America, [your] various tricks will not avail you towards forming a character which you were never intended for ...

13 Chambers to Carey, 26 Mar. 1794: H.S.P., Lea and Febiger collection, incoming correspondence (1785–96), box 4, John Chambers folder; letter dated from Philadelphia, 27 Aug. 1795, as published in *N.S.*, 27 Aug. 1795; *G.U.S.*, 28 Mar. 1796. For a discussion of the 'monarchical' and 'aristocratic' disposition of the Washington and Adams administrations, see Marshall Smelser, 'Jacobin phrenzy: The menace of monarchy, plotocracy, and anglophobia, 1789–1798', in *Review of Politics*, xxi (1959), 239–58.
14 *Aurora*, 11 July 1795.

The American disposition delights in uprightness, and every species of ingeniousness; the outcast [United] Irishman in injustice and every species of low deception. The American uses every effort to promote the welfare of his country, and especially to support the laws and constituted authorities; the abandoned Irishman's chief pride is to destroy his country's decreed rights, to trample down her laws, and overturn her legal power – ferocious by nature, licentious by inclination; no laws divine or human, will deter the one, or restrain the other – Lay these characteristics seriously to heart; they are such as experience will confirm; and say whether you think it possible [that] you [Irish] can become American, by the practices of those arts which now hail you chief of a faction.[15]

For the Federalists, the United Irishmen were not just domestic political challengers. They were also part of an international affiliation which, on one level, actively sought French support for the Irish brotherhood. The French minister for foreign affairs, Charles Delacroix, even suggested that his country might channel 'military stores' to Ireland through Philadelphia while the informer Leonard McNally alleged that plans for the ill-fated French expedition to Bantry Bay (1796) were known and discussed in Philadelphia three months before it actually took place.[16] On another level, Ireland was regarded as only one *milieu* for radical republican activity. The Federalist editor, William Cobbett observed that:

Americans, then, and Britons, and Frenchmen, and men of every country being eligible to the society [of United Irishmen], can any one be silly enough to suppose that the [United Irish] conspiracy had only Ireland in view?

The publication of the XYZ dispatches in April 1798 exacerbated Federalist paranoia, summoned Washington out of retirement and moved America close to war with France. Americans were warned to be 'watchful' lest the United Irishmen, in alliance with their Jacobin friends in France, would 'bring on a revolutionary state' in the new republic. Having reminded his readers of the Bantry Bay expedition, one editor wondered if the United Irishmen would 'give the same invitation for our country'?[17]

15 *G.U.S.*, 5 Dec., 27 Nov. 1798, 7 Mar. 1799; *Porcupine's Gazette* (*P.G.*), 21 Dec. 1798. For a more extensive analysis of the United Irishmen in the greater Philadelphia area, see also Bric, 'Philadelphia polity', ch. 8, and D.A. Wilson, *United Irishmen, United States …* (Dublin, 1998).
16 For Delacroix's suggestion, see R. Barry O'Brien (ed.), *The autobiography of Theobald Wolfe Tone, 1763–1798* (London, 1893), i, p. 240. McNally is quoted in Rupert Coughlan, *Napper Tandy* (Dublin, 1977), p. 111.
17 William Cobbett, *Detection of a conspiracy formed by the United Irishmen with the evident intention of aiding the tyrants of France in subverting the government of the United States of America* in *Porcupine's Works*, viii, pp 203–4; *G.U.S.*, 18 Dec. 1798; *Massachusetts Mercury*, 8 Jan. 1798. For

It was in the light of these concerns that the progress of the 1798 rebellion was reported in the contemporary American press. *The Gazette of the United States* alleged that the cruelties, confusion and violence of the rebellion were a 'consequence of the principles and practices of the United Irishmen'. The more pointed argument was made in John Jay's advice to the secretary of state, Timothy Pickering, that if the United Irishmen were indulged in either Philadelphia or Ireland, America 'would become the theatre of scenes resembling those which have been exhibited by their brethren' in Europe. As the *Gazette* put it on 19 November 1798;

> Our own country [now] fosters in its bosom multitudes of wretches animated by the same infamous principles, and actuated by that same thirst for blood and plunder, which has reduced France to a vast human slaughter-house. The hordes of United Irishmen in America are alone sufficient for a most extensive scene of ruin, and little doubt can be entertained that they are preparing for it.

Federalists suggested that the very independence as well as the security of the new republic would be threatened if 'Irish ways' were allowed to develop in the United States. These were 'utterly inconsistent with any practicable or settled form of Government', and lead to both a diplomatic campaign to keep United Irishmen from emigrating to America and a domestic policy to check their impact on local politics.[18]

Discussion on the aims, real and imagined, of the United Irishmen in America also helped to revive the view that although a republic derived its energy ultimately from its citizens, the polity could be imbalanced and corrupted if the people were too powerful. In John Adams' view this had happened in ancient Rome, where it had precipitated the collapse of what had previously been the greatest republic of all. Therefore as the United Irishmen became more and more associated with the 'new style' of politics during the second half of the 1790s, their activities encouraged not only a sense of paranoia that there were 'wild Irishmen' under every Federalist's bed' but re-animated the debate about the role of the foreign-born in American politics. From 1796, the United Irishmen were allegedly keeping anti-British feeling high in the nation's capital and infusing it into toasts, orations and addresses, contributing to the evolution of a more identifiable 'party' vocabulary for Jeffersonian republicanism. Cobbett's *Porcupine's Gazette* concluded on 12 May 1797 that 'foreign influence

the controversy surrounding the 'XYZ' dispatches, see Manning Dauer, *The Adams Federalists* (Baltimore, 1968).

18 Jay to Pickering, 17 Aug. 1797: Massachusetts Historical Society, Pickering papers; *G.U.S.*, 22 Nov. 1798, 30 Mar. 1799. The final quotation is from Robert Ernst, *Rufus King* (Chapel Hill, 1968), p. 261.

has with us directed, ruled, and managed all our divisions, with a view to produce the greatest possible effect upon our public councils'.[19]

The most controversial activity of this kind took place during October 1797
when an election was held for a state senator to represent part of the greater
Philadelphia area. Although this election was for a relatively minor public office,
at least as office was estimated in the nation's capital, it marked one of the most
powerful appearances to date of two mutually exclusive political organizations
and election machines, and was as significant for broadening Philadelphia's
active polity as that of Swanwick had been for denting the 'old junto' in 1794.
Given that the district included the Liberties as well as other areas of 'new Irish'
strength, it was inevitable that images and counter-images of the United
Irishmen would become prominent features of the contest. The 1797 election
marked not only a milestone of the 'first party system' but it highlighted how far
Philadelphia had come from the politics of 'anti-party'.

The two candidates were the Federalist, Benjamin Morgan and the Jeffersonian, Israel Israel. Israel was an active member of the Presbyterian Church
and had been prominent in the organizations founded to alleviate the distresses
of the yellow fever epidemic of 1793. As a tavern keeper and leading light among
the city's immigrant communities, he personified all that was undesireable in a
public representative in Federalist eyes. Israel brushed off Federalist aspersions
and, 'disorganizer [and] bloody Jacobin' though some deemed him to be, he was
elected by 309 votes. In the 'new Irish' enclaves of the northern Liberties and
Southwark, Israel achieved margins of 534 and 423 respectively over Morgan.
However, objections were lodged that several had voted without 'the necessary
qualifications' and that Israel had been elected only after 'procuring hordes of
United Irishmen to be admitted to the rights of citizenship, in order to influence
the election'. Israel's election was successfully challenged and a second contest
was fixed for Washington's next birthday, 22 February 1798.[20]

The second campaign was fiercely fought. Meetings were held, committees
formed, and support for each of the candidates published in the form of person-
alised letters. One published on behalf of Morgan sums up the attitudes of his
canvassers:

> The supporters of Benjamin R. Morgan are the supporters of the laws,
> the friends of peace ... the sober, discreet, substantial house-keepers, the
> industrious, thriving citizens who possess property ... They are the

19 E.C. Carter II, 'A "Wild Irishman" under every Federalist's bed: Naturalization in Philadelphia,
    1789–1806', in *P.M.H.B.*, xciv (1970), 331–46.
20 *P.G.*, 14 Feb. 1798; *Aurora*, 9, 12 Oct. 1797; *Philadelphia Gazette*, 25 Jan., 17 Feb. 1798; *G.U.S.*,
    19, 20 Feb. 1798. For Israel's involvement in alleviating the yellow fever epidemics, see J.H.
    Powell, *'Bring out your dead': The great plague of yellow fever in Philadelphia in 1793* (Phila-
    delphia, 1949).

fathers of families, who love the country in which they were born, and who exult in handing down to their posterity that independence ... those laws, rights and privileges for which they fought, bled and conquered. They are the friends of Benjamin R. Morgan.

In contrast, Jefferson's adherents were:

Men who hate the constitution, and the civil and moral principles which form the basis of our independence and security ... [T]hey revile ... all that is dear and sacred to freemen ... [T]hey take part with the domestic and foreign enemies of the United States ... [and] they anticipate the time when the floods of licentiousness shall sweep away all the principles that gave [us] peace and security in life, or hope in the hour of dissolution.

In short, 'A Country Elector' concluded, Morgan for one had not been 'poisoned by French politics'.[21]

This was a highly partisan view of the two candidates, but the question as to whether 'every man whose private interests have brought him here, or whose public *crimes* have driven him from his own country, shall the moment he touches the soil of America, possess the power of legislating the rights of property, of personal liberty, and personal security' in America was an emotive one which awakened latent prejudices as well as partisan objections. Republicans rejected such reflections as 'indecent and groundless', and suggested that Israel and his radical Irish supporters were being vilified 'by the instruments of a British faction'. Charge and counter-charge continued, and the castigation of immigrant voters as violent, corrupt and easily bought by alcohol, was rehearsed and repeated. The inspectors of election addressed the question of voter eligibility by announcing that election supervisors would ask electors if they were native to Pennsylvania, and if not, whether they had been resident in the state for at least two years, had ever sworn allegiance to 'any foreign country', had taken the required oaths of citizenship, and had paid the required county or state taxes. In themselves, these questions proved so contentious that the state's chief justice (and Jefferson's friend) Thomas McKean questioned their validity in a broadside circulated on the day before the election. However, the questions were asked. In this charged atmosphere Israel lost the election by 357 votes.[22]

Morgan's election was seen as an important victory in curbing the power of Irish immigrants in Philadelphia politics. However it did not close the issue, and indeed led Pickering to revisit the existing immigration and naturalization laws

21 *G.U.S.*, 22, 15 Feb. 1798.
22 Ibid., 15 Feb. 1798; *Philadelphia Gazette*, 14 Feb. 1798; *American Daily Advertiser*, 21 Feb. 1798; Library Company of Philadelphia (L.C.P.), broadsides collection, Ab (1798) 23, 'Questions to be Put to the Electors', Ab (1798) 8, 'Opinion of Chief Justice McKean'; *Aurora*, 24 Feb. 1798.

to ensure that the suffrage and public office would be free from 'foreign influence'. Although this review had been urged for some years (since at least Swanwick's election), Pickering was now being briefed by Rufus King, John Jay and others to regard the radical Irish as 'pernicious to the order and industry of our people ... [and would] never become useful citizens'. The subsequent debates on the naturalization, alien and sedition laws allowed all these issues to be aired with unprecedented force and divisiveness.[23]

The naturalization act of 1795 had stipulated that immigrants could apply for American citizenship after a five-year residence. By 1797, however, many Federalists were convinced that most of the recently-naturalized citizens voted for Jeffersonian candidates and this coloured their views of the act. Congressman John Allen of Connecticut referred to 'the vast number of naturalizations which lately took place in this city [Philadelphia] to support a particular party in a particular election'. Thus, the local contest between Morgan and Israel impacted on the discussions of the national congress in this vital area. The party-political undertones of the debates were not lost on anyone. Swanwick, for example, rejected one proposal to impose a $20 tax on certificates of naturalization as penalizing the 'poor emigrant'. Another proposal to raise the period of naturalization to at least ten years gave the principal Federalist sponsors, congressmen Harrison Grey Otis and Robert Goodloe Harper, an opportunity to expound on the supposedly dangerous influences of the 'wild Irish'.[24]

Harper asserted that more restrictive measures would enable the United States to 'recover from the mistake [that it] ... fell into when it first began to form its constitutions, of admitting foreigners to citizenship ... [a] mistake ... productive of very great evils to this country'. Harper also made the most often quoted observation in this connection: he 'did not wish to invite hordes of wild Irishmen, nor the turbulent and disorderly of all parts of the world, to come here to disturb our tranquillity'. Harper thus argued that at its simplest, 'strangers ... however acceptable they may be in other respects, could not have the same views and attachments with native citizens'. In the event, although the tax on certificates was fixed at $5, the period of naturalization was extended from five to fourteen years.[25]

The exchanges on the alien and sedition acts developed these and other themes of the debate on the naturalization bill. The Alien Friends Act (22 June

23 Charles King (ed.), *The life and correspondence of Rufus King* (New York, 1894–1900), ii, p. 348.
24 *The debates and proceedings in the Congress of the United States*, fifth Congress (2nd session), 1578, debates of 3 May 1798; (1st session), 422–3, debates of 1 July 1797; (2nd session), 1567–8, debates of 2 May 1798. Swanwick made particular reference to the ways in which 'the poor wanderer, flying from the hearth-tax in Ireland', would be affected by the proposed charges: ibid., p. 424. Unless otherwise noted, all subsequent references to congressional debates are to those of the fifth congress which sat between 15 May 1797 and 3 Mar. 1799.
25 *Debates of Congress* (2nd session), 1567, debates of 2 May 1798; (1st session), 430, debates of 1 July 1798; (2nd session), 1568, debates of 2 May 1798; *Stats. at Large*, i, pp 566–9.

1798) allowed the president to deport any alien he deemed to be dangerous to the peace and safety of the union or whom he suspected – with or without evidence – was 'in treasonable or secret machinations against the government'. It also tightened the conditions under which emigrants entered the United States by obliging ship captains to give detailed reports of the numbers, origin and description of his passengers. The Alien Enemies Act (26 June 1798) proclaimed that resident aliens of a country with which the United States was in a 'declared war' became *ipso facto*, 'alien enemies' and could be 'apprehended, restrained, secured and removed, as alien enemies' by presidential proclamation. The Sedition act (July 1798) also contained proposed fines, periods of imprisonment, or deportation for those who:

> Shall unlawfully combine or conspire together, with intent to oppose any measure or measures of the government of the United States ... counsel, advise or attempt to procure any insurrection, riot, unlawful assembly, or combination ... write, print, utter or publish ... any false, scandalous and malicious writing or writings against the government of the United States ... stir up sedition ... for opposing or resisting any law of the United States, *or any act of the President* ... encourage or abet any hostile designs of any foreign nation.

Given their sweeping powers, both the Alien and Sedition Acts were considered by many contemporaries to constitute an excessive interference with both personal liberty and the liberty of the press, and by two later historians as *Freedom's fetters* and *A crisis in freedom*.[26]

Given the thrust of these laws and the issues that they raised, opposition feelings ran high among Irish immigrants and active Jeffersonian republicans. In the opinion of the editor of the *Aurora*, the Clonmel-educated William Duane, if these provisions were enacted, Irish immigrants would be 'cut off from the prospect of that freedom which was the cardinal inducement of their removal from Europe to the United States'. As such, they led to the 'Plea of Erin', a petition organized by the city's United Irishmen in February 1799. This initiative had two purposes. The first was to appeal against the legislation. The second was to counter the 'unjust impressions' and 'misrepresentations [that had been] incessantly propagated concerning us and our countrymen'. As a result, the so-called 'United Irish riot' ensued and a number of United Irishmen arrested. During the trial that followed, it was suggested that:

---

26 *Stats. at Large*, i, pp 570–2, 577–8; *Debates of Congress* (first session), 1798, debates of 25 June 1798. The text of the Sedition Act is in *Stats. at Large*, i, pp 596–7. See also Smith, *Freedom's fetters* and J.C. Miller, *Crisis in freedom: The Alien and Sedition Acts* (Boston, 1952).

> Aliens have no right whatsoever to … interfere in any respect with the government of this country … the greatest evils this country has ever endured have arisen from the ready admission of foreigners to a participation in the government and internal arrangements of the country … [An open door] to the oppressed of all countries … has been the bane of all countries … [and] had the Americans been left to themselves, we should not this day have been divided and rent into parties.[27]

It is easy to regard these and similar arguments as xenophobic. However, their true importance lies in the fact that they reflect an insecurity about the changing political complexion and developing pluralism of America's capital city. By virtue of their *arriviste* status and visible political organization, the 'new Irish' came to symbolize these changes. John Higham has defined this process as 'nativism', 'an aroused conviction that an intrusive element menaced the unity, and therefore the integrity and survival of the nation itself'. As a result, there was 'intense opposition to an internal minority on the grounds of its foreign [i.e. 'un-American'] connections'. At times of insecurity, it was more usual than not to focus on what was 'anti-American' and to articulate fears for the future in anti-immigrant terms.[28]

For many, the role that Irish immigrants and in particular, the American Society of United Irishmen, played in late eighteenth-century Philadelphia politics gave America its first bout of political nativism. The 'virtue and simplicity of the American character' had been supposedly sullied by the meddling of the 'new Irish'. This circuitous route to debating national identity, focusing on what it was not rather than on what it was, was not peculiar to America. However, as America sought to identify and invent a modern republic, the role of the United Irishmen in the transition from the introspective world of colonial politics to the more dynamic world of the new republic was clear. It helped to associate a new type of citizen with a new type of politics and, as such, to mark out the character of the modern republic.[29]

---

27 William Duane, *A report of the extraordinary transactions which took place at Philadelphia, in February 1799 in consequence of a memorial from certain natives of Ireland to Congress praying an repeal of the Alien Bill* (Philadelphia, 1799), p. 2; Library of Congress, Pennsylvania Broadsides (1799), 'The plea of Erin, or, The case of the natives of Ireland in the United States, fairly displayed'; Francis Wharton, *State trials of the United States* (Philadelphia, 1849).

28 John Higham, *Strangers in the land: Patterns of American nativism 1860–1925* (New York, 1973), pp 4–6.

29 John Adams to Mary Warren: 'Warren-Adams Letters', in *Collections of the Massachusetts Historical Society*, lxxxiii (1925), p. 202. For the ways in which the founding fathers saw the political economy of the new republic, see D.R. McCoy, 'Benjamin Franklin's vision of a republican political economy for America', in *William and Mary Quarterly*, xxxc (1978), 608–28; and Bric, 'Philadelphia Polity', ch. 5.

32

The United Irishmen and the re-invention of Irish America

DAVID WILSON

'Too many United Irishmen arrived here within a few Days', ran the diary entry of the New York printer Hugh Gaine in October 1798.[1] Born in Ireland, Gaine had been a prominent figure in New York's pre-revolutionary Irish community, and served as both treasurer and vice-president of the city's St Patrick Society. In 1776, he had came out against the American Revolution, and turned his *New York Gazette* into one of the leading loyalist newspapers in the country. Like most loyalists who remained in the United States, Gaine resurfaced as a High Federalist during the 1790s and advocated a close Anglo-American alliance against all manifestations of international 'Jacobinism'.[2] As a loyalist Irishman in republican America, he was filled with a kind of double horror when revolutionary democrats from his native country began pouring into his adopted one.

Gaine represents an important and often ignored strand in Irish-American politics. Generally speaking, historians have been happier quoting the Hessian officer who wrote during the War of Independence that he was up against 'nothing more or less than a Scotch Irish Presbyterian rebellion'.[3] Many of the 'Scotch Irish Presbyterians' who were patriots during the American Revolution also embraced the Federalist party in the 1790s. In the trans-Allegheny west, for example, fundamentalist Presbyterians of Irish ethnicity directed religious revivalism into conservative political channels. John McMillan, one of the most influential ministers in the Second Great Awakening, encountered a community of United Irishmen who had emigrated from Saintfield to Washington,

1 Hugh Gaine, 'Journal', 13 Oct. 1798, in *The journals of Hugh Gaine, printer*, ed. P.L. Ford, (New York, 1902), ii, p. 209; see also i, pp 64–5.
2 For connections between American Loyalists and Federalists, see W.N. Nelson, *The American Tory* (Boston, 1992), pp x–xi; H.B. Hancock, *The Loyalists of revolutionary Delaware* (Newark, 1977), pp 97–101, 112–7; Alfred Young, *The Democratic-Republicans of New York* (Chapel Hill, N.C., 1967), pp 566–7; J.E. Cooke, *Tenche Coxe and the Early Republic* (Williamsburg, Va., 1978); E.P. McCaughey, *From loyalist to founding father: The political odyssey of William Samuel Johnson* (New York, 1970).
3 See, for example, J.G. Leyburn, *The Scotch-Irish: A social history* (Chapel Hill, 1962), p. 305.

Pennsylvania: he immediately denounced them as 'taylors, silversmiths, baptists, followers of Tom Paine, with out-casts of all society'.[4] To counter the influence of such people, McMillan aligned himself with the Federalist politician James Ross, also of Irish ethnicity, who supported restrictive naturalization policies and the Alien and Sedition Laws.[5] In its 'Rules and Regulations' of 1798, the American Presbyterian Church adopted its internal version of the Alien Laws, and screened out immigrant ministers who brought the 'vain and pernicious philosophy' of democracy into the country.[6]

Such views were by no means confined to Irish Presbyterians; many Catholic Irish immigrants in the United States also gravitated towards the Federalists. Among them was Thomas Fitzsimons, a wealthy merchant who had helped to finance the American war effort, worked to extend the 'equal rights of citizenship' for American Catholics, became a founding member of the Hibernian Society, and represented Philadelphia in Congress between 1790 and 1794.[7] Fitzsimons worshipped at St Mary's church in Philadelphia, where a substantial majority of his co-religionists shared his Federalist views. In 1799, the United Irishman James Reynolds and three of his friends arrived at the church to gather petitions against the Alien Friends Law; they were driven out by hostile Irish Catholics who objected to their presence on both political and religious grounds. 'I felt myself hurt', complained James Gallagher, 'by the injury and insult done to my religion, making that a place of political meetings; and more so because I did not observe a single Catholic among them.'[8]

The conservative dimension of Irish-American politics was reinforced by the influx of Irish loyalists into the United States during and immediately after the 1790s. Claiming to have special knowledge of the conspiratorial machinations of Irish republicans, they warned Americans that the United Irishmen concealed revolutionary intentions beneath the cloak of patriotism, and should be looked upon 'as so many serpents within your bosom'. The Federalist press teemed with Irish-derived stories about United Irish secret societies with blood-thirsty oaths and passwords, and insisted that the American Society of United Irishmen was following similar procedures in pursuit of similar ends.[9] There was, in fact, a

4 *Washington Reporter*, 30 Jan. 1809. See also C.C. Cleveland, *The Great Revival in the West, 1797–1805* (Chicago, 1916; rpt. Gloucester, Mass., 1959); P.W. Conkin, *Cane Ridge: America's Pentecost* (Madison, Wi., 1990); J.B. Boles, *The Great Revival* (Lexington, Ky., 1972); T.L. Birch, *Seemingly experimental religion* (Washington, Pa., 1806).

5 *Washington Reporter*, 19 Sept. 1808; K.T. Phillips, *William Duane: Radical journalist in the age of Jefferson* (New York and London, 1989), pp 84–91.

6 *Minutes of the General Assembly of the Presbyterian Church in the United States of America 1798–1820* (Philadelphia, 1847), pp 148–9, 152–3, 172–3, 179–81, 202.

7 D.N. Doyle, *Ireland, Irishmen and Revolutionary America* (Cork, 1981), p. 190.

8 William Duane, *A Report of the extraordinary transactions which took place at Philadelphia, in February 1799* (Philadelphia, 1799), p. 7; *Gazette of the United States*, 11 Feb. 1799.

9 See, for example, *Gazette of the United States*, 21–22 Nov., 18 Dec. 1798; *Porcupine's Gazette*, 21 Nov. 1798.

Federalist-Irish loyalist alliance that persisted up to the War of 1812 and beyond. In 1814, the Irish immigrant William Heazleton wrote from Pittsburgh to his cousin in County Tyrone that the 'blagaird runaway united Irish men makes a Great fuss here but Getting out of creditt rapaidly. [T]hey are the onely people that I dislike for their bad Conduct and lying Stories that the[y] propagate against Ireland but the[y] are Coming fast down as the real americans dont like them on any acct. [W]hat I mean by Real Americans is the better Sort of people Call[ed] Federlists [*sic*].'[10]

It is clear, then, Irish America was by no means synonymous with radical republicanism. There were Irish Presbyterians who had opposed the Revolution, made peace with the new regime, and supported the Federalists. There were Irish Presbyterians and Irish Catholics who had supported the Revolution despite rather than because of its democratic tendencies, and who also moved into the Federalist camp. And there were recently-arrived loyalists who described themselves as the 'Anti-Jacobin Irish', inhabiting the border zone between High Federalism and Toryism. By becoming Federalists, these different groups were aligning themselves with 'Real Americans', and presenting the United Irishmen as a menacing alien presence. From this perspective, it is not surprising that some of the most virulent 'nativist' rhetoric directed towards the United Irishmen actually came from Irish loyalist immigrants.[11]

One of the most significant achievements of the United Irishmen in the United States was to obliterate politically the Federalist-Irish loyalist alliance. So total was their victory that today it takes an effort of will to remember that such an alliance ever existed, let alone that it was once in the political ascendant. By the time the United Irishmen had finished, the Federalists had become 'un-American', conservative Irish immigrants had become 'un-Irish', and Irish America had become exclusively associated with democratic republican nationalism.

Central to this process was the United Irishmen's close identification with the American revolutionary tradition, particularly in its Jeffersonian and Paineite ideological forms. In his *History of Virginia*, John Daly Burk argued that the American Revolution was the fulfilment of democratic destiny; similarly, his play *Bunker-Hill* featured banners that connected the 'spirit of '76' with slogans such as 'The Rights of Man', 'Liberty and Equality', and 'Hatred to Royalty'.[12] The Irish, it was argued, were in the vanguard of this struggle. 'We glory in the belief', wrote James Reynolds and William Duane, 'that of the Irish residents in the United

---

10 I would like to thank Kerby Miller for supplying me with this reference.
11 This comes out clearly in the New York election of 1807, when the Irish loyalist Stephen Carpenter Cullen complained bitterly that the radical Irish were destroying the true American character, and turning the United States into a 'multifarious heterogeneous compound'. See [New York] *People's Friend*, 2 May 1807.
12 John Burk, *The history of Virginia, from its first settlement to the present day* (Petersburg, Va., 1804–1805); ibid., *Bunker-Hill; or The death of General Warren* (New York, 1797), esp. p. 54.

States, a greater *proportion* partook of the hazards of the field and of the duties of your independent republican councils, than of the native Americans.'[13] Richard Montgomery, their fellow countryman who had fallen during the siege of Quebec in 1775, became a cult figure who exemplified the qualities of Irish courage, sacrifice, respectability and patriotism in the service of the United States.[14]

America and Ireland, argued the United Irish emigrés, were fighting for a common cause against a common enemy. There were pointed reminders that John Adams himself had adopted this position in 1775 when he asserted that America and Ireland were both victims of Britain's 'iniquitous schemes of extirpating liberty from the British empire', and praised the contribution of Irish patriots in 'the cause of humanity and America'. By 1798, the radicals were turning this language back on Adams, and presenting his support for the Alien and Sedition laws as a species of apostacy.[15] From this perspective, the Rising of 1798 was simply an Irish version of the Revolution of 1776. Like the Americans, the Irish had only turned to revolution once reform had failed; like the Americans, the Irish had sought the aid of France in a war of national liberation; like the Americans, the Irish had been denounced as demagogues. 'It is not a little flattering to be denominated rebels', declared one emigré in August 1798, 'by those who set a price upon the head of Washington, and exempted Samuel Adams and John Hancock from an amnesty, for being rebels!'[16] The key difference, in this view, was that Ireland had experienced a much greater degree of oppression than America had ever known; the Irish Revolution, therefore, was even more justified than the American.

In defining Americanism in ideological terms, in arguing that the Irish had been at the heart of the American revolutionary movement, and in viewing the American and Irish revolutions as local variants on the same theme, the United Irishmen in the United States were moving towards assimilation by syllogism. To be American, they argued, was to embrace democratic republicanism; the United Irishmen were the most democratic republican people; therefore, the United Irishmen were the most American people. This made the United Irishmen more American than the Federalists who happened to be born in the country, and even produced a form of reverse nativism that became increasingly powerful after Jefferson's victory in 1800.

13 *A memorial: To the Senate and House of Representatives. The respectful memorial of the subscribers, natives of Ireland, residing within the United States of America* [Philadelphia, 1798], p. 5.
14 See, for example, *Carey's United States Recorder*, 17, 19, 22 May 1798; *Aurora*, 19 Mar. 1807; John Binns, *An oration commemorative of the birth-day of American Independence, delivered before the Democratic Societies of the city and county of Philadelphia, on the 4th of July 1810* (Philadelphia, 1810).
15 [Continental Congress], *An address of the twelve United Colonies of North-America, by their representatives in Congress, to the people of Ireland* (Philadelphia, 1775), pp 4, 10; *Memorial*, op. cit., p. 6.
16 *Aurora*, 14 Aug. 1798.

The Federalists, from this perspective, were British puppets who were carry-ing the 'FOREIGN INFLUENCE' of royalism and aristocracy into the American republic.[17] Just as Britain had adopted divide-and-rule tactics to control Ireland, ran the argument, it was now fomenting divisions between Federalists and Republicans in America. Viewing American politics through Irish lenses, the United Irishmen believed that the Federalists were to the United States what the Orangemen were to Ireland – a faction that supported the British interest, spread the virus of monarchism, and subverted the liberty of the people. As such, they should be crushed rather than conciliated. There should be none of the 'We are all Federalists, we are all Republicans' nonsense, wrote Denis Driscol; Jefferson was behaving like a naive philosopher who did not realize that unless he eradicated the Federalists politically, they would eradicate the Republic.[18] And while it was permissible to criticize Jefferson from the left, criti-cism from the right was not to be tolerated. The people had spoken in 1800, and 'no man but a traitor to the country' could possibly argue with their choice. In attacking the government, it was argued, the Federalists were abusing the liberty of the press. Driscol, for one, had no doubt about the remedy. People who tra-duced Jefferson, he declared, should be '*tarred* and *feathered* and *sent off*, as *scapegoats*; and then we may piously hope that the country will be *saved*'.[19]

The country not only needed to be saved from the Federalists, but also from the foreigners who supported them. John Daly Burk, in a mirror-image of Federalism, blamed conservative British immigrants for America's difficulties, while Driscol railed at the '*Irish orange men*' who were coming into the country. William Duane was equally convinced that British agents were 'fomenting and upholding conspiracy in the bosom of our land'. In his milder moods, he wanted all such 'foreign spies and incendiaries' to be expelled from the country; in his more extreme moments, he wanted them hanged.[20]

By the time of the War of 1812, a striking reversal of roles had occurred, with the United Irishmen now playing the part that the High Federalists had assumed during the Quasi-War with France. During the Quasi-War, the High Federalists had argued that America was threatened from without by French imperialism, and from within by a combination of republican subversives and foreign agitators, not the least of whom were that 'restless, rebellious tribe' of

---

17 William Duane, *Politics for American farmers: Being a series of tracts, exhibiting the blessings of free government, as it is administered in the United States, compared with the boasted stupendous fabric of British monarchy* (Washington, 1807), p. 60.

18 *American Patriot*, 1 Feb. 1803.

19 *Temple of Reason*, 24 Jan. 1801; *American Patriot*, 8 Mar. 1803.

20 J.D. Burk, *An oration, delivered on the fourth of Mar., 1803, at the court-house, in Petersburg: to cel-ebrate the election of Thomas Jefferson, and the triumph of Republicanism* (Petersburg, Va., 1803), p. 12; *American Patriot*, 25 Sept. 1802; Duane, *Politics for American farmers*, p. 22; William Duane to James Madison, 1 Dec. 1809, in 'Letters of William Duane', *Massachusetts Historical Society*, 2nd. ser., xx (1906), 329.

United Irishmen.[21] Now, the boot was on the other foot; the external enemy was Britain, not France; the domestic traitors were Federalists, not republicans; and the foreign agitators were Loyalists, not democrats. Under these circumstances, the United Irishmen were able to identify themselves with American patriotism much more effectively than had been possible during the late 1790s. The War of 1812 allowed them simultaneously to affirm their allegiance to America and to avenge the defeat of the rising of 1798. The fate of America and the fate of Ireland were inseparable. 'This is the hour', declared an Irish Catholic militia officer in Baltimore, 'to humble the British tyrant in the dust, to complete the independence of America, and shatter into pieces the chains of poor unfortunate Ireland. Ireland will be rescued from British bondage on the plains of Canada, if Irishmen will, at this decisive moment, but religiously and gratefully discharge their duty, to both their adopted and native countries.'[22]

Within this general anti-British and anti-Federalist position, the United Irishmen were locked in combat with conservative Irish immigrants. This battle paralleled the broader conflict between Republicans and Federalists, and there is no doubt that the Republican victory of 1800 put not only the Federalists but also the conservative Irish on the defensive. But the intra-Irish struggle was particularly bitter, partly because of its origins in Ireland, and partly because nothing less than the political character of Irish America was at stake. In Philadelphia, radical Irish immigrants contributed to the defeat of Thomas Fitzsimons in the Congressional elections of 1794, and to the election of Thomas McKean as governor of Pennsylvania five years later; the fact that Reynolds and his companions were acquitted on charges of riot and assault after the so-called St Mary's Riot also indicated which way the wind was blowing. In Baltimore, the radical Irish journalists Samuel McCrea and Samuel Kennedy attempted to discredit a conservative Irish rival editor, George Gray, by smearing him as an informer in Ulster and as a British agent in America; both charges were proven to be false, but by that time the damage had been done.[23] And in New York, the state elections of 1807 revealed a major fissure in the city's Irish community.

The New York elections of 1807 have usually been viewed in terms of Thomas Addis Emmet's conflict with Rufus King, and the revenge of the state prisoners

21 William Cobbett, 'Detection of a conspiracy, formed by the United Irishmen', in D.A. Wilson (ed.), *Peter Porcupine in America: Pamphlets on republicanism and revolution* (Ithaca, N.Y., 1994), p. 242. See also J.M. Smith, *Freedom's fetters: The Alien and Sedition Laws and American civil liberties* (Ithaca, 1956), and John C. Miller, *Crisis in freedom: The Alien and Sedition Acts* (Boston, 1952).
22 *Shamrock*, 26 Sept. 1812.
23 Roland Baumann, 'The Democratic-Republicans of Philadelphia: The origins, 1776–1797' (unpublished Ph.D. thesis, Pennsylvania State University, 1970), pp 493–506; Maurice Bric, 'Ireland, Irishmen, and the broadening of the late eighteenth-century Philadelphia polity' (unpublished Ph.D. thesis, Johns Hopkins University, 1990), pp 466–591; William Duane, *A report of the extraordinary transactions which took place at Philadelphia, in February 1799* (Philadelphia, 1799); *American Patriot*, 21, 25 June 1803, 15, 17 Sept. 1803.

for King's successful attempt to keep them out of the United States in 1798.[24] But there was another, less noticed, side to the struggle. One of the candidates on King's 'American Ticket' was Andrew Morris, an Irish immigrant who had helped finance the construction of a Catholic church in the city. In April 1807, the United Irishman John Caldwell proposed in the Hibernian Provident Society that any member who voted for Morris should be expelled from the organisation. Amid fierce debate and angry charges that the Hibernian Provident Society was setting itself up as a dictatorial Jacobin club, thirty members stormed out in protest. They were supported by many of the city's earlier Irish immigrants, and by more recent loyalist arrivals who bristled at attempts to make 'Irishness' synonymous with democratic republicanism. All to no avail: the Federalists were hammered in the elections, and the conservative Irish attempt to 'rescue the national character' from the 'foul aspersions' of the United Irishmen suffered a serious setback.[25]

Although the Irish Federalists had been ousted from the Hibernian Provident Society and defeated politically, they remained a powerful presence in the Friendly Sons of St Patrick. In 1810, they invited the unpopular British minister Francis James Jackson to their St Patrick's Day dinner, much to the disgust of the United Irishmen; the air was thick with denunciations about 'orgies of tories' who disgraced the memory of St Patrick, and who were nothing more than 'West Britainers'. During the War of 1812, though, the balance of power shifted, and United Irishmen such as Emmet, MacNeven, Caldwell and Chambers were in the ascendant.[26]

By this time, the Federalists had been eclipsed, the conservative Irish had been isolated, and the United Irishmen had established themselves as the authentic voice of Irish America. In the process, they identified Irish America with the struggle for national independence back home. During the 1790s, Irish emigrés organised shipments of weapons and ammunition for the movement back home; as early as 1796, they were smuggling gunpowder to Belfast in flax seed cakes – the first recorded instance of what was to become a persistent Irish-American tradition. The United Irishmen in Philadelphia were in close contact with the Irish revolutionaries clustered around Robert Emmet, and sent pikes and cartridges to Ireland shortly before Emmet's attempted coup of 1803.[27]

24 See, for example, Harvey Strum, 'Federalist Hibernophobes in New York, 1807', in *Eire-Ireland*, xvi (1981), 7–13.
25 *Evening Post*, 4, 25 Apr. 1807; *Morning Chronicle*, 14 Apr. 1807; *People's Friend*, 6, 7, 9 Apr. 1807.
26 J.D. Crimmins, St *Patrick's Day: Its celebration in New York and other American places, 1737–1845* (New York, 1902), pp 131–2; R.C. Murphy and L.J. Mannion, *The history of the Society of the Friendly Sons of Saint Patrick in the city of New York 1784 to 1955* (New York, 1962), pp 166–8, 174–8, 194, 219; John Caldwell, 'Particulars of a North County Irish family', P.R.O.N.I., T.3541/5/3, p. 155.
27 James Durham to Revd Clotworthy Soden, 29 May 1798: N.A.I., RP 620/23/129; General Lake to — , 9 Jan. 1797: N.A.I., RP 620/28/75; Phineas Bond to Lord Hawkesbury, 14 Dec. 1803: P.R.O., FO 5/39.

More generally, they contributed to the formation of a distinct Irish identity in the United States by establishing emigration and patriotic societies, politicising St Patrick's Day parades, promoting Irish culture, and supplying their fellow countrymen with news about political events in the Old Country. At the same time, they communicated their case for Irish independence to an American audience with an impressive output of books, pamphlets and newspaper articles. During the 1820s, they organized Friends of Ireland societies to provide moral and monetary support for Daniel O'Connell's campaign for Catholic Emancipation, despite misgivings about his relatively moderate tactics. Within two years of the Catholic Emancipation Act of 1829, William MacNeven reconstituted the Friends of Ireland as a repeal society. Those United Irishmen who lived into the 1840s, such as John Binns, became strong supporters of the Young Ireland movement. After the young Thomas D'Arcy McGee arrived as a political exile in the United States after the Young Ireland rising of 1848, one of the first things he did was to visit Philadelphia and shake hands with John Binns, one of the last of the United Irishmen.[28]

By the time that handshake took place, the character of Irish-American radicalism had changed significantly. Most of the United Irish emigrés had been Protestant; after the war, the Irish nationalist movement in America had become overwhelmingly Catholic. The leading United Irishmen in America had been middle-class economic nationalists who rejected trade unionism and gravitated towards the Whig Party; many of the immigrants who arrived in the post-war period became active in the American labour movement, and generally supported the Jacksonian democrats. Nevertheless, there were remarkable continuities as well as major changes. It is no coincidence that the central tenets and tactics of American Fenians – including not only anglophobia and separatist nationalism, but also fundraising, arms running, and the belief that Ireland could be liberated through an American-based attack on Canada – followed principles and practices that had been well established by the United Irish emigrés who had come to America between 1795 and 1812. Irish-American nationalism begins not with the Famine, not even with the influx of Catholic Irish immigrants during the 1820s, but with the United Irishmen who came into the country well before the War of 1812.

---

28 D.A. Wilson, *United Irishmen, United States: Immigrant radicals in the early republic* (Ithaca and Dublin, 1998), pp 153–71.

33

'A dish with one spoon': American experience and the transformation of three officers of the crown

PETER LINEBAUGH

'We fell in with some savages, and travelled with them to Quebec; they were very kind to us, and said we were "all one brother" – all "one Indian".'

Lord Edward FitzGerald, 2 February 1789.

The Creator either made the land,
Or he did not.
He made it for the dukes and lords,
Or he did not.
He made it for the people,
Or he did not.

Thomas Ainge Devyr, *The odd book of the nineteenth century*
(New York, 1882).

In June 1791 Wolfe Tone said 'we will free ourselves by the aid of … the men of no property'. Two months later across the ocean at the Bois de Caiman, Saint Domingue, commenced the first successful slave revolt in history, reaching a type of conclusion in 1803 as the second independent republic of the western hemisphere: Haiti. Ireland had lost its constitutional independence two years earlier in the Act of Union. In 1791 Volney had meditated on the revolutions of empires.[1] In his spirit, we ask as nations come and go, what abides, what *loas*?

By November 1791, the Dublin United Irish wrote, 'antiquity can no longer defend absurd and oppressive forms against the common sense and common interests of mankind', forgetting only to mention common lands. The United Irish had not yet fully felt the consequences of its reliance upon agrarian commoners. The project of preserving unenclosed, collective, or communal forms of land tenure seemed part of custom ('antiquity') rather than Enlightenment 'com-

---

1 C.F. de Volney, *Les ruines, ou méditation sur les révolutions des empires* … (Paris, 1791).

mon sense'. The 'muted articulation of social, economic or cultural reform within early United Irish rhetoric' derived from a view that the independence and reform of the Irish state out of London's control would be sufficient to ensure a regime of benevolent progress.[2] Yet as the fateful decade progressed the numbers of Irish people abroad without property increased immensely (Tone and Russell believed that 150,000 Irish were engaged by the imperial army and navy); and in the aftermath of the 1798 rebellion and the counter-terror, the forced migration and the destruction of an independent state went hand in hand. Andrew Bryson is an example of the transition from Irish political prisoner to trans-Atlantic proletarian.[3] Prior to embarking from Waterford aboard the convict ship taking him to the West Indies in 1798, he was imprisoned in the former market house without fire or food in the shadow of the gallows. He was in the process of losing his country, his freedom, and his means of subsistence. The political prisoners were permitted neither fire for warmth nor straw for sleeping. They were taunted by men wearing orange. A sympathizer appeared and informed him, 'a tin and spoon are things you will find the want of immediately', and the friend offered to sell him the implements for 1s. instead of the purser's 4s. aboard ship. Thus, the proletarian or man of no property, in market society.

The full meaning of liberation promised the end of slavery and the preservation of the commons. *The Union doctrine, or Poor man's catechism* was published after the military defeat of 1798. Its introductory creed of nine propositions contains four specifically about the land. It goes on:

> It is not possible that God can be pleased to see a whole nation depending on the caprice and pride of a small faction, who can deny the common property in the land to his people, or at least tell them, how much they shall eat, and what kind; and how much they shall wear, and what kind. As we every day experience from the hands of these cruel usurpers, who have formed themselves into a corporation of law-makers, and are constantly exporting our provisions, or curtailing its growth, on the horrid policy of preserving subordination, by degrading our characters, and forcing on us every servile occupation to earn a scanty livelihood in a country capable of the greatest plenty.

Nation and country were not yet abstractions separate from the soil, the earth of livelihood. Nationalism had not yet become that 'imagined community' separated from the actual commons.[4]

---

2 Kevin Whelan, *The tree of liberty: Radicalism, Catholicism and the construction of Irish identity 1760–1830* (Cork, 1996), pp 61, 64.
3 Michael Durey (ed.), *Andrew Bryson's ordeal: An epilogue of the 1798 rebellion* (Cork, 1998).
4 Luke Gibbons, *Transformations in Irish culture* (Cork, 1997), pp 146–7.

The Belfast procession of 14 July 1790 celebrated the French Revolution with an anti-slavery banner depicting 'a Negro boy well dressed and holding high the cap of liberty'.[5] After the fourth edition of Olaudah Equiano's *Narrative* was published in 1792, the list of Irish subscribers contained many of the early United Irish; indeed, they supported and sustained him in an eight-month visit from May 1791 to January 1792. He wrote of his kindly reception 'by persons of all ranks', particularly praising the hospitality in Belfast. This was the thanks he provided his subscribers: yet there were other connections. During the Seven Years War, Equiano messed with an Irishman, Daniel Quin, aboard the *Aetna*, man-of-war. In addition to barbering, the Bible, and comparative ethnology, the Irishman instructed Equiano that 'I was as free as himself or any other man on board'.[6] Julius Scott has re-discovered in the public houses of Kingston during the 1790s locations where musicians from each culture shared one another's tunes.[7] Step dancers met tap dancers. 'A vast number of United Irishmen were landed' in Jamaica and deserted into the mountains to join the maroons.[8] James Napper Tandy wrote in 1802 disapproving of the French suppression of Toussaint L'Ouverture: 'We are all of the same family, black and white, the work of the same creator.'[9]

Long before Samuel Beckett translated the Martinique theorists of *négritude*, Andrew Bryson, the United Irish prisoner who wanted 'a tin and spoon', gave his sister a trenchant critique of the Caribbean picturesque of that island in 1799:[10]

> But allas, when we look into the back ground & see 300 or 400 of our fellow creatures with small howes tearing up the ground that had never been entered by the plough, the eye turns back disgusted, saying that the [beauty of the prospect] is only visionary pleasure while the latter is real misery. But be not too hasty; turn your eyes again; perhaps they may have deceived you in the first look. Hark: 1 2 3 4 5 6 7 8 9 lashes inflicted on a poor old man who has not as much cloathes on him as would cover a pin cushion. And for what? The head of his hoe is loose ...

When the United Irish repeated the catechism concerning the tree of liberty and where it grew (America), where it bloomed (France), and where its seeds might fall (Ireland), the cynical pointed out that the American branch was really a club

5 Dorothy Thompson, *Outsiders: Class, gender, and nation* (London, 1993) p. 134.
6 Olaudah Equiano, *The interesting narrative and other writings*, Vincent Carretta (ed.), (London, 1995), p. 92.
7 Julius Scott, 'The common wind: Currents of Afro-American communication in the era of the Haitian Revolution' (unpublished Ph.D. thesis, Duke University, 1986).
8 Castlereagh, *Memoirs and correspondence*, Charles Vane (ed.), (London, 1850), ii, p. 417.
9 Quoted in Dorothy Thompson, *Outsiders*.
10 Castlereagh, *correspondence*, ii, p. 82. For Beckett's translations, see Nancy Cunard, *Negro anthology* (London, 1934).

to beat the Indians with, or that it was the barbarous stick of slavery. However the meaning of 'America' to the United Irishmen not only referred to the Whig revolutionaries of plantocrats, landlords, and merchants, because in the 1780s it was not yet clear that the political nation, America, was to exclude both Indians and slaves. The decade saw a vast slave revolt from the plantations and a protracted struggle to unify and federate among the different Indian peoples. It was a period of visionaries. William Blake, who favoured generosity and delight against pity and restraint, was such a visionary. In his prophecy called 'America', Orc is the 'lover of wild rebellion and transgressor of God's Law'; he is 'the image of God who dwells in darkness of Africa. His flames arise in America and are driven over Ireland'. Orc was defeated, but Blake did not know this when he wrote the poem in 1793. Nor was Blake the only one who 'saw things', 'with his own eyes'.

Between 1750 and 1820, 30 per cent of the agricultural land of England was enclosed.[11] Levelling had vibrant connotations of direct action against the enclosure of common fields. The destruction of the commoning economy was opposed on the grounds that it created conditions of slavery. Richard Price, the most published contemporary defender of the commons, wrote in 1771 that 'modern policy is, indeed, more favourable to the higher classes of people, and the consequences may in time prove that the whole kingdom will consist of only gentry and beggars, or grandees and slaves'.[12] Price gave a famous sermon on 4 November 1789, a memorial to one revolution and a paean to another. He called it 'A discourse on the love of our country' in which he specifically excluded the 'soil or spot of earth on which we happen to have been born' from his meaning of country which was worked by the lawyer's quill not the spalpeen's spade. Nevertheless it gave Edmund Burke a fright, expressed in *Reflections on the Revolution in France* (1790). A grotesque genealogy of Levelling, Mens Johns, Seekers, Fifth Monarchists, Millenarians, and Anabaptists of Munster prepared Burke's 'aversion to futurity' by 'closing every vista with the gallows', as Marilyn Butler puts it.[13] The Levellers perverted the natural order of things; and, in scarcely coded nastiness, he saw their system as having led to 'a black and savage atrocity of mind'. The revolutionaries however were discovering planetary revolvings, oceanic time, and geological ages with the aid of James Hutton's *Theory of the Earth* (1795) and the people of the countryside. The project of social revolution concerned the planet earth.

English commoning, Irish rundale, hoe-culture of West Africa, long fallow agriculture of the Iroquois, Mosquito fishing, Mayan forestry: Adam Ferguson categorized these as examples from the 'history of rude nations' before the

---

11 J.M. Neeson, *Commoners: Common right, enclosure and social change in England, 1700–1820* (Cambridge, 1993).

12 Richard Price, *Observations on reversionary payments* (Dublin, 1772).

13 Marilyn Butler, *Romantics, rebels and reactionaries: English literature and its background, 1796–1830* (Oxford, 1981).

'establishment of property'.[14] Ferguson had an agenda, but it was not that of our subjects, men who learned to live harmoniously in the disparate habitats of the rivers and forests of the Great Lakes or the rain forest and barrier reef of central America. Each did so with an African American.

I shall consider three United Irish leaders: Thomas Russell ('the man from God knows where'), Lord Edward FitzGerald ('Eghnidal'), and Colonel Edward Marcus Despard ('the unfortunate Edward'). At the end they were men of action who fell to the assassin's bullet or to the gallows of the oppressor. To begin with, they were distinguished officers in the British army. Russell's father was a veteran of Fontenoy, his brother Ambrose was praised for gallantry by the king, and he himself served for four years in India without taint when the British army was at its most corrupt. According to William Cobbett, FitzGerald was 'the only really honest officer he ever knew in the army'.[15] Despard was an accomplished draughtsman, mathematician, and engineer. He was an inspiring leader of men, grandiloquently praised by Nelson. All three had strong opinions or relationships with the African slavery of the New World. In addition, they may introduce us to the experience of commonism. The enemies of the commons, the enclosers ('improvers' as they called themselves in a brilliant piece of public relations) compared the commoners to levellers, to buccaneers, to Indians, and to savages.[16] The project of political, social, and economic equality – communism in short – originated in such experiences. This is a reason why we cannot completely agree when Perry Anderson writes that the Levellers were 'completely effaced'.[17] Russell, FitzGerald and Despard may help us re-open what Edward Thompson called the 'dialogue between social being and social consciousness' and to understand the 'circuits between intellectuality and practical experience'.[18]

Thomas Russell (1767–1803) was born on the Blackwater river in County Cork. Later he lived in what is now County Laois, but only after Despard had left. Russell went to India in 1783, the year Sir William Jones arrived there and formed the Asiatic Society.[19] The chairman of the East India Company was from County Cork. Sir Eyre Coote, who arrived as commander-in-chief in 1779, was also Irish. Bengal's first newspaper was edited by a 'wild Irishman' who was imprisoned for criticizing Hastings, the English drug lord. Russell in India

14 Adam Ferguson, *An essay on the history of civil society* (London, 1767), pp 75, 82.
15 Thomas Moore, *The life and death of Lord Edward FitzGerald* (London, 1831), i, p. 107.
16 E.P. Thompson, *Customs in common* (London, 1991), pp 163, 165. See also J.H. Neeson, *Commoners: Common right, enclosure, and social change in England, 1700–1820* (London, 1993), p. 329.
17 Perry Anderson, *A zone of engagement* (London, 1992), p. 369.
18 E.P. Thompson, *The poverty of theory and other essays* (London, 1978), p. 195.
19 Denis Carroll, *The man from God knows where: Thomas Russell, 1767–1803* (Dublin, 1995); Angus Calder, *Revolutionary empire: The rise of the English-speaking empires from the fifteenth century to the 1780s* (London, 1981).

learnt more than the ways of the garrison and whorehouse. He returned in 1787 and soon he was reading the *History of Paraguay* by the Jesuit, Pierre François Xavier de Carlevoix. The Jesuits had helped to organize thirty towns of 120,000 Guaraní people. They built musical instruments; they operated printing presses; they worked without toil; they refused to leave the land; they were expelled because they opposed slavery. Here was an experience of managed commonism – no money, the land in common, the long house, the round dance. Russell wrote that it was 'beyond compare the best, the happiest, that has ever been instituted'. Indeed it left deep traces, as a century later it was still a living memory[20] – 'through forest paths ablaze with flowers, and across whose clearings the tropic birds darted like atoms cut adrift from the apocalypse ... ' In 1793 Russell was still taking notes on American Indians.[21]

Russell's anti-slavery poems were published in the *Northern Star* and republished in *Paddy's Resource* (1798). In the *Northern Star* he wrote against slavery on St Patrick's Day 1792. Earlier in the *Belfast Newsletter* (2 December 1791) he had written that 'the blood of the African cries to God for the vengeance of these wrongs'. The importance of these poems which he selected (R.R. Madden was mistaken in attributing their actual authorship to Russell) was political: 'The Negro's Complaint' was about expropriation.[22] He compared the hundreds of thousands of Africans dragged from their homes to similar experiences suffered by the Defenders, the cottiers, weavers, and labourers. 'He esteemed the people who lived in small cabins'. To re-string the harp, the Belfast librarian (as he now was) tramped up and down the villages of Antrim and Down in 1795–6. He helped join the United Irish to Defenderism. In *An address to the people of Ireland* (1796) he stated: 'The aristocracy of Ireland, which exists only by our slavery, and is maintained in its pomp and splendour by the sale of our lives, liberties, and properties, will tumble in the dust'. He criticised the war, for 'cloves and nutmegs and contracts and slaves'. Slavery was the issue of 'the greatest consequence on the face of the earth'. The slave trade created barbarism; it prevented civilization. It was 'a system of cruelty, torment, wickedness and infamy ... the work of demons rather than men'. Russell elsewhere wrote:

> It is well known that the traveller will receive in the most wretched cabin in the wildest parts of Ireland all the hospitality that the circumstances of the owner can afford: he will get his share of the milk, if there is any, and of the potatoes; and if he has lost his way he will be guided to the road for miles, and all this without expectation or wish for a reward.

20 R.B.C. Graham, *A vanished Arcadia, being some account of the Jesuits in Paraguay, 1607–1767* (London, 1901).
21 C.J. Woods (ed.), *Journals and memoirs of Thomas Russell, 1791–1795* (Dublin, 1991), p. 78.
22 M.H. Thuente, *The harp re-strung: The United Irishmen and the rise of Irish literary nationalism* (Syracuse, 1994), pp 90–2.

There is the equality of the destitute such as Captain Stedman described of the slaves who shared the single egg. 'Since the poorest negro among them having but an egg scorns to eat it alone, but were 12 others present & every one of them a stranger, he would cut or break it in as many shares …'[23]

Primitive communism arouses unease.[24] The term itself was proposed by Lewis Henry Morgan, whose studies of the Iroquois consoled Marx after the defeat of the Paris commune when in the space of a few days 17,000 fell to the bourgeoisie. A modern anthropologist attempts a definition – 'the core institutions of economic life included collective or common ownership of land and resources, generalised reciprocity in the distribution of food, and relatively egalitarian political relations'. More broadly, what is sharing and where does it end? Is it a type of behaviour, is it a cultural rule, is it the experience of companionship in intimate groups? To Russell the questions were not so different, since the simple duty to neighbour 'in the most extensive sense of the word – embrac[es] the whole family of mankind'. India, Paraguay, Ohio, Guinea, Antrim, and Down were the places where by direct and indirect study Thomas Russell took his ground. Hospitality was the beginning of a praxis of the tin and the spoon.

He died a revolutionary antinomian. Although refused three more days of life to complete his translation of Revelation, Russell was not so rushed that he did not have time to point out a mis-translation in the Epistle to the Hebrews (9:26), objecting to the 'End of the World and shewing from the Greek testament it should be the End of the Age & other Discourse of the same kind'.[25] He had studied rocks, tramping with John Templeton and contemplated geological time. Just what sort of termination was his hanging to be? An incident in history, not the end of the world.

Lord Edward FitzGerald had three places outside of Ireland that were essential to the formation of his identity as a United Irishman. One of these was Paris, where at the Palais Royal on 18 November 1792 he renounced his title and became Citizen Edward. His aunt wrote: 'he is *mad* about the French affairs – the levelling principle – and, indeed, seems entirely engrossed by these subjects'. A second place was Eutaw Springs in South Carolina, and a third was the hydrographic system of the north American continent – the St Lawrence River, the Great Lakes, the Mississippi – along which, if we had to select a decisive point of consciousness transformation, it would be Detroit where his political and cultural identity again underwent a change.

At the battle of Eutaw Creek at a slave plantation on 8 September 1781, in the last engagement of the American Revolution before Yorktown, FitzGerald fell,

---

23 John Gabriel Stedman, *Narrative of a five years' expedition against the revolted negroes of Surinam*, 2 vols (London, 1996), p. 524.

24 R.B. Lee, 'Reflections of primitive communism', in Tim Ingold, David Riches, and James Woodburn (eds), *Hunters and gatherers 1: History, evolution, and social change* (New York, 1988).

25 3 October 1803: N.A.I., RP 620/50.

along with hundreds of British casualties, lying unconscious with a dangerous thigh wound.[26] Tony Small took him to his cabin, and washed and bound his wound. On recovering FitzGerald engaged Tony Small as his servant and they remained in this intimate relation until FitzGerald's assassination seventeen years later ('Tony embodied and brought to life his master's commitment to freedom and equality for all men,' writes Stella Tillyard.)[27] It is a vivid formulation of a striking relationship – the African-American servant, comrade, nurse to the Irish freedom-fighter. Tony Small brought him to life, certainly and literally so. But what does it mean to say that Tony Small *embodied* freedom and equality?

There were two sets of white belligerents and 20,000 black slaves in the triagonal war, as the partisan warfare in the south has been called.[28] 'The specter of emancipation' was raised in the summer of 1779 with the Philipsburg Proclamation promising security to slaves joining the British forces. In July 1780 the slaves on Izard's Savannah River plantation rose in insurrection. Charleston was a centre of resistance to the plantation and a cross-roads of Caribbean consciousness going back to the Stono Rebellion (1740). Terror became a basic component of policy on Lord Cornwallis' orders – houses were burnt and crops destroyed. Twenty thousand slaves deserted the plantations. This was a war of the death-throes of British rule; it also threatened the slave system with extinction. Small was part of this freedom struggle. Thus he embodied freedom because he had fought for it. Jemmy Hope, the socialist weaver of the United Irish, having talked with veterans of the West Indies and its diseases, expressed the meaning of American counter-revolution: 'mankind seemed divided into different species, each preying on the other'.[29]

In June 1788 FitzGerald was in Halifax, Nova Scotia, a place which, like London and Sierre Leone, was a destination of the African-America diaspora. He wrote: 'There are not gentlemen, everybody is on a footing, provided he works, and wants nothing.' He saw whole tracts of land peopled by Irish. His journey across the Maine woods is mapped as the frontispiece to Tom Moore's second volume. It is a peculiarly empty map, suggesting snow, a *tabula rasa*. 'I really would join the savages, and leaving all our fictitious and ridiculous wants, be what nature intended we should be. Savages have all the real happiness in life,' he wrote to his mother.[30] She calls this his 'cult of Indian life', and it would have seemed so in the plush settings of Holland House, or the Malvern Hills, where they studied Rousseau. But, as a modern biographer of Joseph Brant warns, 'the people of the Longhouse were not the noble savage of philosophy and romance'.[31]

26 R.F. Weigley, *The partisan war: The South Carolina campaign of 1780–1782* (London, 1970), p. 68.
27 Stella Tillyard, *Citizen Lord: Edward FitzGerald, 1763–1798* (London, 1997).
28 S.R. Frey, *Water from the rock: Black resistance in a revolutionary age* (Princeton, 1991), ch. 4.
29 *The autobiography of James (Jemmy) Hope* (Belfast, 1998), p. 26.
30 Tillyard, *Citizen Lord*, p. 87.
31 I.T. Kelsay, *Joseph Brant, 1743–1807: Man of two worlds* (Syracuse, 1984), p. 33.

FitzGerald wrote as if indeed they were such because he was writing to his mother. He did not write to her about soldiering, or write to her in pidgin or creole, languages he strove to understand. At Fort Erie he met Thayendanegea, or Joseph Brant, the great Mohawk leader, who had fought for the British. Brant visited London in 1786 and became acquainted with the opposition leader Charles James Fox, who gave him a snuff box, and who was also Lord Edward's cousin. Hence, three years later when Lord Edward arrived in Ontario, Brant, whose confederacy of the Iroquois had suffered a crippling winter and whose members had begun selling land to corporate cheats, was eager to welcome him. The Mohawk, the Irishman, the African American canoed across Ontario to Detroit.

FitzGerald's journey transpired as the US Constitution took effect and at a turning point from peace to war among the Ohio Indians. George Washington was inaugurated in April with feelings which he compared to 'those of a culprit who is going to the place of execution'.[32] 'Hangman' would have expressed the reality more accurately, as Washington raised an army (and reduced their pay) to invade the western lands. The period of treaties was over; 'the last act of the farce' had begun, an American officer commented.[33] In June 1790, General Knox authorized General Harman 'to extirpate, utterly' the Indian banditti, and in September they began to burn Miami villages. Yet the Indian confederacy had formed an effective force which with British allies could have changed the course of history.

Brant was busy preserving one land, one confederacy, 'a dish with one spoon' as he later explained. In the spring of 1789 he struggled to maintain the unity of the Seneca, Mohawk, Cayugas, Onondagas, Oswegos, and Oneidas. Besides these he wished to include Ohio Indians, or the Miamis, Shawnee, Delaware, Wyandot, Sac, Chippewa, Pottawatomy. When Joseph Brant spoke of 'a dish with one spoon' it signified a common, unbounded hunting ground, and it signified a unity and harmony of purpose among native tribes. It was designed to oppose the aggressive, rapacious invasion into the Ohio lands, and the cruel ding-dong of atrocities 'on either side'. 'A dish with one spoon' was thus an extension of the political confederation that the Iroquois devised in the previous generation to new peoples of Ohio and the west. FitzGerald was learning about federation, about defeat, about war, about agriculture.

Losses were rapid and defeat shameful for the US. Little Turk defeated General Harman in 1790, and in 1791 he nearly annihilated the US army on the banks of the Wabash – 'St Clair's Defeat'. The US raised another army, appointed 'Mad' Anthony Wayne to command it, burned villages and destroyed crops in preparation for victory in 1794 at the battle of Fallen Timbers. By 1795 the van-

32 Jared Sparks (ed.), *The writings of George Washington* (Boston, 1834–7), xi, p. 488.
33 Kelsay, *Brant*, p. 425.

quished were observed begging for scraps of food outside the forts.[34] And in 1803 Brant wrote a letter comparing Indians and English:[35]

> We have no law but that written on the heart of every rational creature by the immediate finger of the great Spirit of the universe himself. We have no prisons – we have no pompous parade of courts … we have no robbery under the colour of law – daring wickedness here is never suffered to triumph over helpless innocence – the estates of widows and orphans are never devoured by enterprising sharpers. Our sachems, and our warriors, eat their own bread, and not the bread of wretchedness … The palaces and prisons among you form a most dreadful contrast. Go to the former places, and you will see, perhaps, a deformed piece of earth swelled with pride, and assuming airs, that become none but the Spirit above. Go to one of your prisons – here description utterly fails! … Liberty, to a rational creature, as much exceeds property, as the light of the sun does that of the most twinkling star: but you put them on a level, to the everlasting disgrace of civilization … [is] a sentence that once struck my mind with some force, that 'a bruised reed he never broke'.

The reference is to Isaiah 42:3 in Brant's own translation:

> He will not break a bruised reed
> or snuff out a smoldering wick;
> he will make justice shine on every race
> never faltering, never breaking down,
> he will plant justice on earth
> while coasts and islands wait for his teaching.

The lines would appeal to an Irishman, insular and universal. They are lines of defeat, the reed is bruised, the wick only smolders, but to the Biblical culture (in 1789 Brant sent Biblical translations to Harvard) the reference is powerful rather than defeated. Readers of Isaiah know the coming verses: 'To open the blind eyes, to bring out the prisoners from the prison, and them that sit in darkness out of the prison house'. To the Christian, the passage is prophetic, since Jesus will quote it in the act of the proclamation of justice (Matthew 12:20). The message summarized a decade – the 1790s – of the most extensive prison-building programme until the end of the twentieth century.

In Detroit on 21 June 1789 David Hill, a renowned commander of the Iroquois, gave Lord Edward an Indian name – 'I, David Hill, chief of the Six Nations, give the name of *Eghnidal* to my friend Lord Edward FitzGerald.'

---

34 Wiley Sword, *President Washington's Indian war: The struggle for the Old Northwest, 1790–1795* (Oklahoma, 1985).

35 W.L. Stone, *Life of Joseph Brant-Thayendanegea* (New York, 1838), ii, p. 481.

Eghnidal was made a chief of the Seneca. Fifty years later Lewis Henry Morgan was also renamed by the Seneca in gratitude for his exertions against landsharks. Like FitzGerald, it affected the rest of his life. FitzGerald spent the rest of the year making his way to New Orleans, arriving there in December 1789 by going north to Michilimackinack, and then down the Mississippi. The Seneca chief was carrying a message to the western Indians; he attempted to negotiate with Spain. On St Patrick's Day 1792 the *Northern Star* published the American justification for waging war against the Indians of the Ohio. It is a typical imperialist document of officious self-justification, odious one-sidedness, hypocritical self-righteousness, and spurious anecdotes of cruelty. It complained, incidentally, that the 'property' of the settlers was taken by the Indians, because the Indian villages of the Wabash were havens for runaway slaves. What messages had Tony Small transmitted? At the end in Dublin in May 1798, running from assassins, FitzGerald went by the name of Jamieson, no longer in the company of Tony Small, whose 'unfortunate face prevented him from going to see his dear master'.[36]

Colonel Edward Marcus Despard was born in County Laois in 1752. Feehan describes the agricultural system of that time:

> The native Irish tradition [was] of dispersed farm clusters, in which the *clachan* (house cluster) was the social unit. The cultivated infield in which oats, and perhaps barley, were sown was located close to the *clachan*, and it was divided into strips which were cultivated by family groups, and which were redistributed from year to year; further out from the farm clusters was the outfield on the mountains, moors, or river callows, where the cattle and sheep were grazed and of which the commons of Slieve Bloom are a direct descendant ... .[37]

Enclosure of land proceeded actively in the eighteenth century (Laois was 'the most improved' of any county Arthur Young had seen in Ireland), with attendant phenomena – 'stealing' and poaching became common, the native Irish sank into abject poverty, and social banditry arose out of the Slieve Bloom mountains.[38] The most powerful and ruthless of ascendancy landlords in the county, Charles Coote, complained of 'the irreclaimable barbarity and uncivilization of the peasantry'. The Despards were in the van of these changes: the estate at Donore was famous for its hedges, 'extemely neat, with saddle copings'.[39] Local Whiteboy disturbances in 1761–6 characterized the years of Despard's childhood, as they would the family in later years. 'Living one winter in terror,

---

36 Moore, *Edward FitzGerald*, ii, p. 55.
37 John Feehan, *Laois: An environmental history* (Ballykilcavan, 1983), p. 323.
38 John Feehan, *The landscape of Slieve Bloom: A study of its natural and human heritage* (Dublin, 1979), p. 137.
39 Charles Coote, *Statistical survey of Queen's County* (Dublin, 1801).

we were driven away by rebel Whitefeet, or Blackfeet,' Despard's niece remembers of a later experience.[40] Enclosure of the land accompanied its disenchantment.[41]

Most of Despard's life – the twenty-three years from 1767 to 1790 – were passed in central America: Jamaica, Nicaragua, Honduras or Belize. In Jamaica he led gangs of men, Irish, African, English, in re-siting the artillery batteries of Kingston (had he experience of arranging the proportion of spade and shovel labourers in Ireland?). In Nicaragua, he led thousands of men and boys (including the young Nelson) in the disastrous expedition in 1780, when in order to survive on the San Juan River he relied on the Indians to teach him fishing, hunting and therapeutics. In 1782 he commanded an expedition to the Black River in Honduras at the time of the evacuation of Savannah and Charleston. In Belize after 1784 he was superintendent in its transition from a logwood to a mahogany economy; he incurred the enmity of the planter class by allying with the Indians and former slaves, and conducted a Mosaic-like lottery of land re-distribution. Morgan visited the Maya of the Yucatan as well, finding the lands held and wrought in common.[42] A renegade to the slavocrats, Despard was thrown out of the colony and returned to London with Catherine, his 'common law wife', as Sir Francis Burdett called her.[43]

Catherine and Ned lived in England scarcely ten years; during most of them he was a guest of his majesty – in king's bench prison, Shrewsbury gaol, Newgate, Clerkenwell new prison (here without tin or spoon), Tothill Fields bridewell, and, lastly, Horsemonger Lane gaol. In one of these gaols his path crossed that of Thomas Spence, 'the unfee'd advocate of the disinherited seed of Adam', the eloquent graffiti artist and defender of the commons. Spence spoke also in the idiom of the American Indians – it was not enough to shave the landlords, they must be scalped – and he drew important lessons from the Cherokees: 'the missionaries are dangerous civilizers. They think of nothing but building churches and partitioning lands. This is the way to be sure to make all sorts and conditions of men, and then they piously thank God for making rich and poor.'

Despard was a United Irishmen. He had links with the proletarians of the northern textile districts of England who were resisting the introduction of machinery.[44] Lord Ellenborough when sentencing Despard spoke of how desirable the inequality of property was and accused Despard of wishing to substitute 'a wild scheme of impracticable equality'. He was beheaded as a traitor in

40 Jane Despard, 'Memoranda connected with the Despard family recollections', p. 40, Despard papers.
41 Michael Beames, *Peasants and power: The Whiteboy movement and their control in pre-Famine Ireland* (Brighton, 1983).
42 L.H. Morgan, *Houses and house: Life of the American aborigines* (Washington, 1881), ch. 2.
43 Peter Linebaugh and Marcus Rediker, *The many-headed hydra* (London and Boston, 2000).
44 Roger Wells, *Insurrection* (Gloucester, 1983).

February 1803 in London, along with eight others – two carpenters, a slater, two soldiers, two shoemakers, a sailor. He was charged with conspiring to kill the king, capture parliament, seize the arms of the Tower, take the gold in the Bank, and stop the coaches from leaving Piccadilly. They called parliament 'a den of thieves', and the ministry 'man eaters'. As for Windsor Castle, it was 'fit to teach the Gospel and maintain poor people's children in'.

Awaiting execution, Despard was visited by the Revd William Winkworth; he tried to see what he could surreptitiously discover for the government by offering his spiritual services.

> He replied he had sometimes been at eight different places of worship on the same day, that he believed in a Deity, and that outward forms of worship were useful for political purposes, otherwise he thought the opinions of Churchmen, Dissenters, Quakers, Methodists, Catholics, Savages, or even Atheists, were equally indifferent. I urged the propriety of a public acknowledgement of God, as the supreme governor and universal friend … He then offered some criticism on the words Altar and Ecclesia, which if my memory does not fail me were quotations from Thomas Paine's Age of Reason. I then presented Dr Dodderidge's Evidence of Christianity and begged as a favour that we would read it. He then requested that I would not 'attempt to put shackles on his mind, as his body (pointing to the iron on his leg) was under so painful a restraint, and said that he had as much right to ask me to read the book he had in his hand (a treatise on Logic) as I had to ask him to read mine', and before I could make reply Mrs. Despard and another lady were introduced, and our conversation ended.

Blake had written ten years earlier in 'America':

> That stony law I stamp to dust; and scatter religion abroad
> To the four winds as a torn book, and none shall gather the leaves.

Despard married an African American woman. He brought her back to Europe. Despard's niece later wrote: 'the Negro woman who first lived with him as his housekeeper never could have inflamed a mind like his, and it is likely that it was her fidelity to him in every situation, and to the last, that engaged his confidence and affections'.[45] She defended him with revolutionary pertinacity. She carried messages. She defended his life. She took her pleas to Horatio Nelson. She worried the home secretary. The sheriff of London regarded her as a positive nuisance. She appears to have organized the prisoners' wives. Catherine saw that Despard was buried. Her own story, like the wives and partners of many of the

45 Elizabeth Despard, 'Recollections of the Despard family', p. 22: Despard papers.

United Irishmen, is largely unknown.[46] It is possible that she and Despard formed their liason while he was in Jamaica, as it is there that so many British army officers acquired the mistress, nurse, laundress, and cook who would preserve them. It is also possible that they met while Despard was in Honduras, and that she had central American filiations. For several years he dwelt on the southeastern frontiers of colonial Yucatan where entire towns harboured millenarians and runaways. 'These places ... were supremely alive, swarming with ideas both written and spoken, with pragmatic programs for rebellion.'[47] It is also very possible that, like Tony Small, she came from the mainland, part of the diaspora of former slaves during the American War of Independence. While much information about her is wanting and was intended to be so, she was outstanding in her courage and faithful to the cause of freedom. Luke Gibbon advises us 'to engage fully with the unwritten epitaphs of another era'.[48] We cannot yet do this in her case. But, since she also paid, deliberately, for Despard's last words by losing her widow's pension, these last words were hers too. At the scaffold he charged:

> his Majesty's Ministers ... of destroying a man, because they think he is a friend to truth, to liberty, and to justice, and because he has been a friend to the poor and the oppressed. But, fellow citizens, I hope and trust, notwithstanding my fate, and perhaps the fate of many others who may follow me, that still the principles of liberty, justice, and humanity will triumph over falsehood, despotism, and delusion, and every thing else hostile to the interests of the human race. And now, having said this, I have nothing more to add, but to wish you all that health, happiness, and that freedom which I have ever made it my endeavour, as far as it lay in my power, to procure for every one of you, and for mankind in general.

Now destitute, she was supported in Dublin by Valentine Lawless. Madden spoke to the widow of Valentine Lawless concerning his knowledge of the Emmet conspiracy, but she could tell him nothing of it or of her.[49] Catherine fell into equally dark obscurity.

In a grievous bitter mood Edward Thompson, wrote: 'all that is left were the bones of our more heroic brothers and sisters to bleach on the plains of the past under a hallucinated utopian sun'.[50] Utopia perhaps is part of defeat, a mottled feather in the thinning wing of the old owl of Minerva. The heroic brothers and sisters have left us more, but they also left a utopia. In the summer of 1802 a Deist

---

46 N.J. Curtin, 'Women and eighteenth-century Irish republicanism', in Margaret MacCurtain and Mary O'Dowd (eds), *Women in early modern Ireland* (Edinburgh, 1991), p. 137.
47 G.D. Jones, *Maya resistance to Spanish rule: Time and history on a colonial frontier* (Albuquerque, NM, 1989), p. 234.
48 Gibbons, *Transformations*.
49 T.C.D., Madden papers, MS 873.
50 Thompson, *Poverty of theory*, p. 264.

magazine, the *Temple of Reason,* published in Philadelphia (centre of the United Irish since at least 1795) *Equality: a history of Lithconia.* The narrator sails to an island and meets everyone on the beach as they knock off work for the day. 'I found, that there was no money in the country, that the lands are in common, and that labour is a duty required of every citizen.' The working day is four hours long. There are no markets or towns. There are no rich and poor, no rank or artificial distinctions. 'The whole island may be compared to a city spread over a large garden … ' The laws 'are written in the hearts of the Lithconians'. *Meum et tuum* are abolished; theft is unnecessary. 'The Lithconians are not a people that are progressing from a state of nature to what is vulgarly called civilization; on the contrary, they are progressing from civil society to a state of nature, if they have not already arrived at that state: for in the history of the country, many and surprising revolutions are recorded.' It is not Rousseauist, because the Lithconians welcome machines and their particular hallucination includes rail service.

'The passions and feelings of the multitude', said a spy in 1795, 'were filled with electrical celerity.'[51] We observe a similar celerity among our three 'heroic brothers' and sister (they were a few among many) who, despite swift plurality of consciousness, shared a conception of the dish with one spoon. It had subsequent realizations. Madden's volumes appeared during the intervals of his own struggles against slavery, exposing the 'pawn system' – a disguised slavery – of Sierre Leone, translating within a creole intellectual circle in Cuba, visiting the barracoon called Misericordia of Havana, rushing to New York to meet Cinqué, leader of the *Amistad* mutiny of 1839, with the greeting 'Salaam Aleikoum'. As perhaps it did in Thomas Ainge Devyr, who at age sixteen 'reached Liverpool and I found myself a white slave looking for a master in vain'. In the 1830s land struggle in Donegal he noted 'the fields became a practical common'. He became active in the Chartism of Tom Spence's birthplace, Newcastle. He proposed a jubilee: 'This great work, which, though commenced in Ireland, must be fought out on this side of the ocean.' 'Yes! you are all equal inheritors of the unspeakably grand estate which this fertile globe presents.'[52] In New York city he joined the struggle to make Tomkins Square public.

As perhaps it did in Roger Casement of the Congo in 1890 and the upper Amazon: 'I realised that I was looking at this tragedy with the eyes of another race of people once hunted themselves, whose hearts were based on affection as the root principle of contact with their fellow men, and whose estimate of life was not something to be appraised at its market price.' The Putamayo had led him to Easter Sunday. He wrote of the 30,000 Indians starved or killed: 'their minds were the minds of civilized men and women. They longed for another life

51 Whelan, *Tree of liberty*, p. 64.
52 T.A. Devyr, *The odd book of the nineteenth century* (New York, 1882). Special thanks to Breandán MacSuibhne for this reference.

– they hoped ever for another world.' They were not children of the forest; they were *lost* in the forest from a defeated past which Casement styled 'socialist'.[53]

We need an elasticity in our understanding of communism. It has a European source in the commoning economies, an American one in the Indian land struggles, and an African one in community expropriation. Catherine Despard and Tony Small were thus part of what Paul Gilroy calls the Black Atlantic. Kevin Whelan proposes the Green Atlantic, and if only to include Edward Marcus Despard and Lord Edward FitzGerald the term is needed. While one understands these colour codes, there was a Red Atlantic that was at once prior to the Black and the Green and a product of their conjunction. I do not refer to the bloody-minded insurrection of Burke's nightmare, but to the project of a classless society for whom abolition of poverty and riches was a lived memory, not an utopian delusion, a precious hope, not an insane hallucination. The communist project was asserted in the midst of the night of carnage. Consider Gracchus Babeuf, so often taken to be the founder of modern communism. He had written a history of common lands. The women and children sought his aid in the summer of 1791 when prevented from gathering herbs and foraging in the château park. He defended the peasants of Clermont who cut hay from the common meadow. He analyzed the agrarian law of Rome; he studied the sixteenth-century Anabaptists who frightened Edmund Burke; he even professed high regard for 'the sublime Nazarene legislator'. Thus when he called for *le bonheur commun* or *l'égalité réelle*, the slogans of the Conspiracy of Equals, it was a living experience that he defended, not a bookish plan.[51] In May 1796 Gracchus Babeuf and co-conspirators were arrested and, a year later, guillotined.

Marx's *Ethnological notebooks* composed in 1880–1 expressed his profound interest in the Iroquois. The vitality of the primitive communities excited and elated him. He affirmed a multilinear notion of human development. In *The origin of the family, private property and the state* (1884), Engels praised the democratic assembly of the Iroquois, the women's nomination of the sachem, and the communal ownership of land. The commons were to be found not only in the indigenously doomed or ethnologically distant; in Marx's youth among the dispossessed commoners of the Moselle valley, Marx was stimulated to embark upon the critique of political economy.[55] FitzGerald and Morgan were brothers with the Seneca of western New York state. Thomas Russell, Marx, Engels were students of these people. Tony Small and Catherine Despard sat around the same council fire.

53 Michael Taussig, *Shamanism, colonialism, and the wild man: A study in terror and healing* (Chicago, 1987); Roger Casement, 'The Putamayo Indians', in *Contemporary Review*, cii (September 1912).

54 R.B. Rose, *Gracchus Babeuf: The first revolutionary communist* (Stanford, Ca., 1978).

55 Teodor Shanin (ed.), *Late Marx and the Russian road* (London, 1984); Karl Marx, *Rheinische Zeitung*, 25 October 1842, in Karl Marx and Friedrich Engels, *Collected works*, i (London, 1975), pp 224–64.

BIBLIOGRAPHY

A check-list of publications on the 1790s,
the United Irishmen and the 1798 rebellion, 1900–2002

KEVIN WHELAN

Abercrombie, Nigel, 'The first [Catholic] Relief Act', in Eamon Duffy (ed.), *Challoner and his church: A Catholic bishop in Georgian Britain* (London, 1970), 174–93.

Adams, Gerry, *The politics of Irish freedom* (Dingle and Wolfeboro, NH, 1986) [chapter on Tone and 1798].

Adams, J.R.R., 'Reading societies in Ulster', in *Ulster Folklife*, xxvi (1980), 55–64.

—— *The printed word and the common man: Popular culture in Ulster, 1700–1900* (Belfast, 1987).

—— 'Folk poetry of the Laggan', in *Donegal Ann.* (1989), 84–88.

Addis, S., 'The story of the rising', in McKearney, *Ninety-eight*, 10–13.

Agnew, Jean (ed.), *The Drennan–McTier letters, 1776–1819*, 3 vols (Dublin, 1998-9).

Akenson, D.H. and W.H. Crawford, *Local poets and social history: James Orr, bard of Ballycarry* (Belfast, 1977).

Aldridge, R.B., 'The journal of Captain Joseph Bull' [Killala, 1798] in *Ir. Sword*, viii, 30 (1967), 65–79; 31 (1967), 109–14; 32 (1968), 186–92; 33 (1968), 255–60.

Allen, Harry, 'Did the rebels of North Down and the Ards miss their opportunity in 1797?', in *Familia*, xiv (1998), 13–21.

Andrews, Stuart, *The British periodical press and the French Revolution, 1789–1799* (London, 2000).

Uí Anluain, Caitlín, *'98 in Wexford: A simple account for the young* (Oulart [County Wexford], 1998).

Archer, Patrick, 'Fingal [County Dublin] in 1798', in *Béaloideas*, ix, 2 (1939), 185–218.

—— 'Fingal in 1798', in *Dub. Hist. Rec.*, xl, 1(1987), 66–79; xl, 2 (1987), 108–15.

Armstrong, Deirdre, *The spirit of the north is high: A source-list of material* (Ballynahinch [County Down], 1998).

—— 'An army of phantom soldiers flying the colours of moral force', in Hill, Turner and Dawson, *Down*, 147–61.

Askamore and Ballyellis Comóradh '98: The year of the piker (Askamore [County Wexford], 1998).

Aylmer, Richard, 'The imperial service of William Aylmer, 1800–1814', in *Ir. Sword*, xx, 82 (1997), 207–16.

—— 'The duke of Leinster withdraws from Ireland: October 1797', in *Jn. Kild. Arch. Soc.*, xix, part 1 (2000–1), 151–83.

Baeyens, Jacques, *Sabre au clair: Amable Humbert, général de la république* (Paris, 1981).

Bailie, W.D., 'William Steel Dickson D.D. 1744–1824', in *Ir. Booklore*, ii, 2 (1976), 238–67.

— 'Revd Samuel Barber, 1738–1811: National Volunteer and United Irishman', in Haire, *Challenge and conflict*, 72–95.

— 'William Steel Dickson', in Swords, *Protestant, Catholic and Dissenter*, 45–80.

— 'Presbyterian clergymen and the County Down rebellion of 1798', in Hill, Turner and Dawson, *Down*, 162–86.

[Ballinamuck], *1798 commemoration at Ballinamuck, County Longford, September 11 1938: Souvenir programme* (Longford, 1938).

Ballymoney: An A-Z of the 1798 rebellion (Ballymoney [County Antrim], 1998).

Ballymoney and the rebellion of 1798 (Ballymoney, 1998).

Ballymoney and the rebellion of 1798: A literature review (Ballymoney, 1998).

Ballymurn Comóradh '98 (Ballymurn [County Wexford], 1998*)*.

Bardon, Jonathan, 'An unlikely coalition: The 1798 rebellion in Ulster', in *Omnibus* (Summer, 1998), 14–19.

Barfoot, C.H., 'Why hang O'Quigley? Treason and the press in 1798', in Leerssen et al., *Forging*, 75–102.

Barkley, John, 'The Presbyterian minister in eighteenth-century Ireland', in Haire, *Challenge and conflict*, 46–71.

— 'Late eighteenth-century Belfast and St Mary's Chapel', in *Familia*, ii, 2 (1986), 82–94.

— 'Protestant Christianity as a source of democratic freedoms', in Mackey, *Europe*, 56–68.

Barnard, Toby, 'The uses of 23 October 1641 and Irish Protestant celebrations', in *Eng.Hist.Rev.*, cvi (1991), 889–920.

Barrell, John, *Imagining the king's death: Figurative treason, fantasies of regicide, 1793–1796* (Oxford, 2000).

Barrett, Eamonn, *Reluctant rebel: The story of Cornelius Grogan of Johnstown Castle* (Wexford, 1998).

Barrington, Jonah, *Personal sketches and recollections of his own times* (Dublin, 1998).

Barron, T.J., 'A poitín affray near Ballybay [County Monaghan] in 1797', in *Clogher Rec.*, viii, 2 (1974), 182–93.

Barry, J.Greene, 'Lord Edward FitzGerald's dagger', in *R.S.A.I. Jn.*, i (1911), 376–9.

Barry, J.M., *Pitch cap and triangle: The Cork militia in the Wexford rising* (Cork, 1998).

Bartlett, Thomas, 'An end to moral economy: The Irish Militia disturbances of 1793', in *Past & Present*, lxc (1983), 41–64.

— 'Defenders and Defenderism in 1795', in *I.H.S.*, xxiv (1984–5), 373–94.

— 'Indiscipline and disaffection in the armed forces in Ireland in the 1790s', in Corish, *Radicals, rebels and establishments*, 115–34.

— (ed.), 'An officer's memoirs of Wexford in 1798', in *Wex. Hist. Soc. Jn.*, xii (1988–9), 72–85.

— 'Indiscipline and disaffection in the French and Irish armies during the revolutionary period', in Gough and Dickson, *Ireland*, 179–201.

— '"A people made rather for copies than originals": The Anglo-Irish, 1760–1800', in *Int. Hist. Rev.*, xii (1990), 11–25.

— 'The origins and progress of the Catholic question, 1690–1800', in Power and Whelan, *Endurance and emergence*, 1–19.

— 'General Humbert takes his leave', in *Cathair na Mart*, xi (1991), 98–104.

— 'Militarisation and politicisation in Ireland, 1780–1820', in Bergeron and Cullen, *Culture et pratiques*, 125–36.

— 'The rise and fall of the Protestant nation, 1690–1800', in *Éire-Ireland*, xxvi, 2 (1991), 7–18.

— 'Religious rivalries in France and Ireland in the age of the French Revolution', in *E.C.I.*, vi (1991), 57–76.

— *The fall and rise of the Irish nation: The Catholic question, 1690–1830* (Dublin, 1992).
— 'The burden of the present: Theobald Wolfe Tone, republican and separatist', in Dickson, Keogh and Whelan, *United Irishmen*, 1–15.
— 'From Irish state to British Empire: Reflections on state-building in Ireland, 1690–1830', in *Études Irlandaises*, xxi, 1 (1995), 23–37.
— 'Masters of the mountains: The insurgent careers of Joseph Holt and Michael Dwyer of County Wicklow, 1798–1803', in Hannigan and Nolan, *Wicklow*, 379–410.
— 'Protestant nationalism in eighteenth-century Ireland', in O'Dea and Whelan, *Nations and nationalisms*, 79–88.
— 'Miles Byrne: United Irishman, Irish exile and *beau sabreur*', in Keogh and Furlong, *The mighty wave*, 118–38.
— 'Defence, counter-insurgency and rebellion in Ireland, 1793–1803', in Bartlett and Jeffery, *Military history*, 247–93.
— *Theobald Wolfe Tone* (Dundalk, 1997).
— 'The invasion that never was', in Murphy, *Bantry Bay*, 48–72.
— 'Bearing witness: Female evidences in courts martial convened to suppress the 1798 rebellion', in Keogh and Furlong, *Women of 1798*, 64–86.
— 'The prime informant: The life and times of the Sham Squire Francis Higgins, 1746–1802', in Póirtéir, *Great Irish rebellion*, 125–36.
— 'Éire agus an Fhrainc sna 1790í', in Ó Tuathaigh, *Éirí Amach, 1798*, 41–54.
— (ed.), *Life and times of Theobald Wolfe Tone, compiled and arranged by William Theobald Wolfe Tone* (Dublin, 1998) [repr. of 1826 ed. with introduction and additions].
— 'Lord Edward FitzGerald, 1763–1798', in Thomas Bartlett (ed.), *History and environment* (Dublin, 1998), 7–22.
— 'Repressing the rebellion in County Down', in Hill, Turner and Dawson, *Down*, 187–210.
— 'Theobald Wolfe Tone', in Cullen, *1798*, 55–62.
— 'Informers, informants and information: The secret history of the 1790s', in *Hist. Ire.*, vi, 2 (1998), 23–6.
— 'The brotherhood of affection: The United Irishmen, 1791–95', in Brennan, *Secularisation*, 33–52.
— '"This famous island set in the Virginian sea": Ireland in the British Empire, 1690–1801', in Marshall (ed.), *Oxford history of the British Empire*, ii, 253–75.
— 'Why the history of the 1798 rebellion has yet to be written', in *E.C.I.*, xv (2000), 181–90.
— 'Clemency and compensation: The treatment of defeated rebels and suffering loyalists in the administration of Lord Cornwallis', in Smyth, *Revolution*, 99–127.
— 'The 1798 rebellion in perspective', in Bull et al., *Ireland and Australia, 1798–1998*, 13–23.
— *Acts of union: An inaugural lecture delivered at University College Dublin, 24 February 2000* (Dublin, 2000).
— 'Theobald Wolfe Tone: An eighteenth-century republican and separatist', in *The Republic*, ii (2001), 38–46.
— 'Britishness, Irishness and the Act of Union', in Keogh and Whelan, *Acts of union*, 243–58 [revised version of *Acts of union*].
— 'The life and opinions of Leonard MacNally, 1752–1820: Playwright, barrister, United Irishman and informer', in Hiram Morgan (ed.), *Information, media and power through the ages* (Dublin, 2001), 113–36.
— *Revolutionary Dublin: The letters of Francis Higgins to Dublin Castle, 1795–1801* (Dublin, forthcoming).
— and Keith Jeffery (eds), *A military history of Ireland* (Cambridge, 1996).
— and David W. Hayton (eds), *Penal era and golden age: Essays in Irish history, 1690–1800* (Belfast, 1979).

— Kevin Dawson and Dáire Keogh, *Rebellion: A television history of 1798* (Dublin, 1998).

Bassett, Ray, *The commemoration of the 1798 insurrection: The Australian dimension* (Belfast, 1996).

Bates, Peadar, *1798 rebellion in Fingal: Preparation, outbreak and aftermath* (Loughshinny [County Dublin], 1998).

Battle of Antrim gamebook (Belfast, 1998) [for juvenile readers].

Battle of Carrigmoclear/ Slievenamon 1798 (Carrigmoclear [County Tipperary], 1998).

The battle of Naas 23–4 May 1798: Souvenir of 150th anniversary commemoration (Naas [County Kildare], 1948).

Beames, Michael, *Peasants and power: The Whiteboy movements and their control in pre-Famine Ireland* (Sussex and New York, 1983).

Beatty, John, 'Protestant women of county Wexford and their narratives of the rebellion of 1798', in Keogh and Furlong, *Women of 1798*, 113–36.

— (ed.), *Protestant women's narratives of the Irish Rebellion of 1798* (Dublin, 2001).

Beckett, J[ames] C[amlin], 'Anglo-Irish constitutional relations in the later eighteenth century', in *I.H.S.*, xiv (1964), 20–38.

— 'Introduction', to Crawford and Trainor (eds), *Aspects of Irish social history*, ix-xvi.

Beiner, Guy, 'Negotiations of memory: Rethinking 1798 commemoration', in *Ir. Review*, 26 (2000), 60–70.

— 'Who spoke of '98? An archaeology of social memory', in P.J. Mathews (ed.), *New voices in Irish criticism* (Dublin, 2000), 163–70.

— 'Richard Hayes, seanchas–collector extraordinaire', in *Béaloideas*, 68 (2000), 3–32.

— 'Orality lost: The archives of the Irish Folklore Commission and folk historiography of Bliain na bhFrancach', in Morgan, *Information*, 222–44.

— 'The invention of tradition', in *History Review*, xii (2001), 1–10.

— *To speak of '98: Remembering the Year of the French* (forthcoming).

Bergeron, Louis and L.M. Cullen (eds), *Culture et pratiques politiques en France et en Irelande XVIᵉ -XVIIIᵉ siècle* (Paris, 1991).

Bergin, Noel, *Kilcullen in 1798* (Kilcullen [County Kildare], 1998).

Berlin, Isaiah, *The roots of romanticism* (London, 1999).

Berman, David, 'Enlightenment and counter-enlightenment in Irish philosophy', in *Archiv für Geschichte der Philosophie*, lxiv (1982), 148–65.

— 'The culmination and causation of Irish philosophy', in *Archiv für Gesichte der Philosophie*, lxiv, 3 (1982), 257–79.

— 'Irish philosophy and the American enlightenment during the eighteenth century', in *Éire-Ireland*, xxiv, 1 (1989), 28–39.

— and Patricia O'Riordain (eds), *The Irish Enlightenment and counter-Enlightenment*, 6 vols (Bristol, forthcoming).

Beresford-Ellis, Peter, 'The United Scotsmen and the events of 1798', in Cullen, *1798*, 75–80.

Bertaud, Jean-Paul, 'Forgotten soldiers: The expedition of General Humbert to Ireland in 1798', in Gough and Dickson, *Ireland*, 220–8.

Bewglass, J.H., 'Teacher, pastor and patriot', in *Donegal Ann.* (1969), 1–6 [James Porter].

[Bigger, Francis Joseph], 'The James Hope memorial', in *U.J.A.*, vii (1901), 64.

— 'A rector jury packer [John Cleland?] in County Down in 1795', in *U.J.A.*, xi (1905), 141–2.

— *Remember Orr: The northern leaders of 1798: number one* (Dublin, 1906; new ed., Belfast, 1998).

— 'Ulster exiles on the continent after '98', in *U.J.A.*, xii, 1 (1906), 46.

— 'Hugh O'Donnell, parish priest of Belfast, 1770–1814', in *U.J.A.*, xiii, 4 (1907), 147–51.

— *Rody McCorley: Who fears to speak of '98?* (Belfast, 1907).

— 'A Ballymoney [County Antrim] patriot: Alexander Gamble of '98', in *U.J.A.*, xiv (1908), 158.

— 'Arthur MacMahon, Presbyterian minister of Kilmore and Holywood [County Down], a '98 informer', in *U.J.A.*, xv (1909), 36–41.
— 'An Antrim informer in '98' [Robby Baird], in *U.J.A.*, xv (1909), 47.
— 'Memorials of the patriot dead: [Roddy] MacCorley, [William Steel] Dickson and [Henry Joy] MacCracken', in *U.J.A.*, xv (1909), 93–5.
— 'Oliver Bond', in *U.J.A.*, xv (1909), 186.
— 'The National Volunteers of Ireland, 1782', in *U.J.A.*, xv (1909), 141–8.
— *The Ulster land war of 1770: The Hearts of Steel* (Dublin, 1910).
— 'Rural libraries in Antrim', in *Ir. Book Lover*, xii, 4 (1921), 47–52.
— 'James Porter, 1753–1798 with some notes on *Billy Bluff* and *Paddy's Resource*', in *Ir. Book Lover*, xiii (1922), 125–31.
Binions, Gloria Hurley, *1798–1998 Killanne-Rathnure: A local history* (Killanne [County Wexford], 1997).
Biographical dictionary of modern British radicals, i: *1770–1830*, ed. J.O. Baylen and N.J. Gossman (Hassocks, Sussex, 1979) [entries on T.W. Tone, 488–90: Mathew Tone, 484–8].
Blacam, Aodh de, *The life story of Wolfe Tone set in a picture of his times* (Dublin and London, 1935).
— 'Ninety-eight: The story', in *Capuchin Annual* (1948), 308–52.
— 'Wolfe Tone: Man of Dublin', in *1798 essays*, 16–21.
Black, Eileen, 'John Tennent, 1777–1813: United Irishman and Chevalier de la Legion d' Honneur', in *Ir. Sword*, xiii, 51 (1977), 157-9.
— 'James Hope, 1754–1847: United Irishman', in *Ir. Sword*, xiv, 54 (1980), 65–7.
Blackstock, Allan, 'The social and political implications of the raising of the yeomanry in Ulster, 1796–1798', in Dickson, Keogh and Whelan, *United Irishmen*, 234–43.
— 'A forgotten army: The Irish yeomanry', in *Hist. Ire.*, iv, 4 (1996), 28–33.
— 'A dangerous species of ally: Orangeism and the Irish yeomanry', in *I.H.S.*, xxx (1997), 393–405.
— *An ascendancy army: The Irish yeomanry, 1796–1834* (Dublin, 1998).
— 'The Down yeomanry', in Hill, Turner and Dawson, *Down*, 40–59.
— 'The Armagh paper war: Lord Charlemont and the United Irishmen', in *Seanchas Ard Mhacha*, xvii, 2 (1998), 60–74.
— *Double traitors? The Belfast Volunteers and yeomen, 1778–1828* (Belfast, 2000).
— 'The invincible mass: Loyal crowds in mid-Ulster, 1795–1796', in Peter Jupp and Eoin Magennis (eds), *Crowds in Ireland, 1720–1920* (Basingstoke, 2000), 83–104.
— 'The Knoxes of Dungannon and the Irish yeomanry', in Charles Dillon and Henry Jeffries (eds), *Tyrone: history and society* (Dublin, 2000), 489–509.
— 'The Union and the military, 1801–1830', in *Trans. Royal Hist. Soc.*, sixth series, x (2000), 329–51.
Blanc, Robert, *James McHenry, 1785–1845: Playwright and novelist* (Philadelphia, 1939).
Blanning, T.C., *The culture of power and the power of culture: Old regime Europe, 1660–1789* (Oxford, 2002).
Bloch, Ruth, *Visionary republic: Millennial themes in American thought, 1756–1800* (Cambridge, 1991).
Bocking, Tony, 'The battle of Ballinascarthy [County Cork] 1798: Colonel O'Reilly's communique', in *Bandon Hist. Jn.*, xv (1999), 1–4.
Bodkin, Matthias McDonnell, *Grattan's parliament before and after* (London, 1912; Dublin, 1922).
Bogue, Tom, 'Cork in 1798', in Crowley and Donnabháin, *The battle of Big Cross*, 5–6.
Bolton, G[eoffrey] C., 'Some British reactions to the Irish Act of Union', in *Ec. Hist. Rev.*, xviii, 2 (1965), 367–75.

— *The passing of the Irish Act of Union: A study in parliamentary politics* (Oxford, 1966).

Bolster, Evelyn (ed.), 'The [Francis] Moylan correspondence in Bishop's House, Killarney', in *Collect. Hib.*, xiv (1971), 82–142; xv (1972), 56–110.

Bond, Gordon, 'The siege of Flushing', in *Ir. Sword*, xi, 43 (1973), 118–28.

Booth, Alan, 'The United Englishmen and radical politics in the north-west of England, 1795–1803', in *Int. Rev. Soc. Hist.*, xxxi (1986), 271–97 [Fr James Coigly].

— 'Irish exiles, revolution and writing in England in the 1790s', in Paul Hyland and Neil Sammels (eds), *Irish writing: Exile and subversion* (London, 1991), 64–81.

Bourke, F.S., *The rebellion of 1803: An essay in bibliography* (Dublin, 1933).

— 'Patrick O'Kelly: An historian of the rebellion of 1798', in *Ir. Book Lover*, xxviii (1941), 37–43.

— 'The French invasion of 1798: A forgotten eye witness', in *Ir. Sword*, ii, 8 (1956), 289–94 [Revd Edward Mangin].

Bowes, Leo, 'Roaring Bess': Failed Wicklow rebel', in *Roundwood and District Hist. and Folklore Jn.*, i (1988), 9–11.

— 'Anne Devlin – the heroic housekeeper', in *Roundwood and District Hist. and Folklore Jn.*, iii (1990), 37–9.

Bowles, Michael, 'Lord Edward FitzGerald: A story of the man', in *Capuchin Annual* (1965), 228–40.

Boyce, D.G., 'Weary patriots: Ireland and the making of unionism', in D.G. Boyce and Alan O'Day (eds), *Defenders of the union: A survey of British and Irish unionism since 1801* (London, 2001), 15–38.

Boyce, D.G., Robert Eccleshall and Vincent Geoghegan (eds), *Political discourse in seventeenth- and eighteenth-century Ireland* (London, 2001).

Boyd, Andrew, 'Wolfe Tone: Republican hero or Whig opportunist', in *History Today*, xlviii, 6 (1998), 14–21.

Boydell, Barra, 'The United Irishmen, music, harps and national identity', in *E.C.I.*, xiii (1998), 44–52.

Boylan, Henry, *Theobald Wolfe Tone* (Dublin, 1981; 1997).

Boyle, John, 'Citizen Tone', in *Threshold*, i, 4 (1957), 30–38.

Boyne, Patrick (ed.), *Memoirs of Miles Byrne with ballads of 1798 and Robert Emmet's Speech from the Dock: School edition* (Dublin, [194–]).

Bradley, Patrick, *Bantry Bay: Ireland in the days of Napoleon and Wolfe Tone* (London, 1931).

Brady, John, *Catholics and Catholicism in the eighteenth-century press* (Maynooth [County Kildare], 1966).

— 'Lawrence O'Connor: A Meath schoolmaster', in *Ir. Eccl. Rec.*, xlix (1937), 281–7.

Brady, K.R., 'The brief for the defence of the trial of John and Henry Sheares in 1798', in *R.S.A.I. Jn.*, vii (1937), 1–25.

Brady, Seamus, 'Wolfe Tone and Donegal (with scenes from the pageant at Buncrana, 1948)', in *Donegal Hist. Soc. Jn.*, i, 2 (1948), 129–39.

Brady, Sean, 'Henry Joy McCracken', in McKearney, *Ninety-eight*, 21–4.

Brandt, Eunice, *Memoirs of the Staker Wallace with a genealogy of his family* (Chicago, 1909) [Limerick United Irishman].

Breen, Colin, *Integrated marine investigation on the historic shipwreck* La Surveillante (Coleraine [County Derry], 2001).

Breen, T.M., 'Ideology and nationalism on the eve of the American Revolution: Revisions once more in need of revising', in *Jn. Am. Hist.*, lxxxiv, i (1997), 13–39.

Brennan, John, 'Forgotten heroes of 1798', in *1798 essays*, 37–40.

Brennan, Paul (ed.), *La secularisation en Irlande* (Caen, France, 1998).

Breslin, Hugh (ed.), *The United Irishmen of the Derg* (Castlederg [County Tyrone], 1999).

Brewer, John, 'The eighteenth-century British state: Contexts and issues', in Stone, *Imperial state*, 52–72.

Bric, Maurice, 'The Irish and the evolution of the new politics in America', in P.J. Drudy (ed.), *The Irish in America: Emigration, assimilation and impact* (Cambridge, 1985), 143–68.

— 'Ireland, America and the reassessment of a special relationship 1760–83', in *E.C.I.*, xi (1996), 88–119.

— 'Patterns of Irish emigration to America, 1783–1800', in *Éire-Ireland*, xxvi, 1 and 2 (2001), 10–28.

Brims, John, 'Scottish radicalism and the United Irishmen', in Dickson, Keogh and Whelan, *United Irishmen*, 151–66.

Brock, F.W. Van, 'Dilemma at Killala', in *Ir. Sword*, viii, 33 (1968), 261–73.

— 'A memoir of 1798' [Sergt. Maj. J.B. Thomas], in *Ir. Sword*, ix, 36 (1970), 192–206.

— 'Captain MacSheehy's mission', in *Ir. Sword*, x, 40 (1972), 215–28.

— 'A proposed Irish regiment and standard', in *Ir. Sword*, xi, 45 (1974), 226–33.

— 'Sergeant Byrne's escape 1796', in *Ir. Sword*, xii, 48 (1976), 221–38.

— 'Defeat at Les Platons 1792', in *Ir. Sword*, xiii, 51 (1977), 89–105.

— 'Major General Oliver Harty in Brittany 1799–1800', in *Ir. Sword*, xiv, 57 (1981), 287–315.

— '[Hervey de Montmorency] Morres's memorial 1798', in *Ir. Sword*, xv, 58 (1982), 36–44.

— 'Louis Sherlock in Rome 1797', in *Ir. Sword*, xvi, 62 (1984), 36–47.

Brown, Katharine, 'The James Bones family circle: A United Irishman's southern American heritage', in *Familia*, xiv (1998), 1–12.

Brown, Terence, *The whole Protestant community: The making of an historical myth* (Derry, 1985).

[Browne, Bernard], *Wexford '98 Bicentenary Committee 1798–1998: A calendar of events* (Enniscorthy [County Wexford], 1998).

Browne, Ray B., 'The Paine-Burke controversy in eighteenth-century Irish songs', in Browne, Ray B., et al. (eds), *Studies in Irish culture and literature* (New York, 1970), 80–97.

Brún, Pádraig de, 'A song relative to a fight between the Kerry Militia and some yeomen at Stewartstown, County Tyrone July 1797', in *Kerry Arch. and Hist. Soc. Jn.*, vi (1973), 101–30; repr. in *The Bell*, ii (1987-8), 49–81.

Brunicardi, Niall, 'The military come to Fermoy', in *Ir. Sword*, xvi, 65 (1986), 328–31.

Bryan, Dominic, *Orange parades: The politics of ritual, tradition and control* (London, 2000).

Bull, Philip, 'The centenary of 1798 and old nationalism', in Bull et al., *Ireland and Australia*, 80–9.

Bull, Philip, Frances Devlin-Glass and Helen Doyle (eds), *Ireland and Australia 1798* (Sydney, 2000).

Bunting, Edward, *A general collection of the ancient Irish music* (London, 1796; facs. ed., Belfast, 1996).

Burgess, Eleanor, 'Lord Edward's aunt: How Louisa Conolly and her sisters faced the rebellion', in Keogh and Furlong, *Women of 1798*, 163–76.

Burke, Martin, 'Piecing together a shattered past: The historical writings of the United Irish exiles in America', in Dickson, Keogh and Whelan, *United Irishmen*, 297–306.

— 'The politics and poetics of Irish historiography: Mathew Carey and the *Vindiciae Hibernicae*', in Leerssen et al., *Forging*, 183–94.

Burns, R[obert] E., 'The Irish Penal Code and some of its historians', in *Rev. of Politics*, xxi (1959), 276–99.

— 'The Irish Popery Laws: A study of eighteenth-century legislation and behaviour', in *Rev. of Politics*, xxiv (1962), 485–508.

— *Irish parliamentary politics in the eighteenth century, 1714–1760*, 2 vols (Washington, DC, 1990).

Butler, Hubert, 'Grandmother and Wolfe Tone, being a reappraisal of Wolfe Tone and his philosophy', in *Kilkenny Magazine*, ix (1963), 38–45; x (1963), 78–82.

— *Wolfe Tone and the common name of Irishman* (Gigginstown [County Westmeath], 1985).

— *Grandmother and Wolfe Tone* (Dublin, 1990).

Butler, Marilyn, *Romantics, rebels and reactionaries: English literature and its background, 1796–1830* (Oxford, 1981).

— 'General introduction', to Marilyn Butler and Mitzi Myers (eds), *The novels and selected works of Maria Edgeworth*, 9 vols (London, 1999), i, vii–lxxx.

— 'Maria Edgeworth's histories of the future', in Stephen Collini, Richard Whatmore and Brian Young (eds), *Economy, polity and society: British intellectual history 1750–1950* (Cambridge, 2000), 168–72.

Butler, P.R., 'William Henry Tone', in *Studies*, xxxv (1946), 259–62.

Buttimer, Cornelius, 'Cogadh Sagsana nuadh sonn: Reporting the American Revolution', in *Stud. Hib.*, xxviii (1984), 63–101.

— 'A Cork Gaelic text on a Napoleonic campaign', in *J.C.H.A.S.*, xcv (1990), 107–19.

— 'A Gaelic reaction to Robert Emmet's rebellion', in *J.C.H.A.S.*, xcvii (1992), 36–53.

— 'Remembering 1798', in *J.C.H.A.S.*, ciii (1998), 1–26.

Byrne, Cyril, *Ireland and Newfoundland: The United Irish rising of 1798 and the fencibles' mutiny in St Johns, 1799* ([St. Johns, NF], [1980]).

Byrne, Miles, *Memoirs of Miles Byrne* (Paris, 3 vols, 1863; repr. Shannon, 3 vols in 1, 1972; introduction by R.B. McDowell).

— *Memoirs of Miles Byrne*, 2nd ed., 2 vols (Dublin, 1906).

— *Some notes of an Irish exile of 1798, being the chapters from the memoirs of Miles Byrne relating to Ireland* (Dublin, 1910).

[—], *Miles Byrne and the 1798 battle of Ballygullen remembered* (Monaseed [County Wexford], 1998).

Byrne, Patrick, *Lord Edward FitzGerald* (Dublin, 1955).

[Caldwell, John], 'Exiled to New York: A United Irishman's memories', *in New York Irish History*, xiii (1999), 5-9.

Calkin, Howard, 'American influence in Ireland, 1760–1800', in *Pennsylvania Mag. Hist. and Biog.*, lxxxi (1947), 103–20.

— 'La propagation en Irlande des idées de la Révolution Française', in *Annales Historiques de la Révolution Française*, xxvii (1955), 143–60.

— *Les invasions d'Irlande pendant la Révolution Française* (Paris, 1956).

— 'For and against a Union', in *Éire-Ireland*, xii, 4 (1978), 22–33.

Campbell, Flann, *The Dissenting voice: Protestant democracy in Ulster from Plantation to partition* (Belfast, 1991).

Campbell, Gerald, *Edward and Pamela FitzGerald being some account of their lives compiled from the letters of those who knew them* (London, 1904).

Campbell, Matthew, 'Thomas Moore's wild song: The 1821 *Irish Melodies*', in *Bullán*, iv, 2 (2000), 83–104.

Cannavan, Jan, 'Revolution in Ireland, evolution of woman's rights: Irish women in 1798 and 1848', in Nie and Cannavan, *Studies*, 9–15.

Canny, Nicholas, 'Irish resistance to empire? 1641, 1690 and 1798', in Laurence Stone (ed.), *An imperial state at war: Britain from 1689–1815* (London, 1994), 288–321.

Cantwell, Brian, 'Persons who died in 1798 and 1799', in *The Past*, xvii (1990), 73–6.

Cantwell, Ian, 'The trial of Patrick Murray', in *Roundwood and District Hist. and Folklore Jn.*, ii (1998), 18–22.

— Glendalough estate and the Hugos', in *Roundwood and District Hist. and Folklore Jn.*, iv (1991), 32–4.

— 'After 1798', in *Roundwood and District Hist. and Folklore Jn.*, x (1998), 41–50.

Carlow '98 Bicentenary Committee, 1798–1998: Schedule of events (Carlow, 1998).

Carey, F.P., 'The shrines for the patriot dead', in McKearney, *Ninety-eight*, 59–61.

[Carnew], *The long-handled pikes of the south: Carnew, Coolboy, Shillelagh, and districts, 1798 commemoration* (Carnew [County Wicklow], 1998).

Carr, Peter, 'The dance of the grand whistler: one townland's experience of 1798' [Portavo], in Hill, Turner and Dawson, *Down*, 231–250.

Carroll, Claire, *Circe's cup: Cultural transformations in early modern Ireland* (Cork and Notre Dame, 2001).

Carroll, Denis, *The man from God knows where: Thomas Russell, 1767–1803* (Dublin, 1995).

— *Dublin in 1798: Three illustrated walks* (Dublin, 1998).

— *Unusual suspects: Twelve radical clergymen* (Dublin, 1998) [James Coigly, James Porter, Myles Prendergast, William Steel Dickson].

Carroll, Michael, *Wolfe Tone and the French invasion of 1798* (Bantry [County Cork], 1995).

Carswell, Allan, 'The Scottish fencible regiments in Ireland', in *Ir. Sword*, xxi, 84 (1998), 155-9.

Casey, James, 'Michael Farrell: United Irishman from Ballymahon [County Longford]' [and Trinity College Dublin], in *Teathbha*, ii, 2 (1983), 122–3.

Carter, E.C., 'A wild Irishman under every Federalist's bed: Naturalisation in Philadelphia 1789–1806', in *Pennsylvania Mag. Hist. and Biog.*, xciv (1970), 331–46.

— 'Wild Irishman revisited', in *Proc. Am. Phil. Soc.*, cxxxiii (1989), 175-89.

Cassirer, Raymond, 'United Irishmen in democratic America', in *Ireland Today*, iii, 1 (1938), 131–7.

Ceretta, Manuella, 'La rivoluzione in Irlanda: Studi recenti sugli United Irishmen', in *Il Pensiero Politico*, xxx, 3 (1997), 494–513.

— (ed.), *A difesa dei Cattolici d'Irlanda: Theobald Wolfe Tone* (Milano, 1998).

— *Nazione e popolo nella rivoluzione Irlandese: gli United Irishmen, 1791–1800* (Milano, 1999).

— 'Tolleranza e liberta di coscienza nell'Irlanda del settecento', in Vittorio Dini (ed.), *Tolleranza e liberta* (Milano, 2001), 143–73.

Chambers, George, 'Divided loyalties in the business community of Belfast in 1798', in *Familia*, ii, 10 (1994), 13–38.

Chambers, Liam, *Rebellion in Kildare, 1790–1803* (Dublin, 1998).

— *1798 and Maynooth* (Maynooth [County Kildare], 1998).

— 'The state solicitor's report on the 1803 rebellion in County Kildare', in *Jn. Kild. Arch. Soc.*, xix, part 1 (2000–1), 217–26.

Charles, P., 'Le Corps Irlandais au service de la France sous le Consultat et L'Empire', in *Revue historique des armées*, ii (1976), 25–54.

Chart, D[avid] A[lfred], *Ireland from Union to Catholic Emancipation: A study of social, economic and administrative conditions 1800–1829* (London, 1910).

— 'The Irish levies during the Great French War', in *Eng.Hist.Rev.*, xxxii (1913), 79–102.

— (ed.), *The Drennan letters being a selection from the correspondence which passed between William Drennan and Samuel and Martha McTier, 1776–1819* (Belfast, 1931).

— 'The close alliance between church and state', in W.A. Philips (ed.), *History of the Church of Ireland* (Oxford, 1933), 175–241.

Chathain, Nora Ní, 'Watty Graham, the Maghera [County Derry] patriot', in McKearney, *Ninety-eight*, 53–6.

Childe-Pemberton, William, *The earl-bishop: The life of Frederick Hervey, bishop of Derry, earl of Bristol*, 2 vols (London, 1924: 1925).

Christie, Ian, *Stress and stability in late eighteenth-century Britain* (Oxford, 1984).

Chuquet, Arthur (ed.), *Quatre généraux de la Revolution: Hoche et Desaix, Kleber et Marceau*, 4 vols (Paris, 1911–20).

Claeys, Gregory (ed.), *Political writings of the 1790s*, 8 vols (London, 1995).

Clark, Anna, *The struggle for the breeches: Gender and the making of the British working class* (Berkeley, CA, 1985).

Clarke, Basil, 'Joseph Stock and Killala', in *Éire-Ireland*, xx, i (1985), 58–72.

Clark, Brian and F.G. Thompson, 'Napoleon's Irish legion 1803–1815: The historical record', in *Ir. Sword*, xii, 48 (1976), 164–72.

Clark, Samuel and James Donnelly (eds), *Irish peasants: violence and political unrest, 1780–1914* (Madison, WI, 1983).

Clark, W.B., 'In defense of Thomas Digges', in *Pennsylvania Mag. Hist. and Biog.*, lxxvii (1953), 381–438.

Clark, William Smith, *The Irish stage in the country towns, 1720–1800* (Oxford, 1965).

Clarke, J.C.D., *The language of liberty, 1660–1832* (Cambridge, 1994).

Clarke-Robinson, W., 'James MacHenry', in *U.J.A.*, xiv (1908), 127–32.

Claydon, Tony and Ian MacBride (eds), *Protestantism and national identity* (Cambridge, 1988).

Cleary, Brian, 'Reaping the whirlwind', in *Wex. Hist. Soc. Jn.*, xiv (1992–93), 9–79 [Wexford politics, 1792].

— 'The battle of Oulart Hill: Context and strategy', in Keogh and Furlong, *The mighty wave*, 79–96.

— 'Wexford in 1798: A republic before its time', in Póirtéir, *Great Irish rebellion*, 101–14.

— '1798 i Loch Garman', in Ó Tuathaigh, *Éirí Amach, 1798*, 81–92.

— 'Poblacht Loch Garman: Meitheamh 1798', in Ó Snodaigh, *Fealsúnacht*, 159–68.

— (ed.), *Tulach a' tSolais* [Oulart Hill]: *Souvenir programme* (Oulart [County Wexford], 1998).

— *The battle of Oulart Hill* (Oulart, 1999).

Clesham, Brigid, 'Lord Altamont's letters to Lord Lucan about the Act of Union 1800', in *Galway Arch. & Hist. Soc. Jn.*, 54 (2002), 25–34.

Clifford, Brendan, *The origin and progress of the Irish union (1807) by Thomas Addis Emmet, William James MacNevin and Arthur O'Connor* (Belfast, 1974).

— *Belfast politics by Henry Joy and the Revd William Bruce* (Belfast, 1974).

— *Belfast in the French Revolution* (Belfast, 1989).

— *Aspects of the movement of the United Irishmen* (Belfast, 1991).

— *Scripture politics: Selections from the writings of William Steel Dickson, the most influential United Irishman of the North* (Belfast, 1991).

— *Billy Bluff and the Squire (a satire on the aristocracy) and other writings by the Revd James Porter who was hanged in the course of the United Irishman rebellion of 1798* (Belfast, 1991).

— *The causes of the rebellion in Ireland (1799) and other writings by the Revd Thomas Ledlie Birch* (Belfast, 1991).

— *An argument on behalf of the Catholics of Ireland (1791) by Theobald Wolfe Tone* (Belfast, 1992).

— *Freemasonry and the United Irishmen: Reprints from the* Northern Star, *1792–3* (Belfast, 1992).

— *The origins of Irish Catholic nationalism: Selections from Walter Cox's* Irish Magazine *1807–1815* (Belfast, 1992).

— *Prison adverts and potato diggings: Materials from the public life of Antrim and Down during the years of Government terror which led to the rebellion of 1798* (Belfast, 1992).

— *Edmund Burke and the United Irishmen: A talk given at the Duhallow Heritage Centre 14 Apr. 1993* (Belfast, 1994).

— Orange: A political rhapsody in three cantos *1798 by George Giffard* (Belfast, 1995).

— *Thomas Russell and Belfast with Russell's* Letter to the people of Ireland *(1796) and other writings* (Belfast, 1988; 1997).

— Address to the people of Ireland *by Theobald Wolfe Tone and* Napoleon *by Walter Cox* (Belfast, 1996).

— *Lord Downshire and the United Irishmen: A selection from the Downshire papers, 1793–1799 with a historical review of the British constitution* (Belfast, 1998).

— *William Drennan, 1754–1820* (Belfast, 1998).

— and Pat Muldowney (ed.), *Bolg an tSolar: The Gaelic Magazine, 1795* (Belfast, 1999).

Cloney, Sean, 'The Hessians', in *Wex. Hist. Soc. Jn.*, xiv (1992–3), 113–28.

— 'South-west Wexford in 1798', in *Wex. Hist. Soc. Jn.*, xv (1994–5), 74–97.

— 'A 1798 ambush', in *Wex. Hist. Soc. Jn.*, xvii (1998–99), 235–37 [Arklow, County Wexford].

Cohen, M., 'Irish influences on early American law books: Authors, printers and subjects', in *Ir. Jurist*, xxxvi (2001), 199–213.

Cole, R. Cargill, *Irish booksellers and English writers, 1740–1800* (Whitstable, 1986).

Coleman, John, 'Luke Gardiner 1745-98: An Irish dilettante', in *Ir. Arts Rev.*, xv (1999), 160–8.

Colleran, Gabriel, 'The Year of the French', in Bernard O'Hara (ed.), *Mayo: Aspects of its heritage* (Galway, 1982), 88–95.

Colley, Linda, *Britons: Forging the nation, 1707–1837* (London, 1992).

— 'The reach of the state, the appeal of the nation: Mass arming and political culture in the Napoleonic wars', in Stone, *Imperial state*, 45–61.

— 'Britishness and otherness: An argument', in O'Dea and Whelan, *Nations and nationalisms*, 61–77.

Collins, John T., 'The Emmet family connection with Munster', in *J.C.H.A.S.*, lviii, 188 (1953), 77–80.

Collins, Peter, 'Remembering '98', in *Causeway* (Winter, 1997), 25–8.

— 'The contest of memory: The continuing impact of 1798 commemoration', in *Éire-Ireland*, xxxiv, 2 (1999), 28–50.

— *Who fears to speak of '98? The historical commemoration of 1798* (Belfast, forthcoming).

Come, Donald, 'French threat to British shores, 1793–1798', in *Military Affairs*, xvi, 4 (1952), 174–88.

Comer, Michael,'Humbert in Swinford [County Mayo]' in *Swinford Echoes* (1997), 95–7.

Comerford, Máire, 'Celebrations down south', in McKearney, *Ninety-eight*, 51–2.

Comerford, Patrick, 'Euseby Cleaver, bishop of Ferns and the clergy of the Church of Ireland in the 1798 rebellion in County Wexford', in *Wex. Hist. Soc. Jn.*, xvi (1996–7), 66–94.

— 'The Church of Ireland in County Kilkenny and the diocese of Ossory during the 1798 rising', in *Old Kilk. Rev.*, l (1998), 144–82.

— 'Church of Ireland clergy and the 1798 rising', in Swords, *Protestant, Catholic and Dissenter*, 219–52.

— 'Simon Butler and the forgotten role of the Church of Ireland during the 1798 rising', in *Jn. Butler Soc.*, iv, 2 (2000), 271–79.

Commemorating the founding of the first Society of United Irishmen in County Wexford, 1792–1992: Souvenir programme (Gorey [County Wexford], 1992).

Comóradh '98 in Baile Átha Cliath: '98 commemorative march 14–21 Samhain (Dublin, 1948).

Concannon, Helena, *The women of 'Ninety-Eight* (Dublin, 1920).

Concubhair, P.S., *Discreet and steady men: Kerry's role in '98* (Ballylongford [County Kerry], 1999).

Conlon, Larry, 'The influence of freemasonry in east Cavan during the rebellion of 1798', in *Breifne*, vii (1997), 782–807.

— 'The influence of freemasonry in Meath and Westmeath in the eighteenth century', in *Ríocht na Mídhe*, ix, 3 (1997), 128–57.

— 'Dissension, radicalism and republicanism in Monaghan and the role of freemasonry up to and during the 1798 rebellion', in *Clogher Rec.*, xvi, 3 (1999), 86–111.

Conner, Clifford, *Colonel Despard: The life and death of an English/Irish Jacobin* (Conshocken and London, 1999; 2000).

Conniff, James, 'Edmund Burke's reflections on the coming revolution in Ireland', in *Jn. Hist. Ideas*, xlvii, 1 (1986), 37–59.

Connolly, Claire, 'I accuse Miss Owenson: The *Wild Irish Girl* as media event', in *Colby Quarterly*, June (2000), 98–115.

— 'Introduction', to Maria Edgeworth, *Ennui* (London, 2000), xi–xxxvi.

— 'Reflections on the Act of Union', in John Whale (ed.), *Edmund Burke's* Reflections on the revolution in France: *New interdisciplinary essays* (Manchester, 2000), 168–92.

— 'Writing the union', in Keogh and Whelan, *Acts of union*, 168–92.

Connolly, Frank (ed.), *Re-enactment of the Back Lane parliament 5 December 1998* (Dublin, 1998).

[Connolly, S.J. (ed.)], *The rebellion of 1798: Facsimile documents from the Public Records Office* (Dublin, 1979).

— *Religion, law and power: The making of Protestant Ireland 1660–1770* (Oxford, 1992).

— 'The United Irishmen at Trinity' [review], in *Bullán*, i, 1 (1994), 148–50.

— 'Eighteenth-century Ireland: Colony or Ancien Regime?' in D.G. Boyce and Alan O'Day (eds), *The making of modern Irish history: Revisionism and the revisionist controversy* (London, 1996), 15–33.

— (ed.), *Political ideas in eighteenth-century Ireland* (Dublin, 2000).

— 'The Glorious Revolution in Irish Protestant political thinking', in Connolly (ed.), *Political ideas*, 27–54.

— 'Precedent and principle: The Patriots and their critics', in Connolly (ed.), *Political ideas*, 130–58.

— 'The Irish rebellion of 1798: An end or a beginning?' in Hans-Dieter Metzger (ed.), *Religious thinking and national identity* (Berlin, 2000), 108–22.

— 'Reconsidering the Irish Act of Union', in *Trans. Royal Hist. Soc.*, sixth series, x (2000), 399–408.

Conway, Stephen, *The British Isles and the war of American independence* (Oxford, 2000).

— 'War and national identity in the mid eighteenth-century British Isles', in *Eng.Hist.Rev.*, cxvi (2001), pp 863–93.

[Conwell, Eugene], *Letters from Maynooth: Calendar of letters of the Revd Eugene Conwell, 1774–1805* (Dundalk [County Louth], 1942).

Coogan, Oliver, 'Sectarianism in Meath 1792–98', in *Ríocht na Mídhe*, x (1999), 91–124.

Cookson, J.E., *The Friends of Peace: Anti-war liberalism in England, 1793–1815* (Cambridge, 1982).

— *The British armed nation, 1793–1815* (Oxford, 1997).

Cooper, Bryan, 'A rebel's diary', in *Cornhill Mag.*, new series, xlix, July-Dec. (1920), 490–501 [on T.W. Tone].

Cooney, John (ed.), *The Irish-French alliance: Papers of the first General Humbert summer school* ([Dublin], 1987).

— 'Two French revolutionary soldiers in rebel Ireland', in *Études Irlandaises*, xiii, 2 (1988), 101–7 [Humbert, Sarrazin].

— *Humbert's expedition: A lost cause* (Dublin, 1989).

— 'En campagne avec l'armée d'Humbert', in *Études Irlandaises*, xxiii, 2 (1998), 137–49.

Copeland, Thomas et al. (eds), *The correspondence of Edmund Burke*, 10 vols (Cambridge, 1958–78).

Corbett, Mary Jean, 'Allegories of prescription: Engendering union in *The Wild Irish Girl*', in *Eighteenth-century Life*, xxii, 3 (1998), 92–102.

— *Allegories of union in Irish and English writing, 1790–1870* (Cambridge, 2000).

Corish, Patrick, *The Catholic community in the seventeenth and eighteenth centuries* (Dublin, 1981).

— (ed.), *Radicals, rebels, and establishments* (Belfast, 1985).

— *Maynooth College, 1795–1995* (Dublin, 1995).

— 'James Caulfield, bishop of Ferns 1786–1814', in *Wex. Hist. Soc. Jn.*, xvi (1996–7), 114–25.

— 'Les seminaires Irlandais du continent, la Révolution Française et les origines du Collège de Maynooth', in *Études Irlandaises*, xxiii, 2 (1998), 121–35.

Cornou, Jakez and Bruno Jonin, *L'odyssée du vaisseau* Droits de l'homme *et l'expédition d'Irlande de 1796* (Quimper, 1988).

Corrigan, Mario, *All that delirium of the brave: Kildare in 1798* (Naas [County Kildare], 1997).

Costello, Con, 'Wolfe Tone and Naas', in *Kildare Arch. Soc. Jn.*, xiv (1964–70), 361.

Costello, Nuala (ed.), 'Little's diary of the French landing in 1798', in *Anal. Hib.*, xi (1941), 59–174 [Revd James Little of Lacken, County Mayo].

— 'Journal de l'expédition d'Irlande suivi de notes sur le Général Humbert qui l'a commandé', in *Anal. Hib.*, xi (1941), 5–55 [Jean Louis Jobit's diary of Humbert's expedition to Ireland 1798].

Costigan, Giovanni, 'The tragedy of Charles O'Conor: An episode in Anglo-Irish relations', in *Am. Hist. Rev.*, xlix, 1 (1943), 32–54.

Coughlan, Rupert, *Napper Tandy* (Dublin, 1976).

Cox, Gerard, 'Tone: murder or suicide?', in *1798 essays*, 25–7.

Cox, Liam, 'Westmeath in the 1798 period', in *Ir. Sword*, ix, 34 (1969), 1–15.

Coyle, Eugene, 'From Abbyville to Quebec: The life and times of General Richard Montgomery', in *Dub. Hist. Rec.*, liv, 2 (2001), 146–60.

Craig, Maurice, *The Volunteer earl* (London, 1948) [on Charlemont].

Crawford, W.H.,'The linen triangle in the 1790s', in *Ulster Local Studies*, xviii, 2 (1997), 43–52.

— 'The social structure of Ulster in the eighteenth century', in Cullen and Furet, *Irlande et France*, 117–28.

Crawford, W.H. and Brian Trainor (ed.), *Aspects of Irish social history, 1750–1800* (Belfast, 1969).

Crean, Tom, '1798 – myth versus reality', in *Socialism Today*, xxxiv, (Jan. 1999), 10–16.

Crone, J.S., 'Funeral of Lord Castlereagh in Westminister Abbey 1822', in *U.J.A.*, xii (1906), 95.

— 'Lord Castlereagh's funeral', in *U.J.A.*, xiii (1907), 144.

— '*Songs of the French Revolution* printed at Belfast 1792', in *U.J.A.*, xv (1909), 119–24.

Cronin, Maura, 'Memory, story and balladry: 1798 and its place in popular memory in pre-Famine Ireland', in Geary, *Rebellion and remembrance*, 112–34.

Cronin, Sean, *Wolfe Tone: Wolfe Tone's bicentenary June 1963* (Dublin, 1963).

— *A man of the people: Jemmy Hope* (Drogheda, 1964; new ed. Dublin, 1998).

— *The revolutionaries: The story of twelve great Irishmen* (Dublin, 1971) [includes Wolfe Tone and Robert Emmet].

— *Tone's republic: The case against sectarianism* (Dublin, 1975).

— *For whom the hangman's rope was spun: Wolfe Tone and the United Irishmen* (Dublin, 1991).

— and Richard Roche (eds), *Freedom the Wolfe Tone way* (Tralee [County Kerry], 1973) [introduction by Jack Bennett].

Crooks, Elizabeth, 'Exhibiting 1798: Three recent exhibitions', in *Hist. Ire.*, vi, 4 (1998), 41–5 [National Museum, Ulster Museum, National 1798 Centre].

Crosslé, F.C., *Volunteers and yeomanry of the Newry district* (Belfast, 1934).

Crossman, Virginia, 'The *Shan Van Vocht*: Women, republicanism and the commemoration of the 1798 rebellion', in *Eighteenth-century Life*, xxii, 3 (1998), 128–39.

Crowe, Ian (ed.), *Edmund Burke: his life and legacy* (Dublin, 1997).

Crowley, Tim and Traolach Ó Donnabháin (eds), *The battle of the Big Cross/Cath Beál a' Mhuighe Shálaigh commemorative journal* (Clonakilty [County Cork], 1998).

Culhane, J., 'Traditions of Glin and neighbourhood', in *Kerry Arch. and Hist. Soc. Jn.*, ii (1969), 74–101.

Cuimhnighimeis ar '98, 1798–1948: All-Ireland celebrations at Vinegar Hill 20 June 1948 (Enniscorthy [County Wexford], 1948).

Cullen, Fintan, *Visual politics: The representation of Ireland, 1750–1930* (Cork, 1997).

— 'Lord Edward FitzGerald: The creation of an icon', in *Hist. Ire.*, vi, 4 (1998), 17–20.

— 'Radicals and reactionaries: Portraits of the 1790s in Ireland', in Smyth, *Revolution*, 161–94.

Cullen, Louis M., 'The Hidden Ireland: Reassessment of a concept', in *Stud. Hib.*, ix (1969), 7–48.

— 'The cultural basis of modern Irish nationalism', in Rosalind Mitchison (ed.), *The roots of nationalism* (Edinburgh, 1980), 91–106.

— 'Ireland and France 1600–1900', in Cullen and Furet, *Irlande et France*, 9–20.

— *The emergence of modern Ireland 1600–1900* (London, 1981).

— 'The political structures of the Defenders', in Gough and Dickson, *Ireland*, 117–38.

— 'Catholics under the Penal Laws', in *E.C.I.*, i (1986), 23–36.

— 'The 1798 rebellion in its eighteenth-century context', in Corish, *Radicals, rebels and establishments*, 91–113.

— 'The 1798 rebellion in Wexford: United Irishmen organisation, membership, leadership', in Whelan, *Wexford*, 248–95.

— *The Hidden Ireland: Reassessment of a concept* (Gigginstown [County Westmeath], 1988) [repr. of 1969 article, with notes and translations of the Irish material by Mairín Ní Dhonnchada].

— 'Catholic social classes under the Penal Laws', in Power and Whelan, *Endurance and emergence*, 57–84.

— 'Late eighteenth-century politicisation in Ireland: Problems in its study and its French links', in Bergeron and Cullen, *Culture et pratiques*, 137–58.

— 'Burke, Ireland and revolution', in *Eighteenth-century Life*, xvi, 1 (1992), 22–42.

— 'The internal politics of the United Irishmen', in Dickson, Keogh and Whelan, *United Irishmen*, 179–96.

— 'Politics and rebellion in Wicklow in the 1790s', in Hannigan and Nolan, *Wicklow*, 411–501.

— 'The United Irishmen in Wexford', in Keogh and Furlong, *The mighty wave*, 48–64.

— 'The political troubles of Armagh: A comment', in *I.E.S.H.*, xxiii (1996), 18–23.

— 'Poetry, culture and politics ', in *Studia Celtica Japonica*, viii (1996), 1–26.

— 'The United Irishmen: Problems and issues of the 1790s', in *Ulster Local Studies*, xviii, 2 (1997), 7–27.

— 'Burke's Irish views and writings', in Crowe, *Burke*, 62–75.

— 'The politics of clerical radicalism in the 1790s', in Swords, *Protestant, Catholic and Dissenter*, 274–309.

— 'Rebellion mortality in Wexford in 1798', in *Wex. Hist. Soc. Jn.*, xvii (1998–99), 7–29.

— 'The politics of crisis and rebellion 1792–1798', in Smyth, *Revolution*, 21–38.

— 'Alliances and misalliances in the politics of the Union', in *Trans. Royal Hist. Soc.*, sixth series, x (2000), 221–41.

Cullen, Mary, 'Partners in struggle: The women of 1798', in Póirtéir, *Great Irish rebellion*, 146–59.

— 'United in struggle: The women of 1798', in Finlay, *Radicals*, 20–3.

— (ed.), *1798: 200 years of resonance* (Dublin, 1998).

Cullen, Seamus and Hermann Geissel (eds), *Fugitive warfare: 1798 in north Kildare* (Clane [County Kildare], 1998).

Cummins, Seamus, 'Pike heads and the calico printer: Leixlip in '98', in *Kild. Arch. Soc. Jn.*, xvi (1985–6), 418–31 [John Smyth].

Cunningham, John, 'Belleek, Ballyshannon and Pettigo in the 1790s', in *Ulster Local Studies*, xxxiv, 2 (1997), 95–101; repr. in Mac Annaidh, *Fermanagh*, 78–85.

Curtin, Nancy, 'The transformation of the Society of United Irishmen into a mass-based revolutionary organisation 1794–6', in *I.H.S.*, xxiv (1985), 463–72.
— 'The Belfast uniform: Theobald Wolfe Tone', in *Éire-Ireland*, xx, 2 (1985), 40–69.
— 'Symbols and rituals of United Irish mobilisation', in Gough and Dickson, *Ireland*, 68–82.
— 'Women and eighteenth-century Irish republicanism', in Margaret MacCurtain and Mary O'Dowd (ed.), *Women in early modern Ireland* (Edinburgh, 1991), 133–47.
— 'The United Irish organisation in Ulster 1795-8', in Dickson, Keogh and Whelan, *United Irishmen*, 209–21.
— *The United Irishmen: Popular politics in Ulster and Dublin, 1791–1798* (Oxford, 1994).
— 'Varieties of Irishness: Historical revisionism Irish-style', in *Jn. British Studies*, xxxv, 2 (1996), 195–219.
— 'Matilda Tone and virtuous republican femininity', in Keogh and Furlong, *Women of 1798*, 26–46.
— 'Rebels and radicals: The United Irish in County Down', in Lindsay Proudfoot (ed.), *Down: History and society* (Dublin, 1997), 267-96.
— 'Ideology and materialism: Politicisation and Ulster weavers in the 1790s', in Marilyn Cohen (ed.), *The warp of Ulster's past* (London, 1997), 111–38.
— 'The magistracy and counter-revolution in Ulster 1795–1798', in Smyth, *Revolution*, 39–54.
— 'A perfect liberty: The rise and fall of the Irish Whigs 1789-97', in Boyce, Eccleshall and Geoghegan, *Political discourse*, 270–89.
Curtis, Perry, 'Moral and physical force: The language of violence in Irish nationalism', in *Jn. British Studies*, xxvii, 2 (1988), 150–89.
D'Alton, E.A., 'The French in Mayo 1798', in *Jn. Galway Arch. and Hist. Soc.*, iv (1905–6), 219–25.
Daly, Mary and David Dickson (eds), *The origins of popular literacy in Ireland* (Dublin, 1990).
Davies, Simon, 'The idea of nationalism in Belfast in the late eighteenth-century', in *Enlightenment and Dissent*, vii (1988), 25–33.
— 'The *Northern Star* and the propagation of enlightenment ideals', in *E.C.I.*, v (1990), 143–52.
Davis, Leith, *Acts of union: Scotland and the literary negotiation of the British nation, 1707–1830* (Stanford, CA, 1998).
Davis, Michael (ed.), *Radicalism and revolution in Britain, 1775–1848* (London, 2000).
Davis, William, 'William James MacNevin, chemist and United Irishman', in Wyse Jackson (ed.), *Science*, 7–24.
Dawson, Kenneth, 'The military leadership of the United Irishmen in County Down, 1796–1798', in Hill, Turner and Dawson, *Down*, 20–39.
[Day, Robert], 'Lord Edward FitzGerald', in *J.C.H.A.S.*, xiii (1907), 47–8.
Deane, Marion (ed.), Belmont Castle or suffering sensibility *by Theobald Wolfe Tone and divers hands* (Dublin, 1998).
Deane, Seamus, 'Irish national character 1790–1900', in Tom Dunne (ed.), *The writer as witness* (Cork, 1987), 90–113.
— *The French Enlightenment and revolution in England, 1789–1832* (Harvard, MA, 1988).
— 'Enlightenment', in W.J. McCormack (ed.), *The Blackwell companion to Irish culture* (London, 1999), 198–200.
— *Strange country: Modernity and nationhood in Irish writing since 1790* (Oxford, 1997).
— 'Programme note', in Whelan, *Northern Star*, 18.
— 'Montesquieu and Burke', in Gargett and Sheridan, *Ireland*, 47–66.
— 'Factions and fictions: Burke, colonialism and revolution', in *Bullán*, iv, 2 (2000), 5–26.
De Búrca, Seán, 'An echo of 1798', in *Cathair na Mart*, xix (1999), 47.
Dechamps, Jules, *Les Iles Britanniques et la Révolution Française, 1798–1803* (Bruxelles, 1949).

Denman, Terence, 'Irish recruitment to the British army 1660–1815', in *Ir. Sword*, xx (1996), 148–66.

De Nie, Michael and Jan Cannavan, *Studies on 1798 and 1848* (Fort Lauderdale, FL, 1999).

—— 'The French disease: The British press and 1798', in Nie and Cannavan, *Studies*, 1–8.

De Paor, Liam, 'Contae an Chláir le linn Thomáis Uí Mhiocháin', in Diarmaid Ó Muirithe, *Tomás Ó Miocháin: Filíocht* (Baile Átha Cliath, 1988), 11–32 [another version: 'The world of Brian Merriman: County Clare in 1780', in Liam de Paor, *Landscape with figures* (Dublin, 1998), 37–64].

—— 'The voice of Tone', in *Landscape with figures*, 65–7 [from *Irish Times*, 2 Aug. 1972].

Desbrière, Edouard, *Projets et tentatives de débarquement aux Îles Britanniques, 1793–1805*, 5 vols (Paris, 1900–02).

'Description of a rebel, 1798', in *Ir. Sword*, xv (1982–83), p. 75 [Captain Michael Doorley of County Kildare].

D'Esparbes, Georges, *Le briseur de fers: Invasion du Général Humbert en Irlande. Chants bardique* (Paris, 1908).

de Paor, Liam, 'Oidhreacht 1798', in Ó Tuathaigh, *Éirí amach 1798*, 123–36.

De Valera, Terry, 'Letters of the Sheares brothers', in *Dub. Hist. Rec.*, xliii (1990), 58–68.

Devlin, Cronan (ed.), *1798: A union of wills? Proceedings of Scoil Shlíabh gCuillinn* (Newry [County Down], 1998).

Dickinson, H.E. (ed.), *Britain and the French Revolution, 1789–1815* (London, 1989).

—— 'Irish radicalism in the late eighteenth-century [review article]', in *History*, lxxxii (1997), 266–84.

—— (ed.), *Britain and the American Revolution* (London, 1998).

—— 'The friends of America: British sympathy with the American Revolution', in Davis, *Radicalism*, 1–29.

Dickson, Charles, *The life of Michael Dwyer with some account of his companions* (Dublin, 1944).

—— 'The battle of Vinegar Hill 1798', in *Ir. Sword*, i, 4 (1952–3), 293–5.

—— *The Wexford rising in 1798: Its causes and its course* (Tralee, 1955; repr., London, 1997).

—— *Revolt in the north: Antrim and Down in 1798* (Dublin, 1960; repr., London, 1997).

—— 'Lord Edward FitzGerald', in *1798 essays*, 31–6.

—— 'The battle of New Ross', in G.A. Hayes McCoy (ed.), *The Irish at war* (Cork, 1964), 71–82.

—— 'A note on 1798', in *Ir. Sword*, ix, 35 (1969), 109–12.

—— (ed.), 'A letter from [Mrs Mary Cooke, Woodlands] County Waterford in 1798', in *Ir. Sword*, x (1970), 283–7.

Dickson, David, 'Property and social structure in eighteenth-century south Munster', in Cullen and Furet, *Irlande et France*, 129–38.

—— 'Taxation and disaffection in late eighteenth-century Ireland', in Clark and Donnelly, *Irish peasants*, 37–63.

—— (ed.), *The gorgeous mask: Dublin, 1700–1850* (Dublin, 1987).

—— *New foundations: Ireland 1660–1800* (Dublin, 1987; 2000).

—— 'Henry Flood and the eighteenth-century Irish patriots', in Ciarán Brady (ed.), *Worsted in the game: Losers in Irish history* (Dublin, 1989), 97–110.

—— 'Centres of motion: Irish cities and the origins of popular politics', in Bergeron and Cullen, *Culture et pratiques*, 101–22.

—— 'In the shadow of revolution: Robert Emmet and Wolfe Tone', in David Scott (ed.), *Treasures of the mind: A Trinity College Dublin quatercentenary exhibition* (London, 1992), 33–44.

—— 'Paine and Ireland', in Dickson, Keogh and Whelan, *United Irishmen*, 135–50.

—— 'Introduction', to Musgrave, *Memoirs*, i–xiii.

—— 'The South Munster region in the 1790s', in Murphy, *Bantry Bay*, 85–94.

—— 'The state of Ireland before 1798', in Póirtéir, *Great Irish rebellion*, 15–25.

Dickson, David, Dáire Keogh and Kevin Whelan (eds), *The United Irishmen: Republicanism, radicalism and rebellion* (Dublin, 1993).

Dixon, Roger, 'Francis Bigger: Ulster's Don Quixote', in *Ulster Folklife*, xliii (1997), 40–7.

— 'The northern leaders of 1798', in *Familia*, xiv (1998), 108–12 [review article on Bigger, *Orr*].

— 'Heroes for a new Ireland: Francis Joseph Bigger and the leaders of 1798', in Trefor Owen (ed.), *From Corrib to Cultra: Folklife essays in honour of Alan Gailey* (Belfast, 2000), 29–38.

Doherty, Michael, '1798: one man's views on certain episodes (a fantasy)', in *Bliainiris*, iii, 3 (1995–6), 82–4.

Donald, Diana, *The age of caricature: Satirical prints in the age of George III* (New Haven, CT, 1998).

Donnelly, James, 'The Rightboy movement', in *Studia Hib.*, xvii–xviii (1977–8), 120–202.

— 'The Whiteboy movement 1761–5', in *I.H.S.*, xxi (1978), 20–54.

— 'Propagating the cause of the United Irishmen', in *Studies*, lxix (1980), 5–23.

— 'Hearts of Oak, Hearts of Steel', in *Studia Hib.*, xxi (1981), 7–73.

— 'Irish agrarian rebellion: The Whiteboys of 1769–76', in *R.I.A. Proc.* 83, C (1983), 293–331.

— 'Republicanism and reaction in the 1790s', in *I.E.S.H.*, xi (1984), 94–100 [review article].

— 'Sectarianism in 1798 and in Catholic nationalist memory', in Geary, *Rebellion and remembrance*, 15–37.

— and Kerby Miller (ed.), *Irish popular culture 1650–1850* (Dublin, 1998).

Donohoe, P.A., *1798 rebellion – brave rebels all: Wexford, Wicklow, Carlow, Kildare* (Enniscorthy [County Wexford], 1998).

Donohue, Tony, 'Some recollections of local involvement in the 1798 rebellion: Crossmolina and Addergoole [County Mayo]' in *Bliainiris*, i, 1 (1982), 36–40.

Donovan, Patrick, *Military tattoo commemorating the battle of Ross by the Ross battalion F.C.A. in Barretts Park, New Ross 5–6 June 1948* (New Ross, 1948).

Donovan, Robert Kent, 'The military origins of the Roman Catholic Relief programme of 1788', in *Hist. Jn.*, xxviii, 1 (1985), 79–102.

Dooher, John, 'Strabane [County Tyrone] and the north-west in the decade of rebellion', in *Ulster Local Studies*, xix, 1 (1997), 7–31.

[Doran, Harry and Jimmy Doyle (eds)], *Selected songs and ballads of '98* (Carrigbyrne [County Wexford], 1999).

Dougherty, Jane Elizabeth, 'Mr and Mrs England: The Act of Union and national marriage', in Keogh and Whelan, *Acts of union*, 202–15.

Douglas, Dick, *The only safe place: The Irish state prisoners at Fort George* (Auchtermuchty [Scotland], 2000).

Douglas, Glynn, *Friends and 1798: Quaker witness to non-violence in eighteenth-century Ireland* (Dublin, 1998).

Dowd, B.T., 'James Meehan', in *Jn. Royal Australian Hist. Soc.*, xxviii, part 1 (1942), 108–18.

Dowds, Thomas, *The French invasion of Ireland in 1798: Tireragh [County Sligo]* (Dublin, 1998).

Dowling, Danny, 'South-east Kilkenny in 1798 and the role of William Gaffney', in *Decies*, xxiv (1983), 15–19.

Down district, 1798 Bicentenary Committee: Schedule of events 1998 (Downpatrick, 1998).

Doyle, Danny and Turlough Folan, *The gold sun of Irish freedom: 1798 in song and story* (Cork, 1998).

Doyle, David, *Ireland, Irishmen and Revolutionary America, 1760–1820* (Cork, 1981).

Doyle, Eamon, *The Wexford insurgents of '98 and their march into Meath* (Enniscorthy [County Wexford], 1997).

Doyle, Geraldine, *Boolavogue, 1798–1998: A compilation of articles relating to the United Irishmen's rebellion and the commemoration of that event down through the years* (Boolavogue [County Wexford], 1998).

Doyle, Jerry and Tommy Roche, *The forgotten man of 1798* (Marshalstown [County Wexford], 1998) [James Gallagher].

Doyle, [James], *The pageant of New Ross 5 June 1998: Souvenir programme containing a concise history of the battle of Ross* (New Ross [County Wexford], 1998).

— 'Robert Carthy of Birchgrove', in *Wex. Hist. Soc. Jn.*, xvii (1998–99), 101–20.

— 'Denis Carty, rebel and explorer', in *Bree Parish Jn.* (2000), 16–17.

— 'One of Ogle's Loyal Blues', in *The Past*, xxii (2000), 101–20 [Nathaniel Pidgeon].

Doyle, Jimmy, Thomas O'Shea and Tom Dunne (eds), *Davidstown-Courtnacuddy remembers, 1798* (Davidstown [County Wexford], 1998).

Doyle, Jude, *Fr Philip Roche, commander-in-chief: Life and times of a '98 rebel priest* (Clonroche [County Wexford], 1998).

Doyle, Susanna, *The Emmet family in Dublin, 1770–1803: Two walking tours* (New York, 1998).

— *Georgian Dublin – buildings known to the Emmet family, 1770–1803: Two walking tours* (New York, 1998).

Doyle, William, 'The Union in a European context', in *Trans. Royal Hist. Soc.*, sixth series, x (2000), 167–80.

Drogheda and 1798 (Drogheda [County Louth], 1998).

Duffy, Michael, 'War, revolution and the crisis of the British Empire', in Mark Philp (ed.), *The French Revolution and British popular politics* (Cambridge, 1991), 118–45.

— 'World-wide war and British expansion 1793–1815', in P.J. Marshall (ed.), *The Oxford history of the British Empire*, vol. II: *The eighteenth century* (Oxford, 1998), 184–207.

Dunne, Alan (ed.), *1798 a local perspective: Mountmellick 1798–1998* (Mountmellick [County Laois], 1998).

Dunne, Tom, *Theobald Wolfe Tone, colonial outsider: An analysis of his political philosophy* (Cork, 1982).

— 'Haunted by history: Irish romantic writing 1800–1850', in Porter and Teich, *Romanticism*, 68–91.

— 'Popular ballads, revolutionary rhetoric and politicisation', in Gough and Dickson, *Ireland*, 139–55.

— 'Representations of 1798 in literature', in F.B. Smith (ed.), *Ireland, England and Australia* (Canberra, 1990), 14–40.

— '1798: Memory, history, commemoration', in *Wex. Hist. Soc. Jn.*, xvi (1996–7), 5–39.

— 'In the service of the Republic? Wolfe Tone in Bantry Bay', in Murphy, *Bantry Bay*, 73–84.

— '1798 and the United Irishmen', in *Ir. Review*, xxii (1998), 54–66.

— 'Subaltern voices? Poetry in Irish, popular insurgency and the 1798 rebellion', in *Eighteenth-century Life*, xxii, 3 (1998), 31–44.

— 'Wexford's Comóradh '98: Politics, heritage and history', in *Hist. Ire.*, vi, 2 (1998), 49–53.

— 'Rebel motives and mentalities: The battle for New Ross 5 June 1798', in *Éire-Ireland*, xxxiv, 2 (1999), 5–27.

— 'The memory of the dead: New Ross and Scullabogue 5 June 1798', in *Wex. Hist. Soc. Jn.*, xvii (1998–99), 191–220.

Duffy, Robert, *One hundred years too soon: Hacketstown and 1798* (Hacketstown [County Carlow], 1998).

Dupy, René-Jean, 'Regard d'Edmund Burke sur la Révolution Française', in *Études Irlandaises*, xxii, 2 (1998), 113–20.

Durey, Michael, 'Transatlantic patriots: Political exiles and America in the age of revolutions', in Clive Emsley and James Walvin (eds), *Artists, peasants and proletarians* (London, 1985), 7–31.

— 'Thomas Paine's apostles: Radical emigrés and the triumph of Jeffersonian Republicanism', in *William and Mary Quarterly*, xliv, 4 (1987), 661–88.

— 'Irish Deism and Jefferson's Republic: Denis Driscol in Ireland and America 1793–1810', in *Éire-Ireland*, xxv, 4 (1990), 56–76.

— 'John Hughes, reluctant agent, *provocateur* and millenarian: A note and new documents', in *E.C.I.*, vii (1992), 141–6.

'The Dublin Society of United Irishmen and the politics of the Carey-Drennan dispute 1792–1794', in *Hist. Jn.*, xxxvii, 1 (1994), 89–111.

— *Transatlantic radicals and the early American republic* (Lawrence, KA, 1997).

— *Andrew Bryson's ordeal: An epilogue of the 1798 rebellion* (Cork, 1998).

— 'The fate of the rebels after 1798', in *History Today*, xlviii, 6 (1998), 21–7.

— 'The United Irishmen and the politics of banishment 1798–1807', in Davis, *Radicalism*, 96–109.

— 'Marquess Cornwallis and the fate of Irish rebel prisoners in the aftermath of the 1798 rebellion', in Smyth, *Revolution*, 128–45.

Eccleshall, Robert, 'Anglican political thought in the century after the revolution of 1688', in D.G. Boyce, Robert Eccleshall and Vincent Geoghegan (eds), *Political thought in Ireland since the seventeenth century* (London, 1993), 36–72.

Edwards, Owen Dudley, 'The American image of Ireland: A study of its early phases', in *Perspectives in American History*, iv (1970), 199–282.

— 'The impact of the American Revolution in Ireland', in R.R. Palmer (ed.), *The impact of the American Revolution abroad* (Washington, DC, 1976), 127–59.

Edwards, R.D.,'The minute book of the Catholic Committee 1773–92', in *Arch. Hib.*, ix (1942), 3–172.

— 'The European and American backgrounds of [Daniel] O'Connell's nationalism: The American War of Independence and Irish nationalism', in *Ir. Monthly*, lxxv (1947), 468–73; 509–20; lxvi (1948), 31–6; 129–34; 327–32; 512–21.

— 'Maurice O'Connell and the French expedition to Bantry Bay 1796', in *Ir. Monthly*, lxxv (1947), 413–21.

Egan, Patrick, 'Progress and suppression of the United Irishmen in the western counties in 1798-9', in *Galway Arch. and Hist. Soc. Jn.*, xxv, 3–4 (1953–4), 104–34.

— 'The forebears of William James MacNeven', in Harman Murtagh (ed.), *Irish midland studies* (Athlone [County Westmeath], 1980), 159–67.

Elias, Robert and Eugene Finch (eds), *Letters of Thomas Attwoood Digges, 1742–1821* (Columbia, SC, 1982).

Elliott, Marianne, 'The Despard conspiracy reconsidered', in *Past & Present*, 75 (1977), 46–61.

— 'The origins and transformation of early Irish republicanism', in *Int. Rev. Soc. Hist.*, xxiii, 3 (1978), 405–28.

— 'Irish republicanism in England: The first phase 1797–1799', in Bartlett and Hayton, *Penal era*, 204–21.

— *Partners in revolution: The United Irishmen and France* (London, 1982).

— 'The United Irishman as diplomat', in Corish, *Radicals, rebels, and establishments*, 69–89.

— *Watchmen in Sion: The Protestant idea of liberty* (Derry, 1985).

— 'Ireland', in O. Dann and J. Dinwiddy (eds), *Nationalism in the age of the French Revolution* (London, 1988), 71–86.

— *Wolfe Tone: Prophet of Irish independence* (New Haven and London, 1989).

— 'The role of Ireland in French war strategy 1796–1798', in Gough and Dickson, *Ireland*, 202–19.

— 'Wolfe Tone and the development of a revolutionary culture in Ireland', in Bergeron and Cullen, *Culture et pratiques*, 171–86.

— 'The Defenders in Ulster', in Dickson, Keogh and Whelan, *United Irishmen*, 222–33.

— 'Wolfe Tone and the republican ideal', in Póirtéir, *Great Irish rebellion*, 49–57.

Ellis, Lucy and Joseph Turquan, *La belle Pamela* (London, 1924) [Pamela FitzGerald].

Emerson, Lucius, '1798 artefacts in the Donegal Museum', in *Don. Annual*, l (1998), 60–1.

Emmet, Thomas Addis, *Memoir of Thomas Addis and Robert Emmet with their ancestors and immediate family*, 2 vols (New York, 1915).

Emmet's anniversary celebration, Round Room, Rotunda 4 Mar. 1915 (Dublin, 1915).

English, N.W., 'Two tombstones of the King's German Legion at Tullamore [County Offaly]', in *Ir. Sword*, xii, 49 (1976), 302–3.

Ennis, John, 'The battle of Fooks [Foulkes] Mills [County Wexford]', in *The Past*, vi (1950), 104–17.

Epstein, James, *Radical expression: Political language, ritual and symbol in England 1790–1850* (Oxford, 1994).

Erdman, David, *Commerce des lumières: John Oswald and the British in Paris, 1790–1793* (London, 1987).

Fagan, Patrick (ed.), *Ireland in the Stuart papers*, 2 vols (Dublin, 1995).

— *Divided loyalties: The question of an oath for Irish Catholics in the eighteenth century* (Dublin, 1997).

— *Catholics in a Protestant country: The papist constituency in eighteenth-century Dublin* (Dublin, 1998).

— 'Infiltration of Dublin freemason lodges by United Irishmen and other republican groups', in *E.C.I.*, xiii (1998), 65–85.

Falkiner, C. Litton, 'The French invasion of Ireland in 1798', in *Studies in Irish history and biography, mainly of the eighteenth century* (London, 1902), 250–350 [Bristol, Clare, Castlereagh, Plunkett, Boyle Roche, Thomas Steele].

Faoite, Ailfrid de, *Theobald Wolfe Tone: The man and his work* (Dublin, 1920).

Farrell, Sean, *Rituals and riots: Sectarian violence and political culture in Ulster, 1784–1886* (Kentucky, 2001).

[Farrell, William], see Roger MacHugh.

Farrelly, Brendan and Michael Moore, *Massacre at Gibbet Rath* [County Kildare] *1798* (Dublin, 1998).

Fay, Anne, *Roddy McCorley: A study of evidence* (Ballymena [County Antrim], 1989).

Fee, Aidan, James Glendinning, Anne Laverty and Frank Mayes, 'The United Irishmen in east Tyrone', in *The Bell: Jn. Stewartstown and District Hist. Soc.*, vii (1999), 3–45.

Fenning, Hugh, *The Irish Dominican province, 1698–1797* (Dublin, 1990).

— 'Cork imprints of Catholic historical interest 1723–1804: A provisional checklist', in *J.C.H.A.S.*, c (1995), 129–48.

— 'Troy to Carroll: letters from Dublin to Baltimore 1794–1815', in *Collect. Hib.*, xxxix-xl (1997-8), 176–209.

— 'Dublin imprints of Catholic interest 1760–1769', in *Coll. Hib.*, xlii (2000), 85–119.

— 'Dublin imprints of Catholic interest 1770–1782', in *Collect. Hib.*, xliv (2001), pp 161–208.

— 'Troy to Bray: letters from Dublin to Thurles 1792–1817', in *Archiv. Hib.*, lv (2001), 48–125.

Fenton, Séamus, *Tradition in County Wexford: Its association with '98* (Dublin, [1938].

— 'Why Ireland rose in 1798', in *Ireland-American Rev.*, i, 1 (1938-9), 56–64.

Ferguson, Kenneth, 'The Volunteer movement and the government 1778–1793', in *Ir. Sword*, xiii, 51 (1978–79), 208–16.

— 'The Irish Bar in December 1798', in *Dub. Hist. Rec.*, lii (1999), 32–60.

Ferguson, Niall, *The cash nexus: Money and power in the modern world, 1700–2000* (London, 2001).

Ferguson, Samuel, *William Staveley, apostle of the Convenanters* (ed.) Eull Dunlop (Ballymena [County Antrim], 1997; first ed. Belfast, 1897).

Feughelman, Jean, 'Arthur Devlin, exile 1771–1820: One of the *Tellicherry* five', in *Descent*, xiv, 4 (1984), 170–78.

Fhlóinn, Barbara Ní, 'Echoes of ninety-eight', in *Roscommon Hist. and Arch. Soc. Jn.*, vii (1998), 112–3.

Fíanna: The official organ of Fíanna Éireann. Vol. 1, No. 1: Tone commemoration number (Dublin, 1922).

Finegan, John (ed.), *The Anne Devlin jail journal faithfully written down by Luke Cullen* (Cork, 1968).

— *Anne Devlin: Patriot and heroine* (Cork, 1992).

Finlay, Enda (ed.), *Radicals and revolutionaries: Essays on 1798* (London, 1998).

Fitzgerald, Brian, *Emily, duchess of Leinster, 1731–1814: A study of her life and times* (London, 1949).

— (ed.), *Correspondence of Emily, duchess of Leinster, 1731–1814*, 3 vols (Dublin, 1949–1957).

Fitzgerald, Garret, 'Estimates for baronies of minimum level of Irish-speaking among successive decennial cohorts 1771–1781 to 1861–1871', in *R.I.A. Proc.*, C, lxxxiv (1984), 117–55.

Fitzgerald, Sean, 'Wolfe Tone and Bantry Bay', in *Bantry Hist. Soc. Jn.*, i (1991), 54–65.

FitzGerald, Walter, 'List of portraits of Lord and Lady Edward FitzGerald', in *Kild. Arch. Soc. Jn.*, ii (1896–9), 382–3; iii (1899–1902), 194; 399.

— 'The will of Lord Edward FitzGerald', in *Kild. Arch. Soc. Jn.*, vi (1909–11), 425; ix (1918–22), 463.

Fitzgibbon, Elliot, *Earl of Clare: Mainspring of union* (London, 1960).

Fitzhenry, Edna, *Henry Joy McCracken* (Dublin, 1936).

Fitzpatrick, Michael, *Historic Gorey 4: Reflections of 1798* (Gorey [County Wexford], 1998).

Flood, W.H. Grattan, 'Memoir of Father James Dixon, first prefect-apostolic of Australia', in *I.E.R.*, fourth series, xxx (1911), 193–206.

Flynn, Kathleen and Stan McCormick, *Westmeath, 1798: A Kilbeggan rebellion* (Kilbeggan [County Westmeath], 1998).

Fogarty, Anne, 'Where Wolfe Tone's statue was not: Joyce, 1798 and the politics of memory', in *Études Irlandaises*, xxiv, 2 (1999), 19–32.

Foley, Tadgh and Fiona Bateman (eds), *Irish–Australian studies* (Sydney, 2000).

Folley, Terence, *Eye witness to 1798* (Cork, 1996).

Forde, Frank, 'The Royal Irish Artillery 1755–1800', in *Ir. Sword*, xi, 42 (1973), 32–8.

— 'The Ultonia regiment of the Spanish army', in *Ir. Sword*, xii, 46 (1975), 36–41.

Forde, Walter (ed.), *Shelmalier '98: A history of Castlebridge, Screen and Curracloe in 1798* (Castlebridge [County Wexford], 1998).

— (ed.), *From heritage to hope: Christian perspectives on the 1798 rebellion* (Gorey [County Wexford], 1998).

Foster, Roy, 'Programme note', to *Northern Star*, by Stewart Parker, Rough Magic (Dublin, 1997), 4–5.

Foster, Sarah, 'Buying Irish: Consumer nationalism in eighteenth-century Dublin', in *History Today*, xlvii, 6 (1997), 44–51.

Fowler, Joseph, *Chapters in '98 history* (London, 1938) [introduction by F.P. Stockley: Re-issue of twelve leaflets separately published].

Fox, Charlotte Milligan, *Annals of the Irish harpers* (London, 1911) [based on Edward Bunting manuscripts].

Foy, R.H., *Remembering all the Orrs: The story of the Orr families of Antrim and their involvement in the 1798 rebellion* (Belfast, 1999).

Freyer, Grattan (ed.), *Bishop Stock's narrative of the year of the French, 1798* (Bofeenaun [County Mayo], 1982).

Freyer, Grattan and Sheila Mulloy, 'The unfortunate John Moore', in *Cathair na Mart*, iv, 1 (1985), 51–68.

Froggatt, Peter, 'Dr James MacDonnell M.D. 1763–1845', in *The Glynns*, ix (1981), 17–31.

Fuchs, Michel, 'France and Irish nationalism in the eighteenth century', in O'Dea and Whelan, *Nations and nationalisms*, 119–28.

Fuller, James, 'The Tones, father and son', in *J.C.H.A.S.*, xxxix (1929), 93–101.

Fulton, Pamela (ed.), *The Minerva journal of John Washington Price: A voyage from Cork, Ireland to Sydney, New South Wales, 1798–1800* (Melbourne, 2000).

Furlong, Nicholas, *Fr John Murphy of Boolavogue, 1753–1798* (Dublin, 1991).

— 'County Wexford and the French Revolution', in *Wex. Hist. Soc. Jn.*, xii (1988–89), 62–5.

— 'Local or cosmopolitan? The strategic importance of Wexford in 1798', in Keogh and Furlong, *The mighty wave*, 109–17.

— 'The church and Fr John Murphy of Boolavogue', in Swords, *Protestant, Catholic and Dissenter*, 186–218.

Gahan, Daniel, 'The "Black Mob" and the "Babes in the Woods": Wexford in the wake of the rebellion 1798–1806', in *Wex. Hist. Soc. Jn.*, xii (1991), 92–110.

— 'The military strategy of the Wexford United Irishmen in 1798', in *Hist. Ire.*, i, 4 (1993), 28–32.

— *The people's rising: Wexford, 1798* (Dublin, 1995).

— 'The Scullabogue massacre', in *Hist. Ire.*, iv, 3 (1996), 27–31.

— 'The military planning of the 1798 rebellion in Wexford', in Keogh and Furlong, *The mighty wave*, 97–108.

— *Rebellion! Ireland in 1798* (Dublin, 1997).

— 'New Ross, Scullabogue and the 1798 rebellion in south-western Wexford', in *The Past*, xxi (1998), 3–33.

— 'The outbreak of rebellion in the provinces: northern and central Wexford 23–26 May 1798', in *Wex. Hist. Soc. Jn.*, xvii (1998–99), 61–82.

— 'Class, religion and rebellion: Wexford in 1798', in Smyth (ed.), *Revolution*, 83–98.

Gailey, Frank, 'The Sharon murders, 1797: A traditional account with introduction and notes', in *Donegal Annual*, iii, 3 (1957), 8–16.

Gallagher, James, 'The revolutionary Irish 1800–1804', in *The Push from the Bush*, xix (1985), 2–33.

Gallagher, John, 'Conflict and tragedy in Napoleon's Irish Legion: The Corbet/Sweeney affair', in *Ir. Sword*, xvi, 64 (1986), 145–54.

— 'William Lawless and the defence of Flushing', in *Ir. Sword*, xvii, 68 (1989), 159–64.

Gargett, Graham and Geraldine Sheridan (eds), *Ireland and the French Enlightenment, 1700–1800* (Basingstoke, 1999).

Gargett, Graham, 'Voltaire's reception in Ireland', in Gargett and Sheridan, *Ireland*, 67–89.

Garland, John, 'Nepotism in reverse: The military career of Maurice Jeffrey O'Connell 1768–1850', in *Ir. Sword*, xv, 60 (1983), 189–91.

— 'The army in Ireland 1797', in *Ir. Sword*, xvi, 65 (1986), 334–6.

Garland, Sean, *The lessons of history and what sort of unity: A lecture to be given during Wolfe Tone week in Dublin* (Dublin, 1971).

— *The Workers Party Wolfe Tone Bodenstown commemoration 19 July 1998* (Dublin, 1999).

Garnham, Neal, 'How violent was eighteenth-century Ireland?' in *I.H.S.*, xxx (1997), 377–92.

Garvin, Tom, *The evolution of Irish nationalist politics* (Dublin, 1981).

— 'Defenders, Ribbonmen and others: Underground political networks in pre-Famine Ireland', in C.H. Philpin (ed.), *Nationalism and popular protest in Ireland* (Cambridge, 1987), 219–44.

Gaskell, Hugh (ed.), *Ossian revisited* (Edinburgh, 1991).

Gastey, Général, 'L'étonnante aventure de l'armée d'Irlande', in *Revue Historique de l'Armée* [Paris], iv (1952), 19–36.

Gaynor, Tony, 'The legal challenge to the government in the 1790s', in *Ir. Jurist*, xxxiv (1999), 300–37.

Geary, Laurence (ed.), *Rebellion and remembrance in modern Ireland* (Dublin, 2001).

Gebbie, J.H. (ed.), *An introduction to the Abercorn letters as relating to Ireland* (Omagh [County Tyrone], 1972).

Geoghegan, Patrick, *1798 and the Irish Bar* (Dublin, 1998).

— *The Irish Act of Union: A study in high politics, 1798–1801* (Dublin, 1999).

— 'An act of power and corruption?: The Union debate', in *Hist. Ire.*, viii, 2 (2000), 22–6.

— 'The Catholics and the Union', in *Trans. Royal Hist. Soc.*, sixth series, x (2000), 243–58.

— 'Castlereagh and the making of the Union', in Hanna, *The Union*, 9–20.

— 'The making of the Union', in Keogh and Whelan, *Acts of union*, 34–45.

— *Robert Emmet: A life* (Dublin, 2002).

— *Lord Castlereagh* (Dundalk, 2002).

Gering, August, 'To sing of '98: The United Irishmen and the ballad tradition in [Seamus] Heaney and [Paul] Muldoon', in *L.I.T.*, x (1999), 149–79.

Gibbon, Peter, 'The origins of the Orange Order and the United Irishmen: A study in the sociology of revolution and counter-revolution', in *Economy and Society*, i (1972), 134–63.

— *The origins of Ulster unionism: The formation of popular Protestant politics and ideology in nineteenth-century Ireland* (Manchester, 1975).

Gibbons, Luke, 'A shadowy narrator: History, art and romantic nationalism in Ireland 1750–1850', in Ciaran Brady (ed.), *Ideology and the historians* (Dublin, 1991), 99–127 [about James Barry].

— *Transformations in Irish culture* (Cork and Notre Dame, 1996).

— 'This sympathetic bond: Ossian, Celticism and colonialism', in Terence Brown (ed.), *Celticism* (Amsterdam, 1996), 273–91.

— 'Edmund Burke and our present discontents', in *Hist. Ire.*, v, 4 (1997), 21–5.

— 'The United Irishmen and Moore's Melodies': Programme note for Kathleen Tynan, *Romancing rebellion: 1798 and the songs of Thomas Moore* (Dublin, 1998), 6–8.

— 'The United Irishmen and cultural politics', in Whelan, *Northern Star*, 10–11.

— 'Alternative enlightenments: The United Irishmen, cultural diversity and the republic of letters', in Cullen, *200 years*, 119–28.

— 'Radical memory', in *Index on Censorship*, 5 (1998), 142–3.

— 'Between Captain Rock and a hard place: Art and agrarian insurgency', in Tadgh Foley and Sean Ryder (ed.), *Ideology and Ireland in the nineteenth century* (Dublin, 1998), 23–44.

— 'From Ossian to O'Carolan: The bard as separatist symbol', in Fiona Stafford and Howard Gaskill (eds), *From Gaelic to romantic: Ossianic translations* (Amsterdam, 1998), 227–51.

— 'Republicanism and radical memory: The O'Conors, O'Carolan and the United Irishmen', in Smyth, *Revolution*, 211–37.

— 'Where Wolfe Tone's statue was not: Joyce, monuments and mourning', in Ian MacBride (ed.), *History, memory and Irish culture* (Cambridge, 2001), 139–59.

— '"Subtilized into savages": Edmund Burke, progress and primitivism', in *South Atlantic Qtly.*, C, no 1 (2001), 83–109.

Giblin, Cathaldus (ed.), 'Letters from Sydney of a '98 deportee: Michael Hayes of Wexford 1799–1825', in *The Past*, vi (1950), 45–103.

Gilbert, John T., *Documents relating to Ireland, 1795–1804* (Dublin, 1893; Shannon, repr, 1970) [introduction by Maureen Wall].

Gill, Conrad, *The naval mutinies of 1797* (Manchester, 1913).

Gillett, Eric (ed.), *Elizabeth Ham by herself, 1783–1820* (London, 1945) [1798 in Carlow and Mayo].

[Glendy, John], 'John Glendy of Maghera, County Derry: Presbyterian minister and patriot 1798', in *U.J.A.*, xiii (1907), 101–5.

Glendinning, James, 'Freemasonry in Stewartstown [County Tyrone]', in *The Bell*, vii (1999), 79–83.

Gogan, Liam, 'Death of Tone', in *1798 essays*, 22–4.

Goodall, David, 'A divided family in 1798: The Grays of Whitefort and Jamestown', in *Wex. Hist. Soc. Jn.*, xv (1994–5), 52–66.

— 'Conflicts of loyalty: The Dixons and Le Hunte's cavalry in 1798', in *Wex. Hist. Soc. Jn.*, xvii (1998–99), 83–100.

Goodwin, Albert, *The Friends of Liberty: The English democratic movement in the age of the French Revolution* (London, 1979).

Gough, Hugh, 'Anatomy of a failure', in Murphy, *Bantry Bay*, 9–24.

— 'France and the 1798 rebellion', in Póirtéir, *Great Irish rebellion*, 37–48.

Gough, Hugh and David Dickson (ed.), *Ireland and the French Revolution* (Dublin, 1990).

Gough, Hugh and Giles Le Biez, 'Un républicanism ambigu: L'Irlande et la Révolution Française', in *Annales Historiques de la Révolution Française*, 296 (1994), 321–30.

Gould, Eliga, 'American independence and Britain's counter-revolution', in *Past & Present*, 154 (1997), 107–41.

Gowan, Ogle Robert, *Murder without sin: The rebellion of 1798*, (ed.) J.R. Whitten (Belfast, 1996) [extract from *Orangeism: its origin and history* (Toronto, 1859)].

Graham, Betty, 'The women of '98', in McKearney, *Ninety-eight*, 38–9.

Graham, Col, Perry McIntyre and Anne-Maree Whitaker (eds), *The voyage of the ship* Friend-ship *from Cork to Botany Bay, 1799–1800* (Sydney, 2000).

Graham, Harry, *Splendid failures* (London, 1913) [includes Theobald Wolfe Tone, 1–30].

Graham, Jenny, *The nation, the law and the king: Reform politics in England, 1789–1799*, 2 vols (New York, 2000).

Graham, Thomas, 'An union of power': The United Irish organisation', in Dickson, Keogh and Whelan, *United Irishmen*, 244–55.

— 'Whitelaw's census of Dublin', in *Hist. Ire.*, ii, 3 (1994), 10–15.

— 'Dublin in 1798: The key to the planned insurrection', in Keogh and Furlong, *The mighty wave*, 65–78.

— 'Dublin's role in the 1798 rebellion', in Póirtéir, *Great Irish rebellion*, 58–71.

— 'The United Irishmen and the revolution of 1798', in Cullen, *1798*, 7–14.

— [(ed.)], *Dublin '98 programme* (Dublin, 1998).

— 'The shift in United Irish leadership from Belfast to Dublin 1796–1798', in Smyth, *Revolution*, 55–66.

Gray, Jane, 'Gender and plebian culture in Ulster', in *Jn. Interdisciplinary Hist.*, xxiv, 2 (1993), 251–70.

Gray, John, 'Millennial vision: Thomas Russell re-assessed', in *Linen Hall Rev.*, vi (1989), 5–9.

— 'Reporting the great Belfast debates of 1792', in *Linen Hall Rev.*, ix, 1 (1992), 4–8.

— 'A tale of two newspapers: The contest between the *Belfast News-Letter* and the *Northern Star* in the 1790s', in John Gray and Wesley McCann (eds), *An uncommon bookman: Essays in memory of J.R.R. Adams* (Belfast, 1996), 175–98.

— 'Mary Anne McCracken: Belfast revolutionary and pioneer of feminism', in Keogh and Furlong, *Women of 1798*, 47–63.

— 'The *Northern Star*: That infernal newspaper', in *Causeway* (Winter, 1997), 22–4.

— *The sans-culottes of Belfast: The United Irishmen and the men of no property* (Belfast, 1998).

Greaves, C. Desmond, *Theobald Wolfe Tone and the Irish nation* (London, 1963; Cork, 1989; Dublin, 1991).

Greene, John, *Theatre in Belfast, 1736–1800* (Lehigh, PA, 2000).

Grego, Joseph (ed.), *Cruikshank's watercolours* (London, 1903) [includes illustrations to Maxwell, *History of … 1798*].

Griffin, Patrick, 'Defining the limits of Britishness: The 'New' British History and the meaning of the revolution settlement for Ulster's Presbyterians', in *Jn. British Studies*, xxxix, no 3 (2000), 263–87.

—— *The people with no name: Ireland's Ulster-Scots, America's Scots-Irish and the creation of a British Atlantic world 1689–1764* (Princeton, NJ, 2001).

Griffin, William, 'Irish generals and Spanish politics under Fernando VII', in *Ir. Sword*, x, 38 (1971), 1–9.

—— 'General Charles O'Hara', in *Ir. Sword*, x, 40 (1972), 179–87.

Guckian, Des, *Leitrim and Longford in 1798* (Longford, 1998).

Guiney, Louise, *Robert Emmet* (Dublin, 1904).

Guinness, Patrick, '"Man being in his natural state the most naked and helpless of all Creatures": The meeting book of the Kildare Knot of the Friendly Brothers of St Patrick 1771–1791', in *Kild. Arch. Soc. Jn.*, xix, 1 (2000–01), 116–50.

Guinness, Selina, 'The year of the undead: 1898', in P.J. Mathews (ed.), *New voices in Irish criticism* (Dublin, 2000), 19–26.

Gwynn, Denis Rolleston, *The struggle for Catholic Emancipation, 1750–1829* (London, 1928).

—— 'John Keogh and Catholic Emancipation', in *Studies*, xvii (1928), 177–95.

—— 'Dr Hussey and Edmund Burke', in *Studies*, xvii (1928), 527–46.

—— 'Henry Grattan and Catholic Emancipation', in *Studies*, xviii (1929), 576–92.

—— *John Keogh: The pioneer of Catholic Emancipation* (Dublin, 1930).

Gwynn, Stephen Lucius, *Thomas Moore* (London, 1905).

—— (ed.), *Memoirs of Miles Byrne*, 2 vols (Dublin, 1907).

—— *Henry Grattan and his times* (Dublin, 1939).

Haire, J.L. (ed.), *Challenge and conflict: Essays in Irish Presbyterian history and doctrine* (Antrim, 1981).

Hale, Leslie, *John Philpot Curran: his life and times* (London, 1958).

Hall, Barbara, *A desperate set of villians: The convicts of the* Marquis Cornwallis *transported to Botany Bay, 1796* (Sydney, 2000).

Hall, David, *A battle lost and won: The battle of Antrim* 1798 (Belfast, 1998).

Hammond, Joseph, 'Town Major Henry Charles Sirr', in *Dub. Hist. Rec.*, iv, 1(1941), 14–33; iv, 2 (1942), 58–75.

—— 'Behind the scenes of the Emmet insurrection: Extracts from hitherto unpublished state papers', in *Dub. Hist. Rec.*, vi, 3 (1944), 91–106; vi, 4 (1944), 153–4.

—— 'The Emmet insurrection: Some eye witness accounts', in *Dub. Hist. Rec.*, ix, i (1946–47), 21–28; ix, 2 (1946–47), 59–68; ix, 3 (1946–47), 84–95.

—— Thomas Braughall 1729–1803: Catholic emancipationist', in *Dub. Hist. Rec.*, xiv, 2 (1955–6), 41–9.

—— 'Revd Thomas Gamble and Robert Emmet', in *Dub. Hist. Rec.*, xiv, 4 (1956-8), 98–101.

—— 'Dublin in 1798', in *1798 essays*, 8–12.

Hanna, Robbie (ed.), *The Union: Essays on Ireland and the British connection* (Newtownards [County Down], 2001).

Hannigan, Ken and William Nolan (ed.), *Wicklow: history and society* (Dublin, 1994).

Harbison, Janet, 'The Belfast Harpers' meeting 1792: The legacy', in *Ulster Folklife*, xxxv (1989), 113–28.

Hardy, [Général] (ed.), *Correspondance intime du Général Jean Hardy de 1797 à 1802* (Paris, 1901) [edited by Général Hardy de Pereni].

Hardy, W.J., 'A born rebel', in *Blackwood's Mag.*, clxxxix, 1148 (June 1911), 772–87 [on T.W. Tone].

Harte, Frank, *The year of liberty* [C.D. with accompanying booklet] (Dublin, 1998).

— 'Who fears to sing of '98', in Devlin, *A union of wills?*, 13–34.

— *My name is Napoleon Bonaparte* [C.D. with accompanying booklet] (Dublin, 2001).

Harvey, Hugh Crosbie, *Beauchamp Bagenal Harvey: The reluctant rebel* (Chapel Hill, NC, 1988).

Hawtrey, Florence, *The history of the Hawtrey family*, 2 vols (London, 1903) [Colonel Jonas Watson, 196–217].

Hayes, Richard, *Ireland and Irishmen in the French Revolution* (Dublin, 1932) [preface by Hilaire Belloc].

— *Éire agus Éireannaigh i muirtheacht na Fraince*, (aist.) Séamus Mac Grianna (Baile Átha Cliath, 1933).

— *Irish swordsmen of France* (Dublin, 1934).

— *The last invasion of Ireland: When Connacht rose* (Dublin, 1937; 1939; 1979).

— *Old Irish links with France: Some echoes of exiled Ireland* (Dublin, 1940).

— 'Priests in the independence movement of 1798', in *Ir. Eccl. Rec.*, lxvi (1945), 258–70.

— *Biographical dictionary of Irishmen in France* (Dublin, 1949).

— 'Madgett's Legion', in *Ir. Sword*, i, 2 (1950–1), 142.

— 'A noted Irish soldier', in *Ir. Sword*, i, 4 (1952–3), 335 [Thomas O'Meara].

— 'An officer's account of the French campaign in Ireland in 1798', in *Ir. Sword*, ii, 6 (1955), 110–18; ii, 7 (1955), 161–71[General Sarrazin].

— 'The battle of Castlebar, 1798', in *Ir. Sword*, iii, 11 (1957), 107–14.

— 'The United Irish movement and revolutionary Tone', in *1798 essays*, 4–7.

Hayes-McCoy, G.A.,'The Irish pike', in *Galway Arch. and Hist. Soc. Jn.*, xx, 3 and 4 (1943), 99–128; xxi (1944–5), 44–50.

— 'The Wexford yeomanry and Miles Byrne', in *An Cosantóir*, Jan. (1948), 3–10.

— 'The topography of a battlefield: Arklow, 1798', in *Ir. Sword*, i, 1 (1949–50), 50–6.

— 'Fencible corps in Ireland 1782–1803', in *Ir. Sword*, ii, 6 (1955), 140–3.

— 'Insurgent efforts towards military organisation 1798', in *Ir. Sword*, iii, 12 (1958), 153–8.

— 'A list of the yeomanry corps of Connacht in 1803', in *Ir. Sword*, iii, 12 (1958), 187–93.

— 'The government forces which opposed the insurgents in 1798', in *Ir. Sword*, iv, 14 (1959), 16–28.

— 'The rebellion of 1798', in *1798 essays*, 1–3.

— 'The Irish horse regiments of the eighteenth century', in *Ir. Sword*, ix, 35 (1969), 127–34.

— *Irish battles: A military history of Ireland* (London, 1969) [repr. (Belfast, 1989)].

— *A history of Irish flags from earliest times*, (ed.) Pádraig Ó Snodaigh (Dublin, 1971; 1979).

— 'The French campaign in Connacht and North Leinster 1798' in *Teathbha*, xi, 1 (1980), 33–40.

Hayes, W.J., *Tipperary in the year of the rebellion, 1798* (Roscrea [County Tipperary], 1998).

Hayter-Hames, Jane, *Arthur O'Connor, United Irishman* (Cork, 2001).

Hayton, David W. (ed.), *The Irish parliament in the eighteenth century: The long apprenticeship* (Edinburgh, 2001).

Heatley, Fred, *Henry Joy McCracken and his times* (Belfast, 1967).

Hennet, Leon, *État militaire de France pour l'année, 1793* (Paris, 1903).

Hennig, John, 'Goethe and Lord Bristol', in *U.J.A.*, third series, ix (1947), 101–7 [re their meeting in 1797].

— 'Robert Emmet's military studies', in *Ir. Sword*, i, 2 (1950–1), 148–50.

Henry, Brian, *Dublin hanged: Crime, law enforcement and punishment in late eighteenth-century Dublin* (Dublin, 1994).

Herr, Cheryl, *For the land they loved: Irish political melodramas 1890–1925* (Syracuse, NY, 1991).

Hewitt, Esther (ed.), *Lord Shannon's letters to his son: A calendar of the letters written by the second Earl of Shannon to his son Viscount Boyle, 1790–1802* (Belfast, 1982).

Hewitt, John, 'Portrait of a United Irishman', in *Belfast Municipal Museum and Art Gallery Bulletin*, i, 2 (1949), 29–30 [Walter Graham].

—— *The rhyming weavers and other poets of Antrim and Down* (Belfast, 1974).

Hewitt, Mark, *1798: The year of revolution, Wolfe Tone and the United Irishmen* (Dublin, 1998).

Heyland, Langford (ed.), *The Irish rebellion of 1798 from the journal of Colonel Heyland of Glendaragh* [County Antrim] *with a copy of the address to the United Irishmen by the brothers Sheares and General Humbert's address to the army. Printed in aid of the friends of the Greenock Unionist Bazaar* (Storer, [Scotland], 1913).

Hickey, Patrick, 'Invasion and rebellion: The Mizen peninsula [County Cork] 1796-8', in *Mizen Jn.*, vi (1998), 21–35.

Hill, Barbara, 'The 1798 rebellion in Coleraine and district', in *Familia*, xiv (1998), 14–19.

Hill, Jacqueline, 'National festivals, the state and Protestant ascendancy in Ireland 1790–1829', in *I.H.S.*, xxiv (1984), 30–51.

—— 'Popery and Protestantism, civil and religious liberty: The disputed lessons of Irish history 1690–1812', in *Past & Present*, cxviii (1988), 96–129.

—— 'The meaning and significance of Protestant ascendancy 1787–1840', in *Ireland after the Union* (Oxford, 1989), 1–22.

—— 'Religious toleration and repeal of the Penal Laws: An imperial perspective 1763–1780', in *Archiv. Hib.*, xliv (1989), 98–109.

—— *From patriots to unionists: Dublin civic politics and Irish Protestant patriotism 1660–1840* (Oxford, 1997).

—— 'The Act of Union', in Cullen, *1798*, 47–54.

—— 'Politics and the writing of history: The impact of the 1690s and 1790s on Irish historiography', in Boyce, Eccleshall and Geoghegan, *Political discourse*, 222–39.

—— 'Irish identities before and after the Act of Union', in *Radharc*, ii (2001), 51–74.

—— 'Convergence and conflict in eighteenth-century Ireland', in *Hist. Jn.*, xliv, no 4 (2001), 1039–63.

Hill, Myrtle, Brian Turner and Kenneth Dawson (eds), *The 1798 rebellion in County Down* (Newtownards [County Down], 1998).

Hill, Myrtle, 'The religious context: Protestantism in County Down in 1798', in Hill, Turner and Dawson, *Down*, 60–77.

—— *Millenarian beliefs in Ulster* (Belfast, 2001).

Hiroshi, Takemato, *A bibliography of the Irish writers in the seventeenth and eighteenth centuries* (Osaka [Japan], 1984).

Historical exhibition of '98 relics in the Athenaeum, Enniscorthy June 1938: Souvenir programme (Enniscorthy, 1938).

Hoban, Brendan, 'Dominick Bellew 1745–1812, parish priest of Dundalk and bishop of Killala', in *Seanchas Ard Mhacha*, vi, 2 (1972), 333–71.

Hobson, Bulmer (ed.), *The letters of Wolfe Tone* (Dublin, [1919]).

—— *The life of Wolfe Tone written by himself and completed by his son together with extracts from his political writings* (Dublin, 1920) [abridged and ed. by Bulmer Hobson].

Hogan, Patrick, 'The migration of Ulster Catholics to Connacht 1795–6', in *Seanchas Ard Mhacha*, ix, 2 (1979), 286–301.

—— 'The undoing of Citizen John Moore, President of the provisional government of the Republic of Connacht 1798', in *Galway Arch. and Hist. Soc. Jn.*, xxxix (1981–20), 59–72.

— 'Some observations on contemporary allegations as to Bishop Dominick Bellew's (1745–1813) sympathies during the 1798 rebellion in Connacht', in *Seanchas Ard Mhacha*, x, 2 (1982), 417–25.

— 'The migration of Ulster Catholics to Connaught 1795–1796: An addendum', in *Seanchas Ard Mhacha*, xii, 1 (1986), 252–3.

— 'Casualties sustained by government forces during the Humbert episode August-September 1798', in *Galway Arch. and Hist. Soc. Jn.*, l (1998), 1–9.

Hollingsworth, Brian, *Maria Edgeworth's Irish writings: Language, history, politics* (New York, 1997).

Holmes, Finlay, *Our Irish Presbyterian heritage* (Belfast, 1985).

— 'United Irishmen and Unionists: Irish Presbyterians 1791 and 1886', in W.J. Shiels and Diana Woods (eds), *Studies in church history* (Oxford, 1989), 171–89.

— *Presbyterians and Orangeism, 1795–1995* (Belfast, 1996).

— *The Presbyterian Church in Ireland: A popular history* (Dublin, 2000).

— 'From rebels to unionists: The political transformation of Ulster's Presbyterians', in Hanna, *The Union*, 34–47.

— 'Ulster Presbyterians and 1798', in Seery, Holmes and Stewart, *Presbyterians*, 21–33.

— 'The triumph of evangelicanism in the Synod of Ulster in the early nineteenth century', in Patton, *Ebb and flow*, 9–19.

Holt, Sheila, 'The moving magazine', in *Roundwood and District Hist. and Folklore Jn.*, i (1998), 7.

Homan, Gerlof, 'Palmer vs. Brown: The Society of United Irishmen in the Batavian Republic', in *Éire-Ireland*, xiv, 4 (1979), pp 30–34 [on the informer William Bird].

Hone, J.A., *For the cause of truth: Radicalism in London, 1796–1821* (Oxford, 1982).

Hone, J.M., 'Wolfe Tone', in *Dublin Magazine*, viii, 4 (1933), 33–41.

[Hope, James], *The memoirs of Jemmy Hope: The autobiography of a working-class United Irishman* (Belfast, 1972) [published by B.I.C.O.].

— *The autobiography of James (Jemmy) Hope* (Belfast, 1998).

— *United Irishman: The autobiography of James Hope*, John Newsinger (ed.) (London, 2001).

Howe, Stephen, 'Speaking of '98: History, politics and memory in the bicentenary of the 1798 United Irish uprising', in *History Workshop Jn.*, 47 (1999), 222–39.

[Hughes, Benjamin (ed.)], *Reply of the Right Revd Dr Caulfield bishop of Ferns to charges made against him in connection with the rebellion to which are added memoirs of Dr Caulfield and Fr Corrin, P.P. of Wexford* (Wexford, 1905).

Hughes, Carmel, ' '98 Celebrations in Ballina [County Mayo]', in *Bliainiris*, i, 1 (1982), 59–71.

Hughes, Robert, *The fatal shore: A history of the transportation of convicts to Australia 1787–1868* (New York, 1986).

Hughes, Tommy, 'Fr Manus Sweeney and the Rebellion of 1798', in *Back the road: Recollections of Burrishoole and Newport*, i, 2 (1998), 37–42.

Hume, David, *To right some things that we thought wrong: The spirit of 1798 and Presbyterian radicalism in Ulster* (Lurgan [County Armagh], 1998).

Hyde, H.M., *The rise of Castlereagh* (London, 1933).

Innes, C.L., 'Black writers in eighteenth-century Ireland', in *Bullán*, v, 1 (2000), 81–96.

Inglis, Brian, *The freedom of the press in Ireland, 1784–1841* (London, 1954).

Ireland, Denis (ed.), *Patriot adventurer: Extracts from the memoirs and journals of Theobald Wolfe Tone* (London, 1936).

— 'Protestantism and the Irish nation', in McKearney, *Ninety-eight*, 25–7.

Ireland, John de Courcy, 'Irish seamen in the naval warfare of 1793–1815', in *Ir. Sword*, iv, 14 (1959), 40–42.

— 'Henry MacDonnell, teniente general in the Spanish navy', in *Ir. Sword*, xv, 58 (1982), 23–9.

— 'Some Franco-Irish naval officers', in *Ir. Sword*, xvii, 67 (1987-88), 120–30.

Israel, Jonathan, *Radical enlightenment: Philosophy and the making of modernity 1650–1750* (Oxford, 2001).

Jacob, Rosamund, *The rise of the United Irishmen, 1791–4* (London, 1937).

—— *The rebel's wife* (Tralee, 1957) [semi-fictional treatment of Matilda Tone].

—— 'Tone and the Catholic Committee', in *1798 essays*, 27–30.

Jackson, Alvin, 'Irish rebellion of 1798', in John Cannon (ed.), *The Oxford companion to British history* (Oxford, 1997), 517–8.

Jacotey, Marie-Louise, *Un volontaire de 1792: le Général Humbert ou la passion de la liberté* (Paris, 1980).

James, Alfred, *The voyage of the transport Minerva from Cork to Sydney, August 1799 to January 1800* (Sydney, 1996).

James, Francis, 'Irish colonial trade in the eighteenth century', in *William and Mary Quarterly*, third series, xx, 4 (1963), 574–84.

—— *Lords of the ascendancy: The Irish House of Lords and its members 1600–1800* (Dublin, 1995).

Jenkins, D., 'The correspondence of Charles Brodrick 1761–1822, archbishop of Cashel', in *Ir. Archives Bull.*, ix-x (1979-80), 43–9.

Joannon, Pierre, 'Wolfe Tone in Paris 1796–1797', in Patrick Rafroidi, Guy Fehlman and Maitiú MacConmara (eds), *France-Ireland literary relations* (Lille and Paris, 1974), 83–107.

—— (ed.), *La descente des Français en Irlande 1798: Jean Sarrazin, Jean-Louis Jobit, Louis-Octave Fontaine* (La Vouivre [Paris], 1998).

—— 'Theobald Wolfe Tone à Paris: conspirateur exilé ou ambassadeur incognito', in *Cycnos*, xv, 2 (1998), 5–18.

Johnson, Nuala, 'Sculpting heroic histories: Celebrating the centenary of the 1798 rebellion in Ireland', in *Trans. Inst. Brit. Geog.*, xix (1994), 78–93.

Johnston, E.M., *Great Britain and Ireland, 1760–1800: A study in political administration* (Edinburgh, 1963).

Johnston-Liik, E.M., *History of the Irish parliament, 1692–1800*, 6 vols (Belfast, 2002).

Joly, Agnes, 'Un élève Irlandais de l'école de cavalrie de Saint-Germain: William T. Tone', in *Revue de l'histoire de Versailles et de Seine-en-Oise*, xlv (1943), 41–68: xlvi (1944), 23–71.

Jones, Catherine, ' "Our partial attachments": Tom Moore and 1798', in *E.C.I.*, xiii (1998), 24–43.

Jones, E.H. Stuart, *An invasion that failed: The French expedition to Ireland 1796* (Oxford, 1950).

—— 'Mutiny in Bantry Bay 1799', in *Ir. Sword*, i, 3 (1951–2), 202–9.

Jones, Laura, 'Archibald Hamilton Rowan 1751–1834', in *Ulster Folk and Transport Museum yearbook* (1975–76), [1977], 11–13.

Jong-Ijsselstein, Marie de (ed.), *The diary of Elizabeth Richards, 1798–1825* (Amsterdam, 1999).

Joyce, John, *General Thomas Cloney: A Wexford rebel of 1798* (Dublin, 1988).

—— *Graiguenemanagh and the south Carlow-Kilkenny area in 1798* (Graiguenemanagh [County Kilkenny], 1998).

Jupp, Peter, 'Irish parliamentary elections and the influence of the Catholic vote', in *Hist. Jn.*, x, 2 (1967), 183–96.

—— 'Britain and the Union 1797–1801', in *Trans. Royal Hist. Soc.*, sixth series, x (2000), 197–219.

Karsten, Peter, 'Irish soldiers in the British army 1792–1922: Suborned or subordinate?' in *Jn. Soc. Hist.*, xvii, 1 (1976), 30–64.

Kaser, David, *Joseph Charless: Printer in the western country* (Philadelphia, PA, 1963).

—— 'Bernard Dornin, America's first Catholic bookseller', in David Kaser (ed.), *Books in America's past* (Charlottesville, VA, 1966), 106–28.

Kavanagh, Art, *The battles of 1798: A series* (Bunclody [County Wexford], 1998).

Kavanagh, P.J.,'James Nolan of Knockindrane 1746–1858: Captain of the Myshall rebels in 1798', in *Carloviana*, 45 (1997), 34–7.

Kavanagh, Patrick, *A popular history of the insurrection of 1798* (Dublin, 1870; 1874; 1884; 1898; 1913; 1916; 1918; 1920; 1923).

Kavanaugh, Anne, 'John FitzGibbon, earl of Clare', in Dickson, Keogh and Whelan, *United Irishmen*, 115–23.

— 'Lord Clare and his historical reputation', in *Hist. Ire.*, i, 3 (1993), 22–6.

— *John FitzGibbon, earl of Clare: Protestant reaction and English authority in late eighteenth-century Ireland* (Dublin, 1997).

Keane, Ronan, 'The will of the general: Martial law in Ireland 1535–1924', in *Ir. Jurist*, xxv-xxvii (1990–92), 150–80.

Kee, Robert, *The most distressful country* (London, 1972) [first of three volumes of *The green flag: A history of Irish nationalism*].

Kelleher, Derry, *Seventeen ninety eight: Myth and truth* (Bray [County Wicklow], 1998).

Kelly, Frieda, *A history of Kilmainham Gaol: The dismal house of little ease* (Dublin, 1988).

Kelly, James, 'The origins of the Act of Union: An examination of unionist opinion 1650–1800', in *I.H.S.*, xxv (1987), 236–63.

— 'Interdenominational relations and religious toleration in late eighteenth-century Ireland: The paper war of 1786–1788', in *E.C.I.*, iii (1988), 39–67.

— 'The genesis of the Protestant ascendancy: The Rightboy disturbances of the 1780s and their impact upon Protestant opinion', in O'Brien, *Parliament, politics and people*, 93–127.

— 'Napper Tandy, radical and republican', in James Kelly and Uaitéir Mac Gearailt (ed.), *Dublin and Dubliners* (Dublin, 1990), 1–24.

— *Prelude to Union: Anglo-Irish politics in the 1780s* (Cork, 1992).

— *Henry Grattan* (Dundalk, 1993).

— 'The glorious and immortal memory: Commemoration and Protestant identity in Ireland 1660–1800', in *R.I.A. Proc.*, C, xciv (1994), 25–52.

— 'A wild Capuchin of Cork: Arthur O'Leary 1729–1802', in Moran, *Radical Irish priests*, 39–61.

— 'The politics of "Protestant ascendancy": County Galway 1650–1832', in Gerard Moran and Raymond Gillespie (eds), *Galway: History and society* (Dublin, 1996), 229–70.

— *Henry Flood: Patriots and politics in eighteenth-century Ireland* (Dublin and Notre Dame, 1998).

— 'The limits of legislative independence', in Cullen, *1798*, 37–46.

— 'Popular politics in Ireland and the Act of Union', in *Trans. Royal Hist. Soc.*, sixth series, x (2000), 259–87.

— 'The politics of Volunteering 1778–1793' in *Ir. Sword*, 88 (2000), 139–57.

— 'Conservative Protestant political thought in late eighteenth-century Ireland', in Connolly (ed.), *Political ideas*, 185–220.

— 'A genuine Whig and patriot: Lord Charlemont's political career', in Michael McCarthy (ed.), *Lord Charlemont and his circle* (Dublin, 2001), 7–37.

— 'Public and political opinion in Ireland and the idea of an Anglo-Irish union 1650–1800', in Boyce, Eccleshall and Geoghegan (ed.), *Political discourse*, 110–41.

— 'The Act of Union: its origin and background', in Keogh and Whelan, *Acts of union*, 46–66.

— 'The last will and testament of Henry Flood: Context and text', in *Stud. Hib.*, xxxi (2000–2001), 37–52.

Kelly, Liam, 'Defenderism in Leitrim of the 1790s', in *Breifne*, vi, 24 (1986), 341–54.

— *A flame now quenched: Rebels and Frenchmen in Leitrim, 1793–1798* (Dublin, 1998).

Kelly, Martin, 'Father Mogue Kearns', in *Kild. Arch. Soc. Jn.*, xvii, 3 (1996–7), 348–50.

Kelly, Patrick, 'William Molyneux and the spirit of liberty in eighteenth-century Ireland', in *E.C.I.*, iii (1988), 133–48.

— 'Perceptions of Locke in eighteenth-century Ireland', in *R.I.A. Proc.*, C, lxxxxix (1989), 17–35.

— 'Irish writers and the French Revolution', in *La storia della storiographia Europea sulla rivoluzione francese* (Roma, 1990), 327–49.

Kelly, Richard, 'The trial and execution of Father Quigley', in *Ir. Eccl. Rec.*, xix (1906), 528–36 [James Coigly].

Kennedy, Máire, 'Nations of the mind: French culture in Ireland and the international book trade', in O'Dea and Whelan, *Nations and nationalisms*, 147–60.

— 'The *Encyclopédie* in eighteenth-century Ireland', in *The Book Collector*, xlv (1996), 201–13.

— *French books in eighteenth century Ireland* (Oxford, 2002).

Kennedy, Máire and Geraldine Sheridan, 'The trade in French books in eighteenth- century Ireland', in Gargett and Sheridan, *Ireland*, 173–96.

Kelly, Michael, 'The Bekan area in *The Year of the French*', in M. Corner and N. Ó Muraíle (ed.), *Béacan/Bekan: Portrait of an east Mayo parish* (Castlebar [County Mayo], 1986), 146–7.

Kennedy, Patrick [pseud.], *Father Murphy, patriot priest of Boolavogue* (Dublin, 1989).

Kennedy, William Benjamin, 'The Irish Jacobins', in *Stud. Hib.*, xvi (1976), 109–21.

— 'The United Irishmen and the Great Naval Mutiny of 1797', in *Éire-Ireland*, xxiii, 3 (1990), 7–18.

— 'Without any guarantee on our part: The French Directory's Irish policy', in Lee Kennett (ed.), *The consortium on revolutionary Europe, 1750–1785* (Gainesville, FL,1973), 50–64.

Kenny, Michael, *The 1798 rebellion: Photographs and memoribilia from the National Museum of Ireland* (Dublin, 1996).

— 'Teaghmháil le stair: Ábhair ó bhailiúchán 1798 an Ard Mhúsáeim', in Ó Snodaigh, *Fealsúnacht*, 169–88.

Keogh, Dáire, 'Fr John Martin: An Augustinian friar and the rebellion of 1798', in *Anal. Augustiniana* (1988), 337–57.

— 'Thomas Hussey, bishop of Waterford and Lismore 1797–1803', in Willam Nolan and T.P. Power (eds), *Waterford: History and society* (Dublin, 1992), 403–26.

— 'The most dangerous villian in society: Fr John Martin's mission to the United Irishmen of Wicklow in 1798', in *E.C.I.*, vii (1992), 115–35.

— *'The French disease': The Catholic Church and radicalism in Ireland, 1790–1800* (Dublin, 1993).

— 'The Catholic Church, Archbishop Troy and radicalism 1791–93', in Dickson, Keogh and Whelan, *United Irishmen*, 124–34.

— 'The battle for affection: The Catholic Church and radical politics 1790–1800', in *Bullán*, ii, 1 (1995), 35–43.

— 'Maynooth: A Catholic seminary in a Protestant state', in *Hist. Ire.*, iii, 3 (1995), 43–7.

— 'Archbishop John Thomas Troy 1739–1823', in *Archiv. Hib.*, xlix (1995), 105–10.

— 'Sectarianism in the rebellion of 1798: The eighteenth-century context', in Keogh and Furlong, *The mighty wave*, 37–47.

— 'Christian citizens: The Catholic Church and radical politics 1790–1800', in Swords, *Protestant, Catholic and Dissenter*, 9–19.

— *A patriot priest: The life of Fr James Coigly, 1761–1798* (Cork, 1998).

— 'Bithiúnaigh iad uilig; sagairt agus easpaig i 1798', in Ó Tuathaigh, *Éirí amach, 1798*, 69–80.

— 'The women of 1798', in Cullen, *1798*, 63–8.

— 'Sectarianism and the rebellion of 1798', in Devlin, *A union of wills?*, 35–48.

— 'An unfortunate man: James Coigly 1761–1798', in *Hist. Ire.*, vi, 2 (1998), 27–32.

— 'Scoundrels all: Priests and prelates in '98', in Póirtéir, *Great Irish rebellion*, 137–45.

— 'Catholic responses to the Act of Union', in Keogh and Whelan, *Acts of union*, 159–70.

Keogh, Dáire and Nicholas Furlong (eds), *The mighty wave: The 1798 rebellion in Wexford* (Dublin, 1996).

— (ed.), *The women of 1798* (Dublin, 1998).

Keogh, Dáire and Kevin Whelan (eds), *Acts of union: The causes, contexts and consequences of the Act of Union* (Dublin, 2001).

Kerrigan, Paul, 'The Shannonbridge fortifications', in *Ir. Sword*, xi, 45 (1974), 234–45.

— 'A military map of Ireland of the late 1790s', in *Ir. Sword*, xii, 48 (1976), 247–51.

— 'The capture of the *Hoche* in 1798', in *Ir. Sword*, xiii, 51 (1977), 123–7.

— 'Gunboats and sea fencibles in Ireland in 1804', in *Ir. Sword*, xiv, 55 (1980), 188–91.

— 'The naval attack on Wexford in June 1798', in *Ir. Sword*, xv, 60 (1983), 198–9.

— 'Minorca and Ireland, an architectural connection: The Martello towers of Dublin Bay', in *Ir. Sword*, xv, 60 (1983), 192–6.

— 'A corps of yeomanry gunners in Ireland 1805–6: The Loughlinstown [County Dublin] Gunners', in *Ir. Sword*, xv, 60 (1983), 197–8.

— 'A return of barracks in Ireland in 1811', in *Ir. Sword*, xv, 61 (1983), 277–83.

— *Castles and fortifications in Ireland 1485–1945* (Cork, 1995).

— 'Regiments in the southern division of Ireland commanded by Lt. General Dalrymple 1797', in *Ir. Sword*, xx (1997), 265–71.

— 'The French expedition to Bantry Bay 1796 and the boat from the *Resolue*', in *Ir. Sword*, xxi, 83 (1998), 65–84.

— 'A 1798 pike and notes on the battle of Tara Hill', in *Ir. Sword*, xxi, no 85 (1999), 273–6.

— 'Weapons and tactics of 1798', in *Ir. Sword*, xxi, no. 85 (1999), 252–72.

Kiberd, Declan, 'Republican self-fashioning: The journal of Wolfe Tone', in Kiberd, *Irish classics* (London, 2000), 221–42.

Kidd, Colin, 'Gaelic antiquity and national identity in enlightenment Scotland and Ireland', in *Eng.Hist.Rev.*, cix (1994), 197–214.

— 'North Britishness and the nature of eighteenth-century British patriotism', in *Hist. Jn.*, xxxix, 2 (1996), 361–82.

— *British identities before nationalism: Ethnicity and nationhood in the Atlantic world 1600–1800* (Cambridge, 1999).

Kiernan, T.J., *Transportation from Ireland to Sydney, 1791–1816* (Canberra, 1954).

Killen, John (ed.), *The decade of the United Irishmen: Contemporary accounts, 1791–1801* (Belfast, 1997).

— *The United Irishmen and the government of Ireland, 1791–1801: A Linen Hall exhibition* (Belfast, 1998).

[Kilpatrick, Cecil (ed.)], *The formation of the Orange Order, 1795–98: The edited papers of Col. William Blacker and Col. Robert H. Wallace* (Belfast, 1994).

Kinane, Vincent, 'Literary food for the American market: Patrick Byrne's exports to Mathew Carey', in *Am. Antiq. Soc. Proc.*, civ, 2 (1994), 315–32.

— 'Some late eighteenth and early nineteenth-century Dublin printers' account books: The Graisberry ledgers', in *Six centuries of the provincial book trade* (Winchester, 1990), 139–50.

King, Mary, 'Conjuring past or future?: Versions of Synge's "Play of '98" in *Ir. Review*, 26 (2000), 71–9.

King-Hall, Magdalen, *The edifying bishop: The story of Frederick Hervey, earl of Bristol and bishop of Derry* (London, 1951).

Kinsella, Anna, 'The spirit of '98 awakened', in *Wex. Hist. Soc. Jn.*, xv (1994–5), 34–42.

— '1798 claimed for Catholics: Fr Kavanagh, Fenians and the centenary celebrations', in Keogh and Furlong, *The mighty wave*, 139–56.

— 'Nineteenth-century perspectives: The women of 1798 in folk memory and ballads', in Keogh and Furlong, *Women of 1798*, 187–99.

— 'Who feared to speak in 1898?' in *Wex. Hist. Soc. Jn.*, xvii (1998–99), 221–34.

Kinsella, Mick, Edward Moran and Conor Murphy (eds), *Kilcumney '98: Its origins, aftermath and legacy* (Kilcumney [County Carlow], 1998).

Kirkpatrick, Kathryn, 'Putting down the rebellion: Notes and glosses in *Castle Rackrent* 1800', in *Éire-Ireland*, xxx, 1 (1995), 77-90.

[Kissane, Noel], *Grattan's parliament: Facsimile documents from the National Library of Ireland* (Dublin, 1982).

Knox, Oliver, *Rebels and informers: Stirrings of Irish independence* (London, 1997).

Kraus, Michael, 'America and the Irish revolutionary movement in the eighteenth century', in Richard Morris (ed.), *The era of the American Revolution* (New York, 1939), 332-48.

— 'Across the western sea 1783-1845', in *Jn. British Studies*, i, 2 (1962), 91-114.

Laffan, Moira, *Frascati and the Lord Edward FitzGerald connection* (Foxrock [County Dublin], 1999).

[Lammey, David (ed.)], *Act of Union bicentenary 1801-2001: Exhibition catalogue* (Belfast, 2001).

Landreth, Helen, *The pursuit of Robert Emmet* (Dublin, 1949).

Larkin, John (ed.), *The trial of William Drennan* (Dublin, 1991).

Larkin, Patrick, 'United Irishmen in Magherafelt' [County Derry], in *South Derry Hist. Soc. Jn.*, i, 3 (1982-3), 218-20.

Latimer, William T., *Ulster biographies relating to the rebellion of 1798* (Belfast, 1897; new ed. 1997) [William Steel Dickson, James Hope, Henry Munro, Henry Joy McCracken, Samuel Neilson, James Porter, David Bailie Warden].

— 'David Bailie Warden of Bangor, patriot of 1798', in *U.J.A.*, xiii (1907), 29-38; 143-4.

— 'Revd William Steel Dickson at Keady' [County Armagh] in *U.J.A.*, xvii (1911), 95-6.

Latocnaye, [Jacques Louis], Chevalier de, *A Frenchman's walk through Ireland*, (ed.) John Stevenson (Belfast, 1917); facsimile repr. (ed.) John Gamble (Belfast, 1984).

Lavery, Anne, 'The year of the harp', in *The Bell*, iv (1992), 33-6 [1792 letter re Belfast Harp Festival].

Lawlor, Chris, *The massacre on Dunlavin Green: A story of the 1798 rebellion* (Dunlavin [County Wicklow], 1998).

Le Biez, Gilles, 'Irish news in the French press 1789-98', in Dickson, Keogh and Whelan, *United Irishmen*, 256-68.

Lecky, W.E.H., *Leaders of public opinion in Ireland* (London and New York, 1903: 1912: First ed., London, 1865) [Henry Flood, Henry Grattan, Daniel O'Connell].

— *A history of Ireland in the eighteenth century*, 5 vols (London, 1913) [first ed., London, 1892].

— *A history of Ireland in the eighteenth century* (Chicago, 1972) [edited by L. Perry Curtis].

Lee, Joseph, 'Grattan's parliament', in Brian O'Farrell (ed.), *The Irish parliamentary tradition* (Dublin, 1973), 149-59.

— 'The road to Wexford', in *World of Hibernia*, Spring (1998), 132-42.

— 'Ireland 1798-1998', in Bull et al., *Ireland and Australia*, 331-42.

Leerssen, Joep, *Mere Irish and fíor-Ghaeil: Studies in the idea of Irish nationality, its development and literary expression prior to the nineteenth century* (Amsterdam, 1986; new ed., Cork and Notre Dame, 1996).

— 'Anglo-Irish patriotism and its European context: Notes towards a reassessment', in *E.C.I.*, iii (1988), 7-24.

— *Remembrance and imagination: Patterns in the historical and literary representation of Ireland in the nineteenth century* (Cork and Notre Dame, 1996).

— '1798: The recurrence of violence and two conceptualisations of history', in *Ir. Review*, 22 (1998), 37-45.

— *Hidden Ireland, public sphere* (Galway, 2002).

Leerssen, Joseph, A.H. Van Der Weel and Bart Westerweel (eds), *Forging in the smithy: National identity and representation in Anglo-Irish literary history* (Amsterdam, 1995).

Le Gros, Bernard, 'Burke et l'Irlande', in *Études Irlandaises*, xviii, 2 (1993), 109-22.

Leighton, C.D.A., *Catholicism in a Protestant kingdom: A study of the Irish Ancien Regime* (Dublin, 1994).

Lenehan, John, 'Memories of Ballinamuck [County Longford]' in *Teathbha*, i, 1 (1969), 47–52.

[Lennox, Sarah], *The life and letters of Lady Sarah Lennox, 1745–1826, daughter of Charles, second duke of Richmond and successively the wife of Sir Thomas Charles Bunbury, and of George Napier; also a short political sketch of the years 1760–1763 by Henry Fox*, (ed.) Countess of Ilchester and Lord Stavordale (New York, 1901) [contains material on Lord Edward FitzGerald].

Lett, H.W., 'The wearing of the green', in *U.J.A.*, xii (1906), 143; xiii (1907), 46.

Leyburn, James, 'Presbyterian immigrants and the American Revolution', in *Jn. Presbyterian Hist.*, liv (1976), 19–29.

Lindsay, Deirdre, 'The Fitzwilliam episode revisited', in Dickson, Keogh and Whelan, *United Irishmen*, 176–96.

— 'The Rebellion Papers: An introduction', in *Ulster Local Studies*, xviii, 2 (1997), 28–42.

— 'The Rebellion Papers', in *Hist. Ire.*, vi, 2 (1998), 18–22.

— 'The Defenders', in Cullen, *1798*, 15–26.

Lindsay, John, *The shining life and death of Lord Edward FitzGerald* (London, 1949).

Linebaugh, Peter, *A dish with one spoon: The American experience of slavery and the commons in the transformation of three officers of the English crown into freedom fighters for the United Irish* (Toledo, OH, 1999) [Lord Edward Fitzgerald, Thomas Russell, Edward Marcus Despard].

— 'The red-crested bird and black duck, a story of 1802: Historical materialism, indigenous people and the failed republic', in *The Republic*, ii (2001), 104–25.

Linebaugh, Peter and Marcus Rediker, *The many-headed hydra: The hidden history of the revolutionary Atlantic* (London, 2000).

Little, G.A. (ed.),'The diary of Richard Farrell, barrister-at-law', in *Capuchin Annual*, xv (1944), 326–38 [Dublin Catholic].

Litton, F.J., 'Reluctant rebel: The story of Francis Lysaght esq., United Irishman', in *Dal gCais*, vi (1982), 5–12 [Clare United Irishman].

Livesey, J.C., 'Acts of union and disunion: Ireland in Atlantic and European contexts', in Keogh and Whelan, *Acts of union*, 95–105.

— 'The culture and history of French republicanism: Terror or utopia', in *The Republic*, ii (2001), 47–58.

Lloyd, David, *Ireland after history* (Cork and Notre Dame, 2000).

Lobo, Anne-Catherine, '1798: Une apocalypse?' in *Études Irlandaises*, xxiv, 2 (1999), 127–38.

— 'Une generation plus tard? Quel bilan pour l'Union?' in *Études Irlandaises*, xxv, 2 (2000), 21–33.

Long, Gerald (ed.), *Books beyond the Pale: Aspects of the provincial book trade in Ireland before 1850* (Dublin, 1996).

Loughridge, Adam, *The Covenanters in Ireland*, (Belfast, 1984; 1987).

Love, Walter, 'Edmund Burke and an Irish historiographical controversy', in *History and Theory*, ii, 2 (1962), 180–98.

Lowe, N.F., 'Mary Wollstonecraft and the Kingsborough scandal', in *E.C.I.*, ix (1994), 44–56.

— 'James Barry, Mary Wollstonecraft and 1798', in *E.C.I.*, xii (1997), 60–76.

Lunney, Linde, 'Ulster attitudes to Scottishnesss: The eighteenth-century and after', in Ian Wood (ed.), *Scotland and Ulster* (Edinburgh, 1994), 56–70.

Lynch, Bernadette, 'Wolfe Tone', in *Ir. Universities Hist. Students Congress Bulletin*, iii (1958), 5–17.

Lyons, J.B., 'William Lawless: An Irish and French revolutionary', in *Jn. Ir. Coll. Physicians and Surgeons*, xxiv, 4 (1998), 238–42.

Lyons, Ken, *1798: A commemorative booklet produced by the Castlebar 1798 commemorative committee* (Castlebar [County Mayo], 1998).

Lynch, P.J., 'New light on Lord Edward', in *Ir. Book Lover*, ix (1917), 21–5 [Lady Pamela Campbell's marginalia on Moore's *Life* of her father].

MacAnnallen, Brendan, 'The Brantry Boys [County Tyrone] of '98', in *Dúiche Néill*, xii (1998), 48–75.
— 'The Brantry Boys: Courtmartial transcripts', in *Dúiche Néill*, xii (1998), 76–94.
MacCarthy, Mary, *Fighting Fitzgerald and other papers* (London, 1930) [includes Frederick Hervey].
MacAtasney, Gerard, *Leitrim and the croppies, 1776–1804* (Carrick-on-Shannon [County Leitrim], 1998).
Mac An Bheatha, Proinsías, *Cnoc na hUamha* (Baile Átha Cliath, 1978) [on Henry Joy McCracken].
— *Jemmy Hope: An cheád soisialaí Éireannach* (Cathair na Mart, 1985).
— *Dóchas aduaidh: Bunaí na hÉireannach Aontaithe, 1791* (Baile Átha Cliath, 1991).
Mac Annaidh, Séamus (ed.), *Fermanagh and 1798* (Tempo [County Fermanagh], 2000).
— 'Two Gaelic manuscripts from Fermanagh in 1798', in Mac Annaidh, *Fermanagh*, 66–77.
Mac Aonghusa, Proinsías and Liam Ó Riagáin (ed.), *The best of Tone* (Cork, 1972).
[MacCary, James], 'Notes on the Revd James MacCary of Carrickfergus', in *U.J.A.*, xiv (1908), 139–40.
MacCauley, J.A., 'The battle of Lough Swilly 1798', in *Ir. Sword*, iv, 16 (1960), 166–70.
— 'General Dumouriez and Irish defence', in *Ir. Sword*, ix, 35 (1969), 98–108; ix, 36 (1970), 165–73.
— 'Wolfe Tone: The last phase', in *Ir. Sword*, xi, 44 (1974), 185–92.
Mac Cearnaigh, Seamus, 'Brave Henry Monro', in McKearney, *Ninety-eight*, 57–8.
Mac Craith, Micheál, 'Filíocht Sheacaibíteach na Gaeilge: Ionar gan uaim?', in *E.C.I.*, ix (1994), 57–74.
— 'Foinsí an radacachais in Éirinn', in Ó Tuathaigh, *Éirí Amach, 1798*, 11–28.
MacDermot, Brian, *The Catholic question in Ireland and England, 1798–1822: The papers of Denys Scully* (Dublin, 1988).
MacDermot, Frank, 'The real Wolfe Tone', in *Ireland Today*, ii, 11 (1937), 35–42.
— 'The Jackson episode in 1794', in *Studies*, xxvii (1938), 77–92 [Revd William Jackson].
— 'The church and ninety-eight', in *Ireland Today*, iii, 1 (1938), 41–4.
— *Theobald Wolfe Tone: A biographical study* (London, 1939).
— 'A postscript on Tone', in *Studies*, xxviii (1939), 639–50.
— 'A new life of Tone', in *Ireland-American Review*, i (1939), 371–7.
— 'Memoirs of Arthur O'Connor', in *Ir. Sword*, ii, 5 (1954), 74.
— 'Arthur O'Connor', in *I.H.S.*, xv (1966), 48–69.
— *Theobald Wolfe Tone and his times* (Tralee, 1968; 1969; 1980) [revised paperback ed. of 1939 book].
— *Taking the long perspective: Democracy and terrorism in Ireland* (Dublin, 1991).
MacDonald, Brian, 'The *Northern Star* in south-west Ulster', in *The Spark Review Magazine*, ix (1995), 3–10.
— 'Distribution of the *Northern Star*', in *Ulster Local Studies*, xxviii, 2 (1997), 54–68.
— 'The Monaghan Militia and the tragedy of Blaris Moor', in *Clogher Rec.*, xvi, 2 (1998), 123–43.
— 'Fermanagh in the 1790s', in Mac Annaidh, *Fermanagh*, 11–43.
MacDonagh, Oliver, *States of mind: A study of Anglo-Irish conflict, 1780–1980* (London, 1983).
MacDonagh, Michael (ed.), *The viceroy's postbag: Correspondence hitherto unpublished of the earl of Hardwicke, first lord lieutenant of Ireland after the Union* (London, 1904).
MacGeehin [afterwards Wall], Maureen, 'The Catholic Committee and the Kenmare secession', in *Bulletin Ir. Comm. Hist. Sciences*, liii (Dec. 1947), 3–4.
Mac Giolla, Tomás, *200th anniversary of the founding of the Society of United Irishmen: Lessons for today* (Dublin, 1991).

Mac Giolla Choille, Breandán, *Transportation Ireland to Australia, 1798–1848: State Papers* (Dublin, 1983).

— 'The unfortunate Michael Campbell: A study of two Defender documents 1796', in *Seanchas Ard Mhacha*, xvii, 2 (1998), 32–54.

Mac Giolla Easpaig, Séamus, *Tomás Ruiséil* (Baile Átha Cliath, 1957).

Mac Giolla Fhinnéin, Brian, 'Pádraig Ó Loinsigh: Saol agus saothar', in *Seanchas Ard Mhacha*, xv, 2 (1993), 98–124.

MacGrath, Kevin, 'Two Wexford priests and 1798', in *Ir. Eccl. Rec.* (1948), 1092–8.

Mac Gréine, Pádraig, 'Traditions of 1798: The battle of Ballinamuck', in *Béaloideas*, iv (1934–5), 393–5.

MacHale, Conor, 'Colonel Baron James O'Dowda, Bonniconlon 1765–1798: The real Corney O'Dowd', in *Bliainiris*, ii, 2 (1988–9), 11–20 [original of a character in *The Year of the French*].

MacHale, E., 'Official list of claims for loss and damage in the county of Mayo in the year 1798', in *Bliainiris*, ii, 2 (1988–9), 21–45.

— 'Some Mayo priests of 1798', in *Blianiris: North Mayo Hist. Jn.*, xi, 5 (1991–2), 7–20.

MacHugh, Roger (ed.), *Carlow in 1798* (Dublin, 1949; new ed. Dublin, 1998) [account of William Farrell].

MacLeod, Catriona, *Robert Emmet* (Dublin, 1935).

MacLeod, Emma, *A war of ideas: British attitudes to the war against revolutionary France, 1792–1802* (Aldershot and Brookfield, VT, 1998).

Mac Loinsigh, Seán, 'Revd James Porter', in *Donegal Ann.* (1969), 7–15.

MacManus, Frank, 'The expulsions from Ulster 1795–1797', in Mac Annaidh, *Fermanagh*, 44–65.

MacManus, John, *1798–1998: A political pamphlet* (Bray [County Wicklow], 1998).

MacMaster, Johnston, 'Francis Hutcheson and the social vision of eighteenth-century radical Presbyterianism', in Mac Annaidh, *Fermanagh*, 100–17.

MacManus, M.J., 'Bibliography of Theobald Wolfe Tone', in *Dublin Magazine*, xv, 3 (1940), 52–64 [also issued as a separate publication (Dublin, 1940)].

MacNeill, J.G. Swift, 'The agent *provocateur* in Ireland', in *The Contemporary Review*, 635, Nov. (1918), 527–36 [James MacGuckian, Leonard MacNally, Thomas Reynolds, Samuel Turner, Bernard Duggan].

Mac Réamoinn, Séan (ed.), *The common name of Irishman* (Dublin, 1998) [essays in commemoration of 1798 by the Workers Party].

Mac Siomóin, S., 'Revd James Porter', in McKearney, *Ninety-eight*, 35–7.

Mac Suibhne, Breandán, 'Up not out: Why did north-west Ulster not rise in 1798?' in Póirtéir, *Great Irish rebellion*, 83–100 [also in *Donegal Annual*, l (1998), 15–32].

— 'Na hÓglaigh agus togáil na feiniúlachta Éireannaí in iarthuaisceart Uladh 1778–86', in Ó Snodaigh, *Fealsúnacht*, 7–64.

— 'Whiskey, potatoes and true-born patriot Paddies: Volunteering and the construction of the Irish nation in north-west Ulster 1770–1789', in Peter Jupp and Eoin Magennis (eds), *Crowds in Ireland 1720–1920* (London, 2000), 45–82.

— 'Three drunken nights and a hangover: The Sieges, the Apprentice Boys and Irish national identity 1779–1780', in William Kelly (ed.), *The sieges of Derry* (Dublin, 2001), 85–95.

— *Patriot Paddies: The politics of identity and rebellion in north-west Ulster, 1778–1803* (Cork and Notre Dame, forthcoming).

Mac Suibhne, Peadar, *The priest's grave at French Furze* [County Kildare]: A *victim of the Gibbet Rath massacre* (Naas [County Kildare], 1967).

— *Carlow in 1798* (Carlow, 1974).

— *Kildare in 1798* (Naas [County Kildare], 1978).

McAnally, Henry, 'Jobit, Fontaine, Sarrazin', in *U.J.A.*, third series, ix (1947), 115–20.

— *The Irish militia, 1793–1816: A social and military study* (Dublin and London, 1949).

McBride, Ian, 'William Drennan and the dissenting tradition', in Dickson, Keogh and Whelan, *United Irishmen*, 49–61.

— 'Presbyterians in the Penal Era', in *Bullán*, i, 2 (1994), 73–86.

— *The siege of Derry in Ulster Protestant mythology* (Dublin, 1997).

— 'When Ulster joined Ireland: Anti-Popery, Presbyterian radicalism and Irish republicanism in the 1790s', in *Past & Present*, clvii (1997), 63–93.

— *Scripture politics: Ulster Presbyterianism and Irish radicalism in the late eighteenth century* (Oxford, 1998).

— 'The Irish rebellion of 1798', in *The Historian*, lviv (1998), 25–9.

— 'Reclaiming the rebellion: 1798 in 1998', in *I.H.S.*, xxxi (1999), 395–410 [review article].

— 'The harp without the crown: Nationalism and republicanism in the 1790s', in Connolly (ed.), *Political ideas*, 159–84.

McBride, Jimmy, 'Songs of the United Irishmen in the northwest', in *Donegal Annual*, l (1998), 41–53.

McBride, Lawrence, 'Visualising '98: Irish nationalist cartoons commemorate the revolution', in *Eighteenth-century Life*, xxii, 3 (1998), 103–17.

— 'Nationalist constructions of the 1798 rebellion: The political illustrations of J.D. Reigh', in *Éire-Ireland*, xxiv, 2 (1999), 117–34.

McCabe, Brian, 'Michael Reynolds and the attack on Naas 1798', in *Kild. Arch. Jn.*, xviii, 4 (1998–9), 598–611.

McCabe, John, 'A United Irish family: The McCabes of Belfast', in *Familia*, xii (1997), 1–24 [reprinted in *North Irish roots*, ix, 1 (1998)].

McCabe, Leo, *Wolfe Tone and the United Irishmen: For or against Christ? 1791–1798*, Vol. 1 (London, 1937) [no more published].

McCalman, Iain, 'Erin go bragh: The Irish in British popular radicalism 1790–1840', in Oliver MacDonagh and W.F. Mandle (ed.), *Irish-Australian studies* (Canberra, 1989), 168–84.

— (ed.), *An Oxford companion to the Romantic age: British culture, 1776–1832* (Oxford, 1999).

McCarthy, Patrick, 'Remembering '98: A bibliographic essay', in *Ir. Sword*, xxi, 83 (1998), 232–8.

McCartney, Donald, 'The writing of history in Ireland 1800–30', in *I.H.S.*, x (1956–7), 347–62.

McCavery, Trevor, 'Reformers, reactionaries and revolutionaries: Opinion in north Down and the Ards in the 1790s', in *Ulster Local Studies*, xviii, 2 (1997), 69–94.

— 'A system of terror is completely established: The 1798 rebellion in north Down and the Ards', in Hill, Turner and Dawson, *Down*, 78–102.

— 'Politics, public finance and the British-Irish Act of Union of 1801', *in Trans. Royal Hist. Soc.*, sixth series, x (2000), 353–75.

McClelland, Aiken, 'Thomas Ledlie Birch, United Irishman', in *Belfast Natural Hist. and Phil. Soc., Proc.*, vii (1965), 24–35.

— 'A link with the '98', in *Ulster Folk and Transport Museum Yearbook, 1966–7* [1968], 14–15 [John Nevin].

— 'Preface', to W.G. Lyttle, *Betsy Gray or Hearts of Down*: A *tale of ninety-eight* (repr., Newcastle [County Down], 1968; 1976; 1997).

— 'Thomas Archer [Ballymena] and his gang', in *Ulster Folk and Transport Museum Yearbook 1969–70* [1971], 15–17.

— *The formation of the Orange Order* ([Belfast], [1971]).

— 'Orangeism in County Monaghan', in *Clogher Rec.*, ix, 3 (1978), 384–404.

McCormack, W.J., *The Dublin paper war of 1786–1788* (Dublin, 1993).

— *From Burke to Beckett: Ascendancy, tradition and betrayal in literary history* (Cork, 1994).

— *The pamphlet debate on the Union between Britain and Ireland 1797–1800* (Dublin, 1996).

— 'Introduction', to *The parliamentary register*, v–xi.

McCoy, Gerard, 'Patriots, Protestants and papists: Religion and the ascendancy 1714–60', in *Bullán*, i, 1 (1994), 105–117.

McCoy, Jack, *Ulster's Joan of Arc: An examination of the Betsy Gray story* (Bangor [County Down], 1989).

McCracken, L.J., 'The United Irishmen', in T.D. Williams (ed.), *Secret societies in Ireland* (Dublin, 1973), 58–67.

McDermott, Joe, '1798 and Newport' [County Mayo], in *Back the road: Recollections of Burrishoole and Newport*, i, 2 (1998), 8–11.

— 'The tree of liberty', in *Back the road: Recollections of Burrishoole and Newport*, i, 2 (1998), 5.

McDougall, Warren, 'Smugglers, reprinters and hot pursuers: The Irish-Scottish book trade and copyright prosecutions in the eighteenth century', in R. Myers and M. Harris (ed.), *The Stationers Company and the book trade 1550–1990* (Winchester, 1997), 151–83.

McDowell, R[obert] B[rendan], 'The Irish government and the provincial press', in *Hermathena*, liii (1939), 54–68.

— 'The personnel of the Dublin Society of United Irishmen', in *I.H.S.*, ii (1940–1), 1–53.

— 'United Irish plans of parliamentary reform 1793', in *I.H.S.*, iii, 9 (1942), 39–59.

— *Irish public opinion, 1750–1800* (London, 1944).

— (ed.), 'Proceedings of the Dublin Society of United Irishmen', in *Anal. Hib.*, xvii (1949), 3–143.

— 'The Fitzwilliam episode', in *I.H.S.*, xvi (1966), 115–30.

— *Ireland in the age of imperialism and revolution, 1760–1801* (Oxford, 1979).

— 'The age of the United Irishmen', in Moody and Vaughan, *New history of Ireland*, iv, 289–373.

— 'Burke and Ireland', in Dickson, Keogh and Whelan, *United Irishmen*, 102–14.

— (ed.), *Proceedings of the Dublin Society of United Irishmen* (Dublin, 1998).

— *Grattan: A life* (Dublin, 2001).

McEldowney, J.F., 'Legal aspects of the Irish Secret Fund 1793–1833', in *I.H.S.*, xxv (1988), 129–37.

McEvoy, Brendan, 'The United Irishmen in County Tyrone', in *Seanchas Ard Mhacha*, iii, 2 (1959), 283–314; iv, 1 (1960–61), 1–32; v, 1(1969), 37–65.

— 'Father James Quigley, priest of Armagh and United Irishman', in *Seanchas Ard Mhacha*, v, 2 (1970), 247–68.

— 'The Peep of Day Boys and Defenders in County Armagh', in *Seanchas Ard Mhacha*, xii,1 (1986), 123–63; xii, 2 (1987), 60–127.

— *The United Irishmen in County Tyrone* (Armagh, 1998) [repr. in book form of the articles cited above].

McFarland, E.W., *Protestants first: Orangeism in nineteenth-century Scotland* (Edinburgh, 1990).

— *Ireland and Scotland in the age of revolution: Planting the green bough* (Edinburgh, 1994).

McGinty, Margaret, 'Thomas Russell', in *Dúiche Néill*, viii (1993), 119–32.

McGleenon, C.F., 'Lord Gosford versus the Patriots: The Armagh by-election of 1794–5 and its sequel', in *Seanchas Ard Mhacha*, xvii, 2 (1998), 55–9.

— 'Lord Arthur Gosford and Armagh politics 1790–1800', in A.J. Hughes and W. Neely (eds), *Armagh: History and society* (Dublin, 2001), 609–38.

McGuffie, T.H., 'A sketch-map of Castlebar 27 August 1798', in *Jn. Soc. Army Hist. Research*, xxvi, 107 (1948), 88–90.

— 'Robert Emmet's insurrection', in *Ir. Sword*, i, 4 (1952–3), 322–3.

McHale, Conor, *Colonel Baron James Vippler O'Dowda of Bonniconlon, 1765–1798* ([Sligo], 1991).

McHugh, John, 'James Hope, weaver of Templepatrick [County Antrim]', in McKearney, *Ninety-eight*, 33–4.

McHugh, Roger J., *Henry Grattan* (Dublin, 1936: New York, 1937).

McIlvanney, Liam, 'Robert Burns and the Ulster-Scots literary revival of the 1790s', in *Bullán*, iv, 2 (2000), 125–44.

McIlrath, B., 'Classon Porter', in *Ulster Local Studies*, xv (1993), 13–37.

McKay, Russell, 'The fortification of Lough Swilly and Lough Foyle', in *Donegal Ann.* (1977), 40–68.

—— 'H.M.S. *Donegal* (formerly *La Hoche*)', in *Donegal Ann.* (1978), 369–70.

McKearney, Seamus (ed.), *Ninety-eight: A booklet of short stories, biographies, articles and ballads published to commemorate the one hundred and fiftieth anniversary of the insurrection of 1798* (Belfast, 1948).

McKelvie, Colin, 'Notes towards a bibliography of William Hamilton Maxwell 1792–1850', in *Ir. Booklore*, iii, 1 (1976), 32–42.

McKeown, J.R., 'The man from God knows where', in McKearney, *Ninety-eight*, 44–6. [Thomas Russell]. .

McKernan, Anne, 'War, gender and industrial innovation: Recruiting women weavers in early nineteenth-century Ireland', in *Jn. Soc. Hist.*, Fall (1994), 110–24.

McLoughlin, Thomas, 'Wolfe Tone and national independence', in *Contesting Ireland: Irish voices against England in the eighteenth century* (Dublin, 1999), 211–38.

McMahon, Sean, *Wolfe Tone* (Cork, 2001).

McMillan, William, 'Presbyterian ministers and the Ulster rising', in Swords, *Protestant, Catholic and Dissenter*, 81–117.

McNally, N., 'The men of '98', in *Jn. Australian Catholic Hist. Soc.*, iii, part 1 (1969), 24–46.

McNally, Patrick, '"The whole people of Ireland": Patriotism, national identity and nationalism in eighteenth-century Ireland', in Scott Brewster et al. (ed.), *Ireland in proximity* (London, 1999), 28–41.

McNally, Vincent, 'John Thomas Troy, archbishop of Dublin and the establishment of Saint Patrick's College Maynooth 1791–95', in *Cath. Hist. Rev.*, lxvii (1981), 565–88.

—— *Reform, revolution and reaction: Archbishop John Thomas Troy and the Catholic Church in Ireland, 1787–1817* (Lanham, MD, 1995).

McNeill, Mary, *The life and times of Mary Ann McCracken, 1770–1866* (Dublin, 1960; new ed., Belfast, 1988; 1997).

McPeake, B.Y., 'Letters of General Lake in 1798', in *Ir. Sword*, i, 4 (1952–3), 284–7.

McSkimmin, Samuel, *Annals of Ulster from 1790 to 1798*, (ed.) E[lizabeth] J. McCrum (Belfast, 1906) [first ed. Belfast, 1849; second ed. Belfast, 1853].

McTernan, J.C., 'Bartholomew Teeling 1774–1798: A hero of 1798', in *Corran* [County Mayo] *Herald*, 31 (1998-9), 14–16.

Mackey, James (ed.), *The cultures of Europe: The Irish contribution* (Belfast, 1994).

Madden, Richard Robert, *The United Irishmen: Their lives and times with several additional memoirs and authentic documents heretofore unpublished; the whole matter newly arranged and revised* (ed.), James J. O'Neill (Dublin, 1920).

—— *The United Irishmen: Their lives and times*, (ed.) Vincent Fleming O'Reilly, 12 vols (New York, 1916) [known as the 'Shamrock' edition].

Madders, Ambrose, *'98 diary: Ireland in rebellion* (Wexford, 1997).

Magee, John, 'The United Irish movement in Saintfield and Ballynahinch [County Down]', in *Seanchas Dhroim Mór* (1984), 5–14.

Magee, Sean, *Dublin's street index 1798 extracted from Whitelaw's census* (Dún Laoghaire, 1998).

Magennis, Eoin, 'A Presbyterian insurrection?: Reconsidering the Hearts of Oak disturbances of July 1763', in *I.H.S.*, xxxi (1998), 165–87.

—— 'County Armagh Hearts of Oak', in *Seanchas Ard Mhacha*, xvii, 2 (1998), 19–31.

Maguire, W.A., 'Arthur MacMahon, United Irishman and French soldier', in *Ir. Sword.*, ix, 36 (1970), 207–15.

—— 'Lord Donegall and the Hearts of Steel', in *I.H.S.*, xxi, 84 (1979), 351–76.

—— (ed.), *Up in arms! The 1798 rebellion in Ireland: A bicentenary exhibition* (Belfast, 1998).

Mahaffy, Belinda, *The United Irishmen in east Donegal* (Lifford [County Donegal], 1998).

Malcolm, Elizabeth, 'From light infantry to constabulary: The military origins of the Irish police 1798–1850', in *Ir. Sword*, xxi, 84 (1998), 163–75.

[Malcomson, A.P.W. (ed.)], *The United Irishmen: Facsimile documents from the Public Record Office of Northern Ireland* (Belfast, 1971; 1976).

— *The 1798 Rebellion: Facsimile documents from the Public Record Office of Northern Ireland* (Belfast, 1971).

— *The Act of Union: Facsimile documents from the Public Record Office of Northern Ireland* (Belfast, 1971).

— *The Penal Laws: Facsimile documents from the Public Record Office of Northern Ireland* (Belfast, 1971; 1976).

— *Irish elections, 1750–1832: Facsimile documents from the Public Record Office of Northern Ireland* (Belfast, 1971).

— *The extraordinary career of the second earl of Massereene, 1743–1805* (Belfast, 1972).

— (ed.), *Irish official papers in Great Britain: Private collections. Vol. 1* (Belfast, 1973).

— *Isaac Corry, 1755–1813: An adventurer in the field of politics* (Belfast, 1975).

— *An Anglo-Irish dialogue: A calendar of the correspondence between John Foster and Lord Sheffield, 1774–1824* (Belfast, 1976).

— *John Foster: The politics of the Anglo-Irish ascendancy* (Oxford, 1978; Belfast, 1981).

— 'The parliamentary traffic of this country', in Bartlett and Hayton, *Penal era*, 137–61.

— 'A lost natural leader: John James Hamilton, first marquis of Abercorn', in *R.I.A. Proc.*, C., lxxxviii (1988), 64–86.

— (ed.), *Irish official papers in Great Britain: Private collections. Vol. 2* (Belfast, 1990).

— 'The Irish peerage and the Act of Union', in *Trans. Royal Hist. Soc.*, sixth series, x (2000), 289–327.

— *Archbishop Charles Agar: Churchmanship and politics in Ireland, 1760–1810* (Dublin, 2002).

— [and Geraldine Hume], *Robert Emmet and the insurrection of July 1803: Facsimile documents from the Public Record Office of Northern Ireland* (Belfast, 1971).

[Mallow and District 1798 Commemoration Committee], *The Mallow conspiracy* (Kanturk [County Cork], 1999).

Mannion, John, 'Trans-Atlantic disaffection: Wexford and Newfoundland 1798–1800', in *Wex. Hist. Soc. Jn.*, xvii (1998–99), 30–61.

Mansergh, Daniel, 'The Union and the importance of public opinion', in Keogh and Whelan, *Acts of union*, 126–39.

— '"As much support as it needs": Social, class and regional attitudes to the Union', in *E.C.I.*, xv (2000), 77–97.

Mansergh, Martin, 'The significance of the 1798 commemoration', in Cullen, *1798*, 129–42.

— 'The rights of man in Ireland: The ideals of 1798', in Devlin, *A union of wills?*, 1–12.

Manwaring, G.E. and Bonamy Dobrée, *The floating republic: An account of the mutinies at Spithead and the Nore in 1797* (London, 1935).

Markey, Eugene, *1798: The Cavan connection* (Bailieborough [County Cavan], 1998).

Marsden, John, 'The union of religious creeds: Theobald Wolfe Tone and the origins of the Irish republican tradition', in *Search*, xii (1994), 25–33.

Marshall, P.J., 'Britain and the world in the eighteenth century: The turn outwards of Britain', in *Trans. Royal Hist. Soc.*, sixth series, xi (2001), 1–16.

Marshall, R.L., 'Maghera in '98', in S.S. McFarland, *Presbyterianism in Maghera* (Maghera [County Derry], 1985).

Martin, Sheila, *Directory of merchants and traders in Dublin in 1798 from the* Gentleman's and Citizen's Almanack (Dublin, 2000).

Mathewson, M.W., *Sir Francis Burdett and his times* (London, 1931).

Maxwell, Jane, 'Sources in Trinity College Dublin for researching the 1798 rebellion', in *Ir. Archives*, v (1998), 3–27 [includes transcript of visitation of T.C.D., 19 Apr. 1798].

Maxwell, William Hamilton, *History of the Irish rebellion in 1798 with memoirs of the Union and Emmet's insurrection in 1803* (London, 1903) [first ed. 1845].

May, W.E., 'The case of Roger Alleyne', in *Ir. Sword*, vii, 26 (1965), 34–6.

Mayes, Frank and Wilfrid Dilworth, 'James Reynolds of Cookstown [County Tyrone]', in *The Bell*, vii (1999), 62–8.

Meagher, John, 'Fr Nicholas Kearns and state prisoners', in *Rep. Nov.* (1955), 197–212.

Meehan, Helen, 'The *Shan Van Vocht*', in *Ulster Local Studies*, xix, 1 (1997), 80–90 [Belfast newspaper 1896–99].

— 'The Donegal Bay area in the 1790s', in *Donegal Annual*, l (1998), 4–14.

— 'The Montgomerys of Crogan and Convoy', in *Donegal Annual*, lii (200), 75–85.

Meenan, P.N., 'The enigma of Wolfe Tone', in *Clio* (1968), 6–8.

Meredith, Robbie, 'The *Shan Van Vocht*: Notes from the North', in Aaron Kelly and Alan Gillis (eds), *Critical Ireland: New essays in literature and culture* (Dublin, 2001), 173–81 [Belfast newspaper 1896–99].

Metscher, Priscilla, *Republicanism and socialism in Ireland: A study in the relationship of politics and ideology from the United Irishmen to James Connolly* (Frankfurt, 1986).

— 'Mary Ann McCracken: A critical Irishwoman within the context of her times', in *Études Irlandaises*, xiv, 2 (1989), 143–58.

— 'The life and campaigns of a radical Belfast woman' [Mary Ann McCracken], in Finlay, *Radicals*, 30–33.

Miller, John, *Crisis in freedom: The Alien and Sedition Acts* (Boston, MA, 1952).

Miller, David W., *Queen's rebels: Ulster loyalism in historical perspective* (Dublin, 1978).

— 'The Armagh troubles 1784–95', in Clark and Donnelly, *Irish peasants*, 155–91.

— 'Presbyterianism and modernisation in Ulster', in *Past & Present*, 113 (1978), 66–90 [repr. in C.H. Philpin (ed.), *Nationalism and popular protest in Ireland* (Cambridge, 1988), 80–109].

— (ed.), *Peep O'Day Boys and Defenders: Selected documents on the County Armagh disturbances, 1784–96* (Belfast, 1990).

— 'Non-professional soldiery 1600–1800', in Bartlett and Jeffery, *Military history*, 315–57.

— Politicisation in revolutionary Ireland: The case of the Armagh troubles', in *I.E.S.H.*, xxiii (1996), 1–17.

— 'Irish Christianity and revolution', in Smyth, *Revolution*, 195–210.

— The origins of the Orange Order in Armagh', in Hughes and Neely, *Armagh*, 583–608.

Miller, Howard, 'The grammar of liberty: American Presbyterians and the first American Constitution', in *Jn. Presbyterian Hist.*, liv (1976), 147–64.

Miller, Kerby, 'No middle ground: The erosion of the Protestant middle class in the south of Ireland in the Pre-Famine period', in *Huntington Library Quarterly*, 49 (1986), 295–306.

— 'Scotch-Irish myths and Irish identities in eighteenth and nineteenth-century America', in Charles Fanning (ed.), *New perspectives on the Irish diaspora* (Carbondale, IL, 2000), 75–92.

— 'Scotch-Irish, black Irish and real Irish: Immigrants and identities in the old south', in Andrew Bielenberg (ed.), *The Irish diaspora* (London, 2000), 139–57.

Miller, Kerby et al., *Irish immigrants in the land of Canaan: Letters and memoirs from colonial and revolutionary America 1675–1815* (New York, 2003).

Milne, King, 'The Elmes letters', in *The Past*, xviii (1992), 31–44.

Mirala, Petri, 'The eighteenth-century masonic lodge as a social unit', in *Ulster Folklife*, xliv (1998), 60–68.

— '"A large mob, calling themselves freemasons": Masonic parades in Ulster', in Jupp and Magennis (ed.), *Crowds*, 117–38.

Mitchell, Martin, *The Irish in the west of Scotland, 1797–1848: Trade unions, strikes and political unrest* (Edinburgh, 1998).

Mitchell, R. Sharpe, 'Robert Emmet and the development of the war rocket', in *Éire-Ireland*, v, 4 (1970), 3–8.

— 'Robert Emmet's rockets', in *Ir. Sword*, ix, 36 (1970), 161–4.

Moloney, Caroline, *The Irish music manuscripts of Edward Bunting (1773–1843): An introduction and catalogue* (Dublin, 2000).

Molony, John Chartres, *Ireland's tragi-comedians* (London and Edinburgh, 1934) [Clare, Tone, FitzGerald, Emmet].

Monagear parish: A rural district in 1798 (Monagear [County Wexford], 1998).

de Montfort, Simon (ed.), 'Mrs [Alice] Pounden's experiences during the 1798 Rising in County Wexford', in *Ir. Ancestor*, viii, 1(1976), 4–8.

Moody, T.W., 'The political ideas of the United Irishmen', in *Ireland Today*, iii, 1 (1938), 15–25.

— (ed.), 'An Irish countryman in the British navy 1809–1815', in *Ir. Sword*, iv, 16 (1960), 149–56; 17 (1960), 228–45; v, 18 (1961), 41–56; 19 (1961), 107–16; 20 (1962), 146–54; 21 (1962), 236–50.

Moody, T.W. and W.E. Vaughan (ed.), *A new history of Ireland*, iv: *Eighteeenth-century Ireland* (Oxford, 1986).

Moody, T.W., R.B. McDowell and C.J. Woods (eds), *The writings of T.W. Tone, volume i: Tone's career in Ireland to June 1795* (Oxford, 1998).

— *The writings of T.W. Tone, volume ii: America, France, and Bantry Bay, August 1795 to December 1796* (Oxford, 2001).

Moore, Andrew, 'The United Irishmen and south-west Sydney: A reconsideration of the Waldersee thesis', in Bull et al., *Ireland and Australia*, 34–47.

Moore, Christopher, 'Lady Louisa Connolly: Mistress of Castletown 1759–1821', in Jane Fenlon, Nicola Figgis and Catherine Marshall (eds), *New perspectives: Studies in art history* (Dublin, 1988), 123–42.

[Moore, John], *Diary of Sir John Moore*, (ed.) Sir J.F.M. Moore, 2 vols (London, 1904) [in Ireland Dec. 1797-June 1799: Irish material, i, 267–332].

Moore, Thomas, *The life and times of Lord Edward FitzGerald* (Dublin, 1909) [abridged version of 1831 ed.].

Moran, Gerard (ed.), *Radical Irish priests 1660–1970* (Dublin, 1998).

[Moravian church], *The 1798 rebellion as recorded in the diaries of Gracehill Moravian Church* (Newtownabbey [County Antrim], 1998).

[Moreau de Jonnes, Alexandre], *Adventures in the Revolution and under the Consulate*, (trans.) Cyril Hammond (London, 1929).

Moriarity, Mary and Catherine Sweeney, *Theobald Wolfe Tone* (Dublin, 1988) [for juvenile readers].

Morley, Vincent, 'Ide-eolaíocht an tSeacaibíteachais in Éirinn agus in Albain', in *Oghma*, ix (1997), 14–24.

— '"Tá an cruatan ar Sheóirse" - folklore or politics?' in *E.C.I.*, xiii (1998), 112–20.

— *Irish opinion and the American Revolution, 1760–1783* (Cambridge, 2002).

Morrow, Andrew, 'Revd Samuel Barber and the Rathfriland [County Down] Volunteers', in *U.J.A.*, xiv (1908), 105–119; xv (1909), 29–35; 125–33; 149–57; xvi (1910), 33–42.

Morton, R. Grenfell, 'Plans for Ulster defence 1795–1797', in *Ir. Sword*, ii, 8 (1956), 270–4.

— 'The rise of the yeomanry', in *Ir. Sword*, viii, 30 (1967), 58–64.

Moylan, Terry, *The age of revolution 1776–1815 in the Irish song tradition* (Dublin, 2000).

— (ed.), *Songs composed during the Irish rebellion of 1798 by the late William Ball Esqr. Dublin* (Ennistymon [County Clare], 2001).

Mullen, Thomas, 'The Hibernia regiment of the Spanish army', in *Ir. Sword*, viii, 32 (1968), 218–25.

Mulloy, Sheila, 'James Joseph MacDonnell, "the best-known of the United Irish chiefs of the west"', in *Cathair na Mart*, v (1985), 67–78.

— 'John Moore of Moorehall 1767-99: The general who wasn't', in *Ir. Sword*, xviii, 73 (1992), 264–70.

— 'Fr Manus Sweeney 1763–1799', in *Cathair na Mart*, xiv (1994), 27–38.

— 'General James Joseph MacDonnell 1763–1848', in *Roscommon Hist. and Arch. Soc. Jn.*, vi (1996), 73–6.

— 'The clergy and the Connacht rebellion', in Swords, *Protestant, Catholic and Dissenter*, 253–72.

— '1798 i gConnachta', in Ó Tuathaigh, *Éirí Amach, 1798*, 107–22.

— 'The radical cleric and the French invasion of Connacht: Fr Manus Sweeney 1762–1799', in Moran, *Radical Irish priests*, 79-90.

Munnelly, Jack, *The French invasion of Connacht* (Killala [County Sligo], 1998).

Munnelly, Tom, '1798 and the balladmakers', in Póirtéir, *Great Irish rebellion*, 160–70.

Murphy, Hilary, 'Memories of Colonel Jonas Watson', in *Wex. Hist. Soc. Jn.*, xv (1994-5), 115–18.

— 'John Henry Colclough', in *Kilmore Parish Jn.*, 26 (1998), 3–5.

— 'Arklow's 1798 memorial', in *Arklow Hist. Soc. Jn.* (1998), 70–2.

Murphy, J.A. (ed.), *The French are in the bay: The French expedition to Bantry Bay in 1796* (Cork, 1996).

Murphy, Kevin, 'South Armagh in the years leading up to the rebellion of 1798', in Devlin, *A Union of wills?*, 49–65.

Murphy, Maureen, 'The noggin of milk: An Old Testament legend and the battle of Ballina-muck', in Keogh and Furlong, *Women of 1798*, 177–86.

Murphy, Rory, *The battle of Newtownbarry 1 June 1798* (Bunclody [County Wexford], 1998).

Murphy, Sean, 'Municipal politics and popular disturbances 1660–1800', in Art Cosgrove (ed.), *Dublin through the ages* (Dublin, 1988), 77–97.

Murphy, Willa, 'A queen of hearts or an old maid?: Maria Edgeworth's fiction of union', in Keogh and Whelan, *Acts of union*, 186–201.

[Murray, Bill (ed.)], *Footsteps of '98: Carrigbyrne Pike Group* (Carrigbyrne [County Wexford], 1997).

— *Footsteps of '98: The sequel* (Carrigbyrne [County Wexford], 2001).

— *The Carrigbyrne Pike Group honour the United Irishmen who were imprisoned and transported from New Geneva barracks, 26 May 2002* (Carrigbyrne [County Wexford], 2002).

Murray, Bill and John Cullen (ed.), *Epitaph of 1798: A photographic record of 1798 memorials on the island of Ireland and beyond* (Carrigbyrne [County Wexford], 2002).

Murray, Kevin, 'The defence of Dublin 1794–5', in *Ir. Sword*, ii, 9 (1956), 332–8.

— 'The defence of Cork 1794–5', in *Ir. Sword*, iii, 10 (1957), 55–6.

Murtagh, Harman, 'General Humbert's campaign in the west', in Póirtéir, *Great Irish rebellion*, 115 24.

Musgrave, Sir Richard, *Memoirs of the different rebellions in Ireland* (4th ed., Fort Wayne, IND, 1995) [first ed. Dublin, 1801].

Myers, Mitzi, 'Like the pictures in a magic lantern: Gender, history and Edgeworth's rebellion narratives', in *Nineteenth-Century Contexts*, xix (1996), 373–412.

— 'War correspondence: Maria Edgeworth and the en-gendering of revolution, rebellion and union', in *Eighteenth-Century Life*, xxii, 3 (1998), 74–92.

[Myshall 1798 committee], *From Myshall Lodge: A selection of letters and documents, 1797–1817* (Myshall [County Carlow], 1998).

[Neilson, John], *Dedication of the monument to John Neilson c.1770–1827, Ballycarry, County Antrim, Ireland: United Irishman, political exile, architect at Monticello and the University of Virginia. Maplewood cemetery, Charlotteville, Virginia, 17 Apr. 1999* (Charlottesville, VA, 1999).

Nevin, Martin (ed.), *The sprig in the window: 1798 in the Leighlin area* (Leighlinbridge [County Carlow], 1998).

[New British History], 'The new British history in Atlantic perspective', in *American Historical Review*, civ (1999), 426–500.

Newman, Gerald, *The rise of English nationalism: A cultural history, 1740–1830* (New York, 1997).

Ní Chinnéide, Síle, *Napper Tandy and the European crisis of 1798–1803* (Dublin, 1963).

Nicolson, Harold, *The desire to please: A study of Hamilton Rowan and the United Irishmen* (London, 1943).

Ninety-eight news: Newsletter of the United Irishmen Commemoration Society [Issues 1–4] (Belfast, 1997–1998).

''98 rebellion in Glenarm and Glencoy [County Antrim]', in *The Glynns*, xxvii (1999), 21–32.

'98: Who fears to speak (Dublin, 1948).

Nolan, William, *The man of Boolavogue* (Ballon [County Carlow], 1998) [Fr John Murphy].

Nybakken, Elizabeth, 'New light on the old side: Irish influences on colonial Presbyterianism', in *Jn. Am. Hist.*, lxviii, 4 (1982), 813–32.

Ó Baoighill, Pádraig, 'Revd James Porter 1753–1798', in *Donegal Annual*, l (1998), 53–60.

Ó Bradaigh, Seán (ed.), *Songs of '98: Bliain na bhFrancach / The year of the French* (Dublin, 1982; 1983; 1997; 1998).

—— *The French Revolution and the Irish struggle* (Longford, 1985).

—— (ed.), *The battle of Ballinamuck: A traditional history by James O'Neill of Crowdrummin* (Aughnacliffe [County Longford], [1986]).

—— *French graves in Connacht* ([n.p., [n.d.]).

Ó Briain, Liam, 'Theobald Wolfe Tone in Galway', in *Ir. Sword*, ii, 7 (1955), 228–9.

[O'Brien, Conor (ed.)], *Aughrim, 1798–1998: Unveiling of commemorative monument 19 September 1998* (Aughrim [County Wicklow], 1998).

O'Brien, Conor Cruise, *The great melody: A thematic biography and commented anthology* (London, 1992) [on Edmund Burke].

O'Brien, Gerard, *Anglo-Irish politics in the age of Grattan and Pitt* (Dublin, 1987).

—— (ed.), *Parliament, politics and people: Essays in eighteenth-century Irish history* (Dublin, 1989).

—— 'The unimportance of public opinion in eighteenth-century Britain and Ireland', in *E.C.I.*, viii (1993), 115–27.

O'Brien, Gillian, 'Spirit, impartiality and independence: The *Northern Star* 1792–97', in *E.C.I.*, xiii (1998), 7–23.

—— 'Camden and the move towards union 1795–1798', in Keogh and Whelan, *Acts of union*, 106–25.

O'Brien, Paul, *Shelley and revolutionary Ireland* (London, 2002).

O'Brien, R. Barry (ed.), *The autobiography of Theobald Wolfe Tone, 1763–1798*, 2 vols (London, 1893; Dublin, 1910; London, 1912).

—— *Irish memories* (London, 1904) [includes John Keogh, John Philpott Curran, Theobald Wolfe Tone].

Ó Broin, Leon, *Emmet* (Baile Átha Cliath, 1954).

—— *The unfortunate Mr Robert Emmet* (Dublin, 1958).

—— *An Maidíneach: Staraí na nÉireannach Aontaoithe* (Baile Átha Cliath, 1971) [life of R.R. Madden].

—— 'R.R. Madden, historian of the United Irishmen', in *Ir. Univ. Rev.*, ii, 1 (1972), 20–33.

Ó Buachalla, Breandán, 'Irish Jacobitism in official documents', in *E.C.I.*, viii (1993), 128–38.

— 'Irish Jacobitism and Irish nationalism: The literary evidence', in O'Dea and Whelan *Nations and nationalisms*, 103–18.

— *Aisling ghéar: Na Stiobhartaigh agus an t-aos léinn, 1603–1788* (Baile Átha Cliath, 1996).

— 'An cúlra ideolaíoch', in Ó Tuathaigh, *Éirí Amach, 1798*, 29–40.

O'Byrne, Cathal, 'Maud Gonne in Belfast long ago', in McKearney, *Ninety-eight*, 54–6.

Ó Cadhain, Mairtín, *Tone inné agus inniú*, (eag.) Beirnedette Ní Rodaigh and Eibhlín Ní Alluráin (Baile Átha Cliath, 1999).

O'Carroll, Paddy, 'Remembering 1798', in Eamonn Slater and Michel Peillon (eds), *Memories of the present: A sociological chronicle of Ireland 1997–1998* (Dublin, 2000), 15–24.

Ó Casaide, Séamus, 'An elegy in Irish and English on John Hoey executed in Drogheda 1798', in *Louth Arch. and Hist. Soc. Jn.*, viii (1933), 61–4.

— *Watty Cox and his publications* (Dublin, 1935; 1954).

Ó Cathain, Diarmuid, 'Charles O'Conor of Belanagare, antiquary and Irish scholar', in *R.S.A.I. Jn.*, cxix (1989), 136–63.

— 'Tomás Ó Cathain: A note on the battle of Ballinamuck', in *Teathbha*, xi, 4 (1997), 276–8.

[Ó] Cearnaigh, Seán, *B'iad a d'adhain an tine bheo* (Baile Átha Cliath, 1998).

— *Ministrí misniúla, 1798* (Baile Átha Cliath, 1998).

Ó Ciardha, Éamonn, *Ireland and the Jacobite cause, 1685–1776: A fatal attachment* (Dublin, 2002).

Ó Ciosáin, Niall, *Print and popular culture in Ireland, 1750–1800* (London, 1977).

— 'Cumainn rúnda agus seicteachas', in Ó Tuathaigh, *Éirí Amach, 1798*, 55–68.

Ó Cochlainn, Rupert, 'Captain Manus O'Donnell. Manus a' phíce', in *Donegal Ann.*, i, 3 (1949), 193–203 [See also Rupert Coughlan].

— 'Napper Tandy's raid on Rutland', in *Donegal Ann.* (1970), 139–60.

Ó Coindealbháin, Séan, 'The United Irishmen in County Cork [I]', in *J.C.H.A.S.*, liii (1948), 115–29.

— 'United Irishmen in County Cork - II', in *J.C.H.A.S.*, liv (1949), 68–83.

— 'United Irishmen in County Cork - III', in *J.C.H.A.S.*, lv (1950), 50–61.

— 'United Irishmen in County Cork - IV', in *J.C.H.A.S.*, lv (1950), 73–90.

— 'United Irishmen in County Cork - V', in *J.C.H.A.S.*, lvi (1951), 18–28.

— 'United Irishmen in County Cork -VI', in *J.C.H.A.S.*, lvi (1951), 95–103.

— 'United Irishmen in County Cork - VII', in *J.C.H.A.S.*, lvii (1952), 87–98.

— 'United Irishmen in County Cork - VIII', in *J.C.H.A.S.*, lviii (1953), 91–6.

— 'A note on the trial of Delegate [Richard] Dry 1797', in *J.C.H.A.S.*, lix (1954), 54–5.

— 'John Swiney, the Cork United Irishman and his duel with Thomas Corbett', in *J.C.H.A.S.*, xl (1955), 22–7.

Ó Conchúir, Breandán, *Scríobhaithe Chorcaí, 1700–1850* (Baile Átha Cliath, 1982).

Ó Conluain, Proinsías, 'The rising road that led nowhere: The years before 1798 in the Blackwater basin' [Tyrone, Armagh, Monaghan], in *Dúiche Néill*, xii (1998), 9–43.

O'Connell, J.W., 'Colonel W. Robert's plans for the defence of the Irish coasts etc 1796–8', in *Galway Arch and Hist. Soc. Jn.*, l (1998), 10–36.

O'Connell, Maurice, 'The political background to the establishment of Maynooth College', in *I.E.R.*, fifth series, lxxxv, 1 (1956), 324–34: 406–15: lxxxvi, 2 (1956), 1–16.

— *Irish politics and social conflict in the age of the American Revolution* (Philadelphia, PA, 1965).

— 'Class conflict in a pre-industrial society: Dublin in 1780', in *Ir. Eccl. Rec.*, cii (1965), 93–106.

— 'The American Revolution and Ireland', in *Éire-Ireland*, xi, 3 (1976), 3–12.

O'Connor, Arthur, *The state of Ireland*, (ed.) James Livesey (Dublin, 1998).

[O'Connor, Maurice], *County Dublin in '98* ([Dublin, 1948?]).

O'Connor, Pat, *The French are at Killala: An account of Humbert's campaign from Kilcummin to Ballinamuck* ([n. p.], 1998).

O'Connor, Thomas, *An Irish theologian in eighteenth-century France: Luke Joseph Hooke, 1714–96* (Dublin, 1995).

— (ed.), *The Irish in continental Europe 1580–1815* (Dublin, 2000).

— (ed.), *Irish migrants in Europe after Kinsale, 1602–1820* (Dublin, 2003).

Ó Crualaoich, Gearóid, 'The French are on the say', in Murphy, *Bantry Bay*, 131–7.

Ó Cuinneagáin, Seosamh, *Lecture on the Tones in a decade of Irish history delivered in the Curragh Concentration Camp 27 Apr. and 4 May 1958* (Enniscorthy [County Wexford], 1970).

Ó Cuiv, Brian, 'Treádlitir ó 1798', in *Éigse*, xi (1964), 57–64 [Pastoral letter by Edmund French, Catholic bishop of Elphin].

O'Day, Edward, 'From Carlow loyalist to Kentucky republican: The emigration odyssey of David Byrne 1797–1827', in *Carloviana*, xliv (1996), 31–5.

O'Dea, Michael, 'Rousseau in eighteenth-century Irish journals', in Gargett and Sheridan, *Ireland*, 90–106.

O'Dea, Michael and Kevin Whelan (ed.), *Nations and nationalisms: France, Britain, Ireland and the eighteenth-century context* (Oxford, 1995).

Ó Donnchadha, Ronán, *Mícheál Óg Ó Longáin: File* (Baile Átha Cliath, 1994).

— 'Mícheál Óg Ó Longáin, file 1798', in Ó Snodaigh, *Fealsúnacht*, 135–48.

[O'Donnell, Frank Hugh], *At the sign of the harp and guillotine: Why Robespierre, Hoche and Wolfe Tone conspired against the Grattan parliament* (London, 1900).

O'Donnell, P[atrick] D., 'Wolfe Tone's Provost prison: Some recent research', in *Ir. Sword*, xi, 42 (1973), 21–31.

— 'Wolfe Tone's death: Suicide or assassination?' in *Ir. Medical News*, Jan.-Mar. (1997), 57–9.

O'Donnell, Ruan, 'General Joseph Holt and the historians', in Bob Reece (ed.), *Irish convicts* (Dublin, 1989), 25–48.

— 'Croppy Biddy Dolan', in E. Burke (ed.), *Cameos* (Dublin, 1990), 26–30.

— 'Roundwood [County Wicklow] in 1798', in *Roundwood and District Hist. and Folklore Jn.*, ii (1990), 6–9 [repr. x (1998), 37–40].

— 'General Joseph Holt', in Bob Reece (ed.), *Exiles from Erin: convict lives in Ireland and Australia* (Dublin, 1991), 27–56.

— 'Michael Dwyer: Wicklow chief', in Bob Reece (ed.), *Irish convict lives* (Sydney, 1993), 13–50 [repr. in Rebecca Pelan (ed.), *Irish-Australian studies* (Sydney, 1994), 206–17].

— 'The Wicklow United Irishmen in New South Wales', in *Wicklow Hist. Soc. Jn.*, i, 7 (1994), 46–53; ii, 1(1995), 10–20.

— 'The rebellion of 1798 in County Wicklow', in Hannigan and Nolan, *Wicklow*, 341–78.

— '"Desperate and diabolical characters": Defenders and United Irishmen in early New South Wales 1793–1800', in Richard Davis et al. (ed.), *Irish-Australian studies* (Sydney, 1996), 360–72.

— *The rebellion in Wicklow, 1798* (Dublin, 1998).

— *Exploring Wicklow's rebel past, 1798–1803: history, folklore and sites* (Wicklow, 1998).

— *1798 diary* (Dublin, 1998).

— 'Bridget 'Croppy Biddy' Dolan: Wicklow's anti-heroine of 1798', in Keogh and Furlong, *Women of 1798*, 87–112.

— 'Kings County in 1798', in William Nolan and Timothy O'Neill (eds), *Offaly: History and society* (Dublin, 1998), 485–514.

— 'Three rebellions? The position of Ulster in 1798', in Finlay (ed.), *Radicals*, 40–3.

— 'Philip Cunningham: Clonmel's insurgent leader of 1798', in *Tipp. Hist. Jn.* (1998), 150–7.

— 'The Devil's own: Joseph Holt and the 1798 rebellion in County Wicklow', in Bartlett, *History and environment*, 94–119.

— (ed.), *Insurgent Wicklow 1798: The story as written by Luke Cullen* (Bray [County Wicklow], 1998).

— 'Keeping up the flame: General Joseph Holt', in *Hist. Ire.*, vi, 2 (1998), 39–43.

— 'Edward Fitzgerald of Newpark', in *Wex. Hist. Soc. Jn.*, xvii (1998-99), 121–43.

— *Aftermath: Post-rebellion insurgency in Wicklow 1799–1803* (Dublin, 2000).

— 'Hellship: Captain Richard Brookes and the voyage of the *Atlas* I', in Foley and Bateman (ed.), *Irish Australian studies*, 164–74.

— 'Foreign enemies and internal rebels: The French war and the United Irishmen in New South Wales', in Geary (ed.), *Rebellion and remembrance*, 38–50.

— 'The Union and internal security', in Keogh and Whelan, *Acts of union*, 216–42.

— *Robert Emmet and the rising of 1803* (Dublin, forthcoming).

O'Donnell, Ruan and Bob Reece, '"A clean beast": Crofton Croker's fairy tale of General Holt', in *E.C.I.*, vii (1992), 7–42.

— 'A valuable man: James Meehan, United Irishman', in Bull et al., *Ireland and Australia*, 48–63.

O'Donnell, Ruan and Henry Cairns (ed.), *Ballads and poems of the Wicklow rebellion 1798* (Bray [County Wicklow], 1998).

O'Donnell, Terence, 'Napper Tandy and Donegal', in *Donegal Ann.* (1968), 300–12.

O'Donoghue, D.J., *Life of Robert Emmet* (Dublin, 1902).

O'Donohue, Patrick, 'The Holy See and Ireland 1780–1803', in *Archiv. Hib.*, xxxiv (1976–7), 99–108.

— 'John Thomas Troy, archbishop of Dublin 1785–1823: A man of his time', in James Kelly and Uaitéir Mac Gearailt (eds), *Dublin and Dubliners* (Dublin, 1990), 25–35.

Ó Dubhthaigh, Seán, 'Ríocárd Bairéad: File Iorrais [County Mayo] 1740–1819', in *Bliainiris*, i, 2 (1983), 18–22.

Ó Duibhir, Pól, 'The French are on the sea: A military history of Killiney Bay from 1793–1815', in *Ir. Sword*, xii, 46 (1975), 55–61.

— 'Captain John Warneford Armstrong and the Sheares brothers', in *Ir. Sword*, xiii (1977), 70–71.

Ó Duigeanáin, Peadar, 'Ballinamuck and '98', in *Teathbha*, i, 1(1969), 41–6.

O'Dwyer, Barry, 'Michael Dwyer and the 1807 plan of insurrection', in *Jn. Royal Australian Hist. Soc.*, lxix, part 2 (1983), 73–82.

Ó Faoláin, Seán, *The autobiography of Theobald Wolfe Tone* (London and New York, 1937) [abridged and edited].

— 'Rebel by vocation: An essay on Wolfe Tone', in *The Bell*, xiii, 2 (1946), 97–114.

— 'The rebels', in *The Irish*, revised ed. (London, 1969), 91–103 [on T.W. Tone].

O'Farrell, Padraic (ed.), *The '98 reader* (Dublin, 1998).

O'Flaherty, Eamonn, 'The Catholic Convention and Anglo-Irish politics 1791–1793', in *Archiv. Hib.*, xl (1985), 14–34.

— 'Irish Catholics and the French Revolution', in Gough and Dickson, *Ireland*, 52–67.

O'Flanagan, Michael, *When they followed Henry Joy* (Dublin, 1997).

— *Emmet, Hope and Russell 1803* (Dublin, 2002).

Ó Gallchobhair, Mícheál, 'Ar bhás an Athar Mánus Mhac Suibhne 1763–1799', in *Béaloideas*, ix (1940), 237–8.

Ó Gadhra, Nollaig, '1798 i gCúige Uladh', in Ó Tuathaigh, *Éirí Amach 1798*, 93–106.

O'Halloran, Clare, 'Irish re-creations of the Gaelic past: The challenge of Macpherson's *Ossian*', in *Past & Present*, cxxiv (1989), 69–95.

— 'Ownership of the past: Antiquarian debate and ethnic identity in Scotland and Ireland', in S.J. Connolly, R.A. Houston and R.J. Morris (eds), *Conflict, identity and economic development: Ireland and Scotland 1600–1939* (Preston, 1995), 135–47.

— 'An English orientalist in Ireland: Charles Vallancey 1726–1812', in Leerssen et al., *Forging*, 161–74.

Ó hAnnracháin, Eoghan, 'Who were the Wild Geese?' in *Études Irlandaises*, xxv, 1 (2000), 105–23.

O'Hara, Aidan, 'The attempted United Irish rising in Newfoundland 1800', in *Hist. Ire.*, viii, 1 (2000), 18–21.

O'Hegarty, Patrick Sarsfield, *Henry Grattan* (Dublin, 1922).

O'Higgins, Paul, *A bibliography of Irish trials and other legal proceedings* (Abingdon, 1986).

— 'Wright v. Fitzgerald revisited', in *Modern Law Review*, xxv (1962), 413–22.

Uí hÓgáin, Rionach, 'Béaloideas 1798 thiar', in Ó Tuathaigh, *Éirí amach 1798*, 137–54.

Ó hÓgartaigh, Margaret, 'Edward Hay, historian of 1798', in *E.C.I.*, xiii (1998), 121–34.

— 'Making history and defining the nation: Nineteenth-century interpretations of 1798', in Bull et al., *Ireland and Australia*, 24–33.

— 'Edward Hay: Wexford historian of 1798', in *Wex. Hist. Soc. Jn.*, xvii (1998–99), 159–75.

O'Keeffe, Diarmuid, '1798 in south Tipperary', in *Tipp. Hist. Jn.* (1990), 109–20.

O'Keefe, Timothy J., 'The 1898 efforts to celebrate the United Irishmen: The '98 centennial', in *Éire-Ireland*, xxiii, 2 (1988), 51–73.

— 'Who fears to speak of '98?: The rhetoric and rituals of the United Irishmen centennial 1898', in *Éire-Ireland*, xxvii, 3 (1992), 67–91.

O'Kelly, Francis, 'Wolfe Tone's novel', in *Ir. Book Lover*, xxiii, 2 (1935), 47-8 [*Belmont Castle*].

Old Ballymena: A history of Ballymena during the 1798 rebellion (Ballymena [County Antrim], 1938).

O'Leary, Paul, *Immigration and integration: The Irish in Wales 1798–1922* (Cardiff, 2000).

Ollivier, Sophie, 'Les historiens Irlandais et le bicentenaire de 1798', in *Études Irlandaises*, xxiv, 2 (1999), 139–53.

— 'Presence and absence of Wolfe Tone during the centenary commemoration of the 1798 rebellion', in Geary, *Rebellion and remembrance*, 175–84.

Ó Loinsigh, Séamus, 'The burning of Ballinagh', in *Breifne*, ii, 7 (1964), 60–4 [County Cavan, 1794].

— 'The rebellion of 1798 in Meath', in *Ríocht na Mídhe*, iv, 2–5 (1966–71), 33–50, 3–28, 30–54, 62–75.

— *The 1798 rebellion in Meath* (Nobber [County Meath], 1997).

O'Mahony, Colman, *In the shadows: Life in Cork 1750–1930* (Cork, 1997).

O'Mahony, John, 'The love-letters of Lord Edward', in *New Ireland Rev.*, xiii, July (1900), 270–3.

O'Mahony, T.H.D., *Edmund Burke and Ireland* (Oxford, 1960).

Oman, Carola, *Sir John Moore* (London, 1953).

Ó Mearain, Lorcain, 'A letter of 1799', in *Clogher Rec.*, x, 1 (1979), 51 [from John O'Neill on the *Minerva*].

Ó Moghráin, Pádraig, 'Gearr-chúntas ar an Athair Mánus Mac Suibhne', in *Béaloideas*, xvii (1947), 3–57.

— *An tAthair Mánus Mac Suibhne, sagart ó Mhuigh Eo in Éirí Amach 1798: Father Manus Sweeney, a Mayo priest in the rebellion of 1798*, (ed. and trans.), Sheila Mulloy (Westport [County Mayo], 1999).

Ó Mórdha, Pilíb, 'The lament for John Connolly', in *Clogher Rec.*, ix, 3 (1978), 377–83.

Ó Mórdha, Séamus, 'Dán faoi mhuirteacht na Fraince', in *Éigse*, vii (1953–4), 202–4.

— 'Charlotte Brookes: Her background and achievement', in *Breifne*, vi, 24 (1986), 320–40.

Ó Muirgheasa, Einrí, *Dhá cheád de cheoltaibh Uladh* (Baile Átha Cliath, 1934).

Ó Muirí, Réamonn, 'The killing of Thomas Birch, United Irishman, Mar. 1797 and the meeting of the Armagh freeholders 19 Apr. 1797', in *Seanchas Ard Mhacha*, x, 2 (1982), 267–319.

— 'Lt. John Lindley St Leger, United Irishman', in *Seanchas Ard Mhacha*, xi, 1 (1983–4), 133–201.

— 'A 1798 courtmartial with reference to Arthur O'Neill, harper', in *Seanchas Ard Mhacha*, xii, 2 (1987), 138–48.

— 'Newry and the French Revolution', in *Seanchas Ard Mhach*a, xiii, 2 (1989), 102–20.

— 'Fr James Coigly', in Swords, *Protestant, Catholic and Disssenter*, 118–64.

— 'An tAthair Séamas Ó Coigligh', in Ó Snodaigh, *Fealsúnacht*, 95–108.

— 'Armagh city in 1798', in *Seanchas Ard Mhacha*, xvii, 2 (1998), 75–82.

— 'Dean Warburton's reports on the United Irishmen in County Armagh', in Hughes and Neely (ed.), *Armagh*, 639–92.

Ó Murchadha, Tadhg, 'Mícheál Óg Ó Longáin 1766–1837', in Séamas Pender (ed.), *Féilscríbhinn Torna* (Corcaigh, 1947), 11–17.

Ó Murthile, Seosamh, 'Éire rúnda na gCosantóirí', in *1798 essays*, 41–8.

O 'Neill, Kevin, 'Almost a gentlewoman: Gender and adolescence in the diary of Mary Shackleton', in Mary O'Dowd and Sabine Wichert (ed.), *Chattel, servant or citizen: Women's status in church, state and society* (Belfast, 1995), 91–102.

— 'Mary Shackleton Leadbeater: Peaceful rebel', in Keogh and Furlong, *Women of 1798*, 137–62.

O'Neil, Phil, 'The convict priests of '98 in Australia', in *Catholic Bulletin*, x, 9 (Sept. 1920), 538–40.

O'Neill, Philip, *The Barrow uncrossed: Fr Peter O'Neill and the events in east County Cork during the 1798 rebellion* (Dublin, 1998).

Ó Raghallaigh, Deasmún, 'William James MacNeven 1763–1841', in *Studies*, xxx (1930), 247–59.

— [O'Reilly, Desmond], 'An Irish-American chemist: William James MacNeven', in *Chymia*, xi (1949), 17–26.

O'Reilly, Stan, 'Wicklow rebels of 1798: William Michael Byrne', in *Wicklow Hist. Soc., Jn.*, i, 7 (1994), 16–18.

[O'Reilly, Vincent], 'Books from the libraries of Theobald Wolfe Tone and William Sampson added to the Society's collection', in *The Recorder: Bull. Amer. Ir. Hist Soc.*, ii, 3 (1924), 5–15.

Orr, Philip, 'Doing history: A re-interpretation of the life of the United Irishman Archibald Hamilton Rowan 1751–1834', in Hill, Turner and Dawson, *Down*, 211–30.

Ó Ruaidhrí, Seaghán, *Bliad[h]ain na b[h]Franncac[h]* (Baile Át[h]a Cliat[h], 1907).

Ó Saothraí, Séamas [see also James Seery], *Mna calma '98* (Baile Átha Cliath, 1966).

— 'Walter Graham of Maghera [County Derry], United Irishman', in *Ulster Local Studies*, ix, 18 (1989), 8–15.

— *Heroines of 1798* (Bray [County Wicklow], 1998).

— 'Banlaochra 1798', in Ó Snodaigh, *Fealsúnacht*, 109–34.

O'Shaughnessy, Peter (ed.), *A rum story: The adventures of Joseph Holt, thirteen years in New South Wales 1800–1812* (Perth, 1988).

— 'General Joe of '98', in *Roundwood and District Hist. and Folklore Jn.*, iii (1990), 24–30 [on Joseph Holt].

— 'Joseph Holt', in *Roundwood and District Hist. and Folklore Jn.*, vi (1987), 2–16.

— (ed.), *Rebellion in Wicklow: General Holt's personal account of 1798* (Dublin, 1998).

O'Sheehan, J., *The story of Theobald Wolfe Tone* (Dublin, 1925).

Ó Siochfhradha, Pádraig (trans.), *Beatha Theobald Wolfe Tone mar do frith 'na scribhinní agus i scribhinní a mhic* (Baile Átha Cliath, 1932; 1937) [translation of the 1826 *Life*].

— 'Lá marbhaithe na bhfear sa Daingean [County Kerry] 1793', in *Béaloideas*, iv, 2 (1933), 147–50.

Ó Sionóid, T.D., *Ninety-eight: A dramatic symposium* (Enniscorthy [County Wexford], [1938]).

Ó Snodaigh, Aongus (eag.), *Fealsúnacht, feall agus fuil: Aistí ar ghnéithe de stair '98* (Baile Átha Cliath, 1998).

Ó Snodaigh, Pádraig [Oliver Snoddy], 'The Limerick City Militia and the battle of Collooney, 1798', in *North Munster Antiquarian Jn.*, ix, 3(1964), 117–22.

— 'Notes on the Volunteers, militia, yeomanry and Orangemen of County Cavan', in *Breifne*, iii, 2 (1968), 320–39.

— 'Notes on the Volunteers, militia, yeomanry and Orangemen of County Donegal', in *Donegal Annual*, viii, 1 (1969), 49–73.

— 'Notes on the Volunteers, militia, yeomanry and fencibles of County Limerick', in *Ir. Sword*, x, 39 (1971), 125–40.

— 'Notes on the Volunteers, militia, Orangemen and yeomanry of County Roscommon', in *Ir. Sword*, xii, 46 (1975), 15–35.

— 'The Volunteers, militia, yeomanry and Orangemen of County Waterford', in *An Cosainteóir*, xxxv, 9 (1975), 319–22; xxxv, 10 (1975), 341–7.

— 'Fencible corps in Ireland', in *Ir. Sword*, xii (1975), 64–5.

— 'Notes on the Volunteers, militia, yeomanry and Orangemen of County Louth', in *Louth Arch. and Hist. Soc. Jn.*, xviii, 4 (1976), 279–94.

— 'Notes on the Volunteers, militia, yeomanry and Orangemen of County Kildare', in *Kild. Arch. Soc., Jn.*, xv (1971–76), 258–69.

— 'Notes on the Volunteers, militia, yeomanry and Orangemen of County Monaghan', in *Clogher Rec.*, ix, 2 (1977), 142–66.

— 'Notaí ar Óglaigh, ar cheitearnaigh, ar mhilistigh is ar Órastaigh Chontae na Gaillimhe', in *Galvia*, xi (1977), 1–31; xii (1978), 1–26.

— 'Notes on the Volunteers, militia, yeomanry and Orangemen of County Meath', in *Ríocht na Mídhe*, vi, 4 (1978–9), 3–32.

— *'98 and Carlow: A look at the historians* (Carlow, 1979).

— 'The Volunteers of '82: A citizen army or armed citizens?' in *Ir. Sword*, xv (1982–3), 177–88.

— 'Notes on the Volunteers, militia, yeomanry and Orangemen of County Longford', in *Teathbha*, xi, 2 (1983), 83–100.

— 'Notes on the Volunteers, militia, yeomanry and Orangemen of County Wexford', in *The Past*, xiv (1983), 5–48.

— 'Class and the Irish Volunteers', in *Ir. Sword*, xvi (1986), 165–84.

— 'Notes on the yeomanry of Tyrone', in *Dúiche Néill*, iii (1988), 97–114.

— *Ceatharlach i 1798: Amharc ar na staraí* (Baile Átha Cliath, 1991) [translation of 1979 pamphlet].

— *The Irish Volunteers 1715–1793: A list of the units* (Dublin, 1995).

— *Dilseóirí na Gaillimhe: Faoi airm agus éide i 1798, roimhe agus ina dhiaidh* (Baile Átha Cliath, 1998).

— 'Fir Bhuí Thír Éogháin: An culrá mileata', in Ó Snodaigh, *Fealsúnacht*, 65-94.

Ó Súilléabháin, Fionntáin, *Towards the mountains of liberty: 1798 at the northern tip of Wexford* (Kilanerin [County Wexford], 1998).

— *Kilcashel/Cill Chaisil 1798–1998* (Kilcashel [County Wexford], 1998).

O'Sullivan, Harold, 'The background to and the events of the insurrection of '98 in Dundalk and north Louth', in *Louth Arch. and Hist. Soc. Jn.*, xxiv, 2 (1998), 165-95.

O'Toole, E.H., 'The medal for Collooney 1798', in *Orders and Medals* [Journal for the Orders and Medals Research Society], xxiv, 1 (1985), 19–23.

Ó Tuathaigh, Gearóid (eag.), *Éirí amach 1798 in Éirinn* (Indreabhán [County Galway], 1998).

Ó Tuathail, Pádraig, 'Wicklow traditions of 1798 told by Mrs O'Toole of Ballycumber, Ballinglen, County Wicklow', in *Béaloideas*, v, 2 (1935), 154–88.

Ó hUid, Tarlach, 'Glóir agus náire '98', in McKearney, *Ninety-eight*, 47-9.

Ó hUiginn, Brian [Brian Higgins] (ed.), *The Wolfe Tone Annual* (Dublin, 1932–62).

— *Wolfe Tone weekly* (Dublin, 1937–39).

— *Wolfe Tone and his comrades: Issued to commemorate the 150th anniversary of the rising of 1798* (Dublin, 1948) [special issue of *Wolfe Tone Annual*].

Outram, Dorinda, 'Holding the future at bay: The French Revolution and modern Ireland', in *Ir. Review*, vi (1989), 1–6.

Owen, Patricia and Frances Owen, *A rebel hand: Nicholas Delaney of 1798 from Ireland to Australia: The story of a Wicklow rebel* (London, 1998).

Owens, David, 'The United Irishmen and the 1798 rebellion', in *Arklow Hist. Soc. Jn.* (1998), 84–9.

Owens, Gary, 'Nationalist monuments in Ireland 1870–1914: Symbolism and ritual', in Raymond Gillespie and B.P. Kennedy (ed.), *Ireland: Art into history* (Dublin, 1994), 103–17.

Paineau-Prevot, Catherine (ed.), *Recits [sic] de mes souvenirs et campagnes dans l'armée francaise et divers documents sur la famille Tone par William Theobald Wolfe Tone* (La Vouivre [Paris], 1997).

Pakenham, Thomas, *The year of liberty: The history of the great Irish rebellion of 1798* (London, 1969; repr. 1972; 1991; 1993; 1997; 2000).

— *The year of liberty: The great Irish rebellion of 1798* (London, 1997; New York, 1998) [abridged by Toby Buchan].

Palmer, R.R., *The age of the democratic revolution: A political history of Europe and America 1760–1800*, 2 vols (Princeton, NJ, 1959–64).

Parkhill, Trevor, 'Here come the French', in *Causeway* (Winter, 1997), 18–21.

The Parliamentary Register or history of the proceedings and debates of the House of Commons in Ireland 9 October 1781–18 May 1797, 17 vols (Bristol, 2001) [facsimile reprint].

Parsons, Lynn, 'The mysterious Mr [Thomas] Digges', in *William and Mary Quarterly*, third series, xxii, 3 (1965), 486–92.

Paseta, Senia, '1798 in 1898: The politics of commemoration', in *Ir. Review*, xxii (1998), 46–53.

Paterson, T.G.F., 'Lisburn [County Antrim] and its neighbourhood in 1798', in *U.J.A.*, i (1938), 193–8.

— 'County Armagh Volunteers of 1778–1793', in *U.J.A.*, iv (1941), 101–27; v (1942), 31–61; vi (1943), 69–105; vii (1944), 76–95.

— 'The Volunteer companies of Ulster 1778–93', in *Ir. Sword*, vii, 27 (1965), 90–116; 28 (1966), 204–30; 29 (1966), 308–12; viii, 30 (1967), 23–32; 31 (1967), 92–7; 32 (1968), 210–7.

Patterson, James, 'Continued Presbyterian resistance in the aftermath of the rebellion of 1798 in Antrim and Down', in *Eighteenth-Century Life*, xxii, 3 (1998), 45–61.

— 'White terror: Counter-revolutionary violence in south Leinster 1798–1801', in *E.C.I.*, xv (2000), 38–53.

Patton, W. Donald (ed.), *Ebb and flow: Essays in church history in honour of R. Finlay G. Holmes* (Belfast, 2002).

Paupié, A., 'Une déscente en Irlande en 1798,: Journal du Capitane Jobit', in *Bulletin de la Société de Géographie de Rochefort*, xxviii (1906), 155–76.

Payne, Eithne, 'A letter from Henry Sheares to his wife', in *J.C.H.A.S.*, ciii (1998), 27–30.

Pearse, H.W., 'The French raid in Ireland 1798 and short sketches of other attempts and landings on the coast of the United Kingdom', in *Journal of the United Service Institution*, 53 (1909),1153–73.

Pearse, Pádraig, 'Theobald Wolfe Tone: An address delivered at the grave of Wolfe Tone in Bodenstown churchyard 22 June 1913', in *How does she stand?: Three addresses* (Dublin, 1915), 1–7 [repr. from *Gaelic-American*].

— *The separatist ideal* (Dublin, 1916) [on Tone's political philosophy].

Pender, Assumpta, *1798–1998: Killanne, Rathnure, Templeudigan* (Killanne [County Wexford], 1998).

Perkins, Harold, *The convict priests* [James Harold, James Dixon, Peter O'Neill] (Rosanna [Aus.], 1983).

Perkins, Sonya, 'Contemporary writings on the western rebellion of 1798', in *Retrospect* (1993), 18–26.

Petrie, Charles, 'Ireland in Spanish and French strategy 1558–1815', in *Ir. Sword*, vi, 24 (1964), 154–65.

Phillips, J.W., *Printing and bookselling in Dublin 1670–1800* (Dublin, 1998).

Pittion, Jean-Paul, *Taking liberties: Estampes satiriques de la Révolution françaises* (Dublin, 1989).

Plehn, Warner, 'Lexical polarities as linguistic reflexion of social life in Wolfe Tone's writings', in Dorothea Siegmund-Schultze (ed.), *Irland: gesellschaft and kultur*, VI (Halle, 1989), 271–7.

Pocock, J.G.A. (ed.), *The variety of British political thought 1500–1800* (Cambridge, 1991).

— 'Protestant Ireland: The view from a distance', in Connolly (ed.), *Political ideas*, 221–30.

— 'The Union in British history', in *Trans. Royal Hist. Soc.*, sixth series, x (2000), 181–96.

Pollard, Mary, 'John Chambers, printer and United Irishman', in *Ir. Book Lore*, iii (1964), 1–22.

— 'Control of the press in Ireland through the King's printer patent 1600–1800', in *Ir. Book Lore*, iv (1980), 79–95.

— *Dublin's trade in books, 1550–1800* (Oxford, 1989).

— *A dictionary of members of the Dublin book trade, 1550–1800* (London, 2000).

Póirtéir, Cathal (ed.), *The great Irish rebellion of 1798* (Cork, 1998).

[Pollock, Diane], *1798 commemorative service of reconciliation, Mountainstown and Castletown* (Mountainstown [County Meath], 1998).

Porter, Norman, 'The ideas of 1798', in Cullen, *1798*, 105–13.

Porter, Roy (ed.), *The enlightenment in national context* (Cambridge, 1981).

Porter, Roy and Michael Teich (eds), *Romanticism in national context* (Cambridge, 1988).

Postgate, Raymond, *Robert Emmet* (London, 1931).

— *Story of a year: 1798* (London, 1969) [Ireland, pp 114–65].

Powell, John S., *Portarlington* [County Laois] *and 1798* (York, 1998).

Powell, Thomas, 'An economic factor in the Wexford rebellion of 1798', in *Stud. Hib.*, xvi (1976), 140–57.

Power, Pat, 'A chronology for the rebellion of 1798', in *Arklow Hist. Soc. Jn.* (1998), 4–21.

— *The rebellion of 1798 in County Wicklow: Education pack* (Wicklow, 1998).

— 'The battle of Arklow', in *Wicklow Hist. Jn.*, ii, 4 (1998), 15–35.

— *People of Wicklow 1798: The rebellion* (Dún Laoghaire, 1999).

Power, Patrick C., 'Tipperary courtmartials 1798 to 1801', in *Tipp. Hist. Jn.* (1993), 135–47.

— *The courts martial of 1798-99* (Naas [County Kildare], 1998).

Power, Patrick (ed.), 'A Carrickman's [James Ryan] diary 1787–1809', in *Waterford and South-East Ire. Arch. Soc. Jn.*, xiv (1911), 97–102; 145–50: xv (1912), 30–37; 62–70; 124–37: xvi (1916), 18–27; 74–85; 176–82: xvii (1917), 4–16; 120–27.

Power, T[homas] P., *Land, politics and society in eighteenth-century Tipperary* (Oxford, 1993). .

— 'Electoral politics in Waterford city 1692–1832', in William Nolan and T.P. Power (eds), *Waterford: History and society* (Dublin, 1992), 227–64.

Power, T[homas] P. and Kevin Whelan (eds), *Endurance and emergence: Catholics in Ireland in the eighteenth century* (Dublin, 1990).

A programme of the military pageant by the Tara '98 Commmittee in the Show Grounds Navan 2–3 October 1948 (Navan [County Meath], 1945).

Puirséil, Séamus, *Henry Flood* (Baile Átha Cliath, 1973).

Purdon, H.S., 'The battle of Antrim', in *U.J.A.*, viii (1902), 96.

Pursell, C.W., 'Thomas Digges and William Pearce: An example of the transit of technology', in *William and Mary Quarterly*, third series, xxi (1964), 551–60.

Putnam, W. [pseud.], 'Theobald Wolfe Tone', in McKearney, *Ninety eight*, 16–20.

Quinn, James, 'The United Irishmen and social reform', in *I.H.S.*, xxxi (1998), 188–201.

—— 'Theobald Wolfe Tone and the historians', in *I.H.S.*, xxxii (2000), 113–28 [review article].

—— 'Thomas Russell, United Irishman', in *Hist. Ire.*, x, 1 (2002), 24–8.

—— *Soul on fire: A life of Thomas Russell 1767–1803* (Dublin, 2002).

'Raphoe obelisk, County Donegal', in *County Donegal Hist. Soc. Jn.*, i, 3 (1949), 210–11 [commemorating the Volunteers].

[Ranson, Joseph (ed.)], 'A '98 diary by Mrs Barbara Newton Lett', in *The Past*, v (1949), 117–49.

Redmond, John Edward, *The truth about '98* (Dublin, 1918).

Redmond, Seán, *Partners in revolt: The United Irishmen 1792–98 and the British reform movement* (Dublin, 1999).

Reece, Bob, *The origins of Irish convict transportation to New South Wales* (London, 2001).

Rees, Jim (ed.), *The trial of Billy Byrne of Ballymanus* [County Wicklow](Arklow, 1996).

—— 'A list of compensation claims arising from the rebellion of 1798', in *Arklow Hist. Soc. Jn.* (1998), 90–2.

—— 'The confessions of A.B.' [Thomas Murray], in *Arklow Hist. Soc. Jn.* (1998), 29–36.

Refaussé, Raymond, 'The bishop of Ferns [Euseby Cleaver] versus the rector of Killegney [James Gordon]: A contemporary exchange on the historiography of the 1798 rebellion', in *Ir. Archives*, v (1998), 23–7.

Rehill, Pádraig (ed.), *Ballinamuck bicentenary 1798–1998* (Longford, 1998).

Reid, Archie (ed.), *The liberty tree: The story of the United Irishmen in and around the borough of Newtownabbey* (Newtownabbey [County Antrim], 1998).

Reid, Horace, 'The battle of Ballynahinch: An anthology of documents', in Hill, Turner and Dawson, *Down*, 123–46.

—— 'The legend of Betsy Gray', in Mac Annaidh, *Fermanagh*, 86–99.

Reilly, Eileen, 'Who fears to speak of '98?: The rebellion in historical novels 1880–1914', in *Eighteenth-century Life*, xxii, 3 (1998), 118–27.

—— 'Rebel, muse and spouse: The female in '98 fiction', in *Éire-Ireland*, xxxiv, 2 (1999), 135–54.

Reynolds, John, *Footprints of Emmet* (Dublin, 1903).

Richtarik, Marilyn, 'Stewart Parker and *Northern Star*', in Whelan, *Northern Star*, 8–9.

Rivoallan, Anatole, 'Un patriote Irlandais: Theobald Wolfe Tone 1763–1798', in *Annales de Bretagne*, lxxiv (1967), 279–97.

Roberts, P.E.W., 'Caravats and Shanavests: Whiteboyism and faction-fighting in east Munster 1802–1811', in Clark and Donnelly, *Irish peasants*, 64–101.

Robb, Colin Johnston, 'When the United Irish society was born', in McKearney, *Ninety-eight*, 6–9.

Robbins, Caroline, '"When is it that colonies may turn independent": An analysis of the environment and politics of Francis Hutcheson 1694–1746', in *William and Mary Quarterly*, third series, xi, 2 (1954), 214–51.

—— *The eighteenth-century commonwealthman: Studies in the transmission, development and circumstances of English liberal thought from the restoration of Charles II until the war with the thirteen colonies* (New York, 1968).

Robinson, Kenneth, *North Down and Ards in 1798* (Bangor [County Down], 1998).

Robinson, Nicholas, *Edmund Burke: A life in caricature* (Yale, 1996).

—— 'Marriage against inclination: The Union in caricature', in Keogh and Whelan, *Acts of union*, 140–58.

Robinson, Philip, 'Hanging ropes and buried secrets', in *Ulster Folklife*, xxxii (1986), 4–15 [on freemasonry].

Roche, Gerry, *Oration at Wolfe Tone commemoration, Bodenstown 1 July 1979* (Dublin, 1979) [Irish Republican Socialist Party].

Roche, Richard (ed.), *The French Revolution and Wexford: Souvenir record Bastille Day Enniscorthy 2 July 1989* (Enniscorthy [County Wexford], 1989).

— *Here's their memory: A record of the United Irish in County Wexford in 1798* (Wexford, 1998).

Roddy, Christine, *Defying tradition: New Light ministers and the rebellion of 1798* (Belfast, 2000).

Rodgers, Nini, 'Equiano in Belfast: A study of the anti-slavery ethos in a northern town', in *Slavery and Abolition*, xviii, 2 (1997), 73–89.

— 'Ireland and the Black Atlantic in the eighteenth century', in *I.H.S.*, cxxvi (2000), 174–92.

— *Equiano and anti-slavery in Belfast* (Belfast, 2000).

— 'Two Quakers and a Utilitarian: The reaction of three Irish women writers to the problem of slavery 1789–1807', in *R.I.A. Proc.*, C, 4 (2000), 137–57 [Maria Edgeworth, Mary Leadbetter, Mary Birkett].

Rogers, Patrick, *The Irish Volunteers and Catholic Emancipation 1778–93: A neglected phase of Irish history* (London, 1934).

— 'A Protestant pioneer of Catholic Emancipation', in *Down and Connor Hist. Soc. Jn.*, vi (1934), 14–23 [William Todd Jones].

Romani, Roberto, 'British views on Irish national character 1800–1846: An intellectual history', in *Hist. Eur. Ideas*, xxiii, 5–6 (1997), 193–219.

Ronan, Myles, 'Archbishop Troy's correspondence with Dublin Castle 1797–1810', in *Archiv. Hib.*, xi (1944), 1–30.

— (ed.), *Insurgent Wicklow 1798: The story as told by the Revd Brother Luke Cullen O.D.C with additional material from other manuscripts* (Wexford, 1938; Dublin, 1948).

— 'Archbishop Murray 1768–1852', in *Ir. Ecc. Rec.*, lxxvii (1952), 241–9 [Daniel Murray, Catholic archbishop of Dublin].

— (ed.), *Personal recollections of Wexford and Wicklow insurgents of 1798 as collected by the Revd Luke Cullen 1798–1859* (Enniscorthy [County Wexford], 1958).

— 'An Augustinian priest's [John Martin] mission to the Wexford insurgents', in *1798 essays*, 13–15.

Roslea martyrs bicentenary 1797–1997 (Roslea [County Fermanagh], 1998).

Ross, Noel, 'The diary of Marianne Fortescue 1797–1800', in *Louth Arch. and Hist. Soc. Jn.*, xxiv, 2 (1998), 222–48; xxiv, 3 (1999), 357–79.

[Rowan, Archibald Hamilton], *The autobiography of Archibald Hamilton Rowan*, (ed.) W.H. Drummond (Shannon, 1972): [first ed., Dublin, 1840].

Roxby, P.M., *Henry Grattan, being the Gladstone prize essay in the University of Oxford* (London, 1902).

Royle, Edward, *Revolutionary Britannia? Reflections on the threat of revolution in Britain 1789–1848* (Manchester, 2000).

Royle, Edward and James Walvin, 'Mutiny and rebellion 1796–1799', in *English radicals and reformers 1760–1848* (Lexington, KY, 1982), 80–92.

Rubsamen, Walter, *Irish ballad operas and burlesques* (New York, 1974) [includes A. McClaren, *What news from Bantry Bay or the faithful Irishman: A comic opera* [1798].

Rudé, George, 'Early Irish rebels in Australia', in *Historical Studies*, xvi (1974–5), 17–35.

Rudebusch, Eckhard, *Irland im zeitalter der revolution: Politik und publizistik der United Irishmen 1791–98* (Frankfurt-am-Main, 1989).

Rushe, Denis Carolan, 'William [*recté* John] Arnold, minister of Ballybay, first Presbyterian congregation, County Monaghan', in *U.J.A.*, xiv (1908), 32.

Ryan, F.W., 'A projected invasion of Ireland in 1811', in *Ir. Sword*, i, 2 (1950–51), 136–41.

Ryder, Seán, 'Young Ireland and the 1798 rebellion', in Geary, *Rebellion and remembrance*, 135–47.

— 'Speaking of '98: Young Ireland and republican memory', in *Éire-Ireland*, xxxiv, 2 (1999), 51–69.

Sack, J.J., *From Jacobite to conservative: Reaction and orthodoxy in Britain c.1760–1832* (Cambridge, 1993).

Sadleir, T.U., 'The family of Tone, the ancestors of Theobald Wolfe Tone', in *Kild. Arch. Soc. Jn.*, xii (1943), 326–9.

[St Mullins], *Souvenir programme of the commemoration of the 150th anniversary of the '98 rising held at St. Mullins* [Carlow] *on 25 July 1948 containing a short account of the part played by local heroes in the rising* (Carlow, 1948).

Scobie, Ian Hamilton Mackay, *An old Highland fencible regiment of foot or Mackay's Highlanders 1794–1802 with an account of its services in Ireland during the rebellion of 1798* (Edinburgh and London, 1914).

Scott, Sam, 'The French Revolution and the Irish regiments in France', in Gough and Dickson, *Ireland*, 14–27.

Seery, James, 'The Presbyterian Church and the United Irishmen', in Seery, Holmes and Stewart, *Presbyterians*, 5–19 [see also Séamus Ó Saothraí].

Seery, James, Finlay Holmes and A.T.Q. Stewart, *Presbyterians, the United Irishmen and 1798* (Belfast, 2000).

Senior, Hereward, *Orangeism in Britain and Ireland 1795–1836* (London, 1966).

Seoighe, Mainchín, *Staker Wallace: His life, times and death* (Cill Fhionáin [Kilfinnane, County Limerick], 1994).

Servières, Georges, 'Un épisode de l'éxpedition d'Irlande: l'extradition et la mise en liberté de Napper Tandy', in *Révue Historique*, xciii (1907), 46–73.

1798: Essays in commemoration (Dublin, [1960]).

1796–1798: Les années des Français en Irlande: Actes du colloque international Brest 1–6 Juin 1998 (Brest, 1999).

Sheedy, Kieran, *Upon the mercy of the government: The story of the surrender, imprisonment and transportation to New South Wales of Michael Dwyer and his Wicklow comrades* (Dublin, 1988).

—— *The* Tellichery *five: The transportation of Michael Dwyer and the Wicklow rebels* (Dublin, 1997).

—— *The United Irishmen of County Clare* (Ennis [County Clare], 1998).

—— 'The United Irishmen in County Clare', in *The Other Clare*, xxii (1998), 14–21.

Sheehan, Seán, *The great hearts of 1798* (Enniscorthy [County Wexford], 1988).

Sheehy, Edward, 'Tone and the United Irishmen', in *Ireland Today*, ii, 12 (1937), 37–42.

—— 'Theobald Wolfe Tone', in *Ireland Today*, ii, 6 (1937), 78–80.

Sherlock, William, 'Bodenstown graveyard: A place of Irish pilgrimage', in *Kild. Arch. Soc. Jn.*, vi (1909–11), 223–9 [Tone's burial place].

Sherman, Paul, 'From Ireland's Vinegar Hill to Australia's Vinegar Hill', in Foley and Bateman, *Irish-Australian studies*, 217–23.

Shields, Hugh, 'Some songs and ballads in use in the province of Ulster in 1845', in *Ulster Folklife*, xvii (1971), 3–65, xviii (1972), 34–65 [Kilwarlin, County Down].

Shine, Michael, 'The North Cork Militia', in *Mallow Field Club Jn.*, xvi (1998), 53–83.

Shulim, Joseph, 'John Daly Burk: Irish revolutionist and American patriot', in *Trans. Am. Phil. Soc.*, liv, 6 (1964), 1–60.

Sheridan, Geraldine, 'Irish literary review magazines and enlightenment France 1730–1790', in Gargett and Sheridan, *Ireland*, 21–46.

Sibbett, Robert M., *The formation of the Orange Order* (Belfast, 1914–15; London, 1939).

—— *Orangeism in Ireland and throughout the empire*, 2 vols (Belfast, 1914–15; 1938).

—— *The sunshine patriots: The 1798 rebellion in Antrim and Down* (Belfast, 1997) [repr. from *Orangeism* (Belfast, 1938)].

Sigerson, George, *The last independent parliament of Ireland with an account of the survival of the nation and its lifework* (Dublin, 1918).

Simms, Brendan, 'The Irish rebellion 1798', in *The Month*, xxxi, 9–10 (1998), 376–80.

Simms, Samuel, 'Revd James O'Coigley, United Irishman', in *Down and Connor Hist. Soc. Jn.*, viii (1937), 41–75.

— 'A select bibliography of the United Irishmen 1791–1798', in *I.H.S.*, i, 2 (1938), 158–80.

Sinnott, Anne, Kathy Frayne and Carmel Whitty (eds), *Exploring 1798: An introduction to sources and an educational pack for students* (Wexford, 1998).

Sirr, Harry, *Ipsissima verba: Strictures on Dr R.R. Madden's* United Irishmen *and Mr W.J. Fitz-Patrick's* Sham Squire *with reference to the notices of Major Sirr* (London, 1911).

Skrine, Helen, 'A glimpse of [Beauchamp] Bagenal Harvey', in *Wex. Hist. Soc. Jn.*, xiv (1992–3), 92–100.

Small, Stephen, 'The twisted roots of Irish patriotism: Anglo-Irish political thought in the late eighteenth century', in *Éire-Ireland*, xxxv, 3–4 (2000–2001), 187–216.

Smith, A.W., 'Irish rebels and English radicals 1798–1820', in *Past & Present*, vii (1955), 78–85.

Smith, Brian, '1798 political pensions', in *The Past*, xxi (1998), 34–8.

Smith, James Morton, 'William Duane and the *Aurora*', in *Penn. Mag. Hist. and Biog.*, lxxvii (1953), 123–55.

— 'The enforcement of the Alien Friends Act of 1798', in *Missisippi Valley Hist. Jn.*, xli, 1 (1954), 85–104.

— *Freedom's fetters: The Alien and Sedition Laws and American civil liberties* (Ithaca, NY, 1956).

Smyth, Denis, *Men of liberty from MacArt's Fort to Boulavogue: A history of the society of United Irishmen* (Belfast, 1988).

— *Thomas Paine and the Rights of Man* (Belfast, 1991).

Smyth, James, 'The Belfast of 1798', in McKearney, *Ninety-eight*, 40–43.

Smyth, Jim, 'Dublin's political underground in the 1790s', in O'Brien, *Parliament, politics and people*, 93–127.

— 'Popular politicisation, Defenderism and the Catholic question', in Gough and Dickson, *Ireland*, 109–16.

— *The men of no property: Irish radicals and popular politics in the late eighteenth century* (London, 1992).

— 'Freemasonry and the United Irishmen', in Dickson, Keogh and Whelan, *United Irishmen*, 167–75.

— 'The men of No Popery: The origins of the Orange Order', in *Hist. Ire.*, ii, 3 (1995), 48–53.

— 'Anti-Catholicism, conservatism and conspiracy: Sir Richard Musgrave's *Memoirs of the different rebellions in Ireland*, in *Eighteenth-Century Life*, xxii, 3 (1998), 62–73.

— 'The men of No Popery', in Cullen, *1798*, 27–36.

— 'A tale of two generals: Cumberland and Cornwallis', in *Hist. Ire.*, vii, 3 (1999), 32–6.

— (ed.), *Revolution, counter revolution and union: Ireland in the 1790s* (Cambridge, 2000).

— 'The Act of Union and public opinion', in Smyth, *Revolution*, 146–60.

[Smyth, Peter], *The Volunteers 1778–1784: Facsimile documents from the Public Record Office of Northern Ireland* (Belfast, 1974).

— 'The Volunteers and parliament 1779–84', in Bartlett and Hayton, *Penal era*, 115–36.

— 'Our cloud-cap't Grenadiers: The Volunteers as a military force', in *Ir. Sword*, xiii, 52 (1978–79), 185–207.

Souvenir programme of the 1798 commemoration at Ballinamuck, County Longford 11 September 1938 (Longford, 1938).

St Mark, J.J., 'Wolfe Tone letter 1795', in *Éire-Ireland*, vi, 4 (1971), 15–16 [letter to Pierre-Auguste Adet].

— 'Wolfe Tone's diplomacy in America, August-December 1795', in *Éire-Ireland*, vii, 4 (1972), 3–11.

— 'The disappearance of Arthur Tone', in *Éire-Ireland*, xx, 3 (1985), 56–70.

— 'Matilda and William Tone in New York and Washington after 1815', in *Éire-Ireland*, xxii, 4 (1987), 4–10.

— 'The Oswald mission to Ireland from America [*recte* France] 20 February to 8 June 1793', in *Éire-Ireland*, xxiii, 2 (1988), 25–38.

Stafford, Fiona, *The sublime savage: James Macpherson and the poems of Ossian* (Edinburgh, 1988).

— 'Tales of the times of old: The legacy of Macpherson's *Ossian*', in Mackey, *Europe*, 40–55.

Stanley, Heather, *The United Irishmen and the 1798 rebellion: Sources checklist for P.R.O.N.I.* (Belfast, 1998).

Steen, L.J., *The battle of the Hill of Tara 26 May 1798* (Trim [County Meath], 1991).

Stewart, A[nthony] T[erence] Q[uincey], '"A stable unseen power": Dr William Drennan and the origins of the United Irishmen', in John Bossy and Peter Jupp (ed.), *Essays presented to Michael Roberts* (Belfast, 1976), 80–92.

— *The narrow ground: Aspects of Ulster 1609–1969* (London, 1977).

— 'The harp new-strung: nationalism, culture and the United Irishmen', in Oliver MacDonagh and W.F. Mandle (ed.), *Ireland and Irish-Australia* (London, 1986), 258–69.

— *A deeper silence: The hidden roots of the United Irish movement* (London, 1993).

— *The summer soldiers: The 1798 rebellion in Antrim and Down* (Belfast, 1995).

— '1798 in the north', in *Hist. Ire.*, vi, 2 (1998), 33–8.

— '1798 in Antrim and Down', in Póirtéir, *Great Irish rebellion*, 72–82.

— 'The ghost of Betsy Gray', in Hill, Turner and Dawson, *Down*, 251–7.

— '1798 and the modesty of history', in Seery, Holmes and Stewart, *Presbyterians*, 34–46.

— *The shape of Irish history* (Belfast, 2001) [see 122–37].

Stewart, David and Lt. Gen. MacMahon, 'Revd Arthur MacMahon', in *U.J.A.*, xv (1909), 134–40.

Stewart, David, *The Seceders in Ireland* (Belfast, 1950).

[Stewart, J.W.], 'A list of the Justices of the Peace in the several counties in Ireland 1797-98', in *U.J.A.*, xvii (1901), 138–41.

Stewart, John Hall, 'The fall of the Bastille on the Dublin stage November 1789', in *R.S.A.I. Jn.*, lxxxiv (1954), 78–91.

— 'The French Revolution on the Dublin stage 1790–94', in *R.S.A.I. Jn.*, xci (1961), 183–92.

— 'The Irish press and the French Revolution', in *Journalism Quarterly*, xxxviv (1962), 507–18.

Stookey, Byron, 'William James MacNevin: Versatile professor', in *Bull. New York Ac. Medicine*, xli, 10 (1965), 1037–51.

Strum, Harvey, 'Federalist Hibernophobes in New York 1807', in *Éire-Ireland*, xvi (1981), 7–13.

Sullivan, T.D. and A.M. Sullivan (ed.), *Speeches from the dock or protests of Irish patriotism: Speeches delivered after conviction by Theobald Wolfe Tone, William Orr* (New York, 1900).

Syndergaard, Rex, 'The Fitzwilliam crisis and Irish nationalism', in *Éire-Ireland*, vii (1973), 34–41.

— 'Wild Irishmen and the Alien and Sedition Act', in *Éire-Ireland*, ix, 1 (1974), 14–24.

Synnott, P.N., 'The 1798 rising: Some records from County Kildare', in *Kild. Arch. Soc. Jn.*, xv, 5 (1975), 448–67.

Sweetman, William, 'Edward Hay', in *The Past*, xv (1984), 55–68.

— 'Jeremiah Fitzhenry: A chief who knew how to command', in *Wex. Hist. Soc. Jn.*, xvii (1998-99), 144–58.

Swords, Liam, *The green cockade: The Irish in the French Revolution 1789–1815* (Dublin, 1989).

— (ed.), *Protestant, Catholic and Dissenter: The clergy and 1798* (Dublin, 1997).

— 'Irish priests and students in revolutionary France', in Swords, *Protestant, Catholic and Dissenter*, 20–44.

Symes, J.G., *The Castle Hill rebellion of 1804* (Sydney, 1990).

Taylor, George, *A history of the rise, progress and suppression of the rebellion in the county of Wexford in the year 1798* (Dublin, 1907) [first ed. 1798].

Taylor, Ida, *The life of Lord Edward FitzGerald 1763–1798* (London, 1903; New York, 1904).

[Teeling, Charles Hamilton], *Stair eirghe-amach na n-Éireannach i 1798* (eag.), Tadgh Ó Rabhartaigh (Baile Átha Cliath, 1941) [translation of *The history of the Irish rebellion 1798*].

— *Personal narrative of the Irish rebellion of 1798 and Sequel to 'The history of the Irish rebellion'* (Shannon, 1972) [repr. of Glasgow, 1876 ed. [introduction by R. Grenfell Morton].

Tesch, Pieter, 'Presbyterian radicalism', in Dickson, Keogh and Whelan, *United Irishmen*, 33–48.

— *Laois and Kilkenny 1798* (Wolfhill [County Laois], 1998).

Thom, Martin, *Republics, nations and tribes* (London, 1995).

Thomas, D. (ed.), *State trials: 1: Treason and libel* (London, 1972).

Thompson, Ann, 'Thomas Paine and the United Irishmen', in *Études Irlandaises*, xvi, 1 (1991), 109–19.

Thompson, Dorothy, 'Ireland and the Irish in English radicalism before 1850', in *Outsiders: class, gender and nation* (London, 1993), 103–43.

— 'Seceding from the Seceders: The decline of the Jacobin tradition in Ireland 1790–1850', in *Outsiders*, 134–63.

Thompson, E.P., *The making of the English working class* (London, 1978).

— *Customs in common* (London, 1991).

— *The Romantics: England in a revolutionary age* (New York, 1997).

Thompson, Glenn, 'The Bank of Ireland yeomanry', in *Ir. Sword*, xiv, 57 (1981), 269–70.

— *The uniforms of 1798–1803* (Dublin, 1998).

Thuente, Mary Helen, 'The literary significance of the United Irishmen', in Michael Kennealy (ed.), *Irish literature and culture* (London, 1992), 35–54.

— 'Thomas Moore and the United Irishmen', in *Ireland of the Welcomes*, xl, 5 (1991), 22–7.

— *The harp restrung: The United Irishmen and the rise of literary nationalism* (Syracuse, NY, 1994).

— 'Liberty, Hibernia and Mary Le More: United Irish images of women', in Keogh and Furlong, *Women of 1798*, 9–25.

— 'William Sampson: United Irish satirist and songwriter', in *Eighteenth-Century Life*, xxii, 3 (1998), 19–30.

— 'The Belfast laugh: The context and significance of United Irish satires', in Smyth, *Revolution*, 67–82.

Tierney, Martin, 'William Aylmer 1772–1820', in *Ir. Sword*, vi, 23 (1963), 103–7.

Tigges, Wim, 'Public, private and poetic: Wolfe Tone's autobiographical writings', in Leerssen et al., *Forging*, 59–74.

Tillyard, Stella, *Citizen Lord: Edward FitzGerald 1763–1798* (London, 1998).

— *Aristocrats: Caroline, Emily, Louisa and Sarah Lennox 1740–1832* (London, 1994).

Timmons, Martin, 'The trial of Neal Devitt', in *Roundwood and District Hist. and Folklore Jn.*, i (1988), 18–19.

Tohall, Patrick, 'The Diamond fight of 1795 and the resultant expulsions', in *Seanchas Ard Mhacha*, iii, 1 (1958), 17–50.

Tóibín, Nioclás (trans.), *Deoraidhe Gaedhil ag eachtradh ar bhliaina 1798* [*Memoirs of Miles Byrne*], 2 vols (Baile Átha Cliath, 1937).

Tóibín, Pádraig (ed.), *Songs and ballads of '98* (Enniscorthy [County Wexford], 1938).

Tone, Frank Jerome, *History of the Tone family* (Niagara Falls, NY, [1944].

[Tone, Theobald Wolfe], *An address to the people of Ireland* (London, 1969).

— *An argument on behalf of the Catholics of Ireland* (Cork, London and Belfast, 1969; Belfast, 1973).

— *Life and adventures of Theobald Wolfe Tone* (London, 1920).

— *The Spanish war* (Dublin, 1915) [re-isued by Cumann Na mBan].

— *Souvenir programme of commemoration week 17 June–22 June 1963* (Dublin, 1963).

— *Wolfe Tone today: issued to mark the bicentenary of the birth of the father of Irish republicanism* (Belfast, 1963).

— *Wolfe Tone memorial: Conditions for competition* (Dublin, 1964).

— *The Wolfe Tone memorial* (Dublin, 1964) [history of Wolfe Tone Memorial Committee].

— *Wolfe Tone memorial Committee: Presentation of awards and opening of public exhibition of sub-mitted designs* (Dublin, 1964).

— *Wolfe Tone songbook* (n.p., n.d.).

— *Wolfe Tone* ([London], n.d.) [issued by Irish Communist Group].

Toner, Gregory, 'The battle of Saintfield', in Hill, Turner and Dawson, *Down*, 103–22.

Topliss, Ian, 'Mary Wollstonecraft's and Maria Edgeworth's modern ladies', in *Études Irlandaises*, vi (1981), 13–31.

Townshend, Charles, 'Martial law: Legal and administrative problems of civil emergency in Britain and the empire 1800–1940', in *Hist. Jn.*, xxv, 1 (1982), 167–95.

Trumpener, Katie, *Bardic nationalism: The romantic novel and the British empire* (Princeton, NJ, 1997).

Turner, Larry, 'Andrew Byrne: "Intelligent, honest, sober and industrious"', in Bob Reece (ed.), *Irish convict lives* (Sydney, 1993), 80–108.

[Turner, Llewelyn], *The memories of Sir Llewelyn Turner: memories serious and light of the Irish rebellion of 1798; Welsh judges, admirals and sea-fights; municipal work and notable persons in North Wales; strange crimes and great events* (ed.) J.E. Vincent (London, 1903).

Turpin, John, 'Oliver Sheppard's 1798 memorials', in *Ir. Arts Rev.* (1991), 71–80.

— '1798, 1898 and the political implications of Sheppard's monuments', in *Hist. Ire.*, vi, 2 (1998), 44–8.

Twomey, Deirdre, 'Who fears to speak of ninety-eight?', in *Yeats Annual*, xiv (2001), 209–64 [W.B. Yeats and the Centenary].

Twomey, Richard J., *Jacobins and Jeffersonians: Anglo-American radicalism in the United States, 1790–1820* (New York, 1989).

Tynan, Katherine, *Lord Edward* (Dublin, 1916).

Tynan, Kathleen, *Romancing rebellion: 1798 and the songs of Thomas Moore* (Dublin, 1998).

Tyrrell, John, 'Weather and warfare: Bantry 1796 revisited', in *Hist. Ire.*, iv, 4 (1996), 34–8.

— 'The weather and political destiny', in Murphy, *Bantry Bay*, 25–47.

— *Weather and warfare: A climatic history of the 1798 rebellion* (Cork, 2001).

Urdail, Medbhín Ní, *The scribe* [Míchéal Óg Ó Longáin] *in eighteenth and nineteenth-century Ireland: Motivations and milieu* (Munster, 2000).

Val, Séamas de, 'The '98 memorial at Buaile Mhaodhóg' [Boolavogue] in *The Past*, x (1973–74), 39–44.

— *Oulart in '98: A brief account* (Oulart [County Wexford], 1986).

— (ed.), 'A letter of 1798', in *The Past*, xvii (1990), 71–2 [Anne Elgee to Revd John Elgee].

— 'Beirt sagart 1798', in Ó Snodaigh, *Fealsúnacht*, 149–58 [Philip Roche, John Redmond].

— 'George Taylor's experiences in the insurrection of 1798', in *The Past*, xxi (1998), 49–58.

— 'Some letters relating to the battle of Bunclody 1 June 1798', in *The Past*, xxi (1998), 39–44.

Vance, Norman, 'Celts, Carthaginians and constitutions: Anglo-Irish literary relations 1780–1820', in *I.H.S.*, xxii (1981), 216–38.

— 'Text and tradition: Robert Emmet's Speech from the Dock', in *Studies*, lxxi (1982), 185–91.

— 'Volunteer thought: William Crawford of Strabane', in Boyce, Eccleshall and Geoghegan, *Political discourse*, 257–69.

Vinegar Hill day, Enniscorthy 21 June 1998: Souvenir record (Enniscorthy [County Wexford], 1998).

Waldersee, James, 'Father James Dixon and the 1798 rising', in *Jn. Religious Hist.*, vi, 1 (1970), 28–40.

Walker, Brian Mercer, 'The lessons of Irish history: The continuing legacy of the 1798 rebellion and the United Irishmen', in *Past and present: history, identity and politics in Ireland* (Belfast, 2000), 29–78.

Wall, Maureen, 'The United Irish movement', in J.L. McCracken (ed.), *Historical Studies*, v (London, 1965), 122–40.

— *Catholic Ireland in the eighteenth century: collected essays of Maureen Wall*, (ed.) Gerard O'Brien (Dublin, 1994).

Wallace, Anthony, *Jefferson and the Indians: The tragic fate of the first Americans* (Harvard, MA, 1999).

Wallace, Hugh Robert, 'Royal Downshire Militia: Extracts from order books etc.', in *U.J.A.*, xii, 4 (1906), 145–55; xiii, 1 (1907), 24–8; xiii, 2 (1907), 59–69.

— *A short history of the Irish Volunteers with a guide to the Irish Volunteer, yeomanry and militia relics* (Belfast, 1938).

Waller, Hardress, 'The Royal Irish Artillery 1756–1801', in *Ir. Sword*, xvi, 65 (1986), 284–324.

Walsh, John, *Frederick Augustus Hervey 1730–1803: Fourth earl of Bristol and bishop of Derry* (Maynooth [County Kildare], 1972).

Walsh, Paul, 'Wolfe Tone and the Irish Catholics', in *Ir. Theol. Qtly.*, xvii, 65 (1922), 1–11; 66, 155–68; 68, 305–16.

Walsh, T.J., 'Francis Moylan: bishop of Cork 1735–1815', in *J.C.H.A.S.*, lv, 182 (1950), 98–110.

Walsh, Walter, 'Religion, ethnicity, and history: Clues to the cultural construction of law', in Ronald Bayor and Timothy Meagher (eds), *The New York Irish* (Baltimore, MD, 1995), 48–69 [on William Sampson].

— 'Redefining radicalism: A historical perspective', in *George Washington Law Review*, lix (1991), 638–82.

Waters, John, 'Reading Isaac Weld: The enlightened gentleman in Ireland and the politics of culture after the Act of Union', in *Radharc*, ii (2001), 101–31.

Waters, Ormonde, 'Revd James Porter: Dissenting minister of Greyabbey [County Down] 1753–1798', in *Seanchas Ard Mhacha*, xiv, 1(1990), 80–101.

Weber, Paul, *On the road to rebellion: The United Irishmen and Hamburg, 1796–1803* (Dublin, 1997).

— 'The United Irishmen and Hamburg', in *Hist. Ire.*, v, 3 (1997), 26–30.

Wells, Roger, *Insurrection: The British experience 1795–1803* (Gloucester, 1983).

— 'The Irish Famine of 1799–1801', in Andrew Charlesworth (ed.), *Marketing, market cultures and popular protest in eighteenth-century Britain and Ireland* (Liverpool, 1996), 163–93.

Welply, W.H., 'Curran and his kinsfolk', in *Notes and Queries*, cxciv (1949), 266–8; 290–94; 338–41; 384–7.

Westerkamp, Marilyn, 'Absentee landlords and squatter rights: The Scots-Irish back country and the American Revolution', in Mackey, *Europe*, 69–86.

Wharton, W.J., 'A note on Grey Abbey [County Down] today', in *Donegal Ann.* (1969), 16–17 [James Porter].

Wheeler, H.F.B. and A.M. Broadley, *The war in Wexford: An account of the rebellion in the south of Ireland in 1798 told from original documents* (London, 1910).

Whelan, Eamonn (ed.), *Clonegal 1798–1998: A pictorial journal of the bicentennial commemorations* (Clonegal [County Carlow], 1998).

Whelan, Kevin, 'Events and personalities in the history of Newcastle 1600–1850', in Peter O'Sullivan (ed.), *Newcastle Lyons: A parish of the Pale* (Dublin, 1986), 63–80.

— 'The religious factor in the 1798 rebellion in County Wexford', in Patrick Flanagan, Paul Ferguson and Kevin Whelan (eds), *Rural Ireland 1600–1900* (Cork, 1987), 60–74.

— (ed.), *Wexford: History and society* (Dublin, 1987; 2001).

— 'The role of the Catholic priest in the 1798 rebellion in County Wexford', in Whelan, *Wexford*, 296–315.

— 'James Edward Devereux and the Devereux family of Carrigmennan', in Lory Kehoe (ed.), *Glynn 1789–1989* (Glynn [County Wexford], 1989), 35–46.
— 'Captain Edward Sweetman', in *Ir. Sword*, xvii (1989), 219–20.
— 'Politicisation in County Wexford and the origins of the 1798 rebellion', in Gough and Dickson, *Ireland*, 156–78.
— 'The Catholic community in eighteenth-century County Wexford', in Power and Whelan, *Endurance and emergence*, 129–70.
— 'Catholics, politicisation and the 1798 rebellion', in Réamonn Ó Muiri (ed.), *Irish church history today* (Armagh, 1990), 63–83.
— 'Catholic mobilisation in Ireland 1750–1800', in Bergeron and Cullen, *Culture et pratiques*, 235–58.
— 'The United Irishmen, the Enlightenment and popular culture', in Dickson, Keogh and Whelan, *United Irishmen*, 269–95.
— 'United and disunited Irishmen: The discourse of sectarianism in the 1790s', in O'Dea and Whelan, *Nations and nationalisms*, 231–47.
— 'An underground gentry? Catholic midddlemen in eighteenth-century Ireland', in *E.C.I.*, x (1995), 7–68.
— 'Reinterpreting the 1798 rebellion in County Wexford', in Keogh and Furlong, *The mighty wave*, 9–36.
— 'The origins of the Orange Order', in *Bullán*, ii, 2 (1996), 19–37.
— 'The republic in the village: The dissemination and reception of popular political literature in the 1790s', in Long, *Books beyond the Pale*, 101–40.
— *The tree of liberty: Radicalism, Catholicism and the construction of Irish identity 1760–1830* (Cork and Notre Dame, 1996; 1998).
— 'Bantry Bay: The wider context', in Murphy, *Bantry Bay*, 95–119.
— *Fellowship of freedom: The United Irishmen and 1798* (Cork, 1998).
— 'Three revolutions and a failure', in Póirtéir, *Great Irish rebellion*, 26–36.
— (ed.), *Northern Star programme* (Belfast, 1998).
— '1798: The politics of memory', in Whelan, *Northern Star*, 14–15.
— 'The Wexford priests in 1798', in Swords, *Catholic, Protestant and Dissenter*, 165–85.
— 'The politics of memory', in Cullen, *1798*, 143–60.
— 'Introduction,' Bigger, *Remember Orr*, ii–iv.
— 'Introduction,' *Memoirs of Miles Byrne*, v–xxv.
— 'Sectarianism and secularism in nineteenth-century Ireland', in Brennan, *Secularisation*, 71–90.
— 'An poblachtas: oidhreacht na nÉireannach Aontaoithe', in *Oghma*, x (1998), 8–18.
— 'Introduction to *The Poor Man's Catechism*', in *Labour History* [Sydney] 75 (1998), 22–37.
— (ed.), *Clonegal* [County Carlow] *in 1798* (Enniscorthy [County Wexford], 1998).
— 'New light on Lord Edward FitzGerald', in *Hist. Ire.*, vii, 4 (1999), 40–44.
— 'Elizabeth Richards and the Wexford rebellion 1798', in de Jong-Ijsselstein, *Diary*, 9–13.
— 'Writing Ireland, reading England,' foreword to Sydney Owenson, *The wild Irish girl*, (eds), Claire Connolly and Stephen Copley (London, 2000)), ix–xxiv [first ed. 1807].
— 'The other within: Ireland, Britain and the Act of Union', in Keogh and Whelan, *Acts of union*, 13–33.
— 'The memories of "The Dead"', in *Yale Jn. Criticism*, xv, 1 (2002), 59–97 [Joyce and 1798].
— and Thomas Bartlett (ed.), *Memoirs of Miles Byrne* (Enniscorthy [County Wexford], 1998).
— [and Mark Leslie], *Fellowship of freedom: The United Irishmen and the rebellion of 1798* (Dublin, 1998) [C.D. Rom].
Whelan, Margaret, 'Edward Hay: Wexford historian of 1798', in *Wex. Hist. Soc. Jn.*, xvii (1998-99), 159–75 [See also Margaret Ó hÓgartaigh].

Whitaker, Anne-Maree, *Unfinished revolution: United Irishmen in New South Wales 1800–1810* (Sydney, 1994).
— 'James Meehan: nearly Australia's third surveyor-general', in *Descent*, June (1994), 66–70.
— 'From swords to ploughshares? The 1798 Irish rebels in New South Wales', in *Labour History* [Sydney], 75 (1998), 9–21 [also in *Saothar*, xxii (1998), 13–22].
Who fears to speak of '98? (Dublin, 1938).
Wickham, Tom (ed.), *The Three Rocks remembered 1798–1998* (Wexford, 1998).
Wicklow commemorating 1798–1998: Calendar of events [ed. Joan Kavanagh] (Wicklow, 1998).
Wilcox, William, 'Lord Lansdowne on the French Revolution and the Irish rebellion', in *Jn. Modern Hist.*, xvii, 1 (1945), 29–36.
Wilkinson, David, 'The Fitzwilliam episode 1795: A re-interpretation of the role of the Duke of Portland', in *I.H.S.*, xix (1995), 315–39.
— 'How did they pass the union? Secret service expenditure in Ireland 1799–1800', in *History*, 82 (1997), 233–51.
Williams, T. Desmond, *Secret societies in Ireland* (Dublin and New York, 1973).
Williams, Tom, 'Taghmon [County Wexford] in 1798', in *Taghmon Hist. Soc. Jn.*, ii (1997), 63–82.
— 'Edward Roche of Garrylough', in *Wex. Hist. Soc. Jn.*, xvii (1998–99), 176–90.
Wilsdon, Bill, *The sites of the 1798 rising in Antrim and Down* (Belfast, 1997).
Wilson, David, 'William Cobbett and the language of sectarianism: The Philadelphia Irish during the French Revolution', in C.J. Houston and Joseph Leydon (eds), *Ireland: The haunted ark* (Toronto, 1996), pp 39–52.
— *United Irishmen, United States: Immigrant radicals in the early republic* (Ithaca, NY and Dublin, 1998).
Wilson, Kathleen, *The sense of the people: Politics, culture and imperialism in England 1715–1785* (Cambridge, 1995).
Wooding, Jonathan, 'The sacral nationalism of the Australian '98 centenary', in Geary, *Rebellion and remembrance*, 196–213.
Wood, Stephen, 'Guernsey and the '98: A fragment from the rebellion', in *Ir. Sword*, xxi, 84 (1998), 160–2 [arrest of John Cormick].
Woods, C.J.,'The secret mission to Ireland of Captain Bernard MacSheehy, an Irishman in the French service 1796 ', in *J.C.H.A.S.*, lxxviii (1973), 93–108.
— 'The contemporary editions of Tone's *Arguments on behalf of the Catholics*', in *Ir. Book-lore*, ii, 2 (1976), 217–26.
— 'Tone's grave at Bodenstown: memorials and commemorations 1798–1913', in Dorothea Siegmund-Schultze (ed.), *Irland: gesellschaft und kultur*, vi (Halle, 1989), 138–48.
— 'The place of Thomas Russell in the United Irish movement', in Gough and Dickson, *Ireland*, 83–100.
— 'The authorship of a letter [by Thomas Russell?] received by Tone in America in 1795', in *E.C.I.*, v (1990), 192–4.
— *Journals and memoirs of Thomas Russell 1791–95* (Dublin, 1991).
— 'United Ireland and Young Ireland meet: Charles Harte's account of a meeting with Matilda Tone', in *Hist. Ire.*, vi, 3 (1998), 11–12.
Woodward, L.,'Les projets de descente en Irland et les refugies Irlandais et Anglais en France sous La Convention', in *Annales historiques de La Revolution Français*, viii (1931), 1–30.
Wright, Frank, *Two lands on one soil: Ulster politics before Home Rule* (Dublin, 1996).
Wright, Julia, 'Courting public opinion: handling informers in the 1790s', in *Éire-Ireland*, xxii (1997-98), 144–69.
— '"The nation begins to form": Competing nationalisms in Morgan's *The O'Briens and the O'Flahertys*', in *E.L.H.*, lxvi (1999), 939–58 [1827 novel about 1798].

Wyse-Jackson, Patrick (ed.), *Science and engineering in Ireland in 1798: A time of revolution* (Dublin, 2000).

York, N.L., *Neither kingdom nor nation: The Irish quest for constitutional rights 1698–1800* (Washington, DC, 1994).

— 'American revolutionaries and the illusion of Irish empathy', in *Éire-Ireland*, xxi, 2 (1996), 13–30.

— 'The impact of the American Revolution on Ireland', in Dickinson, *Britain and the American Revolution*, 205–33.

Young, Arthur, *A tour in Ireland with general observations on the state of that Kingdom made in the years 1776, 1777 and 1798 and brought down to the end of 1779*, 2 vols (repr. Shannon, 1970) [introduction by J.B. Ruane] [first ed., London, 1780].

Zimmerman, Georges-Denis, *Songs of Irish rebellion: Political street ballads and rebel songs 1780–1900* (Dublin, 1967: 2002).

Zimmern, Alfred, *Henry Grattan* (Oxford, 1902).

Zuylen, Alfons Prayon Van, *Korte staatkundige geschiedenis van het Iersche volk: Ierland voor de unie met Engeland; Lord Edward FitzGerald en de Iersche opstand van 1798; Ierland sedert de unie* (Gent, 1901).

THESES

Atkinson, Norman, Sir Laurence Parsons, second earl of Rosse 1758–1841, Ph.D., T.C.D., 1962.

Barry, Arthur, The sources for the Irish rebellion of 1798, M.A., Boston College, 1933.

Beiner, Guy, 'To speak of '98': The social memory and vernacular historiography of Bliain na bhFrancach - the Year of the French, Ph.D., U.C.D., 2000.

Benbow, Mark, The republican conspiracy: The United Irishmen and France 1791–1798, M.A., Wright State [Ohio], 1983.

Beresford, Marcus de la Poer, Ireland in the French strategy 1691–1789, M.Litt, T.C.D., 1975.

Blackstock, Alan, The origins and development of the Irish Yeomanry 1796–1807, Ph.D., Q.U.B., 1993.

Bric, Maurice, Ireland, Irishmen and the broadening of the late eighteenth-century Philadelphia polity, Ph.D., John Hopkins, 1990.

Brims, John, The Scottish democratic movement in the age of the French Revolution, Ph.D., Edinburgh, 1983.

Brooke, Peter, Controversies in Ulster Presbyterianism 1790–1836, Ph.D., Cambridge, 1980.

Burke, Thomas, Irish Catholics and the legislative Union, M.A., U.C.D., 1943.

Cerretta, Manuela, Nazione e popolo nel pensiero politico Irlandese: gli United Irishmen 1791–1800, Ph.D., Torino, 1999.

Chambers, Liam, Politics and rebellion in County Kildare 1790–1803, M.A., Maynooth, 1996.

Champion, Michael, Irish nationalism and identity: A study of commemoration, interpretation and the politics of memory, M.A., North Carolina, 1999.

Charles, Robert, United Irishmen, Defenders and the rebellion, M.A., Concordia, 1975.

Clarke, Joseph, The Dublin newspaper press and the French Revolution 1788–1793: The case of *Faulkner's Dublin Journal* and the *Dublin Evening Post*, M.A., U.C.D., 1990.

Curtin, Nancy, The origins of Irish republicanism: The United Irishmen in Dublin and Ulster 1791–1798, Ph.D., Wisconsin, 1988.

Dickson, David, An economic history of the Cork region in the eighteenth century, Ph.D., T.C.D., 1977.

Doorne, C.J., Mutiny and sedition in the Home Commands of the Royal Navy 1783–1803, Ph.D., London, 1998.

De Valera, Anne, Antiquarian and historical investigations in Ireland in the eighteenth century, M.A., U.C.D., 1978.

Duggan, Mary, County Carlow 1791–1801: A study in the era of revolution, M.A., U.C.D., 1969.

Ensko, Senan, Thomas Paine and Ireland: The reaction of public opinion 1791–1794, M.A., U.C.D., 1990.

Fearon, Mel, Les influences de la Révolution Americaine et de la Révolution française sur le patriotism Irlandais, Ph.D., Versailles, 2001.

Ferguson, Kenneth, The army in Ireland from the Restoration to the Act of Union, Ph.D., T.C.D., 1982.

Fleming, George, The causes of the Irish rebellion of 1798 compared with the causes of the American Revolution, M.A., Catholic University of America, 1939.

Gaynor, Tony, The politics of law and order in Ireland 1794–99, Ph.D., T.C.D., 1999.

Goto, Hiroto, The dawn of anti-imperialism: The radicals and their liberal project for the modernisation of Ireland in the 1780s–1790s, Ph.D., T.C.D., 1998.

Grant, Suzanne, The Irish experiment: A question of empire, M.A., San Diego, 1968.

Hamilton, Albert, The movement for Irish Roman Catholic relief 1790–1793, Ph.D., Notre Dame, 1967.

Haydon, Colin, Anti-Catholicism in eighteenth-century England c.1714–1780, D.Phil., Oxford, 1985.

Henry, Brian, Crime, law enforcement and punishment in Dublin 1780–95, Ph.D., T.C.D., 1992.

Hill, Colin, William Drennan and the radical movement for Irish reform 1779–1794, M.Litt., T.C.D., 1967.

Hogan, Patrick, Civil unrest in the province of Connaught 1793–1798: The role of the landed gentry in maintaining order, M. Ed., U.C.G., 1976.

Hughes, Mark, Henry Joy's *Belfast Newsletter* and the French Revolution 1789–1793, M.A., U.C.D., 1990.

Hurley, Mary, Thomas Braughall, merchant radicalism and the Catholic question 1783–1803, M.A., U.C.D., 1993.

Kalliomaki, Aki, 'Who dares to write of '98?': The historiography of the 1798 rebellion in Ireland 1798–1868, M.Litt., T.C.D., 2000.

Kennedy, Denis, The Irish Whigs 1789–1795, Ph.D., Toronto, 1971.

Kennedy, Máire, French language books in eighteenth-century Ireland: Dissemination and readership, Ph.D., U.C.D., 1994.

Kennedy, W.B., French projects for the invasion of Ireland 1796–1798, Ph.D., Georgia, 1973.

Keogh, Dáire, The Catholic Church and radicalism in Ireland in the 1790s, Ph.D., T.C.D., 1992.

Kerrane, J.G.O., The background to the 1798 rebellion in County Meath, M.A., U.C.D., 1971.

Kilfeather, Siobhán, 'Strangers at home': Political fictions by women in eighteenth-century Ireland, Ph.D., Columbia, 1989.

Kinsella, Anna, 'Who fears to speak of '98?': The nineteenth-century interpretation of 1798, M.Litt., T.C.D., 1991.

Leichty, Joseph, Irish evangelicalism, Trinity College, Dublin and the mission of the Church of Ireland at the end of the eighteenth century, Ph.D., Maynooth, 1987.

Leighton, Cadoc, Theobald McKenna and the Catholic question, M.A., Maynooth, 1985.

Macafee, William, The population of Ulster 1630–1841: Evidence from mid-Ulster, D. Phil., University of Ulster, 1987.

Mac Suibhne, Breandán, 'Patriot Paddies': The Volunteers and Irish identity in north-west Ulster 1778-86, Ph.D., Carnegie-Mellon, 1998.

McCartney, Donal, Writings on Irish history in the early nineteenth century: A study of Irish public opinion 1800–1830, M.A., U.C.D., 1954.

McCutcheon, Catherine, Imaginative rebellion: Women writers and the Irish nation 1798–1830, M.A., Alberta, 1999.

McNally, Vincent, Archbishop John Thomas Troy and the Catholic question in Ireland 1787–1817, Ph.D., T.C.D., 1976.

Madden, Kyla, The troubled years: Settlement, conflict and rebellion in Forkhill, County Armagh 1788–1798, M.A., Queens [Ontario], 1998.

Mirala, Petri, Freemasonry in Ulster 1733–1815, Ph.D., T.C.D., 1999.

Monaghan, John, A social and economic history of Belfast 1790–1800, M. A., Q.U.B., 1936.

Morley, Vincent, The American Revolution and opinion in Ireland 1760–1783, Ph.D., Liverpool, 1999.

Morris, Catherine, From the margins: Alice Milligan and the Irish cultural revival 1888–1905, Ph.D., Aberdeen, 1999.

Morton, Richard Grenfell, The 1798 rising in Ulster, Ph.D., T.C.D., 1949.

Munn, Mary Josephine, The Irish rebellion of 1798, M.A., Illinois (Urbana-Champaign), 1933.

Murphy, W.G., The life of Dr Thomas Hussey 1746–1802, bishop of Waterford and Lismore, M.A., U.C.C., 1968.

Nelson, John Wallace, The Belfast Presbyterians 1670–1830: An analysis of their political and social interests, Ph.D., Q.U.B., 1985.

O'Brien, Gerard, The exercise of legislative power in Ireland 1782–1800, Ph.D., Cambridge, 1983.

O'Brien, Gillian, 'Spirit, impartiality, independence': The *Northern Star* 1792–1797, M.A., U.C.D., 1997.

O'Brien, Gillian, Lord Camden in Ireland 1795–1798: A study in Anglo-Irish relations, Ph.D., Liverpool, 2002.

Ó Ciardha, Éamonn, A fatal attachment: Ireland and the house of Stuart 1685–1766, Ph.D., Cambridge, 1998.

O'Connor, Catherine, Wexford women: A study of women and the 1798 Rebellion, M.A., University of Limerick, 1998.

O'Connor, Theresa, The more immediate effects of the American Revolution in Ireland, M.A., Q.U.B., 1937.

O'Donnell, Ruan, General Joseph Holt and the rebellion of 1798 in County Wicklow, M.A., U.C.D., 1991.

O'Donnell, Ruan, 'Marked for Botany Bay': The Wicklow United Irishmen and the development of political transportation from Ireland 1791–1806, Ph.D., Australian National University, 1996.

O'Donnell, Katherine, Edmund Burke and the heritage of oral culture, Ph.D., U.C.C., 2001.

O'Donoghue, Patrick, The Catholic Church and Ireland in an age of revolution and rebellion 1782–1803, Ph.D., U.C.D., 1975.

O'Flaherty, Eamonn, The Catholic question in Ireland 1774–1793, M.A., U.C.D., 1981.

O'Halloran, Clare, Golden ages and barbarous nations: Antiquarian debate on the Celtic past in Ireland and Scotland in the eighteenth century, Ph.D., Cambridge, 1991.

O'Rourke [Murphy], Maureen, The battle of Ballinamuck: A study in the dynamics of oral transmission, M.A., Indiana, 1970.

O'Sullivan, Tadhg, Captain Rock in print: Literary representation and Irish agrarian unrest 1824–1833, M.Phil., U.C.C. 1998.

Olliff, Martin, Diplomacy between the French Directory and the United Irishmen 1795–1798, M.A., Auburn, 1979.

Patterson, James, Republicanism, agrarianism and banditry in the wake of the great Irish rebellion of 1798, Ph.D., Fordham, 2000.

Phillips, Malcolm, Charles Fox and Ireland 1775–1798, M.A., Memorial [Newfoundland], 1973.

Powell, Thomas J., The background to the rebellion in County Wexford, M.A., U.C.D., 1970.

Quinn, James, In pursuit of the millenium: The career of Thomas Russell 1790–1803, Ph.D., U.C.D., 1996.

Robinson, Thomas, The life of Thomas Addis Emmet, Ph.D., New York University, 1955.

Rosti, Jennifer, 1798: A year of rebellion in Irish literature, M.A., Virginia Polytechnic Institute, 1980.

Scott, Marty, Wolfe Tone and the rhetoric of Irish nationalism, M.A., North Carolina, 1992.

Sebastian-Coleman, Laura, 'All that delirium of the brave': Wolfe Tone, Irish masculine virtue and national identity, M.A., Rochester, 1992.

Small, Stephen, Republicanism, patriotism and radicalism: Political thought in Ireland 1776–1798, Ph.D., Oxford, 1999.

Smith, David, The Volunteer movement in Ulster: background and development 1745–1785, Ph.D., Q.U.B., 1974.

St. Mark, Joseph J., The red shamrock: United Irishmen and revolution 1795–1803, Ph.D., Georgetown, 1974.

Smyth, James, Popular politicisation in Ireland in the 1790s, Ph.D., Cambridge, 1989.

Stewart, A.T.Q., The transformation of Presbyterian radicalism in the north of Ireland 1792–1825, M.A., Q.U.B., 1956.

Stoddart, P.C., Counter-insurgency and defence in Ireland 1790–1805, D. Phil., Oxford, 1972.

Stone, George, Theobald Wolfe Tone and Irish nationalism, M.A., Eastern Illinois, 1964.

Victory, Isolde, Colonial nationalism in Ireland: From common law to natural right, Ph.D., T.C.D., 1984.

Walsh, Margaret, 'Freedom through difficulty': The *Morning Post*'s reaction to the French Revolution 1788–1793, M.A., U.C.D., 1991.

Whelan, Margaret, Edward Hay, 'styled Mr Secretary Hay': Catholic politics, 1792–1822, M.A., Galway, 1991.

Willis, Stanley, The Steelboys in Ireland and America, M.A., Aberdeen, 1999.

For assistance with this bibliography, I would like to thank Charlotte Ames, Guy Beiner, Manuella Ceretta, Peter Collins, Seamus Deane, Brian MacDonald, Breandán Mac Suibhne, Anthony Malcomson, Kerby Miller, Vincent Morley, Bill Murray, Éamonn Ó Ciardha, Ruan O'Donnell, Pat Power, James Quinn, Matthew Stout, Eamonn Whelan and C.J. Woods.

Index

Compiled by Thomas Bartlett